UNIVERSITY CASEBOOK SERIES®

SENTENCING LAW, POLICY, AND PRACTICE

WAYNE A. LOGAN
Steven M. Goldstein Professor
Florida State University College of Law

MICHAEL M. O'HEAR
Professor of Law
Marquette University Law School

FOUNDATION PRESS

444 Cedar Street, Suite 700
St. Paul, MN 55101
1-877-888-1330

Printed in the United States of America

ISBN: 978-1-64242-311-2

To my parents, Leslie and Muriel Logan

WAL

To my wife, Jennifer Madden O'Hear

MMO

PREFACE

Historically, the criminal justice system curriculum in law schools has focused on three main courses: criminal law, criminal procedure-investigation, and criminal procedure-adjudication (a.k.a. "bail-to-jail"). The list, however, omits another component of major significance: sentencing. In an era when guilty pleas determine the outcome of the vast majority of criminal cases, the sentencing phase assumes utmost importance; it determines the punishment that will be imposed on defendants, which, depending on the jurisdiction, can include death. For law students intent upon pursuing a career in the criminal justice system, learning about the sentencing phase of a criminal case is imperative.

Even beyond its practical value for future prosecutors and defense lawyers, sentencing is a fascinating and critically important subject in its own right, justifying study by all law students. Like the criminal justice system as a whole, sentencing reflects the nation's many social and economic challenges, while creating very significant challenges of its own. Testament to the latter is the recent recognition of the massive human and fiscal consequences flowing from what has been termed "mass incarceration," resulting from the nation's decades-long "get tough" sentencing zeitgeist.

An educated understanding of the issue, however, reveals that the problem manifests itself not only in bodies warehoused in brick-and-mortar prisons and jails. In reality, the majority of individuals convicted of crimes are not physically incapacitated, but rather are under community supervision subject to probation and parole conditions. Furthermore, conceiving of the issue solely in terms of correctional control understates the true impact of penal policies. This is because completing a period of correctional supervision very often does not mean that one's debt to society is fully paid. Rather, for serious and non-serious offenses alike, a conviction can trigger the vast array of collateral consequences today imposed by jurisdictions, such as life-long registration and community notification (for sex offenders), deportation, and lost eligibility for student loans and public housing, which can be more personally debilitating than a prison or jail term or community supervision. Meanwhile, restitution, forfeiture of money and property, fines, fees, surcharges, and costs imposed on convicted individuals often pose major obstacles to successful reentry into society.

The twelve chapters in this book reflect this broader understanding of the sentencing process and its outcomes. While the book examines standard sentencing matters such as penal theory, sentencing guidelines, and the death penalty, it places particular emphasis on community corrections and non-incarcerative sanctions. This "bottom of the pyramid" focus is important both because it reflects the real-world impact of sentencing and because it provides a rich opportunity to examine myriad challenging and critically important issues, which law school casebooks often ignore or fail to fully address.

Ultimately, this book conceives of sentencing as an ongoing governmental experiment in social control, involving irreducibly political choices and resource allocations, which has not gone very well in achieving desired outcomes. The huge human and financial expense of the nation's correctional system is surely one benchmark, but so too are high recidivism rates, the troubling lack of mental health care in the nation's prisons and jails, and continued racial disparities in corrections populations.

Despite the serious problems plaguing the U.S. criminal justice system, the nation is now showing promise of a more constructive path. Political leaders across the political spectrum recognize the need to change the status quo, and policymakers are no longer captive to the pessimistic view embodied in sociologist Robert Martinson's influential 1974 conclusion that "nothing works" in corrections. Some interventions do indeed achieve positive outcomes, which are noted in the following chapters. It is the authors' hope that the materials contained in this book will provide the foundation for the coming generation of lawyers to effectuate the change needed for the nation's sentencing law, policy, and practice to achieve its goals of meting out justice in a fair and effective manner.

WAYNE A. LOGAN
MICHAEL M. O'HEAR

February 2022

ACKNOWLEDGMENTS

The authors are indebted to a great many individuals for their help in the creation of this book. In particular, they thank their cadre of wonderful research assistants, who supported the project in multiple ways: Madison Bedder, Bradley Fehrenbach, Makena Felten, Matthew Kass, Joshua Kundert, and Ruth Nord-Pekar. Also, major thanks are in order for our Foundation Press editor, Ryan Pfieffer, who has exhibited enormous patience and support during the book's long gestation, and our friend and colleague Cecilia Klingele, of the University of Wisconsin Law School, who played an instrumental role in the early stages of the project. Finally, thanks go to the following authors and copyright holders for their permission to use material reprinted in the book.

MODEL PENAL CODE (AM. LAW INST. 1962). © American Law Institute. Reprinted with permission.

MODEL PENAL CODE: SENTENCING (AM. LAW INST., Proposed Final Draft 2017). © American Law Institute. Reprinted with permission.

Paul G. Cassell, *In Defense of Victim Impact Statements*, 6 OHIO ST. J. CRIM. L. 611 (2009). © Paul Cassell, Ohio State Journal of Criminal Law. Reprinted with permission.

Cecelia Klingele, *Changing the Sentence Without Hiding the Truth: Judicial Sentence Modification as a Promising Method of Early Release*, 52 WM. & MARY L. REV. 465 (2010). © Cecelia Klingele, William & Mary Law Review. Reprinted with permission.

Edward J. Latessa & Myrinda Schweitzer, *Community Supervision and Violent Offenders: What the Research Tells Us and How to Improve Outcomes*, 103 MARQ. L. REV. 911 (2020). © Edward J. Latessa, Myrinda Schweitzer. Reprinted with permission.

Wayne A. Logan & Ronald F. Wright, *Mercenary Criminal Justice*, 2014 U. ILL. L. REV. 1175 (2014). © Wayne A. Logan, Ronald F. Wright. Reprinted with permission.

Bruce J. Winick, *Therapeutic Jurisprudence and Problem Solving Courts*, 30 FORDHAM URB. L. J. 1055 (2003). © Fordham Urban Law Journal. Reprinted with permission.

SUMMARY OF CONTENTS

TABLE OF CONTENTS

TABLE OF CASES

The principal cases are in bold type.

TABLE OF STATUTES & GUIDELINES

UNIVERSITY CASEBOOK SERIES®

SENTENCING LAW, POLICY, AND PRACTICE

CHAPTER 1

PURPOSES OF PUNISHMENT

It was early 1763, and the twenty-four-year-old Italian aristocrat Cesare Beccaria faced a dilemma to which many contemporary students can relate—he needed a good paper topic. Beccaria had led a mostly quiet, sheltered life of study in and around Milan, with his formal education culminating in the conferral of a law degree in 1758. After completing his legal studies, he joined a literary club, where he became friends with another young aristocrat, Pietro Verri. Beccaria, Verri, and other young men in their social circle found their intellects awakened by the writings of Montesquieu, Voltaire, and other leading figures of the Enlightenment. Inspired to translate the cutting-edge thinking emerging from France and elsewhere into a program of social reform for backward Italy, Beccaria, Verri, and a few of their friends formed the "Academy of the Fist"—so named for the violent disputes that sometimes broke out within the group.

Members of the Academy individually produced a series of papers on a variety of matters of public concern, with Beccaria's first effort focusing on a question of economic policy. However, that paper's publication in 1762 left him in need of a new topic, which he struggled to find. Growing bored, Beccaria eventually asked Verri for assistance. His friend suggested that he look into penal reform. Although Beccaria had little personal knowledge of the subject, Verri's little brother Alessandro—another member of the Academy—happened to have experience as a prison inspector and shared with Beccaria the grim realities he witnessed. Beccaria agreed to take on the suggested topic, and, in 1764, he completed what is now recognized as a pathbreaking work of enduring importance, the short, impassioned treatise entitled *On Crimes and Punishments*.[1]

Steeped in Enlightenment political philosophy, Beccaria saw law and government as the product of a social contract. In his view, the social contract implied a limited government whose purpose was to protect the liberty and advance the happiness of its citizens. Operating within that framework, Beccaria objected vociferously in his treatise to the use of torture and capital punishment, even though these had been long-established aspects of European criminal justice systems. *See* CESARE

---

[1] The biographical information here is derived from COLEMAN PHILLIPSON, THREE CRIMINAL LAW REFORMERS: BECCARIA, BENTHAM, ROMILLY 3–7 (1923), and Aaron Thomas, *Preface, in* CESARE BECCARIA, ON CRIMES AND PUNISHMENTS AND OTHER WRITINGS xv, xv–xxxii (Aaron Thomas ed., 2008). In recognition of the importance of *On Crimes and Punishments,* Beccaria is routinely credited as the "father of modern criminology." Graeme Newman & Pietro Marongiu, *Penological Reform and the Myth of Beccaria*, 28 CRIMINOLOGY 325, 325 (1990). An intellectual "one-hit wonder," Beccaria accomplished little else of note in his subsequent career as a professor and bureaucrat. *See* PHILLIPSON, *supra*, at 20–22.

BECCARIA, ON CRIMES AND PUNISHMENTS AND OTHER WRITINGS 32–37, 51–57 (Aaron Thomas ed., Aaron Thomas & Jeremy Parzen trans., 2008) (1764). He insisted that the severity of punishments be justified by reference to the common good, and he suggested that governments ought to err on the side of lenience. In his concluding chapter, Beccaria issued this much-quoted challenge to the criminal justice systems of his day: "In order that punishment should not be an act of violence committed by one or many against a private citizen, it is essential that it be public, prompt, necessary, the minimum possible in the given circumstances, proportionate to the crimes, and established by the law." *Id.* at 86.

Figure 1-1. Cesare Beccaria (1738–1794).

Translated into English and crossing the Atlantic in the midst of the tax controversies that would soon spark the Revolutionary War, *On Crimes and Punishments* was widely read and embraced by the generation of Americans who achieved national independence and framed the Constitution—a generation that was also deeply influenced by the same Enlightenment thinking that had so inspired Beccaria. BERNARD BAILYN, THE IDEOLOGICAL ORIGINS OF THE AMERICAN REVOLUTION 26–27 (1967). By 1785, Pennsylvania (and future United States) Attorney General William Bradford could observe that "the name of Beccaria has become familiar in Pennsylvania, his authority has become great, and his principles have spread among all classes of persons and impressed themselves deeply in the hearts of our citizens." Kathryn Preyer, *Cesare Beccaria and the Founding Fathers, in* BLACKSTONE IN AMERICA: SELECTED ESSAYS OF KATHRYN PREYER 239, 246 (Mary Sarah Bilder, Maeva Marcus & R. Kent Newmyer eds., 2009). Beccaria's readers in the revolutionary generation included Thomas Jefferson, John Adams, James Madison, and many others. JOHN D. BESSLER, THE BIRTH OF AMERICAN LAW: AN ITALIAN PHILOSOPHER AND THE AMERICAN REVOLUTION ch. 3 (2014). Notably, in Adams' personal copy of Beccaria's treatise, preserved today in the Boston Public Library, this key assertion—an anticipation of Beccaria's concluding challenge—has been underlined: "Every act of authority of one man over another, for which there is not absolute necessity, is tyrannical." JOHN D. BESSLER, THE BARON AND THE MARQUIS: LIBERTY, TYRANNY, AND THE ENLIGHTENMENT MAXIM THAT CAN REMAKE AMERICAN CRIMINAL JUSTICE ix (2019) (underscoring in the original).

America's legal and political culture remains deeply marked by Enlightenment ideals of individual liberty, rule of law, and limited government in service of the common good. While the exact meaning and relative importance of these ideals may be subject to dispute, their continued vitality suggests that Beccaria's challenge remains timely and important for all those who work in, or are students of, the contemporary American criminal justice system. Criminal punishment represents an extraordinary act of state power relative to the individual—an act whose legitimacy seems at least suspect if not justified by some form of social duty or necessity. But how are we to know if any given sentence can be justified in this way? The question demands some appreciation of the basic purposes of punishment that are commonly invoked by American judges, lawyers, and policymakers. It is these purposes that will be the chief subject of the present chapter.

A. CONVENTIONALLY RECOGNIZED PURPOSES OF PUNISHMENT

Criminal punishment, to echo one influential formulation, involves the *intentional* infliction by legally constituted authorities of pain or some other unpleasant consequence on a person for that person's offense against legal rules. *See* H.L.A. HART, PUNISHMENT AND RESPONSIBILITY: ESSAYS IN THE PHILOSOPHY OF LAW 4–5 (1968). What could justify such a practice by the institutions and agents of government? Furthermore, even assuming that punishment can be justified as a general matter, on what grounds should the specific *type* of unpleasantness that is inflicted in particular cases be determined, e.g., probation versus incarceration? And what considerations should guide decisions about the *duration* and *intensity* of the chosen type of punishment?[2]

[2] Intuitively, it may seem that the same principles should be drawn on in responding to all of these questions, i.e., both in justifying punishment as a general matter and in determining how specific individuals should be punished. However, the legal theorist H.L.A. Hart has argued

Broadly speaking, there are two major—and, to a considerable extent, competing—modern western traditions of thought about such questions: utilitarian and retributive. In the utilitarian tradition, the purpose of punishment, at the most general level, is to maximize the sum total of happiness in the community. For instance, sentencing a defendant to prison for ten years will presumably reduce the defendant's happiness over that time period, but, if the prison term deters, say, one hundred other people from committing serious predatory crimes, then the total amount of happiness in the community may still be higher with the prison term than without it. If so, then the ten-year sentence may potentially be regarded as justified from a utilitarian standpoint.

By contrast, the retributive tradition has tended to view punishment through the lens of *desert*, rather than happiness. The criminal is punished because—and to the extent that—the criminal has done something that deserves punishment. For instance, a person's action that is deliberately harmful to another person may be seen as justifying the imposition of a corresponding harm on the actor, regardless of whether doing so would prevent any crimes in the future. In this sense, the retributive approach is often characterized as *backward*-looking, in contrast to the *forward*-looking nature of the utilitarian approach.

In this section, we will first explore utilitarian purposes of punishment and then retributive. We will conclude by considering victim restoration, which has emerged over the past generation as an increasingly important objective for the criminal justice system.

1. UTILITARIAN PURPOSES OF PUNISHMENT

Cesare Beccaria (1738–1794) is often seen as a key progenitor of modern utilitarianism. *See, e.g.*, CESARE BECCARIA, ON CRIMES AND PUNISHMENTS AND OTHER WRITINGS 9 (Aaron Thomas ed., Aaron Thomas & Jeremy Parzen trans., 2008) (1764) (advocating for "the greatest happiness shared among the greatest number" as the proper aim of public policy). Beccaria, in turn, inspired the English philosopher Jeremy Bentham (1748–1832), who sought to explore more systematically the implications of Beccaria's greatest-happiness principle. Between them, Beccaria and Bentham developed many of the important concepts that continue to shape utilitarian thinking about punishment today.

In principle, the utilitarian greatest-happiness framework might be deployed in any area of public policy. In relation to *penal* policies and practices, the utilitarian objective is often equated with crime-prevention. Thus, for instance, a tough new sentencing law might be viewed as a good one if it results in lower crime rates and if the costs of

---

that these two types of questions may be coherently distinguished and answered by reference to different sets of values. HART, *supra*, at 3. Our discussion of purposes in this chapter will proceed with both types of question in mind, without assuming that a single theoretical framework must be used in answering these questions.

increased sentences are not excessive relative to the crime-reduction benefits. But how might a sentencing law, or for that matter a sentence imposed in a particular case, plausibly reduce future crime? Conventionally, four mechanisms are invoked: general deterrence, specific deterrence, incapacitation, and rehabilitation.

a. GENERAL DETERRENCE

The deterrence purpose of punishment is often expressed through the notion that punishment will "send a message"—communicating to prospective criminals that they are better off staying within the law. More precisely conceptualized, a punishment deters by increasing the expected costs to the perpetrator of committing a crime and thereby eliminating the expected net benefit of the offense. If there is no expected net benefit, there is no incentive to commit the crime.[3]

In a highly simplified model, deterrence is a function of (a) the likelihood that a perpetrator will be caught, and (b) the severity of the punishment that will be imposed if he or she is apprehended. Imagine, for instance, a law that imposes a flat fine of $1000 for shoplifting. Imagine further that we are in a jurisdiction in which 20% of shoplifters are arrested and convicted. The expected penalty for shoplifting would be 20% of $1000, or $200. In this jurisdiction—ignoring various real-world complexities like the cost to the prospective defendant of hiring a lawyer, the possibility of bargaining the prosecutor down to a lesser charge, and so forth—we would expect rational, well-informed citizens to be deterred from shoplifting any items worth $200 or less because there would be no expected net gain from such a crime. In fact, the deterrent effect would be even a little stronger than that. Consider, would it make sense for a person to shoplift a $220 item? No, assuming the stolen item is returned to the store if the shoplifter is caught. This would reduce the expected benefit of the crime. The rationally discounted benefit of $176 ($220 × 80% chance of getting to keep the stolen item) is still less than the expected cost of $200. By this reasoning, a rational prospective shoplifter would be deterred from pilfering anything worth $250 or less.

But what about higher-dollar shoplifting? How can that be deterred? Using the simplified model, there are two possible strategies: increase the apprehension rate above the current 20%, or increase the punishment for those who are caught above the current $1000 fine. In principle, our model suggests that either strategy might be effective. Storeowners could increase the apprehension rate by, say, installing

---

[3] This formulation of the deterrence model may strike some readers as having a flavor of economics. This is no accident. Classical deterrence theory rests on the same model of rationally self-interested decision-making as does classical economics. Thus, we should not be surprised that deterrence, although it had been eclipsed by other purposes of punishment in criminological thinking for most of the twentieth century, staged a late twentieth-century comeback thanks to the work of economists like Gary Becker and law-and-economics scholars like Richard Posner. John F. Pfaff, *Gary Becker's Contributions to Law and Economics, in* PIONEERS OF LAW AND ECONOMICS 152 (Joshua Wright & Lloyd Cohen eds., 2009); Richard A. Posner, *Optimal Sentences for White-Collar Criminals*, 17 AM. CRIM. L. REV. 409 (1980).

more surveillance cameras and hiring more security guards. However, these would be costly measures. It is not hard to imagine storeowners lobbying the legislature to increase the fine instead. And, indeed, this might appear at first blush to be a cost-free strategy.

We might wonder, then, is there any limit to the logic of increased-punishment/reduced-crime? The question has important implications for the work of lawmakers in setting statutory punishment levels for different offenses; of prosecutors in deciding how much punishment to seek through their charging, plea-bargaining, and sentence-recommendation decisions; and of judges in determining punishment severity in those cases in which they have the discretion to do so. Do deterrence interests suggest that all of these actors should generally err on the side of greater severity?

Deterrence was the crime-reduction mechanism most emphasized by Beccaria. Yet, Beccaria cautioned strongly against relying too much on the *severity*, as opposed to the *certainty*, of punishment. He presented three arguments why increased punishments may be ineffective, or even counterproductive, as a crime-reduction strategy. First, he pointed out that more severe punishments can perversely create stronger incentives for criminals to commit additional or more serious crimes in order to avoid apprehension. BECCARIA, *supra*, at 50. Interestingly, the United States Supreme Court echoed this argument in *Kennedy v. Louisiana*, 554 U.S. 407 (2008), in which the Court held that the death penalty cannot constitutionally be imposed in cases of child rape that do not involve a homicide. More specifically, in rejecting the argument that the death penalty is justified on deterrence grounds, the Court observed, "[B]y in effect making the punishment for child rape and murder equivalent, a State that punishes child rape by death may remove a strong incentive for the rapist not to kill the victim. Assuming the offender behaves in a rational way, as one must to justify the penalty on grounds of deterrence, the penalty in some respects gives less protection, not more, to the victim, who is often the sole witness to the crime." *Id.* at 445.

Second, Beccaria argued that harsh punishments may lead to reduced enforcement of the law, suggesting that those who must take responsibility for enforcement may not feel comfortable bringing about sentences that seem unfairly severe. BECCARIA, *supra*, at 51. Ironically, in other words, an attempt to enhance deterrence by increasing *severity* may actually end up undercutting deterrence by reducing *certainty*. Once again, in *Kennedy*, the Supreme Court made a similar point. Noting that many sexual assaults of children are perpetrated by family members or others who are known to the victim, and citing the views of professionals who work with child victims, the Court observed, "[W]hen the punishment is death, both the victim and the victim's family members may be more likely to shield the perpetrator from discovery, thus increasing underreporting. As a result, punishment by death may not result in more deterrence or more effective enforcement." *Kennedy*, 554 U.S. at 445 (citation omitted).

Third, Beccaria argued that harsh punishments may lose much of their deterrent effect as people become accustomed to them. *See* BECCARIA, *supra*, at 50. Consider once again our shoplifting hypothetical. A lawmaker might assert, "These fines are not getting the attention of shoplifters. We need something more dramatic for deterrence. A convicted shoplifter should be forced to spend a day standing in front of the store that he or she victimized carrying a sign that reads, 'I shoplifted.' That public humiliation will really send a message!" If the plan were implemented, it is easy to imagine that there might be some impact the first time a shoplifter was seen carrying such a sign. But what about the second, or tenth, or hundredth time? The shock value would surely decline, and along with it perhaps the deterrent effect.

In light of all of these considerations, Beccaria argued, "One of the greatest checks on crimes is not the cruelty of punishments, but the inevitability of punishment .... The certainty of a punishment, even if it is moderate, will always make a stronger impression than the fear of another more terrible punishment ...." *Id.* at 49.

Modern social science has tended to support Beccaria's reservations about efforts to enhance deterrence by increasing penal severity. Daniel S. Nagin, *Deterrence in the Twenty-First Century*, 42 CRIME & JUST. 199, 201 (2013). This is not to say that deterrence doesn't "work." If a legislature declares that a given act is a crime, we can normally expect that the act will be performed less frequently in the future, especially if the public can see that individuals really do suffer unpleasant consequences for doing the act. The point, rather, is that policy and individual-case decisions in the area of *sentencing*—attaching, say, a five-year instead of a one-year mandatory minimum to a crime, or giving a particular defendant a twenty-year instead of a ten-year prison term—may have considerably weaker deterrent effects than is commonly supposed. *Policing* behavior, insofar as it is the key determinant of the certainty of punishment, may be far more consequential to deterrence. *Id.*[4]

The available empirical research on deterrence was recently reviewed by a distinguished committee of scholars working under the auspices of the National Research Council of the National Academies of Science. The committee concluded that there is some evidence of crime-reduction benefits when there are "small increases in short sentences";

[4] Research suggests that there may be considerable room for improvement in the "certainty" area. Recent data point to an arrest rate amounting to only about 20–25% of the serious victimizing offenses reported to the police each year. Shima Baradaran Baughman, *How Effective Are Police? The Problem of Clearance Rates and Criminal Accountability*, 72 ALA. L. REV. 47, 86 (2020). If nonreported crimes are taken into account, then the arrest rate would fall to only about 10%. *Id.* at 86. And if *convictions* are used as the benchmark, then the success rate of police and prosecutors in establishing accountability for offenses would fall to less than 2%. *Id.* at 95.

however, "the deterrent return to increasing already long sentences is modest at best." COMM. ON CAUSES & CONSEQUENCES OF HIGH RATES OF INCARCERATION, NAT'L RESEARCH COUNCIL OF THE NAT'L ACADS., THE GROWTH OF INCARCERATION IN THE UNITED STATES: EXPLORING CAUSES AND CONSEQUENCES 139 (Jeremy Travis, Bruce Western & Steve Redburn eds., 2014). The committee further noted research suggesting that these modest benefits may sometimes be outweighed by the costs of increased incarceration. *Id.* at 138.

Complementing the concerns raised by Beccaria, we might note some additional weaknesses with our simplified deterrence model. At the most fundamental level, the model presupposes that prospective offenders understand and rationally weigh the actual likelihood of apprehension and the actual level of punishment they would face in the event of apprehension. In reality, though, a great deal of criminal decisionmaking deviates from this ideal. As the National Research Council committee observed,

> [S]uddenly induced rages, feelings of threat and paranoia, a desire for revenge and retaliation, and self-perceptions of brilliance in the grandiose phase of manic-depressive illness all can limit a potential offender's ability to exercise self-control. Also playing a role are personality traits and the pervasive influence of drugs and alcohol: in one study, 32 percent of state prison inmates reported being high on drugs at the time of their crime, and 17 percent committed their crime to get money to buy drugs. The influence of crime-involved peers who downplay the long-term consequences of punishment is relevant as well.

COMM. ON CAUSES & CONSEQUENCES OF HIGH RATES OF INCARCERATION, *supra*, at 133–34. *See also* Timothy C. Barnum, Daniel S. Nagin & Greg Pogarsky, *Sanction Risk Perceptions, Coherence, and Deterrence*, 59 CRIMINOLOGY 195, 198–200 (2021) (summarizing research on cognitive biases that might cause prospective offenders to inaccurately estimate the risk of apprehension).

Does this line of thinking suggest that deterrence should be disregarded as a purpose of punishment in certain sorts of cases—e.g., barroom fights or impulsive robberies perpetrated in order to get money for drugs—but still emphasized in other sorts of cases that more closely conform to the ideal of rational decisionmaking? The United States Sentencing Commission may have had this sort of distinction in mind in setting the penalties for federal tax offenses; the Commission expressly declared that "deterring others from violating the tax laws [was] a primary consideration." U.S. SENT'G COMM'N, U.S. SENTENCING GUIDELINES MANUAL § 2T1 intro. commentary (1987). Does it seem to you that criminal tax evasion really is more likely a product of rational, deliberate choice than street robbery? And, if you agree that deterrence really should govern punishment in tax cases, what exactly would that mean for the type and severity of sentences? The Sentencing Commission thought that deterrence of white-collar criminals could best be achieved through "a short but definite period of confinement." Stephen Breyer, *The Federal Sentencing Guidelines and the Key Compromises Upon Which They Rest*, 17 HOFSTRA L. REV. 1, 22 (1988).[5] Does that seem right to you? What concerns might Beccaria raise about the Sentencing Commission's effort to increase the use of incarceration with white-collar offenders? Why not instead use the logic suggested above in the shoplifting discussion and use a system of fines that would strip the prospective tax evader (or other white-collar criminal) of the expected financial gains of the offense, taking into account the likelihood of apprehension?[6]

b. CONTROL OF THE DANGEROUS: SPECIFIC DETERRENCE, INCAPACITATION, REHABILITATION

If imposing a sentence on a defendant "sends a message," as deterrence theory indicates, we might think about two distinct audiences for that message: the general public and the defendant. The content of the message to both audiences may be essentially the same—commit this crime, and you can expect that something unpleasant will happen to you if you get caught—but there may be a special force to the message as it is delivered in person to the defendant by a stern judge in open court. Indeed, the judge may be able to individualize the deterrent threat so as to amplify its impact with the defendant. Consider, for instance, the judge who gives a defendant probation, but warns that the sentence will certainly be incarceration if the defendant has to return to court for another offense in the future. In a sense, this is just another deterrent threat that works (or not) in the same way that deterrent threats generically do by increasing the expected costs of crime to the perpetrator. Yet, there is an immediacy to the threat that is delivered directly to the defendant that might plausibly trigger distinct psychological responses. For this reason, criminologists have sometimes distinguished between two deterrence mechanisms: general deterrence (the threat delivered to the general public) and specific deterrence (the threat delivered to a specific individual or group of individuals).

The concept of specific deterrence points to a broader class of utilitarian purposes of punishment—those that attempt to reduce or eliminate the individual risk posed by individuals who are regarded as dangerous. In addition to specific deterrence, the two other

---

[5] Stephen Breyer, the author of this much-cited article on the original intent of the federal sentencing guidelines, served as a member of the U.S. Sentencing Commission when the guidelines were drafted. He later became an Associate Justice of the United States Supreme Court.

[6] *Cf.* Richard A. Posner, *Optimal Sentences for White-Collar Criminals*, 17 AM. CRIM. L. REV. 409, 410 (1980) ("[T]he white-collar criminal as I have defined him should be punished only by monetary penalties—by fines (where civil damages or penalties are inadequate or inappropriate) rather than by imprisonment or other 'afflictive' punishments (save as they may be necessary to coerce payment of the monetary penalty).").

conventionally recognized purposes that fit under this heading are incapacitation and rehabilitation. We will consider all three in turn.

i. Specific Deterrence

Are deterrent threats more effective when delivered to a specific person or group of people than in an undifferentiated way to the general public? In theory, the same limitations that diminish general deterrent effects—impaired rationality, perverse incentives to commit more crimes to avoid apprehension, and so forth—might also diminish specific deterrent effects. On the other hand, the specific targeting of deterrent threats could conceivably cause them to be more attention-getting and hence more effective. Yet, since specific deterrent threats in the sentencing context normally focus on individuals who have already been found guilty, there is also this challenge: those who are targeted for specific deterrence have already revealed themselves to be less than ideally responsive to penal threats. The same psychological tendencies that cause a person to discount general threats—e.g., a tendency to emphasize immediate gratification over the potential for some future unpleasantness—may also cause that person to discount specific threats. Additionally, a person's criminal history may carry with it stigma and other consequences that tend to push the person's cost-benefit calculus in an unfavorable direction. For instance, imagine a person convicted of a drug-trafficking felony who is given probation and warned that a worse punishment will follow a repeat offense. The stigma of the felony conviction may make it much harder for the person to obtain lawful employment. A lack of alternative means to earn money may, in turn, make renewed drug-dealing appear to be a rational choice for the person notwithstanding the risk of incarceration.

As with general deterrence, the available research indicates that strong specific deterrent effects may be difficult to achieve through sentencing policies or practices alone. In particular, the research casts doubt on the notion that giving a "taste of prison" to a defendant will reliably make that defendant less likely to reoffend. *See* Daniel S. Nagin, Francis T. Cullen & Cheryl Lero Johnson, *Imprisonment and Reoffending*, 38 CRIME & JUST. 115, 143–177 (2009). It has been suggested, though, that research on specific deterrence should pay closer attention to different crime types, with the thought that some may be more prone to deterrent effects than others. *See* Joel H. Garner, Christopher D. Maxwell & Jina Lee, *The Specific Deterrent Effects of Criminal Sanctions for Intimate Partner Violence: A Meta-Analysis*, 111 J. CRIM. L. & CRIMINOLOGY 227, 234–35 (2020). However, one recent metanalytic review of twenty-one studies regarding the effects of incarceration on intimate partner violence concluded that the evidence pointed more to *increased*, rather than *decreased*, recidivism (i.e., reoffense) risk following use of this sanction. *Id.* at 256–57. Can you think of any reasons why this might be so?

A recent study from Florida highlights the complexity of the psychological and sociological effects of incarceration. Daniel P. Mears et al., *Recidivism and Time Served in Prison*, 106 J. CRIM. L. & CRIMINOLOGY 81 (2016). The researchers gathered data on more than 90,000 individuals who had been released from Florida prisons. After controlling for differences in age, sex, criminal history, offense seriousness, and other variables, the researchers compared the recidivism rates of individuals released after serving various lengths of time. If there were strong, consistent specific deterrent effects, we might expect to see a pattern of declining recidivism the longer an offender spends behind bars before release. After all, longer prison terms send a stronger deterrent message inasmuch as they implicitly threaten similar or worse treatment for future offenses.

However, despite the steadily stronger deterrent message carried by greater time served, the researchers found no consistent relationship between time served and recidivism. Instead, they found quite different effects depending on whether the time served was under one year, between one and two years, or greater than two years. In the first category (less than one year), greater time served was associated with *increased* recidivism—the opposite of what would be predicted based on specific deterrence. For instance, the recidivism rate for those serving one month was about 38%, but the rate for those serving twelve months was about 51%. What do you think might account for the greater recidivism of individuals who served a full year in comparison with those who served only a few months?

By contrast, in the second category (one to two years), greater time served was associated with reduced recidivism, which is consistent with specific deterrence. However, the recidivism rate dropped only modestly across this time interval. Thus, for those released after two years, the recidivism rate of 47% was still higher than that for those released after six months. Finally, for prisoners who served longer than two years, recidivism rates did not seem much affected one way or another by time behind bars at least up to the five-year mark. Over the entire two- to five-year time span, recidivism rates dropped only slightly from the initial 47%. (There were not enough individuals in the sample who served more than five years to permit strong conclusions about the effect of even longer prison terms.)

If much of the specific deterrence research casts doubt on the effectiveness of threatening defendants with increasingly harsh punishments, a notable exception may arguably be found in the law-enforcement strategy known as "focused deterrence" or "pulling levers." In several U.S. cities, the implementation of focused deterrence has been associated with significant reductions in gang-related youth violence. Robin S. Engel, Marie Skubak Tillyer & Nicholas Corsaro, *Reducing Gang Violence Using Focused Deterrence: Evaluating the Cincinnati*

Initiative to Reduce Violence, 30 JUST. Q. 403, 406–12 (2013). The strategy has been described this way:

> First, various law enforcement agencies are coordinated to create meaningful and predictable consequences for groups who engage in violence. . . . Direct and accurate communication of the strategy to the target population is of central importance to increase compliance. This is often done during "offender notification meetings" (also referred to as "call-ins" or "forums"), during which violent group members are warned that if any member of their group commits a homicide, the entire group will become the priority of law enforcement. . . .
>
> Second, assistance for those who want to transition out of the violent lifestyle is often offered in the form of social and job services. . . . Finally, key leaders within communities assist in the development of community engagement activities and strive to create a "moral voice" of the community by delivering a clear message of non-violence and rejecting the norms and narratives of the street which promote violence.

Id. at 406–07.

Although the focused deterrence strategy is credited by some with reducing violence in Boston, Indianapolis, Chicago, and elsewhere, it is hard to say how much of the success is due to specific deterrence—i.e., the threats made at the "notification" meetings that law enforcement will "pull every lever" to punish the targeted individuals if they continue to perpetrate violence—and how much is due to the rehabilitation and community engagement aspects of the strategy. And, if specific deterrence really is playing a role, it is also hard to say whether the specific deterrence achieved is a function of increased severity of punishment, increased certainty of punishment, or both. *See* Edmund F. McGarrell, *Focused Deterrence Violence Prevention at Community and Individual Levels*, 103 MARQ. L. REV. 963, 967, 972–81 (2020) (summarizing theoretical underpinnings of focused deterrence and discussing questions about its effectiveness that have not yet been addressed adequately in the research).

ii. Incapacitation

Specific deterrence works—to the extent that it does—by altering the prospective offender's weighing of the costs and benefits of committing an offense. But, for a variety of reasons we have already touched on, it can be very difficult for the criminal justice system to alter a person's thinking in this way. Thus, when confronted with a person who is thought to be dangerous, the system may instead be drawn to a more direct crime-prevention strategy: incapacitation.

Punishment serves an incapacitation purpose to the extent that it takes away, or at least greatly impedes, the ability of the person to commit additional offenses. Capital punishment is, of course, the ultimate incapacitator. Imprisonment is also often thought of as an incapacitating sentence, although the offender is not *entirely* prevented from committing new offenses while he or she is behind bars—assaults by prisoners are not uncommon in some institutions, while drugs and other contraband may circulate with surprising ease. Still, the physical controls and close surveillance associated with incarceration represent at least a major impediment to reoffending.

Other sorts of punishment may also have an incapacitative dimension. A breath alcohol interlock ignition device makes it harder for DUI offenders to drive drunk. A white-collar offender's felony conviction may cause the offender to lose the professional license—as a stock trader or attorney, for instance—that facilitated the person's misdeeds. Castration of male sex offenders, either surgical or chemical, has also been seen in similar terms. Nonetheless, contemporary discussions of incapacitation as a purpose of punishment almost always center on imprisonment.

Some punishments may plausibly serve both incapacitation and specific-deterrence purposes. For instance, a five-year prison term would deliver a substantial period of incapacitation but might also constitute an efficacious threat of further harsh treatment if the defendant reoffends after release. By contrast, a life or multidecade prison term certainly incapacitates but may provide little further crime-prevention benefit via specific deterrence since the defendant will either never get out of prison or be released at such an advanced age that serious recidivism would be highly unlikely anyway. (Such a sentence might, however, have some *general*-deterrence value. Can you explain why?) On the other side of the severity spectrum, a conventional probationary sentence normally provides little incapacitation but might specifically deter additional crimes by a first-time offender.

Is it ethical to sentence a defendant to prison for incapacitation purposes? Such a sentence may seem to punish a defendant not for the crime that he or she has already committed, but for imagined future crimes that he or she *might* commit. Consider these observations from the law professor Paul Robinson and psychologist John Darley:

> The conditions of prison life can be quite harsh; to go to prison in the United States . . . can mean exposure to a debased, mind-numbing environment . . . . The conditions of confinement upon commitment under the criminal justice system are conditions of punishment. Yet, the justification for confinement under an incapacitation strategy is not punishment but prevention, akin to the system of preventive detention that we use for those with infectious diseases or mental illness that is likely to lead to violent behavior. Systems of preventative detention are morally ambiguous, but certainly we are most comfortable with them when they involve detention conditions that are not punitive in

> nature, involve "treatment" efforts that attempt to remove the elements in the individual that cause the presumed dangerousness, and continually reassess the dangerousness of the individual who is incarcerated. This is not a good description of the workings of the prison system in the United States.

The Utility of Desert, 91 NW. U. L. REV. 453, 467 (1997). In light of such ethical concerns, as well as the costs to the state of protracted incarceration, it may strike you that defendants should not be imprisoned for incapacitation purposes unless there are truly compelling indications that they are likely to commit serious crimes if allowed to remain free.

As popularized in the 1980s, the ideal of "selective incapacitation" reflects the view that incapacitation should be based on statistically supportable determinations of dangerousness. Guyora Binder & Ben Notterman, *Penal Incapacitation: A Situationist Critique*, 54 AM. CRIM. L. REV. 1, 8 (2017). Yet, despite decades of research, questions still remain as to whether individualized recidivism predictions can be made with sufficient accuracy to address ethical and practical (cost-benefit) concerns.[7]

A great deal of research in many fields indicates that predictions of future events tend to be less accurate if they are based on intuition than if they are based on a systematic analysis of what has happened in the past. *See, e.g.*, Stefanía Ægisdóttir, *The Meta-Analysis of Clinical Judgment Project: Fifty-Six Years of Accumulated Research on Clinical Versus Statistical Projection*, 34 COUNSELING PSYCHOLOGIST 341 (2006). In the criminal justice field, this realization has inspired a boom in recent years in "actuarial risk assessment"—that is, the use of standardized algorithms to predict the likelihood that a given defendant will reoffend, making use of a large volume of recidivism data from earlier cases. Jennifer L. Skeem & Christopher T. Lowenkamp, *Risk, Race, and Recidivism: Predictive Bias and Disparate Impact*, 54 CRIMINOLOGY 680, 680–81 (2016). Risk-assessment instruments (RAIs) are now routinely used in some jurisdictions for a variety of criminal justice purposes, including bail determinations, parole, and sentencing.

RAIs may provide an improved basis for distinguishing higher- from lower-risk defendants, but it remains contested whether even the best RAIs are sufficiently accurate to justify the use of lengthy prison sentences for incapacitation purposes. Consider, for instance, the Post

[7] Highlighting one of the difficulties, Guyora Binder and Ben Notterman note that incapacitation, as a purpose of punishment, is inherently "dispositionist." Binder & Notterman, *supra*, at 3. That is, incapacitation "presupposes that past offenders are uniquely dangerous individuals who are destined to offend and reoffend regardless of social context." This presupposition, they argue, "must contend with empirical studies showing that situational forces frequently overwhelm individual disposition; the cause of crime is often dangerous situations rather than dangerous people." Binder and Notterman thus see in incapacitationist approaches a manifestation of the "Fundamental Attribution Error, a pervasive cognitive bias that causes humans to underestimate the power of situational factors and overemphasize disposition or personality." *Id.*

Conviction Risk Assessment (PCRA) instrument that is used in the federal system. Based on fifteen variables, the PCRA assigns defendants to one of four risk categories: low, low/moderate, moderate, or high.[8] Research on tens of thousands of cases indicates that most defendants who are categorized as high-risk are indeed rearrested at some point. Skeem & Lowenkamp, *supra*, at 691 tbl. 2. But, in and of itself, that track record may not necessarily justify incapacitation. After all, an arrest could be for a minor infraction, say, public intoxication or possession of a small quantity of drugs for personal use. Few people would argue that incapacitation is appropriate for such low-level crimes—the costs of incarceration would likely far outweigh the minimal social harm of the crimes that are being prevented. Figure 1-2 provides some sense of the range and frequency of the different crimes that are committed by released prisoners, revealing that the most serious victimizing crimes tend to be quite rare.[9]

Figure 1-2. Percent of released prisoners rearrested within five years for specified offenses. Source: United States Department of Justice Bureau of Justice Statistics.

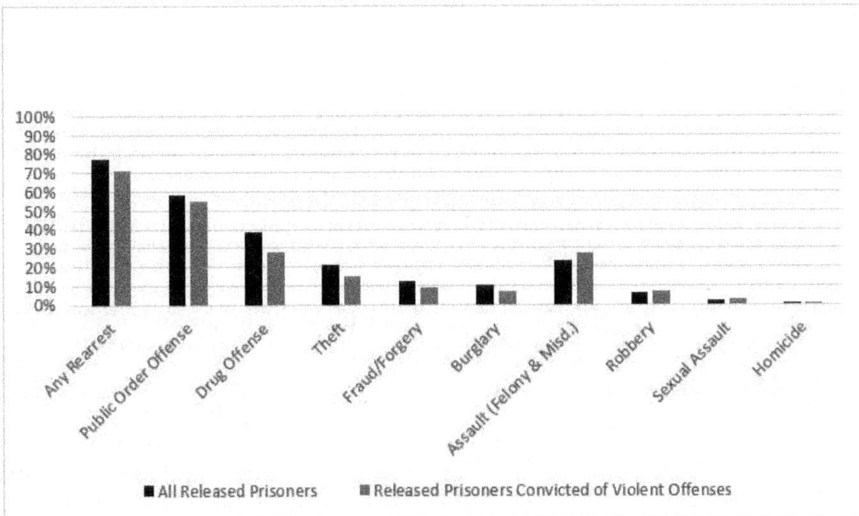

[8] The fifteen variables are: number of prior arrests, age, community supervision violations, varied offending pattern, institutional adjustment problems, violent offense, highest grade completed, unstable recent work history, current unemployment, family problems, unmarried, lack of social support, recent drug problems, recent alcohol problems, and low motivation for change. Jennifer Skeem & Christopher Lowenkamp, *Using Algorithms to Address Trade-Offs Inherent in Predicting Recidivism*, 38 BEHAV. SCI. & L. 259, 265 (2020).

[9] The data come from MATTHEW R. DUROSE, ALEXIA D. COOPER & HOWARD N. SNYDER, U.S. DEP'T OF JUSTICE, RECIDIVISM OF PRISONERS RELEASED IN 30 STATES IN 2005: PATTERNS FROM 2005 TO 2010—SUPPLEMENTAL TABLES: MOST SERIOUS COMMITMENT OFFENSE AND TYPES OF POST-RELEASE ARREST CHARGES OF PRISONERS RELEASED IN 30 STATES IN 2005 tbl.2 (2016). The researchers tracked post-release recidivism of prisoners released in thirty states in 2005. The "public order offense" category includes weapons offenses, driving under the influence, probation and parole violations, obstruction of justice, commercialized vice, disorderly conduct, and other miscellaneous or unspecified offenses.

For purposes of incapacitation, it seems more appropriate to assess the risk of *violent* recidivism, not recidivism generally. With respect to the PCRA, one study found that 21% of the defendants who were classified as "high-risk" were rearrested for a violent crime. *Id.* If this implies that about one in every five defendants in the high-risk category will commit a violent crime in the future, what implications would that have for sentencing? To be sure, one would probably not want to have a neighbor or coworker who has a one-in-five risk of criminal violence, but is the risk really high enough to warrant *imprisonment* on that basis alone? One-in-five is not even "more likely than not"—much less reaching the "beyond a reasonable doubt" standard that is commonly used in the court system for finding facts that result in a loss of liberty. Although RAIs are bringing science to bear in new ways in the sentencing process, the ethical quandaries surrounding incapacitation have hardly been eliminated.[10]

In addition to the ethical concerns, proponents of incapacitation must also contend with the potential for substitution effects. Substitution is easiest to appreciate in relation to remunerative crimes. For instance, if a high-volume drug dealer is imprisoned, other dealers may move quickly to fill the market void. In the end, there may be little or no net reduction in drug trafficking. It has also been theorized that similar effects may stymie efforts to reduce urban gun violence through incapacitation. Wally Hilke, *The Truth Limps After: Sentence Enhancements and the Punishment Paradigm*, 23 UNIV. PA. J. L. & SOC. CHANGE 69 (2020). For instance, if the neighborhood tough is imprisoned, others may compete to step into that position of local status and power—competition that may lead to increased gun-carrying and usage. Similarly, if members of a violent street gang are imprisoned, the gang may recruit others to fill the vacant positions, or other, up-and-coming gangs may seize the opportunity to supplant the crippled gang—potentially leading to an increase, rather than the hoped-for decrease, in gang violence.

One more cautionary note regarding incapacitation is also in order. Even if it can be confidently concluded that a particular defendant presents a high likelihood of violent recidivism that warrants incapacitation *today*, that conclusion would not necessarily justify a prison term of more than a few years. Much research finds a general—albeit not universal—tendency for offenders to reduce their rate of offending as they age and eventually to reach a point of desistance.

---

[10] One important area of controversy regarding RAIs relates to their racial impact. Although none of the leading RAIs treats race as an explicit risk factor, the instruments commonly use other variables like criminal history that are correlated with race. *See, e.g.*, Crystal S. Yang & Will Dobbie, *Equal Protection Under Algorithms: A New Statistical and Legal Framework*, 119 MICH. L. REV. 291, 330 (2020) (comparing eight leading instruments). Despite the potential for racial disparities in RAI risk scores, it remains far from clear that RAIs actually tend to exacerbate the baseline disparities in the criminal justice system. *See* Megan Stevenson, *Assessing Risk Assessment in Action*, 103 MINN. L. REV. 303 (2018). We consider this issue further in Chapter 4.

Patrick Lussier & Jay Healey, *Rediscovering Quetelet, Again: The "Aging" Offender and the Prediction of Reoffending in a Sample of Adult Sex Offenders*, 26 JUST. Q. 827, 828 (2009). This pattern of declining criminal activity has even been found with offenders classified as high-risk. Anthony W. Flores et al., *Time-Free Effects in Predicting Recidivism Using Both Fixed and Variable Follow-Up Periods*, 44 CRIM. JUST. & BEHAV. 121, 122 (2017). As a result, long prison terms of, say, a decade or more are apt to prove excessive in many cases from the standpoint of incapacitation. *See* COMM. ON CAUSES & CONSEQUENCES OF HIGH RATES OF INCARCERATION, NAT'L RESEARCH COUNCIL OF THE NAT'L ACADS., THE GROWTH OF INCARCERATION IN THE UNITED STATES: EXPLORING CAUSES AND CONSEQUENCES 5 (Jeremy Travis, Bruce Western & Steve Redburn eds., 2014).

iii. Rehabilitation

Rehabilitation constitutes a third utilitarian response to the risks of recidivism. A sentence with a rehabilitative purpose aims to eliminate the need for incapacitation. As with specific deterrence, rehabilitation involves a modification of the defendant's thought processes, but potentially at a more fundamental level. For instance, imagine a thief who steals in order to support an addiction to gambling. At sentencing, the judge says, "I am giving you probation on the condition that you enter and stick with a treatment program for gambling." If the program is successful, the defendant will stop stealing—not merely because of a fear of punishment (specific deterrence), but because the underlying motivation for stealing has been alleviated (rehabilitation).

Confidence in the ability of the criminal justice system to promote rehabilitation has periodically waxed and waned. From a relative high point in the middle decades of the twentieth century, support fell in the 1970s and 1980s—the era when "nothing works" became conventional wisdom.[11] Meanwhile, in the political arena, conservatives, directing their attention to rehabilitative programming in prisons, expressed concern that incarceration was "too soft," and liberals worried that the open-ended sentences associated with the rehabilitative approach might result in racial disparities and in prison terms that were longer than deserved. Concerns were also raised that rehabilitative interventions could be overly intrusive into the defendant's autonomy and the private spaces of the defendant's mind—a perspective that was chillingly reflected, for instance, in the popular film and novel *A Clockwork Orange*.

More recently, rehabilitation has regained some of its lost luster. *See, e.g.*, Francis T. Cullen, *Rehabilitation: Beyond Nothing Works*, 42 CRIME & JUST. 299 (2013). To be sure, no rehabilitative program can

[11] This grim assessment was often attributed to a well-known article by the sociologist Robert Martinson, although Martinson's views were not actually so categorically negative as they were often made out to be. *See* Robert Martinson, *What Works? Questions and Answers About Prison Reform*, 35 PUB. INTEREST 22 (1974).

claim anything close to 100% success with all types of defendants. However, careful studies often find that good programs are able to reduce the recidivism rate of participants by about ten percentage points or more, in comparison with untreated defendants who are otherwise similar. Nana A. Landenberger & Mark W. Lipsey, *The Positive Effect of Cognitive-Behavioral Programs for Offenders: A Meta-Analysis of Factors Associated With Effective Treatment*, 1 J. EXPERIMENTAL CRIMINOLOGY 451, 460 (2005). Additionally, public-opinion polling has revealed widespread public support for rehabilitation as an important objective for the criminal justice system. Michael O'Hear & Darren Wheelock, *Imprisonment Inertia and Public Attitudes Toward "Truth in Sentencing,"* 2015 B.Y.U. L. REV. 257.

The leading approach to rehabilitation in the early twenty-first century is described as the "RNR" model, standing for risk-needs-responsivity. D.A. (Don) Andrews, *The Risk-Need-Responsivity (RNR) Model of Correctional Assessment and Treatment*, *in* USING SOCIAL SCIENCE TO REDUCE VIOLENT OFFENDING 127, 128 (Joel A. Dvoskin et al. eds., 2011). The "risk" dimension involves the systematic assessment of defendant risk, as with an actuarial risk assessment instrument (see previous subsection), and the concentration of treatment and supervision resources on relatively high-risk defendants. Indeed, the research indicates that rehabilitative efforts with low-risk defendants are apt to have little positive effect and may even increase risk. (Can you think of any reasons why it might be counterproductive to require a low-risk, first-time defendant to spend, say, thirty hours in group therapy sessions with other convicted defendants?) The "needs" dimension involves an individualized assessment of the defendant's criminogenic needs, i.e., the changeable factors that contribute to the defendant's risk, such as drug dependence. Finally, the "responsivity" dimension involves matching the defendant with appropriate services to address his or her specific criminogenic needs, taking into account considerations that might make the defendant more or less responsive to different sorts of programs, such as age, sex, English language proficiency, education level, and mental illness.

In cases in which the judge wishes to emphasize the utilitarian goal of crime-prevention, the RNR model and related research may have important implications for the way that the sentence is crafted. Judges normally have the authority to condition a probationary sentence on the defendant's participation in rehabilitative treatment, such as anger management or drug abuse programs. However, as already noted, the risk principle indicates that treatment is often ineffective or even counterproductive with low-risk defendants, which suggests that judges might want to take into account each defendant's individual circumstances, rather than automatically requiring everyone who has been convicted of a certain crime to participate in a certain program. Judges should also be aware of the treatment resources in their communities. In smaller communities, for instance, it may not be possible to find programs that address a defendant's criminogenic needs in a manner that is consistent with the responsivity principle. Meanwhile, in big cities, there are apt to be many programs available, but the quality of programs can vary widely, and good programs may have long waiting lists.

A frustrated judge might be inclined to fall back on incarceration when effective treatment in the community seems unlikely. That inclination may be greater if the judge knows that the prison system has programming that would be suitable for the defendant. However, good prison-based programs also often have waiting lists, and there is normally no assurance that a particular defendant will get the treatment that a sentencing judge desires, even if the judge specifically recommends that corrections officials place the defendant in a certain program. Additionally, research suggests that treatment tends to be more effective when delivered in the community than behind bars. *See, e.g.*, Martin Schmucker & Friedrich Losel, *The Effects of Sexual Offender Treatment on Recidivism: An International Meta-Analysis of Sound Quality Evaluations*, 11 J. EXPERIMENTAL CRIMINOLOGY 597, 621 (2015) (discussing research on sex-offender treatment). Can you think of any reasons why this might be so? In the end, if a defendant is to be diverted from prison, the defense lawyer may have a critical role to play in finding and securing a place for the defendant in an appropriate community-based program. If defense counsel is unable or unwilling to play such a role—which may strike some as more akin to social work than lawyering—do you think a prosecutor might ever have a responsibility to help get a defendant into a rehabilitative program as an alternative to incarceration?

c. FINANCIAL AND HUMAN COSTS OF PUNISHMENT

A criminal sentence may have a beneficial crime-prevention effect, but that fact alone does not necessarily make the sentence appropriate from a utilitarian standpoint. Recall Beccaria's ideal—"the greatest happiness shared among the greatest number." If some future crimes are prevented by a sentence, those who would have been victimized otherwise are likely made happier, but the punishment may cause an even greater degree of *un*happiness for others in the community. For instance, imagine a law that requires a sentence of five years in prison for shoplifting. It is likely that the law would deter some prospective shoplifters, thus potentially achieving an overall reduction in crime. However, some other individuals who are exceptionally reckless, desperate, or ignorant might still attempt retail thefts, possibly leading to at least a few of the five-year prison terms actually being imposed. With the annual per-inmate cost of incarceration running in the tens of thousands of dollars, the shoplifting law might conceivably impose fiscal burdens on taxpayers that exceed the value of the additional goods that would have been stolen without the law. Such an imbalance would hardly appear to provide for the "greatest happiness shared among the greatest number."

Making the point that the costs of punishment should also be counted—and not just the benefits—Jeremy Bentham, Beccaria's English admirer, asserted, "[A]ll punishment in itself is evil. Upon the principle of utility, if it at all to be admitted, it ought only to be admitted in as far as it promises to exclude some greater evil." JEREMY BENTHAM, AN INTRODUCTION TO THE PRINCIPLES OF MORALS AND LEGISLATION ch. XIII, § 1, II (1907, reprinting revised edition of 1823). Bentham particularly highlighted four "branches" of the evil of punishment:

> 1. The evil of *coercion*, or *restraint*: or the pain which it gives a man not to be able to do the act, whatever it may be, which by the apprehension of punishment he is deterred from doing. This is felt by those by whom the law is *observed*.
>
> 2. The evil of *apprehension*: or the pain which a man, who has exposed himself to punishment, feels at the thoughts of undergoing it. This is felt by those by whom the law has been *broken*, and who feel themselves in *danger* of its being executed upon them.
>
> 3. The evil of *suffrance*: or the pain which a man feels, in virtue of the punishment itself, from the time when he begins to undergo it. This is felt by those by whom the law is broken, and upon whom it comes actually to be executed.
>
> 4. The pain of sympathy, and the other *derivative* evils resulting to the persons who are in *connection* with the several classes of original sufferers just mentioned.

Id. § 4, XIV. Bentham also noted that there might be cases in which there was some "extraordinary value of the services" of the defendant and the "effect of the punishment would be to deprive the community of the benefit of those services." *Id.*, § 4, XVI(2).

Modern researchers and sentencing policymakers have focused on three areas of punishment costs, which partially overlap with the list of "evils" identified by Bentham. First, there are the harms experienced by the person who is punished—what Bentham referred to as the "evil of suffrance." The nature and severity of the harms will depend to a great extent on whether the person is sentenced to incarceration. Researchers have identified a wide range of potential adverse effects from incarceration, involving such areas as physical health, mental health, family relationships, and post-release job prospects. *See* COMM. ON CAUSES & CONSEQUENCES OF HIGH RATES OF INCARCERATION, NAT'L RESEARCH COUNCIL OF THE NAT'L ACADS., THE GROWTH OF INCARCERATION IN THE UNITED STATES: EXPLORING CAUSES AND CONSEQUENCES chs. 6–8 (Jeremy Travis, Bruce Western & Steve Redburn eds., 2014). On the other hand, while the adverse effects may be less intense, probation and other nonincarcerative sentences are not necessarily experienced as trivial inconveniences. Indeed, some defendants might prefer a short term of incarceration over a longer term of probation, which can entail onerous (and often expensive) conditions. In one study, for instance, nearly one-third of defendants indicated that they would choose one year of prison over three years of probation. Ronald Corbett, *The Burdens of Leniency: The Changing Face of Probation*, 99 MINN. L. REV. 1697, 1711 (2015).

Second, there are the harms experienced by the defendant's family—an aspect of what Bentham called the "derivative evils" of punishment. For instance, the financial aspects of a sentence, including fines and restitution, may represent a devastating economic blow for a family. But incarceration may present the greatest challenge for many families, especially when the defendant has young children. Indeed, more than one-half of prisoners have children under the age of eighteen, and most of these parents report that they were the primary source of financial support and/or daily caregiving for their children prior to their incarceration. LAUREN GLAZE & LAURA MARUSCHAK, U.S. DEP'T OF JUSTICE, PARENTS IN PRISON AND THEIR MINOR CHILDREN 1, 5 (2010). Not surprisingly, then, researchers have found associations between parental incarceration and various adverse outcomes for children, including homelessness; need for food assistance; behavioral problems, including juvenile delinquency; and dropping out of school. *See* COMM. ON CAUSES & CONSEQUENCES OF HIGH RATES OF INCARCERATION, *supra*, ch. 9. Such research findings may call to mind Bentham's concern that punishment may deprive the community of "extraordinary" services that would otherwise be rendered by the defendant. Although it may not be quite what Bentham contemplated, perhaps parenting ought to be considered an extraordinary community service.[12]

Third, and finally, there are the fiscal burdens of punishment that must ultimately be borne by taxpayers. The exact per-inmate costs vary greatly from state to state and, even within states, from institution to institution. One survey found that costs in 2010 ranged from an average of $14,603 per inmate in Kentucky to $60,076 in New York. COMM. ON

---

[12] Some researchers have explored the possibility of another layer of "derivative evils": the cumulative impact of incarceration on those neighborhoods that have been most severely affected by the extraordinarily high rates of incarceration in the United States in the late twentieth and early twenty-first century—neighborhoods that often also experience high rates of poverty and other forms of disadvantage. The continual cycling of residents in and out of prison may create chronic social instability in these neighborhoods and thereby exacerbate other social problems. For instance, Todd Clear asserts, "Concentrated incarceration in those impoverished communities has broken families, weakened the social control capacity of parents, eroded economic strength, soured attitudes toward society, and distorted politics; even after reaching a certain level, it has increased rather than decreased crime." TODD R. CLEAR, IMPRISONING COMMUNITIES: HOW MASS INCARCERATION MAKES DISADVANTAGED NEIGHBORHOODS WORSE 5 (2007). However, researchers have struggled to isolate the independent effects of mass incarceration on neighborhoods, as distinct from the many other interconnected forms of disadvantage that may afflict a community. For a review of the research evidence, see COMM. ON CAUSES & CONSEQUENCES OF HIGH RATES OF INCARCERATION, *supra*, ch. 10.

CAUSES & CONSEQUENCES OF HIGH RATES OF INCARCERATION, *supra*, at 316. Community-based sentences tend to be much less expensive to administer, although the costs may grow proportionately larger with more rigorous forms of supervision, such as electronic monitoring, or the provision of rehabilitative programming. The criminal justice system often tries to shift such financial burdens back to defendants through fees and court costs, but it can be difficult to achieve much success on this front due to the high rates of indigency in the defendant population.

As Bentham observed, the utilitarian approach to punishment cannot be implemented coherently if there is no effort to balance the crime-prevention benefits of punishment against the costs. On the other hand, assessing costs and benefits presents major analytical challenges—both at the level of projecting the potential future consequences of punishment decisions, and in the need to compare fundamentally dissimilar sorts of outcomes. Is it worth $100,000 of incarceration costs to prevent one violent assault? Does the answer depend on the severity of the injuries or who the victim is? And what if the defendant is the primary breadwinner in his or her family—how should the impact of incarceration on the defendant's family be weighed in relation to the other potential costs and benefits? It is not hard to imagine many additional difficult questions that might arise when determining whether a punishment is justified based on costs and benefits.

2. RETRIBUTION (DESERT) AND PROPORTIONALITY

As we have seen, the utilitarian approach to punishment is *forward*-looking. At the level of either policymaking or individual-case decisionmaking, the utilitarian approach involves consideration of the likely future effects of different sentencing options. By contrast, the retributive approach is *backward*-looking—that is, from the retributive perspective, sentences should be based on an evaluation of the blameworthiness of what the defendant did in committing the crime for which he or she is being punished. Put differently, the sentence aims to give the defendant what he or she *deserves*. For this reason, the retributive approach is sometimes referred to as "just deserts."

Retribution requires a sentence that is *proportional* to the severity of the crime—the more blameworthy the defendant's conduct was, the greater should be the punishment.[13] But the flipside is no less important

[13] Some commentators refer to proportionality in a different, forward-looking, utilitarian sense. The goal of "ends-benefits proportionality" has been defined as requiring that "the public and private costs and burdens of a criminal penalty (or of an increased penalty) should not outweigh the expected benefits (or added benefits) of that penalty." RICHARD S. FRASE, JUST SENTENCING: PRINCIPLES AND PROCEDURES FOR A WORKABLE SYSTEM 32 (2013). This is essentially the same as saying that the sentence should be cost-benefit-justified, taking into account the noneconomic costs of the sentence. *Id.* at 33. However, we will use the term "proportionality" exclusively in its backward-looking sense, that is, as referring to a suitable correspondence between the severity of the sentence and the severity of the offense conduct.

to the retributive approach—conduct that had little or no blameworthiness should result in little or no punishment. Meanwhile, conduct that had only moderate blameworthiness should result in only moderate punishment. The concept of proportionality thus implies a measure of restraint in punishment. In this sense, retribution can be contrasted with vengeance, which has been defined as "punishment inflicted by victims *to whatever degree will satisfy them.*" Jeffrie G. Murphy, *Retribution,* 4 REFORMING CRIMINAL JUSTICE: PUNISHMENT, INCARCERATION, AND RELEASE 1, 11 (Erik Luna ed., 2017) (emphasis added). As the philosopher Jeffrie Murphy observes, "[Vengeance] will, of course, often involve inflicting a level of punishment far in excess of what wrongdoers actually deserve as a matter of justice or, if certain victims are committed to the values of love and forgiveness, punishments far less than the wrongdoers actually deserve as a matter of justice." *Id.*

a. IMPLEMENTING DESERT-BASED PROPORTIONALITY

Stated as an abstract proposition, there are probably few people who would disagree that the severity of a punishment should normally be proportionate to the severity of the crime. As we have seen, this was part of Beccaria's reform agenda, and his call for proportionality in punishment resonated widely. *See, e.g.,* GORDON S. WOOD, EMPIRE OF LIBERTY: A HISTORY OF THE EARLY REPUBLIC, 1789–1815, at 492 (2009) (noting efforts by drafters of state constitutions in Revolutionary War era to codify the proportionality ideal). But how exactly does one translate this abstract proposition into practice? What would be a proportionate punishment for armed robbery? For sexual assault? For public intoxication? Upon reflection, the analytical challenges involved in determining a retributively appropriate punishment may strike you as no less daunting than those we have considered in relation to utilitarianism.

Beccaria himself had remarkably little to say about these difficulties beyond indicating that "the true measure of crimes" is "the injury caused to society." CESARE BECCARIA, ON CRIMES AND PUNISHMENTS AND OTHER WRITINGS 20 (Aaron Thomas ed., Aaron Thomas & Jeremy Parzen trans., 2008) (1764). Thomas Jefferson, one of Beccaria's American admirers, tried his hand at crafting a more specific system of proportionate punishment in a proposal he drafted in 1779 for the Virginia Legislature, the so-called "Bill for Proportioning Crimes and Punishments." A modern historian describes some of the notable features this way:

> Murder by poison was punished with death by poison. The body of a convicted challenger in a duel was to be gibbeted [publicly displayed] after being hanged. Perfect symmetry was achieved for other crimes against the person. . . . [R]ape was punished by castration, maiming and disfigurement by retaliation in kind.

Kathryn Preyer, *Cesare Beccaria and the Founding Fathers, in* BLACKSTONE IN AMERICA: SELECTED ESSAYS OF KATHRYN PREYER 239,

243 (Mary Sarah Bilder, Maeva Marcus & R. Kent Newmyer eds., 2009). Convicted of biting off your victim's thumbs in a brawl? Under Jefferson's proposal, you would be sentenced to lose your own thumbs. Nancy J. King, *The Origins of Felony Jury Sentencing in the United States*, 78 CHICAGO-KENT L. REV. 937, 951 (2003). The bill was defeated by a single vote.

Jefferson's bill reflected a certain way of thinking about proportionality that is sometimes called *lex talionis* (literally, the law of retaliation), or, more familiarly, "an eye for an eye." The goal is to inflict on the defendant an injury that is equivalent, or at least closely comparable, to the injury that he or she has caused. However, "talionic" proportionality would encounter a variety of practical and ethical difficulties if it were made the primary guiding principle for contemporary sentencing. In relation to violent crimes, many would feel uncomfortable with the state's intentional infliction of retaliatory violence on its own citizens. Even the death penalty—which might be thought of as the most well-established talionic punishment for violent crime in the United States—has declined markedly in popularity in recent years. In relation to *property* crimes, many perpetrators are indigent and so would be unable to make restitution for what they have taken or damaged. In theory, forced labor—which was part of Jefferson's plan for dealing with property crimes—could work as a type of restitution, but might be costly to administer. And then there are the vast swathes of modern criminal codes dealing with conduct that does not necessarily produce clear, tangible harms—for instance, drug and other vice offenses, DUI, disorderly conduct, bail-jumping, and many business regulatory offenses. Satisfactory talionic punishments might prove especially difficult for such crimes.

Modern thinking about desert and proportionality has moved away from *lex talionis* and, more generally, from the Beccarian emphasis on magnitude of the injury. Instead of injury, the contemporary touchstone for proportionality is the more amorphous concept of *culpability*, or blameworthiness. For instance, the Supreme Court has observed, "With respect to retribution—the interest in seeing that the offender gets his 'just deserts'—*the severity of the appropriate punishment necessarily depends on the culpability of the offender.*" *Atkins v. Virginia*, 536 U.S. 304, 319 (2002) (emphasis added). Importantly, culpability turns to a great extent on the offender's state of mind at the time of the offense. In a culpability-based system of punishment, distinctions can be drawn between offenders who caused seemingly equivalent injuries. Thus, the Supreme Court has decided that retribution can justify capital punishment in some cases of homicide, but not in others—even though in a sense all homicides involve the same type of injury. For instance, the Court has held that retribution cannot justify imposing the death penalty on intellectually disabled individuals who have been convicted of murder, noting that

> [T]hey have diminished capacities to understand and process information, to communicate, to abstract from mistakes and learn from experience, to engage in logical reasoning, to control impulses, and to understand the reactions of others. There is no evidence that they are more likely to engage in criminal conduct than others, but there is abundant evidence that they often act on impulse rather than pursuant to a premeditated plan, and that in group settings they are followers rather than leaders. Their deficiencies do not warrant an exemption from criminal sanctions, but they do diminish their personal culpability.

Id. at 318 (citations omitted).

If culpability is used as the key measure of desert, then sentencers can more readily draw distinctions that may strike you as morally important to recognize, as between provoked, heat-of-passion killings and coolly premeditated assassinations. However, the turn to state of mind comes at a price: punishment may depend on the reconstruction of a person's subjective intentions at a past moment in time—intentions that were not likely openly expressed, may have existed only momentarily, and may not have been entirely clear to the person himself or herself. (Have *you* ever felt puzzled about why you did something you later regretted?) The elusive nature of state of mind was precisely the reason that Beccaria favored injury-based proportionality over intent-based. *See* BECCARIA, *supra*, at 19 ("Intention depends upon the impression objects make at any given time and upon the preceding disposition of the mind; these vary between men and in the same man with the rapid succession of ideas, passions, and circumstances.").

Although there remains no precise, generally accepted method for measuring offense severity, there is widespread agreement as to the basic considerations that make a crime relatively more or less blameworthy. *See* Kevin M. Carlsmith, John M. Darley & Paul H. Robinson, *Why Do We Punish? Deterrence and Just Deserts as Motives for Punishment*, 83 J. PERSONALITY & SOC. PSYCHOL. 284, 285 (2002) (citing studies). Different theorists use different terminology, but the essential points may be expressed through a four-dimensional model of culpability:

- The greater the *harm* caused by a person's conduct, the more culpable he or she is.
- The more *dangerous* a person's conduct—measured by the likelihood that a harm would occur and the severity of that harm—the more culpable he or she is.
- The greater the *intentionality* of the person with respect to the harm or danger—encompassing notions of conscious awareness and deliberateness—the more culpable he or she is.
- The greater the *justification* for the person's conduct—assessed by reference to the presence or perception of

legitimate countervailing benefits—the less culpable he or she is.[14]

This is not to say that all four dimensions are necessarily of equal importance. In particular, contemporary desert theorists tend to place greatest emphasis on the subjective (i.e., state-of-mind) aspects of culpability. Indeed, some go so far as to argue that the occurrence (or non-occurrence) of harm is entirely irrelevant to how much punishment a person deserves. On this view, for instance, the same punishment would be imposed for the crime of *attempted* murder as for a successfully completed murder that is otherwise similar. This position has generated a lively academic debate, although it seems that most laypeople agree that harm does matter. *See, e.g.*, Larry Alexander & Kimberly Kessler Ferzan, *Results Don't Matter*, *in* CRIMINAL LAW CONVERSATIONS 147, 149 (Paul H. Robinson, Stephen P. Garvey & Kimberly Kessler Ferzan, eds., 2009). Courts also tend to see harm as an important part of the retributive calculus. *See, e.g., Kennedy v. Louisiana*, 554 U.S. 407, 442 (2008) (holding that retribution does not justify death penalty for rape of child because the nature of the harm is distinguishable from that of murder; the "goal of retribution . . . reflects society's and the victim's interests in seeing that the offender is repaid for *the hurt he caused*" (emphasis added)).

However culpability is measured in a given case, the modern approach to proportionality emphasizes aligning the *relative* severity of the offender's conduct with the *relative* severity of the punishment. Such a system of "ordinal" proportionality might again be usefully contrasted with *lex talionis*, which seeks to match punishments to offenses based on their inherent character—recall, for instance, Jefferson's proposal to poison the poisoner. Under ordinal proportionality, it is necessary to have an "anchoring point"—an established level of penal severity for the most serious category of offenses. With aggravated murder normally considered to sit atop the scale of offense seriousness, in most U.S. jurisdictions the current anchoring point of penal severity would be either death or life without the possibility of parole (LWOP), depending on the jurisdiction.[15] One might then imagine a culpability-based

---

[14] This model is developed in more detail in Michael M. O'Hear, *Sentencing the Green-Collar Offender: Punishment, Culpability, and Environmental Crime*, 95 J. CRIM. L. & CRIMINOLOGY 133, 156–59 (2004). It is loosely based on the four-factor model set forth in HYMAN GROSS, A THEORY OF CRIMINAL JUSTICE 77–82 (1979). Consistent with leading contemporary approaches to desert theory, this model focuses chiefly on *offense*, as opposed to *offender*, characteristics. Whether, and to what extent, offender characteristics have a role to play in retributive proportionality is a matter of controversy—perhaps most importantly with respect to criminal history. For an overview of the debate over criminal history, see RICHARD S. FRASE, JUST SENTENCING: PRINCIPLES AND PROCEDURES FOR A WORKABLE SYSTEM 181–87 (2013). We consider the use of criminal history and other offender characteristics in more detail in Chapter 4.

[15] Note that the concept of ordinal proportionality does not, in itself, provide a way for determining whether death, LWOP, or some other punishment is the "right" anchoring point. In order to answer that question, we might have recourse, for instance, to utilitarian considerations, or to other, non-ordinal ways of thinking about desert.

ranking of offenses moving down from aggravated murder to, say, criminal trespass or whatever else might sit at the bottom of the culpability scale, and also a parallel ranking of punishments going down from death (or LWOP) to, say, a small fine. Keeping in mind these hypothetical, parallel rankings, ordinal proportionality would aim for a correspondence between culpability and punishment in relative terms. Thus, the second-most-severe offense (non-aggravated murder) would get the second-most-severe sentence (some very long term in prison). A mid-level offense (say, theft from person) would get a mid-level sentence (say, six months in jail). And so forth.

The approach to proportionality described here may provide a helpful way to structure the analysis of what desert demands in a given case, but we still seem a long way from a precise formula for retributive punishment.[16] For one thing, reasonable minds can—and often do—differ on the relative culpability of different offenses. Consider this hypothetical. A paid assassin lies concealed by the side of a quiet country road, expecting her target to arrive soon on his regular morning jog. As the target comes into view, the assassin aims her gun and squeezes the trigger. At just that moment, though, a drunk driver, careening down the road at 80 miles per hour, strikes the jogger from behind. The jogger is saved from the assassin's bullet but dies anyway as a result of the impact from the car. Whose culpability is greater—the assassin who caused no harm, or the drunk driver who accidentally killed? (Recall the debate over whether harm matters to culpability.) Would your answer be affected by knowing that the assassin suffered from a severe mental illness (though not so severe as to satisfy the legal requirements of the insanity defense)? That the assassin believed that the target was a serial child abuser whose death would save many other potential victims from assault? That the drunk driver had multiple prior DUI convictions and was driving with a suspended license? That the drunk driver, although knowing that he had struck the jogger, sped away without rendering aid or calling 911? That the assassin, filled immediately with remorse after pulling the trigger, called 911 and performed CPR until the ambulance arrived in a futile effort to save the jogger's life? Whether, and to what

[16] To be sure, there are some theorists who believe that the concept of ordinal proportionality can be developed and implemented in ways that would assign a clear, specific level of punishment to any given offense. *See, e.g.,* Paul H. Robinson, *Empirical Desert, in* CRIMINAL LAW CONVERSATIONS 29, 31–32 (Paul H. Robinson, Stephen P. Garvey & Kimberly Kessler Ferzan eds., 2009). However, that view has been sharply contested. *See, e.g.,* Michael O'Hear, *Plea Bargaining and Procedural Justice*, 42 GA. L. REV. 407, 441 (2008).

In recognition of differing views regarding the desirability and feasibility of translating the desert ideal into a singular "correct" degree of punishment that must be imposed in each case, theorists distinguish between "positive" and "negative" versions of retribution. Positive retributivism demands that sentences be determined based solely on desert considerations. Negative, or "limiting," retributivism sees desert as a less certain, more flexible concept—a range, not a point. Within the limits set by desert, negative retributivists would permit the consideration of utilitarian or other factors. R.A. DUFF, PUNISHMENT, COMMUNICATION, AND COMMUNITY 137–38 (2001).

extent, any of these considerations should affect desert might well be a matter of sharp dispute.

In addition to such difficulties in assessing the relative severity of an *offense*, there may also be important challenges in evaluating the relative severity of a *punishment*. Of particular note has been a recent academic debate that is based on insights emerging from the field of "positive psychology," or the "science of happiness." Researchers in the field have demonstrated a curious phenomenon called "hedonic adaptation." In essence, long-term happiness is much less affected than most people assume it will be by seemingly major life events, whether good (e.g., winning a lottery) or bad (e.g., becoming permanently disabled). JOHN BRONSTEEN, CHRISTOPHER BUCCAFUSCO & JONATHAN S. MASUR, HAPPINESS AND THE LAW 15–19 (2014). Arguably, this phenomenon might make the achievement of proportionality a much trickier matter. Consider a sentence of imprisonment. Proportionality is normally understood to dictate a longer term behind bars for defendants who acted with greater culpability. For instance, all else being equal, if the robber who only pretends to carry a gun gets five years in prison, then the robber who actually carries a gun and causes a physical injury with it should get an even longer term, say, ten years. But what if, due to hedonic adaptation to prison life, years six through ten are not especially difficult on the inmate? Conceivably the total amount of suffering caused by a ten-year term may be only very little more than that caused by a five-year term. Does that imply that the "bad" robber must get some extremely long term—maybe even life—so as to ensure that his sentence is suitably more severe than that of the "good" robber? And, if so, how is proportionality to be preserved in the relative sentencing of murderers and other defendants whose culpability is even worse than that of the "bad" robber?[17]

In addition to hedonic adaptation, a variety of other personal differences between defendants might cause prison terms of equivalent length to result in quite different levels of actual suffering. For instance, a claustrophobe might find each day behind bars far more psychologically taxing than other inmates. Or a parent with small children at home might find the loss of family connection to be especially devastating. Consider, also, the heightened risk of sexual assault in prison facing

---

[17] Hedonic adaptation might also have implications for deterrence, which also in a sense requires a proper calibration of penal severity, although subject to a potentially important qualification: what matters from a crime-prevention standpoint is not the amount of suffering that is actually experienced by offenders, but the amount that is *anticipated* by prospective offenders. David Gray, *Punishment as Suffering*, 63 VAND. L. REV. 1619, 1626 (2010). If prospective offenders fail to take hedonic adaptation into account, then the phenomenon would not diminish the deterrence benefits of a prison sentence. On the other hand, hedonic adaptation may still have relevance to the "cost" side of the utilitarian cost-benefit analysis, suggesting that what Bentham called the "evil of suffrance" may be rather less than is commonly assumed.

some inmates, based on sex, size, strength, physical appearance, sexual orientation, and physical or mental disability, among other factors.[18]

In response, some theorists argue that the point of retributive proportionality is not to deliver some particular degree of suffering to each convicted defendant, but to communicate a certain level of censure, or condemnation. Dan Markel, Chad Flanders & David Gray, *Beyond Experience: Getting Retributive Justice Right*, 99 CAL. L. REV. 605 (2011). They maintain that different terms of imprisonment can effectively communicate different degrees of censure, regardless of the prisoner's personal experience of suffering behind bars. They invite us to

> imagine an offender who opposes his sentence initially but realizes over time that his experience of incarceration is warranted and in fact serves as an opportunity for personal reform. He pursues self-education, counsels fellow prisoners, apologizes to his victims, and thereafter does good within the prison, deriving a deep sense of contentment. The message of condemnation is not lost on him, nor does his coerced constraint cease to be punishment merely because he subjectively experiences contentment.

Id. at 614. In the end, the debate over the relevance of actual suffering to proportionality may require us to consider with greater depth why exactly it is that sentencers should care about desert.

b. WHY SHOULD DESERT MATTER FOR PUNISHMENT?

At first blush, it may seem absurd to question why desert should matter for punishment. After all, there seems an innate human desire to see people who have acted badly "get what is coming to them." Indeed, neurological researchers have found an association between punishment and stimulation of the reward centers of the brain. Mark R. Fondacaro & Megan J. O'Toole, *American Punitiveness and Mass Incarceration: Psychological Perspectives on Retributive and Consequentialist Responses to Crime*, 18 NEW CRIM. L. REV. 477, 483 (2015). And if people generally *want* punishment for bad actors based on their culpability, doesn't it seem natural—even affirmatively desirable—for government in a democratic society to accommodate this public preference?

On the other hand, just because a preference is widespread and deeply rooted in the human psyche does not necessarily mean that its accommodation should become an explicit objective for the agencies of government. For instance, from a very young age—perhaps even infancy—children categorize people based on race, gender, and other

[18] In a similar spirit, we might also question whether retributive punishment should be reduced if the defendant has already suffered some significant non-state-imposed harm as a result of the crime, e.g., if an armed robber accidentally shoots himself or a drunk driver is severely injured in a car accident. Such "natural punishment" is explicitly recognized as a basis for mitigation in the law of other countries, but not in American law. Raff Donelson, *Natural Punishment*, 100 N.C. L. REV. 557 (2022).

personal characteristics, and show a preference for those who belong to their "group." ALISON GOPNIK, THE PHILOSOPHICAL BABY: WHAT CHILDREN'S MINDS TELL US ABOUT TRUTH, LOVE, AND THE MEANING OF LIFE 218 (2009). Yet, no matter how innate these tendencies, most Americans today would probably reject the idea that government should engage as a matter of course in intentional group-based discrimination. In a system of government that includes a commitment to equal individual rights, public sentiment should not always become public policy.

Indeed, critics of retributive approaches to punishment have argued that retributive impulses are inherently connected to precisely those darker aspects of the human psyche, such as tendencies to cruelty and hatred of those who are different, that should be regarded as especially dubious grounds for government action. *See, e.g.*, James Q. Whitman, *A Plea Against Retributivism*, 7 BUFF. CRIM. L. REV. 85, 106 (2003) ("The very activity of 'blaming' tends to excite people, and indeed to bring out unexpectedly savage and vindictive impulses."). In response, theorists of retributivism have attempted to show that they successfully "resist slavery to emotions like anger and bloodlust in favor of cool reason." David Gray, *Punishment as Suffering*, 63 VAND. L. REV. 1619, 1657 (2010).

Retributive theorists have produced a rich and varied literature in an effort to show why "giving offenders what they deserve" should be regarded not just as a matter of widespread intuitive preference, but also as a permissible—perhaps even an obligatory—basis for official action by the criminal justice system. We cannot hope to do more than scratch the surface of this literature, which might make for a fascinating course in its own right. Our consideration will be limited to just three of the more influential approaches to desert. The approaches contrast with one another to some extent, but you will also probably note several important shared themes.[19]

First, there is the view that the offender has a *right to be punished*. The position has been developed in a variety of different ways, but we

---

[19] Our brief survey largely bypasses what is likely the most historically influential exposition of the retributive point of view, that of the German philosopher Immanuel Kant (1724–1804), a contemporary and vociferous critic of both Beccaria and Bentham. Rejecting their utilitarianism, Kant wrote, "The law concerning punishment is a categorical imperative, and woe to him who rummages around in the winding paths of a theory of happiness looking for some advantage to be gained by releasing the criminal from punishment or reducing the amount of it. . . ." THE METAPHYSICAL ELEMENTS OF JUSTICE (John Ladd trans., 1965) (1798), *reprinted in* WHY PUNISH? HOW MUCH? A READER ON PUNISHMENT 31, 32 (Michael Tonry ed., 2011). Kant famously argued,

> Even if a civil society were to dissolve itself by common agreement of all of its members (for example, if the people inhabiting an island decided to separate and disperse themselves around the world), the last murderer remaining in prison must first be executed, so that everyone will duly receive what his actions are worth and so that the bloodguilt thereof will not be fixed on the people because they failed to insist on carrying out the punishment; for if they fail to do so, they may be regarded as accomplices in this public violation of legal justice.

Id. at 33.

will focus on that of the American philosopher Herbert Morris in his much-cited 1968 article, *Persons and Punishment*, 52 MONIST 475 (1968). Morris argues that the right to be punished derives from a "fundamental human right to be treated as a person." *Id.* at 476. Morris sees in our core criminal law provisions—the prohibitions on violence, theft, and so forth—a set of rules that collectively establish for each person a sphere of freedom from interference by others. But, Morris observes,

> Making possible this mutual benefit is the assumption by individuals of a burden. The burden consists in the exercise of self-restraint by individuals over inclinations that would, if satisfied, directly interfere or create a substantial risk of interference with others in proscribed ways. If a person fails to exercise self-restraint even though he might have and gives in to such inclinations, he renounces a burden which others have voluntarily assumed and thus gains an advantage which others, who have restrained themselves, do not possess.

Id. at 477.

This renunciation of self-restraint, Morris argues, warrants punishment:

> A person who violates the rules has something others have—the benefits of the system—but by renouncing what others have assumed, the burdens of self-restraint, he has acquired an unfair advantage. Matters are not even until this advantage is in some way erased. Another way of putting it is that he owes something to others, for he has something that does not rightfully belong to him. Justice—that is punishing such individuals—restores the equilibrium of benefits and burdens by taking from the individual what he owes, that is, exacting the debt.[20]

Id. at 478. Notably, the Supreme Court has also sometimes discussed retribution in similar terms as a matter of restoring the "moral imbalance" created by an offense. *Graham v. Florida*, 560 U.S. 48, 71 (2010).

Morris emphasizes that just punishment presupposes the offender has *voluntarily* taken *unfair* advantage of the system of burdens and benefits. The offender's *choice* to violate the rules helps to establish the justness of the punishment. In a sense, Morris suggests, "[I]n choosing to do an act violative of the rules an individual has chosen to be punished." Morris, *supra*, at 479. Morris's argument is thus characteristic of retributive thinking more generally in treating choice as a critical prerequisite for punishment—so critical in the minds of some theorists,

---

[20] Does this justification for retributive punishment presuppose that the "equilibrium" that is being restored includes an equitable distribution of the benefits and burdens of social living? If so, are there facets of contemporary American life, such as entrenched wealth inequalities and structural racism, that undermine the legitimacy of retributive punishments?

as we have seen, that actual consequences (i.e., the occurrence or non-occurrence of harm, which may be simply a matter of good or bad luck) cannot justify either increased or decreased punishment.

In contrast to a system that delivers to the offender what "he has brought on himself" through his choices, Morris invites us to consider a system built around the goal of rehabilitation—a system that treats crime not as a choice, but as a sort of mental illness that must be cured. Referring to this as the "therapy system," Morris observes that it would contain no concept of proportionality—a murderer who could be "cured" with a pill would suffer no worse consequence than having to take the pill, while a lifetime of institutionalization might be the consequence for a person who has merely manifested a chronic tendency to "accident proneness." *Id.* at 484. In neither case would the social response to the person's actions be closely tied to what the person has actually chosen. Morris thus argues that the therapy system degrades the importance of human autonomy and effectively treats people like animals. "A person," he asserts, "has a right to institutions that respect his choices. Our [just deserts] punishment system does; our therapy system does not." *Id.* at 486.

Second, there is the *communicative* approach to desert. The Supreme Court itself has sometimes associated retributive punishment with the principle that "[s]ociety is entitled . . . to express its condemnation of [a] crime." *Graham*, 560 U.S. at 71. This intuition that punishment communicates censure has been explored and refined by many desert theorists.[21] We will focus briefly on the thought of one leading contemporary proponent of the communicative approach, the philosopher Antony Duff.

Duff asserts that our criminal laws are, or at least should be, expressions of the core values of our political community about how people should behave toward one another. He argues that a political community "that takes its self-defining values seriously, and that takes its members seriously . . . as citizens who are both bound and protected by those values, cannot ignore violations of those values or the wrongs that citizens do to each other." *Responsibility, Restoration, and Retribution, in* RETRIBUTIVISM HAS A PAST; HAS IT A FUTURE? 63, 72 (Michael Tonry ed., 2011).

When there is a violation of our communal values, and one of our fellow citizens is thereby wronged, Duff contends that we owe a collective duty to the victim. Part of what we owe to victims is to call their

---

[21] The intuition has also been influentially elaborated by a writer working in a different intellectual tradition, the French sociologist Émile Durkheim (1858–1917). Durkeim emphasized the importance of "collective conscience" as a sort of glue that holds society together. He saw criminal punishment as an expression of the collective conscience that was necessary to maintain social cohesion. THE DIVISION OF LABOR IN SOCIETY 108–09 (George Simpson trans., 1933) (1893). *See also* W. John Thomas, *Social Solidarity and the Enforcement of Morality Revisited: Some Thoughts on H.L.A. Hart's Critique of Durkheim*, 32 AM. CRIM. L. REV. 49 (1995).

wrongdoers to account. Moreover, Duff suggests, this is also a duty that "we owe to ourselves collectively in so far as we share those wrongs as their victims' fellow citizens." *Id.* at 73. Further, and reminiscent of Herbert Morris's argument about the offender's "right to be punished," Duff contends that calling the offender to account is also a matter of our collective duty *to the offender*. He observes, "To call someone to account for an alleged wrong . . . [is] to show him a certain kind of respect, or even concern, as a fellow who is, along with us, both bound and protected by the values to which that calling appeals." *Id.*

Duff's theory thus demands public censure for criminal wrongdoers, but why does the censure need to include punishment? Why can't the judge simple deliver a verbal admonition to the offender? Duff contends that a mere scolding from the judge would be too easy for the offender to ignore. The "hard treatment" of criminal punishment "serves as a vehicle for the forceful communication of censure from polity to offender, as a way of focusing the offender's attention on his crime." R.A. Duff, *Guidance and Guidelines*, 105 COLUM. L. REV. 1162, 1183 (2005). Additionally, Duff views punishment not merely as a communication *to* the offender, but also as a communication *from* the offender. He asserts, "What is to be communicated [by the offender] is a kind of symbolic apology, which is given material and thus more forceful expression by the penal 'hard treatment' that the offender undergoes." *Id.* Duff thus favors forms of punishment that demand the offender's active participation—such as community service or probation with required programming—over imprisonment, which he sees as more passive and hence less capable of communicating apology.[22] *Id.* at 1184.

In sum, then, desert-based punishment can be seen as communicative in two senses: the punishment expresses the community's condemnation of the offender's wrongdoing, and also constitutes a sort of "apologetic ritual" on the part of the person who is forced to undergo it. R.A. DUFF PUNISHMENT, COMMUNICATION, AND COMMUNITY 123 (2001). Ultimately, Duff argues, punishment that is appropriately communicative will constitute a sort of "secular penance, which itself serves the aims of repentance, reform, and reconciliation." *Id.* at 80.

Third, and finally, there is the *utilitarian*, or crime-preventive, approach to desert. It may strike you as paradoxical to combine the terms "utilitarian" and "desert," since these are usually discussed as competing purposes of sentencing. From some perspectives, though, these purposes

---

[22] Should we be concerned that many individuals, although forced to undergo a punishment that in some sense communicates apology, will not genuinely feel contrite? You might think here of the parent who "makes" a sullen child apologize after the child has hit a sibling—Duff's view of criminal punishment is not far removed in spirit from such common parental practices. Notwithstanding the potential for insincerity, Duff still sees value in required apologies: "they make clear to the offender what he ought to do (apologize sincerely) and to the victim that the community recognizes and takes seriously the wrong he has suffered." *Responsibility, Restoration, and Retribution, in* RETRIBUTIVISM HAS A PAST; HAS IT A FUTURE? 63, 79 (Michael Tonry ed., 2011).

may be more complementary than contrasting.[23] Perhaps most straightforwardly, there are concerns that, if the criminal justice system does not give offenders their just deserts, then private citizens will be more likely to take matters into their own hands, which may give rise to escalating cycles of vengeance. As Justice Potter Stewart observed, "When people begin to believe that organized society is unwilling or unable to impose upon criminal offenders the punishment they 'deserve,' then there are sown the seeds of anarchy—of self-help, vigilante justice, and lynch law." *Furman v. Georgia*, 408 U.S. 238, 308 (1972) (Stewart, J., concurring).

A more subtle utilitarian justification for desert has been developed by the law professor Paul Robinson, often writing with coauthors.[24] *See, e.g.*, PAUL H. ROBINSON & MICHAEL T. CAHILL, LAW WITHOUT JUSTICE: WHY CRIMINAL LAW DOESN'T GIVE PEOPLE WHAT THEY DESERVE (2006); Paul H. Robinson & John Darley, *The Utility of Desert*, 91 NW. U. L. REV. 453 (1997). Robinson starts with the important, but often overlooked, truth that most people obey the law most of the time, not because they fear formal punishment at the hands of the legal system, but rather because they have internalized the norms of good conduct that are embodied in the law and/or because they fear the *informal* social consequences that can result from being seen as a person who flouts important social norms. Robinson & Darley, *supra*, at 457. (Think, for instance, of the ostracism of a student whom classmates discover to be a cheater, or the impact on a lawyer's career if he or she develops a reputation for dishonesty among his or her professional peers.) Robinson contends that the criminal justice system may best be able to advance utilitarian crime-control objectives by supporting and exploiting these dynamics of self-control and informal social control. Paul H. Robinson, *Empirical Desert, in* CRIMINAL LAW CONVERSATIONS 29, 30 (Paul H. Robinson, Stephen P. Garvey & Kimberly Kessler Ferzan eds., 2009).

More specifically, Robinson argues that the system should strive to criminalize and punish in ways that conform to community views of desert, using a rigorous system of ordinal proportionality, so that the law and the agencies who enforce the law are seen as reliable sources of information about community norms. In this way, the system may strengthen norms that are contested and gain the deference of individuals who are otherwise uncertain about what the norm is in a given situation. Put differently, by consistently giving offenders what they deserve when desert is a matter of clarity and consensus, the commands of the criminal justice system are more likely to be heeded as

---

[23] We have already seen that Beccaria was an advocate of both the utilitarian "greatest happiness" principle and proportionate punishment, albeit an injury-based form of proportionality that most contemporary retributive theorists would find unsatisfactory.

[24] For a thoughtful collection of short critiques of Robinson's theory and a response from Robinson, see CRIMINAL LAW CONVERSATIONS ch. 2 (Paul H. Robinson, Stephen P. Garvey & Kimberly Kessler Ferzan eds., 2009). For additional critical perspectives, see Christopher Slobogin, *Empirical Desert and Preventive Justice: A Comment*, 17 NEW CRIM. L. REV. 376 (2014).

morally authoritative in situations when clarity and consensus are lacking. For instance, if the legal system consistently delivers the deserved punishment to individuals who perpetrate forcible rapes (the profound moral wrongness of which is widely acknowledged), then perhaps the system will have more credibility and receive greater deference when it establishes specific age restrictions for consensual sexual activity between teenagers (an area of relatively less moral consensus).

Finally, in addition to influencing and strengthening informal social controls, Robinson argues that the system's focus on desert may also facilitate the effective functioning of *formal* enforcement mechanisms. "Deviating from a community's intuitions of justice," Robinson contends, "can inspire resistance and subversion among participants—juries, judges, prosecutors, and offenders—where effective criminal justice depends upon acquiescence and cooperation."[25] *Id.* at 29–30.

NOTES & QUESTIONS

1. **"Cool Reason?"** Of the three approaches to desert that we have very briefly summarized, which one seems to you the most persuasive rationale for backward-looking punishments? Are you convinced that any of these approaches really takes retribution out of the realm of "anger and bloodlust" and gives it a firm footing in "cool reason"?

2. **"It Is Morally Right to Hate Criminals."** Or perhaps you are not so convinced that harsh emotional responses to crime have no place in punishment. The eminent English judge and legal theorist Sir James Fitzjames Stephen (1829–1894) famously asserted, "The criminal law . . . proceeds upon the principle that it is morally right to hate criminals, and it confirms and justifies that sentiment by inflicting upon criminals punishments which express it."[26] 2 JAMES FITZJAMES STEPHEN, A HISTORY OF THE CRIMINAL LAW OF ENGLAND 81 (1883), *quoted in* Kenworthey Bilz & John M. Darley, *What's Wrong with Harmless Theories of Punishment*, 79 CHI.-KENT L. REV. 1215, 1218 (2004). Do you agree that punishment should express hatred of criminals? If this view is embraced, isn't there a risk that punishment will devolve into simple cruelty?

3. **Vicious and Virtuous Emotions.** The retributive theorist Michael Moore acknowledges that retributive judgments may be grounded in emotion, but he argues that retributive emotions are not necessarily as

---

[25] A similar observation was made by the arch-utilitarian Jeremy Bentham. *See* JEREMY BENTHAM, AN INTRODUCTION TO THE PRINCIPLES OF MORALS AND LEGISLATION 198–99 (1907, reprinting revised edition of 1823) ("When the people are satisfied with the law, they voluntarily lend their assistance in the execution: when they are dissatisfied, they will naturally withhold that assistance; it is well that they do not take a positive part in raising impediments. This contributes greatly to the uncertainty of the punishment; by which, in the first instance, the frequency of the offence receives an increase.").

[26] The quotation from Stephen has been interpreted in a variety of different ways, with some commentators arguing that Stephen should be viewed as a retributivist and others depicting him as a utilitarian. For a critique of these interpretations, see Marc O. DeGirolami, *Against Theories of Punishment: The Thought of Sir James Fitzjames Stephen*, 9 OHIO ST. J. CRIM. L. 699, 722 (2012).

repellant as critics have made out. Moore contends, "Violations of others' moral rights should make us angry at those who flout that morality, and that anger need not be tainted by cruel, sadistic, fearful, or resentful emotional accompaniments." MICHAEL MOORE, PLACING BLAME: A GENERAL THEORY OF THE CRIMINAL LAW 164 (1997). If it is virtuous to care about others, he questions, "then must it not also be virtuous to feel negatively *in some way* towards flagrant moral violations that hurt others, virtuous to allow such negative feelings to cause retributive judgments?" *Id.* at 144.

In addition to connecting retributive judgments to virtuous feelings of compassion for victims, Moore also connects retributive judgments to virtuous feelings of guilt. He invites us to imagine that we have committed a horrible violent crime that kills an innocent person, and asks us how that would make us feel. He asserts, "My own response, I hope, would be that I would feel guilty unto death. I could not imagine any suffering that could be imposed upon me that would be unfair because it exceeded what I deserved." *Id.* at 145. And if we think that retributive punishment should be imposed on ourselves for own bad acts, Moore challenges, then it would be "elitist and condescending toward others not to grant them the same responsibility and desert." *Id.* at 148–49.

4. **Shaming.** One particularly important context in which the emotions of blaming and punishment have been debated is in relation to "shaming" sanctions, e.g., as a condition of probation, requiring a defendant to wear a sandwich board declaring his or her crime in a public place. Some critics of such practices fear the uncontrollable public emotions that are stirred up by "dangling" an offender before the crowd. James Q. Whitman, *What Is Wrong with Inflicting Shame Sanctions?,* 107 YALE L.J. 1055, 1090 (1998). Shaming may foster a "lynch-mob" mentality and encourage excessive or inappropriate private responses to the offense. We consider shaming sanctions in more detail in Chapter 8.

PROBLEM 1-1: IS A PRISON SENTENCE JUSTIFIED?

It can be challenging to translate the traditional purposes of punishment into a specific sentence in a particular case, especially if the purposes seem to be pushing in opposite directions. Consider, for instance, the facts of *United States v. Blake*, 89 F. Supp. 2d 328 (E.D.N.Y. 2000). The defendant, Summer Blake, faced sentencing for bank robbery. On June 22, 1998, Blake, who was then twenty-one years old, had

> parked her car near a Chase Manhattan Bank in Brooklyn. Entering a nearby building, she walked to the third floor and changed her clothes in a stairwell where she left them. Her new outfit consisted of a pink wig, white sweatshirt, painted blue jeans, and work boots.
>
> Shortly thereafter, she entered the bank and yelled, "This is a stickup." She was brandishing what appeared to be a gun and ordered everyone to the front of the bank. Sheron Nauzo, an assistant manager at Chase, was seated at her desk with a customer when Blake approached her with the gun-like object and

a knife. After Ms. Nauzo assumed a position on the floor, the defendant ordered her to unlock the vault. When she fumbled for her keys, a co-worker unlocked the vault, entered it, and attempted to close the door behind her, leaving Ms. Nauzo and Blake on the other side.

At this point, Blake became agitated and struck at Ms. Nauzo with a knife. Ms. Nauzo was stabbed in the left hand as she attempted to ward off the blow, suffering permanent tendon and nerve damage.

The defendant proceeded behind the teller counter and yelled, "Where's the money?" She then grabbed several rolls of coins and ran from the bank. Witnesses observed her leaving the bank and running in the direction of the building where she had secreted her clothing. They also saw coins falling out of a bag she was carrying.

Members of the civilian Williamsburg Safety Patrol followed Blake to the building and kept it under surveillance until officers from the New York City Police Department arrived. She was located by police in the basement and arrested. When she was discovered, she had stripped down to her underwear. Her clothes and the knife were recovered under the stairwell. The police also recovered the "gun" she had used, which was a toy. No money was recovered from Blake, but $29.75 in coins was found in a lot adjacent to the building.

In a post-arrest statement, Blake admitted her role in the robbery. * * *

Defendant was charged with the crimes of bank robbery (18 U.S.C. § 2113(a)) and assaulting a person or putting his or her life in jeopardy during the commission of the robbery (18 U.S.C. § 2113(d)). She pleaded guilty to both crimes. * * *

Both [of Blake's] parents have a history of drug abuse. Her father apparently still uses narcotics. Beginning at the age of four, Blake would find her mother's drug paraphernalia around the house. * * *

Blake's mother always held a job and financially supported the defendant. Since her mother stopped taking drugs in 1992, she has tried to guide defendant. * * * Her mother, father, other relatives, friends, and a member of the cloth have supported defendant by attending her various appearances in court and in encouraging her rehabilitation attempts.

In October of 1996, when defendant was nineteen, she gave birth to a daughter. Blake's relationship with her child's father ended when she was four months pregnant. At that time, defendant contends that he tried to rape her. He physically assaulted defendant's mother who obtained a restraining order. * * *

Blake's daughter—a pretty and vivacious three year old—lives with defendant and her mother. She is financially supported by them and appears to be a well cared for, intelligent, and happy child.

In April 1997, Blake began a relationship with one Richard Williams that led directly to the crime in question. In August 1997, the defendant began cohabitating with Williams. Physical violence against, and domination of, defendant was endemic. * * *

In March 1998 Blake returned with her daughter to her mother's home. She continued, however, to see Williams; his abuse continued. Williams' financial reliance on Blake also grew. He insisted that she give him $1,800 to obtain his motorcycle which had remained in a repair shop for a year. * * *

The robbery occurred two days after Williams' renewed importuning. The crime's goal was to obtain money to pay for the motorcycle. * * *

Early indications of Blake's psychiatric problems predate the incident. Blake contends that she had previously experienced symptoms of anxiety and depression following a 1997 automobile accident when she was a passenger in a car driven by Williams. She was treated by a psychologist who found her to be "seriously depressed" and recommended psychotherapy. After three visits she terminated treatment. * * *

[Following the bank robbery], Blake was interviewed three times by Dr. Alexandra Bardey, a psychiatrist, in July 1998. Her conclusions were that at the time she committed the crime, Blake suffered from major depression and mixed personality traits with borderline and dependent features. The latter condition is "characterized by fear of abandonment, chaotic relationships, and feelings of emotional emptiness, especially when unattached." As part of this condition, the doctor found that Blake tends to rely on others and is passive and submissive. Moreover, she will go, the doctor opined, to great lengths to maintain a dependent relationship. These traits have, the doctor found, made her prone to being abused. * * *

[Blake] has been in counseling for more than a year and a half. She has attended all of her individual sessions and is an active participant in group therapy.

In addition, defendant has received intense spiritual guidance from Reverend Cheryl G. Anthony of the Judah International Christian Center. Reverend Anthony is one of the many individuals who wrote or appeared in this court on behalf of the defendant.

Sheron Nauzo, the victim of this crime, suffered serious and permanent damage to her hand caused by Blake's knife. In March 1999, she submitted a powerful victim impact statement recounting the incident and her subsequent medical problems. The letter is worth quoting at length.

Ms. Nauzo first described the incident as follows: * * *

> Ms. Blake did severe damage to my left hand, as a result of which I have not been able to return back to work as yet. I had to have a five-hour operation to repair the damage she did to the nerves and tendons in my hand. It's now nine months later, and the feeling still has not fully returned to my thumb, index and middle finger. Neither can I bend the index or thumb fingers fully. The web space between the index and the thumb has shrunken considerably, making it very difficult for me to pick up things, and I have to look forward to the prospect of another operation to correct these problems. * * *
>
> As bad as the physical damage was—the psychological traumas that I suffered and am still suffering were far worse. For the first week after the incident I could not eat nor sleep properly. I kept having panic and anxiety attacks when I closed my eyes. I had nightmares, flashbacks—the works. I have had to seek psychological counseling to deal with the trauma of the attack and am presently still being treated for post-traumatic stress disorder.
>
> My sense of self in the world, as well as a healthy sense of safety in the world, has been drastically altered. I have lost my faith and trust in strangers and my innocence. Sometimes I have difficulty concentrating and experience lots of anger and frustration—hence my inability to return to the world of branch banking. . . . [T]his was a job I did and loved for 16 years with no problems. * * *

[While awaiting sentencing], Blake continued with her education, employment, and therapy. She enrolled at Pace University where she satisfactorily completed her first semester. She is currently attending classes three nights a week. * * *

Blake also sent a letter to the court dated March 2, 2000, expanding on her contrition and feelings of remorse about what she had done to her victim, Ms. Nauzo. The letter reads as follows:

> I am writing to convey my sincerest apologies to Ms. Sheron Nauzo, the other victims of this horrible crime I committed, the institution, the people of that community, but especially Ms. Nauzo. I know and realize that I caused people lives to be changed for the worst on the day of June 22, 1998. I am sincerely sorry and even grieved that I did that awful and even frightful act to the workers of Chase Bank. I have a contrite heart because of the hurt I caused and psychical damaged I did to Ms. Nauzo. I know that the victims are suffering psychologically and even physically in Ms. Nauzo's circumstance. I pray every night for the victims of the bank robbery and their families because it was a day of tragedy for them. Ms. Sharon Nauzo has a right to be angry with me because she did not do anything to deserve what I did to her and I had no right to inflict this pain on her. Thank God, her

> life was not taken because of my malicious actions. I know that she had operations to repair the damages to her hand and she was suppose to have another operation and I hope it went well. I am so sorry that Ms. Nauzo has to go through this. * * * I want to pay all the possible restitution that is necessary for her injuries. I know that it would not make everything right or heal her injuries like her hand, mind, and heart but I feel a need to pay back something I had no right to take away.
>
> * * * I will never allow myself to hurt another human being again. I will continu[e] seeking psychological therapy with Dr. Aponte and contribute to my community through JUDAH International Christian Center until the Court say[s] otherwise. I plead for your mercy in this sentencing and accept whatever sentence you impose.

QUESTIONS

1. **Costs and Benefits.** Do you think Blake should be sentenced to prison? Consider the question first from a utilitarian standpoint. Do you think it likely that any future crimes would be avoided if Blake were imprisoned for, say, three years? If so, would that benefit most likely come from general deterrence, specific deterrence, incapacitation, rehabilitation, or some other mechanism? What seem to you the most important costs of a three-year sentence in *Blake*? Overall, given a choice between the options of either three years in prison or three years of probation, which do you think should be preferred from a utilitarian point of view?

2. **Desert.** Now consider retribution. What would be Blake's "just deserts," taking into account considerations of harm, dangerousness, intent, and justification? What is the image in your mind of a typical robbery? In what ways are the facts in *Blake* aggravated relative to the typical robbery? Mitigated? In trying to come up with a proportionate punishment for Blake, does it help for you to know that the median federal sentence in robbery cases is 92 months in prison? U.S. SENT'G COMM'N, SOURCEBOOK OF FEDERAL SENTENCING STATISTICS tbl. 15 (2019).

3. **Bottom Line.** Putting all of these considerations together, what sentence would you impose if you were the judge in *Blake*?

3. UTILITARIANISM VS. RETRIBUTIVISM: MUST ONE TAKE A SIDE?

Utilitarians and retributivists are often depicted as belonging to warring camps. Over the years, utilitarians have spilled a great deal of ink attacking retributivism, and retributivists have responded in kind. *See, e.g.*, Kenworthey Bilz & John M. Darley, *What's Wrong with Harmless Theories of Punishment*, 79 CHI.-KENT L. REV. 1215, 1217–19 (2004). And there are, to be sure, genuine, deep philosophical differences between some forms of utilitarianism and some forms of retributivism. Earlier, we noted Herbert Morris's complaint that what he called the "therapy system" fails to respect human autonomy and the moral significance of the choices that people make. More broadly, but in the same spirit, retributivists are often heard to charge utilitarians with treating people as "means," not "ends." Some people are to be intimidated (deterrence), caged (incapacitation), and/or manipulated (rehabilitation) so as to make other people happier. Retributivists do not see how this approach to punishment can be reconciled with the ideal of equal respect for the inherent worth and dignity of all human beings.

For their part, utilitarians see a form of cruelty in the retributive insistence that all offenders be given their just punishment even if there is no one who will be made any happier by doing so. They are apt to find nonsensical all of the retributive talk about respecting offenders through punishment. As the law professor Alice Ristroph quips:

> Jails and prisons are unpleasant places where nearly every aspect of a prisoner's life is subject to someone else's control: prisoners are told when (and often, if) they can eat, sleep, shower, read, work, see visitors, and so on. Prisoners are supervised in the shower and at the toilet, strip-searched on occasion, and at all times required to obey the orders of prison officials. With respect like this, who needs insults?

Respect and Resistance in Punishment Theory, 97 CAL. L. REV. 601, 627–28 (2009).

Based on some of the theoretical literature, you may be left with the impression that you must make a seemingly impossible choice: would you rather live in a society that prioritizes justice or happiness? However, the "purist" arguments made by some theoreticians—the arguments that retributive approaches to punishment should be followed to the exclusion of utilitarian, or vice versa—have made little headway with criminal justice policymakers and practitioners. For instance, we have already noted several times in passing the Supreme Court's invocation of a variety of different purposes of punishment, encompassing both retributive and utilitarian approaches. Later in this chapter, we will further consider how policymakers have structured the consideration of diverse purposes at sentencing.

How can we have a sentencing system that embraces both forward-looking utilitarianism and backward-looking retributivism? Perhaps it should not be so surprising that we have a mixed system. Some social science research indicates that laypeople are hardly purists in their thinking about punishment, giving consideration to both utilitarian and retributive approaches, with one or the other weighed more heavily depending on the context. Mark R. Fondacaro & Megan J. O'Toole, *American Punitiveness and Mass Incarceration: Psychological Perspectives on Retributive and Consequentialist Responses to Crime*, 18 NEW CRIM. L. REV. 477, 488–89 (2015). It may not be realistic to expect any greater philosophical purity from policymakers and practitioners than from laypeople.

Moreover, whatever their deep philosophical incompatibilities, utilitarian and retributive approaches may in practice be more complementary than is often assumed. For instance, we have considered Paul Robinson's argument that utilitarian crime-control objectives are best advanced through sentences that reflect popular notions of just punishment. We have also noted various ambiguities in both utilitarian and retributive approaches. Rather than assuming there to be a singular "right" utilitarian or retributive sentence in a given case, it may make more sense to think of a *range* of sentencing outcomes that can be reasonably well-justified on one theory or another. These ranges may be wide enough that there is commonly some overlap between the desert-appropriate sentences and the crime-control-appropriate sentences. (Is this what you found in your analysis of the *Blake* case?) To be sure, academics have no difficulty generating hypotheticals in which utilitarian and retributive approaches would point in starkly different directions. However, such conundrums are not necessarily encountered often in practice.

Even many theorists seem now to have abandoned pure forms of utilitarianism and retributivism. Since the mid-twentieth century, there has been a trend toward "hybrid" approaches that combine backward- and forward-looking in one way or another. Bilz & Darley, *supra*, at 1219–20. One notable hybrid is restorative justice, the topic to which we turn next.

4. VICTIMS AND RESTORATIVE JUSTICE

Thus far, our consideration of purposes of punishment has had little to say about victims. This reflects the traditional orientation of the American criminal justice system, which has emphasized diffuse public interests in crime-prevention and desert over the private interests of the victims of crime. However, with the emergence of a politically powerful victims' rights movement in the United States in the late twentieth-century, policymakers and practitioners increasingly seem to recognize that more consideration ought to be given to victim interests. Julian V. Roberts, *Listening to the Crime Victim: Evaluating Victim Input at Sentencing and Parole*, 38 CRIME & JUST. 347, 347–48 (2009). Often, this enhanced consideration relates more to matters of procedure than substance, for instance, in recognizing a right for victims to speak at sentencing (a topic that we will explore in more depth in Chapter 3). However, some reforms have aimed more directly to alter the substance of sentencing decisions, especially in the area of victim restitution (see Chapter 9). Provocative arguments have been advanced for even more fundamental changes that would place victim restoration at the center of public responses to crime.

The goal of restoring victims might be seen as encompassing both material and psychological dimensions. The material dimension would involve some kind of compensation for the victim, ideally provided by the defendant, to offset the material harm that the victim has experienced. Thus, the vandal who spray paints obscenities on a store window might be required either to compensate the storeowner financially for the cost of removing the paint or to scrape off the paint himself or herself. The drunk driver who causes a collision with another car might be required to pay for the repairs of the other vehicle, as well as any medical care needed by the other driver. In many cases, however, the psychological dimension may be far more important than the material. Recall, for instance, the terrible psychological harm described by the victim in *Blake* (Problem 1-1). Victims may feel degraded by what happened to them or suffer intense, long-term anxiety about the possibility of future victimization. In cases of minor crime, an apology from the defendant may reasonably well address the insult to the victim's dignity, but psychological restoration can be a much more complicated and elusive matter with more serious crimes. Indeed, some victims will carry emotional hurt with them for the rest of their lives and may find patronizing or insulting the use of terms like "healing" and "closure" in reference to their experiences.[27] However, even if a victim cannot be *fully* restored by anything that is done within the criminal justice system, that does not necessarily relieve the system of a responsibility to do what it can to support whatever degree of psychological recovery is possible.

As a purpose of punishment, victim restoration might be assimilated to either utilitarian or retributive frameworks, albeit not without some tension in relation to established ideas about efficient crime-control and just deserts. As a utilitarian matter, the happiness of victims must certainly be taken into account in the business of determining "the greatest happiness shared among the greatest number." At the same time, the utilitarian framework provides no entirely clear basis for regarding the happiness of victims as any more important than the happiness of anyone else. Victim restoration may thus potentially come into conflict with other utilitarian aims. For instance, we earlier noted the view that there may be some particular general-deterrent value to sentences of imprisonment for white-collar defendants. For some of these defendants, however, incarceration will mean the loss of a well-paying job—and with it the ability to pay restitution to victims. Bringing greater attention to victims at sentencing, it should be appreciated, may add another layer of difficulty to the utilitarian cost-benefit tradeoffs.

As to retribution, giving an offender his or her just deserts may be thought of as a symbolic reaffirmation of the victim—an implicit statement by the community that it was indeed the offender who was at

[27] *See, e.g.*, Marilyn Peterson & Mark S. Umbreit, *Exploring "Closure" and the Ultimate Penal Sanction for Survivors of Homicide Victims*, 19 FED. SENT'G RPTR. 105, 105 (2006) ("Studies of family members of homicide victims found that 66% could not find meaning after five years, endured post-homicide distress that did not dramatically lessen over time, and were significantly more likely than other direct crime victims to have lifetime PTSD. In contrast to victims of minor crimes, victims of violent crime suffer significantly more distress including loss of confidence (41% vs. 11%), loss of self-esteem (37% vs. 2%), sleeplessness (27% vs. 9%), and headaches and other physical symptoms (41% vs. 5%)." (citations omitted)).

fault and that the victim should not have had to undergo what he or she experienced—which may help to address the dignitary harms of crime and reassure victims of community support. In this sense, retributive punishment, while not primarily motivated by a desire to relieve victim suffering, may further the ends of victim restoration as a collateral benefit. Indeed, you may have noted that Antony Duff's communicative version of retributivism lays particular emphasis on victims, framing censure of the offender as a duty owed to the victim by the community, and asserting that the victim is also owed a duty of reparations by the offender. This strand of retributive thinking may be especially conducive to victim restoration. Yet, it must not be forgotten that the overriding interest of retributivism lies with just punishment, not the satisfaction of victims *per se*. As we noted earlier, this may be seen as the fundamental difference between retribution and vengeance. In any given case, the punishment that best serves victim restoration may be either more or less than what the offender deserves. Consider, for instance, that victim restoration necessarily requires attending to the harms of the offense, but current thinking about proportionality tends to emphasize the importance of state of mind over harm. Consider also that a majority of violent victimizations in the United States are perpetrated by someone who is known to the victim, with about one in five overall falling into the category of domestic violence. RACHEL E. MORGAN & BARBARA A. OUDEKERK, U.S. DEPT. OF JUSTICE, CRIMINAL VICTIMIZATION, 2018, at 4 (2019). When there is a close relationship between the victim and offender, especially if it is of a familial character, the needs and preferences of the victim by way of punishment may be complicated and idiosyncratic, defying standard formulations of proportionality. A heavy-handed punishment may end up adding to, rather than alleviating, the victim's suffering.

Do you think that the criminal justice system should be more fully centered on the goal of victim restoration? If so, what would such a system look like?

Law professor Randy Barnett once proposed a radical restructuring of the criminal justice system around restitution. ***Restitution:** A New Paradigm of Criminal Justice*, 87 ETHICS 279 (1977). Under his plan, the sentence imposed upon a defendant's conviction would consist of an award of money damages to the victim determined using civil tort principles. If the defendant were unable to pay, then the victim would have a claim on the defendant's future earnings. If even that proved inadequate—for instance, if the defendant were chronically unemployed—then the defendant would be confined to an industrial production facility, where the defendant would have to remain until he had fully worked off the debt to the victim.

Barnett's proposal generated much criticism.[28] What concerns would you have? Do you think these concerns could be addressed effectively?

A more influential, but more diffuse, effort to reimagine criminal justice around the goal of victim restoration has been the "restorative justice" movement, which first appeared in Europe and North America in the 1970s. Mark S. Umbreit et al., *Restorative Justice in the Twenty-First Century: A Social Movement Full of Opportunities and Pitfalls*, 89 MARQ. L. REV. 251, 259 (2005). Restorative justice has been contrasted with the traditional orientation of the American criminal justice system in this way:

> Instead of viewing the state as the primary victim in criminal acts and placing victims, offenders, and the community in passive roles, restorative justice recognizes crime as being directed against individual people. It is grounded in the belief that those most affected by crime should have the opportunity to become actively involved in resolving the conflict.

Id. at 255. The priorities of restorative justice include "[r]epairing harm and restoring losses, allowing offenders to take direct responsibility for their actions, and assisting victims to move beyond vulnerability towards some degree of closure." *Id.*

Although these themes are consistently sounded by restorative justice practitioners and theorists, there is no single model for how to put the ideals of restorative justice into practice. Indeed, these ideals have been incorporated into a diverse range of programs that have been implemented in jurisdictions across the United States and throughout the world. Some of these programs are sponsored by and formally connected to criminal justice agencies, while others operate entirely independently of police, prosecutors, courts, and departments of corrections.

We will focus on two leading restorative-justice models that have been widely adopted and studied. First, *victim-offender dialogues* involve a face-to-face, mediated conversation between the victim and the offender, in which both sides have an opportunity to discuss the offense and its aftermath. The offender may come to a deeper understanding of the consequences of his or her actions and may wish to offer an apology. However, the offender is not required to apologize, and nor is the victim obligated to accept any apology that is offered. The two sides might also try to come to an agreement about how the offender may make amends, for example, by repairing vandalized property. Second, *group conferencing* is in many respects similar to victim-offender dialogues, but also includes community representatives, who are able to describe the broader "ripple effects" of an offense that carry beyond the immediate

---

[28] For an overview of the various questions and concerns, see Michael O'Hear, *Restitution as a Penal Aim*, *in* ENCYCLOPEDIA OF CRIMINOLOGY AND CRIMINAL JUSTICE 4410 (Gerben Bruinsma & David Weisburd eds., 2013).

victim. For instance, in a residential burglary case, the conference might include not only the burglar and the victimized homeowner, but also neighbors who now feel more fearful about threats to their homes. In any event, all participants in the conference are able to share their perspectives. As with dialogues, successful group conferences may culminate with an offer and acceptance of apology and an agreement about how the offender may make amends.

Either model may be implemented in a variety of different ways in relation to court processes. For instance, police or prosecutors might refer a complaint to a restorative justice program in the hope that the victim and offender can work things out without the need for any court involvement. Alternatively, restorative justice might be integrated into court processes: criminal charges might be filed, but then held in abeyance pending the defendant's participation in a program; or, post-conviction, a sentence of probation might be conditioned on the defendant's submission to a dialogue or conferencing process. Finally, dialogues or conferencing might occur after the conclusion of court processes and without any direct implications for the defendant's punishment. A department of corrections, for instance, might sponsor restorative justice opportunities for individuals who are under its supervision.

Would you be concerned about the sincerity of an apology offered by a defendant who might expect thereby to gain a dismissal of charges or a more lenient sentence? Might there still be some value to an apology whose sincerity is in doubt?[29]

A large body of research finds that restorative-justice processes can produce beneficial experiences for the participants. On average, victims and offenders alike rate these processes as fairer than conventional court processes, and outcomes as more satisfactory. Offenders are more likely to apologize and victims to forgive. Additionally, victims who participate in restorative justice are less upset about crime and less afraid of revictimization. For their part, offenders tend to pay more in reparations. There are also some studies that find lower recidivism rates among restorative-justice participants, although it is not yet clear how durable this effect is. Alana Saulnier & Diane Sivasubramaniam, *Restorative Justice: Underlying Mechanisms and Future Directions*, 18 NEW CRIM. L. REV. 510, 517 (2015).

---

[29] *See* Stephanos Bibas & Richard A. Bierschbach, *Integrating Remorse and Apology into Criminal Procedure*, 114 YALE L.J. 85, 143 (2004) ("Even insincere remorse and apologies may be better than none at all. Such expressions vindicate victims, drive home awareness of wrongs, and may ultimately lead offenders to internalize that awareness. . . . The very act of apologizing teaches, which explains why parents make their children apologize (grudgingly) for hitting a sibling or taking a toy. In other words, the ordeal of expressing remorse and apologizing, even if done initially for the wrong reasons, may in time promote genuine repentance. Furthermore, victims may find even half-hearted apologies satisfying, as they vindicate victims and humble offenders." (citations omitted)).

Such research suggests that there may be good *utilitarian* reasons for the criminal justice system to embrace restorative justice, at least with respect to the lower-level sorts of cases as to which it is has most commonly been used—typically property crimes committed by juveniles or first-time offenders. But can restorative justice be defended, or at least tolerated, from a retributive perspective?

As restorative justice gained national and international prominence in the late twentieth and early twenty-first centuries, theorists devoted considerable attention to the compatibility of "restorativism" with retributivism.[30] Important strands of restorative and retributive theorizing do share common themes, particularly in their emphasis on the values of autonomy, equality, dignity, and accountability. There seem especially strong affinities between restorative justice and Antony Duff's communicative version of retributivism, with its view that punishment has, or should have, aspects of apology and reparations, and should aim for reconciliation between offender, victim, and community. *See, e.g.*, Antony Duff, *Restoration and Retribution, in* RESTORATIVE JUSTICE AND CRIMINAL JUSTICE: COMPETING OR RECONCILABLE PARADIGMS? 43 (Andrew von Hirsch et al. eds., 2003).

Yet, Duff has argued forcefully against what he characterizes as radical, or abolitionist, approaches to restorative justice, which conceptualize restorative processes not just as an adjunct to conventional criminal processes—e.g., as a diversion-from-prosecution option for certain low-level cases—but as a *replacement* for the existing criminal justice system. In this radical version of restorative justice,

> [We] think not of crimes that must be condemned and punished, but of "conflicts" or "troubles" that need to be resolved or repaired. We . . . focus not on wrongs whose perpetrators must be prosecuted by the formal force of the law and subjected to the pains of criminal punishment, but on harms that need to be repaired and relationships that need to be restored.

R.A. Duff, *Responsibility, Restoration, and Retribution, in* RETRIBUTIVISM HAS A PAST; HAS IT A FUTURE? 63, 72 (Michael Tonry ed., 2011). Duff argues that crimes are not just a matter of private harm but are also public wrongs that properly concern the wider political community. He thus criticizes restorative justice for its tendency to focus on the harmfulness of the offense to the exclusion of its wrongfulness, and for its reliance on informal private meetings over the public rituals of guilt-adjudication and sentencing. *Id.* at 74.

Do you think that restorative justice has an appropriate role to play in the sentencing process? If so, what exactly should the role be? For instance, would you limit restorative justice to low-level cases? If the

[30] One particularly rich set of essays is collected in the volume RESTORATIVE JUSTICE AND CRIMINAL JUSTICE: COMPETING OR RECONCILABLE PARADIGMS? (Andrew von Hirsch et al. eds., 2003).

victim and offender reached an agreement on how the offender will make amends, should such an agreement ever (or always) be regarded as a substitute for any other court-imposed punishment?[31]

Restorative justice is increasingly codified in American law. Originating as local-level initiatives that were developed without explicit legal authorization, restorative justice programs are now often supported and structured by state statutes. One recent survey identified 264 restorative justice laws in forty-five states and the District of Columbia. Thalia González, *The State of Restorative Justice in American Criminal Law*, 2020 WIS. L. REV. 1147. About one-third of the laws were specific to the juvenile justice system, with the remainder applying to the adult system or both systems. Some laws contemplated that restorative justice would be a pre-adjudication diversion, and others a post-adjudication disposition; most, however, failed to specify how restorative justice should relate to the formal criminal process. Among the statutes that identified a gatekeeper, most authorized the *court* to place the defendant into a restorative justice alternative, with many fewer specifying the prosecutor or the department of corrections.

In reporting the survey results, Professor Thalia González highlighted a number of potentially problematic aspects of the restorative justice laws, including:

- Few states provide a confidentiality guarantee for statements made during a restorative justice process.
- While victim participation is universally voluntary, several laws mandate defendant participation.
- When defendant participation is voluntary, there are no established standards or procedures to ensure informed consent.
- Certain types of crime are often excluded from restorative justice, including sexual offenses, domestic violence, and offenses resulting in serious bodily injury or death.
- Several states mandate that the defendant must pay a fee in order to participate in a restorative justice program ("pay to play").

[31] Consider, for instance, the controversial *Clotworthy* case from New Zealand, described by Professor Paul Robinson as follows:

> During a vicious robbery, Clotworthy stabbed the victim six times, puncturing the victim's lung and diaphragm and seriously disfiguring his face. It was the disfigurement that had the most devastating effect on the victim, for the result was sufficiently repulsive to people that it interfered with his normal social interactions. In the [restorative justice] mediation session, it was agreed that Clotworthy would not go to prison; instead he would work to earn money to pay the fifteen thousand dollars needed for the surgical operation to diminish the victim's disfigurement.

Paul H. Robinson, *Restorative Processes and Doing Justice*, 3 U. ST. THOMAS L.J. 421 (2006). Robinson characterizes this as an "appalling" outcome. Do you agree?

Which of these features of codified restorative justice do you find most concerning, and why?

B. PUTTING PURPOSES TOGETHER

We have considered a number of traditional purposes of punishment that can be fit under the headings of utilitarian or retributive—general and specific deterrence, incapacitation, rehabilitation, just deserts—as well as the increasingly prominent purpose of victim restoration, which might be considered utilitarian or retributive, or possibly as representing a "third way" or hybrid approach. We have noted along the way that these purposes may sometimes seem in tension with one another. In a given case, for instance, desert and general deterrence might point in the direction of incarceration, while rehabilitation and restoration might favor probation. What is to be done in such a case? Many jurisdictions have statutes that provide sentencing judges with a framework for assessing purposes, although the guidance is generally very loose and leaves a great deal to the judge's discretion. We will focus here on three models in particular: the original version of the Model Penal Code ("MPC"), the federal Sentencing Reform Act ("SRA"), and the recently adopted Model Penal Code: Sentencing ("MPC:S").

The Model Penal Code was originally adopted in 1962 by the American Law Institute, a nationally prominent law reform organization, after years of deliberation involving many of the leading criminal-law authorities of the day. Covering not only sentencing, but also substantive criminal law, criminal process, and corrections, the MPC influenced a wave of mid-twentieth-century legal reform efforts across the United States. More recently, the Institute sponsored a lengthy reexamination of the sentencing provisions of the MPC, culminating in the adoption of the MPC:S in 2017.

American Law Institute, Model Penal Code (1962)

Section 1.02. Purposes; Principles of Construction.

(2) The general purposes of the provisions governing the sentencing and treatment of offenders are:

(a) to prevent the commission of offenses;

(b) to promote the correction and rehabilitation of offenders;

(c) to safeguard offenders against excessive, disproportionate or arbitrary punishment; * * *

(e) to differentiate among offenders with a view to a just individualization in their treatment; * * *

(g) to advance the use of generally accepted scientific methods and knowledge in the sentencing and treatment of offenders; * * *

Section 7.01. Criteria for Withholding Sentence of Imprisonment and for Placing Defendant on Probation.

(1) The Court shall deal with a person who has been convicted of a crime without imposing sentence of imprisonment unless, having regard to the nature and circumstances of the crime and the history, character and condition of the defendant, it is of the opinion that his imprisonment is necessary for protection of the public because:

(a) there is undue risk that during the period of a suspended sentence or probation the defendant will commit another crime; or

(b) the defendant is in need of correctional treatment that can be provided most effectively by his commitment to an institution; or

(c) a lesser sentence will depreciate the seriousness of the defendant's crime.

(2) The following grounds, while not controlling the discretion of the Court, shall be accorded weight in favor of withholding sentence of imprisonment:

(a) the defendant's conduct neither caused nor threatened serious harm;

(b) the defendant did not contemplate that his criminal conduct would cause or threaten serious harm;

(c) the defendant acted under a strong provocation;

(d) there were substantial grounds tending to excuse or justify the defendant's criminal conduct, though failing to establish a defense;

(e) the victim of the defendant's criminal conduct induced or facilitated its commission;

(f) the defendant has compensated or will compensate the victim of his criminal conduct for the damage or injury that he sustained;

(g) the defendant has no history of prior delinquency or criminal activity or has led a law-abiding life for a substantial period of time before the commission of the present crime;

(h) the defendant's criminal conduct was the result of circumstances unlikely to recur;

(i) the character and attitudes of the defendant indicate that he is unlikely to commit another crime;

(j) the defendant is particularly likely to respond affirmatively to probationary treatment;

(k) the imprisonment of the defendant would entail excessive hardship to himself or his dependents.

NOTES & QUESTIONS

1. **Purposes of Punishment.** Based on § 1.02(2), would you characterize the MPC's approach to sentencing as more utilitarian or

retributive? The official "explanatory note" that accompanies § 1.02 states that the "dominant theme" in the MPC framework is "the prevention of offenses." Does that help to clarify whether the MPC should be characterized as more utilitarian or retributive? Note, though, that proportionality is not entirely ignored in § 1.02(2). What role does proportionality play in the MPC framework?

2. **Rehabilitation's Heyday.** Adopted in 1962, the MPC is very much a reflection of the expert views on sentencing that prevailed in the middle decades of the twentieth century. As we observed earlier, this was a time period when confidence in the potential of rehabilitative treatment for defendants was especially high. Do you see the emphasis on rehabilitation as a purpose of punishment in § 1.02(2)?

3. **In/Out Decision.** Section 7.01 provides guidance for judges on the "in/out" decision, i.e., whether the defendant will be sentenced to imprisonment or probation. If the defendant is sentenced to prison, the MPC contemplates that a parole board will determine, within certain parameters, when the defendant is released. In a sense, then, the most important decision to be made by the *judge* in this system is "in versus out." (Under § 6.06, the judge could also determine the minimum amount of time before parole release, but in most cases within a relatively narrow range of one-to-two or one-to-three years.) The importance of the in/out decision helps to explain why the MPC includes such a detailed framework for it. Does § 7.01(1) seem consistent with the utilitarian, crime-preventive orientation of § 1.02(2)? The official explanatory note for § 7.01(1) makes clear that that the three factors listed in subsections (a)–(c) correspond with the incapacitative, rehabilitative, and deterrence rationales for punishment, respectively.

4. **A Role for Proportionality.** Of the specific "grounds" listed in § 7.01(2), at least the first five relate to culpability. But note how this subsection is framed: these are grounds for selecting a sentence of probation in lieu of a sentence of imprisonment—in other words, grounds for *lenience*. There is no comparable enumeration of *aggravating* culpability factors that would support imprisonment over probation. This asymmetry is consistent with § 1.02, which speaks about proportionality as a "safeguard" for defendants. Put differently, § 1.02 indicates that proportionality should be taken into account as a ceiling on the severity of punishment but not used to establish a floor.

5. **Extended Terms.** The MPC gives judges the ability to impose an "extended term of imprisonment" when this is "necessary for protection of the public." If certain criteria set forth in § 7.03 are satisfied, then the judge would be authorized to set longer minimum and maximum terms of imprisonment than would normally be available. The public-safety rationale, of course, reflects a utilitarian, incapacitative purpose.

6. **MPC's Influence.** An enormously ambitious undertaking, the MPC's efforts to rationalize and improve American criminal law and process proved more influential in some respects than others. Paul H. Robinson & Markus D. Dubber, *The American Model Penal Code: A Brief Overview*, 10 NEW CRIM. L. REV. 319, 326–29 (2007). The MPC's statement of purposes

(§ 1.02) was moderately influential. Prior to its promulgation, very few states had any formally articulated framework as to purposes of punishment. Michele Cotton, *Back with a Vengeance: The Resilience of Retribution as an Articulated Purpose of Criminal Punishment*, 37 AM. CRIM. L. REV. 1313, 1318–19 (2000). After the MPC's appearance, however, "about half of the states adopted a statutory statement of purposes based on, inspired by, or provoked by that in the MPC." *Id.* at 1319. None adopted the MPC's language verbatim, but about a dozen adopted declarations of purpose that were distinctly utilitarian and omitted retribution as a permissible objective of punishment. *Id.*

Sentencing Reform Act of 1984 (as codified)

18 U.S.C. 3553. Imposition of a sentence

(a) Factors to be considered in imposing a sentence.—The court shall impose a sentence sufficient, but not greater than necessary, to comply with the purposes set forth in paragraph (2) of this subsection. The court, in determining the particular sentence to be imposed, shall consider—

(1) the nature and circumstances of the offense and the history and characteristics of the defendant;

(2) the need for the sentence imposed—

(A) to reflect the seriousness of the offense, to promote respect for the law, and to provide just punishment for the offense;

(B) to afford adequate deterrence to criminal conduct;

(C) to protect the public from further crimes of the defendant; and

(D) to provide the defendant with needed educational or vocational training, medical care, or other correctional treatment in the most effective manner;

(3) the kinds of sentences available; * * *

(6) the need to avoid unwarranted sentence disparities among defendants with similar records who have been found guilty of similar conduct; and

(7) the need to provide restitution to any victims of the offense.

NOTES & QUESTIONS

1. **An Expression of *Its* Time.** As noted, the original sentencing provisions of the MPC reflected midcentury thinking about purposes of punishment. Adopted twenty-two years later, the federal Sentencing Reform Act (SRA) was no less an expression of its time. The SRA was best known for ending discretionary parole release in the federal system, establishing the United States Sentencing Commission, and authorizing the Commission to adopt sentencing guidelines that would be binding on federal judges in most

cases.[32] The SRA was thus emblematic of the late-twentieth-century trend against discretion in the criminal justice system, especially in the areas of sentencing and parole. But, while the SRA was intended to reduce judicial sentencing discretion, it was not designed to eliminate it altogether. For that reason, the language now codified at 18 U.S.C. § 3553(a) had some importance even at the time it was adopted—and then became far more important as a result of the Supreme Court's decision in *United States v. Booker*, 543 U.S. 220 (2005), in which the Court struck down on constitutional grounds a different provision of the SRA that made the federal sentencing guidelines mandatory. (We will discuss this case and its aftermath in more detail in Chapter 3.) In the post-*Booker* system, federal judges are still required to determine the applicable guidelines range in each case and use it as a starting point in the sentencing analysis, but normally may select a sentence outside the range if they wish. Section 3553(a) provides the analytical framework for judges to use in deciding whether to grant a departure or variance from the guidelines sentence.

2. **Parsimony—an Echo of Beccaria.** The statute directs that the court "shall impose a sentence sufficient, but not greater than necessary, to comply with the purposes set forth in paragraph (2) of this subsection." The "not greater than necessary" language reflects what punishment theorists call the "parsimony" principle. We have already seen this principle expressed in Beccaria's mandate that punishment must be "necessary [and] the minimum possible in the given circumstances." But note the balanced phrases of § 3553(a)—punishment has both a ceiling (punishment can be no more than what is "necessary") and a floor (punishment must be "sufficient" to "comply with" the traditionally recognized purposes of punishment). As codified in § 3553(a), parsimony does not necessarily imply that judges should err on the side of lenience.

3. **Just Deserts.** In the framework of § 3553(a), the core purposes are those listed in paragraph (2)—it is these purposes, and only these, that are linked to the key "sufficient" and "necessary" language. Do you see in this list the familiar purposes of deterrence, incapacitation, rehabilitation and just deserts? Comparing this list with the MPC's original sentencing framework, the treatment of desert may strike you as the most notable difference. Whereas the MPC treated desert as merely a limiting consideration, § 3553(a) seems to indicate that desert ("just punishment") is also a positive mandate—this is one of the purposes that sentences must be "sufficient" to "comply with." The SRA's stronger embrace of desert reflects the "retributivist revival" of the late twentieth century. *See* R.A. Duff, *Responsibility, Restoration, and Retribution, in* RETRIBUTIVISM HAS A PAST; HAS IT A FUTURE? 63, 63–66 (Michael Tonry ed., 2011) (describing retributivist revival). As rehabilitation's star waned after the 1960s, retribution's star waxed. Indeed, even in those states that had adopted explicitly utilitarian declarations of purposes in the spirit of the original version of the MPC, "activist" courts nonetheless found that retribution was

---

[32] For an overview of the intellectual origins and legislative history of the SRA, see Michael O'Hear, *The Original Intent of Uniformity in Federal Sentencing*, 74 U. CIN. L. REV. 749, 756–77 (2006). We will consider the federal sentencing guidelines in more detail in Chapter 2.

a permissible objective at sentencing. Michele Cotton, *Back with a Vengeance: The Resilience of Retribution as an Articulated Purpose of Criminal Punishment*, 37 AM. CRIM. L. REV. 1313, 1325 (2000). Moreover, in states that formally adopted or amended statements of purposes after the mid-1970s, retribution was commonly given express approval, as in the SRA. *Id.* at 1355–56. California went so far as to identify desert as "the" purpose for imprisonment, while Pennsylvania declared retribution to be the "primary" aim at sentencing. *Id.*

4. **Rehabilitation.** Rehabilitation is among the purposes endorsed by § 3553(a), but may seem less prominent to you here than it was in the original MPC sentencing framework. The SRA's skeptical view of the ability of the corrections system to foster rehabilitation is more apparent in a separate provision, in which Congress directed, "The court, in determining whether to impose a term of imprisonment, and, if a term of imprisonment is to be imposed, in determining the length of the term, shall consider the factors set forth in section 3553(a) to the extent that they are applicable, *recognizing that imprisonment is not an appropriate means of promoting correction and rehabilitation.*" 18 U.S.C. § 3582(a) (emphasis added).

5. **Individualization and Equality.** Now take a look at the rest of § 3553(a) beyond the core purposes set forth in paragraph (2). These are matters that the judge "shall consider," although there is no requirement that they be given any particular weight in determining the sentence. Of particular note is paragraph (6), which requires consideration of "the need to avoid unwarranted sentence disparities among defendants with similar records who have been found guilty of similar conduct."

This provision might be contrasted with MPC § 1.02(2)(e), which, as we have seen, identifies as a purpose of sentencing the "differentiat[ion] among offenders with a view to a just individualization of treatment." The MPC thus seemed to contemplate highly individualized sentences. This made sense given the MPC's rehabilitative orientation. In such a system, it is important to know who the defendant is as a person because this may potentially affect what treatment approaches will be most effective.

However, such individualization may be in tension with ideals about equality before the law. (The popular image of blindfolded Justice reflects the view that courts should not treat people differently based on who they are.) Indeed, one of the persistent criticisms of the highly discretionary, rehabilitation-focused sentencing system of the mid-twentieth century was that it led to harsher outcomes for racial minorities and the socioeconomically disadvantaged. The SRA reflected the influence of this critique, most importantly in its efforts to curtail sentencing and corrections discretion, but also in § 3553(a)(6), which highlights a "need" to avoid "unwarranted sentencing disparities." Of course, there is a critical ambiguity in the adjective "unwarranted." Consider, for instance, would it be "unwarranted" to give different sentences to two defendants who committed the same crime if the disparity were based on genuine differences in the defendants' rehabilitative potential? Section 3553(a)(6) may permit some continued individualization in sentencing, but, at the very least, it does seem to embody a more skeptical view of individualization than we saw in the MPC.

6. **Restitution.** Paragraph (7) indicates that sentencing judges should take into account the need for defendants to provide restitution, which reflects the growing attentiveness of policymakers to victim-restoration interests by the 1980s.

7. **How Helpful?** If you were a judge, what would you think of the mandates of § 3553(a)? Does the framework seem helpful and appropriate to you? Which do you prefer, § 3553(a) or the original sentencing framework of the MPC? As you read the following case, consider whether your impression of § 3553(a) is changed.

United States v. Stern

590 F. Supp. 2d 945 (N.D. Ohio 2008)

■ O'MALLEY, J.

Before the Court is Defendant Evan M. Stern, who previously pled guilty to possession of child pornography in violation of 18 U.S.C. § 2252(a)(4), a conviction with respect to which the Government and Stern did not reach a plea agreement. In light of the unusual circumstances underlying this conviction, the Court conducted a lengthy initial sentencing hearing during which witnesses testified extensively about the particular facts of this case and about the Defendant himself. The Court did not rule at that hearing, but rather took the matter under advisement to carefully weigh the arguments advanced by both the Government and Stern.

The United States Sentencing Commission's Advisory Sentencing Guidelines ("Guidelines") suggest that a defendant with Stern's offense level and criminal history should be sentenced to a term of imprisonment of between 46 and 57 months. The Court, however, must independently consider the sentencing factors set forth in 18 U.S.C. § 3553(a) to determine whether such a sentence is appropriate in this case. Indeed, the Court is forbidden from assuming that the Guidelines are reasonable as specifically applied to Stern. While the Government argues that 46–57 months represents a just sentence, Stern urges this Court to deviate from the guidelines based on the § 3553(a) factors. Stern, in fact, has asked this Court not to impose any term of imprisonment whatsoever.

As an initial matter, the Court wishes to make clear that it has consistently imposed harsh sentences upon defendants who possess child pornography. Indeed, the Court rarely has disagreed with the Government's recommended sentences in cases involving this crime—and, when it has, it has only deviated marginally from the Government's recommended term. Yet, as more fully explained below, here the Court is faced with an extraordinary and unique case that compels a different result. While any reading of this sentence as a harbinger of future leniency in the absence of such extraordinary circumstances would be mistaken, the Court finds that the sentence the Government urges is more than reasonably necessary to serve all of the sentencing considerations by which this Court must be guided. The Court does not, however, find it appropriate to deviate as far from the Guidelines as is urged by Stern. Accordingly, Stern shall be sentenced to the custody of the Bureau of Prisons for a term of 12 months and 1 day.

BACKGROUND

In 2004, the Pittsburgh Division of the FBI and the Pennsylvania Police Department were jointly investigating file servers dedicated to distributing images involving child pornography and their subscribers. During the course of this investigation, the agencies identified numerous criminal users of child pornography, including Stern, then a student at Kent State.

On October 18, 2005, the FBI went to Stern's home and explained that Stern had been identified as a viewer of child pornography. Stern then admitted to possession of this material and surrendered his computer. At that time, he explained how to access the unlawful files on his computer and stated that he wished to cooperate. The FBI spent nearly a year analyzing the contents of Stern's computer. On August 25, 2006, the FBI completed their forensic analysis and identified in excess of 1000 images as child pornography. Slightly over a year later, on October 15, 2007, the Government charged Stern in a one count information with possession of child pornography, in violation of 18 U.S.C. § 2252(a)(4). * * *

C. Analysis of the § 3553(a) Factors * * *

1. The Nature and Circumstance of the Offense and the Characteristics of the Defendant

A. The Nature and Circumstance of the Offense

The Court finds that possession of child pornography is an exceedingly serious offense, among the most serious class of offenses that do not involve the direct use of violence or coercion on the part of the perpetrator. The Court, accordingly, emphasizes that Stern's crime is a sexual exploitation offense—criminalizing the possession of child pornography is a necessary complement to laws banning production of such items, much of which occurs outside the jurisdictional reach of the Federal Courts.

Laws criminalizing the possession of child pornography are in place to reduce the market for exploitation of the children that are severely victimized by this crime. *United States v. Duhon*, 440 F.3d 711, 719 (5th Cir. 2006) ("Possession of child pornography is not a victimless crime. A child somewhere was used to produce the images downloaded . . . , in large part, because individuals like [the defendant] exist to download the images."). This crime shocks the conscience: "Children are exploited, molested, and raped for the prurient pleasure of [the defendant] and others who support suppliers of child pornography." *United States v. Goff*,

501 F.3d 250, 259 (3d Cir. 2007). The written word seems inadequate to describe the horrors of this crime.

Although it is never easy to differentiate between various levels of unconscionable conduct, it is still true that "possession of pornography is the least serious of the crimes on the continuum of conduct—from possession to distribution to production to predatory abuse—that exploits children." *Baird*, 580 F.Supp.2d at 893; *United States v. Goldberg*, 2008 WL 4542957, at *5–6 (N.D. Ill. Apr. 30, 2008) ("It does sustain a market for child pornography, of course, but that market is unfortunately there regardless of what may happen to [this defendant]."). The individual who possesses child pornography, while demanding punishment, is "considerably less culpable than a producer or distributor of the exploitative materials and is a marginal player in the overall child exploitation scheme." *Id.*; *see also United States v. Honnold*, No. 5:05-CR-0492 (N.D. Ohio Feb. 23, 2006). Here, Stern "never possessed [child pornography] in order to entice a child . . . never produced any of the images . . . never had any improper conduct with an actual child . . . [and] never molested any child." (Doc. 12 at 10.) Indeed, "there is no evidence, direct or indirect, that the defendant ever engaged in the photography of any minors engaged in sexual conduct" or that "the defendant ever engaged in direct or indirect pedophile conduct." *Honnold*, No. 5:05-CR-0492, at 4. There is also no evidence that Stern regularly traded the images he downloaded.

Finally, the files on Stern's computer, while profoundly disturbing, were not as violent as the images found on the computers of many other defendants the Court has encountered in these cases. * * *

B. *The Characteristics of the Defendant*

i. *Stern's Age*

The Court finds several strongly mitigating factors when it considers the individual characteristics of this particular defendant. Most critically, it takes note that Stern was 14-years old when he began to view pornographic images and, at that time, he was looking at images of girls his own age. There is, thus, a fundamental difference between Stern, whose conduct and apparent resultant addiction began during adolescence, and the other defendants convicted of similar crimes who have been sentenced by this Court, other courts in this district, and other courts in the federal system. * * * Indeed, the Court has conducted a review of the scientific literature in this area and believes there is compelling evidence that the judicial system's longstanding principle of treating youth offenders differently than adult offenders is justified in part based on the unformed nature of the adolescent brain. *See, e.g.*, National Institute of Health Publication 4929, The Teenage Brain: A Work In Progress (2008).

This Court does not suggest that this difference removes all culpability, but does believe that there are critical distinctions between Stern and the typical defendant. * * *

On the other hand, however, it is notable that Sterns criminal activities were not confined to his adolescence. Stern did not stop purchasing or viewing pornography until his arrest at age 22, 8 years after his criminal activity first began. Notwithstanding Stern's age, the Court cannot ignore the length of time over which his illegal conduct continued. So too, the Court cannot ignore the fact that, as Stern matured, he not only did not cease his activities, but actually narrowed the focus of his pornographic images to only child pornography. Thus, while there is a difference in culpability between one who starts viewing child pornography as an adult and one who does not stop viewing such material, and while that difference warrants consideration, that consideration is not unlimited.

ii. Stern's Post-Arrest Conduct

Stern's conduct since his arrest also weighs heavily in favor of a downward variance. Stern graduated from Kent State a year after his arrest. The Court finds it noteworthy and predictive of Stern's future behavior that he committed himself to achieving this productive goal irrespective of the immense and deserved public shame that followed his arrest. * * *

Second, Stern sought therapy well in advance of being charged with any crime. Although this factor does not weigh nearly as heavy in Stern's favor as it would had he sought treatment prior to his arrest, the Court nonetheless considers it a positive indication of Stern's commitment to refraining from future criminal conduct. * * *

Third, Stern has been employed for over a year as a computer game designer and is described as a highly talented employee. He has maintained this job despite his conviction for this offense and the looming threat of punishment from this Court. The Court finds this indicative of Stern's current ability to contribute to society, as well as his commitment to leading an exemplary life from this point forward. * * *

Fourth, Stern has maintained normal and productive relationships with his family, his friends, and even a girlfriend. This is likewise compelling; the Court believes that, particularly in contrast to the description of Stern's social behavior while engaged in his criminal activity, this indicates a great likelihood that Stern will continue to be a positive and law-abiding member of society.

The Court is mindful of its obligation to determine whether Stern's behavior is merely a pretextual effort to avoid a harsher sentence. The Court concludes that it is not. As an initial matter, much of Stern's behavior predates the criminal charges against him.

There are, moreover, other factors that support this conclusion. Based on the Court's experience with scores of past defendants, it finds

Stern's professions of remorse and change credible, if obviously well-coached. * * * Finally, Stern's therapist states that Stern recognizes the wrongfulness of his conduct, has insight into the harm it caused, and possesses genuine remorse. The Court finds that this testimony supports a downward variance, particularly given the Court's opportunity to observe other, more empirical, measures of change on the part of Stern. Considering all of these factors together, the Court finds it likely that Stern's turnaround is both genuine and permanent, rather than pretextual or transitory. * * *

2. The Purposes of Sentencing

Federal sentencing law generally asks a court to consider retribution, deterrence, incapacitation, and rehabilitation. * * *

A. The Sentence Must Reflect the Seriousness of the Offense, Promote Respect for the Law, and Provide Just Punishment

As this Court has already stated, there is no question that Stern has committed a serious crime. * * *

Respect for the law is promoted by punishments that are fair, however, not those that simply punish for punishment's sake. * * * There is no reason to believe that respect for the law will increase if a defendant who deserves leniency is sentenced harshly any more than there is reason to believe that respect for the law will increase if a defendant who deserves a harsh punishment receives a slap on the wrist. * * * Similarly, a just punishment for Stern is one that balances the severity of his crime with the individual characteristics of Stern that counsel in favor of leniency. Alternately, however, the Court believes that this crime must be punished with a term of imprisonment, but not a lengthy one. * * *

B. The Sentence Must Afford Adequate Deterrence

Child pornography must be universally condemned, and even a defendant with highly compelling personal characteristics should not be fully excused from such a heinous crime. * * * That said, the sentence contemplated by the Guidelines is greater than necessary to achieve this purpose, in this case. * * *

The Court is mindful that individual factors unique to Stern limit the specific deterrent value of any sentence. In this regard, the Court leans heavily on its finding that Stern's criminal activity began when he was a 14-year old boy looking at pictures of 14-year old girls. The Court does not believe that the parents of future 14-year olds, in considering how closely to monitor their children's use of the internet, will be any less chastened by this Court's sentence merely because it departs from the Guidelines. *Accord. Baird*, 580 F. Supp.2d at 895 ("The mere fact of [the defendant's] prosecution deters others from engaging in this sort of conduct, and a sentence of incarceration will act as a further deterrent to others contemplating such activity. The value of any longer sentence as a deterrent, over and above these other factors, would be marginal.").

C. The Sentence Must Protect the Public from Further Crimes of the Defendant

There is no suggestion that this defendant need be incapacitated. The Court finds it critical that all psychiatrists and psychologists who have examined Stern have found him to pose an exceedingly low risk of recidivism. * * *

D. The Sentence Must Provide the Defendant with Needed Educational or Vocational Training, Medical Care, or Other Correctional Treatment in the Most Effective Manner

There is no suggestion that this defendant would be more fully rehabilitated within the prison system. Indeed, there is great reason to think that this defendant's rehabilitation might be negatively impacted by an excessively long prison stay. * * * One psychologist, for example, stated that he "would be concerned that for [Mr. Stern] to be sentenced to prison potentially has the ability to undo much of what he has done to this point . . . [I]t's hard for me to imagine in my mind that there would be anything positive at all that would occur by him being sentenced there." * * *

The Court believes that prison will be a critical component of rehabilitation for this defendant in one important way. This defendant, although genuinely remorseful, shares many characteristics with other defendants that the court has seen over the years. Some non-trivial percentage of these defendants would have greatly benefitted from a firm "line in the sand" earlier in their lives. Allowing Stern to escape without any prison term might send the wrong message to Stern, who must fully internalize that even the slightest further criminal sexual activity will result in even more substantial incarceration. * * *

6. The Need to Avoid Unwarranted Sentencing Disparities

The Court has carefully considered an extremely wide variety of opinions from across the country as well as the National Guideline Statistics. * * * The Court is deeply troubled by its findings: "anyone seriously concerned about federal sentencing disparities [must begin by] taking a very close look at federal child porn cases." Professor Douglas A. Berman, Is There an Ivy-Leaguer Exception to Federal Child Porn Charges? (October 22, 2008), on-line at http://sentencing.typepad.com. Based on the Court's review of the case law, it is clear that "one would be hard pressed to find a consistent set of principles to explain exactly why some federal child porn defendants face decades in federal prison, some face many years in federal prison, while others only end up facing months." *Id.* * * *

In short, the national sentencing landscape presents a picture of injustice. In the absence of coherent and defensible Guidelines, district courts are left without a meaningful baseline from which they can apply sentencing principles. * * *

The Court, accordingly, has attempted to ensure that its sentence avoids unwarranted sentencing disparities to the greatest degree possible while still hewing to its view that this individual defendant must be punished with a term of imprisonment. The Court acknowledges that the closest factual analogue to this case resulted only in probation. *See Polito*, 215 Fed. Appx. at 356–57. Indeed, the Fifth Circuit affirmed that sentence on facts similar to the ones currently before this Court:

> 1) A substantial amount of time had passed between arrest and sentencing.
>
> 2) Both defendants were arrested while in college.
>
> 3) Neither defendant was found to be a further threat to the community. In particular, neither defendant was found to pose any risk of direct harm to local children.
>
> 4) Both defendants were first-time offenders at the time of their arrest.
>
> 5) After the defendants were arrested, both conducted themselves very positively. Both sought mental health treatment, maintained employment, and avoided further legal difficulties.
>
> 6) In both cases, there was concern that a lengthy term of imprisonment would interrupt substantial positive gains in the defendant's mental health treatment.
>
> 7) Both defendants graduated college in the time since being arrested, but prior to being charged. Polito dropped out of Louisiana State, but later enrolled in a smaller local college, from which he ultimately graduated. Stern was able to continue at Kent State, from which he received a degree.

Id. This Court, however, does not believe that the need to reduce individualized sentencing disparities entirely trumps the Court's independent judgment. In this case, the Court believes jail time is necessary, notwithstanding the contrary result in *Polito*. * * *

7. *The Need to Provide Restitution to any Victims of the Offense*

It is obviously not possible for Stern to provide restitution to his particular victims. Much of the concept of restitution, however, is still a factor in this case. The Court believes that Stern should make "restitution" in the form of community service to those who have suffered from similar crimes. To that end, Stern must complete a very substantial term of community service, preferably assisting battered adult women in a program approved and supervised by the probation office who will be overseeing his lengthy term of supervision.

CONCLUSION

Stern has committed a serious crime and the Court finds it necessary to impose a term of imprisonment on him to make clear that this crime should not and will not go unpunished. The Court finds that Stern is a unique and exceptional defendant for whom the Guidelines are not appropriate. * * * Consequently, as will be confirmed by its formal Judgment, Stern shall be sentenced to the custody of the Bureau of Prisons to be imprisoned for a term of 12 months and 1 day.

NOTES & QUESTIONS

1. **A Well-Justified Sentence?** Consider how the court handled each of the traditional purposes of punishment set forth in § 3553(a)(2). Are you persuaded by the analysis? Do you think a year and a day in prison really is "sufficient, but not greater than necessary, to comply with the purposes" of punishment?

2. **The Conundrum of Child-Pornography Possession.** The *Stern* court noted that cases of possessing child pornography have sharply divided sentencing judges, with some defendants receiving probation and others decades in prison. In part, the controversy stems from uncertainty over how to conceptualize and measure the harm of the offense of simple possession. The *production* of child pornography undoubtedly causes grave harm to many victims, but it is not entirely clear to what extent the *consumer* should be held legally accountable for the full magnitude of those harms. Should familiar legal principles of but-for causation and foreseeability govern, and, if so, how exactly should they be applied? Additionally, and apart from the harms directly caused by production, victims may also suffer ongoing harm from the distribution and viewing of images of their traumatic experiences. But these harms, too, can present assessment difficulties, especially insofar as the defendant may be only one of thousands of viewers who are collectively causing the harm, with no clear way of apportioning responsibility among them. We will return to these difficulties in our discussion of *Paroline v. United States*, 572 U.S. 434 (2014), in Chapter 9.

Complicating matters further is the intuition that people who possess child pornography are at heightened risk of committing hands-on child sex offenses, which may call for an incapacitating sentence. Might prison be warranted for preventive purposes even if the harm proximately caused by the defendant's possession of child pornography was low? On the other hand, there is only weak and inconsistent support in the social-science literature for the assumed possession-abuse connection. *See* Carissa Byrne Hessick, *Disentangling Child Pornography from Child Sex Abuse*, 88 WASH. U. L. REV. 853, 875–79 (2011) (summarizing research). Should policymakers and sentencing judges wait for more definitive proof of the connection before they adopt broadly incapacitative responses to possession offenses?

Despite these difficulties, there has been a marked trend since 1990 toward greater severity in child pornography sentences in both state and federal courts, often as a result of legislatively enacted mandatory minimum prison terms. Hessick, *supra*, at 857–62. Perhaps surprisingly, the application of minimums has in some cases resulted in sentences for possession that are far longer than those that are normally imposed for hands-on offenses.

3. **Disparity.** How did the *Stern* court handle the disparity-avoidance mandate of § 3553(a)(6)? Does the mandate even make any sense as to child pornography possession, given the wildly different ways that judges deal with these offenses?

4. **Restitution.** Note the difficulty highlighted in *Stern* with addressing victim-restoration goals in cases lacking discrete, readily identifiable victims. Are you satisfied with what the court did in *Stern*?

5. **A Different Result Under the MPC?** Do you think the court might have imposed a different sentence on Stern if the original MPC framework were applied, instead of § 3553(a)?

American Law Institute, Model Penal Code: Sentencing (2017)

Section 1.02. Purposes of Sentencing and the Sentencing System.

(2) The general purposes of the provisions on sentencing, applicable to all official actors in the sentencing system, are:

(a) in decisions affecting the sentencing of individual offenders:

(i) to render sentences in all cases within a range of severity proportionate to the gravity of offenses, the harms done to crime victims, and the blameworthiness of offenders;

(ii) when reasonably feasible, to achieve offender rehabilitation, general deterrence, incapacitation of dangerous offenders, restitution to crime victims, preservation of families, and reintegration of offenders into the law-abiding community, provided these goals are pursued within the boundaries of proportionality in subsection (a)(i);

(iii) to render sentences no more severe than necessary to achieve the applicable purposes in subsections (a)(i) and (a)(ii); and

(iv) to avoid the use of sanctions that increase the likelihood offenders will engage in future criminal conduct.

NOTES & QUESTIONS

1. **Limiting Retributivism.** As we saw, 18 U.S.C. § 3553(a)(2) discusses utilitarian and retributive purposes of sentencing on an equal footing and provides no clear mechanism for judges to handle conflicts between the two approaches. By contrast, the Model Penal Code: Sentencing clearly establishes desert as paramount relative to utilitarian considerations. Note the key proviso in § 1.02(2)(a)(ii)—the listed utilitarian purposes can only be pursued "within the boundaries of proportionality in

subsection (a)(i)." Known as "limiting retributivism," this approach to purposes of punishment is closely associated with the law professor Norval Morris (1923–2004). Indeed, the official comment to § 1.02 expressly credits Morris as the inspiration for the "utilitarian within limits" framework.

Of course, this framework only makes sense if one starts with the premise that the demands of desert are imprecise—in other words, that it is more appropriate to think in any given case about a relatively wide *range* of proportionate punishment within which utilitarian considerations can be given some play, rather than there being a singular right answer to the question of what the defendant deserves. In the words of the official commentary, the MPC:S does indeed "embrace[ ] Norval Morris's observation that human moral intuitions about proportionate penalties in individual cases are almost always rough and imprecise." Conceptualized this way, is desert *too* imprecise to function as a meaningful constraint on punishment?

In order to bring greater case-to-case consistency in the assessment of desert, the MPC:S contemplates that a sentencing commission will establish guidelines embodying "presumptive standards for proportionate punishments." However, the sentencing judge may "depart" from the guidelines "when substantial circumstances establish that the presumptive sentence . . . will not best effectuate the purposes stated in § 1.02(2)(a)." MPC:S art. 7.

2. **Desert in the Original MPC.** As we have seen, the MPC's original sentencing framework also conceptualized desert as a constraint on punishment. How was this constraint structured differently than in the MPC:S?

3. **Victim Restoration.** Like 18 U.S.C. § 3553(a), the MPC:S explicitly recognizes restitution as a permissible purpose of punishment (albeit within desert constraints, of course). However, the official commentary indicates that the broader term "restoration" was deliberately avoided: "In contrast with restitution for economic losses, victim 'restoration' is seldom a defined or achievable goal, and has no clear starting or stopping points for implementation. If taken seriously as enforceable statutory language, it is a dangerously open-ended term." Do you agree? Despite this discomfort with the term "restoration," the official commentary endorses continued "experimentation" with restorative-justice programs so long as they are consistent with § 1.02(2), including the prohibition on disproportionate punishments.

4. **Utilitarian Purposes and Feasibility.** The utilitarian purposes listed in § 1.02(2)(a)(ii) are limited not only by proportionality, but also by the "reasonably feasible" constraint. The commentary observes, "Without such a requirement, the Code would invite misuses of utilitarian rationales that are based on hunches, intuitions, bare optimism, fear, or animosity." Given the tenuous connection that we have noted between sentence severity and deterrence, could it *ever* be said that it is "reasonably feasible" for a tough sentence to achieve deterrence? For that matter, given the current state of knowledge about risk assessment and treatment, might there also

be questions about whether incapacitation and rehabilitation purposes can be pursued in ways that are "reasonably feasible?"

5. **Counterproductive Sentences.** Faithfully applying the utilitarian crime-prevention approach, consideration should always be given to the possibility that more severe sentences—whatever their general deterrence or incapacitation benefits—may actually prove counterproductive by leaving the defendant *more* likely to reoffend after release from custody. This may happen, for instance, with a prison sentence that cuts the defendant off from family and other positive social influences on the outside, while stigmatizing the defendant in ways that raise high barriers to lawful employment after release. The MPC:S framework is noteworthy for its explicit attention to such risks. First, the laundry list of utilitarian considerations in § 1.02(2)(a)(ii) includes "preservation of families" and "reintegration of offenders into the law-abiding community." Second, and even more pointedly, § 1.02(2)(a)(iv) identifies as a purpose "avoid[ing] the use of sanctions that increase the likelihood offenders will engage in future criminal conduct."

6. **Parsimony Revisited.** Parsimony puts in an appearance in § 1.02(2)(a)(iii). Do you see how the principle is articulated differently than in 18 U.S.C. § 3553(a)?

7. **How Helpful?** Would the analysis in *Stern* be any easier or more satisfactory using the § 1.02(2)(a) framework than the § 3553(a) framework? Overall, out of the three models we have considered for putting purposes together, which seems to you the most helpful and appropriate?

8. **Prioritization of Purposes.** The MPC:S may strike you as more helpful to judges than § 3553(a) because it establishes a clear relationship between just deserts and utilitarian considerations—desert has primacy, in the sense that utilitarian considerations cannot justify a sentence that lies outside the desert range. The clarity with which the MPC:S defines the relationship between retributive and utilitarian approaches contrasts with the many existing state statutes that, in the same spirit as § 3553(a), are structured more as a laundry list of permissible purposes.[33] Do you think that the MPC:S will inspire many states to rethink their approach to purposes, as the original MPC did in the 1960s?

---

[33] For instance, Hawaii has adopted a laundry list of permissible considerations in the determination of a sentence that essentially replicates § 3553(a)(1)–(3) and (6). Haw. Rev. Stat. Ann. § 706–606. Similarly, the North Dakota Criminal Code identifies as its purposes:

> 1. To ensure the public safety through: a. vindication of public norms by the imposition of merited punishment; b. the deterrent influence of the penalties hereinafter provided; c. the rehabilitation of those convicted of violations of this title; and d. such confinement as may be necessary to prevent likely recurrence of serious criminal behavior. . . .
>
> 3. To prescribe penalties which are proportionate to the seriousness of offenses and which permit recognition of differences in rehabilitation possibilities among individual offenders. . . .

N.D. Cent. Code Ann. § 12.1–01–02.

C. COLLATERAL PURPOSES OF PUNISHMENT

In Section A, we considered the purposes of punishment that are most frequently expressly invoked by sentencing judges and in statutory declarations of the purposes of punishment. However, other purposes also sometimes seem apparent in particular cases or in broad patterns of sentencing outcomes over time. We will consider four such purposes, which might be labeled "collateral"—or perhaps even "covert," since they are, to varying degrees, controversial as a matter of public policy, ethically troublesome, and often disavowed by the actors in the criminal justice system.

1. EFFICIENT FUNCTIONING OF THE CRIMINAL JUSTICE SYSTEM

It is well known that defendants who plead guilty can normally expect more lenient sentences than otherwise similarly situated defendants who are convicted at trial. Depending on how you look at the phenomenon, you might call this differential punishment a "plea benefit" or a "trial penalty." However framed, it clearly plays an important role in the sentencing process. One recent review of the relevant empirical research concluded, "Estimates of the trial tax vary but typically involve two- to sixfold increases in the odds of imprisonment with 15–60 percent longer sentences." Brian D. Johnson, *Trials and Tribulations: The Trial Tax and the Process of Punishment*, 48 CRIME & JUST. 313, 314 (2019). Such differences in punishment based on mode of conviction have raised numerous concerns, including charges that defendants are effectively being penalized for exercising their constitutional right to a trial, and that some innocent defendants are being pressured into entering false pleas of guilt.

How can the differential punishment be justified? Sometimes, the phenomenon is attributed to *rehabilitative* considerations—perhaps the defendant who pleads guilty is exhibiting an acceptance of responsibility that bodes well for his or her prospects of returning to a law-abiding life. However, there is little evidence to support the hope that these defendants actually do recidivate at substantially lower rates than other defendants. *Id.* at 320–21. Alternatively, the plea differential is justified *retributively* on the suppositions that defendants who plead guilty are expressing remorse, and that such remorse reduces culpability. However, the very fact that the defendant gains a sentencing benefit from the plea casts considerable doubt on the extent to which the plea can be fairly regarded as a sincere expression of remorse. Under still another line of thinking, it is appropriate for sentencers to reward guilty pleas because such pleas are beneficial to *victims*—bringing earlier closure to the criminal case and sparing the victim the inconvenience and possible embarrassment associated with trial testimony. However, this fails to account for plea differentials in victimless cases, which tend to be about as large or maybe even larger than in cases involving conventional victimization. *Id.* at 321. A final intriguing, but poorly supported, justification views the differential from the standpoint not of the defendant who pleads guilty, but of the defendant who goes to trial. The assumption is that trials tend to generate "bad facts" that reflect poorly on the defendant's culpability or dangerousness. It is doubted, however, that bad facts are so pervasive and routinely compelling across the broad range of criminal cases as to account fully for the "trial penalty." Moreover, it has been argued that the cases with the worst facts are precisely those in which defendants would be most likely to plead guilty since this minimizes the risk that damaging new information will come to the sentencing judge's attention. *Id.*

The most widely accepted explanation of the plea differential is that prosecutors and judges want to encourage and reward guilty pleas so as to save themselves and their agencies the time and trouble of a trial and all of the related court proceedings. As one judge famously, if cold-bloodedly, declared, "He takes some of my time, I take some of his. That's the way it works." Albert W. Alschuler, *The Trial Judge's Role in Plea Bargaining, Part I*, 76 COLUM. L. REV. 1059, 1089 (1976) (quoting a Chicago trial judge).

The plea differential thus points to government efficiency as a possible purpose of punishment. With limited resources available to the criminal justice system, sentencing practices that reduce the average amount of effort that prosecutors, police, and court personnel must devote to each case should result in greater numbers of cases prosecuted and defendants convicted. Note that this efficiency purpose might be assimilated to both utilitarian and retributive frameworks. From the utilitarian standpoint, more convictions are desirable to the extent that would mean greater *certainty* of punishment (the key to deterrence), increased numbers of dangerous individuals subjected to incapacitation, and increased numbers of treatable individuals subjected to rehabilitation. From the retributive standpoint, more convictions are desirable to the extent that would mean that a greater proportion of the criminally culpable are punished. Of course, the downside of the plea-inducement system from these perspectives is that many defendants will get a reduced degree of punishment that may not be fully commensurate with their desert or with what would be optimal for purposes of deterrence, incapacitation, or rehabilitation.[34]

---

[34] If conceptualized as a trial penalty, the plea differential exists in some tension with the rule that "[t]o punish a person because he has done what the law plainly allows him to do is a due process violation of the most basic sort." Bordenkircher v. Hayes, 434 U.S. 357, 363 (1978). However, for those defendants who go to trial and then receive what seems to them a harsher sentence as a result, it has been difficult to prove a violation of this due-process rule to the satisfaction of reviewing courts. *See, e.g.*, United States v. Gozes-Wagner, 977 F.3d 323, 337 (5th Cir. 2020) ("[I]f the district court plainly stated that it was punishing the defendant more severely than it otherwise would *because* she went to trial, that would clearly amount to a constitutional violation .... But that did not happen here."). *Gozes-Wagner* involved an allegation that a *judge* penalized the defendant for going to trial. When a *prosecutor* through

The encouragement of guilty pleas is not the only way that the efficiency purpose is pursued. For instance, some plea agreements reward the defendant not merely for pleading guilty, but also for providing assistance in the apprehension or prosecution of others. This, too, can help the criminal justice system to punish a greater proportion of the guilty without any greater burdens on police, prosecutor, and court resources. Of course, such cooperation benefits can lead to *false* testimony that convicts the innocent—much as the trial penalty can lead to false guilty pleas. Neither utilitarian nor retributive purposes are *automatically* well-served by an increased number of convictions.

The efficient functioning of *corrections* agencies may also be a consideration for practitioners and policymakers. For instance, as U.S. prison populations exploded in the late twentieth century and state governments were forced to build many expensive new prisons, policymakers grew more interested in developing so-called intermediate sanctions that would—it was hoped—deliver comparable or better crime-reduction benefits at far less cost than conventional imprisonment. We will consider intermediate sanctions in more detail in Chapter 8.

More recently, and with a similar goal of enhancing system efficiency, it has been proposed that sentencing judges be provided with information about the fiscal costs associated with the different sentencing options considered in each case—information that might lead to greater use of lower-cost punishments.[35] Does it trouble you to think that a judge might intentionally give a highly culpable defendant less punishment than he or she deserves in order to save taxpayers' money?

2. GENERATION OF REVENUE

In thinking about efficiency as a purpose of punishment, we imagined goals like increasing the number of convictions or achieving lower recidivism rates while holding constant or perhaps even reducing criminal justice expenditures. But what if criminal sentences could actually help to increase government revenue? Policymakers have long found it hard to resist the temptation to squeeze defendants for funds, and, if anything, there appears a recent trend toward *increasing* the reliance on criminal justice processes as a means to generate cash.

Fines are, of course, the most straightforward way that a criminal sentence results in money for the government. Additionally, forfeiture laws allow the government to seize for its own purposes the proceeds and instrumentalities of criminal activity. This might include, for instance, both the boat used to transport a shipment of drugs into the United

---

his or her charging discretion penalizes a defendant's failure to accept a plea bargain—even explicitly—the Supreme Court has indicated that the Constitution may simply provide no remedy at all. *See Bordenkircher, supra*; Michael O'Hear, *The End of* Bordenkircher*: Extending the Logic of* Apprendi *to Plea Bargaining*, 84 WASH. U. L. REV. 835 (2006).

[35] For a critique of the proposal, see Chad Flanders, *Cost As A Sentencing Factor: Missouri's Experiment*, 77 MO. L. REV. 391 (2012).

States and the money obtained from selling the drugs. Forfeitures can be accomplished as part of a criminal case, although in many jurisdictions the government also has available a civil forfeiture process to achieve the same ends. A host of additional fees can also be levied on defendants, often framed as ways to offset the costs of prosecution and punishment. The law of fines, fees, forfeitures, and the like will be considered in more detail in Chapter 9.

Do you see any ethical problems raised by these practices? Consider the following critical observations.

Wayne A. Logan & Ronald F. Wright, Mercenary Criminal Justice

2014 U. ILL. L. REV. 1175 (2014)

It is often said that a criminal offender owes a debt to society. Lately, though, it seems that a growing number of bill collectors are trying to cash in on that debt. Courts ask for payment of costs, corrections officials demand recovery of incarceration-related expenses, and legislatures levy surcharges for convictions. Even private, for-profit entities get a piece of the action, collecting fees for probation supervision and other services. Some of these collectors knock on the door even before a final bill is due, such as when prosecutors require suspects to pay diversion fees before charges are filed. The payment demands have become so numerous and complex that they have earned their own acronym: LFOs, or "legal financial obligations."

While it might be easy to understand the rationale for each LFO standing alone, taken together they often have debilitating consequences for individuals. Today, it is not uncommon for costs, fees, surcharges, and the like to exceed the amount of restitution or fines that a defendant owes in a given criminal case. Recent academic work and advocacy group studies have condemned LFOs for their economically regressive impact on poor defendants, the barriers they present to reentry, and the racial disparities they reflect.

* * * Today, criminal justice actors increasingly rely on the income from LFOs to fund ordinary system operations and to expand the system's reach. When this happens, courts and other criminal justice actors become mercenaries, in effect working on commission.

The incentives surface at various times, including shortly after arrest, when payments from arrestees can short-circuit the criminal justice process. Demands for payment at a point so early in the process, when institutional oversight is weak, threaten the presumption of innocence. They also raise equal justice concerns.

Yet the troubling effects of LFOs extend beyond individual case outcomes. When the tax-paying public is not asked to fund criminal justice, it gets a distorted message about the real costs of enforcement.

While requiring offenders to internalize the costs associated with their wrongdoing can be justified in principle (for instance, by promoting an offender's acceptance of responsibility), doing so weakens one of the key moderating influences in public safety politics. As one commentator has observed, a "government that can fob off costs on criminals has an incentive to find criminals everywhere."[8]

3. CAREER PRESERVATION AND ADVANCEMENT

In discussions of purposes of punishment, the idea of "sending a message" often figures prominently. A deterrence-oriented sentence is intended to send a message to the defendant (specific deterrence) and/or the public at large (general deterrence). Similarly, retributive purposes are also sometimes conceptualized in communicative terms. In either framework, the "message" that is expressed through the sentence is typically seen as one that is communicated by the sentencer *on behalf of the community*—a message, that is, about the values or intentions of the community. Sometimes, however, punishment seems designed, at least in part, to send a message about the sentencer personally—a message that the sentencer is "tough on crime."

Many judges do have incentives to send this sort of message. In thirty-nine states, trial judges must stand for reelection. Gregory A. Huber & Sanford C. Gordon, *Accountability and Coercion: Is Justice Blind When It Runs for Office?*, 48 AM. J. POL. SCI. 247, 247 (2004). They do so against a backdrop of public-opinion surveys that consistently find large, super-majoritarian support for increasing sentencing severity. Mark D. Ramirez, *Americans' Changing Views on Crime and Punishment*, 77 PUB. OPINION Q. 1006, 1011 (2013). Although other research suggests that public attitudes on this score may reflect widespread misunderstandings about crime and the legal system, and that laypeople appear less punitive when given additional information or asked more nuanced questions, Michael O'Hear & Darren Wheelock, *Violent Crime and Punitiveness: An Empirical Study of Public Opinion*, 103 MARQ. L. REV. 1035, 1051–52 (2020), judges whose careers are on the line may not feel they can count on a uniformly thoughtful, well-informed electorate. Indeed, examples abound of judges who lost their positions after opponents publicized a single sentencing decision that was perceived as unduly lenient. Judges may thus feel a political need to insulate themselves against such attacks when they consider what punishments to impose on defendants, especially defendants who have been convicted of those sorts of major violent and sexual crimes that draw the greatest public attention and indignation. Moreover, similar dynamics may even affect judges in jurisdictions that do not require reelection, for instance, if a judge is eyeing potential appointment to a higher court.

---

[8] *See* Kevin Baker, *Cruel and Unusual Punishment: Why Prisoners Shouldn't Pay Their Debt*, AMER. HERITAGE, July 2006, at 22. * * *

Some empirical research does provide support for the expectation that judges facing reelection may perceive an incentive to send "tough on crime" signals to the electorate. For instance, one study in Washington State concluded that "sentencing of serious offenses becomes more severe as elections approach: sentence lengths increase by about 10% between the beginning and end of a judge's political cycle." Carlos Berdejó & Noam Yuchtman, *Crime, Punishment, and Politics: An Analysis of Political Cycles in Criminal Sentencing*, 95 REV. ECON. & STATISTICS 741, 742 (2013). Notably, the researchers found no increased sentence lengths for less serious crimes, which presumably are of relatively little interest to voters, or with respect to retiring judges in their final term in office.

Are such sentencing patterns a matter of concern? In a democratic system, isn't it desirable for government officials to make decisions that reflect public preferences, including "tough on crime" preferences? If there is a problem, maybe it is with unduly lenient sentences at the start of the judge's term, rather than unduly harsh sentences at the end.

But, on the other hand, one might question whether it is truly consistent with the judicial role to base decisions on perceived public preferences, as opposed to the formally enacted legal frameworks for the decisions. Statutes like 18 U.S.C. § 3553(a) emphasize crime-prevention and desert as purposes of punishment, not the avoidance of career-threatening controversy. To be sure, there may be principled ways of connecting desert to public attitudes, but, as we have seen, modern retributive theorizing suggests that those connections are more subtle than simply ratcheting up the punitiveness in cases that have generated or might generate public outrage. And aren't there risks that a "give the people what they want" approach to sentencing will result in harsher sentences not only for unpopular *offenses*, but also unpopular *offenders*?

Judges are not the only sentencing "deciders" who might be tempted to cater to, or at least seek insulation from, public punitiveness. Legislators, for instance, make policy decisions that can have important consequences for sentencing practice, as in the adoption of new mandatory minimum prison terms. Of course, legislators are much more clearly and appropriately political actors than judges. It may strike you as relatively unproblematic for a legislator to take into account what his or her constituents think when deciding how to vote on a proposed mandatory minimum. Yet, even in this context, there may be concerns about bowing to public attitudes that are uninformed or ill-considered.

Prosecutors, too, may be seen as key deciders, given the practical importance of their charging, plea-bargaining, and sentence-recommendation decisions. In the United States, prosecutors also tend to face at least indirect political pressures, with district attorneys and their equivalents subject to reelection in all but three states—and even in those three states appointed by an elected attorney general. Justin T. Pickett, *Public Opinion and Criminal Justice Policy: Theory and Research*, 2 ANN. REV. CRIMINOLOGY 405, 418–19 (2019). Do you think it is consistent with the prosecutor's role—often characterized as "quasi-judicial"—to take electoral considerations into account in deciding whether to press for harsher sentences in high-profile cases?

4. CONTROL OF THE POOR AND MARGINALIZED

It is well-known that the great majority of the individuals who are prosecuted and punished in the American criminal justice system are economically disadvantaged or otherwise belong to traditionally marginalized social groups. Some research suggests that 80% or more of felony defendants are too poor to afford a lawyer.[36] African-Americans account for about 27% of arrestees, 33% of prisoners, and 30% of probationers. Native-Americans are also arrested and incarcerated at much higher rates than their overall share of the population. Latinx individuals also account for a disproportionate share of prisoners. Individuals with mental illness, another historically marginalized group, are also overrepresented in the criminal justice system.

Figure 1-3. Racial groups as percentage of general population, arrests, and felony convictions.[37]

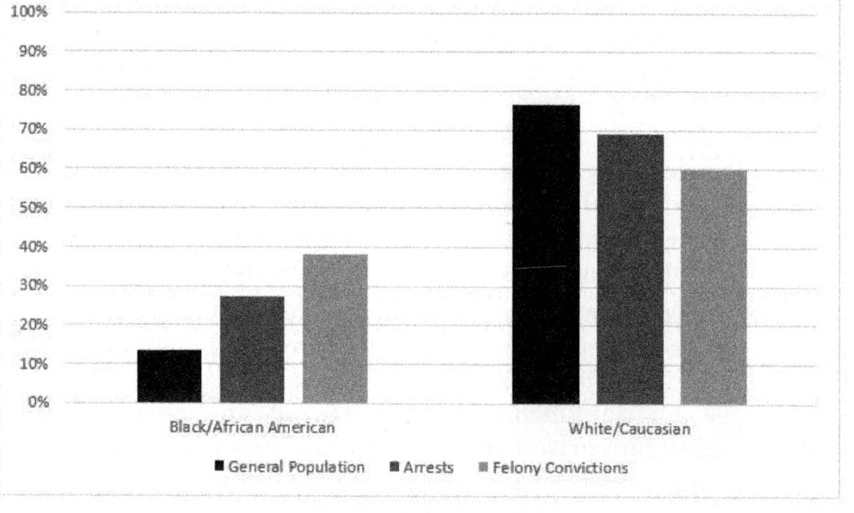

[36] *See, e.g.*, CAROLINE WOLF HARLOW, U.S. DEPT. OF JUSTICE, DEFENSE COUNSEL IN CRIMINAL CASES 1 (2000) (in study of felony cases in large urban counties, finding that about 82% of the defendants were represented by public defenders or assigned counsel).

[37] General population figures are for 2019 and derived from the U.S. Census Bureau, https://www.census.gov/quickfacts/fact/table/US/RHI125219. Black and White percentages are for individuals who identified one race only, and include individuals with Latinx origin. Arrest figures are from the Federal Bureau of Investigation for 2018, https://ucr.fbi.gov/crime-in-the-u.s/2018/crime-in-the-u.s.-2018/tables/table-43. Black and White percentages include individuals with Latinx origin. The data do not permit a separate breakdown of non-Latinx Black and non-Latinx White figures. The felony conviction figures come from SEAN ROSENMERKEL, MATTHEW DUROSE & DONALD FAROLE, JR., U.S. DEP'T OF JUSTICE, FELONY SENTENCES IN STATE COURTS, 2006—STATISTICAL TABLES 17 (2010), https://www.bjs.gov/content/pub/pdf/fssc06st.pdf. The data do not include a separate Latinx category.

Figure 1-4. Racial/ethnic groups as percentage of general population, probationers, and prisoners.[38]

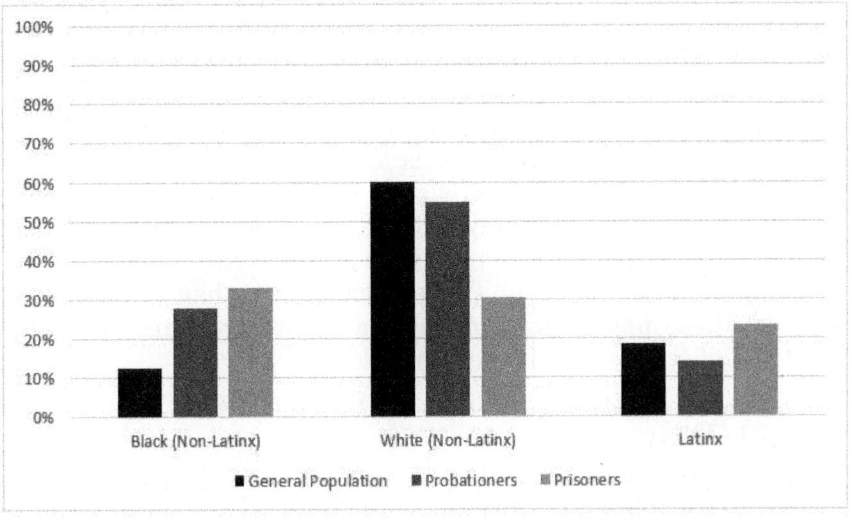

Such patterns naturally raise the question of whether the system's focus on the poor and marginalized is merely incidental to the pursuit of other purposes we have considered, such as crime prevention, or should surveillance and control of the poor and marginalized be recognized as an implicit purpose in and of itself? Such a purpose might reflect a desire to impose white middle-class social values and behavioral norms on the targeted groups, perhaps in a paternalistic hope that these groups would thereby improve their socioeconomic position and become better integrated into "mainstream" American society. Or such a purpose might reflect a desire to ensure that subordinated groups remain subordinated, perhaps in the hope that their labor could be more easily and inexpensively exploited by the dominant group.

Consider a troubling historical example. In 1865, the Thirteenth Amendment formally ended slavery in the United States, but in itself could not eradicate the underlying ideology of White supremacy. White southerners quickly devised a variety of legal and extralegal strategies in an effort to maintain their dominance. For instance, the legal historian Lawrence Friedman describes a first wave of legal responses to emancipation:

> The infamous "Black Codes" of Mississippi, South Carolina, and other southern states blatantly attempted to tie black workers

[38] General population figures are for 2019 and derived from the U.S. Census Bureau, https://www.census.gov/data/tables/time-series/demo/popest/2010s-national-detail.html. Black and White percentages are for individuals who identified one race only, and exclude individuals with Latinx origin. The probation figures come from DANIELLE KAEBLE, U.S. DEPT. OF JUSTICE, PROBATION AND PAROLE IN THE UNITED STATES, 2016, at 17 (2018). The Black and White percentages exclude individuals with Latinx origin. The prison figures come from E. ANN CARSON, U.S. DEP'T OF JUSTICE, PRISONERS IN 2018, at 6 (2020). The Black and White percentages exclude individuals with Latinx origin.

> to the soil, not as slaves (that was illegal), but as peons, or, to give the matter its best face, as contract laborers for white employers. Criminal provisions were a vital part of the codes. A black who quit his job while he was under contract to work was liable to arrest. . . . In Mississippi, under a typical provision, all "freedmen, free negroes and mulattoes" who were over eighteen, and had "no lawful employment or business," were declared to be "vagrants." A vagrant could be fined up to fifty dollars—an enormous sum for a poor ex-slave—and imprisoned up to ten days; if a black could not pay the fine, the sheriff could hire him out to anybody willing to pay it, with a "preference" going to his employer, if he had one. The employer was then entitled to deduct these payments from the black's wages. This was not slavery, of course, but dangerously close.

LAWRENCE M. FRIEDMAN, CRIME AND PUNISHMENT IN AMERICAN HISTORY 94 (1993).

Later, southern states developed an even more horrifying strategy for deploying the criminal justice system so as to extract cheap labor from African-Americans, the so-called "convict-leasing" system. States contracted with private business operators to take custody of convicted defendants—overwhelmingly African-American—who were then sent to work under armed guard in extremely harsh conditions and provided with minimal food, shelter, and medical care. For instance, conditions for convict labor on plantations have been described this way:

> The prisoners ate and slept on bare ground, without blankets or mattresses, and often without clothes. . . . Some who tried to escape were whipped "till the blood ran down their legs"; others had a metal spur riveted to their feet. Convicts dropped from exhaustion, pneumonia, malaria, frostbite, consumption, sunstroke, dysentery, gunshot wounds, and "shackle poisoning" (the constant rubbing of chains and leg irons against bare flesh).

DAVID M. OSHINSKY, "WORSE THAN SLAVERY": PARCHMAN FARM AND THE ORDEAL OF JIM CROW JUSTICE 45 (1997). Mortality rates were shocking. In 1882, for instance, a time when African-Americans were no longer valuable personal chattel of slave owners, 126 out of 735 African-American convicts in Mississippi perished. *Id.* at 46. By contrast, among the White convicts, who were typically held in conventional prisons rather than being leased out, only 2 of 83 died.

Today, it seems easy to recognize that the southern criminal justice system operated in conjunction with a variety of other legal and social mechanisms—lynching, school segregation, poll taxes, restrictive housing covenants, workplace discrimination, bans on interracial marriage, and so forth—to establish a comprehensive system of racial domination in the South up to the middle decades of the twentieth century—the so-called "Jim Crow" system.

Of course, in the wake of *Brown v. Board of Education*, the Civil Rights Act of 1964, and many other legal developments, the doctrinal underpinnings of the old Jim Crow system have been eliminated. Yet, wide racial disparities persist along many important dimensions of American life: income, employment, home-ownership, education, chronic disease, life expectancy—and incarceration. Could it be that those who make or implement our sentencing policies are still contributing to a multifaceted, if somewhat more subtle, contemporary system of racial domination?

Law professor Michelle Alexander, for one, has argued in a bestselling book that our criminal justice system now constitutes a "new Jim Crow." She asserts,

> What has changed since the collapse of Jim Crow has less to do with the basic structure of our society than with the language we use to justify it. In the era of colorblindness, it is no longer socially permissible to use race, explicitly, as a justification for discrimination, exclusion, and social contempt. So we don't. Rather than rely on race, we use our criminal justice system to label people of color "criminals" and then engage in all the practices we supposedly left behind. Today it is perfectly legal to discriminate against criminals in nearly all the ways that it was once legal to discriminate against African Americans. . . . As criminal, you are afforded scarcely more rights, and arguably less respect, than a black man living in Alabama at the height of Jim Crow. We have not ended racial caste in America; we have merely redesigned it.[39]

THE NEW JIM CROW: MASS INCARCERATION IN THE AGE OF COLORBLINDNESS 2 (2010).

In a thoughtful rejoinder, the law professor James Forman, Jr. agrees with much of Alexander's argument, but also suggests that the "new Jim Crow" thesis may in some respects be a misleading or incomplete account of the contemporary phenomenon of mass incarceration. James Forman, Jr., *Racial Critiques of Mass Incarceration: Beyond the New Jim Crow*, 87 N.Y.U. L. REV. 21 (2012). His critique focuses, in part, on the issue of class. He observes, "An essential quality of Jim Crow was its uniform and demeaning treatment of all blacks. Jim Crow was designed to ensure the separation, disenfranchisement, and political and economic subordination of all black Americans—young or old, rich or poor, educated or illiterate." *Id.* at 53. By contrast, he argues, "one of mass incarceration's defining features is that, unlike Jim Crow, its reach is largely confined to the poorest, least-educated segments of the African-American community.

[39] Alexander's account of the loss of rights that follows conviction of a crime emphasizes the so-called "collateral consequences" of a conviction, such as the loss of the right to vote and disqualification from various government benefits programs. We will consider collateral consequences in more detail in Chapter 10.

High school dropouts account for most of the rise in African-American incarceration rates." *Id.* at 54 (citation omitted). Forman further observes, "Many whites—most of them poor and uneducated—are now behind bars. One-third of our nation's prisoners are [non-Latinx] white, and incarceration rates have risen steadily even in states where most inmates are white." *Id.* at 58 (citations omitted). Forman's analysis suggests that, if there is a social control agenda that lies behind contemporary sentencing policies and practices, the agenda may have as much to do with economic and educational disadvantage as with race *per se.*[40]

Many researchers over the years have attempted to assess the impact of race on sentencing outcomes. The best studies make efforts to control for criminal history and offense severity; otherwise, it is hard to say whether racial differences in punishment merely reflect racial differences in offending. To be sure, there is no single, foolproof method for holding offense severity and criminal history constant across a large number of cases. However, many studies over several decades covering multiple jurisdictions and employing a variety of analytical methods consistently point in the same direction: (1) offense severity and criminal history are more important factors in determining sentences than are defendant demographic characteristics; and (2) by small, but statistically significant margins, Black defendants tend to receive more severe sentences than similarly situated White defendants. Ryan D. King & Michael T. Light, *Have Racial and Ethnic Disparities in Sentencing Declined?*, 48 CRIME & JUST. 365, 370–71 (2019). The racial differences are most pronounced as to the "in/out" decision, i.e., whether the defendant will be sentenced to probation or incarceration. Among those who are sentenced to prison, racial differences in sentence *length* tend not to reach statistical significance.[41] It is important, of course, to bear in mind the familiar caveat of social scientists: "correlation does not imply causation." Researchers cannot control for all of the vast range of potentially relevant variables at sentencing. It remains possible that the observed racial differences in sentencing outcomes can be explained by reference to some unobserved, non-racial factors.

Even assuming that race in and of itself makes a difference in some small, but nontrivial, number of cases, that still leaves open the question of why. Is it a matter, for instance, of implicit (unconscious) racial bias, or is there some more intentional racial agenda?

---

[40] In another work, the Pulitzer-Prize winning LOCKING UP OUR OWN: CRIME AND PUNISHMENT IN BLACK AMERICA (2017), Professor Forman has documented the substantial support among Black leaders for the punitive turn in American criminal justice in the 1970s and 1980s in order to address deteriorating conditions in poor Black neighborhoods.

[41] Although Native-Americans, like African-Americans, experience elevated rates of incarceration, the studies that have been conducted on the sentencing of Native-Americans have been comparatively few in number and have produced more mixed results. King & Light, *supra*, at 376–77.

One explanatory theory has particularly drawn the attention of many researchers over the years: the "racial threat" theory. The theory predicts that discrimination against a minority group will grow as it comes to represent a larger percentage of the local population, and hence constitutes a greater threat to the economic and political domination of the majority group. *Id.* at 403. It is claimed that such discrimination may be manifest in a number of different ways, including—some have hypothesized—in more punitive responses to minority crime. However, few studies of sentencing data have found statistically significant correlations between a growing Black population and widening racial disparities in punishment. *See id.* at 406–07 (discussing studies). On the other hand, some research does find a correlation between the size of a state's Black population and the likelihood that it will adopt punitive sentencing laws. Scott W. Duxbury, *Who Controls Criminal Law? Racial Threat and the Adoption of State Sentencing Law, 1975 to 2012*, 86 AM. SOC. REV. 123 (2020). Other research suggests that states with larger black populations are more likely to increase their incarceration rates when rates of violent crime are high. Michael C. Campbell, Matt Vogel & Joshua Williams, *Historical Contingencies and the Evolving Importance of Race, Violent Crime, and Region in Explaining Mass Incarceration in the United States*, 53 CRIMINOLOGY 180 (2015).

Although sentencing researchers have had a longstanding interest in racial dynamics, there has been growing attention in recent years to ethnicity effects, particularly relating to the sentencing of Latinx defendants. The research tends to reach similar conclusions as with race: by small, but statistically significant, margins, Latinx defendants receive harsher sentences than similarly situated white non-Latinx defendants, especially with respect to the in/out decision. King & Light, *supra*, at 371. Notably, though, some research suggests that most or all of the Latinx disparity is driven by harsher punishment for non-citizens. *Id.* at 424. In other words, if Latinx defendants who are U.S. citizens are compared with non-Latinx defendants who are also citizens, there seems comparatively little disparity in sentencing outcomes.

There has been much less research done on the relationship between class and sentencing, which likely results from the fact that criminal justice agencies collect and report measures of defendant socioeconomic status much less consistently than they do information about race and (increasingly) Latinx status. Results from the relatively few studies in this area have been mixed.[42]

---

[42] *Compare* Byungbae Kim, Cassia Spohn & E.C. Hedberg, *Federal Sentencing as a Collaborative Process: Judges, Prosecutors, Judge-Prosecutor Dyads, and Disparity in Sentencing*, 53 CRIMINOLOGY 597, 612 (2015) (in study of three federal district courts, finding no statistically significant relationship between sentencing outcomes and defendant education level), *with* Jill K. Doerner, *The Joint Effects of Gender and Race/Ethnicity on Sentencing Outcomes in Federal Courts*, 25 WOMEN & CRIM. JUST. 313, 326 (2015) (in national study of federal sentences, finding statistically significant relationship between education level and sentence length for Black and non-Latinx White defendants, but not in/out decision).

Many laypeople have strong feelings about the role of race, class, and ethnicity in contemporary criminal punishment. Based on the information presented here, as well as your own sense of things, do you think it would be fair to say that one of the "purposes" of punishment in the United States today is to exert control over people who are poor and/or who belong to historically marginalized racial or ethnic minority groups? To characterize this as a "purpose," of course, implies that there is something intentional or deliberate about the disparities in our criminal justice system.[43] As you consider these disparities, do you think that intentionality actually matters—or should disparities be regarded as a problem regardless of their cause?

[43] In Chapter 4, we will consider the potential role of "implicit" (unconscious) racial bias at sentencing.

CHAPTER 2

SENTENCING SYSTEMS—PAST & PRESENT

The abstractions of penal principles and justifications assume tangible importance the moment a defendant faces sentencing. This chapter examines the various systems that have evolved in the United States for determining and administering criminal punishment. The organization of the chapter reflects two basic observations. The first is that the dramatic changes that have taken place in American sentencing over the past five decades reflect major shifts in political and social sentiment over time. The second is that there is no such thing as an "American sentencing system." Rather, true to the nation's decentralized approach to democratic governance, important variations exist in the laws and practices of the fifty states, the District of Columbia, the federal government, and other jurisdictional entities. While some general trends can be seen in the modern history of American sentencing practices, the differences among jurisdictions can have a critically important impact on sentencing outcomes.

This chapter begins with an overview of the historical evolution of sentencing in the United States and then focuses on the several predominant approaches used today.

A. ORIGINS & EVOLUTION OF SENTENCING PRACTICES IN THE UNITED STATES

Lengthy articles and entire books have been written about the history of American sentencing. By necessity, the account here is abbreviated, intended to provide a foundational understanding of this history and the critically important shifts marking the nation's approach to sentencing.

1. COLONIAL PERIOD TO MID-1800S

During colonial times, sentences were typically determined by the crime of conviction. As the Supreme Court has recounted, early "substantive criminal law tended to be sanction-specific; it prescribed a particular sentence for each offense," and judges imposed the sentence accordingly. *Apprendi v. New Jersey*, 530 U.S. 466, 478 (2000). Following European practice, death sentences were commonly prescribed for felony offenses. However, in the small, close-knit communities of the time, juries played a critical role in mitigating punishment, "calibrat[ing] their verdicts to the seriousness of the crime and the behavior and desert of the criminal." STEPHANOS BIBAS, THE MACHINERY OF CRIMINAL JUSTICE

7 (2012). In this way, community members, players in the courtroom morality plays characteristic of colonial-era criminal justice, often tempered the harsh punishments of the time, which were well known to jurors. In the event jurors could not "massage the facts into a lesser, noncapital charge," they might nullify, acquitting otherwise guilty defendants. And when for whatever reason a jury failed to mitigate, other system actors could intervene by extending "benefit of clergy" (a mechanism originally designed to shield clerics from punishment by lay courts but later made more generally available) or by granting clemency. BIBAS, *supra,* at 7–8; DAVID J. ROTHMAN, THE DISCOVERY OF THE ASYLUM: SOCIAL ORDER AND DISORDER IN THE NEW REPUBLIC 51 (1971).

In a time before the advent of the public prosecutor, as we know the position today, prosecutions were mainly by private citizens. In general, free White men of property sat on juries and acted as judges. Unlike the modern jury, the colonial jury was explicitly permitted to find both the facts and the law. Akhil Reed Amar, *The Bill of Rights as a Constitution,* 100 YALE L.J. 1131, 1193 (1991).

The punishments imposed during the era were often physical in nature and carried out in public. In addition to death, sanctions included mutilation (e.g., one or both ears) and branding (most commonly to the forehead), which then provided notice to others of the person's "record."[1] Moreover, non-lethal punishments shamed convicts, whose humiliation could serve as an object lesson for observers. Public whippings and time spent in the stocks or pillory located in or near the town square, where the convict would be subject to ridicule and scorn, and perhaps pelted with rotten vegetables and the like, served as a vivid reminder of what lay in store for wrongdoers. Executions attracted large crowds and were staged with great pomp and circumstance in fora for all to see. BIBAS, *supra,* at 11.

Colonial jails, to the extent they existed, contained a varied population including debtors, vagrants, individuals awaiting trial, and convicts. Confinement was not considered punishment. Typically, detainees were housed in large rooms, and were not segregated by gender, age, or reason for detention. In the 1790s, however, what one scholar has called "proto-prisons" emerged in response to growing concern over use of the death penalty, shaming, and corporal punishment. Philadelphia's Walnut Street Prison in 1790, followed by New York City's Newgate Prison in 1796, were the most prominent examples. In the 1810s, however, riots, fires, severe overcrowding, and deplorable conditions inspired a major shift in method and philosophy, with the outlines of the modern penitentiary system taking shape. Ashley

---

[1] *See* Steven A. Hatfield, *Criminal Punishment in America: The Colonial to the Modern Era,* 1 U.S. A.F. J. LEGAL STUDIES, 139, 145 (1990) ("The cropping of ears was not always neatly accomplished. Sometimes the ears were nailed to the pillory . . . during the prisoner's stay there. When the prisoner's time was up he was permitted to leave; his ears, however, were expected to stay.").

T. Rubin, *A Neo-Institutional Account of Prison Diffusion*, 49 L. & SOC. REV. 365, 377 (2015).

The revolutionary change came with Auburn Prison, inaugurated in 1821 in upstate New York, and Pennsylvania's Eastern State Penitentiary (in Philadelphia) and Western State Penitentiary (near Pittsburgh), inaugurated in 1829. Although sharing similarities, the institutions took different correctional approaches. Auburn inmates slept in individual cells and during the day worked together in early factory-like environments inside the prison walls.[2] Out of concern that inmates would converse about their misdeeds and perpetuate criminality, officials prohibited inmates from looking at or speaking with one another. The method came to be known as the Congregate or Auburn System. The Separate or Pennsylvania System also housed inmates in individual cells, but inmates did not congregate—they worked, slept, and prayed in their cells, with only a small yard next to each cell provided for exercise. Like Auburn inmates, they were not allowed to speak, except to official visitors such as prison authorities, with rehabilitation as the goal:

> A silent experience, with solitary labor and time for prayer, would enable reformation. Moreover, the [Pennsylvania] System enabled inmates to reenter society unrecognized and unimpeded by stigma: inmates were known by numbers only and, during any egress from their cells, inmates were hooded to protect their identities even from guards.

Rubin, *supra*, at 379.

Proponents of the prisons believed criminals could be reformed if given the opportunity for religious instruction and spiritual reflection in an environment marked by military-like regimentation and manual labor. As historian David Rothman later explained, "The penitentiary, free of corruptions and dedicated to the proper training of the inmate, would inculcate the discipline that negligent parents, evil companions, taverns, houses of prostitution, theaters, and gambling halls had destroyed. Just as the criminal's environment had led him into crime, the institutional environment would lead him out of it." ROTHMAN, *supra*, at 82–83.

In ensuing decades up to the Civil War, other states, often shortly after achieving statehood, gravitated toward use of penitentiaries. In the

---

[2] The idea of using individual cells did not originate in the U.S.:

> [T]he notion of forcibly confining people is ancient, and there is extensive evidence that the Romans had a well-developed system for imprisoning different types of offenders. The first modern correctional facility to use cellular design was the Hospice of San Michele constructed in 1704 at Rome, Italy. Interestingly, the inscription over the main entry, "It is insufficient to restrain the wicked by punishment unless you render them virtuous by corrective discipline," was remarkably similar to much later American epigrams.

Matthew W. Meskell, Note, *The History of Prisons in the United States from 1777 to 1877*, 51 STAN. L. REV. 839, 846 (1999) (citations omitted); *see also* Stephen D. Sowle, *A Regime of Social Death: Criminal Punishment in the Age of Prisons*, 21 N.Y.U. REV. L. & SOC. CHANGE 497 (1994).

South, White convicts were incarcerated, while African-Americans were mainly punished on plantations (by whipping or death), resulting in substantially smaller southern prison populations.[3] By the Civil War, all states had at least one prison, with each (other than Pennsylvania) adopting the Auburn congregate approach, preferred because, among other reasons, it was cheaper; constructing sufficiently large cells for each inmate on the Pennsylvania model was expensive. Rubin, *supra*, at 373, 387–88.

It did not take long to realize that penitentiaries were doing little to achieve their rehabilitative goals. Institutions were overcrowded, filthy, and dangerous places that simply warehoused convicts, who had come to be viewed by some criminologists as irredeemable degenerates needing to be segregated from society. BIBAS, *supra*, at 14.

Reformers urged that the short, determinate sentences then imposed—by juries, flowing directly from their findings of guilt—be replaced by indeterminate sentences in which release was tied directly to successful rehabilitation. Juries were still expected to find facts and determine guilt, but judges determined the sentence, based on a maximum (and sometimes minimum) term of years, with ranges prescribed by legislatures. "Crime was a 'moral disease,' whose cure was delegated to experts in the criminal justice field, one of whom was the judge." Nancy Gertner, *A Short History of American Sentencing: Too Little Law, Too Much Law, or Just Right*, 100 J. CRIM. L. & CRIMINOLOGY 691, 695 (2010) (citation omitted).

In the new system that emerged in the decades following the Civil War, actual time served was largely determined by prison and parole board officials, based on inmate behavior and performance in educational and vocational programs. When they were deemed sufficiently rehabilitated, inmates were released on parole, to the supervision of relatives or employers, and later to supervision agents employed by the government. During the period of release on parole, an inmate's liberty was contingent on his good behavior and compliance with conditions imposed by the parole board. The Elmira Reformatory in New York is credited as the first institution in the U.S. to combine indeterminate sentences with conditional release, a practice that began in 1877. Edward Lindsey, *Historical Sketch of the Indeterminate Sentence and Parole System*, 16 AM. INST. CRIM. L. & CRIMINOLOGY 9, 21–23 (1925).

2. LATE 1800S TO MID-1970S

As states began authorizing indeterminate sentences, Progressive Era values prompted a renewed interest in rehabilitation. Armed with insights from emerging developments in psychology, criminology, and sociology, reformers spearheaded new efforts to transform the criminal

[3] The post-Civil War plight of African-Americans, including their experiences under the "convict-lease" system in the South, was noted in Chapter 1 and is discussed further in Chapter 5.

justice system from the bottom up. Central to the new way of thinking was that deviance resulted not from free choice by individual offenders, but from social, environmental, and psychological causes. With this belief came the conviction that the penal system should be tailored to each individual's background and needs, and should work to "cure" the criminality caused by inequitable social and physiological conditions. Work by social scientists such as Sheldon and Eleanor Glueck laid the foundation for viewing crime as pathological in origin, necessitating therapeutic intervention by the state. Simple regimentation, work, and harsh discipline were no longer seen as sufficient to reform convicts. Instead, would-be delinquents and criminals needed to be identified, retrained when possible, and incapacitated indefinitely when no cure was readily available.

In this medical model of corrections, the job of the court at sentencing was to prescribe a sentence of open-ended duration, typically a minimum and maximum number of years, based on a broad range set by the legislature. Once in prison, psychiatrists and behavioral science experts would design an individualized regimen to rehabilitate, and parole authorities would decide when (or if) an individual's behavior and program progress afforded a basis to think he or she was safe for release to the community. Under this approach, legislatures prescribed only broad ranges of possible imprisonment for offenses, courts selected a minimum and maximum from within that range and correctional authorities thereafter determined the actual time served, based on an inmate's behavior and progress in rehabilitative programming.

Consistent with the tenor of the times, reformers in the early 1900s spearheaded efforts to single out juvenile offenders for specialized disposition and treatment. Inspired by the precept, dating back to Blackstone's *Commentaries*, that youths lacked the moral culpability of adult offenders and the faith that they could be redeemed by therapeutic intervention, social reformers created what today is known as the "juvenile justice system." While special facilities to house juvenile offenders apart from adults had been created in New York City (in 1824) and Chicago (in 1855), the juvenile system is usually thought to have originated in 1899 when the nation's first juvenile court was established in Cook County, Illinois. Over the next twenty-five years most states implemented juvenile courts and created "reform schools" dedicated to rehabilitating youthful offenders. The goal of this system was articulated by Judge Julian Mack, one of Cook County's juvenile court judges:

> The child who must be brought in should, of course, be made to know that he is face to face with the power of the state, but he should at the same time, and more emphatically, be made to feel that he is the object of its care and solicitude. The ordinary trappings of the court-room are out of place in such hearings. The judge on a bench, looking down upon the boy standing at the bar, can never evoke a proper sympathetic spirit. Seated at

> a desk, with the child at his side, where he can on occasion put his arm around his shoulder and draw the lad to him, the judge, without losing his judicial dignity, will gain immensely in the effectiveness of his work.

Julian Mack, *The Juvenile Court*, 23 HARV. L. REV. 104, 120 (1909).

As the foregoing suggests, juvenile court proceedings were informal, non-adversarial, and non-criminal in nature, designed to reorient wayward youths toward a path of law-abidingness. Marked by a philosophy of *parens patriae*, the court was afforded the authority to make decisions affecting the youth much as a responsible parent would be expected to do. To this end, judges prescribed individualized plans of indeterminate duration, designed to promote the rehabilitation and ensure the safety and welfare of the youth coming before the court.

The first decades of the twentieth century also witnessed significant increases in the use of probation, whereby the court suspended jail or prison and allowed the convict to remain physically free in the community subject to satisfying court-prescribed requirements. American probation is thought to have originated in 1841 through the efforts of John Augustus, a Boston cobbler who persuaded his local magistrate to allow him to informally mentor and supervise lower-level offenders in order "to reform criminals and to prevent crime and not to punish maliciously, or from a spirit of revenge." JOHN AUGUSTUS, FIRST PROBATION OFFICER 23 (1939). New York enacted the nation's first statute expressly authorizing adult probation in 1901, and Missouri, Vermont, Illinois, Minnesota, Rhode Island, and New Jersey followed suit shortly thereafter. In other states lacking probation statutes, the probation movement was hobbled by uncertainty over the common law authority of courts to suspend execution or imposition of sentence. This legal question was answered by the U.S. Supreme Court in *Ex parte United States* (*Killits*), 242 U.S. 27 (1916), which held that federal courts (and by inference state courts) lacked inherent authority to suspend sentences for indefinite periods.

The Court's decision prompted more states to enact laws conferring express authority on courts to suspend jail or prison terms and impose probationary conditions. What began as an altruistic endeavor undertaken by a few idealistic souls (often harshly condemned for their soft-hearted indulgence) came to play a linchpin role in Progressive Era efforts to humanize and individualize the sentencing process. Courts used the expansive discretionary authority afforded by these laws to channel offenders into one of two categories: "those who will and who will not reform without punishment." DAVID J. ROTHMAN, CONSCIENCE AND CONVENIENCE: THE ASYLUM AND ITS ALTERNATIVES IN PROGRESSIVE AMERICA 63 (1980). Candidates for prison included those thought too dangerous to be at-large as well as those in need of discipline and training, who were imprisoned "for their own good." Candidates for probation included those who showed a strong chance of rehabilitation and low risk of recidivism. These individuals were expected to maintain employment or pursue education, and often received counseling from probation agents. DAVID DRESSLER, PROBATION AND PAROLE 160–65 (1951). In a statistical pattern that persists in almost every jurisdiction to this day, by the early decades of the 1900s the number of probationers had surpassed the number of prisoners. *See* MAX GRUNHUT, PENAL REFORM: A COMPARATIVE STUDY 297 (1948) (citing data from California and New York).

Emphasis on rehabilitation, and use of open-ended indeterminate sentences, remained the norm well past the twentieth century's midpoint. Low crime rates in the 1950s and early 1960s fueled the optimism of proponents of the Rehabilitative Ideal. As we saw in Chapter 1, faith in the Rehabilitative Ideal was reflected in the landmark Model Penal Code, issued in 1962 by the American Law Institute, as well as the Johnson Administration's "Great Society" programs, which targeted social and economic problems seen as root causes of crime. The view was articulated in the landmark report, *The Challenge of Crime in a Free Society*, published in 1967 by the President's Commission on Law Enforcement and the Administration of Justice:

> [The Commission] has no doubt whatever that the most significant action that can be taken against crime is action designed to eliminate slums and ghettos, to improve education, to provide jobs, to make sure that every American is given the opportunities and the freedoms that will enable him to assume his responsibilities. We will not have dealt effectively with crime until we have alleviated the conditions that stimulate it. To speak of controlling crime only in terms of the work of the police, the courts and correctional apparatus, is to refuse to face the fact that widespread crime implies a widespread failure by society as a whole.

PRESIDENT'S COMMISSION ON LAW ENFORCEMENT AND THE ADMINISTRATION OF JUSTICE, THE CHALLENGE OF CRIME IN A FREE SOCIETY 71–72 (1967).

Starting in the late 1960s, however, the nation underwent a radical change in mood. Significant spikes in reported violent crime rates coupled with alarm over the massive social unrest of the 1960s, made Americans highly receptive to a new "get tough" approach to crime control. *See, e.g.,* TED GEST, CRIME AND POLITICS: BIG GOVERNMENT'S ERRATIC CAMPAIGN FOR LAW AND ORDER (2001); JOHN HAGAN, WHO ARE THE CRIMINALS? THE POLITICS OF CRIME POLICY FROM THE AGE OF ROOSEVELT TO THE AGE OF REAGAN (2010). President Richard Nixon made "law and order" a central theme of his successful 1968 bid for the White House, and thereafter commenced a "war on crime," targeting criminal offenders themselves, rather than the purported social and economic causes of their criminality.

The harsher political climate was fed by several influential books and articles published during this period. In 1973, federal judge Marvin Frankel published his book *Criminal Sentences—Law without Order*, a scathing indictment of indeterminate sentencing philosophy, in which he condemned the carte blanche authority of sentencing judges and the similarly unfettered authority of parole decision makers. Frankel alleged that sentencing was lawless—that decisions governing the deprivation of liberty lacked transparency and were made without reference to any articulable standards.

Frankel's challenge to sentencing practice was soon bolstered when, in 1974, Robert Martinson published *What Works? Questions and Answers about Prison Reform*—a meta-study of empirical work that suggested prison rehabilitative programming failed to "correct" prisoners' behavior. Together, these and other contemporary attacks undermined public confidence in the soundness, plausibility, and fairness of the rehabilitative model of criminal punishment.

As doubts about the soundness of the Rehabilitative Ideal increased, reformers from a variety of philosophical camps stepped forward to fill the vacuum created by the collapse of rehabilitationism. In his influential book *Thinking about Crime* (1975), James Q. Wilson argued that it was time to stop "coddling criminals." He argued that criminals needed to be deterred from committing crimes in the first instance, and the best way to do this was for judges to hand down more severe and certain sentences. Wilson's thinking complemented a report by the American Friends Service Committee, *Struggle for Justice* (1971), which maintained that rehabilitationism had become a covert form of class control, and that a system based on deserved punishment would be fairer than a system in which the state attempted to manipulate convicted individuals' thoughts, values, and families. In 1976, legal theorist Andrew von Hirsch popularized the retributive-based goal of "just deserts" in his influential book *Doing Justice: The Choice of Punishments*. Increasingly, reformers were beginning to believe that short, certain, and predictable sentences would be more equitable and less arbitrary than the longer, more variable indeterminate sentences being imposed by judges exercising broad sentencing discretion, and by parole boards operating without transparency.

3. MID-1970S TO MID-1980S

The foregoing developments set the stage for a period of remarkable change in American sentencing law, policy, and practice. Initially, reformers coalesced around the concern, voiced by Judge Frankel and others, that sentencing procedures and outcomes were too often marked by inconsistency and unfairness. For political liberals, increased certainty and consistency had appeal because it would lessen the prevalence of racial and other forms of unwarranted disparities. "Traditional" sentencing systems, which combined discretionary sentencing with indeterminacy in the release decision came in for particular criticism, with one influential group denouncing coercive, open-ended rehabilitation as a method for "keeping the powerless in line" and the inherent uncertainties of parole decisions as "one of the most painful aspects of prison life." AM. FRIENDS SVC. COMM., STRUGGLE FOR JUSTICE: A REPORT ON CRIME AND PUNISHMENT IN AMERICA 28, 93 (1971). For political conservatives, increasing certainty and consistency held appeal because it promised to enhance the deterrent force of sentences and better ensure "just deserts."

In line with this shift, from 1975 to 1986, many jurisdictions abolished discretionary parole. The era also witnessed the advent of sentencing guidelines, an idea proposed by Judge Frankel in his 1973 book. Frankel envisioned a specialized administrative agency composed of experts that would develop, promulgate, monitor, and revise written guidance for sentencing judges. As Professor Michael Tonry would later write, Frankel "reasoned that legislatures lack the specialized knowledge, staff continuity, and attention spans" necessary to do the job well, and "are too vulnerable to day-to-day political and media influence. He expected appellate courts to review contested sentences and gradually to develop a 'common law of sentencing' to deal with difficult kinds of cases." Michael Tonry, *Fifty Years of American Sentencing Reform: Nine Lessons*, 48 CRIME & JUST. 1, 4 (2019). A notable effort came in 1978 when the Minnesota Legislature created a special independent government commission to devise recommended sentences for judges to impose, except in cases presenting "substantial and compelling" reasons for a different sentence. The Minnesota guidelines, which took effect in 1980, had major influence, spawning similar efforts in multiple other jurisdictions. *See* Robert Weisberg, *The Sentencing Commission Model, 1970s to Present, in* THE OXFORD HANDBOOK OF SENTENCING AND CORRECTIONS 299 (Joan Petersilia & Kevin R. Reitz eds., 2012). We will consider the Minnesota guidelines in more detail later in this chapter.

4. MID-1980S TO LATE 2000S

The period of reflection soon evaporated. Starting in the mid-1980s, the nation underwent a radical transformation in favor of punitive toughness. Even though crime rates soon leveled off and then decreased relative to crime in the 1970s, retribution and heavy reliance on incapacitation dominated policy and practice. Rejecting the individualized release decisions that characterized the Rehabilitative Ideal, many states either abolished or restricted parole release. Determinate "truth-in-sentencing" laws were widely adopted. These laws required individuals sentenced to prison to serve a prescribed minimum percentage of a judge-imposed sentence (often 85%) before becoming eligible for release.

At the same time, many legislatures prescribed mandatory minimum sentences for offenses such as homicides, and drug and weapons offenses. Recidivist sentencing provisions that required lengthy mandatory prison terms for repeat offenders, such as California's harsh "three strikes and you are out" law, gained popularity. Convicted sex offenders became the target of particular concern in the early 1990s, with states adopting sex offender registration and community notification laws (a.k.a. "Megan's Laws") and "sexually violent predator" involuntary commitment programs. As a result of frustration with the apparent inefficacy of the corrections system, "shame" sanctions, such as requiring a person convicted of larceny to wear a sandwich board in public proclaiming "I am a thief," enjoyed popularity. The nation also witnessed a marked increase in laws authorizing or even requiring sentences of life-without-parole for non-capital offenses, including for youthful offenders prosecuted in adult court. In 1999, the number of executions in the U.S. hit 98, the highest number since the reinstatement of capital punishment by the Supreme Court in 1976. Death Penalty Information Center, *Facts about the Death Penalty* (July 1, 2021), https://documents.deathpenaltyinfo.org/pdf/FactSheet.pdf. Meanwhile, in contrast to colonial times, when they served as a check on punitive excess, juries rarely figured in the nation's plea-based system, and when they did play a role, they did so unaware of the sentencing consequences of their decisions. Daniel Epps, *Checks and Balances in the Criminal Law*, 74 VAND. L. REV. 1, 74 (2021).

In the federal system, Congress passed the Sentencing Reform Act of 1984 ("SRA"), which included among other provisions 18 U.S.C. § 3553(a). As you may recall from Chapter 1, § 3553(a) reflected a greater emphasis on desert and uniform treatment of similar cases, and a reduced emphasis on probation and rehabilitation, in comparison with the Model Penal Code. The SRA resulted from a bipartisan congressional effort, fueled by conservatives who thought federal sentences too lenient and liberals concerned about racial and other sentence disparities. Beyond § 3553(a), the SRA abolished discretionary parole release and authorized creation of the U.S. Sentencing Commission, which was to promulgate federal sentencing guidelines. As we will see later in this chapter, the federal guidelines reflected a far more punitive approach than the guidelines in Minnesota and other guidelines states. In contrast to Judge Marvin Frankel's vision, critics charged that the U.S. Commission was not comprised of sentencing experts and independent from partisan influence, but was "stacked" in favor of pro-prosecution interests and subject to regular interventions by Congress. *See, e.g.*, Rachel E. Barkow, *Administering Crime*, 52 UCLA L. REV. 715, 763–69 (2005).

At about the same time that the guidelines were authorized and promulgated, Congress also passed a welter of "get-tough" mandatory minimum sentences and sentence enhancement provisions for recidivists and defendants convicted for gun, violent, and drug crimes. Such laws have heightened the importance of prosecutors' charging decisions and effectively removed sentencing of the covered offenses from regulation by the guidelines. During the time, as Professor Michael Tonry observed in retrospect, sentencing "ceased being something best handled by experts behind closed doors but instead became a central issue in partisan politics." *Sentencing in America, 1975–2025*, 42 CRIME & JUST. 141, 143 (2013).

Legislatures responded to the concerns of influential conservative political thinkers, such as John DiIulio Jr. (who coined the term "superpredator") and former Reagan Administration "Drug Czar" William Bennett (who attributed rising crime to a decline in morality among the young), by increasing punishments. The shift toward greater punitiveness had a palpable effect on the nation's corrections population. Sharp increases in determinate sentences for drug and other crimes, and in the overall likelihood of imprisonment in all cases referred for prosecution, started in the mid-1980s and escalated throughout the 1990s. Viewed as a whole, the rise in prison populations between 1980 and 2009 was broad-based: 51% of prison growth resulted from imprisoning more violent offenders, and 21% drug and 16% property offenders. John P. Pfaff, *Waylaid by a Metaphor: A Deeply Problematic Account of Prison Growth,* 111 MICH. L. REV. 1087, 1089–1106 (2014) (reviewing ERNEST DRUCKER, A PLAGUE OF PRISONS: THE EPIDEMIOLOGY OF MASS INCARCERATION IN AMERICA (2011)).

Between 1978 and 2009, the number of inmates in state and federal prisons increased almost 430%, from 294,000 to 1,556,000. E. ANN CARSON & DANIELA GOLINELLI, U.S. DEP'T OF JUSTICE, PRISONERS IN 2012: TRENDS IN ADMISSIONS AND RELEASES, 1991–2012 (2013). When the expansion in population started in the 1970s, the nation's incarceration rate was roughly 100 per 100,000 U.S. residents, as it had been for the preceding five decades—a lower rate than in several other Western nations. However, from 1973 to 2009, imprisonment rates grew every year. MICHAEL O'HEAR, THE FAILED PROMISE OF SENTENCING REFORM xiii-xv (2017). By 2010, U.S. incarceration had increased five-fold, leaving it with the world's highest imprisonment rate, considerably ahead of second place Russia. ROY WALMSLEY, INSTITUTE FOR CRIMINAL POLICY RESEARCH, WORLD PRISON POPULATION LIST 6–14 (2018). Figure 2-1 illustrates the rapid rise in the nation's adult correctional population, including those held in prisons and those subject to community supervision (probation or parole).

Figure 2-1. U.S. numbers in prison and on community supervision (parole plus probation), 1980–2019. Source: U.S. Department of Justice Bureau of Justice Statistics.

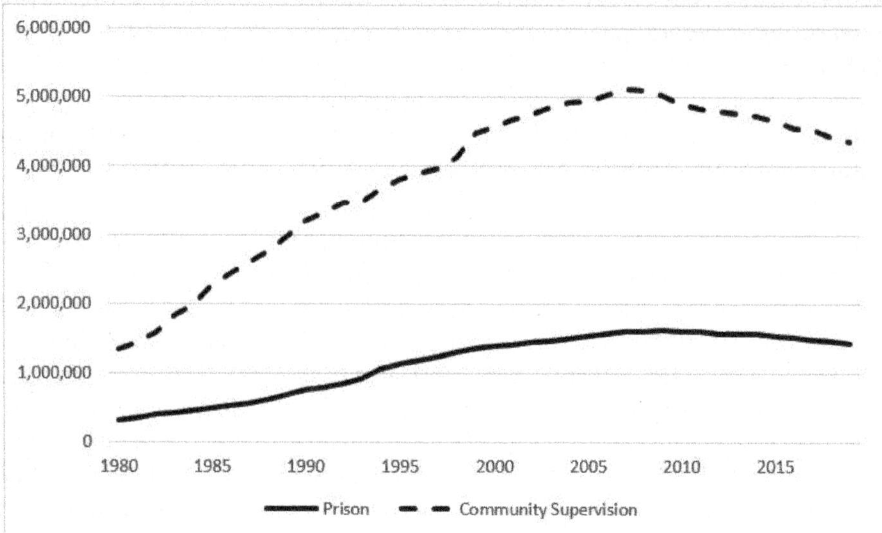

The enormous number of inmates housed in the nation's prisons and jails has over time reflected dramatic racial disparities. In 2009, for instance, an estimated 65% of inmates were African-American or Latinx. According to the National Center on Crime and Delinquency, in 2003, "African Americans were newly admitted to custody at a rate of 5.7 times the rate for Whites. Hispanics were admitted 1.9 times and Native-Americans 4.3 times the rate for Whites." CHRISTOPHER HARTNEY & LIN VUONG, NAT'L COUNCIL ON CRIME & DELINQUENCY, CREATED EQUAL: RACIAL AND ETHNIC DISPARITIES IN THE U.S. CRIMINAL JUSTICE SYSTEM 16 (2009). National statistics, however, only tell part of the story; they mask significant interstate variations. In Wisconsin, for example, African-Americans were 16.7 times more likely than Whites to be incarcerated; in New York, Latinx individuals were 5.7 times more likely than non-Latinx Whites to be incarcerated; and in Minnesota, Native-Americans were 12.3 times more likely than Whites to be incarcerated. *Id.* at 17. In keeping with historic practice, men continued to constitute the overwhelming proportion of inmates; however, a notable aspect of the incarceration spike was a sharp increase in women. NATASHA A. FROST ET AL., INSTITUTE ON WOMEN & CRIMINAL JUSTICE, HARD HIT: GROWTH IN THE IMPRISONMENT OF WOMEN, 1977–2004, at 10 (2006).

Prison statistics, while certainly notable, actually understate the enormity of the American correctional system. This is because, as depicted in Figure 2-1, the number of convicts "doing time on the outside," subject to probation or parole supervision, dwarfs the number of jail and prison inmates. As the nation's inmate populations grew exponentially in number, so did the number of individuals subject to community supervision. Driven by large increases in the proportion of individuals convicted of felony and less serious offenses alike (i.e., "mass conviction"), the nation concomitantly experienced mass probation and mass incarceration. During the 1980s, the nation's probation population grew by an average of 9% per year, doubling in overall number from roughly 1.12 million in 1980 to 2.5 million by yearend 1989. LAUREN E. GLAZE & THOMAS P. BONCZAR, U.S. BUREAU OF JUSTICE STATISTICS, PROBATION AND PAROLE IN THE UNITED STATES, 2010 (2011). Between 1980 and its peak in 2007, the number of probationers grew from 1.1 million to 4.3 million, peaking at a ratio of 1 of every 53 adults. Michelle S. Phelps, *Mass Probation: Toward a More Robust Theory of State Variation in Punishment*, 19 PUNISHMENT & SOC'Y 53, 54 (2017).

Starting in the 1980s, community supervision effectively became an extension of is brick-and-mortar counterpart. Probation, it was hoped, could be transformed into a more cost-effective risk-management solution. Malcolm M. Feeley & Jonathan Simon, *The New Penology: Notes on the Merging Strategy of Corrections and Its Implications*, 30 CRIMINOLOGY 449, 457 (1992). Probation was increasingly dominated by a "Justice Model," marked by conditions designed more to punish and monitor convicts than ensure their rehabilitation. Wayne A. Logan, *The Importance of Purpose in Probation Decision Making*, 7 BUFF. CRIM. L. REV. 171, 191–95 (2003). The concept of "intermediate sanctions," so called because they were a middle ground between conventional supervision and incarceration, also gained currency. An influential 1985 Rand Corporation report made the case for the shift:

> We believe the criminal justice system needs an alternative, intermediate form of punishment for those offenders who are too antisocial for the relative freedom that probation now offers, but not so seriously criminal as to require imprisonment. A sanction is needed that would impose intensive surveillance, coupled with substantial community service and restitution. It should be structured to satisfy public demands that the punishment fit the crime, to show that crime does not pay, and to control potential recidivists.

JOAN PETERSILIA ET AL., GRANTING FELONS PROBATION ix (1985) (citation omitted). In keeping with this shift, jurisdictions started imposing sanctions such as "split sentences" (requiring a brief period in jail to punish and then probation); "shock" incarceration (entailing brief prison or jail terms for less serious offenders); "boot camps"; intensive supervision; house arrest and electronic monitoring; monetary sanctions; and community service.

An expansive literature has sought to explain the nation's growing punitiveness throughout the latter portion of the twentieth century and the early years of the new millennium. One explanation is socio-cultural:

even though violent crime rates began to fall in the 1990s,[4] Americans by then had become angry, fearful, and insecure, susceptible to a climate of "populist punitivism."[5] In this climate, according to Professor Jonathan Simon, political leaders manipulated anxieties to secure and maintain power and advance broader political aims, "governing through crime." *See* JONATHAN SIMON, GOVERNING THROUGH CRIME: HOW THE WAR ON CRIME TRANSFORMED AMERICAN DEMOCRACY AND CREATED A CULTURE OF FEAR (2009). Similar accounts attribute the shift to "late modernity," a destabilized time of economic and social instability, feeding desire for a "culture of control." DAVID GARLAND, THE CULTURE OF CONTROL: CRIME AND SOCIAL ORDER IN CONTEMPORARY SOCIETY (2001). The media, often subscribing to the precept of "if it bleeds, it leads," fostered public anxieties and drove political willingness to adopt harsh policies. *See generally* PETER ENNS, INCARCERATION NATION: HOW THE UNITED STATES BECAME THE MOST PUNITIVE DEMOCRACY IN THE WORLD (2016). An increasingly influential victims' rights movement also likely played a role. MARIE GOTTSCHALK, THE PRISONS AND THE GALLOWS: THE POLITICS OF MASS INCARCERATION IN AMERICA (2006).

At the same time, there is no mistaking that the massive growth in corrections has required equally massive spending, which has an effect of its own. Not only has the growth meant jobs for the constituents of political leaders, it has also meant revenue for business interests, leading to creation of what has been called the nation's "prison industrial complex." Eric Schlosser, *The Prison-Industrial Complex*, ATLANTIC, Dec. 1998, at 51; *see also* KATHERINE BECKETT, MAKING CRIME PAY: LAW AND ORDER IN CONTEMPORARY AMERICAN POLITICS (1997).[6]

Among institutional players, Professor John Pfaff and others have singled out prosecutors; in a plea-bargain-dominated system, the prosecutor's virtually unreviewable power to charge has been a main driver of prison population increases.[7] *See* JOHN F. PFAFF, LOCKED IN:

---

[4] Another example of the counter-cyclical relationship between violent crime and incarceration, marked by declining rates of the former and increased rates of the latter, is found in 1926–1940 period. Jeffery S. Adler, *Less Crime, More Punishment: Violence, Race, and Criminal Justice in Early Twentieth-Century America*, 102 J. AM. HIST. 34, 46 (2015) ("[E]arly twentieth-century tends in crime and punishment eerily presaged late-century developments, particularly in the way a crime panic fueled the explosive development of penal institutions, generated a surge in imprisonment, and contributed to racial disparities in punishment.").

[5] Anthony E. Bottoms, *The Philosophy and Politics of Punishment and Sentencing, in* THE POLITICS OF SENTENCING REFORM (Chris Clarkson & Rod Morgan eds., 1995). *See also* LORD WINDLESHAM, POLITICS, PUNISHMENT AND POPULISM (1998); FRANKLIN E. ZIMRING ET AL., PUNISHMENT AND DEMOCRACY: THREE-STRIKES AND YOU'RE OUT IN CALIFORNIA (2001).

[6] Chapter 5 discusses the important implications of prison location, including its impact on how inmates are counted for purposes of determining legislative representation ("prison gerrymandering").

[7] Central to Pfaff's account is the effect of what he terms the "prosecutorial moral hazard" problem: prosecutors are local actors, at the city or county level, who perform their jobs knowing that the cost of imprisonment falls on the state, which funds the prison system. Notably, California, which boasts the nation's largest prison population, adopted a "realignment" policy in 2011, which had the effect of channeling many more convicts to county-funded jails, which not coincidentally significantly reduced state prison populations. John Pfaff, *Why the Policy Failures of Mass Incarceration Are Really Political Failures*, 104 MINN. L. REV. 2673, 2674–77

THE TRUE CAUSES OF MASS INCARCERATION AND HOW TO ACHIEVE REAL REFORM (2017).

As discussed in Chapter 1, racism—whether overt or implicit—has also been advanced as a prominent catalyst for prison population growth. For instance, according to Professor Michelle Alexander, mass imprisonment resulted from and reflects a "New Jim Crow," a "stunningly comprehensive and well-disguised system of racialized social control."[8]

5. 2010 TO PRESENT

As Figure 2-1 reflects, recent years have witnessed a modest decrease in the nation's correctional populations. At the end of 2019, more than six million individuals were under the supervision of adult correctional systems in the U.S. The figure includes state, local, and federal prison and jail inmates (2.1 million), and those under community supervision based on probation and parole (4.4 million). The figure was about 62,200 fewer than in 2018 and marked the lowest correctional population since 1999. The correctional population has declined an average of 1.3% each year since 2009, accounting for a 12.4% decrease since then (895,200 individuals). In 2019, the rate per 100,000 U.S. adults (2,480) was the lowest since 1991. TODD D. MINTON, U.S. DEP'T OF JUSTICE, CORRECTIONAL POPULATIONS IN THE UNITED STATES, 2019-STATISTICAL TABLES (2021). The 2019 prison and jail incarceration rate (810 per 1000,000) was also down considerably from its peak, falling to a level not seen since 1995.

The continued decline is certainly notable, but the numbers remain high in historic terms. For instance, the prison and jail incarceration rate in 1980 was 310 per 100,000, in comparison with the 810 per 100,000 in 2019. The U.S. is still the world leader in incarceration rate; rates in Western Europe, for instance, are less than a quarter of the U.S. rate. JOHN GRAMLICH, PEW RESEARCH CENTER, AMERICA'S INCARCERATION RATE FALLS TO LOWEST SINCE 1995 (2021). Racial disparity in the nation's prison populations also remains stark: although African-Americans comprise only 13% of the U.S. population, they make up 33%

(2020). For another assessment framing the causal role of prosecutors in mass incarceration, see EMILY BAZELON, CHARGED: THE NEW MOVEMENT TO TRANSFORM AMERICAN PROSECUTORS AND END MAS INCARCERATION (2019). Whether and to what extent a new breed of "progressive prosecutor" can undo mass incarceration has been an important recent topic of debate. *See, e.g.*, Jeffrey Bellin, *Defending Progressive Prosecution: A Review of* Charged *by Emily Bazelon*, 39 YALE L. & POL'Y REV. 218 (2020).

[8] MICHELLE ALEXANDER, THE NEW JIM CROW: MASS INCARCERATION IN THE AGE OF COLOR-BLINDNESS 4 (2010). The start of the tough-on-crime wave coincided with the tail end of the civil rights era, and may be thought of, at least in part, as one aspect of the backlash against the legal, political, and economic gains made by African-Americans in the middle decades of the twentieth century. In comparison with their share of the overall population, African-Americans were disproportionately affected by the surge in incarceration that occurred over the century's final quarter (depicted, for instance, in Figures 1-3 and 1-4 in Chapter 1). *See* MICHAEL TONRY, PUNISHING RACE: A CONTINUING AMERICAN DILEMMA (2001); Loic Wacquant, *Class, Race, and Hyperincarceration in Revanchist America*, 139 DAEDALUS 74 (2010).

of the prison population. E. ANN CARSON, U.S. DEP'T OF JUSTICE, PRISONERS IN 2020–STATISTICAL TABLES 10 (2021).

It is also important to bear in mind that the declines are not uniform, with large decreases in some jurisdictions potentially masking steady or increased numbers in others. Illustrative of state-level variation, at the end of 2019, incarceration rates per 100,000 varied from a low of 133 in Massachusetts to a high of 680 in Louisiana. *State-by-State Data,* THE SENTENCING PROJECT, https://www.sentencingproject.org/the-facts/#map (last visited August 19, 2021). Drilling down further on the data, apparent state-level declines in incarceration may conceal important intrastate variation: sharp reductions in urban areas have driven state decreases; rural and suburban areas often held steady or increased their contributions to prison populations. John Pfaff, *Why the Policy Failures of Mass Incarceration Are Really Political Failures*, 104 MINN. L. REV. 2673, 2689–90 (2020); *see also* Katherine Beckett & Lindsey Beach, *The Place of Punishment in Twenty-First Century America, Understanding the Persistence of Mass Incarceration*, 45 L. & SOC. INQUIRY 1 (2021).

Variation also exists in the use of probation and parole. Overall, in 2019, as in recent years, the national supervised population fell compared to the prior year—by almost 1%. One out of every fifty-nine adults was under community supervision at yearend 2019, down from one in forty-six in 2000. However, the differences among states are striking: in 2019, the probation population decreased in twenty-seven states but rose in twenty-two; the parole population increased in twenty-six states and the federal system, and decreased in twenty-three states and the District of Columbia. BARBARA OUDEKERK & DANIELLE KAEBLE, U.S. DEP'T OF JUSTICE, PROBATION AND PAROLE IN THE UNITED STATES, 2019 (2021). Professor Michelle Phelps has documented that states may utilize high levels of both custody and probation (e.g., Georgia, Idaho, and Texas); high levels of custody and low use of probation (e.g., Missouri, Oklahoma, and Louisiana); low use of custody and high use of probation (e.g., Minnesota, Rhode Island, and Washington); or low use of both probation and custody (e.g., New Hampshire, Maine, and North Dakota). Michelle Phelps, *Mass Probation: Toward a More Robust Theory of State Variation in Punishment*, 19 PUNISHMENT & SOC'Y 53 (2016).

Stark differences also mark the use of capital punishment. Recent years show a very marked decrease in both the number of death sentences and executions. *The Death Penalty in 2020: Year End Report*, DEATH PENALTY INFORMATION CENTER, Dec. 16, 2020, https://deathpenaltyinfo.org/facts-and-research/dpic-reports/dpic-year-end-reports/the-death-penalty-in-2020-year-end-report. But again, geographic variation underlies the decreases. The highest numbers of death row inmates can be found in the South. NAACP LEGAL DEFENSE & EDUCATIONAL FUND, INC., DEATH ROW USA 37–38 (2021). As is true with respect to the use of imprisonment, large variations exist in usage of the death penalty not only between states, but within them at the county level. *Executions by County*, DEATH PENALTY INFORMATION CENTER, https://deathpenaltyinfo.org/executions/executions-overview/executions-by-county (last visited Nov. 4, 2021).

Nonetheless, the tempering, if not reversal, of "penality" is important. Those looking for causes point to a variety of possibilities. One salient factor is the sustained decrease in crime rates.[9] Another is a shift in political consciousness. Arguments long made by those on the political left—that sentencing policy is too harsh, that too many non-violent offenders are imprisoned, and that incarceration is an ineffective and often inhumane method of social control, with serious negative long-term effects on individuals and communities[10]—have begun to resonate with political conservatives. Concern over mass incarceration has given rise to "Right on Crime," a reform-oriented group comprised of high-profile conservatives such as former U.S. House Speaker Newt Gingrich and head of the Americans for Tax Reform Grover Norquist. According to the group's Statement of Principles,

> Conservatives are known for being tough on crime, but we must also be tough on criminal justice spending. That means demanding more cost-effective approaches that enhance public safety. A clear example is our reliance on prisons, which serve a critical role by incapacitating dangerous offenders and career criminals but are not the solution for every type of offender.

Statement of Principles, RIGHT ON CRIME, https://rightoncrime.com/the-conservative-case-for-reform/statement-of-principles/ (last visited Dec. 9, 2021).

The political shift was evidenced at the policy level, for instance, when in 2012 California voters—often a bellwether for the nation—approved major limits on their state's harsh "three strikes" sentencing enhancement law. This move followed California's experiment in "realignment," which reduced the state's prison population by transferring authority over large numbers of convicted felons from state institutions to county jail and probation agencies. *See* Joan Petersilia,

---

[9] Andrew D. Leipold, *Is Mass Incarceration Inevitable?*, 56 AM. CRIM. L. REV. 1579, 1593–95 (2019). As Professor Leipold notes, debate continues among scholars over whether the high prison/low crime rate reflects a perverse systemic dedication to punitiveness or whether the massive increases in incarceration account for the lower crime rates. Examining the available evidence, Leipold concludes that "[t]he preliminary evidence from the states that have engaged in penal reform over the last several years is somewhat ambiguous, but it certainly favors the view that prison rates can be decreased without causing crime to increase." *Id.* at 1596.

[10] DONALD BRAMAN, DOING TIME ON THE OUTSIDE: INCARCERATION AND FAMILY LIFE IN AMERICA (2004); TODD R. CLEAR, IMPRISONING COMMUNITIES: HOW MASS INCARCERATION MAKES DISADVANTAGED COMMUNITIES WORSE (2007); IMPRISONING AMERICA: THE SOCIAL EFFECTS OF MASS INCARCERATION (Mary Patillo et al. eds., 2004). These longstanding criticisms of mass incarceration dovetail with an increasingly prominent abolition movement that seeks not merely a return to historical incarceration norms, but a more fundamental rethinking of the place of incarceration and related phenomena in American life. *See, e.g.,* Dorothy Roberts, *Foreward: Abolition Constitutionalism*, 133 HARV. L. REV. 1 (2019); Dylan Rodríguez, *Abolition as Praxis of Human Being: A Foreword*, 132 HARV. L. REV. 1575 (2019) (introducing symposium issue on abolition).

California Prison Downsizing and Its Impact on Local Criminal Justice Systems, 8 HARV. L. & POL'Y REV. 801 (2014).

These changes are not limited to California. Across the nation, in response to decreased demand, many states have shuttered prison facilities. SENTENCING PROJECT, ON THE CHOPPING BLOCK 2013: STATE PRISON CLOSURES (2013). The new perspective is also evidenced in recent efforts to critically reevaluate the use of "collateral consequences," the extensive array of nominally civil consequences that often attach to convictions (e.g., loss of the right to vote), which have proliferated since the 1990s and impose hardships that can impede reintegration and crime desistance. Collateral consequences are considered in more detail below in Chapter 11.

Whether the broad shift away from get-tough policy will continue is unclear. If the philosophical shift is less than it seems, it could well be that decreasing concern over the fiscal cost of punitiveness will allow for a return to recent historic practice. Indeed, spending on corrections has proven remarkably resilient. As Professor John Pfaff has written:

> Despite the enormous fiscal impact of the 2008 credit crisis, and despite the austerity-laced rhetoric that has infused debates about criminal justice reform since then, states actually spent more on prisons in 2015 and 2016, at least in nominal terms, than ever before; spending did decline a bit from 2010–2013, but it has been rising since. Real spending on prisons is down a bit, but it too has been rising in recent years, and it was higher in 2016 than it was in 2005. As a share of total state expenditures, correctional spending has declined somewhat, but only a bit: from 3.6% of all direct spending in 2005 to 2.9% of all direct spending in 2016. All told, it is a story of relative stability.

Pfaff, *supra*, at 2679.

Moreover, it remains the case that dollars spent on the massive workforces required to operate prisons play a crucial role in local economies, with institutions often located in remote communities with few other opportunities for well-paying jobs. Political actors representing these areas have a major stake in maintaining the status quo. *See generally* JOHN M. EASON, BIG HOUSE ON THE PRAIRIE: RISE OF THE RURAL GHETTO AND PRISON PROLIFERATION (2017). Pressure to keep prison populations high also flows from the reality that very often inmates are "counted" for purposes of legislative districting where they are imprisoned, providing incentives for some elected leaders to resist decreases. Pfaff, *supra*, at 2680.

Yet, there is reason to think that the shift we are now seeing may have staying power. One reason for this lies in the often-overlooked reality that Americans are perhaps not as punitive as the sentencing policy of the last several decades would suggest. *See, e.g.*, Roger Matthews, *The Myth of Punitiveness*, 9 THEORETICAL CRIMINOLOGY 175

(2005). For instance, even during the nation's sharp and sustained spike in corrections populations, Americans continued to feel that rehabilitation should be an integral goal of corrections. Francis T. Cullen, *It's Time to Reaffirm Rehabilitation*, 5 CRIMINOLOGY & PUB. POL'Y 665 (2006). Nor should it be overlooked that the last several decades have also been marked by some progressive innovations. For instance, restorative justice took root during this period (see Chapter 1), as did an array of specialized problem-solving courts (e.g., for drug offenders or domestic abusers), which combine the efforts of legal and treatment professionals to provide intensive community-based treatment, management, and supervision (see Chapter 3). More recently, a handful of states have attempted to address persistent racial disparities in imprisonment by providing for the creation of "racial" or "demographic" impact statements to accompany proposed criminal legislation. Kevin R. Reitz & Cecelia M. Klingele, *Model Penal Code: Sentencing—Workable Limits on Mass Punishment*, 19 CRIME & JUST. 255, 266–67 (2019). It is hoped that such projections will lead to the rejection or modification of proposals that have racially disparate effects.

Another prominent feature of American criminal justice in the early twenty-first century has been a growing reliance on data—systematically collected and analyzed—as a basis for decisionmaking. Much as "big data" has remade many other social endeavors, from political campaigns to retail sales to sports team management ("money ball"), so, too, is criminal justice decisionmaking being reshaped by increasingly sophisticated numbers-crunching. The label "evidence-based decisionmaking" ("EBDM") is often applied to the new data-oriented initiatives, which have touched on all aspects of criminal justice, from policing strategy to diversion-from-prosecution programs to pretrial release to sentencing, community supervision, and parole. *See, e.g.*, Cecelia Klingele, *The Promises and Perils of Evidence-Based Corrections*, 91 NOTRE DAME L. REV. 537 (2015). EBDM is perhaps best exemplified by the increasing use of actuarial risk-assessment instruments (RAIs) in pretrial release, sentencing, and corrections decisions. Intended to make more efficient use of scarce criminal justice resources by focusing incarceration and supervision on those defendants who are most likely to reoffend, the use of RAIs has not been without controversy. We noted some of the strengths and limitations of RAIs in Chapter 1 and will return to the topic again in Chapter 4.

The COVID-19 pandemic drew new attention to the nation's incarcerated population beginning in 2020, as crowded penal facilities proved a fertile ground for transmission of the disease. The public-health threat led to calls for criminal justice officials to be given new authority to grant early release to inmates or to utilize existing authority more aggressively. Jenny E. Carroll, *COVID-19 Relief and the Ordinary Inmate*, 18 OHIO ST. J. CRIM. L. 427 (2021); M. Eve Hanan, *Incarcerated Activism During COVID-19*, 18 OHIO ST. J. CRIM. L. 475 (2021). Some preliminary evidence indicates that significant reductions in incarceration were achieved in some jurisdictions during the pandemic,[11] but it is still too early to say what the overall effect has been on national incarceration rates, much less whether pandemic-related reductions will be sustained after the public-health crisis ends.

B. SENTENCING SYSTEMS TODAY

The remainder of this chapter examines the structure of contemporary sentencing systems in more detail. Professor Kevin Reitz has helpfully suggested some groupings of states based on two characteristics: whether they employ determinate or indeterminate sentencing (i.e., whether they offer discretionary parole release to prisoners) and whether they use sentencing guidelines. The results yield four major groups:

(1) indeterminate systems without guidelines (a.k.a. the "traditional" system);

(2) indeterminate systems with guidelines;

(3) determinate systems without guidelines; and

(4) determinate systems with guidelines.

Kevin R. Reitz, *The "Traditional" Indeterminate Sentencing Model*, *in* THE OXFORD HANDBOOK OF SENTENCING AND CORRECTIONS 270, 274 (Joan Petersilia & Kevin R. Reitz eds., 2012).

The great variety of sentencing systems in practice creates significant challenges for classification. For instance, should a state that uses indeterminate sentencing for most offenses, but not for serious violent offenses, be classified as determinate or indeterminate? Similarly, should a state that has promulgated guidelines for some offenses, but not others, be classified as a guidelines or non-guidelines jurisdiction? Nonetheless, while there will always be some room for debate around the margins, classification seems necessary in order to study the effects of choosing one sentencing system over another. Table 2-1 summarizes classifications made in 2018 by the University of Minnesota's Robina Institute of Criminal Law and Criminal Justice. ALEXIS LEE WATTS, UNIV. OF MINN., IN DEPTH: SENTENCING GUIDELINES AND DISCRETIONARY PAROLE RELEASE (2018).

[11] Through the CARES Act, for instance, Congress in 2020 expanded a preexisting authority for the federal Bureau of Prisons to transfer inmates out of institutions and into home confinement for the final portion of their prison terms. Between March 2020 and December 2021, the BOP placed more than 35,000 federal inmates into home confinement. Christopher H. Schroeder, U.S. Dept of Justice, Mem. Op for Att'y General: Discretion to Continue the Home-Confinement Placements of Federal Prisoners After the COVID-19 Emergency 4 (2021).

Table 2-1. Classification of American sentencing systems (2018). Source: Robina Institute of Criminal Law and Criminal Justice, University of Minnesota.

Indeterminate/ No Guidelines	Indeterminate/ Guidelines	Determinate/ No Guidelines	Determinate/ Guidelines
Alaska	Alabama	Arizona	Delaware
Colorado	Arkansas	California	District of Columbia
Connecticut	Maryland	Illinois	Federal System
Georgia	Massachusetts	Indiana	Florida
Hawaii	Michigan	Maine	Kansas
Idaho	Pennsylvania	New Mexico	Minnesota
Iowa	Tennessee	Wisconsin	North Carolina
Kentucky	Utah		Ohio
Louisiana			Oregon
Mississippi			Virginia
Missouri			Washington
Montana			
Nebraska			
Nevada			
New Hampshire			
New Jersey			
New York			
North Dakota			
Oklahoma			
Rhode Island			
South Carolina			
South Dakota			
Texas			
Vermont			
West Virginia			
Wyoming			

In the sections that follow, we explore in more depth the nature of the determinacy/indeterminacy and guidelines/non-guidelines choices. We also consider the importance of mandatory minimums to a jurisdiction's sentencing system. Finally, we discuss some of the criteria that are used to evaluate contemporary sentencing systems.

1. DETERMINACY

Sentencing systems may be distinguished based on their determinacy. In a highly determinate system, the sentence pronounced by the judge would leave few, if any, important decisions to be made later about the nature and duration of the defendant's punishment. By the conclusion of the sentencing hearing, the defendant, the prosecutor, the victim, and any other interested parties in attendance would have a clear idea about most key aspects of the punishment—and, in particular, about how much time the defendant would have to spend in custody before being returned to the community. By contrast, in a highly indeterminate system, the judge's choice of sentence would establish only loose parameters around the punishment; corrections and/or parole officials would make many important decisions later that might, as a practical matter, do more to determine the overall severity of the punishment than the judge's sentencing decision.

In principle, indeterminacy may come from any of a variety of sources, but, traditionally, the key mechanism of indeterminacy in American sentencing has been the power of parole boards to decide prison release dates. For this reason, those states that no longer provide for discretionary parole release are typically classified as "determinate," while those that continue to offer parole are typically classified as "indeterminate." Today, thirty-four states remain indeterminate in this sense of the term. Kevin R. Reitz & Edward E. Rhine, *Parole Release and Supervision: Crucial Drivers of American Prison Policy*, 3 ANN. REV. CRIMINOLOGY 281, 285 (2020).

In some indeterminate states, the judge pronounces a minimum and maximum sentence, e.g., two to five years, or ten to twenty years. The parole board will later decide on a release date within that range. In other indeterminate states, the judge imposes a sentence of a specified length, but with the understanding that the parole board will likely release the defendant some time before that term is fully served. In such states, the legislature often sets rules for the minimum and/or maximum amounts of time that must be served. For instance, in Georgia, prisoners generally become eligible for parole consideration only after serving one-third of the prison term pronounced by the court. ALEXIS LEE WATTS ET AL., UNIV. OF MINN., PROFILES IN PAROLE RELEASE AND REVOCATION: EXAMINING THE LEGAL FRAMEWORK IN THE UNITED STATES—GEORGIA (2016). At whatever point in the prison term a person is released, he or she will normally have to spend the remainder of the term on community supervision. While in this status, the person will be subject to a variety of special requirements and restrictions, such as maintaining regular employment and avoiding alcohol use. If these rules are violated, the person may be returned to prison.

We will consider the functioning of discretionary parole release in more detail below in Chapters 8 and 12. For present purposes, though, it is important to appreciate that parole boards have been subject to considerable criticism over the years. Some of the important criticisms include:

- Release criteria are vague and open-ended, which leads to decisionmaking that is arbitrary and unpredictable.
- Typically appointed by governors, parole board members often lack any particular expertise in corrections or offender rehabilitation.
- Parole boards lack the time and resources to devote anything more than cursory attention to most cases.
- Parole boards often fail to provide clear, realistic guidance to inmates about what they must do in order to earn release.
- Parole board members often lack job security, which may cause them to be unduly timid in making release decisions.
- Conversely, parole boards may sometimes be too *quick* to release, especially during times of intense prison overcrowding.
- Inconsistent, opaque decisionmaking may undercut the deterrent effect of prison sentences, fostering the belief that actual time served is usually only a small fraction of the sentence imposed.

As noted earlier in this chapter, because the development of parole was rooted in the Rehabilitative Ideal, the criticisms of parole grew especially pointed and influential in the late twentieth century, when confidence in correctional rehabilitation was at an especially low ebb. It was during this time period that many states either abolished discretionary parole or sharply restricted its availability, often in laws that bore the "truth in sentencing" label.

In most of the states that have retained parole, a variety of reforms in recent years have attempted to address some of the criticisms of traditional parole practices. Edward Rhine, Joan Petersilia & Kevin Reitz, *The Future of Parole Release*, 46 CRIME & JUST. 279, 281 (2017). Many states now supplement vague statutory criteria with more specific guidelines, which aim to bring greater consistency and coherence to parole decisions. Many states now also rely on actuarial risk-assessment instruments in order to make better judgments about the public-safety risks posed by parole candidates.

By way of illustration, the Texas Board of Pardons and Paroles currently uses guidelines that assign a score of one to seven to each individual being considered for release. TEX. BD. PARDONS & PAROLES, PAROLE GUIDELINES REPORT FY2020. This score is based on a combination of the "offense severity class" (low, moderate, high, or highest) and the "risk level," which is determined using a risk-assessment instrument. The instrument focuses on ten different factors, including, among others, current age, prior incarcerations, employment history, gang membership, and prison disciplinary record. The instrument is used to classify males as low, moderate, high, or highest risk. (A different algorithm is utilized for females, who are classified as low, moderate, or high.) The combination of highest offense severity class and highest risk level produces an overall guidelines score of one, while the combination of lowest offense severity and lowest risk produces a guidelines score of seven. Other combinations produce scores somewhere between the extremes. Once the score is calculated, parole decisionmakers may take the score into account, but are not required to decide in any particular way based on the score. "Ones" are sometimes granted parole, and "sevens" are sometimes denied. In FY 2020, nearly three-quarters of "sevens" were approved for parole. *Id.* at 9. However, the approval rate dropped to 51% for "sixes" and 37% for "fives."

The states that have abolished discretionary parole release are typically classified as "determinate," but it should be appreciated that no state can boast a system of "100%" determinacy as to the length of prison terms. Retaining some variability in release dates is thought to aid the work of corrections officials in several respects. In particular, such variability may strengthen the incentives for inmates to comply with institutional rules, encourage greater rehabilitative effort by inmates, and facilitate the movement of low-risk inmates out of overcrowded institutions. For these reasons, a variety of "early release" mechanisms are commonly found even in the parole-abolition states. For instance, more than half of all states (including both "determinate" and "indeterminate" jurisdictions), plus the federal system, offer "good-time," which involves awarding inmates credit toward early release based on time spent in the institution without rules violations. Michael O'Hear, *Solving the Good-Time Puzzle: Why Following the Rules Should Get You Out of Prison Early*, 2012 WIS. L. REV. 195, 197. Many states have established "earned-time" systems, which accelerate release based on participation in institutional programming or other desired behaviors.[12] Similarly, forty-nine states now offer "compassionate release" for elderly, disabled, or terminally ill inmates, although these programs tend to be only lightly utilized in practice. MARY PRICE, FAMILIES AGAINST MANDATORY MINIMUMS, EVERYWHERE AND NOWHERE: COMPASSIONATE RELEASE IN THE STATES (2018). A few states also provide mechanisms for judges to reconsider and revise their sentencing decisions based on prisoners' rehabilitative progress or other considerations. Cecelia Klingele, *Changing the Sentence Without Hiding the Truth: Judicial Sentence Modification as a Promising Method of Early Release*, 52 WM. &

[12] Little systematic research has been conducted on whether good-time and earned-time programs function in practice as intended, but a few studies suggest that such programs are capable of reducing rates of institutional misconduct and post-release recidivism. Michael O'Hear, *Good Conduct Time for Prisoners: Why (and How) Wisconsin Should Provide Credits Toward Early Release*, 98 MARQ. L. REV. 487 (2014).

MARY L. REV. 465 (2010). Furthermore, prison officials may be endowed with the authority to order "special action" releases in order to relieve overcrowding, provide furloughs in order to accommodate family or other needs, or move inmates out of prisons and into halfway houses or other community-based "intermediate" sanctions. Governors also typically have broad clemency powers, including the power to "commute" (reduce) prison terms. We will consider some of these early-release mechanisms in more detail in Chapter 12.

In short, the existence of discretionary parole in an "indeterminate" state may mask a relatively high degree of practical determinacy if the parole board operates in an unusually transparent, predictable fashion. Similarly, the *absence* of discretionary parole in a "determinate" state may conceal a relatively *low* degree of practical determinacy if the state has other early-release mechanisms that are used frequently, but without much transparency or predictability.

2. GUIDELINES

Determinacy gets at the predictability of punishment *after* the sentence has been imposed. You might wonder, though, about the predictability of the sentence itself. If the sentence results from a plea bargain, there is a good chance that the terms of the plea bargain will bring some predictability to the sentence. For instance, if the prosecutor agrees to recommend a prison term of a particular length, the judge is not likely to select a much harsher outcome. However, the predictability that results from plea-bargaining may not be entirely desirable from a public-policy standpoint. After all, plea deals may reflect the particular priorities, biases, or personality of the prosecutor, as well as the relative capability and zeal of the defense lawyer. Predictability may *generally* be an attractive characteristic for a sentencing system, but not necessarily if predictability means that sentences are predictably unfair or ill-advised. Similarly, with or without a plea deal, experienced lawyers will often have a pretty good idea going into the sentencing hearing of what the judge will impose, but predictable judicial behavior may also be problematic to the extent that it reflects judicial idiosyncrasies or unfounded beliefs about the purposes of punishment.

Sentencing guidelines aim to achieve a measure of *systemwide* predictability, in which the identities of the specific judge, prosecutor, and defense lawyer assigned to the case matter less to the outcome than in traditional, highly discretionary systems. Statutory sentencing ranges are often quite broad. For instance, under the applicable statutes, a person convicted in federal court of distributing 28 grams of crack cocaine may receive a sentence of anywhere from five to forty years in prison—and of distributing 280 grams, a sentence of anywhere from ten years to life. 21 U.S.C. § 841(b). Such wide statutory ranges practically invite highly disparate outcomes from courtroom to courtroom and case to case. Guidelines thus draw distinctions among defendants who have been convicted of the same offense, e.g., based on their criminal history or on particular ways in which they committed the offense, and establish relatively narrow sentencing ranges on the basis of these distinguishing factors. For instance, under the federal sentencing guidelines, a defendant who was convicted at trial of distributing 28 grams of crack, and who had two prior prison sentences, would likely face a range, not of 5–40 *years* in prison, but of 63–78 *months*.

As noted earlier in this chapter, the concept of sentencing guidelines first gained traction in the 1970s as a response to the perceived problem of unwarranted sentencing disparities. Proponents from the political left tended to emphasize concerns about race- and class-based disparities, while proponents from the right tended to focus on unwarranted *lenience*, which was seen as detrimental to the retributive and deterrent aims of punishment. Some policymakers were also drawn to guidelines as a tool to help restrain the growth (and hence expense) of prison populations. In all, twenty-two states, plus the federal government, adopted sentencing guidelines, although a handful subsequently abandoned the reform. Richard S. Frase, *Forty Years of American Sentencing Guidelines: What Have We Learned?*, 48 CRIME & JUST. 79, 80 (2019).

a. TYPES OF GUIDELINES

Each sentencing guidelines system is unique. A wide range of features serve to distinguish guidelines from one another, and a comprehensive survey of these differences might proceed at some length. *See, e.g.*, RICHARD S. FRASE, JUST SENTENCING: PRINCIPLES AND PROCEDURES FOR A WORKABLE SYSTEM 121–62 (2013) (describing guidelines in Minnesota, Washington, Oregon, Kansas, and North Carolina). For present purposes, we focus on just three important ways in which guidelines differ.

First, guidelines may be *advisory* or *presumptive*. Advisory guidelines offer a recommended range for the sentencing judge, but a party may not appeal a sentence on the ground that it lies outside the range. Without enforceability, the guidelines may, in effect, be disregarded by a sentencing judge who would prefer to handle a case differently than the guidelines propose. By contrast, presumptive guidelines have greater legal force. The judge must provide an explanation for a sentence outside the recommended range, and the sentence may be overturned on appeal if the explanation is found to be inadequate. Leading examples of presumptive guidelines include those operating in Minnesota, Kansas, Oregon, and Washington.[13]

---

[13] As Professor Frase notes, binary advisory/presumptive classifications can be difficult and misleading because there is actually a continuum of varying levels of presumptiveness. Richard S. Frase, *Forty Years of American Sentencing Guidelines: What Have We Learned?*, 48 CRIME & JUST. 79, 99 (2019). Frase places Minnesota, Kansas, Oregon, and Washington on the highly presumptive end of the continuum because there is active appellate review of sentences that meaningfully regulates departures from the guidelines in those states. At the other end of the spectrum would be guidelines jurisdictions that do not permit appeals of departures at all,

In political debates and media coverage, presumptive guidelines are sometimes confused with mandatory minimums. There is not always a crisp dividing line between the two, but presumptive guidelines, at least as the term is used here, can be differentiated from minimums on the basis of three characteristics. First, presumptive guidelines provide more flexibility for the sentencing judge, who is authorized to impose a sentence outside the guidelines range (a.k.a. a "departure" sentence) whenever an unusual, legally permissible consideration is present. Although some mandatory minimum statutes include "safety valve" provisions that permit a below-minimum sentence in some circumstances, these circumstances tend to be quite limited. Second, presumptive guidelines normally cover a wide range of case types, while minimums more specifically target certain types of offenses or offenders. For instance, "three strikes and you are out" laws, which are perhaps the most well-known example of a mandatory minimum, target only certain kinds of repeat offenders who have especially aggravated criminal histories. Finally, presumptive guidelines are drafted by a specialized sentencing commission, while mandatory minimums are the product of ordinary legislative processes (or sometimes a successful ballot initiative).

How frequently judges impose within-guidelines sentences varies considerably from jurisdiction to jurisdiction. Perhaps surprisingly, the "compliance" rates in some advisory jurisdictions are higher than in some presumptive jurisdictions. Frase, *supra,* at 105. On the whole, however, the available research suggests that presumptive guidelines are more effective than advisory guidelines in reducing unwarranted disparities and restraining growth in prison populations. Michael Tonry, *Fifty Years of American Sentencing Reform: Nine Lessons*, 48 CRIME & JUST. 1, 4–5 (2019).

Second, guidelines may be "descriptive" or "prescriptive." In descriptive guidelines, the recommended guidelines ranges are based on average sentences imposed in earlier cases. Descriptive guidelines aim to move outlier judges closer to the norms of their colleagues—without regard to how well the past averages advance the purposes of punishment. By contrast, prescriptive guidelines are based on an overarching normative framework (e.g., retributive proportionality) or a set of ideas about how existing practices should be changed. For instance, as noted in Chapter 1, the federal sentencing guidelines were deliberately intended to increase the use of prison sentences in cases of white-collar crime. To the extent that they present a broader and more direct challenge to existing practices, prescriptive guidelines may provoke stronger judicial resistance than descriptive.

---

including Arkansas, Delaware, the District of Columbia, Maryland, Massachusetts, Utah, and Virginia. The remaining guidelines jurisdictions (see Table 2-1) would fall somewhere between these extremes.

Third, guidelines may or may not be superintended by an *active sentencing commission*. Sentencing guidelines are typically produced by a special commission, but sometimes the commission is discontinued once the guidelines go into effect—or sometimes later as a legislative cost-cutting measure during times of fiscal distress. In the states that maintain an active, well-funded sentencing commission, the commission may engage in such activities as gathering data regarding sentencing trends and departure rates, tracking legislative and caselaw developments that may affect the interpretation or application of the guidelines, training judges and others on use of the guidelines, updating the guidelines based on changes in the law or other needs, and advising the legislature on proposed bills that would affect the guidelines or sentencing practices. Professor Richard Frase argues, "Guidelines need monitoring and updating on a regular basis or they will not achieve their purposes (and will eventually be ignored by judges and others). Given the huge costs and impacts of criminal punishment, creating and retaining a well-funded sentencing commission is money well spent." Richard S. Frase, *Forty Years of American Sentencing Guidelines: What Have We Learned?*, 48 CRIME & JUST. 79, 113–14 (2019).

Commissions are structured in a variety of different ways. There are usually about one to two dozen members, typically including one or more judges and also often including prosecution and defense representatives. *Id.* at 85–86. Other stakeholder groups that may be entitled to representation include corrections officials and crime victims. In some systems, all of the members are appointed by the governor, but most commissions also include individuals appointed by legislative, judicial, and other authorities. Having a balanced commission with broad stakeholder representation may enhance the legitimacy of the commission—and, by extension, the guidelines.

b. FIRST ILLUSTRATION OF PRESUMPTIVE GUIDELINES: THE MINNESOTA SYSTEM

Minnesota became the first state to establish a sentencing commission in 1978. The Minnesota Sentencing Guidelines Commission, which remains active to this day, was created in order to develop and superintend a new system of presumptive sentencing guidelines. The Commission and the guidelines were part of a broader sentencing reform package that also included the abolition of discretionary parole release. Although the abolition of parole does not necessarily require the creation of sentencing guidelines, the two reforms have often been linked together in practice. Do you see why the abolition of parole might strengthen the perceived need for sentencing guidelines?

In designing the state's guidelines system, the Minnesota Sentencing Guidelines Commission made several key policy decisions:

> First, it decided to be "prescriptive" and explicitly to establish its own sentencing priorities . . . . Second, the Commission

> decided to de-emphasize imprisonment as a punishment for property offenders and to emphasize imprisonment for violent offenders . . . . Third, in order to attack sentencing disparities, the Commission established very narrow sentencing ranges . . . and [authorized] departures . . . only when "substantial and compelling" reasons were present. Fourth, the Commission elected to adopt "just deserts" as the governing premise of its policies concerning who receives prison sentences. Fifth, the Commission chose to interpret an ambiguous statutory injunction that it take correctional resources into "substantial consideration" as a mandate that its guidelines not increase prison population beyond existing capacity constraints. This meant that the Commission had to make deliberate trade-offs in imprisonment policies. If the Commission decided to increase the length of prison terms for one group of offenders, it either had to decrease prison terms for another group or to shift the "in/out" line and divert some group of prisoners from prison altogether. Sixth, the Commission forbade consideration at sentencing of many personal factors—such as education, employment, marital status, living arrangements—that many judges believed to be legitimate. This decision resulted from a policy that sentencing decisions not be based on factors that might directly or indirectly discriminate against minorities, women, or low income groups.

MICHAEL H. TONRY, SENTENCING REFORM IMPACTS 48 (1987).

Since their initial launch in 1980, the Minnesota guidelines have been modified from time to time, but much of the original design survives.[14] The centerpiece of the guidelines remains the "grid," which we reprint below.[15]

Minnesota Sentencing Guidelines (2021)

Part 4A. Sentencing Guidelines Grid

Presumptive sentence lengths are in months. Italicized numbers within the grid denote the discretionary range within which a court may sentence without the sentence being deemed a departure. Offenders with stayed felony sentences may be subject to local confinement.

[14] For an overview and evaluation of the first quarter-century of the Minnesota system, see Richard S. Frase, *Sentencing Guidelines in Minnesota, 1978–2003*, 32 CRIME & JUST. 131 (2005).

[15] We reprint here the version of the guidelines grid that became effective on September 15, 2021. The full set of guidelines are available through the website of the Minnesota Sentencing Guidelines Commission at https://mn.gov/sentencing-guidelines/assets/2021Sept15MinnSentencingGuidelinesCommentary_tcm30-497682.pdf.

SEVERITY LEVEL OF CONVICTION OFFENSE (*Example offenses listed in italics*)		CRIMINAL HISTORY SCORE						
		0	**1**	**2**	**3**	**4**	**5**	**6 or more**
Murder, 2nd Degree (Intentional; Drive-By-Shootings)	11	306 *261–367*	326 *278–391*	346 *295–415*	366 *312–439*	386 *329–463*	406 *346–463*	426 *363–480*
Murder, 2nd Degree (Unintentional); Murder, 3rd Degree (Depraved Mind)	10	150 *128–180*	165 *141–198*	180 *153–216*	195 *166–234*	210 *179–252*	225 *192–270*	240 *204–288*
Murder, 3rd Degree (Drugs); Assault, 1st Degree (Great Bodily Harm)	9	86 *74–103*	98 *84–117*	110 *94–132*	122 *104–146*	134 *114–160*	146 *125–175*	158 *135–189*
Agg. Robbery, 1st Degree; Burglary, 1st Degree (w/Weapon or Assault)	8	48 *41–57*	58 *50–69*	68 *58–81*	78 *67–93*	88 *75–105*	98 *84–117*	108 *92–129*
Felony DWI; Financial Exploitation of a Vulnerable Adult	7	36	42	48	54 *46–64*	60 *51–72*	66 *57–76*	72 *62–84*
Assault, 2nd Degree; Burglary, 1st Degree (Occupied Dwelling)	6	21	27	33	39 *34–46*	45 *39–54*	51 *44–61*	57 *49–68*
Residential Burglary; Simple Robbery	5	18	23	28	33 *29–39*	38 *33–45*	43 *37–51*	48 *41–57*
Nonresidential Burglary	4	12	15	18	21	24 *21–28*	27 *23–32*	30 *20–27*
Theft Crimes (Over $5,000)	3	12	13	15	17	19 *17–22*	21 *18–25*	23 *20–27*
Theft Crimes ($5,000 or less); Check Forgery ($251–$2,500)	2	12	12	13	15	17	19	21 *18–25*
Assault, 4th Degree; Fleeing a Peace Officer	1	12	12	12	13	15	17	19 *17–22*

Presumptive commitment to state imprisonment.

Presumptive stayed sentence; at the discretion of the court, up to one year of confinement and other non-jail sanctions can be imposed as conditions of probation.

By way of illustration, consider how the Minnesota guidelines might be applied to Summer Blake (see Problem 1-1). Assume that Blake is convicted under Minnesota law of first-degree aggravated robbery. The basic statutory sentencing range for this offense would permit any term of imprisonment up to twenty years. Minn. Stat. § 609.245. What does the grid call for? You may assume that Blake has no prior convictions and would thus have a criminal history score of 0.

If given the presumptive sentence, how much time would Blake actually serve behind bars? In order to provide for a period of post-prison supervision, a person who receives a commitment sentence is normally released after serving two-thirds of the sentence; the remaining one-third constitutes a term of "supervised release." Minn. Stat. § 244.101. While on supervised release, the person is required to comply with various conditions and may be returned to prison if any conditions are violated. Additionally, the presumptive release at the two-thirds mark of the sentence may be deferred by corrections officials as a sanction for violations of prison rules. These features of the Minnesota system preserve some sentencing indeterminacy notwithstanding the state's abolition of discretionary parole. Why not go "all in" with determinacy?

Note the shaded boxes in the grid. For cases in these boxes, the presumptive term of imprisonment is presumptively stayed—in other words, the defendant is presumptively given a probationary sentence. For cases outside this area of the grid, including Blake's, the presumptive prison term is presumptively executed. Thus, if Blake were to be given probation, this would be considered a "dispositional" departure. If Blake were to be given a prison term, but one that is shorter than the bottom of the guidelines range, this would be considered a "durational" departure.

Might Blake be able to obtain a departure? The Minnesota guidelines state, "The court must pronounce a sentence of the applicable disposition, within the applicable prison range, and within the applicable length of stay, unless there exist identifiable, substantial, and compelling circumstances to support a departure." MINN. SENT'G GUIDELINES COMM'N, MINNESOTA SENTENCING GUIDELINES AND COMMENTARY § 2.D.1 (2020). The guidelines further specify that, "[i]n exercising the discretion to depart from a presumptive sentence, the court must disclose in writing or on the record the particular substantial and compelling circumstances that make the departure more appropriate than the presumptive sentence. The reasons must be stated in the sentencing order or recorded in the departure report and filed with the Commission." § 2.D.1(c).

The guidelines indicate that various factors should *not* be used as grounds for departure, including:

- Race;
- Sex;
- Employment factors, including (1) occupation or impact of sentence on profession or occupation, (2) employment history, (3) employment at time of offense, and (4) employment at time of sentencing; and
- Social factors, including (1) educational attainment, (2) living arrangements at time of offense or sentencing, (3) length of residence, and (4) marital status.

§ 2.D.2. By contrast, the guidelines also provide a nonexclusive list of permissible grounds for departure. Permissible *mitigating* factors include:

- The offender played a minor or passive role in the crime or participated under circumstances of coercion or duress;
- The offender, because of physical or mental impairment, lacked substantial capacity for judgment when the offense was committed;
- Other substantial grounds exist that tend to excuse or mitigate the offender's culpability, although not amounting to a defense; and
- The offender is particularly amenable to probation.

§ 2.D.3(a). Permissible *aggravating* factors include, among others, that the "victim was treated with particular cruelty for which the individual offender should be held responsible." § 2.D.3(b).

Do you think there are any "substantial and compelling circumstances" warranting a departure for Blake, either durational or dispositional, or upward or downward? If so, would the guidelines permit a departure on those grounds?

Overall, does it seem to you that the Minnesota system would help or hinder a judge in reaching a just and appropriate sentence for Blake? And, apart from *Blake*, does the Minnesota guidelines system strike you as well-designed and worthy of emulation by other jurisdictions? What criteria should be used to evaluate the quality of a guidelines system?

The Minnesota sentencing guidelines received renewed national attention in 2021 in connection with the sentencing of former police officer Derek Chauvin for the murder of George Floyd.

State v. Chauvin

2021 WL 2621001 (Minn. Dist. Ct.)
Sentencing Order & Memorandum Opinion
June 25, 2021

■ CAHILL, J.

* * *

In most cases, the maximum sentence a district court may impose is the top of the presumptive sentencing range because the sentencing guidelines mandate that district courts pronounce a sentence within the range on the sentencing guidelines grid. Minn. Sent. Guidelines 2.D.1. However, the Sentencing Guidelines recognize there are cases in which the guidelines sentence may not be appropriate and therefore allow district courts to depart from the presumptive sentence, although departing courts must articulate "substantial and compelling" circumstances justifying the departure. *Id.*; *see also State v. Barthman*, 938 N.W.2d 257, 267, 270 (Minn. 2020). "Substantial and compelling circumstances are those demonstrating that 'the defendant's conduct in the offense of conviction was *significantly* more or less serious than that typically involved in the commission of the crime in question.' "

Barthman, 938 N.W.2d at 270 (emphasis in original); *Tucker v. State*, 799 N.W.2d 583, 586 (Minn. 2011). When such factors are present, the judge "may depart from the presumptive disposition or duration provided in the Guidelines and stay or impose a sentence that is deemed to be more appropriate than the presumptive sentence." Minn. Sent. Guidelines 2.D.1. That includes exceeding the top end of the presumptive range when "there exist identifiable, substantial, and compelling circumstances." *Id.*; *State v. Rourke*, 773 N.W.2d 913, 919 (Minn. 2009).

For a defendant like Mr. Chauvin with zero criminal history points, the guidelines presumptive range for unintentional second-degree murder—the most serious charge of which Mr. Chauvin was found guilty by the jury and on which he is being convicted and sentenced by this Court—is 128 to 180 months, with the presumptive sentence being 150 months. Consideration of a sentence outside the presumptive guidelines range involves a two-stage process:

> (1) In the first stage, either a jury or the district court must make a factual finding that there are one or more aggravating factors present in the commission of the crime apart from the prima facie elements of the charged crime.
>
> (2) In the second stage, the district court is required to explain why the presence of any such aggravating factors creates a substantial and compelling reason to impose a sentence outside the presumptive guidelines range.

Rourke, 773 N.W.2d at 919–20.

As to the first stage, at the conclusion of the trial and after return of the jury's verdicts, Mr. Chauvin agreed to submit the issue of the existence of aggravated sentencing factors to this Court for decision. The State had urged the Court to find the existence of five aggravated sentencing factors in light of the evidence presented during the three-week trial between March 29 and April 15, 2021. In the Court's Verdict and Findings of Fact Regarding Aggravated Sentencing Factors, this Court found that the evidence at trial proved beyond a reasonable doubt the following four aggravated sentencing factors:[1]

(i) That Mr. Chauvin abused a position of trust and authority;

(ii) That Mr. Chauvin treated George Floyd with particular cruelty;

(iii) That children were present during the commission of the offense; and

(iv) That Mr. Chauvin committed the crime as a group with the active participation of three other individuals, former Minneapolis Police Officers Thou Thao, Thomas Lane, and

[1] This Court found that the fifth factor urged by the State, that George Floyd was particularly vulnerable, had not been proved beyond a reasonable doubt.

J. Alexander Kueng, who all actively participated with Mr. Chauvin in the crime in various ways.

The issue now before this Court on sentencing is the second stage: whether any of these four aggravated factors demonstrates that Mr. Chauvin's conduct in connection with the offense for which he has been convicted renders his conduct significantly more serious than that typically involved in the commission of such an offense, and therefore supplies a "substantial and compelling reason" for imposing an aggravated sentence of more than the 180 month top-of-the-guidelines range.

Although this Court found the presence of four aggravating factors, the decision whether to depart durationally upward and impose an aggravated sentence remains within the Court's sound discretion. * * *

II. MR. CHAUVIN'S ABUSE OF A POSITION OF TRUST OR AUTHORITY IS A SUBSTANTIAL AND COMPELLING REASON FOR AN UPWARD DURATIONAL DEPARTURE UNDER THE CIRCUMSTANCES OF THIS CASE.

The Court of Appeals has held that this aggravating factor supplies a "substantial and compelling reason" for an upward departure where the defendant and victim are in a "relationship[ ] fraught with power imbalances that may make it difficult for a victim to protect himself" and the defendant abuses his or her position of trust or authority in committing the crime.[3] *State v. Rourke*, 681 N.W.2d 35, 41 (Minn. App. 2004). That was the situation here.

Mr. Chauvin was employed as a licensed peace officer by the City of Minneapolis. As such, he "held a position of trust and authority with respect to the community and its members." Verdict and Findings of Fact Regarding Aggravated Sentencing Factors ¶ 1(b). The "trust placed in Defendant included trust that anyone arrested would be treated with respect and only with reasonable force and that medical needs would be addressed in a timely fashion." *Id.*

This Court has already concluded that:

(1) Mr. Chauvin "abused his position of authority" by using unreasonable force to hold "a handcuffed George Floyd in a prone position on the street"—"a position that Defendant knew from his training and experience carried with it a danger of positional asphyxia"—for more than nine minutes and forty seconds, "an inordinate amount of time." *Id.* ¶ 1(c).

(2) "Defendant's placement of his knee on the back of George Floyd's neck was an egregious abuse of the authority to subdue

[3] Mr. Chauvin argues that "abuse of a position of trust and authority" is not explicitly included among the aggravated sentencing factors enumerated in the Minnesota Sentencing Guidelines. Minn. Sent. Guidelines 2.D.3(b). However, the list of aggravating factors in the guidelines is expressly noted as nonexclusive, *id.*, and courts have upheld the abuse of position of authority as an aggravating factor in sentencing a defendant.

and restrain because the prolonged use of this maneuver was employed after George Floyd had already been handcuffed and continued for more than four and a half minutes after Mr. Floyd had ceased talking and had become unresponsive." *Id.* ¶ 1(f).

(3) Mr. Chauvin "abused his position of trust and authority by not rendering aid, by declining two suggestions from one of his fellow officers to place George Floyd on his side, and by preventing bystanders, including an off-duty Minneapolis fire fighter, from assisting." *Id.* ¶ 1(d).

(4) That "failure to render aid became particularly abusive after Mr. Floyd had passed out, and was still being restrained in the prone position, with Mr. Chauvin continuing to kneel on the back of Mr. Floyd's neck with one knee and on his back with another knee, for more than two and a half minutes after one of his fellow officers announced he was unable to detect a pulse." *Id.*

Here, by virtue of his position as a police officer, Mr. Chauvin "was in a position to dominate and control" Mr. Floyd. *State v. Bennett*, 1997 WL 526313, at *3 (Minn. App. Aug. 26, 1997). That "position of control" not only allowed Mr. Chauvin to "manipulate the circumstances and commit the crime," *id.*, but also "ma[d]e it difficult" for Mr. Floyd "to protect himself" from Mr. Chauvin's and his co-defendant officers' conduct. *Rourke*, 681 N.W.2d at 41. * * *

III. MR. CHAUVIN'S TREATING GEORGE FLOYD WITH PARTICULAR CRUELTY IS A SUBSTANTIAL AND COMPELLING REASON FOR AN UPWARD DURATIONAL DEPARTURE UNDER THE CIRCUMSTANCES OF THIS CASE.

Mr. Chauvin's particularly cruel treatment of George Floyd is also a separate "[s]ubstantial and compelling" basis for an upward sentencing departure. *Hicks*, 864 N.W.2d at 157. Here, the cruelty of Mr. Chauvin's conduct was "of a kind not usually associated with the commission of the offense[s] in question." *State v. Schantzen*, 308 N.W.2d 484, 487 (Minn. 1981). Mr. Chauvin's "gratuitous infliction of pain," *Tucker*, 799 N.W.2d at 586, and "psychological" cruelty, *State v. Norton*, 328 N.W.2d 142, 146 (Minn. 1982), justify an upward sentencing departure.

This Court has already concluded that:

(1) "[i]t was particularly cruel to kill George Floyd slowly" by inhibiting "his ability to breathe when Mr. Floyd had already made it clear he was having trouble breathing." Verdict and Findings of Fact Regarding Aggravated Sentencing Factors ¶ 2(b).

(2) The "prolonged use" of the prone position was "particularly egregious" because "George Floyd made it clear he was unable to breathe and expressed the view that he was dying as a result of the officers' restraint." *Id.* ¶ 1(c).

(3) Mr. Chauvin manifested his indifference to Mr. Floyd's pleas for his life and his medical distress by, among other things, "not rendering aid"; by "declining two suggestions from one of his fellow officers to place George Floyd on his side"; by "preventing bystanders, including an off-duty Minneapolis fire fighter, from assisting"; by failing to render aid even "after Mr. Floyd had passed out"; and by "continuing to kneel on the back of Mr. Floyd's neck . . . for more than two and a half minutes after one of his fellow officers announced he was unable to detect a pulse." *Id.* ¶ 1(d).

(4) The "slow death of George Floyd occurring over approximately six minutes of his positional asphyxia was particularly cruel in that Mr. Floyd was begging for his life and obviously terrified by the knowledge that he was likely to die but during which the Defendant objectively remained indifferent to Mr. Floyd's pleas." *Id.* ¶ 2(c).

(5) Restraining Mr. Floyd "in the prone position against the hard street surface by kneeling on the back of Mr. Floyd's neck with his other knee in Mr. Floyd's back, all the while holding his handcuffed arms in the fashion Defendant did for more than nine minutes," is "by itself a particularly cruel act." *Id.* ¶ 2(d).

(6) That the "prolonged nature of the asphyxiation" as manifested by the extensive video evidence presented during the trial was also "by itself particularly cruel." *Id.* ¶ 2(e).

These factual findings provide a "[s]ubstantial and compelling" basis for an aggravated sentencing departure, because they demonstrate that Mr. Chauvin's conduct "was significantly more . . . serious than that typically involved in the commission of the crime[s] in question." *Hicks*, 864 N.W.2d at 157. Here, Mr. Chauvin's actions inflicted "gratuitous . . . pain," *Tucker*, 799 N.W.2d at 586, by inhibiting George Floyd's "ability to breathe when Mr. Floyd had already made it clear he was having trouble breathing" and after he "expressed the view that he was dying as a result of the officers' restraint." And Mr. Chauvin's actions caused Mr. Floyd significant "psychological" distress, *Norton*, 328 N.W.2d at 146, because "Defendant objectively remained indifferent to Mr. Floyd's pleas" even as "Mr. Floyd was begging for his life and obviously terrified by the knowledge that he was likely to die."

Mr. Chauvin's prolonged restraint of Mr. Floyd was also much longer and more painful than the typical scenario in a second-degree or third-degree murder or second-degree manslaughter case. The "prolonged nature of the asphyxiation" makes this offense different in kind than, for example, a near-instantaneous death by gunshot, which is one typical scenario for this type of offense. * * *

[Although the court had previously found two additional aggravating factors (presence of children and commission of offense as part of a group), the court determined that these were not appropriate grounds for an upward departure in the particular circumstances of this case.]

VI. THE APPROPRIATE PRISON SENTENCE IS 270 MONTHS.

When a sentencing trial court has found that one or more aggravated factors are present, the court may, in the exercise of its discretion if substantial and compelling circumstances warrant, impose a sentence that is up to "double the presumptive sentence length." *State v. Evans*, 311 N.W.2d 481, 483 (Minn. 1981). The existence of a single aggravating factor is sufficient to justify the imposition of a sentence "double the upper limit of the presumptive range." *Barthman*, 938 N.W.2d at 269, 275. Here, the State is asking this Court to sentence Mr. Chauvin to 360 months, which represents a double upward durational departure from the 180 months at the "top of the box" of the presumptive guidelines range.

Determining the appropriate length of any felony sentence is not a mathematical calculation. Nor should it be a reflexive doubling of the presumptive sentence once aggravating factors are proven and found by the Court to be substantial and compelling. Each sentence should be an application of the law to the facts of the individual case without regard to sympathy, bias, passion, or public opinion. While every case is different and must be considered carefully and individually, examination of sentences imposed in similar cases is also relevant if the Court is to effectuate the Minnesota Sentencing Guidelines policy of reducing sentencing disparity.

Attached to this memorandum is Minnesota Sentencing Guidelines Commission data from the last ten years analyzing aggravated durational departures imposed throughout Minnesota for Murder in the Second Degree (Unintentional Killing during a Felony). The data shows that of all the sentences imposed, 67% were within the presumptive guidelines range. For a defendant with a criminal history score of zero, which is Mr. Chauvin's score, the guidelines sentence is, and has been since 2005, 150 months with a presumptive range of 128 months to 180 months. Any sentence within that range is not a departure.

For all cases where sentences were imposed, 20% of the sentences were aggravated durational departures and 13% were mitigated durational departures (*i.e.* departures imposing less prison time than the sentencing guidelines range). The most common aggravated sentence has been 240 months, followed by 300 months. The average aggravated departure imposed on defendants with a zero criminal history score is 278.2 months.

Drilling deeper into the actual cases, there are only two cases where the defendant's criminal history score is zero, and both "abuse of a position of trust or authority" and "particular cruelty" were cited as aggravating factors. Unlike the instant case, however, those cases involved particularly vulnerable victims, specifically, three-year-old children. The defendant in 27-CR-18-18213 was originally charged with Murder in the First Degree and pleaded guilty to Murder in the Second Degree (Unintentional Killing during a Felony) for an agreed-upon range of 300 to 420 months and was sentenced to 384 months. The defendant in 27-CR-15-25934 pleaded guilty to the charge with an agreed-upon sentence of 300 months. In both cases, the cruelty inflicted on the children was horrific, even more severe than the cruelty inflicted on Mr. Floyd.

Mr. Chauvin did not plead guilty, but he cannot be punished for exercising his constitutional right to a jury trial. Nevertheless, he must be held accountable for the death of Mr. Floyd and for doing so in a manner that was particularly cruel and an abuse of his authority. In consideration of all the facts presented at trial, this Court's experience, and the collective experience of the entire Court over the last ten years, the Court finds the appropriate prison sentence for Mr. Chauvin is 270 months.

NOTES & QUESTIONS

1. **Finding of Facts.** Departure decisions in Minnesota require explicit fact-finding. As the *Chauvin* court put it, "either a jury or the district court must make a factual finding that there are one or more aggravating factors present in the commission of the crime apart from the prima facie elements of the charged crime." What sort of due-process protections do you think should be observed to ensure that such fact-finding is fair and reliable? Since the finding of aggravating facts potentially exposes the defendant to additional punishment, you might think that the defendant should have the same set of (relatively) robust procedural protections for sentencing fact-finding as for the fact-finding that occurs in a trial on guilt or innocence. As we will see in Chapter 3, however, the Supreme Court was slow to recognize procedural rights for defendants at sentencing—even notwithstanding the implementation of new guidelines systems that gave more definite legal significance to sentencing fact-finding than in traditional discretionary systems. Although the Court's 2000 decision in *Apprendi v. New Jersey* (excerpted in Chapter 3) marked an important turning point in this regard, procedural protections at sentencing remain weaker than in criminal trials.

2. **Persistence of Discretion.** Minnesota judges retain discretion to determine whether any aggravating (or mitigating) facts that have been found warrant a sentence outside the guidelines range, and, if so, how far. Doesn't such discretion seem inconsistent with the guidelines' goal of reducing disparities in sentencing?

3. **Abuse of Trust and Cruelty.** The court found that an upward departure was warranted by the presence of two "substantial and compelling" circumstances: Chauvin's abuse of a position of trust and the particular cruelty of the offense. Do you agree that these considerations justified a sentence above the normal guidelines range? Does taking these considerations into account advance any of the purposes of punishment that were discussed in Chapter 1?

4. **Why 270 Months?** The court's finding of "substantial and compelling" circumstances authorized a punishment of anywhere from 180 to 360 months. How exactly did the court select a sentence from within that wide range? Note the court's reliance on sentences imposed in other cases. Using other, similar cases as a benchmark may help to address concerns about disparities in the use of departures. However, you may also recall the sentencing judge's rather unfruitful effort to consider other cases in *United States v. Stern* in Chapter 1. Were you persuaded that the Minnesota court made appropriate use of the other-cases information in *Chauvin*?

5. **Social Context.** The *Chauvin* court pointedly observed, "Each sentence should be an application of the law to the facts of the individual case without regard to sympathy, bias, passion, or public opinion." Perhaps reflecting this point of view, the court made no mention of the extraordinary national social response to the murder of George Floyd. Does this seem appropriate to you? If a crime provokes widespread public anguish and outrage, why should that not be taken into account in determining the sentence? Surely, Chauvin's offense affected many, many more lives than any of the other offenses that the court used for comparison purposes. Do you think that might warrant a longer sentence than was imposed in any of the other cases?

c. SECOND ILLUSTRATION OF PRESUMPTIVE GUIDELINES: PRE-2005 FEDERAL SYSTEM

In Chapter 1, we noted Congress's adoption of the Sentencing Reform Act of 1984, which included the language on purposes of punishment that is now codified as 18 U.S.C. § 3553(a). The SRA also abolished discretionary parole in the federal system, established a sentencing commission, and authorized the creation of federal sentencing guidelines, which went into effect in 1987. In very broad outline, the federal system was similar to Minnesota's—an expert commission drafted guidelines that were centered on a two-dimensional grid; the guidelines had relatively narrow recommended sentencing ranges; and federal sentencing judges could "depart" from these ranges in only limited circumstances. In their specifics, however, the federal guidelines differed sharply from their Minnesota counterparts, perhaps most notably in their complexity and severity.

In an important 2005 decision, *United States v. Booker*, 543 U.S. 220 (2005), the Supreme Court held that the presumptive federal system was unconstitutional, but retained the guidelines in advisory form. We explore *Booker* and its aftermath in more detail in Chapter 3 below. Although *Booker* and its progeny substantially altered the federal guidelines system that had been launched in the mid-1980s, that system remains of interest for several reasons. First, even post-*Booker*, federal sentencing judges are still required to calculate the guidelines range in all cases; *Booker* merely enhanced the discretion of judges to deviate from that range. Second, notwithstanding the formal shift of the federal guidelines from presumptive to advisory, sentencing appeals are still permitted, and the guidelines continue to play an important role as a benchmark in the substantive evaluation of sentences. Indeed, because of the complex and unusual functioning of post-*Booker* appellate review, it may be more accurate to characterize the guidelines today as a presumptive-advisory hybrid, rather than simply advisory. It is clear, in any event, that the practical reality of the post-*Booker* system remains far closer to the pre-*Booker* system than many critics of the guidelines had hoped would be the case when *Booker* was decided. Third, for many practitioners, policymakers, and academic commentators, the pre-*Booker* system continues to be the most familiar exemplar of presumptive sentencing guidelines. When the strengths and weaknesses of presumptive guidelines are discussed, the federal model often figures prominently in the conversation.

We reprint below the guidelines sentencing table (a.k.a. the "grid"). As you can see, the determination of a sentencing range in any given case requires the calculation of a criminal history score and an offense severity level. Determination of the former will be discussed in Chapter 4. As for offense severity, its determination involves a three-part process. First, it is necessary to find the right offense guideline. Using the statutory citation for the offense of conviction, the appropriate guideline can usually be found in Appendix A of the official *Guidelines Manual*.[16] Once located, the offense guideline will specify a "base offense level." Second, adjustments to the base offense level are made in light of the "specific offense characteristics" identified in the offense guideline. The specific offense characteristics are particular acts or circumstances that either mitigate or (more commonly) aggravate offense severity. For instance, if the offense was committed using a firearm, the offense level might be increased by a given amount. Third, additional adjustments are made based on the factors covered in Chapter 3 of the *Guidelines Manual*, such as the defendant's acceptance of responsibility for the offense, which would result in a two- or three-point reduction in the offense level.

---

[16] The most recent edition of the federal *Guidelines Manual* can be found through the website of the United States Sentencing Commission at https://www.ussc.gov/guidelines.

United States Sentencing Guidelines (2021)

Part 5A. Sentencing Table

	Criminal History Category (Criminal History Points)					
Offense Level	**I (0 or 1)**	**II (2 or 3)**	**III (4, 5, 6)**	**IV (7, 8, 9)**	**V (10, 11, 12)**	**VI (13 or more)**
1	0 – 6	0 – 6	0 – 6	0 – 6	0 – 6	0 – 6
2	0 – 6	0 – 6	0 – 6	0 – 6	0 – 6	1 – 7
3	0 – 6	0 – 6	0 – 6	0 – 6	2 – 8	3 – 9
4	0 – 6	0 – 6	0 – 6	2 – 8	4 – 10	6 – 12
5	0 – 6	0 – 6	1 – 7	4 – 10	6 – 12	9 – 15
6	0 – 6	1 – 7	2 – 8	6 – 12	9 – 15	12 – 18
7	0 – 6	2 – 8	4 – 10	8 – 14	12 – 18	15 – 21
8	0 – 6	4 – 10	6 – 12	10 – 16	15 – 21	18 – 24
9	4 – 10	6 – 12	8 – 14	12 – 18	18 – 24	21 – 27
10	6 – 12	8 – 14	10 – 16	15 – 21	21 – 27	24 – 30
11	8 – 14	10 – 16	12 – 18	18 – 24	24 – 30	27 – 33
12	10 – 16	12 – 18	15 – 21	21 – 27	27 – 33	30 – 37
13	12 – 18	15 – 21	18 – 24	24 – 30	30 – 37	33 – 41
14	15 – 21	18 – 24	21 – 27	27 – 33	33 – 41	37 – 46
15	18 – 24	21 – 27	24 – 30	30 – 37	37 – 46	41 – 51
16	21 – 27	24 – 30	27 – 33	33 – 41	41 – 51	46 – 57
17	24 – 30	27 – 33	30 – 37	37 – 46	46 – 57	51 – 63
18	27 – 33	30 – 37	33 – 41	41 – 51	51 – 63	57 – 71
19	30 – 37	33 – 41	37 – 46	46 – 57	57 – 71	63 – 78
20	33 – 41	46 – 57	41 – 51	51 – 63	63 – 78	70 – 87
21	37 – 46	51 – 63	46 – 57	57 – 71	70 – 87	77 – 96
22	41 – 51	57 – 71	51 – 63	63 – 78	77 – 96	84 – 105
23	46 – 57	51 – 63	57 – 71	70 – 87	85 – 105	92 – 115
24	51 – 63	57 – 71	63 – 78	77 – 96	92 – 115	100 – 125
25	57 – 71	63 – 78	70 – 87	84 – 105	100 – 125	110 – 137
26	63 – 78	70 – 87	78 – 97	92 – 115	110 – 137	120 – 150
27	70 – 87	78 – 97	87 – 108	100 – 125	120 – 150	130 – 162
28	78 – 97	87 – 108	97 – 121	110 – 137	130 – 162	140 – 175
29	87 – 108	97 – 121	108 – 135	121 – 151	140 – 175	151 – 188
30	97 – 121	108 – 135	121 – 151	135 – 168	151 – 188	168 – 210
31	108 – 135	121 – 151	135 – 168	151 – 188	168 – 210	188 – 235
32	121 – 151	135 – 168	151 – 188	168 – 210	188 – 235	210 – 262
33	135 – 168	151 – 188	168 – 210	188 – 235	210 – 262	235 – 293
34	151 – 188	168 – 210	188 – 235	210 – 262	235 – 293	262 – 327
35	168 – 210	188 – 235	210 – 262	235 – 293	262 – 327	292 – 365
36	188 – 235	210 – 262	235 – 293	262 – 327	292 – 365	324 – 405
37	210 – 262	235 – 293	262 – 327	292 – 365	324 – 405	360 – life
38	235 – 293	262 – 327	292 – 365	324 – 405	360 – life	360 – life
39	262 – 327	292 – 365	324 – 405	360 – life	360 – life	360 – life
40	292 – 365	324 – 405	360 – life	360 – life	360 – life	360 – life
41	324 – 405	360 – life	360 – life	360 – life	360 – life	360 – life
42	360 – life	360 – life	360 – life	360 – life	360 – life	360 – life
43	life	life	life	life	life	life

KEY:

Zone A	Zone B	Zone C	Zone D

The "zones" indicate the availability of probation or other alternatives to imprisonment. If a case is in Zone A, probation is freely available to the sentencing judge. § 5C1.1. In Zones B and C, there are progressively greater restrictions on the use of alternatives. In Zone D, the guidelines contemplate that a sentence of imprisonment will be imposed, and the length of the term will be at least equal to the bottom of the specified range.

To illustrate the determination of the sentencing range, consider once again the *Blake* case. We reprint below § 2B3.1 of the guidelines, which is the offense guideline for robberies. What is the base offense level? What specific offense characteristics seem to apply to *Blake*? By how much do they increase the offense level? It may help to know that "serious bodily injury" is defined as "injury involving extreme physical pain or the protracted impairment of a function of a bodily member, organ, or mental faculty; or requiring medical intervention such as surgery, hospitalization, or physical rehabilitation." Meanwhile, "permanent or life-threatening bodily injury" is defined as "injury involving a substantial risk of death; loss or substantial impairment of the function of a bodily member, organ, or mental faculty that is likely to be permanent; or an obvious disfigurement that is likely to be permanent." § 1B1.1 app. n.1.

United States Sentencing Guidelines (2021)

§ 2B3.1. Robbery

(a) Base Offense Level: **20**

(b) Specific Offense Characteristics

(1) If the property of a financial institution or post office was taken, or if the taking of such property was an object of the offense, increase by **2** levels.

(2) (A) If a firearm was discharged, increase by **7** levels; (B) if a firearm was otherwise used, increase by **6** levels; (C) if a firearm was brandished or possessed, increase by **5** levels; (D) if a dangerous weapon was otherwise used, increase by **4** levels; (E) if a dangerous weapon was brandished or possessed, increase by **3** levels; or (F) if a threat of death was made, increase by **2** levels.

(3) If any victim sustained bodily injury, increase the offense level according to the seriousness of the injury:

	Degree of Bodily Injury	Increase in Level
(A)	Bodily Injury	Add **2**
(B)	Serious Bodily Injury	Add **4**
(C)	Permanent or Life-Threatening Bodily Injury	Add **6**
(D)	If the degree of injury is between that specified in subdivisions (A) and (B), add **3** levels; or	
(E)	If the degree of injury is between that specified in subdivisions (B) and (C), add **5** levels.	

Provided, however, that the cumulative adjustments from (2) and (3) shall not exceed **11** levels.

(4) (A) If any person was abducted to facilitate commission of the offense or to facilitate escape, increase by **4** levels; or (B) if any person was physically restrained to facilitate commission of the offense or to facilitate escape, increase by **2** levels.

(5) If the offense involved carjacking, increase by **2** levels.

(6) If a firearm, destructive device, or controlled substance was taken, or if the taking of such item was an object of the offense, increase by **1** level.

(7) If the loss exceeded $20,000, increase the offense level as follows:

	Loss (Apply the Greatest)	Increase in Level
(A)	$20,000 or less	no increase
(B)	More than $20,000	Add **1**
(C)	More than $95,000	Add **2**
(D)	More than $500,000	Add **3**
(E)	More than $1,500,000	Add **4**
(F)	More than $3,000,000	Add **5**

Since Blake pled guilty, she would likely receive a three-level reduction for acceptance of responsibility. § 3E1.1. Assuming that no other Chapter 3 adjustments apply and that Blake is in Criminal History Category I, what is her guidelines sentencing range? Would probation or other alternatives to imprisonment be available? Putting aside the possibility of a departure, does it seem to you that the federal guidelines do a better or worse job of handling the *Blake* case than the Minnesota guidelines?

In the pre-*Booker* system, departures were governed by 18 U.S.C. § 3553(b)(1), which stated, "[T]he court shall impose a sentence of the kind, and within the range, [specified by the federal sentencing guidelines] unless the court finds that there exists an aggravating or mitigating circumstance of a kind, or to a degree, not adequately taken into consideration by the Sentencing Commission in formulating the guidelines that should result in a sentence different from that described."[17] The Commission itself provided more detailed guidance regarding a wide range of potential departure grounds in Chapter 5 of the *Guidelines Manual*. Two aspects of this guidance bear particular

[17] Congress adopted an even higher standard for departures for child crimes and sexual offenses in the Prosecutorial Remedies and Other Tools to End the Exploitation of Children Today ("PROTECT") Act of 2003. The relevant provision was codified as 18 U.S.C. § 3553(b)(2).

emphasis. First, § 5K1.1 authorizes downward departures on the basis of the defendant's "substantial assistance in the investigation or prosecution of another person who has committed an offense." However, a sentencing judge may not depart on this ground unless the departure is supported by the government. This provision was frequently cited by guidelines critics who argued that the guidelines empowered prosecutors at the expense of judges. In any event, "substantial assistance" accounted for a large majority of the departures in the pre-*Booker* era. U.S. SENT'G COMM'N, FINAL REPORT ON THE IMPACT OF *UNITED STATES V. BOOKER* ON FEDERAL SENTENCING 51 (2006). Even today, post-*Booker*, § 5K1.1 is noted as the basis for about one-sixth of all sentences that are outside the recommended guidelines range. U.S. SENT'G COMM'N, SOURCEBOOK OF FEDERAL SENTENCING STATISTICS tbl. 33 (2020). Second, the guidelines generally prohibit or discourage the use of a defendant's personal characteristics as a basis for departure. For instance, the guidelines flatly state that race, sex, national origin, religion, and socioeconomic status "are not relevant in the determination of a sentence." § 5H1.10. The guidelines further specify that such factors as employment record and family responsibilities are "not ordinarily relevant in determining whether a departure is warranted." §§ 5H1.5, 5H1.6. We explore both aspects of the guidelines' departure provisions (authorization of departures for substantial assistance, restriction of departures based on personal characteristics) in more detail in Chapter 4 below.

Overall, the percentage of cases with departures varied considerably over the pre-*Booker* time period, but generally ranged between 20% and 35%. FINAL REPORT ON THE IMPACT OF *UNITED STATES V. BOOKER*, *supra*, at 51. More recently, post-*Booker*, about half of sentences have been outside the range. SOURCEBOOK OF FEDERAL SENTENCING STATISTICS, *supra*, tbl. 29. Sentences below the range have always far outnumbered sentences above the range. By way of comparison, about 25% of Minnesota sentences are departures—also overwhelmingly of the *downward* variety. MINN. SENT'G GUIDELINES COMM'N, 2019 SENTENCING PRACTICES: ANNUAL SUMMARY STATISTICS FOR FELONY CASES 26 (2020).

In case you are wondering, the judge in *Blake* did depart downward. In light of "the aberrant nature of this crime, the diminished capacity [Blake] was under at the time of the offense, the effect on family, and the extensive rehabilitation demonstrated by Blake," the judge sentenced her to time served (one month) and five years of supervised release. *United States v. Blake*, 89 F. Supp. 2d 328, 353 (E.D.N.Y. 2000). Importantly, the sentencing judge was Jack Weinstein, who was well-known nationally for his disdain of the federal guidelines and his expansive views regarding the departure power of district judges. Kate Stith, *Weinstein on Sentencing*, 33 FED. SENT'G RPTR. 155 (2021). His approach to departures in *Blake* and other cases should not be regarded as representative of pre-*Booker* practice.

In drafting the federal guidelines, the United States Sentencing Commission made a multitude of important policy choices. The Commission described several of these in the original introduction to the *Guidelines Manual*.

United States Sentencing Guidelines (2021)

§ 1A1. Original Introduction to the Guidelines Manual

3. The Basic Approach (Policy Statement)

To understand the guidelines and their underlying rationale, it is important to focus on the three objectives that Congress sought to achieve in enacting the Sentencing Reform Act of 1984. The Act's basic objective was to enhance the ability of the criminal justice system to combat crime through an effective, fair sentencing system. To achieve this end, Congress first sought honesty in sentencing. It sought to avoid the confusion and implicit deception that arose out of the pre-guidelines sentencing system which required the court to impose an indeterminate sentence of imprisonment and empowered the parole commission to determine how much of the sentence an offender actually would serve in prison. * * *

Second, Congress sought reasonable uniformity in sentencing by narrowing the wide disparity in sentences imposed for similar criminal offenses committed by similar offenders. Third, Congress sought proportionality in sentencing through a system that imposes appropriately different sentences for criminal conduct of differing severity.

Honesty is easy to achieve: The abolition of parole makes the sentence imposed by the court the sentence the offender will serve, less approximately fifteen percent for good behavior. There is a tension, however, between the mandate of uniformity and the mandate of proportionality. Simple uniformity—sentencing every offender to five years—destroys proportionality. Having only a few simple categories of crimes would make the guidelines uniform and easy to administer, but might lump together offenses that are different in important respects. For example, a single category for robbery that included armed and unarmed robberies, robberies with and without injuries, robberies of a few dollars and robberies of millions, would be far too broad.

A sentencing system tailored to fit every conceivable wrinkle of each case would quickly become unworkable and seriously compromise the certainty of punishment and its deterrent effect. For example: A bank robber with (or without) a gun, which the robber kept hidden (or brandished), might have frightened (or merely warned), injured seriously (or less seriously), tied up (or simply pushed) a guard, teller, or customer, at night (or at noon), in an effort to obtain money for other crimes (or for other purposes), in the company of a few (or many) other robbers, for the first (or fourth) time.

The list of potentially relevant features of criminal behavior is long; the fact that they can occur in multiple combinations means that the list of possible permutations of factors is virtually endless. * * *

The larger the number of subcategories of offense and offender characteristics included in the guidelines, the greater the complexity and the less workable the system. Moreover, complex combinations of offense and offender characteristics would apply and interact in unforeseen ways to unforeseen situations, thus failing to cure the unfairness of a simple, broad category system. Finally, and perhaps most importantly, probation officers and courts, in applying a complex system having numerous subcategories, would be required to make a host of decisions regarding whether the underlying facts were sufficient to bring the case within a particular subcategory. The greater the number of decisions required and the greater their complexity, the greater the risk that different courts would apply the guidelines differently to situations that, in fact, are similar, thereby reintroducing the very disparity that the guidelines were designed to reduce.

In view of the arguments, it would have been tempting to retreat to the simple, broad category approach and to grant courts the discretion to select the proper point along a broad sentencing range. Granting such broad discretion, however, would have risked correspondingly broad disparity in sentencing, for different courts may exercise their discretionary powers in different ways. Such an approach would have risked a return to the wide disparity that Congress established the Commission to reduce and would have been contrary to the Commission's mandate set forth in the Sentencing Reform Act of 1984.

In the end, there was no completely satisfying solution to this problem. The Commission had to balance the comparative virtues and vices of broad, simple categorization and detailed, complex subcategorization, and within the constraints established by that balance, minimize the discretionary powers of the sentencing court. * * *

A philosophical problem arose when the Commission attempted to reconcile the differing perceptions of the purposes of criminal punishment. Most observers of the criminal law agree that the ultimate aim of the law itself, and of punishment in particular, is the control of crime. Beyond this point, however, the consensus seems to break down. Some argue that appropriate punishment should be defined primarily on the basis of the principle of "just deserts." Under this principle, punishment should be scaled to the offender's culpability and the resulting harms. Others argue that punishment should be imposed primarily on the basis of practical "crime control" considerations. This theory calls for sentences that most effectively lessen the likelihood of future crime, either by deterring others or incapacitating the defendant.

Adherents of each of these points of view urged the Commission to choose between them and accord one primacy over the other. As a practical matter, however, this choice was unnecessary because in most sentencing decisions the application of either philosophy will produce the same or similar results.

In its initial set of guidelines, the Commission sought to solve both the practical and philosophical problems of developing a coherent sentencing system by taking an empirical approach that used as a starting point data estimating pre-guidelines sentencing practice. It analyzed data drawn from 10,000 presentence investigations, the differing elements of various crimes as distinguished in substantive criminal statutes, the United States Parole Commission's guidelines and statistics, and data from other relevant sources in order to determine which distinctions were important in pre-guidelines practice. After consideration, the Commission accepted, modified, or rationalized these distinctions.

This empirical approach helped the Commission resolve its practical problem by defining a list of relevant distinctions that, although of considerable length, was short enough to create a manageable set of guidelines. Existing categories are relatively broad and omit distinctions that some may believe important, yet they include most of the major distinctions that statutes and data suggest made a significant difference in sentencing decisions. Relevant distinctions not reflected in the guidelines probably will occur rarely and sentencing courts may take such unusual cases into account by departing from the guidelines.

The Commission's empirical approach also helped resolve its philosophical dilemma. Those who adhere to a just deserts philosophy may concede that the lack of consensus might make it difficult to say exactly what punishment is deserved for a particular crime. Likewise, those who subscribe to a philosophy of crime control may acknowledge that the lack of sufficient data might make it difficult to determine exactly the punishment that will best prevent that crime. Both groups might therefore recognize the wisdom of looking to those distinctions that judges and legislators have, in fact, made over the course of time. These established distinctions are ones that the community believes, or has found over time, to be important from either a just deserts or crime control perspective.

The Commission did not simply copy estimates of pre-guidelines practice as revealed by the data, even though establishing offense values on this basis would help eliminate disparity because the data represent averages. Rather, it departed from the data at different points for various important reasons. Congressional statutes, for example, suggested or required departure, as in the case of the Anti-Drug Abuse Act of 1986 that imposed increased and mandatory minimum sentences. In addition, the data revealed inconsistencies in treatment, such as punishing economic crime less severely than other apparently equivalent behavior.

Despite these policy-oriented departures from pre-guidelines practice, the guidelines represent an approach that begins with, and builds upon, empirical data. The guidelines will not please those who wish the Commission to adopt a single philosophical theory and then work deductively to establish a simple and perfect set of categorizations and distinctions. The guidelines may prove acceptable, however, to those who seek more modest, incremental improvements in the status quo, who believe the best is often the enemy of the good, and who recognize that these guidelines are, as the Act contemplates, but the first step in an evolutionary process. After spending considerable time and resources exploring alternative approaches, the Commission developed these guidelines as a practical effort toward the achievement of a more honest, uniform, equitable, proportional, and therefore effective sentencing system.

4. The Guidelines' Resolution of Major Issues (Policy Statement) * * *

(a) Real Offense vs. Charge Offense Sentencing

One of the most important questions for the Commission to decide was whether to base sentences upon the actual conduct in which the defendant engaged regardless of the charges for which he was indicted or convicted ("real offense" sentencing), or upon the conduct that constitutes the elements of the offense for which the defendant was charged and of which he was convicted ("charge offense" sentencing). A bank robber, for example, might have used a gun, frightened bystanders, taken $50,000, injured a teller, refused to stop when ordered, and raced away damaging property during his escape. A pure real offense system would sentence on the basis of all identifiable conduct. A pure charge offense system would overlook some of the harms that did not constitute statutory elements of the offenses of which the defendant was convicted.

The Commission initially sought to develop a pure real offense system. After all, the pre-guidelines sentencing system was, in a sense, this type of system. The sentencing court and the parole commission took account of the conduct in which the defendant actually engaged, as determined in a presentence report, at the sentencing hearing, or before a parole commission hearing officer. The Commission's initial efforts in this direction, carried out in the spring and early summer of 1986, proved unproductive, mostly for practical reasons. To make such a system work, even to formalize and rationalize the status quo, would have required the Commission to decide precisely which harms to take into account, how to add them up, and what kinds of procedures the courts should use to determine the presence or absence of disputed factual elements. The Commission found no practical way to combine and account for the large number of diverse harms arising in different circumstances; nor did it find a practical way to reconcile the need for a fair adjudicatory procedure with the need for a speedy sentencing process given the potential existence of hosts of adjudicated "real harm" facts in many typical cases. The effort proposed as a solution to these problems required the use of, for example, quadratic roots and other mathematical operations that the Commission considered too complex to be workable. In the Commission's view, such a system risked return to wide disparity in sentencing practice.

In its initial set of guidelines submitted to Congress in April 1987, the Commission moved closer to a charge offense system. This system, however, does contain a significant number of real offense elements. For one thing, the hundreds of overlapping and duplicative statutory provisions that make up the federal criminal law forced the Commission to write guidelines that are descriptive of generic conduct rather than guidelines that track purely statutory language. For another, the guidelines take account of a number of important, commonly occurring real offense elements such as role in the offense, the presence of a gun, or the amount of money actually taken, through alternative base offense levels, specific offense characteristics, cross references, and adjustments.

The Commission recognized that a charge offense system has drawbacks of its own. One of the most important is the potential it affords prosecutors to influence sentences by increasing or decreasing the number of counts in an indictment. Of course, the defendant's actual conduct (that which the prosecutor can prove in court) imposes a natural limit upon the prosecutor's ability to increase a defendant's sentence. Moreover, the Commission has written its rules for the treatment of multicount convictions with an eye toward eliminating unfair treatment that might flow from count manipulation. For example, the guidelines treat a three-count indictment, each count of which charges sale of 100 grams of heroin or theft of $10,000, the same as a single-count indictment charging sale of 300 grams of heroin or theft of $30,000. Furthermore, a sentencing court may control any inappropriate manipulation of the indictment through use of its departure power. * * *

(b) Departures

The sentencing statute permits a court to depart from a guideline-specified sentence only when it finds "an aggravating or mitigating circumstance of a kind, or to a degree, not adequately taken into consideration by the Sentencing Commission in formulating the guidelines that should result in a sentence different from that described." 18 U.S.C. § 3553(b). The Commission intends the sentencing courts to treat each guideline as carving out a "heartland," a set of typical cases embodying the conduct that each guideline describes. When a court finds an atypical case, one to which a particular guideline linguistically applies but where conduct significantly differs from the norm, the court may consider whether a departure is warranted. Section 5H1.10 (Race, Sex, National Origin, Creed, Religion, and Socio-Economic Status), § 5H1.12 (Lack of Guidance as a Youth and Similar Circumstances), the third sentence of § 5H1.4 (Physical Condition, Including Drug or Alcohol Dependence or Abuse), the last sentence of § 5K2.12 (Coercion and Duress), and § 5K2.19 (Post-Sentencing Rehabilitative Efforts) list several factors that the court cannot take into account as grounds for departure. With those specific exceptions, however, the Commission does not intend to limit the kinds of factors, whether or not mentioned anywhere else in the guidelines, that could constitute grounds for departure in an unusual case. * * *

(c) Plea Agreements

Nearly ninety percent of all federal criminal cases involve guilty pleas and many of these cases involve some form of plea agreement. Some commentators on early Commission guideline drafts urged the Commission not to attempt any major reforms of the plea agreement process on the grounds that any set of guidelines that threatened to change pre-guidelines practice radically also threatened to make the federal system unmanageable. Others argued that guidelines that failed to control and limit plea agreements would leave untouched a "loophole" large enough to undo the good that sentencing guidelines would bring.

The Commission decided not to make major changes in plea agreement practices in the initial guidelines, but rather to provide guidance by issuing general policy statements concerning the acceptance of plea agreements in Chapter Six, Part B (Plea Agreements). * * *

(d) Probation & Split Sentences

The statute provides that the guidelines are to "reflect the general appropriateness of imposing a sentence other than imprisonment in cases in which the defendant is a first offender who has not been convicted of a crime of violence or an otherwise serious offense. * * * " 28 U.S.C. § 994(j). Under pre-guidelines sentencing practice, courts sentenced to probation an inappropriately high percentage of offenders guilty of certain economic crimes, such as theft, tax evasion, antitrust offenses, insider trading, fraud, and embezzlement, that in the Commission's view are "serious."

The Commission's solution to this problem has been to write guidelines that classify as serious many offenses for which probation previously was frequently given and provide for at least a short period of imprisonment in such cases. The Commission concluded that the definite prospect of prison, even though the term may be short, will serve as a significant deterrent, particularly when compared with pre-guidelines practice where probation, not prison, was the norm. * * *

NOTES & QUESTIONS

1. **Uniformity.** According to the Commission, one of the core objectives of the new guidelines systems was to achieve "reasonable uniformity in sentencing by narrowing the wide disparity in sentences imposed for similar criminal offenses committed by similar offenders." Because it is not entirely clear what makes offenses and offenders "similar," direct measurement of disparity has proven difficult. Nonetheless, a substantial body of research performed on the pre-*Booker* federal system tended to confirm that the presumptive federal guidelines reduced *judge*-created sentencing disparities.

For instance, in connection with the fifteenth anniversary of the guidelines' implementation, the Commission issued a comprehensive assessment of the guidelines' impact along various dimensions. The Commission summarized its finding regarding disparity as follows:

> The effect of the guidelines on unwarranted disparity is best evaluated by comparing, among judges who receive similar types of cases, the amount of variation in sentences before and after guidelines implementation. Researchers both inside and outside the Commission have made this comparison using the "natural experiment" created by the random assignment of cases to judges in many courthouses. The most recent and best of these studies found significant reductions in the unwarranted influence of judges on sentencing under the guidelines compared to the preguidelines era.
>
> Studies of disparity divide judges' influence into "primary judge effects" (greater severity or leniency among judges in all types of cases, represented by differences in their average sentence) and "interaction effects" (greater severity or leniency in particular types of cases). Two judges with similar average sentences may greatly differ in their treatment of particular offenses. Interaction effects can reduce or even cancel the primary judge effect, with one judge sentencing drug offenses more severely than "white collar" offenses and another doing the opposite.
>
> In the Commission's study, the influence[s] of several different factors were compared, including the primary judge effect, interaction effects, city effects, as well as the general type of offense involved and whether an offender had any prior criminal conviction. General offense type accounted for the most variation in sentences both before and after guidelines implementation (between 15% & 20%) followed by interaction effects, city effects, and judge effects. The primary judge effect was relatively small in both the preguidelines and guidelines era, but was reduced by between a third and half under the guidelines (e.g., from 2.32% to 1.24% among judges who sentenced in both time periods). Interaction effects were about three to five times larger than primary judge effects. Interaction effects were reduced for most judges under the guidelines, although not among judges who sentenced in both time periods. The influence of judges was reduced by the guidelines for drug, fraud, firearm, and larceny offenses, though immigration or robbery offenses did not show a reduction. Notably, regional differences in drug trafficking cases were increased from the preguidelines to the guidelines era.

U.S. SENT'G COMM'N, FIFTEEN YEARS OF GUIDELINES SENTENCING x–xi (2004). Do these data prove that the guidelines were a success?

2. **Proportionality & Complexity.** Another core objective of the Commission was to achieve proportionality in punishment. In the Commission's view, guidelines that sought to ensure maximum

proportionality would have to establish a particular weight to be assigned to each aggravating factor that can arise in each context in which a particular crime may be committed. However, the Commission concluded that this would make for unworkable, overly complicated guidelines. The Commission thus described its approach as a compromise of sorts—striking a balance between the competing objectives of proportionality and administrability. Nonetheless, the federal guidelines proved to be far more complex than any state guidelines. Recall, for instance, how many more facts must be found to calculate a guidelines range for robbery in the federal than in the Minnesota system.

3. **Empirical Approach.** The original Commission included proponents of both the "just deserts" approach to punishment (law professor Paul Robinson) and the utilitarian approach to punishment (economics professor Michael Block). Michael O'Hear, *The Original Intent of Uniformity in Federal Sentencing*, 74 U. CIN. L. REV. 749, 778 (2006). The Commission was unable to settle on either approach. In order to break the impasse, the Commission utilized what it referred to as the "empirical" approach. What are you able to gather about the Commission's methodology? Does this seem a satisfactory way to resolve the "philosophical dilemma"?

To use the terminology suggested earlier in this chapter, the federal guidelines may have a "descriptive" foundation, but they are not purely descriptive. Based on the excerpt from the *Guidelines Manual*, do you also see some indications of prescriptiveness?

4. **Severity.** Where the Commission was prescriptive, its efforts to change established practices were generally in the direction of greater severity. *Id.* at 783. To some extent, these changes had been required, or at least encouraged, by the Sentencing Reform Act, particularly with respect to violent offenses, drug offenses, and repeat-offenders. *Id.* at 775–76. The Commission further chose to increase sentences for white-collar offenses. *Id.* at 783. Subsequent changes to the guidelines also tended to increase severity, often as a result of congressional mandate or pressure. *See, e.g.*, Frank O. Bowman III, Pour Encourager les Autres? *The Curious History and Distressing Implications of the Criminal Provisions of the Sarbanes-Oxley Act and the Sentencing Guidelines Amendments That Followed*, 1 OHIO ST. J. CRIM. L. 373 (2004). The Commission also felt obliged to accommodate the mandatory minimums that Congress adopted with some frequency in the late twentieth century.

Cumulatively, these severity-enhancing measures seem to have contributed to a notable increase in the frequency and length of prison sentences in the federal system. Over the first handful of years after the guidelines' implementation, the proportion of sentenced federal defendants who received straight probation dropped from 29% to just 14%. U.S. SENT'G COMM'N, FIFTEEN YEARS OF GUIDELINES SENTENCING, *supra*, at 43. Similarly, the average length of prison terms more than doubled from 26 to 59 months. *Id.* at 46.

The well-known story of the increase in severity in the federal system following the implementation of guidelines has caused guidelines to be perceived in some quarters as having an inherent tendency toward harshness. However, the assumption does not seem borne out by state-level experiences. For instance, between 1980 and 2000, the overall national prison population quadrupled. As rapid as that growth was, the federal prison population grew even more quickly, increasing by a multiple of six. By contrast, the Minnesota prison population "merely" tripled—a sharp increase, to be sure, but still representing a slower rate of growth than the national norm. As noted in the previous section, Minnesota's guidelines were designed to restrain growth in imprisonment. No such objective was apparent in the design of the federal guidelines.

It may be that certain distinctive features of federal lawmaking and the federal criminal justice system tend to push federal guidelines in the direction of greater severity. For instance, federal lawmakers, in contrast to the lawmakers in many states, are under no legal obligation to maintain a balanced budget. This may leave federal lawmakers less sensitive than their state counterparts to the costs associated with a fast-rising prison population—and hence more likely to accommodate public demands for tougher sentencing laws.

5. **Real-Offense Sentencing.** The Commission indicated that it initially tried to develop a pure "real-offense" guidelines system. What does that mean? In light of the complexity of the proposed pure system, the Commission chose to compromise and move a bit in the direction of a "charge-offense" system. Nonetheless, as adopted, the federal guidelines are still exceptionally "real." Consider, for instance, all of the distinctions the guidelines make in robbery cases, which may result in starkly different sentences among individuals who have all been formally convicted of precisely the same offense. What seem to you the advantages and disadvantages of the real-offense approach in comparison with the charge-offense approach?

6. **Heartland.** The Commission indicated that the guidelines were intended to apply to the "heartland" of typical cases. If courts encountered a case outside the heartland, they were authorized to depart (assuming that what made the case atypical was not a prohibited factor, such as the defendant's race or religion). But how exactly was a district judge to know whether a case was outside the heartland? Summer Blake wore a pink wig when she committed her robbery. That is surely highly unusual. Would that suffice to take the case outside the heartland for departure purposes? Although pink wigs are atypical, it is somewhat less unusual for people to wear a disguise when they commit a robbery. If it could be demonstrated that only 30% of robbers wear a disguise, would that be enough to take the case outside the heartland? 20%? 10%? Would it matter if disguises were common in the district where the crime was committed, but much less common nationally?

7. **The Plea-Bargaining "Loophole."** The guidelines do not directly regulate plea-bargaining in the federal system. As the Commission observed, critics charged that unregulated plea bargaining would create a " 'loophole' large enough to undo the good that sentencing guidelines would bring." Do you see how?

Concerns have persisted about the impact of plea bargaining and prosecutorial discretion on the guidelines' ability to minimize unwarranted sentencing disparities. The Commission itself voiced some of these concerns in the *Fifteen-Year Report*:

> The [Sentencing Reform Act] focused primarily on sentencing, but Congress, the Commission, and other observers recognized that sentencing could not be considered in isolation. Decisions regarding what charges to bring, decline, or dismiss, or what plea agreements to reach can all affect the fairness and uniformity of sentencing. Congress directed the Commission to develop mechanisms to monitor and, if necessary, control some of the negative effects of plea bargaining, particularly through policy statements establishing standards for judicial review and rejection of plea agreements that undermine the guidelines. In addition, the Commission developed the real offense system of relevant conduct and multiple count rules to reduce the effects of charging variations on the sentencing of offenders who engage in similar conduct. . . .
>
> [A] variety of evidence developed throughout the guidelines era suggest that the mechanisms and procedures designed to control disparity arising at presentencing stages are not all working as intended and have not been adequate to fully achieve uniformity of sentencing.
>
> The Commission, as well as outside observers, have reported that plea bargaining is reintroducing disparity into the system. The Commission in 1989, 1995, and again in 2000 compared descriptions of the offense conduct contained in samples of presentence reports with the conduct for which the offenders were charged and sentenced. Each time a large proportion of qualifying offenders (in some cases large majorities) were not charged with potentially applicable penalty statutes. While some offenders are charged in a manner that results in sentences above the guideline range that would otherwise apply to the case, in other cases the charges selected cap the statutory range below the guideline range that would properly apply to the offender's real offense conduct. Charging decisions that limit the normal operation of the guidelines result in sentences that are disproportionate to the seriousness of the offense and disparate among offenders who engage in similar conduct.
>
> Surveys of judges and probation officers have suggested other forms of plea bargaining, such as fact bargaining, that can result in disparity. A majority of chief probation officers reported in a survey sponsored by the Commission's Probation Officer's Advisory Group that the facts included in plea agreements were complete and accurate in the majority of cases. However, 43 percent reported this was true just half the time or less. Probation officers in some districts reported that prosecutors tried to limit information used in applying the guidelines in some cases. The Federal Judicial Center found in a nationwide survey that more than a quarter of

> responding judges reported that plea stipulations understated the offense conduct somewhat or very frequently, while another 12 percent said they did so about half the time. Judges reported that they did sometimes "go behind" the plea agreements to examine underlying conduct, but they reported doing so "infrequently."
>
> Field studies in several districts have demonstrated other ways that plea bargaining can result in sentencing disparity. An early study sponsored by the Commission estimated that plea agreements circumvented the guidelines in 20 to 35 percent of cases through charge, fact, or date bargaining. Some commentators have called circumvention of the guidelines through plea agreements a form of "hidden departure," in which prosecutors and courts create incentives for guilty pleas and defendant cooperation beyond the incentives contained in the guidelines themselves. In some cases, the sentence recommended in plea agreement appears to the parties and to the court more fair and effective at achieving the purposes of sentencing than the sentence required by strict pursuit of every potentially applicable charge or sentence enhancement.

U.S. SENT'G COMM'N, FIFTEEN YEARS OF GUIDELINES SENTENCING, *supra*, at xi–xiii. Without tighter regulation of prosecutors, is there any point in having sentencing guidelines?

3. MANDATORY MINIMUMS

In addition to degree of indeterminacy and the use of guidelines, state sentencing systems may also be distinguished based on the prevalence and severity of mandatory minimum prison terms. Mandatory minimums are legislatively enacted, often as an ad hoc political response to a high-profile crime or a public perception of worsening crime rates. In some jurisdictions, the mandatory minimums may be few in number and narrowly targeted, in which case their overall impact on plea-bargaining, sentencing, and corrections may be modest. In other jurisdictions, mandatory minimums are more expansive and often play an important role in the disposition of criminal cases. A prosecutor's power to charge or dismiss mandatory-minimum counts may greatly amplify the prosecutor's leverage in plea bargaining. Moreover, in a given jurisdiction, mandatory minimums may significantly limit the power of the sentencing commission to set sentencing policy, of the judge to utilize departure mechanisms or otherwise exercise discretion in determining punishment, and of the parole board to set release dates. To consider a jurisdiction's sentencing system without regard to the practical impact of its mandatory minimums may create a misleading sense of the true balance of power between the jurisdiction's key sentencing actors.

The federal system illustrates a jurisdiction in which mandatory minimums play a particularly important role. One study found that nearly 22% of sentenced federal defendants in 2016 had been convicted under a statute carrying a mandatory minimum, with the figure reaching as high as 32% in some earlier years. U.S. SENT'G COMM'N, OVERVIEW OF MANDATORY MINIMUM PENALTIES IN THE FEDERAL CRIMINAL JUSTICE SYSTEM 29 (2017). In the federal system, there are some limited circumstances in which a judge might be able to sentence below a mandatory minimum, which we will explore in more detail in Chapter 4. As a result, about 39% of the defendants who were subject to a minimum in 2016 actually received a lower sentence. *Id.* at 30.

Mandatory minimums exert an especially strong influence over federal drug sentences. Indeed, more than two-thirds of the federal defendants who were subject to a minimum in 2016 had been convicted of drug crimes. *Id.* at 34. Such figures reflect the enduring importance of the Anti-Drug Abuse Act of 1986, which included five- and ten-year mandatory minimums that were designed to cover a large share of drug-trafficking cases. In 2020, about two-thirds of sentenced federal drug defendants were subject to a mandatory minimum, including the more than 40% who were subject to a mandatory minimum of a decade or more. U.S. SENT'G COMM'N, 2020 SOURCEBOOK OF FEDERAL SENTENCING STATISTICS tbl. D-11. However, over half of the defendants who were convicted under a minimum statute received some form of relief that permitted a sentence below the minimum. *Id.* fig. D-2. We will further discuss the federal drug minimums in Chapter 4.

We have already noted what has probably been the nation's most well-known mandatory minimum of the past generation—the California "three strikes and you are out" law. Adopted in 1994, the law mandates a life sentence for individuals who have two prior "serious felony" convictions and who are then convicted of a new felony, even if the new felony is not "serious." A three-strikes life term is parole-eligible, but not until after twenty to twenty-five years (depending on good behavior in prison). Because simple theft could in some circumstances be treated as a felony in California, there were several much-publicized examples of defendants receiving mandatory life sentences for seemingly trivial offenses, such as stealing a slice of pizza or shoplifting a few videotapes. MICHAEL O'HEAR, THE FAILED PROMISE OF SENTENCING REFORM 5 (2017). Importantly, the same law also has a "two-strikes" provision that doubles the otherwise-applicable sentence upon conviction of a *second* serious felony. Over the first decade after the law's adoption, more than 87,000 individuals were sentenced as either two- or three-strikers. *Id.* at 176. Accounting for more than one-quarter of the state's entire prison population by 2004, these sentences helped to fuel an overcrowding crisis of staggering dimensions.

The California three-strikes law is often held up as an example of what is wrong with mandatory minimums. This rigid, draconian law can result in sentences that seem impossible to defend from a "just deserts" perspective. Moreover, while there is some evidence that the law may have had some modest crime-reduction benefits, it is highly questionable whether these benefits outweigh the law's heavy social costs. *See* COMM. ON CAUSES & CONSEQUENCES OF HIGH RATES OF INCARCERATION, NAT'L RESEARCH COUNCIL OF THE NAT'L ACADS., THE GROWTH OF INCARCERATION IN THE UNITED STATES: EXPLORING CAUSES AND CONSEQUENCES 138 (Jeremy Travis, Bruce Western & Steve Redburn eds., 2014). Indeed, the concerns about three-strikes proved sufficiently great that California voters softened some of its provisions through ballot initiatives adopted in 2012 and 2014. O'HEAR, *supra*, at 186–88.

Although mandatory minimums have been the subject of much critical commentary, *see, e.g.*, Erik Luna, *Mandatory Minimums, in* 4 REFORMING CRIMINAL JUSTICE 117 (2017), it should be appreciated that very few, if any, other mandatory minimum statutes are quite so extreme in their impact as the California three-strikes law. Indeed, even other three-strikes laws tend to be much more narrowly targeted. Although the California law was one of two dozen three-strikes laws adopted during a national wave of tough-on-crime legislating in the early and mid-1990s, a 1998 study found that the great majority of the three-strikes laws in other states had been applied only quite infrequently—in several states, barely a handful of times. California's was far and away the most heavily utilized. WALTER DICKEY & PAM STIEBS HOLLENHORST, THREE STRIKES LAWS: FIVE YEARS LATER (1998).

C. WHICH SYSTEM IS BEST?

Focusing on two major system-design questions—should the system utilize discretionary parole? should the system utilize sentencing guidelines?—we have suggested that policymakers face a choice among four types of sentencing system: determinate/guidelines, determinate/no guidelines, indeterminate/guidelines, and indeterminate/no guidelines (a.k.a. "traditional"). Much ink has been spilled on the advantages and disadvantages of both parole and guidelines. The debate often centers on two questions: how much discretionary power should be entrusted to which actors in the criminal justice system, and what is the impact of system design on incarceration rates? Additionally, the debate over guidelines also raises the question of whether the guidelines currently in use have succeeded in reducing unwarranted sentencing disparities. We consider each question in turn.

1. DISCRETION & ITS DISCONTENTS

There is a long tradition of discomfort with criminal justice discretion in western political thought. To give one citizen discretionary power over the life, liberty, or property of another may seem hard to square with core Enlightenment political ideals, including the rule of law and equal rights before the law. That the citizen with power acts in the name of the polity, perhaps subject to some form of democratic accountability, may or may not provide much reassurance.

The influential eighteenth-century Italian theorist Cesare Beccarria, whom we encountered in Chapter 1, wrote forcefully against discretion. He advocated for a system of simple, clear criminal laws that would leave nothing for the courts to do beyond the finding of facts. If judges were given any broader role, then arbitrariness would necessarily result. In language foreshadowing Judge Marvin Frankel's critique of judicial sentencing discretion two centuries later, Beccaria observed that application of the law in a system that permits judicial "interpretation"

> will then be the result of the good or bad logic of the judge; and this will depend on his good or bad digestion; on the violence of his passions; on the rank and condition of the abused, or on his connections with the judge; and on all those circumstances which change the appearance of objects in the fluctuating mind of man. . . . We see the same crimes punished in a different manner at different times in the same tribunals; the consequence of not having consulted the constant and invariable voice of the laws, but the erring instability of arbitrary interpretation.

CESARE BECCARIA, ON CRIMES AND PUNISHMENTS AND OTHER WRITINGS ch. 4 (Aaron Thomas ed., Aaron Thomas & Jeremy Parzen trans., 2008) (1764).

Beccaria linked his call for discretion-free criminal justice to a system of deliberately mild, proportionality-based punishments. *See id.* ch. 27. However, if the criminal code shows less restraint than Beccaria demanded, it is not so clear that the elimination of discretion is either feasible or desirable. When punishments are seen as excessive, those who work in the criminal justice system will find ways to blunt the system's severity, whether or not they are formally endowed with discretion to do so. Earlier in this chapter, for instance, we noted the tendency of American juries in Beccaria's own day to soften harsh, nominally mandatory penal laws by acquitting defendants of capital offenses notwithstanding the evidence. Beccaria himself called for lenient punishments, in part, because he recognized the difficulties of securing consistent enforcement of harsh laws. *Id.* at 51.

Nor is it clear how a discretion-free system could function in a jurisdiction with an expansive criminal code that covers a vast range of human conduct—at least in the absence of a highly oppressive (and expensive) police-state apparatus. Full enforcement of contemporary American codes is simply unimaginable. In light of resource constraints and political realities, police and prosecutors must do a great deal of picking and choosing in developing and implementing their enforcement priorities. In Chapter 1, for instance, we noted that resource constraints are often cited as a leading explanation for plea bargaining, in which defendants are often offered more lenient outcomes than would occur after a trial.

Taking the expansiveness and severity of contemporary American criminal law as a given—as well as limitations on the number of police officers, prosecutors, courtrooms, and jail cells—then *some* criminal justice discretion seems inevitable. However, that observation leaves open the important questions of *how much* discretion should be exercised, and *by whom*.

In thinking about sentencing system design, it may be helpful to imagine that there is a fixed quantity of discretion in the system that must be allocated among three actors: prosecutor, judge, and parole board. Different design choices result in different allocations of power. When a jurisdiction abolishes or severely restricts discretionary parole release, then discretion is effectively shifted from the parole board to the "upstream" actor, the sentencing judge. Similarly, when a jurisdiction adopts presumptive sentencing guidelines or mandatory minimums, discretion seems to be shifted further upstream from the judge to the prosecutor, who can control the application of guidelines or minimums through charging and plea-bargaining decisions.[18]

Are there good reasons to favor putting discretion in the hands of one actor at the expense of another? Discussion of this issue often focuses on the two questions of *competence* and *legitimacy*.

Consider the parole board first. The parole board has at least one particular competence-related advantage over the prosecutor and judge. The board is able to assess whether it would be sufficiently safe to release a prisoner in real time, making use of the prisoner's record of good (or bad) behavior and rehabilitative progress while in the institution, as well as the latest evaluations of the prisoner's mental and physical health. By contrast, at the time of sentencing a judge or prosecutor would have little reliable basis for deciding whether a defendant could be safely released, say, after five years or should be given six years instead. On the other hand, if retributive approaches to punishment are emphasized over utilitarian, it is not clear that the parole board has any particular competence advantages over the other actors.[19] And, even if rehabilitation and incapacitation are accepted as important objectives, the theoretical advantages of parole boards are sometimes undermined in practice by the traditional shortcomings noted earlier in this chapter—lack of appropriate expertise on the board, insufficient resources, risk aversion, and so forth.

---

[18] Surveys of judges indicate that many *perceive* a shift of power to prosecutors under presumptive guidelines, but there has been little effort by researchers to objectively confirm or quantify this perceived transfer. Oren Gazal-Ayal, Hagit Turjeman & Gideon Fishman, *Do Sentencing Guidelines Increase Prosecutorial Power? An Empirical Study*, 76 L. & CONTEMP. PROBS 131, 137 (2013).

[19] Notably, researchers find that, in practice, parole boards tend to give at least as much weight to offense seriousness as they do to rehabilitative progress. Amelia Courtney Hritz, *Parole Board Decision Making and Constitutional Rights*, 17 ANN. REV. L. & SOC. SCI. 335, 336, 345 (2021).

How do the decisions of criminal justice actors acquire legitimacy? Two important possibilities to consider are (1) the decisionmaker's democratic accountability, and (2) the decisionmaker's use of a fair, transparent process in arriving at the decision—what is sometimes called "procedural justice." Parole boards do not fare especially well by these standards. Parole board members are not elected, even if their appointment by an elected governor may give their decisions some measure of second-hand legitimacy. It should not be surprising that some proponents of "truth in sentencing" have characterized parole board members as unaccountable, out-of-touch bureaucrats. *See, e.g.*, MICHAEL O'HEAR, WISCONSIN SENTENCING IN THE TOUGH-ON-CRIME ERA ch. 5 (2017). Parole boards, moreover, do not have an especially strong reputation for due process. Edward Rhine, Joan Petersilia & Kevin Reitz, *The Future of Parole Release*, 46 CRIME & JUST. 279 (2017).

Consider next the judge. Experienced judges who have a large set of prior cases to draw upon for comparison purposes may seem reasonably competent to assess a defendant's just deserts. There may be greater concerns that the judge's legal training and experience are not as well-suited to implementing the utilitarian purposes of punishment. To be sure, the judge will quickly gain some sense of recidivism risk by observing all of the "repeat customers" in his or her courtroom. However, the judge's knowledge base may be skewed in various ways. For instance, the defendants who succeed on probation and never return to court may quickly recede from memory, while those who fail will be constantly in view, perhaps creating an exaggerated sense of the frequency of failure. Likewise, the judge would have little way of knowing if he or she has unnecessarily incapacitated a defendant who would have been safe to release—while the opposite sort of mistake (that is, failing to incapacitate someone who then commits a major new offense) will be all too painfully apparent. On the other hand, the increasing use of risk-assessment instruments (RAIs) at sentencing may somewhat alleviate these concerns.

Judges may seem especially appealing from a legitimacy standpoint. In thirty-nine states, trial judges must stand for reelection, Gregory A. Huber & Sanford C. Gordon, *Accountability and Coercion: Is Justice Blind When It Runs for Office?*, 48 AM. J. POL. SCI. 247, 247 (2004), which establishes the sort of direct democratic accountability that parole boards lack. (Importantly, though, there may be subtle costs to democratic accountability; in Chapter 1, we noted evidence that judges tend to ratchet up the severity of their sentences as election day approaches.) Judges' use of standard, adversarial courtroom processes may also be appealing from a procedural-justice standpoint. To be sure, as we will see in Chapter 3, sentencing processes tend to be rather less formal and offer fewer constitutional protections for defendants than trials on guilt or innocence. Nonetheless, due-process rights remain at least somewhat more robust in sentencing than in parole hearings.

What about prosecutors? Perhaps the greatest contrast between judges and prosecutors as discretionary actors lies in the extremely informal, "behind-closed-doors" character of most prosecutorial charging and plea-bargaining decisions. Michael O'Hear, *Plea Bargaining and Procedural Justice*, 42 GA. L. REV. 407 (2008). The minimal due-process protections for defendants in relation to these critical prosecutorial decisions may diminish their legitimacy. Prosecutors may also tend to be somewhat younger and less experienced than judges, which may bear upon their relative competence, although an effective system of training and supervision for junior lawyers in the prosecutor's office may alleviate these concerns. Further to competence, the judge may have considerably more information available about the case and the defendant at the time of sentencing than is available to the prosecutor at the earlier charging and plea-bargaining stages of the criminal process. (We will explore the presentencing investigation in more detail in Chapter 3.) Finally, it is sometimes suggested that prosecutors, due to their often close working relationship with police officers and crime victims or perhaps the inherent nature of their role in the adversarial criminal process, are more prone than judges to unwarranted antidefendant biases.

Which actor or actors do you think should play the predominant role in determining punishment? Does your answer depend on knowing more about the actors, e.g., whether the judges are elected or not, or whether the parole board makes its decisions based on published guidelines? Regardless of the relative merits of different actors, do you think it is important for there to be robust "checks and balances" in the determination of punishment? What are the implications of your answers to these questions for the broad structural questions on which we focus: whether there should be discretionary parole release, and whether there should be sentencing guidelines?

2. SYSTEM DESIGN & SENTENCE SEVERITY

Determinate sentencing and sentencing guidelines became prominent features on the American criminal justice landscape in the late twentieth century at about the same time that the national imprisonment rate swelled to record highs. As a result, both types of reforms came to be seen by some critics of mass incarceration as tough-on-crime measures that had an inherent tendency to put more defendants into prison and keep them there for longer periods of time. Opponents of these reforms argued that, by reducing discretion in the system and/or shifting discretion "upstream" to the prosecutor, determinacy and guidelines left insufficient room for the consideration of mitigating aspects of the defendant's background and character. An "unbalanced" emphasis on the offense in comparison to the offender, it was charged, would naturally tend to increase severity.

Whatever the theoretical plausibility of the charge, the available evidence provides, at most, weak and inconsistent support for the expectation that curtailing the discretion of judges and parole boards will result in greater imprisonment. Indeed, the evidence suggests that, if anything, the adoption of determinate sentencing and guidelines together may be more likely to *restrain* than enhance imprisonment growth—although the variability of experiences across jurisdictions indicates that change in either direction is possible. We have already noted the stark contrast between Minnesota and the federal system; although both jurisdictions abolished discretionary parole and then implemented presumptive guidelines in the 1980s, Minnesota's prison population grew more slowly than the national average between 1980 and 2000, while the federal prison population grew more swiftly.

In comparison with other "reform" jurisdictions, which experience—Minnesota or federal—was more the outlier? When it comes to determinate sentencing, Kevin Reitz and Edward Rhine offer the following observations:

> [I]ndeterminate states were the main sites of the mass-incarceration buildup. During the high-crime decades from the early 1970s through the early 1990s, the rehabilitative intentions of parole release were superseded by punitive impulses, risk aversion, and incapacitation policy. Over this period, parole boards became stingier in their release rates, turning into parole-denial boards. At the end of 2009, nine out of ten states with the highest standing imprisonment rates were indeterminate jurisdictions. From 1980 to 2009, nine of the top ten prison-growth states were indeterminate jurisdictions.
>
> States that abolished parole-release discretion tended to be comparatively low-growth states during the prison buildup era.

Parole Release and Supervision: Crucial Drivers of American Prison Policy, 3 ANN. REV. CRIMINOLOGY 281, 285 (2020) (citations omitted).

States that combined determinate sentencing with guidelines (presumptive or advisory) did especially well in restraining imprisonment growth. Seven of the ten states in this category experienced below-average rates of growth during the buildup era. Richard S. Frase, *Forty Years of American Sentencing Guidelines: What Have We Learned?*, 48 CRIME & JUST. 79, 107 (2019). Other reform combinations were not so closely associated with penal restraint. Professor Richard Frase reports as follows:

- Out of six states in the determinate/no guidelines category, only one experienced below-average growth, and
- Out of eight states in the indeterminate/guidelines category, only three experienced below-average growth.

Id. at 107 n.34.

The relative success of determinate/guidelines states in restraining imprisonment growth belies any strong claims that discretion-reducing reforms must necessarily lead to greater severity. Nonetheless, simple comparisons of imprisonment trends in states with and without a given reform should be taken with a grain of salt. The correlation of a reform and low imprisonment growth does not imply causation. For instance, non-reform states might, as a matter of simple coincidence, have had faster-growing *crime* rates than reform states, which might in turn have driven increases in imprisonment; if crime trends were accounted for, the reform states might actually turn out to be harsher than their non-reform counterparts.

In order to evaluate reforms more rigorously, a number of researchers have attempted multistate comparisons that control for crime rate and other potentially confounding variables. Results have been mixed, with some studies finding no statistically significant relationship between imprisonment rates and the reform or reforms being assessed, others finding a positive relationship, and still others finding a negative relationship. Mark G. Harmon, *Opening the Door for More: Assessing the Impact of Sentencing Reforms on Commitments to Prison Over Time*, 41 AM. J. CRIM. JUST. 296, 300–02 (2016) (summarizing prior studies). *See, e.g.*, Michael C. Campbell, Matt Vogel & Joshua Williams, *Historical Contingencies and the Evolving Importance of Race, Violent Crime, and Region in Explaining Mass Incarceration in the United States*, 53 CRIMINOLOGY 180 (2015) (finding no statistically significant relationship between a state's imprisonment rate and whether the state has determinate sentencing); William Spelman, *Crime, Cash, and Limited Options: Explaining the Prison Boom*, 8 CRIMINOLOGY & PUB. POL'Y 29 (2009) (finding positive relationship between truth-in-sentencing laws and prison populations, negative relationship between presumptive guidelines and prison populations, and no statistically significant relationship between three-strikes laws and prison populations).

By way of illustration, Professor Mark Harmon's study evaluated the impact of six different sentencing reforms on annual prison admissions, using data from all fifty states over the time period from 1972 to 2008. Harmon, *supra*. After controlling for arrest rates (violent and drug crime), poverty and unemployment rates, racial demographics, and political leanings, Harmon found no standalone impact from advisory guidelines, presumptive guidelines, or determinate sentencing, but did find a relationship between "truth-in-sentencing" laws, which restrict parole eligibility without necessarily eliminating it altogether, and increased commitments to prison. *Id.* at 309. On the other hand, when presumptive guidelines were combined with determinate sentencing, the two reforms together were associated with relatively *lower* prison admissions—consistent with Professor Frase's observations. However, even when considered in combination with other reforms, *advisory* guidelines had no discernible relationship with prison admissions.

Harmon's study complements other controlled analyses that similarly suggest a restraining effect from the combination of presumptive guidelines and determinate sentencing. *See* Reitz & Rhine, *supra*, at 285 (citing studies). Beyond that, however, it is difficult to discern other clear patterns in the empirical research, which has produced a mishmash of inconsistent or odd findings. Harmon's study, for instance, points to a restraining effect from determinate sentencing when combined with presumptive guidelines, but an imprisonment-*enhancing* effect from truth in sentencing—even though determinate sentencing and truth in sentencing are overlapping reforms that both target parole-board discretion.[20]

In order to understand the impact of a reform on imprisonment, it may be more important to know the underlying *purpose* of the reform than the general type of reform. Robert C. Kenter et al., *Reconsidering State Variation in Incarceration Rates*, 48 POLITICS & POL'Y 1029 (2020). For instance, as we have seen, Minnesota and the federal system both adopted presumptive guidelines, but with rather different outcomes. The relatively lenient Minnesota guidelines reflect the underlying purpose of bringing greater fairness to sentencing without exceeding prison capacity constraints, while the more severe federal guidelines reflect the underlying purpose of ensuring harsher punishment for various large categories of federal offenders. The underlying purpose of a reform may influence the way that policymakers fill in the details of the reform, which may in turn determine its real-world impact. Even beyond that, purpose may influence the way that residual discretion is exercised in the system. For instance, if the legislature adopts an important new law that is seen as "tough on crime," elected judges and prosecutors may take that as an indication that the political mood favors more punitive responses to crime across the board. Conversely, the adoption of a law that is intended to restrain costly imprisonment growth may be seen as a signal that softer approaches have become more politically acceptable.

In sum, the evidence suggests that broad system-design choices (determinate versus indeterminate, guidelines versus no guidelines) may have some effect on the system's overall severity, but the direction and strength of the effect likely depend on a complex array of factors that are not yet well-understood. If restraint is desired, the particular combination of determinacy and presumptive guidelines seems a promising one, but even that is hardly foolproof (see the pre-*Booker* federal system).

---

[20] Why might the elimination of parole tend to slow growth in prison populations? Professor Frase suggests that

> the availability of parole encourages judges to impose unreasonably severe prison terms in reliance on the unreliable and often illusory possibility of parole release. The variable nature of parole release policy also makes it much more difficult for legislators to predict and take political responsibility for the prison bed and fiscal impacts of severe sentencing laws.

Frase, *supra*, at 109.

3. GUIDELINES & DISPARITY

While the overall amount of punishment delivered may be an important consideration in evaluating a jurisdiction's sentencing system, fairness in the distribution of that punishment among defendants also certainly matters. As indicated in the introduction of the federal *Guidelines Manual* (reprinted above), one of the chief objectives of the federal guidelines system was "uniformity," that is, the avoidance of unwarranted disparities in the treatment of similarly situated defendants. Guidelines are not the only aspect of system design that might enhance uniformity. For instance, one argument that is sometimes made in favor of parole is that a statewide parole board may smooth out the disparities that inevitably result when sentencing is handled by an ideologically diverse, decentralized judiciary. For instance, the board may advance uniformity through relatively liberal treatment of inmates who had unusually harsh judges and relatively conservative treatment of inmates who had unusually lenient judges. Yet, while disparity concerns figure occasionally in the parole debate,[21] they arise more commonly as a justification for guidelines.

When Judge Frankel first proposed guidelines in the 1970s, their capacity to reduce disparities was a matter of theoretical conjecture. A half-century later, there is now a considerable body of empirical evidence to inform the debate. Research has focused particularly on two types of disparity: inter-judge disparities (that is, disparities that result from the identity of the judge) and racial disparities (that is, disparities that result from the race of the defendant).

The federal guidelines have been studied most extensively. As noted in the discussion of the federal guidelines earlier in this chapter, researchers found that some reduction in inter-judge sentencing disparities did occur following the implementation of the federal guidelines. Yet, as also noted above, evidence pointed to a corresponding increase in *prosecutor*-created disparities. The presumptive federal guidelines shifted discretion upstream to prosecutors, giving greater importance to "charging and plea-bargaining [decisions] that could not be controlled by Department of Justice policies and that went unchecked by judicial review." Paul J. Hofer, *Federal Sentencing After* Booker, 48 CRIME & JUST. 137, 161 (2019).

Efforts to quantify the impact of the federal guidelines on racial disparities have proven more difficult. (For a discussion of the technical problems, see *id.* at 164–65.) The implementation of the guidelines coincided with a sharp divergence in the average sentence lengths

[21] The opacity of the parole process in many jurisdictions makes systematic research regarding disparity and bias difficult. Amelia Courtney Hritz, *Parole Board Decision Making and Constitutional Rights*, 17 ANN. REV. L. & SOC. SCI. 335, 349 (2021). The relatively few studies that have been published over the past thirty years tend to find indications of unwarranted racial disparities and/or other forms of arbitrariness. *See id.* at 346–47 (summarizing studies).

imposed on Black and White defendants in federal court. U.S. SENT'G COMM'N, FIFTEEN YEARS OF GUIDELINES SENTENCING 116 (2004). Whereas average sentences had been about equal for the two groups in the mid-1980s, the average for Black defendants was almost twice as long as the average for White defendants by the mid-1990s. This was a highly ironic development, given that the guidelines had been adopted, in part, to address longstanding perceptions of unequal treatment for Black defendants. As always, though, a simple comparison of averages can be misleading without appropriate statistical controls.

Researchers have attempted to isolate race effects by controlling for offense type, criminal history, and other variables. Studies of the pre-*Booker* federal system sometimes found statistically significant race effects, and other times not. Hofer, *supra*, at 165. The Commission observed,

> Offense-to-offense and year-to-year fluctuations in racial and ethnic effects are difficult to reconcile with theories of enduring stereotypes, powerlessness, or overt discrimination affecting sentencing of minorities under the guidelines. . . .
>
> Perhaps the best conclusion is that if discrimination affects the decisions of even some judges in some cases, the number of cases affected is small and the size of the effect is relatively minor compared to the consistent importance of the seriousness of the offense and the criminal history of the offender.

U.S. SENT'G COMM'N, *supra*, at 125, 127.

On the other hand, even if the presumptive guidelines system seemed largely to neutralize the impact of whatever racial biases were held by sentencing judges, there remained considerable concern that the guidelines themselves contained baked-in tendencies to produce racial disparities—tendencies that might not be revealed in the multivariate regression studies that were designed to ferret out *judge*-created disparities. Such studies attempt to hold constant offense severity and criminal history, but what if current offense severity (largely controlled by prosecutors) and criminal history (largely a function of police and prosecutor decisions on earlier occasions) themselves embody racial biases? And, moreover, what if legislative decisions about maximum and minimum sentences for different offenses—decisions that establish the framework within which guidelines must operate—also have racialized effects? Thus, the Commission itself suggested that "[judicial] discrimination contributes less to the gap between majority and minority offenders than do certain of the sentencing rules themselves, some of which may arguably represent an institutionalized unfairness that is a greater cause for concern than is discrimination by individual judges." *Id.* at 127.

The most important "structural disparity" in the pre-*Booker* guidelines was the guidelines' much harsher treatment of crack cocaine than powder cocaine offenses, which was to some extent dictated by mandatory-minimum laws. The guidelines' crack-powder disparity had sizeable racial consequences because Black defendants accounted for a much larger share of crack than powder cases. For instance, the Commission observed, "In 2002, 81 percent of the offenders sentenced for trafficking the crack form of cocaine were African American. The average length of imprisonment for crack cocaine was 119 months, compared to 78 months for the powder form of the drug." *Id.* at 131. When the Commission proposed even just softening, not eliminating, the crack-powder disparity, the Commission calculated that the proposal would by itself close the overall gap in average Black-White sentence lengths in the federal system by more than nine months. *Id.* at 132. We will consider the crack-powder disparity in more detail in Chapter 4.

In sum, while there is reason to think that judge-created racial disparities under the presumptive federal guidelines were not large, there is also reason to suspect that any progress made on the judicial front was offset by structural (and perhaps also prosecutor-created) disparities.[22]

Much less research has been conducted on racial disparities in state guidelines systems. The research that has been done—chiefly in the form of single-state studies focusing on Minnesota, Ohio, or Pennsylvania—generally echoes the federal research in finding that judge-created racial disparities are small and/or reduced after the implementation of guidelines, especially presumptive guidelines, but also in questioning whether the guidelines themselves create structural disparities. Frase, *supra*, at 111–12.

One of the few extant multistate studies attempted a comparison of states with presumptive guidelines, advisory guidelines, and no guidelines. Xia Wang et al., *Assessing the Differential Effects of Race and Ethnicity Outcomes Under Different Sentencing Systems*, 59 CRIME & DELINQUENCY 87 (2013). After controlling for sex, age, criminal record, offense type, and other variables, the researchers found a statistically significant relationship between defendant race and whether a prison sentence was imposed in no-guidelines states, but not in either presumptive or advisory guidelines states. On the other hand, the researchers found evidence of *ethnicity* effects in advisory guidelines states, as well as no-guidelines states, but not in presumptive guidelines states. More specifically, Latinx defendants were at higher risk of receiving a prison sentence in advisory and no-guidelines states, but not in presumptive states. Additionally, when looking at *jail* sentences, in comparison to probation, Black and Latinx defendants were at higher

[22] This dynamic seems to have continued in the post-*Booker* era. *See, e.g.*, Jeffrey T. Ulmer, Noah Painter-Davis & Leigh Tinik, *Disproportional Imprisonment of Black and Hispanic Males: Sentencing Discretion, Processing Outcomes, and Policy Structures*, 33 JUST. Q. 641 (2016) (finding that analysis of data from 2005–2009 "strongly suggests that most of Federal imprisonment disproportionality is determined by processes prior to the sentencing decision"). We will explore the practical effects of *Booker* in more detail in Chapter 3.

risk of incarceration in advisory than in presumptive states. However, when it came to the *length* of jail and prison terms, the researchers found no evidence of either race or ethnicity effects in any of the three categories of states. The results are summarized in Table 2-2. Overall, the study suggests—but does not, of course, conclusively prove—that advisory guidelines may modestly reduce the impact of race on sentencing, and that presumptive guidelines may have a somewhat stronger effect in reducing both race and ethnicity disparities.

Table 2-2. Race and ethnicity effects on sentences. Source: Wang et al., *supra*.

	No Guidelines	Advisory Guidelines	Presumptive Guidelines
Race effects: prison sentence (in-out)	Yes	No	No
Race effects: jail sentence (in-out)	Yes	Yes	No
Race effects: length of prison sentence	No	No	No
Race effects: length of jail sentence	No	No	No
Ethnicity effects: prison sentence (in-out)	Yes	Yes	No
Ethnicity effects: jail sentence (in-out)	Yes	Yes	No
Ethnicity effects: length of prison sentence	No	No	No
Race effects: length of jail sentence	No	No	No

PROBLEM 2-1: WRITING ON A BLANK SLATE

If you could reconstruct from scratch the sentencing system of your state, what would the system look like? What do you see as the key pluses and minuses of each of the four basic categories we have considered (traditional, indeterminate/guidelines, determinate/no guidelines, determinate/guidelines)? In designing your preferred system, consider not only the choice among these four categories, but also the second-order questions that must be answered. For instance, if your preferred system includes guidelines, would your guidelines be advisory or presumptive, and why? What other important choices must be made in establishing the framework for a guidelines system? For a parole system?

CHAPTER 3

SENTENCING PROCESS

As lawyers may appreciate better than most, process matters. This is no less true of sentence-determinations than of any other decisions made in the legal system. The rules of procedure may have a large impact on the substantive quality of the decisions reached. For instance, rules of procedure may either facilitate or obstruct the flow of relevant information to the decisionmaker, with predictable consequences for the likelihood of erroneous fact-finding or otherwise misguided decisions. Moreover, even beyond their influence on the substantive quality of decisions, rules of procedure may also play an important role in determining whether those who are affected by a legal decision feel that they have been treated fairly. Indeed, research on "procedural justice" suggests that legal decisions are more likely to be accepted and regarded as legitimate by all sides if the process is seen as balanced and respectful. Michael M. O'Hear, *Plea Bargaining and Procedural Justice*, 42 GA. L. REV. 407 (2008).

In this chapter, we consider sentencing processes—how sentencing deciders (usually judges) obtain the information that they use to determine punishment; how lawyers and other stakeholders convey opinions and arguments to the decider; and how the burdens of proof are structured when factual disputes must be resolved. We first provide an overview of the sentencing process, focusing on subconstitutional rules of procedure and conventions of practice. Next, we consider the constitutional procedural rights of defendants in relation to sentencing. Finally, we conclude with sections exploring victims' rights at sentencing and the new procedural model that has been developed in the so-called "problem solving courts."

A. OVERVIEW OF THE SENTENCING PROCESS

The specifics of the sentencing process can vary a great deal from jurisdiction to jurisdiction, and even within jurisdictions, from courthouse to courthouse and judge to judge. In broad outline, however, the process consistently includes certain basic components that we outline below. For purposes of this overview, we focus particularly on noncapital felony sentencing. *Capital* sentencing involves distinct processes, which we will consider in Chapter 7. On the other end of the severity spectrum, *misdemeanor* sentencing is apt to be less formal than felony sentencing and is more likely to involve alternatives to conventional processes, such as referral to a restorative justice program or a problem solving court. We briefly consider some of the distinctive procedural aspects of misdemeanor sentencing at the end of this section.

1. PLEA BARGAINING

Plea bargaining is normally thought of as a distinct process from sentencing. However, in many cases, plea bargaining plays such an important role in shaping the sentence that the two processes really ought to be considered in tandem.

Guilty pleas are, of course, the most common way by far that a criminal case progresses to sentencing. In the federal system, for instance, nearly 98% of convictions result from a guilty plea, as opposed to a trial verdict. MARK MOTIVANS, U.S. DEPT. OF JUSTICE, FEDERAL JUSTICE STATISTICS, 2015–2016, at 9 (2019). The breakdown in state courts appears to be similar.[1] To be sure, not all of these guilty pleas involve an explicit quid pro quo agreement between prosecution and defense, but such deals are probably the norm in most U.S. jurisdictions.

Most plea deals involve a *charge* bargain, a *sentence* bargain, or both. In a charge bargain, in return for the defendant's guilty plea to one or more charges, a prosecutor will dismiss or refrain from filing one or more other charges. For instance, if a defendant has been charged with perpetrating a string of five burglaries in a neighborhood, the prosecutor might agree to dismiss two of the burglary charges in return for the defendant's guilty plea to the remaining three. Or, if the defendant has been charged with armed robbery, the prosecutor might agree to reduce the charge to simple robbery in return for the defendant's plea. Even though such charge bargains are often contrasted with sentence bargains, a reduction or dismissal of charges will normally have implications for the sentence, and it is often with an eye to sentencing that the defendant will agree to a proposed charge bargain. The sentencing exposure—i.e., the maximum sentence, or worst-case scenario—of the defendant who is convicted of three burglaries will normally be less than that of the defendant who is convicted of five, as with the defendant who is convicted of simple, rather than armed, robbery.

Note, though, that the anticipated sentencing benefits of a charge bargain to the defendant may sometimes prove illusory. For instance, because few defendants receive the maximum possible sentence, and since sentences on multiple counts are often imposed to run concurrently (i.e., at the same time), it is possible that our hypothetical serial burglar would get exactly the same prison term whether formally convicted of three offenses or five. Indeed, the sentencing judge might even take the two dismissed charges into account in determining the defendant's sentence, as long as the overall punishment remained within the maximum established by the three convictions. If the dismissal of a charge relieves the defendant of a mandatory *minimum*, rather than

---

[1] For instance, in one study of seventy-five large urban counties, researchers found that 98% of felony convictions came by way of a plea. BRIAN A. REAVES, U.S. DEP'T OF JUSTICE, FELONY DEFENDANTS IN LARGE URBAN COUNTIES, 2009—STATISTICAL TABLES 24 tbl.21 (2013).

simply reducing the *maximum* exposure, the plea deal may prove more directly consequential for the sentence.

Given that the bottom-line impact of a charge bargain on the sentence may be uncertain, some defendants might prefer to negotiate the sentence directly. And, for that matter, some prosecutors might also like to have greater control over the sentence, for instance, to ensure prison time for defendants who are thought to require incapacitation or to ensure sufficiently large plea discounts so that defendants will continue to enter into plea deals. In general, however, it is not possible for the defendant and prosecutor, acting on their own, to strike a deal that will absolutely guarantee a particular sentence. In the system of separation of powers that governs criminal litigation, determination of individual sentences is normally seen as a distinctly *judicial* function.

In some jurisdictions, the uncertainty can potentially be overcome by including the judge in the plea negotiations; this way, if the judge is willing to tip his or her hand, all sides may have a clearer sense of what will happen at sentencing under a proposed deal. However, direct judicial participation in actual plea bargaining is prohibited in about twenty states, as well as the federal system and the District of Columbia. Rachel Broder, *Fair and Effective Administration of Justice: Amending Rule 11(c)(1) to Allow for Judicial Participation in Plea Negotiations*, 88 TEMP. L. REV. 357, 370–71 (2016). Moreover, even to the extent that participation is allowed, judges may sometimes prefer to keep their options open until the time of the sentencing hearing.[2]

Even in the absence of judicial participation, prosecutors and defendants often attempt to negotiate regarding the sentence, either in addition to or in lieu of a charge bargain. A sentence bargain will typically involve a promise by the prosecutor to take a certain position at sentencing or to refrain from taking a position that the defendant would regard as unfavorable. In our burglary example, for instance, the prosecutor might agree to recommend three short jail terms, all to run concurrently. Of course, the judge would not be obligated to accede to the prosecutor's recommendation, but judges don't often impose sentences that are substantially more severe than what the prosecutor requests. (Why do you think this might be so?) Alternatively, the prosecutor might agree to "stand silent" at sentencing, that is, not to make any recommendation at all. The defendant might be satisfied with such a deal because his or her request for leniency would presumably carry more weight with the judge if the prosecutor were not actively advocating for something harsher.

---

[2] Professors Nancy King and Ronald Wright have documented a recent flowering of new forms of judicial involvement in plea negotiations. They argue that the "many benefits of judicial input [into plea deals]—a counterweight to intransigent prosecutors, a safeguard against overstretched defense counsel, and a source of more complete information for defendants during negotiations and for judges deciding sentences—can be compelling." Nancy J. King & Ronald F. Wright, *The Invisible Revolution in Plea Bargaining: Managerial Judging and Judicial Participation in Negotiations*, 95 TEX. L. REV. 325, 329 (2016).

What if the defendant or the prosecutor insisted on more certainty as to the sentence? In the federal system, Federal Rule of Criminal Procedure 11(c)(1)(C) does contemplate that a plea deal may establish the specific sentence to be imposed. However, the judge need not accept such a deal. Fed. R. Crim. P. 11(c)(3)(A). If the judge is uncomfortable with the agreed-upon sentence and rejects the deal, then the defendant must be given an opportunity to withdraw his or her guilty plea. Fed. R. Crim. P. 11(d)(2)(A).

Plea deals may be rejected on a number of other grounds. For instance, as a matter of constitutional law, the defendant's plea must be knowing and voluntary. Court rules may also require the showing of a factual basis for the plea and give the court discretion to reject conditional guilty pleas or no-contest (*nolo contendere*) pleas. *See, e.g.*, Fed. R. Crim. P. 11(a)(2)–(3), (b)(2)–(3). Normally, a hearing is held with the defendant present in court in order to confirm that the requirements for a valid plea have been satisfied. Once the defendant's guilty (or no-contest) plea is accepted, the plea hearing may move directly into a sentencing hearing. Often, though, the judge will want to conduct the sentencing at a later date, especially if the judge contemplates the preparation of a presentence report ("PSR")—a subject to which we will turn shortly.

The American plea-bargaining process has been subject to numerous criticisms, not the least of which are those relating to transparency and accountability. Consider these observations from Professor Jenia Turner:

> Unlike the trials it replaces, plea bargaining occurs privately and off the record. Victims and the public are excluded from the negotiations, and even the defendant is typically absent. Plea offers are often not documented, and the final plea agreements are not always in writing or placed on record with the court. Plea hearings—at which a judge reviews the validity of a defendant's guilty plea—are public, but they tend to be brisk, rote affairs that often fail to reveal all of the concessions exchanged between the parties. As a result, plea bargaining is largely shielded from outside scrutiny, and critical plea-related data are missing.

Transparency in Plea Bargaining, 96 NOTRE DAME L. REV. 973, 975 (2021) (citations omitted). Turner recommends several reforms, including the following requirements: (1) that all plea agreements be reduced to writing and put on the record; (2) that all plea *offers* also be placed on the record if the offer is rejected by the defendant and the case is set for trial; and (3) that all charges, plea offers, and final sentences be entered into a searchable digital database. *Id.* at 976–77. What do you think might be said for and against such proposals?

In recent years, many states and the federal government have adopted laws that require prosecutors to inform victims of plea agreements and to consider their views of a proposed deal. However, prosecutors do not always adhere to the letter and spirit of these laws. A notable example involves the case of Jeffrey Epstein, the billionaire financier charged with sexually assaulting and trafficking dozens of underage girls. Epstein was able to negotiate a nonprosecution agreement (NPA) with federal prosecutors that spared him federal prosecution and resulted in a lenient state sentence based on a plea agreement with state prosecutors. Epstein's lawyers were also able to negotiate that the deal be kept secret from both the public and the alleged victims until it was too late for objections to be raised.

One of the victims, Courtney Wild, sought relief under the federal Crime Victims' Rights Act (CVRA), enacted in 2004, which provides a crime victim "[t]he reasonable right to confer with the attorney for the Government in the case." 18 U.S.C. § 3771(a)(5). Ms. Wild sought to enforce the CVRA, maintaining that the right "to confer" can attach even before formal criminal charges are filed when an NPA is brokered. Ultimately, the Eleventh Circuit Court of Appeals, sitting *en banc*, declined to rule on that issue and instead held that the CVRA provides a victim no ability to file a "freestanding civil suit seeking judicial enforcement of her rights under the CVRA in the absence of any underlying proceeding." *In re Wild*, 994 F.3d 1244, 1252 (11th Cir. 2021). Concluding, the Court stated:

> We are aware, of course, that many will misunderstand today's decision. To be clear, the question before us is not whether Jeffrey Epstein was a bad man. By all accounts, he was. Nor is the question before us whether, as a matter of best practices, prosecutors should have consulted with Ms. Wild (and other victims) before negotiating and executing Epstein's NPA. By all accounts—including the government's own—they should have. Our sole charge is to determine, on the facts before us, whether the CVRA provides Ms. Wild with a private right of action to enforce her rights outside of the context of a preexisting criminal proceeding. Despite our sympathy for Ms. Wild—and the courage that she has shown in pursuing this litigation—we find ourselves constrained to hold that it does not.

Id. at 1269. *See generally* Elizabeth N. Jones, *The Ascending Role of Crime Victims in Plea-Bargaining and Beyond*, 117 W. VA. L. REV. 97 (2014); Zulkifl M. Zargar, Note, *Secret* Faits Accomplis*: Declination Decisions, Nonprosecution Agreements, and the Crime Victim's Right to Confer*, 89 FORDHAM L. REV. 343 (2020).

Like the CVRA, many state-level victims' rights laws provide victims with a right to speak at a plea hearing and/or confer with the government regarding a proposed plea deal. However, such laws have been criticized for failing to ensure that victim input is obtained early enough so that it can genuinely influence the process, as well as a lack of effective enforcement mechanisms. OFFICE FOR VICTIMS OF CRIME, U.S. DEP'T OF JUSTICE, VICTIM INPUT INTO PLEA AGREEMENTS 2 (2002); Jones, *supra*. As a stronger alternative, why not simply provide the victim with a veto over any proposed plea deal? For a proposal along these lines, see GEORGE P. FLETCHER, WITH JUSTICE FOR SOME: VICTIMS' RIGHTS IN CRIMINAL TRIALS 248 (1995).

The rights of victims and their role in other parts of the sentencing process are further discussed at the end of the chapter.

2. PRESENTENCE INVESTIGATION & REPORT

In a system that assigned a specific penalty to each offense, there would be no need for additional information to be gathered between the determination of guilt and the imposition of the sentence. (You might recall from Chapter 1, for instance, Thomas Jefferson's proposed system of talionic punishments in 1779—castrate the rapist, poison the poisoner, and so forth.) In contemporary American sentencing, however, the judge normally has discretion to select the punishment from a range of options. In order to select the most appropriate sentence in light of the authorized purposes of punishment, the judge will typically want to know some background information about the defendant, including, for instance, the defendant's criminal history, employment status and prospects, family support and responsibilities, mental health and substance abuse issues, and educational attainment. (Do you see how such considerations might relate to some of the purposes of punishment we considered in Chapter 1?) The judge might also like to know more about the circumstances and consequences of the defendant's current criminal conduct than is available through the formal charging documents.

How is the judge to obtain such supplemental information? If the defendant has been convicted after a trial, the judge will have likely learned quite a bit about the circumstances of the offense from the trial evidence. As we have seen, however, most convictions are based on a guilty plea, not a trial verdict. Of course, the judge's consideration of the plea, especially insofar as the judge must ensure there is a factual basis for it, will require the judge to learn *something* about the offense. Other pretrial proceedings, such as the determination of bail or a suppression hearing, may result in the judge gaining additional information about the crime and the defendant's background. Still, the amount of information available to the judge at the time the guilty plea is accepted may fall far short of what the judge views as necessary to determine the defendant's likelihood of reoffense, rehabilitative needs, just deserts, and so forth.

Defense counsel has an obvious incentive to supply the judge with *mitigating* information for sentencing purposes—to explain, for instance, that the crime was aberrational and unlikely to be repeated, that the defendant was acting under the influence of mental illness or extreme economic pressures, or that the defendant is remorseful and has attempted to make voluntary restitution to the victim. Similarly, the prosecutor will often see it as part of his or her role to supply the judge with *aggravating* information—to show, for instance, the severity of the psychological impact on the victim, the prior occasions when the defendant has been given a break and yet failed to turn his or her life around, or the defendant's leadership role in inducing others to assist the commission of the offense.

Should the judge be satisfied with the adequacy of the adversarial process to develop the information necessary for sentencing? Not necessarily. Busy lawyers, trained to focus on the elements of the offense and the evidence necessary to prove (or disprove) those elements at trial, may not have the time or patience to engage in a more open-ended exploration of the full range of facts that may potentially prove relevant at sentencing. Their adversarial zeal, moreover, may be tempered by a desire to adhere to the letter and spirit of a plea deal. (For instance, what motivation would a prosecutor have to discover and present aggravating information if the prosecutor is already committed to supporting a sentence of probation?) It may be desirable, then, for the adversarial process to be supplemented by a systematic presentence investigation conducted by a neutral party—preferably one who has some experience in working with people who have been convicted of crimes and some basis for recognizing the factors that are relevant to their risk and rehabilitative needs.

In the federal system, for instance, the preparation of a detailed presentence investigation report by a probation officer is made the default—a report is prepared as a matter of course unless the court finds that one is unnecessary. Federal Rule of Criminal Procedure 32 details the process.

Federal Rules of Criminal Procedure

Rule 32. Sentencing and Judgment.

(c) PRESENTENCE INVESTIGATION.

(1) *Required Investigation.*

(A) *In General.* The probation officer must conduct a presentence investigation and submit a report to the court before it imposes sentence unless:

(i) 18 U.S.C. § 3593(c) or another statute requires otherwise; or

(ii) the court finds that the information in the record enables it to meaningfully exercise its sentencing authority under 18 U.S.C. § 3553, and the court explains its finding on the record.

(B) *Restitution.* If the law permits restitution, the probation officer must conduct an investigation and submit a report that contains sufficient information for the court to order restitution.

(2) *Interviewing the Defendant.* The probation officer who interviews a defendant as part of a presentence investigation must,

on request, give the defendant's attorney notice and a reasonable opportunity to attend the interview.

(d) PRESENTENCE REPORT.

(1) *Applying the Advisory Sentencing Guidelines.* The presentence report must:

(A) identify all applicable guidelines and policy statements of the Sentencing Commission;

(B) calculate the defendant's offense level and criminal history category;

(C) state the resulting sentencing range and kinds of sentences available;

(D) identify any factor relevant to:

(i) the appropriate kind of sentence, or

(ii) the appropriate sentence within the applicable sentencing range; and

(E) identify any basis for departing from the applicable sentencing range.

(2) *Additional Information.* The presentence report must also contain the following:

(A) the defendant's history and characteristics, including:

(i) any prior criminal record;

(ii) the defendant's financial condition; and

(iii) any circumstances affecting the defendant's behavior that may be helpful in imposing sentence or in correctional treatment;

(B) information that assesses any financial, social, psychological, and medical impact on any victim;

(C) when appropriate, the nature and extent of nonprison programs and resources available to the defendant;

(D) when the law provides for restitution, information sufficient for a restitution order; * * *

(F) a statement of whether the government seeks forfeiture under Rule 32.2 and any other law; and

(G) any other information that the court requires, including information relevant to the factors under 18 U.S.C. § 3553(a).

(3) *Exclusions.* The presentence report must exclude the following:

(A) any diagnoses that, if disclosed, might seriously disrupt a rehabilitation program;

(B) any sources of information obtained upon a promise of confidentiality; and

(C) any other information that, if disclosed, might result in physical or other harm to the defendant or others.

(e) DISCLOSING THE REPORT AND RECOMMENDATION.

(1) *Time to Disclose.* Unless the defendant has consented in writing, the probation officer must not submit a presentence report to the court or disclose its contents to anyone until the defendant has pleaded guilty or nolo contendere, or has been found guilty.

(2) *Minimum Required Notice.* The probation officer must give the presentence report to the defendant, the defendant's attorney, and an attorney for the government at least 35 days before sentencing unless the defendant waives this minimum period.

(3) *Sentence Recommendation.* By local rule or by order in a case, the court may direct the probation officer not to disclose to anyone other than the court the officer's recommendation on the sentence.

(f) OBJECTING TO THE REPORT.

(1) *Time to Object.* Within 14 days after receiving the presentence report, the parties must state in writing any objections, including objections to material information, sentencing guideline ranges, and policy statements contained in or omitted from the report.

(2) *Serving Objections.* An objecting party must provide a copy of its objections to the opposing party and to the probation officer.

(3) *Action on Objections.* After receiving objections, the probation officer may meet with the parties to discuss the objections. The probation officer may then investigate further and revise the presentence report as appropriate.

(g) SUBMITTING THE REPORT. At least 7 days before sentencing, the probation officer must submit to the court and to the parties the presentence report and an addendum containing any unresolved objections, the grounds for those objections, and the probation officer's comments on them.

Sample Federal Presentence Report[3]

UNITED STATES DISTRICT COURT
FOR THE EASTERN DISTRICT OF WISCONSIN

United States of America	)	
	)	
vs.	)	Presentence Investigation Report
	)	

[3] This is a hypothetical report reflecting the structure and types of information that are often found in a PSR.

Timothy John Smith) Docket No.: ______________

Sentence Date: January 4, 2021

Offense: Conspiracy to Distribute in Excess of 50 Grams of Methamphetamine (21 U.S.C. §§ 846, 841(a)(1), and 841(b)(1)(A)(viii))—10 years to life/$10,000,000.00 fine

Release Status: Detained since March 17, 2019

Detainers: None

Codefendants:

THOMAS, Jason Winston	Appeared on May 3, 2019, and pled guilty to conspiracy to distribute in excess of 50 grams of methamphetamine. Sentenced on August 3, 2020, to 110 months imprisonment and 4 years supervised release.
JONES, Lilly Bethany	Appeared on November 18, 2019, and pled guilty to conspiracy to distribute in excess of 50 grams of methamphetamine. Sentenced on April 12, 2020, to 72 months imprisonment and 5 years supervised release.

Related Cases: None

Date Report Prepared: November 15, 2020

Identifying Data:

Date of Birth:	August 31, 1980
Age:	40
Race:	White
Hispanic Origin:	Non-Hispanic Origin
Sex:	Male
SS#:	987-65-432
FBI#:	123456
Education:	11th grade
Dependents:	None
Citizenship:	United States

Legal Address:	327 Elm Street Racine, WI
Aliases:	None

Interview Dates With Defendant: September 22, 2020; October 28, 2020

PART A. THE OFFENSE

Charge(s) and Conviction(s)

1. On March 17, 2019, a one count criminal complaint was filed in the U.S. District Court, Eastern District of Wisconsin, charging **Timothy J. Smith** with conspiracy to distribute in excess of 50 grams of methamphetamine.
2. On March 17, 2019, the defendant appeared before Magistrate Judge Susan Rogers and was temporarily detained.
3. On March 25, 2019, the defendant appeared before Magistrate Judge Nathan Stone for a detention hearing and was detained.
4. On April 5, 2019, a one count indictment was filed charging **Timothy J. Smith** with conspiracy to distribute in excess of 50 grams of methamphetamine.
5. In August 2020, the defendant appeared before the Court for a bench trial and on September 2, 2020, the defendant was found guilty.

The Offense Conduct

6. According to the government, beginning in November of 2018, **Timothy J. Smith** worked with Jason W. Thomas and Lilly B. Jones to distribute methamphetamine. Ms. Jones, who lives in Chicago, Illinois, acted as the source of the drugs. **Mr. Smith** was at the center of the conspiracy, maintaining the connection with Ms. Jones, ordering the drugs, controlling the proceeds, and supervising Mr. Thomas, who distributed methamphetamine for **Mr. Smith.**
7. In January of 2019, the Drug Enforcement Agency (DEA) received a tip from a confidential informant that **Mr. Smith** and Mr. Thomas were distributing methamphetamine in the Racine area. On March 3, 2019, Special Agent (SA) Janine Baker contacted Mr. Thomas to determine if he would agree to sell her methamphetamine. In a series of phone calls, the two agreed to a twenty-gram transaction. The purported purpose of the deal was to provide SA Baker with a "sample" of the conspiracy's methamphetamine. If the quality was good, SA Baker indicated that she would be interested in purchasing much larger quantities in the future. During negotiations, Mr. Thomas went to **Mr. Smith**'s house, where **Mr. Smith** apparently determined through Ms. Jones that the drugs would be available and set the time and place of the transaction.

8. On March 5, 2019, SA Baker met Mr. Thomas in the parking lot of a grocery store and purchased twenty grams of methamphetamine from him. During the purchase, **Mr. Smith** and Ms. Jones were riding around in a car in the area. Mr. Thomas carried a phone with him during the sale. A call was placed by **Mr. Smith** to Mr. Thomas, and the line was kept open so that **Mr. Smith** could monitor the transaction.
9. After the deal, Mr. Thomas met Ms. Jones and **Mr. Smith** in the parking lot of a nearby fast-food restaurant, where Mr. Thomas handed over to **Mr. Smith** the proceeds of the drug sale. **Mr. Smith** then paid Ms. Jones a portion of the money for supplying the drugs and Mr. Thomas another portion of the money for his role in the transaction. **Mr. Smith** kept the remainder as his profit.
10. On March 12, 2019, SA Baker had more phone contact with Mr. Thomas to arrange the purchase of forty grams of methamphetamine. The two agreed to meet on March 17, 2019, at the same location.
11. On March 17, 2019, Mr. Thomas and Ms. Jones met SA Baker at the agreed upon time and place. Mr. Thomas gave a package of methamphetamine to SA Baker, at which time SA Baker gave a signal and DEA agents converged on Mr. Thomas and Ms. Jones. They were taken into custody. Mr. Thomas told the agents that he had obtained the drugs from **Mr. Smith** at his home.
12. Shortly thereafter, agents obtained a search warrant for **Mr. Smith**'s home. They executed the warrant during the evening of March 17, 2019. They found a scale with methamphetamine residue, eight grams of marijuana, and a handgun. They also found **Mr. Smith**, whom they placed under arrest.
13. After his arrest and with the advice of counsel, Mr. Thomas initially agreed to cooperate. In debriefings done under a proffer letter and pursuant to U.S.S.G. § 1B1.8, Mr. Thomas said that he had been socially acquainted with **Mr. Smith** in the early 2000's. However, Mr. Thomas was arrested and sentenced to prison in 2007 in connection with a different drug conspiracy. Mr. Thomas did not see **Mr. Smith** again until 2018.
14. In April of 2018, Mr. Thomas was working in a clothing store in Racine. **Mr. Smith** went into the store to make a purchase, which was the first time Mr. Thomas had seen **Mr. Smith** in about eleven years. The two conversed for several minutes and made arrangements to meet at a neighborhood bar after Mr. Thomas got off work. When they met later, the two discussed their need for money. **Mr. Smith** indicated that he had a connection in Chicago who could supply drugs. He asked Mr. Thomas if he would like to help him distribute drugs. Mr. Thomas initially declined to become involved in drug dealing again.

15. Mr. Thomas and **Mr. Smith** continued to meet socially from time to time for the next few months. In October of 2018, Mr. Thomas lost his job at the clothing store. When **Mr. Smith** learned of this, he again encouraged Mr. Thomas to join him in dealing drugs. **Mr. Smith** described his Chicago connection, Ms. Jones, and indicated that he was already making some money selling methamphetamine in the Racine area. Mr. Thomas agreed to help. In November of 2018, he began to work regularly for **Mr. Smith**, helping to transport and distribute drugs that were supplied to **Mr. Smith** by Ms. Jones.

16. According to Mr. Thomas, **Mr. Smith** was purchasing about 100 grams of methamphetamine per week from Ms. Jones. Sometimes, Mr. Thomas and **Mr. Smith** drove to Chicago to pick up the drugs. Other times, Ms. Jones would bring the drugs to Racine. Either way, they stored and packaged the drugs at **Mr. Smith**'s home. Buyers were instructed to call Mr. Thomas when they were ready to make a purchase. Mr. Thomas negotiated the details of the transactions with the buyers under the supervision of **Mr. Smith**. For small deals with known customers, Mr. Thomas obtained the drugs from **Mr. Smith** and completed the transaction himself. For other deals, **Mr. Smith** or Ms. Jones would either accompany Mr. Thomas in person or monitor the transaction via cellphone. Whatever money Mr. Thomas obtained from buyers was turned over to **Mr. Smith**, who then returned a portion to Mr. Thomas.

Victim Impact

17. Here the community is the victim so no direct victim impact statement is available.

[CALCULATION OF GUIDELINES OFFENSE LEVEL OMITTED]

PART B. DEFENDANT'S CRIMINAL HISTORY

Juvenile Adjudications

35. None known.

Adult Criminal Convictions

	Date of Arrest	Conviction/Court	Date Sentence Imposed/Disposition
36.	March 2, 2004 (Age 23)	Battery; Ashland County Circuit Court; Ashland, WI (Case No. 2004CM97)	March 10, 2004: Probation

37. Copies of the arrest report and court file have been requested, but not yet received. The defendant could not recall the details of this offense.

38.	July 7, 2006 (Age 25)	Possession with Intent to Deliver Controlled Substance; Milwaukee	January 30, 2007: 90 days jail; 2 years

		County Circuit Court: Milwaukee, WI (Case No. 2006CF589)	probation; $1000.00 fine

39. According to the complaint, a car driven by the defendant was stopped for speeding. A consensual search of the car revealed 5 grams of methamphetamine hidden under a seat.

40.	October 14, 2007 (Age 27)	Possession with Intent to Deliver Controlled Substance; Milwaukee County Circuit Court: Milwaukee, WI (Case No. 2007CF1211)	<u>November 29, 2008:</u> 3 years prison; 3 years extended supervision

41. According to the complaint, an undercover agent purchased 7 grams of methamphetamine from the defendant.

42.	July 5, 2009 (Age 28)	Battery of Prison Guard; Dodge County Circuit Court; Juneau, WI (Case No. 2009CF285)	<u>September 12, 2010:</u> 1.5 years prison; 1 year extended supervision

43. According to the complaint, a fight broke out between two inmates at the institution where the defendant was incarcerated for his 2008 sentence. The defendant attempted to intervene on behalf of one of the combatants. When a guard ordered the defendant to stand aside, the defendant punched the guard in the face and chest.

[CALCULATION OF GUIDELINES CRIMINAL HISTORY SCORE OMITTED]

<u>Traffic Convictions</u>

48. **Mr. Smith** was fined on October 5, 2005, by the Chicago Police Department in Illinois for improper traffic lane usage. He was also fined on January 17, 2006, by the Chicago Police Department for an improper turn signal.

<u>Other Criminal Conduct</u>

49. None known.

<u>Pending Charges</u>

50. None known.

<u>Other Arrests</u>

	Date of Arrest	Charge	Agency	Disposition
51.	January 1, 2004 (Age 23)	Possession of Marijuana	Ashland County Sheriff's Dept.	<u>February 20, 2004</u>: Dismissed

PART C. OFFENDER CHARACTERISTICS

Personal and Family Data

52. **Mr. Smith** was born August 31, 1980, in Ashland, Wisconsin, the only child produced by the relationship of James and Mary Smith. **Mr. Smith**'s parents separated when he was an infant. **Mr. Smith** moved with his mother to Racine, Wisconsin, while his father remained in Ashland. **Mr. Smith**'s mother married her current husband, Daniel Pipps, in 1984. Since Ashland is a six-hour drive from Racine, **Mr. Smith**'s contact with his biological father while growing up was limited to two weeks each summer.

53. By all accounts, supervision and discipline were lacking in **Mr. Smith**'s home when he was a child. Both his mother and stepfather worked irregular hours outside the home in a series of food-service and bartending jobs. The maternal grandmother attempted to provide supervision in the home when no one else was available but was physically frail and often bedridden. **Mr. Smith** was described as being an unruly child. He began experimenting with alcohol and drugs as a youth. In brief, although **Mr. Smith**'s material needs were met, he did not have the benefit of good parenting.

54. **Mr. Smith**'s father, James Smith, resides in Ashland, Wisconsin. He is a retired schoolteacher. **Mr. Smith**'s stepfather, Daniel Pipps, resides with **Mr. Smith**'s mother in Kenosha, Wisconsin. They own and operate a tavern in Kenosha.

55. **Mr. Smith** has one half-sibling, Alonzo Pipps, age 33, who has been incarcerated in an Illinois state prison since a drug trafficking conviction in 2016.

56. On November 7, 2002, **Mr. Smith** married Elizabeth Westman in Ashland. They divorced on April 13, 2007. The marriage resulted in the birth of one child, Courtney Smith, age 15. Mr. Smith has not seen his daughter since his October 2007 arrest. While he was in prison following that arrest, his ex-wife and daughter moved to Florida and their whereabouts are unknown.

Physical Condition

57. **Mr. Smith** stands 5 feet 11 inches tall and weighs 180 pounds. He has brown hair and brown eyes. He has a tattoo of his daughter's name, "Courtney," on his left shoulder.

58. **Mr. Smith** describes his overall health as generally good. He denies current or recent use of prescription medication, or the need for a physician's care. He experiences asthma from time to time, dating to adolescence, with difficulty most often during hot weather.

Mental and Emotional Health

59. **Mr. Smith** has periodically received counseling for depression and substance abuse since about age 15. He indicates that he attempted suicide after the breakup of his marriage in 2007. He has not

received any counseling since his most recent release from prison in 2012. He admits that he has continued to feel depressed from time to time and is somewhat depressed over his current legal predicament.

Substance Abuse

60. **Mr. Smith** has a long history of substance abuse dating back to age 13. He started using alcohol as a youth and reports that he is an alcoholic. He has also been a periodic abuser of opioid drugs, which he first obtained by stealing painkillers that were prescribed for his maternal grandmother. He reports using his grandmother's pills regularly while he was in high school. He also began using marijuana in high school.

61. After **Mr. Smith** left high school and moved to Ashland to live with his father, he discontinued his use of opioids, but continued to consume alcohol on a daily basis and marijuana occasionally. When he was married, at the urging of his wife, he sought counseling for his alcoholism and greatly reduced his alcohol consumption. However, after his marriage ended, he resumed his previous drinking habits. He also experimented with heroin and methamphetamine. He reports periodic efforts to "get clean" since then but has repeatedly relapsed. He indicates that at the time of his current arrest, he had been sober for four months.

62. Urine surveillance was not conducted during the presentence investigation as **Mr. Smith** has been in continuous custody.

Education, Vocational, and Special Skills

63. **Mr. Smith** attended Racine North High School through the eleventh grade. School records indicate that he was a "B" student in ninth grade, but that his grades the following two years dropped to C's, D's, and F's. After the eleventh grade, with the agreement of his parents, **Mr. Smith** moved to Ashland to live with his father. It was hoped that the change of scenery would help **Mr. Smith** with his substance abuse problems and that he would be able to complete high school in Ashland. However, he never enrolled in school in Ashland, and has completed no additional formal education.

Employment Record

64. **Mr. Smith** was employed from July of 1997 until January of 2007 as a machine operator by the Quigley Manufacturing Corporation in Ashland, Wisconsin. The employer was contacted and verified his employment. Records from the Social Security Administration indicate that **Mr. Smith** earned $20,000 in 2006, his final full year of employment with Quigley Manufacturing. **Mr. Smith** reports that he was fired as a result of his felony conviction and incarceration in early 2007.

65. **Mr. Smith** was incarcerated continuously between October 2007 and March 2012. Since his release in 2012, **Mr. Smith** reports that he has worked as a seasonal laborer (April to October) at Benton Construction Company in Racine for $8 per hour. A verification request was sent, but not returned. Social Security records do not indicate any income for **Mr. Smith** in these years. **Mr. Smith** also reports that most Friday and Saturday nights he helps out at Danny's Place, the tavern owned by his mother and stepfather in Kenosha. In return, according to **Mr. Smith**, his mother assists with some of his living expenses. However, **Mr. Smith**'s mother indicates that she helps him out "because he is my son"; she denies that any payments she has made to him are in return for his work at the tavern, which she describes as "occasional—just whenever he is around and feels like helping out."

66. **Mr. Smith** also indicates that, between 2012 and 2016, he supplemented his legal income by transporting drugs for his stepbrother Alonzo, whom he reports was a "big drug dealer in Chicago." The stepbrother was convicted of drug trafficking in Illinois state court in 2016 and has been incarcerated since then.

<u>Financial Condition: Ability to Pay</u>

67. **Mr. Smith** has no known assets other than a few personal effects and clothing. Prior to his current arrest, he lived in a rented home, from which he has since been evicted for nonpayment of rent. Similarly, his vehicle, a 2019 Toyota 4RUNNER, was repossessed for nonpayment during his period of pretrial detention.

PART D. SENTENCING OPTIONS [OMITTED]

PART E. FACTORS THAT MAY WARRANT DEPARTURE

70. None

PART F. FACTORS THAT MAY WARRANT A SENTENCE OUTSIDE OF THE ADVISORY GUIDELINE SYSTEM

71. None

PART G. PROPOSED SUPERVISION CONDITIONS [OMITTED]

NOTES & QUESTIONS

1. **Presentence Investigation as Default.** Rule 32 indicates that a presentence investigation "must" be performed unless one of the indicated exceptions applies. (The statute cited in the first exception, 18 U.S.C. § 3593(c), establishes a different presentence process for *capital* cases.) Not all states have adopted the federal approach in this area. *See, e.g.,* Wis. Stat. § 972.15(1) ("After a conviction the court *may* order a presentence investigation . . . ." (emphasis added)). The American Law Institute's Model Penal Code: Sentencing ("MPC:S") requires a presentence investigation in

some situations, but not always.[4] Do you see any reasons why a PSR should not be completed in *every* case?

In recent years, funding constraints seem to have resulted in a reduced production of PSRs in some jurisdictions. The researchers in one recent study reported, "In several states, presentence reports seem to be vanishing from routine use. . . . [For example, judges] don't often order presentence reports in some counties in Oregon, Maryland, or Florida . . ., and use them in only about half or fewer of felony cases in Missouri." Nancy J. King & Ronald F. Wright, *The Invisible Revolution in Plea Bargaining: Managerial Judging and Judicial Participation in Negotiations*, 95 TEX. L. REV. 325, 377–78 (2016).

2. **Role of Defense Counsel.** Rule 32(c)(2) requires that the defendant's lawyer be given an opportunity to attend the defendant's interview. Does this seem to you a good use of attorney time? Do you think it would be malpractice for the lawyer *not* to attend if given the opportunity? Not all states are as generous as the federal system in giving defense counsel a chance to attend the presentence interview. Given the importance of the content of a PSR, do you think this should be a matter of constitutional right?[5]

In its *Standards for Criminal Justice*, the American Bar Association addresses the role of the defense lawyer in relation to the presentence interview this way:

> Counsel should explain to his or her client the importance to the judge's sentencing decision of the presentence report. Counsel should also impress upon the client the significance of statements made by the client to the court or administrative personnel involved in the preparation of this report. Ordinarily, when it is possible and otherwise permissible, counsel should attend such presentence interviews. The nature of the sentence guidelines used in some jurisdictions may make counsel's attendance at such interviews necessary to provide the client with a complete and effective defense.

AM. BAR ASS'N, STANDARDS FOR CRIMINAL JUSTICE std.4–8.1 cmmnt. (3d ed. 1993).

An important tactical question in some cases is whether the defendant should invoke his or her right to remain silent in connection with the presentence interview. We consider application of the Fifth Amendment privilege to sentencing later in this chapter.

3. **Content of the PSR.** Rule 32(d) identifies certain types of information that must be included in the PSR. Do you see how these various

---

[4] More specifically, § 7.07(1) states that "the court shall order a presentence investigation report whenever a defendant has been convicted of a felony and the court is contemplating a sentence of incarceration or a period of probation in excess of the time served by the defendant while awaiting conviction and sentencing on the felony offense."

[5] *Compare* State v. Kauk, 691 N.W.2d 606, 609 (S.D. 2005) (finding no Sixth Amendment right to counsel during presentence interview), *with* State ex rel. Russell v. Jones, 647 P.2d 904, 907 (Or. 1982) (holding that Sixth Amendment prohibits state from barring defense counsel from presentence interview).

types of information required by Rule 32(d)(2) are connected to the purposes of punishment specified in 18 U.S.C. § 3553(a)? The text of the statute was reprinted in Chapter 1. State rules for PSR content vary, but often cover much the same ground as the federal rule.

4. **Disclosure to the Defense.** Traditionally, there has been some resistance to the disclosure of PSRs to the defendant. Can you see why? On the other hand, nondisclosure creates risks that a defendant may be sentenced on the basis of incorrect information in the PSR that the defendant could rebut if given the opportunity. In its current form, Rule 32 mostly comes down on the side of disclosure, establishing a specific process by which the defendant may review the PSR and register objections. Yet, the federal disclosure regime is not without its limitations. Note in particular the "exclusions" from the report mandated by Rule 32(d)(3). What purpose do they serve? Are they fair to the defendant?

5. **Third-Party Disclosure.** Even as restrictions on disclosure of the PSR to the defendant have been relaxed, PSRs still tend to be regarded as confidential documents that should not normally be released more broadly to third parties, e.g., to the media. In the federal system, Rule 32 does not speak directly to third-party disclosure, but courts have adopted a "strong presumption" against such broader release. *See, e.g., In re Morning Song Bird Food Litig.*, 831 F.3d 765, 773 (6th Cir. 2016); *United States v. Schlette,* 842 F.2d 1574, 1579 (9th Cir. 1988). In considering a third-party request for a PSR, courts weigh the interests supporting release in relation to the countervailing interests, including "the privacy interests of the defendant, the defendant's family, and the crime victim." *United States v. Corbitt,* 879 F.2d 224, 229–30 (7th Cir. 1989).

6. ***United States v. Smith.*** Is there anything surprising to you about the *Smith* PSR? How would you feel about the report if you were Smith's lawyer? Smith's prosecutor? Smith himself? If you were the judge, what parts of the report would you regard as most helpful? Least helpful? Is there any information that you would like to see added to the report?

3. SENTENCING HEARING

In many cases in which a PSR is prepared and the parties have a fair opportunity to respond in writing, it may be possible for the judge to issue a reasonably well-informed sentencing decision "on the papers" and forego an in-person hearing. Nonetheless, the in-person sentencing hearing is among the most well-established traditions in American criminal process.

Sometimes, the hearing serves factfinding purposes, with live-witness testimony, cross-examination by the lawyers, and credibility determinations by the judge. For instance, in a multidefendant case, there may be a factual dispute about which defendant was the ringleader. The presentation of evidence by each side at the sentencing hearing may help the judge to sort out who played what role in the offense, which may have a bearing, for instance, on culpability and just punishment. When there are important factual disputes like this to be resolved, trial-type procedures with live-witness testimony are often thought to promote accuracy in factfinding.

Yet, the tradition of the in-person sentencing hearing plainly rests on more than just factfinding needs. Indeed, in many cases, there are no well-delineated factual disputes of real importance that must be resolved at sentencing. The judge's decision does not center on the finding of facts, but on determining the *significance* of facts that are either not disputed or have already been formally established through a plea or trial verdict. Even in these cases, though, it is almost always simply taken for granted that there will be a sentencing hearing. Do you see any purposes that might be served by a hearing in such cases?

Among other possibilities, there may be some symbolic value to the public ritual of pronouncing sentence. Consider this description of what two authors (one a former federal district judge) characterize as the "traditional" federal sentencing hearing:

> [T]he complex interplay of various actors, characteristic of the adjudicatory stage, resolved itself into a single axis of tension between the defendant, now convicted, and the judge, robed and seated behind the high bench. No longer serving primarily as an arbiter between the parties, the judge was called upon to exercise the ultimate authority of the state.
>
> Those present . . . witnessed a ritual of undeniable moral significance. It was critical that this proceeding took the form of a face-to-face encounter between individuals. The sentencing judge might have a wide audience: victims, their families and friends, the family and friends of the defendant, the general public, and even the appellate courts . . . . But the judge *addressed* only one person when imposing a sentence and ordering the entry of the judgment of conviction. The meaning of this solemn confrontation was clear: only a person can pass moral judgment, and only a person can be morally judged.

Kate Stith & José A. Cabranes, *Judging Under the Federal Sentencing Guidelines*, 91 NW. U. L. REV. 1247, 1253 (1997).

Most sentencing hearings include certain basic components and follow a somewhat standardized process. In the federal system, much of this is laid out in Rule 32.

Federal Rules of Criminal Procedure

Rule 32. Sentencing and Judgment.

(i) SENTENCING.

(1) *In General.* At sentencing, the court:

(A) must verify that the defendant and the defendant's attorney have read and discussed the presentence report and any addendum to the report;

(B) must give to the defendant and an attorney for the government a written summary of—or summarize *in camera*—any information excluded from the presentence report under Rule 32(d)(3) on which the court will rely in sentencing, and give them a reasonable opportunity to comment on that information;

(C) must allow the parties' attorneys to comment on the probation officer's determinations and other matters relating to an appropriate sentence; and

(D) may, for good cause, allow a party to make a new objection at any time before sentence is imposed.

(2) *Introducing Evidence; Producing a Statement.* The court may permit the parties to introduce evidence on the objections. If a witness testifies at sentencing, Rule 26.2(a)–(d) and (f) applies. If a party fails to comply with a Rule 26.2 order to produce a witness's statement, the court must not consider that witness's testimony.

(3) *Court Determinations.* At sentencing, the court:

(A) may accept any undisputed portion of the presentence report as a finding of fact;

(B) must—for any disputed portion of the presentence report or other controverted matter—rule on the dispute or determine that a ruling is unnecessary either because the matter will not affect sentencing, or because the court will not consider the matter in sentencing; * * *

(4) *Opportunity to Speak.*

(A) *By a Party.* Before imposing sentence, the court must:

(i) provide the defendant's attorney an opportunity to speak on the defendant's behalf;

(ii) address the defendant personally in order to permit the defendant to speak or present any information to mitigate the sentence; and

(iii) provide an attorney for the government an opportunity to speak equivalent to that of the defendant's attorney.

(B) *By a Victim.* Before imposing sentence, the court must address any victim of the crime who is present at sentencing and must permit the victim to be reasonably heard.

NOTES & QUESTIONS

1. **Factfinding and Live-Witness Testimony.** In general, Rule 32 requires the sentencing judge to resolve any factual disputes that arise from the presentence process. To that end, the parties may call witnesses to testify at sentencing. Under Rule 32(i)(2), the party that calls a witness may be required upon request to disclose prior statements of that witness pursuant to Rule 26.2, which may serve as a check on false or misleading testimony.

Note how Rule 32(i)(3)(A) underscores the importance of the presentence process and, in particular, the need for the lawyers to review the PSR carefully and lodge timely objections.

Although the factfinding portion of the sentencing hearing may in some respects resemble a conventional trial, the normal rules of evidence may be substantially relaxed. In the federal system, "the [sentencing] court may consider relevant information without regard to its admissibility under the rules of evidence applicable at trial, provided that the evidence has sufficient indicia of reliability to support its probable accuracy." U.S. Sent'g Guidelines § 6A1.3. Why might it make sense to dispense with the trial rules at sentencing?

What burden of proof should be used in the resolution of factual disputes? In the federal system, the United States Sentencing Commission, like the judges and policymakers in many states, has embraced the civil "preponderance of the evidence" standard, instead of the more demanding "beyond a reasonable doubt" standard that normally applies at criminal trials. U.S. Sent'g Guidelines § 6A1.3 cmmnt. However, as we will see later in this chapter, the Supreme Court has ruled that, in certain circumstances, the higher standard must be used for sentencing factfinding.

2. **Right of the Defendant to Be Heard.** Rule 32(i)(4)(A) assures the lawyers an opportunity to speak at sentencing. Consistent with long tradition in American criminal process, the Rule also gives the defendant a *personal* right to speak at sentencing, i.e., not merely through defense counsel. A defendant's unsworn statement at sentencing is referred to as "allocution." If you were a defense lawyer, what sort of advice would you give your client about speaking to the court at sentencing? Do you think you might ever advise a client to waive allocution? Do you think that might be your normal practice?

Now consider allocution from the judge's perspective. How much weight would you give to the defendant's statement, if any? Would you reduce the sentence of the defendant who tearfully—and, as far as you can tell, sincerely—expresses remorse over his or her crime? Would you *increase* the sentence of the defendant who steadfastly protests his or her innocence, even though the evidence of guilt seems overwhelming? Would you penalize a defendant for making statements that are false or contradictory, or for projecting a "hard," unrepentant demeanor? Would you be confident in your ability to account appropriately for the impact of depression, anxiety, intellectual disability, age, sex, and cultural background in your evaluation of the quality of the defendant's allocution performance? *See* Michael O'Hear, *Remorse, Cooperation, and "Acceptance of Responsibility": The Structure, Implementation, and Reform of Section 3E1.1 of the Federal Sentencing Guidelines*, 91 NW. U. L. REV. 1507, 1548–53 (1997) (arguing that consideration of remorse at sentencing has potential for discriminatory impact as to defendants who are mentally ill or belong to a racial minority group).[6]

[6] Despite such concerns, many judges indicate that allocution plays a role in their sentencing decisions. For instance, in one survey of federal judges, more than 80% said that

If allocution is risky for some defendants and of questionable value to the judge, why has it remained a regular part of sentencing hearings? The *ABA Standards for Criminal Justice* suggest one possibility: "The policy behind the right of allocution has more to do with maximizing the perceived equity of the process than with conveying information on which courts may rely in making findings of fact." AM. BAR ASS'N, STANDARDS FOR CRIMINAL JUSTICE std. 18–5.17 cmmnt. (3d ed. 1993).[7]

3. **Victim Allocution.** American practice has long accorded the defendant an opportunity to make a statement at sentencing. More recently, it has also become common for victims to be given a parallel opportunity to speak, as provided in Rule 32(i)(4)(B). We explore victims' rights in relation to sentencing later in this chapter.

4. **Role of Defense Counsel.** As we have already seen, the defendant's lawyer may have an important role to play in monitoring the presentence investigation, correcting or contextualizing harmful information in the PSR, and advising the defendant with respect to allocution. Yet, this hardly exhausts the services that counsel might provide in relation to sentencing. The *ABA Standards*, for instance, identify the following duties:

> Defense counsel should present to the court any ground which will assist in reaching a proper disposition favorable to the accused. If a presentence report or summary is made available to defense counsel, he or she should seek to verify the information contained in it and should be prepared to supplement or challenge if it necessary. If there is no presentence report or if it is not disclosed, defense counsel should submit to the court and the prosecutor all favorable information relevant to sentencing and in an appropriate case, with the consent of the accused, be prepared to suggest a program of rehabilitation based on defense counsel's exploration of employment, educational, and other opportunities made available by community services.

AM. BAR ASS'N, *supra*, std.4–8.1(b).

The commentary to this standard further specifies, "Where appropriate, counsel should also make every effort to assist his or her client in obtaining drug or alcohol counseling." Do you see why this might help the client to receive a more favorable sentencing outcome? But, on the other hand, do the *Standards* contemplate a set of sentencing-related duties for defense counsel that cross the line between lawyering and social work? Or, given the practical realities of the criminal justice system and the difficult life circumstances of most defendants, perhaps the notion of a line separating defense work from

---

allocution was at least "somewhat important" in their own determination of punishment. Mark W. Bennett & Ira P. Robbins, *Last Words: A Survey and Analysis of Federal Judges' Views on Allocution in Sentencing*, 65 ALA. L. REV. 735, 757 (2014).

7 Some critics object to the pressures placed on the allocuting defendant to stick to a standard contrition "script," when objections to injustices in the criminal legal system might be more in order. *See* M. Eve Hanan, *Talking Back in Court*, 96 WASH. L. REV. 493, 503 (2021) ("[T]he allocution is part of the play, a speech designed to validate the proceedings through the defendant's acceptance of the judgment and punishment."). *See also* M. CATHERINE GRUBER, "I'M SORRY FOR WHAT I'VE DONE": THE LANGUAGE OF COURTROOM APOLOGIES 160 (2014).

social work doesn't make sense. Might that have implications for the way that lawyers are trained?

What if defense counsel fails to prepare adequately for sentencing or to advocate effectively at the hearing? Should defendants ever be given a "do-over"? Later in this chapter, when we cover the defendant's constitutional rights at sentencing, we will consider whether and under what circumstances poor defense lawyering might violate the Sixth Amendment right to effective assistance of counsel.

5. **Role of Prosecutor.** In cases in which there is no joint recommendation as to the sentence, defense counsel can normally be expected to press for an outcome that is on the low end of what might reasonably be imposed. If not barred by a plea agreement, should the prosecutor respond in kind and press for a sentence on the high end? That would seem consistent with the generally adversarial structure of criminal litigation. However, the *ABA Standards* caution, prosecutors should not make sentence severity "the index" of their effectiveness; rather, the prosecutor "should seek to assure that a fair and informed judgment is made on the sentence and to avoid unfair sentence disparities." AM. BAR ASS'N, *supra*, std. 3–6.1.

How do you think a prosecutor should go about determining what position to take at sentencing? Should prosecutors focus on the same purposes of punishment as judges? Should it matter to the prosecutor that the victim wants a sentence at or near the maximum?

6. **Explanation of Sentence.** After the witnesses testify, the lawyers present their recommendations and arguments, and the defendant and victim offer whatever statements they wish to make, the judge customarily concludes the sentencing hearing by stating what the defendant's sentence will be. Typically, the judge also provides some explanation of the sentence by reference to the authorized purposes of punishment. However, the depth and analytical rigor of such explanations varies considerably from judge to judge and case to case. Sometimes, a sentence explanation is so thinly reasoned that the sentence is overturned on appeal, but such cases are quite rare.[8] With a lack of consistent appellate policing of the quality of sentence explanations, the Wisconsin Supreme Court has observed the persistence of a "mechanical form of sentencing": "for some [sentencing judges], merely uttering the facts, invoking sentencing factors, and pronouncing a sentence is deemed sufficient." *State v. Gallion*, 678 N.W.2d 197, 200, 205 (Wis. 2004). By contrast, the explanation in *United States v. Stern*, excerpted in Chapter 1, illustrates a more thoughtful effort to work through the purposes of punishment in a systematic fashion.[9]

---

[8] For two unusual examples, see United States v. Webb, 965 F.3d 262 (4th Cir. 2020); McCleary v. State, 182 N.W.2d 512 (Wis. 1971).

[9] For an argument that "the failure to expressly connect punishment with its purposes has devastating moral and practical effects," see Marah Stith McLeod, *Communicating Punishment*, 100 B.U. L. REV. 2263, 2267 (2020). Professor McLeod asserts,

> Most importantly, the act of giving reasons for punishment humanizes and dignifies offenders as reasoning beings. Because punishment involves moral condemnation as well as suffering, it carries a special risk of demeaning and dehumanizing offenders. The explanation of punishment helps counteract that risk by affirming the dignity of

7. **Factfinding and Sentencing Guidelines.** In the traditional, highly discretionary sentencing process, factfinding can have an amorphous quality. It is not always clear in advance what facts will be deemed important by the judge, nor even in retrospect what facts actually were relied on. For instance, a judge might impose a prison term based on "the need to protect the community from future crimes by this defendant" and allude in a general way to the defendant's "prior record" without specifically identifying what prior bad acts the judge found the defendant to have perpetrated. The defendant's rap sheet might, for example, include a couple of arrests that did not lead to the filing of criminal charges. The defendant might wonder if the judge used those arrests against her, and, if so, on what basis the judge determined that the alleged offenses actually occurred when they were never proven in court. And, indeed, the judge may not have made any self-conscious determination that the alleged offenses did occur, but instead used the arrests in a looser sense as a poor reflection on the defendant's character—further evidence that the defendant is a troublemaker or has a tendency to get mixed up in questionable activities, regardless of the truth of the specific allegations.

Guidelines can give the factfinding that occurs at sentencing a more focused, explicit quality. In a jurisdiction with sentencing guidelines, like the federal system, the lawyers are able to know in advance many of the facts that will be important in determining the sentence and can tailor their presentation of evidence and arguments accordingly. And, when the lawyers put specific facts into dispute that have a requisite weight in the sentencing calculus, the judge can be expected to resolve the dispute in a more-or-less transparent manner. Factfinding may be similarly influenced by the application of sentence enhancement statutes that raise the minimum or maximum sentence based on the existence of specified facts, such as the defendant having a certain number of prior convictions or the defendant's use of a firearm in the commission of the present offense.

As guidelines and enhancement statutes became a more widespread and important feature of American sentencing in the late twentieth century, and as sentencing factfinding accordingly became more self-conscious and explicit, increased attention was focused on the reliability and fairness of these factfinding processes. These processes tended to be much less formal, and with many fewer constitutional protections for defendants, than the factfinding that occurred in conventional criminal trials. Some critics argued that these differences were unjustifiable and that sentencing factfinding should incorporate more of the familiar trial-type procedural rights for defendants. (Note how Rule 32 takes a middle-ground position between the traditional informality of sentencing factfinding and a full-blown trial.) In the next part of this chapter, we will see that the advocates for enhanced constitutional protections had some success in the Supreme Court, but that this was mostly limited to the application of presumptive sentencing

---

> the offender as a reasoning moral agent whose suffering must be premised on legitimate goals.

Id. at 2267–68. Is it appropriate for judges to express anger? *See* Terry A. Maroney, *Angry Judges*, 65 VAND. L. REV. 1207, 1210 (2012).

guidelines and enhancement statutes. The factfinding that underlies discretionary sentencing choices is still only loosely regulated, at least as a matter of constitutional law, and, in many cases, continues to be more implicit than explicit.

8. **Jury Sentencing.** Our discussion of sentencing process has thus far assumed that the decider is a judge, and a judge alone. As we will discuss later in the chapter, in certain limited circumstances, the Constitution may require that a jury perform some kinds of sentencing factfinding. Additionally, juries are commonly involved in capital sentencing—also as a matter of constitutional right. Outside the capital context, though, juries in most U.S. jurisdictions rarely have any role to play after the determination of guilt. However, a half-dozen states (Virginia, Kentucky, Missouri, Arkansas, Texas, and Oklahoma) do authorize jury sentencing on a more generalized basis. Nancy J. King & Rosevelt L. Noble, *Felony Jury Sentencing in Practice: A Three-State Study*, 57 VAND. L. REV. 885, 886 (2004).

Professors Nancy King and Rosevelt Noble observe that jury sentencing in these states varies in some important ways:

> Jury sentencing states differ as to whether or not trial is bifurcated into guilt and punishment phases; whether or not the prosecutor can veto a defendant's choice to be sentenced by a judge instead of jury; whether or not judicial sentencing is bounded by sentencing guidelines; which felony offenses and offenders may be sentenced by juries; which sentencing options are available to jurors; whether or not the sentences that juries impose are subject to parole; and what information jurors are permitted to learn about punishment options, the offense, and the offender.

Id. at 891–92.

King and Noble argue that limitations on the information and options provided to sentencing juries may prevent them from serving effectively as a " 'community-based barometer' of punishment." *Id.* at 888. For instance, sentencing juries are often deprived of rehabilitation-oriented alternatives to incarceration that would be available to a sentencing judge. However, despite such limitations, King and Noble suggest that the institution of the sentencing jury may nonetheless play some useful functions. In particular, they note that fear of the severity of sentencing juries may encourage defendants to plead guilty or consent to a bench trial so as to avoid jury-sentencing, and that use of sentencing juries may spare elected judges from political accountability for sentences that are perceived as too lenient. *Id.* at 889. Do these seem good reasons to preserve the institution of jury sentencing? And why not provide sentencing juries with the full range of options given to sentencing judges? For an argument in support of non-binding "advisory" sentences by juries, see Kurt A. Holtzman, Comment, *Criminal Advisory Juries: A Sensible Compromise for Jury Sentencing Advocates*, 16 NW. J. L. & SOC. POL'Y 164 (2021).

9. **Aspirations and Realities.** Rule 32 seems to contemplate a well-informed, deliberative sentencing process, with ample opportunity for both

sides to present information to the judge and to challenge assertions made by the other side. However, the realities of sentencing in busy urban courtrooms may fall far short of such ideals. The following sentencing transcript—typical in some respects, unusual in others—illustrates some of the potential shortfalls.

State v. Taylor

Circuit Court for Milwaukee County
Case No. 2015-CF-1080
Sentencing Hearing
June 2, 2016

[The underlying facts in this case were described by an appellate court as follows:

> M.N., a City of Greenfield police officer, was on patrol in a marked squad car early on the morning of March 7, 2015. At approximately 2:15 a.m., he approached a vehicle idling in the parking lot of a closed Greenfield business and made contact with the driver. M.N. smelled marijuana and directed the driver, subsequently identified as Taylor, to remain in his vehicle. Taylor, however, began opening and closing the driver's-side door. M.N. called for backup from additional officers.
>
> As events unfolded, Taylor started driving, which "forced [M.N.] to jump into [Taylor's] vehicle to avoid being run over," and Taylor then drove his vehicle into M.N.'s squad car.
>
> M.N. struggled with Taylor inside his vehicle and eventually arrested him. M.N. sustained a cut to his face and abrasions to his leg and was conveyed to a hospital for treatment. A search of Taylor's vehicle incident to the arrest uncovered several grams of cocaine.
>
> The State charged Taylor with possession of cocaine, causing soft tissue injury to an officer while resisting the officer, and second-degree recklessly endangering safety as a repeat offender.
>
> To support the claim that Taylor was a repeat offender, the State alleged that Taylor had a prior conviction for second-degree recklessly endangering safety, and the State attached to the complaint in the instant matter a copy of a 2013 criminal complaint filed in Fond du Lac County. According to the 2013 complaint, Taylor fled from a traffic officer and led police on a high speed chase. When he finally stopped his vehicle, an officer approached Taylor's vehicle on foot. The officer's arms were "in the driver's door" when Taylor accelerated, dragging the officer some distance before the officer eventually fell onto the roadway within inches of the vehicle's tires. Taylor subsequently

abandoned his vehicle in a snowbank. When police searched the vehicle, they found twenty grams of marijuana.

In March 2016, Taylor decided to resolve the charges in the instant case with a plea agreement. Pursuant to its terms, he pled guilty to second-degree recklessly endangering safety as a repeat offender and to causing soft tissue damage to an officer while resisting the officer. The State agreed to recommend a global disposition of one and one-half years of initial confinement and four and one-half years of extended supervision. The State also moved to [dismiss] the charge of possessing cocaine.

State v. Taylor, 939 N.W.2d 883, 2020 WI App 10, ¶¶ 2–5 (2020). "Extended supervision" refers to a period of community supervision for the defendant following imprisonment. The defendant may be subject to a variety of conditions while on supervision, the violation of which may result in a return to prison.]

TRANSCRIPT OF PROCEEDINGS

[Proceedings commenced at 8:49 a.m.]

The Clerk: State of Wisconsin versus Kevin Taylor, 15-CF-1080. Appearances, please.

Ms. Parthum: Irene Parthum appearing for the State. Good morning, Your Honor.

Mr. Last: Mr. Taylor appears in person in custody with Attorney Matt Last. Good morning, Your Honor.

Ms. Parthum: Your Honor, the last time that we were here the defendant entered a plea. There was a stipulation to the amount of restitution that was being sought by the City of Greenfield * * * and that was in the amount of $2600. But the defendant was not stipulating to the amount of damage to the squad vehicle. And that was submitted by Captain Dave Patrick, who is now Assistant Chief Dave Patrick, who is present today. There is a restitution worksheet that has a request for $1542.10, and it has receipts attached for the parts and replacement.

And we did subpoena Assistant Chief Patrick. I appreciate him coming this morning on that issue. I was hoping we could take care of that first so he could go to his other duties and then we could proceed to sentencing, if that's acceptable to the Court and the other party. * * *

The Court: Fine. I'll hear from the chief from the department relative to restitution, please.

(Whereupon, Assistant Chief Dave Patrick was sworn and testified as follows.) * * *

DIRECT EXAMINATION

Q (Parthum): Thank you. Chief Patrick, how are you employed?

A (Patrick): I work for the City of Greenfield Police Department.
* * *

Q: And at the time that a victim impact statement was submitted in case number 15-CF-1080 regarding a Kevin Taylor, which was relative to a Greenfield Police Department report number 15-000701, were you ranked as a captain at that time?

A: I was.

Q: And did you submit a victim impact statement dated March 30th of 2015?

A: I did.

Q: Do you have a copy of that in front of you?

A: I do.

Q: And the victim impact statement that was submitted was regarding squad car damage and a push bar for a squad car with receipts totaling $1542.10. How did you arrive at that amount?

A: From the receipts—the actual receipts paid from Hiller Ford and—I believe it was John Paul's. Yeah, and John Paul's. * * *

Q: Okay. State doesn't have any further questions of this witness.

The Court: Counsel?

CROSS EXAMINATION

Q (Last): Just briefly. So regarding the damage to—it appears that there was damage to the push bar and to the actual squad itself. Is that correct?

A: That's correct. * * *

Q: Okay. And then regarding specifically the push bar, the damage to that, the push bar, did that need to be replaced altogether or were there just repairs that were done on the push bar?

A: It needed to be completely replaced.

Q: And do you know the extent of the damage to the push bar that would have required it to be completely replaced?

A: They get bent. I mean, we have to replace them. It seems like one out of three accidents they just get destroyed where the car can't be realigned—and the bolts—you know, once they take it off if the push bar is bent, they take it off to do the repairs to the front bumper. You know, nothing lines up anymore to put it back on. * * *

Mr. Last: Okay. I have nothing further. * * *

The Court: All right. You can step down, Officer. Thank you.

Ms. Parthum: Thank you. Chief.

As far as the offense is concerned, Your Honor, this was an incident that was charged for the prior DA on this caseload. There was a video. I don't know if the Court wishes to review that. I do have it in my file.

The defendant was parked in a lot of a closed business. Based upon that and the time of night—or I should say the time of morning. It was 2:12 a.m. that he was parked in this closed business at Layton Plaza on a strip mall. And the officer, being diligent in his duties, went to check that out and figure out if somebody was trying to break into this place. It was at the intersection of Layton and South 76th Street.

The officer approached and he was standing inside the area of the passenger door talking to the defendant. And the defendant threw the car into reverse and—rather forcefully. And so the car—Officer Noah had to jump into the car to avoid getting hit and run over by the car. He hit his head inside the car, cut his leg, got a bruise. As well, he had to be hospitalized. You see that the squad was damaged as well.

As it turns out, the defendant had money on his person and 2.86 grams of crack. That did not get charged by the issuing DA and I'm not certain why that was. But it's obviously good reason for the defendant to not want to come into custody of police officers.

[The prosecutor then described Taylor's 2013 case, which was resolved through a plea deal and resulted in four years of probation.]

So he got a pretty substantial reduction there. But it sounds pretty similar in nature as far as this incident where he tries to throw the car into reverse to basically get away from the police officer.

[The prosecutor then discussed a 2009 misdemeanor case in which Taylor pled guilty to criminal damage to property and received a two-year probationary sentence.]

I think under the circumstances the State's recommendation is fair. This was highly dangerous behavior. The defendant obviously was up to criminal behavior because he had cocaine on his person. He could have had that in addition charged. And the officer was placed in great risk. He suffered soft tissue injury as a result of this and he was in danger. And there was loss to the—to the City of Greenfield as well. When all the officer was doing was what we expect officers to do, what we ask them to do, at 2:00 in the morning when he's on his own and pretty much in a position of complete—wouldn't say helplessness; but he's certainly in a position where somebody else is up to no good and does something suddenly. He can get very badly injured and doesn't have a lot of people around there to be able to come to his aid.

So I think under the circumstances this is a prison case. I would ask the Court to make the restitution payable by withholding of 25% of prison wages for everything above and beyond the $2500 that was already posted [as bail]. It could have been forfeited to the county. But it was more important, I thought, to ask that it be held for restitution so that the city would be made whole because they have relatively finite resources as well. * * *

Thank you, Judge.

The Court: Thank you. Counsel?

Mr. Last: Thank you, Your Honor.

We would be on behalf of Mr. Taylor asking the Court to sentence him to a period of 13 to 14 months initial confinement followed by two to two-and-a-half years of extended supervision. Mr. Taylor recognizes that the actions in this case do warrant that additional incarceration is necessary. He's ready and willing to face up to that. He understands there needs to be a punishment component for his behavior and is willing to accept that today as he did when he entered into his pleas in this case.

Mr. Taylor is 23 years old, about to turn 24. This case has been pending since March of last year. Mr. Taylor was on supervision at the time this offense occurred. He subsequently waived his revocation hearing, was revoked on his supervision, and has been serving his sentence on that during the majority of this case. As counsel indicated, he did complete that sentence on February 16th of this year and since then has been out for a period of time on bail but has been in custody for a total of 93 days since that revocation is done. The revocation was for—not surprising—picking up the new criminal case and the allegations in this.

Mr. Taylor is a young man. He unfortunately is not someone who completed high school. He stopped going in the eleventh grade. The reason he stopped going to high school was at that time his girlfriend became pregnant and his daughter was born. Mr. Taylor made the decision to stop going to school and try to find employment so that he could help support his daughter. He subsequently has been working on finishing school. When I last spoke with Mr. Taylor, he indicated that he was four credits short of completing his GED. He has—while he was in custody on the revocation, he completed two of his tests. And I believe he has two tests remaining to obtain his GED. So he is working on that.

He's an individual who does have somewhat of a work history. As I indicated, he started working around the age of 17 when he was [in] the eleventh grade. He worked at McDonald's for a year. He was doing various jobs there. In addition to working at McDonald's for a year, he was also working at Precision Casting off and on for a period of two-and-a-half years. His role with that company dealt with—they did wax injections and he helped set up the dyes and he was the lead person on the second shift at his highest point working with them. He also did warehouse work for a company called Wisconsin Expo in Germantown, and he also worked various temp jobs.

While he was out on bail on this case after serving the revocation sentence for the period of time that he was out, he was working at a company called Bayers Cardboard Company in Waukesha. That was a temp service. He was making boxes, cardboard boxes there. And also working at Legacy Bakery in Waukesha.

So he's an individual who in his past before this case has showed a desire to work. While out on bail on this case, he's showed a desire to get back into work and provide for himself. He has indicated to me that upon his release, whenever that is, he does have a family friend who runs a temp agency and that family friend has indicated to Mr. Taylor that jobs will be available for him when he gets out.

Mr. Taylor does know that he likely is going to be remaining in custody today. He's prepared and ready for that. Upon his release, his plan is to reside with his mother in Milwaukee. She's indicated that he can stay with her while he gets back onto his feet, get some employment, start getting some money so that he can afford a place for himself.

He has expressed interest in—once he does complete his GED of trying to go to [technical college] and do a welding program there. That's something that he thinks would be interesting to him and something potentially he could do that would help support him.

He does have two children. His son is 3 now and his daughter is 5. Prior to being taken into custody, he was residing with his child's mother and they were living together at that time. Mr. Taylor was trying to get some money together so they could get a nice place together.

He did in his past have some [drug] issues, mostly marijuana. Mr. Taylor has expressed that he believes that he's past that point in his life. He wants to stay away from drugs. He wants to be employed, stay employed, and not be someone who's back in front of the court every year or two.

So for all those reasons, I would ask the Court to consider a sentence in this case of 13 to 14 months initial confinement followed by two to two-and-a-half years of extended supervision. I would ask the Court to grant Mr. Taylor the 93 days custody credit. Thank you, Your Honor.

Ms. Parthum: And if I misspoke, Your Honor, the count 3, it was not that it wasn't charged. That was the cocaine and that was [dismissed]. I'm sorry if I misspoke.

The Court: Right. Counsel, what's your client's position on the restitution?

Mr. Last: Your Honor, the restitution as to the medical expenses we would stipulate to. We have no issue paying those. As to the squad damage, I would just ask the Court, the issue that Mr. Taylor has is the dollar amount from looking at the pictures and the testimony. I guess the main issue more for us is the push bar having to be completely replaced, so I would ask the Court to consider restitution in the amount of just the damage to that for the vehicle itself.

The Court: Does your client want to make a statement?

Mr. Last: No, Your Honor.

The Court: Any family members want to make a statement?

Mr. Last: No, Your Honor.

The Court: For the record, the Court has reviewed the documentation in the file and I've read the complaint. I also read the attached complaint which was from the 2013 case. The 2013 case, as the State noted is very, very similar to this case. That's the case where he was also ultimately convicted of recklessly endangering safety.

In fashioning a fair and appropriate sentence, the Court's looking at the gravity of the offense, the defendant's character, the need to protect the public, along with things like punishment, deterrence, and rehabilitation.

Looking at the defendant's character, I'd say it's, at best, poor. I'm being charitable when I say it's poor. We have someone who's 22 years old when this offense occurred. He's 23 now. He has multiple criminal contacts, multiple criminal violations. At the time of this offense, he's on supervision for a case that, when reading the 2013 complaint in Fond du Lac County, is very, very similar. For instance, in some ways, they're almost borderline identical. Nothing's identical, but they're very similar.

In that case, in 2013, he gets stopped by a police officer when he's speeding, at one point in time, 70-plus miles an hour in a 55 zone, and another time 75 miles an hour in a 45 mile zone. And upon requesting the driver to exit the vehicle, the driver put his vehicle in drive and sped away. In this case, he put the vehicle in reverse and attempted to speed away. That would be what they refer to as a distinction without a difference.

As the State noted going back all the way to 2009, so seven years, he was convicted of misdemeanor criminal damage to property. So basically from the minute Mr. Taylor's been treated as an adult—in Wisconsin, age 17—through today, through this offense, he's been breaking the law and committing dangerous acts; not so much the criminal damage to property, of course, but two counts of recklessly endangering safety, both times involving police officers, both times involving some form of fleeing; maybe not technically fleeing, but some at least common sense version of fleeing an officer.

In this case, he injures an officer, fortunately not severely. But he slams his car in reverse when the second officer approaches the vehicle. The officer, sadly, but somewhat ironically, ends up having to jump out of the way by getting into the defendant's vehicle. The defendant still doesn't stop until the officer basically gains control, I'm sure by overpowering Mr. Taylor of the shifter, and slams the car's brakes and puts the car in park. A very, very dangerous situation.

In terms of Mr. Taylor's character, he obviously has no respect for authority, no respect in particular for police. It's painfully evident. He's been raised poorly. Anyone who's done all these things by his age, all these crimes, all these offenses—some people maybe make mistakes. But Mr. Taylor is making them over and over and over again.

He pled guilty in this case. He gets some credit for that. He has a sporadic work history, so that's somewhat positive. On the other hand, he sits on his revocation on the other case, bails out. I'm sure it was not his money. And then [violates a bail condition], ends up back in custody, once again proving he has no respect for authority, for officers, for judges, for the courts, or anyone.

Mr. Taylor is a serious danger to the community. If Mr. Taylor were released today or tomorrow, I'm confident that he would within the next probably few weeks, if not few months, be out having drugs in his possession. In this case it was noted the possession of cocaine was dismissed. He also at the time of the stop had marijuana in his car or at least marijuana roaches and blunts. Not surprisingly in his 2013 case, he had THC, marijuana, and possession of drug paraphernalia in that case. Those were at least the charges. It looks like they were dismissed. But he had drugs in that case as well.

Not graduated from high school. He's not completed a GED. But he has managed to impregnate—is it one or two women, counsel?

Mr. Last: One, Your Honor. And Your Honor, if I may—

The Court: No. You're done.

Mr. Taylor is a menace to society. He's a threat—and he sits here shaking his head and rolling his eyes at me as if, "Who cares what the judge says," and "How can you say that, Judge?" He sits here and forces his attorney to bring in an officer from the Department of Greenfield to squabble over $400 in restitution. That is a sure sign of lack of respect for authority and lack of accountability, lack of apology. There's been no apology in this case, no accountability, no showing of remorse whatsoever. * * *

He has pled guilty. I recognize that. That's a positive. He's had some sporadic temp jobs. That's a positive. Sporadic work over the last number of years. He has two children. I really don't have anything to say about that in particular.

* * * He caused approximately $1500 in damages to the car and about $1600 approximately in medical bills for the emergency room, x-rays, and medical bills to the officer. That should not be lost either in terms of the gravity of this offense, the fact that he injured a police officer. * * *

I think Mr. Taylor is, as I said, a danger to the public. He's likely to reoffend. Not just possibility to reoffend, which I guess everyone is in some sense or in some way, shape, or form. But he's likely to reoffend. He needs to be punished. He needs to be incarcerated. He needs to be rehabilitated, but his rehabilitation needs to be in an institutional setting.

And, frankly, he deserves more punishment than the State is recommending. He's facing ten years on the second-degree reckless injury, six years on the resisting an officer. Mr. Taylor certainly needs to go to prison and pay, literally and figuratively, for his actions. At some point hopefully in the next number of years, Mr. Taylor will mature and stop breaking the law. I think, candidly, that's doubtful. I'm skeptical of whether or not that's gonna happen. Hopefully the [Department of Corrections] and his time in custody can have some effect on Mr. Taylor, who again, shows no remorse; if anything, shows disdain as he sits here for the entire process, squabbles over $400 in restitution, restitution that some of which will be governed by the bail which the Court kept. Some will be covered hopefully by his prison wages, earnings, or funds. But restitution he'll certainly have to pay.

For someone that now is on his second serious felony at the age of 23, multiple criminal contacts, multiple criminal convictions, injures a police officer, shows no remorse whatsoever, which is a negative, squabbles over restitution. When you're gonna have a total restitution in the thousands of dollars he's worried about $400 and whether or not the push bar for the squad needed to be replaced or damaged or whether we can just touch it up with paint, preposterous. And it speaks to Mr. Taylor's utter lack of character, utter lack of empathy. Utter lack of maturity.

I'm sentencing Mr. Taylor as follows. On his first count of second-degree reckless injury, six years in prison; three years of initial confinement, three years of extended supervision. That count and that sentence is consecutive to any other case, consecutive to any other sentence.

On count 2, he's sentenced to two years in prison; one year of initial confinement, one year of extended supervision. I'm not gonna let him injure an officer and think it's a joke, which is where this matter currently stands. That matter is consecutive.

He's going to serve a total of four years in custody, four years of extended supervision. With all due respect to the DA's Office, that negotiation or that recommendation in this case was light.

* * * The conditions of extended supervision are as follows. First of all, he's not allowed to operate a motor vehicle unless he has a valid driver's license. But he's not even allowed to operate any motor vehicle for at least two years while he's on extended supervision. He should never be behind the wheel. He's a danger to the community and a danger when he sets foot in a car. Whether it's rolling joints in the front seat, having cocaine, allegedly or apparently, or the way he operates his vehicle. No driving of any vehicles and no allowance for him to have a license for the first two years of extended supervision. After that, no operating a vehicle without a valid driver's license.

He's to have [drug assessment and] treatment. He's to have random drug tests and random urine screens, also random breathalyzers. While he's on extended supervision he's to complete a GED or HSED. He's to pay all costs, fees, and surcharges. He's to cooperate with the Department of Corrections. He's to be employed full-time. That means a minimum of 40 hours per week. Not 35 hours, not 36—40 hours per week. If he's not employed 40 hours per week, I expect him occupied 40 hours per week in a vocational training program or he can be doing some of the 250 hours of community service which is also added as part of his sentence; 250 hours which is lenient as that works out to less than ten hours a month, more like five hours a month, while he's on extended supervision. 250 hours of community service.

* * * While he's in prison I'm authorizing up to 25% of his prison wages, earnings, funds, or monies of any sort—not just his wages—but any money that's put in his books, anything he earns; 25% of that goes first to restitution, then to costs, fees, and surcharges. Any restitution that's not been paid or costs, fees, and surcharges that are not paid during the term of extended supervision results in a civil judgment.

Because this matter is a felony, Mr. Taylor, you're not allowed to own or possess a firearm or handgun ever for the rest of your life. You are also not allowed to vote in any election until your civil rights are restored. They will be restored after you've completely served your entire sentence. But until then you're not allowed to vote in any election. And you are not allowed to own or possess a firearm, a gun, at any time for the rest of your life.

* * * I'm keeping the $2,500 bail [for restitution]. The money, about $150, that was confiscated is also kept by the Court and used [for restitution]. * * *

[Proceedings concluded at 9:31 a.m.]

NOTES & QUESTIONS

1. **A Well-Informed Decision?** No PSR was prepared in *Taylor*, and neither side submitted a sentencing memorandum to the court in advance of the hearing. Note, too, that the sentencing judge was new to the case, filling in for a different judge who had handled the change of plea hearing and other pretrial matters. Without any prior involvement in the case, on what sources of information did the judge rely? Do these seem adequate to you?

2. **Factfinding, Witness Testimony, and Vindictiveness.** For the most part, the facts in *Taylor* were uncontested, both as to the crime and the defendant's background. There was, however, something of a factual dispute regarding the need to replace the push bar on the damaged squad car. (A push bar allows a squad car to break through barriers or to move damaged vehicles.) Note the prosecutor's use of live witness testimony to resolve the dispute.

Note, too, the judge's evident displeasure with the defendant for raising the issue, which the judge interprets as "a sure sign of lack of respect for authority." Does it seem to you that Taylor may have been penalized for challenging the state's restitution claim? If so, does that possibility trouble you? These questions may remind you of the discussion of the "trial penalty" phenomenon from Chapter 1, i.e., the tendency for defendants who are convicted at trial to receive more severe sentences than otherwise similar defendants who plead guilty.

On appeal, Taylor argued that his sentence was improperly increased as punishment for his restitution challenge. However, the appellate court determined that the sentencing judge had "directly linked" Taylor's conduct in raising the challenge to Taylor's "character and lack of remorse," which were proper sentencing factors. 2020 WI App 10, ¶¶ 18–21. On that basis, Taylor's sentence was affirmed. Does the appellate court's approach make it too easy for vindictive judges to punish defendants for exercising their litigation rights at sentencing? Isn't it always possible to characterize any litigation efforts by the defendant as indicating a "lack of remorse"? The appellate court did, however, deliver a light rebuke to the sentencing judge in a footnote, "remind[ing] the circuit court to choose its words with care when imposing sentence to ensure that the defendant fully understands the reasoning underlying the sentencing decision." *Id.* ¶ 27 n.4.

3. **Prosecutor's Role.** On what sorts of information did the prosecutor focus in her presentation? How did this information differ from that presented by defense counsel? Do you think the prosecutor should have addressed other aspects of the defendant's background besides his criminal history? What was the prosecutor's sentencing recommendation? How well do you think she supported that recommendation? What purpose or purposes of punishment seem emphasized by the prosecutor?

4. **Defense Lawyer's Role.** What do you think the defense lawyer was trying to accomplish in his presentation to the court? What was his sentencing recommendation? How well do you think he supported the recommendation? Do you think it was wise for Taylor to decline his opportunity to make a statement himself?

5. **The Plea Bargain.** What were the terms of Taylor's plea deal? Did he receive the anticipated benefit from the bargain? The judge seems to have shown little deference to the state's sentence recommendation. Would you have given that recommendation greater weight if you were the judge?

6. **The Sentence.** What sentence did the judge impose? What purposes of punishment seemed paramount in the judge's mind, and what factual considerations were most heavily emphasized? How well do you think the judge justified the sentence? What sentence would you have imposed?

7. **Character.** The judge seemed to place great emphasis on the defendant's character. On what basis did the judge determine the defendant's character to be "poor"? Do these seem adequate grounds? And why should poor character matter at sentencing anyway? Is the term simply used as a synonym for recidivism risk? If not, what business does the criminal justice system have punishing on the basis of bad character? If you have studied evidence law, you will appreciate that character evidence is permitted at trial in only very limited forms for very limited purposes. *See* Fed. R. Evid. 404, 405. Character may be far more open for exploration and evaluation at sentencing, although the reasons why character is regarded as

relevant to punishment are not always articulated very clearly. Should we concerned about the possibility that character judgments may be influenced by such problematic factors as socioeconomic status, race, ethnicity, sex, age, or mental illness?

8. **Family Responsibilities.** As we will see in Chapter 4, a defendant's family responsibilities are sometimes regarded as a mitigating factor at sentencing. Taylor, however, received no apparent benefit from his parental responsibilities, which were noted by the judge, if anything, in a disparaging fashion. Should having children ever be treated as an *aggravating* sentencing factor? Would that conflict with a fundamental right to procreate? *Cf. Skinner v. Oklahoma ex rel. Williamson,* 316 U.S. 535 (1942) (overturning state law requiring sterilization of certain individuals on the basis of criminal convictions).

9. **Conditions of Supervision.** At a felony sentencing, attention is usually focused on the questions of whether the defendant will be imprisoned and, if so, for how long. However, the judge also normally establishes conditions for community supervision, either as an aspect of a probation sentence in lieu of imprisonment or as a second phase of the sentence that occurs after release from prison. These conditions may eventually prove highly consequential to the defendant, not least of all because their violation may result in the defendant's return to prison. Taylor, himself, for instance, was revoked from probation and imprisoned for his earlier, 2013 felony conviction.

What conditions were set by the judge in Taylor's 2016 sentence? Do these seem well-justified to you?

In setting conditions of release, sentencing judges often seem to enter that gray zone between measures specifically intended to prevent repeat criminal offending and more generalized efforts to improve the defendant's character and life prospects. How convinced are you that getting a GED and working 40 hours per week—"not 35 hours, not 36"—will materially reduce Taylor's recidivism risk? We will consider conditions of release in more detail below in Chapter 8.

10. **Follow the Money.** Court records indicate that Taylor was ordered to pay $4,083.27 in all. Note the efforts undertaken by both the prosecutor and the judge at sentencing to set up a structure for payment of the financial aspects of the sentence. Most of this sum reflected restitution awards in favor of parties that could, at least in principle, sue Taylor civilly for compensation for their economic losses. By virtue of the sentence, however, the court assumes responsibility for securing their reimbursement. In a sense, the criminal justice system becomes a collection agency.

Given the impoverished state of many defendants, obtaining full repayment of fines, restitution, court costs, and so forth can be difficult or impossible. (Taylor himself was represented by a court-appointed lawyer, indicating that he was too poor to afford a lawyer on his own.) Although many imprisoned defendants have opportunities to work for pay while incarcerated, the compensation rates tend to be quite low. For instance, at the institution where Taylor served much of his prison sentence, pay rates ranged from $0.12 to $0.42 per hour. FOX LAKE CORRECTIONAL INSTITUTION, INMATE HANDBOOK AND RESOURCE GUIDE 36 (2012). As of mid-2021, court records indicated that Taylor still owed $1,064.73 from the amount assessed at his 2016 sentencing. The financial aspects of sentencing are considered in more detail below in Chapter 9.

4. MISDEMEANOR SENTENCING

Law school courses, like the media and the public, tend to focus on felony, rather than misdemeanor, processes, which is understandable for a number of reasons. (The technical definitions vary somewhat from state to state, but "felonies" are conventionally understood to be those criminal offenses that carry a potential term of incarceration exceeding one year, while "misdemeanors" are those offenses carrying lesser penalties.) Few law students dream of someday litigating or adjudicating misdemeanors. Indeed, in some states, much of the misdemeanor-level caseload is managed in courts in which defense lawyers rarely appear and in which even the individuals filling the roles of prosecutor and judge may not be legally trained.[10] Legal professionals, to the extent they are involved in the misdemeanor process, tend to view the cases as low-stakes affairs that rarely warrant large investments of time and effort. Many misdemeanor defendants themselves also often have a "let's get it over with" mentality, especially if they are unable to make bail and are thus stuck behind bars while their cases are pending. And in the relatively few cases in which the defendant is ready, willing, and able to fight the charge tooth and nail, the formal litigation process tends to be considerably more streamlined and with fewer procedural rights for defendants than in felony cases—and hence to provide considerably less grist for law school casebooks.

Although the average misdemeanor case may seem far less consequential than the average felony case, the cumulative importance of misdemeanor cases to the American criminal justice system—and indeed to American society more broadly—should not be underestimated. There are about 13 million misdemeanor cases filed annually in the United States, which is more than triple the number of felony cases.

---

[10] Lawyer-free proceedings are especially associated with municipal courts. Such courts—also known by a variety of other names, including "police court" and "town court"—are established by units of local government and operate with varying degrees of independence from the regular state court system. They are typically given jurisdiction over misdemeanor cases and municipal ordinance violations. One recent study found about 7,500 municipal courts in thirty states, collectively handling more than 3.5 million nontraffic misdemeanor cases annually. Alexandra Natapoff, *Criminal Municipal Courts*, 134 HARV. L. REV. 964, 966 (2021). Rules vary from state to state, and sometimes within states, as to whether municipal court prosecutors and judges must be attorneys.

The Supreme Court has indicated that municipal courts may be excused from some of the usual constitutional criminal process requirements if the convicted defendant is given an opportunity to request a trial *de novo* in a higher court. North v. Russell, 427 U.S. 328, 337 (1976). However, the available data suggest that fewer than 1% of municipal court misdemeanor convictions are appealed in this manner, Nancy J. King & Michael Heise, *Misdemeanor Appeals*, 99 B.U. L. REV. 1933, 1943–44 (2019), which means there may be little effective check on the power of those municipal courts that are operating outside constitutional due-process norms.

Sandra G. Mayson & Megan T. Stevenson, *Misdemeanors by the Numbers*, 61 B.C. L. REV. 971, 975 (2020). (This figure excludes non-DUI traffic offenses, which are treated as criminal in some states, but not in others.) The sentence in most of these cases will include some combination of fine, court fees, probation, and/or term of incarceration of one month or less. *See id.* at 1012–13 (summarizing misdemeanor sentencing data from eight jurisdictions).

Such penalties, it should be emphasized, can have a devastating impact on people, especially the poor and working-class individuals who are so disproportionately represented in misdemeanor dockets, and on their families. As Professors Sandra Mayson and Megan Stevenson observe, "Probation is intrusive, and failure to comply with all conditions of probation can land a person back in jail. Even short jail sentences can be highly destabilizing: a few days in jail can lead a person to lose her job, housing, or custody of her children." *Id.* at 974. A failure to pay fines and fees can also result in jailing. Moreover, a misdemeanor conviction may also trigger various burdensome "collateral consequences." Depending on the jurisdiction and the offense, these consequences might include loss of eligibility for government aid programs, loss of driver's license, loss of eligibility to work in certain fields, triggering of sex offender registration and community notification (i.e., "Megan's Laws"), and deportation. (Collateral consequences of criminal convictions are considered in more detail below in Chapter 11.) Finally, a defendant's misdemeanor record increases the likelihood that any subsequent arrest will be prosecuted as a felony.

In relation to punishment, five overlapping aspects of the misdemeanor process warrant closer consideration at present. First, the amount of court and lawyer time devoted to each case tends to be relatively low, with correspondingly less generation of sentencing-relevant information regarding the defendant and the crime. For instance, one recent study found a misdemeanor trial rate of less than 1% in seven of the eight jurisdictions evaluated. Mayson & Stevenson, *supra*, at 1004 n.118. Also, in seven of the eight, more than three-quarters of the cases were resolved within six months of filing, with a substantial minority resolved within two weeks. *Id.* at 1004. Another study of twenty-one counties in Florida found that almost 70% of defendants pled guilty at their first appearance in court, and more than 80% of these arraignments were completed in three minutes or less. ALISA SMITH & SEAN MADDAN, NAT'L ASS'N CRIM. DEFENSE LAWYERS, THREE-MINUTE JUSTICE: HASTE AND WASTE IN FLORIDA'S MISDEMEANOR COURTS 15 (2011).

Similarly, Professor Issa Kohler-Hausmann's study of New York City found that about two-thirds of misdemeanors in the early 2000s were disposed of at arraignment, which usually occurred within twenty-four hours of arrest. MISDEMEANORLAND: CRIMINAL COURTS AND SOCIAL CONTROL IN AN AGE OF BROKEN WINDOWS POLICING 124–25 (2018). In a typical six-hour shift, a court would handle between 100 and 200 arraignments. Prosecutors would spend about two to five minutes reviewing the paperwork for each case before deciding on a plea offer. For their part, defense lawyers often met their clients for the first time at arraignment, sometimes speaking for just a few minutes in a small interview room or a hallway in the courthouse.

How will the information available to the lawyers and judge in the cases described by Kohler-Hausmann differ from, say, what you saw above in the *United States v. Smith* PSR—or even in the *State v. Taylor* sentencing? What are the implications of these information gaps for the determination of an appropriate punishment?

Second, in many cases, the defendant has no attorney at all, or an attorney who cannot realistically be expected to present a robust mitigation case to the prosecutor or judge. The federal constitution guarantees a court-appointed lawyer for indigent defendants in all felony cases, but only in some misdemeanor cases.[11] Many, but not all, states provide a broader right to counsel than the federal minimum. However, researchers have documented a variety of significant impediments to defendants' ability to exercise whatever right to counsel they may have, including application fees, counsel fees, lack of notice of the right, and the need to make a second trip to court in order to obtain a lawyer. DIANE DEPIETROPAOLO PRICE ET AL., NAT'L ASS'N CRIM. DEFENSE LAWYERS, SUMMARY INJUSTICE: A LOOK AT CONSTITUTIONAL DEFICIENCIES IN SOUTH CAROLINA'S SUMMARY COURTS 11–12 (2016); SMITH & MADDAN, *supra*, at 15, 18. Thus, for instance, in the Florida study noted above, two-thirds of the defendants appeared without a lawyer at arraignment—the crucial court proceeding at which the great majority of cases were resolved. SMITH & MADDAN, *supra*, at 15. Meanwhile, a different study of misdemeanor cases in Virginia found that only about 55% to 60% of defendants were represented. Mayson & Stevenson, *supra*, at 1002. With all of these unrepresented defendants, do prosecutors and judges need to think differently about the nature of *their* roles? On the other hand, it does seem that misdemeanor representation is much closer to universal in some other jurisdictions. *Id.*

Yet, even in those jurisdictions, having a lawyer is not necessarily the same thing as having an *effective* lawyer. Despite the significant short- and long-term adverse consequences of misdemeanor convictions, misdemeanor criminal defense is notorious for its "meet 'em and plead 'em" practitioners who put only minimal time into their cases and develop little sense of the potential mitigation arguments that might be made in plea bargaining or at sentencing. This form of practice results, in no small part, from the enormous caseloads that confront defense lawyers in some jurisdictions. As Professor Alexandra Natapoff points out, "The American

---

[11] The right to counsel attaches in those misdemeanor cases in which a term of incarceration is imposed, whether or not the sentence is suspended. Alabama v. Shelton, 535 U.S. 654 (2002).

Bar Association recommends that no lawyer maintain a caseload of more than three hundred misdemeanor cases per year. But in Dallas, public defenders juggle 1,200 misdemeanors a year; in Chicago, Atlanta, and Miami, annual caseloads exceed 2,000." ALEXANDRA NATAPOFF, PUNISHMENT WITHOUT CRIME: HOW OUR MASSIVE MISDEMEANOR SYSTEM TRAPS THE INNOCENT AND MAKES AMERICA MORE UNEQUAL 68–69 (2018). In such circumstances, it may be hard to make the time for even one substantial conversation with the client, let alone interview family members or others who might provide helpful information. On the other hand, even if defense counsel could collect substantially more information about their cases and clients, it cannot be assumed that the prosecutors and judges in misdemeanor courts, who often face intense docket pressures of their own, would be willing and able to give careful attention to whatever defense counsel might like to say by way of mitigation.[12]

Third, pretrial detention looms large as a determinant of misdemeanor punishment. This is true in at least two senses. First, the detention that occurs while the defendant's case is pending will often be the only incarceration that the defendant experiences in relation to a misdemeanor charge. Although this period in custody is not formally framed as "punishment," that fine point of law may be lost on many defendants, who often find themselves held in the same grim facilities that are also used to hold sentenced defendants. Moreover, even as a formal matter, pretrial detention can retroactively become punishment if the judge imposes a "time served" sentence. Second, pretrial detention exerts pressure on the defendant to accept whatever plea deal is offered by the prosecutor, especially if the defendant expects to receive no additional incarceration in the sentence. In such cases, acceptance of the plea deal offers the hope of immediate freedom—a powerful inducement to plea, given the harsh conditions often experienced in jail, as well as the fears of job loss, housing loss, and other potential costs of protracted detention. It should not be a surprise, for instance, that the Florida study found that the single most important predictor of whether a defendant would plead guilty at arraignment was whether the defendant was in custody. SMITH & MADDAN, *supra*, at 15.

---

[12] Whether represented or not, Professor M. Eve Hanan observes that the defendant only rarely "talks back" to the judge in misdemeanor cases. *Talking Back in Court*, 96 WASH. L. REV. 493 (2021). By this, she means that defendants are normally compliant and refrain from speaking in ways "that might disrupt or challenge authority," as by asserting that a fine would impose an unfair hardship on the defendant's family. *Id.* at 496. Hanan attributes defendant acquiescence not only to fear that the judge might punish "talking back" with a harsher sentence, but also to the subtle pressures created by courtroom culture; "[d]isplaying orderliness and agreeability is paramount in courtrooms." *Id.* at 558. Hanan notes, moreover, that defense lawyers "are susceptible to the same power dynamics as defendants." *Id.* at 559. Are there reasons to wish that defendants and defense lawyers felt freer to talk back? *See id.* at 501 ("Silence prevents defendants from contesting aspects of the proceedings that are unfair or harmful to them. This may lead to worse outcomes in their cases . . . . Talking back illuminates criminal legal practices that are unjust, serving as an important check on institutional power.").

Pretrial detention practices vary considerably by jurisdiction. In some places, the majority of arrested defendants are released without having to post bond; in others, virtually no defendants get out without putting up money. Mayson & Stevenson, *supra*, at 1009. When bond is required, the amounts in misdemeanor cases are often under $1000, but even that level may be impossible for many defendants to meet. One study of Philadelphia, Louisville, and rural Kentucky found that, even with bond amounts of $500 or less, close to half of defendants remained in custody for at least three days. *Id.* at 1010. Given the importance of pretrial detention to the resolution of misdemeanor cases, doesn't it appear that socioeconomic status may be playing an uncomfortably large role in determining punishment severity?

Fourth, in a large share of misdemeanor cases, there is no formal imposition of sentence. Again, practices vary wildly, but in some jurisdictions, diversions, dismissals, and deferred adjudications are the norm. Thus, for instance, one study found a misdemeanor conviction rate of only 27% in Chicago and 38% in San Antonio. *Id.* at 1005. In New York City, the conviction rate is under 20%. KOHLER-HAUSMANN, *supra*, at 68. If there is no conviction, there is, as a formal matter, no sentence. Does this mean there is no punishment? Not necessarily.

Fifth, to a great extent in many misdemeanor cases, "the process is the punishment." This phrase was Professor Malcolm Feeley's famous characterization of the misdemeanor court in New Haven, Connecticut, in the 1970s. THE PROCESS IS THE PUNISHMENT: HANDLING CASES IN A LOWER CRIMINAL COURT (1979). What was true in New Haven a half-century ago remains true in many courthouses across the country today. With or without a conviction and sentence, being a misdemeanor defendant can be a quite unpleasant experience. This is most obviously true for those defendants who are stuck in jail for any significant period of time while their cases are pending. But even for those who are not arrested, or who manage a prompt release, the burdens of the process may be substantial. Court dates are apt to involve a lot of waiting around and may be highly inconvenient for defendants who have inflexible job or family responsibilities. Court personnel, sometimes including the defendant's own court-appointed lawyer, may treat the defendant in a brusque or demeaning fashion. The defendant may feel compelled to hire a private lawyer or be required to bear other fees, such as a bail bondsman's fee or an application fee for a public defender. Moreover, the dismissal of charges is often conditioned on a defendant's participation in some form of programming, such as an anger management course or drug treatment. Programming of this sort may involve yet more meetings at inconvenient times and places, the payment of yet more fees, and perhaps additional burdens, such as regular drug testing for several weeks or months. To be sure, all of these sorts of burdens are often experienced in felony cases, too. However, they may be more important to take into account in the misdemeanor context because they are more likely to approach or even exceed the burdens associated with the formally imposed sentence.

In this chapter, we are primarily concerned with the processes that are, or ideally should be, followed *prior to* the determination of punishment, either to enhance the substantive quality of the sentencing decision or to enhance the perceived fairness and legitimacy of the decision. The "process as punishment" perspective presents a challenge to this way of thinking. The sorts of burdens we are considering here are routinely imposed with very few, if any, due-process protections. If these burdens constitute most or all of what defendants normally experience as punishment in a misdemeanor court, does that reality trigger a responsibility on the part of the lawyers and judges to be ever-mindful of these burdens, to minimize the gratuitous indignities and inconveniences of the process, and to take care that the most substantial burdens—such as programs involving many required meetings—are only imposed in cases in which they are justified in light of the recognized purposes of punishment? Or are these unrealistic expectations in the sort of high-volume misdemeanor courtrooms that Kohler-Hausmann describes?

The latter question may, in turn, prompt consideration of whether current misdemeanor caseloads are justified. Of particular concern is the prosecution of offenses that are widely regarded as involving little or no inherent harm or danger, such as marijuana possession, trespass, or disorderly conduct—especially to the extent that these prosecutions seem to focus disproportionately on racial or ethnic minority groups. In their study of misdemeanor cases in eight varied jurisdictions, Mayson and Stevenson found that four offenses constituted the majority of cases in most of the jurisdictions: DUI, assault, theft, and marijuana possession. Mayson & Stevenson, *supra*, at 1009. They characterize the first three as "mini-felonies" and suggest that they "seem relatively objective in the scheme of things." *Id.* at 1021. The prevalence of these offenses may arguably cut against the view of misdemeanor prosecutions as a system for maintaining control over marginalized social groups without regard to traditional criminal-law notions of individual culpability and proportionate punishment. On the other hand, marijuana possession charges may cut the other way. Mayson and Stevenson also observed "sizable numbers of . . . public-order cases, including disorderly conduct, resisting arrest, and trespass," which may further heighten concerns. *Id.* at 1022.

B. CONSTITUTIONAL PROCEDURAL RIGHTS AT SENTENCING

Given all of the jurisdiction-to-jurisdiction variations we have noted, you might wonder whether the Constitution sets any minimal requirements for sentencing procedure that must be observed across all U.S. jurisdictions. Prior to 2000, a reasonable answer might have been, "Yes, but the constitutional rights in this area are so sparse and weak as to warrant little discussion." Since then, the answer has grown considerably more complex. Before turning to the more recent cases, though, we will consider the Supreme Court's important decision in *Williams v. New York*, which set the tone for constitutional rights at sentencing for much of the twentieth century.

1. RIGHT TO CONFRONT ACCUSERS

Williams v. New York

337 U.S. 241 (1949)

■ BLACK, J.

A jury in a New York state court found appellant guilty of murder in the first degree. The jury recommended life imprisonment, but the trial judge imposed sentence of death. In giving his reasons for imposing the death sentence the judge discussed in open court the evidence upon which the jury had convicted stating that this evidence had been considered in the light of additional information obtained through the court's "Probation Department, and through other sources." * * *

The Court of Appeals of New York affirmed the conviction and sentence over the contention that as construed and applied the controlling penal statutes are in violation of the due process clause of the Fourteenth Amendment of the Constitution of the United States "in that the sentence of death was based upon information supplied by witnesses with whom the accused had not been confronted and as to whom he had no opportunity for cross-examination or rebuttal." * * *

The narrow contention here makes it unnecessary to set out the facts at length. The record shows a carefully conducted trial lasting more than two weeks in which appellant was represented by three appointed lawyers who conducted his defense with fidelity and zeal. The evidence proved a wholly indefensible murder committed by a person engaged in a burglary. The judge instructed the jury that if it returned a verdict of guilty as charged, without recommendation for life sentence, "The Court must impose the death penalty," but if such recommendation was made, "the Court may impose a life sentence." The judge went on to emphasize that "the Court is not bound to accept your recommendation."

About five weeks after the verdict of guilty with recommendation of life imprisonment, and after a statutory pre-sentence investigation report to the judge, the defendant was brought to court to be sentenced. Asked what he had to say, appellant protested his innocence. After each of his three lawyers had appealed to the court to accept the jury's recommendation of a life sentence, the judge gave reasons why he felt that the death sentence should be imposed. He narrated the shocking details of the crime as shown by the trial evidence, expressing his own complete belief in appellant's guilt. He stated that the pre-sentence investigation revealed many material facts concerning appellant's background which though relevant to the question of punishment could not properly have been brought to the attention of the jury in its consideration of the question of guilt. He referred to the experience appellant "had had on thirty other burglaries in and about the same vicinity" where the murder had been committed. The appellant had not been convicted of these burglaries although the judge had information that he had confessed to some and had been identified as the perpetrator of some of the others. The judge also referred to certain activities of appellant as shown by the probation report that indicated appellant possessed "a morbid sexuality" and classified him as a "menace to society." The accuracy of the statements made by the judge as to appellant's background and past practices were not challenged by appellant or his counsel, nor was the judge asked to disregard any of them or to afford appellant a chance to refute or discredit any of them by cross-examination or otherwise.

The case presents a serious and difficult question. The question relates to the rules of evidence applicable to the manner in which a judge may obtain information to guide him in the imposition of sentence upon an already convicted defendant. Within limits fixed by statutes, New York judges are given a broad discretion to decide the type and extent of punishment for convicted defendants. Here, for example, the judge's discretion was to sentence to life imprisonment or death. To aid a judge in exercising this discretion intelligently the New York procedural policy encourages him to consider information about the convicted person's past life, health, habits, conduct, and mental and moral propensities. The sentencing judge may consider such information even though obtained outside the courtroom from persons whom a defendant has not been permitted to confront or cross-examine. It is the consideration of information obtained by a sentencing judge in this manner that is the basis for appellant's broad constitutional challenge to the New York statutory policy.

Appellant urges that the New York statutory policy is in irreconcilable conflict with the underlying philosophy of a second procedural policy grounded in the due process of law clause of the Fourteenth Amendment. That policy as stated *In re Oliver*, 333 U.S. 257, 273, is in part that no person shall be tried and convicted of an offense unless he is given reasonable notice of the charges against him and is afforded an opportunity to examine adverse witnesses. That the due process clause does provide these salutary and time-tested protections where the question for consideration is the guilt of a defendant seems entirely clear from the genesis and historical evolution of the clause.

Tribunals passing on the guilt of a defendant always have been hedged in by strict evidentiary procedural limitations. But both before and since the American colonies became a nation, courts in this country and in England practiced a policy under which a sentencing judge could exercise a wide discretion in the sources and types of evidence used to assist him in determining the kind and extent of punishment to be imposed within limits fixed by law. Out-of-court affidavits have been used frequently, and of course in the smaller communities sentencing judges naturally have in mind their knowledge of the personalities and backgrounds of convicted offenders. * * *

In addition to the historical basis for different evidentiary rules governing trial and sentencing procedures there are sound practical reasons for the distinction. In a trial before verdict the issue is whether a defendant is guilty of having engaged in certain criminal conduct of which he has been specifically accused. Rules of evidence have been fashioned for criminal trials which narrowly confine the trial contest to evidence that is strictly relevant to the particular offense charged. These rules rest in part on a necessity to prevent a time consuming and confusing trial of collateral issues. They were also designed to prevent tribunals concerned solely with the issue of guilt of a particular offense from being influenced to convict for that offense by evidence that the defendant had habitually engaged in other misconduct. A sentencing judge, however, is not confined to the narrow issue of guilt. His task within fixed statutory or constitutional limits is to determine the type and extent of punishment after the issue of guilt has been determined. Highly relevant—if not essential—to his selection of an appropriate sentence is the possession of the fullest information possible concerning the defendant's life and characteristics. And modern concepts individualizing punishment have made it all the more necessary that a sentencing judge not be denied an opportunity to obtain pertinent information by a requirement of rigid adherence to restrictive rules of evidence properly applicable to the trial.

Undoubtedly the New York statutes emphasize a prevalent modern philosophy of penology that the punishment should fit the offender and not merely the crime. The belief no longer prevails that every offense in a like legal category calls for an identical punishment without regard to the past life and habits of a particular offender. This whole country has traveled far from the period in which the death sentence was an automatic and commonplace result of convictions—even for offenses today deemed trivial. Today's philosophy of individualizing sentences makes sharp distinctions for example between first and repeated offenders. Indeterminate sentences, the ultimate termination of which are sometimes decided by nonjudicial agencies have to a large extent taken the place of the old rigidly fixed punishments. The practice of probation which relies heavily on non-judicial implementation has been accepted as a wise policy. Execution of the United States parole system rests on the discretion of an administrative parole board. Retribution is no longer the dominant objective of the criminal law. Reformation and rehabilitation of offenders have become important goals of criminal jurisprudence.

Modern changes in the treatment of offenders make it more necessary now than a century ago for observance of the distinctions in the evidential procedure in the trial and sentencing processes. For indeterminate sentences and probation have resulted in an increase in the discretionary powers exercised in fixing punishments. In general, these modern changes have not resulted in making the lot of offenders harder. On the contrary a strong motivating force for the changes has been the belief that by careful study of the lives and personalities of convicted offenders many could be less severely punished and restored sooner to complete freedom and useful citizenship. This belief to a large extent has been justified.

Under the practice of individualizing punishments, investigation techniques have been given an important role. Probation workers making reports of their investigations have not been trained to prosecute but to aid offenders. Their reports have been given a high value by conscientious judges who want to sentence persons on the best available information rather than on guesswork and inadequate information. To deprive sentencing judges of this kind of information would undermine modern penological procedural policies that have been cautiously adopted throughout the nation after careful consideration and experimentation. We must recognize that most of the information now relied upon by judges to guide them in the intelligent imposition of sentences would be unavailable if information were restricted to that given in open court by witnesses subject to cross-examination. And the modern probation report draws on information concerning every aspect of a defendant's life. The type and extent of this information make totally impractical if not impossible open court testimony with cross-examination. Such a procedure could endlessly delay criminal administration in a retrial of collateral issues.

The considerations we have set out admonish us against treating the due-process clause as a uniform command that courts throughout the Nation abandon their age-old practice of seeking information from out-of-court sources to guide their judgment toward a more enlightened and just sentence. New York criminal statutes set wide limits for maximum and minimum sentences. Under New York statutes a state judge cannot escape his grave responsibility of fixing sentence. In determining whether a defendant shall receive a one-year minimum or a twenty-year maximum sentence, we do not think the Federal Constitution restricts the view of the sentencing judge to the information received in open court. The due-process clause should not be treated as a device for freezing the evidential procedure of sentencing in the mold of trial procedure. So to treat the due-process clause would hinder if not preclude all courts—state and federal—from making progressive efforts to improve the administration of criminal justice.

[The dissenting opinions of JUSTICES MURPHY and RUTLEDGE are omitted.]

NOTES & QUESTIONS

1. **Right of Confrontation.** The Sixth Amendment states that "[i]n all criminal prosecutions, the accused shall enjoy the right . . . to be confronted with the witnesses against him." The right of confrontation is among the most practically important *trial* rights of the criminal defendant, particularly insofar as it encompasses a right to cross-examine the government's witnesses. With some limited exceptions, this right generally precludes convicting a defendant on the basis of hearsay—that is, out-of-court statements made by witnesses who are not subject to in-court cross-examination. This is seen by many as an important safeguard against wrongful convictions. In the famous words of John Henry Wigmore, cross-examination is "beyond any doubt the greatest legal engine ever invented for the discovery of truth." 3 JOHN HENRY WIGMORE, EVIDENCE § 1367 (2d ed. 1923).

Yet, in *Williams*, the Supreme Court authorized sentencing courts to dispense with cross-examination. Thus, as a constitutional matter, there is nothing inherently impermissible about a judge increasing a defendant's sentence on the basis of hearsay. This ruling opens a wide gap between trial practice and sentencing practice. What justifies the ruling? Is the Court saying that truth doesn't matter at sentencing? That cross-examination is not, after all, so crucial to truth-finding as Wigmore and others have suggested?

2. **Confrontation and the PSR.** In order to better appreciate the practical significance of *Williams*, it might help to take another look at the PSR in *United States v. Smith*. What would be left of the PSR if all of the hearsay were removed? And isn't the PSR itself, as an out-of-court writing, inherently hearsay? How would sentencing hearings change if the information currently conveyed to the sentencing judge through the PSR had to be presented through live witnesses in court subject to standard trial-type confrontation? Do you think defendants, on the whole, would benefit from such a system? How would the *Williams* Court answer that question?

3. **Relic from a Different Sentencing Era?** Although Williams' argument focused particularly on his right to cross-examine his accusers, the Court's broadly worded opinion not only rejected Williams' specific constitutional claim, but also cast doubt more generally on procedural rights at sentencing. Justice Black, writing for the Court, embraced an informal approach to sentencing that sharply distinguished sentencing procedures from trial procedures. His reasoning was premised on the assumption that informality would normally *help* defendants, even though it may have hurt Williams himself. This assumption, in turn, rested on the belief that sentencing judges would use of the wealth of (hearsay) information contained in PSRs to fashion *rehabilitative* sentences. Justice Black could not have foreseen the harshly punitive, anti-rehabilitative turn that American sentencing policies would take in the final quarter of the twentieth century. Perhaps he and his colleagues in the *Williams* majority would have recognized a greater need for procedural formality if they had contemplated contemporary sentencing guidelines and enhancement statutes; in these

systems, the judge's factfinding frequently serves to aggravate, not mitigate, the punishment. Still, *Williams* remains good law as to confrontation rights at sentencing, at least outside the death-penalty context. For an argument that confrontation rights should be extended to sentencing, as some other Sixth Amendment rights have been, see Shaakirrah R. Sanders, *The Value of Confrontation As a Felony Sentencing Right*, 25 WIDENER L.J. 103 (2016).

4. **The Rest of the Story.** Williams was convicted largely on the basis of a confession that was obtained from him following eighteen hours of continuous police interrogation without a lawyer present. In 1963, he was ordered released by a federal court that determined his confession had been coerced. *U. S. ex rel. Williams v. Fay*, 323 F.2d 65 (2d Cir. 1963). Later, he received $120,000 in damages for malicious prosecution and false arrest. Maneka Sinha, *Junk Science at Sentencing*, 89 GEO. WASH. L. REV. 52, 92 (2021). Does this subsequent history affect the way you view the Supreme Court's decision in his case?

5. **Death Is Different.** In the five decades following *Williams*, the Supreme Court generally adhered to a minimalist view of constitutional rights at sentencing. Beginning in the 1970s, however, the Court adopted a markedly different approach in death-penalty cases. We will consider the special constitutional requirements that apply to capital sentencing proceedings in Chapter 7.

2. RIGHTS TO JURY TRIAL & PROOF BEYOND A REASONABLE DOUBT

Apprendi v. New Jersey

530 U.S. 466 (2000)

■ STEVENS, J.

A New Jersey statute classifies the possession of a firearm for an unlawful purpose as a "second-degree" offense. N.J. Stat. Ann. § 2C:39–4(a) (West 1995). Such an offense is punishable by imprisonment for "between five years and 10 years." § 2C:43–6(a)(2). A separate statute, described by that State's Supreme Court as a "hate crime" law, provides for an "extended term" of imprisonment if the trial judge finds, by a preponderance of the evidence, that "[t]he defendant in committing the crime acted with a purpose to intimidate an individual or group of individuals because of race, color, gender, handicap, religion, sexual orientation or ethnicity." N.J. Stat. Ann. § 2C:44–3(e) (West Supp. 1999–2000). The extended term authorized by the hate crime law for second-degree offenses is imprisonment for "between 10 and 20 years." § 2C:43–7(a)(3).

The question presented is whether the Due Process Clause of the Fourteenth Amendment requires that a factual determination authorizing an increase in the maximum prison sentence for an offense from 10 to 20 years be made by a jury on the basis of proof beyond a reasonable doubt.

I

At 2:04 a.m. on December 22, 1994, petitioner Charles C. Apprendi, Jr., fired several .22-caliber bullets into the home of an African-American family that had recently moved into a previously all-white neighborhood in Vineland, New Jersey. Apprendi was promptly arrested and, at 3:05 a.m., admitted that he was the shooter. After further questioning, at 6:04 a.m., he made a statement—which he later retracted—that even though he did not know the occupants of the house personally, "because they are black in color he does not want them in the neighborhood."

A New Jersey grand jury returned a 23-count indictment charging Apprendi with four first-degree, eight second-degree, six third-degree, and five fourth-degree offenses. The charges alleged shootings on four different dates, as well as the unlawful possession of various weapons. None of the counts referred to the hate crime statute, and none alleged that Apprendi acted with a racially biased purpose.

The parties entered into a plea agreement, pursuant to which Apprendi pleaded guilty to two counts (3 and 18) of second-degree possession of a firearm for an unlawful purpose and one count (22) of the third-degree offense of unlawful possession of an antipersonnel bomb; the prosecutor dismissed the other 20 counts. Under state law, a second-degree offense carries a penalty range of 5 to 10 years; a third-degree offense carries a penalty range of between 3 and 5 years. As part of the plea agreement, however, the State reserved the right to request the court to impose a higher "enhanced" sentence on count 18 (which was based on the December 22 shooting) on the ground that that offense was committed with a biased purpose, as described in § 2C:44–3(e). Apprendi, correspondingly, reserved the right to challenge the hate crime sentence enhancement on the ground that it violates the United States Constitution.

At the plea hearing, the trial judge heard sufficient evidence to establish Apprendi's guilt on counts 3, 18, and 22; the judge then confirmed that Apprendi understood the maximum sentences that could be imposed on those counts. Because the plea agreement provided that the sentence on the sole third-degree offense (count 22) would run concurrently with the other sentences, the potential sentences on the two second-degree counts were critical. If the judge found no basis for the biased purpose enhancement, the maximum consecutive sentences on those counts would amount to 20 years in aggregate; if, however, the judge enhanced the sentence on count 18, the maximum on that count alone would be 20 years and the maximum for the two counts in aggregate would be 30 years, with a 15-year period of parole ineligibility.

After the trial judge accepted the three guilty pleas, the prosecutor filed a formal motion for an extended term. The trial judge thereafter held an evidentiary hearing on the issue of Apprendi's "purpose" for the shooting on December 22. Apprendi adduced evidence from a psychologist and from seven character witnesses who testified that he did not have a reputation for racial bias. He also took the stand himself, explaining that the incident was an unintended consequence of overindulgence in alcohol, denying that he was in any way biased against African-Americans, and denying that his statement to the police had been accurately described. The judge, however, found the police officer's testimony credible, and concluded that the evidence supported a finding "that the crime was motivated by racial bias." Having found "by a preponderance of the evidence" that Apprendi's actions were taken "with a purpose to intimidate" as provided by the statute, the trial judge held that the hate crime enhancement applied. Rejecting Apprendi's constitutional challenge to the statute, the judge sentenced him to a 12-year term of imprisonment on count 18, and to shorter concurrent sentences on the other two counts.

Apprendi appealed, arguing, *inter alia,* that the Due Process Clause of the United States Constitution requires that the finding of bias upon which his hate crime sentence was based must be proved to a jury beyond a reasonable doubt, *In re Winship,* 397 U.S. 358 (1970). Over dissent, the Appellate Division of the Superior Court of New Jersey upheld the enhanced sentence. 698 A.2d 1265 (1997). Relying on our decision in *McMillan v. Pennsylvania,* 477 U.S. 79 (1986), the appeals court found that the state legislature decided to make the hate crime enhancement a "sentencing factor," rather than an element of an underlying offense—and that decision was within the State's established power to define the elements of its crimes. * * *

We granted certiorari and now reverse.

II

It is appropriate to begin by explaining why certain aspects of the case are not relevant to the narrow issue that we must resolve. First, the State has argued that even without the trial judge's finding of racial bias, the judge could have imposed consecutive sentences on counts 3 and 18 that would have produced the 12-year term of imprisonment that Apprendi received; Apprendi's actual sentence was thus within the range authorized by statute for the three offenses to which he pleaded guilty. The constitutional question, however, is whether the 12-year sentence imposed on count 18 was permissible, given that it was above the 10-year maximum for the offense charged in that count. The finding is legally significant because it increased—indeed, it doubled—the maximum range within which the judge could exercise his discretion, converting what otherwise was a maximum 10-year sentence on that count into a minimum sentence. The sentences on counts 3 and 22 have no more relevance to our disposition than the dismissal of the remaining 18 counts. * * *

III

In his 1881 lecture on the criminal law, Oliver Wendell Holmes, Jr., observed: "The law threatens certain pains if you do certain things, intending thereby to give you a new motive for not doing them. If you persist in doing them, it has to inflict the pains in order that its threats may continue to be believed."[2] New Jersey threatened Apprendi with certain pains if he unlawfully possessed a weapon and with additional pains if he selected his victims with a purpose to intimidate them because of their race. As a matter of simple justice, it seems obvious that the procedural safeguards designed to protect Apprendi from unwarranted pains should apply equally to the two acts that New Jersey has singled out for punishment. Merely using the label "sentence enhancement" to describe the latter surely does not provide a principled basis for treating them differently.

At stake in this case are constitutional protections of surpassing importance: the proscription of any deprivation of liberty without "due process of law," Amdt. 14, and the guarantee that "[i]n all criminal prosecutions, the accused shall enjoy the right to a speedy and public trial, by an impartial jury," Amdt. 6. Taken together, these rights indisputably entitle a criminal defendant to "a jury determination that [he] is guilty of every element of the crime with which he is charged, beyond a reasonable doubt." *United States v. Gaudin*, 515 U.S. 506, 510 (1995). * * *

Any possible distinction between an "element" of a felony offense and a "sentencing factor" was unknown to the practice of criminal indictment, trial by jury, and judgment by court as it existed during the years surrounding our Nation's founding. As a general rule, criminal proceedings were submitted to a jury after being initiated by an indictment containing "all the facts and circumstances which constitute the offence, . . . stated with such certainty and precision, that the defendant . . . may be enabled to determine the species of offence they constitute, in order that he may prepare his defence accordingly . . . and *that there may be no doubt as to the judgment which should be given*, if the defendant be convicted." J. Archbold, Pleading and Evidence in Criminal Cases 44 (15th ed. 1862) (emphasis added). The defendant's ability to predict with certainty the judgment from the face of the felony indictment flowed from the invariable linkage of punishment with crime. * * *

We should be clear that nothing in this history suggests that it is impermissible for judges to exercise discretion—taking into consideration various factors relating both to offense and offender—in imposing a judgment *within the range* prescribed by statute. We have often noted that judges in this country have long exercised discretion of this nature in imposing sentence *within statutory limits* in the individual

[2] O. Holmes, The Common Law 40 (M. Howe ed.1963).

case. See, *e.g.*, *Williams v. New York*, 337 U.S. 241, 246 (1949). As in *Williams*, our periodic recognition of judges' broad discretion in sentencing—since the 19th-century shift in this country from statutes providing fixed-term sentences to those providing judges discretion within a permissible range—has been regularly accompanied by the qualification that that discretion was bound by the range of sentencing options prescribed by the legislature.

The historic link between verdict and judgment and the consistent limitation on judges' discretion to operate within the limits of the legal penalties provided highlight the novelty of a legislative scheme that removes the jury from the determination of a fact that, if found, exposes the criminal defendant to a penalty *exceeding* the maximum he would receive if punished according to the facts reflected in the jury verdict alone. * * *

IV

* * * *Almendarez-Torres v. United States*, 523 U.S. 224 (1998), represents at best an exceptional departure from the historic practice that we have described. In that case, we considered a federal grand jury indictment, which charged the petitioner with "having been 'found in the United States . . . after being deported,' " in violation of 8 U.S.C. § 1326(a)—an offense carrying a maximum sentence of two years. Almendarez-Torres pleaded guilty to the indictment, admitting at the plea hearing that he had been deported, that he had unlawfully reentered this country, and that "the earlier deportation had taken place 'pursuant to' three earlier 'convictions' for aggravated felonies." The Government then filed a presentence report indicating that Almendarez-Torres' offense fell within the bounds of § 1326(b) because, as specified in that provision, his original deportation had been subsequent to an aggravated felony conviction; accordingly, Almendarez-Torres could be subject to a sentence of up to 20 years. Almendarez-Torres objected, contending that because the indictment "had not mentioned his earlier aggravated felony convictions," he could be sentenced to no more than two years in prison.

Rejecting Almendarez-Torres' objection, we concluded that sentencing him to a term higher than that attached to the offense alleged in the indictment did not violate the strictures of *Winship* in that case. Because Almendarez-Torres had *admitted* the three earlier convictions for aggravated felonies—all of which had been entered pursuant to proceedings with substantial procedural safeguards of their own—no question concerning the right to a jury trial or the standard of proof that would apply to a contested issue of fact was before the Court. * * * Both the certainty that procedural safeguards attached to any "fact" of prior conviction, and the reality that Almendarez-Torres did not challenge the accuracy of that "fact" in his case, mitigated the due process and Sixth Amendment concerns otherwise implicated in allowing a judge to determine a "fact" increasing punishment beyond the maximum of the statutory range.

Even though it is arguable that *Almendarez-Torres* was incorrectly decided, and that a logical application of our reasoning today should apply if the recidivist issue were contested, Apprendi does not contest the decision's validity and we need not revisit it for purposes of our decision today to treat the case as a narrow exception to the general rule we recalled at the outset. Given its unique facts, it surely does not warrant rejection of the otherwise uniform course of decision during the entire history of our jurisprudence.

[In sum, other] than the fact of a prior conviction, any fact that increases the penalty for a crime beyond the prescribed statutory maximum must be submitted to a jury, and proved beyond a reasonable doubt. With that exception, we endorse the statement of the rule set forth in the concurring opinions in [*Jones v. United States*, 526 U.S. 473 (1999)]: "[I]t is unconstitutional for a legislature to remove from the jury the assessment of facts that increase the prescribed range of penalties to which a criminal defendant is exposed. It is equally clear that such facts must be established by proof beyond a reasonable doubt."

V

The New Jersey statutory scheme that Apprendi asks us to invalidate allows a jury to convict a defendant of a second-degree offense based on its finding beyond a reasonable doubt that he unlawfully possessed a prohibited weapon; after a subsequent and separate proceeding, it then allows a judge to impose punishment identical to that New Jersey provides for crimes of the first degree, based upon the judge's finding, by a preponderance of the evidence, that the defendant's "purpose" for unlawfully possessing the weapon was "to intimidate" his victim on the basis of a particular characteristic the victim possessed. In light of the constitutional rule explained above, and all of the cases supporting it, this practice cannot stand. * * *

[The concurring opinions of JUSTICES SCALIA and THOMAS and the dissenting opinions of JUSTICES O'CONNOR and BREYER are omitted.]

NOTES & QUESTIONS

1. **Two Constitutional Rights for the Price of One.** In *Apprendi*, the Court found that the sentencing process used to implement New Jersey's hate crimes statute violated two constitutional rights of the defendant: the right to a trial by jury and the right to factfinding beyond a reasonable doubt. Based on the Court's reasoning, what specific aspect of the sentencing decision in this case triggered these two rights? Which right do you think has more practical value to a defendant?

2. **What About *Patterson*?** The principal dissent, authored by Justice O'Connor, emphasized the tension between the majority's holding and the Court's earlier decision in *Patterson v. New York*, 432 U.S. 197 (1977). At issue in *Patterson* was a New York homicide statute, under which the defendant was convicted of second-degree murder. Justice O'Connor described the New York law this way:

> [T]he fact that a person intentionally killed another while under the influence of extreme emotional disturbance distinguished the reduced offense of first-degree manslaughter from the more serious offense of second-degree murder. Thus, the presence or absence of this one fact was the defining factor separating a greater from a lesser punishment. Under New York law, however, the State did not need to prove the absence of extreme emotional disturbance beyond a reasonable doubt. Rather, state law imposed the burden of proving the presence of extreme emotional disturbance on the defendant, and required that the fact be proved by a preponderance of the evidence.

Apprendi, 530 U.S. at 530 (O'Connor, J., dissenting). Patterson challenged this system as a violation of his right to have every element of the offense proven beyond a reasonable doubt. In rejecting his argument, the Court expressly "decline[d] to adopt as a constitutional imperative, operative countrywide, that a State must disprove beyond a reasonable doubt every fact constituting any and all affirmative defenses related to the culpability of an accused." *Patterson*, 432 U.S. at 210. How can this principle be reconciled with the rule in *Apprendi*? If a legislature can place *on the defendant* the burden of proof for a fact that affects punishment, why can't the legislature keep the burden on the state, but at a lower level than beyond a reasonable doubt?

3. **What About *Williams*?** In *Apprendi*, the Court cited *Williams* with apparent approval and suggested that the judicial factfinding in that case was constitutionally permissible. How can *Apprendi* be reconciled with *Williams*?

4. **Prior Convictions.** The rule in *Apprendi* specifically carves out prior convictions from the general requirement of jury factfinding beyond a reasonable doubt. This may have reflected a reluctance on the part of the Court to overturn its then-recent decision in *Almendarez-Torres v. United States*—a case that is discussed at length in the *Apprendi* excerpt above. What were the facts in *Almendarez-Torres*? How did the *Apprendi* majority attempt to distinguish the earlier decision? Are you persuaded? Does it seem to you that Apprendi's sentencing was any unfairer than that of Almendarez-Torres?

5. **Waiver.** At first blush, it might seem to you that *Apprendi* would result in the empaneling of a large number of sentencing juries. However, *Apprendi* rights are no less waivable than the rights of criminal defendants generally are. *Apprendi* considerations may thus be folded into plea bargaining. For instance, a defendant might consent to the application of a sentence enhancement without a trial, perhaps in return for some mitigating consideration from the state. Alternatively, the state might agree not to seek the application of a particular sentence enhancement, perhaps in return for the defendant's guilty plea to another charge. In practice, in many or most cases in which it applies, *Apprendi* might best be thought of as just another bargaining chip for the defendant—or, perhaps even more accurately, as a factor that modestly diminishes the *state*'s ability to use threatened sentence enhancements as bargaining chips.

6. **Mandatory Minimums.** *Apprendi* dealt with a sentence enhancement statute that increased the *maximum* possible punishment that could be imposed on the defendant. What about a statute that increases the *minimum*? Earlier, in *McMillan v. Pennsylvania,* 477 U.S. 79 (1986), the Court considered the constitutionality of Pennsylvania's Mandatory Minimum Sentencing Act, which provided that anyone convicted of certain enumerated felonies was subject to a mandatory minimum sentence of five years in prison if the sentencing judge found by a preponderance of the evidence that the defendant "visibly possessed a firearm" during the commission of the offense. The Court found *Patterson, supra,* to be controlling. Consistent with *Patterson*'s view that legislatures have a mostly free hand in defining what counts as an offense "element" that must be proven beyond a reasonable doubt, the Pennsylvania legislature could properly decide that visible possession of a firearm should be a "sentencing factor" subject to the preponderance standard, rather than an element. Fourteen years later, in *Apprendi*, the Court expressed some skepticism of *McMillan*, but declined to overturn the precedent—effectively opening a gap in the treatment of maximum- and minimum-enhancing statutes. Finally, in *Alleyne v. United States*, 570 U.S. 99 (2013), the Court effectively overruled *McMillan* and extended the *Apprendi* rule to minimums. Which decision do you think was of more practical importance to defendants, *Apprendi* or *Alleyne*?

7. **Fines.** In *Southern Union v. United States*, 567 U.S. 343 (2012), the Supreme Court extended the *Apprendi* rule to the imposition of criminal fines. A defendant, in other words, has a right to a jury trial on facts that increase the potential size of a fine. The Court has not yet determined whether restitution or forfeiture orders that are made part of a criminal sentence are similarly subject to *Apprendi*'s limitations. William M. Acker, Jr., *The Mandatory Victims Restitution Act Is Unconstitutional. Will the Courts Say So After* Southern Union v. United States?, 64 ALA. L. REV. 803 (2013).

8. **Concurrent Versus Consecutive Sentences.** In *Oregon v. Ice*, 555 U.S. 160 (2009), the Court upheld a statute that directed judges to impose concurrent sentences in multicount cases unless the judge found certain aggravating facts to be present. In so doing, the Court refused to extend *Apprendi*, concluding that judicial factfinding in relation to the concurrent/consecutive decision does not constitute "encroachment on the jury's traditional domain."

9. **Judge or Jury—Who's Better?** *Apprendi* did not consider the policy question—is it better, putting to one side considerations of history or doctrinal coherence, to have a judge or a jury find the facts that determine the sentence? From the standpoint of accuracy, anyway, there are some reasons to think that judges might be better, but also some reasons to think that juries might be better. Can you imagine the arguments that might be made both ways? In one review of the social science literature, two scholars opine, "Both judges and juries have advantages and disadvantages as reliable re-creators of past events. Given our current limited data, one might conclude that juries, on balance, may have a slight advantage over judges as

factfinders, not because of an actual superiority in reliable factfinding, but because they are perceived as being superior, and that perception can have important practical benefits for the effective operation of a sentencing system." Paul H. Robinson & Barbara A. Spellman, *Sentencing Decisions: Matching the Decisionmaker to the Decision Nature*, 105 COLUM. L. REV. 1124, 1145 (2005). What do you suppose these "practical benefits" are? And how should they be weighed against the greater administrative burdens of jury decision-making?

10. **Guidelines.** Perhaps the most important question left open by *Apprendi* was its application to sentencing guidelines. The Court first considered the constitutionality of a state guidelines system in *Blakely v. Washington*, 542 U.S. 296 (2004), and then of the federal system in *United States v. Booker*.

United States v. Booker

543 U.S. 220 (2005)

■ STEVENS, J.

The question presented in each of these cases is whether an application of the Federal Sentencing Guidelines violated the Sixth Amendment. In each case, the courts below held that binding rules set forth in the Guidelines limited the severity of the sentence that the judge could lawfully impose on the defendant based on the facts found by the jury at his trial. In both cases the courts rejected, on the basis of our decision in *Blakely v. Washington,* 542 U.S. 296 (2004), the Government's recommended application of the Sentencing Guidelines because the proposed sentences were based on additional facts that the sentencing judge found by a preponderance of the evidence. We hold that both courts correctly concluded that the Sixth Amendment as construed in *Blakely* does apply to the Sentencing Guidelines. In a separate opinion authored by Justice BREYER, the Court concludes that in light of this holding, two provisions of the Sentencing Reform Act of 1984 (SRA) that have the effect of making the Guidelines mandatory must be invalidated in order to allow the statute to operate in a manner consistent with congressional intent.

I

Respondent Booker was charged with possession with intent to distribute at least 50 grams of cocaine base (crack). Having heard evidence that he had 92.5 grams in his duffel bag, the jury found him guilty of violating 21 U.S.C. § 841(a)(1). That statute prescribes a minimum sentence of 10 years in prison and a maximum sentence of life for that offense. § 841(b)(1)(A)(iii).

Based upon Booker's criminal history and the quantity of drugs found by the jury, the Sentencing Guidelines required the District Court Judge to select a "base" sentence of not less than 210 nor more than 262 months in prison. See United States Sentencing Commission, Guidelines

Manual §§ 2D1.1(c)(4), 4A1.1 (Nov. 2003) (USSG). The judge, however, held a post-trial sentencing proceeding and concluded by a preponderance of the evidence that Booker had possessed an additional 566 grams of crack and that he was guilty of obstructing justice. Those findings mandated that the judge select a sentence between 360 months and life imprisonment; the judge imposed a sentence at the low end of the range. Thus, instead of the sentence of 21 years and 10 months that the judge could have imposed on the basis of the facts proved to the jury beyond a reasonable doubt, Booker received a 30-year sentence. * * *

II * * *

In *Blakely v. Washington,* 542 U.S. 296 (2004), we dealt with a determinate sentencing scheme similar to the Federal Sentencing Guidelines. There the defendant pleaded guilty to kidnaping, a class B felony punishable by a term of not more than 10 years. Other provisions of Washington law, comparable to the Federal Sentencing Guidelines, mandated a "standard" sentence of 49-to-53 months, unless the judge found aggravating facts justifying an exceptional sentence. Although the prosecutor recommended a sentence in the standard range, the judge found that the defendant had acted with " 'deliberate cruelty' " and sentenced him to 90 months. *Id.,* at 300.

* * * [T]he requirements of the Sixth Amendment were clear. The application of Washington's sentencing scheme violated the defendant's right to have the jury find the existence of " 'any particular fact' " that the law makes essential to his punishment. 542 U.S., at 301. That right is implicated whenever a judge seeks to impose a sentence that is not solely based on "facts reflected in the jury verdict or admitted by the defendant." *Id.,* at 303. We rejected the State's argument that the jury verdict was sufficient to authorize a sentence within the general 10-year sentence for class B felonies, noting that under Washington law, the judge was *required* to find additional facts in order to impose the greater 90-month sentence. Our precedents, we explained, make clear "that the 'statutory maximum' for *Apprendi* purposes is the maximum sentence a judge may impose *solely on the basis of the facts reflected in the jury verdict or admitted by the defendant.*" *Ibid.* (emphasis in original). The determination that the defendant acted with deliberate cruelty, like the determination in *Apprendi* that the defendant acted with racial malice, increased the sentence that the defendant could have otherwise received. Since this fact was found by a judge using a preponderance of the evidence standard, the sentence violated Blakely's Sixth Amendment rights.

As the dissenting opinions in *Blakely* recognized, there is no distinction of constitutional significance between the Federal Sentencing Guidelines and the Washington procedures at issue in that case. This conclusion rests on the premise, common to both systems, that the relevant sentencing rules are mandatory and impose binding requirements on all sentencing judges.

If the Guidelines as currently written could be read as merely advisory provisions that recommended, rather than required, the selection of particular sentences in response to differing sets of facts, their use would not implicate the Sixth Amendment. We have never doubted the authority of a judge to exercise broad discretion in imposing a sentence within a statutory range. See *Apprendi,* 530 U.S., at 481; *Williams v. New York,* 337 U.S. 241, 246 (1949). Indeed, everyone agrees that the constitutional issues presented by these cases would have been avoided entirely if Congress had omitted from the SRA the provisions that make the Guidelines binding on district judges; it is that circumstance that makes the Court's answer to the second question presented possible. For when a trial judge exercises his discretion to select a specific sentence within a defined range, the defendant has no right to a jury determination of the facts that the judge deems relevant.

The Guidelines as written, however, are not advisory; they are mandatory and binding on all judges. While subsection (a) of § 3553 of the sentencing statute lists the Sentencing Guidelines as one factor to be considered in imposing a sentence, subsection (b) directs that the court "*shall* impose a sentence of the kind, and within the range" established by the Guidelines, subject to departures in specific, limited cases. (Emphasis added.) Because they are binding on judges, we have consistently held that the Guidelines have the force and effect of laws.

The availability of a departure in specified circumstances does not avoid the constitutional issue, just as it did not in *Blakely* itself. The Guidelines permit departures from the prescribed sentencing range in cases in which the judge "finds that there exists an aggravating or mitigating circumstance of a kind, or to a degree, not adequately taken into consideration by the Sentencing Commission in formulating the guidelines that should result in a sentence different from that described." 18 U.S.C. § 3553(b)(1) (2000 ed., Supp. IV). At first glance, one might believe that the ability of a district judge to depart from the Guidelines means that she is bound only by the statutory maximum. Were this the case, there would be no *Apprendi* problem. Importantly, however, departures are not available in every case, and in fact are unavailable in most. In most cases, as a matter of law, the Commission will have adequately taken all relevant factors into account, and no departure will be legally permissible. In those instances, the judge is bound to impose a sentence within the Guidelines range. * * *

Booker's case illustrates the mandatory nature of the Guidelines. The jury convicted him of possessing at least 50 grams of crack in violation of 21 U.S.C. § 841(b)(1)(A)(iii) based on evidence that he had 92.5 grams of crack in his duffel bag. Under these facts, the Guidelines specified an offense level of 32, which, given the defendant's criminal history category, authorized a sentence of 210-to-262 months. See USSG § 2D1.1(c)(4). Booker's is a run-of-the-mill drug case, and does not present any factors that were inadequately considered by the

Commission. The sentencing judge would therefore have been reversed had he not imposed a sentence within the level 32 Guidelines range.

Booker's actual sentence, however, was 360 months, almost 10 years longer than the Guidelines range supported by the jury verdict alone. To reach this sentence, the judge found facts beyond those found by the jury: namely, that Booker possessed 566 grams of crack in addition to the 92.5 grams in his duffel bag. The jury never heard any evidence of the additional drug quantity, and the judge found it true by a preponderance of the evidence. Thus, just as in *Blakely,* "the jury's verdict alone does not authorize the sentence. The judge acquires that authority only upon finding some additional fact." 542 U.S., at 305. There is no relevant distinction between the sentence imposed pursuant to the Washington statutes in *Blakely* and the sentences imposed pursuant to the Federal Sentencing Guidelines in these cases. * * *

IV

All of the foregoing supports our conclusion that our holding in *Blakely* applies to the Sentencing Guidelines. We recognize * * * that in some cases jury factfinding may impair the most expedient and efficient sentencing of defendants. But the interest in fairness and reliability protected by the right to a jury trial—a common-law right that defendants enjoyed for centuries and that is now enshrined in the Sixth Amendment—has always outweighed the interest in concluding trials swiftly. * * *

[The Court's separate opinion regarding remedy, as well as the dissenting-in-part opinions of JUSTICES STEVENS, SCALIA, THOMAS, and BREYER are omitted.]

NOTES & QUESTIONS

1. **State Guidelines: *Blakely*.** As discussed in the *Booker* excerpt, the Court's earlier decision in *Blakely* held that Washington's sentencing guidelines system was unconstitutional insofar as it permitted a judge to impose a sentence above the guidelines range on the basis of the judge's own finding of an aggravating fact like "deliberate cruelty." The Court ruled that the defendant had a Sixth Amendment right to a jury trial on such aggravating facts. Importantly, Blakely's sentence was unconstitutional even though it was within the statutory maximum that was generically associated with his crime of conviction. *Apprendi* established that the defendant has a right to a jury trial on any fact that increases the statutory maximum. In effect, *Blakely* then held that the top of the guidelines range should be treated as a statutory maximum for Sixth Amendment purposes in a system of presumptive sentencing guidelines.

In addition to the Washington system, *Blakely*'s reasoning cast a constitutional shadow over the guidelines systems in at least a dozen other states. John F. Pfaff, *The Future of Appellate Sentencing Review:* Booker *in the States*, 93 MARQ. L. REV. 683, 700 (2009). Most responded by incorporating a mechanism for jury factfinding within their guidelines systems, while the remainder either abandoned their guidelines or shifted their system from presumptive to advisory. As the Court confirmed in *Booker* (through Justice Breyer's opinion for the "remedy majority"), the factfinding in an *advisory* system does not trigger the right to a jury trial. In an advisory system, the judge has sufficient discretion to select a sentence anywhere in the generic statutory range so that the top of the guidelines range cannot be regarded as the functional equivalent of an alternate statutory maximum.

Notably, in the states that did add a jury-trial mechanism, there is little evidence of a substantial increase in jury trials. Frank O. Bowman, III, *Debacle: How the Supreme Court Has Mangled American Sentencing Law and How It Might Yet Be Mended*, 77 U. CHI. L. REV. 367, 461–62 (2010). In Minnesota, for instance, it is estimated that *Blakely* resulted in only about twenty-seven jury trials of sentence-affecting facts per year. *Id.* at 463. This likely reflects a combination of two considerations: (1) the jury-trial rights under *Apprendi* and *Blakely* are waivable and can be bargained around by the defendant and prosecutor, and (2) as indicated in *Apprendi*, guidelines enhancements based on the fact of a prior conviction remain outside the jury-trial right. Indeed, in presumptive-guidelines states, sentence enhancements on grounds other than criminal history are rare. *See* Nancy J. King, *Handling Aggravating Facts After* Blakely*: Findings From Five Presumptive-Guidelines States*, 99 N.C. L. REV. 1241, 1255 tbl. 1 (2021). Additionally, some of these states have adopted questionable, narrowing interpretations of *Blakely* that further reduce the range of fact-finding decisions that are subject to the jury-trial right. *Id.* at 1257–64.

2. **Federal Guidelines: *Booker*.** There was little basis for distinguishing the presumptive guidelines in the federal system from those of Washington State. Indeed, it was only a matter of months before the Supreme Court confirmed in *Booker* that the federal guidelines also ran afoul of the Sixth Amendment. Can you explain in your own words why Freddie Booker's sentence was unconstitutional?

Having found the federal guidelines system unconstitutional, the Court then had to decide on a remedy. The analysis turned on the question of what Congress would have wanted as its "Plan B" if it had known that its preferred system of jury-free presumptive guidelines was unconstitutional. Perhaps Congress, for instance, would not have wanted any guidelines at all in light of the new constitutional constraints on their use. If so, then the most appropriate remedy might be to invalidate the whole statute that authorized the guidelines. Instead, by a slim 5–4 majority, the Court settled on a narrower remedy that retained the guidelines but changed their status from presumptive to merely advisory. The crux of the new system was the modified standard for appellate review of sentences—"reasonableness." Sentencing judges would still have to calculate a guidelines range in each case but could more freely select a sentence above or below the range. As long as the sentence imposed was reasonable relative to the basic statutory purposes of punishment (discussed in Chapter 1), the appellate court should affirm.

Booker left unanswered many questions about reasonableness review. There was a delicate balance to be struck. On the one hand, if reasonableness review imposed no meaningful constraints on the sentencing judge's discretion, that might seem an abandonment of Congress's effort to bring greater uniformity to federal sentencing. On the other hand, if reasonableness review were too rigorous, then the effect might be to reestablish an unconstitutional system in which judges were required to justify harsh sentences on the basis of specific aggravating facts—facts that would have been found by the judge himself or herself, rather than a jury.

3. **Reasonableness Review, Elaborated.** In an important trilogy of cases in 2007, the Supreme Court substantially clarified the new system of reasonableness review. First, in *Rita v. United States*, 551 U.S. 338 (2007), the Court held that when reviewing federal sentences for reasonableness, appellate courts *may* (but are not required to) apply a rebuttable presumption of reasonableness in favor of a sentence falling within a properly calculated guidelines range. However, the converse is not permissible—appellate courts are *not* to presume that a sentence that falls *outside* of the guidelines is *unreasonable*.

Second, in *Kimbrough v. United States*, 552 U.S. 85 (2007), the Court indicated that a sentencing judge may deviate from a guidelines range even on the basis of a policy disagreement with the guidelines. After Kimbrough's conviction of crack cocaine and weapons offenses, the trial judge imposed a sentence of 15 years (the minimum allowable by statute), rather than adhering to the guideline range of 19 to 22 years, reflecting the judge's stated disagreement with the guidelines' highly controversial 100:1 crack-to-powder cocaine ratio (that is, treating one gram of crack as the equivalent of 100 grams of powder, which was widely criticized as racially discriminatory). On appeal, the Fourth Circuit reversed, holding that imposing a sentence "outside the guidelines range is *per se* unreasonable when it is based on a disagreement with the sentencing disparity for crack and powder cocaine offenses." However, the Supreme Court rejected this reasoning, determining that the Fourth Circuit's approach gave too much weight to the "advisory" guidelines. However, the Court has left open the question of whether there should be closer appellate review of sentences that reflect a judge's rejection of policy choices made by the Sentencing Commission. *Peugh v. United States*, 569 U.S. 530, 537 n.2 (2013).

Third, the Court further elaborated on the role of the guidelines in reasonableness review in *Gall v. United States*, 552 U.S. 38 (2007). In *Gall*, the Court upheld as reasonable the sentencing judge's downward variance from the guidelines range of 30–37 months in prison to 36 months of probation. The judge had particularly cited the defendant's voluntary withdrawal from an ecstasy distribution conspiracy and the fact that he had lived productively and crime-free for years prior to being charged for his role in the conspiracy. The Supreme Court's opinion in *Gall* described the roles of district and appellate courts in post-*Booker* sentencing this way:

> In reviewing the reasonableness of a sentence outside the Guidelines range, appellate courts may . . . take the degree of variance into account and consider the extent of a deviation from the Guidelines. We reject, however, an appellate rule that requires "extraordinary" circumstances to justify a sentence outside the

> Guidelines range. We also reject the use of a rigid mathematical formula that uses the percentage of a departure as the standard for determining the strength of the justifications required for a specific sentence.
>
> . . . [A] district court should begin all sentencing proceedings by correctly calculating the applicable Guidelines range. As a matter of administration and to secure nationwide consistency, the Guidelines should be the starting point and the initial benchmark. The Guidelines are not the only consideration, however. Accordingly, after giving both parties an opportunity to argue for whatever sentence they deem appropriate, the district judge should then consider all of the [statutory sentencing] factors to determine whether they support the sentence requested by a party. In so doing, he may not presume that the Guidelines range is reasonable. He must make an individualized assessment based on the facts presented. If he decides that an outside-Guidelines sentence is warranted, he must consider the extent of the deviation and ensure that the justification is sufficiently compelling to support the degree of the variance. We find it uncontroversial that a major departure should be supported by a more significant justification than a minor one. After settling on the appropriate sentence, he must adequately explain the chosen sentence to allow for meaningful appellate review and to promote the perception of fair sentencing. . . .
>
> Regardless of whether the sentence imposed is inside or outside the Guidelines range, the appellate court must review the sentence under an abuse-of-discretion standard. It must first ensure that the district court committed no significant procedural error, such as failing to calculate (or improperly calculating) the Guidelines range, treating the Guidelines as mandatory, failing to consider the [statutory sentencing] factors, selecting a sentence based on clearly erroneous facts, or failing to adequately explain the chosen sentence—including an explanation for any deviation from the Guidelines range. Assuming that the district court's sentencing decision is procedurally sound, the appellate court should then consider the substantive reasonableness of the sentence imposed under an abuse-of-discretion standard. When conducting this review, the court will, of course, take into account the totality of the circumstances, including the extent of any variance from the Guidelines range. . . . It may consider the extent of the deviation, but must give due deference to the district court's decision that the [statutory] factors, on a whole, justify the extent of the variance. The fact that the appellate court might reasonably have concluded that a different sentence was appropriate is insufficient to justify reversal of the district court.

Id. at 46–51.

Do you think the *Gall* formulation gives due regard to the constitutional rights recognized in *Apprendi* and *Blakely*? How might you argue to the contrary? Note that the Court in *Gall* might have simply said, "Advisory means advisory. Trial judges are free to select a sentence anywhere they wish within the statutory range, without regard to the guidelines. And, in reviewing the reasonableness of sentences, appellate courts may not use the guidelines as a benchmark." Would that have been a better approach?

Although *Rita*, *Kimbrough*, and *Gall* resolved some important questions regarding appellate review of federal sentences post-*Booker*, important ambiguities remain, and a number of notable circuit splits in this area have emerged. Carissa Byrne Hessick, *The Sixth Amendment Sentencing Right and Its Remedy*, 99 N.C. L. REV. 1195 (2021).

4. **Safe Harbor for the States.** The 2007 trilogy established the parameters of appellate review for the federal system. However, while these cases are not binding on the states, they do seem to establish a sort of constitutional safe harbor for states that would like to have advisory guidelines combined with meaningful appellate review. If you were a legislator in a guidelines state, which approach would you prefer—presumptive guidelines with a jury-trial mechanism and rigorous appellate enforcement of the guidelines, or advisory guidelines with reasonableness review as approved in *Rita*, *Kimbrough*, and *Gall*? Might your answer depend on the content of the guidelines at issue? For a highly complex set of guidelines with many aggravating sentencing factors, like the federal guidelines, jury trials might seem hopelessly impractical. By contrast, all existing state guidelines are much simpler than the federal guidelines and might therefore seem easier to administer as presumptive guidelines in an *Apprendi*-compliant fashion.

5. ***Booker*'s Impact.** In the two years prior to *Blakely*, about 70% of federal sentences were within the then-presumptive guidelines range. U.S. SENT'G COMM'N, REPORT ON THE CONTINUING IMPACT OF *UNITED STATES V. BOOKER* ON FEDERAL SENTENCING 58 (2012). That figure dropped to about 60% during the time period between *Booker* and *Gall*. Then, in the wake of *Gall*, which was widely seen as favoring an even more deferential approach to appellate review than had prevailed in the immediate aftermath of *Booker*, the proportion of within-range sentences dropped even further to about 54%. Does this mean that *Booker* and *Gall* rendered the guidelines meaningless?

Consider a different way of viewing the data. Throughout the whole pre-*Booker* through post-*Gall* time period, a majority of the sentences outside the guidelines range were below-range sentences that were sponsored by the government, which typically happens pursuant to a plea or cooperation deal. Since the government is unlikely to appeal a below-range sentence that it has sponsored, changes to the appellate standard of review are unlikely to have a large impact one way or the other on the prevalence of below-range sentences in these cases. The real test of the impact of *Booker* and *Gall* is the frequency of below-range sentences that are opposed by the government and as to which the sentencing judge might reasonably fear an appeal. (*Above*-range sentences have always been quite rare.) Comparing pre-*Booker* to post-*Gall* time periods, the ratio of within-range sentences to non-government-sponsored below-range sentences fell sharply from 12:1 to 3:1, which suggests that the Supreme Court's decisions really did make a difference.

Still, even a 3:1 ratio means that the judge imposes a within-range sentence in the great majority of cases in which the government does not support a below-range option. Why do you suppose that federal judges did not make greater use of their enhanced discretion under *Booker* and *Gall*?

In Chapter 2, we noted research indicating that inter-judge disparities in the federal system declined after the adoption of the guidelines in their original, presumptive form. As might be expected, post-*Booker* research suggests that inter-judge disparities rebounded somewhat after the guidelines became "advisory." Paul J. Hofer, *Federal Sentencing After* Booker, 48 CRIME & JUST. 137, 163 (2019). However, it should be recalled that the presumptive system was criticized based on its potential to exacerbate *prosecutor*-created disparities and based on certain structural features (e.g., the especially harsh treatment of crack cocaine offenses) that contributed to racial disparities. To some extent, the increased post-*Booker* judge-created disparities may reflect the efforts of some judges to correct for prosecutorial and structural disparities. Whether racial disparities have increased post-*Booker* is a matter of some dispute; some statistical models find increased disparities, and others do not. *Id.* at 165–71.

3. PRIVILEGE AGAINST SELF-INCRIMINATION

Mitchell v. United States

526 U.S. 314 (1999)

■ KENNEDY, J.

Two questions relating to a criminal defendant's Fifth Amendment privilege against self-incrimination are presented to us. The first is whether, in the federal criminal system, a guilty plea waives the privilege in the sentencing phase of the case, either as a result of the colloquy preceding the plea or by operation of law when the plea is entered. We hold the plea is not a waiver of the privilege at sentencing. The second question is whether, in determining facts about the crime which bear upon the severity of the sentence, a trial court may draw an adverse inference from the defendant's silence. We hold a sentencing court may not draw the adverse inference.

I

Petitioner Amanda Mitchell and 22 other defendants were indicted for offenses arising from a conspiracy to distribute cocaine in Allentown, Pennsylvania, from 1989 to 1994. According to the indictment, the leader of the conspiracy, Harry Riddick, obtained large quantities of cocaine and resold the drug through couriers and street sellers, including petitioner. Petitioner was charged with one count of conspiring to distribute five or more kilograms of cocaine, in violation of 21 U.S.C. § 846, and with three counts of distributing cocaine within 1,000 feet of a school or playground, in violation of § 860(a). In 1995, without any plea agreement, petitioner pleaded guilty to all four counts. She reserved the right to contest the drug quantity attributable to her under the conspiracy count, and the District Court advised her the drug quantity would be determined at her sentencing hearing.

Before accepting the plea, the District Court made the inquiries required by Rule 11 of the Federal Rules of Criminal Procedure. Informing petitioner of the penalties for her offenses, the District Judge advised her, "the range of punishment here is very complex because we don't know how much cocaine the Government's going to be able to show you were involved in." The judge told petitioner she faced a mandatory minimum of one year in prison under § 860 for distributing cocaine near a school or playground. She also faced "serious punishment depending on the quantity involved" for the conspiracy, with a mandatory minimum of 10 years in prison under § 841 if she could be held responsible for at least 5 kilograms but less than 15 kilograms of cocaine. By pleading guilty, the District Court explained, petitioner would waive various rights, including "the right at trial to remain silent under the Fifth Amendment."

After the Government explained the factual basis for the charges, the judge, having put petitioner under oath, asked her, "Did you do that?" Petitioner answered, "Some of it." She indicated that, although present for one of the transactions charged as a substantive cocaine distribution count, she had not herself delivered the cocaine to the customer. The Government maintained she was liable nevertheless as an aider and abettor of the delivery by another courier. After discussion with her counsel, petitioner reaffirmed her intention to plead guilty to all the charges. * * * [T]he District Court accepted the plea.

In 1996, 9 of petitioner's original 22 codefendants went to trial. Three other codefendants had pleaded guilty and agreed to cooperate with the Government. They testified petitioner was a regular seller for ringleader Riddick. At petitioner's sentencing hearing, the three adopted their trial testimony, and one of them furnished additional information on the amount of cocaine petitioner sold. According to him, petitioner worked two to three times a week, selling 1½ to 2 ounces of cocaine a day, from April 1992 to August 1992. Then, from August 1992 to December 1993 she worked three to five times a week, and from January 1994 to March 1994 she was one of those in charge of cocaine distribution for Riddick. On cross-examination, the codefendant conceded he had not seen petitioner on a regular basis during the relevant period.

Both petitioner and the Government referred to trial testimony by one Alvitta Mack, who had made a series of drug buys under the supervision of law enforcement agents, including three purchases from petitioner totaling two ounces of cocaine in 1992. Petitioner put on no evidence at sentencing, nor did she testify to rebut the Government's evidence about drug quantity. Her counsel argued, however, that the three documented sales to Mack constituted the only evidence of sufficient reliability to be credited in determining the quantity of cocaine attributable to her for sentencing purposes.

After this testimony at the sentencing hearing the District Court ruled that, as a consequence of her guilty plea, petitioner had no right to remain silent with respect to the details of her crimes. The court found credible the testimony indicating petitioner had been a drug courier on a regular basis. Sales of 1½ to 2 ounces twice a week for a year and a half put her over the 5-kilogram threshold, thus mandating a minimum sentence of 10 years. "One of the things" persuading the court to rely on the testimony of the codefendants was petitioner's "not testifying to the contrary."

The District Judge told petitioner:

> I held it against you that you didn't come forward today and tell me that you really only did this a couple of times. . . . I'm taking the position that you should come forward and explain your side of this issue.
>
> Your counsel's taking the position that you have a Fifth Amendment right not to. . . . If he's—if it's determined by a higher Court that he's right in that regard, I would be willing to bring you back for resentencing. And if you—if—and then I might take a closer look at the [codefendants'] testimony.

The District Court sentenced petitioner to the statutory minimum of 10 years of imprisonment, 6 years of supervised release, and a special assessment of $200.

The Court of Appeals for the Third Circuit affirmed the sentence. * * *

II

The Government maintains that petitioner's guilty plea was a waiver of the privilege against compelled self-incrimination with respect to all the crimes comprehended in the plea. We hold otherwise and rule that petitioner retained the privilege at her sentencing hearing.

A

It is well established that a witness, in a single proceeding, may not testify voluntarily about a subject and then invoke the privilege against self-incrimination when questioned about the details. The privilege is waived for the matters to which the witness testifies, and the scope of the "waiver is determined by the scope of relevant cross-examination," *Brown v. United States,* 356 U.S. 148, 154–155 (1958). * * *

The justifications for the rule of waiver in the testimonial context are evident: A witness may not pick and choose what aspects of a particular subject to discuss without casting doubt on the trustworthiness of the statements and diminishing the integrity of the factual inquiry. As noted in *Rogers,* a contrary rule "would open the way to distortion of facts by permitting a witness to select any stopping place in the testimony," 340 U.S., at 371. It would, as we said in *Brown,* "make of the Fifth Amendment not only a humane safeguard against judicially coerced self-disclosure but a positive invitation to mutilate the truth a party offers to tell," 356 U.S., at 156. The illogic of allowing a witness to offer only self-selected testimony should be obvious even to the witness, so there is no unfairness in allowing cross-examination when testimony is given without invoking the privilege.

We may assume for purposes of this opinion, then, that if petitioner had pleaded not guilty and, having taken the stand at a trial, testified she did "some of it," she could have been cross-examined on the frequency of her drug deliveries and the quantity of cocaine involved. The concerns which justify the cross-examination when the defendant testifies are absent at a plea colloquy, however. The purpose of a plea colloquy is to protect the defendant from an unintelligent or involuntary plea. The Government would turn this constitutional shield into a prosecutorial sword by having the defendant relinquish all rights against compelled self-incrimination upon entry of a guilty plea, including the right to remain silent at sentencing.

There is no convincing reason why the narrow inquiry at the plea colloquy should entail such an extensive waiver of the privilege. Unlike the defendant taking the stand, who "cannot reasonably claim that the Fifth Amendment gives him . . . an immunity from cross-examination on the matters he has himself put in dispute," *id.,* at 155–156, the defendant who pleads guilty puts nothing in dispute regarding the essentials of the offense. Rather, the defendant takes those matters out of dispute, often by making a joint statement with the prosecution or confirming the prosecution's version of the facts. Under these circumstances, there is little danger that the court will be misled by selective disclosure. In this respect a guilty plea is more like an offer to stipulate than a decision to take the stand. Here, petitioner's statement that she had done "some of" the proffered conduct did not pose a threat to the integrity of factfinding proceedings, for the purpose of the District Court's inquiry was simply to ensure that petitioner understood the charges and that there was a factual basis for the Government's case. * * *

Of course, a court may discharge its duty of ensuring a factual basis for a plea by "question[ing] the defendant under oath, on the record, and in the presence of counsel about the offense to which the defendant has pleaded." Rule 11(c)(5). We do not question the authority of a district court to make whatever inquiry it deems necessary in its sound discretion to assure itself the defendant is not being pressured to offer a plea for which there is no factual basis. A defendant who withholds information by invoking the privilege against self-incrimination at a plea colloquy runs the risk the district court will find the factual basis inadequate. At least once the plea has been accepted, statements or admissions made during the preceding plea colloquy are later admissible against the defendant, as is the plea itself. A statement admissible against a defendant, however, is not necessarily a waiver of the privilege against self-incrimination. Rule 11 does not prevent the defendant from relying upon the privilege at sentencing. * * *

B

The centerpiece of the Third Circuit's opinion is the idea that the entry of the guilty plea completes the incrimination of the defendant, thus extinguishing the privilege. Where a sentence has yet to be imposed, however, this Court has already rejected the proposition that "incrimination is complete once guilt has been adjudicated," *Estelle v. Smith,* 451 U.S. 454, 462 (1981), and we reject it again today. * * *

It is true, as a general rule, that where there can be no further incrimination, there is no basis for the assertion of the privilege. We conclude that principle applies to cases in which the sentence has been fixed and the judgment of conviction has become final. If no adverse consequences can be visited upon the convicted person by reason of further testimony, then there is no further incrimination to be feared.

Where the sentence has not yet been imposed a defendant may have a legitimate fear of adverse consequences from further testimony. As the Court stated in *Estelle:* "Any effort by the State to compel [the defendant] to testify against his will at the sentencing hearing clearly would contravene the Fifth Amendment." 451 U.S., at 463. *Estelle* was a capital case, but we find no reason not to apply the principle to noncapital sentencing hearings as well. "The essence of this basic constitutional principle is 'the requirement that the State which proposes to convict *and punish* an individual produce the evidence against him by the independent labor of its officers, not by the simple, cruel expedient of forcing it from his own lips.' " *Id.,* at 462 (emphasis in original) (quoting *Culombe v. Connecticut,* 367 U.S. 568, 581–82 (1961)). * * *

The Fifth Amendment by its terms prevents a person from being "compelled in any criminal case to be a witness against himself." U.S. Const., Amdt. 5. To maintain that sentencing proceedings are not part of "any criminal case" is contrary to the law and to common sense. * * * Petitioner faced imprisonment from one year upwards to life, depending on the circumstances of the crime. To say that she had no right to remain silent but instead could be compelled to cooperate in the deprivation of her liberty would ignore the Fifth Amendment privilege at the precise stage where, from her point of view, it was most important. * * *

III

The Government suggests in a footnote that even if petitioner retained an unwaived privilege against self-incrimination in the sentencing phase of her case, the District Court was entitled, based on her silence, to draw an adverse inference with regard to the amount of drugs attributable to her. The normal rule in a criminal case is that no negative inference from the defendant's failure to testify is permitted. *Griffin v. California,* 380 U.S. 609, 614 (1965). We decline to adopt an exception for the sentencing phase of a criminal case with regard to factual determinations respecting the circumstances and details of the crime. * * *

The concerns which mandate the rule against negative inferences at a criminal trial apply with equal force at sentencing. Without question, the stakes are high: Here, the inference drawn by the District Court from petitioner's silence may have resulted in decades of added imprisonment. The Government often has a motive to demand a severe sentence, so the central purpose of the privilege—to protect a defendant from being the unwilling instrument of his or her own condemnation—remains of vital importance. * * *

The rule against adverse inferences is a vital instrument for teaching that the question in a criminal case is not whether the defendant committed the acts of which he is accused. The question is whether the Government has carried its burden to prove its allegations while respecting the defendant's individual rights. The Government retains the burden of proving facts relevant to the crime at the sentencing phase and cannot enlist the defendant in this process at the expense of the self-incrimination privilege. Whether silence bears upon the determination of a lack of remorse, or upon acceptance of responsibility for purposes of the downward adjustment provided in § 3E1.1 of the United States Sentencing Guidelines (1998), is a separate question. It is not before us, and we express no view on it.

By holding petitioner's silence against her in determining the facts of the offense at the sentencing hearing, the District Court imposed an impermissible burden on the exercise of the constitutional right against compelled self-incrimination. * * *

■ SCALIA, J., dissenting.

I agree with the Court that Mitchell had the right to invoke her Fifth Amendment privilege during the sentencing phase of her criminal case. In my view, however, she did not have the right to have the sentencer abstain from making the adverse inferences that reasonably flow from her failure to testify. I therefore respectfully dissent.

The majority muses that the no-adverse-inference rule has found "wide acceptance in the legal culture" and has even become "an essential feature of our legal tradition." Although the latter assertion strikes me as hyperbolic, the former may be true—which is adequate reason not to overrule these cases, a course I in no way propose. It is not adequate reason, however, to extend these cases into areas where they do not yet apply, since neither logic nor history can be marshaled in defense of them. The illogic of the *Griffin* line is plain, for it runs exactly counter to normal evidentiary inferences: If I ask my son whether he saw a movie I had forbidden him to watch, and he remains silent, the import of his silence is clear. * * *

Which brings me to the greatest—the most bizarre—inconsistency of all: the combination of the rule that the Court adopts today with the balance of our jurisprudence relating to sentencing in particular. "[C]ourts in this country and in England," we have said, have "practiced a policy under which a sentencing judge [can] exercise a wide discretion in the sources and types of evidence used to assist him in determining the kind and extent of punishment to be imposed within limits fixed by law." *Williams v. New York, supra,* at 246. "[A] sentencing judge 'may appropriately conduct an inquiry broad in scope, largely unlimited either as to the kind of information he may consider, or the source from which it may come.' " *Nichols v. United States,* 511 U.S. 738, 747 (1994) (quoting *United States v. Tucker,* 404 U.S. 443, 446 (1972)). "Few facts available to a sentencing judge," we have observed, "are more relevant to 'the likelihood that [a defendant] will transgress no more, the hope that he may respond to rehabilitative efforts to assist with a lawful future career, [and] the degree to which he does or does not deem himself at war with his society' " than a defendant's willingness to cooperate. *Roberts v. United States,* 445 U.S. 552, 558 (1980). Today's opinion states, in as inconspicuous a manner as possible at the very end of its analysis (one imagines that if the statement were delivered orally it would be spoken in a very low voice, and with the Court's hand over its mouth), that its holding applies only to inferences drawn from silence "in determining the facts of the offense." "Whether silence bears upon the determination of a lack of remorse, or upon acceptance of responsibility for purposes of the downward adjustment provided in § 3E1.1 of the United States Sentencing Guidelines (1998), is a separate question" on which the majority expresses no view. Never mind that we have said before, albeit in dicta, that "[w]e doubt that a principled distinction may be drawn between 'enhancing' the punishment imposed upon the petitioner and denying him the 'leniency' he claims would be appropriate if he had cooperated." *Roberts, supra,* at 557, n.4.

Of course the clutter swept under the rug by limiting the opinion to "determining facts of the offense" is not merely application of today's opinion to § 3E1.1, but its application to *all* determinations of acceptance of responsibility, repentance, character, and future dangerousness, in both federal and state prosecutions—that is to say, to what is probably the *bulk* of what most sentencing is all about. If the Court ultimately decides—in the fullness of time and after a decent period of confusion in the lower courts—that the "no inference" rule is indeed *limited* to "determining facts of the offense," then we will have a system in which a state court *can* increase the sentence of a convicted drug possessor who refuses to say how many ounces he possessed—not because that suggests he possessed the larger amount (to make such an inference would be unconstitutional!) but because his refusal to cooperate suggests he is unrepentant.

NOTES & QUESTIONS

1. **Silence and the No-Adverse-Inferences Rule.** Everyone knows criminal defendants have a Fifth Amendment "right to remain silent," but does this right prevent a judge or prosecutor from suggesting to a jury that a defendant's silence may be interpreted as an implicit admission of guilt? In *Griffin v. California,* 380 U.S. 609, 615 (1965), the Supreme Court squarely held that the Fifth Amendment "forbids either comment by the prosecution on the accused's silence or instructions by the court that such silence is evidence of guilt." In *Mitchell,* the Court then extended the *Griffin* no-adverse-inference rule from trial to sentencing—sort of. In dissent, Justice Scalia suggested that the *Mitchell* holding may leave out "the *bulk* of what most sentencing is all about." What exactly did he mean by this?

2. **Remorse in the Lower Courts.** *Mitchell* indicated that a defendant's silence may not be used against him or her for the purpose of determining the facts of his or her criminal conduct but left open whether silence could be taken as evidence of the defendant's lack of remorse. In the wake of *Mitchell,* lower courts have divided over this open question. The New Hampshire Supreme Court provided a helpful survey of some of the decisions on both sides of the question in *State v. Burgess,* 943 A.2d 727 (N.H. 2008). Ultimately, the *Burgess* court itself took the position that "a sentencing court may not draw a negative inference of lack of remorse from a defendant's silence at sentencing." *Id.* at 738. In the court's view, the practice of inferring a lack of remorse from silence, and then increasing the sentence based on lack of remorse, created a "cruel trilemma": the defendant must either "admit wrongdoing and jeopardize his post-trial remedies, testify falsely and risk a perjury conviction, or remain silent and risk obtaining a greater sentence." *Id.* at 736. However, the court limited its holding "to situations where a defendant maintains his innocence throughout the criminal process and risks incriminating himself if he expresses remorse at sentencing." *Id.* at 738. The court also noted that its holding "does not preclude a court from considering other evidence besides a defendant's silence that indicates a defendant's lack of remorse." *Id.*

3. **Added Punishment Versus Lost Leniency.** Some post-*Mitchell* lower-court decisions distinguish between increasing punishment based on silence and denying leniency. *Mitchell* itself might be seen as an increased-punishment case insofar as the sentencing judge used silence to infer the defendant's guilt of a certain volume of drug-dealing that triggered a mandatory minimum prison term. By contrast, when a defendant's silence is used as a basis to deny probation, this is sometimes characterized as merely a form of lost leniency that does not raise Fifth Amendment problems.

Consider, for instance, *State v. Hernandez,* 295 P.3d 451 (Ariz. Ct. App. 2013). After her conviction for a sexual offense, Hernandez declined to make any statement about her offense to the probation officer preparing her presentence investigation report. Based on her refusal to discuss the offense, the probation officer opined that Hernandez would not be able to participate successfully in sex offender treatment programs—a view that was cited by the sentencing judge as a basis for denying probation and ordering

Hernandez imprisoned. On appeal, Hernandez argued that she was effectively punished for exercising her right to remain silent. However, the Court of Appeals of Arizona "concluded the Fifth Amendment does not preclude a sentencing court from considering a defendant's refusal to answer questions about the offense in determining whether he or she is a suitable candidate for probation. . . . Because Hernandez had no right to a suspension of sentence or placement on probation, the trial court neither abused its discretion nor violated the Fifth Amendment by declining to grant her that leniency." *Id.* at 454.

Note, however, that other courts have questioned such logic. For instance, the New Hampshire Supreme Court has expressed "doubt that a principled distinction may be drawn between 'enhancing' the punishment imposed upon the defendant and denying him the 'leniency' he claims would be appropriate if he had expressed remorse." *Burgess*, 943 A.2d at 737 (citation and internal quotation marks omitted). Framed either way, the court suggested, the defendant may effectively still face the same cruel trilemma in deciding whether to remain silent.

4. **Out-of-Court Presentence Interviews.** *Mitchell* dealt with a defendant who was apparently penalized for failing to testify at her sentencing hearing. In ruling in the defendant's favor, the Supreme Court affirmed that the right to remain silent applies at such hearings. What about at presentence investigation interviews with a probation officer? Or the expert psychological evaluations that are sometimes performed in aid of sentencing? In *Estelle v. Smith*, 451 U.S. 454 (1981), a pre-*Mitchell* decision, the Supreme Court indicated that the right to remain silent may also extend to out-of-court interviews that are used in determining a sentence. At Smith's capital sentencing hearing, the State relied on an expert psychiatric evaluation in arguing that Smith presented a risk of additional criminal violence in the future. The evaluation was based, in part, on the expert's out-of-court interview of Smith. On appeal, Smith argued that use of the interview against him violated the Fifth Amendment because he was not notified that he had a right to remain silent during the interview, i.e., he was not given his *Miranda* warnings. The Supreme Court agreed, holding that a "criminal defendant, who neither initiates a psychiatric evaluation nor attempts to introduce any psychiatric evidence, may not be compelled to respond to a psychiatrist if his statements can be used against him at a capital sentencing proceeding." *Id.* at 468.

Although this holding was framed in relation to capital sentencing, the Court, as we have seen, later stated that *Estelle*'s reasoning applied with "full force" in *Mitchell*, which was a noncapital case. *Mitchell*'s reliance on *Estelle* casts doubt on efforts to limit *Estelle* to the capital context. Nor is there any apparent reason to distinguish psychological evaluations like the one at issue in *Estelle* from other sorts of presentence investigation interviews.

5. **Remorse Revisited.** Does *Estelle* help to resolve the ongoing debate over whether silence can be used against a defendant on a lack-of-remorse theory? The Fourth Circuit has suggested as much:

> [In *Estelle*] the Supreme Court found that the Fifth Amendment prohibited using a defendant's unwarned statement to prove . . . future dangerousness. Future dangerousness and lack of remorse are similar factors that pertain to character rather than to circumstances of criminal conduct. Accordingly, at least for the purpose of capital sentencing, *Estelle* belies any supposed distinction created by *Mitchell* between circumstances of criminal conduct and characteristics of the defendant. . . . Thus, *Estelle* and *Mitchell* together suggest that the Fifth Amendment may well prohibit considering a defendant's silence regarding . . . lack of remorse.

United States v. Caro, 597 F.3d 608, 630 (4th Cir. 2010).

6. **Section 3E1.1 of the Federal Sentencing Guidelines.** In the same passage in which the *Mitchell* Court declined to take a position on the use of silence for remorse-determination purposes, the Court also expressly left open "[w]hether silence bears upon the determination of . . . acceptance of responsibility for purposes of the downward adjustment provided in § 3E1.1 of the United States Sentencing Guidelines (1998)." Section 3E1.1 plays a prominent role in the federal sentencing guidelines system. The provision is designed to provide a reduction in sentence length of about one-quarter to one-third in cases in which the judge determines that the defendant accepted responsibility for the offense. In practice, judges routinely provide the acceptance discount when the defendant pleads guilty, but sometimes even these defendants are denied the discount—often on the ground that the defendant lacked sufficient remorse for the offense. Michael O'Hear, *Remorse, Cooperation, and "Acceptance of Responsibility": The Structure, Implementation, and Reform of Section 3E1.1 of the Federal Sentencing Guidelines*, 91 NW. U. L. REV. 1507, 1510–11 (1997).

The U.S. Sentencing Commission has promulgated official commentary on § 3E1.1 that attempts to address the Fifth Amendment problem. Application Note 1(a) states that "a defendant is not required to volunteer, or affirmatively admit, relevant conduct beyond the offense of conviction in order to obtain a reduction . . . . A defendant may remain silent in respect to relevant conduct beyond the offense of conviction without affecting his ability to obtain a reduction under this subsection." The Commission thus draws a distinction between the offense of conviction, as to which an affirmative admission can be required as the price of the acceptance discount, and any other criminal conduct ("relevant conduct"), as to which the defendant may remain silent without fear of losing the § 3E1.1 adjustment.

7. **Waiver.** The *Mitchell* majority observed, "We may assume for purposes of this opinion, then, that if petitioner had pleaded not guilty and, having taken the stand at a trial, testified she did 'some of it,' she could have been cross-examined on the frequency of her drug deliveries and the quantity of cocaine involved." 526 U.S. at 322. The defendant's decision to testify constitutes a waiver of the right to remain silent and opens the door to cross-examination by the government. However, the scope of the waiver is limited by the scope of the testimony. A defendant's testimony about her drug-dealing, for instance, does not necessarily permit the government to ask her

questions about an unrelated drunk-driving case. Nor, if the defendant refused to answer such questions, would it seem permissible for the sentencing judge in the drug-dealing case to infer the truth of the drunk-driving charge based on the defendant's silence.

PROBLEM 3-1: RIGHT TO REMAIN SILENT?

Police officers responded to a call about a suspected residential burglary in progress. Upon their arrival at the house in question, they saw Adam exiting from a window. He was wearing a full backpack. Adam ran when he saw the police but was apprehended in an alley a few minutes later. A search of the backpack revealed a number of valuables that were later identified as belonging to the owner of the house. In some bushes just a few feet away from the place of arrest, officers also found a loaded handgun. An investigation revealed that (a) the handgun bore Adam's fingerprints, and (b) the handgun had been reported stolen from another home in the same neighborhood about a week earlier. Adam was charged with the crime of armed burglary, which carries a sentence of five to twenty years.

At trial, Adam testified in his own defense. He admitted that he broke into the home and stole the valuables that were in his backpack, but he denied that he was carrying a weapon at the time. Effective cross-examination of the State's fingerprint expert exposed some slight shakiness in the identification of Adam's fingerprints on the gun. In the end, the jury acquitted Adam of armed burglary, but convicted him of the lesser-included offense of simple burglary, which carries a sentence of one to ten years.

At sentencing, Judge Bentham asked Adam, "Were you the one who stole that gun?" Adam responded, "On the advice of counsel, I invoke my Fifth Amendment right to remain silent." Later, in imposing sentence, Judge Bentham declared, "You may have been able to pull the wool over the jury's eyes about that gun, but I am not impressed. Your silence today about the gun speaks volumes. I'd normally give a two-year sentence for a burglary of this sort, but I am tacking on two extra years for the theft of the gun, which goes to show what a dangerous person you are, plus an additional two years for not owning up to what you did." Violation of *Mitchell*? How might you argue in the affirmative as defense counsel? How might you respond for the State?

4. OTHER PROCEDURAL RIGHTS AT SENTENCING

In this section, we more briefly outline a few additional procedural rights at sentencing. First, in most cases, the defendant has a *right to counsel* at sentencing, *Mempa v. Rhay*, 389 U.S. 128 (1967)—including for indigent defendants a right to court-appointed counsel.[13] Moreover, the defendant's right to a lawyer encompasses a right to *effective assistance of counsel*. In order to obtain a resentencing on the basis of ineffective assistance, the defendant must normally satisfy a two-part

[13] The right to court-appointed counsel is recognized in felony cases and in misdemeanor cases in which a sentence of incarceration is imposed, including a suspended sentence of incarceration. Alabama v. Shelton, 535 U.S. 654 (2002).

test, showing that (1) counsel's performance was unreasonable under prevailing professional norms (the so-called "performance prong"), and (2) there was a reasonable probability of a different outcome but for counsel's unprofessional errors (the "prejudice prong"). The United States Supreme Court has further specified,

> A fair assessment of attorney performance requires that every effort be made to eliminate the distorting effects of hindsight, to reconstruct the circumstances of counsel's challenged conduct, and to evaluate the conduct from counsel's perspective at the time. Because of the difficulties inherent in making the evaluation, a court must indulge a strong presumption that counsel's conduct falls within the wide range of reasonable professional assistance; that is, the defendant must overcome the presumption that, under the circumstances, the challenged action might be considered sound trial strategy. * * *
>
> [S]trategic choices made after thorough investigation of law and facts relevant to plausible options are virtually unchallengeable; and strategic choices made after less than complete investigation are reasonable precisely to the extent that reasonable professional judgments support the limitations on investigation.

Strickland v. Washington, 466 U.S. 668, 689, 690–91 (1984) (internal quotation marks and citation omitted). These general standards apply equally to claims of ineffectiveness at sentencing as to claims of ineffectiveness at trial.

The standards are demanding, but defendants do sometimes prevail. By way of illustration, consider *Williams v. Taylor*, 529 U.S. 362 (2000), a death-penalty case. In ruling in the defendant's favor, the Supreme Court observed,

> The record establishes that counsel did not begin to prepare for [the sentencing] phase of the proceeding until a week before the trial. They failed to conduct an investigation that would have uncovered extensive records graphically describing Williams' nightmarish childhood, not because of any strategic calculation but because they incorrectly thought that state law barred access to such records. Had they done so, the jury would have learned that Williams' parents had been imprisoned for the criminal neglect of Williams and his siblings, that Williams had been severely and repeatedly beaten by his father, that he had been committed to the custody of the social services bureau for two years during his parents' incarceration (including one stint in an abusive foster home), and then, after his parents were released from prison, had been returned to his parents' custody.
>
> Counsel failed to introduce available evidence that Williams was "borderline mentally retarded" and did not

> advance beyond sixth grade in school. They failed to seek prison records recording Williams' commendations for helping to crack a prison drug ring and for returning a guard's missing wallet, or the testimony of prison officials who described Williams as among the inmates "least likely to act in a violent, dangerous or provocative way." Counsel failed even to return the phone call of a certified public accountant who had offered to testify that he had visited Williams frequently when Williams was incarcerated as part of a prison ministry program, that Williams "seemed to thrive in a more regimented and structured environment," and that Williams was proud of the carpentry degree he earned while in prison.
>
> [These omissions] clearly demonstrate that trial counsel did not fulfill their obligation to conduct a thorough investigation of the defendant's background.
>
> We are also persuaded . . . that counsel's unprofessional service prejudiced Williams . . . .
>
> [T]he graphic description of Williams' childhood, filled with abuse and privation, or the reality that he was "borderline mentally retarded," might well have influenced the jury's appraisal of his moral culpability.

Id. at 395–98 (internal citations omitted).

Although *Williams* was a capital case, the Supreme Court has indicated that the same basic standards also apply in noncapital sentencing proceedings. For instance, in *Glover v. United States*, 531 U.S. 198, 203 (2001), the Court held that an attorney error resulting in an increase in prison time from six to twenty-one months would be sufficient to satisfy the prejudice prong.

Very rarely, in truly extreme cases of attorney neglect, the defendant may be excused from satisfying the prejudice prong of the two-part *Strickland* test. For instance, in *Lewis v. Zatecky*, 993 F.3d 994, 1006 (7th Cir. 2021), the Seventh Circuit held that Lewis, the defendant, was entitled to a resentencing when his lawyer's effort at sentencing consisted, in its entirety, of "utter[ing] two short sentences: 'Judge, I'm going to defer to Mr. Lewis if he has any comments. I don't have anything to add.' " Characterizing this performance as effectively an abandonment of the client, the Seventh Circuit ruled that prejudice could simply be presumed.

Second, the defendant has a limited *right to discovery* in relation to sentencing. In particular, the Supreme Court has held, "[T]he suppression by the prosecution of evidence favorable to an accused . . . violates due process where the evidence is material either to guilt *or to punishment*, irrespective of the good faith or bad faith of the prosecution." *Brady v. Maryland*, 373 U.S. 83, 87 (1963) (emphasis added). For instance, in *Cone v. Bell*, 556 U.S. 449 (2009), a capital case, the Supreme

Court considered whether the state violated the *Brady* rule by failing to disclose a variety of witness statements and other evidence that would have lent support to the defendant's position "that he habitually used excessive amounts of drugs, that his addiction affected his behavior during his crime spree, and that the State's arguments to the contrary were false and misleading." Even though this evidence was not material to Cone's guilt, the Court nonetheless concluded, "Because the evidence suppressed at Cone's trial may well have been material to the jury's assessment of the proper punishment in this case, we conclude that a full review of the suppressed evidence and its effect is warranted." *Id.* at 475. The case was remanded for the lower courts to determine whether the evidence was, in fact, material, i.e., whether there was "a reasonable probability that, had the evidence been disclosed, the result of the proceeding would have been different." *Id.* at 470. Note that the materiality requirement for alleged discovery violations parallels the prejudice prong that must be satisfied when the defendant alleges ineffective assistance of counsel.

Third, the defendant has a *right to the prosecutor's performance as promised in a plea deal.* For instance, in *Santobello v. New York*, 404 U.S. 257 (1971), the defendant agreed to plead guilty to a gambling offense carrying a one-year maximum; in return, the prosecutor agreed to make no recommendation to the court regarding the sentence. There followed some unusual delays in the case following the acceptance of the defendant's plea. Finally, the case proceeded to sentencing before a new judge and with new lawyers on both the prosecution and defense sides. Apparently unaware of the terms of the plea deal, the new prosecutor recommended the maximum one-year prison term, which the judge then imposed. Although there seemed no bad intent on the part of the state, the Supreme Court held, "[W]hen a plea rests in any significant degree on a promise or agreement of the prosecutor, so that it can be said to be part of the inducement or consideration, such promise must be fulfilled." *Id.* at 262. However, the Court left it up to the lower courts to decide the remedy—that is, whether the defendant would get a resentencing in front of a new judge or be permitted to withdraw his guilty plea.

While the courts will enforce the *letter* of a plea deal, they will not necessarily concern themselves with the *spirit*. Consider, for instance, *United States v. Benchimol*, 471 U.S. 453 (1985). The defendant agreed to plead guilty to mail fraud in return for the government's promise to recommend probation with restitution. However, the presentence report incorrectly indicated that the government would stand silent as to punishment. At the sentencing hearing, the defendant's lawyer informed the court of the actual terms of the deal. The prosecutor then simply stated, "That is an accurate representation." An appellate court concluded that the government had breached the plea deal because it "made no effort to explain its reasons for agreeing to recommend a lenient sentence but rather left an impression with the court of less-than-enthusiastic support for leniency." However, the Supreme Court reversed, observing, "It may well be that the Government in a particular case might commit itself to 'enthusiastically' make a particular recommendation to the court, and it may be that the Government in a particular case might agree to explain to the court the reasons for the Government's making a particular recommendation. But respondent does not contend, nor did the Court of Appeals find, that the Government had in fact undertaken to do either of these things here." *Id.* at 455.

Fourth, the defendant has a limited *right to be sentenced pursuant to the law as it existed at the time of the offense*, that is, without regard to subsequent amendments that make sentences harsher. As the Supreme Court has put it, "The Constitution forbids the passage of ex post facto laws, a category that includes '[e]very law that changes the punishment, and inflicts a greater punishment, than the law annexed to the crime, when committed.'" *Peugh v. United States*, 569 U.S. 530, 532–33 (2013) (quoting *Calder v. Bull,* 3 Dall. 386, 390 (1798)). Thus, in *Peugh v. United States*, the Court held that the defendant had to be sentenced under the version of the federal sentencing guideline for fraud that existed in 1999–2000, the time of his offense, rather than the much harsher version that had been adopted by the time of his sentencing in 2010. Notably, the Court reached this conclusion even though the federal guidelines were only advisory in 2010, leaving the judge with discretion to select a more lenient sentence than what the guidelines recommended. The Court observed,

> [T]he fact that the sentencing authority exercises some measure of discretion will * * * not defeat an ex post facto claim. On the other hand, we have made it clear that mere speculation or conjecture that a change in law will retrospectively increase the punishment for a crime will not suffice to establish a violation of the Ex Post Facto Clause. The touchstone of this Court's inquiry is whether a given change in law presents a sufficient risk of increasing the measure of punishment attached to the covered crimes. The question when a change in law creates such a risk is a matter of degree; the test cannot be reduced to a single formula.

Id. at 539 (citations and internal quotation marks omitted). Why do you suppose the Constitution prohibits the retroactive application of new sentencing laws?

Note that the Supreme Court has distinguished procedural changes in sentencing law from substantive for ex post facto purposes. For instance, in *Dobbert v. Florida*, 432 U.S. 282 (1977), the Court approved a retroactive change in Florida's death-penalty law that permitted judges to override a jury's recommendation of mercy. The Court observed, "Even though it may work to the disadvantage of a defendant, a procedural change is not ex post facto." *Id.* at 293.

Note further that, if the law is made more *lenient*, defendants are not necessarily entitled to be sentenced under the more favorable law. *United States v. Prophet*, 989 F.3d 231, 239 (3d Cir. 2021). For instance, in the federal system, the United States Sentencing Commission sometimes adopts softening amendments to the sentencing guidelines; under 28 U.S.C. § 994(u), the Commission may choose whether or not to give retroactive effect to such amendments.

NOTES & QUESTIONS

1. **Trial Versus Sentencing.** We have outlined above several defendant rights at sentencing that are well-established in the Supreme Court's jurisprudence. In the notes that follow, we touch on a few additional rights whose status at sentencing is less clear. Much of the case law in this area is animated by the difficult questions of whether and in what respects there are fundamental differences in the nature of a guilt-innocence trial and a sentencing hearing, and whether and to what extent any such differences justify reduced procedural protections for the defendant at sentencing. Recall the case with which we began our consideration of constitutional due process at sentencing, *Williams v. New York*, which took the position that there are stark differences in the nature of the proceedings, and that defendants are accordingly entitled to few, if any, due process rights at sentencing. However, *Apprendi v. New Jersey* and its progeny have blurred the distinction between trial and sentencing, at least with respect to factfinding that shifts the minimum required or maximum permissible sentence. Yet, for discretionary choices within an established sentencing range, notions of constitutional due process seem to have evolved comparatively little from the time of *Williams*. Additionally, the case law in this area is also marked by debate and uncertainty over whether heightened procedural protections recognized first in capital cases should be extended to noncapital sentencing.

2. **Right to Notice.** The Sixth Amendment gives defendants a right to "be informed of the nature and cause of the accusation." Should there be an analogous constitutional right of notice as to the adverse information used against the defendant at sentencing? In *Gardner v. Florida*, 430 U.S. 349 (1977), a badly fractured Supreme Court overturned a death sentence based on the state's failure to disclose to the defendant portions of a presentence investigation report. Writing for a plurality, Justice Stevens concluded that the defendant was "denied due process of law when the death sentence was imposed, at least in part, on the basis of information which he had no opportunity to deny or explain." *Id.* at 362. Although other justices preferred to ground the holding in the Eighth Amendment, rather than the Due Process Clause, there seemed a solid majority behind the view that the information on which a death sentence is based must be disclosed to the defendant or the defendant's lawyer for potential rebuttal. However, the Court has never squarely held that this notice requirement also applies in noncapital cases.

The closest the Court came was in *Burns v. United States*, 501 U.S. 129 (1991). In that case, the Court considered whether a federal judge could impose a sentence above the applicable federal sentencing guidelines range without giving the defendant advance notice of an intention to do so. Holding in the negative, the Court relied chiefly on the Federal Rules of Criminal Procedure. However, the Court also noted, "[W]ere we to read Rule 32 to dispense with notice, we would then have to confront the serious question whether notice in this setting is mandated by the Due Process Clause." *Id.* at 138. Taking this cue from *Burns*, several lower courts have subsequently found a sentencing right to notice in noncapital cases. *See* Alan C. Michaels, *Trial Rights at Sentencing*, 81 N.C. L. REV. 1771, 1811 (2003) (collecting cases).

More recently, in *Irizarry v. United States*, 553 U.S. 708 (2008), the Court indicated that the constitutional concerns identified in *Burns* were limited to the particular federal sentencing system in place at the time. Sentenced after the federal guidelines were transformed from mandatory to advisory, Irizarry was given a prison term longer than what the guidelines recommended. He objected that he was provided with no advance notice of the judge's intention to sentence above the guidelines, as required by *Burns*. However, the Court held that the "due process concerns that motivated [*Burns*] to require notice in a world of mandatory Guidelines no longer provide a basis for this Court to extend the rule set forth in *Burns*." *Id.* at 714. *Irizarry* thus suggests that constitutional notice rights may not apply with respect to the considerations that lead a judge to bump up a sentence within a discretionary range.

3. **Right to Allocute and Present a Sentencing "Defense."** As we have seen, the defendant has at least a limited right to remain silent at sentencing. Is the reverse also true? In other words, does the defendant have a constitutional right to speak (allocute) at sentencing? The Supreme Court has never directly answered this question, and the lower courts have split over it. Michaels, *supra*, at 1845.

At *trial*, there is a recognized constitutional right for defendants to testify in their own defense, which has been connected to broader rights to call witnesses and present a defense. *Arkansas v. Rock,* 483 U.S. 44 (1987). Whether either of these broader rights (that is, to call witnesses and present a defense) applies at sentencing has also been left unaddressed by the Supreme Court. Lower courts indicate that the defendant does have a right to rebut evidence used against him or her at sentencing, but the lower courts have generally rejected claims that the defendant has a right to call witnesses. Michaels, *supra*, at 1846.

4. **Right to Be Sentenced Based on Accurate Information.** The Supreme Court has indicated that a sentence based on inaccurate information may in some circumstances violate the Due Process Clause, but the Court has not yet clearly held that such a sentence would be *categorically* unconstitutional. The leading Supreme Court decision is *Townsend v. Burke*, 334 U.S. 736 (1948), in which the Court reversed a sentence that was based on inaccurate information about the defendant's criminal history. However, in so holding, the Court seemed to emphasize that the defendant had not been represented by a lawyer at the sentencing. *See, e.g., id.* at 740–41 ("Consequently, on this record we conclude that, *while disadvantaged by lack*

of counsel, this prisoner was sentenced on the basis of assumptions concerning his criminal record which were materially untrue. Such a result, whether caused by carelessness or design, is inconsistent with due process of law, and such a conviction cannot stand." (emphasis added)).

Another frequently cited Supreme Court decision in this area is *United States v. Tucker*, 404 U.S. 443 (1972), in which the Court overturned a sentence that was based on two prior convictions that were subsequently held to be unconstitutional because of a denial of the defendant's right to counsel in the earlier cases. The Court analogized the situation to *Townsend* insofar as both defendants were "sentenced on the basis of assumptions concerning [their] criminal record[s] which were materially untrue." *Id.* at 447. However, the Court also noted that the "misinformation" in *Tucker* was of "constitutional magnitude," *id.*, and stated that a ruling in favor of the defendant was necessary in order to prevent "[e]rosion of the *Gideon* principle" (i.e., the right to counsel), *id.* at 449. Thus, *Tucker*, no less than *Townsend*, leaves open the question of whether a sentence based on inaccurate information implicates the Due Process Clause *in the absence of a denial of counsel*.

Despite these limitations, *Townsend* and *Tucker* have sometimes been cited by lower courts more broadly for the proposition that the defendant does have a due-process right to be sentenced on the basis of accurate information. *See, e.g., United States v. Hill*, 915 F.3d 669, 674 (9th Cir. 2019) (citing *Townsend* and *Tucker*); *United States v. Gonzalez-Castillo*, 562 F.3d 80, 83 (1st Cir. 2009) (citing *Townsend*). However, at least one of these courts has limited relief to cases in which the sentencing judge "made it abundantly clear that (the challenged information) was the basis for its sentence." *Hill*, 915 F.3d at 674 (citation omitted). Thus, a mere "passing reference" to misinformation would not suffice. *Id.*

5. **Right to Be Present.** Although the Supreme Court has not yet squarely addressed the question, the lower courts generally hold that the defendant has a constitutional right to be physically present at the sentencing hearing. *See, e.g., United States v. Diggles*, 957 F.3d 551, 557–58 (5th Cir. 2020); Michaels, *supra*, at 1839–40 (collecting cases). Note, however, that the right may be deemed waived if the defendant voluntarily chooses not to attend the sentencing, e.g., by absconding. *See, e.g., Harrison v. State*, 707 N.E.2d 767, 785–86 (Ind. 1999); *State v. Anderson*, 929 P.2d 1107, 1109 (Utah 1996). In such cases, sentencing *in absentia* may be permitted.

6. **Right to Public Sentencing.** The defendant's right to a public trial is protected by the Sixth Amendment. Although there is little case law directly on point, there are some lower-court decisions suggesting that this trial right may also extend to sentencing. *United States v. Thompson*, 713 F.3d 388, 394 (8th Cir. 2013); Michaels, *supra*, at 1832. Members of the press and public may also have a distinct First Amendment right to attend a sentencing hearing. *United States v. Alcantara*, 396 F.3d 189, 196 (2d Cir. 2005). However, the public-trial right is not absolute, and limited closures of the courtroom during sentencing may be permissible if justified by a

sufficiently strong state interest, such as protecting a witness from potential retaliation. *Thompson*, 713 F.3d at 396.

7. **Exclusionary Rules.** At trial, the government may be precluded from using evidence obtained in violation of the defendant's rights under the Fourth or Fifth Amendments. In *Estelle v. Smith*, 451 U.S. 454 (1981), discussed above, the Supreme Court held that a statement taken in violation of the defendant's Fifth Amendment *Miranda* rights could not be used against the defendant at sentencing. Although some might read *Estelle* as limited to the death-penalty context, the Court's reliance on *Estelle* in the subsequent noncapital case of *Mitchell v. United States*, 526 U.S. 319 (1999), excerpted above, suggests that *Estelle* should be read to have broader application. There is also some lower-court authority supporting the extension of the Fifth Amendment exclusionary rule to sentencing. Michaels, *supra*, at 1851.

By contrast, the lower courts have more consistently resisted application of the Fourth Amendment exclusionary rule in sentencing proceedings. *See, e.g., United States v. Ryan*, 236 F.3d 1268 (10th Cir. 2001) (holding that drugs seized in violation of motorist's Fourth Amendment rights were properly considered at sentencing in arriving at proper offense level for motorist's other, unrelated drug offenses). One possible exception involves circumstances indicating that the police violated the defendant's Fourth Amendment rights with the *intent* of securing an enhanced sentence. *See, e.g., United States v. Kim*, 25 F.3d 1426, 1435 & n. 8 (9th Cir. 1994).

8. **Right to Individualized Sentence.** In *Woodson v. North Carolina*, 428 U.S. 280 (1976), the Supreme Court considered the constitutionality of a statute mandating capital punishment for *all* defendants convicted of first-degree murder. A fractured Court held that the statute violated the Eighth Amendment, with the key opinion authored by Justices Stewart, Powell, and Stevens. They wrote,

> A process that accords no significance to relevant facets of the character and record of the individual offender or the circumstances of the particular offense excludes from consideration in fixing the ultimate punishment of death the possibility of compassionate or mitigating factors stemming from the diverse frailties of humankind. It treats all persons convicted of a designated offense not as uniquely individual human beings, but as members of a faceless, undifferentiated mass to be subjected to the blind infliction of the penalty of death.
>
> This Court has previously recognized that "(f)or the determination of sentences, justice generally requires consideration of more than the particular acts by which the crime was committed and that there be taken into account the circumstances of the offense together with the character and propensities of the offender." Consideration of both the offender and the offense in order to arrive at a just and appropriate sentence has been viewed as a progressive and humanizing development. While the prevailing practice of individualizing sentencing

> determinations generally reflects simply enlightened policy rather than a constitutional imperative, we believe that in capital cases the fundamental respect for humanity underlying the Eighth Amendment requires consideration of the character and record of the individual offender and the circumstances of the particular offense as a constitutionally indispensable part of the process of inflicting the penalty of death.

Id. at 303–04 (citations omitted).[14]

Woodson thus seemed to establish a right to individualized sentencing, and a corresponding rejection of mandatory punishment, in relation to the death penalty. Later, in *Harmelin v. Michigan*, 501 U.S. 957 (1991), the Court considered the constitutionality of a statute mandating life without the possibility of parole for certain drug offenses. In rejecting the defendant's invocation of *Woodson*, the Court declared, "We have drawn the line of required individualized sentencing at capital cases, and see no basis for extending it further." *Id.* at 996.

Yet, extend it further the Court eventually did in *Miller v. Alabama*, 567 U.S. 460 (2012). In this case, the Court rejected mandatory life without the possibility of parole for juvenile offenders:

> Such mandatory penalties, by their nature, preclude a sentencer from taking account of an offender's age and the wealth of characteristics and circumstances attendant to it. Under these schemes, every juvenile will receive the same sentence as every other—the 17-year-old and the 14-year-old, the shooter and the accomplice, the child from a stable household and the child from a chaotic and abusive one .... In meting out the death penalty, the elision of all these differences would be strictly forbidden .... [A] similar rule should apply when a juvenile confronts a sentence of life (and death) in prison.

Id. at 476–77. While *Miller* represented a breakthrough of sorts in extending the right to individualized sentencing for the first time beyond the death penalty, the Court took pains to limit its holding to juveniles and to reaffirm that *Harmelin* remains good law for adult defendants. *Id.* at 482.

9. **Double Jeopardy.** In *Bullington v. Missouri*, 451 U.S. 430 (1981), a jury convicted the defendant of capital murder, but then sentenced him to life imprisonment in lieu of the death penalty. The defendant successfully appealed his conviction and was awarded a second trial. The state indicated that it intended once again to try to obtain a death sentence at the new trial. However, the Supreme Court ruled that such an effort would violate the Double Jeopardy Clause. In effect, the Court ruled, the first jury's decision acquitted the defendant of death, and the Constitution prohibited the state from forcing the defendant to face that sentencing possibility a second time.

Later, in *Monge v. California*, 524 U.S. 721 (1998), the Court held that the double-jeopardy protection of *Bullington* was strictly limited to the capital context. Monge's prison sentence had been doubled under a

[14] *Woodson* is considered in more detail in Chapter 7.

California sentence-enhancement law based on evidence that he had previously been convicted of an armed assault. However, a state appeals court ruled that the evidence had been insufficient to support the enhancement. Was the state permitted a second opportunity to prove the prior incident? Yes, the Supreme Court ruled. The state's failure to prove that a *noncapital* sentence enhancement applies is not the equivalent of an acquittal of the enhancement for double-jeopardy purposes.

Monge fits within a line of Supreme Court decisions that have generally minimized the ability of defendants to invoke double-jeopardy protections at sentencing. For instance, the Court has indicated that recidivism statutes that increase punishment based on prior convictions do not amount to unconstitutional double-punishment for the earlier offenses. *United States v. Watts,* 519 U.S. 148, 154 (1997) (*per curiam*). Similarly, the Court has permitted a sentencing judge to take into account criminal conduct of which the defendant was *acquitted* by a jury when selecting a sentence from within a statutory range. *Id.* at 155. The Court has also held that government appeals of sentences do not violate the Constitution, even though the Double Jeopardy Clause generally limits the ability of the government to appeal adverse *trial* outcomes. *United States v. DiFrancesco*, 449 U.S. 117 (1980).

10. **Purpose of Process.** Why do we provide any due process rights to defendants at sentencing, and on what basis might we wish to see more? In the case law and the commentary, much of the discussion of sentencing due process seems premised on the assumption that process exists only to enhance the *substantive* quality of decisions about punishment. Substantive quality might include such considerations as whether the sentence was based on factfinding that was accurate and complete, whether the sentence credibly advanced the approved purposes of punishment, and whether the benefits of the sentence were sufficient to justify the costs. Due process rights for the defendant might help to support substantively good decisions by, for instance, giving the defendant an opportunity to demonstrate that adverse factual allegations made by the prosecutor or contained in a PSR are false, or by allowing the defendant to present important mitigating information that would not otherwise be available to the judge.

But there may be more to due process than just enhancing the substantive quality of sentences. Consider *Mitchell* and the no-adverse-inferences rule. Do you think it would normally be incorrect to infer guilt from silence? Justice Scalia, for one, thought it perfectly obvious that the defendant who declines to speak is likely covering something up. *Mitchell v. United States,* 526 U.S. 314, 332 (1999) (Scalia, J., dissenting). However, even if you share that instinct, you might nonetheless feel that the no-adverse-inferences rule should still be maintained at sentencing. Regardless of accuracy interests, it may strike you as fundamentally unfair to tell defendants that they have a right to remain silent, but then use their silence against them.

As we saw in Chapter 1, there is a long tradition in sentencing theory of viewing just deserts as a valid end in itself, without regard to whether a desert-based sentence will prevent any future crimes or otherwise produce any desired consequences. It is possible to think about due process in a similar fashion. Perhaps there are certain procedural rights that should be observed at sentencing simply because to do otherwise would be unjust. Respecting these rights may be seen as a matter of treating others as we would wish to be treated ourselves, or of recognizing the shared humanity and essential dignity of all people.[15]

Social science provides an alternative way of thinking about the value of "procedural justice." A large body of research now indicates that adverse decisions made by legal actors (such as the judge's imposition of a sentence) are more likely to be accepted as legitimate if made through a process that is seen as fair and respectful. Tom R. Tyler & E. Allan Lind, *Procedural Justice, in* HANDBOOK OF JUSTICE RESEARCH IN LAW 65, 65 (Joseph Sanders & V. Lee Hamilton eds., 2001). The perceived legitimacy of legal decisionmakers, in turn, promotes cooperation with legal authorities and the internalization of a sense of obligation to obey the law. Tom R. Tyler, *Procedural Justice, Legitimacy, and the Effective Rule of Law,* 30 CRIME & JUST. 283, 286, 297 (2003). In this way, procedural justice at sentencing may reinforce the substantive goals of punishment—again, without regard to whether the process is affirmatively contributing to the substantive quality of the decisions. More specifically, the research indicates that the key components of procedural justice are whether the person affected by a decision has a meaningful opportunity to tell his or her side of the story ("voice"), and whether the decisionmaker conveys a sense of concern regarding the person's welfare, is perceived as unbiased, and treats the person with dignity and respect.[16]

Among the different procedural rights discussed so far in this chapter, which do you think are most important for the purpose of enhancing the *substantive* quality of sentencing decisions? Which seem most important from a *procedural* justice standpoint?

PROBLEM 3-2: "SHALL CONSIDER AS AN AGGRAVATING FACTOR"

A Wisconsin statute, Wis. Stat. § 973.017, includes the following provisions:

> **(5)** AGGRAVATING FACTORS; VIOLENT FELONY COMMITTED AGAINST ELDER PERSON.
>
> **(a)** In this subsection:
>
> **1.** "Elder person" means any individual who is 62 years of age or older.

[15] An influential "dignitary" theory of process is more fully sketched out in JERRY L. MASHAW, DUE PROCESS IN THE ADMINISTRATIVE STATE (1985).

[16] The many empirical studies on procedural justice do not always employ uniform terminology to describe the components of procedural justice. *See, e.g.*, Michael M. O'Hear, *Plea Bargaining and Procedural Justice*, 42 GA. L. REV. 407, 421 n.38 (2008) (identifying and reconciling inconsistencies in terminology in several studies). The four-factor model presented here is adapted from Tom R. Tyler & Hulda Thorisdottir, *A Psychological Perspective on Compensation for Harm: Examining the September 11 Victim Compensation Fund*, 53 DEPAUL L. REV. 355, 380 (2003). A similar four-factor model has also been used by other legal scholars. *See, e.g.*, Ric Simmons, *Big Data and Procedural Justice: Legitimizing Algorithms in the Criminal Justice System*, 15 OHIO ST. J. CRIM. L. 573, 575–76 (2018).

2. "Violent felony" means [various battery and sexual assault offenses, reckless injury, or robbery].

(b) When making a sentencing decision concerning a person convicted of a violent felony, the court shall consider as an aggravating factor the fact that the victim of the violent felony was an elder person. This paragraph applies even if the person mistakenly believed that the victim had not attained the age of 62 years. * * *

(9) AGGRAVATING FACTORS NOT AN ELEMENT OF THE CRIME. The aggravating factors listed in this section are not elements of any crime. A prosecutor is not required to charge any aggravating factor or otherwise allege the existence of an aggravating factor in any pleading for a court to consider the aggravating factor when making a sentencing decision.

Ann is charged with robbery of Bill. Ann's lawyer, Cassandra, negotiates a plea deal with Dennis, the prosecutor. In return for Ann's guilty plea to the charged offense, Dennis agrees that "the State will not recommend incarceration as the sentence." Ann's guilty plea is accepted by Judge Ellen, and the case is set for sentencing following the preparation of a presentence report.

The PSR author contacts Bill in order to collect victim impact information. Bill states that he was "just a little shaken up" by the robbery and has "mostly gotten over it." He does not wish to make a statement in court at sentencing. Bill also provides some basic personal information about himself for the PSR, including his age (62). The PSR author recommends a sentence of probation.

The PSR is shared with Cassandra and Dennis prior to sentencing. However, neither reviews the PSR with any care since they both expect a sentence of probation based on the plea deal.

At the sentencing hearing, Cassandra argues for probation based on Ann's lack of prior convictions and good behavior while on pretrial release. Dennis states, "Robbery is a serious offense, for which I normally seek a prison term. However, under the particular circumstances of this case, I will not oppose what the defendant requests." Ann declines the opportunity to allocute.

Judge Ellen flips through the pages of the PSR while Cassandra and Dennis make their remarks. The information about Bill's age catches her eye. She states, "I'd be inclined to impose probation here, but the victim's age is a concern. State law says that I must treat this as an aggravating factor. I think that tips me in favor of incarceration. Surely, Dennis, the State supports protecting the elderly from predatory crimes like this one?" Dennis, who had not paid attention to the victim's age before sentencing, responds, "Well, of course, we want to protect the elderly. If that is something the court feels must be taken into account today, the State would not object."

Cassandra objects, "We had a deal. Everyone understood this was going to be a probation sentence." Judge Ellen responds, "Do you dispute the victim's age?" Cassandra concedes that she has no information to the contrary.

Judge Ellen declares, "I find this victim to be 62 years old, which I am required to treat as an aggravating factor. In light of the victim's age, I do not think that a sentence of probation adequately reflects the seriousness of the offense. Therefore, I am imposing a sentence of 18 months in prison."

1. Did this process violate any of Ann's constitutional rights? What constitutional arguments might be made in Ann's favor? What responses might be made by the State? Is there any more information you would like to have in order to assess the constitutionality of the sentencing process?

2. What if the aggravating factor statute was adopted and took effect between the time of the robbery and the sentencing—would that affect your constitutional analysis?

3. What if the robbery occurred the day before Bill turned 62, so that he was actually 61 at the time of the offense? Assume that the PSR does not make this fact clear.

4. Imagine a variation on the facts. Ann strikes Bill during the robbery, resulting in an injury that requires medical attention. At Ann's sentencing for robbery, Dennis points out Bill's age, as reported in the PSR, and asks the court to apply the aggravating factor statute. However, the court declines, stating, "I would need some verification of the victim's age beyond this second-hand report in the PSR." Later, Dennis decides to charge Ann with battery for striking Bill during the robbery. Ann is convicted, and the case proceeds to sentencing. Would the Double Jeopardy Clause bar Dennis from attempting to prove Bill's age again, using stronger evidence this time?

C. VICTIM IMPACT STATEMENTS AND VICTIM RIGHTS AT SENTENCING

Paul G. Cassell, In Defense of Victim Impact Statements

6 OHIO ST. J. CRIM. L. 611 (2009)

I. BRIEF HISTORY OF THE MODERN CRIME VICTIMS' RIGHTS MOVEMENT AND VICTIM IMPACT STATEMENTS

To put the debate about victim impact statements into context, some history may be useful. The start of the crime victims' rights movement is conventionally placed in the 1970s, when various groups became concerned about the treatment of victims in the nation's criminal justice system. The movement sprung from disparate sources. "Law and order" conservatives decried the seemingly single-minded focus of the judicial system on the rights of criminal defendants and inattention to countervailing interests. But concern was by no means limited to the political right. For example, advocates for the poor condemned the fact that the government did nothing to ameliorate the financial consequences of crime on indigent victims. The civil rights movement worried about the victims of racial violence in the South and the inability of those victims to force effective criminal prosecutions. And feminists criticized the treatment of rape victims, who were often themselves placed on trial during rape prosecutions.

Responding to these groups, in the 1970s lawmakers began to enact legislation addressing these victim-related problems in the criminal justice system. For example, legislators passed crime victims compensation schemes and rape shield provisions. But while these progressive efforts on particular issues were widely applauded, no comprehensive effort to review the treatment of crime victims in the American criminal justice system was made until 1982. That year, President Reagan appointed a task force on the victims of crime. Following public hearings around the country, the Task Force released an influential report.

The Task Force concluded that the criminal justice system had "lost the balance that has been the cornerstone of its wisdom" and recommended various reforms to expand the role of crime victims. Of particular interest here are the Task Force's recommendations regarding victim impact statements. The Task Force recommended that "[v]ictims, no less than defendants, are entitled to have their views considered" at sentencing. The Task Force, therefore, called for legislation that would require victim impact statements at sentencing and for such a statement to be included in all pre-sentence reports provided to judges. * * *

In addition to recommending victim impact statements and other particular reforms, the Task Force also called for an amendment to the United States Constitution protecting crime victims' rights. The proposed amendment, to be added to the Sixth Amendment, would have read: "Likewise, the victim, in every criminal prosecution shall have the right to be present and to be heard at all critical stages of judicial proceedings."

The crime victims' movement's dream became to pass such a federal constitutional amendment, which would comprehensively protect victims' rights throughout the country. But realizing that securing such an amendment was a daunting task, the crime victims' movement decided to organize to promote such amendments to state constitutions. After succeeding in the states, the victims' movement then planned to return to the task of obtaining a federal constitutional amendment.

The movement had considerable success in promoting victims' rights in the states. Beginning in 1982, thirty-two states adopted victims' rights amendments to their own state constitutions. * * *

After making considerable progress to protect victims' rights at the state level, victims' advocates decided to make an effort for federal constitutional protection in 1995. * * *

While the proposed Victims' Rights Amendment always had significant backing in Congress, it could never attract the required two-thirds support. As a result, in 2004 the victims' movement decided to instead press for a far-reaching federal statute protecting victims' rights in the federal criminal justice system. In exchange for backing off from the federal amendment in the short term, victims' advocates received near universal congressional support for a "broad and encompassing" statutory victims' bill of rights.[23] This "new and bolder" approach not only created a string of victims' rights, but also provided funding for victims' legal services and created remedies when victims' rights were violated. The federal legislation is noteworthy here because it included (among other things) a guaranteed right for all victims in federal cases to be "reasonably heard" at any sentencing.

II. AN EXAMPLE OF A VICTIM IMPACT STATEMENT

As a result of these efforts by the crime victims' rights movement, it is now virtually universal law that crime victims can deliver a victim impact statement at sentencing. But what does such a statement actually look like? One way to proceed would be in the arid language of a law school hypothetical. This seems unsatisfactory, given that a considerable part of the debate about the statements centers on their emotional content. Consider, then, a real world example of a victim impact statement.

The example comes from my hometown of Salt Lake City, Utah. On February 12, 2007, six persons were gunned down and many more injured in the so-called "Trolley Square Massacre." The shooter was Salejman Talovic, who obtained two firearms and much ammunition before entering the Trolley Square Shopping Center, intending to kill as many people as possible. Talovic obtained one of his firearms from Mackenzie Hunter. In a hurried transaction in a parking lot, Talovic paid $800 for a stolen handgun. Talovic had earlier asked Hunter to help him buy the handgun because, as a juvenile, he could not buy one. When Hunter asked Talovic why he wanted the handgun, Talovic said it was for a bank robbery.

One of the victims of the Trolley Square massacre was Vanessa Quinn. She was a young woman in the prime of her life. She grew up in Cincinnati, Ohio, and was the first person in her family to earn a college degree. * * *

After the murder of Vanessa and the other Trolley Square victims, the U.S. Attorney's Office in Utah began a criminal investigation into how Talovic got the guns he used to perpetrate the massacre. In May 2007, the Office indicted Mackenzie Hunter for the illegal sale of the handgun to Talovic. The indictment charged that Hunter knew that Talovic was a juvenile who could not lawfully purchase handguns and, moreover, that Hunter made the sale with knowledge that the handgun

[23] 150 CONG. REC. S4261 (daily ed. Apr. 22, 2004) (statement of Sen. Feinstein).

would be used in a violent crime. On November 1, 2007, Hunter elected to plead guilty to a reduced misdemeanor charge—illegal sale of a handgun to a minor, but without knowledge of how it would be used.

The next day, *The Salt Lake Tribune* ran an article about the desire of some of the crime's victims to give statements at sentencing. The article particularly described the plight of Sue and Kenny Antrobus, Vanessa's parents. They wanted to give a victim impact statement at Hunter's sentencing—but the U.S. Attorney's Office thought that the court would not permit it. Coincidentally, that day was my last day on the job as a federal district court judge—a position that I was leaving to do pro bono crime victims' litigation. I was put in touch with the Antrobuses and agreed to represent them pro bono in their efforts to deliver a victim impact statement.

So here is what a victim impact statement actually looks like:

> My name is Susan Antrobus[.] I am the mother of Vanessa Quinn, who was murdered at Trolley Square Mall February 12, 2007. I am writing this letter to you in hopes that you can understand why I feel the need to give an impact statement on behalf of my daughter Vanessa. . . .
>
> How has this affected my family[?] [T]o be honest I don't know yet, I can only tell you how it has affected us to this point in time. My Mom gave up her fight for life, 6 weeks after Vanessa was taken from us, and my youngest daughter Susanna had a miscarriage the same night my Mom passed away. My husband and I cry every day, we struggle to get through each and every day, you wake up with it, you carry it through your day and it goes to bed with you every night. All you can do is hope tomorrow will be a little easier [than] today. February 12 has never ended for us; it feels like one long continuous day that will never end. . . .
>
> If you're old enough at 18 to give your life up for this country, you're old enough to know what you're doing when you sell an illegal weapon to a minor. I am asking and pleading with this court to give Mr. Hunter the maximum sentence to send a message to the people of this country and people like Mr. Hunter, that if you chose to engage in [selling] illegal weapons to minors you will be held responsible for your actions, and maybe some people would get it. . . .
>
> It cost us 7,000 dollars to lay our daughter Vanessa to rest. . . .
>
> I think I deserve to give an impact statement, since Vanessa is not here to speak for herself, I don't think 10 minutes is asking for much considering what we've lost for a life time. . . .

Was Sue Antrobus able to give this impact statement? Before I tell you the "rest of the story" about whether she was able to give a victim impact statement, this example puts us in a good position to consider the main issue I want to address in this essay—should she be able to give a victim impact statement?

III. JUSTIFICATIONS FOR VICTIM IMPACT STATEMENTS

What are the justifications for allowing victims and their representatives, like Sue Antrobus, to give victim impact statements? * * *

A. *Providing Information to the Sentencer*

A victim impact statement provides information to the sentencer.[31] * * * [The] sentencers (both judges and juries) need to know the harm caused by the criminal to determine a proper sentence. For example, the widely-cited factors governing federal sentencing include the "seriousness of the offense." Obviously more serious—i.e., more harmful—offenses require more stringent penalties. * * *

Examples of detailed information that a victim might provide about the defendant's crime are legion. For example, if the defendant physically injured the victim, the victim could describe the nature and extent of the injuries—facts that are clearly relevant to sentencing under virtually any conceivable sentencing scheme. * * * For financial crimes, victims can provide information about their losses and often can describe the sophistication of the defendant's scheme—factors relevant to sentencing.

A related, secondary point is that a victim impact statement can contain important information about restitution. Restitution is often an option at sentencing and, at least in the federal system, is required for violent crimes and some other serious offenses. This can be important for victims, like the Antrobuses. The Antrobuses lived on an extremely limited income, yet had to pay $7,000 in funeral expenses for Vanessa, which they covered only by pulling money out of their very modest retirement account.

B. *Benefiting the Victim* * * *

Giving victims a chance to participate in the rite of allocution can have important benefits for the victim. Professor Mary Giannini observes that by delivering a victim impact statement in court,

> the victim gains access to a forum that directly and individually acknowledges her victimhood.
>
> The moment of sentencing is among the most public, formalized, and ritualistic parts of a criminal case. By giving victims a clear and uninterrupted voice at this moment on par with that of defendants and prosecutors, a right to allocute

---

[31] For simplicity, in this article I will assume the victim is presenting an impact statement about the harm of the crime, setting aside the potentially more complicated issues that arise when victims seek to give their opinion on the proper sentence.

signals both society's recognition of victims' suffering and their importance to the criminal process.[44]

There may be therapeutic aspects to a victim giving a victim impact statement. As one victim explained the process, "The Victim Impact Statement allowed me to construct what had happened in my mind. I could read my thoughts. . . . It helped me to know that I could deal with this terrible thing."[45] Another victim said, "[W]hen I read [the victim impact statement] [in court] it healed a part of me—to speak to [the defendant] and tell him how much he hurt me."[46] * * * And, if the judge acknowledges what the victim has said in the statement, the judge's words can be (as one victim put it) "balm for her soul."[48] * * *

The point should not be overstated. Occasionally the claim is made that victim impact statements will automatically bring "closure" to victims from a crime. It is not clear that "closure" ever really occurs after a violent crime—especially when extreme violence is at issue. But victim impact statements need not deliver total closure to nonetheless be a desirable part of the criminal justice process. * * *

C. *Explaining the Crime's Harm to the Defendant*

In many jurisdictions, a victim can elect to deliver an impact statement in open court, in the presence of not only the judge but also the defendant. This is a rite that has nothing to do with the ultimate sentence imposed, but rather is a chance for a victim "to look [the] . . . defendant in the eye and let him know the suffering his misconduct has caused."[56] * * *

[I]f a victim impact statement helps a defendant understand and gain empathy towards the victim, it may serve as the first step towards his effective rehabilitation. A victim impact statement can thus be justified because it may be beneficial for the offender. * * *

D. *Improving the Perceived Fairness of Sentencing*

A final justification for victim impact statements is that they help to improve the perceived fairness of the process. * * *

The point here is not that, merely because the defendant gets to allocute, the victim should do so as well. Such a claim might be subject to the rejoinder that the criminal justice system gives some rights to the defendant alone. For example, the defendant uniquely possesses a right

---

[44] Mary Margaret Giannini, *Equal Rights for Equal Rites?: Victim Allocution, Defendant Allocution, and the Crime Victims' Rights Act*, 26 YALE L. & POL'Y REV. 431 (2008) (quoting Richard A. Bierschbach, *Allocution and the Purposes of Victim Participation Under the CVRA*, 19 FED. SENT'G REP. 44, 46–47 (2006)).

[45] ELLEN K. ALEXANDER & JANICE HARRIS LORD, IMPACT STATEMENTS: A VICTIM'S RIGHT TO SPEAK, A NATION'S RESPONSIBILITY TO LISTEN 22 (1994) (quoting victim).

[46] Paul G. Cassell, *Balancing the Scales of Justice: The Case for and the Effects of Utah's Victims' Rights Amendment*, 1994 UTAH L. REV. 1373, 1395 n.107.

[48] Amy Propen & Mary Lay Schuster, *Making Academic Work Advocacy Work: Technologies of Power in the Public Arena*, 22 J. BUS. & TECH. COMM. 299, 318 (2008).

[56] Kenna v. U.S. Dist. Court for C.D. Cal., 435 F.3d 1011, 1017 (9th Cir. 2006).

to remain silent and the benefit of a presumption of innocence. The point here is that the defendant is allowed to speak at sentencing because this opportunity is critical to the legitimacy of the proceeding. * * * By the same token, allowing victims the same opportunity assures perceived fairness. In other words, victim impact evidence is appropriate not merely because defendants have this opportunity; rather, it is appropriate for the same reason as defendants get it. * * *

V. CONCLUSION

* * * I want to return briefly to the story of Sue Antrobus. Was she allowed to give a victim impact statement at the sentencing of the man who criminally sold the murder weapon used to kill her daughter Vanessa?

Since the prosecution was being handled in federal court, the federal victims' rights law (the Crime Victims' Rights Act) applied. This law gives crime victims (and, if they are deceased, their representatives) the right to be "reasonably heard at . . . sentencing." In Sue's case, no doubt existed that she and her husband Ken were Vanessa's representatives. But was Vanessa a "crime victim"? Obviously, when Sulejman Talovic murdered her, she was a victim of his crime. But he was never prosecuted, as an off-duty police officer managed to kill him on the night of the massacre. So the only criminal prosecution was for Hunter's illegal sale of the murder weapon to Talovic. Was she a victim of that crime?

The Crime Victims' Rights Act defines a "victim" as a "person directly and proximately harmed as a result of the commission of a Federal offense." Vanessa was "directly" harmed by Hunter's crime when the handgun he illegally sold was used to kill her. Whether she was "proximately" harmed by the crime is the sticking point. In the district court, her pro bono lawyers argued that the term should be interpreted consistently with notions of "proximate" cause in tort law. Basic tort law principles permit a defendant to be held accountable for actions that lead to a crime by another person where the defendant could reasonably foresee that crime. Given that Hunter and Talovic apparently talked about a bank robbery during the sale of the weapon, Sue Antrobus's lawyers argued that foreseeability of misuse of the gun was established.

The district court, however, saw things differently:

> The actions of Talovic were an independent, intervening cause which broke the necessary chain of causation. While the court does not want to minimize in any way the harm suffered by those who were killed, injured, or had loved ones killed or injured by Talovic, that harm is not sufficiently connected to Hunter's offense of unlawfully selling a firearm to a minor for this court to consider Hunter's actions to be the direct and proximate cause of the harm.

The district court therefore held that Vanessa Quinn was not a "victim" under the CVRA and that her mother, Sue Antrobus, had no right to give an impact statement at sentencing.

The district court also recognized (as Sue Antrobus's attorneys had argued) that it had discretion to hear from Sue Antrobus. The court, however, concluded that it had already read the materials submitted by her. In view of that "adequate" understanding of Sue Antrobus's position, the court found no need to exercise its discretion in favor of allowing her to speak. The district court then sentenced Hunter to fifteen months in prison, at the low end of the applicable Guideline range. And Sue Antrobus was not able to speak. * * *

But in concluding this article, I want to focus on the district court's remarkable conclusion that there was no need to exercise its discretion to allow Sue to speak because it already understood her position. This is a crabbed view of the purposes of victim impact statements—assuming they exist solely for the benefit of the court. Instead, as I have tried to explain, victim impact statements serve broader ends. They not only provide information to judges, but also give possible therapeutic benefits to victims, educate defendants about the harms of their crime, and ensure that the sentencing process is viewed as fair by the broader public. * * *

NOTES & QUESTIONS

1. **Widespread Recognition of Victims' Rights.** Today, thirty-five states include victims' rights amendments in their state constitutions, and all fifty states, as well as the federal government, enshrine rights in statutory law. Paul G. Cassell & Margaret Garvin, *Protecting Crime Victims in State Constitutions: The Example of the New Marsey's Law in Florida*, 110 J. CRIM. L. & CRIMINOLOGY 99, 105 (2020). Although one of the main priorities of the victims' rights movement has been securing an opportunity for victims to provide an impact statement at *sentencing*, victims also generally have the right to participate in various other aspects of the criminal process, from bail determinations through parole-release decisions.[17]

2. **Why a "Right"?** Even in the absence of a formally recognized right, victim voices might still be heard at sentencing. Probation officers might often find it helpful to interview victims as part of the presentence investigation and to include information from victims regarding harm in the PSR. *See, e.g.*, Fed. R. Crim. P. 32(d)(2) ("The presentence report must also contain the following: . . . (B) information that assesses any financial, social, psychological, and medical impact on any victim . . . ."). For their part, prosecutors might also have an interest in presenting a victim impact statement at sentencing, either in written or oral form, and judges would normally have discretion to accept and consider such a statement. Why not

[17] Particular issues arising from the use of victim statements in *capital* sentencing are considered in Chapter 7.

trust these court actors to provide an adequate opportunity for victims to be heard?

3. **The Case for Victim Impact Statements.** What are the justifications that Professor Cassell offers for victim impact statements? Are you persuaded? If you were the judge in the *Hunter* case that Cassell discusses, would you have permitted Sue Antrobus to speak at the sentencing?

4. **Harm, Culpability, and the Uncertain Potential for Disproportionate Sentences.** Note Professor Cassell's easy equation of offense seriousness with harm ("Obviously more serious—*i.e., more harmful*—offenses require more stringent penalties.") Yet, as discussed in Chapter 1, resulting harm is only one aspect of an offense's blameworthiness. One of the recurring criticisms of victim statements is that the emotionally charged presentation of resulting harm evidence may overwhelm consideration of all of the other relevant information that is presented at sentencing—and especially of the countervailing factors that might mitigate punishment.

The existing social science research does not provide a clear answer to the question of whether victim statements result in an overemphasis on harm relative to other sentencing factors or, more generally, in punitiveness and disproportionately severe sentences. Impact statements seem capable of triggering strong emotions, but strong emotions are not necessarily contrary to a thoughtful consideration of all of the available evidence. For instance, while anger tends to short-circuit thorough decision-making, sadness may have the opposite effect. Susan A. Bandes & Jessica M. Salerno, *Emotion, Proof and Prejudice: The Cognitive Science of Gruesome Photos and Victim Impact Statements*, 46 ARIZ. ST. L.J. 1003, 1045 (2014). Furthermore, the nature and strength of emotional responses to a victim statement may depend, at least in part, on the race, sex, and other personal characteristics of the victim and the audience. *Id.* at 1039–40. A number of mock-jury studies have found a relationship between exposure to victim impact evidence and support for harsher sentences, but such studies are sometimes criticized as artificial exercises that are too divorced from the real-life dynamics of actual legal decision-making to provide much useful insight. *Id.* at 1035–36, 1050–53. Moreover, other researchers have found no overall increase in sentence severity after the adoption of victim impact statement laws. *See* Cassell & Garvin, *supra,* at 118 n.20 (citing studies).

If impact statements have little discernible effect on outcomes in most cases, some of the concerns about disproportionality might be alleviated. But, on the other hand, would that mean that impact statements are a waste of time? Not necessarily. Recall that Cassell offers several additional justifications for statements beyond simply their informational value in helping judges to make better decisions. As we saw earlier in this chapter, there are arguments to be made in favor of *defendant* procedural rights at sentencing even if these rights do not enhance the substantive quality of the decisions made. Cassell suggests that there are parallel arguments to be made in favor of *victim* procedural rights.

5. **Connection with Restorative Justice.** As we saw in Chapter 1, proponents of "restorative justice" urge a more victim-centric approach to criminal justice, in which, among other things, the victim has an opportunity to explain to the offender the impact of the offender's actions. Restorative justice processes are typically envisioned as out-of-court dialogues or conferences that include the possibility of back-and-forth exchanges involving victim, offender, and perhaps a few supporters and community representatives. Although such processes would in many respects look quite different than a victim statement delivered in court as part of a formal sentencing hearing, Cassell's claim that impact statements may deliver therapeutic benefits for the victim and rehabilitative benefits for the defendant echoes similar claims that have been made for restorative justice. For an argument that restorative justice should be expressly included in the rights that are recognized for victims, see Lynn S. Branham, *The Overlooked Victim Right: According Victim-Survivors a Right of Access to Restorative Justice*, 98 DENV. L. REV. FORUM 1 (2021).

6. **Connection with Procedural Justice.** Professor Cassell further argues that the victim's right to make an impact statement enhances the perceived fairness and legitimacy of the sentencing process. As noted earlier in this chapter, research on "procedural justice" suggests that perceptions of fairness and legitimacy in legal decision-making increase the likelihood that decisions will be accepted and, more generally, support law-abidingness and cooperation with the authorities. Perhaps then, by virtue of procedural-justice dynamics, the victim's right to make a statement may be capable of advancing the crime-control objectives of sentencing without regard to whether there are substantive effects on the sentences imposed. On the other hand, shouldn't we be concerned about the possibility that defendants may sometimes perceive the process as less fair to them when victim impact statements are made?

7. **Equal Justice for All Victims?** The ability of a victim to offer a compelling impact statement—or any statement at all—may depend in part on the victim's socioeconomic status and education level. Moreover, some victims—e.g., prisoners, the undocumented, the severely mentally or physically disabled—may be unable to provide a statement or fear serious repercussions if they attempt one. Consider, too, that some homicide victims led lonely, isolated lives—who will step forward to say something about them when it comes time for the killer to be sentenced? For a discussion of the racial factors at play, functioning to elevate "ideal" victims, see Italy Ravid, *Inconspicuous Victims*, 25 LEWIS & CLARK L. REV. 529 (2021).

A common criticism of victim impact statements is that they may contribute to unjustifiable differences in sentences based on the personal characteristics of the victim. For instance, the drunk driver who runs down a hard-working, middle-class parent of three may spend years longer in prison than the otherwise-identical drunk driver who runs down a homeless loner, even though the identity of the victim of this sort of crime is normally a matter of happenstance. Of course, these sorts of victim-based disparities may occur even without impact statements, but there are concerns that victim participation in the sentencing process may tend to exacerbate such disparities.

To be sure, such concerns rest on the uncertain assumption that victim statements affect sentencing outcomes. Moreover, even if there are significant disparity problems that ought to be addressed, it does not necessarily follow that impact statements should be excluded. One alternative, for instance, might be to provide more funding for victim advocates to help disadvantaged victims present more effective statements.

8. **Crime Victims' Rights Act.** As Cassell notes, when efforts to achieve a federal victims' rights constitutional amendment came up short, proponents turned their attention to federal statutory reform, resulting in the adoption of the Crime Victims' Rights Act in 2004. The statute governs criminal litigation in the federal courts. Much of the CVRA echoes similar state laws. Key provisions are reprinted below.

Crime Victims' Rights Act of 2004 (as codified)

18 U.S.C. § 3773. Crime victims' rights

(a) Rights of crime victims.—A crime victim has the following rights:

(1) The right to be reasonably protected from the accused.

(2) The right to reasonable, accurate, and timely notice of any public court proceeding, or any parole proceeding, involving the crime or of any release or escape of the accused.

(3) The right not to be excluded from any such public court proceeding, unless the court, after receiving clear and convincing evidence, determines that testimony by the victim would be materially altered if the victim heard other testimony at that proceeding.

(4) The right to be reasonably heard at any public proceeding in the district court involving release, plea, sentencing, or any parole proceeding.

(5) The reasonable right to confer with the attorney for the Government in the case.

(6) The right to full and timely restitution as provided in law.

(7) The right to proceedings free from unreasonable delay.

(8) The right to be treated with fairness and with respect for the victim's dignity and privacy.

(9) The right to be informed in a timely manner of any plea bargain or deferred prosecution agreement.

(10) The right to be informed of the rights under this section and the services described in section 503(c) of the Victims' Rights and Restitution Act of 1990 (42 U.S.C. 10607(c)) and provided contact information for the Office of the Victims' Rights Ombudsman of the Department of Justice.

(b) Rights afforded.—

(1) In general.—In any court proceeding involving an offense against a crime victim, the court shall ensure that the crime victim is afforded the rights described in subsection (a). Before making a determination described in subsection (a)(3), the court shall make every effort to permit the fullest attendance possible by the victim and shall consider reasonable alternatives to the exclusion of the victim from the criminal proceeding. The reasons for any decision denying relief under this chapter shall be clearly stated on the record. * * *

(c) Best efforts to accord rights.—

(1) Government.—Officers and employees of the Department of Justice and other departments and agencies of the United States engaged in the detection, investigation, or prosecution of crime shall make their best efforts to see that crime victims are notified of, and accorded, the rights described in subsection (a).

(2) Advice of attorney.—The prosecutor shall advise the crime victim that the crime victim can seek the advice of an attorney with respect to the rights described in subsection (a). * * *

(d) Enforcement and limitations.—

(1) Rights.—The crime victim or the crime victim's lawful representative, and the attorney for the Government may assert the rights described in subsection (a). A person accused of the crime may not obtain any form of relief under this chapter.

(2) Multiple crime victims.—In a case where the court finds that the number of crime victims makes it impracticable to accord all of the crime victims the rights described in subsection (a), the court shall fashion a reasonable procedure to give effect to this chapter that does not unduly complicate or prolong the proceedings.

(3) Motion for relief and writ of mandamus.—The rights described in subsection (a) shall be asserted in the district court in which a defendant is being prosecuted for the crime or, if no prosecution is underway, in the district court in the district in which the crime occurred. The district court shall take up and decide any motion asserting a victim's right forthwith. If the district court denies the relief sought, the movant may petition the court of appeals for a writ of mandamus. The court of appeals may issue the writ on the order of a single judge pursuant to circuit rule or the Federal Rules of Appellate Procedure. The court of appeals shall take up and decide such application forthwith within 72 hours after the petition has been filed, unless the litigants, with the approval of the court, have stipulated to a different time period for consideration. In deciding such application, the court of appeals shall apply ordinary standards of appellate review. In no event shall proceedings be stayed or subject to a continuance of more than five days for purposes of

enforcing this chapter. If the court of appeals denies the relief sought, the reasons for the denial shall be clearly stated on the record in a written opinion.

(4) Error.—In any appeal in a criminal case, the Government may assert as error the district court's denial of any crime victim's right in the proceeding to which the appeal relates.

(5) Limitation on relief.—In no case shall a failure to afford a right under this chapter provide grounds for a new trial. A victim may make a motion to re-open a plea or sentence only if—

(A) the victim has asserted the right to be heard before or during the proceeding at issue and such right was denied;

(B) the victim petitions the court of appeals for a writ of mandamus within 14 days; and

(C) in the case of a plea, the accused has not pled to the highest offense charged.

This paragraph does not affect the victim's right to restitution as provided in title 18, United States Code.

(6) No cause of action.—Nothing in this chapter shall be construed to authorize a cause of action for damages or to create, to enlarge, or to imply any duty or obligation to any victim or other person for the breach of which the United States or any of its officers or employees could be held liable in damages. Nothing in this chapter shall be construed to impair the prosecutorial discretion of the Attorney General or any officer under his direction.

(e) Definitions.—For the purposes of this chapter: * * *

(2) Crime victim.—

(A) In general.—The term "crime victim" means a person directly and proximately harmed as a result of the commission of a Federal offense or an offense in the District of Columbia.

(B) Minors and certain other victims.—In the case of a crime victim who is under 18 years of age, incompetent, incapacitated, or deceased, the legal guardians of the crime victim or the representatives of the crime victim's estate, family members, or any other persons appointed as suitable by the court, may assume the crime victim's rights under this chapter, but in no event shall the defendant be named as such guardian or representative. * * *

NOTES & QUESTIONS

1. **"Right to Be Reasonably Heard."** The CVRA establishes a right for the victim to be heard in connection with sentencing proceedings but leaves the details remarkably vague. The Federal Rules of Criminal Procedure provide only slightly greater clarity: "Before imposing sentence,

the court must address any victim of the crime who is present at sentencing and must permit the victim to be reasonably heard." Fed. R. Crim. P. 32(i)(4)(B). Both the CVRA and Rule 32 qualify the right to be heard through use of the term "reasonably," which effectively leaves it to the courts to determine what the specific limitations will be.

2. **Written or Oral?** The CVRA does not expressly indicate whether the victim's statement should be in written or oral form. In a notable decision issued not long after the CVRA's adoption, the Ninth Circuit reviewed the statute's legislative history and found "a clear congressional intent to give crime victims the right to *speak* at proceedings covered by the CVRA," including the sentencing hearing. *Kenna v. U.S. Dist. Court for C.D. Cal.*, 435 F.3d 1011, 1016 (9th Cir. 2006) (emphasis added). The appellate court further observed, "Limiting victims to written impact statements, while allowing the prosecutor and the defendant the opportunity to address the court, would treat victims as secondary participants in the sentencing process. The CVRA clearly meant to make victims full participants." *Id.* The Ninth Circuit's ruling implies that victims in federal cases have a right to choose a written or oral statement.

Why do you suppose a sentencing judge might prefer to receive impact statements in written form? Why might some victims prefer an in-court oral presentation? Which form do you think best advances the underlying purposes of victims' rights laws?

In many states, the law expressly gives victims the option of choosing the form of the statement. *See, e.g.,* Ariz. Stat. § 13–4428(B); Minn. Stat. § 611A.038(a). In practice, most victim input is probably conveyed in written form through the PSR. MPC:S § 7.07C cmmnt. (g). When the victim statement is oral, it is often in the form of unsworn allocution, without any opportunity for cross-examination by the defendant. *Id.*

3. **Sentence Recommendation.** States are divided on the question of whether victim statements may include a recommendation as to the sentence. *See* MPC:S § 7.07C rptr. note (j) (surveying state laws). (In capital cases, the Eighth Amendment may impose special restrictions on sentence recommendations, as we will see in Chapter 7.) The MPC:S has taken the minority position in explicitly barring sentence recommendations. § 7.07C(7). The official commentary asserts, "Among the values and interests that support victim participation in sentence proceedings, none suggests that the victim is competent to speak to the overall penalty that should be imposed." Do you agree? If you think a victim should be permitted to recommend a particular sentence, do you think the victim should have a right to appeal if the judge imposes a lesser punishment?[18]

Note that, contrary to popular perceptions, crime victims do not always favor the most punitive sentencing options. Most striking, perhaps, are the cases in which the family member of a homicide victim indicates opposition

---

[18] *See* Cooper v. Dist. Court, 133 P.3d 692, 702–03 (Alaska Ct. App. 2006) ("[T]he question before us is whether, if a crime victim's procedural rights have been honored but the victim is dissatisfied with the sentencing judge's substantive decision, the victim may independently seek appellate review of that decision. American courts are unanimous in answering 'no' to this question.").

to the death penalty.[19] More generally, public defender Benji McMurray has argued that defense lawyers too quickly assume that victim interests are necessarily opposed to defendant interests. *The Mitigating Power of a Victim Focus at Sentencing*, 19 FED. SENT'G RPTR. 119 (2006). He suggests that defense lawyers may sometimes aid their clients by attempting to facilitate reconciliation with the victim prior to sentencing. Doing so may not only carry inherent benefits for both sides but also lead to more favorable (or at least less unfavorable) victim impact statements. As an illustration, consider the case of Summer Blake that was described in Problem 1-1. As you may recall, Blake apologized to her victim and offered to pay restitution for the victim's injury. The victim, who initially recommended the maximum possible sentence for Blake, later softened her position and indicated that she would be satisfied to leave the punishment to the court's discretion. *United States v. Blake,* 89 F. Supp. 2d 328, 336 (E.D.N.Y. 2000).

4. **Access to PSR.** If the victim has a right to opine on the sentence, does that also imply that the victim should have a right of access to the PSR? For instance, how can a victim possibly weigh the full range of permissible sentencing considerations if the victim does not have a reasonably complete picture of the defendant's background? On the other hand, do you see any concerns about sharing the PSR in its entirety with the victim?

The CVRA does not provide an express right of access for victims to the PSR, and claims that such a right is implied in the statute have thus far met with little success. *See, e.g., In re Siler*, 571 F.3d 604, 610 (6th Cir. 2009).

5. **Defendant's Right to Challenge the Victim Statement.** As discussed earlier in this chapter, there has been much debate and litigation over the defendant's right to view and challenge allegations made in a PSR. Parallel issues arise with respect to victim impact statements. State laws vary as to defendants' rights in this area, including such specific questions as: must written victim statements be disclosed to the defendant in advance of sentencing, must the victim who speaks in court be placed under oath, may the defendant cross-examine the victim, and may the defendant present rebuttal witnesses? *See* MPC:S § 7.07C rptr. note (j) (surveying state laws). Apart from the varying state laws, the federal Constitution may arguably impose certain minimal requirements, but the caselaw is not entirely clear or well-developed. *Cf. State v. Blackmon*, 908 P.2d 10, 12 (Az. Ct. App. 1995) (holding that defendant had due-process right to cross-examine victim who gave statement at sentencing hearing). As a matter of policy, do you think that victims *should* be permitted to offer unsworn statements free from the fear of potential cross-examination?

6. **Attorney for the Victim?** It cannot be taken for granted that a lay victim will be able to ascertain and enforce his or her legal rights. Who will provide any necessary legal assistance? To some extent, the CVRA presses prosecutors into this service, mandating that they "shall make their best efforts to see that crime victims are notified of, and accorded, the rights

[19] *See, e.g.,* Wayne A. Logan, *Victim Impact Evidence in Federal Capital Trials,* 19 FED. SENT'G RPTR. 5, 8–9 (2006) (noting how some survivors who provided statements in connection with sentencing of 9/11 terror attack defendant signaled their opposition to the death penalty).

described in subsection (a)." Prosecutors are also expressly authorized to "assert the rights described in subsection (a)." Yet, implicitly recognizing that the prosecutor cannot always be counted on to act as *de facto* attorney for the victim, the CVRA also directs the prosecutor to "advise the crime victim that the crime victim can seek the advice of an attorney with respect to the rights described in subsection (a)." But what if the victim cannot afford an attorney? Should the victim be given a right to court-appointed counsel, much as indigent defendants have?

7. **Cases with Large Numbers of Victims.** Cases with large numbers of victims, such as those involving mass shootings or large-scale frauds, can strain a court's ability to accommodate all of the impact statements that victims might like to offer. In these cases, the CVRA specifically authorizes the court to "fashion a reasonable procedure to give effect to this chapter that does not unduly complicate or prolong the proceedings." Obscured by the deceptively simple "reasonableness" mandate, the process of streamlining voluminous victim evidence may involve many difficult and even hurtful choices.

Consider this critical assessment of the process in *United States v. Moussaoui*, a capital prosecution that grew out of the 9/11 terrorist attacks:

> [T]he selection process aggravates relations between victims and the entity theoretically seeking to vindicate their interests—government. With mass killings, the government necessarily must choose from among many potential witnesses. In *Moussaoui*, this pool was especially large as the government created an unprecedented database of 8000 individuals adversely affected by 9/11 and interviewed each individual who wished to speak about the impact of 9/11 on their lives. As a result of this process . . . several hundred victims expressed an interest in testifying at Moussaoui's sentencing hearing . . . . [T]he government proposed "45 stories of victim impact," the "minimum amount of victim impact testimony necessary to convey the unprecedented level of death and injury caused" . . . . The winnowing process of "worthy" witnesses . . . has the obvious potential to alienate those not selected.

Wayne A. Logan, *Confronting Evil: Victims' Rights in an Age of Terror*, 96 GEO. L. J. 721, 750–51 (2008). In mass-killing capital cases, like *Moussaoui*, particular concerns have been raised about government efforts to favor victims who support the death penalty over those who are opposed. *Id.* at 749.

8. **Expedited Litigation Rules.** The recognition of victims' rights may result in substantial disruptions to the criminal process. For instance, litigation over victim claims may slow down the resolution of cases in the trial court and, at the appellate level, threaten the finality of judgments entered below. Do you see how the CVRA addresses these concerns? The CVRA's expedited litigation processes seem capable of keeping criminal cases on track for timely resolution notwithstanding disputes over victims'

rights. But don't these processes seem potentially quite disruptive in their own ways?

9. **Definition of "Victim."** Note the CVRA's open-ended definition of who counts as a "victim": "a person directly and proximately harmed as a result of the commission of a Federal offense or an offense in the District of Columbia." This is similar to what is found in most states. *See* MPC:S § 7.07C reptr. note (c) (surveying state laws). Although such definitions may be quite capacious, they do have some limits—recall, for instance, Professor Cassell's discussion of why the sentencing judge in *Hunter* decided that Sue Antrobus did not qualify. As suggested by the analysis in *Hunter*, the definition of "victim" may require difficult and uncertain determinations of proximate causation. Could an emergency responder who experienced psychological distress from assisting a severely injured crime victim also count as a "victim" himself or herself? *See, e.g.,* Wayne A. Logan, *Victim Impact Evidence in Federal Capital Trials*, 19 FED. SENT'G RPTR. 5, 7 (2006) (noting that sentencing hearing of Oklahoma City bombing defendant included "gripping evidence on the emotional harms suffered by professional emergency rescue workers and police").

10. **Scope of "Impact."** The CVRA imposes no express limitations on the types of impact that might be included in a victim statement, although the definition of "victim" may imply that victims should confine themselves to harms that were "directly and proximately" caused by the defendant's criminal conduct. Could a victim impact statement include information about the effect of a major crime on a whole community? *See, e.g., id.* (noting that sentencing hearing in *Moussaoui*, the 9/11 case, included statements about the impact of the terror attack on New York City).

D. PROBLEM SOLVING COURTS

As we saw in *Williams v. New York*, it is sometimes thought that rehabilitative aims justify, or maybe even necessitate, a relatively informal approach to the sentencing process. Decided in 1949, *Williams* reflected the prevailing mid-twentieth-century view that rehabilitation should play a central role in the determination of punishment. Later in the twentieth century, rehabilitation seemed to be eclipsed in importance by other purposes of punishment. By the late 1990s, however, there was increasing evidence that the pendulum had begun to swing back in favor rehabilitation. Perhaps most importantly, a new model of "problem solving court" was growing swiftly in popularity. In the excerpt below, Professor Bruce Winick describes the conceptual origins of this model and the broad range of social problems the model has been used to address. As you read the excerpt, consider how the roles of judge, prosecutor, and defense lawyer might be different in a problem solving court, and how the operations of such a court might be in tension with familiar ideals of due process.

Bruce J. Winick, Therapeutic Jurisprudence and Problem Solving Courts

30 FORDHAM URB. L. J. 1055 (2003)

Recently, a range of new kinds of problems, many of which are social and psychological in nature, have appeared before the courts. These cases require the courts to not only resolve disputed issues of fact, but also to attempt to solve a variety of human problems that are responsible for bringing the case to court. Traditional courts limit their attention to the narrow dispute in controversy. These newer courts, however, attempt to understand and address the underlying problem that is responsible for the immediate dispute, and to help the individuals before the court to effectively deal with the problem in ways that will prevent recurring court involvement.

The new courts, increasingly known as problem solving courts, are specialized tribunals established to deal with specific problems, often involving individuals who need social, mental health, or substance abuse treatment services. These courts also include criminal cases involving individuals with drug or alcoholism problems, mental health problems, or problems of family and domestic violence. The juvenile court is the forerunner of these specialized courts; it was started in Chicago in 1899 as an attempt to provide a rehabilitative approach to the problem of juvenile delinquency, rather than the punitive approach of the adult criminal court. The modern antecedents of this movement are the drug treatment courts, founded in Miami in 1989.

The drug treatment court was a response to the recognition that processing nonviolent drug possession charges in the criminal courts and then sentencing the offender to prison did not succeed in changing the offender's addictive behavior. Criminal court dockets had become swollen with these drug cases, and the essentially retributivist intervention of the criminal court and prison seemed to do little to avoid repetition of the underlying problem. The result was a "revolving door effect in which [drug offenders typically] resumed their drug-abusing behavior after [being] released from prison." Instead of relying on the traditional criminal justice approach, the drug treatment court emphasized the offender's rehabilitation, and placed the judge as a member of the treatment team. Offenders accepting diversion to the drug treatment court, or pleading guilty and agreeing to participate in the drug treatment court as a condition of probation, agreed to several conditions[:] to remain drug-free, "to participate in a prescribed course of drug treatment, to submit to periodic drug testing in order to monitor their compliance [with the treatment plan], and to report [periodically] to court for judicial supervision of their progress."

These courts' success in helping many addicts to end their addiction and to avoid re-involvement with the criminal court led to a tremendous growth in the number of drug courts nationally and internationally, with the result that, as of December 2000, there were 697 such courts in America, and many more in the planning stage. Indeed, there now are juvenile drug treatment courts, which specialize in juveniles with drug abuse problems, and dependency drug treatment courts, that deal with families with drug problems that are charged with child abuse or neglect.

Other specialized treatment courts or problem solving courts, as they are now known, include domestic violence courts, which attempt to protect the victims of domestic violence, to motivate perpetrators of domestic violence to attend batterer's intervention programs, and to monitor compliance with court orders and treatment progress. More than two hundred domestic violence courts now exist.

Reentry courts are another form of problem solving courts. These courts were designed to assist offenders that are released from prison into a form of judicially-supervised parole, to effect a successful integration into the community. A recently proposed application of the reentry court model deals with sex offenders and attempts to manage the risk of their reoffending through close supervision and monitoring through the use of polygraph examinations.

Another example is the dependency court, a branch of family court that deals with issues of child abuse and neglect. This is a civil court that adjudicates whether child abuse or neglect has occurred, and when it has, it attempts to provide services designed to avoid its repetition. When such services appear fruitless, the dependency court works to terminate parental rights and arrange foster care for the child.

Teen court, sometimes known as youth court, is another problem solving court. This court deals with cases involving juveniles charged with minor offenses. In addition, it allows other juveniles who have been through the teen court process, and who have received special training, to play the role of prosecutor, defense attorney, or member of the jury. This special process provides the juveniles charged with minor offenses with the ability to see their behavior from the victims' or society's perspective and to receive an inoculation of empathy training.

One of the most recent types of problem solving courts to emerge is the mental health court, started in 1997 in Broward County, Florida. The mental health court is a misdemeanor criminal court designed to deal with people arrested for minor offenses whose major problem is mental illness rather than criminality. This is a revolving door category of patients who are periodically committed to mental hospitals where they are treated with psychotropic medication. Due to the use of medication, they experience sufficient improvement, which allows hospitals to discharge them, but, when they are back in the community, they fail to take their medication. As a result, they frequently decompensate, sometimes committing minor offenses that result in their arrest. Mental health courts seek to divert them from the criminal justice system and to persuade them to voluntarily accept treatment while in the community.

In addition, they link them with treatment resources, and provide social service support and judicial monitoring to ensure treatment compliance.

All of these courts grew out of the recognition that traditional judicial approaches have failed, at least in the areas of substance abuse, domestic violence, certain kinds of criminality, child abuse and neglect, and mental illness. These are all recycling problems, the reoccurrence of which traditional interventions did not succeed in bringing to a halt. The traditional judicial model addressed the symptoms, but not the underlying problem. The result was that the problem reemerged, constantly necessitating repeated judicial intervention. All these areas involved specialized problems that judges of courts of general jurisdiction lacked expertise in. Moreover, they involved treatment or social service needs that traditional courts lacked the tools to deal with.

In response to these failures, courts decided that they needed new judicial approaches. These new approaches involve a collaborative, interdisciplinary approach to problem solving where the judge plays a leading role. Not only is the judge a leading actor in the therapeutic drama, but also the courtroom itself becomes a stage for the acting out of many crucial scenes. On this stage, the judge also assumes the role of director, coordinating the roles of many of the actors, providing a needed motivation for how they will play their parts, and inspiring them to play them well.*

NOTES & QUESTIONS

1. **Problem Solving Courts Within the Criminal Process.** As Professor Winick indicates, specialized problem solving courts (PSCs) can be connected to the conventional criminal process in a variety of different ways. Most commonly, a defendant enters a PSC by one of three different routes: (1) as a pre-conviction (or possibly even a pre-charging) diversion from conventional adjudication; (2) as a post-conviction diversion from conventional sentencing; or (3) as an aspect of a formally imposed sentence, e.g., as a condition of probation. Some PSCs are structured so as to take defendants through only one of these different pathways, while others are more flexible and take defendants via multiple routes.

2. **Defendant Incentives.** Defendant participation in a PSC is voluntary. Why would a defendant choose such an option, which may involve a multitude of onerous requirements, such as weekly court dates, weekly counseling sessions, and regular drug tests? For some, participation may seem a helpful opportunity to access needed social services, such as drug addiction treatment, that can otherwise be difficult for low-income individuals to obtain. For many participants, though, the primary incentive is the hope of a better resolution of their legal problems. Depending on how the PSC is structured, successful participation may save the individual from a criminal conviction or, failing that, at least from a sentence of

* This article was originally published in Volume 30 of the *Fordham Urban Law Journal* and is republished with permission.

incarceration. Individuals who are eligible for a PSC will weigh the potential costs and benefits of participation in relation to the expected outcome they would experience through conventional case-processing. The relative appeal of the PSC option will thus vary considerably from court to court, which may help to explain why some PSCs have long waiting lists, while others have unused slots. MICHAEL O'HEAR, THE FAILED PROMISE OF SENTENCING REFORM 32 (2017). Note that defense lawyers may have a critical role to play in ensuring that prospective PSC participants make well-informed choices about entry into the court.

3. **Determination of Eligibility.** PSCs normally have a variety of eligibility criteria. It is common, for instance, for defendants who are charged with a violent crime to be categorically excluded by PSC rules. Beyond such objective criteria, however, it is also common to give a judge and/or a prosecutor discretion to decide who can participate. As noted above, this decision is sometimes part of the formal sentencing process. Often, however, the defendant enters the PSC as an alternative to conventional adjudication and sentencing. Will the "decider" (judge and/or prosecutor) have enough information at that point to make substantively good decisions? And will the defendant have a meaningful opportunity to be heard in the judge/prosecutor decision-making process? The answers to such questions may differ a great deal from PSC to PSC.

The due-process concerns here overlap substantially with the due-process concerns noted earlier in this chapter in relation to misdemeanor case-processing. Indeed, PSCs normally focus on low-level criminality, and are an increasingly common part of the diversion/dismissal repertoire that is used to resolve a majority of misdemeanor cases in some jurisdictions.

4. **Program Requirements.** Every PSC has its own requirements, but certain components are common, including a multiphase structure involving close supervision at the start and then decreasing court contacts over time as treatment milestones are achieved. By way of illustration, consider the requirements of the drug treatment court in Waukesha County, Wisconsin, a large suburban jurisdiction[20]:

Phase 1

- Meet weekly with case manager
- Attend drug court weekly
- Undergo assessments for treatment needs
- Submit to random drug tests at least three times per week
- Attend at least one self-help support group meeting
- Attend one meeting of drug court alumni group
- Develop relationship with assigned mentor
- Stay current with financial obligations, including court costs and program fees

[20] These requirements are set forth in WIS. COMM'TY SVCS., WAUKESHA COUNTY DRUG TREATMENT COURT PARTICIPANT HANDBOOK (2019).

- Movement to next phase requires at least 14 consecutive days of sobriety

Phase 2

- Meet weekly with case manager
- Attend drug court every two weeks
- Attend counseling sessions as directed
- Submit to random drug tests at least three times per week
- Attend two self-help support meetings per week
- Attend one meeting of drug court alumni group per month
- Obtain a sponsor
- Work toward employment or some other approved community activity
- Stay current with financial obligations, including court costs and program fees
- Movement to next phase requires at least 30 consecutive days of sobriety

Phase 3

- Meet with case manager every two weeks
- Attend drug court once per month
- Attend counseling sessions as directed
- Submit to random drug tests at least twice per week
- Attend three self-help support meetings per week
- Attend one meeting of drug court alumni group per month
- Maintain weekly contact with sponsor
- Work toward employment or some other approved community activity
- Complete autobiography
- Stay current with financial obligations, including court costs and program fees
- Movement to next phase requires at least 45 consecutive days of sobriety

Phase 4

- Meet with case manager every two weeks
- Attend drug court every four weeks
- Attend counseling sessions as directed
- Submit to random drug tests at least twice per week
- Attend two self-help support meetings per week
- Attend one meeting of drug court alumni group per month
- Maintain weekly contact with sponsor

- Work toward employment or some other approved community activity
- Develop aftercare treatment plan
- Stay current with financial obligations, including court costs and program fees
- Movement to next phase requires at least 60 consecutive days of sobriety

Phase 5

- Meet with case manager every four weeks
- Attend drug court every four weeks
- Submit to random drug tests at least twice per week
- Attend two self-help support meetings per week
- Attend one meeting of drug court alumni group per month
- Maintain weekly contact with sponsor
- Work toward employment or some other approved community activity
- Develop continuing care and relapse prevention plans
- Complete essay on why you are an appropriate candidate for graduation
- Stay current with financial obligations, including court costs and program fees
- Graduation requires at least 90 consecutive days of sobriety

How well do you think *you* would be able to keep track of all of these meetings and other requirements?

5. **Graduated Sanctions.** In Professor Winick's account, PSCs are designed to address stubbornly recurring criminal behavior that is tied to some difficult underlying social or psychological problem of the defendant. With such defendants, simply entering a PSC and commencing treatment is unlikely to bring an immediate end to troubling behavior. Thus, an important challenge for any PSC is developing a system for appropriately responding to program violations or other misconduct by participants. The preferred approach is "graduated sanctions"—that is, responding with some relatively mild punishment for the first violation or two, and then gradually increasing the severity of responses to subsequent missteps. Michael O'Hear, *Drug Courts as Communicative Punishment, in* RETRIBUTIVISM HAS A PAST: HAS IT A FUTURE? 234, 238 (Michael Tonry ed., 2011). At the high end of sanctions would be a short stint of "motivational jail"; return to an earlier, more onerous phase of the PSC process; or termination from the program and a return to the regular criminal process, which might result in a sentence to incarceration.

Although the principle of graduated sanctions seems widely accepted, judges have considerable discretion in determining how aggressively to move up the sanctions ladder. Practices can vary widely from one courtroom to the next. In some PSCs, jailing is a commonly used sanction, and participants might realistically expect to spend several weeks behind bars before completing the program. *See, e.g.,* Denise C. Gottfredson et al., *Effectiveness of Drug Treatment Courts: Evidence From a Randomized Trial*, 2 CRIMINOLOGY & PUB. POL'Y 171, 183 (2003) (presenting data from Baltimore drug court). Indeed, it is not unheard of for participants to spend more time incarcerated while in a PSC than they would have if they had refused entry and remained in the conventional court system—an ironic outcome for programs that are often framed as an *alternative* to incarceration.

As with the decisions about who enters the PSC, sanctioning decisions are typically made with few formal procedural protections for the participants. A particular area of concern has been a tendency for traditional understandings of the attorney-client relationship and adversarial process to break down in the PSC. *See, e.g.,* NAT'L ASS'N OF CRIM. DEFENSE LAWYERS, AMERICA'S PROBLEM-SOLVING COURTS: THE CRIMINAL COSTS OF TREATMENT AND THE CASE FOR REFORM 30–38 (2009). As Winick observes, the PSC employs "a collaborative, interdisciplinary approach to problem solving." The defense lawyer is normally expected to be one of the collaborators—a member of the "team." Some defense lawyers complain of pressure to go along with the team's view of what best serves the client's therapeutic needs, rather than to advocate for the client's stated preferences. *Id.* at 33. Relatedly, key decisions are often made at private, off-the-record team meetings without the client—and often without even the lawyer—being present. *Id.* at 31. Courtroom proceedings are conceptualized less as decision-making processes than as a sort of theater—"a stage," as Winick puts it, "for the acting out of many crucial scenes" in the "therapeutic drama." A key feature of this drama is the direct interaction between judge and client, without a lawyer playing the accustomed mediating role. However, such direct interaction may pose significant dangers of misunderstanding, especially for those PSC participants who suffer impediments to effective communication, such as educational, intellectual, or linguistic deficits.

Do you think the due-process concerns are alleviated by the facts that entry into the PSC is voluntary and that sanctioning is imposed within the context of a therapeutic intervention that is intended to improve the sanctioned person's well-being?

6. **Proportionality.** Should the PSC be conceptualized as a *punishment* for the underlying criminal offense that caused the participant to enter the legal system, or as an *alternative to punishment* that aims to deliver social services in lieu of punitive hard treatment? PSC proponents tend to favor the latter view, but the punishment-services dichotomy can be overstated. For one thing, as we saw in Chapter 1, rehabilitation is widely considered a core purpose of punishment and is traditionally weighed in conventional sentencing processes alongside desert and other objectives. For another, the PSC itself tends to involve plenty of hard treatment for participants, not only in the form of sanctioning, but also in the onerous basic requirements of the program—frequent court appearances, mandatory counseling sessions, drug tests, and the like. (Here, you might recall the "process as punishment" view discussed earlier in this chapter.)

To the extent that the PSC is fairly regarded as punishment, it may be difficult to reconcile the PSC with ideals of proportionality. The amount of hard treatment experienced by PSC participants is a function, not of the severity of their underlying offense, but of their compliance with and success in the treatment regimen. Compliance and success determine not only the amount of sanctioning that the participant experiences, but also the length of time that the participant is subject to basic program requirements—PSC "graduation" is based on the achievement of treatment milestones. One participant might spend, say, 6–12 months longer in the program, with 1–2 months more jail time, than another participant who was originally charged with precisely the same offense. Importantly, sanctions are often based on violations that are not inherently criminal, e.g., showing up late for a court date or refusing to speak candidly during a counseling session.

Moreover, concerns have been raised that treatment success may be determined, to a considerable extent, by socioeconomic status. RYAN S. KING & JILL PASQUARELLA, THE SENTENCING PROJECT, DRUG COURTS: A REVIEW OF THE EVIDENCE 6 (2009). (Can you imagine any of the reasons why this might be so?) Such socioeconomic effects may, in turn, help to explain the much higher success rates of White than Black participants in some PSCs. Michael O'Hear, *Rethinking Drug Courts: Restorative Justice as a Response to Racial Injustice*, 20 STAN. L. & POL'Y REV. 463, 480 (2009).

7. **Continued Growth in PSC Numbers.** Winick notes the explosive growth in the number of PSCs nationwide in the 1990s. That growth has continued into the twenty-first century. Drug treatment courts are the most well-established and widespread form of PSC. By 2015, there were about 3,400 drug treatment courts in the United States, with about half focused on adult clients and the remainder on juveniles. MICHAEL O'HEAR, THE FAILED PROMISE OF SENTENCING REFORM 29 (2017). Other types of PSCs—mental health courts, reentry courts, DUI courts, and the like—have also been gaining in prominence. Perhaps the fast-growing type of PSC in recent years has been veterans' court. The number of specialized courts for veterans in the United States increased from 25 in 2009 to 461 in 2016. Barry C. Edwards, Ramon Hinojosa & Komysha Hassan, *How to Transform the Judicial System: Lesson From the Institutionalization of Veterans' Treatment Court*, 21 N.Y.U. J. LEGIS. & PUB. POL'Y 841, 850 (2019).

8. **But Do They Work?** Drug treatment courts have been extensively studied. Given the large number of such courts in existence, the wide variety of settings in which they are found, differences in entry criteria and procedures, varying treatment strategies and sanctioning practices, and other potentially important court-to-court differences, it should not be surprising that researchers have found widely varying success rates. Simply calling a court a "treatment court" and subjecting participants to a regimen of counseling and regular drug tests under judicial supervision does not seem to guarantee any better outcomes than are achieved by conventional criminal courts. However, the weight of research evidence now seems to support the view that a well-designed, well-run, adequately funded treatment court can help participants to reduce their drug use and criminal activity over a sustained period of time.

For instance, one leading study sponsored by the National Institute of Justice compared the outcomes of 1,100 drug court participants at 23 different sites with those of 600 drug-involved individuals at 6 sites lacking a drug court. SHELLI B. ROSSMAN ET AL., URBAN INST., THE MULTI-STATE ADULT DRUG COURT EVALUATION (2011). Eighteen months after entry into the drug court, 29% of the participant group tested positive for drug use, as compared with 46% of the comparison group. Additionally, a lower percentage of participants reported criminal activity in the past year, by a margin of 40% to 53%. There has been comparatively little rigorous research performed on other types of PSCs, but some studies provide grounds for optimism that the PSC model may also work outside the drug context. *See, e.g.*, Virginia Aldigé Hiday, Heathcote W. Wales & Bradley Ray, *Effectiveness of Short-Term Mental Health Court: Criminal Recidivism One Year Postexit*, 37 L. & HUM. BEHAVIOR 401 (2013).

9. **What Did It Cost?** Even assuming that establishing a PSC would carry social *benefits*, that does not necessarily mean that doing so would represent good policy. What do you think some of the important social *costs* might be?

CHAPTER 4

SENTENCING FACTORS

In Chapter 1, we considered the various commonly recognized purposes of punishment. In any given case, if the judge is to craft a sentence that furthers these purposes, the judge will almost always want to know more information than simply the name and elements of the crime of conviction. The various types of information that are relevant to sentencing may be referred to as *sentencing factors*. Even based on just a passing familiarity with the purposes of punishment, it would probably be easy to generate a list of dozens of sentencing factors that seem at least plausibly linked to one or more of the purposes.

Upon closer analysis, however, you may perceive important difficulties with many of the sentencing factors that are most familiar or obvious. Some may rest, for instance, on unproven intuitions about recidivism risk or rehabilitative prospects. Thus, as noted in Chapter 1, a defendant's decision to plead guilty—while a commonly cited sentencing factor in practice—may not actually be a reliable indicator that the defendant is "on the road to rehabilitation," as is sometimes asserted. Meanwhile, other factors defy easy categorization as aggravating or mitigating; in other words, the same factor may seem aggravating from the standpoint of one purpose of punishment but mitigating from the standpoint of another. For instance, a seventeen-year-old defendant's young age may indicate a heightened recidivism risk, at least in the near term, but also a diminished culpability. Finally, some factors may seem problematic insofar as they correlate with other considerations that are plainly improper, such as race.

In this chapter, we survey several of the most important sentencing factors. First, we assess what may be the most widely embraced sentencing factor in practice, criminal history. Next, we consider an array of other defendant characteristics, including family relationships, mental impairment, and socioeconomic status. We then examine offense-severity factors, including role in the offense, quantitative factors, and motive. We conclude with a consideration of post-offense assistance to the authorities and the handling of multicount cases.

A. CRIMINAL HISTORY & RECIDIVISM RISK

Criminal history often plays a central role in American sentencing decisions. Sentencing guidelines, for instance, commonly require calculation of a criminal history score, as you may recall from the Minnesota and federal "grids" reprinted in Chapter 2. Additionally, there are many mandatory minimum statutes that enhance sentences on the basis of prior convictions, such as the "three strikes and you are out" statutes that were adopted by about half of all states in the 1990s. And, even in the absence of some mandatory weight for criminal history, judges routinely take prior convictions into account in their exercise of sentencing discretion. Indeed, empirical researchers consistently find that prior record and offense severity are the most important determinants of sentencing outcomes. Michael Cassidy & Jason Rydberg, *Analyzing Variation in Prior Record Penalties Across Conviction Offenses*, 64 CRIME & DELINQUENCY 831, 834 (2018). For instance, one study of 863 felony cases in Texas found that each prior felony conviction was associated, on average, with a 12% increase in the length of prison terms. Theodore R. Curry, *The Conditional Effects of Victim and Offender Ethnicity and Victim Gender on Sentences for Non-Capital Cases*, 12 PUNISHMENT & SOC'Y 438, 450 (2010).

1. JUSTIFICATIONS FOR CONSIDERING CRIMINAL HISTORY

Although policymakers and practitioners generally seem to take "prior record enhancements" (PREs) for granted, they are controversial among theorists. *See* Rhys Hester et al., *Prior Record Enhancements at Sentencing: Unsettled Justifications and Unsettling Consequences*, 47 CRIME & JUST. 209 (2018). PREs are particularly difficult to square with desert-based approaches to punishment (i.e., retribution), since these approaches tend to emphasize the harm and blameworthiness of the immediate crime.

Despite the apparent tension between desert and PREs, several theorists have attempted to reconcile the two. For instance, a prior conviction might increase a defendant's culpability to the extent that the prior conviction put the defendant on *notice* of the wrongfulness of his conduct. *See, e.g.*, Andrew von Hirsch, *Desert and Previous Convictions*, *in* PRINCIPLED SENTENCING: READINGS IN THEORY AND POLICY 191, 193 (Andrew von Hirsch & Andrew Ashworth eds., 1998). The defendant's subsequent repetition of the conduct may then be seen as more blameworthy because more willful or defiant. However, the notice argument seems only to justify a substantial increase in punishment for a *second* conviction. After the first conviction, the defendant is fully on notice. It is hard to see how a second, third, or fourth conviction somehow establishes *more* notice and hence more culpability for subsequent offenses. Moreover, the notice argument also seems inapplicable to major crimes whose wrongfulness should be obvious to everyone. Does it really seem that the second-time armed robber should get more punishment than a first-timer simply because the second-timer is now on notice that armed robbery is wrong? Finally, notice arguments may also be inapplicable if the second conviction is for a crime dissimilar to the first. A defendant's conviction for shoplifting, for instance, seems to provide little enhanced notice of the wrongfulness of driving while intoxicated. *See* Aaron J. Rappaport, *Rationalizing the Commission: The Philosophical Premises of the U.S. Sentencing Guidelines*, 52 EMORY L.J. 557, 597–98 (2003).

Under an alternative approach, we might think about prior convictions not as a basis for increased punishment, but rather as a matter of *progressive loss of mitigation*. According to Professor Andrew von Hirsch, a leading proponent of this view, first-timers should receive a punishment discount in recognition of the essential human frailty that we all share. *See, e.g., Proportionality and Progressive Loss of Mitigation: Some Further Reflections, in* PREVIOUS CONVICTIONS AT SENTENCING: THEORETICAL AND APPLIED PERSPECTIVES 1, 11 (Julian V. Roberts & Andrew von Hirsch eds., 2010). On this view, some tolerance should be shown when a person first errs, but subsequent lapses are entitled to diminishing (or perhaps no) forgiveness. The tolerance for initial offenses, von Hirsch contends, partly reflects an expectation that the defendant "will respond by desisting. If he does not, he (gradually) loses the discount, depending [on] the frequency of his subsequent reoffending." *Id.* at 10.

However, as with the notice theory, the loss-of-mitigation theory seems to provide a justification only for drawing a distinction between first-timers and second-timers, and perhaps to a lesser extent second- and third-timers. Neither theory seems to justify further aggravation of punishment beyond the first few offenses, as is commonly done in guidelines systems, or the sharp increases in punishment that are often required under three-strikes and other "habitual criminality" laws. Nor does it seem that "tolerance for human frailty" could justify a discount even for first-time offenses whose extreme culpability takes them well outside the realm of normal human error. *See* Mirko Bagaric, *The Punishment Should Fit the Crime—Not the Prior Convictions of the Person Who Committed the Crime: An Argument for Less Impact Being Accorded to Previous Convictions in Sentencing*, 51 SAN DIEGO L. REV. 343, 373–74 (2014).

Other efforts have been made to justify the use of criminal history at sentencing on desert grounds, but none has gained widespread acceptance among theorists. (For a recent canvassing and critique of these theories, see Hester et al., *supra*.) Moreover, as with the notice and loss-of-mitigation approaches, other theories also generally provide greater support for modest PREs after the first offense or two than for continued enhancement with further recidivism or for draconian PREs that give greater weight to criminal history than to the severity of the instant offense.

Many of these efforts to justify PREs rely, explicitly or implicitly, on certain ideas about desert and character. The thinking seems to be that criminal history is an indicator of bad character, that a person's good or bad character is to some extent within the person's control, and that added punishment is to some extent deserved when a person of bad character fails to take steps to address his or her problematic behavioral propensities. For instance, a person who recognizes that his or her friends are a bad influence and are contributing to his or her repeated criminality might be blamed for failing to jettison those friends in favor of a more pro-social peer group. As the convictions mount, more severe punishment may be deserved as a result of the person's failure to take steps to diminish his or her criminal propensities by moving on from the bad influences.[1]

But is this too simplistic a model of character? Doesn't it seem that a person's character may to a considerable extent be *outside* his or her control due to genetic predispositions, poor parenting, mental disorder, traumatic life experiences, socioeconomic disadvantage, and so forth? Punishing bad character may thus seem uncomfortably close to punishing status, which is unconstitutional. Hester et al., *supra*, at 223 (citing *Robinson v. California*, 370 U.S. 660 (1962)). Moreover, even if most defendants have sufficient control over their propensities to warrant *some* incremental punishment for bad character, that does not necessarily mean that *large* increases in punishment are justified—especially if individual control over character tends not to be strong and society tends not to give much support to individual self-improvement efforts, as by providing mental health care, stable housing, or vocational training for people who cannot afford these services on their own.

In sum, if desert is prioritized as the dominant purpose of punishment, it may be hard to justify giving much weight to prior convictions. In particular, the most widely cited retributive justifications for PREs would support only modest record-based increases in punishment—and even these only after the first few offenses.

By contrast, utilitarian approaches are more amenable to PREs. In general, a defendant's prior convictions support an inference that the defendant is more likely to commit additional crimes in the future. The defendant's record may thus call for a sterner specific-deterrent message, longer-term incapacitation, or a requirement that the defendant participate in rehabilitative programming.[2] On the other hand, it is possible—and indeed perhaps commonplace—to push this crime-prevention reasoning too far. More prior convictions do not inevitably justify more punishment, even on a purely utilitarian basis.

Many of the key limiting considerations were covered in the discussion of utilitarian purposes of punishment in Chapter 1. They include:

- Incarceration may perversely increase recidivism risk for some defendants;

---

[1] This illustration echoes the "omission theory" of Professor Youngjae Lee, although he himself does not frame his approach as character-based. *See Recidivism As Omission: A Relational Account*, 87 TEX. L. REV. 571 (2009).

[2] The U.S. Supreme Court has relied on such utilitarian justifications in turning aside a constitutional challenge to a long "three-strikes" sentence. *See* Ewing v. California, 538 U.S. 11, 29 (2003) ("The [defendant's] sentence is justified by the State's public-safety interest in incapacitating and deterring recidivist felons . . . ."). *Ewing* is excerpted and discussed in Chapter 6 below.

- Incarceration is costly for society, not only in a fiscal sense, but also in the human impact on defendants' families and others;
- Rehabilitative programming may be more effective for many defendants if administered in the community;
- Desistance from crime ("aging out") is the norm for most defendants, which suggests that long-term incapacitation will only rarely be cost-benefit justified; and
- Crime-reduction benefits from incarceration may be offset by substitution effects as others step into the defendant's shoes.

Taking into account all of these retributive and utilitarian considerations, Professors Rhys Hester, Richard Frase, Julian Roberts, and Kelly Lyn Mitchell have proposed that the PREs in sentencing guidelines be reformed along the following lines:

> Recommended custody-duration enhancements should not increase at a steady or uniform rate as the criminal history score rises. Retributive and risk-based rationales justify a substantial difference in penalty severity between first offenders and low-history repeat offenders * * *; however, the pace of enhancement should be much more modest as offender scores continue to rise.
>
> To limit the costs and other adverse effects of prior record enhancements and, in particular, to maintain proportionality between sentence severity and conviction offense seriousness, the recommended duration for highest-history offenders should not be more than two times greater than the recommended sentence for no-history (or lowest-history) offenders. This "doubling" limit ensures that an offender's prior record never counts more than his current crime.
>
> Judges should have authority to adjust the sentence upon a finding that the offender's criminal history score does not accurately reflect the risk of serious recidivism; * * *.
>
> A particularly strong basis to mitigate sentences, even for offenders with a number of prior convictions, would exist in [cases in] which the court finds that, notwithstanding his most recent crime, the offender has made substantial efforts to address the causes of his offending.

Hester et al., *supra*, at 244–45. Do these seem sensible suggestions to you? Note that the proposed "doubling" limit would represent a change from existing law in many jurisdictions. See, for instance, the Minnesota and federal guidelines grids reprinted in Chapter 2.

NOTES & QUESTIONS

1. **Criminal History and Race.** A person's prior record is partly a function of the person's past behavior, and partly a function of choices that have been made by police, prosecutors, and others. Much criminal activity never comes to the attention of the authorities, and much of what does is handled in ways that do not create a record of an arrest or a conviction. However, some groups in society may be more likely to benefit from official inattention or lenience than others. Thus, for instance, two young men who engage in a similar course of adolescent irresponsibility may end up with sharply contrasting official criminal histories if one lives in a heavily policed inner-city neighborhood and the other lives in a lightly policed suburb. The potential for such disparities has been a recurring source of criticism of PREs, particularly insofar as they may fuel disproportionately severe sentences for Black defendants.

In one study in Minnesota, for instance, researchers found that Black defendants were almost 50% more likely to receive a prison sentence than White defendants, and that more than half of the difference in outcomes could be traced to criminal history. Hester et al., *supra*, at 238. Of course, it is very hard to know the extent to which differences in the prior records of Black and White defendants reflect differences in policing and other official practices, as opposed to differences in the defendants' own behavior.

In its provision regarding the use of criminal history in sentencing guidelines, the Model Penal Code: Sentencing ("MPC:S") mandates that the sentencing commission "shall give due consideration to the danger that the use of criminal-history provisions to increase the severity of sentences may have disparate impacts on racial or ethnic minorities, or other disadvantaged groups." § 6B.07(1)(c). If consideration of priors significantly increases racial disparities in imprisonment, do you think that criminal history should be categorically prohibited for use as a sentencing factor, regardless of its utility as a possible indicator of recidivism risk?

2. **Criminal History and Diversions.** In addition to increasing the severity of formally imposed sentences, prior convictions can also disqualify defendants from the diversion programs that often serve as an alternative to conventional sentencing, especially in lower-level cases. For instance, one recent survey found that nine states categorically excluded individuals with a prior violent-crime conviction from participation in drug-treatment courts. Michael O'Hear, *Third-Class Citizenship: The Escalating Legal Consequences of Committing a "Violent" Crime*, 109 J. CRIM. L. & CRIMINOLOGY 165, 192 n.193 (2019). Depending on the state, such a conviction might also statutorily disqualify an individual from entry into other sorts of problem solving courts, such as mental health or veterans' courts, as well as various non-PSC diversions. *Id.* at 192–93. Even when there is no categorical bar, a repeat offender might still be excluded from a diversion program as a matter of judicial or prosecutorial discretion. Such policies and practices may be hard to reconcile with the RNR model discussed in Chapter 1, which indicates that rehabilitative efforts should focus on higher-risk individuals.

3. **Actuarial Risk Assessment.** If criminal history is used at sentencing mainly as a proxy for recidivism risk, then perhaps it would be better to replace existing PREs with more scientific methods for assessing and managing risk. Recall, for instance, the earlier discussion of actuarial risk-assessment instruments (RAIs) from Chapter 1. RAIs are based on the identification of variables that are correlated with recidivism through the systematic analysis of a large number of actual cases. Typically, criminal history plays an important role in driving RAI scores, but the incorporation of other variables into RAI algorithms is thought to produce more accurate risk-assessment than would be possible through prior record alone.

RAIs are used at all at stages of the criminal process, from bail determinations through decisions about the administration of prison and community supervision. RAIs have been used at the sentencing stage in at least twenty jurisdictions. Erin Collins, *Punishing Risk*, 107 GEO. L.J. 57, 60 (2018). Although a small number of states attach a particular legal significance to risk scores, "most jurisdictions that authorize actuarial sentencing simply direct that the risk information be provided to a judge in advance of sentencing without any guidance on how it should—or should not—be used." *Id.* at 68.

Despite their increasingly widespread use, RAIs are hardly free from controversy. *See, e.g.*, Christopher Slobogin, *Introduction to Special Issue on Implementing Post-Conviction Risk Assessment*, 38 BEHAV. SCI. & L. 187 (2020) (providing overview of special issue exploring legal, technical, and ethical problems with use of RAIs at sentencing). Among other concerns, you might consider RAIs in light of the due-process ideals that were discussed in Chapter 3. It is one thing to enhance a sentence on the basis of prior convictions, which are established through a trial verdict or a defendant's formal plea of guilty or no contest. It is another to enhance the sentence on the basis of the "findings" of a probation officer (or other person charged with filling out an RAI form) regarding such matters as whether the defendant has a history of alcohol or drug problems.

Also of concern is the use in some RAIs of personal characteristics over which the defendant has little or no control. For instance, being male is generally associated with higher recidivism risk than being female. Some RAIs accordingly use defendant sex as a variable in their risk-assessment algorithms. It may seem unfair to impose relatively longer sentences on males on the basis of their sex. On the other hand, if sex were excluded as an RAI factor, then female defendants would tend to be evaluated as higher risk than they actually are, which may also seem unfair. Note, however, that the use of some personal characteristics in an RAI, including sex, might constitute a "suspect" or "quasi-suspect" classification that would trigger heightened constitutional scrutiny. *See* Crystal Yang & Will Dobbie, *Equal Protection Under Algorithms: A New Statistical and Legal Framework*, 119 MICH. L. REV. 291, 302–04 (2020) (summarizing key constitutional principles and noting dearth of case law on their application to RAIs).

The strongest objections to RAIs, however, have focused on their potential to exacerbate racial disparities. *See, e.g.*, Bernard E. Harcourt, *Risk as a Proxy for Race: The Dangers of Risk Assessment*, 27 FED. SENT'G RPTR.

237 (2015); Sonja B. Starr, *Evidence-Based Sentencing and the Scientific Rationalization of Discrimination*, 66 STAN. L. REV. 803 (2014). Race itself is very rarely, if ever, utilized as an explicit factor in contemporary RAIs, but RAIs do commonly give weight to various factors that tend to be correlated with race, such as education, employment, and criminal history. *See* Yang & Dobbie, *supra*, at 330. Indeed, it has been suggested that very little would be left to include in the algorithms if all race-correlated variables were purged, given the pervasive influence of race in American life today. *Id.* at 298. Thus, if priority is placed on designing RAIs so as to achieve parity in average risk scores across racial groups, there may need to be significant tradeoffs in the accuracy of the instruments.[3]

Racial critiques of RAIs should also take into account the existence of racial disparities in the traditional, more intuitive approaches to risk assessment. It is possible that any racial disparities following the introduction of an RAI in a jurisdiction may actually be less than those that existed previously. Thus far, little research has been conducted on whether RAIs tend to increase or decrease racial disparities. Most, but not all, of the small number of available studies find an *improvement* in outcomes (e.g., less jailing) for people of color when an RAI is used. Desmarais & Zottola, *supra*, at 812. *Cf.* Megan Stevenson, *Assessing Risk Assessment in Action*, 103 MINN. L. REV. 303, 309 (2018) (finding no change in racial disparities in pretrial release in Kentucky after introduction of pretrial risk assessment). But perhaps it is cold comfort if RAIs simply do no worse, or maybe slightly better, than the status quo. Are persistent racial disparities in sentencing—whether using intuitive or actuarial risk assessment—a reason to abandon the whole project of risk-based sentencing? What would the alternative be—purely backwards-looking desert-based sentencing? Do you think desert judgments would be any less prone to racial disparities than risk assessments?

Professor Sandra Mayson argues that an appreciation of the racial disparities in risk scores should not lead to a rejection of RAIs, but to a fundamental change in the way that the criminal justice system responds to risk. She writes:

---

3 It is not clear, however, that equality ideals necessarily call for equal risk scores across racial groups. If defendants in one racial group recidivate more frequently than defendants in another racial group, then disparities in their average risk scores might not be unwarranted. An alternative way of thinking about racial fairness in this context would focus on whether risk scores are equally predictive across racial groups. On this view, we should want there to be comparable recidivism rates between Black defendants who are evaluated as high risk and White defendants who are evaluated as high risk. The available research indicates that some RAIs perform fairly well in this regard. Sarah L. Desmarais & Samantha A. Zottola, *Violence Risk Assessment: Current Status and Contemporary Issues*, 103 MARQ. L. REV. 793, 810 (2020). For instance, a study of the federal Post Conviction Risk Assessment (PCRA) instrument found that Blacks who were categorized as high risk were rearrested 62% of the time, while the rearrest rate for high-risk Whites was 66%. Jennifer L. Skeem & Christopher T. Lowenkamp, *Risk, Race, and Recidivism: Predictive Bias and Disparate Impact*, 54 CRIMINOLOGY 680, 680–81 (2016). Similarly, Blacks categorized as low risk were rearrested 12% of the time, while the comparable figure for low-risk Whites was 10%. The researchers also looked for differences in *violent* rearrest rates, finding that high-risk Blacks were rearrested 23% of the time for violent offenses, while high-risk Whites were rearrested for such offenses 19% of the time. Overall, it is hard to see a pattern of predictive bias in the PCRA that favors one group over the other.

> Given the nature of prediction, a racially unequal past will necessarily produce racially unequal outputs. To adapt a computer-science idiom, "bias in, bias out." To be more specific, if the thing that we undertake to predict—say arrest—happened more frequently to black people than to white people in the past data, then a predictive analysis will project it to happen more frequently to black people than to white people in the future. * * *
>
> If the data fairly represent the incidence of serious crime * * *, the place to redress racial disparity is not in the measurement of risk, but in the *response* to it. Risk assessment must reflect the past; it need not dictate the future. The default response to risk could be supportive rather than coercive. In the long term, a supportive response to risk would help to redress the conditions that produce risk in the first place. In the short term, it would mitigate the disparate racial impact of prediction. Counterintuitively, algorithmic assessment could play a valuable role in a system that targets the risky for support rather than for restraint.

Sandra G. Mayson, *Bias in, Bias Out*, 128 YALE L.J. 2218, 2224, 2226 (2019). As an example of a "supportive" response, Mayson points to a problem-solving court that has been developed in the Eastern District of Pennsylvania for individuals returning from prison who pose a medium-to-high risk for violent recidivism. *Id.* at 2291.

4. **Bad and Good.** If a defendant's prior bad acts (convictions) are taken into account at sentencing, then why not also the defendant's prior *good* acts? *See* U.S. Sent'g Guidelines § 5H1.11 (stating that a defendant's "[m]ilitary, civic, charitable, or public service; employment-related contributions; and similar prior good works are not ordinarily relevant" for determining whether to impose a sentence below the federal guidelines range). For an argument that greater symmetry in the treatment of prior bad and good acts may be warranted, see Carissa Byrne Hessick, *Why Are Only Bad Acts Good Sentencing Factors?*, 88 B.U. L. REV. 1109 (2008).

2. WHICH PRIORS SHOULD COUNT AND TO WHAT EXTENT?

Thus far, we have considered criminal history as a sentencing factor in a broadly conceptual fashion. However, when jurisdictions attempt to codify PREs into guidelines or statutes, they confront a host of difficult technical questions about what exactly should count as a "prior" and how much weight different kinds of priors should be given. The remainder of this part will give you a taste of some of these technical issues. We focus particularly on federal law, which includes numerous PREs, both in the sentencing guidelines and in more narrowly targeted sentence-enhancement statutes. Although our attention will be on the federal system, it should be appreciated that the questions raised by federal PREs represent pervasive challenges in the use of criminal history as a sentencing factor. Even judges in highly discretionary state systems must confront these sorts of issues as they consider criminal history on a case-by-case basis—although the issues tend to get much less explicit attention when priors do not have some clearly predetermined weight.

United States Sentencing Guidelines (2021)

§ 4A1.1. Criminal History Category

The total points from subsections (a) through (e) determine the criminal history category in the Sentencing Table in Chapter Five, Part A.

(a) Add **3** points for each prior sentence of imprisonment exceeding one year and one month.

(b) Add **2** points for each prior sentence of imprisonment of at least sixty days not counted in (a).

(c) Add **1** point for each prior sentence not counted in (a) or (b), up to a total of 4 points for this subsection.

(d) Add **2** points if the defendant committed the instant offense while under any criminal justice sentence, including probation, parole, supervised release, imprisonment, work release, or escape status.

(e) Add **1** point for each prior sentence resulting from a conviction of a crime of violence that did not receive any points under (a), (b), or (c) above because such sentence was treated as a single sentence, up to a total of 3 points for this subsection.

NOTES & QUESTIONS

1. **Counting Criminal History Points.** Perhaps the simplest way to assign defendants a criminal history score would be to give each defendant one point for each prior conviction. The federal sentencing guidelines use a somewhat more complicated formula. What might be said in favor of the guidelines' approach? Are there any other approaches that you think might have merit? Note that, in the guidelines' system, two defendants with precisely the same set of prior convictions might have quite different criminal history scores if one was luckier than the other in drawing more lenient sentencing judges in the earlier cases. Do you see how? Is there any way to design a system that would avoid such disparities?

2. **New Offense Committed While Under Sentence for Old.** Imagine two defendants, A and B, who are both convicted at the same time of misdemeanor assault for their parts in a bar fight. A is given one year of probation, while B is given two. Eighteen months later, A and B are arrested for drug offenses and prosecuted in federal court. How many criminal history points do A and B have? Is the difference justified?

3. **Effect on Sentencing Range.** Continuing with the hypothetical, A and B are convicted in their federal case of conspiracy to distribute a small quantity of heroin, along with their coconspirator C. C has two prior drug trafficking felony convictions, which resulted in sentences of three and five years in prison, respectively. C was on parole at the time of the current offense. Assume that all three have an offense level of eighteen. What is the

advisory sentencing range for A, B, and C? (In order to answer this question, you will need to consult the federal sentencing table reprinted in Chapter 2). How would you characterize the effect of criminal history on the ranges of these three hypothetical defendants? Based on this example, do the guidelines seem to give too much or too little weight to prior convictions, or does the weight seem about right?

4. **Multiple Counts in Earlier Case.** In the problem from the previous note, what if C's two prior drug convictions had come in a single case and the sentences were imposed to run concurrently, i.e., at the same time—would that be one sentence or two for purposes of § 4A1.1? In § 4A1.2(a)(2), the guidelines specify,

> Prior sentences always are counted separately if the sentences were imposed for offenses that were separated by an intervening arrest (i.e., the defendant is arrested for the first offense prior to committing the second offense). If there is no intervening arrest, prior sentences are counted separately unless (A) the sentences resulted from offenses contained in the same charging instrument; or (B) the sentences were imposed on the same day. Treat any prior sentence covered by (A) or (B) as a single sentence.

Why do you suppose the guidelines ascribe so much importance to an intervening arrest?

5. **Decay Period.** An important question for any method of weighing criminal history is whether to recognize a decay period, i.e., whether to treat some convictions as too old to count. It seems clear enough that certain priors—say, a fifty-year-old misdemeanor conviction—have no bearing on the appropriate sentence for a new offense. But, on the other hand, where exactly should the line be drawn—how old is too old? One body of empirical research suggests that a person with some criminal history who manages to go seven years without a fresh arrest is only slightly more likely to commit a crime than are people of the same age who do not have any criminal history. *See* Michael O'Hear, *Early Release for Prisoners Convicted of Violent Crimes: Can Anyone Escape the Incapacitation-Retribution Catch-22?*, 52 CONN. L. REV. 653, 668–70 (2020) (summarizing studies). Arguably, then, convictions should no longer count for criminal-history scoring after seven years.

The federal sentencing guidelines do incorporate a decay period, but it is considerably longer than seven years for most prior sentences. Under § 4A1.2(e), a sentence of longer than one year and one month counts if it was imposed within fifteen years of the current offense. Shorter sentences count if they were imposed within ten years of the current offense. Somewhat shorter decay periods apply to some offenses that were committed when the defendant was under the age of eighteen.

Most state-level guidelines in the U.S. also recognize a decay period, although the specifics vary considerably from state to state. MPC:S § 6B.07 cmmnt. (e). The MPC:S calls for a decay period of ten years or less, and recommends that priors near the end of the decay period be given less weight than more recent priors. *Id.*

6. **Juvenile Adjudications.** Section 4A1.2(d) makes clear that delinquency adjudications in a juvenile court should be counted in the criminal-history scoring, subject to an accelerated decay rule of five years. Most state-level guidelines in the U.S. also count juvenile adjudications. MPC:S § 6B.07 cmmnt. (d). The MPC:S would also permit the use of juvenile cases, "but only when the procedural safeguards attending the adjudications were comparable to those of a criminal trial." § 6B.07(2).

7. **Flexibility and Discretion.** The guidelines establish a fairly mechanical process for calculating the criminal-history score, but also recognize that the rules may sometimes produce scores that substantially over- or understate the seriousness of a defendant's earlier criminal activity. Section 4A1.3 thus expressly recognizes the sentencing judge's authority to depart upward or downward on the ground that the calculated criminal-history score misrepresents "the seriousness of the defendant's criminal history or the likelihood that the defendant will commit other crimes." Additionally, as you may recall from Chapter 3, in the wake of the Supreme Court's decisions in *Booker* and *Kimbrough*, sentencing judges have even more discretion to reject the guidelines' system for weighing prior sentences. What arguments do you think defense lawyers might make in support of requests for a downward departure under § 4A1.3 or a *Booker* variance from the calculated criminal-history score?

8. **Uncounseled Prior Convictions.** As we noted in Chapter 3, the constitutional right to counsel does not extend to misdemeanor cases in which no sentence of incarceration is imposed. *See Alabama v. Shelton*, 535 U.S. 654 (2002). If a prior conviction was obtained in a case in which the defendant did not have legal representation available, there may be concerns about the reliability of the conviction. However, the Supreme Court has rejected arguments that it is unconstitutional to use an uncounseled prior conviction against a defendant for sentencing purposes in a subsequent case if the defendant was not constitutionally entitled to counsel in the prior case. *Nichols v. United States*, 511 U.S. 738 (1994). Note the irony: it is unconstitutional to sentence an indigent defendant to prison if no lawyer has been made available to the defendant, but there is no constitutional problem with using the uncounseled prior conviction as a ground for imposing or extending a prison term in a later case.

3. HABITUAL CRIMINALITY STATUTES

In addition to sentencing guidelines provisions like § 4A1.1, many jurisdictions also have statutes that increase maximum or minimum sentences for particular groups of defendants based on their prior convictions. Often, such statutes require the defendant to have a certain number of prior "felonies," "violent felonies," "serious felonies," or the like. Such statutes are sometimes called "habitual criminality" or "recidivism" laws. A familiar example is the "three strikes and you are out" statutes that were adopted in about the half the states in the 1990s. Another notable example from the federal system is the Armed Career Criminal Act, or "ACCA," which is the subject of the next case.

Taylor v. United States

495 U.S. 575 (1990)

■ BLACKMUN, J.

In this case we are called upon to determine the meaning of the word "burglary" as it is used in § 1402 of Subtitle I (the Career Criminals Amendment Act of 1986) of the Anti-Drug Abuse Act of 1986, 18 U.S.C. § 924(e). This statute provides a sentence enhancement for a defendant who is convicted under 18 U.S.C. § 922(g) (unlawful possession of a firearm) and who has three prior convictions for specified types of offenses, including "burglary."

I

Under 18 U.S.C. § 922(g)(1), it is unlawful for a person who has been convicted previously for a felony to possess a firearm. A defendant convicted for a violation of § 922(g)(1) is subject to the sentence-enhancement provision at issue, § 924(e):

> "(1) In the case of a person who violates section 922(g) of this title and has three previous convictions by any court . . . for a violent felony or a serious drug offense, or both . . . such person shall be fined not more than $25,000 and imprisoned not less than fifteen years. . . .
>
> "(2) As used in this subsection—
>
> . . . . .
>
> "(B) the term 'violent felony' means any crime punishable by imprisonment for a term exceeding one year . . . that—
>
> "(i) has as an element the use, attempted use, or threatened use of physical force against the person of another; or
>
> "(ii) is burglary, arson, or extortion, involves use of explosives, or otherwise involves conduct that presents a serious potential risk of physical injury to another."

In January 1988, in the United States District Court for the Eastern District of Missouri, petitioner Arthur Lajuane Taylor pleaded guilty to one count of possession of a firearm by a convicted felon, in violation of § 922(g)(1). At the time of his plea, Taylor had four prior convictions. One was for robbery, one was for assault, and the other two were for second-degree burglary under Missouri law.

The Government sought sentence enhancement under § 924(e). Taylor conceded that his robbery and assault convictions properly could be counted as two of the three prior convictions required for enhancement, because they involved the use of physical force against persons, under § 924(e)(2)(B)(i). Taylor contended, however, that his burglary convictions should not count for enhancement, because they did not involve "conduct that presents a serious potential risk of physical injury to another," under § 924(e)(2)(B)(ii). His guilty plea was conditioned on the right to appeal this issue. The District Court, pursuant to § 924(e)(1), sentenced Taylor to 15 years' imprisonment without possibility of parole.

The United States Court of Appeals for the Eighth Circuit, by a divided vote, affirmed Taylor's sentence. It ruled that, because the word "burglary" in § 924(e)(2)(B)(ii) "means 'burglary' however a state chooses to define it," the District Court did not err in using Taylor's Missouri convictions for second-degree burglary to enhance his sentence. * * *

The word "burglary" has not been given a single accepted meaning by the state courts; the criminal codes of the States define burglary in many different ways. On the face of the federal enhancement provision, it is not readily apparent whether Congress intended "burglary" to mean whatever the State of the defendant's prior conviction defines as burglary, or whether it intended that some uniform definition of burglary be applied to all cases in which the Government seeks a § 924(e) enhancement. And if Congress intended that a uniform definition of burglary be applied, was that definition to be the traditional common-law definition, or one of the broader "generic" definitions articulated in the Model Penal Code and in a predecessor statute to § 924(e), or some other definition specifically tailored to the purposes of the enhancement statute?

II

Before examining these possibilities, we think it helpful to review the background of § 924(e). Six years ago, Congress enacted the first version of the sentence-enhancement provision. Under the Armed Career Criminal Act of 1984, any convicted felon found guilty of possession of a firearm, who had three previous convictions "for robbery or burglary," was to receive a mandatory minimum sentence of imprisonment for 15 years. Burglary was defined in the statute itself as "any felony consisting of entering or remaining surreptitiously within a building that is property of another with intent to engage in conduct constituting a Federal or State offense."

The Act was intended to supplement the States' law enforcement efforts against "career" criminals. The House Report accompanying the Act explained that a "large percentage" of crimes of theft and violence "are committed by a very small percentage of repeat offenders," and that robbery and burglary are the crimes most frequently committed by these career criminals. * * * [T]he Senate Report stated that burglary was included because it is one of "the most common violent street crimes," and "[w]hile burglary is sometimes viewed as a non-violent crime, its character can change rapidly, depending on the fortuitous presence of the occupants of the home when the burglar enters, or their arrival while he is still on the premises." * * *

Only five months later, § 924(e) again was amended, into its present form, by § 1402 of Subtitle I (the Career Criminals Amendment Act of 1986) of the Anti-Drug Abuse Act of 1986. This amendment effected three changes that, taken together, give rise to the problem presented in this case. It expanded the predicate offenses triggering the sentence enhancement from "robbery or burglary" to "a violent felony or a serious drug offense"; it defined the term "violent felony" to include "burglary"; and it deleted the pre-existing definition of burglary. * * *

The legislative history as a whole suggests that the deletion of the 1984 definition of burglary may have been an inadvertent casualty of a complex drafting process. * * *

III

These observations about the purpose and general approach of the enhancement provision enable us to narrow the range of possible meanings of the term "burglary."

A

First, we are led to reject the view of the Court of Appeals in this case. It seems to us to be implausible that Congress intended the meaning of "burglary" for purposes of § 924(e) to depend on the definition adopted by the State of conviction. That would mean that a person convicted of unlawful possession of a firearm would, or would not, receive a sentence enhancement based on exactly the same conduct, depending on whether the State of his prior conviction happened to call that conduct "burglary."

For example, Michigan has no offense formally labeled "burglary." It classifies burglaries into several grades of "breaking and entering." See Mich.Comp.Laws § 750.110 (1979). In contrast, California defines "burglary" so broadly as to include shoplifting and theft of goods from a "locked" but unoccupied automobile. See Cal.Penal Code Ann. § 459 (West Supp.1990); *United States v. Chatman*, 869 F.2d 525, 528–529, and n. 2 (CA9 1989) (entry through unsecured window of an unoccupied auto, and entry of a store open to the public with intent to commit theft, are "burglary" under California law); see also Tex.Penal Code Ann. §§ 30.01–30.05 (1989 and Supp.1990) (defining burglary to include theft from coin-operated vending machine or automobile).

Thus, a person imprudent enough to shoplift or steal from an automobile in California would be found, under the Ninth Circuit's view, to have committed a burglary constituting a "violent felony" for enhancement purposes—yet a person who did so in Michigan might not. * * *

We think that "burglary" in § 924(e) must have some uniform definition independent of the labels employed by the various States' criminal codes.

B

Some Courts of Appeals have ruled that § 924(e) incorporates the common-law definition of burglary, relying on the maxim that a statutory term is generally presumed to have its common-law meaning. * * *

The problem with this view is that the contemporary understanding of "burglary" has diverged a long way from its common-law roots. Only a few States retain the common-law definition, or something closely resembling it. Most other States have expanded this definition to include entry without a "breaking," structures other than dwellings, offenses committed in the daytime, entry with intent to commit a crime other than a felony, etc. * * *

Also, interpreting "burglary" in § 924(e) to mean common-law burglary would not comport with the purposes of the enhancement statute. The arcane distinctions embedded in the common-law definition have little relevance to modern law enforcement concerns. * * *

C

Petitioner suggests another narrowing construction of the term "burglary," more suited to the purpose of the enhancement statute:

> "Burglary is any crime punishable by a term of imprisonment exceeding one year and consisting of entering or remaining within a building that is the property of another with intent to engage in conduct constituting a Federal or State offense that has as an element necessary for conviction conduct that presents a serious risk of physical injury to another."

As examples of burglary statutes that would fit this definition, petitioner points to first-degree or aggravated-burglary statutes having elements such as entering an occupied building; being armed with a deadly weapon; or causing or threatening physical injury to a person. This definition has some appeal, because it avoids the arbitrariness of the state-law approach, by restricting the predicate offense in a manner congruent with the general purpose of the enhancement statute.

We do not accept petitioner's proposal, however, for two reasons. First, it is not supported by the language of the statute or the legislative history. Petitioner essentially asserts that Congress meant to include as predicate offenses only a subclass of burglaries whose elements include "conduct that presents a serious risk of physical injury to another," over and above the risk inherent in ordinary burglaries. But if this were Congress' intent, there would have been no reason to add the word "burglary" to § 924(e)(2)(B)(ii), since that provision already includes any crime that "involves conduct that presents a serious potential risk of physical injury to another." We must assume that Congress had a purpose in adding the word "burglary" to H.R. 4885 before enacting it into law. The most likely explanation, in view of the legislative history, is that Congress thought that certain general categories of property crimes—namely burglary, arson, extortion, and the use of explosives—so often presented a risk of injury to persons, or were so often committed by career criminals, that they should be included in the enhancement statute even though, considered solely in terms of their statutory elements, they do not necessarily involve the use or threat of force against a person.

Second, if Congress had meant to include only an especially dangerous subclass of burglaries as predicate offenses, it is unlikely that it would have used the unqualified language "*is* burglary . . . or otherwise involves conduct that presents a serious potential risk" in § 924(e)(2)(B)(ii) (emphasis added). Congress presumably realized that the word "burglary" is commonly understood to include not only aggravated burglaries, but also run-of-the-mill burglaries involving an unarmed offender, an unoccupied building, and no use or threat of force. * * *

D

* * * We believe that Congress meant by "burglary" the generic sense in which the term is now used in the criminal codes of most States.

Although the exact formulations vary, the generic, contemporary meaning of burglary contains at least the following elements: an unlawful or unprivileged entry into, or remaining in, a building or other structure, with intent to commit a crime. * * *

IV

There remains the problem of applying this conclusion to cases in which the state statute under which a defendant is convicted varies from the generic definition of "burglary." If the state statute is narrower than the generic view, e.g., in cases of burglary convictions in common-law States or convictions of first-degree or aggravated burglary, there is no problem, because the conviction necessarily implies that the defendant has been found guilty of all the elements of generic burglary. And if the defendant was convicted of burglary in a State where the generic definition has been adopted, with minor variations in terminology, then the trial court need find only that the state statute corresponds in substance to the generic meaning of burglary.

A few States' burglary statutes, however, as has been noted above, define burglary more broadly, e.g., by eliminating the requirement that the entry be unlawful, or by including places, such as automobiles and vending machines, other than buildings. One of Missouri's second-degree burglary statutes in effect at the times of petitioner Taylor's convictions included breaking and entering "any booth or tent, or any boat or vessel, or railroad car." Also, there may be offenses under some States' laws that, while not called "burglary," correspond in substantial part to generic burglary. We therefore must address the question whether, in the case of a defendant who has been convicted under a nongeneric-burglary statute, the Government may seek enhancement on the ground that he actually committed a generic burglary.

This question requires us to address a more general issue—whether the sentencing court in applying § 924(e) must look only to the statutory definitions of the prior offenses, or whether the court may consider other evidence concerning the defendant's prior crimes. The Courts of Appeals uniformly have held that § 924(e) mandates a formal categorical approach, looking only to the statutory definitions of the prior offenses, and not to the particular facts underlying those convictions. We find the reasoning of these cases persuasive.

First, the language of § 924(e) generally supports the inference that Congress intended the sentencing court to look only to the fact that the defendant had been convicted of crimes falling within certain categories, and not to the facts underlying the prior convictions. Section 924(e)(1) refers to "a person who . . . has three previous convictions" for—not a person who has committed—three previous violent felonies or drug offenses. Section 924(e)(2)(B)(i) defines "violent felony" as any crime punishable by imprisonment for more than a year that "has as an element"—not any crime that, in a particular case, involves—the use or threat of force. Read in this context, the phrase "is burglary" in § 924(e)(2)(B)(ii) most likely refers to the elements of the statute of conviction, not to the facts of each defendant's conduct.

Second, as we have said, the legislative history of the enhancement statute shows that Congress generally took a categorical approach to predicate offenses. There was considerable debate over what kinds of offenses to include and how to define them, but no one suggested that a particular crime might sometimes count towards enhancement and sometimes not, depending on the facts of the case. If Congress had meant to adopt an approach that would require the sentencing court to engage in an elaborate factfinding process regarding the defendant's prior offenses, surely this would have been mentioned somewhere in the legislative history.

Third, the practical difficulties and potential unfairness of a factual approach are daunting. In all cases where the Government alleges that the defendant's actual conduct would fit the generic definition of burglary, the trial court would have to determine what that conduct was. In some cases, the indictment or other charging paper might reveal the theory or theories of the case presented to the jury. In other cases, however, only the Government's actual proof at trial would indicate whether the defendant's conduct constituted generic burglary. Would the Government be permitted to introduce the trial transcript before the sentencing court, or if no transcript is available, present the testimony of witnesses? Could the defense present witnesses of its own and argue that the jury might have returned a guilty verdict on some theory that did not require a finding that the defendant committed generic burglary? If the sentencing court were to conclude, from its own review of the record, that the defendant actually committed a generic burglary, could the defendant challenge this conclusion as abridging his right to a jury trial?

Also, in cases where the defendant pleaded guilty, there often is no record of the underlying facts. Even if the Government were able to prove those facts, if a guilty plea to a lesser, nonburglary offense was the result of a plea bargain, it would seem unfair to impose a sentence enhancement as if the defendant had pleaded guilty to burglary.

We think the only plausible interpretation of § 924(e)(2)(B)(ii) is that, like the rest of the enhancement statute, it generally requires the trial court to look only to the fact of conviction and the statutory definition of the prior offense. This categorical approach, however, may permit the sentencing court to go beyond the mere fact of conviction in a narrow range of cases where a jury was actually required to find all the elements of generic burglary. For example, in a State whose burglary statutes include entry of an automobile as well as a building, if the indictment or information and jury instructions show that the defendant was charged only with a burglary of a building, and that the jury necessarily had to find an entry of a building to convict, then the Government should be allowed to use the conviction for enhancement.

We therefore hold that an offense constitutes "burglary" for purposes of a § 924(e) sentence enhancement if either its statutory definition substantially corresponds to "generic" burglary, or the charging paper and jury instructions actually required the jury to find all the elements of generic burglary in order to convict the defendant.

In Taylor's case, most but not all the former Missouri statutes defining second-degree burglary include all the elements of generic burglary. Despite the Government's argument to the contrary, it is not apparent to us from the sparse record before us which of those statutes were the bases for Taylor's prior convictions. We therefore vacate the judgment of the Court of Appeals and remand the case for further proceedings consistent with this opinion.

NOTES & QUESTIONS

1. **Dangerousness of Burglary.** In the ACCA, Congress defined burglary as a "violent felony," even though the offense does not include any of the elements that are normally associated with a violent crime, such as "use of force against the person of another" or "intentionally cause bodily harm." Based on the legislative history discussed in *Taylor*, it appears that Congress categorized burglary as "violent" because of its *potential* to result in bodily harm. Why might this seem a realistic concern? And, in any event, why is there so much discussion in *Taylor* of the dangerousness of burglary? After all, the case involved a sentence imposed for a firearms offense, not a burglary.

2. **Purpose of the ACCA.** What was the purpose of the ACCA? Does it seem reasonably well-designed to achieve that purpose?

3. **The ACCA Versus the Guidelines.** The original version of the ACCA was adopted in 1984 as just one part of a much larger bill. The same legislation also created the United States Sentencing Commission and

authorized the Commission to draft presumptive sentencing guidelines. Why do you think Congress felt it was also necessary to adopt the new mandatory minimum? Why not simply leave it to the Commission to deal with the threat of "career criminals" through the guidelines?

In 1984, of course, Congress could not have known precisely how the Commission would deal with criminal history in the guidelines, which were not promulgated until 1987. If Congress had anticipated the adoption of § 4A1.1 in its current form, do you think Congress should have or would have viewed the ACCA as unnecessary?

In the event, Congress actually employed a belt-and-suspenders approach to address concerns regarding dangerous recidivists. Not only did Congress enact the ACCA, but, in the same statute, also directed the Commission to "assure that the guidelines will specify a sentence to a term of imprisonment at or near the maximum term authorized" for defendants convicted of drug trafficking or a violent felony who have two or more prior convictions for drug trafficking or a violent felony. 28 U.S.C. § 944(h). The Commission complied with this directive through the "career offender" provision of the guidelines, § 4B1.1, which, when applicable, overrides § 4A1.1 and automatically places the defendant in the highest criminal-history category. Again, does it seem to you that § 4A1.1 is insufficient to deal with the targeted recidivism threat?

4. **What Counts as "Burglary"?** Burglary is a relatively high-volume felony. In 2014, for instance, as counted by the Federal Bureau of Investigation, there were about 238,000 burglary arrests in the United States, in comparison with only 94,000 arrests for robbery and fewer than 11,000 arrests for murder or nonnegligent manslaughter. Interpretation of the term "burglary" in the ACCA may thus have a large impact on the statute's practical reach.

In *Taylor*, the Supreme Court made two important decisions about what counts as burglary in the ACCA. First, the Court decided that the offense should be understood in its modern "generic" form. According to the Court, what are the elements of generic burglary? What alternative interpretations did the Court consider, and why were they rejected?

Second, the Court adopted the "categorical" approach to determining whether a prior conviction counts. Under this approach, the sentencing court is to examine the elements of the crime of which the defendant was convicted, not the defendant's actual conduct. For instance, imagine a defendant who was charged under state law with a generic burglary, but who entered into a plea deal that resulted in a dismissal of the burglary charge and a conviction of theft. In a later ACCA case, could a federal prosecutor use the burglary as an ACCA predicate by proving that what the defendant actually did satisfied the elements of burglary? No, the Supreme Court indicated in *Taylor*—the federal prosecutor can rely only on the statutory elements of the formal offense of conviction. But doesn't this formalistic analysis mean that many dangerous recidivists will slip through the ACCA net based on arbitrary choices made by state legislatures in drafting burglary statutes and by state prosecutors in charging and resolving burglary cases? How did the *Taylor* Court justify its adoption of the categorical approach? For a critique of the categorical approach, see Eric S. Fish, *The Paradox of Criminal History*, 42 CARDOZO L. REV. 1373 (2021).

5. **Prior Record Enhancements and the Federalism Problem.** Although *Taylor* deals with only one specific recidivism statute, the basic problem confronted by the Court is an important, recurring challenge for all recidivism laws in our fractured national system of criminal justice. Every state, as well as the federal government, has its own body of substantive criminal law. Sometimes, different labels are applied by different jurisdictions to the same crime. Other times, a single label is employed by different jurisdictions to cover crimes with differing elements. It may seem easy enough for a state legislature to draft a recidivism statute that attaches appropriate weights to earlier convictions from that state, but what is to be done with out-of-jurisdiction priors? A statute cannot possibly be drafted to account in a specific way for all of the terminological variation across all U.S. jurisdictions.

Taylor exemplifies one solution to the federalism problem—identify a generic benchmark version of an offense and compare the elements of prior convictions with that benchmark. Section 4A1.1 of the guidelines exemplifies a different solution—ignore offense labels and elements entirely, and judge the seriousness of priors instead by the sentence imposed. Does either approach seem clearly better to you than the other? Note that these two approaches do not exhaust the possibilities. Can you think of other "solutions" to the federalism problem?

Broadly speaking, differing approaches may be characterized as "external" or "internal." *See* Wayne A. Logan, *Horizontal Federalism in an Age of Criminal Justice Interconnectedness*, 154 U. PA. L. REV. 257 (2005). Jurisdictions that take an external approach defer to the labels and judgments of other jurisdictions. If the other state called what the defendant did "burglary," then the current forum state will treat it as burglary for purposes of its recidivism statute. If the other state classified the defendant's crime as a felony, then the forum state will do the same. And so forth.

Internal approaches, by contrast, peak below the labels and judgments assigned by other authorities, attempting to ascertain and evaluate what the defendant actually did by reference to the forum jurisdiction's chosen criteria. *Taylor* illustrates. In applying the ACCA, federal courts are not to defer to the "burglary" labels assigned to prior convictions by state law but are instead to evaluate what the defendant did by reference to uniform federal criteria, i.e., the generic elements of burglary.

The internal approach holds out the hope of greater coherence in the application of a jurisdiction's recidivism law, since the forum jurisdiction is not bound by all of the idiosyncrasies that appear in the laws of other jurisdictions. But the internal approach also raises a difficult practical challenge: how can a sentencing judge in the forum jurisdiction know what the defendant did in the earlier case—conduct that presumably occurred far away and possibly many years ago. In principle, court files from the earlier case can be obtained and reviewed—that is, if they are not so old that they have been lost or shredded—but court files are often very skimpy, especially if the defendant pled guilty. Moreover, there is a looming constitutional problem. As we saw in our discussion of *Apprendi* in Chapter 3, the defendant has no right to a jury trial on the fact of a prior conviction, but if the application of a recidivism law requires more facts than just the formal elements that a jury found or that a defendant agreed to in a plea, then the defendant may have a right to have those facts found by a jury. These concerns help to explain why the "categorical" method is often used with the internal approach, as exemplified in *Taylor*. Under *Taylor*, the federal sentencing judge can peek below the surface of the state-law label, but not very far. The categorical method alleviates some of the practical difficulties with the internal approach—but at the cost of a formalistic analysis that may, as suggested in the previous note, miss many defendants who actually engaged in burglarious conduct.

Note that *Taylor* is not a constitutional decision. Although the Supreme Court adopted the internal approach and the categorical method for purposes of the federal ACCA, states are free to adopt different approaches for their recidivism laws. Indeed, one survey of state laws found a fairly even split: twenty-eight jurisdictions were found to use a version of the internal approach, while twenty-two were found to use the external. Logan, *supra*, at 269, 276.

6. **The Residual Clause.** Look again at the text of the ACCA, as quoted in *Taylor*. The "or otherwise" language that appears at the end of 18 U.S.C. 924(e)(2)(B)(ii) is a flexible residual clause that might potentially help to deal with the ACCA's federalism problem—that vast array of differently worded state-law crimes that might signal a defendant's violent tendencies but that cannot possibly all be identified specifically in the definition of "violent felony." Phrased in varying ways, such residual clauses are common in statutes that particularly target violent recidivism risk. Michael O'Hear, *Third-Class Citizenship: The Escalating Legal Consequences of Committing a "Violent" Crime*, 109 J. CRIM. L. & CRIMINOLOGY 165, 177–78 (2019). However, the ACCA's residual clause proved difficult for the federal courts to apply in a consistent, predictable way, partly as a result of the categorical method and the need to classify offenses based on their elements alone as presenting "a serious potential risk of physical injury to another." Eventually, in 2015, a frustrated Supreme Court declared the residual clause void for vagueness. The Court observed,

> Two features of the residual clause conspire to make it unconstitutionally vague. In the first place, the residual clause leaves grave uncertainty about how to estimate the risk posed by a crime. It ties the judicial assessment of risk to a judicially imagined "ordinary case" of a crime, not to real-world facts or statutory elements. How does one go about deciding what kind of conduct the "ordinary case" of a crime involves? A statistical analysis of the state reporter? A survey? Expert evidence? Google? Gut instinct? * * *
>
> At the same time, the residual clause leaves uncertainty about how much risk it takes for a crime to qualify as a violent felony. It

> is one thing to apply an imprecise "serious potential risk" standard to real-world facts; it is quite another to apply it to a judge-imagined abstraction.

Johnson v. United States, 576 U.S. 591, 597–98 (2015) (citations and internal quotation marks omitted).[4]

7. ***Mathis*: Application of the Categorical Method.** After Richard Mathis's guilty plea in federal court to illegal possession of a firearm, the government requested that he be sentenced under the ACCA based on his five prior convictions of burglary under Iowa law. *Mathis v. United States*, 579 U.S. 500 (2016). The relevant Iowa burglary law covers unlawful entry into "any building, structure, [or] land, water, or air vehicle." Do you see how this statute is broader than generic burglary under *Taylor*?

In an authoritative ruling on the state law, the Iowa Supreme Court has held that "any building, structure, [or] land, water, or air vehicle" defines a single, indivisible locational element; a jury does not need to decide which kind of location was entered by the defendant. In other words, a jury might convict even if members of the jury could not agree that what the defendant entered (say, a mobile home resting on cinder blocks) counts as a "structure" or a "vehicle."

In Mathis's case, the federal sentencing judge reviewed records from the earlier burglary proceedings and determined that Mathis had indeed burgled "structures." On that basis, the judge imposed a fifteen-year ACCA sentence on Mathis. Acceptable under *Taylor*? No, the Supreme Court decided. If the defendant has been convicted of a crime with a single element that can be satisfied under state law in a variety of different ways, a federal sentencing judge cannot for ACCA purposes dig deeper into the state court records to determine in which way the defendant actually satisfied the element. By contrast, if the element at issue is "divisible"—and thus requires a jury to agree on the way in which the element was satisfied—then the federal sentencing judge can engage in a review of a limited set of court records to clarify which prong actually was proven (or, in a guilty-plea case, admitted by the defendant) in state court.[5] Whether an element is divisible or indivisible is a question of state law.

8. **Challenging Priors.** What if an ACCA defendant admits to the *existence* of his or her prior convictions, but contends that those convictions were obtained in violation of his or her constitutional rights? It might seem unfair to hold an improper conviction against the defendant, especially if the constitutional violation undermined the reliability of the conviction. However, the Supreme Court has generally prohibited ACCA defendants from advancing such claims in their federal sentencing proceedings. *Custis*

---

[4] The Court has also wrestled with the question of whether a defendant's conviction on multiple counts in a single case should be treated as a single conviction for ACCA purposes. *See* Wooden v. United States, 142 S. Ct. 1063, 1067 (2022) ("Convictions arising from a single criminal episode . . . can count only once under ACCA.").

[5] In a guilty-plea case, the review is limited to "the terms of the charging document, the terms of a plea agreement or transcript of colloquy between judge and defendant in which the factual basis for the plea was confirmed by the defendant, or to some comparable judicial record of this information." Shepard v. United States, 544 U.S. 13, 26 (2005).

v. United States, 511 U.S. 485 (1994). The Court has indicated that defendants should instead seek whatever post-conviction relief is available in the court system in which the challenged conviction occurred. The Court has recognized only a narrow exception for claims that the defendant was denied his or her right to a lawyer in the earlier case.

Note that the Court's holdings in this regard apply only to the federal ACCA. Other habitual offender laws have sometimes been interpreted so as to permit "collateral" challenges to the validity of prior convictions. *See, e.g., People v. Soto,* 54 Cal. Rptr. 2d 593 (Cal. Ct. App. 1996).

B. DEFENDANT CHARACTERISTICS

1. OVERVIEW

There is a widespread consensus that sentencing should take into account *what the defendant did* in relation to the crime of conviction, but much less consensus over whether and how sentencing should take into account *who the defendant is*—his or her habits, beliefs, physical health and appearance, mental health, family background and relationships, lifestyle, education, employment, and so forth. Criminal history comprises the most notable exception. Most commentators and practitioners seem in agreement that a defendant's prior record should matter—although, as we have seen, there is no consensus even as to this when it comes to the *why* and the *how*. In any event, criminal history differs from many other defendant characteristics in a way that is arguably quite important—that is, the defendant had some control over the development of his or her prior record. This contrasts, for instance, with the defendant's age, race, ethnicity, or disadvantaged upbringing.

Taking into account a defendant's characteristics may seem inconsistent with the popular ideal of blindfolded Justice, who adjudicates disputes without any regard to the wealth or social status of the disputants. As the late Judge Marvin Frankel observed in his influential book about sentencing, "There is dignity and security in the assurance that each of us—plain or beautiful, rich or poor, black, white, tall, curly, whatever—is promised treatment as a bland, fungible 'equal' before the law." CRIMINAL SENTENCES: LAW WITHOUT ORDER 11 (1973). Frankel's comment might remind you of the importance of unbiased treatment to perceptions of procedural justice, as discussed in Chapter 3.

The use of defendant characteristics at sentencing may further implicate constitutional values, as well as concerns about the perpetuation of historical injustices. The Equal Protection Clause of the Fourteenth Amendment limits the ability of state actors—including sentencing judges—to treat individuals differently on the basis of their personal characteristics, although the doctrine is far more restrictive when it comes to some characteristics (e.g., race or religion) than others (e.g., education or income level). Adopted in the wake of the Civil War in the hope of protecting formerly enslaved individuals in the South, the

Fourteenth Amendment is a reminder of the long history of discriminatory practices in the United States that were once taken for granted by many Americans, but that are now widely condemned as unjust and intolerable. An important concern overshadowing the use of some defendant characteristics at sentencing is the fear that doing so perpetuates enduring legacies of past discrimination. Indeed, we noted in the previous section that the use of criminal history is sometimes criticized on precisely this basis, in light of evidence that Black defendants seem on average to have more extensive prior records than White defendants.

Sentencing practices that compound historical injustices would seem to demand, at a minimum, some compelling justification. But how about considering personal characteristics in ways that are *beneficial* to historically disadvantaged groups? There is evidence, for instance, that female defendants tend on average to receive more lenient sentences than males who are convicted of the same crimes. *See* Jill K. Doerner, *The Joint Effects of Gender and Race/Ethnicity on Sentencing Outcomes in Federal Courts*, 25 WOMEN & CRIM. JUST. 313, 314 (2015) (citing studies). On the face of it, do such sex disparities strike you as a matter of pressing concern? Would you feel differently if it were the *men* receiving more lenient sentences? *Cf.* Ion Meyn, *Race-Based Remedies in Criminal Law*, 63 WM. & MARY L. REV. 219 (2021) (arguing that measures designed to help disadvantaged racial groups in the criminal justice system may be able to withstand strict scrutiny more successfully than affirmative action measures in education or employment contexts).

Your feelings about the use of defendant characteristics at sentencing might be affected by your views about the proper purposes of punishment. If you would emphasize general deterrence, for instance, it is hard to see much place in the analysis for the characteristics of a particular defendant; your main interests would probably lie in the costs, benefits, and likelihood of apprehension of the offense *as a general matter*. Some approaches to retribution might result in somewhat greater attention to defendant characteristics. In particular, insofar as deserved punishment rests on the defendant's *choice* to act wrongfully, a judge operating in the retributive mode might be interested in knowing about personal characteristics, such as poverty or mental illness, that illuminate the range of options that were realistically available to the defendant and the defendant's ability to appreciate the likely consequences of his or her actions.

However, defendant characteristics are most likely to consistently play a leading role at sentencing if the judge focuses primarily on assessing and managing the defendant's recidivism risk. It would be important, for instance, for the judge to know whether the defendant's criminality is connected to some underlying mental health or other personal problem that could be addressed through rehabilitative programming. But how much should sentencing judges be concerned that some of the defendant characteristics that correlate with risk and amenability to rehabilitation—e.g., educational attainment, employment history, and homelessness—may also be correlated with race and family background? Sentencing that focuses narrowly on risk and rehabilitation might inadvertently compound past disadvantage.

This preliminary overview should give you some sense of why defendant characteristics have proven such a controversial set of sentencing factors. Perhaps not surprisingly, the law seems to send mixed messages about the consideration of defendant characteristics.

Sentencing Reform Act of 1984 (as codified)

18 U.S.C. § 3553. Imposition of a sentence

(a) Factors to be considered in imposing a sentence.—* * * The court, in determining the particular sentence to be imposed, shall consider—

(1) * * * the history and characteristics of the defendant * * *

28 U.S.C. § 994. Duties of the [U.S. Sentencing] Commission

(d) The [Sentencing] Commission in establishing categories of defendants for use in the guidelines and policy statements governing the imposition of sentences of probation, a fine, or imprisonment, governing the imposition of other authorized sanctions, governing the size of a fine or the length of a term of probation, imprisonment, or supervised release, and governing the conditions of probation, supervised release, or imprisonment, shall consider whether the following matters, among others, with respect to a defendant, have any relevance to the nature, extent, place of service, or other inciden[ce] of an appropriate sentence, and shall take them into account only to the extent that they do have relevance—

(1) age;

(2) education;

(3) vocational skills;

(4) mental and emotional condition to the extent that such condition mitigates the defendant's culpability or to the extent that such condition is otherwise plainly relevant;

(5) physical condition, including drug dependence;

(6) previous employment record;

(7) family ties and responsibilities;

(8) community ties;

(9) role in the offense;

(10) criminal history; and

(11) degree of dependence upon criminal activity for a livelihood.

The Commission shall assure that the guidelines and policy statements are entirely neutral as to the race, sex, national origin, creed, and socioeconomic status of offenders.

(e) The Commission shall assure that the guidelines and policy statements, in recommending a term of imprisonment or length of a term of imprisonment, reflect the general inappropriateness of considering the education, vocational skills, employment record, family ties and responsibilities, and community ties of the defendant.

American Law Institute, Model Penal Code: Sentencing (2017)

§ 6B.06. Eligible Sentencing Considerations.

(2) Except as provided in this Section, the [sentencing] commission shall give no weight to the following factors when formulating any guidelines provision that affects the severity of sentences:

> **(a)** an offender's race, ethnicity, gender, sexual orientation or identity, national origin, religion or creed, and political orientation or belief * * *

(4) Notwithstanding the provisions of subsection (2)(a):

> **(a)** the personal characteristics of offenders may be included as considerations within the guidelines when indicative of circumstances of hardship, deprivation, vulnerability, or handicap, but only as grounds to reduce the severity of sentences that would otherwise be recommended * * *

NOTES & QUESTIONS

1. **"Shall Consider?"** The mandate of 18 U.S.C. § 3553—the sentencing judge "shall consider . . . the history and characteristics of the defendant"—seems an unqualified endorsement of taking personal characteristics into account, but Congress sent a rather more equivocal message through 28 U.S.C. § 994. The latter statute provides a laundry list of defendant characteristics and directs that the Sentencing Commission should incorporate them into the federal sentencing guidelines "only to the extent that they do have relevance." Section 994 further requires neutrality as to "race, sex, national origin, creed, and socioeconomic status," and indicates that it is generally inappropriate to consider "the education, vocational skills, employment record, family ties and responsibilities, and community ties of the defendant" in making incarceration decisions.

Section 994 is framed as a set of instructions to the Sentencing Commission—"guidelines for the guidelines," as it were. In complying with the "shall consider" mandate of § 3553, do you think sentencing judges should take into account the skeptical view of defendant characteristics that was expressed in § 994?

2. **What the Commission Did.** The Sentencing Commission took an even more restrictive approach to defendant characteristics than was mandated by Congress. Notable pronouncements of the guidelines going beyond the explicit limitations of § 994 include the following:

- "Drug or alcohol dependence or abuse ordinarily is not a reason for a downward departure." § 5H1.4.
- "Addiction to gambling is not a reason for a downward departure." § 5H1.4.
- "Civic, charitable, or public service; employment-related contributions; and similar prior good works are not ordinarily relevant in determining whether a departure is warranted." § 5H1.11.
- "Lack of guidance as a youth and similar circumstances indicating a disadvantaged upbringing are not relevant grounds in determining whether a departure is warranted." § 5H1.12.

Note the subtle distinction between characteristics that are "not a reason" for departure (or, to similar effect, "not relevant") and characteristics that are "*ordinarily* . . . not a reason" (or "not *ordinarily* relevant").

Do you agree with all of these provisions? For instance, what of the restriction on taking charitable *service* into account? Should this be understood also to discourage the consideration of charitable *donations*? Would allowing consideration of donations lead wealthy defendants to make "investments" in their future liberty? *See* Jessica Bowes, *Freedom Futures: Charitable Donations in White Collar Sentencing*, 106 IOWA L. REV. 873 (2021).

Of course, in a post-*Booker* world, the Commission's restrictions on use of personal characteristics are not strictly binding. If you were a sentencing judge, would you be inclined to adhere to these provisions anyway?

3. **Disparate Impact.** In constitutional equal protection law, a distinction is often made between discriminatory intent and disparate impact. While intentional discrimination on the basis of various suspect or "quasi-suspect" classifications—race, sex, national origin, and the like—is normally barred, state action that merely produces a disparate impact on one group or another does not in itself violate the Equal Protection Clause. Yet, even though the Constitution does not prohibit unintended disparate impacts, policymakers may nonetheless wish to avoid or minimize them, especially insofar as historically disadvantaged groups are the ones who are adversely affected.

Against this backdrop, what are we to make of the mandate in § 994(d) that the "Commission shall assure that the guidelines and policy statements are entirely neutral as to the race, sex, national origin, creed, and socioeconomic status of offenders?" Should it be enough for the Commission to decree, as it has, that these factors "are not relevant in the determination of a sentence"? § 5H1.10. Or should the Commission go further and assess whether any of the hundreds of facially neutral factors included in the guidelines have a disparate impact in any of the areas in which neutrality is required (race, sex, etc.)? For instance, as suggested in the previous section, a *racial* disparate impact review might have important implications for the way that criminal history is handled in the guidelines. And what about the judges, prosecutors, and defense lawyers—do *they* have any sort of obligation to try to avoid or minimize disparate impacts at sentencing? *Cf.* 18 U.S.C. § 3553(a)(6) (requiring sentencing judge to consider "the need to avoid unwarranted sentence disparities among defendants with similar records who have been found guilty of similar conduct").

4. **Tripartite Framework.** The treatment of personal characteristics in the guidelines suggests a tripartite framework. Personal characteristics might be classified as forbidden, discouraged, or fully open for consideration. If discouraged, the characteristic should only be taken into account in unusual circumstances or for purposes other than determining the severity of the punishment. For instance, a discouraged factor might be used as a basis for selecting a particular rehabilitative program as a condition of the defendant's probation, but not for the basic choice between probation and incarceration.

Given a personal characteristic that has some plausible connection with a recognized purpose of punishment, what might justify treating that characteristic as forbidden or discouraged? Some possible considerations might be:

- Whether the characteristic is in the constitutional "danger zone" of suspect or quasi-suspect classifications (e.g., race, sex, and national origin);
- Whether the characteristic is correlated with a suspect or quasi-suspect classification (e.g., household wealth in the United States is currently correlated with race);
- Whether consideration of the characteristic is otherwise likely to exacerbate patterns of socioeconomic disadvantage;
- The extent to which the characteristic is beyond a defendant's control;
- The strength and certainty of the connection between the characteristic and a recognized purpose of punishment; and
- The presence of ambiguity as to whether the characteristic should be treated as aggravating or mitigating (e.g., addiction might be mitigating from a retributive standpoint, but aggravating from a risk-management point of view).

How would you classify some of the characteristics listed in 28 U.S.C. § 994(d) in the tripartite framework, e.g., age and education?

State laws vary considerably as to whether personal characteristics are classified as forbidden, discouraged, or open. To the extent that these matters are not addressed by state law, judges have discretion to decide for themselves how to handle different characteristics—subject, of course, to constitutional restrictions on the explicit, intentional use of certain classifications.

5. **Model Penal Code: Sentencing.** How would you describe the differences in the treatment of personal characteristics in federal law in comparison with MPC:S § 6B.06 (reprinted above)? Which approach do you prefer? While § 6B.06 is directed to the sentencing commission, the MPC:S has an identically worded mandate for sentencing judges (§ 7.03).

Note further that the MPC:S seems more cognizant than federal law of the potential for the use of defendant characteristics to adversely affect disadvantaged groups. For instance, the MPC:S mandates, "The commission shall give due consideration to the danger that the use of criminal-history provisions to increase the severity of sentences may have disparate impacts on racial or ethnic minorities, or other disadvantaged groups." § 6B.07(1)(c). Additionally, the MPC:S elsewhere declares that its general purposes, "applicable to all official actors in the sentencing system," include the elimination of "inequities in sentencing across population groups." § 1.02(2)(b)(iii). The sentencing commission is also required to "investigate the existence of discrimination or inequities in the sentencing and corrections systems across population groups, including groups defined by race, ethnicity, and gender, and search for the means to eliminate such discrimination or inequities." § 6A.05(2)(f). A few states have already adopted similar directives for their commissions. *See* MPC:S § 6A.05 reptr. note (b)(4) (surveying state laws).

6. **Victim Characteristics.** The consideration of a *victim*'s personal characteristics for sentencing purposes raises concerns that parallel those raised by the consideration of a *defendant*'s personal characteristics, e.g., victims who have a high socioeconomic status may get more "justice" than low-status victims. As noted in Chapter 3, this has been one of the recurring criticisms of victim impact statements.

7. **Death Penalty.** As detailed below in Chapter 7, the constitutional proportionality rules for the death penalty give a determinative weight in some circumstances to certain personal characteristics: youth, intellectual disability, and severe mental illness. In death sentencing, *victim* characteristics are also sometimes considered, such as whether the victim was a child or a police officer.

2. FAMILY RESPONSIBILITIES

Many defendants are primary or secondary caregivers for children, parents, spouses, or others. Defendants who have such roles often argue that their family responsibilities should be regarded as a mitigating factor at sentencing, and especially as a reason for a community sentence in lieu of incarceration. As noted in Chapter 1, it is possible to fit the familial impact of different sentencing options into the utilitarian framework for punishment. In principle, the crime-prevention benefits of a sentence might be weighed against, for instance, the psychological and other harm caused by separating a child from his or her parent.

Despite such theoretical justifications for taking family responsibilities into account at sentencing, doing so is hardly free from controversy. Can you imagine some of the arguments that are made against giving a break to defendant-caregivers?

The federal sentencing guidelines have placed family responsibilities into the "discouraged" category. § 5H1.6. However, prior to *Booker*, the lower federal courts struggled to articulate clear, consistent standards as to the facts that would justify a below-range sentence on the basis of this "not ordinarily relevant" factor. In 2003, the Sentencing Commission promulgated official commentary in the hope of clarifying matters. The Commission decreed that no downward departure from the guidelines range should be permitted on the basis of lost family caretaking or support unless all of the following circumstances were present:

> (i) The defendant's service of a sentence within the applicable guideline range will cause a substantial, direct, and specific loss of essential caretaking, or essential financial support, to the defendant's family.
>
> (ii) The loss of caretaking or financial support substantially exceeds the harm ordinarily incident to incarceration for a similarly situated defendant. For example, the fact that the defendant's family might incur some degree of financial hardship or suffer to some extent from the absence of a parent through incarceration is not in itself sufficient as a basis for departure because such hardship or suffering is of a sort ordinarily incident to incarceration.
>
> (iii) The loss of caretaking or financial support is one for which no effective remedial or ameliorative programs reasonably are available, making the defendant's caretaking or financial support irreplaceable to the defendant's family.
>
> (iv) The departure effectively will address the loss of caretaking or financial support.

Id., App. Note 1(B).

Of course, *Booker* deprived this restrictive commentary of at least some of its legal force. Federal district judges now have substantially more freedom to take family responsibilities into account—but perhaps not unlimited freedom. Consider the two contrasting post-*Booker* decisions excerpted below.

United States v. Bueno

549 F.3d 1176 (8th Cir. 2008)

■ WOLLMAN, J.

This case is before us for the second time. In the first appeal, we * * * vacated the sentence and remanded the case for resentencing. *United States v. Bueno,* 443 F.3d 1017 (8th Cir.2006). We now affirm the sentence imposed following our remand.

As set forth in our opinion in the first appeal, Bueno pleaded guilty to possessing with intent to distribute five kilograms or more of powder cocaine in violation of 21 U.S.C. §§ 841(a)(1) and (b)(1)(A). The district court reduced Bueno's United States Sentencing Guidelines (U.S.S.G.) offense level from thirty to twenty-one, which resulted in a sentencing range of thirty-seven to forty-six months, granted a downward departure from the Guidelines, and sentenced Bueno to eighteen months of imprisonment and three years of supervised release.

In reaching our decision to vacate the sentence, we rejected Bueno's contention that the fact that his wife was suffering from lupus and rheumatoid arthritis and that Bueno was her primary caregiver constituted extraordinary family ties and responsibilities that would warrant a downward departure from the Guidelines range under U.S.S.G. § 5H1.6. Noting that this is a disfavored reason for granting a departure, and citing *Koon v. United States,* 518 U.S. 81, 95 (1996), we distinguished our decision in *United States v. Haversat,* 22 F.3d 790 (8th Cir. 1994), in which we held that such a departure was warranted because of potentially life-threatening psychiatric problems that the defendant's wife suffered and of whose treatment plan the defendant was an irreplaceable part. *Bueno,* 443 F.3d at 1023. Rather, we likened Bueno's situation to that which existed in *United States v. VanHouten,* 307 F.3d 693 (8th Cir. 2002), in which we held that the defendant's failure to present evidence that his mother's condition was life-threatening or that his care was a necessary part of her medical treatment defeated his claim for a downward departure under § 5H1.6. * * *

I.

At resentencing, Bueno submitted extensive documentation in support of his claim for downward departure under § 5H1.6, including Mrs. Bueno's fourteen-page declaration describing her physical condition. Among other things, she has suffered from lupus since 1981, a condition that is getting progressively worse. Following Mrs. Bueno's left hip replacement surgery in June of 2006, Bueno was trained by a nurse to administer the twice-daily intravenous injections of antibiotics required to treat the open sore that developed at the surgery site, including the cleaning of the wound site and the flushing of the IV lines. The 2006 hip replacement surgery was the fifth such surgery on Mrs. Bueno's left hip and has left her unable to attend to her post-toilet personal hygiene, to shower or bathe by herself, or to get to the bathroom unassisted. The lupus has rendered her unable to brush her teeth, open or close most medication bottles, to clothe or unclothe herself, or to stand or walk. She has been confined to a wheelchair since 2003. She has difficulty holding things such as eating or kitchen utensils, jars, bottles, or containers. She is subject to falls and cannot rise from the floor without assistance. She suffers from grand mal seizures, during the occurrence of which she loses bowel and bladder control. Her declaration states that she needs her husband's assistance to perform all of the everyday functions required for survival, including the proper administration of the 40 pills that she is required to take each day; that he is her only care provider before and after his working day activities; and that he often comes home from work during the day to care for her when necessary. Further, the declaration states that Mrs. Bueno experiences panic attacks that render her claustrophobic, and that she has been hospitalized 20 to 25 times since Bueno's April 2004 sentencing date. She avers that neither her daughter nor her sixteen-year-old son is able to provide the personal and medical assistance that she requires to cope with her physical and emotional problems.

In addition to Mrs. Bueno's self-description of her physical and emotional problems, Bueno submitted the July 13, 2006, evaluation and consultation report of Allen I. Salick, M.D. * * *. [The report] states:

> [Mrs. Bueno's] condition is life threatening and her long-term prognosis is not good. She is kept alive by her husband. His treatment is irreplaceable and necessary because not only does she require constant attendance to monitor her medication and to help her with all of her disabilities and weaknesses, but he also has a very serious positive effect on her emotions. Without him, in my opinion, she would be severely depressed and probably suicidal.
>
> Her Central Nervous System Lupus has left her with a seizure disorder. Obviously when she has a seizure she loses consciousness and becomes incontinent and she needs somebody with her, someone like her husband, all the time. This lady is incapable of living alone or taking care of herself, not just on the basis of her central nervous system, but also with her muscle disease and her severe inanition.
>
> . . . .
>
> I tried to keep this discussion in terms that a layperson could understand. [Mrs. Bueno] has a life threatening condition with a very poor long-term prognosis. It is a miracle that she survived to date. I think that she never would have been able to do this without the constant attendance of her husband. I certainly recommend from a humanitarian point of view, that he be allowed to continue this. I am also concerned about her emotions as she is taking psychotropic medications and seeing a psychologist. In my opinion, her husband is providing very significant psychiatric support for this lady.

Bueno also submitted the July 14, 2006, special psychological report prepared by Marge Cohen, Ph.D., a licensed psychologist who had performed a psychological evaluation on Mrs. Bueno earlier that day. In Dr. Cohen's opinion, Mrs. Bueno suffers from severe psychiatric problems. Her mental health issues, including major depressive disorder, single episode-severe with suicidal ideation and panic disorder without agoraphobia, are life-threatening. Dr. Cohen summarized her evaluation as follows:

> In sum, Mayra Bueno's husband, Mario, is emotionally indispensable to her in helping her cope with her emotional symptoms and physical symptoms of Lupus and he is irreplaceable in her treatment. * * *

After considering the above-described evidence, as well as Bueno's testimony at the resentencing hearing, the district court found that Mrs. Bueno was in fact suffering from life-threatening diseases and maladies and that Bueno was the only person who could provide the continual care that she required. Accordingly, the district court imposed upon Bueno a sentence of five years probation, the conditions of which include house arrest with electronic monitoring, if that additional condition was determined by the United States Probation Office to be required, with Bueno being given the freedom to leave the home to go to work and to provide the necessary care to his wife. * * *

II.

At the outset, one could well ask how, in light of our earlier determination that an eighteen-month sentence constituted an unreasonable departure from the applicable Guidelines range, it could plausibly be contended that a sentence of five years' probation is not equally an unreasonable sentence. The short answers are the substantially more detailed evidence submitted at resentencing regarding Mrs. Bueno's physical and emotional condition and the Supreme Court's December 10, 2007, opinion in *Gall v. United States.* * * *

With respect to the question of sufficiency of the additional evidence submitted at resentencing to support the district court's finding that extraordinary circumstances existed that warranted such a substantial departure under § 5H1.6, one would be justified in asking how, in the face of such circumstances, Bueno found it possible to leave his ailing wife's side and drive from his home in California to St. Louis. *See Bueno,* 443 F.3d at 1021. Likewise, one could view with skepticism medical reports that give the appearance of having been lawyer-drafted to replicate that which we found to be sufficient evidence of truly exceptional family circumstances in *Haversat* and in *United States v. Spero,* 382 F.3d 803 (8th Cir. 2004). It was for the district court to raise such questions, however, and it obviously credited [the findings in the medical reports submitted on Bueno's behalf]. All in all, then, we conclude that the district court's finding that exceptional family circumstances exist that render Bueno's caretaking an irreplaceable, indispensable part of Mrs. Bueno's well-being and [of] her caregiving regime to be adequately supported by the additional evidence submitted at resentencing.

We turn, then, to the second intervening event that paints this case in a light different from [that] in which it appeared during the first appeal, that being the Court's decision in *Gall,* for were it not for that decision, which highlighted the importance of the advisory nature of the Guidelines following the Court's decision in *United States v. Booker*, we would find it difficult, if not [nigh] well impossible, to affirm what can only be described as a most substantial departure from the applicable Guidelines range. *Gall* told us in unmistakably clear language that once it has been determined that the district court committed no significant procedural error in calculating the applicable Guidelines range, the appellate court's sole remaining role is to consider the substantive reasonableness of the sentence under an abuse-of-discretion standard, one that eliminates from the process of appellate review the appellate court's own view of what sentence would have been appropriate. * * *

Although the sentence imposed in this case stretches the allowable downward departure under § 5H1.6 to its very limits, we cannot say that it is unreasonable, and thus it is affirmed.

United States v. Christman

607 F.3d 1110 (6th Cir. 2010)

■ MARTIN, J.

Richard Christman pled guilty to two counts of possessing child pornography in January 2005 pursuant to a plea agreement calling for dismissal of the remaining counts against him, four counts of distribution of child pornography. The district court sentenced him to 57 months in prison, a within-Guidelines sentence at the bottom of the 57–71 month recommended range. [This original sentence was later vacated by the court of appeals on procedural grounds.]

At re-sentencing, the district court, over the prosecution's objection, sentenced Christman to five days in prison—that is, the time that he had spent in custody when first arrested—and fifteen years of supervised release. The court found that this sentence was warranted because Christman had severe back pain, he was his elderly, ailing mother's primary caregiver, his family believed that he was remorseful, he was a musician and composer, and he had complied with the restrictions of his release on bail. The government appeals, arguing that the district court's imposition of the nominal prison term cannot reasonably be justified by the factors identified at re-sentencing.

For the reasons set forth below, we find that the sentence was substantively unreasonable, VACATE the new sentence, and REMAND for re-sentencing in light of this opinion. * * *

A. Reliance on Inappropriate Factors * * *

Under the Guidelines, a "defendant's family ties and responsibilities, [section] 5H1.6, his or her education and vocational skills, section 5H1.2, and his or her military, civic, charitable, or public service record, section 5H1.11," [*Koon v. United States*, 518 U.S. 81, 95 (1996)], are discouraged factors that are " 'not ordinarily relevant to the determination of whether a sentence should be outside the applicable guideline range.' " *Id.* (quoting 1995 U.S.S.G. ch. 5, pt. H, intro. comment). Moreover, the Guidelines suggest that only "in exceptional cases" should the court consider such circumstances. U.S.S.G. ch. 5, pt. H, intro. comment. Of course, "[a]fter *Booker*, . . . the fact that a factor is discouraged or forbidden under the guidelines does not automatically make it irrelevant when a court is weighing statutory factors apart from the guidelines." *United States v. Husein*, 478 F.3d 318, 326 (6th Cir. 2007). Nevertheless, section 3553(a)(5) "requires that the district court consider applicable policy statements issued by the Sentencing Commission, and the Guidelines' disfavored view towards age and physical condition is, therefore, relevant to our reasonableness review." [*United States v. Burton*, 230 Fed.Appx. 505, 510 (6th Cir. 2007)]. * * *

The district court also found that the fact that Christman had, while on bail pending his appeal, become the primary caregiver to his elderly mother, was a mitigating factor under section 5H1.6 (family ties and responsibilities). * * *

Here, defendant argues that "Christman can be relieved but not replaced." However, in and of itself, this is not sufficient. When "there are feasible alternatives of care that are relatively comparable to what the defendant provides, the defendant cannot be irreplaceable." *United States v. Pereira,* 272 F.3d 76, 83 (1st Cir. 2001). There is a feasible alternative available: should his siblings be unable to provide care, a nursing home can provide the around-the-clock care that Christman provides to his mother and that his family believes to be necessary. While this is, of course, a substantial hardship to his mother, it is difficult to see how placement in a nursing home is necessarily a death sentence upon her, as the district court argues. Unlike in *Husein*, it has not been argued that Christman's family cannot afford to place his mother in a nursing home, just that they would prefer not to, so cost is not a relevant consideration here; they argue only that "her quality of life would be greatly diminished." As the government notes, many adults provide care for their aged parents or their young children. However, as long as alternate arrangements for care can be made, which in the case of children may include foster care, a situation analogous to placement in a nursing home, this does not argue for mitigation unless extraordinary circumstances exist. To say otherwise would be to invite gross sentencing disparities based solely on whether one has a young child or an infirm dependent. As no extraordinary circumstances appear here, either as argued by Christman's attorney or in the statements of Christman's family at the sentencing hearing, we find that the district court abused its discretion in weighing this factor so heavily in favor of mitigation. * * *

NOTES & QUESTIONS

1. **"Irreplaceable."** The Sentencing Commission indicates that a defendant should not get a below-range sentence on the basis of his or her family caregiving or support responsibilities unless he or she is "irreplaceable." *Bueno* and *Christman* seem to come out differently, at least in part, due to the differing success of the two defendants in satisfying the irreplaceability standard. Are you convinced that Bueno was irreplaceable and Christman not?

Is irreplaceability the right standard—or even a meaningful standard? In a nation that has at least some minimal semblance of a social safety net, won't the government always be available as a last resort to provide whatever care and support are truly necessary? Note, for instance, the suggestion in *Christman* that a parent can always be replaced through the foster care system. But, viewed differently, might it not also be said that almost *every* member of a family plays a unique role in that family and would be missed if removed through incarceration? The court in *Bueno* emphasized that the defendant met the emotional, and not just the physical, needs of his wife. But if emotional attachments are taken into account, doesn't it seem likely that most defendants could be seen as making contributions to family members that would be extremely difficult or impossible to replace?

2. **Role of Defense Counsel.** Bueno's lawyer seems to have put some considerable effort into presenting a compelling family-responsibilities case. (Note the snarky comment in the Eighth Circuit's opinion about medical reports "giv[ing] the appearance of having been lawyer-drafted to replicate that which we found to be sufficient evidence of truly exceptional family circumstances in" earlier cases.) Not all defense lawyers will be willing and able to go to such lengths. Should we be concerned that taking into account family responsibilities—and perhaps other mitigating defendant characteristics that also require a substantial presentation of evidence—may exacerbate sentencing disparities related to lawyering quality?

3. **Moral Hazard and the Risk of Erroneous Adjudication.** Among sentencing factors, family responsibilities may be somewhat unusual in the extent to which the defendant and people close to the defendant are in possession of the key information. There may be some temptation for the defendant and his or her family members to exaggerate the importance of the defendant's role, or for the defendant to assume a greater role in anticipation of sentencing. Such actions could potentially lead to erroneous fact-finding by the sentencing judge. In *Bueno*, the Eighth Circuit seemed to have some suspicions along these lines ("one would be justified in asking how, in the face of such circumstances, Bueno found it possible to leave his ailing wife's side and drive from his home in California to St. Louis") but declined in the end to substitute its view of the facts for that of the district judge.

4. **Weight of the Guidelines After *Booker* and *Gall*.** In *Bueno*, the Eighth Circuit leaves the impression that it would have decided the case differently prior to the Supreme Court's decision in *Gall*, even notwithstanding the defendant's beefed-up evidence of family

responsibilities. In Chapter 3, we noted that *Gall* reinforced *Booker*'s mandate for deferential appellate review of federal sentences. Post-*Gall*, the analysis in *Bueno* suggests, it is mostly up to district judges to decide how much weight, if any, to give to the guidelines' restrictive position on family responsibilities. By contrast, in *Christman*, the Sixth Circuit seems to demand that district judges pay greater heed to the guidelines' categorization of family responsibilities as a discouraged factor. Is *Christman* consistent with *Booker* and *Gall*?

5. **"Gross Sentencing Disparities."** In requiring a showing of "extraordinary circumstances" for a family-responsibilities departure, the *Christman* court asserts, "To say otherwise would be to invite gross sentencing disparities based solely on whether one has a young child or an infirm dependent." The reference to disparities seems an invocation of 18 U.S.C. § 3553(a)(6), which instructs sentencing judges to consider "the need to avoid unwarranted sentence disparities among defendants with similar records who have been found guilty of similar conduct." But is it truly "unwarranted" to give disparate treatment to two defendants based on differing family responsibilities? For instance, if A has no dependents, while B is the sole caregiver for a small child, would it be "unwarranted" to sentence A to prison, while giving B probation in order to save the child from a foster-care placement?

6. **Too Close to a Constitutional Danger Zone?** In contemporary American society, family caregiving responsibilities are not evenly divided between the sexes. For instance, nearly 82% of the unmarried solo parents living with a child are women. GRETCHEN LIVINGSTON, PEW RESEARCH CENTER, THE CHANGING PROFILE OF UNMARRIED PARENTS 3 (2018). Similarly, in a survey of state prisoners who lived with their minor children prior to incarceration, 77% of the female inmates, but only 26% of the male inmates, reported that they provided most of the daily care for their kids. LAUREN E. GLAZE & LAURA M. MARUSCHAK, U.S. DEP'T OF JUSTICE, PARENTS IN PRISON AND THEIR MINOR CHILDREN 5 (2010). Such data suggest that a uniformly applied family responsibilities "discount" would disproportionately benefit female defendants. Given the heightened historical and constitutional concerns regarding sex discrimination in the United States, does the risk of sex-based sentencing disparities lend support to the Sentencing Commission's restrictive position on family responsibilities as a sentencing factor? Should it matter that women—the group that would benefit the most from a less restrictive position—have been more typically the ones who are disadvantaged by sex discrimination?

7. **Disposition Versus Duration.** At sentencing, family responsibilities seem more likely to be relevant—if they are relevant at all—to the disposition question (prison versus community supervision) than to the duration question (how long a term should be served). For instance, a defendant's caregiving role might supply a compelling justification for imposing a probationary sentence, but not for reducing, say, a fifteen-year prison term to a ten-year prison term. (Do you see why not?) Having decided to take family responsibilities into account, it is not surprising that the

district judges in both *Bueno* and *Christman* effectively imposed community sentences.

If a judge feels that a sentence of incarceration is necessary in a given case based on the seriousness of the offense or other considerations, can you imagine anything the judge might do to minimize the adverse impact on dependents?

8. **Model Penal Code: Sentencing.** The MPC:S takes a somewhat different view of family responsibilities than the guidelines. As one of its general purposes, the MPC:S includes, "when reasonably feasible, to achieve . . . preservation of families . . ., provided [this goal is] pursued within the boundaries of proportionality." § 1.02(2)(a)(ii). Do you prefer this approach to that of the guidelines?

9. **Dysfunctional Family Relationships.** It should not be assumed that a dependent would always be *harmed* by removing a caregiver from the home. Most obviously, if the caregiver has been convicted of abusing the dependent, it might seem perverse to treat the abuser's family responsibilities as a basis for keeping him or her out of prison. But what if the judge has reason to believe that a person who has been convicted of a different sort of crime—say, burglary or tax evasion—is also harming someone in his or her home? If you think that family well-being can appropriately be taken into account as a *mitigating* consideration at sentencing, why not also—where the facts warrant—as an *aggravating* consideration?

10. **Support *from* Family.** A defendant's family relationships may be relevant in different ways than those considered in *Bueno* and *Christman*. For instance, we have considered the potential significance of the support that a defendant *gives* to his or her family members, but it may also matter if a defendant *receives* family support. In particular, family support may affect the defendant's recidivism risk and rehabilitative potential. Can you think of any reasons why that might be so? Courts are sometimes willing to "take a chance" with the defendant who has a supportive family.[6] But does this practice create unwarranted disparities between those defendants who are fortunate in their family backgrounds and those who are not?

3. MENTAL ILLNESS AND INTELLECTUAL DISABILITY

Mental impairments of one form or another are a pervasive aspect of the American criminal justice system. For instance, surveys indicate that more than one-half of incarcerated individuals report either current symptoms of serious psychological distress or a mental illness diagnosis at some time in the past. JENNIFER BRONSON & MARCUS BERZOFSKY, U.S. DEP'T OF JUSTICE, INDICATORS OF MENTAL HEALTH PROBLEMS REPORTED BY PRISON AND JAIL INMATES, 2011–2012 (2017). Additionally, nearly one-quarter report a cognitive disability, defined as having "serious

---

[6] *See, e.g.*, United States v. Stall, 581 F.3d 276 (6th Cir. 2009) (finding no abuse of discretion by district judge in imposing a below-guidelines sentence on the basis of defendant's support from family and friends, which judge thought increased likelihood that therapy would be effective).

difficulty concentrating, remembering, or making decisions" due to a "physical, mental, or emotional problem," and a similar percentage report having attended special education classes. LAURA MARUSCHAK, JENNIFER BRONSON & MARIEL ALPER, U.S. DEP'T OF JUSTICE, DISABILITIES REPORTED BY PRISONERS (2021). Of course, in certain extreme forms, a person's mental impairment may preclude a criminal conviction entirely, by virtue of either the insanity defense or the requirement that a defendant be competent to stand trial. But what of lesser forms of impairment that do not preclude conviction—under what circumstances, if any, should they be taken in account in determining the sentence?

In *Atkins v. Virginia*, 536 U.S. 304 (2002), the Supreme Court held that the Eighth Amendment bars the use of capital punishment with intellectually disabled individuals.[7] This holding grew out of the Court's "narrowing jurisprudence," which "seeks to ensure that only the most deserving of execution are put to death." *Id.* at 319. (We will consider this jurisprudence in more detail in Chapter 7.) In finding that the intellectually disabled are not among the "most deserving," the Court considered the potential justifications for a death sentence and found them inapplicable to the intellectually disabled:

> With respect to retribution—the interest in seeing that the offender gets his "just deserts"—the severity of the appropriate punishment necessarily depends on the culpability of the offender. * * * [I]n *Godfrey v. Georgia,* 446 U.S. 420 (1980), we set aside a death sentence because the petitioner's crimes did not reflect "a consciousness materially more 'depraved' than that of any person guilty of murder." *Id.,* at 433. If the culpability of the average murderer is insufficient to justify the most extreme sanction available to the State, the lesser culpability of the intellectually disabled offender surely does not merit that form of retribution. * * *
>
> With respect to deterrence—the interest in preventing capital crimes by prospective offenders—"it seems likely that 'capital punishment can serve as a deterrent only when murder is the result of premeditation and deliberation,' " *Enmund v. Florida,* 458 U.S. 782, 799 (1982). Exempting the intellectually disabled from that punishment will not affect the "cold calculus that precedes the decision" of other potential murderers. *Gregg v. Georgia,* 428 U.S. 153, 186 (1976) (joint opinion of Stewart, Powell, and Stevens, JJ.). Indeed, that sort of calculus is at the opposite end of the spectrum from behavior of intellectually disabled offenders. The theory of deterrence in capital sentencing is predicated upon the notion that the increased

[7] In *Atkins*, the Court used the term "mentally retarded," but subsequent decisions by the Court have employed the term "intellectual disability" to describe the same condition. We have substituted the currently preferred term in the excerpts below.

> severity of the punishment will inhibit criminal actors from carrying out murderous conduct. Yet it is the same cognitive and behavioral impairments that make these defendants less morally culpable—for example, the diminished ability to understand and process information, to learn from experience, to engage in logical reasoning, or to control impulses—that also make it less likely that they can process the information of the possibility of execution as a penalty and, as a result, control their conduct based upon that information. Nor will exempting the intellectually disabled from execution lessen the deterrent effect of the death penalty with respect to offenders who are not intellectually disabled. Such individuals are unprotected by the exemption and will continue to face the threat of execution. Thus, executing the intellectually disabled will not measurably further the goal of deterrence.

Id. at 319–20. The Court further observed,

> The reduced capacity of intellectually disabled offenders provides a second justification for a categorical rule making such offenders ineligible for the death penalty. The risk "that the death penalty will be imposed in spite of factors which may call for a less severe penalty," *Lockett v. Ohio,* 438 U.S. 586, 605 (1978), is enhanced, not only by the possibility of false confessions, but also by the lesser ability of intellectually disabled defendants to make a persuasive showing of mitigation in the face of prosecutorial evidence of one or more aggravating factors. Intellectually disabled defendants may be less able to give meaningful assistance to their counsel and are typically poor witnesses, and their demeanor may create an unwarranted impression of lack of remorse for their crimes. * * * [M]oreover, reliance on intellectual disability as a mitigating factor can be a two-edged sword that may enhance the likelihood that the aggravating factor of future dangerousness will be found by the jury. Intellectually disabled defendants in the aggregate face a special risk of wrongful execution.

Id. at 320–21.

The Court characterized the individuals protected by its holding as having "not only subaverage intellectual functioning, but also significant limitations in adaptive skills such as communication, self-care, and self-direction that became manifest before age 18." *Id.* at 318. Doesn't it seem, however, that the concerns raised by the Court with respect to culpability, deterrability, and risk of error might also apply to a broader class of individuals suffering other sorts of mental impairment?

NOTES & QUESTIONS

1. **Extension to Noncapital Cases?** *Atkins* is firmly rooted in the Supreme Court's distinctive Eighth Amendment capital sentencing jurisprudence. The Court has not indicated that intellectually disabled defendants have any special Eighth Amendment protections in *noncapital* cases. However, in *Graham v. Florida,* 560 U.S. 48 (2010) (excerpted in Chapter 6), the Court held on Eighth Amendment grounds that the diminished culpability of *juvenile* defendants precluded the sentence of life without the possibility of parole (LWOP) for such defendants in nonhomicide cases. The Court discussed the impulsiveness and immature decisionmaking abilities of young people in ways that were reminiscent of the discussion of intellectual disability in *Atkins*. Putting together *Graham* and *Atkins*, should LWOP be constitutionally prohibited for intellectually disabled defendants in nonhomicide cases?

2. **Definition of Intellectual Disability.** In *Atkins*, the Court indicated that it would leave the definition of intellectual disability to the states. However, twelve years later, in *Hall v. Florida*, 572 U.S. 701 (2014), the Court took a more activist position. The defendant, Hall, scored 71 on an IQ test—just slightly above the cutoff of 70 that Florida had set in its definition of intellectual disability. Other evidence indicated that Hall's mental functioning was at the level of a toddler or four-year old, but the state's inflexible IQ rule precluded consideration of anything else, and Hall's death sentence was affirmed in the state-court system. In the U.S. Supreme Court, though, Florida's rule was rejected as inconsistent with established medical practice in using IQ scores and diagnosing intellectual disability. The Court held:

> Intellectual disability is a condition, not a number. Courts must recognize, as does the medical community, that the IQ test is imprecise. This is not to say that an IQ test score is unhelpful. It is of considerable significance, as the medical community recognizes. But in using these scores to assess a defendant's eligibility for the death penalty, a State must afford these test scores the same studied skepticism that those who design and use the tests do, and understand that an IQ test score represents a range rather than a fixed number. A State that ignores the inherent imprecision of these tests risks executing a person who suffers from intellectual disability.
>
> This Court agrees with the medical experts that when a defendant's IQ test score falls within the test's acknowledged and inherent margin of error, the defendant must be able to present additional evidence of intellectual disability, including testimony regarding adaptive deficits.

Id. at 723 (citations omitted). The Court seemed to regard the relevant margin of error as +/– 5 IQ points, suggesting that any defendant with a tested IQ of 75 or lower should be permitted to present additional evidence of intellectual disability.

3. **What About Adult-Onset or Temporary Mental Impairments?** The Supreme Court has noted that "the medical community defines intellectual disability according to three criteria: significantly subaverage intellectual functioning, deficits in adaptive functioning (the inability to learn basic skills and adjust behavior to changing circumstances), and *onset of these deficits during the developmental period.*" *Hall*, 572 U.S. at 710 (emphasis added). It is not clear, though, why the latter criterion, adopted for medical purposes, should limit the constitutional protection provided for mental impairment.[8] Serious intellectual and adaptive functioning deficits may develop during a person's adult years, for instance, as a result of traumatic brain injury or dementia. At whatever age such deficits first become manifest, as long as they were present at the time the offense was committed, doesn't it seem that the concerns raised in *Atkins* regarding diminished culpability, increased risk of wrongful execution, and so forth would be equally compelling? *See, e.g.*, Laura Snodgrass & Brad Justice, *"Death Is Different": Limits on the Imposition of the Death Penalty to Traumatic Brain Injuries*, 26 DEV. MENTAL HEALTH L. 81 (2007) (arguing that constitutional protections should be extended to individuals suffering from traumatic brain injury).

Temporary or episodic mental impairments present greater difficulties. For instance, the Model Penal Code recognizes involuntary intoxication as an affirmative defense to criminal liability. MPC § 2.08. Thus, if a person is forcibly drugged and then commits a crime, the person may be able to avoid conviction entirely, but only if the person's mental impairment rises to the same level that would be necessary to satisfy the requirements of the insanity defense. What if the impairment—involving, say, a paranoid delusion about the victim—was not quite great enough to satisfy the insanity standard, but still played a major causal role in the commission of the crime—should the defendant's condition at least entitle the defendant to constitutional protection from the death penalty? Note that some of the mitigated culpability concerns highlighted by the Court in *Atkins* might be present, but—assuming the defendant recovers from the forced intoxication by the time legal proceedings commence—perhaps not the concerns about wrongful execution.

Still greater difficulties arise if the impairment resulted from the defendant's own voluntary choices, e.g., drinking alcohol to excess. Courts and policymakers have been much more reluctant to recognize voluntary than involuntary intoxication as a mitigating condition. *See, e.g.*, Fla. Stat. § 921.0026(3) ("[T]he defendant's substance abuse or addiction, including intoxication at the time of the offense, is not a mitigating factor [under the departure statute] and does not, under any circumstances, justify a downward departure from the permissible sentencing range."). But is such reluctance always justified? After all, voluntary intoxication is not *per se* unlawful, and there seems no societal consensus that it is inherently a moral

---

[8] In state law, the "developmental period" is typically equated with the first seventeen years of life, although a few states recognize ages of onset as late as twenty-two. Margaret S. Russell et al., *Intellectual Disability and the Death Penalty: Florida's Wrongs Should Be Made Right*, 45 NOVA L. REV. 1, 22–24 (2020).

wrong, either. Moreover, the line between voluntary and involuntary intoxication is not always clear-cut. What about an addicted individual who consumes intoxicants in order to avoid terrible withdrawal symptoms, for instance, or the young person who drinks as a result of intense peer pressure? How about the person who becomes intoxicated as a result of consuming a prescribed medication? Should mental impairments in these scenarios be regarded as mitigating?

4. **Subconstitutional Law.** *Atkins* is a constitutional decision. In general, as a matter of subconstitutional law, sentencing judges are free, but not required, to treat mental impairments as mitigating in a much wider range of circumstances. For instance, in a noncapital case of aggravated assault, the judge might decide to impose a more lenient sentence based on the defendant's traumatic brain injury, or the defendant's involuntary or perhaps even voluntary intoxication. However, just because a judge can make such a decision does not mean that the judge should do so. In any given case, mental impairment should be connected to a recognized purpose of punishment before it is used as a sentencing factor.

The retributive ground for mitigation seems clearest. Mental impairment may affect one's ability to process sensory information, appreciate the consequences of one's actions, communicate effectively with others, and control impulses—all of which may tend to diminish the blameworthiness of any criminal conduct that results from the impairment. Even accepting this proposition, however, many difficult questions remain, including how severe the impairment should be in order to justify a sentence reduction, how the size of the reduction should be determined, and whether a formal diagnosis of a medically recognized disorder should be required. Also uncertain is how to weigh the defendant's carelessness or culpability in producing the impairment, for instance, in cases of voluntary intoxication or when the defendant has chosen not to take a medication that was prescribed to treat the defendant's mental condition.

In some cases, there may also be good utilitarian grounds for taking mental impairments into account. If the defendant is receiving therapy in the community for his or her mental condition, the judge might decide that rehabilitative purposes would best be served by a probationary sentence that would allow for continuity in the defendant's treatment. A judge might also decide that a defendant's precarious mental condition would make the experience of incarceration exceptionally difficult for the defendant to bear, which might, in the utilitarian weighing of costs and benefits, also support a probationary sentence in lieu of incarceration.[9]

5. **Mental Impairment as Aggravator.** *Atkins* treats a certain type of mental impairment as a mitigating factor. Might mental impairments be

---

[9] Similarly, the particular hardships caused by incarceration for the mentally ill may also affect the length of the term that is thought necessary for retributive purposes. *See* Michael Mullan, *How Should Mental Illness Be Relevant to Sentencing?*, 88 MISS. L. J. 255, 270 (2019) ("[M]ental illness is relevant to the sentencing decision as it dramatically changes the offender's prison experience. For those with mental illness, incarceration is not only more likely, but is a vastly different and harsher experience."). We consider the effect of incarceration on mentally ill individuals in more detail in Chapter 5.

appropriately regarded as *aggravating* in some cases? The case for aggravating treatment would seem to be strongest with a mental condition that predisposes a defendant to violence and that cannot be managed effectively through community-based treatment. However, care should be taken not to increase sentence severity on the basis of unfounded stereotypes regarding mental illness and crime. Professor Stephen Morse sums up the relevant research this way:

> Investigation of good studies discloses a far weaker connection between major mental disorder and criminality than many people stereotypically assume. Most people with mental disorder do not engage in serious criminal behavior and are more likely to be victims of violence than perpetrators. The rate of serious criminal behavior among people with major mental disorder is approximately the same as the population as a whole—about 3% to 4%—unless the person is also abusing substances, which does increase the rate. This is unsurprising because people with serious disorders do have higher rates of substance-use problems, probably because they are self-medicating to deal with the pain of mental disorder and related problems. Nonetheless, even in this co-morbid population—people with major mental disorder and substance abuse—the rate of serious criminal behavior is low. Moreover, the association between psychotic states and violent behavior is weak and inconsistent. The strongest association between mental disorder and violent conduct is self-harm, especially suicide by gun.

Mental Disorder and Criminal Justice, in 1 REFORMING CRIMINAL JUSTICE: PUNISHMENT, INCARCERATION, AND RELEASE 251, 260 (Erik Luna ed., 2017) (citations omitted).

6. **Federal Guidelines.** The federal sentencing guidelines handle mental impairments in an equivocal manner. Section 5H1.3 reads:

> **Mental and Emotional Conditions (Policy Statement)**
>
> Mental and emotional conditions may be relevant in determining whether a departure is warranted, if such conditions, individually or in combination with other offender characteristics, are present to an unusual degree and distinguish the case from the typical cases covered by the guidelines.
>
> In certain cases a downward departure may be appropriate to accomplish a specific treatment purpose.
>
> Mental and emotional conditions may be relevant in determining the conditions of probation or supervised release; e.g., participation in a mental health program.

However, § 5K2.13 somewhat narrows this authorization to depart:

> **Diminished Capacity (Policy Statement)**
>
> A downward departure may be warranted if (1) the defendant committed the offense while suffering from a significantly reduced mental capacity; and (2) the significantly reduced mental capacity contributed substantially to the commission of the offense.

> Similarly, if a departure is warranted under this policy statement, the extent of the departure should reflect the extent to which the reduced mental capacity contributed to the commission of the offense.
>
> However, the court may not depart below the applicable guideline range if (1) the significantly reduced mental capacity was caused by the voluntary use of drugs or other intoxicants; (2) the facts and circumstances of the defendant's offense indicate a need to protect the public because the offense involved actual violence or a serious threat of violence; (3) the defendant's criminal history indicates a need to incarcerate the defendant to protect the public; or (4) the defendant has been convicted of an offense under chapter 71 [obscenity], 109A [sexual abuse], 110 [sexual exploitation and other abuse of children], or 117 [transportation for illegal sexual activity], of title 18, United States Code.

7. **Irresistible Impulses.** If you have taken a substantive criminal law class, you may appreciate that the insanity defense distinguishes between cognitive defects, which relate to the brain's acquisition and processing of information, and volitional defects, which relate to control over behavior. For instance, the Model Penal Code permits the insanity defense to be used when, due to a mental disease or defect, a person "lacks substantial capacity to appreciate the criminality (wrongfulness) of his conduct [cognitive prong] or to conform his conduct to the requirements of law [volitional prong]." MPC § 4.01(1). The volitional prong, sometimes referred to as the "irresistible impulse" standard, has been by far the more controversial of the two, and is now accepted in only a minority of U.S. jurisdictions. Criticisms have centered on the practical difficulty of distinguishing between an irresistible impulse and an impulse that was merely not resisted. *See, e.g., United States v. Lyons*, 731 F.2d 243 (5th Cir. 1984) (rejecting volitional prong for purposes of federal insanity defense).

For its part, *Atkins* seems to make no distinction between cognitive and volitional defects, citing, for instance, the intellectually disabled person's diminished capacities both "to understand and process information" and "to control impulses." Similarly, the federal sentencing guidelines would permit a diminished capacity downward departure in circumstances both of impaired ability to "understand the wrongfulness of the behavior comprising the offense or to exercise the power of reason" (cognitive impairment) and of impaired ability to "control behavior that the defendant knows is wrongful" (volitional). § 5K2.13 app. n.1.

Do you agree that volitional defects should be treated as a mitigating factor at sentencing? This might have especially important implications for defendants whose criminal conduct resulted from addiction.[10]

---

[10] Returning to the realm of constitutional law, the Supreme Court famously struggled with the Eighth Amendment implications of addiction in *Powell v. Texas*, 392 U.S. 514 (1968), failing to produce either a majority opinion or a clear answer to the question of whether there might be some circumstances in which it would be unconstitutional to punish an alcoholic for drinking.

8. **Neuroimaging Evidence.** Increasingly sophisticated neuroimaging evidence is starting to change the way that mental impairment issues are litigated at sentencing. Consider this assessment from Professor Maneka Sinha:

> Typically, neuroscience evidence takes the form of neuroimaging data, computer-generated images of the brain, or nonimaging evidence resulting from tests administered by a medical professional in order to attempt to measure an individual's brain function as compared to normal brain function. Both imaging and nonimaging data seek to shed light on brain operation and functioning. But neuroimaging allows visualization of injuries and other abnormalities in a brain; it allows us to *see* brain damage.
>
> Neuroimaging can support a defendant's arguments to mitigate his sentence by highlighting physical causes for, or contributors to, the offending conduct in question and is, therefore, increasingly being offered as mitigating evidence in sentencings, especially in capital cases. While not yet regularly used by prosecutors against defendants, there is concern that prosecutors, especially in the capital context, will introduce neuroscience evidence to support the argument that defendants are likely to commit future crimes and, thus, more severe penalties or death sentences are appropriate.

Junk Science at Sentencing, 89 GEO. WASH. L. REV. 52, 76–77 (2021). Professor Sinha expresses concern about the potential for scientifically unsound uses of neuroimaging evidence. She notes, for instance, that there is "an expectation that every brain structure controls a particular aspect of behavior and that, as a result, an injury to a particular structure would impact a specific type of behavior. But the degree to which a behavior is regulated by a specific structure varies significantly, both in general and from person to person." *Id.* at 77–78. Neuroimaging evidence may ultimately present the same challenge as more traditional medical diagnostic evidence on mental impairment—the risk that evidence presenting a façade of certainty and sophistication may ultimately obscure, rather than illuminate, the key questions about culpability and risk.

To the extent that imaging evidence is deemed reliable and indicates that a defendant is predisposed to act violently, how should this information affect the sentence, taking into account the traditional purposes of punishment discussed in Chapter 1?

4. SOCIOECONOMIC STATUS

Socioeconomic status (SES) is a somewhat amorphous category that may encompass a number of overlapping sentencing factors. SES implicates not only income and wealth, but also various types of intangible human capital that may help a person to be able to generate income and wealth—education, specialized skills, work history, connections to the wealthy and powerful, reputation, celebrity, privileged family background, social media followers, and so forth. Depending on the circumstances, either high or low SES may plausibly be relevant to sentencing under both retributive and utilitarian approaches to punishment. However, use of SES factors at sentencing strikes many as starkly inconsistent with the "blind Justice" ideal, especially when high-SES defendants are shown lenience that would not be accorded low-SES defendants.

In the federal system, as we have already noted, Congress mandated that the Sentencing Commission "shall assure that the [sentencing] guidelines and policy statements are entirely neutral as to the . . . socioeconomic status of offenders." 28 U.S.C. § 994(d). Congress further directed that the guidelines "reflect the general inappropriateness of considering" various SES-related factors, including education, vocational skills, employment record, and community ties of the defendant. 28 U.S.C. § 994(e). However, Congress gave no such mandates to sentencing judges. Should they feel freer to take SES factors into account, especially post-*Booker*?

United States v. Boucher

937 F.3d 702 (6th Cir. 2019)

■ STRANCH, J.

Senator Rand Paul was mowing his lawn when he stopped to gather a few limbs in his path. Without warning, Rene Boucher—Paul's next-door neighbor, whom he had not spoken with in years—raced toward Paul and attacked him from behind. The impact broke six of Paul's ribs, caused long-lasting damage to his lung, and led to several bouts of pneumonia. Boucher later pleaded guilty to assaulting a member of Congress in violation of 18 U.S.C. § 351(e). Although his Guidelines sentencing range was 21 to 27 months in prison, the district court sentenced him to 30 days' imprisonment. On appeal, the Government argues that Boucher's sentence was substantively unreasonable. We agree and therefore **VACATE** his sentence and **REMAND** for resentencing.

I. BACKGROUND

A. Factual Background

[Boucher's attack apparently resulted not from political differences, but, rather, from Boucher's frustration over Paul's placement of yard debris on several occasions close to or over the property line dividing the two neighbors' backyards.]

B. Procedural History

The Warren County Attorney initially charged Boucher with Fourth Degree Misdemeanor Assault under Kentucky law. He was taken into custody for a few days, after which the FBI intervened and the state charges were dropped. The Government then indicted Boucher on one count of assaulting a member of Congress in violation of 18 U.S.C. § 351(e). Boucher pleaded guilty. * * *

At his sentencing hearing, Boucher called three witnesses. The first was Amy Milliken, the Warren County Attorney. Milliken testified that "many times in assault fourth cases, where . . . you're looking at someone older, [ ] who has ties in the community, [ ] who has a job, [ ] who is productive, [and] who has no criminal history, we have somewhat of a standard plea . . . and that would generally be 30 days in the Warren County Regional Jail." But she also clarified that misdemeanor assault charges were appropriate for only "minor" injuries, and she did not know "the extent of [Paul's] injuries" when she charged Boucher with Fourth Degree Misdemeanor Assault. * * *

Boucher's second witness was Jim Skaggs, one of the developers of the gated community where Boucher and Paul live. Skaggs testified that "we had absolutely no problems" with Boucher, who "always paid his homeowner's dues and kept a neat place." He had "no complaints" about Boucher as a neighbor but conceded that if he "had broken ribs, maybe [he would] feel differently about it." Boucher's final witness was Father John Thomas, the priest at his church. Thomas testified that Boucher was "a friendly, open, kind, faithful person." He recalled that Boucher had visited sick parishioners "a couple of times" and had "helped with preparation for those who [were] interested in learning more about the Catholic faith."

Boucher and his counsel also spoke. Boucher told the court that he was "sincerely sorry" for the assault, apologized to Paul and his family, offered to pay for Paul's medical expenses, and assured the court that he would "never do . . . anything like this again." He added that he would "prefer not to go to jail for this situation" and "plead[ed] for the mercy of the court and forgiveness." Boucher's counsel made a similar plea for leniency. Citing Milliken's testimony, he argued that "if anyone else in Warren County [had gotten] involved in a scuffle over yard trash, . . . we would be in the Warren District Court" and "the resolution would be a 30-day jail sentence . . . ." Counsel also emphasized Boucher's status in the community:

> A felony conviction carries with it, Judge, a very real stigma, and maybe to some people a felony conviction isn't that big of a deal, but for a person who has become board certified in two specialties, who's 60 years old, who is a devout member of his church, who's the father of two wonderful children, and who lives in the nicest neighborhood in Warren County, by my evaluation, a felony conviction is a very real punishment in and of itself.

In lieu of live testimony, the Government responded by introducing two victim impact statements—one from Paul and another from his wife, Kelley. * * *

The district court nevertheless sentenced Boucher to 30 days in prison. The court's rationale rested primarily on two observations. * * * The court described the attack as an "isolated," "first-time action," and felt there was a "spontaneity about when it happened" that suggested Boucher would not "get [himself] involved in anything like this" again.

Second, the court announced that Boucher had an "excellent background." He was "an educated person" who had "gone by 60 years of . . . a good life from the letters that the court ha[d] reviewed" and "from the witnesses who testified," including his pastor and the developer of the gated community. The court also mentioned that Boucher had no criminal history, had served in the military, had "raised two children who [were] doing very well," and had "participated in the community in [his medical] practice and in [his] church."

After weighing these factors, the court decided that a within-Guidelines sentence would not "serve any purpose." It sentenced Boucher to 30 days in prison along with 100 hours of community service, one year of supervised release, and a $10,000 fine. On appeal, the Government argues that this sentence was substantively unreasonable.

II. ANALYSIS

A. Substantive Reasonableness * * *

The Supreme Court's guidance and our own precedents offer two principal takeaways. First, when a district court varies above or below the Guidelines, we "must consider the extent of the deviation and ensure that the justification is sufficiently compelling to support the degree of the variance." *Gall*, 552 U.S. at 50. "The farther the judge's sentence [varies] from the guidelines sentence . . . the more compelling the justification based on factors in section 3553(a) must be." *United States v. Aleo*, 681 F.3d 290, 302 (6th Cir. 2012). Second, in looking for that compelling justification, a key question is whether the defendant's case falls within "the heartland to which the Commission intends individual Guidelines to apply." *Kimbrough*, 552 U.S. at 109. If the district court reasonably explains why the defendant's case falls outside the heartland, then the sentence "may attract greatest respect." *Id.* But "a sentence that [varies] from the advisory range in a 'mine-run case' warrants 'closer review.'" *United States v. Herrera-Zuniga*, 571 F.3d 568, 582 (6th Cir. 2009) (quoting *Kimbrough*, 552 U.S. at 109).

Here, the district court sentenced Boucher to 30 days' imprisonment, though his Guidelines range was 21 to 27 months. That represented an eight-step decrease in Boucher's total offense level and a 95% reduction from the lowest end of his recommended sentence. Although we do not reduce substantive reasonableness review to "a rigid mathematical formula," *Gall*, 552 U.S. at 47, the size of the variance remains relevant to our analysis. *See id.* at 50. The question, then, is whether the district court gave a "sufficiently compelling" reason for the dramatic downward variance in this case. *Id.*

B. The § 3553(a) Factors

[The Sixth Circuit found the offense to be a "garden variety assault" that was not shown to be outside the "heartland" of cases covered by the assault guideline. The court also faulted the sentencing judge for not addressing the severity of the injuries suffered by the victim, or the need to deter other attacks on members of Congress.]

3. History and Characteristics

The district court also commended Boucher's "excellent background." It spotlighted his education, medical practice, reputation in the community, involvement in his church, lack of criminal history, military background, and two children who "are doing very well." In its "Statement of Reasons" submitted after sentencing, the court repeated that Boucher was "a 60 year old highly educated medical doctor, Army veteran, father, church member, and good standing community member with no criminal history."

While these factors might distinguish Boucher from a mine-run defendant convicted of assault, they are almost all disfavored as grounds for a below-Guidelines sentence.[3] Congress has instructed the Sentencing Commission to "assure that the guidelines and policy statements, in recommending a term of imprisonment . . . reflect the general inappropriateness of considering the education, vocational skills, employment record, family ties and responsibilities, and community ties of the defendant." 28 U.S.C. § 994(e). The Guidelines' policy statements do just that. *See* USSG § 5H1.2 ("Education and vocational skills are not ordinarily relevant [to a defendant's sentence.]"); *id.* § 5H1.5 ("Employment record is not ordinarily relevant."); *id.* § 5H1.6 ("[F]amily ties and responsibilities are not ordinarily relevant."); *id.* § 5H1.11 ("Civic, charitable, or public service . . . and similar good works are not ordinarily relevant."); *id.* § 5H1.1 (noting age "may be relevant" only if "present to an unusual degree"). And although a defendant's criminal record is relevant to "determining the applicable criminal history category," *id.* § 5H1.8, it is usually not a proper reason for a variance precisely because the Guidelines already take it into account.

These factors are disfavored for good reason. To prioritize a defendant's education, professional success, and standing in the community would give an additional leg up to defendants who are already in a privileged position. Indigent defendants are less likely to impress a sentencing court with their education, employment record, or local reputation. But they are no less deserving of a reasonable and compassionate sentence. That is why Congress and the Guidelines oppose a class-based system where accumulated wealth, education, and status serve as credits against a criminal sentence.

---

[3] The lone exception is Boucher's military service, which "may be relevant" under the guidelines if it is "present to an unusual degree." USSG § 5H1.11. That was arguably the case here—Boucher served in the Army for eight years and achieved the rank of Major.

This is not to say that sentencing courts are prohibited from weighing factors disfavored under the Guidelines. These factors may, for example, still "be relevant insofar as they bear some connection to permissible considerations." *United States v. Stall*, 581 F.3d 276, 289 (6th Cir. 2009). A defendant's personal or professional success after his last incarceration, while not always relevant in isolation, might demonstrate an honest effort to turn his life around. But while "the fact that a factor is discouraged or forbidden under the guidelines does not automatically make it irrelevant when a court is weighing statutory factors apart from the guidelines," Section 3553(a)(5) still "requires that the district court consider applicable policy statements issued by the Sentencing Commission, and the Guidelines' disfavored view toward [these factors] is, therefore, relevant to our reasonableness review." *Christman*, 607 F.3d at 1119. The district court did not acknowledge that Congress and the Guidelines view these factors with suspicion or explain what unusual circumstances justified relying on them here. These simple markers of privilege did not warrant an extreme variance in Boucher's case. *See id.* (holding that the district court erred by citing the defendant's "educational background and skill" as mitigating factors without identifying what "unusual circumstances" warranted reliance on those factors).

4. Unwarranted Sentence Disparities

The last key factor is the need to avoid unwarranted sentence disparities. *See* 18 U.S.C. § 3553(a)(6). * * *

The most recent Commission data shows that federal defendants with a criminal history category of I who were convicted of assault received an average sentence of 26 months' imprisonment and a median sentence of 21 months. See U.S. Sentencing Commission, Length of Imprisonment for Offender in Each Criminal History Category by Primary Offense Category, Table 14 (2017). * * *

Despite these comparators, the district court failed to address the risk of sentence disparities. Of course, a sentence may be substantively reasonable even when the court does not squarely address this factor. But the risk of disparity is more acute in mine-run cases like this one. And that risk intensifies when the defendant receives a sentence well outside the Guidelines range. The unremarkable nature of this case—coupled with the court's substantial variance from the Guidelines—warranted a more careful discussion about the relationship between Boucher's sentence and the danger of unjustified disparities. * * *

NOTES & QUESTIONS

1. **"Simple Markers of Privilege."** What were the personal characteristics cited by the district court in granting Boucher a below-guidelines sentence? Can you justify treating these characteristics as mitigating by reference to any of the standard purposes of punishment? The Sixth Circuit seemed to dismiss them all as "simple markers of privilege."

Does that seem fair to you, or do you think that important distinctions might be made between these personal characteristics?

2. **Disparity—Warranted or Unwarranted?** The Sixth Court also indicated that Boucher's sentence was in tension with the mandate of 18 U.S.C. § 3553(a)(6) for judges to "avoid unwarranted sentence disparities among defendants with similar records who have been found guilty of similar conduct." While Boucher's sentence certainly was much more lenient than the norm for defendants with minimal criminal history who are convicted of assault in federal court, such disparities are not disfavored *per se*. Rather, the statute is concerned with *unwarranted* disparities. Boucher's sentence might fairly be characterized as disparate, but that merely begs the question of whether Boucher's unusual characteristics—that is, for a person convicted of assault—warranted his unusually lenient sentence.[11]

3. **General Deterrence.** The Sixth Circuit noted Congress's interest in "protecting our elected representatives from harm," and faulted the district court for failing to explain why that interest did not warrant a within-range sentence. *Boucher*, 937 F.3d at 710. This line of analysis highlights important tensions between the aim of general deterrence and the practice of reducing sentences on the basis of a defendant's mitigating personal characteristics. Do you think a due regard for general deterrence requires that defendant characteristics be ignored at sentencing?[12]

4. **Leveling up or Leveling down.** *Boucher* strikes an egalitarian chord. In principle, egalitarian aims can be advanced in any one of three ways: high-status people may be treated like low ("leveling down"), low-status people may be treated like high ("leveling up"), or both groups may meet somewhere in the middle. *Boucher* seems to embrace the leveling down strategy—the high-status defendant is to be treated like everyone else who is convicted of assault in federal court. Might it be preferable to try to some leveling up? The Sixth Circuit itself seems to gesture in this direction through its assertion that indigent defendants "are no less deserving of a reasonable and compassionate sentence"—although it is hard to see how the holding in *Boucher* does anything to further this end.[13]

---

[11] In a portion of the opinion not reprinted above, the Sixth Circuit rejected an argument that state-court assault sentences should be used as a benchmark to determine whether Boucher's sentence was disparate. The Sixth Circuit stated, "The only disparities relevant in this case are those among federal defendants on a national scale." *Boucher*, 937 F.3d at 712. Some commentators, however, have taken a different view about the relevance of state-court practices in the sentencing of crimes that are commonly prosecuted in state courts. *See, e.g.*, Michael O'Hear, *National Uniformity/Local Uniformity: Reconsidering the Use of Departures to Reduce Federal-State Sentencing Disparities*, 87 IOWA L. REV. 721 (2002).

[12] Note that this view may be in tension with the discussion of general deterrence in *Atkins*. In that case, the Supreme Court asserted, "Nor will exempting the intellectually disabled from execution lessen the deterrent effect of the death penalty with respect to offenders who are not intellectually disabled. Such individuals are unprotected by the exemption and will continue to face the threat of execution." *Atkins*, 536 U.S. at 320. By analogy, couldn't it be argued that giving high-SES defendants a break at sentencing will not lessen the deterrent effect of the sentencing guidelines with respect to the much larger number of prospective assaulters who are not high-status?

[13] The French Revolution supplies a macabre illustration of leveling up. In early modern Europe, the method of execution in capital cases was based on status: commoners were hung, while aristocrats were beheaded. The French Revolution brought a new spirit of egalitarianism to France, which affected a great many aspects of social life—including executions. In this area,

5. **Suffered Enough Already?** Boucher's lawyer argued that a severe sentence was unnecessary because, for a person of Boucher's status, "a felony conviction is a very real punishment in and of itself." Does that seem a convincing argument to you?

In a similar vein, cases with high-SES defendants sometimes attract more media attention than otherwise-similar cases involving low-SES defendants. (For an extreme example, think O.J. Simpson.) With close media attention may come particularly acute feelings of humiliation for the defendant. Would this strengthen the "suffered enough already" argument? *See* Mirko Bagaric & Peter Isham, *A Rational Approach to the Role of Publicity and Condemnation in the Sentencing of Offenders*, 46 FLA. ST. U. L. REV. 239 (2019) (arguing that publicity should be irrelevant to sentencing).

On the other hand, note that unusually high media attention for a case might arguably support giving the defendant a *more* severe sentence for deterrence purposes—it is possible that a much larger number of prospective offenders will become aware of the punishment in a high-profile case than in more ordinary cases.

6. **The Many Benefits of High SES.** *Boucher* illustrates a number of the potential benefits enjoyed by defendants who have a high SES. Note, for instance, the state prosecutor's description of a relatively lenient "standard plea [deal]" offered to the defendant who is older, has ties in the community and a job, is "productive," and has no criminal history. Additionally, Boucher was able to offer to pay Paul's medical expenses—a gesture that is apt to be viewed favorably as a sign of remorse. One wonders, too, whether a defendant who is educated and belongs to the same socioeconomic class as the judge is able to make a greater impact than most other defendants through his or her allocution. High-SES defendants are also more likely to benefit from high-status character witnesses, as Boucher did. And this is to say nothing of the potential advantages of a well-paid defense lawyer. On the whole, even if a judge scrupulously avoids using the "markers of privilege" as explicit sentencing factors, there may nonetheless be important *indirect* effects of high SES that tend to produce better sentencing outcomes for high-status than low-status defendants.

Even more fundamentally, of course, high-SES individuals are better-positioned than low-SES individuals to avoid committing crimes in the first place. Education, wealth, family connections, and so forth may provide relatively easy access to well-paid lawful employment, credit on reasonable terms to help deal with financial emergencies, professional counseling and prescription medications to deal with psychic distress, and lawyers and civil courts to deal with disputes. Are efforts to suppress the explicit use of factors connected to high SES at sentencing merely a fig leaf to cover much deeper-seated inequities in American criminal justice?

---

the leaders of the Revolution chose to level up, meaning that *everyone* was accorded the privilege of decapitation. Today, we tend to view the guillotine with horror, but, in its historical context, it represented a new recognition of the equal dignity of all condemned individuals. JAMES Q. WHITMAN, HARSH JUSTICE: CRIMINAL PUNISHMENT AND THE WIDENING DIVIDE BETWEEN AMERICA AND EUROPE 113 (2003).

7. **Victim Status.** The Sixth Circuit indicated that Boucher should not be advantaged by his status at sentencing but seemed untroubled by the likelihood that he was disadvantaged by his *victim*'s status. After all, if Paul were not a member of Congress, Boucher would not have ended up in federal court subject to the federal sentencing guidelines. Is there any reason to view victim status more favorably as a sentencing factor than defendant status? Should we be concerned by perceptions that rich victims get "more justice" than poor victims?

8. **Military Service.** Not all of Boucher's personal characteristics cited by the district court are necessarily linked to high SES, including his status as a military veteran. As the Sixth Circuit observed in footnote 3, past military service is somewhat unusual among defendant characteristics in that its use as a sentencing factor is not discouraged by the guidelines. Is this treatment of military service by the guidelines justified? Why, for instance, should Boucher's service to the military count more favorably for sentencing purposes than his service to his church?[14]

9. **High SES as an Aggravating Factor.** Various factors associated with high SES, such as good education and employment, are also associated with reduced recidivism risk, which is normally regarded as a mitigating consideration from a utilitarian standpoint. But, viewed from a retributive standpoint, do you think high SES might actually be *aggravating*? High SES individuals tend to have more and better options than low SES individuals for dealing with the needs and challenges they experience in life. Does that make them more blameworthy when they choose to engage in criminal conduct?[15] Consider Boucher. Surely the residents of what Boucher's lawyer called "the nicest neighborhood in Warren County" have access to the civil courts to deal with their property disputes. By contrast, the residents of some less privileged neighborhoods would likely view civil litigation as far more daunting and unaffordable. Does that make Boucher's choice to use violence in connection with his property dispute more blameworthy than a similar choice made by a homeowner in a working-class neighborhood?

---

[14] With more than 100,000 veterans currently serving time in state and federal prisons in the United States, the treatment of military service as a sentencing factor is of no small importance. LAURA M. MARUSCHAK, JENNIFER BRONSON & MARIEL ALPER, U.S. DEP'T OF JUSTICE, VETERANS IN PRISON (2021). About three-quarters of these veterans received an honorable discharge from the military, and about one-quarter were combat veterans.

An honorable discharge from the military has been recognized as a mitigating factor in some jurisdictions. *See, e.g.*, N.C.G.S. § 15A–1340.16(e)(14); State v. Clemons, 696 N.E.2d 1009 (Ohio 1998); *cf.* Demps v. Dugger, 874 F.2d 1385, 1390 (11th Cir. 1989) (finding that military service not resulting in honorable discharge lacked mitigating force). However, courts have also found that a special skill obtained in the military can be an *aggravating* factor if the skill played a role in the crime. *See, e.g.*, United States v. Runyon, 707 F.3d 475, 475 503–04 (4th Cir. 2013) (deeming permissible in capital trial non-statutory aggravating evidence that defendant used skills earned in armed forces to commit killing).

[15] Note that many high-SES defendants possess special skills, which, in some cases, are used to facilitate their offenses. Think, for instance, of an accountant who uses his or her accounting skills to facilitate a tax fraud. Use of a special skill is recognized as an aggravating factor in the federal sentencing guidelines (§ 3B1.3). However, this provision is sometimes also used with defendants who do not seem to fit the typical high-SES profile. *See, e.g.*, United States v. Berry, 717 F.3d 823 (10th Cir. 2013) (holding that special-skills enhancement warranted for defendant who used his truck-driving skills to transport marijuana).

10. **Low SES as Sentencing Factor.** Much the same debate might be had over *low* SES as a sentencing factor, but to some extent in mirror image form. For instance, various factors associated with low SES would tend to make risk look greater, but the relatively fewer and poorer options available to low SES individuals might be seen as mitigating culpability in some cases.

Consider *State v. Taylor*, the case from Chapter 3 involving reckless injury to a police officer. Although we do not get a complete picture of Taylor's life circumstances, the fact that he had a court-appointed lawyer, as well as his education level (high school dropout) and limited work history, strongly suggest a low SES. Do you think Taylor's SES should have been regarded as mitigating, aggravating, or neither?

11. **Low SES and Mental Impairment.** There may be some overlap between low SES and mental impairment as sentencing factors. Low SES can create chronic stress, as a person must continually struggle to meet basic day-to-day needs. Such stress, in turn, has been associated in psychological research with adverse effects on a person's capacity for cognition and self-control. *See* Elisabeth Winston Lambert, *A Way Out of the "Rotten Social Background" Stalemate: "Scarcity" and Stephen Morse's Proposed Generic Partial Excuse*, 21 U. PA. J. L. & SOC. CHANGE 297, 321–23 (2018) (discussing studies). In light of these psychological dynamics, Lambert proposed that a sentence discount be recognized for financially distressed defendants who can show a causal connection between their poverty-related mental impairments and their offense.

> For example, [researchers] suggest that the "tunneling" effects of scarcity [that is, the tendency to become preoccupied with a need that is not being met] can lead people to misread or overlook other people's social cues. A misread social cue might be a logical explanation for an act of otherwise inexplicable violence. Scarcity also inhibits impulse control and the ability to appropriately moderate emotional responses. These particular impairments might logically explain certain crimes of recklessness, or crimes of violence driven by emotional overreactions. As a third example, scarcity has been shown to cause steep time discounting, meaning that the individual inappropriately prioritizes the present over the future, focusing on meeting the present need or drive without adequate consideration for future consequences. Steep time discounting might logically explain some theft and property crimes.

Id. at 327 (citations omitted). Lambert notes, however, that defendants would likely have a hard time taking advantage of such a sentence discount without the use of expert witnesses, *id.* at 328, which might create a dilemma for the many indigent defendants who are unable to obtain expert assistance. Given the pervasiveness of poverty among criminal defendants, do you think it might make more sense to "bake" the mitigating tendencies of low SES into standard sentencing ranges rather than trying to sort these effects out on a case-by-case basis?

12. **After Remand.** At Boucher's resentencing, a new judge imposed a sentence of eight months' imprisonment followed by six months of home

confinement. *Sen. Rand Paul's Attacker Receives Longer Prison Sentence*, DETROIT NEWS, July 28, 2020. Does that seem about right to you?

5. RACE AND IMPLICIT BIAS

As we have seen, Congress has mandated that the federal sentencing guidelines be "entirely neutral" as to the defendant's race. 28 U.S.C. § 994(d). Even without such a mandate, it might violate the Equal Protection Clause if sentencing laws or sentencing judges treated race as an explicit factor to be considered in determining an individual's punishment. *Cf. Johnson v. California*, 543 U.S. 499 (2005) (holding that state policy of segregating new prison inmates by race was subject to strict scrutiny). Yet, for all of the legal discouragement of race-based sentencing, it nonetheless appears that race matters. We noted the relevant research in Chapter 1. Although race does not seem to play a large role at sentencing if offense severity and criminal history are held constant, the statistical evidence points to small, but significant, racial differences in sentencing outcomes, especially as to in/out decisions (i.e., probation versus incarceration). Ryan D. King & Michael T. Light, *Have Racial and Ethnic Disparities in Sentencing Declined?*, 48 CRIME & JUST. 365, 370–71 (2019). Although ethnicity has been studied much less extensively than race, some research suggests that Latinx ethnicity may similarly play a small, but significant, role in the determination of punishment. *Id.* at 371. Other research, however, indicates that these ethnicity effects may be driven largely or entirely by differences in the sentencing of citizens versus noncitizens. *Id.* at 424.

The troubling persistence of racial disparities in sentencing may result, at least in part, from some combination of indirect effects and implicit bias. Indirect racial effects result from the correlations between race and various legally permissible, facially neutral sentencing factors. For instance, we considered the racial effects of taking criminal history into account as a sentencing factor earlier in this chapter.

Implicit, or unconscious, bias may also play a role. The underlying research has been described as follows:

> Implicit social cognition is a branch of psychology that studies how mental processes that occur outside of awareness and that operate without conscious control can affect judgments about and behaviors toward social groups. These unconscious processes are simply an extension of the way humans think and process information. Briefly stated, our mental processes facilitate decisionmaking by making automatic associations between concepts. For example, people might automatically associate "doctor" with "hospital" and other related ideas. These associations are linked in our minds because they often occur together.

> Implicit racial biases refer to the unconscious associations we make about racial groups. The existence of these biases is consistent with the conclusion of more general research that we automatically and unconsciously use heuristics to cope with the enormous amount of information that bombards us. . . . Like all unconscious mental processes, implicit racial biases are unintentional because they are not planned responses; involuntary, because they occur automatically in the presence of an environmental cue; and effortless, in that they do not deplete an individual's limited information processing resources.

L. Song Richardson & Phillip Atiba Goff, *Implicit Racial Bias in Public Defender Triage*, 122 YALE L.J. 2626, 2629–30 (2013) (citations omitted).

The presence of widespread, unconscious, negative feelings or associations regarding African-Americans can be seen through research using Implicit Association Tests (IATs). In its most common form, an IAT is a short computerized test that determines the speed with which people sort various words and images, thereby revealing the presence of unconscious associations that can either facilitate or impede the sorting, depending on how the sorting task is structured.[16] The test has been taken millions of times, with results consistently showing a moderate preference for Whites over Blacks among Whites, regardless of their age, education level, or political ideology. Nor does it appear that lawyers or judges are immune from these tendencies. *See* Joseph J. Avery & Joel Cooper, *Racial Bias in Post-Arrest and Pretrial Decision Making: The Problem and a Solution,* 29 CORNELL J.L. & PUB. POL'Y 257, 259 (2019) (summarizing IAT studies conducted on judges and criminal defense lawyers). Of particular concern in this context are unconscious associations between Blackness and criminality, inculcated by the media and otherwise.[17]

The uncertain question is whether, and to what extent, unconscious positive or negative racial associations affect real-world legal

---

[16] You can take an on-line IAT yourself through Harvard University's Project Implicit website, https://implicit.harvard.edu/implicit/takeatest.html. The website also contains additional information about the history and theory of the IAT, as well as a treasure trove of fascinating IAT research results.

[17] As Professor Jelani Jefferson Exum points out, this association may have a complex causal relationship with racial disparities in the criminal justice system, both contributing to the disparities and being reinforced and exacerbated by the disparities. *Sentencing Disparities and the Dangerous Perpetuation of Racial Bias*, 26 WASH. & LEE J. CIVIL RTS. & SOC. JUST. 491 (2020).

Note that implicit *racial* bias substantially overlaps with, but is also conceptually distinct from, biases against people who have darker skin tone or more Afrocentric features. *See* Mark W. Bennett, *The Implicit Racial Bias in Sentencing: The Next Frontier,* 126 YALE L.J. FORUM 391, 402–04 (2017). Varying skin tones and facial features are found not only *across* racial groups, but also *within* racial groups. Thus, even if there were overall neutrality between Blacks and Whites, that neutrality could potentially mask unfair discrimination within each group based on having darker skin or more Afrocentric features. These forms of bias are less well-known to judges than conventional racial bias and are thus less likely to be consciously corrected for in judicial decisionmaking.

decisionmaking. At least two studies have attempted to uncover relationships between a judge's IAT score and the sentence that he or she would impose in a *hypothetical* case. In one study, the participating judges were asked to consider three hypothetical criminal cases. Jeffrey J. Rachlinski et al., *Does Unconscious Racial Bias Affect Trial Judges?*, 84 NOTRE DAME L. REV. 1195 (2009). In the first two scenarios, the judges were to select a sentence. No race was given for the defendant, but the judges were subliminally primed with either Black- or White-associated words. In both scenarios, the judges who showed a preference for Whites on an IAT tended to select more lenient punishments if primed with the White-associated words. On the other hand, in the third scenario, in which the judges were asked to convict or acquit, and in which the defendant's race was made explicit, there was no statistically significant correlation between IAT scores and case dispositions. The results suggest that judges may be able to compensate for their unconscious racial biases if they are consciously aware of the potential impact of those biases on their decisions.

In the second study, the researchers sought to determine the effect of implicit biases against Jewish people and people of Asian descent. Justin D. Levinson et al., *Judging Implicit Bias: A National Empirical Study of Judicial Stereotypes*, 69 FLA. L. REV. 63, 66 (2017). Based on an IAT test, the participating judges from both state and federal courts were found to possess implicit biases against both groups. The researchers found an association between pro-Christian, anti-Jewish bias and lenience toward a hypothetical Christian defendant but did not find a similar tendency for anti-Asian bias to affect sentencing outcomes.

Together, the two studies provide some (rather modest) support for the hypothesis that implicit bias may potentially influence sentencing outcomes. However, it is important to remember that these studies deal with hypotheticals, not actual cases. Real-world sentencing may be quite different, although it is far from clear which way these differences would cut. On the one hand, real cases involve real stakes for the people involved, which may motivate judges to sentence with greater care, giving more attention to the risk of biased decisionmaking. On the other hand, the stresses and strains of high-volume courtrooms may drain judges of their cognitive resources, making it all the more likely they will fall back on unconscious racial associations as a sort of decisionmaking shortcut. You may recall, in particular, the description in Chapter 3 of sentencing processes in misdemeanor cases, which are perhaps the most prone to be influenced by group-based stereotypes because of the speed with which decisions must be rendered and limitations on the availability of individualized information about the defendants.

Professor M. Eve Hanan cautions that remorse determinations also raise particular concerns. "Because the decision whether to believe a defendant's expression of remorse is profoundly subjective," she contends, "it is a fertile area in which implicit bias can flourish and lead to sentencing disparity." *Remorse Bias*, 83 MO. L. REV. 301, 306 (2018). She argues,

> Whether because of language and demeanor that differs from the court's cultural expectations or through a priori biased character assessments, sentencing authorities are likely to view African-American defendants' expressions of remorse as insincere. Moreover, to the extent that the judge sees the defendant as inherently criminal and dangerous, she will perceive any display of remorse as "forensically resourceful" or manipulative.

Id. at 329.

Even if judges are normally able to compensate for their implicit biases, sentences may still be warped by the biases of other courtroom actors. As we have seen, prosecutors can shape sentences through their charging, plea-bargaining, and sentence-recommendation decisions. However, prosecutors are possibly even more prone to implicit-bias effects than judges insofar as their decisions are made more quickly, earlier in the case with less information available about the defendant, and with less public accountability. *See* Elayne E. Greenberg, *Unshackling Plea Bargaining from Racial Bias*, 111 J. CRIM. L. & CRIMINOLOGY 93 (2020); Robert J. Smith & Justin D. Levinson, *The Impact of Implicit Racial Bias on the Exercise of Prosecutorial Discretion*, 35 SEATTLE U. L. REV. 795 (2012). Much less research has been conducted on racial disparities in plea bargaining than in sentencing, but one recent study of nearly 50,000 cases in Dane County, Wisconsin, found that White defendants were more likely than Black defendants to receive a reduction from their initial charge, controlling for defendant sex, age, and criminal history. Carlos Berdejó, *Criminalizing Race: Racial Disparities in Plea-Bargaining*, 59 B.C. L. REV. 1187 (2018). These disparities were particularly pronounced in misdemeanor and low-level felony cases, as well as cases in which the defendant had no prior convictions. These results are consistent with the suspicion that race may be used as a proxy for recidivism risk in less serious cases that are disposed of with less careful attention. *See id.* at 1241.

Probation officers may make their implicit biases felt through their presentence reports. The participation of victims in the sentencing process may also be affected by their unconscious group-based stereotypes. And even defense lawyers may vary their efforts as a result of race. As Professors L. Song Richardson and Phillip Atiba Goff observe, "[D]espite the existence of dedicated and committed [public defenders], the lack of adequate resources coupled with unmanageable caseloads make it virtually impossible to provide zealous and effective representation to every client." *Implicit Racial Bias in Public Defender Triage,* 122 YALE L.J. 2626, 2631–32 (2013). They express concern that the inevitable PD "triage" process may be adversely influenced in a variety of ways by implicit biases, for instance, through the lawyer's assessment that a Black client lacks credibility and therefore is unlikely to achieve a favorable case outcome regardless of the lawyer's level of effort.

What, if anything, do you think should be done to reduce the effects of implicit racial bias on sentences? Do concerns about implicit bias change the way you think about remorse or other commonly utilized sentencing factors?

Many ideas have been suggested for reducing the effects of implicit racial bias on real-world legal decisionmaking, but little rigorous research has been conducted to evaluate the effectiveness of different approaches. We note here just a few of the reforms that have been proposed in relation to sentencing. First, prosecutorial offices and courts could systematically collect and disseminate racial disparity data, and mandate that prosecutors and judges prioritize the reduction of such disparities. Jelani Jefferson Exum, *Sentencing Disparities and the Dangerous Perpetuation of Racial Bias*, 26 WASH. & LEE J. CIVIL RTS. & SOC. JUST. 491, 522 (2020). Second, judges, prosecutors, and probation officers could be required to attend training on the concept of implicit bias, with the training to include taking IATs. Mark W. Bennett, *The Implicit Racial Bias in Sentencing: The Next Frontier,* 126 YALE L.J. FORUM 391, 404 (2017). Third, photographs of defendants could be eliminated from presentence reports to reduce the racial "priming" of the judge reading the report. *Id.* Fourth, docket pressures on judges could be eased. Hanan, *supra,* at 351. Fifth, judges could be encouraged to keep and utilize detailed notes about each case, rather than simply relying on their memories. *Id.* at 354 (citing Minn. Judicial Branch, *Implicit Bias Bench Card*). Sixth, district attorney offices could prioritize hiring a more diverse set of prosecutors. Smith & Levinson, *supra,* at 825. Seventh, and finally, district attorney offices could hire intake coordinators who would be responsible for scrubbing all racially identifying information from case files before charging decisions are made. *Id.* Which of these ideas, if any, strike you as both helpful and feasible?

C. OFFENSE SERIOUSNESS FACTORS

A large body of empirical research indicates that the two most important determinants of sentence severity in practice tend to be criminal history and offense seriousness. Michael Cassidy & Jason Rydberg, *Analyzing Variation in Prior Record Penalties Across Conviction Offenses*, 64 CRIME & DELINQUENCY 831, 834 (2018). At some level, offense seriousness may appear intuitive and obvious. Everyone knows that murder is more serious than armed robbery, and armed robbery more serious than shoplifting, right? However, statutory sentencing ranges for felony offenses tend to be quite wide, which invites consideration of the many ways in which a single statutory offense, like armed robbery, might be differentiated as to seriousness. A given armed robber might carry a knife, an unloaded gun, or a loaded gun; might or might not wear a mask; might or might not cause physical injury; might operate alone or with others; and so forth. Any of these considerations could be seen as a sentencing factor that mitigates or aggravates offense seriousness, and hence calls for a relatively lower or higher sentence within the statutory range. However, it is not always clear which aspects of the commission of a given crime should be regarded as relevant to punishment, nor how much weight to give to particular offense factors. Should the armed robber who carried a *loaded* gun get one more month in prison than the otherwise-similar armed robber who carried an *unloaded* gun? One more year? Five more years? Ten more years? If the robber made off with the victim's wallet, should it matter at all for sentencing that the wallet happened to contain $10 versus $100 or $1000?

Although it is hardly a matter of scientific precision, the framework suggested in Chapter 1 for thinking about just deserts may be a good starting point for assessing which offense factors should "count" for sentencing purposes. This framework looks to the harm caused by the crime, the dangerousness of the crime, the intentionality or deliberateness of the harmful or dangerous conduct, and the presence of any justification for the conduct. From this standpoint, for instance, there might be a good retributive rationale for treating victim injury as an aggravating offense factor in a robbery case.[18]

Offense factors might also be regarded as relevant in light of utilitarian considerations. Of particular note might be the concept of marginal deterrence, which was also discussed in Chapter 1—the idea that additional punishment should be imposed if a crime is committed in ways that increase its dangerous or make more difficult the apprehension of the perpetrator. For instance, marginal deterrence might justify a more severe sentence for the loaded, as opposed to the unloaded, firearm, or for the wearing of a mask. Additionally, if a crime is perpetrated in a sadistic or gratuitously reckless fashion, that might be seen as an indicator that the perpetrator is an especially dangerous individual who is in greater need of incapacitation.

At all events, though, an offense factor should not be given any weight at sentencing unless there is some rational connection between that factor and at least one of the recognized purposes of punishment.

1. ROBBERY

Please review the federal sentencing guideline for robbery (§ 2B3.1), which was reprinted in Chapter 2. This guideline highlights a number of the commonly cited offense seriousness factors—as well as a few of more questionable relevance.

---

[18] As discussed in Chapter 7, in Payne v. Tennessee, 501 U.S. 808 (1991), the Court held that in a capital sentencing decision it is permissible to consider the victim's characteristics and the impact of the murder on the victim's family.

NOTES & QUESTIONS

1. **Connecting Factors to Purposes.** What offense seriousness factors are made relevant by § 2B3.1? Can you connect each of these to a purpose of punishment? Do the relative weights of the different factors seem appropriate?

2. **Sentencing Robbery Cases in a Discretionary System.** In many state-court systems, the sentencing judge will have no particular guidance for sentencing robbery cases, only a wide statutory range of, say, probation to twenty years in prison. If you were a new judge sentencing your first robbery case in a discretionary system, would you find the federal guideline to be a helpful resource—at least as a sort of checklist of what is relevant?

3. **Victim Status.** Note that it matters in the robbery guideline who the victim is—robberies that target a financial institution or post office are sentenced more harshly than, say, an otherwise-similar robbery of a convenience store or gas station. Whether, and under what circumstances, victim status should be regarded as a relevant offense factor is a debatable matter. In Chapter 3, we noted a Wisconsin statute that requires the sentencing judge in violent felony cases to treat victim age (62 or older) as an aggravating factor. Does that seem justified by reference to any legitimate purpose of punishment? Or consider the sentencing transcript in *State v. Taylor*, also discussed in Chapter 3. The judge in that case seemed to place emphasis on the fact that the victim was a police officer. Do you think that warrants harsher punishment?

Lurking in the background, as we suggested earlier, is the concern that some victims may unfairly get "more justice" than others. For instance, there is troubling evidence that the death penalty is more likely to be imposed in murder cases if the victim was White than if the victim was Black. Katherine Beckett & Heather Evans, *Race, Death, and Justice: Capital Sentencing in Washington State, 1981–2014*, 6 COLUM. J. RACE & L. 77, 85 (2016).

4. **Marginal Deterrence.** Aspects of the robbery guidelines seem to fit neatly into a marginal deterrence framework, such as the abduction/restraint enhancement (§ 2B3.1(b)(4)). But how much marginal deterrence is actually feasible for the person who has committed himself or herself to a robbery and is already facing a quite severe punishment if caught—even without any special penal add-ons? In this regard, consider the observations of Richard Wright, William Sabol, and Thaddeus Johnson, which are based on interviews with 86 armed robbers:

> Virtually all would-be robbers are born into deplorable social circumstances. . . .
>
> Would-be offenders are attracted to street life partly because they regard their legitimate prospects as grim and see no value in long-range planning. . . .
>
> But street life participation can only be sustained via regular infusions of cash, thereby setting in motion the instigating conditions for predatory crime. The problem is that as fast as

> offenders get their hands on more cash, they spend it with reckless abandon in a desperate attempt to, in their words, keep the party going. As a result, they are almost perpetually in need of additional funds. . . .
>
> The threat of legal sanctions rests on an assumption that would-be offenders perceive themselves as having freedom to choose whether or not to commit any given crime. This assumption flies in the face of what we know about the immediate context in which robbers "decide" to offend, with most of them believing that their desperate need for cash cannot be deferred or met through more conventional means. This is not to say that such offenders are unmindful of the risk of arrest and prosecution, but rather that the perceived urgency of their immediate situation serves to attenuate the link between law-breaking and potential sanctions. . . .
>
> Some offenders go so far as to drink or use drugs before an offense in a deliberate attempt to dull the impact of threatened sanctions, thereby allowing them to proceed without worrying about the potential consequences.

Robbery, Recidivism, and the Limits of the Criminal Justice System, 103 MARQ. L. REV. 1179, 1184–87 (2020) (citations omitted).

5. **A Closer Look at a Few Offense Factors.** As with defendant characteristics, there are a great many offense seriousness factors that might be considered in more detail, but space permits a deeper dive into only a few. We begin with the defendant's role in a group offense.

2. ROLE IN THE OFFENSE

If multiple people are involved in the commission of a crime, with some playing a substantially more important role than others in planning or executing the offense, there seems a natural tendency to favor harsher sentences for the more important participants than for the bit players. The federal sentencing guidelines codify this intuition through specific aggravating and mitigating role adjustments. As indicated in the case that follows, the aggravating role provision (§ 3B1.1) is important not only for its direct effect on the determination of a guidelines sentencing range, but also because an aggravating role adjustment categorically precludes a defendant from taking advantage of the "safety valve" of 18 U.S.C. § 3553(f), which in certain circumstances might otherwise permit a judge to sentence below a statutory mandatory minimum.

United States Sentencing Guidelines (2021)

§ 3B1.1. Aggravating Role

Based on the defendant's role in the offense, increase the offense level as follows:

(a) If the defendant was an organizer or leader of a criminal activity that involved five or more participants or was otherwise extensive, increase by **4** levels.

(b) If the defendant was a manager or supervisor (but not an organizer or leader) and the criminal activity involved five or more participants or was otherwise extensive, increase by **3** levels.

(c) If the defendant was an organizer, leader, manager, or supervisor in any criminal activity other than described in (a) or (b), increase by **2** levels.

§ 3B1.2. Mitigating Role

Based on the defendant's role in the offense, decrease the offense level as follows:

(a) If the defendant was a minimal participant in any criminal activity, decrease by **4** levels.

(b) If the defendant was a minor participant in any criminal activity, decrease by **2** levels.

In cases falling between (a) and (b), decrease by **3** levels.

United States v. Irlmeier

750 F.3d 759 (8th Cir. 2014)

■ SMITH, J.

Randy and Paul Irlmeier each pleaded guilty to one count of conspiracy to manufacture at least 100 marijuana plants, in violation of 21 U.S.C. §§ 846 and 841(b)(1)(B)(vii). The district court sentenced both defendants to 60 months' imprisonment—the mandatory minimum. The district court determined that their sentences warranted an aggravating role enhancement pursuant to U.S.S.G. § 3B1.1, which precluded them from obtaining safety-valve relief under 18 U.S.C. § 3553(f). * * *

I. *Background*

In October 2010, the Iowa Division of Narcotics Enforcement and the Audubon County Sheriff's Department executed a search warrant at Randy Irlmeier's ("Randy") farm in Coon Rapids, Iowa. Officers discovered a marijuana-grow operation. Officers found marijuana plants, an elaborate lighting and ventilation system, a calendar used to track the plants' growth, and tools and supplies used to cultivate the plants. Officers also found an outbuilding on the property that served as a drying room for the marijuana. In total, authorities seized almost 13 kilograms of marijuana from Randy's farm.

When interviewed, Randy identified his nephew, Paul Irlmeier ("Paul"), as someone who assisted him with the marijuana-grow operation. Thus, officers obtained a search warrant for Paul's farm in Audubon, Iowa, later that same day. Officers found over 116 grams of marijuana on the property.

* * * Both Randy and Paul pleaded guilty to conspiracy to manufacture at least 100 marijuana plants, in violation of 21 U.S.C. §§ 846 and 841(b)(1)(B)(vii). The statutory mandatory minimum for this offense is 60 months' imprisonment. The government dropped the remaining counts.

Both of their presentence reports (PSRs) recommended a total offense level of 23 and a criminal history category of I. Included in the calculation of each offense level was a four-level enhancement under U.S.S.G. § 3B1.1(a) for being an organizer or leader of criminal activity. Most importantly, this enhancement precluded both defendants from receiving statutory safety-valve relief. As a result, the PSRs calculated their Guidelines ranges to be 46–57 months. Because the mandatory minimum is 60 months, the Guidelines recommendation became 60 months.

Randy and Paul objected to the PSRs' determination that they were leaders or organizers of this criminal activity. [After a hearing, the district court overruled Randy and Paul's objections and imposed the mandatory minimum sentence of 60 months.]

II. *Discussion*

On appeal, both Randy and Paul dispute the district court's application of the aggravating role enhancement. * * *

According to 18 U.S.C. § 3553(f), a defendant may be eligible for a "safety valve." The so-called safety valve allows the district court to avoid imposing a mandatory minimum sentence. The safety valve, if applicable, would benefit defendants like Randy and Paul who were convicted of a crime under 21 U.S.C. §§ 841 and 846. *Id.* The statute enumerates five other eligibility requirements. *Id.* The only eligibility requirement at issue in this case is whether "the defendant was [ ] an organizer, leader, manager, or supervisor of others in the offense, as determined under the sentencing guidelines." * * *

As the district court noted, the precise level of enhancement is immaterial here. The relevant inquiry is whether the defendants qualify under *any* of these subsections [of § 3B1.1] such that they are an organizer, leader, manager, or supervisor and thus ineligible for safety-valve relief. * * *

The Guidelines also note:

> In distinguishing a leadership and organizational role from one of mere management or supervision, titles such as "kingpin" or "boss" are not controlling. Factors the court should consider include the exercise of decision making authority, the nature of participation in the commission of the offense, the recruitment of accomplices, the claimed right to a larger share of the fruits of the crime, the degree of participation in planning or organizing the offense, the nature and scope of the illegal activity, and the degree of control and authority exercised over

> others. There can, of course, be more than one person who qualifies as a leader or organizer of a criminal association or conspiracy. This adjustment does not apply to a defendant who merely suggests committing the offense.

U.S.S.G. § 3B1.1 cmt. n. 4. Although the purpose of comment note four is to help distinguish between leadership and management roles, we have considered the comment note instructive in determining whether a defendant qualifies for the safety valve. *See United States v. Gamboa,* 701 F.3d 265, 267 (8th Cir. 2012).

The government must demonstrate by a preponderance of the evidence that the defendants warrant the enhancement. "Merely distributing or selling drugs is not sufficient for the enhancement." *Id.* Nonetheless, we define "organizer" and "leader" broadly and "manager" and "supervisor" quite liberally. *United States v. Lopez,* 431 F.3d 313, 317–18 (8th Cir. 2005). In fact, defendants are subject to this enhancement even where they manage or supervise only one other participant in the conspiracy. *Id.* at 318. Furthermore, the enhancement "may apply even if the management activity was limited to a single transaction." *Lopez,* 431 F.3d at 318. The "defendant[s] must direct or enlist the aid of others." *Id.*

Additionally, "[w]e have never construed the terms . . . so narrowly as to restrict application of the enhancement solely to the organizer who first instigated the criminal activity." *United States v. Noe,* 411 F.3d 878, 889 (8th Cir. 2005). In fact, the defendant need not be the only leader or organizer, and the defendant need not lead or organize all of the participants. *Id.* Finally, we have previously rejected a defendant's contention that others helped him in furtherance of the conspiracy *sua sponte* and without coordination where it was clear that the defendant was the "driving force" behind the crime. *United States v. Rodgers,* 122 F.3d 1129, 1133–34 (8th Cir. 1997). * * *

A. *Paul Irlmeier*

Paul contends that "[w]hile the definition of organizer or leader may be broad, there must also be a point where the action taken [by coconspirators] is so insignificant that it does not constitute control over the person" such that a defendant cannot be considered a leader or organizer. However, our review of the record confirms that Paul qualifies for the U.S.S.G. § 3B1.1 enhancement so as to preclude safety-valve relief. First, the government presented testimony from Paul's ex-wife, Traci Irlmeier ("Traci"). Traci explained how Paul directed or ordered her to water marijuana plants. Traci also watched their children while Paul harvested marijuana; bought products like Ziploc bags, potting soil, and a food saver machine; watered Randy's marijuana plants; and transplanted marijuana plants, all at Paul's request and in furtherance of the conspiracy. Paul recruited Traci and directed her activities in the conspiracy. The district court did not err in determining that he was at least a supervisor of the operation. One transaction or occurrence is sufficient to qualify for the enhancement. Paul's conduct toward Traci is sufficient for Paul to qualify for the enhancement. * * *

B. *Randy Irlmeier*

In arguing against the enhancement, Randy avers that "the activity of any of the coconspirators was done voluntarily, without direction, instruction, or influence" such that the district court should not have applied the aggravating role enhancement. Randy references an occasion where Randy's girlfriend, Janice Wolfe, and her sister, Linda Southwell, traveled from their homes in South Carolina to visit Randy at his Iowa farm. During the visit, Wolfe and Southwell assisted Randy in cutting marijuana plants on one occasion. Wolfe testified that she cut the plants by voluntarily imitating Randy, for he never solicited her help in cutting the plants or instructed her how to cut them. Southwell testified that she did not remember receiving any invitation or instructions from Randy regarding the marijuana cutting. One of Randy's customers, Gene Weitl, also participated in this marijuana-cutting soiree, but he could not remember receiving any invitation or instructions from Randy. The district court apparently accepted these testimonies as true[.]

Thus, Randy questions whether the aggravating role enhancement applies where the coconspirators participated voluntarily and without his direction or instruction.

We need not answer this question because other facts demonstrate that Randy qualifies for the aggravating role enhancement. First, Traci testified that Paul watered Randy's marijuana plants occasionally while Randy was out of town because watering was part of Paul's "responsibility" to Randy. One can reasonably infer that Paul was responsible for this activity because of Randy's instruction. Additionally, Weitl testified that Randy asked him to retrieve a bag of marijuana from another building and deliver it to Randy, which Weitl did. Weitl also testified that he helped drill holes in the field for Randy so that Randy could plant marijuana. Randy's actions seem comparably more supervisory than the defendant in *Lopez* who merely asked his roommate to serve as a lookout on one occasion. *See* 431 F.3d at 318. Although not overwhelming, the evidence reflecting Randy's supervisory authority is sufficient. * * *

NOTES & QUESTIONS

1. **Purpose of Aggravating Role Enhancement.** In what ways does § 3B1.1 advance any of the standard purposes of punishment? Is there any greater culpability for the person who obtains the assistance of others in committing a crime than for the person who commits the same crime solo? Consider, for instance, the case of Paul Irlmeier, who obtained various rather mundane forms of assistance from his ex-wife Traci in his marijuana growing operation. Isn't the size of his crop the main determinant of his culpability? How is the social harm of his crime any different depending on whether he produced that crop alone or with help?

It might be argued that an organizer or manager causes greater harm, and is hence more culpable, for drawing others into a "life of crime" or exposing them to danger or legal liability. This argument would seem most compelling when the underlings have been procured through coercion, trickery, or psychological manipulation, or when juveniles have been roped in. There might or might not have been some pressure, deceit, or manipulation with Traci Irlmeier, but note that there is no indication in the Eighth Circuit's analysis that such facts would matter in the application of § 3B1.1. Indeed, the court indicated that the enhancement could even apply when others join a criminal activity *sua sponte.* In a similar vein, you might also consider Randy Irlmeier's "volunteers." Does it seem to you that there is enough added culpability on the part of the organizer/manager in such scenarios to warrant a longer prison sentence?

Perhaps utilitarian considerations might provide a stronger basis for § 3B1.1. It is commonly thought that coordinated groups of criminals pose a greater threat than individual criminals operating in isolation from one another. Groups potentially benefit from a division of labor and specialization of roles, permitting them to achieve greater sophistication and efficiency than "lone wolves." For this reason, the criminal who has demonstrated a capacity and willingness to attract and utilize associates may present elevated risks of serious criminal activity in the future—and hence may warrant a more severe sentence today for incapacitative purposes. Similarly, § 3B1.1 might conceivably deter individuals from trying to enlist others into their criminal activities in the first place.

In *Irlmeier*, the real question was whether the district court could sentence below a mandatory minimum. However, if there had been no minimum in play, the defendants might conceivably have sought a downward departure or variance under *Booker* in order to offset their aggravating role enhancements. If you were the district judge, would you grant such a variance—or are you convinced there were good reasons to extend Paul and Randy's prison sentences on the basis of the help they obtained from others?

2. **Mitigating Role Adjustment of § 3B1.2.** In the federal guidelines, offense severity factors are normally framed as aggravating and serve to *increase* sentence length when they are present. Section 3B1.2 is thus unusual in recognizing a factor that *decreases* offense severity and sentence length. The opaque terms "minimal" and "minor" participant are given somewhat greater clarity in the section's application notes:

> This section provides a range of adjustments for a defendant who plays a part in committing the offense that makes him substantially less culpable than the average participant in the criminal activity. * * *
>
> In determining whether to apply subsection (a) or (b), or an intermediate adjustment, the court should consider the following non-exhaustive list of factors:
>
> > (i) the degree to which the defendant understood the scope and structure of the criminal activity;

(ii) the degree to which the defendant participated in planning or organizing the criminal activity;

(iii) the degree to which the defendant exercised decision-making authority or influenced the exercise of decision-making authority;

(iv) the nature and extent of the defendant's participation in the commission of the criminal activity, including the acts the defendant performed and the responsibility and discretion the defendant had in performing those acts;

(v) the degree to which the defendant stood to benefit from the criminal activity.

For example, a defendant who does not have a proprietary interest in the criminal activity and who is simply being paid to perform certain tasks should be considered for an adjustment under this guideline.

The fact that a defendant performs an essential or indispensable role in the criminal activity is not determinative. Such a defendant may receive an adjustment under this guideline if he or she is substantially less culpable than the average participant in the criminal activity.

The application notes seem to lay particular emphasis on the diminished culpability of the minimal or minor participant as the basis for a reduced sentence. Do you think there might also be good utilitarian grounds for § 3B1.2?

3. **Captain and Crew.** For an illustration of the application of § 3B1.2, consider *United States v. Arias-Mercedes*, 901 F.3d 1 (1st Cir. 2018). Arias-Mercedes and two other men, Concepción and Mercedes, were charged with attempting to smuggle a large quantity of cocaine into the United States aboard a twenty-foot vessel that was intercepted *en route* from the Dominican Republic to Puerto Rico. Arias-Mercedes pled guilty and sought a mitigating role adjustment. He pointed to the greater responsibility of Mercedes, who captained the vessel. Arias-Mercedes himself had no role in planning or organizing the venture, but only served as a crewman. Nonetheless, the district court denied an adjustment, and the First Circuit affirmed. The latter court emphasized two considerations. First, Arias-Mercedes "exercised a modicum of decisionmaking authority in steering and navigating the vessel toward its destination." Second, Arias-Mercedes "stood to benefit from the criminal activity. He was paid handsomely to traverse the Caribbean Sea and, in addition, received what he had sought all along: passage to the United States." Thus, the mere fact of being in a subordinate position in the criminal endeavor did not entitle Arias-Mercedes to an adjustment in light of his (fairly minimal) decisionmaking authority and his expectation of substantial benefits from the endeavor.

4. **The Courier Problem.** The person who acts as a courier for drugs or other contraband presents a recurring problem for § 3B1.2. Courts have resisted categorical rules in this area. *See, e.g., United States v. Nkome*, 987 F.3d 1262, 1277 (10th Cir. 2021) ("[W]e have consistently held that courier

or mule status does not invariably qualify a defendant for a mitigating-role adjustment." (citations and internal quotation marks omitted)). The Second Circuit, for instance, indicates that the "inquiry is highly fact-intensive and, in cases involving drug couriers, necessarily depends on such factors as the nature of the defendant's relationship to other participants, the importance of the defendant's actions to the success of the venture, and the defendant's awareness of the nature and scope of the criminal enterprise." *United States v. Kerr*, 752 F.3d 206, 223 (2d Cir. 2014) (citation and internal quotation marks omitted).

On the one hand, couriers play an essential role in the commission of some crimes, such as the importation of drugs across national borders, which might make couriers seem inappropriate for a mitigating role adjustment. On the other hand, their work may involve little decisionmaking authority, little knowledge of the overall drug distribution scheme, and little compensation. Consider, for instance, the facts of *United States v. Silva-De Hoyos*, 702 F.3d 843 (5th Cir. 2012) The defendant was arrested at the U.S.-Mexico border after 12.36 kilograms of cocaine were found hidden in the vehicle he was driving. He claimed that he did not know the amount or type of drugs in the car, and that he only agreed to serve as a courier because of threats made to his family by a Mexican drug trafficker. Law enforcement agents found this statement credible, and it seems that no contrary evidence was presented. Nonetheless, citing the importance of the defendant's role to the criminal scheme, the district court denied him a § 3B1.2 adjustment, and the Fifth Circuit affirmed.

3. QUANTITATIVE FACTORS

The harm caused or intended by a defendant is often regarded as an important—if not the *most* important—offense-severity factor. In certain kinds of cases, harm may seem reasonably closely correlated with some quantifiable variable. Theft of money presents perhaps the clearest, least controversial example—the specific amount of money taken often appear a reasonably fair measure of the harm done. A theft of $10,000 will normally seem a significantly more serious offense than a theft of $1,000, which will, in turn, normally seem a significantly more serious offense than a theft of $10. Note, though, that even in the context of monetary theft, focusing exclusively on the quantitative variable may sometimes be misleading. For instance, stealing $1000 from a working-class family living from paycheck to paycheck may have a far more devastating impact than stealing $10,000 from a more well-to-do family. Additionally, some thefts inflict a psychological harm on the victim that is as great or greater than the economic harm, as sometimes occurs when the theft involves a betrayal of trust. Nonetheless, offense severity for theft and other property crimes is often assessed based largely on a number—the dollar value of what the victim lost or the defendant intended to take.

As with property offenses, the sentencing of drug trafficking offenses may also be driven by a number, that is, the quantity of drugs involved in the offense. Here, too, that number may at first blush seem a reasonable proxy for harm. Doesn't the defendant who distributes, say, one *gram* of heroin likely cause far less damage to society than the defendant who distributes one *kilogram*? However, such simplistic numerical comparisons may be confounded by a variety of other considerations, including drug purity and role in the offense.

In a discretionary sentencing system, a judge is able to put the numbers into context. Greater concerns are raised by the use of quantitative factors in a presumptive or mandatory sentencing scheme, which normally involves drawing artificial lines along a continuum—cross a line and you face a more severe sentence. By way of illustration, consider the loss table in the federal robbery guideline, § 2B3.1(b)(7), reprinted in Chapter 2. There seems little practical difference between a robbery that nets $20,000 and an otherwise-identical robbery that nets $21,000, but the latter crosses a line in the loss continuum that triggers a higher sentencing range. Indeed, some arbitrariness seems inevitable with any sentencing scheme that attempts to draw quantitative distinctions. A certain amount of arbitrariness on the margins can probably be justified on the basis of the relative predictability and consistency offered by objective sentencing factors. Consider, for instance, whether you think it would be better for the loss component of the robbery guideline to be structured in the same sort of qualitative fashion as are the role-in-the-offense guidelines. You might imagine a scheme, for instance, in which the judge would have to classify the loss as "minimal," "minor," "moderate," "aggravated," or "extreme."

While the occasional arbitrariness around the margins in some quantitative schemes may seem an acceptable trade-off for greater predictability and consistency, the line-drawing in other schemes may strike you as unfair or ill-advised in a more fundamental way. For instance, over the past half-century, there has probably been no line-drawing exercise in the federal sentencing system that has been more controversial than that for crack cocaine offenses. The relevant history and policy concerns were outlined by the Supreme Court in *Kimbrough v. United States*, 552 U.S. 85 (2007):

> Under the statute criminalizing the manufacture and distribution of crack cocaine, 21 U.S.C. § 841, and the relevant Guidelines prescription, § 2D1.1, a drug trafficker dealing in crack cocaine is subject to the same sentence as one dealing in 100 times more powder cocaine. . . .
>
> Crack and powder cocaine are two forms of the same drug. Powder cocaine, or cocaine hydrochloride, is generally inhaled through the nose; it may also be mixed with water and injected. *See* United States Sentencing Commission, Special Report to Congress: Cocaine and Federal Sentencing Policy 5, 12 (Feb. 1995) (hereinafter 1995 Report). Crack cocaine, a type of cocaine base, is formed by dissolving powder cocaine and baking soda in boiling water. The resulting solid is divided into single-dose

"rocks" that users smoke. The active ingredient in powder and crack cocaine is the same. The two forms of the drug also have the same physiological and psychotropic effects, but smoking crack cocaine allows the body to absorb the drug much faster than inhaling powder cocaine, and thus produces a shorter, more intense high.

Although chemically similar, crack and powder cocaine are handled very differently for sentencing purposes. The 100-to-1 ratio yields sentences for crack offenses three to six times longer than those for powder offenses involving equal amounts of drugs. See United States Sentencing Commission, Report to Congress: Cocaine and Federal Sentencing Policy iv (May 2002) (hereinafter 2002 Report). This disparity means that a major supplier of powder cocaine may receive a shorter sentence than a low-level dealer who buys powder from the supplier but then converts it to crack.

The crack/powder disparity originated in the Anti-Drug Abuse Act of 1986 (1986 Act). The 1986 Act created a two-tiered scheme of five- and ten-year mandatory minimum sentences for drug manufacturing and distribution offenses. Congress sought "to link the ten-year mandatory minimum trafficking prison term to major drug dealers and to link the five-year minimum term to serious traffickers." 1995 Report 119. The 1986 Act uses the weight of the drugs involved in the offense as the sole proxy to identify "major" and "serious" dealers. . . .

Crack cocaine was a relatively new drug when the 1986 Act was signed into law, but it was already a matter of great public concern: "Drug abuse in general, and crack cocaine in particular, had become in public opinion and in members' minds a problem of overwhelming dimensions." 1995 Report 121. Congress apparently believed that crack was significantly more dangerous than powder cocaine . . . .

Based on these assumptions, the 1986 Act adopted a "100-to-1 ratio" that treated every gram of crack cocaine as the equivalent of 100 grams of powder cocaine. The 1986 Act's five-year mandatory minimum applies to any defendant accountable for 5 grams of crack or 500 grams of powder, 21 U.S.C. § 841(b)(1)(B)(ii), (iii); its ten-year mandatory minimum applies to any defendant accountable for 50 grams of crack or 5,000 grams of powder, § 841(b)(1)(A)(ii), (iii).

While Congress was considering adoption of the 1986 Act, the Sentencing Commission was engaged in formulating the Sentencing Guidelines. In the main, the Commission developed Guidelines sentences using an empirical approach based on data about past sentencing practices, including 10,000 presentence investigation reports. . . .

> The Commission did not use this empirical approach in developing the Guidelines sentences for drug-trafficking offenses. Instead, it employed the 1986 Act's weight-driven scheme. The Guidelines use a drug quantity table based on drug type and weight to set base offense levels for drug-trafficking offenses. In setting offense levels for crack and powder cocaine, the Commission, in line with the 1986 Act, adopted the 100-to-1 ratio. The statute itself specifies only two quantities of each drug, but the Guidelines "go further and set sentences for the full range of possible drug quantities using the same 100-to-1 quantity ratio." 1995 Report 1. . . .
>
> Although the Commission immediately used the 100-to-1 ratio to define base offense levels for all crack and powder offenses, it later determined that the crack/powder sentencing disparity is generally unwarranted. . . . In a series of reports, the Commission identified three problems with the crack/powder disparity.
>
> First, the Commission reported, the 100-to-1 ratio rested on assumptions about "the relative harmfulness of the two drugs and the relative prevalence of certain harmful conduct associated with their use and distribution that more recent research and data no longer support." *Ibid.* . . .
>
> Second, the Commission concluded that the crack/powder disparity is inconsistent with the 1986 Act's goal of punishing major drug traffickers more severely than low-level dealers. Drug importers and major traffickers generally deal in powder cocaine, which is then converted into crack by street-level sellers. But the 100-to-1 ratio can lead to the "anomalous" result that "retail crack dealers get longer sentences than the wholesale drug distributors who supply them the powder cocaine from which their crack is produced." *Id.,* at 174.
>
> Finally, the Commission stated that the crack/powder sentencing differential "fosters disrespect for and lack of confidence in the criminal justice system" because of a "widely-held perception" that it "promotes unwarranted disparity based on race." 2002 Report 103. Approximately 85 percent of defendants convicted of crack offenses in federal court are black; thus the severe sentences required by the 100-to-1 ratio are imposed "primarily upon black offenders." *Ibid.*

Id. at 91, 94–98.

In *Kimbrough*, the Court held that district judges may reject the guidelines' 100-to-1 ratio. However, the Court did not *require* judges to impose below-guidelines sentences in crack cases. Moreover, *Kimbrough* did nothing to free sentencing judges from the *statutory* 100:1 ratio that was built into the five- and ten-year mandatory minimum sentences of the Anti-Drug Abuse Act of 1986. Congress finally responded to longstanding criticisms of the statutory 100:1 ratio in the Fair Sentencing of 2010, which raised the minimum-triggering quantities for crack distribution. Although the Obama Administration initially pressed for equalization of crack and powder penalties, the final version of the legislation embodied a compromise 18:1 ratio. MICHAEL O'HEAR, THE FAILED PROMISE OF SENTENCING REFORM 123–24 (2017). By that time, the Sentencing Commission had already moderated, but not eliminated, the disparate treatment of crack and powder in the guidelines. *Id.* at 121.

NOTES & QUESTIONS

1. **Weight-Based Drug Sentencing.** Weight-based drug sentencing became established in federal law in the 1980s. MICHAEL O'HEAR, WISCONSIN SENTENCING IN THE TOUGH-ON-CRIME ERA 171 (2017). As indicated in *Kimbrough*, the idea in setting weight-based statutory sentencing ranges was to distinguish "major drug dealers" from other "serious traffickers," and serious traffickers from even lower-level participants in the drug trade. In theory, Congress could have pursued this aim through *qualitative*, rather than *quantitative*, distinctions. For instance, a judge or jury's finding that the defendant was a "major drug dealer" might have been made the trigger for the ten-year minimum, rather than a finding that the defendant was responsible for a particular weight of drugs. Congress's decision to use the quantitative approach was consistent with its general emphasis in the 1980s on achieving greater consistency and transparency in sentencing decisions. Recall, in particular, that this was the decade when Congress eliminated federal parole and authorized creation of the federal sentencing guidelines.

In hindsight, it may have been unfortunate that Congress chose to establish a new weight-based approach to drug sentencing in the mid- and late 1980s, when public concern regarding drugs was reaching a fever-pitch. For instance, in public opinion surveys, the mention of drugs as the nation's top problem peaked in 1990 and fell steadily thereafter. PRINCETON SURVEY RESEARCH ASSOCIATES INT'L, NCSC SENTENCING ATTITUDES SURVEY: A REPORT OF THE FINDINGS 13 (2006). In the political environment of the 1980s, Congress understandably seemed to err on the side of severity in structuring the new weight-based scheme. For the most part, the punitiveness of the 1980s has remained locked into the federal statutory sentencing ranges even as public attitudes have shifted in favor of more rehabilitative responses to drug crime. Moreover, as *Kimbrough* noted, the Sentencing Commission followed Congress's lead in establishing its weight-based system for the federal sentencing guidelines. Many states likewise imitated the federal model.

2. **Does *Kimbrough* Have Broader Implications for Quantitative Sentencing Factors in the Guidelines?** *Kimbrough* held that a district court may impose a below-guidelines sentence even in a "mine-run" (that is, typical or heartland) case based the court's disagreement with the severity of the crack guidelines. Would a district court be permitted to do the same in a case involving a *different* quantitative guideline?

Of course, post-*Booker*, there is little question that a below-guidelines sentence could be imposed if the court identified something about the case that was factually unusual and relevant to the purposes of punishment. It is the mine-run cases that present the greater difficulty. For instance, public attitudes and state policies regarding marijuana have changed dramatically over the past decade or two. Yet, the federal guidelines continue to call for substantial terms of imprisonment in many marijuana cases, depending largely on the weight of marijuana involved. By way of illustration, recall the *Irlmeier* case from the previous section, in which the marijuana growers faced guidelines ranges of 46–57 months in prison. Could a district court in a mine-run marijuana case impose a below-guidelines sentence simply on the ground that the guidelines treat marijuana offenses too harshly as a general matter?

Kimbrough did not provide an entirely clear answer to this question. Parts of the opinion that emphasize the advisory nature of the guidelines post-*Booker* might imply broad authority on the part of district courts to select a below-guidelines sentence on nearly any articulated ground that can be rationally related to the purposes of punishment. On the other hand, *Kimbrough* took some pains to recount the unique history and particular criticisms of the crack guidelines. These guidelines, the Court observed, "do not exemplify the [Sentencing] Commission's exercise of its characteristic institutional role" as an expert agency but were instead simply a matter of following Congress's (ill-advised) cues. Do such observations imply that district courts should generally go along with other guidelines that were developed by the Commission in its more "characteristic" fashion?[19]

However much additional flexibility there is in the application of the *guidelines* post-*Booker*, it is important to recall that the weight-based *statutory minimums* remain binding and constitute an important sentencing floor in many federal drug cases. The "safety valve" of 18 U.S.C. § 3553(f) permits sentences below the minimum in certain cases, but a defendant may be disqualified from the safety valve by criminal history, use of violence, possession of a firearm, or (as we saw in *Irlmeier*) an aggravating role in the offense, among other limitations. Do you think the safety valve should be liberalized, or would that undermine the benefits of having the seemingly objective weight-based system?

3. **Finding the Quantity.** Quantitative sentencing factors provide a reassuring appearance of objectivity, but that objectivity may be an illusion if the underlying fact-finding processes are unreliable. In the drug area, a particular concern has been the need in many cases to rely on the testimony

[19] The guideline for possession of child pornography, § 2G2.2, is another that been found by several district courts not to reflect the work of the Commission in its characteristic institutional role. *See, e.g., United States v. Beiermann*, 599 F. Supp. 2d 1087, 1100 (N.D. Iowa 2009) ("[N]umerous district courts ha[ve] read *Kimbrough* to permit a sentencing court to give little deference to the guideline for child pornography cases on the ground that the guideline did not exemplify the Sentencing Commission's exercise of its characteristic institutional role and empirical analysis, but was the result of congressional mandates, often passed by Congress with little debate or analysis." (citing eleven earlier district court decisions)).

of the defendant's coconspirators to determine quantity.[20] Coconspirators usually have their own liability to worry about, which may give them an incentive to blame-shift or, in the interest of obtaining a favorable cooperation agreement, to exaggerate their knowledge of the workings of the conspiracy. You might recall, for instance, *Mitchell v. United States*, the self-incrimination case from Chapter 3, in which the key quantity decision was made mostly on the basis of testimony from three of the defendant's coconspirators, all of whom had cut deals with the government.

In many guilty-plea cases, the defendant actually stipulates to the drug quantity. In such cases, your concerns about unfairness to the defendant may be alleviated—but only to the extent that you regard the underlying plea-bargaining as fair. A recurring criticism of mandatory minimums, which are commonly in play in federal drug distribution cases, is that they give too much leverage to prosecutors and effectively coerce some defendants into conceding litigable issues. *See* Ronald F. Wright, *Trial Distortion and the End of Innocence in Federal Criminal Justice*, 154 U. PA. L. REV. 79, 153 (2005).

4. **Mixtures and Purity.** Should purity matter in the application of the weight-based system? Imagine two individuals, A and B, who each sell five grams of what purports to be heroin. The crimes of A and B are identical in all respects, except that A's "heroin" is 80% pure, while B's has been more diluted with various inert substances and is only 40% pure. Should the harm of the two crimes be regarded as equivalent since the weight of the two mixtures was the same? Or is A's crime twice as harmful since the amount of actual heroin she sold was twice as great? Or does some third approach seem preferable?

In general, federal law disregards purity and bases sentences on the weight of the *mixture*. *See, e.g., Chapman v. United States*, 500 U.S. 453, 461 (1991) ("Congress adopted a 'market-oriented' approach to punishing drug trafficking, under which the total quantity of what is distributed, rather than the amount of pure drug involved, is used to determine the length of the sentence."). The guidelines generally reflect this approach, although with methamphetamine and a few other drugs, a sentence may be increased through an alternative calculation based on the "actual" drug quantity. § 2D1.1(c). Upward departures are also expressly authorized in cases involving drugs of "unusually high purity." § 2D1.1 cmt. n.27(C).

Note that disregarding purity may benefit some defendants who are higher on the distribution chain in comparison to those who are closer to the retail purchaser, since drugs may be mixed with other substances as they move through the distribution chain in order to increase profits or facilitate street sales.

5. **Conspiracies.** Drug distribution conspiracies may involve multiple individuals who play a wide variety of different roles. In a large-scale conspiracy, there are apt to be some participants who have little or no knowledge about—let alone ability to control—what other participants are

[20] Review question: under what circumstances would the defendant have a right to a jury trial on drug quantity?

doing. This presents some difficulty for the weight-based system. Should each conspirator be held accountable for the full quantity of drugs that the group as a whole distributed or attempted to distribute, for only that quantity with which the individual conspirator was directly involved, or for some in-between quantity?

The guidelines take a middle-ground position. Under the guidelines' "relevant conduct" provision, a person's sentence is based on the conduct of coconspirators only if the conduct falls "within the scope of the jointly undertaken criminal activity," is committed "in furtherance of that criminal activity," and is "reasonably foreseeable in connection with that criminal activity." § 1B1.3 cmt. n.3(A) (2018).

Should the same approach be used in determining *statutory* sentencing ranges? This question has divided the federal circuits into two camps. *See United States v. Collazo,* 984 F.3d 1308, 1335–36 (9th Cir. 2021) (en banc) (summarizing circuit split). Some circuits utilize the guidelines' reasonable foreseeability standard, reasoning that it is in line with traditional substantive criminal law rules regarding liability for coconspirators' offenses. *See, e.g., United States v. Stoddard,* 892 F.3d 1203, 1221 (D.C. Cir. 2018). Other circuits see no basis for a reasonable foreseeability requirement in the text of the relevant statute and hold that each conspirator should be liable for the full quantity of drugs attributed to the conspiracy as a whole. *See, e.g., Collazo,* 984 F.3d at 1336.

Does either approach fairly capture the defendant's culpability? As we have seen, many commentators would particularly associate a defendant's blameworthiness with his or her *mens rea,* asking what harm the defendant intended or expected from his or her conduct. Yet, even that which is "reasonably foreseeable" is not necessarily actually anticipated. Invoking the criminal law's traditional emphasis on *mens rea,* a group of Ninth Circuit judges, dissenting from a recent en banc opinion, argued that in order to trigger the weight-based mandatory minimums in a drug conspiracy case, the government should have to prove that the individual defendant "knowingly or intentionally" distributed whatever the triggering quantity was. *Collazo,* 984 F.3d at 1338 (Fletcher, J., dissenting). The majority countered that "the imposition of an additional burden on the government to prove the conspirator's knowledge of drug type and quantity would serve only to make it more difficult to obtain convictions on charges of conspiracy, a policy with no apparent purpose." *Id.* at 1333 (internal quotation marks and citation omitted). Do you agree that no purpose would be served by the dissenters' proposed rule?

As with many other controversial aspects of the weight-based approach, the rules for dealing with conspiracies might seem less problematic if there were more robust mitigating-role adjustments available, including with respect to the statutory minimums.

6. **Entrapment.** Quantitative sentencing factors can invite government manipulation. In the drug area, for instance, an undercover agent might encourage a suspect to engage in more or larger sales in order

to bring the suspect over a threshold into a higher guidelines range or so as to trigger a weight-based statutory minimum.

Two provisions of the guidelines address what is variously called "sentence entrapment" or "sentence factor manipulation."[21] First, the guidelines provide,

> If, in a reverse sting (an operation in which a government agent sells or negotiates to sell a controlled substance to a defendant), the court finds that the government agent set a price for the controlled substance that was substantially below the market value of the controlled substance, thereby leading to the defendant's purchase of a significantly greater quantity of the controlled substance than his available resources would have allowed him to purchase except for the artificially low price set by the government agent, a downward departure may be warranted.

§ 2D1.1 cmt. n.27(A). Second, in cases which the defendant agreed to buy or sell a quantity of drugs, the amount agreed to is generally the governing quantity, but if "the defendant establishes that the defendant did not intend to provide or purchase, or was not reasonably capable of providing or purchasing, the agreed-upon quantity of the controlled substance, the court shall exclude from the offense level determination the amount of controlled substance that the defendant establishes that the defendant did not intend to provide or purchase or was not reasonably capable of providing or purchasing." § 2D1.1 cmt. n.5.

In addition to these guidelines provisions, some courts indicate that factor manipulation may be taken into account in the post-*Booker* sentencing analysis under 18 U.S.C. § 3553(a). *See, e.g., United States v. Knox*, 573 F.3d 451, 452 (7th Cir. 2009). Some courts further indicate that, in some circumstances, manipulation may violate the Due Process Clause. For instance, the Eighth Circuit holds that unconstitutional sentence manipulation "occurs when the government unfairly exaggerates the defendant's sentencing range by engaging in a longer-than-needed investigation and, thus, increasing the drug quantities for which the defendant is responsible." *United States v. Torres*, 563 F.3d 731, 734 (8th Cir. 2009). However, the caselaw in this area is marked by much inter-circuit variation and has been characterized as simply "chaotic." Molly F. Spakowski, Comment, *Crafted from Whole Cloth: Reverse Stash-House Stings and the Sentencing Factor Manipulation Claim*, 67 BUFF. L. REV. 451, 481 (2019).

7. **Methamphetamine Sentencing.** Even as criticism of federal crack sentencing policy swelled in the 1990s and early 2000s, Congress and the Sentencing Commission repeatedly increased penalties for methamphetamine offenses. When Congress finally softened crack penalties in 2010, it did nothing to reduce meth sentences—thus opening a sizable gap

[21] The two terms are sometimes used synonymously by the courts, and sometimes differentiated from one another, but not in entirely consistent ways. *See* Molly F. Spakowski, Comment, *Crafted from Whole Cloth: Reverse Stash-House Stings and the Sentencing Factor Manipulation Claim*, 67 BUFF. L. REV. 451, 479–92 (2019) (summarizing caselaw from each federal circuit).

in the treatment of crack and meth. Meth sentences are now said to be more than five times greater than the sentences for comparable crack offenses, with even larger disparities for offenses involving the crystalline form of methamphetamine ("ice"). Lex A. Coleman, *Crack 2.0: Federal Methamphetamine Policy, the Crack/Meth Sentencing Disparity, and the Meth/Meth-Mixture Ratio—Why Drug Type, Quantity, and Purity Remain "Incredibly Poor Proxies" for Sentencing Culpability Under 21 U.S.C. § 841(b) and U.S.S.G. § 2D1.1*, 34 FED. SENT'G REP. 29, 30 (2021).

Since 2009, meth cases have surpassed marijuana, cocaine, and crack cases in number to become by far the largest share of the federal drug enforcement docket. Jake J. Smith, *Why Are Federal Meth Sentences Getting Longer?*, 34 FED. SENT'G REP. 44, 45 (2021). Over the same time period, the median federal meth sentence increased from 72 to 78 months—even as the median crack sentence fell from 96 to 60 months. *Id.*

The weight-based meth minimums and guidelines have been subject in recent years to many of the same criticisms that motivated crack sentencing reform, albeit without the particular racial concerns that were so prominent in the crack area. For a history and critique of federal meth sentencing policy, see Coleman, *supra*.

8. **Other Quantitative Guidelines.** Although the weight-based drug guidelines have attracted the most critical comment over the years, quantitative provisions are found throughout the federal guidelines. For instance, § 2B1.1, the guideline for fraud and a number of other economic offenses, relies heavily on a complex loss table with sixteen different categories, ranging from $6,500 or less to more than $550 million. The guideline covering receipt of child pornography, § 2G2.2, includes enhancements based on the number of images received, with categories ranging from under 10 to 600 or more. The guideline for unlawful receipt, possession, or transportation of firearms, § 2K2.1, similarly includes an enhancement for the number of firearms involved, with categories ranging from under 3 to 200 or more. Many further illustrations could be supplied. Such provisions have contributed much to the federal guidelines' reputation for being overly complex and mechanical.

4. MOTIVE & HATE CRIMES

Motive is not usually an issue in determining criminal liability. If a person steals drugs from a pharmacy, the person's guilt does not depend on whether the drugs were stolen to save a sick child or for resale on the black market. However, such considerations of motive may play an important role in determining the sentence. From a retributive standpoint, motive may be relevant to determining whether there was some partial justification for the crime, which could reduce culpability. Understanding the defendant's motive may also shed light on the deliberateness of the defendant's criminal conduct. From a utilitarian standpoint, motive may provide insight into the defendant's recidivism risk and the likelihood that the defendant would benefit from rehabilitative treatment. For instance, in order to most effectively manage a residential burglar's recidivism risk it might be very helpful to know whether the burglary was motivated by a need to obtain money in order to support a drug habit, by a wish to impress juvenile peers, or by a malicious desire to harm the victim homeowner. *See generally* Carissa Byrne Hessick, *Motive's Role in Criminal Punishment*, 80 S. CAL. L. REV. 89 (2006) (discussing reasons why motive might be relevant at sentencing and arguing for more systematic consideration of this factor).

The federal sentencing guidelines contain no general motive provision, but specific motive issues are handled in a variety of different guidelines. For instance, § 5K2.11 provides as follows:

> Sometimes, a defendant may commit a crime in order to avoid a perceived greater harm. In such instances, a reduced sentence may be appropriate, provided that the circumstances significantly diminish society's interest in punishing the conduct, for example, in the case of a mercy killing. Where the interest in punishment or deterrence is not reduced, a reduction in sentence is not warranted. For example, providing defense secrets to a hostile power should receive no lesser punishment simply because the defendant believed that the government's policies were misdirected.

For additional illustrations of the use of motive as a sentencing factor in the guidelines, see, for instance, § 2B2.1(b)(3) (in burglary guideline, increasing offense level if taking of "firearm, destructive device, or controlled substance . . . was an object of the offense"); § 2B5.3(b)(4) (in guideline for criminal copyright and trademark infringements, decreasing offense level if "the offense was not committed for commercial advantage or private financial gain"); § 2G2.2(b)(3) (in guideline for distribution of child pornography, increasing offense level if distribution was for pecuniary gain or "was intended to persuade, induce, entice, coerce, or facilitate the travel of, the minor to engage in prohibited sexual conduct"); § 3A1.4(a) (increasing offense level if offense was intended to promote a "federal crime of terrorism," defined in part by 18 U.S.C. § 2332b(g)(5) as an offense that "is calculated to influence or affect the conduct of government by intimidation or coercion, or to retaliate against government conduct").

In the remainder of this section, we will focus on one particular motive-based type of sentence enhancement. "Hate-crime" enhancements are triggered when a victim was targeted as a result of some protected personal characteristic. You may recall, for instance, that such an enhancement was at issue in *Apprendi v. New Jersey*, the pathbreaking Supreme Court case the expanded procedural rights for defendants at sentencing. For another illustration, consider the hate-crime provision of the federal guidelines:

> If the finder of fact at trial or, in the case of a plea of guilty or nolo contendere, the court at sentencing determines beyond a reasonable doubt that the defendant intentionally selected any

> victim or any property as the object of the offense of conviction because of the actual or perceived race, color, religion, national origin, ethnicity, gender, gender identity, disability, or sexual orientation of any person, increase by 3 levels.

§ 3A1.1(a).

A common criticism of hate-crimes legislation has been that such laws may threaten core freedoms of thought and expression. The Supreme Court considered a constitutional challenge raising such concerns in the following case.

Wisconsin v. Mitchell

508 U.S. 476 (1993)

■ REHNQUIST, C.J.

Respondent Todd Mitchell's sentence for aggravated battery was enhanced because he intentionally selected his victim on account of the victim's race. The question presented in this case is whether this penalty enhancement is prohibited by the First and Fourteenth Amendments. We hold that it is not.

On the evening of October 7, 1989, a group of young black men and boys, including Mitchell, gathered at an apartment complex in Kenosha, Wisconsin. Several members of the group discussed a scene from the motion picture "Mississippi Burning," in which a white man beat a young black boy who was praying. The group moved outside and Mitchell asked them: "Do you all feel hyped up to move on some white people?" Shortly thereafter, a young white boy approached the group on the opposite side of the street where they were standing. As the boy walked by, Mitchell said: "You all want to fuck somebody up? There goes a white boy; go get him." Mitchell counted to three and pointed in the boy's direction. The group ran toward the boy, beat him severely, and stole his tennis shoes. The boy was rendered unconscious and remained in a coma for four days.

After a jury trial in the Circuit Court for Kenosha County, Mitchell was convicted of aggravated battery. That offense ordinarily carries a maximum sentence of two years' imprisonment. But because the jury found that Mitchell had intentionally selected his victim because of the boy's race, the maximum sentence for Mitchell's offense was increased to seven years under § 939.645. That provision enhances the maximum penalty for an offense whenever the defendant "[i]ntentionally selects the person against whom the crime . . . is committed . . . because of the race, religion, color, disability, sexual orientation, national origin or ancestry of that person. . . ." The Circuit Court sentenced Mitchell to four years' imprisonment for the aggravated battery.

Mitchell unsuccessfully sought postconviction relief in the Circuit Court. Then he appealed his conviction and sentence, challenging the constitutionality of Wisconsin's penalty-enhancement provision on First

Amendment grounds. The Wisconsin Court of Appeals rejected Mitchell's challenge, but the Wisconsin Supreme Court reversed. The Supreme Court held that the statute "violates the First Amendment directly by punishing what the legislature has deemed to be offensive thought." It rejected the State's contention "that the statute punishes only the 'conduct' of intentional selection of a victim." According to the court, "[t]he statute punishes the 'because of' aspect of the defendant's selection, the *reason* the defendant selected the victim, the *motive* behind the selection." And under *R.A.V. v. St. Paul,* 505 U.S. 377 (1992), "the Wisconsin legislature cannot criminalize bigoted thought with which it disagrees."

The Supreme Court also held that the penalty-enhancement statute was unconstitutionally overbroad. It reasoned that, in order to prove that a defendant intentionally selected his victim because of the victim's protected status, the State would often have to introduce evidence of the defendant's prior speech, such as racial epithets he may have uttered before the commission of the offense. This evidentiary use of protected speech, the court thought, would have a "chilling effect" on those who feared the possibility of prosecution for offenses subject to penalty enhancement. Finally, the court distinguished antidiscrimination laws, which have long been held constitutional, on the ground that the Wisconsin statute punishes the "subjective mental process" of selecting a victim because of his protected status, whereas antidiscrimination laws prohibit "objective acts of discrimination." * * *

The State argues that the statute does not punish bigoted thought, as the Supreme Court of Wisconsin said, but instead punishes only conduct. While this argument is literally correct, it does not dispose of Mitchell's First Amendment challenge. To be sure, our cases reject the "view that an apparently limitless variety of conduct can be labeled 'speech' whenever the person engaging in the conduct intends thereby to express an idea." *United States v. O'Brien,* 391 U.S. 367, 376 (1968). Thus, a physical assault is not by any stretch of the imagination expressive conduct protected by the First Amendment.

But the fact remains that under the Wisconsin statute the same criminal conduct may be more heavily punished if the victim is selected because of his race or other protected status than if no such motive obtained. Thus, although the statute punishes criminal conduct, it enhances the maximum penalty for conduct motivated by a discriminatory point of view more severely than the same conduct engaged in for some other reason or for no reason at all. Because the only reason for the enhancement is the defendant's discriminatory motive for selecting his victim, Mitchell argues (and the Wisconsin Supreme Court held) that the statute violates the First Amendment by punishing offenders' bigoted beliefs.

Traditionally, sentencing judges have considered a wide variety of factors in addition to evidence bearing on guilt in determining what sentence to impose on a convicted defendant. The defendant's motive for committing the offense is one important factor. Thus, in many States the commission of a murder, or other capital offense, for pecuniary gain is a separate aggravating circumstance under the capital sentencing statute.

But it is equally true that a defendant's abstract beliefs, however obnoxious to most people, may not be taken into consideration by a sentencing judge. *Dawson v. Delaware,* 503 U.S. 159 (1992). In *Dawson,* the State introduced evidence at a capital sentencing hearing that the defendant was a member of a white supremacist prison gang. Because "the evidence proved nothing more than [the defendant's] abstract beliefs," we held that its admission violated the defendant's First Amendment rights. *Id.,* at 167. In so holding, however, we emphasized that "the Constitution does not erect a *per se* barrier to the admission of evidence concerning one's beliefs and associations at sentencing simply because those beliefs and associations are protected by the First Amendment." *Id.,* at 165. Thus, in *Barclay v. Florida,* 463 U.S. 939 (1983) (plurality opinion), we allowed the sentencing judge to take into account the defendant's racial animus towards his victim. The evidence in that case showed that the defendant's membership in the Black Liberation Army and desire to provoke a "race war" were related to the murder of a white man for which he was convicted. Because "the elements of racial hatred in [the] murder" were relevant to several aggravating factors, we held that the trial judge permissibly took this evidence into account in sentencing the defendant to death. *Id.,* at 949, and n. 7. * * *

Mitchell argues that the Wisconsin penalty-enhancement statute is invalid because it punishes the defendant's discriminatory motive, or reason, for acting. But motive plays the same role under the Wisconsin statute as it does under federal and state antidiscrimination laws, which we have previously upheld against constitutional challenge. Title VII of the Civil Rights Act of 1964, for example, makes it unlawful for an employer to discriminate against an employee "*because of* such individual's race, color, religion, sex, or national origin."

Nothing in our decision last Term in *R.A.V.* compels a different result here. That case involved a First Amendment challenge to a municipal ordinance prohibiting the use of " 'fighting words' that insult, or provoke violence, 'on the basis of race, color, creed, religion or gender.' " 505 U.S., at 391. Because the ordinance only proscribed a class of "fighting words" deemed particularly offensive by the city—*i.e.,* those "that contain . . . messages of 'bias-motivated' hatred," 505 U.S., at 392, we held that it violated the rule against content-based discrimination. But whereas the ordinance struck down in *R.A.V.* was explicitly directed at expression (*i.e.,* "speech" or "messages"), the statute in this case is aimed at conduct unprotected by the First Amendment.

Moreover, the Wisconsin statute singles out for enhancement bias-inspired conduct because this conduct is thought to inflict greater individual and societal harm. For example, according to the State and its *amici,* bias-motivated crimes are more likely to provoke retaliatory crimes, inflict distinct emotional harms on their victims, and incite community unrest. The State's desire to redress these perceived harms provides an adequate explanation for its penalty-enhancement provision over and above mere disagreement with offenders' beliefs or biases. As Blackstone said long ago, "it is but reasonable that among crimes of different natures those should be most severely punished, which are the most destructive of the public safety and happiness." 4 W. Blackstone, Commentaries *16.

Finally, there remains to be considered Mitchell's argument that the Wisconsin statute is unconstitutionally overbroad because of its "chilling effect" on free speech. Mitchell argues (and the Wisconsin Supreme Court agreed) that the statute is "overbroad" because evidence of the defendant's prior speech or associations may be used to prove that the defendant intentionally selected his victim on account of the victim's protected status. Consequently, the argument goes, the statute impermissibly chills free expression with respect to such matters by those concerned about the possibility of enhanced sentences if they should in the future commit a criminal offense covered by the statute. We find no merit in this contention.

The sort of chill envisioned here is far more attenuated and unlikely than that contemplated in traditional "overbreadth" cases. We must conjure up a vision of a Wisconsin citizen suppressing his unpopular bigoted opinions for fear that if he later commits an offense covered by the statute, these opinions will be offered at trial to establish that he selected his victim on account of the victim's protected status, thus qualifying him for penalty enhancement. * * * This is simply too speculative a hypothesis to support Mitchell's overbreadth claim.

The First Amendment, moreover, does not prohibit the evidentiary use of speech to establish the elements of a crime or to prove motive or intent. Evidence of a defendant's previous declarations or statements is commonly admitted in criminal trials subject to evidentiary rules dealing with relevancy, reliability, and the like. Nearly half a century ago, in *Haupt v. United States,* 330 U.S. 631 (1947), we rejected a contention similar to that advanced by Mitchell here. Haupt was tried for the offense of treason, which, as defined by the Constitution (Art. III, § 3), may depend very much on proof of motive. To prove that the acts in question were committed out of "adherence to the enemy" rather than "parental solicitude," *id.,* at 641, the Government introduced evidence of conversations that had taken place long prior to the indictment, some of which consisted of statements showing Haupt's sympathy with Germany and Hitler and hostility towards the United States. We rejected Haupt's argument that this evidence was improperly admitted. While "[s]uch testimony is to be scrutinized with care to be certain the statements are not expressions of mere lawful and permissible difference of opinion with our own government or quite proper appreciation of the land of birth," we held that "these statements . . . clearly were admissible on the question of intent and adherence to the enemy." *Id.*, at 642. * * *

NOTES & QUESTIONS

1. **Prevalence of Hate-Crime Laws and Hate Crimes.** By 2016, hate-crime laws have been adopted in forty-five states and the District of Columbia. Sara Ainsworth & Nadia Bryan, *Hate Crime Regulation and Challenges*, 17 GEO. J. GENDER & L. 303, 317 (2016). All of these laws covered crimes motivated by racial, religious, or ethnicity bias, but many also addressed other types of bias, including disability bias (thirty-two states), sexual orientation bias (thirty-one states), gender bias (twenty-eight states), age bias (thirteen states), transgender or gender identity bias (eleven states), and political affiliation bias (six states). *Id.* at 317–20.

Survey research indicates that the United States averages about 250,000 hate crimes per year, based on *victim* perceptions of whether the crime was motivated by bias in the areas of race, gender, gender identity, religion, disability, sexual orientation, or ethnicity. MADELINE MASUCCI & LYNN LANGTON, U.S. DEP'T OF JUSTICE, HATE CRIME VICTIMIZATION, 2004–2015 (2017). More than 90% are violent crimes, including the 62% that were simple assaults. Only 42% were reported to the police. Nearly half of the incidents involved racial bias, and more than one-third ethnicity bias. Although the absolute number of violent hate crimes is large, the survey research indicates that they account for only about 4% of all violent victimizations.

2. **Purpose and Reach of Hate-Crime Laws.** Can hate-crime sentence enhancements be justified based on the conventional purposes of punishment? Imagine that Mitchell beat his victim in, say, a road-rage incident without any racial overtones. Would he deserve any different punishment than on the actual facts? Assuming that the victim's physical injuries were the same in both variations, can you think of any ways in which there might nonetheless have been more or different harm in the hate-crime scenario? What did the *Mitchell* Court suggest about this? And would there be any utilitarian rationale for a harsher punishment in the hate-crime scenario?

Can you foresee any practical problems in the investigation and prosecution of cases? Bias may seem relatively clear when, for instance, a person used a racial epithet when committing a crime, but what if no words were uttered? Also, when does a person's reliance on a stereotype cross into the realm of a hate crime? For instance, if people who belong to hypothetical ethnic group X are thought to carry large amounts of cash, would targeting a member of X for robbery on the basis of that stereotype qualify?

3. ***Dawson v. Delaware.*** Although the defendant's First Amendment arguments were rejected in *Mitchell*, the Supreme Court did nothing to cast any doubt on its earlier decision in *Dawson v. Delaware*, 503 U.S. 159 (1992), which indicated that the First Amendment does impose some limitations on what factors may be considered at sentencing. Dawson was convicted of murder. At his capital sentencing hearing, the prosecution introduced

evidence that Dawson was a member of the Aryan Brotherhood, which was identified as a "white racist prison gang." Dawson was subsequently sentenced to death. On appeal to the U.S. Supreme Court, Dawson argued that he was effectively punished for his association with the Aryan Brotherhood—an association, he contended, that was protected by the First Amendment. The Court agreed that Dawson's sentencing has been unconstitutional. On the one hand, the Court held that "the Constitution does not erect a *per se* barrier to the admission of evidence concerning one's beliefs and associations at sentencing simply because those beliefs and associations are protected by the First Amendment." *Id.* at 165. But, on the other hand, the prosecution in Dawson's case had gone too far because the Aryan Brotherhood evidence was "totally without relevance to Dawson's sentencing proceeding." *Id.*

The Court elaborated:

> Even if the Delaware group to which Dawson allegedly belongs is racist, those beliefs, so far as we can determine, had no relevance to the sentencing proceeding in this case. For example, the Aryan Brotherhood evidence was not tied in any way to the murder of Dawson's victim. . . In the present case, . . . the murder victim was white, as is Dawson; elements of racial hatred were therefore not involved in the killing.
>
> Because the prosecution did not prove that the Aryan Brotherhood had committed any unlawful or violent acts, or had even endorsed such acts, the Aryan Brotherhood evidence was also not relevant to help prove any aggravating circumstance. In many cases, for example, associational evidence might serve a legitimate purpose in showing that a defendant represents a future danger to society. A defendant's membership in an organization that endorses the killing of any identifiable group, for example, might be relevant to a jury's inquiry into whether the defendant will be dangerous in the future. Other evidence concerning a defendant's associations might be relevant in proving other aggravating circumstances. But the inference which the jury was invited to draw in this case tended to prove nothing more than the abstract beliefs of the Delaware chapter. Delaware counters that even these abstract beliefs constitute a portion of Dawson's "character," and thus are admissible in their own right under Delaware law. Whatever label is given to the evidence presented, however, we conclude that Dawson's First Amendment rights were violated by the admission of the Aryan Brotherhood evidence in this case, because the evidence proved nothing more than Dawson's abstract beliefs. Delaware might have avoided this problem if it had presented evidence showing more than mere abstract beliefs on Dawson's part, but on the present record one is left with the feeling that the Aryan Brotherhood evidence was employed simply because the jury would find these beliefs morally reprehensible. Because Delaware failed to do more, we cannot find the evidence was properly admitted as relevant character evidence.

> Nor was the Aryan Brotherhood evidence relevant to rebut any mitigating evidence offered by Dawson. We have held that a capital defendant is entitled to introduce any relevant mitigating evidence that he proffers in support of a sentence less than death. But just as the defendant has the right to introduce any sort of relevant mitigating evidence, the State is entitled to rebut that evidence with proof of its own. In this case, Dawson's mitigating evidence consisted of testimony about his kindness to family members, as well as evidence regarding good time credits he earned in prison for enrolling in various drug and alcohol programs. Delaware argues that because Dawson's evidence consisted of "good" character evidence, it was entitled to introduce any "bad" character evidence in rebuttal, including that concerning the Aryan Brotherhood. The principle of broad rebuttal asserted by Delaware is correct, but the argument misses the mark because, as stated above, the Aryan Brotherhood evidence presented in this case cannot be viewed as relevant "bad" character evidence in its own right.

Id. at 166–68.

On what basis was *Dawson* seemingly distinguished in *Mitchell*? Are you persuaded?

4. ***R.A.V. v. St. Paul.*** The *Mitchell* Court also had to distinguish *R.A.V. v. St. Paul,* 505 U.S. 377 (1992). What was the ordinance that the Court held unconstitutional in *R.A.V.*? How was *R.A.V.* distinguished in *Mitchell*?

5. **Evidentiary Use of Defendant's Protected Speech.** In order to prove a defendant's bias against people who belong to a particular group, a prosecutor may wish to introduce into evidence statements made by the defendant on earlier occasions regarding that group. This can, in practical effect, mean that a defendant receives additional punishment as a result of his or her constitutionally protected speech. However, the *Mitchell* Court seemed untroubled by this possibility, declaring, "The First Amendment, moreover, does not prohibit the evidentiary use of speech to establish the elements of a crime or to prove motive or intent."

How broadly should this language be interpreted? Professor Dan Coenen argues that *Mitchell* does not necessarily foreclose all First Amendment challenges to the use of prior speech as evidence against a defendant. *Free Speech and the Law of Evidence*, 68 DUKE L. J. 639 (2019). He observes that Mitchell brought a facial challenge to the Wisconsin hate-crimes statute, seeking total invalidation of the statute, rather than an "as-applied" challenge complaining of a particular improper use of the statute. Based on his interpretation of a long line of other First Amendment cases, including *Dawson v. Delaware, supra,* Coenen contends that courts should give more serious consideration to as-applied challenges, weighing the value of the evidence against the free-speech costs, particularly with regard to a defendant's prior speech on matters of public concern.

What if Mitchell had posted on Facebook—if an anachronism may be indulged—that "all Whites are bigots" one month before the assault? Should the state be permitted to introduce that post against him as evidence? What if, instead, his Facebook post had said, "Since most Whites harbor implicit biases against Blacks, we have to elect more Black judges if we ever want a fair court system?" Note that the contemporary world of social media creates a potentially rich treasure trove of biased-motive evidence for prosecutors in hate-crime cases. If *Mitchell* were decided today, perhaps the Court would not have so quickly dismissed the defendant's concerns regarding the potential evidentiary use of a defendant's First-Amendment-protected speech.

6. **Actual Motivation Versus Perceived Motivation.** Should hate-crime laws focus on the defendant's *actual* motivation or the victim's *perception* of the defendant's motivation? Taking the latter approach might lessen the need for prosecutors to engage in the constitutionally awkward business of utilizing a defendant's First-Amendment-protected speech as evidence. However, almost all hate-crime laws take the actual-motivation approach and doing otherwise may raise constitutional problems of its own.

Consider, for instance, a New Jersey statute that criminalized certain intimidating behavior if the victim "reasonably believed" that the defendant committed the offense on account of the victim's race. *See State v. Pomianek*, 110 A.3d 841, 843 (N.J. 2015) (citing N.J.S.A. 2C:16–1(a)(3)). The New Jersey Supreme Court determined that the statute violated the constitutional vagueness doctrine, a component of the Due Process Clause jurisprudence that requires fair notice of what conduct violates the law. The court reasoned,

> [The] defendant here could not readily inform himself of a fact and, armed with that knowledge, take measures to avoid criminal liability. Defendant was guilty of a crime under *N.J.S.A.* 2C:16–1(a)(3) even if he had no intent to commit bias intimidation, so long as the victim reasonably believed that defendant targeted him on account of his race or color. Of course, a victim's reasonable belief about whether he has been subjected to bias may well depend on the victim's personal experiences, cultural or religious upbringing and heritage, and reaction to language that is a flashpoint to persons of his race, religion, or nationality. A tone-deaf defendant may intend no bias in the use of crude or insensitive language, and yet a victim may reasonably perceive animus. The defendant may be wholly unaware of the victim's perspective, due to a lack of understanding of the emotional triggers to which a reasonable person of that race, religion, or nationality would react. Nothing in the history of the bias-intimidation statute suggests that the Legislature intended to criminalize conduct through the imposition of an amorphous code of civility or criminalize speech that was not intended to intimidate on the basis of bias.

Id. at 854.

How effectively, you might wonder, does even the *actual-motivation* approach protect the defendant who is "tone-deaf," but not genuinely motivated by improper bias? After all, juries are asked to determine subjective motivation by drawing "reasonable inferences" from the defendant's words and actions. Isn't there a risk that jurors, just like victims, will erroneously impute motives to the defendant on the basis of their own "personal experiences, cultural or religious upbringing and heritage," which may differ quite significantly from the defendant's?

D. POST-OFFENSE CONDUCT AND ASSISTANCE TO THE AUTHORITIES

1. POST-OFFENSE CONDUCT GENERALLY

A and B are high school seniors. They have never been in trouble before, but they jointly decide to rob a convenience store for "kicks" and a little spending money. However, the store clerk proves resistant. At B's urging, A strikes the clerk in the head with a baseball bat. Just then, a police officer enters the store. From that moment, A and B follow sharply divergent paths. A, overcome with remorse, immediately drops the bat, surrenders to the officer, and spontaneously confesses to what he has done. Meanwhile, B runs out a backdoor and goes into hiding. Eventually, with A's assistance and after no small amount of effort, the authorities are able to locate and arrest B. While being questioned by the police, B denies any role in the robbery. He claims that he was in the store to purchase a snack and ran away because he was afraid he would be unfairly blamed for participating in the crime.

A and B are both charged with one count of attempted armed robbery and one count of aggravated assault of the clerk. A pleads guilty at the first opportunity without the benefit of a plea deal. A also sends all of his meager savings to the clerk in order to offset some of the clerk's medical expenses from the assault, along with a heartfelt letter of apology.

B continues to deny responsibility. His case goes to trial, where he again states that he had no involvement in the robbery. He is nonetheless convicted by a jury, based in large part on testimony provided by A.

As A and B face sentencing, each has been convicted of precisely the same offenses. Should their punishment also be identical?

The hypothetical illustrates differences in *post-offense conduct* and invites you to consider whether and to what extent such differences should be regarded as valid sentencing factors.

From a purely retributive standpoint, it is not entirely clear that A and B should receive different sentences. They are being punished for the same offenses, and it was only after the offenses were completed that their behavior veered in different directions. To be sure, some of B's post-offense actions could be prosecuted as crimes in their own right, for instance, as obstruction of justice or perjury. But would it be fair to punish B for these crimes, which have never been formally charged, let alone proven in court beyond a reasonable doubt? If we keep our focus on the actual crimes of conviction, we must consider if there is some way to view the post-offense conduct so that it reflects back on the culpability of the robbery and assault. It is possible, for instance, that A's immediate post-offense indications of remorse reveal that his participation in the crimes was not entirely deliberate but may instead have been a matter of following B's lead or otherwise getting carried away by the emotions of the moment. However, great care must be exercised when inferring time-of-offense mental states from later conduct. Was A genuinely remorseful, or is it just that he realized the "jig was up" and was trying to curry favor with law enforcement to minimize the legal consequences of his crimes? Were B's actions in running away and denying responsibility the sign of a cold-blooded, calculating criminal, or indications that he was so overcome with shame that he was incapable of publicly owning up to what he did?

Even if post-offense conduct sheds little light on the blameworthiness of the offense, there is another sense in which it may be relevant to how much punishment is deserved. Positive post-offense conduct may be seen as a partial payment of the defendant's "debt to society," or as a type of atonement for the offense, that diminishes the retributive need for punishment in the formally imposed sentence. In the hypothetical, for instance, A has made some meaningful sacrifices that benefit others—he has voluntarily surrendered money and his right to a jury trial, and provided active assistance to the authorities in apprehending and prosecuting B. Given how much more he has already done than B to atone for his offenses, there might be good retributive grounds for giving him a more lenient sentence than B.

It is easier to justify taking post-offense conduct into account in the forward-looking utilitarian framework. After all, the deterrence strand of utilitarian thinking assumes the appropriateness of calibrating punishments so as to discourage undesirable—and, by extension, to encourage desirable—future behavior. If the As of the world consistently receive more lenient punishments than the Bs, we might reasonably hope that future suspects and defendants will be more likely to follow A's path than B's. To be sure, we have attempted to problematize the deterrence punishment model, principally on the basis that to many prospective criminals the likelihood of receiving *any* punishment seems sufficiently low or remote that the *amount* of punishment hardly registers as an important consideration. However, this calculus may be quite different in the post-offense, and especially the post-apprehension, context. With punishment now looming more imminently, minimizing the amount of punishment is apt to become a rather more salient consideration as the suspect or defendant contemplates his or her options. Defense counsel—who is much more likely to be present post-offense than pre-offense—can also help to ensure that the defendant understands the likely sentencing consequences of choosing one course of action over another.

Post-offense conduct is also often seen as relevant to the defendant's "character" and recidivism risk. Thus, at sentencing, A might be regarded as already on the road to rehabilitation and much less likely to reoffend than B. Does that seem plausible to you? Would you feel differently about that judgment if A had a prior conviction for armed robbery?

However well-justified, post-offense conduct is routinely considered by prosecutors and judges in relation to sentencing. We have already noted, for instance, the large volume of empirical research making clear that the defendant who insists on a trial can normally expect to pay a high price at sentencing if convicted. *See* Brian D. Johnson, *Trials and Tribulations: The Trial Tax and the Process of Punishment*, 48 CRIME & JUST. 313, 314 (2019) ("Estimates of the trial tax vary but typically involve two- to sixfold increases in the odds of imprisonment with 15–60 percent longer sentences.").

The federal sentencing guidelines give substantial weight to post-offense conduct through a set of important provisions, including:

- § 3C1.1—increases offense level by two if defendant obstructs justice
- § 3C1.2—increases offense level by two if defendant recklessly endangers another during flight from a law enforcement officer
- § 3E1.1—decreases offense level by two or three if defendant demonstrates acceptance of responsibility for offense
- § 5K1.1—authorizes downward departure if defendant provides substantial assistance to the authorities
- § 5K2.16—authorizes downward departure if defendant voluntarily discloses offense to the authorities prior to its discovery
- § 5K3.1—authorizes downward departure pursuant to a district's early disposition program; such programs establish a process for rapid resolution of cases, including prompt guilty pleas

We will consider § 5K1.1 in more detail in the next section. For more information about § 3E1.1, you may refer back to the notes following *Mitchell v. United States* in Chapter 3.

Should we be concerned that when prosecutors and judges seek to reward cooperative post-offense conduct—or to punish uncooperative post-offense conduct—they may be elevating their own convenience over the public interest in retribution and efficient crime prevention? If the As of the world receive large sentencing discounts for their post-offense conduct, their punishment may fall short of their just deserts or fail to effectively address their recidivism risk. And if the Bs of the world must pay large sentencing premiums for their post-offense conduct, their punishment may exceed their just deserts, increase their recidivism risk, or simply waste scarce correctional resources. The concerns here dovetail with those raised in Chapter 1 in the discussion of the trial penalty and system efficiency as a purpose of punishment. *Some* recognition of post-offense conduct at sentencing may be justifiable but determining precisely *how much* calls for a complex and uncertain balancing of many considerations. Might prosecutors and judges, as a matter of their own self-interest, have a tendency to err on the side of giving too much weight to cooperative post-offense conduct?

2. ASSISTANCE IN THE INVESTIGATION OR PROSECUTION OF OTHERS

Sentencing Reform Act of 1984 (as codified)

18 U.S.C. § 3553. Imposition of a sentence

(e) Limited authority to impose a sentence below a statutory minimum.—Upon motion of the Government, the court shall have the authority to impose a sentence below a level established by statute as a minimum sentence so as to reflect a defendant's substantial assistance in the investigation or prosecution of another person who has committed an offense. Such sentence shall be imposed in accordance with the guidelines and policy statements issued by the Sentencing Commission pursuant to section 994 of title 28, United States Code.

United States Sentencing Guidelines (2021)

§ 5K1.1. Substantial Assistance to Authorities

Upon motion of the government stating that the defendant has provided substantial assistance in the investigation or prosecution of another person who has committed an offense, the court may depart from the guidelines.

(a) The appropriate reduction shall be determined by the court for reasons stated that may include, but are not limited to, consideration of the following:

(1) the court's evaluation of the significance and usefulness of the defendant's assistance, taking into consideration the government's evaluation of the assistance rendered;

(2) the truthfulness, completeness, and reliability of any information or testimony provided by the defendant;

(3) the nature and extent of the defendant's assistance;

(4) any injury suffered, or any danger or risk of injury to the defendant or his family resulting from his assistance;

(5) the timeliness of the defendant's assistance.

NOTES & QUESTIONS

1. **Why Reward the Snitch?** In 18 U.S.C. § 3553(e), Congress permits a sentence below an otherwise-applicable statutory minimum for the

defendant who provides "substantial assistance" in the investigation or prosecution of someone else. (This provision complements the "safety valve" statute, 18 U.S.C. § 3553(f), discussed above in the role-in-the-offense material, which also permits a below-minimum sentence in certain circumstances.) Similarly, § 5K1.1 of the federal sentencing guidelines authorizes a departure below an otherwise-applicable guidelines range on the basis of substantial assistance.[22] How can these provisions be justified?

Most commonly, the substantial-assistance discount is defended as a tool that helps police and prosecutors to do their jobs more effectively and efficiently. By giving one defendant a break, it may be possible to convict other lawbreakers who would have otherwise escaped justice or at least required considerably more time and effort to investigate and prosecute.

Other justifications are also sometimes suggested. For instance, Dean Michael Simons has defended the substantial-assistance discount on retributive terms:

> The retributive aspects of cooperation manifest themselves in two ways. First, for many cooperators, cooperation itself is punishment. At a minimum, the cooperator is alienated from the defendants against whom he cooperates. Typically, a cooperator will cooperate against his accomplices in a shared criminal enterprise. Thus, he must turn against—betray, if you will—the very people with whom he may be closest. More broadly, the "common disdain" in which cooperators are held often means that the cooperator is ostracized not only from his accomplices, but also from other communities that may be important to him. Thus, cooperation can be viewed as extra punishment .... The cooperator who suffers this extra punishment, then, may deserve less traditional punishment than a similarly situated noncooperating defendant.
>
> Second, for some cooperators, cooperation can be a vehicle through which the defendant experiences atonement.... [E]ven for those defendants who start cooperating for purely selfish reasons, cooperation can become (voluntarily or not) a means of expiation. Whether the cooperator desires it or not, the cooperation process forces a cooperator to express remorse and to make reparation, if not directly to his victim, then to society. So even for the selfish cooperator, cooperation can bring a defendant towards atonement. Thus, to the extent that expiation lessens a defendant's "just desert" ..., a cooperator may deserve a lesser sentence than a noncooperator ....

Retribution for Rats: Cooperation, Punishment, and Atonement, 56 VAND. L. REV. 1, 4 (2003).

It is also sometimes argued that the pro-social actions of cooperators are indicative of greater rehabilitative potential, or that the prospect of criminal collaborators turning on one another for sentencing benefits discourages the formation of criminal organizations. Do you find these justifications

[22] Likewise, Federal Rule of Criminal Procedure 35(b) authorizes a post-sentencing reduction in sentence on the basis of a defendant's post-sentencing substantial assistance.

persuasive? *See* Mirko Bagaric et al., *Should We Flip on Flippers: A Rational Approach to Providing Penalty Reductions to Criminal Informers*, 87 TENN. L. REV. 121, 160–61 (2019) (arguing they are not).

2. **Downsides of the Discount.** The substantial-assistance provisions are among the more controversial aspects of federal sentencing law. What do you think some of the objections would be?

One of the most common criticisms is that rewarding "snitches" can create too great an incentive for defendants to provide false statements about others, potentially leading to wrongful convictions. For instance, according to the Innocence Project, jailhouse informants have been implicated in about one out of every five cases of DNA-based exonerations, which would make them one of the leading causes of wrongful convictions in the United States. INNOCENCE PROJECT, INFORMING INJUSTICE: THE DISTURBING USE OF JAILHOUSE INFORMANTS (2019). Besides eliminating cooperation discounts entirely, can you think of any other safeguards that might help to address this problem? *See, e.g.*, Bagaric et al., *supra*, at 165 (discussing Illinois law that provides for pretrial hearing to assess reliability of jailhouse informants).

3. **Prosecutor's Motion and Judicial Review.** Both substantial-assistance provisions—statute and guideline—require a prosecutor's motion. It is unusual for a prosecutor to be given such explicit control over a mitigating sentencing factor. On the one hand, this approach seems to make some sense if the point of the discount is to facilitate the work of law-enforcement agencies; after all, a law-enforcement official is probably better-positioned than a judge to assess the value of a defendant's cooperation to law enforcement. On the other hand, when prosecutors hold so much power, there is a risk that some defendants may be treated unfairly—especially if there is no accountability for the way that the power is exercised.

In *Wade v. United States*, 504 U.S. 181 (1992), the Supreme Court considered whether a prosecutor's refusal to file a substantial-assistance motion is subject to judicial review. Wade, the defendant, had provided information to law enforcement that led to the arrest of another drug dealer, but the prosecutor in his case declined to file a motion under 18 U.S.C. § 3553(e), and Wade was accordingly subject to a ten-year mandatory minimum. In addressing Wade's appeal, the Supreme Court first noted that both § 3553(e) and § 5K1.1 give "the Government a power, not a duty, to file a motion when a defendant has substantially assisted." *Id.* at 185. Yet, the Court also reasoned,

> Because we see no reason why courts should treat a prosecutor's refusal to file a substantial-assistance motion differently from a prosecutor's other decisions, we hold that federal district courts have authority to review a prosecutor's refusal to file a substantial-assistance motion and to grant a remedy if they find that the refusal was based on an unconstitutional motive. Thus, a defendant would be entitled to relief if a prosecutor refused to file a substantial-assistance motion, say, because of the defendant's race or religion.

Id. at 185–86. The Court further specified that a defendant "would be entitled to relief if the prosecutor's refusal to move was not rationally related to any legitimate Government end." *Id.* at 186. At the same time, the Court indicated that a substantial threshold showing of impropriety might be required before a defendant would be entitled even to discovery or a hearing on a prosecutor's refusal to support a substantial-assistance discount; "generalized allegations of improper motive" would not be enough. *Id.* Wade himself failed to meet this standard, leading to the affirmance of his sentence.[23]

4. **Cooperation Process.** The business of earning a substantial-assistance discount can be a long, complicated process for the defendant, full of risk and uncertainty. The process often begins with a "proffer session," in which the defendant shares the information that he or she has with the government, without any guarantee that the government will provide any benefit in return. As indicated in *Wade, supra*, the government has almost unlimited discretion at this stage to decide that the defendant's offered assistance is insufficient to warrant a substantial-assistance motion.

Among other risks to the defendant, the proffer session is apt to include a great deal of self-incrimination. To be sure, proffer sessions are typically intertwined with plea bargaining, and Federal Rule of Evidence 410 prohibits the use of a defendant's plea-bargaining statements against the defendant at trial. However, defendants are often required to sign a "proffer waiver" in which they surrender their right to keep their statements out of evidence. (The fact that such waivers are routinely signed by defendants is a powerful indicator of the extreme imbalance in negotiating leverage between the two sides, which in the federal system results to a great extent from sentencing law—mandatory minimums and the sentencing guidelines.) In *United States v. Mezzanatto*, 513 U.S. 196 (1995), the Supreme Court ruled that a proffer waiver permitted the government to use a defendant's proffer statements in order to impeach the defendant's testimony at trial. Moreover, at least nine federal circuits have extended *Mezzanatto* to permit proffer statements to be used against a defendant *substantively*, that is, not limited to impeachment purposes. *See* Christopher B. Mueller, *"Make Him an Offer He Can't Refuse"*—Mezzanatto *Waivers As Lynchpin of Prosecutorial Overreach*, 82 MO. L. REV. 1023, 1028 n.5 (2017). With a waiver signed, the federal defendant who participates in a proffer session may practically guarantee his or her conviction of something, either through a plea deal or a trial verdict.[24]

---

[23] In *Wade*, the defendant never entered into a plea agreement with the government. However, even if a plea agreement is in place, most federal circuits have held that judicial review of the prosecutor's refusal to file a substantial-assistance motion should still be governed by the deferential *Wade* (bad motive) standard. A minority of courts distinguish *Wade* when an agreement is in place and hold that a prosecutor's refusal warrants a judicial remedy if the prosecutor acted in bad faith. *See* Colin Miller, *Plea Agreements As Constitutional Contracts*, 97 N.C. L. REV. 31 (2018); Lucius T. Outlaw III, *A Net for a Cooperator's Leap of Faith: The Due Process Need for Universal Acceptance of Bad Faith Review of Prosecutors' Substantial Assistance Determinations in Federal Sentencing*, 104 MARQ. L. REV. 661 (2021).

[24] States are divided as to the validity of proffer waivers. Mueller, *supra*, at 1028–29.

As a defendant ponders whether and how to cooperate, a major source of anxiety may be the threat that a codefendant will "flip" more quickly. If multiple individuals have been implicated in a criminal activity, the government is unlikely to offer a substantial-assistance discount to all of them. The first cooperator is often the most valuable, providing the key information to the government that forces other defendants to give up the fight and take deals of their own. Subsequent cooperators may be offered far less favorable terms—or not offered any deal at all. If—feeling the pressure to be first—multiple defendants step forward to cooperate at about the same time, the prosecutor has the luxury of conducting multiple proffer sessions to decide which defendant would be the most valuable for investigation or litigation purposes going forward.

Once the prosecutor decides that a particular defendant appears to be a suitable cooperation partner, the two sides will enter into a cooperation agreement, which is typically reduced to writing in the federal system and often also includes a plea agreement. Once again reflecting the prosecutor-defendant power imbalances, cooperation agreements often seem rather one-sided, obligating the defendant to provide ongoing assistance to the government, e.g., in testifying against others at multiple legal proceedings, while leaving the government with maximum freedom to decline to file a substantial-assistance motion if the defendant's cooperation is found unsatisfactory, e.g., if the defendant's testimony is determined not to be entirely truthful. The cooperation agreement may also require the defendant to engage in potentially dangerous undercover activities, e.g., meeting with criminal confederates while wearing a "wire." Moreover, in order to maintain the government's leverage, the cooperator may be required to plead guilty promptly to some or all of the charges he or she faces but wait for sentencing until after all of the required assistance is fully provided. R. Michael Cassidy, *"Soft Words of Hope:"* Giglio, *Accomplice Witnesses, and the Problem of Implied Inducements*, 98 NW. U. L. REV. 1129, 1146 (2004).

From start to finish, then, the cooperation process may be fraught with strategic gamesmanship, not only between prosecution and defense, but also between defendants. Does this seem a sensible, fair way to determine punishment?

Note that, post-*Booker*, the sentencing judge may have some ability to offset arbitrariness in the determination of who gets a substantial-assistance motion. A defendant who makes a good-faith effort to provide assistance, but who falls short of what the prosecutor deems "substantial," could have his or her efforts credited anyway. *See United States v. Robinson*, 741 F.3d 588, 599 (5th Cir. 2014) ("We now join our sister circuits in expressly holding that a sentencing court has the power to consider a defendant's cooperation under § 3553(a), irrespective of whether the Government files a § 5K1.1 motion."). However, a downward variance from the guidelines range under *Booker* would not provide relief from a statutory minimum.

5. **Size of the Discount.** While the prosecutor serves as the gatekeeper for a substantial assistance discount in the federal system, it is the judge who has the final say over whether the discount is granted and, if so, how large it will be. There is no precise formula for determining the size

of the benefit, although § 5K1.1 does list a handful of factors for the court to consider. Data from the U.S. Sentencing Commission indicate that the average reduction in sentence length for a § 5K1.1 departure is 54.4%—in other words, the sentence is cut by more than half. SOURCEBOOK OF FEDERAL SENTENCING STATISTICS tbl. 37 (2020). This amounts to an average reduction of 53 months in prison, or 4.5 years. Given such a large benefit, there should be little surprise that so many defendants are willing to subject themselves to the risk and uncertainty of the cooperation process.

Although the overall average discount is quite sizeable, some research indicates that defendants who are Black or Latinx tend to receive smaller sentence reductions than otherwise-similar White defendants. Celesta A. Albonetti, *Sentencing of Federal Cocaine Trafficking/Manufacturing Defendants: Assessing Direct and Conditioning Effects of Defendant's Race/ Ethnicity and Gender on Length of Imprisonment*, 21 J. GENDER RACE & JUST. 1 (2017).

6. **Frequency of Substantial-Assistance Departures.** Nationally, a § 5K1.1 departure was granted in 8.2% of sentenced federal criminal cases in fiscal year 2020. SOURCEBOOK, *supra*, tbl. 30. However, this national figure conceals considerable district-to-district variation. On the low end, for instance, the substantial-assistance rate was only 1.2% in the District of New Mexico, 1.6% in the District of Arizona, and 1.8% in the District of South Dakota. On the high end, the rate was 35.3% in District of North Dakota, 27.8% in the Eastern District of Tennessee, and 27.4% in the District of Hawaii. To some extent, such variations reflect differences in the criminal dockets of different districts. For instance, U.S. Attorney Offices that particularly target group criminality, such as drug-trafficking organizations or complex white-collar offenses, will naturally have more reason to utilize the § 5K1.1 tool. But the wide district-level variations also probably owe something to the way that different office cultures have developed over time. Consider this observation from a veteran federal criminal defense lawyer:

> There have been many cases in which a client was given the benefit of a 5K1.1 motion by simply providing a statement at the time of arrest and others that were denied the same motion who participated in numerous proffer sessions over long periods of time. The difference between these cases was not the truthfulness or the helpfulness of these clients, but rather the jurisdiction in which they found themselves being prosecuted.

Drew Findling, *Location, Location, Location: Just as in Real Estate, for Cooperating Defendants, Location Is Everything*, 43 CHAMPION 5, 6 (2019). Does it seem fair to you that defendants in some districts find it so much harder to obtain substantial-assistance motions than defendants in other districts?

7. **Role in the Offense.** There may, in practice, be some tension between the goals of rewarding assistance to the authorities and ensuring that higher-level actors in a criminal organization are sentenced more severely than lower-level. The difficulty is that leaders and managers are likely to have much more complete information about the organization's

activities than the lower-level participants. As a result, their cooperation is apt to be more valuable to law enforcement, and, hence, more likely to be recognized as a mitigating factor at sentencing.

8. **State Law.** Assistance to the authorities is widely recognized as an appropriate sentencing factor in state law, albeit usually without the formal codification found in federal law. *See* Bagaric et. al., *supra* (summarizing caselaw in California, Texas, and New York). Florida, by contrast, *statutorily* authorizes a downward departure if the "defendant cooperated with the state to resolve the current offense or any other offense." Fla. Stat. Ann. § 921.0026(2)(i). However, the Florida courts have specified that "[c]ooperation requires more than a confession to the authorities after arrest and guilty plea." *State v. Johnson*, 193 So. 3d 32, 34 (Fla. Dist. Ct. App. 2016). The courts further indicate that a departure may be denied if the information supplied by a defendant regarding others did not lead to an arrest, prosecution, or conviction. *State v. Pita*, 54 So. 3d 557, 562 (Fla. Dist. Ct. App. 2011).

E. ADDITIONAL OFFENSES

When a defendant has been convicted and faces sentencing on multiple counts, two important questions arise—one (mostly) of form and the other of substance. The formal question is whether the sentences imposed on each count should run consecutively or concurrently. The substantive question is how to count the distinct harms of the different offenses so as to arrive at an overall sentence in the case that fairly reflects the overall seriousness of the entire course of criminal conduct for which the defendant has been convicted.

As to the formal question, judges traditionally had nearly unfettered discretion to choose consecutive or concurrent sentencing. Most states preserve that discretion today, although a few have opted to establish a rebuttable presumption one way or the other, that is, in favor of either the consecutive or concurrent approach. *Oregon v. Ice*, 555 U.S. 160, 163 (2009).

Oregon law, for instance, generally favors concurrent sentences, but provides that consecutive sentences are permissible in certain circumstances:

> The court has discretion to impose consecutive terms of imprisonment for separate convictions arising out of a continuous and uninterrupted course of conduct only if the court finds:
>
> (a) That the criminal offense for which a consecutive sentence is contemplated was not merely an incidental violation of a separate statutory provision in the course of the commission of a more serious crime but rather was an indication of defendant's willingness to commit more than one criminal offense; or

> (b) The criminal offense for which a consecutive sentence is contemplated caused or created a risk of causing greater or qualitatively different loss, injury or harm to the victim or caused or created a risk of causing loss, injury or harm to a different victim than was caused or threatened by the other offense or offenses committed during a continuous and uninterrupted course of conduct.

Or. Rev. Stat. Ann. § 137.123(5).

Under *Apprendi,* does the defendant have a constitutional right to a jury trial on the factual issues raised by (a) or (b)? The Supreme Court ruled to the contrary in *Oregon v. Ice.* Noting that the concurrent/consecutive decision was traditionally up to the judge, the Court held, "There is no encroachment here by the judge upon facts historically found by the jury, nor any threat to the jury's domain as a bulwark at trial between the State and the accused." *Ice,* 555 U.S. at 169. *Ice* thus seems to provide states with considerable leeway in structuring the consecutive/concurrent decision without fear of triggering jury-trial rights.

Assuming a judge has discretion to sentence consecutively or concurrently, on what basis should the judge make this decision? As long as a sufficiently severe sentence for the entire course of conduct can be imposed within the maximum sentence for the most serious offense of conviction, consecutive sentences will normally be unnecessary. For instance, recall from the previous section the hypothetical defendant B, who attempted to commit an armed robbery and then fled from police. He might be convicted of the offenses of attempted armed robbery (count 1), carrying a maximum sentence of twenty years, and flight (count 2), carrying a maximum sentence of three years. As a first-time offender, B would be highly unlikely to receive a sentence for attempted armed robbery that is at or near the twenty-year maximum, leaving plenty of room for the sentence on count 1 also to include punishment for the much less serious crime of flight. If the count 1 sentence is structured in this way, then the count 2 sentence should be made concurrent so that the overall sentence in the case is not excessive relative to the overall severity of the criminal conduct. This sort of approach is probably the most common in practice. MPC:S § 6B.08 cmmnt. (b).

On the other hand, if the judge is able to ensure that the sentences on each count add up to an appropriate overall sentence for the entire course of conduct, there seems no compelling reason to choose the concurrent over the consecutive approach. That is why the concurrent/consecutive question is characterized as one of form, not substance—in most cases, it is likely that an appropriate overall sentence can be achieved through either approach.

This brings us to the substantive question—when multiple counts reflect multiple harms caused, intended, or risked by the defendant, how should these different harms be viewed collectively so as to determine an appropriate overall sentence?

Justice Stephen Breyer, who played a key role in establishing the federal guidelines' architecture as a member of the United States Sentencing Commission before he joined the Supreme Court, invites our consideration of several hypotheticals:

- The defendant injures one person (or six people) in a brawl.
- The defendant sells 100 (or 600) grams of cocaine.
- The defendant robs one bank (or six banks).
- The defendant, driving recklessly, causes an accident that kills one person (or six people).

Stephen Breyer, *The Federal Sentencing Guidelines and the Key Compromises Upon Which They Rest*, 17 HOFSTRA L. REV. 1, 25 (1988). In each variation of each hypothetical, the defendant seems to cause six times as much harm. Most people, according to Breyer, see the variations as warranting more punishment, but not six times as much punishment. This intuition, favoring diminishing marginal punishment as the harm is increased, is reflected in the guidelines.

More specifically, the guidelines use two different approaches. The first is for counts involving fungible items such as drugs or money. In this scenario, the guidelines call for adding "the fungible items that are the subject of the several counts and punish[ing] the offender as if there were a single count involving the total amount. Since the Commission's punishments for most drug and money crimes are determined by tables that increase punishment at a rate less than proportional to the amounts of drugs or money, collapsing the counts and using the tables produces a result that [increases punishment], but at a less than proportional rate." *Id.* at 27.

The second approach covers situations in which the subject matters of the different counts are not fungible. Breyer explains,

> This situation would arise, for example, where count one charges an assault and count two charges a robbery. In that event, the Commission's rules involve two operations. Operation One requires separating the subject matters of all counts into separate events. The rules for collapsing subject matters into single events require that two or more acts which are part of a *single* transaction involving a *single* victim (robbing and assaulting one person at one time, for example) count as *one* event; but *two* acts involving *two* victims (or one victim on two occasions) will count as *two* events. Operation Two involves assigning a score, in units, to each separate event. The units are then added and measured against a punishment scale that assigns more, but declining, additional amounts of punishment. The upshot is that a bank robber who robs *six* banks will receive roughly *twice* as much (not *six* times as much) punishment as the robber who robs one bank.

Id. at 27–28. Does this seem an appropriate approach to you?

If you are interested in the technical details of how the Commission's solution to the multicount problem is implemented, see Part 3D of the guidelines; warning—this is among the most complicated aspects of the federal system! For an overview of how the multicount problem is handled in some state guidelines, see RICHARD S. FRASE, JUST SENTENCING: PRINCIPLES AND PROCEDURES FOR A WORKABLE SYSTEM 199–200 (2013).

Logically, it seems that there should be some sort of relationship between the treatment of multiple convictions in a single case and prior convictions from earlier cases, but it can be difficult to work out what that relationship should be. Consider the following four scenarios, each of which involves two burglary convictions. Out of the following scenarios, which should get the most and least severe cumulative punishments, that is, for the two burglaries combined?

1) *D* burgles a residence, is convicted and sentenced to probation, successfully completes the probation, and then is convicted of a new residential burglary.

2) *D* burgles a residence, is convicted and sentenced to probation, and then commits a new burglary while still on probation.

3) *D* is arrested and charged with burglary of a residence; while out on bail, *D* commits a new burglary.

4) *D* commits two burglaries in a single evening.

PROBLEM 4-1: SENTENCING SMITH

Review the PSR from *United States v. Smith* in Chapter 3. Using what you have learned about sentencing factors, can you calculate a guidelines range for the defendant? Here is the recommended process:

- Determine the offense level based on the drug quantity table in § 2D1.1(c) of the federal sentencing guidelines (to simplify things, don't worry about the "actual" weight of the meth in this case)
- Consider whether the adjustments of §§ 3B1.1 and 3E1.1 apply
- Determine the criminal history score using § 4A1.1
- Use the grid in Part 5A to determine the sentencing range

You may find the relevant guidelines in the current edition of the *Guidelines Manual*, which is available at the website of the U.S. Sentencing Commission (https://www.ussc.gov/guidelines).

Can you think of any plausible arguments Smith might make for a below-range sentence? What sentence would you impose if you were the judge? Don't forget that there is a ten-year mandatory minimum that applies.

CHAPTER 5

DOING TIME

"[T]he Constitution does not mandate comfortable prisons."
Rhodes v. Chapman, 452 U.S. 337, 349 (1981)

Previous chapters focused on the justifications of punishment and the mechanics of its imposition. Here, in Chapter 5, we focus on the experience of incarceration, and its impact on inmates and others, as well as the federal constitutional limits on government's custodial authority.

Whatever else their penal justification, prisons and jails serve the basic function of isolating their populations from free society. They are neither intended to be, nor are, pleasant places to be. As one author described prison life:

> Organized gangs, predatory inmates, endemic violence, simmering personal disputes, indifferent or abusive prison guards, insufficient surveillance, ethnic wars, dysfunctional cellmates, serious overcrowding, rampant disease, certifiable insanity, wretched physical circumstances, and a merciless pecking order make every jail sentence a daily ordeal of danger, humiliation, and insecurity.

ROBERT A. FERGUSON, INFERNO: AN ANATOMY OF AMERICAN PUNISHMENT 15–16 (2014). Wilbert Rideau, a prison journalist who spent decades in Louisiana's Angola Prison, described his life as entailing being "assaulted psychologically and emotionally, [in a] way in which you are robbed of any dignity as a human being and told in countless ways that you don't matter." WILBERT RIDEAU, IN THE PLACE OF JUSTICE: A STORY OF PUNISHMENT AND DELIVERANCE 338 (2010). The total control purposefully exercised by an institution results in a feeling of total vulnerability. Sharon Dolovich, *Cruelty, Prison Conditions, and the Eighth Amendment*, 84 N.Y.U. L. REV. 881, 912–13 (2009).

As a preliminary matter, it is important to distinguish the two most basic physical institutions used in corrections: the jail and the prison. A jail typically houses individuals awaiting trial and those serving shorter sentences, usually less than one year. Typically, jails are operated by local governments such as a city or county.[1] Prisons, which are operated by the federal government and states, typically house individuals convicted of offenses requiring in excess of a year of incarceration. Prisons, as will be discussed, entail some important variations, ranging from minimum to maximum security, including among the latter the "supermax" penitentiary operated by the U.S. Government. Located in

[1] The overwhelming majority of the jailed population resides in county, not municipal, jails. Gerald G. Gaes, *Current Status of Prison Privatization Research on American Prisons and Jails*, 18 CRIMINOLOGY & PUB. POL'Y 269, 271–72 (2019).

Florence, Colorado, it holds inmates in single cells for twenty-three hours a day. Generally speaking, the term prison will be used here, other than in particular circumstances when prison and jail environments differ.

A. HISTORY

In relative historical terms, prisons are a recent invention. Up through the late 1700s, persons convicted of serious crimes usually were subject to physical punishment, such as drawing and quartering, maiming, branding, whipping, or hanging. Others were subject to physical banishment from the jurisdiction or public shaming in a pillory.

Although involuntary physical confinement in some shape or form dates back to ancient and medieval times, prison as we know it today first began to take shape in 1770s England, and even more recognizably in early 1800s America. With states turning away from the widespread use of the death penalty, imported from England, two correctional approaches came into use. As discussed in Chapter 2, one was on display in Auburn, New York, the other at two institutions in Pennsylvania. Although both systems sought to reform their wayward charges, in silence, Auburn used a "congregate" system and Pennsylvania prisons (most notably the Eastern State Penitentiary in Philadelphia) used an individualized approach. *See generally* David J. Rothman, *Perfecting the Prison: United States, 1789–1865, in* THE OXFORD HISTORY OF THE PRISON: THE PRACTICE OF PUNISHMENT IN WESTERN SOCIETY at 100, 106 (Norval Morris & David J. Rothman eds., 1998).

The efforts gained world renown, prompting the French in particular to dispatch Alexis de Tocqueville, author of the landmark two-volume study *Democracy in America* (1835, 1840), to visit America. His rather positive findings on the enterprise contrasted with the view of Charles Dickens, visiting several years later, who was considerably less impressed. Dickens called the Pennsylvania system he observed "cruel and wrong." He added:

> I believe that very few men are capable of estimating the immense amount of torture and agony that this dreadful punishment, prolonged for years, inflicts upon the sufferers. . . . I hold this slow and daily tampering with the mysteries of the brain, to be immeasurably worse than any torture of the body.

Rothman, *supra*, at 111 (quoting Dickens).

In the era following the Civil War, corrections experienced a marked shift. Rothman writes that "[p]risons in the post-Civil War era became modern, that is, characterized by overcrowding, brutality, and disorder. . . . Massive walls enclosed prison space, and heavy gates swung open to admit a steady stream of convicts." *Id.* at 113. Another historian, Edgardo Rotman, notes that after the Civil War the construction and design of new penitentiaries was driven by limited state budgets—"by how to confine the largest number of [prisoners] at the lowest possible cost"—rather than the most effective means of satisfying their ostensible rehabilitative purpose. As the focus on rehabilitation waned, the American penitentiary became known for its "pervasive overcrowding, corruption, and cruelty." Prison administrators blamed the cruel conditions on the prison system's need to control the growing immigrant population that filled the nation's prisons:

> Prisoners were often living three and four to a cell designed for one, and prison discipline was medieval-like in character, with bizarre and brutal punishments commonplace in state institutions. Wardens did not so much deny this awful reality as explain it away, attributing most of the blame not to those who administered the system but to those who experienced it. Because the prisons were filled with immigrants who were ostensibly hardened to a life in crime and impervious to American traditions, those in charge had no choice but to rule over [prisoners] with an iron hand. In fact, the closing decades of the nineteenth century were the dark ages for America's prisons.

Edgardo Rotman, *The Failure of Reform: United States, 1865–1965, in* THE OXFORD HISTORY OF THE PRISON: THE PRACTICE OF PUNISHMENT IN WESTERN SOCIETY at 150, 152 (Norval Morris & David J. Rothman eds., 1998).

Today, the nation's corrections system bears scant resemblance to that of the early-to-mid nineteenth century. An obvious difference is scale. The system consists of several hundred state prisons and jails, dozens of federal prisons (called "federal correctional institutions"), and many privately operated institutions. There are separate facilities for men, women, and juveniles, which collectively house over two million individuals.

No less important, the animating purpose of American corrections has changed considerably over time. At the outset, as noted, reformation was the primary motivation, and this remained the focus for a long time. Vocational training and educational opportunities (including college, to some extent) were available. Indeterminate sentencing regimes dominated, with actual time served dependent on "back-end" parole decision makers determining whether and when inmates were fit for release. Starting in the 1970s, however, what was termed the "rehabilitative ideal" fell out of favor. Of particular importance was a 1974 article by sociologist Robert Martinson entitled *What Works?—Questions and Answers About Prison Reform*, 35 PUB. INT. 22 (1974). In his article, Martinson canvassed over two hundred studies of rehabilitation programs and reached the pessimistic answer to his query: not much if anything worked in reducing recidivism.

As history would have it, around this time a shift was occurring amid politicians and policy makers. Law and order advocates, mainly conservative Republicans, and individuals concerned about sentencing disparity and unfairness, mainly liberal Democrats, converged in their view that a change in philosophy and practice was needed. As discussed in Chapter 2, out of this convergence came determinate sentencing, sentencing commissions and guidelines, and mandatory minimum sentences, which along with other factors drove an enormous increase in incarceration. Today, perhaps to a greater extent than ever before, incapacitation is a dominant penal justification of American sentencing and corrections. Next the discussion turns to the many ways in which this shift is reflected in the corrections system and the daily lives of its inhabitants.

B. LIFE IN CONFINEMENT[2]

Justice Anthony Kennedy was correct when in August 2003 he told an American Bar Association audience that "[o]ne day in prison is longer than almost any day you and I have had to endure." *Speech Delivered by Justice Anthony M. Kennedy at the American Bar Association Annual Meeting*, Aug. 2003, *reprinted in* 16 FED. SENT'G REP. 126 (2003). Prison has been called a "total institution," a concept popularized by sociologist Erving Goffman in his seminal 1961 book *Asylums: Essays on the Social Situation of Mental Patients and Other Inmates*. Prisons are largely self-contained, physically separated from the outside world; tightly scheduled; and closely monitored by authorities. Moreover, they provide inhabitants a new institutional identity (manifest in prison garb) and largely strip them of autonomy.[3]

In general, prison life is routinized and boring. The sameness, however, is prone to interruption by violence and intimidation. An initially uneventful day can quickly and without notice turn into one with a violent melee or a lockdown enabling officers to conduct searches for weapons and/or contraband. "It is not a daily round of threats, fights, plots, and 'shanks' (prison-made knives)—though you have to be constantly careful to avoid situations or behavior that might lead to violence. A sense of impending danger is always with you; you must be careful to move around people rather than against or through them." Norval Morris, *The Contemporary Prison, in* THE OXFORD HISTORY OF THE PRISON 202, 203 (Norval Morris & David J. Rothman eds., 1995). Meanwhile, there is constant noise, scrutiny by guards, often unsanitary conditions, and no personal privacy.[4]

---

[2] Conditions experienced by death row inmates, convicted of capital crimes, are discussed in Chapter 7.

[3] For a fascinating archive of in-house prisoner-operated newspapers, containing commentary and news of prison life, often motivated by a desire to reach the outside world, see Kate McQueen, *Introducing American Prison Newspapers: 1800–2020: Voices from the Inside*, Sept. 22, 2021, https://daily.jstor.org/introducing-the-american-prison-newspapers-collection/?utm_term=Read%20More&utm_campaign=jstordaily_09232021&utm_content=email&utm_source=Act-On+Software&utm_medium=email. *See also* JAMES M. MORRIS, JAILHOUSE JOURNALISM: THE FOURTH ESTATE BEHIND BARS (2002).

[4] For an illuminating description of prison life, from an individual who served twenty-five years in New York prisons, see Mika'il DeVeaux, *The Trauma of the Incarceration Experience*,

Predictably, the security classification of an institution can affect prison life. Typically, a minimum security facility, which usually houses those believed to pose the least risk of escape or harming others, is least restrictive. Inmates might be housed in non-secure dormitories, able to freely walk the grounds, and work outside the prison. There might be a single perimeter or no fence and no guard watch tower. In the federal system, such facilities have been given the moniker "club fed," suggestive of their relatively nice environs and less regimented life. Medium security prisons, where most inmates live, typically house individuals convicted of non-violent crimes, but who still pose security risk, either from the outset or by exhibiting a problematic institutional history. Maximum security prisons, which house inmates convicted of violent crimes and who have the most problematic disciplinary histories, impose the greatest limits on personal freedom.

The composition of inmate populations can have a significant impact on institutional environment. Research suggests, for instance, that inmates serving longer sentences most want to secure and maintain better living conditions and privileges, which disciplinary infractions can deny. Such inmates might have a stabilizing effect that contributes to a calmer, more positive overall environment. Derek Kreager et al., *Where "Old Heads" Prevail: Inmate Hierarchy in a Men's Prison Unit*, 82 AMER. SOC. REV. 685 (2017).

The culture of supervision maintained by corrections officers at particular institutions can vary and is also important. Officers possess near-complete control and power over inmates, which allows them to maintain the correctional power structure. Some are known as tough and rule-enforcement oriented and others as more indulgent, while still others (perhaps most problematically) are inconsistent. Informal supervision practices can have a great impact on inmate life, such as imposing shortened access to the recreation yard. Some officers, moreover, have been known to engage in inappropriate behavioral control methods. *See, e.g.*, Bryan Pietsch, *Jail Employees Face Charges After Using "Baby Shark" Song to Punish Inmates*, N.Y. TIMES, Oct. 6, 2020. In North Carolina, a warden and guard were suspended in 2012 after allegations that "guards had forced [inmates] to rub hot sauce on their genitals, kiss deadly snakes, and imitate sex acts." Robbie Brown, *North Carolina: Warden and Guard Suspended*, N.Y. TIMES, Dec. 4, 2012.

The life of an officer, much like that of an inmate, has a daily rhythm, which can unpredictably be punctuated by highly stressful and dangerous situations. Writer Ted Conover served as a corrections officer for a year in New York's maximum security prison Sing. Describing his

48 HARV. C.R.—C.L. L. REV. 257 (2013). For an interesting discussion of how inmates come to perceive the passage of time differently, and how this affects the human psyche, see Dominique Moran, *"Doing Time" in Carceral Space: Timespace and Carceral Geography*, 94 HUM. GEOG. 305 (2012).

work, Conover writes that "I have always thought of [it] as an assembly line in a poorly run explosives factory. Tedium, tedium, tedium, then-*bang*—you'd be missing your hands." TED CONOVER, NEWJACK: GUARDING SING SING 250 (2000).

1. SOLITARY CONFINEMENT

Solitary confinement is another major factor affecting the experience of imprisonment. Early in the nation's history, as noted above, solitary confinement of a kind was used in Pennsylvania. The idea was to separate the wayward criminal convicts from others to encourage introspection and repentance. Due to checks and balances in the system, however, only rarely did individuals experience extended periods of isolated confinement. *See* David M. Shapiro, *Solitary Confinement in the Young Republic*, 133 HARV. L. REV. 542 (2019).

Today, solitary confinement is used to a far greater extent and for far longer durations. Individuals (including juveniles) languish for years and even decades in isolation. The shift began in the 1980s with a particular incident in 1983 serving as a particular catalyst: two officers at the federal prison in Marion, Indiana, were stabbed, prompting an extended lockdown of inmates in their cells. Other prison systems soon followed suit by expanding solitary confinement and constructing supermaxes, prisons designed for long-term isolation. Today, over forty states and the federal governments operate supermax facilities. *Id.* at 574.

Solitary confinement is variously referred to as the "hole" or the "box," as well as by more formal terms such as disciplinary segregation, special housing, administrative segregation, and special or intensive management. Inmates are placed in these isolated environments for many possible reasons, such as punishment for violation of rules and protection from other inmates. Although focus is most commonly upon state and federal prisons, isolation is also frequently used in jails, such as New York City's Rikers Island. Craig Haney et al., *Examining Jail Isolation: What We Don't Know Can Be Profoundly Harmful*, 96 PRISON J. 126 (2016). *See also generally* Jules Lobel, *Mass Solitary and Mass Incarceration: Explaining the Dramatic Rise in Prolonged Solitary in America's Prisons*, 115 NW. U. L. REV. 159 (2020).

Usually, inmates get at most one hour outside their small concrete cell each day and take their meals alone after receiving them through a slot in the door. Human contact is limited to officers, through a speaker or telephone. Guards facilitate showers and opening of doors by remote buttons in a control room. On the rare occasion inmates interact with other humans, such as for medical attention, it is often through a video teleconference.

It is estimated that inmates in solitary confinement constitute 2–8% of the U.S. prison population, but they account for almost half of all inmate suicides. The extended sensory deprivation and loss of human interaction can have devastating short- and long-term mental and emotional consequences, even adverse neurological effects. Isolation can produce mental illness in previously heathy inmates and significantly worsen preexisting psychiatric conditions. Severe depression, hallucinations, headaches, weight loss, and spatial disorientation are also common consequences. Shapiro, *supra,* at 580–81; *see also* Craig Haney, *The Science of Solitary: Expanding the Harmfulness Narrative,* 115 NW. U. L. REV. 211 (2020).

2. OVERCROWDING

As the nation's imprisonment rates rose in the 1980s, new places of confinement were constructed, but the effort failed to accommodate the ever-increasing flow of inmates, longer sentences imposed, and decreases in early release opportunities. By the early 1990s, state prisons nationwide on average operated at 118% of their capacity and federal prisons at over 150% of their capacity. CHRISTOPHER MUMOLA & ALLEN BECK, U.S. DEP'T OF JUSTICE, PRISONERS IN 1996 (1997). At the end of 2019, twenty-one states and the federal government had a total number of prisoners in custody that met or exceeded their capacity. E. ANN CARSON, U.S. DEP'T OF JUSTICE, PRISONERS IN 2019, at 24 (2020).

Overcrowding has many negative effects. Predictably, stuffing more humans into a space than it is intended to accommodate imposes significant emotional and psychological strain. It also fosters disorder and unrest. As psychiatrist Terry Kupers has written:

> In crowded, noisy, unhygienic environments, human beings tend to treat each other terribly. Imagine sleeping in a converted gymnasium with 150 to 200 prisoners. There are constant lines to use the toilets and phones, and altercations erupt when one irritable prisoner thinks another has been on the phone too long. There are rows of bunks blocking the view, so beatings and rapes can go on in one part of the dorm while officers sit at their desks in another area. The noise level is so loud that muffled screams cannot be heard. Meanwhile the constant noise and unhygienic conditions cause irritability on everyone's part. Individuals who are vulnerable to attack and sexual assault—for example, smaller men, men suffering from serious mental illness, and gay or transgender persons—have no cell to retreat to when they feel endangered.

Terry A. Kupers, *Prison and the Decimation of Pro-Social Life Skills, in* THE TRAUMA OF PSYCHOLOGICAL TORTURE (Almerindo Ojeda ed., 2008).

Overcrowding also impedes or renders unavailable basic services for inmates, such as medical and mental health care, and increases suicide rates and psychiatric commitments. *See* Craig Haney, *The Wages of Prison Overcrowding: Harmful Psychological Consequences and*

Dysfunctional Correctional Reactions, 22 WASH. U. J. L. & POL'Y 265 (2006); Evelyn Malave, Note, *Prison Health Care After the Affordable Care Act: Envisioning an End to the Policy of Neglect*, 89 N.Y.U. L. REV. 700 (2004).

For corrections staff, overcrowding makes an already difficult job more so. The ability of staff to monitor and control inmates is overtaxed, making them more stressed and fearful. Joseph L. Martin et al., *"They Can Take Us Over Any Time They Want": Correctional Officers' Responses to Prison Crowding*, 92 PRISON J. 88 (2012).

3. GANGS

Over the past fifty years gangs have come to play a central organizing role in the corrections ecosystem. When discussing gangs in this context, it is important to recognize that prison and streets gangs, while having some membership overlap, are quite distinct. As one ethnographic study relates:

> Gang membership and leadership structures in prison are rigid and not susceptible to the changes common amongst street gangs. Environments affect how gangs manage conflict. Violence and crime in the street gang is chaotic while prison gang violence and crime is controlled by gang leaders due to a mutual need for violence reduction within correctional facilities. Lastly, while street gangs experience an antagonistic relationship with law enforcement because of formal policies such as stop and frisk and informal policies such as harassment of identified gang members, prison gangs have a complicated relationship with correctional staff that is determined by the type of correctional officer present in a facility.

Jennifer M. Ortiz, *Gangs and Environment: A Comparative Analysis of Prison and Street Gangs*, 2 AM. J. OF QUAL. RES. 97 (2018).

In relative historical terms, prison gangs are a recent development. For much of the twentieth century, inmates lived by what was known as the "Convict's Code," a central creed of which was "no snitching"—meaning no talking to authorities about inmate activities. Violation of the Code resulted in criticism, ostracism, physical violence, and sometimes death. The influence of the Code began to wane, however, in the 1970s amid rapid expansion of inmate populations, including those who were younger and more ethnically diverse. Younger inmates were less experienced with the Code and more prone to challenge the established order and hierarchy. During the time as well, racial and ethnic fault lines began dividing prison communities.

The demise of the Code made life less predictable for inmates. Spontaneous and uncoordinated acts of violence became more prevalent and the need for personal security increased. Out of this world rose what is regarded as the first prison gang, in California: the "Mexican Mafia," comprised of Mexican-American inmates who were victimized by black and white inmates. Thereafter, gangs of all kinds developed in prisons, and efforts by authorities to thin their ranks by transfer to other institutions served only to disperse their presence.

Today, gangs provide inmates an opportunity for collective security, most often based on race or ethnicity (e.g., the "Aryan Brotherhood," "Black Guerilla Family"). In some institutions, gangs figure centrally in order maintenance, serving as the de facto disciplinary authority in place of, or in conjunction with, guards. They can provide inmates a means of survival, protecting them from physical and sexual predation. Gangs are also a conduit for the entry of illicit drugs, weapons, and other contraband from outside, sold for profit and dominance within and beyond prison walls. *See generally* DAVID C. PYROOZ & SCOTT H. DECKER, COMPETING FOR CONTROL: GANGS AND THE SOCIAL ORDER OF PRISONS (2019).

Testament to the integral role that gangs and race/ethnicity more generally play in modern prison life is the equal protection challenge heard by the Supreme Court in *Johnson v. California*, 543 U.S. 499 (2005). The plaintiffs in the case challenged an unwritten policy in California of racially segregating inmates in double cells for their first sixty days in a new facility. The state maintained that doing so was a racially neutral policy "necessary to prevent violence caused by racial gangs." The Court did not reach the merits of the equal protection claim, stating only that strict scrutiny applied to the race-based segregation strategy.

4. GEOGRAPHIC LOCATION

Prisons are often located in remote rural areas considerable distances away from inmates' home communities. They are major employers in their communities, and are advocated for by powerful local politicians, which in significant part explains their location and slim political prospects for decommission. *See generally* Eric Schlosser, *The Prison-Industrial Complex*, THE ATLANTIC, Dec. 1998. A similar phenomenon explains the proliferation and sustainment of county-operated jails. As one commentator recently noted:

> [the] sheriffs and [local government actors] make jail construction happen, often for reasons that have little to do with local public safety. They are responsible for proposing, justifying the need for, obtaining support (whether from the electorate or other sources) to fund, and determining the size of an expansion. . . . And they participate in a bedspace market that generates revenue . . . and fuels jail growth.

Aaron Littman, *Jails, Sheriffs, and Carceral Policymaking*, 74 VAND L. REV. 861, 865 (2021). *See also* JACOB KANG-BROWN & RAM SUBRAMANIAN,

VERA INST. OF JUSTICE, OUT OF SIGHT: THE GROWTH OF JAILS IN RURAL AMERICA (2017).[5]

Location can have a major impact on an inmate's life. Doing time in an institution that is far away from home makes it harder for visits from family and others. Steven Koh, *Geography and Justice: Why Prison Location Matters in U.S. and International Theories of Criminal Punishment*, 46 VAND. J. TRANSNAT'L L. 1267 (2013). This is important because a large body of research makes clear the importance to successful reentry of inmates maintaining family and social support systems while incarcerated. *See, e.g.*, Susan McNeeley & Grant Duwe, *Keep Your Friends Close and Your Enemies Closer: Prison Visitation, Spatial Distance, Concentrated Disadvantage of Visitor Neighborhoods, and Offender Recidivism*, 37 JUST. QTLY. 571 (2020).

The characteristics of a particular prison can also significantly affect inmate life. Living in a Southern prison in the summer, for instance, can be especially unpleasant when, as in Texas, air conditioning is rarely if ever used. Mary E. Adair, *Beat the Heat: Texas's Need to Reduce Summer Temperatures in Offender Housing*, 51 ST. MARY'S L.J. 707 (2020). Furthermore, some prisons are more violent than others. A U.S. Department of Justice report, for instance, recently found that Alabama inmates were routinely subject to physical harm and death, at the hands of fellow inmates and guards. U.S. DEP'T OF JUSTICE, INVESTIGATION OF ALABAMA'S STATE PRISONS FOR MEN (2019). A reporter for the *New York Times* said of the thousands of photos from inside Alabama prisons she viewed:

> The contraband is scary enough: Homemade knives with grips whittled to fit particular hands. Homemade machetes. And homemade armor, with books and magazines for padding. Then there is the blood: In puddles. In toilets. Scrawled on the wall in desperate messages. Bloody scalps, bloody footprints, blood streaming down a cheek like tears. And the dead: a man kneeling like a supplicant, hands bound behind his back with white fabric strips and black laces. Another, hanging from a twisted sheet in the dark, virtually naked, illuminated by a flashlight beam. These were ugly scenes from inside an American prison, apparently taken as official documentation of violence and rule violations.

---

[5] A recent story concerning Alabama jails highlighted another instance of the entrepreneurial wherewithal of sheriffs, noting that "Alabama has a Depression-era law that allows sheriffs to 'keep and retain' unspent money from jail food-provision accounts. Sheriffs across the state take excess money as personal income—and, in the event of a shortfall, are personally liable for covering the gap." One sheriff used his $750,000 surplus to buy a $740,000 beach house. Camilia Domonoske, Nat. Pub. Radio, *Alabama Sheriff Legally Took $750,000 Meant To Feed Inmates, Bought Beach House*, Mar. 14, 2018, https://www.npr.org/sections/thetwo-way/2018/03/14/593204274/alabama-sheriff-legally-took-750-000-meant-to-feed-inmates-bought-beach-house.

Shaila Dewan, *Inside America's Black Box: A Rare Look at the Violence of Incarceration*, N.Y. TIMES, Mar. 30, 2019.

It is also important to note that inmates can be transferred outside the jurisdiction that sentenced them. In the federal corrections system, inmates are commonly shuttled around the nation's different institutions. One might be convicted in Atlanta, Georgia, and perhaps begin serving one's sentence there, but later serve time in Kansas or California. States also engage in what has been called the "prisoner trade." Vermont, for instance, outsources a sixth of its state prison population, and Hawaii houses around half of its prisoners on the mainland. At various points in the last decade, Wyoming exported a third of its prison population, and California shipped out roughly 10,000 prisoners. Until 2019, La Palma Correctional Facility, a private prison in Arizona, held only people serving California time. Emma Kaufman, *The Prisoner Trade*, 133 HARV. L. REV. 1815 (2020).

States transfer inmates for a variety of reasons, including to alleviate overcrowding, reduce staffing costs, impose discipline, and mitigate risk of harm by particular inmates. Professor Kaufman notes that

> out-of-state imprisonment is relatively new. Exporting prisoners was illegal in many states until the mid-twentieth century and was uncommon everywhere until states built the infrastructure required to move and monitor prisoners. Then states started to share prison beds, to swap prisoners, and to pay private companies to hold prisoners across state lines. Slowly, state borders grew less salient to the practice of punishment.

Id. at 1818. Being shipped out of state can pose even greater personal hardships and logistical challenges than a facility's rural location. The Supreme Court, however, has held that an inmate has no due process right to remain in the polity that imposed sentence. *Olim v. Wakinekona*, 461 U.S. 238 (1983). Several states have constitutional prohibitions on banishment, yet with the exception of West Virginia, state supreme courts have held that interstate transfer is permissible. Kaufman, *supra*.[6]

[6] Professor Kaufman notes that despite the constitutionality of interstate transfer, the practice presents a number of important legal questions:

> If a prisoner remains in the constructive custody of his home state after an interstate transfer, who is the proper custodian when a prisoner brings a habeas claim? Which state's officers can be sued for violations of a prisoner's constitutional rights? Is a prisoner governed by the security classification, grievance procedures, and disciplinary rules of his home state or the state where he is confined? When is medical care sufficiently unusual or serious to warrant payment by a sending state? Who decides when a prisoner is eligible for parole or other forms of discretionary early release? Which state's criminal code applies when a prisoner commits a crime in an out-of-state prison? The list goes on.

Kaufman, *supra*, at 1831.

One final ramification of physical location worthy of attention is of a less personal nature. Inmates are usually counted by the U.S. Census Bureau as residents of their incarceration location during confinement, not their home residence. This is important because the degree of democratic representation in state legislatures is usually tied to population size, which means that locales with prisons experience a corresponding increase in political power. The outcome has been referred to as "prison gerrymandering," which benefits the often rural and predominantly white jurisdictions where prisons are located. In response, a few states (e.g., New York and California) have enacted laws requiring population assessments to be determined by inmates' last known home. *See* Michael Skocpol, Note, *The Emerging Constitutional Law of Prison Gerrymandering*, 69 STAN. L. REV. 1473 (2017).[7]

Gerrymandering, of course, is a common occurrence. Is there reason to think, however, that it is more problematic when based on the counting of prison populations? Do you think elected political leaders in such a system represent the interests of their "constituents" behind prison walls (who are very likely not allowed to vote, as discussed in Chapter 11)? If you favor allowing inmates to vote, should their vote pertain to where they are incarcerated, i.e., local elections? What are the pros and cons of such a policy?

Another outgrowth of using prison as a residence situs is that it can affect funding by the state and federal governments. According to Professor Pam Karlan, the incarceration of roughly 26,000 individuals from Chicago in downstate prisons in the 2000 census would result in a loss to the city of $88 million in government aid over the coming decade. Pamela S. Karlan, *Convictions and Doubts: Retribution, Representation, and the Debate Over Felon Disenfranchisement*, 56 STAN. L. REV. 1147 (2004).

Critics of prison gerrymandering assert that it creates a situation akin to the infamous "Three-Fifths" Clause contained in the original Constitution, which treated enslaved African-Americans as less than full persons: although they were not allowed to vote, they were counted as three-fifths of a person for political representation purposes, increasing the political power of slave states. Are you persuaded?

5. PRISON LABOR

Prison labor has a long history in the U.S. Early on, inmates not facing the death penalty were subjected to hard labor, in the name of deterrence (specific and general), whether done in public or inside, and rehabilitation, inculcating habits of industry and sobriety. In the rapidly industrializing North, "carceral capitalism" figured centrally in the early-

[7] For a recent decision permitting a proposed initiative petition that would create a new state constitutional provision allowing for possible reallocation of prisoners to their home addresses for purposes of redistricting, see *In re* Petition Initiative No. 426, 465 P.3d 1244 (Okla. 2020).

mid nineteenth century. "Through the contract system, states sold their property rights in convicts' labor to some of the period's largest corporations in exchange for substantial revenues—often up to 150 percent the costs of carceral administration. Facing tortuous punishment for refusal to work, inmates toiled for private companies who built factories inside of state and federal prisons." Genevieve LeBaron, *Rethinking Prison Labor: Social Discipline and the State in Historical Perspective*, 15 J. OF LABOR & SOC'Y 327, 333 (2012). "By the 1880s, between 75 and 95 percent of Northern prisoners worked in large-scale industrial factories producing the equivalent of over US $30 billion (in 2005 dollars) a year in goods." *Id.* at 334. The advantages to businesses were substantial:

> Companies paid no rent for buildings, storage, or insurance, and paid only low (if any) costs for labor supervision and discipline (as these were tasks shared by the state). Perhaps most significantly, prison contractors purchased convict labor well below free-market rates. Although it varied by state, the per diem price of a prison laborer was anything from one-fifth and one-third the daily wage of a free local laborer in the same industry. In the case of a Massachusetts shoe contract, for example, the per diem rate of state prison labor was US $0.15 per prisoner per day, compared with the US $2.40 that a free cobbler would have cost per day.

Id. at 336.

In the South a distinct system of prison labor emerged in the wake of the Civil War. Faced with the loss of labor provided by enslaved African-Americans, governments and business interests seized upon key language in the Thirteenth Amendment, which while outlawing slavery, allowed involuntary servitude "as a punishment for crime whereof the party shall have been duly convicted." Under what was known as the convict lease system, private businesses, such as those mining coal or phosphate, growing cotton, or extracting resin from pine trees to manufacture turpentine, would "lease" inmates from the state to perform work beyond prison walls. Inmates toiled fifteen to seventeen hours a day and slept and ate in shackles in "rolling iron cages" that were moved about based on need. LeBaron, *supra*, at 338. The conditions were atrocious, subsistence at best, and inmates themselves were treated as fungible: "it was profitable to literally work the prisoners to death because procuring new ones did not interfere with profits. In Mississippi, not a single leased convict lived long enough to serve a sentence of ten years or more," and at death their unclaimed bodies were purchased by a medical school for student training. *Id.* at 339.[8] The private companies

[8] For a provocative historical reexamination of the Thirteenth Amendment, arguing that its Northern Republican Framers believed that convicted individuals retained protection against any servitude inflicted not as a punishment for crime, but for some non-penological end, such as raising state revenue or generating private profits, see James G. Pope, *Mass*

paid fees to the state and were responsible for the care of inmates, who were usually African-American males arrested on weak or fabricated charges of vagrancy or loitering. Unable to pay the fine imposed ($25, for example), the individuals were indentured to private businesses.[9]

In institutions like Parchman Farm, in Mississippi, and Angola Penitentiary, in Louisiana, which still exist today, inmates performed field work and other tasks under conditions strongly reminiscent of antebellum plantations, this time benefitting the state, not only private business interests. The Supreme Court of Virginia, in an 1871 case involving the murder trial of a leased state convict, memorably described prisoners as "slaves of the State." *Ruffin v. Commonwealth*, 62 Va. (21 Gratt.) 790 (1871).

Today, prison labor plays a core role in prison life. Inmates perform a broad variety of work: they maintain the institution, such as by working in the prison kitchen or laundry, or producing food by field and agricultural work; perform public works, such as building or repairing roads, picking up trash or fighting forest fires; produce goods or services for use outside the prison (e.g., making auto license plates and road signs); and provide products for private companies (e.g., garments).

States are free to set their prison pay scale with very little or no payment. In eight states (Alabama, Arkansas, Florida, Georgia, Mississippi, Oklahoma, South Carolina, and Texas) for some jobs no pay is provided. Nationwide, the typical inmate earns between $0.14 and $0.63 per hour, and prison work does not constitute covered employment under federal social security law; nor are inmates "employees" under the federal Fair Labor Standards Act, which among other things ensures increased pay for overtime work. Stephanie McMahon, *Inmates May Work, But Don't Tell Social Security*, 72 S. C. L. REV. 757 (2021).

Whether inmates feel coerced to perform work is a subject of concern. In Texas prisons, able inmates are required to work and if they refuse they lose privileges and possibly good-time credits. Under the system, "Texas Correctional Industries" recently generated more than $70 million a year for the prison system. Chris Tomlinson, *Prison Labor Isn't Just a Problem in China. It Happens in Texas, Too*, HOUS. CHRON., Aug. 27, 2021.

What would an advocate of prison labor today argue—perhaps that it allows the state to recoup expenses of incarceration or provides a skill? What if the low-skill work inmates undertake does not provide them with marketable skills? Does the age-old rationale that work instills discipline and combats the corrosive effect of idleness suffice? What are your views?

Incarceration, Convict Leasing, and the Thirteenth Amendment: A Revisionist Account, 94 N.Y.U. L. REV. 1465 (2019).

[9] For an in-depth look at the era, see DOUGLAS A. BLACKMON, SLAVERY BY ANOTHER NAME: THE RE-ENSLAVEMENT OF BLACK AMERICANS FROM THE CIVIL WAR TO WORLD WAR II (2008); MATTHEW MANCINI, ONE DIES, GET ANOTHER: CONVICT LEASING IN THE AMERICAN SOUTH, 1866–1928 (1996).

6. PHYSICAL HARM AND DEATH

Although day-to-day prison life is mostly marked by routinized sameness and boredom, inmates often face intimidation, serious physical harm, and death. The threat emanates from fellow prisoners and corrections officers alike.[10] Studies suggest that up to 66% of inmates experience physical victimization during incarceration, with many instances believed to go unreported due to concern over reprisal. *See* Teresa Braga et al., *How Dark Are Dark Figures? Official and Self-Report Rates of Inmate-on-Inmate Victimization*, 14 VICTIMS & OFFENDERS 745 (2019); Nancy Wolf et al., *Physical Violence Inside Prisons: Rates of Victimization*, 34 CRIM. JUST. & BEHAV. 588 (2007).

The risk of physical harm can be enhanced among particular subpopulations. LGBTQ inmates, for instance, are especially vulnerable to physical abuse and mistreatment, by both staff and other prisoners. VALERIE JENNESS ET AL., VIOLENCE IN CALIFORNIA CORRECTIONAL FACILITIES: AN EMPIRICAL EXAMINATION OF SEXUAL ASSAULT (2007). Also, as has become rather commonly known, inmates convicted of sexually assaulting children are often singled out by fellow inmates for harassment, intimidation, and violence. Charles Schwaebe, *Learning to Pass: Sex Offenders' Strategies for Establishing a Viable Identity in the General Prison Population*, 49 INT'L J. OFF. THERAPY & COMP. CRIMINOLOGY 614 (2005).

Homicides, statistically speaking, are a relatively rare occurrence (almost 90% of deaths in state and federal prisons in 2019 were the result of illness). However, homicides are on the rise: the 143 homicides in state prisons in 2019 were nearly four times the number reported in 2001. E. ANN CARSON, U.S. DEP'T OF JUSTICE, MORTALITY IN STATE AND FEDERAL PRISONS, 2001–2019, STATISTICAL TABLES (2021). For discussion of the possible causes and correlates of prison homicides, see Matt DeLisi & H. Daniel Butler, *Murder as Importation: An Empirical Study of the Continuity of Homicide Offending from Community to Confinement*, 24 HOMICIDE STUD. 398 (2020).

Violence not only affects those directly experiencing physical harm. One study of recently released adult male inmates in Ohio, for instance, found that almost all reported witnessing violence while they were incarcerated. Benjamin C. Hattem, Note, *Carceral Trauma and Disability Law*, 72 STAN. L. REV. 995 (2020). For discussion of the impact of witnessing such violence, see Diane C. Daquin et al., *Vicarious Victimization in Prison: Examining the Effects of Witnessing Victimization While Incarcerated on Offender Reentry*, 43 CRIM. JUST. & BEHAV. 1018 (2016).

---

[10] Prison staff also face significant risk of physical assault. *See* Srinivas Konda et al., *U.S. Correctional Officers Killed or Injured on the Job*, 75 CORR. TODAY 122 (2013).

7. SEXUAL VICTIMIZATION

Sexual abuse of inmates is disturbingly common. To be "punked" in prison is for a male to be forced into a sexually submissive role; to be "turned out" is to be raped, resulting in a perceived change in sexual appearance or orientation. In 2015, there were almost 25,000 sexual abuse reports in state and federal prison and jails. Of the reported victimizations, 58% were by staff on inmates and 42% were by fellow inmates. From 2012–2014 the number of sexual assault allegations nearly tripled. RAMONA R. RANTALA, U.S. DEP'T OF JUSTICE, SEXUAL VICTIMIZATION REPORTED BY ADULT CORRECTIONAL AUTHORITIES, 2012–15 (2018). Female inmates are at particular risk for sexual assault by male guards. Elena M. Stern, Comment, *Accessing Accountability: Exploring Criminal Prosecution of Male Guards for Sexually Assaulting Female Inmates in U.S. Prisons*, 167 U. PA. L. REV. 733 (2019).[11] As with physical violence, concern exists that the actual rates of sexual assault are under-reported, due to stigmatization and fear of reprisal. Chandra Bozelko, *Why We Let Prison Rape Go On*, N.Y. TIMES, Apr. 17, 2015.

Sexual victimization is a particular risk for gay and transgender inmates. A 2007 study conducted in the California prison system found that 67% percent of inmates who identified as LGBTQ reported being sexually assaulted by another inmate during their incarceration, a rate 15 times higher than the inmate population overall. JENNESS ET AL., *supra*. A report by Human Rights Watch observed that "many gay inmates—even those who are openly gay outside of prison—carefully hide their sexual identities while incarcerated. . . because inmates who are perceived as gay by other inmates face a very high risk of sexual abuse." HUMAN RIGHTS WATCH, NO ESCAPE: MALE RAPE IN U.S. PRISONS 52 (2001).

The risk faced by LGBTQ populations can prompt institutions to take special precautions. One strategy is to house individuals separately from the general population. Often, this takes the form of protective custody, a form of solitary confinement. According to one commentator, the resulting isolation is problematic: while it might promote safety, it "force[s] vulnerable prisoners into the cruel position of having to choose between personal safety and the satisfaction of other basic and urgent human needs, above all, those of community and fellow human contact." Sharon Dolovich, *Strategic Segregation in the Modern Prison*, 48 AM. CRIM. L. REV. 1, 4 (2011). As a result, perversely, use of isolation might discourage reporting of abuse in the first instance. On the challenges and difficulties posed more generally, see Jessica Szuminski, Note, *Behind the Binary Bars: A Critique of Prison Placement Policies for Trans-*

---

[11] Of note, in some federal judicial circuits consent can serve as a defense to an Eighth Amendment sexual assault claim brought by an inmate against an officer. Nika Arzoumanian, Comment, *Consent Behind Bars: Should It Be a Defense Against Inmates' Claims of Sexual Assault?*, 2019 U. CHI. LEGAL F. 415.

Gender, Non-Binary, and Gender Non-Conforming Prisoners, 105 MINN. L. REV. 477 (2020).

Sexual assault is likely under-reported, due both to fear of reprisal (by an offending fellow inmate or guard) and stigmatization. Hannah Brenner et al., *Bars to Justice: The Impact of Rape Myths on Women in Prison*, 17 GEO. J. GENDER & L. 521, 555 (2016).

In response to nationwide concern over sexual assault in prisons, Congress in 2003 unanimously passed the Prison Rape Elimination Act. The PREA was intended, inter alia, to promote increased reporting and impose enforceable best practices standards for reducing the incidence of assaults. For a discussion of whether and how the PREA has proved beneficial, see Brenda V. Smith, *Promise and Peril: PREA's Efforts to Regulate an End to Prison Rape*, 57 AM. CRIM. L. REV. 1599 (2020).

NOTES & QUESTIONS

1. **Role of Defense Counsel.** Skilled criminal defense counsel will do their best to marshal a client toward a less dangerous or unpleasant prison, to the extent it exists. Inmates, of course, are regularly transported from one institution to another during their imprisonment term. To the extent the latter does not occur, or even if does, should the time spent in a more problematic prison environment "count" more when devising a sentence? How likely is it that a corrections system will publicly acknowledge such inter-institutional differences?

2. **Judicial Consideration of Conditions?** In *Farmer v. Brennan*, 511 U.S. 825 (1994), a trans woman, was placed in the general male prison population and was beaten and raped. The Court rejected the inmate's Eighth Amendment cruel and deliberate indifference challenge. Justice Thomas, in his solo concurring opinion, wrote that "conditions of confinement are not punishment in any recognized sense of the term, unless imposed as part of a sentence. . . .[B]ecause the unfortunate attack that befell petitioner was not part of his sentence, it did not constitute 'punishment' under the Eighth Amendment." *Id.* at 859 (Thomas, J., concurring). Earlier, in *Rhodes v. Chapman*, 452 U.S. 337 (1981), Justice Powell wrote for the majority that "[t]o the extent that [prison] conditions are restrictive and even harsh, they are part of the penalty that criminal offenders pay for their offense against society." Justice Kennedy, in the American Bar Association speech noted earlier, acknowledged that imprisonment seeks "to degrade and demean the prisoner." And prison rape is often seen as a just deserts punishment. I. Bennett Capers, *Real Rape Too*, 99 CAL. L. REV. 1259 (2011).

No sentencing judge, of course, would specifically impose the most dire aspects of prison life on a convicted individual. Does the foregoing alter your view on whether a sentence should reflect not only the known intended deprivations of prison life, but also its less common but equally known recurring hardships?

3. **Judicial Consideration of Personal Impact?** More generally, should the subjective experience of a given individual be considered when

determining a prison sentence? For instance, presume Inmate has been diagnosed as suffering from claustrophobia, a medically recognized situational anxiety disorder triggered by an irrational and intense fear of closed or crowded place. Or that Inmate is physically weak or disabled, making him more susceptible to abuse and possible violence. What if Inmate was convicted of a sexual offense involving a child, a subpopulation known to be singled out for particular disdain in prisons? Law enforcement, and sometimes other governmental actors convicted of crimes, also often face unique challenges, and threats, behind prison walls.

Should these personal or situational characteristics be considered? What would a retributivist argue? A proponent of deterrence? Would concern over the sentence disparity that would inevitably be created be outweighed by other concerns? The questions have prompted an interesting academic debate in recent years. *See, e.g.*, Christopher Wildeman et al., *The Hedonic Consequences of Prison Revisited*, 104 J. CRIM. L. & CRIMINOLOGY 133 (2014).

4. **State Versus Federal.** Historically, until the 1930s, federal criminal law was quite modest in its scope, concerning such rare crimes as treason. Today, however, it is quite common for federal criminal law to overlap with state criminal law, for instance regarding drug and firearm offenses, robbery, and kidnapping. At the same time, state and federal prisons can significantly differ in their conditions (with the latter often thought "softer"). If an individual is disadvantaged, in relative terms by the jurisdictional channeling, should this be the basis for a constitutional challenge of some kind?

8. PHYSICAL AND MENTAL HEALTH

Infectious diseases, including hepatitis C, tuberculosis, and HIV/AIDS, are more prevalent in prisons, which operate in confined space and are very often overcrowded. LÉON DIGARD ET AL., VERA INSTITUTE OF JUSTICE, RETHINKING RESTRICTIVE HOUSING: LESSONS FROM FIVE U.S. JAIL AND PRISON SYSTEMS (2018). Outbreaks of methicillin-resistant staphylococcus aureus (MRSA) occurred in California, Georgia, Mississippi, and Texas institutions due to limited medical care, lack of access to hygienic supplies, and overcrowding. *See* Bianca Malcolm, *The Rise of Methicillin-Resistant Staphylococcus Aureus in U.S. Correctional Populations*, 17 J. CORR. HEALTH CARE 254 (2011).

The nation's recent experience with the COVID pandemic starkly highlighted the difficulties presented. Crowded, confined prison spaces, where social distancing is challenging at best, proved fertile vectors for transmission. As of late 2020, almost 2,000 inmates died of the virus, and thousands more contracted it. Madeline Carlisle & Josiah Bates, *With Over 275,000 Infections and 1,700 Deaths, COVID-19 Has Devastated the U.S. Prison and Jail Population*, TIME MAG., Dec. 28, 2020.

Officials, faced with the dual institutional obligations of incarceration and maintaining the health of inmates, are placed in unenviable positions. Measures such as quarantine are less feasible behind the walls, and solitary confinement, as discussed, can have very negative effects on individuals. For discussion of these and other issues, see David H. Cloud et al., *Medical Isolation and Solitary Confinement: Balancing Health and Humanity in US Jails and Prisons During COVID-19*, 35 J. INTERN. MED. 2738 (2020); Andre G. Montoya-Barthelemy et al., *COVID-19 and the Correctional Environment: The American Prison as a Focal Point for Public Health*, 58 AM. J. PREV. MED. 888 (2020).

More generally, many inmates have preexisting health problems, aggravated by poor or nonexistent health care they received prior to prison. Hypertension, diabetes, asthma, and other serious diseases can get worse in prison and render inmates susceptible to other medical problems. Andrew P. Wilper et al., *The Health and Health Care of US Prisoners: Results of a Nationwide Survey*, 99 AM. J. PUB. HEALTH 666 (2009).[12]

Medical care in prisons is often sub-par. A foremost reason is lack of funding, which can vary significantly among states. Louisiana, which has the nation's highest imprisonment rate, spends the least, averaging \$2,173 per person in fiscal year 2015. California had the highest per capita rate: \$19,796. The national average was \$5,720. PEW CHARITABLE TRUST, PRISON HEALTH CARE SPENDING VARIES DRAMATICALLY BY STATE (2017).

Lack of funds will obviously impact the extent of supplies available and the quality of medical staff. But even in California health care can be alarmingly poor. In *Brown v. Plata*, 563 U.S. 493 (2011), inmates at several severely overcrowded California prisons brought a class action challenging, inter alia, poor medical care. In granting relief the Court provided the following account:

> Prisoners suffering from physical illness . . . receive severely deficient care. California's prisons were designed to meet the medical needs of a population at 100% of design capacity and so have only half the clinical space needed to treat the current population. A correctional officer testified that, in one prison, up to 50 sick inmates may be held together in a 12-by-20-foot cage for up to five hours awaiting treatment. The number of staff is inadequate, and prisoners face significant delays in access to care. A prisoner with severe abdominal pain died after a 5-week delay in referral to a specialist; a prisoner with " 'constant and extreme' " chest pain died after an 8-hour delay in evaluation by a doctor; and a prisoner died of testicular cancer after a "failure of MDs to work up for cancer in a young man with 17 months of

[12] Because inmates often come from disadvantaged communities, where consistent access to quality health care can be difficult, it cannot be said with certainty that prison causes the higher rates of serious medical conditions in inmate populations. However, as two researchers found, while "the contribution of prisons to illness is unknown, the shortcomings in treatment and aftercare provision contribute to adverse outcomes." Seena Fazel & Jacques Baillargeon, *The Health of Prisoners*, 377 LANCET 956 (2011).

> testicular pain." Doctor Ronald Shansky, former medical director of the Illinois state prison system, surveyed death reviews for California prisoners. He concluded that extreme departures from the standard of care were "widespread," and that the proportion of "possibly preventable or preventable" deaths was "extremely high." Many more prisoners, suffering from severe but not life-threatening conditions, experience prolonged illness and unnecessary pain.

Id. at 504.

Mental disorders are also common among inmates. According to Bureau of Justice Statistics, in 2011–2012 about 14% of state and federal prisoners and 26% jail inmates reported experiences that met the threshold for serious psychological distress in the last thirty days (versus 5% in the general population). The Bureau also reported that 37% of prisoners and 44% of jail inmates had been told in the past by a mental health professional that they had a mental disorder. Among these individuals, a large percentage of prisoners (24%) and jail inmates (31%) reported they had a major depressive disorder. Women reported higher rates of recent serious psychological distress, in both prison (20.5% vs. 14% for men) and jail (32% vs. 25%). JENNIFER BRONSON & MARCUS BERZOFSKY, U.S. DEP'T OF JUSTICE, INDICATORS OF MENTAL HEALTH PROBLEMS REPORTED BY PRISONERS AND JAIL INMATES, 2011–12 (2017).

One factor believed to contribute to the troublingly high rates is the de-institutionalization effort starting in the 1950s that resulted in the shuttering of many large mental institutions. The large institutions were to be replaced by smaller, community-based treatment options. The resources and the political will needed to effectuate the shift, however, never materialized, leaving mentally ill individuals without help, leading to their ensnarement in the criminal justice system. Deinstitutionalization, it has been observed, is perhaps most accurately described as trans-institutionalization, whereby individuals who formerly would have been placed in psychiatric institutions have found themselves in prisons and jails. Over time, the number of individuals with serious mental illness increased as the number of beds in psychiatric facilities decreased. *See* Andrea Segal et al., *County Jail or Psychiatric Hospital? Ethical Challenges in Correctional Health Care*, 28 QUAL. HEALTH RES. 963 (2018).

In *Brown v. Plata*, discussed *supra*, in addition to noting the troubling medical health care situation in California state prisons, the majority described the system's mental health care difficulties:

> Prisoners in California with serious mental illness do not receive minimal, adequate care. Because of a shortage of treatment beds, suicidal inmates may be held for prolonged periods in telephone-booth-sized cages without toilets. A psychiatric expert reported observing an inmate who had been held in such a cage for nearly 24 hours, standing in a pool of his

> own urine, unresponsive and nearly catatonic. Prison officials explained they had " 'no place to put him.' " Other inmates awaiting care may be held for months in administrative segregation, where they endure harsh and isolated conditions and receive only limited mental health services. Wait times for mental health care range as high as 12 months.

Plata, 563 U.S. at 504–04. Professor Craig Haney, a leading researcher who has spent decades studying the issue, recently commented on the acute problem, and the ill-suited nature of the prison environment for housing individuals suffering from serious mental illnesses:

> The fact that there are presently about 10 times more identified mentally ill persons in prisons and jails in the United States than in mental hospitals is tragic for a number of reasons. But to get to the tragic crux of the matter, let me simply say that, if any one of us were challenged to devise an environment that was uniquely ill suited to address the needs of psychologically vulnerable persons—those formally diagnosed with mentally illness as well as the broader group of emotionally fragile persons or those who are especially prone to unstable behavior (perhaps as the result of an extensive history of trauma, severe forms of material or economic deprivation, or other background "risk factors' 'from which they have suffered)—we would be hard pressed to come up with anything worse than the modern American prison. Prisons are fraught with danger, dehumanization, and deprivation, and pervaded by all of the negative emotions that those things engender. They are the very antithesis of a treatment-oriented milieu that promotes openness, caring, and mutual concern.

Craig Haney, *"Madness" and Penal Confinement: Some Observations on Mental Illness and Prison Pain*, 19 PUNISH. & SOC'Y 310, 311 (2017).

Prisons and jails alike face the challenge but the problem is perhaps most acute in jails, operated by local governments that often lack the resources of states. The Cook County Jail, in Chicago, has been called the city's "largest mental health facility." After drastic budget cuts left many residents without access to mental health care, the city's massive jail was flooded with individuals with serious mental health problems, becoming the "de facto mental health hospital." It is estimated that 35% of the jail's population suffers from mental illness. Jailers, not trained mental health professionals, were asked to fill the need, with clinicians and social workers in short supply. LILI HOLZER-GLIER, VERA INSTITUTE OF JUSTICE, INSIDE THE MASSIVE JAIL THAT DOUBLES AS CHICAGO'S LARGEST MENTAL HEALTH FACILITY (2016).

Imprisoned individuals also suffer high rates of illicit drug dependence or use. According to Bureau of Justice Statistics data, in 2002 up to 60% of prison and jail inmates met DSM-IV criteria for drug dependence or abuse, a rate grossly disproportional to that of the general population (about 8%). As with mental health services, drug treatment services fall far short of what is needed, and that which is provided is often deficient. Redonna K. Chandler et al., *Treating Drug Abuse and Addiction in the Criminal Justice System*, 301 J. AM. MED. ASS'N 183 (2009).

Tragically, high rates of mental illness align with high prison suicide rates. In *Brown v. Plata*, the Court observed that

> In 2006, the suicide rate in California's prisons was nearly 80% higher than the national average for prison populations; and a court-appointed Special Master found that 72.1% of suicides involved "some measure of inadequate assessment, treatment, or intervention, and were therefore most probably foreseeable and/or preventable."

Plata, 563 U.S. at 504.

NOTES & QUESTIONS

1. **Inside/Outside?** When discussing health care in prisons, one matter worth noting is that very often inmates, who most frequently hail from disadvantaged communities with limited health care, are constitutionally entitled to health care in prison (*see infra*). As a result, theoretically, those convicted of crimes and serving time in prison receive better health care than law-abiding citizens on the outside. Does/should this affect your view on whether jurisdictions should take more ambitious steps in ensuring provision of quality health care to inmates?

2. **The Government's Dime?** Imagine that Inmate, who has long struggled with gender identity, is serving a ten-year prison sentence for burglary. Presume that the expensive gender-conforming surgical procedure and post-operative treatment would not be covered by Medicare, Medicaid, or private insurance on the outside, and would have to be paid by Inmate "out of pocket." Should the prison (i.e., the government) be required to pay for the procedure and treatment, when Inmate, if before or after prison, lacked the financial means to get them? For discussion of the issue see Samantha Braver, Note, *Circuit Court Dysphoria: The Status of Gender Confirmation Surgery Requests by Incarcerated Transgender Individuals*, 120 COLUM. L. REV. 2235 (2020).

C. ELDERLY IN PRISONS

Crime, criminologists have long noted, is a "young man's game." What they mean is that, viewing the population as a whole, involvement in criminal activity mainly involves males and diminishes with age. Those doing time, however, are increasingly elderly. From 1993 to 2013, U.S. prison populations experienced a 400% increase in the number of adults age fifty-five or older and it was estimated that 10% of all inmates are in that age range. E. ANN CARSON, U.S. DEP'T OF JUSTICE, AGING OF THE STATE PRISON POPULATION, 1993–2013 (2016). According to a report by Human Rights Watch, between 2007 and 2010 federal and state prisoners age sixty-five or older grew ninety-four times faster than the total prisoner population. During the period, the cohort increased by 63%, while the total prison population grew by .7%. HUMAN RIGHTS WATCH, OLD BEHIND BARS: THE AGING PRISON POPULATION IN THE UNITED STATES (2012).

Today, the elderly prison population accounts for approximately 16% of the total prison population. By 2030, it is expected that inmates fifty-five years of age and older will represent approximately one-third of the total prison population. Johnny Thach, Note, *Not Far Enough: The Rising Elderly Prison Population and Criminal Justice and Prison Reform Following the First Step Act of 2018,* 26 CARDOZO J. EQUAL RTS. & SOC. JUST. 631 (2020).

Although the U.S. population in general itself is graying, the sharp increase in older inmates is chiefly explained by two factors: (1) the increasing imposition of lengthy prison terms and (2) the steady increase in the rate of older adults entering prison. As for the latter, the number of prisoners fifty-five or older sentenced to state prison increased 400% between 1993 and 2013. Testament to the impact of lengthier prison terms, 40% of state prisoners age fifty-five or older in 2013 had been imprisoned for ten years or more, compared to 9% in 1993. CARSON, *supra.*

Chronic medical problems of elderly inmates impose major fiscal and logistical challenges to the corrections system. With aging comes increased likelihood of the onset of chronic medical problems such as heart, lung, kidney, and liver disease; dementia and Alzheimer's disease; diabetes; and emphysema. Because inmates are in government custody, the government has a constitutional obligation to provide medical care (as discussed later in this Chapter). A 2012 report by the American Civil Liberties Union estimates that inmate health care costs amount to roughly $16 billion a year. ACLU, AT AMERICA'S EXPENSE: MASS INCARCERATION OF THE ELDERLY (2012).

Caring for the elderly also has very costly brick-and-mortar consequences. Many jurisdictions have built and operate new building spaces dedicated to providing medical help and hospice care. Institutions must also install ramps and shower handles and make other structural changes to accommodate inmates' physical challenges. Inmates who cannot perform daily personal tasks, such as getting out of bed, using the restroom, showering, or walking to medicine or food lines, are often placed in new assisted living areas that require staffing. Aggravating matters, infirm inmates can be vulnerable to abuse from younger and healthier inmates.

In response, what is known as "compassionate" or "geriatric conditional" release is becoming increasingly common.[13] The policy is justified on humanitarian grounds—aged inmates are able to live their last days on the outside, perhaps with family or loved ones. Early release also makes fiscal sense—corrections departments avoid the cost of providing care (although, of course, the cost of care for an indigent elderly individual could well be paid by federal government Medicare or Medicaid).

Early release, however, can be a fraught political proposition. Even if actual risk of criminal recidivism of the aged and infirm might be low, releasing individuals convicted of serious offenses like homicide and rape will not likely be politically popular. Whether governments—and taxpayers—are willing to shoulder the burdens of caring for geriatric prison populations will remain a major public policy question for decades to come. Beyond the public policy questions, is there a constitutional basis to challenge continued imprisonment of inmates with irreversible debilitating diseases? *See, e.g.*, Rachel E. Lopez, *The Unusual Cruelty of Nursing Homes Behind Bars?*, 32 FED. SENT'G REP. 264 (2020).

D. WOMEN'S INSTITUTIONS

Women's prisons were rare until the 1870s. Women in early prisons were taught to cook and sew, and most were released on parole to work as domestic servants, where it was assumed that the master of the house would ensure their subsequent good behavior. While the prisons emphasized the virtues of traditional femininity, their conditions were often quite poor. For instance, New York's Mount Pleasant Female Prison, established in 1835, routinely subjected inmates to straitjackets and gagging. A mid-1840s report from an Ohio women's prison reported that "the women fight, scratch, pull hair, curse, swear and yell, and to bring them to order a keeper has frequently to go among them with a horsewhip." Nicole H. Rafter, *Prisons for Women, 1790–1980*, 5 CRIME & JUST. 129, 145 (1983).

Conditions have improved since then but multiple inquiries in recent years have revealed troubling situations, in prisons such as the Julia Tutwiler Prison for Women in Alabama and the Lowell Correctional Institution in Florida. Of Tutwiler one reporter wrote:

> For a female inmate, there are few places worse than the Julia Tutwiler Prison for Women.
>
> Corrections officers have raped, beaten and harassed women inside the aging prison here for at least 18 years, according to an unfolding Justice Department investigation.

[13] In 2018, the First Step Act was enacted, which facilitates the early release of federal prisoners. The Act is discussed at length in Chapter 12. For discussion of opportunities for compassionate release in state institutions see FAMILIES AGAINST MAND. MINIMUMS, EVERYWHERE AND NOWHERE: COMPASSIONATE RELEASE IN THE STATES (2018).

> More than a third of the employees have had sex with prisoners, which is sometimes the only currency for basics like toilet paper and tampons.

Kim Severson, *Troubles at Women's Prison Test Alabama*, N.Y. TIMES, March 1, 2014.

The female incarcerated population, as a whole, differs from the male population in many respects. Females are more likely sentenced for non-violent crimes, such as theft and drug offenses. Incarcerated women are also significantly more likely to have reported a history of childhood physical and/or sexual abuse. Melissa S. Jones, *Life as She Knows It: Intimate Partner Violence Among Women Prisoners*, 85 CHILD ABUSE & NEG. 68 (2018).

When one considers the nation's ascending imprisonment rates over the past several decades, one striking data point is the marked increase in the number of female inmates. In 1980, just over 26,000 women were incarcerated in U.S. prisons and jails; by year-end 2019, the number had risen more than 700%—to almost 222,500. The increase was twice as high as that of men since 1980. Drug convictions have been a major driver of the increase. The proportion of incarcerated females convicted of drug offenses has increased from 12% in 1986 to 26% in 2018. Sentencing Project, *Fact Sheet: Incarcerated Women and Girls* (2020). *See also generally* Spencer K. Beall, *"Lock Her Up!": How Women Have Become the Fastest Growing Population in the American Carceral State*, 23 BERKELEY J. CRIM. L. 1 (2018).

Pregnant inmates can experience unique difficulties. The daily stresses and deprivations of prison life can take their toll, quality prenatal care is not always available, and women have been shackled during labor and childbirth. Priscilla A. Ocen, *Punishing Pregnancy: Race, Incarceration, and the Shackling of Pregnant Prisoners*, 100 CAL. L. REV. 1239 (2012). Post-partum difficulties very often go undiagnosed, and when they are, they go untreated. And because the vast majority of prisons have no facility for newborns or infants, "giving birth means saying goodbye." Alysia Santo, *The Separation,* THE MARSHALL PROJECT (May 6, 2020). *See also generally* Lauren Kuhlik & Carolyn Sufrin, *Pregnancy, Systematic Disregard, and Carceral Institutions*, 14 HARV. L. & POL'Y REV. 417 (2020).

Tens of thousands of incarcerated women are parents of children on the outside. U.S. CIV. RTS. COMM'N, BRIEFING REPORT, WOMEN IN PRISON: SEEKING JUSTICE BEHIND BARS 78–86 (2020). Journalist Andi Rierden was granted access to a Connecticut women's prison for over three years, and provided this account of one inmate's experience with family visits:

> Two weeks in segregation, with no visitors, nothing but stone-cold walls, a window to a parking lot, a pot to pee in, and thoughts, thoughts, thoughts. . . . Two weeks later [BeBe, the

inmate] emerges from segregation, from the cell block of her mind, raw, humiliated, ashamed. Her two children visit. They are very young, under ten. They still think they are visiting their mommy in the hospital. It is the lie a lot of inmates spin. BeBe prays they never learn the truth. "When will you be better, mommy?" they ask her. Soon babies, soon.

ANDI RIERDEN, THE FARM: LIFE INSIDE A WOMEN'S PRISON 125 (1997).

Women behind bars often receive less vocational training and other programming efforts that can facilitate successful reentry. According to a U.S. Civil Rights Commission Report, women "in prison are often offered work or program opportunities such as cleaning, domestic work, and 'female-coded' occupations, rather than the same chances as incarcerated men to learn new skills." U.S. CIV. RTS. COMM'N, *supra*, at 4.

The female inmate population has attracted increased public attention in recent years, due in significant part to the popular book and television series *Orange Is the New Black*. For a collection of compelling essays by women inmates see INSIDE THIS PLACE, NOT OF IT: NARRATIVES FROM WOMEN'S PRISONS (Robin Levi & Ayelet Waldman eds., 2017).

E. EXPERIMENTAL TESTING ON INMATES

One issue that is often overlooked is the historical use of inmates in medical and other experiments. As a very large, set-apart, captive population, subject to the discipline and control of authority, prison populations have significant appeal as experimental test subjects. However, obvious concern exists over the informed and voluntary consent of the inmate population, given the inherently coercive atmosphere of prison and its deprivations (enhancing, for instance, desire for money paid for being a subject).

Nevertheless, for decades prisoners have served as populations for a large range of experiments. One well-known example concerned the experiments conducted on inmates at Holmesburg Prison in Philadelphia from 1951 to 1974. The experiments were overseen by dermatologist Doctor Albert Kligman, who initially was summoned to the penitentiary to treat an outbreak of athlete's foot among inmates. Upon seeing the multitude of inmates Kligman reportedly remarked "All I saw before me were acres of skin. . . . It was like a farmer seeing a fertile field for the first time." The inmates, who participated for modest amounts of money, signed up in droves. Some tests concerned cosmetics and toiletries such as shampoo, others included the administration of radioactive materials and the toxic chemical dioxin (to test the human effects of Agent Orange, used by the military), and even mind-altering drugs on behalf of the U.S. Army and the CIA. ALLEN M. HORNBLUM, ACRES OF SKIN: HUMAN EXPERIMENTS AT HOLMESBURG PRISON: A STORY OF ABUSE AND EXPLOITATION IN THE NAME OF MEDICAL SCIENCE (1998).

Multiple other examples of experimentation exist. For instance, in the 1960s and 1970s in Oregon and Washington State scientists used inmates to determine the effect of irradiation on male fertility. Hong Truong et al., *Radiation Effect on Male Spermatogenesis and Fertility—The Science and Ethical Consideration of the Oregon and Washington Radiation Experiments on Prison Inmates*, 121 UROLOGY 33 (2018). By 1972 more than 90% of drug toxicity testing was conducted on prisoners. Ruth Faden, *Prisoners: Captive Research Population, in* THE HUMAN RADIATION EXPERIMENTS: FINAL REPORT OF THE PRESIDENT'S ADVISORY COMMITTEE (1996). *See also generally* Laura I. Appleman, *The Captive Lab Rat: Human Medical Experimentation in the Carceral State*, 61 B.C. L. REV. 1 (2020).

Today, experimentation on prisoners is regulated by federal law (45 C.F.R. sec. 46, subpart C), but leeway exists; for instance, the regulations only pertain to federally funded research. Osagie K. Obasogie, *Prisoners as Human Subjects: A Closer Look at the Institute of Medicine's Recommendations to Loosen Current Restrictions on Using Prisoners in Scientific Research*, 6 STAN. J. C.R. & C.L. (2010). According to some commentators, limits should not be imposed:

> Participating in science and enjoying benefits from the advancement of science are human rights. Some have even described participation in research as a duty. At a minimum, contributions to science are a form of community service that should be acknowledged and facilitated. Restoring participatory research rights for prisoners could enable the development of innovative accelerated rehabilitative disposition programs that inspire STEM careers. Furthermore, it could enable prisoners, despite physical separation from society, to have positive, shared experiences with family and friends who participate in research together and additionally function as one way to mend, preserve, or strengthen their connections with society. Finally, . . . as precision medicine and integration of research in healthcare become standard practice, continued "protection" of prisoners from research activities might constitute a deliberate indifference to their human and constitutionally protected right to adequate healthcare.

Elaine Huang et al., *Barred From Better Medicine? Reexamining Regulatory Barriers to the Inclusion of Prisoners in Research*, 4 J. L. & BIOSCIENCES 159, 170 (2017). Another point advanced in favor of testing is that women, African-Americans, and Latinx individuals are generally underrepresented in medical research, and that testing of these inmate populations would promote greater universality of test results. Sharona Hoffman, *Beneficial and Unusual Punishment: An Argument in Support of Prisoner Participation in Clinical Trials*, 33 IND. L. REV. 475 (2000).

Another medical-related question is whether inmates should be allowed to donate bodily organs, not in exchange for money, but rather for a reduction in sentence. In 2007, legislation in South Carolina was proposed (but not enacted) that would reduce prison sentences by 180 days for the donation of a kidney. Emily C. Lee, *Trading Kidneys for Prison Time: When Two Contradictory Legal Traditions Intersect, Which One Has the Right-of-Way?*, 43 U. SAN FRAN. L. REV. 507 (2009). More recently, two sisters in Mississippi serving life sentences (for armed robbery) were released after serving sixteen years on the condition that the younger sister donate a kidney to her ailing sibling. Mississippi Governor Haley Barbour authorized the release, stating that he acted because he believed the women no longer posed a safety risk and to relieve the state of the cost of dialysis treatment, which was approximately $200,000 a year. Timothy Williams, *Jailed Sisters Are Released for Kidney Transplant*, N.Y. TIMES, Jan. 7, 2011. *See also generally* Amanda Bersinger & Lisa Milot, *Posthumous Organ Donation as Prisoner Agency and Rehabilitation*, 65 DEPAUL L. REV. 1193 (2016). Several states (e.g., Arizona, Texas, and Utah) allow inmates to donate their organs while incarcerated if they die of natural causes while incarcerated. *See id.* at 807–09.

Presuming that you are concerned that a sentence reduction raises concern over coercion, would you favor a policy with no *quid pro quo*? Or is the prison environment itself inherently coercive, undercutting any prospect of free and informed consent? For an argument against the practice, see Whitney Hinkle, *Giving Until It Hurts: Prisoners Are Not the Answer to the National Organ Shortage*, 35 IND. L. REV. 593 (2002); in favor of the practice, see R. Bisi Adeyemo, Note/Comment, *Don't Break My Heart, My Achy Breaky Heart: A Call for Legislation to Expressly Grant Inmates the Right to Donate Their Non-Vital Organs*, 60 HOW. L.J. 781 (2017).

What of death row inmates? Should there be a limit on their donating an organ, for instance to a family member or the loved one of the homicide victim? Does/should it matter whether the medical procedure and donation occur during the inmate's life or posthumously? For arguments in favor of donation, see Shu S. Lin et al., *Prisoners on Death Row Should Be Accepted as Organ Donors*, 93 J. THORACIC SURGERY 1773 (2012). For discussion of alleged organ "harvesting" from executed individuals in China, see Wendy A. Rogers et al., *Smoke and Mirrors: Unanswered Questions and Misleading Statements Obscure the Truth About Organ Sources in China*, 42 J. MED. ETHICS 552 (2016). Should death row inmates be eligible to *receive* donated organs? *See* Ryan Kilkenny, Note, *Prisoners Are People: The Right of Death-Row Inmates to Receive Lifesaving Organ Donations*, 72 RUTGERS U. L. REV. 837 (2020).

NOTES & QUESTIONS

1. **Drawing Lines.** Are you persuaded that limits should be imposed on medical experimentation? What about non-medical experimentation, such as regarding a new kind of hair shampoo? Should there be a total ban,

based on principled objection, or should certain kinds of experimentation (e.g., medical) be allowed? Something that might warrant mention is that when several inmate-subjects in the Holmesburg dermatology experiments testified before Congress they mentioned being upset at losing a source of income. Mark Hilberman, *"Acres of Skin,"* 25 J. OF MED. ETHICS 353 (1999). Are personal autonomy interests of inmates actually worthy of more deference, inasmuch as they otherwise have so little control over their lives and decision-making?

2. **Distinctiveness of the Population.** Inmates are not allowed to participate in experimental treatments, which might extend or improve the quality of life. Hoffman, *supra*. Many inmates suffer from chronic conditions such as HIV and hepatitis, and experiments might benefit them (as well as the outside population). Should this affect the policy decision?

3. **A Matter of Perspective?** What is your view on the organ donation question? One bioethicist condemned the Mississippi deal noted earlier, stating that "[e]ither out of ignorance or out of indifference, [the Governor] shifted what had been a gift into compensation. [The Governor] turned it into a business contract." Williams, *supra*. Is your response: "So what, if that is true. The result was a win for all parties concerned?"

F. PRIVATE CORRECTIONAL INSTITUTIONS[14]

One of the most important policy changes in the past several decades involves the increase in the use of private prisons. At year-end 2019, private companies held 7% of the nation's state prison population and 16% of the federal (roughly 116,000 prisoners). Five states house more than 20% of their prison population in privately operated facilities: Montana (47%), New Mexico (36%), Tennessee (29%), Oklahoma (25%), and Oklahoma (24%). On the other hand, eighteen states in 2019 did not have any private prisons at all. E. ANN CARSON, U.S. DEP'T OF JUST., PRISONERS IN 2019 (2020).

American corrections has a long history of privatization, dating back at least to the "convict-lease" system in the post-Civil War American South (*see supra*). The orientation took on added gusto in the early 1980s, amid strains imposed by the nation's rising incarceration rates and the idea that private prisons could be operated more cheaply, a view aligned with increasing interest in privatization of government services more generally.

Private and publicly traded companies alike house inmates and they secure large profits for doing so. The public companies CoreCivic (formerly Corrections Corporation of America) and the GEO Group have a combined market capitalization of almost $5.8 billion and control over 75% of the private prison business. In 2015 alone, the companies generated over $360 million in profits. Laura I. Appleman, *Cashing In on*

[14] Chapters 8 and 9 discuss the increasing privatization of community-based corrections, such as with the electronic monitoring of probationers, and the array of interesting and important policy questions it presents.

Convicts: Privatization, Punishment, and the People, 2018 UTAH L. REV. 579, 583–84.

As the prison privatization movement has grown so too have reports of the companies providing sub-standard living conditions and care. Moreover, companies frequently provide insufficient numbers of staff, and those on site are often poorly trained and paid, resulting in high rates of violence, unrest, and prisoner escapes. Appleman, *supra*. For an insider account by a journalist working undercover in a private prison, see SHANE BAUER, AMERICAN PRISON: A REPORTER'S UNDERCOVER JOURNEY INTO THE BUSINESS OF PUNISHMENT (2018).

Whether privatization actually saves taxpayers money is a key question. On this question, Professor Laura Appleman writes:

> [R]epeated investigations have found that . . . privatizers base their contracts on imaginary costs and a set formula, saving state and local governments little if any money in the long run. In part, this is because private prisons can often cherry-pick the least expensive, least dangerous prisoners for their facilities, leaving a state's public prisons with the sickest and most violent inmates, the most expensive and most difficult to house. Even when a prison facility is outsourced, the state must continue to be involved. Generally, the state is tasked with overseeing and administering private prisons in the correctional system, creating additional governmental cost, even if state employees aren't staffing or running the prisons. . . .
>
> Occupancy requirements are another way that privatizing corrections can cost a state as much as running public facilities. A large majority of private prison contracts . . . require the state or local government to guarantee a minimum number of bodies in prison or jail beds, or else require payment to make up for empty prison cells. . . . These quotas make state taxpayers responsible for guaranteeing profits for private prison companies, instead of saving them money, as was promised.

Appleman, *Cashing In*, *supra*, at 610–11.

NOTES & QUESTIONS

1. **Prison as Non-Delegable Function?** If privatization of corrections does not provide budgetary savings, a major argument in its favor is neutralized. But beyond the cost-savings issue, and presuming that private companies can perform the job safely and adequately, is the delegation of punishment and operation of a correctional system objectionable in principle? Is there something unique about punishment and the operation of a correctional system that should preclude outsourcing? Or is the domain like any other government service?

2. **Modify the Incentive Structure?** Professor John Pfaff recently asserted that private and public prisons are "more similar than different"

and much of the criticism of private prisons could be mitigated by contracts that temper their wherewithal to secure profit maximization. According to Professor Pfaff, "[i]If states wrote different contracts—ones that did not pay per prisoner per diem rates but instead based funding on goals such as reduced recidivism risks—then the private prisons would focus on things other than just warehousing people. Importantly, some places, most notably Australia and New Zealand, but also Pennsylvania, have started to experiment with exactly this sort of idea." John F. Pfaff, *The Incentives of Private Prions*, 52 ARIZ. ST. L.J. 991, 992 (2020). Does this change your view of privatization?

3. **Staying Power.** If private prisons have not lived up to the expectations of advocates, what explains their staying power?

G. FAITH AND CHARACTER-BASED INSTITUTIONS

Another notable development in corrections strategy in recent years concerns the growth in faith-based institutions. In a sense, religious focus in prison programming is nothing new. As noted earlier, the nation's earliest prisons in New York and Pennsylvania had a heavy religious orientation. In describing modern-day programs one commentator recently noted:

> These programs exist at Federal Bureau of Prisons institutions, as well as state prisons and jails. They may be run by a church; a non-profit organization; or a private corporation . . . and their funding schemes vary widely. Many faith-based rehabilitation programs are directed at drug or alcohol abusers, while others are offered to criminal offenders in general. They vary in capacity, duration, and of course method.

Laney Ellison, Comment, *Faith-Based Rehabilitation Programs and the Establishment Clause: What Lower Courts Are Getting Wrong in the Absence of Supreme Court Precedents and How to Fix It*, 22 LEWIS & CLARK L. REV. 271, 276 (2018). For an in-depth look at one such program in Florida, where 2,600 inmates statewide participate, see Tori Schneider, *Faith, Character & Corrections: Extraordinary Program Guides Inmates' Journey to the "Free World,"* TALLAHASSEE DEMOCRAT, Nov. 24, 2019. *See also generally* TANYA ERZEN, GOD IN CAPTIVITY: THE RISE OF FAITH-BASED PRISON MINISTRIES IN THE AGE OF MASS INCARCERATION (2017).

A question that comes to mind is whether the programs violate the First Amendment's Establishment Clause. In challenges, courts focus on whether participation in the program is coerced and whether refusal results in adverse consequences. *See, e.g., Inouye v. Kemna*, 504 F.3d 705, 710 (9th Cir. 2007) (addressing forced participation in Alcoholics/ Narcotics Anonymous program, "substantially based in religion," as a prerequisite to parole).

Another question is whether faith-based programs are effective in reducing post-prison recidivism. Researchers addressing the issue must take account of a possible significant self-selection effect: that participants in the programs, in general, are already motivated to successfully reenter society. According to a review of studies undertaken on the question, "[t]hose few empirical studies that approach methodological validity either fail to show that faith-based prisons reduce recidivism or provide weak evidence in their favor." Alexander Volokh, *Do Faith-Based Prisons Work?*, 63 ALA. L. REV. 43, 45 (2011).

H. IMPACT ON FAMILIES AND COMMUNITIES

As noted in Chapter 2, today over two million individuals are incarcerated in state, local, and federal prisons and jails, making the U.S. a world leader in imprisonment. The number, stark as it is, however, does not convey the full human impact of the nation's resort to mass incarceration. Imprisonment most directly affects those held in physical captivity; however, much like tossing a pebble in a pond generates ripples, the incarceration of each individual impacts others. An inmate is very often a family member or significant other of one or more individuals living on the outside. A large literature highlights the near and long-term negative physical, psychological, educational, and financial effects of having an incarcerated parent,[15] an impact that disproportionately affects individuals hailing from disadvantaged communities already struggling with poor housing and education. *See* Amy B. Cyphert, *Prisoners of Fate: The Challenges of Creating Change for Children of Incarcerated Parents*, 77 MD. L. REV. 385 (2018).[16]

These external effects are very important and significant. An inmate's time in prison or jail might well deprive others of money, and therefore life necessities such as food or shelter. Personal connections are frayed and very often destroyed during time away; once healthy marriages, for instance, can end. Most inmates have minor age children, who are deprived of adult supervision and money for food, clothing, shelter, and other needs. The children of single parent female inmates are left in the care of others, which has major negative effects on the mothers, children, and those required to care for them. In the event no adult is available, a child might become a ward of the state, which is rarely a positive experience. Moreover, research shows that children of incarcerated parents are more likely to engage in criminal activity. *See,*

---

[15] In Kentucky, for instance, 13% of children have a parent who was or is incarcerated. It is conservatively estimated that 5.1 million children have had a parent in prison or jail at some point. ANNE E. CASEY FOUNDATION, A SHARED SENTENCE: THE DEVASTATING TOLL OF PARENTAL INCARCERATION ON KIDS, FAMILIES, AND COMMUNITIES (2016).

[16] One aspect of this financial impact, recently attracting media attention, is the significant cost involved in speaking over the phone to a loved one in prison. Such calls cost many times more than a call in the free world, imposing large debts on inmates and their loved ones, while providing states with a significant source of revenue. *See* Clint Smith, *The Lines of Connection*, ATLANTIC MAG., July 21, 2021.

e.g., Qianwei Zhao et al., *Maternal Incarceration and the Intergenerational Transmission of Imprisonment: A Nationwide Study*, 118 CHILD. & YOUTH SERVS. REV. 105461 (2020). For in-depth description of the challenges faced, see DONALD BRAMAN, DOING TIME ON THE OUTSIDE: INCARCERATION AND FAMILY LIFE IN URBAN AMERICA (2004); MEGAN COMFORT, DOING TIME TOGETHER: LOVE AND FAMILY IN THE SHADOW OF PRISON (2008).

Research on the sheer scale of imprisonment highlights its impact on entire communities. The impact is especially pronounced in poorer, socially disadvantaged communities that are home to a majority of the nation's inmates. Robert Sampson & Charles Loeffler, *Punishment's Place: The Local Concentration of Mass Incarceration*, 139 DAELAUS 20 (2010). Criminologist Todd Clear has summarized the many deleterious health, sociological, safety, and economic effects that concentrated incarceration has on communities. *See* Todd R. Clear, *The Effects of High Imprisonment Rates on Communities*, 37 CRIME & JUST. 97 (2008). Research has also shown that the reduced availability of males, as a result of mass imprisonment, has a negative effect on marriage in particular communities. Kerwin Kofi & Ming Ching Luoh, *Male Incarceration, the Marriage Market, and Female Outcomes*, 92 REV. ECON. & STAT. 614 (2010).

I. A BRIEF HISTORY OF PRISONERS' RIGHTS LITIGATION

The care and treatment of inmates has long been the subject of constitutional challenge. The Supreme Court has stated that "[t]here is no iron curtain drawn between the Constitution and the prisons of this country." *Wolff v. McDonnell*, 418 U.S. 539, 555–56 (1974). Yet, as the quote provided at the chapter's outset attests, imprisonment in the U.S. is not intended to be, nor is, pleasant. The question becomes where the constitutional line is to be drawn. The history of corrections reform litigation is generally thought to consist of several phases.

"Hands-Off" Era

Up until the mid-twentieth century, federal courts rejected prisoners' constitutional claims. The reasons for their doing so included separation of powers (imprisonment was a concern of the executive and legislative branches), federalism (punishment of state inmates was a state concern), and lack of competence (administration of prisons is best handled by wardens and other experts).

"Prisoners' Rights" Era

Starting in the 1960s, federal courts warmed to the idea of acceding to constitutional claims. A key development was the Supreme Court's decision in *Monroe v. Pape*, 365 U.S. 167 (1961), which allowed individuals to bring federal constitutional claims under 42 U.S.C. § 1983 against state and local actors. During this time as well, incorporation doctrine resulted in the application of almost all parts of the Bill of Rights to state and local, not only federal, governmental action. *See, e.g., Robinson v. California*, 370 U.S. 660 (1962) (incorporating the Cruel and Unusual Punishments Clause of the Eighth Amendment).

In the late 1960s, prison conditions were the frequent subject of successful constitutional claims in the lower federal courts, based mainly on the Eighth and Fourteenth Amendments, focusing mainly on the treatment of inmates and prison conditions in the South. In many instances, cases were filed by the growing cadre of public interest lawyers (today, often called "cause lawyers") who took on cases either pro bono or with financial support from government and private foundation grants.

One of the more notable decisions was that of the Eighth Circuit Court of Appeals in *Jackson v. Bishop*, 404 F.2d 571 (8th Cir. 1968), which held that use of "the strap" as a disciplinary method by Arkansas prison authorities violated the Eighth Amendment. Judge (and later Justice) Harry Blackmun described the strap as made

> of leather and from 3 1/2 to 5 1/2 feet in length, about 4 inches wide, and 1/4 inch thick. Each has a wooden handle 8 to 12 inches long. . . . Whipping is the primary disciplinary measure used in the Arkansas system. Prisoners there have few privileges which can be withheld from them as punishment. Facilities for segregation and solitary confinement are limited.

Id. at 575. A year before, a federal trial court described use by Arkansas guards of the "Tucker telephone," a hand-cranked device used to administer electric shocks to sensitive parts of the body. *Jackson v. Bishop*, 268 F. Supp. 804 (E.D. Ark. 1967).[17]

In the 1960s and 1970s the Supreme Court issued numerous decisions identifying or expanding federal constitutional rights of inmates. *See, e.g., Procunier v. Martinez*, 416 U.S. 396 (1974) (limiting the authority of officials to censor inmate mail); *Cruz v. Beto*, 405 U.S. 319 (1972) (recognizing free exercise of religion among inmates); *Younger v. Gilmore*, 404 U.S. 15 (1971) (requiring that prisons provide an adequate law library); *Johnson v. Avery*, 393 U.S. 483 (1969) (invalidating rule that limited the ability of prisoners to assist one another in filing claims).

The litigation achieved marked success in improving prison conditions and the treatment of prisoners. In many instances, facilities remained under lower federal court supervision and monitors for many years, to better ensure compliance with injunctions and consent decrees. *See* MALCOLM M. FEELEY & EDWARD L. RUBIN, JUDICIAL POLICY MAKING

[17] Alabama, as of 1995, chained inmates together in work squads, and for discipline used a "hitching post": "a horizontal bar 'made of sturdy, nonflexible material,' placed between 45 and 57 inches from the ground. Inmates are handcuffed to the hitching post in a standing position and remain standing the entire time they are placed on the post. Most inmates are shackled to the hitching post with their two hands relatively close together and at face level." Hope v. Pelzer, 536 U.S. 730, 733 n.1 (2002) (citations omitted).

AND THE MODERN STATE: HOW THE COURTS REFORMED AMERICA'S PRISONS (1998); Margo Schlanger, *Civil Rights Injunctions Over Time: A Case Study of Jail and Prison Court Orders*, 81 N.Y.U. L. REV. 550 (2006).

"Hands-Off" Redux

The last, and current, era started in the late 1980s and has been marked by significant limits placed on prisoner constitutional claims, with institutional deference playing a key role. As the Supreme Court stated in *Turner v. Safley*, 482 U.S. 78 (1987), "courts are ill equipped to deal with the increasingly urgent problems of prison administration and reform . . . all of which are peculiarly within the province of the legislative and administrative branches of government." *Id.* at 84. In many instances, across a broad range of constitutional claims, the Court imposed significant limits on the ability of inmates to secure relief, including:

- *Hudson v. Palmer*, 468 U.S. 517 (1984): inmates cannot assert a Fourth Amendment privacy claim regarding the search of their cells.
- *Wilson v. Seiter*, 501 U.S. 294 (1991): conditions-related claims, such as overcrowding or unsanitary facilities, require a showing that conditions objectively failed to meet basic human needs and that prison officials were deliberately indifferent to such harms (i.e., actual knowledge of a substantial risk of serious harm).
- *Hudson v. McMillian*, 503 U.S. 1 (1992): claim of excessive force by officer requires showing of objectively unreasonable force and asks "whether force was applied in a good faith effort to maintain or restore discipline or maliciously and sadistically for the very purpose of causing harm."
- *Farmer v. Brennan*, 511 U.S. 825 (1994): claim based on failure to protect a prisoner from third-party violence requires showing of an objectively substantial risk of serious harm to the prisoner and deliberate indifference by the official.

In 1996, Congress significantly limited prisoner litigation with its passage of the Prison Litigation Reform Act (PLRA), which imposed major procedural hurdles and limits on damages and injunctive relief available to inmates. For discussion of its impact see Margo Schlanger, *Trends in Prisoner Litigation, as the PLRA Enters Adulthood*, 5 U.C. IRVINE L. REV. 153 (2015).

A notable exception to this retrenchment came in *Brown v. Plata*, 563 U.S. 493 (2011). In *Plata*, a 5–4 majority applying the PLRA held that California's overcrowded prisons violated the Eighth Amendment right to constitutionally adequate physical and mental health care. The majority upheld a three-judge court's order requiring the state to decrease overcrowding to no more than 137.5% of design capacity (down from double capacity), amounting to a reduction of as many as 46,000 prisoners, by December 31, 2013.

NOTES & QUESTIONS

1. **The Prison Experience.** In light of the material covered in this chapter, if you were a judge, would the information provided affect how you think about incarceration as a sentencing option? If so, how? Similarly, has the material altered your views about how well incarceration is likely to advance the traditional purposes of punishment discussed in Chapter 1?

2. **Special Populations.** On the basis of the materials in this chapter, do you believe that there any particular defendant subpopulations that should be sentenced differently?

CHAPTER 6

CONSTITUTIONAL LIMITS ON PUNISHMENT (NON-CAPITAL)

As discussed in Chapter 1, punishment imposed by government requires a justification. To be lawful, moreover, the sentencing proceeding culminating in punishment must also satisfy any constitutional requirements and limits, as covered in Chapter 3. This chapter examines the substantive constitutional limits regarding punishment, in particular non-capital sentences.

In the U.S., several constitutional provisions regulate governmental authority to punish. As a starting point, the text of the Constitution itself prohibits Congress and state legislatures from enacting ex post facto laws and bills of attainder. *See* U.S. CONST. art. I, §§ 9 (regarding Congress) & 10 (regarding state legislatures). The ex post facto provisions prohibit laws that retroactively create offenses or enhance punishment. *See, e.g., Smith v. Doe*, 538 U.S. 84 (2003) (holding that sex offender registration and community notification law did not retroactively enhance punishment of previously convicted sex offenders).[1] A bill of attainder is a law declaring a person, or a group of persons, guilty of a crime, and punishing them without a trial. *See, e.g., Brown v. United States*, 381 U.S. 437 (1965) (holding that federal law making it a crime for a member of the Communist Party to serve as an officer or as an employee of a labor union was an invalid bill of attainder).

The Constitution's amendments provide several other bases for challenges to punishment that will be examined here. The first we will examine is the Eighth Amendment, which inter alia prohibits "cruel and unusual punishments." Over the years, the Eighth Amendment has figured in multiple challenges to use of the death penalty, which will be examined in Chapter 7. Here, the focus will be upon prison sentences, a matter of enormous importance given the nation's resort to very lengthy prison terms in recent decades, including life without parole, as well as physical punishment, which while certainly less common, has figured in some cases.[2]

---

[1] For more on the Ex Post Facto Clause, see WAYNE A. LOGAN, THE EX POST FACTO CLAUSE: ITS HISTORY AND ROLE IN A PUNITIVE SOCIETY (2022). Its counterpart is the common law doctrine of lex mitior, which requires that criminal defendants whose prosecutions are not final enjoy the retroactive benefit of laws that either decriminalize conduct or reduce punishment for it. According to one author's count, twenty-two U.S. jurisdictions today reject the doctrine; ten partly reject it and partly embrace it; and eighteen wholly embrace it. Peter Westen, *Lex Mitior: Converse of Ex Post Facto and Window into Criminal Desert*, 18 NEW CRIM. L. REV. 167, 170 (2015).

[2] *Robinson v. California*, 370 U.S. 660 (1962), imposed another limit on government authority to punish—one based on personal status or condition. In *Robinson*, the Court invalidated a California statute making addiction to narcotics a crime (a misdemeanor).

The other constitutional provision that we will focus upon concerns ensuring equal protection of the law, governing sentences imposed in state and federal court alike. In state court cases, the Fourteenth Amendment of the U.S. Constitution explicitly commands that "[n]o State shall . . . deny to any person within its jurisdiction the equal protection of the laws." In federal court cases, the Due Process Clause of the Fifth Amendment guards against unequal treatment. *See González-Maldonado v. MMM Healthcare, Inc.*, 693 F.3d 244, 247 n.2 (1st Cir. 2012) (stating that "the Due Process Clause of the Fifth Amendment is treated as containing an equal protection component that binds the federal government in the same way that the Equal Protection Clause [of the Fourteenth Amendment] binds the states").

A. LIMITS ON IMPRISONMENT

As discussed in Chapter 5, sentencing convicted individuals to prison emerged as the primary method of punishment only relatively recently, in the mid-nineteenth century. Since then, and especially since the 1980s, as Chapter 2 recounted, prison sentences have radically grown in both number and length. Today, the U.S. by far leads the world in use of long prison sentences, including lengthy terms of years and life without parole. At this point, we are accustomed to the practice, but it is important to keep in mind the actual human consequences of imprisonment, however heinous the crime(s) serving as its basis. As federal judge Gerard Lynch once said, imposition of an even comparatively short prison term of seventy-eight months "is hardly trivial: imagine being sent away from your family when your daughter was eleven, and returning on her eighteenth birthday; or consider going to jail with your mother aged seventy-five, and guessing whether she'll still be living at nearly eight-two, when you get out." Gerard E. Lynch, *Sentencing Eddie*, 91 J. CRIM. L. & CRIMINOLOGY 547, 565 (2001). Whether and how the judiciary is to regulate the length of prison sentences is the subject to which we now turn, focusing first on adult and then juvenile offenders.

Robinson was not under the influence of drugs at the time of his arrest, and the only evidence against him was the testimony of the arresting officer who observed scars and needle marks on his arms. The Court struck down the statute, conceiving of it as one imposing punishment based solely on the presence of a particular condition or status, rather than punishment for a criminal act (such as possession of illegal narcotics).

1. SENTENCE PROPORTIONALITY LIMITS—ADULTS

Ewing v. California

538 U.S. 11 (2003)

[JUSTICE O'CONNOR, in a plurality opinion joined by CHIEF JUSTICE REHNQUIST and JUSTICE KENNEDY.]

In this case, we decide whether the Eighth Amendment prohibits the State of California from sentencing a repeat felon to a prison term of 25 years to life under the State's "Three Strikes and You're Out" law.

I

A

California's three strikes law reflects a shift in the State's sentencing policies toward incapacitating and deterring repeat offenders who threaten the public safety. * * *

B

California's current three strikes law consists of two virtually identical statutory schemes "designed to increase the prison terms of repeat felons." When a defendant is convicted of a felony, and he has previously been convicted of one or more prior felonies defined as "serious" or "violent" sentencing is conducted pursuant to the three strikes law. Prior convictions must be alleged in the charging document, and the defendant has a right to a jury determination that the prosecution has proved the prior convictions beyond a reasonable doubt.

If the defendant has one prior "serious" or "violent" felony conviction, he must be sentenced to "twice the term otherwise provided as punishment for the current felony conviction." If the defendant has two or more prior "serious" or "violent" felony convictions, he must receive "an indeterminate term of life imprisonment." [Ewing was in the latter category and therefore eligible for parole only after serving 25 years.]

C

On parole from a 9-year prison term, petitioner Gary Ewing walked into the pro shop of the El Segundo Golf Course in Los Angeles County on March 12, 2000. He walked out with three golf clubs, priced at $399 apiece, concealed in his pants leg. A shop employee, whose suspicions were aroused when he observed Ewing limp out of the pro shop, telephoned the police. The police apprehended Ewing in the parking lot.

Ewing is no stranger to the criminal justice system. In 1984, at the age of 22, he pleaded guilty to theft. The court sentenced him to six months in jail (suspended), three years' probation, and a $300 fine. In 1988, he was convicted of felony grand theft auto and sentenced to one year in jail and three years' probation.

[The Court recounted Ewing's several convictions and sentences from 1990 through September 1993.]

In October and November 1993, Ewing committed three burglaries and one robbery at a Long Beach, California, apartment complex over a 5-week period. He awakened one of his victims, asleep on her living room sofa, as he tried to disconnect her video cassette recorder from the television in that room. When she screamed, Ewing ran out the front door. On another occasion, Ewing accosted a victim in the mailroom of the apartment complex. Ewing claimed to have a gun and ordered the victim to hand over his wallet. When the victim resisted, Ewing produced a knife and forced the victim back to the apartment itself. While Ewing rifled through the bedroom, the victim fled the apartment screaming for help. Ewing absconded with the victim's money and credit cards.

On December 9, 1993, Ewing was arrested on the premises of the apartment complex for trespassing and lying to a police officer. The knife used in the robbery and a glass cocaine pipe were later found in the back seat of the patrol car used to transport Ewing to the police station. A jury convicted Ewing of first-degree robbery and three counts of residential burglary. Sentenced to nine years and eight months in prison, Ewing was paroled in 1999.

Only 10 months later, Ewing stole the golf clubs at issue in this case. He was charged with, and ultimately convicted of, one count of felony grand theft of personal property in excess of $400. As required by the three strikes law, the prosecutor formally alleged, and the trial court later found, that Ewing had been convicted previously of four serious or violent felonies for the three burglaries and the robbery in the Long Beach apartment complex.

At the sentencing hearing, Ewing asked the court to reduce the conviction for grand theft, a "wobbler" under California law, to a misdemeanor so as to avoid a three strikes sentence. Ewing also asked the trial court to exercise its discretion to dismiss the allegations of some or all of his prior serious or violent felony convictions, again for purposes of avoiding a three strikes sentence.

In the end, the trial judge determined that the grand theft should remain a felony. The court also ruled that the four prior strikes for the three burglaries and the robbery in Long Beach should stand. As a newly convicted felon with two or more "serious" or "violent" felony convictions in his past, Ewing was sentenced under the three strikes law to 25 years to life.

The California Court of Appeal affirmed in an unpublished opinion. Relying on our decision in *Rummel v. Estelle*, 445 U.S. 263 (1980), the court rejected Ewing's claim that his sentence was grossly disproportionate under the Eighth Amendment. Enhanced sentences under recidivist statutes like the three strikes law, the court reasoned, serve the "legitimate goal" of deterring and incapacitating repeat offenders. The Supreme Court of California denied Ewing's petition for review, and we granted certiorari. We now affirm.

II

A

The Eighth Amendment, which forbids cruel and unusual punishments, contains a "narrow proportionality principle" that "applies to noncapital sentences." * * *

In *Rummel*, we held that it did not violate the Eighth Amendment for a State to sentence a three-time offender to life in prison with the possibility of parole. Like Ewing, Rummel was sentenced to a lengthy prison term under a recidivism statute. Rummel's two prior offenses were a 1964 felony for "fraudulent use of a credit card to obtain $80 worth of goods or services," and a 1969 felony conviction for "passing a forged check in the amount of $28.36." His triggering offense was a conviction for felony theft—"obtaining $120.75 by false pretenses."

This Court ruled that "[h]aving twice imprisoned him for felonies, Texas was entitled to place upon Rummel the onus of one who is simply unable to bring his conduct within the social norms prescribed by the criminal law of the State." The recidivism statute "is nothing more than a societal decision that when such a person commits yet another felony, he should be subjected to the admittedly serious penalty of incarceration for life, subject only to the State's judgment as to whether to grant him parole." We noted that this Court "has on occasion stated that the Eighth Amendment prohibits imposition of a sentence that is grossly disproportionate to the severity of the crime." But "[o]utside the context of capital punishment, successful challenges to the proportionality of particular sentences have been exceedingly rare." Although we stated that the proportionality principle "would . . . come into play in the extreme example . . . if a legislature made overtime parking a felony punishable by life imprisonment," we held that "the mandatory life sentence imposed upon this petitioner does not constitute cruel and unusual punishment under the Eighth and Fourteenth Amendments." * * *

[I]n *Solem v. Helm*, 463 U.S. 277 (1983), we held that the Eighth Amendment prohibited "a life sentence without possibility of parole for a seventh nonviolent felony." The triggering offense in *Solem* was "uttering a 'no account' check for $100." We specifically stated that the Eighth Amendment's ban on cruel and unusual punishments "prohibits . . . sentences that are disproportionate to the crime committed," and that the "constitutional principle of proportionality has been recognized explicitly in this Court for almost a century." The *Solem* Court then explained that three factors may be relevant to a determination of whether a sentence is so disproportionate that it violates the Eighth Amendment: "(i) the gravity of the offense and the harshness of the penalty; (ii) the sentences imposed on other criminals in the same jurisdiction; and (iii) the sentences imposed for commission of the same crime in other jurisdictions."

Applying these factors in *Solem*, we struck down the defendant's sentence of life without parole. We specifically noted the contrast between that sentence and the sentence in *Rummel*, pursuant to which the defendant was eligible for parole. Indeed, we explicitly declined to overrule *Rummel*. * * *

Eight years after *Solem*, we grappled with the proportionality issue again in *Harmelin*. *Harmelin* was not a recidivism case, but rather involved a first-time offender convicted of possessing 672 grams of cocaine. He was sentenced to life in prison without possibility of parole. A majority of the Court rejected Harmelin's claim that his sentence was so grossly disproportionate that it violated the Eighth Amendment. The Court, however, could not agree on why his proportionality argument failed. Justice Scalia, joined by the Chief Justice, wrote that the proportionality principle was "an aspect of our death penalty jurisprudence, rather than a generalizable aspect of Eighth Amendment law." He would thus have declined to apply gross disproportionality principles except in reviewing capital sentences.

Justice Kennedy, joined by two other Members of the Court, concurred in part and concurred in the judgment. Justice Kennedy specifically recognized that "[t]he Eighth Amendment proportionality principle also applies to noncapital sentences." He then identified four principles of proportionality review—"the primacy of the legislature, the variety of legitimate penological schemes, the nature of our federal system, and the requirement that proportionality review be guided by objective factors"—that "inform the final one: The Eighth Amendment does not require strict proportionality between crime and sentence. Rather, it forbids only extreme sentences that are 'grossly disproportionate' to the crime." Justice Kennedy's concurrence also stated that *Solem* "did not mandate" comparative analysis "within and between jurisdictions."

The proportionality principles in our cases distilled in Justice Kennedy's concurrence guide our application of the Eighth Amendment in the new context that we are called upon to consider.

B

For many years, most States have had laws providing for enhanced sentencing of repeat offenders. Yet between 1993 and 1995, three strikes laws effected a sea change in criminal sentencing throughout the Nation. These laws responded to widespread public concerns about crime by targeting the class of offenders who pose the greatest threat to public safety: career criminals. As one of the chief architects of California's three strikes law has explained: "Three Strikes was intended to go beyond simply making sentences tougher. It was intended to be a focused effort to create a sentencing policy that would use the judicial system to reduce serious and violent crime."

Throughout the States, legislatures enacting three strikes laws made a deliberate policy choice that individuals who have repeatedly engaged in serious or violent criminal behavior, and whose conduct has not been deterred by more conventional approaches to punishment, must be isolated from society in order to protect the public safety. Though three strikes laws may be relatively new, our tradition of deferring to state legislatures in making and implementing such important policy decisions is longstanding.

Our traditional deference to legislative policy choices finds a corollary in the principle that the Constitution "does not mandate adoption of any one penological theory." A sentence can have a variety of justifications, such as incapacitation, deterrence, retribution, or rehabilitation. Some or all of these justifications may play a role in a State's sentencing scheme. Selecting the sentencing rationales is generally a policy choice to be made by state legislatures, not federal courts.

When the California Legislature enacted the three strikes law, it made a judgment that protecting the public safety requires incapacitating criminals who have already been convicted of at least one serious or violent crime. Nothing in the Eighth Amendment prohibits California from making that choice. To the contrary, our cases establish that "States have a valid interest in deterring and segregating habitual criminals." Recidivism has long been recognized as a legitimate basis for increased punishment.

California's justification is no pretext. Recidivism is a serious public safety concern in California and throughout the Nation. According to a recent report, approximately 67 percent of former inmates released from state prisons were charged with at least one "serious" new crime within three years of their release. In particular, released property offenders like Ewing had higher recidivism rates than those released after committing violent, drug, or public-order offenses. * * *

The State's interest in deterring crime also lends some support to the three strikes law. We have long viewed both incapacitation and deterrence as rationales for recidivism statutes: "[A] recidivist statute['s] . . . primary goals are to deter repeat offenders and, at some point in the life of one who repeatedly commits criminal offenses serious enough to be punished as felonies, to segregate that person from the rest of society for an extended period of time." Four years after the passage of California's three strikes law, the recidivism rate of parolees returned to prison for the commission of a new crime dropped by nearly 25 percent. Even more dramatically [according to a government report]:

> An unintended but positive consequence of 'Three Strikes' has been the impact on parolees leaving the state. More California

> parolees are now leaving the state than parolees from other jurisdictions entering California. This striking turnaround started in 1994. It was the first time more parolees left the state than entered since 1976. This trend has continued and in 1997 more than 1,000 net parolees left California.

To be sure, California's three strikes law has sparked controversy. Critics have doubted the law's wisdom, cost-efficiency, and effectiveness in reaching its goals. This criticism is appropriately directed at the legislature, which has primary responsibility for making the difficult policy choices that underlie any criminal sentencing scheme. We do not sit as a "superlegislature" to second-guess these policy choices. It is enough that the State of California has a reasonable basis for believing that dramatically enhanced sentences for habitual felons "advance[s] the goals of [its] criminal justice system in any substantial way."

III

Against this backdrop, we consider Ewing's claim that his three strikes sentence of 25 years to life is unconstitutionally disproportionate to his offense of "shoplifting three golf clubs." We first address the gravity of the offense compared to the harshness of the penalty. At the threshold, we note that Ewing incorrectly frames the issue. The gravity of his offense was not merely "shoplifting three golf clubs." Rather, Ewing was convicted of felony grand theft for stealing nearly $1,200 worth of merchandise after previously having been convicted of at least two "violent" or "serious" felonies. Even standing alone, Ewing's theft should not be taken lightly. His crime was certainly not "one of the most passive felonies a person could commit." *Solem*, *supra*, at 296. To the contrary, the Supreme Court of California has noted the "seriousness" of grand theft in the context of proportionality review. Theft of $1,200 in property is a felony under federal law, and in the vast majority of States. * * *

In imposing a three strikes sentence, the State's interest is not merely punishing the offense of conviction, or the "triggering" offense: "[I]t is in addition the interest . . . in dealing in a harsher manner with those who by repeated criminal acts have shown that they are simply incapable of conforming to the norms of society as established by its criminal law." To give full effect to the State's choice of this legitimate penological goal, our proportionality review of Ewing's sentence must take that goal into account. Ewing's sentence is justified by the State's public-safety interest in incapacitating and deterring recidivist felons, and amply supported by his own long, serious criminal record. Ewing has been convicted of numerous misdemeanor and felony offenses, served nine separate terms of incarceration, and committed most of his crimes while on probation or parole. His prior "strikes" were serious felonies including robbery and three residential burglaries. To be sure, Ewing's sentence is a long one. But it reflects a rational legislative judgment, entitled to deference, that offenders who have committed serious or violent felonies and who continue to commit felonies must be incapacitated. The State of California "was entitled to place upon [Ewing] the onus of one who is simply unable to bring his conduct within the social norms prescribed by the criminal law of the State." Ewing's is not "the rare case in which a threshold comparison of the crime committed and the sentence imposed leads to an inference of gross disproportionality."

We hold that Ewing's sentence of 25 years to life in prison, imposed for the offense of felony grand theft under the three strikes law, is not grossly disproportionate and therefore does not violate the Eighth Amendment's prohibition on cruel and unusual punishments. The judgment of the California Court of Appeal is affirmed.

■ JUSTICE SCALIA, concurring in the judgment.

In my opinion in *Harmelin v. Michigan*, 501 U.S. 957 (1991), I concluded that the Eighth Amendment's prohibition of "cruel and unusual punishments" was aimed at excluding only certain modes of punishment, and was not a "guarantee against disproportionate sentences." Out of respect for the principle of stare decisis, I might nonetheless accept the contrary holding of *Solem v. Helm*—that the Eighth Amendment contains a narrow proportionality principle—if I felt I could intelligently apply it. This case demonstrates why I cannot.

Proportionality—the notion that the punishment should fit the crime—is inherently a concept tied to the penological goal of retribution. "[I]t becomes difficult even to speak intelligently of 'proportionality,' once deterrence and rehabilitation are given significant weight,"—not to mention giving weight to the purpose of California's three strikes law: incapacitation. In the present case, the game is up once the plurality has acknowledged that "the Constitution does not mandate adoption of any one penological theory," and that a "sentence can have a variety of justifications, such as incapacitation, deterrence, retribution, or rehabilitation." That acknowledgment having been made, it no longer suffices merely to assess "the gravity of the offense compared to the harshness of the penalty," that classic description of the proportionality principle (alone and in itself quite resistant to policy-free, legal analysis) now becomes merely the "first" step of the inquiry. Having completed that step (by a discussion which, in all fairness, does not convincingly establish that 25-years-to-life is a "proportionate" punishment for stealing three golf clubs), the plurality must then add an analysis to show that "Ewing's sentence is justified by the State's public-safety interest in incapacitating and deterring recidivist felons."

Which indeed it is—though why that has anything to do with the principle of proportionality is a mystery. Perhaps the plurality should revise its terminology, so that what it reads into the Eighth Amendment is not the unstated proposition that all punishment should be reasonably proportionate to the gravity of the offense, but rather the unstated proposition that all punishment should reasonably pursue the multiple purposes of the criminal law. That formulation would make it clearer than ever, of course, that the plurality is not applying law but evaluating policy. Because I agree that petitioner's sentence does not violate the Eighth Amendment's prohibition against cruel and unusual punishments, I concur in the judgment.

[The concurring opinion of JUSTICE THOMAS and the dissents of JUSTICES STEVENS and BREYER, joined by JUSTICES SOUTER and GINSBURG, have been omitted.]

NOTES & QUESTIONS

1. **Threshold Test.** In his *Ewing* dissent, Justice Breyer summarized the proportionality test used by the Court in non-capital cases, based on Justice Kennedy's concurring opinion in *Harmelin v. Michigan*:

> [C]ourts faced with a "gross disproportionality" claim must first make "a threshold comparison of the crime committed and the sentence imposed." If a claim crosses that threshold—itself a rare occurrence—then the court should compare the sentence at issue to other sentences "imposed on other criminals" in the same, or in other, jurisdictions. The comparative analysis will "validate" or invalidate "an initial judgment that a sentence is grossly disproportionate to a crime."

Ewing, 538 U.S. at 37 (Breyer, J., dissenting) (citations omitted). The *Ewing* plurality, however, only applied the first step—the "threshold comparison" of gravity of the offense and the punishment imposed. As Justice Breyer noted, satisfying this first step is "a rare occurrence," and to his mind too demanding:

> A threshold test that blocked every ultimately invalid constitutional claim—even strong ones—would not be a threshold test but a determinative test. And, it would be a determinative test that failed to take account of highly pertinent sentencing information, namely, comparison with other sentences. Sentencing comparisons are particularly important because they provide proportionality review with objective content. By way of contrast, a threshold test makes the assessment of constitutionality highly subjective. And, of course, so to transform that threshold test would violate this Court's earlier precedent.

Id. at 43 (Breyer, J., dissenting).

2. **Supreme Deference.** The outcome and supporting rationales in *Ewing v. California* highlight the Court's reluctance to critically scrutinize legislative determinations of punishment proportionality in challenges to prison term length.[3] Summarizing the Court's prior case law, *Ewing* instructs that the Eighth Amendment prohibits only "extreme sentences that are 'grossly disproportionate' to the crime." Moreover, as Justice O'Connor stated for the plurality, the Court does not sit as a " 'superlegislature' to

[3] In the same term as *Ewing*, the Court affirmed on habeas corpus review a sentence imposed on another California defendant of two consecutive sentences of 25 years to life for stealing approximately $150 of videotapes, when the defendant had three prior felony convictions. Lockyer v. Andrade, 538 U.S. 63 (2003).

second-guess [legislative] policy choices." The Eighth Amendment "proportionality principle" comes into play only " 'in the extreme example . . . if a legislature made overtime parking a felony punishable by life imprisonment.' " Do you agree that the constitutional oversight role of the Court should be so limited? If you disagree, can you identify a test for when the Court should intervene, other than the overtime parking scenario identified by the Court?

The importance of devising such a standard has been heightened by the Court's gravitation toward originalism as a method of constitutional interpretation.[4] As you likely know, originalism is a method of constitutional interpretation often embraced by conservative jurists, as contrasted from living constitutionalism, often embraced by more liberal jurists. Justices Thomas and Scalia, in particular, have invoked original understanding as a basis to conclude that the Eighth Amendment contains no proportionality requirement (while it does potentially regulate *methods* of punishment). Recently, however, an increasing body of scholarship suggests that during and before the Framing Era proportionality figured centrally in judicial review of punishments. *See, e.g.*, John F. Stinneford, *Rethinking Proportionality Under the Cruel and Unusual Punishments Clause*, 97 VA. L. REV. 899 (2011).

3. **Retributive Considerations.** The *Ewing* Court cites deterrence and incapacitation as the main policy goals of California in enacting the law challenged. What of retribution? Is there a retributive justification for the very heavy punishment imposed—25 years to life? In this vein, how does the Court assess the gravity of Ewing's last offense, on which his challenge is based? What, precisely, is Ewing being punished for?

4. **Impact of Three Strikes.** The California "three strikes" law, and other recidivist enhancement laws like it, impose a harsher punishment because of a prior conviction. One clear effect of California's law was a major increase in the state's prison population, which contributed to an overcrowding crisis and, eventually, a profound restructuring of the state's entire criminal-justice system. *See* MICHAEL O'HEAR, THE FAILED PROMISE OF SENTENCING REFORM 173–86 (2017). An extensive academic literature had grown up around the politics and effectiveness of the three-strikes law. Some research finds modest reductions in crime associated with the law, but at a large and arguably unjustified human and fiscal cost. *See* COMM. ON CAUSES & CONSEQUENCES OF HIGH RATES OF INCARCERATION, NAT'L RESEARCH COUNCIL OF THE NATIONAL ACADEMIES, THE GROWTH OF INCARCERATION IN THE UNITED STATES: EXPLORING CAUSES AND CONSEQUENCES 135–36 (Jeremy Travis, Bruce Western & Steve Redburn eds., 2014). In light of the foregoing, was the Supreme Court right in deferring to legislative judgment, which can often be driven by "tough-on-crime" politics?

[4] In a recent death penalty case, for instance, a majority of the Court relied on what it regarded as the "original and historical understanding of the Eighth Amendment." Bucklew v. Precythe, 139 S. Ct. 1112, 1122 (2019).

5. **State Constitutions.** The Eighth Amendment of the U.S. Constitution is not the only potential basis for challenging a prison sentence. State constitutions also contain provisions that can be invoked. While some state provisions mirror the language of the Eighth Amendment, many have provisions with language possibly providing more protection. *See* Richard S. Frase, *Limiting Excessive Prison Sentences Under Federal and State Constitutions*, 11 U. PA. J. CONST. L. 39, 64–66 (2008).

Consistent with federalism principles, states are free to interpret their constitutional provisions in a manner that provides their citizens more protection than that provided by the federal constitution as interpreted by the U.S. Supreme Court. However, as is the case with state constitutional law more generally, states very often eschew the opportunity and hew to the federal constitutional baseline (what is known as the "lockstep" approach). The Florida Constitution contains a provision expressly providing that "[t]he prohibition against cruel or unusual punishment, and the prohibition against cruel and unusual punishment, shall be construed in conformity with decisions of the United States Supreme Court which interpret the prohibition against cruel and unusual punishment provided in the Eighth Amendment to the United States Constitution." FLA. CONST. art. I, § 17. Mississippi also takes a limited approach. According to the Mississippi Supreme Court, the U.S. Supreme Court in *Harmelin* "overruled the bulk of the law created in *Solem*," meaning that a sentence is not constitutionally excessive so long as it is within the range of punishment permitted by statutory law. *Jackson v. State*, 740 So. 2d 832, 835 (Miss. 1999).

Summing up his survey of state constitutional provisions, Professor Frase observes that

> [t]he reluctance of state courts to grant broader protection against excessive penalties under state constitutions is surprising given the frequency with which expanded criminal procedure rights are recognized by state courts in other contexts. For example, many courts have given citizens greater protection from searches and seizures under state provisions worded similarly or even identically to the Fourth Amendment.

Frase, *supra*, at 66.

Some states, however, exercise their right to adopt a more expansive approach in assessing excessiveness. Michigan exemplifies this tendency, as reflected in how the state subsequently addressed a proportionality challenge against the same drug sentencing provision upheld in *Harmelin v. Michigan*. In *Harmelin*, the U.S. Supreme Court rejected the defendant's challenge to his mandatory life without parole sentence based on his possession of 672 grams of cocaine. The following year, in another case, the Michigan Supreme Court held that even if the sentence did not violate the Eighth Amendment, it did violate the state constitution's Cruel or Unusual Punishment Clause. *People v. Bullock*, 485 N.W.2d 866, 872 (Mich. 1992).

In justifying its conclusion, the *Bullock* Court emphasized the textual and historical differences between the state and federal provisions:

First * * * the Michigan provision prohibits "cruel or unusual" punishments, while the Eighth Amendment bars only punishments that are both "cruel and unusual." This textual difference does not appear to be accidental or inadvertent. Language providing that "no cruel or unusual punishments shall be inflicted" was included in Article II of the Northwest Ordinance of 1787. Michigan's first Constitution, adopted in 1835, provided that "cruel and unjust punishments shall not be inflicted." Const. 1835, art. 1, § 18 (emphasis added). The Constitution of 1850 provided that "cruel or unusual punishment shall not be inflicted. . . ." Identical language was adopted as part of the 1908 and 1963 Constitutions. * * * This Court, in *People v. Lorentzen*, 194 N.W.2d 827 (Mich. 1972), took specific note of this difference in phraseology and suggested that it might well lead to different results with regard to allegedly disproportionate prison terms. "The prohibition of punishment that is unusual but not necessarily cruel carries an implication that unusually excessive imprisonment is included in that prohibition." As this Court noted in [People v. Collins, 475 N.W.2d 684 (1981)], a "significant textual difference [ ] between parallel provisions of the state and federal constitutions" may constitute a "compelling reason" for a different and broader interpretation of the state provision. * * *

Second, while two members of the *Harmelin* majority maintained that the historical circumstances and background of the adoption of the Eighth Amendment preclude the notion that the federal clause contains a "proportionality principle" (opinion of Scalia, J., joined by Rehnquist, C.J.), such a conclusion cannot be reached with regard to the framing and adoption of the Michigan Constitution of 1963. Whatever the legal terms "cruel" and "unusual" were understood to mean in 1791 when the Eighth Amendment was ratified—or in 1689 when its antecedent, the English Bill of Rights, was adopted—by 1963 those words had been interpreted and understood by the United States Supreme Court and by this Court for more than half a century to include a prohibition on grossly disproportionate sentences. *See Weems v. United States*, 217 U.S. 349, 366–367 (1910); *Harmelin*, 111 S. Ct. at 2710 (White, J., dissenting); *People v. Mire*, 173 138 N.W. 1066 (Mich. 1912).

This would constitute another "compelling reason" under *Collins* for a broader view of state constitutional protection, in that "history provide[s] reason to believe that those who framed and adopted the state provision had a different purpose in mind," different, at any rate, from the historical understanding asserted by Justice Scalia. * * *

Finally, this Court, in interpreting Const. 1963, art. 1, § 16, has long followed an approach more consistent with the reasoning of the *Harmelin* dissenters than with that of the *Harmelin* majority. Twenty years ago, in *People v. Lorentzen*, we struck down,

> under both the Eighth Amendment and Const. 1963, art. 1, § 16, a mandatory minimum sentence of twenty years in prison (reducible to approximately ten years by earning "good time") for selling any amount of marijuana. * * *
>
> We believe the precedential weight of *Lorentzen* and its antecedents, as a matter of Michigan law, constitutes a very compelling reason not to reflexively follow the latest turn in the United States Supreme Court's Eighth Amendment analysis.

Id. at 872–75.

For other examples of more expansive state constitutional perspectives, see, e.g., *People v. Miller*, 781 N.E.2d 300, 307–09 (Ill. 2002) (interpreting what is known as state's "proportionate penalties clause," which inter alia focuses upon whether a punishment is "so cruel, degrading or so wholly disproportioned to the offense committed as to shock the moral sense of the community"); *Conner v. State*, 626 N.E.2d 803, 806 (Ind. 1993) (construing state provision providing that "[a]ll penalties shall be proportioned to the nature of the offense" and noting that the "provision goes beyond the protection against cruel and unusual punishment contained in the Eighth Amendment to the U.S. Constitution"). *See also generally* William W. Berry III, *Cruel State Punishments*, 98 N.C. L. REV. 1201 (2020) (surveying different verbiage in state constitutional provisions and arguing in favor of broader state coverage).

2. SENTENCE PROPORTIONALITY LIMITS—LWOP FOR KIDS

Since the early 1900s, when the juvenile justice system originated in Chicago, Illinois, youthful offenders have been relegated to a special regime. They are "adjudicated" (not "prosecuted") in juvenile court, usually receive sentences to juvenile institutions until they reach a particular age (e.g., twenty-one), and usually have their adjudicative records sealed. *See generally* Barry C. Feld, *Competence and Culpability: Delinquents in Juvenile Courts, Youths in Criminal Courts*, 102 MINN. L. REV. 473 (2017). Many juvenile offenders accused of especially serious offenses, such as homicide, however, are prosecuted in adult court, and can receive very lengthy (non-capital) sentences that are served in adult prisons. This section examines the constitutional limits on the sentencing of this latter group of individuals.

Graham v. Florida

560 U.S. 48 (2010)

■ KENNEDY, J.

The issue before the Court is whether the Constitution permits a juvenile offender to be sentenced to life in prison without parole for a nonhomicide crime. The sentence was imposed by the State of Florida. Petitioner challenges the sentence under the Eighth Amendment's Cruel and Unusual Punishments Clause. * * *

I

Petitioner is Terrance Jamar Graham. He was born on January 6, 1987. Graham's parents were addicted to crack cocaine, and their drug use persisted in his early years. Graham was diagnosed with attention deficit hyperactivity disorder in elementary school. He began drinking alcohol and using tobacco at age 9 and smoked marijuana at age 13.

In July 2003, when Graham was age 16, he and three other school-age youths attempted to rob a barbeque restaurant in Jacksonville, Florida. One youth, who worked at the restaurant, left the back door unlocked just before closing time. Graham and another youth, wearing masks, entered through the unlocked door. Graham's masked accomplice twice struck the restaurant manager in the back of the head with a metal bar. When the manager started yelling at the assailant and Graham, the two youths ran out and escaped in a car driven by the third accomplice. The restaurant manager required stitches for his head injury. No money was taken.

Graham was arrested for the robbery attempt. Under Florida law, it is within a prosecutor's discretion whether to charge 16- and 17-year-olds as adults or juveniles for most felony crimes. Graham's prosecutor elected to charge Graham as an adult. The charges against Graham were armed burglary with assault or battery, a first-degree felony carrying a maximum penalty of life imprisonment without the possibility of parole; and attempted armed robbery, a second-degree felony carrying a maximum penalty of 15 years' imprisonment.

On December 18, 2003, Graham pleaded guilty to both charges under a plea agreement. Graham wrote a letter to the trial court. After reciting "this is my first and last time getting in trouble," he continued, "I've decided to turn my life around." Graham said, "I made a promise to God and myself that if I get a second chance, I'm going to do whatever it takes to get to the [National Football League]." The trial court accepted the plea agreement. The court withheld adjudication of guilt as to both charges and sentenced Graham to concurrent 3-year terms of probation. Graham was required to spend the first 12 months of his probation in the county jail, but he received credit for the time he had served awaiting trial, and was released on June 25, 2004.

Less than six months later, on the night of December 2, 2004, Graham again was arrested [for participating] in a home invasion robbery [and an attempted robbery]. * * * His two accomplices were Meigo Bailey and Kirkland Lawrence, both 20-year-old men. * * * [At the time Graham] was 34 days short of his 18th birthday. * * *

The trial court held a sentencing hearing. Under Florida law the minimum sentence Graham could receive absent a downward departure by the judge was 5 years' imprisonment. The maximum was life imprisonment. Graham's attorney requested the minimum nondeparture sentence of 5 years. A presentence report prepared by the Florida

Department of Corrections recommended that Graham receive an even lower sentence—at most 4 years' imprisonment. The State recommended that Graham receive 30 years on the armed burglary count and 15 years on the attempted armed robbery count.

After hearing Graham's testimony, the trial court explained the sentence it was about to pronounce:

> Mr. Graham, as I look back on your case, yours is really candidly a sad situation. You had, as far as I can tell, you have quite a family structure. You had a lot of people who wanted to try and help you get your life turned around including the court system, and you had a judge who took the step to try and give you direction through his probation order to give you a chance to get back onto track. And at the time you seemed through your letters that that is exactly what you wanted to do. And I don't know why it is that you threw your life away. I don't know why.
>
> But you did, and that is what is so sad about this today is that you have actually been given a chance to get through this, the original charge, which were very serious charges to begin with .... The attempted robbery with a weapon was a very serious charge.
>
> .....
>
> [I]n a very short period of time you were back before the Court on a violation of this probation, and then here you are two years later standing before me, literally the—facing a life sentence as to—up to life as to count 1 and up to 15 years as to count 2.
>
> And I don't understand why you would be given such a great opportunity to do something with your life and why you would throw it away. The only thing that I can rationalize is that you decided that this is how you were going to lead your life and that there is nothing that we can do for you. And as the state pointed out, that this is an escalating pattern of criminal conduct on your part and that we can't help you any further. We can't do anything to deter you. This is the way you are going to lead your life, and I don't know why you are going to. You've made that decision. I have no idea. But, evidently, that is what you decided to do. * * *
>
> I have reviewed the statute. I don't see where any further juvenile sanctions would be appropriate. I don't see where any youthful offender sanctions would be appropriate. Given your escalating pattern of criminal conduct, it is apparent to the Court that you have decided that this is the way you are going to live your life and that the only thing I can do now is to try and protect the community from your actions.

The trial court found Graham guilty of the earlier armed burglary and attempted armed robbery charges. It sentenced him to the maximum sentence authorized by law on each charge: life imprisonment for the armed burglary and 15 years for the attempted armed robbery. Because Florida has abolished its parole system a life sentence gives a defendant no possibility of release unless he is granted executive clemency. * * *

II

[The Court noted that its cases involving proportionality challenges fall into categories: those concerning (1) a term of years, based on particular circumstances of the case and (2) categorical restriction on use of the death penalty, which considers the nature of the offense and/or the characteristics of the defendant. The case at bar, however, required consideration of "an issue the Court has not considered previously: a categorical challenge to a term-of-years sentence."]

III

A

The analysis begins with objective indicia of national consensus. * * * Six jurisdictions do not allow life without parole sentences for any juvenile offenders. Seven jurisdictions permit life without parole for juvenile offenders, but only for homicide crimes. Thirty-seven States as well as the District of Columbia permit sentences of life without parole for a juvenile nonhomicide offender in some circumstances. Federal law also allows for the possibility of life without parole for offenders as young as 13. Relying on this metric, the State and its amici argue that there is no national consensus against the sentencing practice at issue.

This argument is incomplete and unavailing. * * * "There are measures of consensus other than legislation." Actual sentencing practices are an important part of the Court's inquiry into consensus. Here, an examination of actual sentencing practices in jurisdictions where the sentence in question is permitted by statute discloses a consensus against its use. Although these statutory schemes contain no explicit prohibition on sentences of life without parole for juvenile nonhomicide offenders, those sentences are most infrequent. [According to research] * * * there are 124 juvenile nonhomicide offenders serving life without parole sentences. A significant majority of those, 77 in total, are serving sentences imposed in Florida. The other 46 are imprisoned in just 10 States—California, Delaware, Iowa, Louisiana, Mississippi, Nebraska, Nevada, Oklahoma, South Carolina, and Virginia. * * * Thus, only 11 jurisdictions nationwide in fact impose life without parole sentences on juvenile nonhomicide offenders—and most of those do so quite rarely—while 26 States, the District of Columbia, and the Federal Government do not impose them despite apparent statutory authorization. * * *

The sentencing practice now under consideration is exceedingly rare. And "it is fair to say that a national consensus has developed against it."

B

Community consensus, while "entitled to great weight," is not itself determinative of whether a punishment is cruel and unusual. In accordance with the constitutional design, "the task of interpreting the Eighth Amendment remains our responsibility." The judicial exercise of independent judgment requires consideration of the culpability of the offenders at issue in light of their crimes and characteristics, along with the severity of the punishment in question. In this inquiry the Court also considers whether the challenged sentencing practice serves legitimate penological goals.

Roper [*v. Simmons*, 543 U.S. 551 (2005)], which outlawed use of the death penalty on persons under age 18 at the time of the offense] established that because juveniles have lessened culpability they are less deserving of the most severe punishments. As compared to adults, juveniles have a " 'lack of maturity and an underdeveloped sense of responsibility' "; they "are more vulnerable or susceptible to negative influences and outside pressures, including peer pressure"; and their characters are "not as well formed." These salient characteristics mean that "[i]t is difficult even for expert psychologists to differentiate between the juvenile offender whose crime reflects unfortunate yet transient immaturity, and the rare juvenile offender whose crime reflects irreparable corruption." Accordingly, "juvenile offenders cannot with reliability be classified among the worst offenders." A juvenile is not absolved of responsibility for his actions, but his transgression "is not as morally reprehensible as that of an adult." * * *

No recent data provide reason to reconsider the Court's observations in *Roper* about the nature of juveniles. * * * [D]evelopments in psychology and brain science continue to show fundamental differences between juvenile and adult minds. For example, parts of the brain involved in behavior control continue to mature through late adolescence. Juveniles are more capable of change than are adults, and their actions are less likely to be evidence of "irretrievably depraved character" than are the actions of adults. It remains true that "[f]rom a moral standpoint it would be misguided to equate the failings of a minor with those of an adult, for a greater possibility exists that a minor's character deficiencies will be reformed." These matters relate to the status of the offenders in question; and it is relevant to consider next the nature of the offenses to which this harsh penalty might apply.

The Court has recognized that defendants who do not kill, intend to kill, or foresee that life will be taken are categorically less deserving of the most serious forms of punishment than are murderers. There is a line "between homicide and other serious violent offenses against the individual." Serious nonhomicide crimes "may be devastating in their harm . . . but 'in terms of moral depravity and of the injury to the person and to the public,' . . . they cannot be compared to murder in their 'severity and irrevocability.' " * * * Although an offense like robbery or rape is "a serious crime deserving serious punishment," those crimes differ from homicide crimes in a moral sense.

It follows that, when compared to an adult murderer, a juvenile offender who did not kill or intend to kill has a twice diminished moral culpability. The age of the offender and the nature of the crime each bear on the analysis.

As for the punishment, life without parole is "the second most severe penalty permitted by law." It is true that a death sentence is "unique in its severity and irrevocability," * * * [T]he sentence alters the offender's life by a forfeiture that is irrevocable. It deprives the convict of the most basic liberties without giving hope of restoration, except perhaps by executive clemency—the remote possibility of which does not mitigate the harshness of the sentence. * * *

The Court has recognized the severity of sentences that deny convicts the possibility of parole. * * * [In] *Solem*, the only previous case striking down a sentence for a term of years as grossly disproportionate, the defendant's sentence was deemed "far more severe than the life sentence we considered in *Rummel*," because it did not give the defendant the possibility of parole.

Life without parole is an especially harsh punishment for a juvenile. Under this sentence a juvenile offender will on average serve more years and a greater percentage of his life in prison than an adult offender. A 16-year-old and a 75-year-old each sentenced to life without parole receive the same punishment in name only. This reality cannot be ignored.

The penological justifications for the sentencing practice are also relevant to the analysis. Criminal punishment can have different goals, and choosing among them is within a legislature's discretion. It does not follow, however, that the purposes and effects of penal sanctions are irrelevant to the determination of Eighth Amendment restrictions. A sentence lacking any legitimate penological justification is by its nature disproportionate to the offense. With respect to life without parole for juvenile nonhomicide offenders, none of the goals of penal sanctions that have been recognized as legitimate—retribution, deterrence, incapacitation, and rehabilitation—provides an adequate justification.

Retribution is a legitimate reason to punish, but it cannot support the sentence at issue here. Society is entitled to impose severe sanctions on a juvenile nonhomicide offender to express its condemnation of the crime and to seek restoration of the moral imbalance caused by the offense. But "[t]he heart of the retribution rationale is that a criminal sentence must be directly related to the personal culpability of the criminal offender." And as *Roper* observed, "[w]hether viewed as an attempt to express the community's moral outrage or as an attempt to right the balance for the wrong to the victim, the case for retribution is not as strong with a minor as with an adult." The case becomes even weaker with respect to a juvenile who did not commit homicide. *Roper* found that "[r]etribution is not proportional if the law's most severe penalty is imposed" on the juvenile murderer. The considerations underlying that holding support as well the conclusion that retribution does not justify imposing the second most severe penalty on the less culpable juvenile nonhomicide offender.

Deterrence does not suffice to justify the sentence either. *Roper* noted that "the same characteristics that render juveniles less culpable than adults suggest . . . that juveniles will be less susceptible to deterrence." Because juveniles' "lack of maturity and an underdeveloped sense of responsibility" [they often make] impetuous and ill-considered actions and decisions, they are less likely to take a possible punishment into consideration when making decisions. This is particularly so when that punishment is rarely imposed. * * * Even if the punishment has some connection to a valid penological goal, it must be shown that the punishment is not grossly disproportionate in light of the justification offered. Here, in light of juvenile nonhomicide offenders' diminished moral responsibility, any limited deterrent effect provided by life without parole is not enough to justify the sentence.

Incapacitation, a third legitimate reason for imprisonment, does not justify the life without parole sentence in question here. Recidivism is a serious risk to public safety, and so incapacitation is an important goal. But while incapacitation may be a legitimate penological goal sufficient to justify life without parole in other contexts, it is inadequate to justify that punishment for juveniles who did not commit homicide. To justify life without parole on the assumption that the juvenile offender forever will be a danger to society requires the sentencer to make a judgment that the juvenile is incorrigible. The characteristics of juveniles make that judgment questionable. * * *

Here one cannot dispute that this defendant posed an immediate risk, for he had committed, we can assume, serious crimes early in his term of supervised release and despite his own assurances of reform. Graham deserved to be separated from society for some time in order to prevent what the trial court described as an "escalating pattern of criminal conduct," but it does not follow that he would be a risk to society for the rest of his life. * * * A life without parole sentence improperly denies the juvenile offender a chance to demonstrate growth and maturity. Incapacitation cannot override all other considerations, lest the Eighth Amendment's rule against disproportionate sentences be a nullity.

Finally there is rehabilitation, a penological goal that forms the basis of parole systems. The concept of rehabilitation is imprecise; and its utility and proper implementation are the subject of a substantial, dynamic field of inquiry and dialogue. It is for legislatures to determine what rehabilitative techniques are appropriate and effective.

A sentence of life imprisonment without parole, however, cannot be justified by the goal of rehabilitation. The penalty forswears altogether the rehabilitative ideal. By denying the defendant the right to reenter the community, the State makes an irrevocable judgment about that person's value and place in society. This judgment is not appropriate in light of a juvenile nonhomicide offender's capacity for change and limited moral culpability. A State's rejection of rehabilitation, moreover, goes beyond a mere expressive judgment. As one amicus notes, defendants serving life without parole sentences are often denied access to vocational training and other rehabilitative services that are available to other inmates. For juvenile offenders, who are most in need of and receptive to rehabilitation, the absence of rehabilitative opportunities or treatment makes the disproportionality of the sentence all the more evident.

In sum, penological theory is not adequate to justify life without parole for juvenile nonhomicide offenders. This determination; the limited culpability of juvenile nonhomicide offenders; and the severity of life without parole sentences all lead to the conclusion that the sentencing practice under consideration is cruel and unusual. This Court now holds that for a juvenile offender who did not commit homicide the Eighth Amendment forbids the sentence of life without parole. This clear line is necessary to prevent the possibility that life without parole sentences will be imposed on juvenile nonhomicide offenders who are not sufficiently culpable to merit that punishment. Because "[t]he age of 18 is the point where society draws the line for many purposes between childhood and adulthood," those who were below that age when the offense was committed may not be sentenced to life without parole for a nonhomicide crime.

A State is not required to guarantee eventual freedom to a juvenile offender convicted of a nonhomicide crime. What the State must do, however, is give defendants like Graham some meaningful opportunity to obtain release based on demonstrated maturity and rehabilitation. * * * It bears emphasis, however, that while the Eighth Amendment prohibits a State from imposing a life without parole sentence on a juvenile nonhomicide offender, it does not require the State to release that offender during his natural life. Those who commit truly horrifying crimes as juveniles may turn out to be irredeemable, and thus deserving of incarceration for the duration of their lives. The Eighth Amendment does not foreclose the possibility that persons convicted of nonhomicide crimes committed before adulthood will remain behind bars for life. It does prohibit States from making the judgment at the outset that those offenders never will be fit to reenter society. * * *

D

There is support for our conclusion in the fact that, in continuing to impose life without parole sentences on juveniles who did not commit homicide, the United States adheres to a sentencing practice rejected the world over. This observation does not control our decision. The judgments of other nations and the international community are not dispositive as to the meaning of the Eighth Amendment. But " '[t]he climate of international opinion concerning the acceptability of a particular punishment' " is also " 'not irrelevant.' " The Court has looked beyond our Nation's borders for support for its independent conclusion that a particular punishment is cruel and unusual.

Today we continue that longstanding practice in noting the global consensus against the sentencing practice in question. A recent study concluded that only 11 nations authorize life without parole for juvenile offenders under any circumstances; and only 2 of them, the United States and Israel, ever impose the punishment in practice. An updated version of the study concluded that Israel's "laws allow for parole review of juvenile offenders serving life terms," but expressed reservations about how that parole review is implemented. But even if Israel is counted as allowing life without parole for juvenile offenders, that nation does not appear to impose that sentence for nonhomicide crimes; all of the seven Israeli prisoners whom commentators have identified as serving life sentences for juvenile crimes were convicted of homicide or attempted homicide.

Thus, as petitioner contends and respondent does not contest, the United States is the only Nation that imposes life without parole sentences on juvenile nonhomicide offenders. We also note, * * * that Article 37(a) of the United Nations Convention on the Rights of the Child, * * * ratified by every nation except the United States and Somalia, prohibits the imposition of "life imprisonment without possibility of release . . . for offences committed by persons below eighteen years of age." As we concluded in *Roper* with respect to the juvenile death penalty, "the United States now stands alone in a world that has turned its face against" life without parole for juvenile nonhomicide offenders. The State's amici stress that no international legal agreement that is binding on the United States prohibits life without parole for juvenile offenders and thus urge us to ignore the international consensus. These arguments miss the mark. The question before us is not whether international law prohibits the United States from imposing the sentence at issue in this case. The question is whether that punishment is cruel and unusual. In that inquiry, "the overwhelming weight of international opinion against" life without parole for nonhomicide offenses committed by juveniles "provide[s] respected and significant confirmation for our own conclusions." *Roper*, *supra*, at 572. * * *

The Court has treated the laws and practices of other nations and international agreements as relevant to the Eighth Amendment not because those norms are binding or controlling but because the judgment of the world's nations that a particular sentencing practice is inconsistent with basic principles of decency demonstrates that the Court's rationale has respected reasoning to support it.

The Constitution prohibits the imposition of a life without parole sentence on a juvenile offender who did not commit homicide. A State need not guarantee the offender eventual release, but if it imposes a sentence of life it must provide him or her with some realistic opportunity to obtain release before the end of that term. The judgment of the First District Court of Appeal of Florida is reversed, and the case is remanded for further proceedings not inconsistent with this opinion.

[Concurring opinion of JUSTICE STEVENS, joined by JUSTICES GINSBURG and SOTOMAYOR, omitted.]

■ ROBERTS, C.J., concurring in the judgment.

I agree with the Court that Terrance Graham's sentence of life without parole violates the Eighth Amendment's prohibition on "cruel and unusual punishments." Unlike the majority, however, I see no need to invent a new constitutional rule of dubious provenance in reaching that conclusion. Instead, my analysis is based on an application of this Court's precedents, in particular (1) our cases requiring "narrow proportionality" review of noncapital sentences and (2) our conclusion in *Roper v. Simmons*, 543 U.S. 551 (2005), that juvenile offenders are generally less culpable than adults who commit the same crimes.

These cases expressly allow courts addressing allegations that a noncapital sentence violates the Eighth Amendment to consider the particular defendant and particular crime at issue. * * * [H]ere Graham's juvenile status—together with the nature of his criminal conduct and the extraordinarily severe punishment imposed—lead me to conclude that his sentence of life without parole is unconstitutional. * * *

Today, the Court views *Roper* as providing the basis for a new categorical rule that juveniles may never receive a sentence of life without parole for nonhomicide crimes. I disagree. * * * A life sentence is of course far less severe than a death sentence, and we have never required that it be imposed only on the very worst offenders, as we have with capital punishment. Treating juvenile life sentences as analogous to capital punishment is at odds with our longstanding view that "the death penalty is different from other punishments in kind rather than degree." It is also at odds with *Roper* itself. * * * Indeed, *Roper* explicitly relied on the possible imposition of life without parole on some juvenile offenders. * * *

In short, our existing precedent already provides a sufficient framework for assessing the concerns outlined by the majority. Not every juvenile receiving a life sentence will prevail under this approach. Not every juvenile should. But all will receive the protection that the Eighth Amendment requires.

Applying the "narrow proportionality" framework to the particular facts of this case, I conclude that Graham's sentence of life without parole violates the Eighth Amendment. * * * [The Chief Justice thereafter applied the three *Harmelin* factors and concluded that the life without parole sentence imposed on Graham was unconstitutional.] * * *

The fact that Graham cannot be sentenced to life without parole for his conduct says nothing whatever about [other] offenders * * * who commit nonhomicide crimes far more reprehensible than the conduct at issue here. The Court uses Graham's case as a vehicle to proclaim a new constitutional rule—applicable well beyond the particular facts of Graham's case—that a sentence of life without parole imposed on any juvenile for any nonhomicide offense is unconstitutional. This categorical conclusion is as unnecessary as it is unwise.

A holding this broad is unnecessary because the particular conduct and circumstances at issue in the case before us are not serious enough to justify Graham's sentence. In reaching this conclusion, there is no need for the Court to decide whether that same sentence would be constitutional if imposed for other more heinous nonhomicide crimes. * * *

[T]here is nothing inherently unconstitutional about imposing sentences of life without parole on juvenile offenders; rather, the constitutionality of such sentences depends on the particular crimes for which they are imposed. But if the constitutionality of the sentence turns on the particular crime being punished, then the Court should limit its holding to the particular offenses that Graham committed here, and should decline to consider other hypothetical crimes not presented by this case.

In any event, the Court's categorical conclusion is also unwise. Most importantly, it ignores the fact that some nonhomicide crimes * * * are especially heinous or grotesque, and thus may be deserving of more severe punishment. * * *

Our system depends upon sentencing judges applying their reasoned judgment to each case that comes before them. * * *

I would not, however, reach the same conclusion in every case involving a juvenile offender. Some crimes are so heinous, and some juvenile offenders so highly culpable, that a sentence of life without parole may be entirely justified under the Constitution. * * *

■ THOMAS, J., dissenting, joined in part by JUSTICES SCALIA and ALITO.

The Court holds today that it is "grossly disproportionate" and hence unconstitutional for any judge or jury to impose a sentence of life without parole on an offender less than 18 years old, unless he has committed a homicide. Although the text of the Constitution is silent regarding the permissibility of this sentencing practice, and although it would not have offended the standards that prevailed at the founding, the Court insists that the standards of American society have evolved such that the Constitution now requires its prohibition.

The news of this evolution will, I think, come as a surprise to the American people. Congress, the District of Columbia, and 37 States allow judges and juries to consider this sentencing practice in juvenile nonhomicide cases, and those judges and juries have decided to use it in the very worst cases they have encountered.

The Court does not conclude that life without parole itself is a cruel and unusual punishment. It instead rejects the judgments of those legislatures, judges, and juries regarding what the Court describes as the "moral" question whether this sentence can ever be "proportiona[te]" when applied to the category of offenders at issue here.

I am unwilling to assume that we, as Members of this Court, are any more capable of making such moral judgments than our fellow citizens. Nothing in our training as judges qualifies us for that task, and nothing in Article III gives us that authority. * * *

As has been described elsewhere at length, there is virtually no indication that the Cruel and Unusual Punishments Clause originally was understood to require proportionality in sentencing. * * * [T]he Clause does not expressly refer to proportionality or invoke any synonym for that term, even though the Framers were familiar with the concept, as evidenced by several founding-era state constitutions that required (albeit without defining) proportional punishments. In addition, the penal statute adopted by the First Congress demonstrates that proportionality in sentencing was not considered a constitutional command. * * *

For the first time in its history, the Court [today] declares an entire class of offenders immune from a noncapital sentence using the categorical approach it previously reserved for death penalty cases alone. * * *

Today's decision eviscerates that distinction. "Death is different" no longer. * * * The Court now claims * * * [the power] to declare that "less culpable" persons are categorically exempt from the "second most severe penalty." No reliable limiting principle remains to prevent the Court from immunizing any class of offenders from the law's third, fourth, fifth, or fiftieth most severe penalties as well. * * *

[E]ven if it were relevant, none of this psychological or sociological data is sufficient to support the Court's " 'moral' " conclusion that youth defeats culpability in every case.

The Court responds that a categorical rule is nonetheless necessary to prevent the " 'unacceptable likelihood' " that a judge or jury, unduly swayed by " 'the brutality or cold-blooded nature' " of a juvenile's nonhomicide crime, will sentence him to a life-without-parole sentence for which he possesses " 'insufficient culpability.' " I find that justification entirely insufficient. The integrity of our criminal justice system depends on the ability of citizens to stand between the defendant and an outraged public and dispassionately determine his guilt and the proper amount of punishment based on the evidence presented. That process necessarily admits of human error. But so does the process of judging in which we engage. As between the two, I find far more "unacceptable" that this Court, swayed by studies reflecting the general tendencies of youth, decree that the people of this country are not fit to decide for themselves when the rare case requires different treatment. * * *

That is especially so because, in the end, the Court does not even believe its pronouncements about the juvenile mind. If it did, the categorical rule it announces today would be most peculiar because it leaves intact state and federal laws that permit life-without-parole sentences for juveniles who commit homicides. The Court thus acknowledges that there is nothing inherent in the psyche of a person less than 18 that prevents him from acquiring the moral agency necessary to warrant a life-without-parole sentence. Instead, the Court rejects overwhelming legislative consensus only on the question of which acts are sufficient to demonstrate that moral agency.

The Court is quite willing to accept that a 17-year-old who pulls the trigger on a firearm can demonstrate sufficient depravity and irredeemability to be denied reentry into society, but insists that a 17-year-old who rapes an 8-year-old and leaves her for dead does not. Thus, the Court's conclusion that life-without-parole sentences are "grossly disproportionate" for juvenile nonhomicide offenders in fact has very little to do with its view of juveniles, and much more to do with its perception that "defendants who do not kill, intend to kill, or foresee that life will be taken are categorically less deserving of the most serious forms of punishment than are murderers." * * *

Both the Court and the concurrence claim their decisions to be narrow ones, but both invite a host of line-drawing problems to which courts must seek answers beyond the strictures of the Constitution. The Court holds that "[a] State is not required to guarantee eventual freedom to a juvenile offender convicted of a nonhomicide crime," but must provide the offender with "some meaningful opportunity to obtain release based on demonstrated maturity and rehabilitation." But what, exactly, does such a "meaningful" opportunity entail? When must it occur? And what Eighth Amendment principles will govern review by the parole boards the Court now demands that States empanel? The Court provides no answers to these questions, which will no doubt embroil the courts for years.

The ultimate question in this case is not whether a life-without-parole sentence "fits" the crime at issue here or the crimes of juvenile nonhomicide offenders more generally, but to whom the Constitution assigns that decision. The Florida Legislature has concluded that such sentences should be available for persons under 18 who commit certain crimes, and the trial judge in this case decided to impose that legislatively authorized sentence here. * * *

[Dissenting opinion of JUSTICE ALITO omitted.]

NOTES & QUESTIONS

1. **Categorical Rule.** In *Graham v. Florida,* a closely divided Court eschewed the judicial deference shown legislative determinations evidenced in *Ewing v. California.* After *Graham,* neither Congress nor state legislatures can impose a sentence of life without parole on a juvenile offender who committed a non-homicide offense. Previously, the Court in *Roper v. Simmons,* 543 U.S. 551 (2005), relied on social science research highlighting the developmental distinctiveness of juveniles, as compared to adults, to impose a categorical prohibition on the execution of juveniles. Assuming arguendo that the studies relied upon by the Court are accurate, with respect to juveniles in general, do they warrant a categorical rule that prohibits life without parole on all juveniles who have committed non-homicide offenses—including juveniles who demonstrate more maturity than a typical juvenile? In this sense, do you agree with concurring opinion of Chief Justice Roberts?

2. **Thomas Dissent.** Are your persuaded by Justice Thomas's dissent, which parallels the judicial deference exhibited in *Ewing*? And what of his point that the Court

> does not even believe its pronouncements about the juvenile mind. If it did, the categorical rule it announces today would be most peculiar because it leaves intact state and federal laws that permit life-without-parole sentences for juveniles who commit homicides. * * *
>
> The Court is quite willing to accept that a 17-year-old who pulls the trigger on a firearm can demonstrate sufficient depravity and irredeemability to be denied reentry into society, but insists that a 17-year-old who rapes an 8-year-old and leaves her for dead does not.

Graham, 560 U.S. at 119 (Thomas, J., dissenting).

3. **"Meaningful Opportunity" for Release.** Even if one agrees with the result and reasoning in *Graham,* Justice Kennedy's opinion for the plurality includes a major proviso: "[a] State is not required to guarantee eventual freedom to a juvenile offender convicted of a nonhomicide crime," but must provide the offender with "some meaningful opportunity to obtain release based on demonstrated maturity and rehabilitation." *Id.* at 75. What qualifies as "meaningful opportunity to obtain release" went undefined.

So, presumably, a state could impose a sixty-year minimum sentence on a seventeen-year-old; what then, as the dissent notes, does it mean to provide a "meaningful opportunity to obtain release" and when must the opportunity occur (perhaps before a designated age, such as seventy)? Faced with such questions, some legislatures adopted criteria. In California, for instance, parole eligibility is set at the twenty-five-year point, Cal. Penal Code § 3051(b), and statutory law provides criteria the parole authority is to consider, *id.* § 4801(c).

4. **Impact of Scientific Findings.** The *Graham* Court drew a line in the sand, so to speak, at the chronologic age of eighteen. Why eighteen? Is it

because that is the age young people can vote and be drafted into military service? Research suggests that in actuality the frontal cortex of the brain, the crucial area of the brain in question, is not fully formed until individuals reach their early to mid-twenties. Beth Colgan, *Constitutional Line Drawing at the Intersection of Childhood and Crime*, 9 STAN. J. C.R. & C.L. 79, 85 (2013). Should the Court defer to this finding—obliging use of an even later age to trigger Eighth Amendment proportionality concern? What do you see as the benefits and detriments of expansion? What systemic effect would the change have, for instance concerning resources and plea bargaining? Should this have any bearing on how the constitutional question is handled?

5. **De Facto Life Terms.** After *Graham*, courts have addressed challenges to what might be called "de facto" life terms for juveniles convicted in adult court of non-homicides. In *People v. Caballero*, 282 P.3d 291 (Cal. 2012), the California Supreme Court invalidated on Eighth Amendment grounds a 110-year sentence imposed upon a sixteen-year-old convicted of three counts of attempted murder. *See also, e.g., Budder v. Addison*, 851 F.3d 1047, 1049 (10th Cir. 2017) (invalidating a 155-year sentence consisting of three life-with-parole sentences plus twenty years imposed on a juvenile non-homicide offender, who had to serve 131.75 years before becoming eligible for parole); *Moore v. Biter*, 725 F.3d 1184, 1191–92 (9th Cir. 2013) (finding sentence of 254 years with no opportunity for parole eligibility within defendant's lifetime "materially indistinguishable from a life sentence without parole"); *State v. Moore*, 76 N.E.3d 1127, 1128–29 (Ohio 2017) (stating that "a term-of-years prison sentence that exceeds a defendant's life expectancy violates the Eighth Amendment. . . when it is imposed on a juvenile nonhomicide offender").

In so holding, the courts reason that de facto LWOP sentences defy *Graham*'s requirement that non-homicide juvenile defendants receive "some meaningful opportunity to obtain release based on demonstrated maturity and rehabilitation," and preclude a "meaningful opportunity to obtain release." Not all courts agree, however. *See, e.g., Bunch v. Smith*, 685 F.3d 546, 550 (6th Cir. 2012) (upholding a non-homicide juvenile offender's consecutive, fixed-term sentence of 89 years, reasoning that *Graham* did not apply to juveniles convicted of multiple non-homicide offenses). The latter view aligns with a technical view of a "life" term without parole, but do you agree that it aligns with what might be called the "spirit" of *Graham*?

6. **Mandatory LWOP.** Two years after *Graham*, the Court in *Miller v. Alabama*, 567 U.S. 460 (2012) held that the Eighth Amendment barred *mandatory* (as opposed to discretionary) sentences of life without parole for juvenile defendants (in *Miller*, two fourteen-year-olds)—including those who commit homicides. Echoing *Graham*, the five-member *Miller* Court emphasized that "youth matters" and reasoned that a mandatory life without parole sentence was improper because it prevents a sentencing court from taking "account of an offender's age and the wealth of characteristics and circumstances attendant to it." *Id.* at 476. "By making youth (and all that accompanies it) irrelevant to imposition of that harshest prison sentence [LWOP], such a scheme poses too great a risk of disproportionate punishment." *Id.* at 479. "[C]hildren are different," *id.* at 480, so sentencing

schemes that preclude consideration of that fact by mandating LWOP for juveniles are invalid under the Eighth Amendment. *Id.* at 489.

The *Miller* Court identified four factors that a judge is to consider when imposing a LWOP sentence: (1) "Immaturity, impetuosity, and a failure to appreciate risks and consequences"; (2) "family and home environment"; (3) "circumstances of the homicide offense, including the extent of [the juvenile's] participation in the conduct and the way familial and peer pressure may have affected him"; and (4) the possibility of rehabilitation. *Id.* at 477.

In so holding, the majority resisted imposing a categorical bar, maintaining that life without parole "will be uncommon," and required that a sentencing court "take into account how children are different, and how those differences counsel against irrevocably sentencing them to a lifetime in prison." *Id.* at 479–80. *Miller*, in short, did not preclude a life without parole sentence; it only prohibited its mandatory imposition.

Much as with non-homicide cases, controlled by *Graham*, courts have addressed claims that a de facto life term for a homicide is subject to *Miller*. In *McKinley v. Butler*, 809 F.3d 908 (7th Cir. 2016), for instance, Judge Richard Posner applied the logic of *Miller* to vacate a 100-year sentence imposed on a juvenile, reasoning that the sentencing court "did not consider the Supreme Court's 'children are different' statement in *Miller*," and that:

> [I]t is such a long term of years (especially given the unavailability of early release) as to be—unless there is a radical increase, at present unforeseeable, in longevity within the next 100 years—a de facto life sentence, and so the logic of *Miller* applies. . . .
>
> [T]he "children are different" passage . . . from *Miller v. Alabama* cannot logically be limited to de jure life sentences, as distinct from sentences denominated in numbers of years yet highly likely to result in imprisonment for life.

Id. at 911. However, the Eighth Circuit in *United States v. Jefferson*, 816 F.3d 1016 (8th Cir. 2016), held that *Miller* did not apply to non-mandatory de facto life sentences, in *Jefferson* a 600-month sentence imposed for a homicide, reasoning that "[t]he Court in *Miller* did not hold that the Eighth Amendment categorically prohibits imposing a sentence of life without parole on a juvenile offender." *Id.* at 1018–19.

7. **Parole Hearings.** In *Miller*, the Court contemplated that states could remedy a violation by offering parole hearings to juveniles serving life sentences. The Fourth Circuit, addressing a case where the juvenile had several opportunities for parole, which were denied, determined that Eighth Amendment protections were not triggered so long as parole hearings were available. *Bowling v. Dir., Va. Dep't of Corr.*, 920 F.3d 192, 198 (4th Cir. 2019). Concern exists, however, that parole proceedings typically do not provide meaningful opportunity for release of juveniles. *See, e.g.*, Amelia Courtney Hritz, *Board to Death: De Facto Juvenile Life without Parole*, 47 AM. J. CRIM. L. 47 (2020) (discussing results of study showing very low rates of parole release and contending that parole hearings do not accommodate concerns raised in *Graham* and *Miller*).

8. **Retroactivity.** In 2016, the Court in *Montgomery v. Louisiana*, 577 U.S. 190 (2016), held that *Miller* was a new substantive constitutional rule that should be applied retroactively, affecting not only cases on direct but also collateral review. *Montgomery*, moreover, identified what has become known as a "incorrigibility standard," allowing a court to impose life without parole on the "rare juvenile offender whose crime reflects irreparable corruption." *Id.* at 209.

In the wake of *Miller* and *Montgomery*, jurisdictions have been required to resentence some two thousand juvenile offenders. The resentencings have posed significant logistical and budgetary challenges to state and local justice systems, with different case outcomes often reflecting varied criteria, procedures, and evidence presented. *See* Emily Komp, Comment, *Resentencing Juveniles: States' Implementation of* Miller *and* Montgomery *Through Resentencing Hearings*, 53 UIC J. MARSHALL L. REV. 311 (2020).

9. **Gauging Incorrigibility.** The determination of "incorrigibility" has been affected by an even more recent Supreme Court decision, *Jones v. Mississippi*, 141 S. Ct. 1307 (2021). In *Jones*, a fifteen-year-old convicted of homicide argued that the sentencing court erred by imposing a LWOP sentence because it failed to make a factual finding of permanent incorrigibility or, at the very least, to provide an on-the-record explanation of the sentence containing an "implicit finding" of permanent incorrigibility. The Court disagreed, holding that *Miller* does not require a separate factual finding of permanent incorrigibility before a LWOP sentence can be imposed.

Writing for the 6–3 majority, Justice Kavanaugh stated that "a sentencing explanation is. . . not necessary to ensure that the sentencer in juvenile life-without-parole cases considers the defendant's youth." *Id.* at 1320. A court is only required to *consider* the offender's youth and attendant circumstances prior to imposing a life without parole sentence. Moreover, "unless the record affirmatively reflects otherwise, the trial court will be deemed to have considered the relevant criteria, such as mitigating circumstances, enumerated in the sentencing rules." *Id.* at 1321.

Justice Sotomayor, joined by Justices Breyer and Kagan, dissented. She argued that the Court "abandon[ed]" *Miller* and *Montgomery* by permitting juveniles to be sentenced to life without parole if the sentence is not mandatory and when the sentencer has discretion to impose a lesser punishment without determining whether the juvenile was one of the rare children who were incorrigible. *Id.* at 1328 (Sotomayor, J., dissenting). *See also United States v. Grant*, 9 F.4th 186, 197 (3d Cir. 2021) (en banc) (noting that the Supreme Court has "guaranteed to juvenile homicide offenders only a sentencing procedure in which the sentencer must weigh youth as a mitigating factor. The Court has not guaranteed particular outcomes for either corrigible or incorrigible juvenile homicide offenders. . . . Such individualized consideration is all that *Miller* requires."); *Holmes v. State*, 859 S.E.2d 475, 481 (Ga. 2021) ("In short, *Jones* clarified that although the Eighth Amendment requires that, before sentencing a juvenile murderer to LWOP, a trial court must hold a sentencing hearing where the defendant's age and characteristics of children are considered, neither *Miller* nor

Montgomery requires a sentencer to say anything on the record about youth and its attendant characteristics before imposing a LWOP sentence.").

10. **Abandonment of LWOP?** Should LWOP—what Pope Francis has called "a death penalty in disguise"[5]—be abandoned altogether, for juveniles and adults? In framing your answer, it might be useful to know that LWOP itself is a relatively new sentence. In 1990, thirty-two states and the District of Columbia had LWOP statutes, whereas today all U.S. jurisdictions but one authorize LWOP, and over 40,000 individuals are so sentenced. Much like the death penalty, the punishment views the condemned individual as beyond possible redemption and rehabilitation, yet LWOP receives considerably less appellate scrutiny, and for many the hopelessness of LWOP is worse than death. For an argument in favor of abolition, see William W. Berry III, *Life-With-Hope Sentencing: The Argument for Replacing Life-Without-Parole Sentences with Presumptive Life Sentences*, 76 OHIO ST. L.J. 1051 (2015).

11. **LWOP and Death with Dignity.** Nine states and the District of Columbia authorize individuals suffering from terminal illnesses to a "death with dignity" with the assistance of a physician. Four jurisdictions expressly disallow inmates from availing themselves of the right. *See* Brittany L. Deitch, *Life Without Parole as Death Without Dignity*, 72 ALA. L. REV. 327 (2020). "Although the exclusion of prisoners from death with dignity applies to all incarcerated persons," Professor Deitch writes, "the ban disproportionately impacts LWOP prisoners, who know with practical certainty that they will die in prison. The states' preclusion of inmates from enjoying the freedom of choice, autonomy, and dignity that nonincarcerated citizens are entitled to exercise over the time and manner of their deaths constitutes an additional, unjustifiable condition of punishment." *Id.* at 327–28. *See also* id. 331–32 ("Undeniably, LWOP inmates are condemned to die in prison. However, these death-with-dignity jurisdictions impose the additional punishment of prohibiting these prisoners from exercising autonomy in their death. Instead, these prisoners will suffer as they succumb to a terminal illness. In other words, 'life in prison' in these jurisdictions includes stripping the prisoner of the dignity that free citizens enjoy."). If you were a legislator, would you endorse an exclusion? If so, on what basis?

B. PHYSICAL PUNISHMENT AS CRUEL AND UNUSUAL PUNISHMENT

Unlike during the nation's early history, physical punishment is a rarity in the contemporary criminal justice system, and is condemned even by members of the Court who otherwise view the Eighth Amendment as of little utility in limiting governmental power to punish. *See, e.g., Graham v. Florida*, 560 U.S. 48, 99 (2010) (Thomas, J., dissenting) (citations omitted) ("It is by now well established that the Cruel and Unusual Punishments Clause was originally understood as

[5] Pope Francis, Bishop of Rome, *Address to the Delegates of the International Association of Penal Law* (Oct. 23, 2014), http://www.vatican.va/content/francesco/en/speeches/2014/october/documents/papa-francesco_20141023_associazione-internazionale-diritto-penale.html.

prohibiting torturous 'methods of punishment,' . . . specifically methods akin to those that had been considered cruel and unusual at the time the Bill of Rights was adopted."). The following case provides a modern-day example of a judicial limit imposed on government-desired use of physical punishment.

State v. Brown

326 S.E.2d 410 (S.C. 1985)

■ PER CURIAM.

These cases involve attempts by three defendants to gain suspended sentences conditioned upon their completion of surgical castration. Petitioner Roscoe James Brown moves for the issuance of a writ of mandamus to compel the execution of the suspended sentence. Appellants Michael Braxton and Mark Vaughn seek dismissal of their appeals so that they too may have their suspended sentences carried out. At oral argument, counsel for all three defendants conceded that our disposition of these cases should be the same as to all of them. We hold that the suspension of the sentences conditioned upon castration is void and remand for resentencing.

Appellants Vaughn and Braxton and petitioner Brown pled guilty to first degree criminal sexual conduct, in connection with a brutal sexual assault. Vaughn and Brown also pled guilty to criminal conspiracy. The trial judge heard evidence in aggravation and mitigation of punishment. Each defendant was then sentenced on the criminal sexual conduct charge as follows:

> On the indictments charging each of you with criminal sexual conduct in the first degree, the sentence of the Court is that you be confined in the custody of the State Board of Corrections for a period of thirty years, which is the maximum sentence I can impose, provided however, that upon each of you voluntarily agreeing to be castrated and upon the successful completion of that surgical procedure, the balance of this sentence will be suspended and you'll be placed on probation for a period of five years.

Vaughn and Brown were each given a five year concurrent sentence on the conspiracy charge, suspended upon the same condition imposed in the criminal sexual conduct sentence. * * *

At common law, trial courts have no general power to suspend sentences, but such authority may be conferred by the legislature. * * * The authority to suspend sentences in felony cases is contained in S.C.Code Ann. § 24–21–410 (1976). * * *

Section 24–21–410 was intended to give trial judges the power to suspend sentences upon the conditions they deem fit and proper. They are allowed a wide, but not unlimited, discretion in imposing conditions of suspension or probation and they cannot impose conditions which are illegal and void as against public policy. * * *

The public policy of this State is derived by implication from the established law of the State, as found in its Constitution, statutes, and judicial decisions. * * * Article I, § 15, of our Constitution prohibits the infliction of cruel and unusual punishment. * * * Castration, a form of mutilation, is prohibited by Article I, § 15. *See Davis v. Berry*, 216 F. 413 (D.C. Iowa 1914); *Mickle v. Henrichs*, 262 F. 687 (D.C. Nev.1918).

Accordingly, we remand all three cases to the lower court for resentencing in accordance with this opinion. Brown's petition for writ of mandamus is denied. The appeals of Vaughn and Braxton are dismissed.

[Concurrence of JUSTICE NESS omitted.]

NOTES & QUESTIONS

1. **Procedural Route of *Brown*.** In terms of constitutional doctrine, *Brown* is important, but it also entailed an interesting subsidiary issue, which might not have occurred to you when reading the case: how did the matter get to the South Carolina Supreme Court? The defendants wished to proceed with the physical castration, in return for suspension of the lengthy prison sentences that would otherwise be imposed. It turns out that the Court had a writ of mandamus before it from one of the three defendants who was trying to get the lower court to go forward with the castration and suspended sentence.

In a later unrelated case, *American Civil Liberties of Arkansas, Inc. v. State*, 5 S.W.3d 418 (Ark. 1999), the Arkansas Supreme Court held that the ACLU lacked standing to intervene and challenge use of physical castration, in lieu of a prison sentence, stating that "such a sentence does not involve the unique and irreversible penalty of death, which is different in kind from any other punishment." *Id.* at 420. Do you disagree—should a group, such as the ACLU, be allowed to intervene in what the *Brown* Court called a case involving a "form of mutilation"?

2. **A Non-Waivable Right?** Should an individual, such as Brown, be allowed to waive any constitutional objection and consent to the procedure? Although the U.S. Supreme Court has not directly addressed the question, lower courts have held that the protection cannot be waived. *See, e.g., Brown*, 326 S.E.3d at 411 (invalidating castration because a state "cannot impose conditions which are illegal and void as against public policy"); *see also, e.g., LaGrand v. Stewart*, 173 F.3d 1144, 1148 (9th Cir. 1999). However, assuming a waiver is informed and consensual, should courts accede to the individual's wish? Purely as a matter of personal autonomy, it would appear that doing so is proper. Are there any downsides to allowing waiver of constitutional protections? Does or should the ongoing debate over assisted suicide have any bearing on the question? For more on the waiver question see Jeffrey L. Kirchmeier, *Let's Make a Deal: Waiving the Eighth Amendment by Selecting a Cruel and Unusual Punishment*, 32 CONN. L. REV. 615 (2000).

3. **Physical Castration as an Option.** Despite constitutional concerns, several states make physical castration an option for convicted sex offenders. California, Florida, and Montana allow for voluntary castration (along with chemical castration, involving drugs designed to reduce sexual drive), as does Texas, but Texas does not allow for it in return for a reduced sentence. *See* Lystra Batchoo, Note, *Voluntary Surgical Castration of Sex Offenders: Waiving the Eighth Amendment Protection for Cruel and Unusual Punishment*, 72 BROOK. L. REV. 689, 699–701 (2007). According to the author:

> Sex offenders who volunteer for surgical castration often do so because they believe their chances of an early release from prison will increase and the likelihood of re-offending will decrease. In these cases, courts must determine whether the procedure is an effective substitute to the more traditional punishment of prolonged incarceration.
>
> If the court considers the procedure an effective substitute, the sex offender might gain his release from prison or a lighter prison sentence. Of paramount consideration is whether the sex offender is likely to commit more sex crimes. A number of courts have granted sex offenders their freedom for undergoing the procedure or given drastically reduced sentences.

Id. at 699.

As discussed in Chapter 11, individuals convicted of sex offenses are arguably the most disdained subpopulation in modern society, triggering a range of unique sanctions, including registration and community notification (a.k.a. "Megan's Laws") and indefinite involuntary commitment (a.k.a. "sexually violent predator" laws). Does their uniqueness warrant special constitutional consideration? Whatever its possible value as a deterrent, does any expressive benefit experienced by society as a result of physically castrating convicted sex offenders justify its use?

4. **Physical Punishment as an Alternative.** It is widely accepted that imprisonment is a less than ideal method of punishment. Not only is it very expensive and its effectiveness as a deterrent to crime questioned, it has serious immediate and long-term consequences on individuals and communities. Professor Graeme Newman has argued that physical punishment, for instance by brief but sharp electric shocks, is actually an attractive alternative to prison. For instance, it might be a better deterrent to criminal activity than imprisonment and would avoid its enormous expense and negative collateral effects on others. GRAEME NEWMAN, JUST AND PAINFUL: A CASE FOR THE CORPORAL PUNISHMENT OF CRIMINALS (1983).

If corporal punishment is wrong in principle, how is it that executions—which obviously have a physical component in their administration and ultimate effect—are permitted? And why should government be prohibited from using corporal punishment, especially when it is consented to by a convicted individual, yet parents are permitted to physically strike their children as a form of discipline? For more on the question, see, e.g., Ole Martin Moen, *Judicial Corporal Punishment*, 17 J. ETHICS & SOC. PHIL. 27

(2020); Geoffrey Scarre, *Corporal Punishment*, 6 ETHICAL THEORY & MORAL PRAC. 295 (2003).

C. EQUAL PROTECTION

As noted at the outset, the Fifth and Fourteenth Amendments of the U.S. Constitution ensure that criminal defendants are accorded equal protection of the law.[6] To successfully raise an equal protection claim, an individual must establish that they are being treated differently by the government, and thereby disadvantaged, than other similarly situated individuals. The following case is one of the few instances in which the Supreme Court has addressed such a claim in relation to criminal punishment.

Skinner v. State of Oklahoma ex rel. Williamson

316 U.S. 535 (1942)

■ DOUGLAS, J.

This case touches a sensitive and important area of human rights. Oklahoma deprives certain individuals of a right which is basic to the perpetuation of a race—the right to have offspring. Oklahoma has decreed the enforcement of its law against petitioner, overruling his claim that it violated the Fourteenth Amendment. Because that decision raised grave and substantial constitutional questions, we granted the petition for certiorari.

The statute involved is Oklahoma's Habitual Criminal Sterilization Act. That Act defines an 'habitual criminal' as a person who, having been convicted two or more times for crimes 'amounting to felonies involving moral turpitude' either in an Oklahoma court or in a court of any other State, is thereafter convicted of such a felony in Oklahoma and is sentenced to a term of imprisonment in an Oklahoma penal institution. Machinery is provided for the institution by the Attorney General of a proceeding against such a person in the Oklahoma courts for a judgment that such person shall be rendered sexually sterile. Notice, an opportunity to be heard, and the right to a jury trial are provided. The issues triable in such a proceeding are narrow and confined. If the court or jury finds that the defendant is an 'habitual criminal' and that he 'may be rendered sexually sterile without detriment to his or her general health', then the court 'shall render judgment to the effect that said defendant be rendered sexually sterile' * * * by the operation of vasectomy in case of a male and of salpingectomy in case of a female. Only one other provision of the Act is material here and that is [section 195] which provides that "offenses arising out of the violation of the

[6] State constitutions also contain equal protection provisions. *See, e.g.*, CAL. CONST. art. I, § 7(a).

prohibitory laws, revenue acts, embezzlement, or political offenses, shall not come or be considered within the terms of this Act."

Petitioner was convicted in 1926 of the crime of stealing chickens and was sentenced to the Oklahoma State Reformatory. In 1929 he was convicted of the crime of robbery with fire arms and was sentenced to the reformatory. In 1934 he was convicted again of robbery with firearms and was sentenced to the penitentiary. He was confined there in 1935 when the Act was passed. In 1936 the Attorney General instituted proceedings against him. Petitioner in his answer challenged the Act as unconstitutional by reason of the Fourteenth Amendment. A jury trial was had. The court instructed the jury that the crimes of which petitioner had been convicted were felonies involving moral turpitude and that the only question for the jury was whether the operation of vasectomy could be performed on petitioner without detriment to his general health. The jury found that it could be. A judgment directing that the operation of vasectomy be performed on petitioner was affirmed by the Supreme Court of Oklahoma by a five to four decision.

Several objections to the constitutionality of the Act have been pressed upon us. It is urged that the Act cannot be sustained as an exercise of the police power in view of the state of scientific authorities respecting inheritability of criminal traits. It is argued that due process is lacking because under this Act, unlike the act upheld in *Buck v. Bell*, 274 U.S. 200 [1927], the defendant is given no opportunity to be heard on the issue as to whether he is the probable potential parent of socially undesirable offspring. It is also suggested that the Act is penal in character and that the sterilization provided for is cruel and unusual punishment and violative of the Fourteenth Amendment. We pass those points without intimating an opinion on them, for there is a feature of the Act which clearly condemns it. That is its failure to meet the requirements of the equal protection clause of the Fourteenth Amendment.

We do not stop to point out all of the inequalities in this Act. A few examples will suffice. In Oklahoma grand larceny is a felony. Larceny is grand larceny when the property taken exceeds $20 in value. Embezzlement is punishable "in the manner prescribed for feloniously stealing property of the value of that embezzled." Hence he who embezzles property worth more than $20 is guilty of a felony. A clerk who appropriates over $20 from his employer's till and a stranger who steals the same amount are thus both guilty of felonies. If the latter repeats his act and is convicted three times, he may be sterilized. But the clerk is not subject to the pains and penalties of the Act no matter how large his embezzlements nor how frequent his convictions. A person who enters a chicken coop and steals chickens commits a felony; and he may be sterilized if he is thrice convicted. If, however, he is a bailee of the property and fraudulently appropriates it, he is an embezzler. Hence no matter how habitual his proclivities for embezzlement are and no matter how often his conviction, he may not be sterilized. Thus the nature of the two crimes is intrinsically the same and they are punishable in the same manner. Furthermore, the line between them follows close distinctions—distinctions comparable to those highly technical ones which shaped the common law as to "trespass" or "taking." There may be larceny by fraud rather than embezzlement even where the owner of the personal property delivers it to the defendant, if the latter has at that time "a fraudulent intention to make use of the possession as a means of converting such property to his own use, and does so convert it." *Bivens v. State*, 120 P. 1033, 1036 [(Okla. 1912)]. If the fraudulent intent occurs later and the defendant converts the property, he is guilty of embezzlement. [*Id.*] Whether a particular act is larceny by fraud or embezzlement thus turns not on the intrinsic quality of the act but on when the felonious intent arose—a question for the jury under appropriate instructions. [*Id.*]

It was stated in *Buck v. Bell*, that the claim that state legislation violates the equal protection clause of the Fourteenth Amendment is "the usual last resort of constitutional arguments." Under our constitutional system the States in determining the reach and scope of particular legislation need not provide "abstract symmetry." *Patsone v. Pennsylvania*, 232 U.S. 138 [(1914)]. They may mark and set apart the classes and types of problems according to the needs and as dictated or suggested by experience. *See People of State of New York ex rel. Bryant v. Zimmerman*, 278 U.S. 63 [(1928)]. It was in that connection that Mr. Justice Holmes, speaking for the Court in *Bain Peanut Co. v. Pinson*, 282 U.S. 499 [(1931)], stated, "We must remember that the machinery of government would not work if it were not allowed a little play in its joints." Only recently we reaffirmed the view that the equal protection clause does not prevent the legislature from recognizing "degrees of evil," that "the Constitution does not require things which are different in fact or opinion to be treated in law as though they were the same." * * * Thus, if we had here only a question as to a State's classification of crimes, such as embezzlement or larceny, no substantial federal question would be raised. * * * For a State is not constrained in the exercise of its police power to ignore experience which marks a class of offenders or a family of offenses for special treatment. Nor is it prevented by the equal protection clause from confining "its restrictions to those classes of cases where the need is deemed to be clearest." *Miller v. Wilson*, 236 U.S. 373 [(1915)]. As stated in *Buck v. Bell*, "the law does all that is needed when it does all that it can, indicates a policy, applies it to all within the lines, and seeks to bring within the lines all similarly situated so far and so fast as its means allow."

But the instant legislation runs afoul of the equal protection clause, though we give Oklahoma that large deference which the rule of the foregoing cases requires. We are dealing here with legislation which involves one of the basic civil rights of man. Marriage and procreation are fundamental to the very existence and survival of the race. The power to sterilize, if exercised, may have subtle, farreaching and devastating effects. In evil or reckless hands it can cause races or types which are inimical to the dominant group to wither and disappear. There is no redemption for the individual whom the law touches. Any experiment which the State conducts is to his irreparable injury. He is forever deprived of a basic liberty. We mention these matters not to reexamine the scope of the police power of the States. We advert to them merely in emphasis of our view that strict scrutiny of the classification which a State makes in a sterilization law is essential, lest unwittingly or otherwise invidious discriminations are made against groups or types of individuals in violation of the constitutional guaranty of just and equal laws. The guaranty of "equal protection of the laws is a pledge of the protection of equal laws." *Yick Wo v. Hopkins*, 118 U.S. 356 [(1886)]. When the law lays an unequal hand on those who have committed intrinsically the same quality of offense and sterilizes one and not the other, it has made as an invidious a discrimination as if it had selected a particular race or nationality for oppressive treatment. * * *

Sterilization of those who have thrice committed grand larceny with immunity for those who are embezzlers is a clear, pointed, unmistakable discrimination. Oklahoma makes no attempt to say that he who commits larceny by trespass or trick or fraud has biologically inheritable traits which he who commits embezzlement lacks. * * * We have not the slightest basis for inferring that that line has any significance in eugenics nor that the inheritability of criminal traits follows the neat legal distinctions which the law has marked between those two offenses. In terms of fines and imprisonment the crimes of larceny and embezzlement rate the same under the Oklahoma code. Only when it comes to sterilization are the pains and penalties of the law different. The equal protection clause would indeed be a formula of empty words if such conspicuously artificial lines could be drawn. In *Buck v. Bell*, *supra*, the Virginia statute was upheld though it applied only to feebleminded persons in institutions of the State. But it was pointed out that "so far as the operations enable those who otherwise must be kept confined to be returned to the world, and thus open the asylum to others, the equality aimed at will be more nearly reached." Here there is no such saving feature. Embezzlers are forever free. Those who steal or take in other ways are not. If such a classification were permitted, the technical common law concept of a "trespass'. . . based on distinctions which are 'very largely dependent upon history for explanation" (Holmes, The Common Law, p. 73) could readily become a rule of human genetics. * * *

■ STONE, C.J., concurring.

I concur in the result, but I am not persuaded that we are aided in reaching it by recourse to the equal protection clause.

If Oklahoma may resort generally to the sterilization of criminals on the assumption that their propensities are transmissible to future generations by inheritance, I seriously doubt that the equal protection clause requires it to apply the measure to all criminals in the first instance, or to none. * * *

Moreover, if we must presume that the legislature knows—what science has been unable to ascertain—that the criminal tendencies of any class of habitual offenders are transmissible regardless of the varying mental characteristics of its individuals, I should suppose that we must likewise presume that the legislature, in its wisdom, knows that the criminal tendencies of some classes of offenders are more likely to be transmitted than those of others. And so I think the real question we have to consider is not one of equal protection, but whether the wholesale condemnation of a class to such an invasion of personal liberty, without opportunity to any individual to show that his is not the type of case which would justify resort to it, satisfies the demands of due process.

There are limits to the extent to which the presumption of constitutionality can be pressed, especially where the liberty of the person is concerned (*see United States v. Carolene Products Co.*, 304 U.S. 144, 152, n.4 [(1938)]) and where the presumption is resorted to only to dispense with a procedure which the ordinary dictates of prudence would seem to demand for the protection of the individual from arbitrary action. Although petitioner here was given a hearing to ascertain whether sterilization would be detrimental to his health, he was given none to discover whether his criminal tendencies are of an inheritable type. Undoubtedly a state may, after appropriate inquiry, constitutionally interfere with the personal liberty of the individual to prevent the transmission by inheritance of his socially injurious tendencies. *Buck v. Bell*, 274 U.S. 200. But until now we have not been called upon to say that it may do so without giving him a hearing and opportunity to challenge the existence as to him of the only facts which could justify so drastic a measure.

Science has found and the law has recognized that there are certain types of mental deficiency associated with delinquency which are inheritable. But the State does not contend—nor can there be any pretense—that either common knowledge or experience, or scientific investigation, has given assurance that the criminal tendencies of any class of habitual offenders are universally or even generally inheritable. In such circumstances, inquiry whether such is the fact in the case of any particular individual cannot rightly be dispensed with. Whether the procedure by which a statute carries its mandate into execution satisfies due process is a matter of judicial cognizance. A law which condemns, without hearing, all the individuals of a class to so harsh a measure as the present because some or even many merit condemnation, is lacking in the first principles of due process. And so, while the state may protect itself from the demonstrably inheritable tendencies of the individual which are injurious to society, the most elementary notions of due process would seem to require it to take appropriate steps to safeguard the liberty of the individual by affording him, before he is condemned to an irreparable injury in his person, some opportunity to show that he is without such inheritable tendencies. The state is called on to sacrifice no permissible end when it is required to reach its objective by a reasonable and just procedure adequate to safeguard rights of the individual which concededly the Constitution protects.

■ JACKSON, J., concurring.

I join the CHIEF JUSTICE in holding that the hearings provided are too limited in the context of the present Act to afford due process of law. I also agree with the opinion of Mr. Justice DOUGLAS that the scheme of classification set forth in the Act denies equal protection of the law. I disagree with the opinion of each in so far as it rejects or minimizes the grounds taken by the other.

Perhaps to employ a broad and loose scheme of classification would be permissible if accompanied by the individual hearings indicated by the CHIEF JUSTICE. On the other hand, narrow classification with reference to the end to be accomplished by the Act might justify limiting individual hearings to the issue whether the individual belonged to a class so defined. Since this Act does not present these questions, I reserve judgment on them.

I also think the present plan to sterilize the individual in pursuit of a eugenic plan to eliminate from the race characteristics that are only vaguely identified and which in our present state of knowledge are uncertain as to transmissibility presents other constitutional questions of gravity. This Court has sustained such an experiment with respect to an imbecile, a person with definite and observable characteristics where the condition had persisted through three generations and afforded grounds for the belief that it was transmissible and would continue to manifest itself in generations to come. *Buck v. Bell*, 274 U.S. 200 [1927].

There are limits to the extent to which a legislatively represented majority may conduct biological experiments at the expense of the dignity and personality and natural powers of a minority—even those who have been guilty of what the majority define as crimes. But this Act falls down before reaching this problem, which I mention only to avoid the implication that such a question may not exist because not discussed. On it I would also reserve judgment.

NOTES & QUESTIONS

1. ***Buck v. Bell.*** *Skinner* was not the first time the Court addressed a claim involving forced sterilization. As the opinion for the Court by Justice Douglas noted, *Buck v. Bell*, 274 U.S. 200 (1927) addressed a challenge in the non-criminal context, involving the forced sterilization of a woman deemed "feeble minded" who had the potential to bear "socially inadequate offspring." *Id.* at 207. The Court, by an 8–1 vote, rejected the challenge. Aligning himself with eugenics theory, then embraced by many progressive thinkers, Justice Oliver Wendell Holmes infamously declared that "three

generations of imbeciles is enough." Further, Holmes reasoned that equal protection was the "last resort of constitutional arguments." *Id.* at 208.

Skinner of course addressed a challenge to government use of forced sterilization (in Skinner's case, a vasectomy) in a criminal case. The Oklahoma Sterilization Act targeted persons convicted and incarcerated for three "felonies involving moral turpitude," on the condition that the sterilization procedure would not be a detriment to the individual's "general health." Skinner had been convicted once of stealing chickens and twice of armed robbery, and was thus subject to sterilization. Skinner himself was poor and disabled, having lost one of his feet in an accident. However, he was not allowed to argue before the advisory board that he committed his crimes out of exigency rather than "moral turpitude." Paul A. Lombardo, *Medicine, Eugenics, and the Supreme Court: From Coercive Sterilization to Reproductive Freedom*, 13 J. CONTEMP. HEALTH L. & POL'Y 1, 15–16 (1996).

Ignoring Justice Holmes's prior dismissal of equal protection, the Court invalidated the statute on equal protection grounds because a person convicted of larceny three times would be subject to forced sterilization, yet a person convicted of embezzlement three times would not. What accounts for the shift in the constitutional treatment of sterilization? One factor might be that by 1942, when *Skinner* was decided, to some extent Americans had awakened to the racial eugenic-inspired "medical" atrocities engaged in by Nazi Germany. *See* Mary Ziegler, *Reinventing Eugenics: Reproductive Choice and Law Reform After World War II*, 14 CARDOZO J.L. & GENDER 319, 325 (2008). *See also* Michael von Cranach, *The Killing of Psychiatric Patients in Nazi Germany Between 1939–1945*, ISR. J. PSYCH. RELATED SCI. 1, 8–18 (2003) (discussing Nazis' early and sustained sterilization of individuals with cognitive impairments and mental illness).

Justice Robert Jackson concurred with both Justice Douglas's equal protection rationale and the due process rationale favored by Chief Justice Harlan Fiske Stone in his concurring opinion. At one point, Jackson wrote that "[t]here are limits to the extent to which a legislatively represented majority may conduct biological experiments at the expense of the dignity and personality and natural powers of a minority—even those who have been guilty of what the majority defines as crimes." *Id.* at 546 (Jackson, J., concurring). Notably, not long after *Skinner*, in 1945–1946, Justice Jackson took a leave from the Court and served as Chief United States Prosecutor at the Nuremberg trials of Nazi war criminals, which laid bare Nazi atrocities.

It is important to recognize that *Skinner* did not overrule *Buck*. The majority and both concurrences distinguished *Buck* from *Skinner*. Writing for the Court, Justice Douglas advanced a subtle distinction:

> In *Buck v. Bell*, the Virginia statute was upheld though it applied only to feeble-minded persons in institutions of the State. But it was pointed out that "so far as the operations enable those who otherwise must be kept confined to be returned to the world, and thus open the asylum to others, the equality aimed at will be more nearly reached." Here there is no such saving feature. Embezzlers are forever free. Those who steal or take in other ways are not.

Skinner, 316 U.S. at 542 (citations omitted).

Skinner was decided before the Eighth Amendment was incorporated and imposed upon the states (*Robinson v. California*, 370 U.S. 660 (1962)), whereas the terms of the Fourteenth Amendment's Equal Protection Clause expressly apply to the states. If an Eighth Amendment cruel and unusual punishment challenge were brought today against a law similar to the Oklahoma Act, what arguments might the Court find persuasive?

2. **Post-*Skinner*.** It might come as a surprise to learn that involuntary sterilizations, sanctioned by state law, occurred well into the twentieth century. "Of the states with eugenic sterilization laws as of 1968, the feeble-minded or mentally deficient were subject to sterilization in all 27, the mentally ill in 25, epileptics in 14, habitual criminals in 7, and 'moral degenerates and sexual perverts' in 7.' " Jana Leslie-Miller, *From* Bell *to* Bell: *Responsible Reproduction in the Twentieth Century*, 8 MD. J. CONTEMP. LEGAL ISSUES 123, 133 (1997) (citation omitted). The state laws resulted in over 60,000 involuntary sterilizations, with Virginia, North Carolina, California, and Oregon operating perhaps the most active programs. North Carolina's program alone targeted 7,600 individuals between 1929 and 1974; by the late 1960s, more than 60% of those sterilized were black, and 99% were female. Michael G. Silver, Note, *Eugenics and Compulsory Sterilization Laws: Providing Redress for the Victims of a Shameful Era in United States History*, 72 GEO. WASH. L. REV. 862, 887 (2004). Justice Thurgood Marshall in 1985 described the laws as "a regime of state-mandated segregation and degradation . . . that in its virulence and bigotry rivaled, and indeed paralleled, the worst excesses of Jim Crow." *City of Cleburne v. Cleburne Living Ctr., Inc.*, 473 U.S. 432, 462 (1985) (Marshall, J., dissenting).

3. **Lobotomies.** It is also worth noting that U.S. jurisdictions (and indeed other nations) subjected individuals to involuntary prefrontal lobotomies for a considerable period of time during the twentieth century. *See generally* MICAL RAZ, THE LOBOTOMY LETTERS: THE MAKING OF AMERICAN PSYCHOSURGERY (2013). A statement contained in a 1948 *Yale Law Journal* article extolled the technique's promise: " '[P]sychosurgery has startling implications for rehabilitation . . . and it is proving successful in an increasing number of cases. Perfection of so relatively simple and inexpensive a rehabilitative technique as the prefrontal lobotomy promises to be a major contribution to the cure of criminals.' " Francis X. Shen, *The Overlooked History of Neurolaw*, 85 FORDHAM L. REV. 667, 681 (2016) (citation omitted). Presuming its efficacy in curtailing violent impulses, for argument's sake, should such a "cure" be categorically prohibited as a constitutional matter? *Cf.* ANTHONY BURGESS, A CLOCKWORK ORANGE (2d ed. 1986) (describing form of aversive conditioning therapy whereby inmate is injected with a serum, strapped to a chair, and forced to watch films involving brutally violent and sadistic behavior, similar to that he had previously committed).

4. ***Skinner*'s Progeny.** Since being decided, *Skinner* has only rarely figured in equal protection challenges to criminal provisions. One instance is *McLaughlin v. Florida*, 379 U.S. 184 (1964). In *McLaughlin*, the Court struck down a statute providing that "[a]ny negro man and white woman, or

any white man and negro woman, who are not married to each other, who shall habitually live in and occupy in the nighttime the same room shall each be punished by imprisonment not exceeding twelve months, or by fine not exceeding five hundred dollars." *Id.* at 185. Because the law singled out for criminalization only the behavior of interracial couples, not others engaging in the same conduct, the law violated equal protection. *Id.* at 194.

5. **Jurisdictional Variation.** As *Skinner* acknowledges, governments are afforded latitude in punishing offenses differently based on perceived seriousness. As the Supreme Court later stated, a legislature is not "required to hew the line of logical exactness where the statutory distinction challenged is merely one which sets apart offenses subject to penalties of differing degrees of severity, not one which divides the lawful from the unlawful." *McGowan v. Maryland*, 366 U.S. 420, 542 (1961). For instance, a jurisdiction can make the theft of livestock a more serious offense than theft of other items without reference to the value of the property taken. *See, e.g., State v. Clark*, 632 P.2d 841 (Utah 1981). A court can also take into account specific characteristics of the jurisdiction in imposing sentence. *See, e.g., United States v. Ortiz*, 789 F.3d 15, 19 (1st Cir. 2015) (citation omitted) ("Geographic considerations can be relevant at sentencing, as 'the incidence of particular crimes in the relevant community appropriately informs and contextualizes the relevant need for deterrence.' ").

Despite academic arguments in favor of deeming persons convicted of crimes as a suspect classification, requiring heightened constitutional scrutiny,[7] sentencing laws in general are subject only to rational basis scrutiny, the least demanding form of review. However, because equal protection requires like treatment of persons who are similarly situated, in some circumstances a challenge is sustainable. For instance, when two criminal statutes prescribe different penalties for identical conduct, a defendant convicted and sentenced under the harsher statute is denied equal protection of the laws. *See, e.g., People v. Watkins*, 126 P.3d 309 (Colo. App. 2005). The same is true of a municipal and state law, proscribing the same conduct. *See, e.g., City of Seattle v. Hogan*, 766 P.2d 1134 (Wash. App. 1989).[8] And even under rational basis review a law can be invalidated when a court finds that the legislature failed to satisfy the undemanding standard. *See, e.g., People v. Noyan*, 232 Cal.App.4th 657 (Cal. App. 2015) (holding that statute sentencing to state prison those convicted of knowingly smuggling a controlled substance into a custodial facility, and statute sentencing to jail those convicted of smuggling a contraband non-controlled substance, lacked rational basis).

---

[7] *See, e.g.*, Ben Geiger, Comment, *The Case for Treating Ex-Offenders as a Suspect Class*, 94 CALIF. L. REV. 1191 (2006).

[8] For discussion of intrastate disparity in the death penalty context, which to date has not been regarded as constitutionally problematic, see Andrew Ditchfield, Note, *Challenging the Intrastate Disparities in the Application of Capital Punishment Statutes*, 95 GEO. L.J. 801 (2007). For discussion of intrastate disparity in application of the California three-strikes law, later upheld in *California v. Ewing*, see Joshua Bowers, Comment, *"The Integrity of the Game Is Everything": The Problem of Geographic Disparity in Three Strikes*, 76 N.Y.U. L. REV. 1164, 1172–80 (2001).

However, different defendants convicted of the same offense need not be treated equally, with sentence differences being permissibly based for instance on varied participation or distinct individual background. *See, e.g., People v. Fern*, 723 N.E.2d 207 (Ill. 1999). Similarly, repeat-offender statutes of various kinds routinely survive equal-protection attacks. *See, e.g., State v. Rowe*, 609 P.2d 1348 (Wash. 1980).

What of inter-jurisdictional variation in punishment for the identical crime? In the state-federal context, no equal protection problem exists. *See, e.g., United States v. Moore*, 543 F.3d 891, 897 (7th Cir. 2008) (recognizing that "two defendants, one charged in federal court and the other in state court, who are otherwise identical in all material respects, are not similarly situated at the sentencing stage, where they may face very different penalties. That the federal defendant may face harsher punishment than his state counterpart, or vice versa, simply does not raise equal protection concerns."). What of state-state variation, such when one state makes possession of a certain amount of marijuana a felony and another a misdemeanor, or even decriminalizes or legalizes it? There, again, such differences are tolerated in a federalist system. *See, e.g., People v. Parker*, 359 N.E.2d 348 (N.Y. 1976). And what of sentence differences arising when a serious offense is committed by a Native-American on tribal land, when governing federal law is more severe than state law for the same or similar offense? *See, e.g., United States v. Deegan*, 605 F.3d 625, 635 (8th Cir. 2010), *reh'g en banc denied*, 634 F.3d 428 (8th Cir. 2010) (upholding 121-year sentence for second-degree murder, imposed on a Native-American woman for the death of her baby, and stating that problematic disparity "refers only to disparities among *federal* defendants").

6. **Equal Protection and Race.** As noted above, for Fourteenth Amendment equal protection purposes, criminal defendants and individuals convicted of crime do not qualify as a suspect classification, and legal challenges concerning them are subject to undemanding rational basis scrutiny (not more demanding strict or intermediate scrutiny). A classification based on race, however, most certainly does qualify as a suspect classification and triggers strict scrutiny. Accordingly, a claim alleging race as a basis for a heightened penalty would appear to implicate the old aphorism " 'strict' in theory and fatal in fact," i.e., that the demanding standard of review inevitably leads to invalidation of the challenged law.[9]

To date, however, this categorical approach has not been followed in cases alleging racial discrimination. As discussed in Chapter 7, in the capital punishment context the Supreme Court has denied a challenge that the imposition of the death penalty is driven by race, based on statistics showing that African-American defendants with White victims faced a considerably higher chance of being sentenced to death. *See McCleskey v. Kemp*, 481 U.S. 279 (1987). The Court held that with an equal protection claim the petitioner

---

[9] The famous phrase was coined by Professor Gerald Gunther in his article *The Supreme Court, 1971 Term—Foreword: In Search of Evolving Doctrine on a Changing Court: A Model for a Newer Equal Protection*, 86 HARV. L. REV. 1, 8 (1972).

must prove that the decision makers in his actual case acted with discriminatory purpose, which McCleskey failed to do.

Later, in *United States v. Armstrong*, 517 U.S. 456 (1996), the Court held that in order to obtain discovery to support a selective prosecution claim based on race an individual must satisfy a heavy burden: they "must demonstrate that the . . . prosecutorial policy 'had a discriminatory effect and that it was motivated by a discriminatory purpose.' To establish a discriminatory effect in a race case, the claimant must show that similarly situated individuals of a different race were not prosecuted." *Id.* at 465 (citations omitted). In *Armstrong*, the defendants challenged their "crack" cocaine prosecutions under federal law, contending that they, like other African-American defendants, but unlike Whites, were singled out for prosecution and possible sentencing under the law's much harsher punishment. The Court held that the defendants failed to provide "some evidence" that "similarly situated defendants of other races could have been prosecuted, but were not." *Id.* at 469.

Fortunately, we no longer live in a time of explicit racial distinction being drawn in the criminal law, such as evident in the infamous "Black Codes" existing in the American South after the Civil War. *See* RANDALL KENNEDY, RACE, CRIME AND THE LAW 84–85 (1997). Today, rather than facial discrimination on the basis of race, challenges are typically based on discriminatory impact. Does *Armstrong* impose too high a burden—requiring evidence of non-prosecution—to satisfy a petitioner's burden?

7. **Race and Mitigation.** Can, or should, race figure to *lower* a sentence? In *United States v. Grisanti*, 943 F.3d 1044 (7th Cir. 2019), the Seventh Circuit considered the question. In *Grisanti*, the defendant was convicted of federal child pornography offenses and at sentencing asked the court to rely on the "Child Pornography Offender Risk Tool," the "Correlates of Admission of Sexual Interest in Children" assessment, and other research to argue that he was unlikely to recidivate because, inter alia, he is "white, employed, and had no previous criminal history." The Seventh Circuit held that the sentencing court properly refused to rely on the information adduced by the defendant, stating:

> Subject to constitutional limits, sentencing judges have broad discretion about the information they may consider when deciding on an appropriate sentence. . . . But imposing different sentences based on race would violate the Equal Protection Clause of the Fourteenth Amendment and the Sentencing Guidelines. . . . The Supreme Court in other contexts has permitted consideration of race to offset negative effects of past discrimination and to combat harmful stereotypes. . . . On the other hand, the use of actuarial tools that use race as a factor for assessing probabilities of future crimes, like the studies cited by Grisanti, carry "the potential to reify, rather than ameliorate, extant racial disparities.". . . The Supreme Court has also recognized that some sentencing differentials "foster[ ] disrespect for and lack of confidence in the criminal justice system because of a widely-held perception that [they] promote[ ] unwarranted disparity based on race."

Id. at 1053 (citations omitted). Do you agree—should any available social science research suggesting lower, or higher, risk of recidivism not be considered by the sentencing court?

8. **Equal Protection and Gender.** What of equal protection claims based on gender? Early on, such claims were regularly denied. *See, e.g., Ex parte Brady*, 157 N.E. 69, 72 (Ohio 1927) (rejecting challenge to law allowing for the indeterminate sentencing of females while subjecting males to determinate sentences, stating that "[s]uch classification is not unreasonable because, with a view to reformation, it provides corrective treatment for a female different from the male offender").

Later, courts became less tolerant of sex-based sentencing disparities, for men and women alike. One instance, which was condemned by the Fourth Circuit Court of Appeals, involved a trial judge who imposed a ten-year sentence on a female and fifteen-year sentence on the male co-defendant, when the two were convicted of the same crime and the judge stated that "I just don't believe in punishing women who participated in a crime with the men on the same basis as a man. . . . [B]ecause of your age and the fact that you are a woman, the Court will not incarcerate you for quite as long as I did your co-defendant." *United States v. Maples*, 501 F.2d 985, 986 (4th Cir. 1974). *See also, e.g., Commonwealth v. Daniel*, 243 A.2d 400 (Pa. 1968) (invalidating law providing separate procedure for sentencing women resulting in indeterminate sentence when general law concerning men allowed for determinate, lesser sentence). For further discussion of the evolution, see Carissa Hessick, *Race and Gender as Explicit Sentencing Factors*, 14 J. GENDER, RACE & JUST. 127 (2010).

Yet there are modern-day instances where courts, relying on what are seen as different harms associated with a crime, condone varied treatment of males and females. *See, e.g., Michael M. v. Superior Court of Sonoma Cty.*, 450 U.S. 464, 471 (1981) (upholding statutory rape law providing that only males, not also females, are criminally liable because females are not similarly situated, because only they "become pregnant, and they suffer disproportionately the profound physical, emotional and psychological consequences of sexual activity"); *Liberta v. Kelly*, 839 F.2d 77 (2d Cir. 1988) (upholding harsher statutory penalties for forcible rape committed by men against women, noting particular harm the offense can cause female victims). Presuming that such differences exist, do you think the law should nonetheless be applied in a gender-neutral fashion?

D. "PUBLIC POLICY"

Formal constitutional claims do not exhaust the gamut of bases to challenge a punishment. A good example is found in the use of banishment, an age-old criminal sanction. England regularly banished convicted individuals to other countries, including Australia and parts of the United States, and early American colonies also exiled individuals.[10] Also, viewers of westerns will recognize as familiar the phrase "get out of

---

10 *See generally* Matthew D. Borrelli, Note, *Banishment: The Constitutional and Public Policy Arguments Against This Revived Ancient Punishment*, 36 SUFFOLK U. L. REV. 469 (2003).

town by sundown." And today, courts often impose limited geographic bans on individuals as terms of probation. (*See* Chapter 8.) Perhaps surprisingly, the U.S. Supreme Court has never weighed in on the issue. The following case examines the propriety of banishment.

People v. Baum

231 N.W. 95 (Mich. 1930)

■ POTTER, J.

Defendant was convicted of a violation of the liquor law, and sentenced to pay a fine of $500 and $500 costs. In addition, defendant 'must leave the state of Michigan within 30 days and not return for period of probation,' which was fixed at five years. The sole question presented is the validity of this sentence, it being claimed by defendant it violates chapter 11 of Act No. 175, Public Acts 1927, article 2, §§ 9, 15, and 16, of the Constitution of Michigan, and section 1 of Amendment 14 of the Constitution of the United States.

Banishment and deportation were not cruel and unusual punishments at common law. * * * Deportation of the nationals of foreign countries is a popular method of punishing undesirable aliens who commit crimes against the United States. The American states are not supreme, independent, sovereign states in relation to those things delegated by the people to the federal government, though the states are all in the Union on the basis of equality of political rights. Independent national states have a right to protect their political institutions, their people, and their independent existence by excluding legally and forcibly undesirable foreigners. This is the basis of the laws of the United States restricting immigration. To permit one state to dump its convict criminals into another would entitle the state believing itself injured thereby to exercise its police and military power, in the interest of its own peace, safety, and welfare, to repel such an invasion. It would tend to incite dissension, provoke retaliation, and disturb that fundamental equality of political rights among the several states which is the basis of the Union itself. Such a method of punishment is not authorized by statute, and is impliedly prohibited by public policy.

In *State v. Baker*, 58 S. C. 111, 36 S. E. 501, 502 [1900], defendant was tried and convicted of grand larceny and sentenced to be confined in the state penitentiary for seven years. The sentence then continued:

> 'After you have served five years, you will be released, with the understanding that you leave the state, and never set foot in it again. If you do return, after notice on you by the state and a cause shown, you will be called back to serve out the full term (additional two years), so as to make seven years; otherwise, you will be discharged after service of five years.'

In reversing, [the court stated]: "We do not recognize the circuit judge as possessing any right to impose such a sentence as is involved in the perpetual banishment of the defendant from the state set out in the sentence."* * *

NOTES & QUESTIONS

1. **Spurring Self-Banishment?** At one point in *Ewing*, discussed earlier, Justice O'Connor cited a report by the California Attorney General noting that the "three strikes" law had "[a]n unintended but positive consequence"—"the impact on parolees leaving the state." In other words, the law appeared to encourage migration out of California of those possibly subject to the law. Should this motivation, and effect, be condoned by the Court? Does it matter that such a policy could promote a "race to the bottom" (or "top," depending on your policy perspective) as states compete in enacting ever-harsher penalties? Is the impact of the California law effectively banishment and, if so, is this problematic? Do you agree with the policy concern expressed in *Baum* about "dump[ing]," or should a state be able to exile individuals convicted of crime? Does/should it matter that the state is motivated by financial considerations—saving costs associated with incarceration and other punishment-related expenses—as opposed to getting rid of an "undesirable"?

The Supreme Court, in a case invalidating on Fourteenth Amendment privileges and immunities grounds a state law limiting the amount of public assistance provided to newcomers, *Saenz v. Roe*, 526 U.S. 489 (1999), posited that

> Citizens of the United States, whether rich or poor, have the right to choose to be citizens "of the State wherein they reside." U.S. Const., Amdt. 14, § 1. The States, however, do not have any right to select their citizens. The Fourteenth Amendment, like the Constitution itself, was, as Justice Cardozo put it, "framed upon the theory that the peoples of the several states must sink or swim together, and that in the long run prosperity and salvation are in union and not division."

Id. at 510–11 (citation omitted). Do states have a mutual obligation to address, on their own, the criminal propensities of their residents? *See* Wayne A. Logan, *Constitutional Collectivism and Ex-Offender Residence Exclusion Laws*, 92 IOWA L. REV. 1 (2006).

2. **State Constitutional Provisions.** In addition to being disfavored by courts, a number of state constitutions expressly forbid interstate banishment (*see, e.g.*, ALA. CONST. art. I, § 30; ARK. CONST. art. II, § 21; MD. CONST. art. XXIV; OHIO CONST. art. I, § 12; TEX. CONST. art. I, § 20). *Intra*state banishment is also at times disfavored. *See, e.g.*, *Crabtree v. State*, 112 P.3d 618, 622 (Wyo. 2005) (overturning banishment from county after concluding that county-wide banishment implicates the same public policy concerns as interstate banishment because "banishment from an entire county will incite dissention and provoke retaliation among counties just as it would among states").

The Georgia Constitution has a rather unusual provision permitting banishment from all but a single county of the state (avoiding a challenge to a technical banishment from the state, which is banned by the state constitution). *See* Jason S. Alloy, Comment, *"158 County Banishment" in Georgia: Constitutional Implications under the State Constitution and the Federal Right to Travel*, 36 GA. L. REV. 1083 (2002). In *Terry v. Hamrick*, 663 S.E.2d 256 (Ga. 2008), the Georgia Supreme Court held that a probation condition banishing the petitioner from all counties within the state—except one—did not violate the state constitutional prohibition against banishment beyond state limits and that the condition was logically related to the rehabilitative purpose of the sentence pronounced (a common express requirement of probation, as noted in Chapter 8).

If you were a resident of the receiving county how would you feel? And what if the county singled out is rural, with comparatively little public transportation, few employment opportunities, and meager support services, all important for reentry: how willing would an individual be to locate there, as opposed to simply leaving the state?

3. **Legal Pluralism?** Native American tribes, sovereign governments, have on occasion banished tribal members from their reservations. *See generally* Patrice H. Kunesh, *Banishment as Cultural Justice in Contemporary Tribal Legal Systems*, 37 N.M. L. REV. 85 (2007).[11] In *Poodry v. Tonawanda Band of Seneca Indians*, 85 F.3d 874 (2d Cir. 1996), the Second Circuit addressed a claim involving five members of the Seneca Nation who had been disenrolled from the tribe and permanently banished by the tribal government because they "engaged in 'unlawful activities,' including 'actions to overthrow, or otherwise bring about the removal of, the traditional government' of the Tonawanda Band." *Id.* at 889.

The technical question before the court was whether the petitioners were entitled to federal review of the tribe's action under the Indian Civil Rights Act of 1968. In answering in the affirmative the court stated that the sanction was an extraordinary and severe punishment and noted: "This is especially true at a time when some Indian tribal communities have achieved unusual opportunities for wealth, thereby unavoidably creating incentives for dominant elites to 'banish' irksome dissidents for 'treason.'" *Id.* at 897. Furthermore, while acknowledging that tribes are unique political and cultural entities, the Court cautioned that "there is simply no room in our constitutional order for the definition of basic rights on the basis of cultural affiliations, even with respect to those communities whose distinctive 'sovereignty' our country has long recognized and sustained." *Id.* at 900–01. What are your thoughts—should tribes, sovereigns, be able to banish members without federal government oversight?

---

[11] There have also been instances of banishment from reservations of non-Native individuals. *See* Halley Petersen, Note, *Banishment of Non-Natives By Alaska Native Tribes, A Response to Alcoholism and Drug Addiction*, 35 ALASKA L. REV. 267 (2018).

CHAPTER 7

CAPITAL PUNISHMENT

Capital punishment has long been and remains a controversial subject among Americans. In terms of its constitutionality, proponents note that the Fifth Amendment expressly refers to "capital" crimes and the prohibition of being "twice put in jeopardy of life or limb," and that the death penalty was regularly used at the nation's origin. Meanwhile, opponents point to the Supreme Court's plurality decision in *Trop v. Dulles*, 356 U.S. 86, 101 (1958) stating that the Eighth Amendment's prohibition of "cruel and unusual punishments" must be assessed in terms of "evolving standards of decency," compelling that capital punishment be discontinued. In terms of policy, proponents maintain that both retribution and deterrence justify continued use of the death penalty; meanwhile, opponents maintain that capital punishment does not deter killings and that retribution, to the extent it remains a valid penal justification in contemporary society, can be satisfied by non-capital punishment, such as life without parole.

This chapter examines the wide array of issues concerning the nation's use of what is termed the "ultimate penalty."

A. BACKGROUND

For decades, proponents and opponents of the death penalty have been at loggerheads. Of late, however, a shift has been taking place in the national debate regarding the death penalty, as demonstrated by several data points:

- In 2020, 17 individuals were executed, the least since 1991 (in 1999, there were 98).
- Between 1998 and 2020 the number of death sentences annually imposed by judges and juries dropped sharply: from 295 to 18.
- Since 2007, at least eleven states have renounced use of the death penalty (Colorado, Connecticut, Delaware, Illinois, Maryland, New Hampshire, New Mexico, New York, Virginia, and Washington) and in at least three other states governors imposed moratoria (California, Oregon, and Pennsylvania).
- Public support of the death penalty has been declining: whereas in the 1990s support was 70–80%, by 2018 support was just over 50%.

- In 2009, the American Law Institute withdrew its endorsement of the Model Penal Code's death penalty provisions.[1]

Many reasons account for the shift. Among the most significant are:

- **Cost:** Contrary to the belief of many, capital cases are far more costly than non-capital cases. In Florida, for instance, enforcing the death penalty costs Florida $51 million a year above what it would cost to punish all first-degree murderers with life in prison without parole. The forty-four executions Florida carried out between 1976 and 2000 amounted to $24 million for each execution.
- **Innocence and error:** Concern persists over the possible execution of a factually innocent individual. Since 1973, more than 180 individuals have been released from death row due to doubts about their guilt. Studies, moreover, highlight the high error and reversal rates of capital sentences. *See, e.g.,* James S. Liebman et al., *Capital Attrition: Error Rates in Capital Cases*, 1973–1995, 78 TEX. L. REV. 1839, 1862–63 (2000) (reporting that 685 death sentences initially imposed at trial were overturned on appeal); Bradley A. MacLean & H.E. Miller, Jr., *Tennessee's Death Penalty Lottery*, 13 TENN. J. L. & POL'Y 85, 146 (2018) (noting in Tennessee a death penalty case reversal rate of 23% based on inadequate representation). However, Justice Scalia has written that the error detection and reversal rates are evidence of the "success" of the criminal justice system, not its "failure." *Kansas v. Marsh*, 548 U.S. 163, 193 (Scalia, J., concurring).[2]
- **Inadequate legal counsel:** Although indigent capital defendants have long been constitutionally entitled to counsel, it is widely acknowledged that many receive sub-par legal assistance. Not only do capital cases require specialized training, which counsel often lack, but defenders are very often poorly paid and struggle with large case overloads. As a consequence, death is too often imposed on those saddled with the worst lawyer, rather than the "worst of the worst." *See generally* Stephen B. Bright, *Neither Equal Nor Just: The Rationing and Denial of Legal*

---

[1] Data provided in this section were drawn from the Death Penalty Information Center, *Facts About the Death Penalty* (updated July 1, 2021), https://deathpenaltyinfo.org/ [hereinafter DPIC, *Fact Sheet*].

[2] Disagreement exists over whether factually innocent individuals have actually been put to death. *Compare, e.g.,* Joshua Marquis, *The Myth of Innocence*, 95 J. CRIM. L. & CRIMINOLOGY 517–18 (2005), *with* JAMES S. LEIBMAN & COLUM. DE LUNA PROJECT, THE WRONG CARLOS: ANATOMY OF A WRONGFUL EXECUTION (2014).

Services to the Poor When Life and Liberty Are at Stake, 1997 ANN. SURV. AM. L. 783 (1999).

- **Racial disparity:** Concern has long existed that the death penalty is infected by racial disparities, especially regarding African-American males. One of the most prominent and consistent findings is that there is a much greater statistical likelihood that death will be imposed when the defendant is African-American and the victim is White.
- **Geographic disparity:** Within states with the death penalty, and among federal judicial districts, wide disparity can exist on use of the death penalty. Fewer than 2% of counties in the U.S. account for more than 50% of the nation's death-row population. Meanwhile, more than 80% of U.S. counties have no one on death row and since 1976 more than 80% of U.S. counties have not executed anyone.
- **Outlier international status:** Almost all nations that the U.S. aligns with, including Canada and Western European nations, long ago abandoned use of the death penalty, leaving the U.S. in the company of countries such as North Korea, Syria, and Pakistan. America's continued use of the death penalty has strained its diplomatic relations with other nations and resulted in the refusal by some to extradite individuals who might face death. Editorial, *Europe's View of the Death Penalty*, N.Y. TIMES, May 13, 2001.
- **Questions about deterrence:** Whether the death penalty deters murders has been debated for decades, with no clear answer. *Compare* John J. Donohue, *Empirical Analysis and the Fate of Capital Punishment*, 11 DUKE J. CONST. L. & PUB. POL'Y 51, 58 (2016) (stating that it is "widely accepted" that the death penalty does not provide "any added deterrent beyond that afforded by a sentence of life imprisonment"), *with* Paul M. Zimmerman, *State Executions, Deterrence, and the Incidence of Murder*, 7 J. APPLIED ECON. 163 (2004) (finding deterrent effect). However, a blue-ribbon committee of researchers tasked with evaluating the large literature on deterrence in the modern death penalty era concluded that widespread research design flaws undercut the reliability of studies. *See* COMMITTEE ON DETERRENCE AND THE DEATH PENALTY, NATIONAL ACADEMY OF SCIENCE, DETERRENCE AND THE DEATH PENALTY 2 (2012) (concluding "claims that research demonstrates that capital punishment decreases or increases the homicide rate by a specified amount or has no

> effect on the homicide rate should not influence policy judgments about capital punishment").

Opponents also raise other concerns, including that the mere existence of the death penalty as an option unduly empowers the government to extract guilty pleas[3] and that the complex body of law regulating the death penalty, much of it resulting from the myriad capital decisions of the Supreme Court, actually provides only the illusion of regulation, serving to legitimize the continued resort to capital punishment. Carol Steiker & Jordan Steiker, *Sober Second Thoughts: Reflections on Two Decades of Constitutional Regulation of Capital Punishment*, 109 HARV. L. REV. 355, 438 (1995).

Despite the foregoing, capital punishment remains in effect in twenty-seven states, as well as in the U.S. federal and military systems.[4] For proponents, deterrence remains a possibility, and retribution—taking a life for a life unlawfully taken—continues to enjoy considerable influence. As Justice Potter Stewart wrote in *Gregg v. Georgia*, 428 U.S. 153, 184 (1976), "[T]he decision that capital punishment may be the appropriate sanction in extreme cases is an expression of the community's belief that certain crimes are themselves so grievous an affront to humanity that the only adequate response may be the penalty of death." The death penalty, moreover, is thought to provide potent expressive force, in sociological terms, as sociologist Emile Durkheim maintained with punishment more generally, promoting social solidarity by forcefully denouncing killings. Finally, the death penalty fully incapacitates, unlike its alternatives, life in prison or life without possibility of parole—executed individuals pose no further lethal threat to others (in free society or prison).[5]

The Supreme Court, for its part, has refused to conclude that the death penalty is unconstitutional in principle. It has instead, in the words of Justice Harry Blackmun, continued to "tinker with the machinery of death," and in most terms decides one or more capital cases. As noted, more than half of the states (including the large population states of California, Florida, and Texas), the federal government, and the military retain capital punishment as an option. And the Court has acknowledged that continued use of the death penalty would be

---

[3] WELSH S. WHITE, THE DEATH PENALTY IN THE EIGHTIES 46–47 (1987).

[4] The death rows vary considerably in their number. While several states such as Texas, Florida, and California have well over one hundred death row inmates, in nine jurisdictions death row populations number less than ten. DPIC, *Fact Sheet*, *supra*.

By far, Southern states lead the nation in the number of individuals executed since the death penalty was reinstated in 1976. Well over 50% of executions have occurred in the South: 1,257 of 1,540. Of these 1,257 executions, Texas alone accounts for almost half (573). Death Penalty Information Center, *Executions By State and Region Since 1976*, https://deathpenaltyinfo.org/executions/executions-overview/number-of-executions-by-state-and-region-since-1976.

[5] For centuries, proponents and opponents have debated the morality of the death penalty. For a useful collection of the competing views, see DEBATING THE DEATH PENALTY: SHOULD AMERICA HAVE CAPITAL PUNISHMENT (Hugo Bedeau & Paul Cassell eds., 2004).

impossible if its imposition was free of the possibility of error. *Kansas v. Marsh*, 548 U.S. 163, 181 (2006).

Viewed in the broader context of sentencing as a whole, solely in terms of number, the death penalty does not warrant being the subject of a stand-alone chapter in this volume. As of July 2021, state death rows contained roughly 2500 individuals, a small proportion of the serious felony sentences imposed annually, and an even smaller fraction of the larger multitude of less serious offenses that dominate the nation's criminal dockets. However, as noted at the outset, continued use of the death penalty, which is unique in its gravity and finality, justifies independent attention in itself. So, too, do the many unique and interesting constitutional, moral, philosophical, and policy questions that arise out its use.

B. DECISION-MAKING PROCEDURES IN THE CAPITAL PROCESS

As noted at the outset, the death penalty has been imposed from the outset of (indeed, even before) the nation's origin. Although at various times during the nation's history individual states abolished use of the death penalty (for instance, Michigan in 1846 for all crimes other than treason), the abolitionist cause was invigorated during the civil rights era, bearing the unmistakable earmarks of the NAACP's orchestrated campaign to dismantle state-sponsored segregation. Like the civil rights activists, abolitionists sought recourse in the courts in the hope of achieving wholesale constitutional invalidation, in lieu of piecemeal and possibly ephemeral legislative victories. In the early 1960s, abolitionist lawyers working under the auspices of the NAACP Legal Defense and Educational Fund crafted a "moratorium strategy," dedicated to attacking the procedures used in capital trials. Because "death is different" from other penalties, the lawyers argued, capital trials should be characterized by greater procedural protections and rights for the accused. Invoking this mantra, from 1963–1972 the campaign achieved a de facto if not de jure cessation of capital punishment, as legal challenges to then-common features of the capital system created a "logjam" and brought executions to a virtual stop. *See* JACK GREENBERG, CRUSADERS IN THE COURTS: HOW A DEDICATED BAND OF LAWYERS FOUGHT FOR THE CIVIL RIGHTS REVOLUTION 440–56 (1994).

In 1972, in *Furman* v. *Georgia*, 408 U.S. 238 (1972), the Court by a 5–4 vote, with several lengthy concurrences but no majority opinion, invalidated capital punishment as then practiced. Although only two justices (Brennan and Marshall) categorically condemned use of the death penalty, the prevailing sentiment of others was that the lack of sentencing guidance in state death regimes risked unfair and "capricious" executions in violation of the Eighth and Fourteenth Amendments. With its multiple opinions, *Furman* remains one of the longest decisions in the Court's history, and its result was sweeping: the death sentences of over 600 individuals were invalidated and the capital regimes of some forty jurisdictions were rendered constitutionally suspect. MICHAEL MELTSNER, CRUEL AND UNUSUAL: THE SUPREME COURT AND CAPITAL PUNISHMENT 292–93 (1973).

With *Furman*, abolitionists succeeded in setting the death penalty on constitutional terrain, much as civil rights activists had done with racial segregation in *Brown v. Board of Education*. The legal victory, as in *Brown*, suggested that the movement's tactical decision to focus on judicial relief, as opposed to battling the death penalty on the legislative and public opinion fronts, was wise. Nonetheless, because *Furman* focused only on the methods of capital schemes, not the per se constitutionality of capital punishment itself, abolitionists braced themselves for a resurgence of state capital laws, which soon came. The approaches, intended to redress *Furman*'s concern over arbitrariness, adopted one of two basic strategies. The first mandated death for specified crimes, such as killing a police officer. The second afforded enhanced guidance to sentencers and imposed heightened procedural protections and requirements.

In 1976, the Court addressed the first approach in *Woodson v. North Carolina*, 428 U.S. 280 (1976), and *Roberts v. Louisiana*, 428 U.S. 325 (1976), deeming it invalid for three reasons. First, mandating death for a conviction failed to comport with contemporary societal values. Second, a mandatory death penalty statute merely "paper[ed] over" the problem of unfettered jury discretion and the arbitrary and capricious infliction of the death penalty. Third, a mandatory death penalty failed to provide for individualized capital sentencing, which the Court held the Eighth Amendment required.

The other approach, however, passed muster in *Gregg v. Georgia*, 428 U.S. 153 (1976); *Proffitt v. Florida*, 428 U.S. 242 (1976); and *Jurek v. Texas*, 428 U.S. 262 (1976). In *Gregg* and *Proffitt* the Court approved similar capital sentencing statutes in Georgia and Florida that contained mechanisms designed to channel juror discretion and promote consistency in death decisions. The laws did so by limiting the number of death eligible crimes, bifurcating the guilt and death decision-making phases, requiring jurors to weigh aggravating and mitigating circumstances in deciding whether death was warranted, and ensuring appellate oversight. The Court held that the new regimes adequately addressed *Furman*'s concern over the arbitrary and capricious imposition of death.

In *Jurek*, the Court backed the somewhat different approach of Texas, which unlike Georgia and Florida did not rely on aggravating and mitigating circumstances in the sentencing phase. Instead, Texas limited the crimes eligible for death to five specific types of murder and required juries to answer specific questions concerning the deliberate nature of the crime, the likelihood the defendant would be dangerous in the future, and the existence of provocation by the victim. The Court condoned the approach because it structured juror discretion and assured individualized sentencing.

With the decisions, the Court placed its constitutional imprimatur on the death penalty and backed the basic capital punishment system that continues to this day. In *Gregg*, the most expansive of the three decisions, the Court concluded that the death penalty, in principle, did not violate the Eighth and Fourteenth Amendments, given its long history in the U.S., and that retribution and deterrence were not impermissible justifications in support of its use. Indeed, with respect to retribution, the Court stated that "capital punishment is an expression of society's moral outrage at particularly offensive conduct. This function may be unappealing to many, but it is essential in an ordered society that asks its citizens to rely on legal processes rather than self-help to vindicate their wrongs." *Gregg*, 428 U.S. at 186. And despite the "inconclusive" results of studies on whether the death penalty deters killings, the Court concluded that deterrence was "a complex factual issue the resolution of which properly rests with the legislatures, which can evaluate the results of statistical studies in terms of their own local conditions and with a flexibility of approach that is not available to the courts." *Id.*

Turning to the constitutionality of the actual Georgia regime, the Court concluded that it passed muster:

> The basic concern of *Furman* centered on those defendants who were being condemned to death capriciously and arbitrarily. Under the procedures before the Court in that case, sentencing authorities were not directed to give attention to the nature or circumstances of the crime committed or to the character or record of the defendant. Left unguided, juries imposed the death sentence in a way that could only be called freakish. The new Georgia sentencing procedures, by contrast, focus the jury's attention on the particularized nature of the crime and the particularized characteristics of the individual defendant. While the jury is permitted to consider any aggravating or mitigating circumstances, it must find and identify at least one statutory aggravating factor before it may impose a penalty of death. In this way the jury's discretion is channeled. No longer can a jury wantonly and freakishly impose the death sentence; it is always circumscribed by the legislative guidelines. In addition, the review function of the Supreme Court of Georgia affords additional assurance that the concerns that prompted our decision in *Furman* are not present to any significant degree in the Georgia procedure applied here.

Id. at 206–07.

Today, several decades after *Gregg* lifted the Court's constitutional ban on the death penalty, capital laws vary considerably, but admit of a few generalities. One is that capital trials are bifurcated—first guilt is determined, then the decision whether death is warranted is made, typically by the same jury, on the basis of mitigating and aggravating factors (the latter usually specified by statute). Also, capital laws must "channel the sentencer's discretion by 'clear and objective standards' that provide 'specific and detailed guidance.' " *Godfrey v. Georgia*, 446 U.S. 20, 428 (1980) (citations omitted). Another requirement is that unless a defendant opts for a judge, juries, often referred to as the "conscience of the community," must determine whether the aggravating facts in support of death exist, beyond a reasonable doubt. *Ring v. Arizona*, 536 U.S. 584 (2002). *See also Hurst v. Florida*, 577 U.S. 92 (2016) (holding that capital sentencing scheme, under which an advisory jury makes a recommendation to a judge, and the judge makes the critical findings needed for imposition of a death sentence, violates the Sixth Amendment right to jury trial).[6] Although proportionality review among death cases is not constitutionally required, automatic appellate review of death sentences is available. Also, while most capital jurisdictions require that jurors be unanimous in deciding to impose death,[7] this is not always the case.[8]

In terms of mechanics during the sentencing phase, most jurisdictions adopt one of two approaches: weighing or non-weighing. In non-weighing jurisdictions (e.g., Texas), also known as "threshold" schemes, aggravating factors serve the threshold function of narrowing the class of death-eligible defendants. After finding one or more aggravating circumstances, the sentencer has unlimited discretion in deciding whether or not to impose death. In weighing jurisdictions (e.g., Florida), by contrast, an aggravating factor must first be found and death can be imposed if the aggravating factors outweigh the mitigating evidence,[9] which cannot be limited to statutorily specified factors

---

[6] It is worth noting that the preeminent place of jurors in capital cases differs from their limited to non-existent role in sentencing in less serious cases (see Chapter 3). Is that to say that we believe jurors are equipped to make life and death decisions in homicide cases but not those involving burglary, robbery, drug possession, and other non-capital cases?

[7] *See* Death Penalty Information Center, *Life Verdict or Hung Jury? How States Treat Non-Unanimous Jury Votes in Capital Sentencing Proceedings*, Jan. 27, 2018, https://deathpenaltyinfo.org/stories/life-verdict-or-hung-jury-how-states-treat-non-unanimous-jury-votes-in-capital-sentencing-proceedings.

[8] *See* Ala. Code § 13A–5–46(f) (2020) ("The decision of the jury to return a verdict recommending a sentence of life imprisonment without parole must be based on a vote of a majority of the jurors. The decision of the jury to recommend a sentence of death must be based on a vote of at least 10 jurors."); State v. Poole, 297 So. 3d 487 (Fla. 2020) (holding that state law does not require a unanimous jury recommendation of death, overruling prior precedent holding otherwise). Notwithstanding the Supreme Court of Florida's decision, state law, at this time, requires unanimity. *See* Fla. Stat. § 921.14(2)(c). *Cf.* Andrew E. Taslitz, *Daredevil and the Death Penalty*, 1 OHIO ST. J. CRIM. L. 699, 711 (2004) ("Traditional Jewish law prohibits a jury from imposing a death sentence where the verdict is unanimous, for fear that where there is no doubt, there is no serious deliberative judgment.").

[9] In *Kansas v. Marsh*, 548 U.S. 163 (2006), the Court upheld a law that required imposition of the death penalty when the jury concludes that the aggravating and mitigating evidence are in equipoise. Justice Souter, in a dissent joined by three of his colleagues, thought the provision was unconstitutional, stating that the law "[p]roduces a death sentence exactly when a sentencing impasse demonstrates as a matter of law that the jury does not see the

(although several states include a non-exhaustive list of factors as warranting consideration).[10]

Furman, *Gregg*, and many other cases make clear the critical importance of guiding or structuring death sentencing decisions through such means as statutorily specified aggravating circumstances. Yet, the Court has also made clear that the sentencer (judge or jury) cannot be precluded from considering any relevant mitigating circumstances when deciding whether death is warranted. *See, e.g., Hitchcock v. Dugger*, 481 U.S. 393 (1987) (holding that a defendant has a right to adduce, and have the sentencer consider, evidence of mitigating circumstances not specified in the capital statute); *Eddings v. Oklahoma*, 455 U.S. 104 (1982) (sentencing judge improperly refused to consider evidence of the defendant's troubled youth and emotional difficulties). *See also Lockett v. Ohio*, 438 U.S. 586, 605 (1978) ("Given that the imposition of death . . . is so profoundly different from all other penalties, we cannot avoid the conclusion that an individualized decision is essential in capital cases. The need for treating each defendant in a capital case with that degree of respect due the uniqueness of the individual is far more important than in noncapital cases.").

The Court has acknowledged that "some tension" exists between the imperative of individualization and the need to impose limits on the exercise of discretion in death decisions. *Tuilaepa v. California*, 512 U.S. 967, 973 (1994). The tension has troubled several members of the Court. To Justice Scalia, "[t]o acknowledge that 'there perhaps is an inherent tension' . . . is rather like saying that there was perhaps an inherent tension between the Allies and the Axis Powers in World War II. . . . They cannot be reconciled." *Walton v. Arizona*, 497 U.S. 639, 664 (1990) (Scalia, J., concurring). Four years later, at the end of his time on the Court, Justice Blackmun—who in many instances during his time on the Court rejected constitutional challenges in death penalty cases—wrote that he would no longer "tinker with the machinery of death." *Callins v. Collins*, 510 U.S. 1141, 1145 (1994) (Blackmun, J., dissenting from denial of certiorari). Elaborating, Blackmun reasoned that

> Twenty years have passed since this Court declared that the death penalty must be imposed fairly, and with reasonable consistency, or not at all, see *Furman v. Georgia*, 408 U.S. 238 (1972), and, despite the effort of the States and courts to devise legal formulas and procedural rules to meet this daunting challenge, the death penalty remains fraught with arbitrariness, discrimination, caprice, and mistake. This is not to say that the problems with the death penalty today are

---

evidence as showing the worst sort of crime committed by the worst sort of criminal, in a combination heinous enough to demand death." *Id.* at 207 (Souter, J., dissenting).

[10] Another approach is to pose particular sentencing questions. In Texas, for instance, the sentencer is asked "whether there is a probability that the defendant would commit criminal acts of violence that would constitute a continuing threat to society." If yes, the sentencer is asked whether mitigating evidence supports a life sentence.

> identical to those that were present 20 years ago. Rather, the problems that were pursued down one hole with procedural rules and verbal formulas have come to the surface somewhere else, just as virulent and pernicious as they were in their original form. Experience has taught us that the constitutional goal of eliminating arbitrariness and discrimination from the administration of death, *see Furman v. Georgia*, can never be achieved without compromising an equally essential component of fundamental fairness—individualized sentencing. *See Lockett v. Ohio*, 438 U.S. 586 (1978).

Id. at 1143–44.

> For more than 20 years I have endeavored—indeed, I have struggled—along with a majority of this Court, to develop procedural and substantive rules that would lend more than the mere appearance of fairness to the death penalty endeavor. Rather than continue to coddle the Court's delusion that the desired level of fairness has been achieved and the need for regulation eviscerated, I feel morally and intellectually obligated simply to concede that the death penalty experiment has failed. It is virtually self-evident to me now that no combination of procedural rules or substantive regulations ever can save the death penalty from its inherent constitutional deficiencies. The basic question—does the system accurately and consistently determine which defendants "deserve" to die?—cannot be answered in the affirmative. . . . The problem is that the inevitability of factual, legal, and moral error gives us a system that we know must wrongly kill some defendants, a system that fails to deliver the fair, consistent, and reliable sentences of death required by the Constitution.

Id. at 1145–46. Elsewhere in his opinion Blackmun wrote that "[i]t seems that the decision whether a human being should live or die is so inherently subjective—rife with all of life's understandings, experiences, prejudices, and passions—that it inevitably defies the rationality and consistency required by the Constitution." *Id.* at 1153.[11]

Judges and juries, of course, play key roles in the death decision-making process. But so do prosecutors. Not every murder in a death penalty jurisdiction triggers a capital charge; for resource reasons, if

---

[11] The Court voiced this same concern in the term before *Furman* was decided, stating that "[t]o identify before the fact those characteristics of criminal homicides and their perpetrators which call for the death penalty, and to express these characteristics in language which can be fairly understood and applied by the sentencing authority, appear to be tasks which are beyond present human ability." McGautha v. California, 402 U.S. 183, 204 (1971). In rejecting a due process challenge to California's law, the Court stated that "[i]n light of history, experience, and the present limitations of knowledge, we find it quite impossible to say that committing to the untrammeled discretion of the jury the power to pronounce life or death in a capital case is offensive to anything in the Constitution." *Id.* at 207. In 1976, however, with *Gregg* and other capital cases decided, the Court began its now multi-decade quest to regulate the capital sentencing process.

nothing else, charging discretion must be exercised in winnowing the number of death cases brought in a jurisdiction. The unavoidable discretion, and the equally unavoidable political repercussions of its exercise by prosecutors, has, as noted earlier, resulted in significant geographic per capita variation in death cases within the same capital jurisdiction.

Does such jurisdictional variation raise constitutional concern? Does the fact that prosecutors are often popularly elected matter? Is the variation a proper reflection of local democratic preferences? Should death charging decisions be centralized at the state level? *See* Adam M. Gershowitz, *Statewide Capital Punishment; The Case for Eliminating Counties' Role in Capital Punishment*, 63 VAND. L. REV. 307 (2010). *See also generally* Robert J. Smith, *The Geography of the Death Penalty and Its Ramifications*, 92 B.U. L. REV. 227 (2012).

As with civil and criminal cases more generally, advocacy by counsel can figure centrally in capital trials. Defense counsel, for their part, do their best to "humanize" their clients, and convince the sentencing authority that they are not the "worst of the worst," by introducing mitigating evidence of redeeming personal qualities and hardships in life (such as a brain injury suffered as the result of parental abuse). Prosecutors, of course, seek to show that the individual convicted of a capital crime deserves to die, based on the sentencer's "reasoned moral response" to the killing and defendant's culpability.

PROBLEM 7-1: ARGUMENTS THAT GO TOO FAR?

The following exercise provides examples of prosecution closing arguments in the sentencing phase of capital trials that arguably exceed constitutional constraints. Which if any do you find problematic and why?

- "[L]ook at [the knife] and think about what it would feel like if it went two inches into your neck."

* * *

- "Just put yourself in her shoes . . . . [P]ut yourselves where she was. And you're in that little daybed in the middle of the night . . . [H]e pushes you down on the bed, covers your little face with a pillow, starts to suffocate you, smother you, . . . [a]nd you're twisting and turning and gasping for breath, . . . [a]nd it goes on and it goes on and it goes on until you're unconscious."

* * *

- "Throughout their remarks, [defense counsel] attempted to . . .spar[e] you the truth. They said 'Thou shalt not kill.' If that applies to him, it applies to you, insinuating that your decision is the final decision and that they're gonna take [defendant] out in the front of this Courthouse in moments and string him up and that is terribly, terribly unfair. For they know, as I know, and as Judge Baker has told you, that the decision you render is automatically reviewable by the Supreme Court. Automatically, and I think it's unfair and I don't mind telling them so."

* * *

- "You know, it's not always wrong to kill. It's maybe always difficult to kill; but if you kill in self-defense, that's not wrong. If you kill in a just war, that is not wrong. It's right. If somebody is going to kill your child and you have a chance to kill them to prevent it, would you do it? Of course. Kill [the defendant]."

* * *

- "I want to respond to some of the things argued by [defense counsel]. He told you that it's absurd to talk about life and death, that the law is absurd, that you are playing God, that it's revenge. . . . [Defense counsel] says don't play God. Let every person be in subjection to the governing authorities for there is no authority except from God and those which are established by God. Therefore, he who resists authority has opposed the ordinance of God, and they who have opposed will receive condemnations upon themselves for rulers are not a cause of fear for good behavior, but for evil. Do you want to have no fear of authority? Do what is good and you will have praise for the same for it is a minister of God to you for good. But if you do what is evil, be afraid for it does not bear the sword for nothing for it is a minister of God an avenger who brings wrath upon one who practices evil."
- "You are not playing God. You are doing what God says. This might be the only opportunity to wake him up. God will destroy the body to save the soul. Make him get himself right."
- "Don't be fooled by what's to come [in defense's rebuttal]. Let him have the opportunity to get his soul right. That's the only way to get his attention. You are not playing God. God ordains authority."

* * *

Post-*Furman*, capital punishment has been marked by an increasingly complex body of laws intended to structure and inform death decisions. Statutory law specifies which crimes are capital in nature (i.e., death-eligible). If the defendant is found guilty of such a crime, the jury (or a judge, if jury is waived) must decide whether the defendant should be sentenced to death, based on an assessment of statutorily specified aggravating circumstances (e.g., the killing was "heinous, atrocious, or cruel"), which increase the reprehensibility of the killing, and mitigating circumstances (e.g., the defendant's difficult upbringing), presented by the defense in favor of a non-death sentence. *See Zant v. Stephens*, 462 U.S. 862, 877 (1983) (a death penalty scheme must "genuinely narrow the class of persons eligible for the death penalty and must reasonably justify the imposition of a more severe sentence on the defendant compared to others found guilty of murder"); *see also id.* at 878 ("[S]tatutory aggravating circumstances play a constitutionally necessary function. . . : they circumscribe the class of persons eligible for the death penalty.").

As noted earlier, jurisdictions differ in how the actual death decision is made. However, all jurisdictions have aggravating factors that jurors must apply when deciding if death is to be imposed. The factors themselves often contain quite expansive language, which has been subject to constitutional challenge. In one early challenge, *Godfrey v. Georgia*, 446 U.S. 420 (1980), the Court found unconstitutionally vague a statutory aggravator that the killing "was outrageously or wantonly vile, horrible or inhuman in that it involved . . . depravity of mind." To the Court, the defendant's killing of his wife and mother-in-law, while culpable homicides, could not "be said to have reflected a consciousness materially more 'depraved' than that of any person guilty of murder. His victims were killed instantaneously." *Id.* at 433. As a result, there was "no principled way to distinguish this case, in which the death penalty was imposed, from the many cases it was not." *Id.*

Other challenges to broad language have been less successful, especially when complemented by a limiting instruction provided by a court. In *Proffitt v. Florida*, 428 U.S. 242 (1976), for instance, the Court rejected a challenge to the state's "especially heinous, atrocious or cruel" aggravating circumstance when the state supreme court provided the limiting construction—a "conscienceless or pitiless crime which is unnecessarily torturous to the victim." Is that to say that a killing can be done in a "necessarily" torturous manner? *See also Arave v. Creech*, 507 U.S. 463 (1993) (rejecting challenge to aggravator that the "defendant exhibited utter disregard for human life," when the state supreme court limited its application to "cold-blooded, pitiless slayers").

In a Missouri case, *State v. Butler*, 951 S.W.2d 600 (Mo. 1997), the jury was asked to apply a statutory aggravator that singled out a murder that is "outrageously or wantonly vile, horrible or inhuman in that it involved . . . depravity of mind." Previously, the state supreme court had construed the phrase "depravity of mind" to involve considerations including "the brutality of defendant's conduct." In *Butler*, where the defendant was charged with killing his wife to collect insurance proceeds, by shooting her twice in the head, the court held that the requirement was satisfied, stating: "A gunshot wound to the head is an excessive act of physical abuse. The victim was shot twice in the head. Thus, the defendant committed repeated and excessive acts of physical violence on the victim." *Id.* at 606.

Statutory provisions, of course, are difficult to craft with precision, even when life and death is in the balance. But a considerable body of research suggests that even rather understandable provisions can create interpretive difficulty and cause confusion among capital jurors. One informative source illustrating the problem is the series of studies undertaken in the 1990s as part of the Capital Jury Project, which interviewed capital jurors in several states, including Florida, North Carolina, Pennsylvania, South Carolina, and Virginia. Among other findings the research indicated that capital jurors often:

- do not understand what mitigation evidence is and the role it is to play in death decisions, and can confuse it with aggravating evidence[12];
- operate under the mistaken assumption that the law required a death sentence if the defendant is found guilty[13] or if they found heinousness or dangerousness[14]; and
- wrongly believe that the defense must prove the existence of a mitigating circumstance beyond a reasonable doubt.[15]

Other notable findings of the Project include that jurors often determine that death is justified before the sentencing phase begins[16]; jurors' race, religion, and gender affect their death penalty decisions[17]; jurors believe that defendants receiving the death penalty will not actually be executed[18]; and when life without parole is the alternative to death, jurors either do not know about it or do not believe it actually means that the defendant will never be released on parole.[19]

C. VICTIM IMPACT EVIDENCE IN CAPITAL TRIALS

As noted, the Court has made clear that the Eighth Amendment requires that capital defendants be permitted to present, and have juries consider, relevant mitigating evidence in favor of rendering a sentence less than death. At the same time, to improve the reliability of the death sentencing process and reduce the risk of its arbitrariness, laws provide jurors with statutory aggravating circumstances favoring death.

---

[12] Ursula Bentele & William J. Bowers, *How Jurors Decide Death: Guilt Is Overwhelming, Aggravation Requires Death; and Mitigation Is No Excuse*, 66 BROOKLYN L. REV. 1011 (2001); Marla Sandys, *Cross-Overs: Capital Jurors Who Change Their Minds About the Punishment: A Litmus Test for Sentencing Guidelines*, 70 IND. L.J. 1183, 1220 (1995).

[13] William J. Bowers et al., *Foreclosing Impartiality in Capital Sentencing: Jurors' Predispositions, Attitudes and Premature Decision-Making*, 83 CORNELL L. REV. 1476 (1998); William S. Geimer & Jonathan Amsterdam, *Why Jurors Vote Life or Death: Operative Factors in Ten Florida Death Penalty Trials*, 15 AM. J. CRIM. L. 1 (1989).

[14] Theodore Eisenberg et al., *Jury Responsibility in Capital Sentencing: An Empirical Study*, 44 BUFF. L. REV. 339 (1996)

[15] John Blume et al., *Lessons from the Capital Jury Project, in* BEYOND REPAIR? AMERICA'S DEATH PENALTY (2003); Theodore Eisenberg & Martin T. Wells, *Deadly Confusion: Juror Instructions in Capital Cases*, 79 CORNELL L. REV. 1 (1993); James Luginbuhl & Julie Howe, *Discretion in Capital Sentencing Instructions: Guided or Misguided?*, 70 IND. L.J. 1161 (1995).

[16] William J. Bowers et al., *The Capital Sentencing Decision: Guided Discretion, Reasoned Moral Judgment, or Legal Fiction, in* AMERICA'S EXPERIMENT WITH CAPITAL PUNISHMENT: REFLECTIONS ON THE PAST, PRESENT, AND FUTURE OF THE ULTIMATE PENAL SANCTION (2d ed. 2003); Wanda D. Foglia, *They Know Not What They Do: Unguided and Misguided Decision-Making in Pennsylvania Capital Cases*, 20 JUST. Q. 187 (2003); Bowers et al., *Foreclosed Impartiality*, *supra*.

[17] William Bowers et al., *Death Sentencing in Black and White: An Empirical Analysis of the Role of Juror's Race and Jury Racial Composition*, 3 U. PA. J. CONST. L. 171 (2001); Theodore Eisenberg et al., *Forecasting Life and Death: Juror Race, Religion and Attitude Toward the Death Penalty*, 30 J. LEGAL STUD. 277, 286 (2001); Stephen P. Garvey, *The Emotional Economy of Capital Sentencing*, 75 N.Y.U. L. REV. 26 (2000).

[18] Eisenberg et al., *supra*; Garvey, *supra;* Austin Sarat, *Violence, Representation and Responsibility in Capital Trials: The View from the Jury*, 70 IND. L. REV. 1137 (1995).

[19] Theodore Eisenberg & Stephen P. Garvey, *The Deadly Paradox of Capital Jurors*, 74 S. CAL. L. REV. 371 (2001).

Ultimately, the sentence imposed "should reflect a reasoned moral response to the defendant's background, character, and crime rather than mere sympathy or emotion." *California v. Brown*, 479 U.S. 538, 545 (1987) (O'Connor, J., concurring). In the decision excerpted below, *Payne v. Tennessee*, the Court addressed whether, and how, a murder victim's personal traits, and the impact of the murder on survivors, should figure in death penalty decision-making.

Payne v. Tennessee

501 U.S. 808 (1991)

■ REHNQUIST, C.J.

In this case we reconsider our holdings in *Booth v. Maryland*, 482 U.S. 496 (1987), and *South Carolina v. Gathers*, 490 U.S. 805 (1989), that the Eighth Amendment bars the admission of victim impact evidence during the penalty phase of a capital trial.

Petitioner, Pervis Tyrone Payne, was convicted by a jury on two counts of first-degree murder and one count of assault with intent to commit murder in the first degree. He was sentenced to death for each of the murders and to 30 years in prison for the assault.

The victims of Payne's offenses were 28-year-old Charisse Christopher, her 2-year-old daughter Lacie, and her 3-year-old son Nicholas. The three lived together in an apartment in Millington, Tennessee, across the hall from Payne's girlfriend, Bobbie Thomas. * * *

Payne passed the morning and early afternoon [of June 27, 1987] injecting cocaine and drinking beer. * * * Sometime around 3 p.m., Payne * * * entered the Christophers' apartment, and began making sexual advances towards Charisse. Charisse resisted and Payne became violent. A neighbor who resided in the apartment directly beneath the Christophers heard Charisse screaming, " 'Get out, get out,' as if she were telling the children to leave." The noise briefly subsided and then began, " 'horribly loud.' " The neighbor called the police after she heard a "blood curdling scream" from the Christopher's apartment.

When the first police officer arrived at the scene, he immediately encountered Payne, who was leaving the apartment building, so covered with blood that he appeared to be " 'sweating blood.' " The officer confronted Payne, who responded, " 'I'm the complainant.' " When the officer asked, " 'What's going on up there?' " Payne struck the officer with [an] overnight bag, dropped his tennis shoes, and fled.

Inside the apartment, the police encountered a horrifying scene. Blood covered the walls and floor throughout the unit. Charisse and her children were lying on the floor in the kitchen. Nicholas, despite several wounds inflicted by a butcher knife that completely penetrated through his body from front to back, was still breathing. Miraculously, he survived, but not until after undergoing seven hours of surgery and a transfusion of 1,700 cc's of blood—400 to 500 cc's more than his estimated normal blood volume. Charisse and Lacie were dead.

Charisse's body was found on the kitchen floor on her back, her legs fully extended. She had sustained 42 direct knife wounds and 42 defensive wounds on her arms and hands. The wounds were caused by 41 separate thrusts of a butcher knife. None of the 84 wounds inflicted by Payne were individually fatal; rather, the cause of death was most likely bleeding from all of the wounds.

Lacie's body was on the kitchen floor near her mother. She had suffered stab wounds to the chest, abdomen, back, and head. The murder weapon, a butcher knife, was found at her feet. Payne's baseball cap was snapped on her arm near her elbow. Three cans of malt liquor bearing Payne's fingerprints were found on a table near her body, and a fourth empty one was on the landing outside the apartment door. * * *

[Payne was convicted in the guilt phase of his capital trial and presented mitigating evidence from his mother and father, a girlfriend who spoke highly of him, and a clinical psychologist specializing in criminal court evaluation work.]

The State presented the testimony of Charisse's mother, Mary Zvolanek. When asked how Nicholas had been affected by the murders of his mother and sister, she responded:

> He cries for his mom. He doesn't seem to understand why she doesn't come home. And he cries for his sister Lacie. He comes to me many times during the week and asks me, Grandmama, do you miss my Lacie. And I tell him yes. He says, I'm worried about my Lacie.

In arguing for the death penalty during closing argument, the prosecutor commented on the continuing effects of Nicholas' experience, stating:

> But we do know that Nicholas was alive. And Nicholas was in the same room. Nicholas was still conscious. His eyes were open. He responded to the paramedics. He was able to follow their directions. He was able to hold his intestines in as he was carried to the ambulance. So he knew what happened to his mother and baby sister.
>
> There is nothing you can do to ease the pain of any of the families involved in this case. There is nothing you can do to ease the pain of Bernice or Carl Payne, and that's a tragedy. There is nothing you can do basically to ease the pain of Mr. and Mrs. Zvolanek, and that's a tragedy. They will have to live with it the rest of their lives. There is obviously nothing you can do for Charisse and Lacie Jo. But there is something that you can do for Nicholas.

> Somewhere down the road Nicholas is going to grow up, hopefully. He's going to want to know what happened. And he is going to know what happened to his baby sister and his mother. He is going to want to know what type of justice was done. He is going to want to know what happened. With your verdict, you will provide the answer.

In the rebuttal to Payne's closing argument, the prosecutor stated:

> You saw the videotape this morning. You saw what Nicholas Christopher will carry in his mind forever. When you talk about cruel, when you talk about atrocious, and when you talk about heinous, that picture will always come into your mind, probably throughout the rest of your lives. . . .
>
> No one will ever know about Lacie Jo because she never had the chance to grow up. Her life was taken from her at the age of two years old. So, no there won't be a high school principal to talk about Lacie Jo Christopher, and there won't be anybody to take her to her high school prom. And there won't be anybody there—there won't be her mother there or Nicholas' mother there to kiss him at night. His mother will never kiss him good night or pat him as he goes off to bed, or hold him and sing him a lullaby. . . .
>
> [Petitioner's attorney] wants you to think about a good reputation, people who love the defendant and things about him. He doesn't want you to think about the people who love Charisse Christopher, her mother and daddy who loved her. The people who loved little Lacie Jo, the grandparents who are still here. The brother who mourns for her every single day and wants to know where his best little playmate is. He doesn't have anybody to watch cartoons with him, a little one. These are the things that go into why it is especially cruel, heinous, and atrocious, the burden that that child will carry forever."

The jury sentenced Payne to death on each of the murder counts.

[The Supreme Court of Tennessee affirmed the conviction and sentence.]

We granted certiorari to reconsider our holdings in *Booth* and *Gathers* that the Eighth Amendment prohibits a capital sentencing jury from considering "victim impact" evidence relating to the personal characteristics of the victim and the emotional impact of the crimes on the victim's family.

In *Booth,* the defendant robbed and murdered an elderly couple. As required by a state statute, a victim impact statement was prepared based on interviews with the victims' son, daughter, son-in-law, and granddaughter. The statement, which described the personal characteristics of the victims, the emotional impact of the crimes on the family, and set forth the family members' opinions and characterizations of the crimes and the defendant, was submitted to the jury at sentencing. The jury imposed the death penalty. The conviction and sentence were affirmed on appeal by the State's highest court.

This Court held by a 5-to-4 vote that the Eighth Amendment prohibits a jury from considering a victim impact statement at the sentencing phase of a capital trial. The Court made clear that the admissibility of victim impact evidence was not to be determined on a case-by-case basis, but that such evidence was per se inadmissible in the sentencing phase of a capital case except to the extent that it "relate[d] directly to the circumstances of the crime." In *Gathers*, decided two years later, the Court extended the rule announced in Booth to statements made by a prosecutor to the sentencing jury regarding the personal qualities of the victim. [In *Gathers*, the Court deemed improper a prosecutor's closing argument referencing the positive traits and religiosity of the murder victim, a homeless, self-styled "Reverend Minister."] * * *

Booth and *Gathers* were based on two premises: that evidence relating to a particular victim or to the harm that a capital defendant causes a victim's family do not in general reflect on the defendant's "blameworthiness," and that only evidence relating to "blameworthiness" is relevant to the capital sentencing decision. However, the assessment of harm caused by the defendant as a result of the crime charged has understandably been an important concern of the criminal law, both in determining the elements of the offense and in determining the appropriate punishment. Thus, two equally blameworthy criminal defendants may be guilty of different offenses solely because their acts cause differing amounts of harm. "If a bank robber aims his gun at a guard, pulls the trigger, and kills his target, he may be put to death. If the gun unexpectedly misfires, he may not. His moral guilt in both cases is identical, but his responsibility in the former is greater." *Booth*, 482 U.S., at 519 (Scalia, J., dissenting). The same is true with respect to two defendants, each of whom participates in a robbery, and each of whom acts with reckless disregard for human life; if the robbery in which the first defendant participated results in the death of a victim, he may be subjected to the death penalty, but if the robbery in which the second defendant participates does not result in the death of a victim, the death penalty may not be imposed. *Tison v. Arizona*, 481 U.S. 137, 148 (1987). * * *

Wherever judges in recent years have had discretion to impose sentence, the consideration of the harm caused by the crime has been an important factor in the exercise of that discretion. * * *

We have held that a State cannot preclude the sentencer from considering "any relevant mitigating evidence" that the defendant proffers in support of a sentence less than death. *Eddings v. Oklahoma*, 455 U.S. 104, 114 (1982). Thus we have, as the Court observed in *Booth*, required that the capital defendant be treated as a " 'uniquely individual human bein[g].'" *Booth*, 482 U.S. at 504 (quoting *Woodson v. North Carolina*, 428 U.S., at 304). But it was never held or even suggested in any of our cases preceding *Booth* that the defendant, entitled as he was to individualized consideration, was to receive that consideration wholly apart from the crime which he had committed. The language quoted from *Woodson* in the *Booth* opinion was not intended to describe a class of evidence that could not be received, but a class of evidence which must be received. * * * This misreading of precedent in *Booth* has, we think, unfairly weighted the scales in a capital trial; while virtually no limits are placed on the relevant mitigating evidence a capital defendant may introduce concerning his own circumstances, the State is barred from either offering "a quick glimpse of the life" which a defendant "chose to extinguish," *Mills v. Maryland*, 486 U.S. 367, 397 (1988) (Rehnquist, C.J., dissenting), or demonstrating the loss to the victim's family and to society which has resulted from the defendant's homicide.

The *Booth* Court reasoned that victim impact evidence must be excluded because it would be difficult, if not impossible, for the defendant to rebut such evidence without shifting the focus of the sentencing hearing away from the defendant, thus creating a " 'mini-trial' on the victim's character." In many cases the evidence relating to the victim is already before the jury at least in part because of its relevance at the guilt phase of the trial. But even as to additional evidence admitted at the sentencing phase, the mere fact that for tactical reasons it might not be prudent for the defense to rebut victim impact evidence makes the case no different than others in which a party is faced with this sort of a dilemma. * * *

Payne echoes the concern voiced in Booth's case that the admission of victim impact evidence permits a jury to find that defendants whose victims were assets to their community are more deserving of punishment than those whose victims are perceived to be less worthy. As a general matter, however, victim impact evidence is not offered to encourage comparative judgments of this kind—for instance, that the killer of a hardworking, devoted parent deserves the death penalty, but that the murderer of a reprobate does not. It is designed to show instead each victim's "uniqueness as an individual human being," whatever the jury might think the loss to the community resulting from his death might be. The facts of *Gathers* are an excellent illustration of this: The evidence showed that the victim was an out of work, mentally handicapped individual, perhaps not, in the eyes of most, a significant contributor to society, but nonetheless a murdered human being.

Under our constitutional system, the primary responsibility for defining crimes against state law, fixing punishments for the commission of these crimes, and establishing procedures for criminal trials rests with the States. * * *

The States remain free, in capital cases, as well as others, to devise new procedures and new remedies to meet felt needs. Victim impact evidence is simply another form or method of informing the sentencing authority about the specific harm caused by the crime in question, evidence of a general type long considered by sentencing authorities. We think the *Booth* Court was wrong in stating that this kind of evidence leads to the arbitrary imposition of the death penalty. In the majority of cases, and in this case, victim impact evidence serves entirely legitimate purposes. In the event that evidence is introduced that is so unduly prejudicial that it renders the trial fundamentally unfair, the Due Process Clause of the Fourteenth Amendment provides a mechanism for relief. *See Darden v. Wainwright*, 477 U.S. 168, 179–83 (1986). Courts have always taken into consideration the harm done by the defendant in imposing sentence, and the evidence adduced in this case was illustrative of the harm caused by Payne's double murder.

We are now of the view that a State may properly conclude that for the jury to assess meaningfully the defendant's moral culpability and blameworthiness, it should have before it at the sentencing phase evidence of the specific harm caused by the defendant. "[T]he State has a legitimate interest in counteracting the mitigating evidence which the defendant is entitled to put in, by reminding the sentencer that just as the murderer should be considered as an individual, so too the victim is an individual whose death represents a unique loss to society and in particular to his family." *Booth*, 482 U.S. at 517 (White, J., dissenting). By turning the victim into a "faceless stranger at the penalty phase of a capital trial," *Gathers*, 490 U.S. at 821 O'Connor, J., dissenting), *Booth* deprives the State of the full moral force of its evidence and may prevent the jury from having before it all the information necessary to determine the proper punishment for a first-degree murder.

The present case is an example of the potential for such unfairness. The capital sentencing jury heard testimony from Payne's girlfriend that they met at church; that he was affectionate, caring, and kind to her children; that he was not an abuser of drugs or alcohol; and that it was inconsistent with his character to have committed the murders. Payne's parents testified that he was a good son, and a clinical psychologist testified that Payne was an extremely polite prisoner and suffered from a low IQ. None of this testimony was related to the circumstances of Payne's brutal crimes.

In contrast, the only evidence of the impact of Payne's offenses during the sentencing phase was Nicholas' grandmother's description—in response to a single question—that the child misses his mother and baby sister. Payne argues that the Eighth Amendment commands that the jury's death sentence must be set aside because the jury heard this testimony. But the testimony illustrated quite poignantly some of the harm that Payne's killing had caused; there is nothing unfair about allowing the jury to bear in mind that harm at the same time as it considers the mitigating evidence introduced by the defendant. * * *

Under the aegis of the Eighth Amendment, we have given the broadest latitude to the defendant to introduce relevant mitigating evidence reflecting on his individual personality, and the defendant's attorney may argue that evidence to the jury. Petitioner's attorney in this case did just that. For the reasons discussed above, we now reject the view—expressed in *Gathers*—that a State may not permit the prosecutor to similarly argue to the jury the human cost of the crime of which the defendant stands convicted. We reaffirm the view expressed by Justice Cardozo in *Snyder v. Massachusetts*, 291 U.S. 97, 122 (1934): "[J]ustice, though due to the accused, is due to the accuser also. The concept of fairness must not be strained till it is narrowed to a filament. We are to keep the balance true."

We thus hold that if the State chooses to permit the admission of victim impact evidence and prosecutorial argument on that subject, the Eighth Amendment erects no per se bar. A State may legitimately conclude that evidence about the victim and about the impact of the murder on the victim's family is relevant to the jury's decision as to whether or not the death penalty should be imposed. There is no reason to treat such evidence differently than other relevant evidence is treated.

Payne and his amicus argue that despite these numerous infirmities in the rule created by *Booth* and *Gathers*, we should adhere to the doctrine of stare decisis and stop short of overruling those cases. Stare decisis is the preferred course because it promotes the evenhanded, predictable, and consistent development of legal principles, fosters reliance on judicial decisions, and contributes to the actual and perceived integrity of the judicial process. * * * Nevertheless, when governing decisions are unworkable or are badly reasoned, "this Court has never felt constrained to follow precedent." Stare decisis is not an inexorable command; rather, it "is a principle of policy and not a mechanical formula of adherence to the latest decision." This is particularly true in constitutional cases, because in such cases "correction through legislative action is practically impossible." *Burnet v. Coronado Oil & Gas Co.*, 285 U.S. 393, 407 (1932) (Brandeis, J., dissenting).

Booth and *Gathers* were decided by the narrowest of margins, over spirited dissents challenging the basic underpinnings of those decisions. They have been questioned by Members of the Court in later decisions, and have defied consistent application by the lower courts. * * * Reconsidering these decisions now, we conclude, for the reasons heretofore stated, that they were wrongly decided and should be, and now are, overruled. We accordingly affirm the judgment of the Supreme Court of Tennessee.

■ O'CONNOR, J., concurring, joined by JUSTICES WHITE and KENNEDY.

In my view, a State may legitimately determine that victim impact evidence is relevant to a capital sentencing proceeding. A State may decide that the jury, before determining whether a convicted murderer should receive the death penalty, should know the full extent of the harm caused by the crime, including its impact on the victim's family and community. A State may decide also that the jury should see "a quick glimpse of the life petitioner chose to extinguish," *Mills v. Maryland*, 486 U.S. 367, 397 (1988) (Rehnquist, C.J., dissenting), to remind the jury that the person whose life was taken was a unique human being.

Given that victim impact evidence is potentially relevant, nothing in the Eighth Amendment commands that States treat it differently than other kinds of relevant evidence. * * * The possibility that this evidence may in some cases be unduly inflammatory does not justify a prophylactic, constitutionally based rule that this evidence may never be admitted. Trial courts routinely exclude evidence that is unduly inflammatory; where inflammatory evidence is improperly admitted, appellate courts carefully review the record to determine whether the error was prejudicial. * * *

I agree with the Court that *Booth v. Maryland* and *Gathers* were wrongly decided. The Eighth Amendment does not prohibit a State from choosing to admit evidence concerning a murder victim's personal characteristics or the impact of the crime on the victim's family and community. Booth also addressed another kind of victim impact evidence—opinions of the victim's family about the crime, the defendant, and the appropriate sentence. As the Court notes in today's decision, we do not reach this issue as no evidence of this kind was introduced at petitioner's trial. * * *

[Concurring opinion of JUSTICE SCALIA, joined by JUSTICES O'CONNOR and KENNEDY, omitted.]

■ SOUTER, J., concurring, joined by JUSTICE KENNEDY.

I join the Court's opinion addressing two categories of facts excluded from consideration at capital sentencing proceedings by *Booth v. Maryland* and *South Carolina v. Gathers*: information revealing the individuality of the victim and the impact of the crime on the victim's survivors. As to these two categories, I believe *Booth* and *Gathers* were wrongly decided. * * *

[Justice Souter disputed that a defendant must be aware of the positive traits of his victim(s). This is because] such detailed foreknowledge does not exhaust the category of morally relevant fact. One such fact that is known to all murderers and relevant to the blameworthiness of each one was identified by the *Booth* majority itself when it barred the sentencing authority in capital cases from considering "the full range of foreseeable consequences of a defendant's actions." Murder has foreseeable consequences. When it happens, it is always to distinct individuals, and, after it happens, other victims are left behind. Every defendant knows, if endowed with the mental competence for criminal responsibility, that the life he will take by his homicidal behavior is that of a unique person, like himself, and that the person to be killed probably has close associates, "survivors," who will suffer harms and deprivations from the victim's death. Just as defendants know that they are not faceless human ciphers, they know that their victims are not valueless fungibles; and just as defendants appreciate the web of relationships and dependencies in which they live, they know that their victims are not human islands, but individuals with parents or children, spouses or friends or dependents. Thus, when a defendant chooses to kill, or to raise the risk of a victim's death, this choice necessarily relates to a whole human being and threatens an association of others, who may be distinctly hurt. The fact that the defendant may not know the details of a victim's life and characteristics, or the exact identities and needs of those who may survive, should not in any way obscure the further facts that death is always to a "unique" individual, and harm to some group of survivors is a consequence of a successful homicidal act so foreseeable as to be virtually inevitable. * * *

■ MARSHALL, J., dissenting, joined by JUSTICE BLACKMUN.

Power, not reason, is the new currency of this Court's decisionmaking. Four Terms ago, a five-Justice majority of this Court held that "victim impact" evidence of the type at issue in this case could not constitutionally be introduced during the penalty phase of a capital trial. *Booth v. Maryland*, 482 U.S. 496 (1987). By another 5–4 vote, a majority of this Court rebuffed an attack upon this ruling just two Terms ago. *South Carolina v. Gathers*, 490 U.S. 805 (1989). Nevertheless, having expressly invited respondent to renew the attack, 498 U.S. 1076 (1991), today's majority overrules *Booth* and *Gathers* and credits the dissenting views expressed in those cases. Neither the law nor the facts supporting *Booth* and *Gathers* underwent any change in the last four years. Only the personnel of this Court did. * * *

As the majorities in *Booth* and *Gathers* recognized, the core principle of this Court's capital jurisprudence is that the sentence of death must reflect an " 'individualized determination' " of the defendant's " 'personal responsibility and moral guilt' " and must be based upon factors that channel the jury's discretion " 'so as to minimize the risk of wholly arbitrary and capricious action.' " The State's introduction of victim-impact evidence * * * violates this fundamental principle. Where, as is ordinarily the case, the defendant was unaware of the personal circumstances of his victim, admitting evidence of the victim's character and the impact of the murder upon the victim's family predicates the sentencing determination on "factors . . . wholly unrelated to the blameworthiness of [the] particular defendant." *Booth*, 482 U.S. at 504; *Gathers*, 490 U.S. at 810. And even where the defendant was in a position to foresee the likely impact of his conduct, admission of victim-impact evidence creates an unacceptable risk of sentencing arbitrariness. As Justice Powell explained in *Booth*, the probative value of such evidence is always outweighed by its prejudicial effect because of its inherent capacity to draw the jury's attention away from the character of the defendant and the circumstances of the crime to such illicit considerations as the eloquence with which family members express their grief and the status of the victim in the community. I continue to find these considerations wholly persuasive, and I see no purpose in trying to improve upon Justice Powell's and Justice Brennan's exposition of them. * * *

■ STEVENS, J., dissenting, joined by JUSTICE BLACKMUN.

The novel rule that the Court announces today represents a dramatic departure from the principles that have governed our capital sentencing jurisprudence for decades. * * * Our cases provide no support whatsoever for the majority's conclusion that the prosecutor may introduce evidence that sheds no light on the defendant's guilt or moral culpability, and thus serves no purpose other than to encourage jurors to decide in favor of death rather than life on the basis of their emotions rather than their reason.

Until today our capital punishment jurisprudence has required that any decision to impose the death penalty be based solely on evidence that tends to inform the jury about the character of the offense and the character of the defendant. * * * Thus, if a defendant, who had murdered a convenience store clerk in cold blood in the course of an armed robbery, offered evidence unknown to him at the time of the crime about the immoral character of his victim, all would recognize immediately that the evidence was irrelevant and inadmissible. Evenhanded justice requires that the same constraint be imposed on the advocate of the death penalty. * * *

Today's majority has obviously been moved by an argument that has strong political appeal but no proper place in a reasoned judicial opinion. Because [prior precedent] recognizes the defendant's right to introduce all mitigating evidence that may inform the jury about his character, the Court suggests that fairness requires that the State be allowed to respond with similar evidence about the victim. This argument is a classic non sequitur: The victim is not on trial; her character, whether good or bad, cannot therefore constitute either an aggravating or a mitigating circumstance.

Even if introduction of evidence about the victim could be equated with introduction of evidence about the defendant, the argument would remain flawed in both its premise and its conclusion. The conclusion that exclusion of victim impact evidence results in a significantly imbalanced sentencing procedure is simply inaccurate. Just as the defendant is entitled to introduce any relevant mitigating evidence, so the State may rebut that evidence and may designate any relevant conduct to be an aggravating factor provided that the factor is sufficiently well defined and consistently applied to cabin the sentencer's discretion.

The premise that a criminal prosecution requires an even-handed balance between the State and the defendant is also incorrect. The Constitution grants certain rights to the criminal defendant and imposes special limitations on the State designed to protect the individual from overreaching by the disproportionately powerful State. Thus, the State must prove a defendant's guilt beyond a reasonable doubt. Rules of evidence are also weighted in the defendant's favor. For example, the prosecution generally cannot introduce evidence of the defendant's character to prove his propensity to commit a crime, but the defendant can introduce such reputation evidence to show his law-abiding nature. Even if balance were required or desirable, today's decision, by permitting both the defendant and the State to introduce irrelevant evidence for the sentencer's consideration without any guidance, surely does nothing to enhance parity in the sentencing process.

III

Victim impact evidence, as used in this case, has two flaws, both related to the Eighth Amendment's command that the punishment of death may not be meted out arbitrarily or capriciously. First, aspects of the character of the victim unforeseeable to the defendant at the time of his crime are irrelevant the defendant's "personal responsibility and moral guilt" and therefore cannot justify a death sentence.

Second, the quantity and quality of victim impact evidence sufficient to turn a verdict of life in prison into a verdict of death is not defined until after the crime has been committed and therefore cannot possibly be applied consistently in different cases... Open-ended reliance by a capital sentencer on victim impact evidence simply does not provide a "principled way to distinguish [cases], in which the death penalty [i]s imposed, from the many cases in which it [i]s not." *Godfrey v. Georgia*, 446 U.S. 420, 433 (1980) (opinion of Stewart, J.).

The majority attempts to justify the admission of victim impact evidence by arguing that "consideration of the harm caused by the crime has been an important factor in the exercise of [sentencing] discretion." This statement is misleading and inaccurate. It is misleading because it is not limited to harm that is foreseeable. It is inaccurate because it fails to differentiate between legislative determinations and judicial sentencing. It is true that an evaluation of the harm caused by different kinds of wrongful conduct is a critical aspect in legislative definitions of offenses and determinations concerning sentencing guidelines. There is a rational correlation between moral culpability and the foreseeable harm caused by criminal conduct. Moreover, in the capital sentencing area, legislative identification of the special aggravating factors that may justify the imposition of the death penalty is entirely appropriate. But the majority cites no authority for the suggestion that unforeseeable and indirect harms to a victim's family are properly considered as aggravating evidence on a case-by-case basis. * * *

Irrelevant victim impact evidence that distracts the sentencer from the proper focus of sentencing and encourages reliance on emotion and other arbitrary factors necessarily prejudices the defendant.

The majority's apparent inability to understand this fact is highlighted by its misunderstanding of Justice Powell's argument in *Booth* that admission of victim impact evidence is undesirable because it risks shifting the focus of the sentencing hearing away from the defendant and the circumstances of the crime and creating a " 'mini-trial' on the victim's character." *Booth* found this risk insupportable not, as today's majority suggests, because it creates a "tactical" "dilemma" for the defendant, but because it allows the possibility that the jury will be so distracted by prejudicial and irrelevant considerations that it will base its life-or-death decision on whim or caprice.

IV

The majority thus does far more than validate a State's judgment that "the jury should see 'a quick glimpse of the life petitioner chose to extinguish.' " Instead, it allows a jury to hold a defendant responsible for a whole array of harms that he could not foresee and for which he is therefore not blameworthy. Justice Souter argues that these harms are sufficiently foreseeable to hold the defendant accountable because "[e]very defendant knows, if endowed with the mental competence for criminal responsibility, that the life he will take by his homicidal behavior is that of a unique person, like himself, and that the person to be killed probably has close associates, 'survivors,' who will suffer harms and deprivations from the victim's death." But every juror and trial judge knows this much as well. Evidence about who those survivors are and what harms and deprivations they have suffered is therefore not necessary to apprise the sentencer of any information that was actually foreseeable to the defendant. Its only function can be to "divert the jury's attention away from the defendant's background and record, and the circumstances of the crime." *See Booth*, 482 U.S. at 505.

Arguing in the alternative, Justice Souter correctly points out that victim impact evidence will sometimes come to the attention of the jury during the guilt phase of the trial. He reasons that the ideal of basing sentencing determinations entirely on the moral culpability of the defendant is therefore unattainable unless a different jury is empaneled for the sentencing hearing. * * * The fact that a good deal of such evidence is routinely and properly brought to the attention of the jury merely indicates that the rule of *Booth* may not affect the outcome of many cases.

In reaching our decision today, however, we should not be concerned with the cases in which victim impact evidence will not make a difference. We should be concerned instead with the cases in which it will make a difference. In those cases, defendants will be sentenced arbitrarily to death on the basis of evidence that would not otherwise be admissible because it is irrelevant to the defendants' moral culpability. The Constitution's proscription against the arbitrary imposition of the death penalty must necessarily proscribe the admission of evidence that serves no purpose other than to result in such arbitrary sentences. * * *

The fact that each of us is unique is a proposition so obvious that it surely requires no evidentiary support. What is not obvious, however, is the way in which the character or reputation in one case may differ from that of other possible victims. Evidence offered to prove such differences can only be intended to identify some victims as more worthy of protection than others. Such proof risks decisions based on the same invidious motives as a prosecutor's decision to seek the death penalty if a victim is white but to accept a plea bargain if the victim is black. *See McCleskey v. Kemp*, 481 U.S. 279, 366 (Stevens, J., dissenting).

Given the current popularity of capital punishment in a crime-ridden society, the political appeal of arguments that assume that increasing the severity of sentences is the best cure for the cancer of crime, and the political strength of the "victims' rights" movement, I recognize that today's decision will be greeted with enthusiasm by a large number of concerned and thoughtful citizens. The great tragedy of the decision, however, is the danger that the "hydraulic pressure" of public opinion that Justice Holmes once described—and that properly influences the deliberations of democratic legislatures—has played a role not only in the Court's decision to hear this case, and in its decision to reach the constitutional question without pausing to consider affirming on the basis of the Tennessee Supreme Court's rationale, but even in its resolution of the constitutional issue involved. Today is a sad day for a great institution.

NOTES & QUESTIONS

1. **Reading *Payne*.** As discussed in Chapter 3, victim impact evidence (VIE) has long figured in non-capital sentencing. *Payne v. Tennessee* extended its use to capital sentencing. *Payne* remains one of the Court's more controversial decisions. Not only did the Court reverse two of its very recent precedents but it provided the government a significant new evidentiary tool in the sentencing phase of capital trials.

Do you agree with the majority's conclusion that harm—in particular the positive traits of the murder victim and the impact of their murder on survivors—should figure in deciding whether the death penalty is warranted? Does doing so create the risk that death will be imposed for "more worthy" victims? Can (and should) the fact that a victim has wonderful personal qualities, and has survivors willing to take the stand to articulate these qualities, possibly affect prosecutorial charging decisions? If so, to the extent that the death penalty is imposed to vindicate the loss associated with a murder, does such a view effectively diminish the societal loss of a perhaps less esteemed individual when no VIE is available or the jury rejects a death sentence?

2. **A Non Sequitur?** Justice Stevens, in his dissent, writes that "the Court suggests that fairness requires that the State be allowed to respond with similar evidence about the victim. This argument is a classic non sequitur: The victim is not on trial; her character, whether good or bad, cannot therefore constitute either an aggravating or a mitigating

circumstance." *Payne*, 501 U.S. at 859 (Stevens, J., dissenting). Do you agree?

3. **Limits on VIE.** *Payne* allows for a " 'quick glimpse of the life' " of the victim and evidence concerning "the impact of the murder on the victim's family," cautioning that due process will prohibit "unduly prejudicial" VIE. To date, however, the Court has provided no other guidance on the parameters of VIE, and death penalty jurisdictions have expanded the scope of who can provide VIE (beyond family members), the number of VIE witnesses, what qualifies as VIE (beyond impact of the immediate family), and the forms VIE can take (e.g., videos of victims singing or their funerals, their artwork). *See, e.g.,* Alexander H. Updergrove, Note, *Victim Impact Evidence in Capital Cases: Regulating the Admissibility of Photographs and Videos in the* Payne *Era*, 34 NOTRE DAME J.L. ETHICS & PUB. POL'Y 167 (2020). Illustrative of the broad spectrum of VIE is Florida's law, which permits impact on the "community's members." Fla. Stat. § 921.141(8) ("Such evidence shall be designed to demonstrate the victim's uniqueness as an individual human being and the resultant loss to the community's members by the victim's death.").

4. **Prior Knowledge of Defendant?** One of the more interesting areas of disagreement in *Payne* is whether VIE is inapt because often the defendant does not know of the victim's positive traits and the impact the murder will have on others. Justice Souter, in his concurring opinion, stated that:

> Murder has foreseeable consequences. When it happens, it is always to distinct individuals, and, after it happens, other victims are left behind. Every defendant knows, if endowed with the mental competence for criminal responsibility, that the life he will take by his homicidal behavior is that of a unique person . . . and that the person to be killed probably has close associates, "survivors," who will suffer harms and deprivations from the victim's death. . . . [J]ust as defendants appreciate the web of relationships and dependencies in which they live, they know that their victims are not human islands. . . . Thus, when a defendant chooses to kill, or to raise the risk of a victim's death, this choice necessarily relates to a whole human being and threatens an association of others, who may be distinctly hurt.

Payne, 501 U.S. at 838 (Souter, J., concurring). Justice Stevens, in his dissent, countered that "every juror and trial judge knows that humans are unique" and "[e]vidence about who those survivors are and what harms and deprivations they have suffered is therefore not necessary to apprise the sentencer of any information that was actually foreseeable to the defendant." Stevens added, quoting *Booth*, that "[i]ts only function can be to 'divert the jury's attention away from the defendant's background and record, and the circumstances of the crime.' " *Id.* at 865 (Stevens, J., dissenting). Who has the better argument?

5. **VIE and Mass Killings.** One notable, and obviously exceptional, example of the use of VIE is found in capital trials for mass killings, mounted

in the wake of the terrorist attacks on September 11, 2001 and in Oklahoma City in 1995. In both, the massive death toll and human suffering was obvious and well-known, yet in both cases prosecutors mounted dozens of VIE witnesses (including first responders) providing gripping and highly emotional testimony. In such cases does VIE perhaps play a distinct role? *See* Wayne A. Logan, *Confronting Evil: Victims' Rights in an Age of Terror*, 96 GEO. L.J. 721 (2008).

6. **VIE and Defense Counsel.** Is it relevant that as a practical matter defense counsel usually will not (and indeed usually cannot) contest VIE—for instance, the sadness experienced by a grieving mother of a murder victim, or the positive traits of a victim? And, as Justice Stevens noted, why cannot defense counsel adduce evidence of any negative traits of a victim?

7. **Relevance of Victim Views.** One interesting potential ramification of *Payne* concerns any views the murder victim might have concerning capital punishment. Should a particular murder victim's opposition to capital punishment matter—in a prosecutor's charging decision or in jurors' death decisions? For discussion of the question, including how such information might be compared to "living wills" to guide medical professionals on end-of-life decisions, see Wayne A. Logan, *Declaring Life at the Crossroads of Death: Victims' Anti-Death Penalty Views and Prosecutors' Charging Decisions*, 18 CRIM. JUST. ETHICS 41 (1999).

8. **Survivors' Sentiments.** Finally, it is worth noting that *Payne* left intact *Booth*'s prohibition of opinions of the victim's family regarding the crime, the defendant, and the appropriate sentence. However, courts have not always zealously enforced the prohibitions. *See* Wayne A. Logan, *Opining on Death: Witness Sentence Recommendations in Capital Trials*, 41 B.C. L. REV. 517 (2000).

D. RACIAL DISCRIMINATION AND THE DEATH PENALTY

Allegations of racial discrimination have long plagued application of the death penalty. In the post-Civil War period, not only were African-Americans the common target of lynching, primarily but not exclusively in the South, but the "Slave Codes" in existence for decades before the Civil War, and "Black Codes" thereafter, made specific crimes punishable by death when committed by Blacks, but not when committed by Whites (e.g., sexual assault of a white woman). John D. Bessler, *The Inequality of America's Death Penalty: A Crossroads for Capital Punishment at the Intersection of the Eighth and Fourteenth Amendments*, 73 WASH. & LEE L. REV. ONLINE 487, 506–07, 530–33 (2017). According to Professors Carol and Jordan Steiker, the death penalty's "original sin," was "the stain of racial discrimination." CAROL S. STEIKER & JORDAN M. STEIKER, COURTING DEATH: THE SUPREME COURT AND CAPITAL PUNISHMENT 3 (2016).

As noted earlier, the NAACP, the nation's leading African-American civil rights organization, played a key role in the effort in the 1960s to abolish the death penalty, spearheading a "moratorium" on its use nationwide. A central feature of its litigation strategy was the amassing and analysis of data on capital rape cases prosecuted in eleven southern states between the 1940s and 1965, which showed sharply higher death sentences for blacks in general, with the rate rising up to eighteen times as many death sentences when the defendant was Black and the victim was White. DAVID C. BALDUS ET AL., EQUAL JUSTICE AND THE DEATH PENALTY: A LEGAL AND EMPIRICAL ANALYSIS 250–51 (1990).

In *Furman*, counsel from the NAACP for two of the rape defendants referenced the data in arguing that the death penalty was "unusual" under the Eighth Amendment. MICHAEL MELTSNER, CRUEL AND UNUSUAL: THE SUPREME COURT AND CAPITAL PUNISHMENT 268–77 (1973). Of the five majority opinions, however, only three acknowledged that racial minorities were the disproportionate target of the death penalty (the opinions of Justices Marshall, Douglas, and Stewart). Meanwhile, Justice Powell, in his dissent, dismissed racial disparity in death sentences as being the result of historical practices largely no longer in existence. *Furman*, 408 U.S. at 450 (Powell, J., dissenting). Powell also noted that "[i]f a Negro defendant . . . could demonstrate that members of his race were being singled out for more severe punishment than others charged with the same offense, a constitutional violation might be established." *Id.* at 449. Such evidence might "point the way to a means of raising the equal protection challenge that is more consonant with precedent and the Constitution's mandates than the several courses pursued by today's concurring opinions." *Id.* at 450.

In *McCleskey v. Kemp*, which follows, a race-based equal protection challenge against the death penalty came before the Court, with a 5–4 majority, in an opinion authored by Justice Powell, rejecting the claim.

McCleskey v. Kemp

481 U.S. 279 (1987)

■ POWELL, J.

This case presents the question whether a complex statistical study that indicates a risk that racial considerations enter into capital sentencing determinations proves that petitioner McCleskey's capital sentence is unconstitutional under the Eighth or Fourteenth Amendment.

I

McCleskey, a black man, was convicted of two counts of armed robbery and one count of murder in the Superior Court of Fulton County, Georgia, on October 12, 1978. McCleskey's convictions arose out of the robbery of a furniture store and the killing of a white police officer during the course of the robbery. * * *

The jury convicted McCleskey of murder. At the penalty hearing, the jury heard arguments as to the appropriate sentence. * * * The jury recommended that he be sentenced to death on the murder charge and to consecutive life sentences on the armed robbery charges. The court followed the jury's recommendation and sentenced McCleskey to death.

[The Supreme Court of Georgia denied McCleskey's appeal and he filed a habeas corpus with the Federal District Court for the Northern District of Georgia.]. * * * His petition raised 18 claims, one of which was that the Georgia capital sentencing process is administered in a racially discriminatory manner in violation of the Eighth and Fourteenth Amendments to the United States Constitution. In support of his claim, McCleskey proffered a statistical study performed by Professors David C. Baldus, Charles Pulaski, and George Woodworth, and (the Baldus study) that purports to show a disparity in the imposition of the death sentence in Georgia based on the race of the murder victim and, to a lesser extent, the race of the defendant. The Baldus study is actually two sophisticated statistical studies that examine over 2,000 murder cases that occurred in Georgia during the 1970's. * * *

Baldus subjected his data to an extensive analysis, taking account of 230 variables that could have explained the disparities on nonracial grounds. One of his models concludes that, even after taking account of 39 nonracial variables, defendants charged with killing white victims were 4.3 times as likely to receive a death sentence as defendants charged with killing blacks. According to this model, black defendants were 1.1 times as likely to receive a death sentence as other defendants. Thus, the Baldus study indicates that black defendants, such as McCleskey, who kill white victims have the greatest likelihood of receiving the death penalty.

[The District Court denied both the Eighth and Fourteenth Amendment claims, the Eleventh Circuit Court of Appeals affirmed, and the Court granted certiorari.]

II

McCleskey's first claim is that the Georgia capital punishment statute violates the Equal Protection Clause of the Fourteenth Amendment. He argues that race has infected the administration of Georgia's statute in two ways: persons who murder whites are more likely to be sentenced to death than persons who murder blacks, and black murderers are more likely to be sentenced to death than white murderers. As a black defendant who killed a white victim, McCleskey claims that the Baldus study demonstrates that he was discriminated against because of his race and because of the race of his victim. In its broadest form, McCleskey's claim of discrimination extends to every actor in the Georgia capital sentencing process, from the prosecutor who sought the death penalty and the jury that imposed the sentence, to the State itself that enacted the capital punishment statute and allows it to remain in effect despite its allegedly discriminatory application. We agree with the Court of Appeals, and every other court that has considered such a challenge, that this claim must fail.

A

Our analysis begins with the basic principle that a defendant who alleges an equal protection violation has the burden of proving "the existence of purposeful discrimination." A corollary to this principle is that a criminal defendant must prove that the purposeful discrimination "had a discriminatory effect" on him. Thus, to prevail under the Equal Protection Clause, McCleskey must prove that the decisionmakers in his case acted with discriminatory purpose. He offers no evidence specific to his own case that would support an inference that racial considerations played a part in his sentence. Instead, he relies solely on the Baldus study. McCleskey argues that the Baldus study compels an inference that his sentence rests on purposeful discrimination. McCleskey's claim that these statistics are sufficient proof of discrimination, without regard to the facts of a particular case, would extend to all capital cases in Georgia, at least where the victim was white and the defendant is black.

The Court has accepted statistics as proof of intent to discriminate in certain limited contexts. * * *

But the nature of the capital sentencing decision, and the relationship of the statistics to that decision, are fundamentally different from the corresponding elements in the venire-selection or Title VII cases. Most importantly, each particular decision to impose the death penalty is made by a petit jury selected from a properly constituted venire. Each jury is unique in its composition, and the Constitution requires that its decision rest on consideration of innumerable factors that vary according to the characteristics of the individual defendant and the facts of the particular capital offense. Thus, the application of an inference drawn from the general statistics to a specific decision in a trial and sentencing simply is not comparable to the application of an inference drawn from general statistics to a specific venire-selection or Title VII case. In those cases, the statistics relate to fewer entities, and fewer variables are relevant to the challenged decisions.

Another important difference between the cases in which we have accepted statistics as proof of discriminatory intent and this case is that, in the venire-selection and Title VII contexts, the decisionmaker has an opportunity to explain the statistical disparity. Here, the State has no practical opportunity to rebut the Baldus study. "[C]ontrolling considerations of . . . public policy" * * * dictate that jurors "cannot be called . . . to testify to the motives and influences that led to their verdict." Similarly, the policy considerations behind a prosecutor's traditionally "wide discretion" suggest the impropriety of our requiring prosecutors to defend their decisions to seek death penalties, "often years after they were made." Moreover, absent far stronger proof, it is unnecessary to seek such a rebuttal, because a legitimate and unchallenged explanation for the decision is apparent from the record: McCleskey committed an act for which the United States Constitution and Georgia laws permit imposition of the death penalty.

Finally, McCleskey's statistical proffer must be viewed in the context of his challenge. McCleskey challenges decisions at the heart of the State's criminal justice system. "[O]ne of society's most basic tasks is that of protecting the lives of its citizens and one of the most basic ways in which it achieves the task is through criminal laws against murder." Implementation of these laws necessarily requires discretionary judgments. Because discretion is essential to the criminal justice process, we would demand exceptionally clear proof before we would infer that the discretion has been abused. The unique nature of the decisions at issue in this case also counsels against adopting such an inference from the disparities indicated by the Baldus study. Accordingly, we hold that the Baldus study is clearly insufficient to support an inference that any of the decisionmakers in McCleskey's case acted with discriminatory purpose.

B

McCleskey also suggests that the Baldus study proves that the State as a whole has acted with a discriminatory purpose. He appears to argue that the State has violated the Equal Protection Clause by adopting the capital punishment statute and allowing it to remain in force despite its allegedly discriminatory application. * * * For this claim to prevail, McCleskey would have to prove that the Georgia Legislature enacted or maintained the death penalty statute because of an anticipated racially discriminatory effect. In *Gregg v. Georgia, supra*, this Court found that the Georgia capital sentencing system could operate in a fair and neutral manner. There was no evidence then, and there is none now, that the Georgia Legislature enacted the capital punishment statute to further a racially discriminatory purpose.

Nor has McCleskey demonstrated that the legislature maintains the capital punishment statute because of the racially disproportionate impact suggested by the Baldus study. As legislatures necessarily have wide discretion in the choice of criminal laws and penalties, and as there were legitimate reasons for the Georgia Legislature to adopt and maintain capital punishment, we will not infer a discriminatory purpose on the part of the State of Georgia. Accordingly, we reject McCleskey's equal protection claims.

III

[The Court thereafter addressed McCleskey's Eighth Amendment claim, first concluding that application of the death penalty in his case was not a disproportionate punishment and that penalty was imposed pursuant to Georgia law, which the *Gregg* Court held passed muster as a facial matter under the Eighth Amendment. The Court thereafter addressed McCleskey's claim that the Baldus study showed that the Georgia capital system was racially discriminatory, and therefore arbitrary and capricious and thus excessive in his case.]

To evaluate McCleskey's challenge, we must examine exactly what the Baldus study may show. * * * Statistics at most may show only a likelihood that a particular factor entered into some decisions. There is, of course, some risk of racial prejudice influencing a jury's decision in a criminal case. There are similar risks that other kinds of prejudice will influence other criminal trials. The question "is at what point that risk becomes constitutionally unacceptable," *Turner v. Murray,* 476 U.S. 28, 36, n. 8 (1986). McCleskey asks us to accept the likelihood allegedly shown by the Baldus study as the constitutional measure of an unacceptable risk of racial prejudice influencing capital sentencing decisions. This we decline to do.

Because of the risk that the factor of race may enter the criminal justice process, we have engaged in "unceasing efforts" to eradicate racial prejudice from our criminal justice system. Our efforts have been guided by our recognition that "the inestimable privilege of trial by jury . . . is a vital principle, underlying the whole administration of criminal justice. "Specifically, a capital sentencing jury representative of a criminal defendant's community assures a " 'diffused impartiality' " in the jury's task of "express[ing] the conscience of the community on the ultimate question of life or death."

Individual jurors bring to their deliberations "qualities of human nature and varieties of human experience, the range of which is unknown and perhaps unknowable." The capital sentencing decision requires the individual jurors to focus their collective judgment on the unique characteristics of a particular criminal defendant. It is not surprising that such collective judgments often are difficult to explain. But the inherent lack of predictability of jury decisions does not justify their condemnation. * * *

McCleskey's argument that the Constitution condemns the discretion allowed decisionmakers in the Georgia capital sentencing system is antithetical to the fundamental role of discretion in our criminal justice system. Discretion in the criminal justice system offers substantial benefits to the criminal defendant. Of course, "the power to be lenient [also] is the power to discriminate," K. Davis, Discretionary Justice 170 (1973), but a capital punishment system that did not allow for discretionary acts of leniency "would be totally alien to our notions of criminal justice." *Gregg v. Georgia,* 428 U.S. at 200, n. 50.

C

At most, the Baldus study indicates a discrepancy that appears to correlate with race. Apparent disparities in sentencing are an inevitable part of our criminal justice system. The discrepancy indicated by the Baldus study is "a far cry from the major systemic defects identified in *Furman*," *Pulley v. Harris,* 465 U.S. at 54. As this Court has recognized, any mode for determining guilt or punishment "has its weaknesses and the potential for misuse." Specifically, "there can be 'no perfect procedure for deciding in which cases governmental authority should be used to impose death.' " Despite these imperfections, our consistent rule has been that constitutional guarantees are met when "the mode [for determining guilt or punishment] itself has been surrounded with safeguards to make it as fair as possible." Where the discretion that is fundamental to our criminal process is involved, we decline to assume that what is unexplained is invidious. In light of the safeguards designed to minimize racial bias in the process, the fundamental value of jury trial in our criminal justice system, and the benefits that discretion provides to criminal defendants, we hold that the Baldus study does not demonstrate a constitutionally significant risk of racial bias affecting the Georgia capital sentencing process.

V

Two additional concerns inform our decision in this case. First, McCleskey's claim, taken to its logical conclusion, throws into serious question the principles that underlie our entire criminal justice system. The Eighth Amendment is not limited in application to capital punishment, but applies to all penalties. Thus, if we accepted McCleskey's claim that racial bias has impermissibly tainted the capital sentencing decision, we could soon be faced with similar claims as to other types of penalty. Moreover, the claim that his sentence rests on the irrelevant factor of race easily could be extended to apply to claims based on unexplained discrepancies that correlate to membership in other minority groups, and even to gender. Similarly, since McCleskey's claim relates to the race of his victim, other claims could apply with equally logical force to statistical disparities that correlate with the race or sex of other actors in the criminal justice system, such as defense attorneys, or judges. Also, there is no logical reason that such a claim need be limited to racial or sexual bias. If arbitrary and capricious punishment is the touchstone under the Eighth Amendment, such a claim could—at least in theory—be based upon any arbitrary variable, such as the defendant's facial characteristics, or the physical attractiveness of the defendant or the victim, that some statistical study indicates may be influential in jury decisionmaking. As these examples illustrate, there is no limiting principle to the type of challenge brought by McCleskey. The Constitution does not require that a State eliminate any demonstrable disparity that correlates with a potentially irrelevant factor in order to operate a criminal justice system that includes capital punishment. As we have stated specifically in the context of capital punishment, the Constitution does not "plac[e] totally unrealistic conditions on its use." *Gregg v. Georgia*, 428 U.S., at 199, n. 50.

Second, McCleskey's arguments are best presented to the legislative bodies. It is not the responsibility—or indeed even the right—of this Court to determine the appropriate punishment for particular crimes. * * * It is the ultimate duty of courts to determine on a case-by-case basis whether these laws are applied consistently with the Constitution. Despite McCleskey's wide-ranging arguments that basically challenge the validity of capital punishment in our multiracial society, the only question before us is whether in his case, the law of Georgia was properly applied. We agree with the District Court and the Court of Appeals for the Eleventh Circuit that this was carefully and correctly done in this case. * * *

■ BRENNAN, J., dissenting, joined by JUSTICE MARSHALL and, in all but Part I, JUSTICES BLACKMUN and STEVENS.

I

Adhering to my view that the death penalty is in all circumstances cruel and unusual punishment forbidden by the Eighth and Fourteenth Amendments, I would vacate the decision below insofar as it left undisturbed the death sentence imposed in this case. The Court observes that "[t]he *Gregg*-type statute imposes unprecedented safeguards in the special context of capital punishment," which "ensure a degree of care in the imposition of the death penalty that can be described only as unique." Notwithstanding these efforts, murder defendants in Georgia with white victims are more than four times as likely to receive the death sentence as are defendants with black victims. Nothing could convey more powerfully the intractable reality of the death penalty. * * *

Even if I did not hold this position, however, I would reverse the Court of Appeals, for petitioner McCleskey has clearly demonstrated that his death sentence was imposed in violation of the Eighth and Fourteenth Amendments. * * *

II

At some point in this case, Warren McCleskey doubtless asked his lawyer whether a jury was likely to sentence him to die. A candid reply to this question would have been disturbing.

First, counsel would have to tell McCleskey that few of the details of the crime or of McCleskey's past criminal conduct were more important than the fact that his victim was white. Furthermore, counsel would feel bound to tell McCleskey that defendants charged with killing white victims in Georgia are 4.3 times as likely to be sentenced to death as defendants charged with killing blacks. In addition, frankness would compel the disclosure that it was more likely than not that the race of McCleskey's victim would determine whether he received a death sentence: 6 of every 11 defendants convicted of killing a white person would not have received the death penalty if their victims had been black, while among defendants with aggravating and mitigating factors comparable to McCleskey's, 20 of every 34 would not have been sentenced to die if their victims had been black. Finally, the assessment would not be complete without the information that cases involving black defendants and white victims are more likely to result in a death sentence than cases featuring any other racial combination of defendant and victim. The story could be told in a variety of ways, but McCleskey could not fail to grasp its essential narrative line: there was a significant chance that race would play a prominent role in determining if he lived or died.

The Court today holds that Warren McCleskey's sentence was constitutionally imposed. It finds no fault in a system in which lawyers must tell their clients that race casts a large shadow on the capital sentencing process. The Court arrives at this conclusion by stating that the Baldus study cannot "prove that race enters into any capital sentencing decisions or that race was a factor in McCleskey's particular case." Since, according to Professor Baldus, we cannot say "to a moral certainty" that race influenced a decision, we can identify only "a likelihood that a particular factor entered into some decisions," and "a discrepancy that appears to correlate with race." This "likelihood" and "discrepancy," holds the Court, is insufficient to establish a constitutional violation. * * * The Court's evaluation of the significance of petitioner's evidence is fundamentally at odds with our consistent concern for rationality in capital sentencing, and the considerations that the majority invokes to discount that evidence cannot justify ignoring its force.

III

A

It is important to emphasize at the outset that the Court's observation that McCleskey cannot prove the influence of race on any particular sentencing decision is irrelevant in evaluating his Eighth Amendment claim. Since *Furman v. Georgia*, the Court has been concerned with the risk of the imposition of an arbitrary sentence, rather than the proven fact of one. Furman held that the death penalty "may not be imposed under sentencing procedures that create a substantial risk that the punishment will be inflicted in an arbitrary and capricious manner." * * *

As a result, our inquiry under the Eighth Amendment has not been directed to the validity of the individual sentences before us. * * *

Defendants challenging their death sentences thus never have had to prove that impermissible considerations have actually infected sentencing decisions. We have required instead that they establish that the system under which they were sentenced posed a significant risk of such an occurrence. McCleskey's claim does differ, however, in one respect from these earlier cases: it is the first to base a challenge not on speculation about how a system might operate, but on empirical documentation of how it does operate.

The Court assumes the statistical validity of the Baldus study, and acknowledges that McCleskey has demonstrated a risk that racial prejudice plays a role in capital sentencing in Georgia. Nonetheless, it finds the probability of prejudice insufficient to create constitutional concern. Close analysis of the Baldus study, however, in light of both statistical principles and human experience, reveals that the risk that race influenced McCleskey's sentence is intolerable by any imaginable standard.

B

The Baldus study indicates that, after taking into account some 230 nonracial factors that might legitimately influence a sentencer, the jury more likely than not would have spared McCleskey's life had his victim been black. * * *

Furthermore, even examination of the sentencing system as a whole, factoring in those cases in which the jury exercises little discretion, indicates the influence of race on capital sentencing. * * * The rate of capital sentencing in a white-victim case is thus 120% greater than the rate in a black-victim case. * * *

These adjusted figures are only the most conservative indication of the risk that race will influence the death sentences of defendants in Georgia. Data unadjusted for the mitigating or aggravating effect of other factors show an even more pronounced disparity by race. The capital sentencing rate for all white-victim cases was almost 11 times greater than the rate for black-victim cases. Furthermore, blacks who kill whites are sentenced to death at nearly 22 times the rate of blacks who kill blacks, and more than 7 times the rate of whites who kill blacks. In addition, prosecutors seek the death penalty for 70% of black defendants with white victims, but for only 15% of black defendants with black victims, and only 19% of white defendants with black victims. * * *

McCleskey's statistics have particular force because most of them are the product of sophisticated multiple-regression analysis. Such analysis is designed precisely to identify patterns in the aggregate, even though we may not be able to reconstitute with certainty any individual decision that goes to make up that pattern. Multiple-regression analysis is particularly well suited to identify the influence of impermissible considerations in sentencing, since it is able to control for permissible factors that may explain an apparent arbitrary pattern. * * *

The statistical evidence in this case thus relentlessly documents the risk that McCleskey's sentence was influenced by racial considerations. This evidence shows that there is a better than even chance in Georgia that race will influence the decision to impose the death penalty: a majority of defendants in white-victim crimes would not have been sentenced to die if their victims had been black. * * *

C

Evaluation of McCleskey's evidence cannot rest solely on the numbers themselves. We must also ask whether the conclusion suggested by those numbers is consonant with our understanding of history and human experience. Georgia's legacy of a race-conscious criminal justice system, as well as this Court's own recognition of the persistent danger that racial attitudes may affect criminal proceedings, indicates that McCleskey's claim is not a fanciful product of mere statistical artifice.

For many years, Georgia operated openly and formally precisely the type of dual system the evidence shows is still effectively in place. The criminal law expressly differentiated between crimes committed by and against blacks and whites, distinctions whose lineage traced back to the time of slavery. * * *

This Court has invalidated portions of the Georgia capital sentencing system three times over the past 15 years. * * *

This historical review of Georgia criminal law is not intended as a bill of indictment calling the State to account for past transgressions. Citation of past practices does not justify the automatic condemnation of current ones. But it would be unrealistic to ignore the influence of history in assessing the plausible implications of McCleskey's evidence. * * *

The ongoing influence of history is acknowledged, as the majority observes, by our " 'unceasing efforts' to eradicate racial prejudice from our criminal justice system." These efforts, however, signify not the elimination of the problem but its persistence. * * *

The discretion afforded prosecutors and jurors in the Georgia capital sentencing system creates such opportunities. No guidelines govern prosecutorial decisions to seek the death penalty, and Georgia provides juries with no list of aggravating and mitigating factors, nor any standard for balancing them against one another. Once a jury identifies one aggravating factor, it has complete discretion in choosing life or death, and need not articulate its basis for selecting life imprisonment. The Georgia sentencing system therefore provides considerable opportunity for racial considerations, however subtle and unconscious, to influence charging and sentencing decisions. * * *

[W]e have demanded a uniquely high degree of rationality in imposing the death penalty. A capital sentencing system in which race more likely than not plays a role does not meet this standard. It is true that every nuance of decision cannot be statistically captured, nor can any individual judgment be plumbed with absolute certainty. Yet the fact that we must always act without the illumination of complete knowledge cannot induce paralysis when we confront what is literally an issue of life and death. Sentencing data, history, and experience all counsel that Georgia has provided insufficient assurance of the heightened rationality we have required in order to take a human life.

IV

The Court cites four reasons for shrinking from the implications of McCleskey's evidence: the desirability of discretion for actors in the criminal justice system, the existence of statutory safeguards against abuse of that discretion, the potential consequences for broader challenges to criminal sentencing, and an understanding of the contours of the judicial role. While these concerns underscore the need for sober deliberation, they do not justify rejecting evidence as convincing as McCleskey has presented.

The Court maintains that petitioner's claim "is antithetical to the fundamental role of discretion in our criminal justice system." It states that "[w]here the discretion that is fundamental to our criminal process is involved, we decline to assume that what is unexplained is invidious."

Reliance on race in imposing capital punishment, however, is antithetical to the very rationale for granting sentencing discretion. * * * The decision to impose the punishment of death must be based on a "particularized consideration of relevant aspects of the character and record of each convicted defendant." * * * Considering the race of a defendant or victim in deciding if the death penalty should be imposed is completely at odds with this concern that an individual be evaluated as a unique human being. Decisions influenced by race rest in part on a categorical assessment of the worth of human beings according to color, insensitive to whatever qualities the individuals in question may possess. Enhanced willingness to impose the death sentence on black defendants, or diminished willingness to render such a sentence when blacks are victims, reflects a devaluation of the lives of black persons. * * *

The Court also declines to find McCleskey's evidence sufficient in view of "the safeguards designed to minimize racial bias in the [capital sentencing] process." *Gregg v. Georgia* upheld the Georgia capital sentencing statute against a facial challenge. * * *

It has now been over 13 years since Georgia adopted the provisions upheld in *Gregg*. Professor Baldus and his colleagues have compiled data on almost 2,500 homicides committed during the period 1973–1979. * * * [The study] produced striking evidence that the odds of being sentenced to death are significantly greater than average if a defendant is black or his or her victim is white. The challenge to the Georgia system is not speculative or theoretical; it is empirical. As a result, the Court cannot rely on the statutory safeguards in discounting McCleskey's evidence, for it is the very effectiveness of those safeguards that such evidence calls into question. * * *

The Court next states that its unwillingness to regard petitioner's evidence as sufficient is based in part on the fear that recognition of McCleskey's claim would open the door to widespread challenges to all aspects of criminal sentencing. Taken on its face, such a statement seems to suggest a fear of too much justice. Yet surely the majority would acknowledge that if striking evidence indicated that other minority groups, or women, or even persons with blond hair, were disproportionately sentenced to death, such a state of affairs would be repugnant to deeply rooted conceptions of fairness. The prospect that there may be more widespread abuse than McCleskey documents may be dismaying, but it does not justify complete abdication of our judicial role. The Constitution was framed fundamentally as a bulwark against governmental power, and preventing the arbitrary administration of punishment is a basic ideal of any society that purports to be governed by the rule of law.

In fairness, the Court's fear that McCleskey's claim is an invitation to descend a slippery slope also rests on the realization that any humanly imposed system of penalties will exhibit some imperfection. Yet to reject McCleskey's powerful evidence on this basis is to ignore both the qualitatively different character of the death penalty and the particular repugnance of racial discrimination, considerations which may properly be taken into account in determining whether various punishments are "cruel and unusual." * * *

It hardly needs reiteration that this Court has consistently acknowledged the uniqueness of the punishment of death. * * * As a result, the degree of arbitrariness that may be adequate to render the death penalty "cruel and unusual" punishment may not be adequate to invalidate lesser penalties. What these relative degrees of arbitrariness might be in other cases need not concern us here; the point is that the majority's fear of wholesale invalidation of criminal sentences is unfounded.

The Court also maintains that accepting McCleskey's claim would pose a threat to all sentencing because of the prospect that a correlation might be demonstrated between sentencing outcomes and other personal characteristics. * * * Race is a consideration whose influence is expressly constitutionally proscribed. * * * Furthermore, we have explicitly acknowledged the illegitimacy of race as a consideration in capital sentencing, *Zant v. Stephens*, 462 U.S. 862, 885 (1983). That a decision to impose the death penalty could be influenced by race is thus a particularly repugnant prospect, and evidence that race may play even a modest role in levying a death sentence should be enough to characterize that sentence as "cruel and unusual."

Certainly, a factor that we would regard as morally irrelevant, such as hair color, at least theoretically could be associated with sentencing results to such an extent that we would regard as arbitrary a system in which that factor played a significant role. As I have said above, however, the evaluation of evidence suggesting such a correlation must be informed not merely by statistics, but by history and experience. One could hardly contend that this Nation has on the basis of hair color inflicted upon persons deprivation comparable to that imposed on the basis of race. Recognition of this fact would necessarily influence the evaluation of data suggesting the influence of hair color on sentencing, and would require evidence of statistical correlation even more powerful than that presented by the Baldus study. * * *

Furthermore, the Court's fear of the expansive ramifications of a holding for McCleskey in this case is unfounded because it fails to recognize the uniquely sophisticated nature of the Baldus study. * * * Acceptance of petitioner's evidence would therefore establish a remarkably stringent standard of statistical evidence unlikely to be satisfied with any frequency. * * *

[The dissent of JUSTICE BLACKMUN, joined by JUSTICES MARSHALL and STEVENS, and joined in part by JUSTICE BRENNAN, is omitted.]

[The dissent of JUSTICE STEVENS, joined by JUSTICE BLACKMUN, is omitted.]

NOTES & QUESTIONS

1. **"Fear of Too Much Justice"?** *McCleskey*, decided in 1987, remains one of the Court's more controversial capital punishment decisions. Among the findings of the Baldus study was that defendants in Georgia charged with killing a White victim were 4.3 times more likely to get death than when their victims were Black, and that Black capital defendants with White victims faced a higher likelihood of death. The majority seemingly accepted the validity of the Baldus study yet held that neither the Fourteenth Amendment equal protection nor the Eighth Amendment cruel and unusual punishment claims were actionable.[20]

Was the majority's refusal based, as Justice Brennan put it in dissent, on a "fear of too much justice"? Are you persuaded that a finding by the Court of unconstitutional racial disparity could be cabined—based on the axiom that "death is different" and the acknowledged high quality of the Baldus study? Brennan reasoned that "surely the majority would acknowledge that if striking evidence indicated that other minority groups, or women, or even persons with blond hair, were disproportionately sentenced to death, such a state of affairs would be repugnant to deeply rooted conceptions of fairness." *McCleskey*, 481 U.S. at 339 (Brennan, J., dissenting). Do you find the analogy persuasive?

2. **What More Is Needed?** In the majority's view, what evidence would a petitioner such as McCleskey need to adduce to establish an equal protection claim? In a recent study, augmenting the dataset analyzed by Baldus, researchers found that *executions* (not only death sentences) also showed racial effect, with condemned individuals with White victims experiencing considerably higher execution rates:

> Specifically, 2.26% (22/972) of the defendants who were convicted of killing a white victim were ultimately executed, compared to just 0.13% (2/1503) of the defendants convicted of killing a Black victim. Thus, the overall execution rate is a staggering seventeen times greater for defendants convicted of killing a white victim.

Scott Phillips & Justin Marceau, *Whom the State Kills*, 55 HARV. C.R.-C.L. L. REV. 585, 587 (2020). Recall that the Baldus study found that the odds of a death sentence were 4.3 times greater when the victim was White. Do you think the study by Philips and Marceau, showing that the execution rate is seventeen times higher, would persuade the Supreme Court to reconsider *McCleskey*?

---

[20] Later research has confirmed that a statistically significant disparity exists on the race of the victim and that there is an even greater disparity based on the combination of the race of the defendant and race of the victim. Steven F. Shatz & Terry Dalton, *Challenging the Death Penalty with Statistics:* Furman, McCleskey, *and a Single County Study*, 34 CARDOZO L. REV. 1227, 1250–51 (2013).

3. **Inevitably of Bias.** The majority acknowledged that "[a]pparent disparities in sentencing are an inevitable part of our criminal justice system." *McCleskey*, 481 U.S. at 312. Because the capital system is operated by humans there is an inevitable risk of arbitrariness and bias. Does this recognition counsel in favor of the abolition of capital punishment? If so, why not also life without parole, society's second-heaviest punishment?

4. **Gender Bias?** *McCleskey* considered social science findings regarding the race of the victim in capital trials. Research has also shown a gender bias—a "female victim effect" in which murders with female victims are punished more severely than those with male victims. *See* Caisa E. Royer et al., *Victim Gender and the Death Penalty*, 82 UMKC L. REV. 429 (2014) (concluding that "victim gender is strongly related to many case and victim characteristics that appear to influence the sentencer. These factors include things that are relevant to both the character of the victim (such as vulnerability) and the heinousness of the crime (such as the method of the homicide)."). Does this finding simply bolster the majority's view of the acceptability of inevitable disparities or does it strengthen the dissent's concern over the unconstitutional vicissitudes of death decision making?

5. **Second Thoughts?** After leaving the Court, Justice Powell, authority of the five-member majority opinion in *McCleskey*, regretted his decision in the case. Indeed he rued all his votes in favor of capital punishment, stating that "I have come to think that capital punishment should be abolished." JOHN C. JEFFRIES, JR., JUSTICE LEWIS F. POWELL, JR. 451 (1994). If Justice Powell had sided with the dissent, and McCleskey had prevailed, would the capital system have been sustainable thereafter? If so, what changes might have been required to pass constitutional muster?

E. CATEGORICAL LIMITS ON DEATH

As discussed in Chapter 6, the Supreme Court has effectively adopted a hands-off approach when addressing Eighth Amendment challenges to the proportionality of prison sentences (at least for adults). The Court has not been so reluctant to intervene in death penalty challenges. Since lifting the bar on capital punishment in 1976 the Court has held that use of the death penalty is categorically barred, as a disproportionate sentence, in the following situations:

- the defendant does not commit a homicide, reasoning inter alia that if the defendant did not kill, his culpability does not warrant the death penalty:

  Kennedy v. Louisiana, 554 U.S. 407 (2008) (rape of a child); *Coker v. Georgia*, 433 U.S. 584 (1977) (rape of an adult woman)

- the defendant is intellectually disabled:

  Atkins v. Virginia, 536 U.S. 304 (2002) ("mildly mentally retarded" defendant with an I.Q. of 59)[21]

- the defendant was a juvenile at the time of the killing:

  Roper v. Simmons, 543 U.S. 551 (2005) (individuals less than 18 years of age at time of the capital crime(s) cannot be executed)

- the defendant did not play a significant role in the killing:

  Tison v. Arizona, 481 U.S. 137 (1987) (defendant with major participation in the felony committed (resulting in death), combined with reckless indifference to human life, is sufficient to satisfy culpability for death); *Enmund v. Florida*, 458 U.S. 782 (1982) (when defendant does not himself kill, attempt to kill, or intend that killing take place or that lethal force will be employed, defendant cannot be executed)

The following decision illustrates the methodology used by the Court in assessing whether a categorical prohibition of the death penalty is warranted.

Kennedy v. Louisiana

554 U.S. 407 (2008)

■ KENNEDY, J.

* * * Patrick Kennedy, the petitioner here, seeks to set aside his death sentence under the Eighth Amendment. He was charged * * * with the aggravated rape of his then-8-year-old stepdaughter. After a jury trial petitioner was convicted and sentenced to death under a state statute authorizing capital punishment for the rape of a child under 12 years of age. This case presents the question whether the Constitution bars respondent from imposing the death penalty for the rape of a child where the crime did not result, and was not intended to result, in death of the victim. We hold the Eighth Amendment prohibits the death penalty for this offense. The Louisiana statute is unconstitutional.

I.

Petitioner's crime was one that cannot be recounted in these pages in a way sufficient to capture in full the hurt and horror inflicted on his

[21] In subsequent decisions, the Court elaborated on when and how the exception applies. *See* Moore v. Texas, 137 S. Ct. 1039 (2017) (test used to assess mental disability must reflect current medical and clinical understandings of condition); Hall v. Florida, 572 U.S. 701 (2014) (state cannot refuse to entertain other evidence of intellectual disability when a defendant has an IQ score above 70). For a constitutional originalist take, finding that the Court's view of the categorical prohibition of executing individuals with mental disabilities significantly understates the actual historical breadth of the protected population, when the Eighth Amendment was adopted, see Michael Clemente, Note, *A Reassessment of Common Law Protections for "Idiots,"* 124 YALE L.J. 2746 (2015).

victim or to convey the revulsion society, and the jury that represents it, sought to express by sentencing petitioner to death. At 9:18 a.m. on March 2, 1998, petitioner called 911 to report that his stepdaughter, referred to here as L.H., had been raped. He told the 911 operator that L.H. had been in the garage while he readied his son for school. Upon hearing loud screaming, petitioner said, he ran outside and found L.H. in the side yard. Two neighborhood boys, petitioner told the operator, had dragged L.H. from the garage to the yard, pushed her down, and raped her. Petitioner claimed he saw one of the boys riding away on a blue 10-speed bicycle.

When police arrived at petitioner's home between 9:20 and 9:30 a.m., they found L.H. on her bed, wearing a T-shirt and wrapped in a bloody blanket. She was bleeding profusely from the vaginal area. Petitioner told police he had carried her from the yard to the bathtub and then to the bed. Consistent with this explanation, police found a thin line of blood drops in the garage on the way to the house and then up the stairs. Once in the bedroom, petitioner had used a basin of water and a cloth to wipe blood from the victim. This later prevented medical personnel from collecting a reliable DNA sample.

L.H. was transported to the Children's Hospital. An expert in pediatric forensic medicine testified that L.H.'s injuries were the most severe he had seen from a sexual assault in his four years of practice. A laceration to the left wall of the vagina had separated her cervix from the back of her vagina, causing her rectum to protrude into the vaginal structure. Her entire perineum was torn from the posterior fourchette to the anus. The injuries required emergency surgery. * * *

[For just over a week the victim and the defendant persisted in their account that two neighborhood boys had raped the victim. Investigators, however, soon focused on the defendant as the culprit and arrested him. At trial, defendant was convicted of aggravated rape, involving a child less than twelve years of age, a capital crime under state law, with testimony presented that he had also previously sexually abused an eight-year-old girl.]

II.

* * * [C]apital punishment must "be limited to those offenders who commit 'a narrow category of the most serious crimes' and whose extreme culpability makes them 'the most deserving of execution.' " *Roper, supra*, at 568. Though the death penalty is not invariably unconstitutional, see *Gregg v. Georgia*, 428 U.S. 153 (1976), the Court insists upon confining the instances in which the punishment can be imposed.

Applying this principle, we held in *Roper* and *Atkins* that the execution of juveniles and mentally retarded persons are punishments violative of the Eighth Amendment because the offender had a diminished personal responsibility for the crime. The Court further has held that the death penalty can be disproportionate to the crime itself where the crime did not result, or was not intended to result, in death of the victim. In *Coker*, 433 U.S. 584, for instance, the Court held it would be unconstitutional to execute an offender who had raped an adult woman. And in *Enmund v. Florida*, 458 U.S. 782 (1982), the Court overturned the capital sentence of a defendant who aided and abetted a robbery during which a murder was committed but did not himself kill, attempt to kill, or intend that a killing would take place. On the other hand, in *Tison v. Arizona*, 481 U.S. 137 (1987), the Court allowed the defendants' death sentences to stand where they did not themselves kill the victims but their involvement in the events leading up to the murders was active, recklessly indifferent, and substantial.

In these cases the Court has been guided by "objective indicia of society's standards, as expressed in legislative enactments and state practice with respect to executions." *Roper*, 543 U.S., at 56; *see also Coker, supra*, at 593–597 (plurality opinion) (finding that both legislatures and juries had firmly rejected the penalty of death for the rape of an adult woman); *Enmund*, 458 U.S., at 788 (looking to "historical development of the punishment at issue, legislative judgments, international opinion, and the sentencing decisions juries have made"). The inquiry does not end there, however. Consensus is not dispositive. Whether the death penalty is disproportionate to the crime committed depends as well upon the standards elaborated by controlling precedents and by the Court's own understanding and interpretation of the Eighth Amendment's text, history, meaning, and purpose.

Based both on consensus and our own independent judgment, our holding is that a death sentence for one who raped but did not kill a child, and who did not intend to assist another in killing the child, is unconstitutional under the Eighth and Fourteenth Amendments.

III.

A.

The existence of objective indicia of consensus against making a crime punishable by death was a relevant concern in *Roper, Atkins, Coker*, and *Enmund*, and we follow the approach of those cases here. The history of the death penalty for the crime of rape is an instructive beginning point.

In 1925, 18 States, the District of Columbia, and the Federal Government had statutes that authorized the death penalty for the rape of a child or an adult. Between 1930 and 1964, 455 people were executed for those crimes. To our knowledge the last individual executed for the rape of a child was Ronald Wolfe in 1964.

In 1972, *Furman* invalidated most of the state statutes authorizing the death penalty for the crime of rape; and in *Furman*'s aftermath only six States reenacted their capital rape provisions. Three States—Georgia, North Carolina, and Louisiana—did so with respect to all rape offenses. Three States—Florida, Mississippi, and Tennessee—did so with respect only to child rape. All six statutes were later invalidated under state or federal law.

Louisiana reintroduced the death penalty for rape of a child in 1995. Under the current statute, any anal, vaginal, or oral intercourse with a child under the age of 13 constitutes aggravated rape and is punishable by death. * * * Five States have since followed Louisiana's lead: [Georgia, Montana, Oklahoma, South Carolina, and Texas]. Four of these States' statutes are more narrow than Louisiana's in that only offenders with a previous rape conviction are death eligible. Georgia's statute makes child rape a capital offense only when aggravating circumstances are present, including but not limited to a prior conviction.

By contrast, 44 States have not made child rape a capital offense. As for federal law, Congress in the Federal Death Penalty Act of 1994 expanded the number of federal crimes for which the death penalty is a permissible sentence, including certain nonhomicide offenses; but it did not do the same for child rape or abuse. Under 18 U.S.C. § 2245, an offender is death eligible only when the sexual abuse or exploitation results in the victim's death. * * *

The evidence of a national consensus with respect to the death penalty for child rapists, as with respect to juveniles, mentally retarded offenders, and vicarious felony murderers, shows divided opinion but, on balance, an opinion against it. Thirty-seven jurisdictions—36 States plus the Federal Government—have the death penalty. As mentioned above, only six of those jurisdictions authorize the death penalty for rape of a child. Though our review of national consensus is not confined to tallying the number of States with applicable death penalty legislation, it is of significance that, in 45 jurisdictions, petitioner could not be executed for child rape of any kind. That number surpasses the 30 States in *Atkins* and *Roper* and the 42 States in *Enmund* that prohibited the death penalty under the circumstances those cases considered.*

C.

Respondent insists that the six States where child rape is a capital offense, along with the States that have proposed but not yet enacted applicable death penalty legislation, reflect a consistent direction of change in support of the death penalty for child rape. Consistent change might counterbalance an otherwise weak demonstration of consensus. *See Atkins*, 536 U.S. at 315 ("It is not so much the number of these States that is significant, but the consistency of the direction of change"); *Roper*, 543 U.S., at 565 ("Impressive in *Atkins* was the rate of abolition of the death penalty for the mentally retarded"). But whatever the significance

* When issued and announced on June 25, 2008, the Court's decision neither noted nor discussed the military penalty for rape under the Uniform Code of Military Justice. *See* 10 U.S.C. §§ 856 (2000 ed.), 920 (2000 ed. and Supp. V); Manual for Courts-Martial, United States, Part IV, Art. 120, ¶ 45.f(1), p. IV–78 (2008). In a petition for rehearing respondent argues that the military penalty bears on our consideration of the question in this case. For the reasons set forth in the statement respecting the denial of rehearing, we find that the military penalty does not affect our reasoning or conclusion.

of consistent change where it is cited to show emerging support for expanding the scope of the death penalty, no showing of consistent change has been made in this case.

Respondent and its amici identify five States where, in their view, legislation authorizing capital punishment for child rape is pending. It is not our practice, nor is it sound, to find contemporary norms based upon state legislation that has been proposed but not yet enacted. There are compelling reasons not to do so here. [The court thereafter noted that the proposals failed to become law for various reasons.]

Aside from pending legislation, it is true that in the last 13 years there has been change toward making child rape a capital offense. This is evidenced by six new death penalty statutes, three enacted in the last two years. But this showing is not as significant as the data in *Atkins*, where 18 States between 1986 and 2001 had enacted legislation prohibiting the execution of mentally retarded persons. Respondent argues the instant case is like *Roper* because, there, only five States had shifted their positions between 1989 and 2005, one less State than here. But in *Roper*, we emphasized that, though the pace of abolition was not as great as in *Atkins*, it was counterbalanced by the total number of States that had recognized the impropriety of executing juvenile offenders. * * * Here, the total number of States to have made child rape a capital offense after *Furman* is six. This is not an indication of a trend or change in direction comparable to the one supported by data in *Roper*. The evidence here bears a closer resemblance to the evidence of state activity in *Enmund*, where we found a national consensus against the death penalty for vicarious felony murder despite eight jurisdictions having authorized the practice.

D.

There are measures of consensus other than legislation. Statistics about the number of executions may inform the consideration whether capital punishment for the crime of child rape is regarded as unacceptable in our society. These statistics confirm our determination from our review of state statutes that there is a social consensus against the death penalty for the crime of child rape.

Nine States—Florida, Georgia, Louisiana, Mississippi, Montana, Oklahoma, South Carolina, Tennessee, and Texas—have permitted capital punishment for adult or child rape for some length of time between the Court's 1972 decision in *Furman* and today. Yet no individual has been executed for the rape of an adult or child since 1964, and no execution for any other nonhomicide offense has been conducted since 1963.

Louisiana is the only State since 1964 that has sentenced an individual to death for the crime of child rape; and petitioner and Richard Davis, who was convicted and sentenced to death for the aggravated rape of a 5-year-old child by a Louisiana jury in December 2007, are the only two individuals now on death row in the United States for a nonhomicide offense.

After reviewing the authorities informed by contemporary norms, including the history of the death penalty for this and other nonhomicide crimes, current state statutes and new enactments, and the number of executions since 1964, we conclude there is a national consensus against capital punishment for the crime of child rape.

IV.

A.

As we have said in other Eighth Amendment cases, objective evidence of contemporary values as it relates to punishment for child rape is entitled to great weight, but it does not end our inquiry. "[T]he Constitution contemplates that in the end our own judgment will be brought to bear on the question of the acceptability of the death penalty under the Eighth Amendment." *Coker, supra,* at 597. We turn, then, to the resolution of the question before us, which is informed by our precedents and our own understanding of the Constitution and the rights it secures.

It must be acknowledged that there are moral grounds to question a rule barring capital punishment for a crime against an individual that did not result in death. These facts illustrate the point. Here the victim's fright, the sense of betrayal, and the nature of her injuries caused more prolonged physical and mental suffering than, say, a sudden killing by an unseen assassin. The attack was not just on her but on her childhood. For this reason, we should be most reluctant to rely upon the language of the plurality in Coker, which posited that, for the victim of rape, "life may not be nearly so happy as it was," but it is not beyond repair. Rape has a permanent psychological, emotional, and sometimes physical impact on the child. We cannot dismiss the years of long anguish that must be endured by the victim of child rape.

It does not follow, though, that capital punishment is a proportionate penalty for the crime. * * * Evolving standards of decency that mark the progress of a maturing society counsel us to be most hesitant before interpreting the Eighth Amendment to allow the extension of the death penalty, a hesitation that has special force where no life was taken in the commission of the crime. * * *

Our concern here is limited to crimes against individual persons. We do not address, for example, crimes defining and punishing treason, espionage, terrorism, and drug kingpin activity, which are offenses against the State. As it relates to crimes against individuals, though, the death penalty should not be expanded to instances where the victim's life was not taken. We said in *Coker* of adult rape:

> We do not discount the seriousness of rape as a crime. It is highly reprehensible, both in a moral sense and in its almost total contempt for the personal integrity and autonomy of the

> female victim . . . . Short of homicide, it is the 'ultimate violation of self.' . . . [But] [t]he murderer kills; the rapist, if no more than that, does not. . . . We have the abiding conviction that the death penalty, which 'is unique in its severity and irrevocability,' is an excessive penalty for the rapist who, as such, does not take human life. 433 U.S., at 597–598 (plurality opinion) (citation omitted).

* * * Consistent with evolving standards of decency and the teachings of our precedents we conclude that, in determining whether the death penalty is excessive, there is a distinction between intentional first-degree murder on the one hand and nonhomicide crimes against individual persons, even including child rape, on the other. The latter crimes may be devastating in their harm, as here, but "in terms of moral depravity and of the injury to the person and to the public," *Coker*, 433 U.S. at 598, they cannot be compared to murder in their "severity and irrevocability." *Ibid.*

In reaching our conclusion we find significant the number of executions that would be allowed under respondent's approach. The crime of child rape, considering its reported incidents, occurs more often than first-degree murder. * * * Approximately 5,702 incidents of vaginal, anal, or oral rape of a child under the age of 12 were reported nationwide in 2005; this is almost twice the total incidents of intentional murder for victims of all ages (3,405) reported during the same period. Although we have no reliable statistics on convictions for child rape, we can surmise that, each year, there are hundreds, or more, of these convictions just in jurisdictions that permit capital punishment. As a result of existing rules, only 2.2% of convicted first-degree murderers are sentenced to death. But under respondent's approach, the 36 States that permit the death penalty could sentence to death all persons convicted of raping a child less than 12 years of age. This could not be reconciled with our evolving standards of decency and the necessity to constrain the use of the death penalty.

It might be said that narrowing aggravators could be used in this context, as with murder offenses, to ensure the death penalty's restrained application. We find it difficult to identify standards that would guide the decisionmaker so the penalty is reserved for the most severe cases of child rape and yet not imposed in an arbitrary way. Even were we to forbid, say, the execution of first-time child rapists, or require as an aggravating factor a finding that the perpetrator's instant rape offense involved multiple victims, the jury still must balance, in its discretion, those aggravating factors against mitigating circumstances. In this context, which involves a crime that in many cases will overwhelm a decent person's judgment, we have no confidence that the imposition of the death penalty would not be so arbitrary as to be "freakis[h]," *Furman, supra*, at 310. We cannot sanction this result when the harm to the victim, though grave, cannot be quantified in the same way as death of the victim.

It is not a solution simply to apply to this context the aggravating factors developed for capital murder. The Court has said that a State may carry out its obligation to ensure individualized sentencing in capital murder cases by adopting sentencing processes that rely upon the jury to exercise wide discretion so long as there are narrowing factors that have some " 'common-sense core of meaning . . . that criminal juries should be capable of understanding.' " *Tuilaepa*, 512 U.S. at 975. * * * All of these standards have the potential to result in some inconsistency of application.

[T]he resulting imprecision and the tension between evaluating the individual circumstances and consistency of treatment have been tolerated where the victim dies. It should not be introduced into our justice system, though, where death has not occurred.

* * * [W]e have spent more than 32 years articulating limiting factors that channel the jury's discretion to avoid the death penalty's arbitrary imposition in the case of capital murder. Though that practice remains sound, beginning the same process for crimes for which no one has been executed in more than 40 years would require experimentation in an area where a failed experiment would result in the execution of individuals undeserving of the death penalty. Evolving standards of decency are difficult to reconcile with a regime that seeks to expand the death penalty to an area where standards to confine its use are indefinite and obscure.

B

Our decision is consistent with the justifications offered for the death penalty. * * *

* * * The goal of retribution, which reflects society's and the victim's interests in seeing that the offender is repaid for the hurt he caused, does not justify the harshness of the death penalty here. In measuring retribution, as well as other objectives of criminal law, it is appropriate to distinguish between a particularly depraved murder that merits death as a form of retribution and the crime of child rape.

There is an additional reason for our conclusion that imposing the death penalty for child rape would not further retributive purposes. * * * In considering the death penalty for nonhomicide offenses this inquiry necessarily also must include the question whether the death penalty balances the wrong to the victim.

It is not at all evident that the child rape victim's hurt is lessened when the law permits the death of the perpetrator. Capital cases require a long-term commitment by those who testify for the prosecution, especially when guilt and sentencing determinations are in multiple proceedings. In cases like this the key testimony is not just from the family but from the victim herself. * * *

Society's desire to inflict the death penalty for child rape by enlisting the child victim to assist it over the course of years in asking for capital punishment forces a moral choice on the child, who is not of mature age to make that choice. The way the death penalty here involves the child victim in its enforcement can compromise a decent legal system; and this is but a subset of fundamental difficulties capital punishment can cause in the administration and enforcement of laws proscribing child rape.

There are, moreover, serious systemic concerns in prosecuting the crime of child rape that are relevant to the constitutionality of making it a capital offense. The problem of unreliable, induced, and even imagined child testimony means there is a "special risk of wrongful execution" in some child rape cases. This undermines, at least to some degree, the meaningful contribution of the death penalty to legitimate goals of punishment. Studies conclude that children are highly susceptible to suggestive questioning techniques like repetition, guided imagery, and selective reinforcement.

Similar criticisms pertain to other cases involving child witnesses; but child rape cases present heightened concerns because the central narrative and account of the crime often comes from the child herself. She and the accused are, in most instances, the only ones present when the crime was committed. And the question in a capital case is not just the fact of the crime, including, say, proof of rape as distinct from abuse short of rape, but details bearing upon brutality in its commission. These matters are subject to fabrication or exaggeration, or both. Although capital punishment does bring retribution, and the legislature here has chosen to use it for this end, its judgment must be weighed, in deciding the constitutional question, against the special risks of unreliable testimony with respect to this crime.

With respect to deterrence, if the death penalty adds to the risk of nonreporting, that, too, diminishes the penalty's objectives. Underreporting is a common problem with respect to child sexual abuse. Although we know little about what differentiates those who report from those who do not report, one of the most commonly cited reasons for nondisclosure is fear of negative consequences for the perpetrator, a concern that has special force where the abuser is a family member. The experience of the amici who work with child victims indicates that, when the punishment is death, both the victim and the victim's family members may be more likely to shield the perpetrator from discovery, thus increasing underreporting. As a result, punishment by death may not result in more deterrence or more effective enforcement.

In addition, by in effect making the punishment for child rape and murder equivalent, a State that punishes child rape by death may remove a strong incentive for the rapist not to kill the victim. Assuming the offender behaves in a rational way, as one must to justify the penalty on grounds of deterrence, the penalty in some respects gives less protection, not more, to the victim, who is often the sole witness to the crime. It might be argued that, even if the death penalty results in a marginal increase in the incentive to kill, this is counterbalanced by a marginally increased deterrent to commit the crime at all. Whatever balance the legislature strikes, however, uncertainty on the point makes the argument for the penalty less compelling than for homicide crimes.

Each of these propositions, standing alone, might not establish the unconstitutionality of the death penalty for the crime of child rape. Taken in sum, however, they demonstrate the serious negative consequences of making child rape a capital offense. These considerations lead us to conclude, in our independent judgment, that the death penalty is not a proportional punishment for the rape of a child.

V

Our determination that there is a consensus against the death penalty for child rape raises the question whether the Court's own institutional position and its holding will have the effect of blocking further or later consensus in favor of the penalty from developing. The Court, it will be argued, by the act of addressing the constitutionality of the death penalty, intrudes upon the consensus-making process. By imposing a negative restraint, the argument runs, the Court makes it more difficult for consensus to change or emerge. The Court, according to the criticism, itself becomes enmeshed in the process, part judge and part the maker of that which it judges.

These concerns overlook the meaning and full substance of the established proposition that the Eighth Amendment is defined by "the evolving standards of decency that mark the progress of a maturing society." Confirmed by repeated, consistent rulings of this Court, this principle requires that use of the death penalty be restrained. * * * [R]esort to the penalty must be reserved for the worst of crimes and limited in its instances of application. In most cases justice is not better served by terminating the life of the perpetrator rather than confining him and preserving the possibility that he and the system will find ways to allow him to understand the enormity of his offense. Difficulties in administering the penalty to ensure against its arbitrary and capricious application require adherence to a rule reserving its use * * * for crimes that take the life of the victim.

The judgment of the Supreme Court of Louisiana upholding the capital sentence is reversed. This case is remanded for further proceedings not inconsistent with this opinion.

[Dissent of JUSTICE ALITO, joined by the CHIEF JUSTICE and JUSTICES SCALIA and THOMAS, is omitted.]

NOTES & QUESTIONS

1. **Categorical Prohibition.** Are you persuaded that a categorical prohibition is necessary? Is the majority correct in its assessment that child rape is a crime that "in many cases will overwhelm a decent person's

judgment," effectively resulting in mandatory death sentences? Or is that the point—that the crime itself is so heinous that death should be an option? If death were an option, could the predicted visceral response among jurors be tempered by requiring the presence of particular aggravating factors (e.g., the defendant is a child rape recidivist, the victim also suffered significant physical injury, multiple victims)?

2. **Critiquing *Kennedy*.** At one point in his opinion Justice Kennedy notes that child rapes are far more common than homicides and reasons that the increased number of possible death sentences cannot "be reconciled with our evolving standards of decency and the necessity to constrain the use of the death penalty." *Kennedy*, 554 U.S. at 439. Is this reasoning persuasive? As Justice Alito wrote in dissent: "With respect to the question of moral depravity, is it really true that every person who is convicted of capital murder and sentenced to death is more morally depraved than every child rapist?" *Id.* at 466 (Alito, J., dissenting). Also, accepting that the child victim does not die, in a biological sense, should *Coker* control as precedent—is raping a child itself a categorically more heinous crime, possibly justifying death?

3. **Place of Policy.** One of the striking aspects of the majority opinion is its rather extensive discussion of policy ramifications—e.g., that the death penalty will perhaps deter reporting of child sexual abuse, that child victims will be further traumatized by death prosecutions, that child victim testimony might be unreliable, and that punishing "child rape by death may remove a strong incentive for the rapist not to kill the victim." *Id.* at 445. However, are such concerns more properly assessed by legislatures, which the Court often insists are better equipped and qualified to make informed policy decisions? *See Kennedy*, 554 U.S. at 462 (Alito, J., dissenting) ("These policy arguments, whatever their merits, are simply not pertinent to the question whether the death penalty is 'cruel and unusual' punishment. The Eighth Amendment protects the right of an accused. It does not authorize this Court to strike down federal or state criminal laws on the ground that they are not in the best interests of crime victims or the broader society.") Or does the political climate in which death-eligibility decisions are made, especially regarding a heinous crime like child rape, oblige judicial oversight?

4. **Evolving Standards and Deference.** *Kennedy* is representative of the Court's methodology in Eighth Amendment categorical challenges to the death penalty: lending significant weight in its evolving standards of decency analysis to current laws, legislative trends, and jury sentencing decisions.[22] At the end of his opinion, Justice Kennedy seeks to respond to the claim that the Court's holding will

---

[22] One of the enduring controversies in the Court's death penalty caselaw concerns how it determines whether a "national consensus" exists against a particular application of the death penalty, when determining whether it comports with evolving standards of decency. For instance, should the denominator be all U.S. jurisdictions or only death penalty jurisdictions? Although the Court endorses the quantitative method as "objective," one's choice will obviously affect the percentage of states engaging in the particular practice. And even if the smaller denominator of death penalty states is used, the Court's use of the term "consensus" is debatable. *See, e.g.*, Roper v. Simmons, 543 U.S. 551, 609 (2005) (Scalia, J., dissenting) (stating

> have the effect of blocking further or later consensus in favor of the penalty from developing. The Court, it will be argued, by the act of addressing the constitutionality of the death penalty, intrudes upon the consensus-making process. By imposing a negative restraint, the argument runs, the Court makes it more difficult for consensus to change or emerge. The Court, according to the criticism, itself becomes enmeshed in the process, part judge and part the maker of that which it judges.

Kennedy, 554 U.S. at 446. Do you agree with the view Justice Kennedy seeks to rebuff? Should the Court refrain from second-guessing state legislative judgments, much as it has in the non-capital sentencing realm regarding adults (*see* Chapter 6), allowing states to perhaps serve as "laboratories" of democratic experimentation, as Justice Brandeis envisioned with social and economic laws more generally?

5. **International Norms.** When evaluating whether use of the death penalty comports with evolving standards of decency, the Court will at times consider international legal norms. For instance, in *Roper v. Simmons*, 543 U.S. 551 (2005), which banned use of the death penalty for offenders under the age of eighteen at the time of offense, the Court noted "the stark reality that the United States is the only country in the world that continues to give official sanction to the juvenile death penalty," and surveyed at length laws and covenants condemning the practice. *Id.* at 575. The Court did offer the caveat that international opposition was not "controlling, for the task of interpreting the Eighth Amendment remains our responsibility," but the opposition clearly figured in its ultimate decision. In dissent, Justice Scalia, joined by Chief Justice Roberts and Justice Thomas, challenged the consideration of international norms, noting inter alia the distinct content and history of U.S. constitutional provisions. Do you agree with Justice Scalia or does the moral gravity of the death penalty, and its use by a nation that considers itself a leader of the world order, oblige consideration of what is arguably an established rule of customary international law?

PROBLEM 7-2

Imagine that you represent Neil Doolittle, who faces a capital charge in Florida based on his importation of a large amount of cocaine that the state believes resulted in the death of a user. *See* Fla. Stat. § 893.135 (making it a capital crime to import 300 kilograms or more of cocaine when knowing that "the probable result of such importation would be the death of any person"). What arguments would you make in favor of the law's constitutional infirmity, based on *Kennedy v. Louisiana*? What arguments can the state make in defense of the law's constitutionality?

---

in response to the majority's finding that a national consensus exists "because 18 States—or 47% of States that permit capital punishment—now have legislation prohibiting the execution of offenders under 18" that "[w]ords have no meaning if the views of less than 50% of death penalty States can constitute a national consensus"). For more on the question, see Robert J. Smith et al., *The Way the Court Gauges Consensus (and How to Do It Better)*, 35 CARDOZO L. REV. 2397 (2014).

F. EXECUTION METHODS

Over the centuries, a variety of techniques, some straining the bounds of human imagination, have been employed to execute condemned individuals. Among the most prominent methods were burning, stoning, impalement, strangulation, decapitation (for instance, by guillotine), shooting by firing squad, and hanging. Until the nineteenth century, executions were carried out in public, usually by means of hanging, to impress upon the populace the might of the reigning authority and to strike fear in the hearts of witnesses. STUART BANNER, THE DEATH PENALTY: AN AMERICAN HISTORY 9–13 (2002). In time, however, executions became a less public phenomenon, taking place behind prison walls. *See generally* NIGEL CAWTHORNE, PUBLIC EXECUTIONS FROM ROME TO THE PRESENT DAY (2006).

One reason for this was that executions were a common form of public entertainment, which often took a gruesome turn when hangings were botched. At times, those in attendance felt sympathy "for a fellow human being who would die shortly," BANNER, *supra*, at 29, and critics maintained that public executions had a brutalizing effect on the increasingly large and rowdy crowds in attendance. *Id.* at 148–50. By the late nineteenth century public hanging survived only in a few southern states, where "the mounting frequency of lynchings [of blacks] prevented whites from becoming too sensitive to the public display of violence." *Id.* at 154. By the end of the nineteenth century, however, public hangings were discontinued in most southern states. *Id.* at 155. Hanging in general, moreover, became controversial for many reasons, including its association with vigilante mob justice and lynching. *See generally* FRANKLIN M. ZIMRING, THE CONTRADICTIONS OF AMERICAN CAPITAL PUNISHMENT (2003).

About the time executions were removed from open public view,[23] there arrived a new execution method: electrocution, in a specially designed chair equipped to send high voltages of electricity into the body of the condemned.[24] Auburn Prison in New York State, in addition to being one of the nation's oldest penitentiaries, was the site of the nation's first electrocution execution (in 1890). Believed to be more humane and

---

[23] Professor Stuart Banner writes of the shift from public to private executions:

> By excluding the [public] crowd . . . the move into the jail yard changed the character of capital punishment. Executions lost much of their symbolic meaning. The community was no longer gathered to make its statement of condemnation. . . . [W]ith executions conducted behind closed doors, before a small group of the well connected, out of the public eye, the *people* were no longer punishing the criminal. Now the government was doing the punishing, and the people were reading about it later.

BANNER, *supra*, at 168 (emphasis in original).

[24] For a fascinating history regarding the advent of electrocution as an execution method, involving the rather crafty undertakings of Thomas Edison, who was engaged in a heated competition with fellow inventor George Westinghouse over whose approach to the new technology of electricity would triumph in the marketplace, see BANNER, *supra*, at 181.

effective than hanging,[25] electrocution remained the execution method of choice until the 1990s, when several botched executions in Florida (including the 1990 execution of Jesse Joseph Tafero[26]) and elsewhere, prompted consideration of another method. A similar outcry drove the demise of the poison gas chamber, which while initiated as a more humane method in the 1920s, also was largely discontinued due to its protracted achievement of death and association with Nazi genocides in World War II. Death by firing squad remained an option, with Gary Gilmore, a condemned murderer in Utah, volunteering to be subject to it in January 1977, becoming the first post-*Furman* inmate to be executed (with his final words being "Let's do it!"). While certainly cheaper, to the minds of some the firing squad too closely resembled murder, the crime condemned inmates were themselves found guilty of committing.

In an effort to find a less controversial method governments soon gravitated toward another option: intravenous injection of lethal drugs. In 1977, Texas and Oklahoma became the first states to adopt the new method, and in 1982 a Texas inmate became the first to die by lethal injection. To carry out the execution, an inmate was strapped to a gurney and injected with three drugs: a barbiturate to produce unconsciousness (sodium thiopental), then a muscle relaxant to paralyze the lungs (pancuronium), and last a drug to stop the heart (potassium chloride).

For the last several years lethal injection has been the primary execution method in the U.S. Today, all states provide it as a primary method, with hanging, firing squad, and electrocution serving as alternatives in several states. Since executions resumed after *Gregg* in 1976, lethal injection by far has been the most commonly method employed: 1360 have died by lethal injection, followed by 163 by electrocution, 11 by gas chamber, 3 by hanging, and 3 by firing squad.

---

[25] Again, Stuart Banner recounts actual occurrences in support, here about the failure of hanging in the late nineteenth century to do the job:

> From the 1870s on, every year or two brought another celebrated case of a hanged person believed to be still alive. . . . In North Carolina Jack Lambert was reported to have been seen walking around on the Sunday after his hanging, and was rumored to have been revived with an electric battery, brandy, and aromatic spirits of ammonia. Locals demanded that Lambert's grave be opened and his body exhibited. As Coleman Blackburn's relatives took him to the cemetery to be buried in Mississippi, they heard scratching on the inside of the coffin lid and discovered that Blackburn was still breathing. He was revived and hanged a second time.

BANNER, *supra*, at 175.

[26] As Professor Deborah Denno described the execution, based on news reports:

> His execution was "gruesome." For four minutes, the hooded executioner applied three 2,000-volt jolts of electricity to Tafero's body. Until the last jolt Tafero "continued to clench his fists, nod, convulse and appear to breathe deeply . . . as if he were alive." Tafero's execution was particularly controversial because the jolts sparked a fire on his head with six- to twelve-inch flames that filled the execution chamber with smoke. The fire also caused ashes, "flames and smoke clouds to fly from [Tafero's bobbing] head during each of the three surges" while "his throat produced gurgling sounds."

Deborah W. Denno, *Is Electrocution an Unconstitutional Method of Execution? The Engineering of Death Over the Century*, 35 WM. & MARY L. REV. 551, 554–55 (1994) (citations omitted).

Death Penalty Information Center, *Facts About the Death Penalty* (Dec. 9, 2021), https://documents.deathpenaltyinfo.org/pdf/FactSheet.pdf.

Since its first use, lethal injection has undergone significant changes. Among the most significant reasons is the inability to secure the drugs needed because of the reluctance of pharmaceutical companies to provide them. The problem is especially pronounced with companies based in Europe, where almost all governments long ago abandoned the death penalty and laws are in place forbidding companies from providing products for use in U.S. death chambers. *See* James Gibson & Corinna B. Lain, *Death Penalty Drugs and the International Moral Marketplace*, 103 GEO. L.J. 1215 (2015). The lack of drugs has resulted in execution delays and prompted jurisdictions to modify their "drug cocktails" and pursue other sources, including drug "compounding" pharmacies that mix small batches of drugs upon order, which can lack necessary safety standards for producing safe, sterile drugs and avoid regulation by the federal Food and Drug Administration. Some states sought drugs from "gray markets" overseas, with even more questionable safety protocols. Faced with pressure from death penalty abolitionists, jurisdictions have enacted laws preventing disclosure of their drug sources and injection protocols. The shifts have heightened the risk of "botched" executions and inspired expensive and time-consuming litigation, often resulting in stays of execution. Eric Berger, *Courts, Culture, and the Lethal Injection Stalemate*, 62 WM. & MARY L. REV. 1, 23–29 (2020).[27]

Early on, the Supreme Court had relatively little involvement. In *Wilkerson v. Utah*, 99 U.S. 130 (1878), for instance, the Court stated in dictum that the firing squad was not cruel and unusual punishment (when the Eighth Amendment Clause was not yet applicable to the states). Wilkerson was later executed in botched fashion when marksmen missed their mark (the heart, indicated by a piece of paper) and Wilkerson died by blood loss on the ground as long as 27 minutes later. In *In re Kemmler*, 136 U.S. 436 (1890), the Court declined to address an Eighth Amendment challenge to electrocution, concluding that the Amendment did not apply to the states, and therefore left unexamined the state's assertion that electrocution produced "instantaneous, and, therefore, painless death," which in Kemmler's case later proved questionable.[28] In *Malloy v. South Carolina*, 237 U.S. 180 (1915), the

---

[27] Another concern relates to the common lack of involvement of trained medical professionals in executions. *See* Berger, *supra*, at 45–48 (noting that the ethical positions of many physician and nurse associations condemn their involvement, yet some do participate, and in some instances executions occur without their involvement, raising the risk of "botched" executions).

[28] *See* Denno, *supra*, at 600 (citations omitted):

> After the current had been released for seventeen seconds and the attending physician pronounced Kemmler dead, Kemmler's body twitched a half minute later. Officials believed that Kemmler was still alive, but had to wait several minutes until the current could be reapplied. This second contact lasted for seventy seconds, during which Kemmler's hair and flesh began to burn.
>
> The three doctors who conducted the autopsy about three hours after the execution concluded that Kemmler became "instantly unconscious" by the first jolt and remained

Court rejected an ex post facto challenge to a change in execution method, from hanging to electrocution (i.e., the change did not constitute a retroactive increase in punishment). And, in *Francis v. Resweber*, 329 U.S. 459 (1947), the Court held that execution after a failed initial attempt did not constitute cruel and unusual punishment under the Eighth Amendment or Double Jeopardy under the Fifth Amendment, presuming that violation of the two prohibitions would violate the Due Process Clause of the Fourteenth Amendment.

Not until 2008, in *Baze v. Rees*, 553 U.S. 35 (2008), six decades later, did the Court again address a constitutional challenge, for the first time under the Eighth Amendment (incorporated in *Robinson v. California* (1962)) to an execution method—lethal injection. *Baze*, *Glossip v. Gross*, 576 U.S. 863 (2015), and *Bucklew v. Precythe*, 139 S. Ct. 1112 (2019), continued the Court's uniform rejection of challenges to execution methods, and provide the analytic framework for the assessment of challenges. In *Bucklew*, the Court rejected an inmate's as-applied claim that Missouri's protocol, involving injection of a single drug (the sedative pentobarbital), would cause him excruciating pain due to his rare medical condition.[29]

Writing for the five-member majority rejecting the claim, Justice Gorsush emphasized at the outset that "the Eighth Amendment does not guarantee a prisoner a painless death—something that, of course, isn't guaranteed to many people, including most victims of capital crimes." Rather, relying on language in *Baze*, and applying a test consistent with the "original and historic understanding of the Eighth Amendment," Gorsuch wrote that the Constitution only bars methods of execution that "superadd terror, pain, or disgrace" to a death sentence. *Bucklew*, 139 S. Ct. at 1124. To answer whether the criteria are satisfied in a particular case, Gorsush, borrowing from *Baze* and *Glossip*, stated that a petitioner must identify a "feasible and readily implemented alternative method of execution [that] the State [has] refused to adopt without a legitimate reason, even though it would significantly reduce a substantial risk of severe pain." *Id.* at 1129.

Ultimately, the Court rejected Bucklew's suggestion of using nitrogen hypoxia as an alternative, deeming its use insufficiently supported to qualify as a "readily implemented alternative method." Furthermore, Bucklew failed to show that Missouri lacked a "legitimate"

---

so during the entire procedure, confirming that his death was "painless." There was, however, "[e]xtensive charring" of Kemmler's body at the points where the electrodes attached. Moreover, one doctor described as "awful" the four-and-one-half minute interim between the first and the last application of current. "I want never again to witness anything like that. You may kill a man—but kill him."

For more on "botched" executions see AUSTIN SARAT, GRUESOME SPECTACLES: BOTCHED EXECUTIONS AND AMERICA'S DEATH PENALTY (2014).

[29] Justice Breyer, in a dissent, joined by Justices Ginsburg, Sotomayor, and Kagan, described Bucklew's medical condition as involving "tumors that grow in his throat [that might] rupture during his execution, causing him to sputter, choke, and suffocate on his own blood for up to several minutes before he dies." *Bucklew*, 139 S. Ct. at 1136 (Breyer, J., dissenting).

reason for maintaining its current method, with Gorsuch noting the dearth of evidence of the alternative's viability because no other state had used it. *Id.* Finally, even if Bucklew had satisfied the readily available alternative requirement, he failed to show that it would "significantly reduce a substantial risk of severe pain," with Justice Gorsuch adding that "[a] minor reduction in risk is insufficient; the difference must be clear and considerable." *Id.* at 1130.

NOTES & QUESTIONS

1. **Changing Methods.** As noted, the Court has yet to invalidate an execution method on constitutional grounds, including several refusals to invalidate use of lethal injection. Despite this, death penalty jurisdictions continue to revise the drugs used in executions. In significant part, as noted, the changes are due to shifting availability of the drugs themselves, which of course presents the risk that new drugs will have perhaps unforeseen adverse consequences. At the same time, jurisdictions wary of an actual successful challenge to lethal injection, have enacted laws providing what Professor Deborah Denno calls "constitutional substitutes" such as electrocution and the firing squad, resulting in the reintroduction of what might be seen as outmoded (yet constitutional) methods. Deborah W. Denno, *Back to the Future with Execution Methods, in* THE EIGHTH AMENDMENT AND ITS FUTURE IN A NEW AGE OF PUNISHMENT (Meghan J. Ryan & William W. Berry, 2020). From the perspective of a capital punishment opponent, is this a desirable evolution?

2. **Deference to States.** *Bucklew* makes clear that the Court will show considerable deference to state decisions regarding execution methods. In this respect, the Court's Eighth Amendment jurisprudence on execution methods parallels that concerning sentence lengths for adults convicted of crimes. *See, e.g., Harmelin v. Michigan*, 501 U.S. 957 (1991).

3. **Should Executions Be Televised?** As noted, today, unlike in past centuries, executions in the U.S. take place behind prison walls. Furthermore, laws and regulations impose strict limits on who can sit in the viewing area of death chambers. Over the years, litigation seeking to force jurisdictions to allow filming of executions and public access to recordings has repeatedly failed, with officials citing, inter alia, the inmate's need for privacy, and courts deferring to their position. Presuming the condemned inmate consents to the filming, do you agree that filming, and broader public access to executions, should be prohibited? What arguments are in favor and against the practice?

4. **Executioners.** In addition to veiling the identify of drug makers, jurisdictions hide the identity of executioners, to shield them from possible negative notoriety in their communities.[30] Should transparency be the norm when the government undertakes arguably the most grave action it can

[30] For discussion of the trauma experienced by executioners, sometimes resulting in their becoming death penalty opponents, see John D. Bessler, *Torture and Trauma: Why the Death Penalty Is Wrong and Should Be Strictly Prohibited by American and International Law*, 58 WASHBURN L.J. 1, 45–47 (2019).

possibly undertake: the execution of one of its citizens? *See* Ellyde Roko, Note, *Executioner Identities: Toward Recognizing a Right to Know Who Is Behind the Hood*, 75 FORDHAM L. REV. 2791 (2007). Protocols are also often put in place making it hard to determine which executioner out of a group actually caused the death (for instance, having three buttons to activate electrocution, two of which are "dummies"), to mitigate possible trauma. Alexandra L. Klein, *Nondelegating Death*, 81 OHIO ST. L.J. 923, 933–39 (2020).

G. LIFE ON DEATH ROW

Much like Damocles, death row inmates, absent a successful appeal, await their preordained fate. After an individual is sentenced to death

> a date of execution is typically set by the trial court judge. That date is immediately stayed pending appeals. Once appeals and clemency requests are exhausted, there is no legal impediment to execution. The next step is the issuance of the death warrant. A death warrant is not automatic. Instead, individuals sentenced to death wait on death row until a government official, typically the trial prosecutor, the chief prosecutor in the jurisdiction, or another executive requests or signs a death warrant. The death warrant authorizes the prison department or warden to execute the defendant.

Joanmarie Ilaria Davoli, *Playing Politics with Executions: Abuse of Executive Discretion*, 30 GEO. MASON U. CIV. RTS. L.J. 307, 318–19 (2020).[31]

As one might expect, the atmosphere on death row is not pleasant. Like the prison environment more generally (see Chapter 5), conditions are usually spartan, the food poor, and opportunities for freedom from omnipresent surveillance few. Often condemned individuals are housed with one another. They are allowed out of their cells for periods of time but are contained in small groups in dayrooms on the pod or tier in which they are housed, in complete isolation from the larger prison population. As described by one author:

> The dayrooms are complete with glass-encased control modules that are manned around the clock; these modules supplement

---

[31] For discussion of the process by which inmates sentenced to death are actually selected and sequenced for execution, a process referred to as "execution selection," see Lee Kavorsky, *The American Execution Queue*, 71 STAN. L. REV. 1163 (2019). Professor Kavorsky relates that

> U.S. jurisdictions maintain no pretense of avoiding arbitrary decisionmaking when they construct their execution queues. There is no federal law on execution selection, and state law usually governs only ministerial authority to seek and set execution dates. Norms and legal rules tell us how the bell will toll, but almost nothing about when or for whom. There are virtually no constraints on execution selection, inviting a raft of questions about the role of chance and arbitrary decisionmaking in the most visible acts of state killing. As a descriptive matter, why is the process permitted to remain so underregulated? As a normative matter, should execution selection even be analyzed as "punishment"? And how should institutions respond?

Id. at 1165.

> the bars and locks that keep the dayroom areas securely segregated from the rest of the prison. Surveillance is unremitting. As a result, the dayrooms serve less as a respite from the prisoners' cells and more as an extension of those cells, yielding a kind of group solitary confinement. Movement outside the dayrooms is fully controlled at all times, with prisoners handcuffed, shackled, and escorted under heavy guard. It is as if the prisoners drag the death row environment around with them wherever they go, like the chains that bind their hands and feet during their rare excursions within the prison. Officers and inmates alike describe this death row as a cold, lonely, and often frightening world.

ROBERT JOHNSON, CONDEMNED TO DIE: LIFE UNDER SENTENCE OF DEATH x–xi (1981). Johnson writes of a particular inmate:

> Not a day passes that I do not fight just to get out of bed. And in the late hours of the night, it takes much strength just to keep a grip on my sanity. I have spent many hours, at my window, standing on my toilet at the air vent, pleading with men who were considering suicide. . . . I have been on that very edge myself.

Id.

Most often, however, death row inmates do not live in a congregate setting, but rather live in near total solitary confinement. Gabriella Robles, *Condemned to Death—and Solitary Confinement*, THE MARSHALL PROJECT, July 23, 2017, https://www.themarshallproject.org/2017/07/23/condemned-to-death-and-solitary-confinement (noting that 61% of death row inmates are isolated for twenty or more hours per day). The use of solitary death row confinement has recently come under fire. In *Porter v. Clarke*, 923 F.3d 348 (4th Cir. 2019), the Fourth Circuit held that Virginia's practice of isolating inmates for between twenty-three and twenty-four hours a day violated the Eighth Amendment.

Condemned inmates can spend decades on death row. The extended waiting, in the psychologically stressful and deprived environment, has given rise to what has been referred to as "death row syndrome," motivating inmates to forego or suspend challenges and "volunteer" for execution. *See* Amy Smith, *Not 'Waiving' But Drowning: The Anatomy Of Death Row Syndrome And Volunteering For Execution*, 17 B.U. PUB. INT. L.J. 237 (2008).

To the minds of many, including several justices on the Supreme Court, the extended delays amount to justice denied, for survivors and the governments seeking to implement their death penalty provisions, and are a function of inmates gaming the capital system. Attributing the delays to defense strategic delays and foot-dragging, however, has been contested as a factual matter. This is especially so since the enactment of the Antiterrorism and Effective Death Penalty Act (AEDPA) in 1996, which imposed significant limits such as filing deadlines and prohibition of "second or successive" applications for relief. *See* Lee Kovarsky, *Delay in the Shadow of Death*, 95 N.Y.U. L. REV. 1319 (2020). Justice Breyer in particular has opined that the extended stays on death row should serve as a possible basis for an Eighth Amendment challenge.[32] *See, e.g.*, *Knight v. Florida*, 528 U.S. 990, 993 (1999) (Breyer, J., dissenting from denial of certiorari) (stating that it "is difficult to deny the suffering inherent in a prolonged wait for execution"). *See also* Jacob Leon, Bucklew v. Pecythe's *Return to the Original Meaning of "Unusual": Prohibiting Extensive Delays on Death Row*, 68 CLEV. ST. L. REV. 485, 606 (2020) (noting that inmates in 2013 spent an average of 15.5 years on death row, amounting to 6100% more time than condemned parties experienced in the eighteenth century, buttressing an originalist claim of Eighth Amendment unconstitutionality).

Finally, in a few cases the Supreme Court has been asked whether the Eighth Amendment prohibits execution of individuals who are beset with particular conditions after being sentenced to death, rendering them constitutionally incompetent to be executed. In *Ford v. Wainwright*, 477 U.S. 399 (1986), the Court held that the Eighth Amendment precluded execution of Ford, who suffered "pervasive delusion[s]" associated with "[p]aranoid [s]chizophrenia." The plurality opinion authored by Justice Marshall was not very specific in its supporting reasoning, stating only that "the execution of an insane person simply offends humanity"; that it "provides no example to others"; that "it is uncharitable to dispatch an offender into another world, when he is not of a capacity to fit himself for it"; that "madness is its own punishment"; and that executing an insane person serves no retributive purpose. *Id.* at 407–08.

In *Panetti v. Quarterman*, 551 U.S. 930 (2007), the Court elaborated on the rationale behind prohibiting the execution of an individual whose mental illness deprives him of the capacity to understand that he is being punished for commission of a crime. Expert testimony suggested that Panetti rationally understood the state's reason for executing him (for an atrocious murder), but Panetti believed that the state's real reason was that "forces of darkness" sought to "to stop him from preaching." The Court held that "[a] prisoner's awareness of the State's rationale for an execution is not the same as a rational understanding of it." *Id.* at 933. The Court reversed the lower court's determination of competence but stated that it did "not attempt to set down a rule governing all competency determinations," and remanded for further development and analysis of the claim. *Id.* at 962.

Most recently, in *Madison v. Alabama*, 139 S. Ct. 718 (2019), the Court stated that dementia (resulting from a stroke, after decades spent on death row) preventing an inmate's ability to remember the killing he

[32] The assertion is often called a "*Lackey* claim," which takes its name from an opinion suggesting as much by Justice Stevens respecting the denial of certiorari in *Lackey v. Texas*, 514 U.S. 1045 (1995) (Stevens, J., memorandum respecting denial of certiorari).

committed could prevent him from possessing the "rational understanding" of his impending execution required by *Ford* and *Panetti*. The Court first held that a person lacking memory of his crime may yet rationally understand why the State seeks to execute him, allowing for a finding of execution competency. This is because

> *Panetti* asks about understanding, not memory—more specifically, about a person's understanding of why the State seeks capital punishment for a crime, not his memory of the crime itself. And the one may exist without the other. Do you have an independent recollection of the Civil War? Obviously not. But you may still be able to reach a rational—indeed, a sophisticated—understanding of that conflict and its consequences. Do you recall your first day of school? Probably not. But if your mother told you years later that you were sent home for hitting a classmate, you would have no trouble grasping the story. And similarly, if you somehow blacked out a crime you committed, but later learned what you had done, you could well appreciate the State's desire to impose a penalty. Assuming, that is, no other cognitive impairment, loss of memory of a crime does not prevent rational understanding of the State's reasons for resorting to punishment. And that kind of comprehension is the *Panetti* standard's singular focus.

Id. at 727. The Court also held that a person suffering from dementia may be unable to rationally understand the reasons for his sentence; if so, his execution is barred. "What matters is whether a person has the 'rational understanding' *Panetti* requires—not whether he has any particular memory or any particular mental illness." *Id.* at 726–27. Ultimately, the Court concluded

> [p]sychosis or dementia, delusions or overall cognitive decline are all the same under *Panetti*, so long as they produce the requisite lack of comprehension. . . . The *Panetti* standard concerns, once again, not the diagnosis of such illness, but a consequence—to wit, the prisoner's inability to rationally understand his punishment.

Id. at 728.

Assuming a condemned party is found incompetent to be executed, based on *Ford-Panetti-Madison*, is the execution forever forestalled? Not necessarily: the state might subject the individual to involuntary medication to restore competency, e.g., make him better in order to execute him. As of this writing, the Supreme Court has not addressed whether doing so comports with the Eighth Amendment but at least one court has condoned the practice. *See Singleton v. Norris*, 319 F.3d 1018, 1026–27 (8th Cir. 2003) (approving of involuntary administration of antipsychotic medication that protected the inmate or others from danger, and had the side effect of making the inmate competent to be executed). For discussion of the issue, see Brian D. Shannon & Victor R.

Scarano, *Incompetency to Be Executed: Continuing Ethical Challenges & Time for a Change in Texas*, 45 TEX. TECH. L. REV. 419 (2013).

CHAPTER 8

COMMUNITY SUPERVISION

It is often said that we live in an era of mass incarceration in the United States. It is certainly true that the number of prisoners in the United States reached unprecedented levels in the first decade of the twenty-first century and remains quite high relative to both international and U.S. historical norms. Yet, at any given time, there are far more Americans on community supervision than behind bars. Viewed altogether, the present correctional system might be best described as one of *mass supervision*.

The supervised population may be roughly divided into two components: those who are on probation, and those who are on parole. Probationers have been sentenced to a period of supervision in the community *in lieu of imprisonment*, while parolees have been assigned to a period of community supervision *after their release from prison*.[1] As might be expected, parolees tend to have more serious current offenses and criminal histories than probationers. Yet, both forms of community supervision share many key features in common, including:

- Conditional liberty—probationers and parolees must comply with certain conditions in order to remain in the community;
- Supervision—probationers and parolees are assigned to a correctional agent who has responsibility for monitoring their compliance with conditions and supporting their rehabilitation; and
- Sanctioning and revocation for violations—when conditions are violated, the probationer or parolee is subject to sanctions, including the possibility of revocation (which normally implies that the person will be incarcerated).

Figure 8-1 depicts trends in imprisonment and community supervision in the United States since the mid-1990s. The parole population is consistently a little lower, and the probation population consistently a lot higher, than the prison population. The total supervised population peaked at about 5.1 million in 2007, while the prison population peaked at 1.6 million two years later.[2] By 2019, the prison

[1] We employ conventional understandings of the terms "probation" and "parole" here, but, as with many other aspects of sentencing law, readers should appreciate that there is considerable state-to-state variation in the terminology and organization of community supervision.

[2] The prison figures exclude individuals who are held in local jails, which includes both sentenced individuals who are serving short terms of incarceration and defendants who are detained pending resolution of their cases. In 2009, the U.S. jail population was about 767,4000. LAURA S. MARUSCHAK & TODD D. MINTON, U.S. DEP'T OF JUSTICE, CORRECTIONAL POPULATIONS

population had dropped about 11% from its peak, and the supervised population had dropped about 15%.[3]

Figure 8-1. U.S. numbers in prison, on parole, on probation, and on community supervision (parole plus probation), 1994–2019. Source: U.S. Department of Justice Bureau of Justice Statistics.

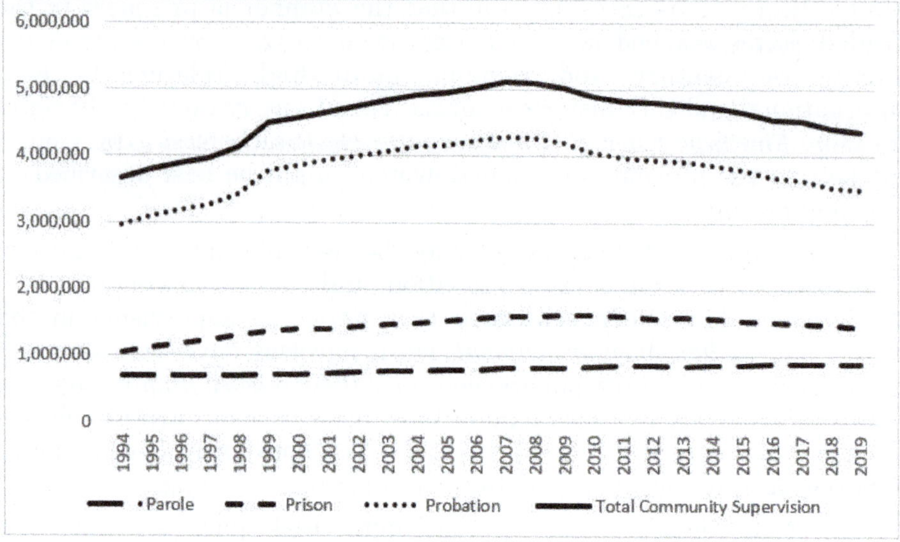

In Chapter 5, we considered contemporary conditions of incarceration in the United States, which tend to be rather grim. It is often simply assumed that community supervision is far "softer" than time behind bars and would be greatly preferred by all or nearly all defendants. Although there is a measure of truth to these beliefs, it is easy to overstate the softness of community supervision. Release conditions and supervision practices may be perceived as quite oppressive by some defendants, and the threat of revocation can create a persistent sense of insecurity. As one of us has written,

> No longer is probation synonymous with the "soft" enterprise of rehabilitating offenders. Rather, in tandem with the expanded array of techniques coming into use over time, which by design and effect have considerably more onerous effects, probation today is animated by a far richer gamut of purposes—including the punishment, deterrence and incapacitation of offenders, and the restoration of victims and communities to their pre-crime status.

IN THE UNITED STATES, 2017–2018 (2020). The combined jail and inmate population of 2.4 million was still less than half the supervised population.

[3] The supervision population, like the prison population, is marked by sharp racial disparities. African-Americans constitute 30% of the probation group and 37% of the parole group, despite accounting for only about 13% of the general U.S. population. DANIELLE KAEBLE & MARIEL ALPER, U.S. DEP'T OF JUSTICE, PROBATION AND PAROLE IN THE UNITED STATES, 2017–2018, at 20, 27 (2020).

Wayne A. Logan, *The Importance of Purpose in Probation Decision Making*, 7 BUFF. CRIM. L. REV. 171, 172 (2003). *See also* Ronald P. Corbett, Jr., *The Burdens of Leniency: The Changing Face of Probation*, 99 MINN. L. REV. 1697, 1708 (2015) (discussing recent increases in number and range of supervision conditions).

Perhaps, then, it should not be surprising that one survey found that nearly one-third of defendants would prefer one year of prison over three years of probation. Corbett, *supra*. Indeed, in at least a few jurisdictions, it is not uncommon for defendants to request an incarceration sentence in lieu of probation. Nancy J. King, *Handling Aggravating Facts After* Blakely*: Findings From Five Presumptive-Guidelines States*, 99 N.C. L. REV. 1241, 1269 (2021). As you read the material in this chapter, see if you can identify more specifically some of the features of probation and parole that might cause community supervision to be perceived as so onerous, and consider whether these features seem more likely to enhance or diminish the effectiveness of supervision.

We proceed by first considering the basic pathways to community supervision: the probationary sentence and conditional release from prison (parole). Next, we focus on the experience of community supervision, including conditions, supervision practices, and revocation. Finally, we turn our attention to so-called "intermediate sanctions," which are said to lie somewhere between conventional supervision and full-blown incarceration.

A. PATHWAYS TO COMMUNITY SUPERVISION

1. PROBATION

John Augustus, a public-spirited Boston shoemaker, is often credited with inventing probation in the 1840s. Moved by a sense of compassion for the poor, Augustus developed a regular practice of bailing out indigent defendants and helping them to address the underlying difficulties in their lives, such as unemployment or alcoholism. When it came time for the defendant to return to court, Augustus would report on the defendant's rehabilitative progress; if satisfactory, the court would impose a nominal fine rather than a term of incarceration. SAMUEL WALKER, POPULAR JUSTICE: A HISTORY OF AMERICAN CRIMINAL JUSTICE 93–94 (2d ed. 1998).

In truth, even before the 1840s, American criminal justice had already developed a variety of different mechanisms by which some less serious defendants might be spared the full rigor of the law, subject to their success in avoiding future criminal entanglements. These mechanisms included, for instance, conditional executive clemency and the peace-bond system, in which the defendant or the defendant's family or friends would pledge a sum of money as a guaranty of the defendant's good behavior. LAWRENCE M. FRIEDMAN, CRIME AND PUNISHMENT IN

AMERICAN HISTORY 38–39 (1993). However, Augustus's proto-probation initiative represented an advance of sorts over earlier practices, particularly insofar as he provided a more direct and regularized form of supervision for those whom he took under his wing. WALKER, *supra*, at 94–95. Augustus's work in Boston pointed the way to the contemporary system of bureaucratized probation, in which supervision is normally provided by full-time professional probation officers (POs)—a system that first emerged in the late nineteenth century and spread across the country in the early twentieth.

Today, the imposition of a probationary sentence is normally a matter of judicial discretion, subject in some jurisdictions to sentencing guidelines that might either encourage or discourage probation in different cases based on offense severity or criminal history. Additionally, depending on the jurisdiction, mandatory minimum statutes may take probation off the table as an option for many defendants.

Why might a judge choose probation over incarceration for a given defendant? Probation might be preferred by the judge based on any number of considerations, including that the defendant's crime was not sufficiently serious to warrant incarceration, that incarceration would be counterproductive to the defendant's rehabilitation, or that the social costs of incarceration would likely outweigh any benefits. On the other hand, hanging over the decision may be a fear that the defendant will commit another crime, perhaps even more serious, while free in the community. In one study of large urban jurisdictions, 13% of the individuals charged with murder were on probation for another offense at the time of their murder arrest. BRIAN A. REAVES, U.S. DEPT. OF JUSTICE, FELONY DEFENDANTS IN LARGE URBAN COUNTIES, 2009—STATISTICAL TABLES 10 (2013). These worst-case scenarios represent only a very small percentage of probation cases, but an understandable desire to avoid such outcomes may discourage risk-averse judges and prosecutors from taking chances with any but the lowest-risk defendants.

In the federal system, probation is statutorily authorized for all but the most serious offenses, unless the case is one in which probation is expressly precluded by law. 18 U.S.C. § 3561(a). The term of probation may be anything from one to five years for a felony, or anything up to five years for a misdemeanor. 18 U.S.C. § 3561(c).

Within these broad statutory parameters, the federal sentencing guidelines aim to narrow the scope of judicial discretion. Under § 5B1.1(a), straight probation is authorized only for cases falling into "Zone A" of the guidelines sentencing table (a.k.a. the "grid," reprinted in Chapter 2). These are the cases that present the least serious combinations of offense level and criminal history. Probation is also permitted for cases in Zone B, but only if it is combined with additional special restrictions, such as house arrest. Under § 5B1.2 of the guidelines, if the offense level is six or greater, the term of probation must be at least one year but not more than five years; otherwise, the term can be no longer than three years.

The implementation of the guidelines in the late 1980s was associated with a sharp drop in the use of probation in the federal system. Between 1987 and 1991, the proportion of sentenced federal defendants who received straight probation dropped from 29% to just 14%. U.S. SENT'G COMM'N, FIFTEEN YEARS OF GUIDELINES SENTENCING 43 (2004). However, the guidelines were hardly the sole cause for this change; the 1980s and 1990s also witnessed the adoption of many mandatory minimums, changing prosecutorial priorities, and the ascendance more generally of "tough on crime" attitudes.

Since then, the Supreme Court's decision in *Booker v. United States* has widened the discretion of federal judges to choose probation. However, perhaps surprisingly, probation remains a relatively unusual sentence in the federal system. In fiscal year 2020, only 6% of sentenced federal defendants received straight probation, while an additional 1.7% received probation combined with other alternatives. U.S. SENT'G COMM'N, 2020 SOURCEBOOK OF FEDERAL SENTENCING STATISTICS fig. 6.

The recently adopted Model Penal Code: Sentencing authorizes probation for any felony or misdemeanor "when necessary to hold offenders accountable for their criminal conduct, promote their rehabilitation and reintegration into law-abiding society, or reduce the risk that they will commit new offenses." § 7.02(3). Notably, the MPC:S cautions that probation "should not be viewed as a default sanction when other sanctions are not imposed." § 7.02(3)(b).

The MPC:S limits the length of probation terms more strictly than federal law. For a felony conviction, probation may be no longer than three years; for a misdemeanor, probation is limited to one year.[4] What might be said in favor of the MPC:S's relatively tight limits on term length?

Although probation or some functional equivalent of probation is available in all states, there is wide variation in how it is structured. In some states, as in the federal system and the MPC:S, probation is simply another sentencing option, like incarceration or a fine. In other states, probation is not a sentence in its own right but effectively results when a sentence of incarceration is imposed and then conditionally suspended. In still other states, probation is structured as a post-conviction stay of sentencing. Some states provide the judge with a choice between two or more of these options. Adding further to the variety, the required (or permissible) structure may differ depending on whether the offense is a felony or misdemeanor. Also, in some states, probation may be imposed as part of a "split sentence," in which it is combined with a period of

[4] The MPC:S calls for the development of presumptive sentencing guidelines to address the use of probation, including the length of terms and the conditions that ought to be imposed. *See* § 6.03(4). Sentencing guidelines currently cover probation in just a handful of states, *id.* cmmnt. g, as well as the federal system.

incarceration. Moreover, although the probation decision is most commonly made after conviction and prior to incarceration, a few states permit defendants to be placed with their consent on probation *pre-*conviction as a sort of pretrial diversion, and a few others permit the judge to place a defendant on probation *after* the defendant has already served a few weeks or months behind bars. The latter option is referred to as "earned" or "shock" probation. Finally, in some states, terms like "community control" or "community custody" are used to describe some or all of what would be called "probation" in most other states. For a detailed summary of the probation law of twenty-one states, see KELLY LYN MITCHELL ET AL., UNIV. OF MINN., PROFILES IN PROBATION REVOCATION: EXAMINING THE LEGAL FRAMEWORK IN 21 STATES (2014).

Maximum term lengths for probation also vary considerably. For instance, one recent study found a range from one year (Washington) to ten years (Texas) for felonies, and a range from six months (Florida) to five years (California, Colorado, Mississippi, Ohio, and Oregon) for misdemeanors. ALEXIS LEE WATTS, UNIV. OF MINN., PROBATION IN-DEPTH: THE LENGTH OF PROBATION SENTENCES (2016). Additionally, some states authorize lifetime probation for certain offenses of special concern, such as sexual crimes against children. In a handful of states, the maximum probation term for an offense is the same as the maximum incarceration term, while in two other states (Colorado and Massachusetts) there is no upper bound on the length of felony probation terms.

However structured, probation is most commonly imposed in misdemeanor cases, but is also used with some regularity even in felony cases. One study of large urban jurisdictions found that probation was the most severe sanction for about one-quarter of convicted felony defendants. REAVES, *supra*, at 29. Many additional felony defendants received split sentences that combined probation with a term of incarceration. Even in cases of *violent* felonies, probation was the most severe sanction for 16% of the convicted defendants.

U.S. probation populations tend to be quite high by international standards. As of yearend 2019, there were 1,364 individuals on probation in the United States for every 100,000 adult residents. BARBARA OUDEKERK & DANIELLE KAEBLE, U.S. DEP'T OF JUSTICE, PROBATION AND PAROLE IN THE UNITED STATES, 2019, at 22 (2021). State rates ranged from lows of 330 (New Hampshire) and 381 (Alaska) to highs of 5,042 (Georgia) and 2,620 (Idaho). By contrast, European nations average under 300 probationers per 100,000 residents. MARIEL ALPER, ALESSANDRO CORDA & KEVIN REITZ, UNIV. OF MINN., AMERICAN EXCEPTIONALISM IN PROBATION SUPERVISION (2016).

2. DISCRETIONARY PAROLE AND OTHER POST-PRISON SUPERVISION

Like probation, parole developed through a process of fits and starts over the nineteenth and early twentieth centuries. As imprisonment became a standard felony punishment, governors were increasingly asked to exercise their powers of clemency to shorten terms of incarceration. Pardons and commutations became common means by which prisoners obtained early release, but the process was criticized as ad hoc and arbitrary, with politically connected defendants heavily favored. WALKER, *supra*, at 103. Reformers called for early release to be linked in a more systematic fashion to demonstrated rehabilitative progress. Various approaches were attempted in different states before regular, individualized assessment of inmates by a specialized parole board became the dominant model in the first half of the twentieth century.

Importantly, early release by the parole board was *conditional* release. The former prisoner who violated parole rules could be promptly returned to prison. Over time, bureaucratic agencies were developed to supervise parolees in the community. Much as *probationers* were assigned to a probation officer, *parolees* were assigned to a parole officer. Indeed, in some jurisdictions, a single agency handled both types of community supervision. Reflecting this overlap, we will use the acronym PO to refer to any community supervision officer, whether in the probation or the parole context.

The classic parole system combined two mechanisms with distinct, but complementary, purposes. First, parole included a mechanism for the discretionary release of prisoners by an executive agency (the parole board). This mechanism was thought to incentivize prisoners' rehabilitative effort and compliance with institutional rules. Additionally, for corrections officials, discretionary parole sometimes proved a welcome safety valve to help deal with severe institutional overcrowding. Second, parole also included a mechanism for the supervision of released prisoners in the community. It was hoped that POs would help to keep parolees on the positive rehabilitative trajectory they had established in prison, and, if they faltered, return them to the institution before they did much harm.

The first mechanism, discretionary release, fell into some disrepute in the late twentieth century. From the political left came charges that parole-board decisions were arbitrary and racially biased. From the political right came charges that parole-board decisions were unduly lenient and failed to adequately ensure either just punishment or public safety. Lending strength to these criticisms was academic research that cast doubt on the effectiveness of prison-based rehabilitative programming. If prisons were incapable of rehabilitating inmates, it was not clear on what basis parole boards should be making release decisions.

Maine became the first state to abolish discretionary parole release in 1975. By 2000, fourteen more states and the federal government had followed suit, while twenty other states had otherwise curtailed the availability of parole for at least some categories of prisoners. MICHAEL O'HEAR, THE FAILED PROMISE OF SENTENCING REFORM 6 (2017).

a. DISCRETIONARY PAROLE RELEASE

Although discretionary parole is no longer as ubiquitous a feature of American criminal justice as it was in the mid-twentieth century, it continues to play an important role in a majority of states.[5] In these states, the prison term announced by the judge does not determine when precisely the defendant will be released, but instead establishes parameters within which the parole board exercises discretion.

The specifics vary considerably from state to state. For instance, in Georgia, prisoners generally become eligible for parole consideration after serving one-third of the prison term pronounced by the court, with most up for reconsideration at least every five years if release is denied. Once release is obtained, the person's term of supervision in the community is equal to the unexpired portion of the person's prison term. ALEXIS LEE WATTS ET AL., UNIV. OF MINN., PROFILES IN PAROLE RELEASE AND REVOCATION: EXAMINING THE LEGAL FRAMEWORK IN THE UNITED STATES—GEORGIA (2016). By contrast, in Nevada, the sentencing judge determines a minimum and maximum period of imprisonment in each case. For instance, a defendant might be sentenced to one to twenty years in prison, or seven to eight years in prison. The defendant then becomes eligible for parole consideration after the minimum term has been served, with reconsideration normally occurring within three years if there is a denial the first time. If the maximum term is three years or more, the person *must* be released on parole for at least the final twelve months of the sentence unless the Board of Parole Commissioners decides otherwise for public safety reasons. Once released, the person's term of community supervision will generally be equal to the unexpired portion of the maximum prison term. ALEXIS LEE WATTS, EDWARD E. RHINE & STEVEN GRAZIANO, UNIV. OF MINN., PROFILES IN PAROLE RELEASE AND REVOCATION: EXAMINING THE LEGAL FRAMEWORK IN THE UNITED STATES—NEVADA (2018).

Parole boards have often been criticized as lacking in professionalism. Edward Rhine, Joan Petersilia, and Kevin Reitz recapitulate some of the standard complaints:

> The institutional structure of paroling authorities is shaped profoundly by how members and chairs are appointed and by

---

[5] In a modest reversal of the anti-parole trend of the late twentieth century, several states have liberalized their parole rules in recent years. *See, e.g.*, Laura S. Abrams, Kaylyn Canlione & D. Michael Applegarth, *Growing Up Behind Bars: Pathways to Desistance for Juvenile Lifers*, 103 MARQ. L. REV. 745, 750 (2020) (describing series of parole expansion laws adopted in California between 2012 and 2017, applying to individuals who were under the age of twenty-five at the time of their offense).

> the absence of meaningful statutory qualifications informing their selection. Significant uniformity is found across most states. Direct gubernatorial appointments, usually subject to legislative confirmation, account for membership on the majority of parole boards (43) or appointment as chair (37). In most states especially where the governor is the sole appointing authority, the chair and members of the parole board may be removed as easily as they are appointed.
>
> It has been a longstanding criticism that few formal credentials are required for appointment to the parole board, whether educational, experience-based, or otherwise. The majority of states specify at most vague educational requirements or relevant work experience. . . .
>
> Once appointed, institutional vulnerability and personal job insecurity push parole boards toward risk aversion in their decision making. The external scrutiny of parole decisions varies with time and can change quickly. Board members are acutely aware that there is little price to pay for keeping offenders in prison beyond their release eligibility dates and potential catastrophe if even one releasee commits a horrible crime.

The Future of Parole Release, 46 CRIME & JUST. 279, 286 (2017). These tendencies toward risk aversion by parole boards may help to explain a seeming paradox: even though discretionary parole is often assumed to be a "lenient" system, the states retaining discretionary parole have generally experienced faster prison growth than the abolition states. *Id.* at 280. Today, the states that retain discretionary parole include most of the states with the highest imprisonment rates. *Id.*

If sentencing procedures tend to be much less formal than criminal trials, parole board procedures are far less formal still.[6] Hearings tend to be quite brief, with times typically in the range of three to twenty minutes each.[7] The Supreme Court has recognized no constitutional right to counsel at parole proceedings, and only a handful of states provide lawyers for indigent prisoners. Rules of evidence do not apply. Prisoners have no right to confront adverse witnesses and may not even be

---

[6] The Supreme Court has indicated that parole release decisions do not inherently trigger constitutional due process protections, although the particular structure of the parole system in a given state may establish a constitutionally cognizable liberty interest in release. *Greenholtz v. Nebraska Penal Inmates,* 442 U.S. 1 (1979). *But see Sandin v. Conner*, 515 U.S. 472 (1995) (criticizing *Greenholtz's* methodology for establishing protectable liberty interest). Even to the extent that due process rights exist, however, they are not likely robust. *See Greenholtz,* 442 U.S. at 14 ("Merely because a statutory expectation [in parole release] exists cannot mean that in addition to the full panoply of due process required to convict and confine there must also be repeated, adversary hearings in order to continue the confinement.").

[7] Fordham Law School has compiled an illuminating, searchable database of parole documents from New York State, including hearing transcripts. The Parole Information Project is available at https://ir.lawnet.fordham.edu/nys_parole_dd/.

permitted to review their files to ensure accuracy. Even the burdens of proof are not clearly established in many states. *Id.* at 312–14.

The statutory criteria for parole decisions tend to be open-ended and vague, echoing the statutory criteria for sentencing decisions. Indeed, most parole boards are empowered to reevaluate the very same factors considered by the sentencing judge and reach different conclusions as to their significance. *Id.* at 298. However, there is a recent trend toward more systematic approaches to parole decisionmaking, with a majority of boards now using parole guidelines (analogous to sentencing guidelines), risk-assessment instruments, and/or other policy-driven decision instruments. *Id.* at 281. By way of illustration, you may recall the risk-assessment system used by the Texas Board of Pardons and Paroles, which was described in Chapter 2. Yet, despite efforts to bring greater attention to risk and rehabilitation, empirical researchers continue to find that offense seriousness often plays a dominant role in parole board decisions, which means, among other things, that defendants who committed major violent offenses may struggle to obtain release notwithstanding strong evidence of reform or advanced age and infirmity. Amelia Courtney Hritz, *Parole Board Decision Making and Constitutional Rights*, 17 ANN. REV. L. & SOC. SCI. 335, 336, 345 (2021).

One particularly controversial (and related) aspect of contemporary parole board practice has been the consideration of victim impact statements. All discretionary parole states now give victims a right to submit a statement to the paroling authorities, much as they are able to do at sentencing. Although only a small percentage of victims take advantage of this opportunity, some research finds that when victims do participate, the likelihood of a denial of release increases. *Id.* at 317. As you may recall from the discussion of victim impact statements at sentencing in Chapter 3, victim influence over punishment raises concerns about the potential for unwarranted disparities in the treatment of different defendants.[8]

In 2019, at least 178,074 individuals were granted discretionary parole release in the United States, which accounted for at least 43% of the individuals who entered post-prison community supervision. BARBARA OUDEKERK & DANIELLE KAEBLE, U.S. DEP'T OF JUSTICE, PROBATION AND PAROLE IN THE UNITED STATES, 2019, at 29 (2021).[9]

[8] Also controversial is the insistence of the parole board in some cases that the defendant admit his or her offense and express remorse. *See, e.g.*, Tom Robbins, *He Says He's No Murderer. That's Why He's Still in Prison*, N.Y. TIMES, Dec. 2, 2021 (describing case of "model inmate" denied parole because he refused to admit guilt). Such an insistence puts the wrongfully convicted defendant to a difficult choice—either forego parole release or admit guilt and thereby potentially lose any chance of having the wrongful conviction reversed.

[9] We say "at least" because information is not available regarding about 6% of the releases to post-prison supervision.

b. OTHER PATHWAYS TO POST-PRISON SUPERVISION

Discretionary release by a parole board is not the only pathway to post-prison community supervision. For instance, in some states with discretionary parole the law mandates release by some definite time prior to the expiration of the maximum prison term. Thus, as we noted above, in Nevada prisoners must generally be released no later than 12 months prior to the maximum length of their prison terms. Such mandates reflect the view that some transitional phase between imprisonment and full liberty in the community helps to ease the former prisoner's reintegration into society and may reduce the likelihood of recidivism. Mandatory releases accounted for more than 20% of entries into post-prison supervision in 2019.

Mandatory release rules like Nevada's ensure a transitional phase of community supervision in many states that retain discretionary parole release. How about in abolition states? The approach adopted by many is to require the *judge* to set a term of post-prison supervision at the time of sentencing. Consider, for instance, how this was handled in the federal system.

Sentencing Reform Act of 1984 (as codified)

18 U.S.C. § 3583. Inclusion of a term of supervised release after imprisonment

(a) In general.—The court, in imposing a sentence to a term of imprisonment for a felony or a misdemeanor, may include as a part of the sentence a requirement that the defendant be placed on a term of supervised release after imprisonment * * *.

(b) Authorized terms of supervised release.—Except as otherwise provided, the authorized terms of supervised release are—

(1) for a Class A or Class B felony, not more than five years;

(2) for a Class C or Class D felony, not more than three years; and

(3) for a Class E felony, or for a misdemeanor (other than a petty offense), not more than one year.

(c) Factors to be considered in including a term of supervised release.—The court, in determining whether to include a term of supervised release, and, if a term of supervised release is to be included, in determining the length of the term and the conditions of supervised release, shall consider the factors set forth in [18 U.S.C. § 3553(a) with the exception of § 3553(a)(2)(A)].

United States Sentencing Guidelines (2021)

§ 5D1.1. Imposition of a Term of Supervised Release

(a) The court shall order a term of supervised release to follow imprisonment * * * when a sentence of imprisonment of more than one year is imposed. * * *

§ 5D1.2. Term of Supervised Release

(a) Except as provided [elsewhere], if a term of supervised release is ordered, the length of the term shall be:

(1) At least two years but not more than five years for a defendant convicted of a Class A or B felony.

(2) At least one year but not more than three years for a defendant convicted of a Class C or D felony.

(3) One year for a defendant convicted of a Class E felony or a Class A misdemeanor.

NOTES & QUESTIONS

1. **Permissive or Mandatory?** Under 18 U.S.C. § 3583(a), whether to impose any term of "supervised release" is generally within the sentencing judge's discretion. However, the guidelines mandate supervised release in almost all cases in which a prison term of more than one year is imposed. The guidelines also give the judge less discretion as to the length of the supervised release term.

Although § 3583 mostly leaves supervised release to the judge's discretion, other statutes mandate minimum terms of supervised release in certain kinds of cases. For instance, the weight-based drug sentencing statutes that we considered in Chapter 4 require not only minimum prison terms, but also minimum terms of post-prison supervision. Thus, a defendant convicted of distributing at least 500 grams of cocaine would face not only a minimum of five years in prison, but also a minimum of four years of supervised release—with both minimums doubling if there has been a prior conviction for a serious drug or violent felony. 21 U.S.C. § 841(b)(1)(B).

2. **Timing of Recidivism.** In thinking about the optimal length of supervision terms, an important consideration might be the timing of post-prison recidivism. The evidence indicates that the first year home is a difficult one for many former prisoners, with relatively high risks of reoffense. After the first year, however, recidivism rates tend to decrease.

For instance, in one of the most ambitious studies of its kind, the U.S. Department of Justice's Bureau of Justice Statistics tracked prisoners released in thirty states in 2005 over a nine-year period. MARIEL ALPER, MATTHEW R. DUROSE & JOSHUA MARKMAN, U.S. DEP'T OF JUSTICE, 2018 UPDATE ON PRISONER RECIDIVISM: A 9-YEAR FOLLOW-UP PERIOD (2005–2014) (2018). Overall, 83% of the former inmates were rearrested at least once during that time period, but first rearrests were markedly skewed toward the earlier years of the study. Figure 8-2 depicts the proportion of the released prisoners who had a first rearrest each year. Out of all of those who were ever rearrested, 53% were rearrested during their first year out of prison, and 82% were rearrested in the first three years. Out of those who managed to get through six years without a rearrest, only 19% were ever rearrested within the nine-year timeframe. Moreover, rates of rearrest for a *violent* offense—the most concerning type of new crime—fell steadily each year from 9% in year one to 5% in year nine. Do these figures suggest that the enhanced supervision terms called for in statutes like 21 U.S.C. § 841 may be unnecessary? On the other hand, is there any harm in keeping low-risk former prisoners on supervision?

Figure 8-2. Percent of former prisoners experiencing first rearrest, by years since release. Source: U.S. Department of Justice Bureau of Justice Statistics.

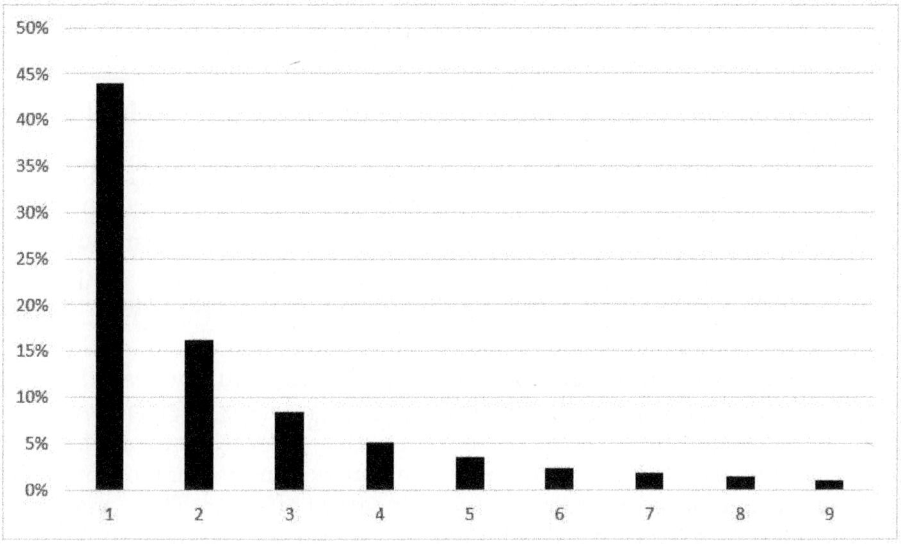

The data might also have implications for supervision terms in traditional discretionary parole systems. In these systems, the supervision term is equal to the unexpired portion of the maximum prison term imposed by the judge. Thus, a defendant who received a long prison term, but who did well in prison and was granted parole early in his or her term, might spend many years on supervision. Indeed, ironically, this individual might spend much longer on supervision than other prisoners who did poorly in prison and had to wait longer to secure release—even though those prisoners would presumably present a higher risk of reoffense.

3. **Why Set the Term and Conditions of Supervised Release at the Time of Sentencing?** Section 3583 contemplates that the judge, at the time of sentencing, will establish both the period of supervision and the conditions with which the defendant must comply, much as the judge does when imposing a sentence of probation. Note, however, a crucial distinction between probation and supervised release: probation begins immediately, but supervised release does not commence until after the defendant's term

of imprisonment is over, which may be several years in the future. In setting the term and conditions of *probation*, the sentencing judge should (at least in principle) possess all of the most important information that is relevant to the term and conditions. However, in setting the term and conditions of *supervised release*, the sentencing judge can only speculate as to the life changes that will occur while the defendant is in prison. The judge does not know, for instance, whether the defendant will benefit from rehabilitative programming behind bars, develop a new or deeper religious faith, develop problematic connections with other inmates, display new proclivities toward violence, or develop or overcome an addiction or mental illness. To be sure, § 3583(e) does authorize judicial modification of terms and conditions post-sentencing. Still, there is likely some inertia once terms and conditions are set forth in a judgment. Do you think it would be better to leave terms and conditions open until the time of release?

4. **Desert.** In § 3583(c), Congress directed sentencing judges, in setting terms and conditions, to take into account the same purposes and other considerations that are generally mandated for federal sentencing under § 3553(a), but specifically carved out § 3553(a)(2)(A), which addresses "just punishment." The implication seems to be that supervised release should be structured primarily for utilitarian ends. *See* U.S. SENT'G COMM'N, FEDERAL OFFENDERS SENTENCED TO SUPERVISED RELEASE 9 (2010) ("The legislative history indicates that § 3553(a)(2)(A) was not included for consideration under 18 U.S.C. § 3583(c) because the primary purpose of supervised release is to facilitate the integration of offenders back into the community rather than to punish them.").

5. **Lifetime Supervision.** Guideline § 5D1.2(b) authorizes a *life* term of supervised release for certain terrorism offenses or sex offenses involving minors. Lifetime supervision is part of the network of harsh post-imprisonment sanctions that have become increasingly common over the past generation for individuals who commit sexual offenses. These measures are considered in more detail in Chapter 11. Do you think that lifetime supervision would *ever* be an appropriate sentence?

6. **Model Penal Code: Sentencing.** The MPC:S makes postrelease supervision discretionary in all cases, subject to any relevant sentencing guidelines. §§ 6.09(2), (4). As with probation, the MPC:S cautions that postrelease supervision "should not be viewed as a default sanction to follow a term of incarceration." § 7.02(6)(b). The commentary observes, "[P]ostrelease supervision is often imposed on offenders for whom it makes little sense. For many minor felons, first-time offenders, and those for whom age, health, or other personal attributes make recidivism unlikely, ongoing state supervision serves little purpose—other than to impose the contingent liability of revocation and re-incarceration. A primary evil of gratuitous supervision is that it drains resources that could be channeled more effectively into other cases." § 7.02 cmmnt. d.

The MPC:S caps felony supervision at five years. § 7.02(6). The commentary explains,

> For the mass of parolees, a supervision period no longer than one or two years should be sufficient, particularly if energy and resources now wasted on much longer supervision terms are reallocated to the most critical, early months following release. The Code's choice of a five-year period is informed by criminological research into the behavior of prison releasees. The first year following exit from prison is when most reoffending occurs, with diminishing rates of criminal involvement in subsequent years.

§ 7.02 cmmnt. g.

7. **By the Numbers.** Supervised release in the federal system and similar state systems accounts for about 25% of all individuals entering postrelease supervision. BARBARA OUDEKERK & DANIELLE KAEBLE, U.S. DEP'T OF JUSTICE, PROBATION AND PAROLE IN THE UNITED STATES, 2019, at 29 (2021). As we observed with respect to probation, rates of post-prison supervision in the United States are high by international standards. As of yearend 2019, there were 343 individuals on post-prison supervision per 100,000 adult residents. *Id.* at 27. By contrast, the European average is about 77 per 100,000. MARIEL ALPER, ALESSANDRO CORDA & KEVIN REITZ, UNIV. OF MINN., AMERICAN EXCEPTIONALISM IN PAROLE SUPERVISION (2016).

8. **A Word on Terminology.** As we noted earlier, the classic American parole system included two distinct components: (1) a mechanism for the discretionary release of prisoners based on individualized assessments by an executive agency, and (2) a period of conditional liberty and supervision following release from prison. Today, the first component has been eliminated in more than a dozen states and the federal system. However, the second component remains alive and well in nearly all U.S. jurisdictions. Many of the jurisdictions that eliminated the first component have developed new terms like "supervised release" or "extended supervision" to describe the second component. Nonetheless, the term "parole" remains in widespread use nationally to denote any type of postrelease supervision, whether entered into through the discretionary decision of a parole board or otherwise. We will adhere to this convention.

c. SPECIAL CHALLENGES OF PRISONER REENTRY

As we consider the law and policy of community supervision over the remainder of this chapter, we will generally not distinguish between probation and parole. However, it is important for readers to appreciate that parolees face a distinct set of challenges, especially at the outset of their period of supervision. New parolees are, more or less by definition, individuals who are emerging from a protracted period of incarceration. Their relationships with family and friends on the outside may have been strained or broken by the long absence. They may struggle with the transition from a highly structured institutional life to one in which there are many more choices to be made and temptations to be resisted. Some returning prisoners are fortunate to have a job waiting for them, but many more do not. Some research points to an unemployment rate of about 50% even for those who have been out for a full year. COMM. ON

CAUSES & CONSEQUENCES OF HIGH RATES OF INCARCERATION, NAT'L RESEARCH COUNCIL OF THE NAT'L ACADS., THE GROWTH OF INCARCERATION IN THE UNITED STATES: EXPLORING CAUSES AND CONSEQUENCES 233 (Jeremy Travis, Bruce Western & Steve Redburn eds., 2014). Some returning prisoners are fortunate to have stable housing waiting for them, but others do not. It is estimated that about 10% of former prisoners experience homelessness. Susan Turner, *Reentry*, *in* REFORMING CRIMINAL JUSTICE: PUNISHMENT, INCARCERATION, AND RELEASE 341, 355 (Erik Luna ed., 2017). As noted in Chapter 5, imprisonment may cause trauma and mental illness, or exacerbate preexisting mental conditions. Returning prisoners may also experience stigma that impairs their ability to secure employment, housing, and positive social relationships.[10]

The particular challenges of prisoner reentry are increasingly well-documented in a burgeoning body of research literature. *See, e.g.*, Turner, *supra*. Importantly, many of the difficulties experienced by returning prisoners, such as unemployment, homelessness, and weak family ties, are also correlated with recidivism. This may help to explain high rates of rearrest following release—44% in the first year alone (Fig. 8-2 above). The law tends not to draw sharp distinctions between probation and parole status, but parolees often present an especially daunting set of risks and needs. Supervision policies and practices that make sense for probationers are not necessarily as well-suited for parolees, and vice versa. In this respect, and in others, the supervised population presents tremendous diversity. One-size-fits-all approaches to supervision might warrant some skepticism.

B. EXPERIENCE OF COMMUNITY SUPERVISION

1. CONDITIONS

18 U.S.C. § 3563. Conditions of probation

(a) Mandatory conditions.—The court shall provide, as an explicit condition of a sentence of probation—

(1) for a felony, a misdemeanor, or an infraction, that the defendant not commit another Federal, State, or local crime during the term of probation;

(2) for a felony, that the defendant also abide by at least one condition set forth in subsection (b)(2) or (b)(12), unless the court has imposed a fine under this chapter, or unless the court finds on the

---

[10] A recent review of the social science literature has identified and assessed several distinct "mechanisms" of stigma experienced by the formerly incarcerated. Zoe R. Feingold, *The Stigma of Incarceration Experience*, 27 PSYCH., PUB. POL'Y & L. 550, 551 (2021). "Enacted" stigma is the direct experience of discrimination from others. "Perceived" stigma is the perception of negative attitudes in society toward the formerly incarcerated. "Anticipated" stigma is the expectation of rejection by others based on one's status as formerly incarcerated. And "internalized" stigma is the application of the negative attitudes of others to oneself.

record that extraordinary circumstances exist that would make such a condition plainly unreasonable, in which event the court shall impose one or more of the other conditions set forth under subsection (b);

(3) for a felony, a misdemeanor, or an infraction, that the defendant not unlawfully possess a controlled substance;

(4) for a domestic violence crime as defined in § 3561(b) by a defendant convicted of such an offense for the first time that the defendant attend a public, private, or private nonprofit offender rehabilitation program that has been approved by the court, in consultation with a State Coalition Against Domestic Violence or other appropriate experts, if an approved program is readily available within a 50-mile radius of the legal residence of the defendant;

(5) for a felony, a misdemeanor, or an infraction, that the defendant refrain from any unlawful use of a controlled substance and submit to one drug test within 15 days of release on probation and at least 2 periodic drug tests thereafter (as determined by the court) for use of a controlled substance, but the condition stated in this paragraph may be ameliorated or suspended by the court for any individual defendant if the defendant's presentence report or other reliable sentencing information indicates a low risk of future substance abuse by the defendant;

(6) that the defendant—

(A) make restitution [under specified statutes]; and

(B) pay the assessment imposed in accordance with § 3013 [$100 for felony conviction];

(7) that the defendant will notify the court of any material change in the defendant's economic circumstances that might affect the defendant's ability to pay restitution, fines, or special assessments;

(8) for a person required to register under the Sex Offender Registration and Notification Act, that the person comply with the requirements of that Act; and

(9) that the defendant cooperate in the collection of a DNA sample from the defendant if the collection of such a sample is authorized pursuant to § 3 of the DNA Analysis Backlog Elimination Act of 2000.

If the court has imposed and ordered execution of a fine and placed the defendant on probation, payment of the fine or adherence to the court-established installment schedule shall be a condition of the probation.

(b) Discretionary conditions.—The court may provide, as further conditions of a sentence of probation, to the extent that such conditions are reasonably related to the factors set forth in § 3553(a)(1) and (a)(2) and to the extent that such conditions involve only such deprivations of liberty or property as are reasonably necessary for the purposes indicated in § 3553(a)(2), that the defendant—

(1) support his dependents and meet other family responsibilities;

(2) make restitution [under a different statute than specified in (a)(6) above]

* * *

(4) work conscientiously at suitable employment or pursue conscientiously a course of study or vocational training that will equip him for suitable employment;

(5) refrain, in the case of an individual, from engaging in a specified occupation, business, or profession bearing a reasonably direct relationship to the conduct constituting the offense, or engage in such a specified occupation, business, or profession only to a stated degree or under stated circumstances;

(6) refrain from frequenting specified kinds of places or from associating unnecessarily with specified persons;

(7) refrain from excessive use of alcohol, or any use of a narcotic drug or other controlled substance * * * without a prescription by a licensed medical practitioner;

(8) refrain from possessing a firearm, destructive device, or other dangerous weapon;

(9) undergo available medical, psychiatric, or psychological treatment, including treatment for drug or alcohol dependency, as specified by the court, and remain in a specified institution if required for that purpose;

(10) remain in the custody of the Bureau of Prisons during nights, weekends, or other intervals of time, totaling no more than the lesser of one year or the term of imprisonment authorized for the offense, during the first year of the term of probation or supervised release;

(11) reside at, or participate in the program of, a community corrections facility * * * for all or part of the term of probation;

(12) work in community service as directed by the court;

(13) reside in a specified place or area, or refrain from residing in a specified place or area;

(14) remain within the jurisdiction of the court, unless granted permission to leave by the court or a probation officer;

(15) report to a probation officer as directed by the court or the probation officer;

(16) permit a probation officer to visit him at his home or elsewhere as specified by the court;

(17) answer inquiries by a probation officer and notify the probation officer promptly of any change in address or employment;

(18) notify the probation officer promptly if arrested or questioned by a law enforcement officer;

(19) remain at his place of residence during nonworking hours and, if the court finds it appropriate, that compliance with this condition be monitored by telephonic or electronic signaling devices * * *;

(20) comply with the terms of any court order or order of an administrative process pursuant to the law of a State, the District of Columbia, or any other possession or territory of the United States, requiring payments by the defendant for the support and maintenance of a child or of a child and the parent with whom the child is living;

(21) be ordered deported by a United States district court, or United States magistrate judge, pursuant to a stipulation entered into by the defendant and the United States under § 238(d)(5) of the Immigration and Nationality Act, except that, in the absence of a stipulation, the United States district court or a United States magistrate judge, may order deportation as a condition of probation, if, after notice and hearing pursuant to such section, the Attorney General demonstrates by clear and convincing evidence that the alien is deportable;

(22) satisfy such other conditions as the court may impose; or

(23) if required to register under the Sex Offender Registration and Notification Act, submit his person, and any property, house, residence, vehicle, papers, computer, other electronic communication or data storage devices or media, and effects to search at any time, with or without a warrant, by any law enforcement or probation officer with reasonable suspicion concerning a violation of a condition of probation or unlawful conduct by the person, and by any probation officer in the lawful discharge of the officer's supervision functions.

NOTES & QUESTIONS

1. **The Laundry List.** Section 3563 admittedly makes for some tedious reading, but it is important to appreciate the nature and sheer number of conditions that may be imposed on a probationer. Similar laundry lists are also found in state law. *See, e.g.,* Fiona Doherty, *Obey All Laws and Be Good: Probation and the Meaning of Recidivism*, 104 GEO. L. J. 291 (2016) (describing standard probation conditions adopted by sixteen different U.S. jurisdiction). Reviewing the federal list of mandatory and discretionary conditions, are there are any that strike you as especially onerous or potentially unfair? Note that the imposition of these conditions may subject a person to punishment, including revocation and incarceration, for behaviors that are not normally treated as criminal, such as excessive use of alcohol.

What do you suppose the point is of condition (a)(1)—don't violate any more criminal laws? After all, if the defendant commits another crime while on probation, he or she could be charged with the new offense in a new case. Note that the federal version of this condition is somewhat narrower than many state counterparts, some of which require probationers to obey *all* laws, civil and criminal alike. Doherty, *supra*, at 302.

Under § 3563, the judge does not have an entirely free hand with respect to the discretionary conditions; they are authorized only to the extent that they are "reasonably necessary for the purposes indicated in § 3553(a)(2)"—the basic federal purposes-of-punishment provision that we have encountered repeatedly.

2. **Conditions in the Guidelines.** Section 5B1.3 of the federal sentencing guidelines includes its own lengthy list of conditions, which mostly echo or expand upon the statutory laundry list. Some of the notable conditions that are recommended as "standard" conditions include:

- "The defendant shall answer truthfully the questions asked by the probation officer."[11]
- "The defendant shall live at a place approved by the probation officer. If the defendant plans to change where he or she lives or anything about his or her living arrangements (such as the people the defendant lives with), the defendant shall notify the probation officer at least 10 days before the change."
- "The defendant shall allow the probation officer to visit the defendant at any time at his or her home or elsewhere . . . ."
- "The defendant shall work full time (at least 30 hours per week) at a lawful type of employment, unless the probation officer excuses the defendant from doing so."
- "The defendant shall not communicate or interact with someone the defendant knows is engaged in criminal activity. If the defendant knows someone has been convicted of a felony, the defendant shall not knowingly communicate or interact with that person without first getting the permission of the probation officer."

§ 5B1.3(c).

3. **Supervised Release.** Conditions of supervised release in the federal system are governed by 18 U.S.C. § 3583(d), which closely tracks

[11] Conditions like these, which are also common in state supervision, may strike you as being in tension with the defendant's Fifth Amendment privilege against self-incrimination. Imagine, for instance, a PO asking a client, "Have you committed any crimes since our last meeting?" If the client had committed a crime, he or she might feel compelled to confess; otherwise, the client would be in violation of a condition of release and potentially subject to revocation. The Supreme Court faced a similar situation in *Minnesota v. Murphy*, 465 U.S. 420 (1984). The Court indicated that a PO's client may invoke the Fifth Amendment privilege and decline to answer questions from the PO that would result in self-incrimination. However, if the client does not invoke the privilege, any self-incrimination may be used against the client in a subsequent criminal proceeding. Additionally, the Court indicated that the PO normally need not to deliver the *Miranda* warnings before questioning a client because the client is not "in custody" when participating in a regular PO meeting.

§ 3563, including both mandatory and discretionary conditions. Similarly, § 5D1.3 of the guidelines, covering supervised release conditions, mirrors § 5B1.3, covering probation conditions.

4. **Problem: *United States v. Smith*.** Imagine that you are the sentencing judge in *United States v. Smith*, the case for which a hypothetical PSR was provided in Chapter 3. You intend to sentence Smith to the mandatory minimum prison term of ten years. Based on the offense of conviction, Smith is also subject to a mandatory five-year term of supervised release. Which of the discretionary conditions listed in 18 U.S.C. § 3563(b) would you impose to go along with the supervised release?

5. **Model Penal Code: Sentencing.** In contrast to federal law, the MPC:S includes no mandatory conditions for probation or postrelease supervision, but instead puts all conditions in the hands of the sentencing judge. The MPC:S further specifies, "No condition or set of conditions may be attached to a probation sanction that would place an unreasonable burden on the offender's ability to reintegrate into the law-abiding community." § 6.03(9). *See also* § 6.09(9) (postrelease supervision). The commentary explains:

> Although no data are maintained, reports from the field suggest that the average number of conditions has been growing in recent years. When these become too numerous or complex they can interfere with offenders' work and family obligations. Corrections professionals report that many probationers are unable to comply with them. Overburdensome sentence conditions can also have negative effects on the system as a whole. Probation agencies and courts in many jurisdictions cannot hope to respond effectively to all violations. Instead, according to knowledgeable observers, enforcement tends to be excessively lenient over the course of numerous transgressions, and then excessively harsh when an offender's repeated missteps have exhausted the patience of the probation officer and the court. The result can be a system that lacks credibility in the eyes of offenders, is demoralizing, and sacrifices the public-safety benefits of a more sensible reintegrative approach.

§ 6.03 cmmnt. j.

The MPC:S instructs that, in setting the term and conditions of supervision, the sentencing judge "should consult reliable risk- and needs-assessment instruments, when available." §§ 6.03(4), 6.09(4). You may recall that risk-assessment instruments were discussed above in Chapter 4. Some such instruments not only provide a risk score, but also identify each defendant's criminogenic needs, i.e., the risk factors, such as substance abuse, that could be targeted for treatment. It is not hard to imagine how a needs assessment could be taken into account in setting conditions of supervision, e.g., the defendant whose substance abuse contributes to his or her offending might be required to obtain substance-abuse treatment. But what if the defendant lacks reasonable access to a quality treatment program that would be suitable for his or her particular circumstances? The concerns raised by the MPC:S regarding unrealistic conditions suggest that attempting to address criminogenic needs through supervision conditions may sometimes do more harm than good.

6. **Conditions in a System of Discretionary Parole.** Both federal law and the MPC:S contemplate that a *judge* will establish the conditions of post-prison supervision at the time of sentencing. However, in a state with discretionary parole release, conditions are normally set by the parole board. Standard conditions in nearly all states include:

- Obey all federal, state, and local laws;
- Notify the PO of any change in residence;
- Report to the PO as directed and answer all reasonable inquiries by the PO; and
- Comply with requests for drug testing.

EBONY L. RUHLAND ET AL., UNIV. OF MINN., THE CONTINUING LEVERAGE OF RELEASING AUTHORITIES: FINDINGS FROM A NATIONAL SURVEY 36 (2017). Other standard conditions found in many states include maintaining gainful employment, not associating with people who have a criminal record, and abstaining from alcohol. A survey in 2008 found that each state has, on average, about nineteen standard conditions of parole release. Lawrence F. Travis & James Stacey, *A Half Century of Parole Rules: Conditions of Parole in the United States, 2008*, 38 J. CRIM. JUST. 604 (2010). Moreover, any number of additional special conditions may be layered on top of the standard conditions at the discretion of the parole board.

7. **Vagueness.** If you were told to abide by the conditions in § 3563, would you have a clear understanding of what was expected of you? Some state standard conditions seem even vaguer than the federal. For instance, Rhode Island tells its probationers to "keep the peace and remain on good behavior," while Georgia mandates "general good behavior." Doherty, *supra*, at 304. Similarly, probationers in some counties in Texas are told to "avoid persons or places of disreputable or harmful character." *Id.* at 307. However, constitutional challenges to such probation conditions on due process (vagueness) grounds have generally not been successful. *See id.* at 305 (discussing cases). In effect, these broad mandates to "be good" delegate discretion to the PO to determine what kinds of behavior will be treated as a violation. Such discretion provides much flexibility for the PO to deal with unusual cases, but do you see any downsides?

8. **Humane or Insidious?** Community supervision is typically seen as a more humane alternative to incarceration. However, an appreciation of the number and scope of the conditions that are commonly imposed on supervisees may suggest a less benign point of view. The degree of control asserted by the state over the supervised individual's life is quite extraordinary, extending well into the zone of private behavior that we normally regard as none of the state's business. To be sure, given the tight resource constraints of supervision agencies, there is a considerable gap between the control that is *asserted* and the control that is effectively *exercised*. Most violations likely pass undetected, and many of the violations

that are detected result in no meaningful state response. Should this allay concerns about state overreach?

Or consider this perspective. Our prisons and jails already tend to be overcrowded, and simply could not handle any but a small fraction of the individuals who are currently on supervision. (Recall Figure 8-1 above, depicting a supervised population that is about three times larger than the existing prison population.) Seen in this light, supervision is not really an alternative to incarceration at all. Instead, the true significance of supervision is that it permits the criminal justice system to assert control over the lives of a far larger number of individuals for a far longer period of time than the system would otherwise be capable of doing through incarceration alone. New technologies, moreover, enable more efficient and accurate tracking of supervisees beyond prison walls ("techno-corrections"). The subject individuals, of course, tend to be socioeconomically disadvantaged and disproportionately members of racial and ethnic minority groups. In Chapter 1, we noted the critical perspective that the system has a covert agenda of controlling the poor and marginalized without regard to traditional purposes of punishment. Should community supervision be seen in this light?

9. **The Role of Private Sector Businesses.** Private sector businesses have come to play a very significant role in community supervision. In Georgia, for instance, as of 2012, three dozen for-profit companies were providing supervision services, tacking on "enrollment" and other surcharges that can together exceed the fines and court costs imposed on supervisees. When more time on probation brings more revenue for the contractors, an obvious moral hazard threat arises—one borne out in the practice of one provider requesting that defendants serve their sentences consecutively, not concurrently. The incentive system is reinforced when firms tie their evaluation of individual officer performance to the amount of money secured from probationers, not to the officer's provision of service or the behavior of probationers. Wayne A. Logan & Ronald F. Wright, *Mercenary Criminal Justice*, 2014 U. ILL. L. REV. 1175, 1214.

10. **The Three R's and "Evidence-Based" Corrections.** Carl Wicklund, a former executive director of the American Probation and Parole Association, has recommended that supervision conditions comply with the "three R's." They should be "*realistic*—few in number and attainable; *relevant*—tailored to individual risks and needs; and *research-based*—supported by evidence that they can change behavior and improve public safety and offender reintegration." Edward Rhine, Joan Petersilia & Kevin Reitz, *The Future of Parole Release*, 46 CRIME & JUST. 279, 324 (2017).

These values, which are also reflected in the MPC:S's treatment of supervision conditions, have the *potential* to make supervision less intrusive and onerous. On the other hand, it should not be taken for granted that a more scientifically grounded (a.k.a "research-" or "evidence-based") approach will *necessarily* be more humane. Although few of the conditions that are currently in widespread use have been rigorously tested for risk-reduction benefits, it cannot be known what conditions will be supported by future research. Among other concerns, an uncritical embrace of whatever earns the label "evidence-based" may ultimately lead to a supervision system that involves *greater*, not less, state control over the lives of the poor and marginalized.[12] For a critique of the recent trend toward increased reliance on research and data in the criminal justice system, see Cecelia Klingele, *The Promise and Perils of Evidence-Based Corrections*, 91 NOTRE DAME L. REV. 537 (2016).

11. **Rationales.** Over time, three rationales have been advanced to justify probation conditions, although, as Professor Fiona Doherty notes, reason exists to question their continued validity:

> *The Benevolent Supervisor Theory*. Many of the current conditions of probation are relics of an era in which the probation officer was meant to be an enlightened and benevolent figure: a person who could humanely elevate members of the disadvantaged classes. But if courts once counted on the benevolent intentions of probation officers, however paternalistic that framework might have been, modern day probation systems focus heavily on enforcement and deterrence, not on a mission of benevolence. The public (or rather, public safety) has displaced the probationer as the true client of probation systems.
>
> *The Privilege Theory*. Although probation was once considered a special act of grace, it is now often the default sentence, rather than a discounted sentence. And courts are increasingly using probation as a method of supplementing incarceration, rather than as a method of avoiding incarceration altogether.
>
> *The Contract Theory*. This theory rests heavily on the validity of the privilege theory: a person agrees to be bound by the requirements of probation in return for the privilege of being on probation. To the extent that probation can be conceptualized as a contract, however, it is a contract of adhesion, rather than a negotiated contract. And the only way to opt out of the contract is to insist on incarceration, even if no one else would be incarcerated for the same crime.

Doherty, *supra*, at 297.

12. **Alternatives to the Alternative.** For a wide swath of criminal behavior, probation seems the more-or-less reflexively chosen sentence if incarceration is not imposed. Professor Cecelia Klingele argues that more consideration should be given to alternative dispositions:

> [T]here is a class of individuals for whom unconditional discharge—that is, conviction without further sanction—is sufficient punishment. While the concept of unconditional discharge as a

---

[12] Recall, for instance, the discussion of problem-solving courts in Chapter 3. As noted there, participation in a PSC can be connected to the criminal process in a variety of different ways, including as a condition of probation. Research provides sufficient support for the recidivism-reduction benefits of PSCs that they are routinely characterized as "evidence-based." Yet, they are highly intrusive and, for many participants, end up involving far greater burdens than would have been experienced through the conventional criminal process. PSCs have also been criticized on due process and racial disparity grounds. In the end, it remains controvertible whether PSCs have made for a more just and humane criminal justice system.

> freestanding punishment may seem foreign to modern ears, it is a sanction that still exists in the laws of several New England states, and it has been reintroduced in [the MPC:S].
>
> The process of being charged and convicted is inherently punitive and carries with it a lasting stigma. Conviction often brings with it serious consequences, both formal and informal. In addition to the social stigma that attaches to being a "convict," the formal legal consequences of conviction often include disenfranchisement, limits on occupational licensing, [loss of] public benefits eligibility, and a host of other noncriminal, but nonetheless punitive, sanctions that may endure for a lifetime. For many minor and first-time offenders, no sanction other than conviction itself may be needed to punish and deter: the shame and stigma of conviction will be adequate.

Rethinking the Use of Community Supervision, 103 J. CRIM. L. & CRIMINOLOGY 1015, 1055–56 (2013) (citations omitted). If unconditional discharge is unsatisfactory in a given case, Professor Klingele suggests that a fine, or even a short jail term, may be preferable to a term of probation with onerous conditions that the defendant is unlikely to satisfy. *Id.* at 1159.

13. **Idiosyncratic Conditions.** Thus far, we have focused on standard conditions of supervision—that is, conditions that are, by virtue of statutes or guidelines, mandated or recommended for all defendants or certain specified categories of defendants. However, judges (and parole boards) generally also have discretion to impose additional conditions that they believe to be appropriate in light of the crime and the individual circumstances of the defendant. Even if such conditions seem quite idiosyncratic or oppressive, they are often affirmed on appeal. *See* Andrew Horwitz, *Coercion, Pop-Psychology, and Judicial Moralizing: Some Proposals for Curbing Judicial Abuse of Probation Conditions*, 57 WASH. & LEE L. REV. 75 (2000). By way of illustration, consider the following case.

United States v. Gementera

379 F.3d 596 (9th Cir. 2004)

■ O'SCANNLAIN, J.

We must decide the legality of a supervised release condition that requires a convicted mail thief to spend a day standing outside a post office wearing a signboard stating, "I stole mail. This is my punishment."

I

Shawn Gementera pilfered letters from several mailboxes along San Francisco's Fulton Street on May 21, 2001. A police officer who observed the episode immediately detained Gementera and his partner in crime, Andrew Choi, who had been stuffing the stolen letters into his jacket as Gementera anxiously kept watch. After indictment, Gementera entered a plea agreement pursuant to which he pled guilty to mail theft, and the government dismissed a second count of receiving a stolen U.S. Treasury check.

The offense was not Gementera's first encounter with the law. Though only twenty-four years old at the time, Gementera's criminal history was lengthy for a man of his relative youth, and it was growing steadily more serious. At age nineteen, he was convicted of misdemeanor criminal mischief. He was twice convicted at age twenty of driving with a suspended license. At age twenty-two, a domestic dispute led to convictions for driving with a suspended license and for failing to provide proof of financial responsibility. By twenty-four, the conviction was misdemeanor battery. Other arrests and citations listed in the Presentence Investigation Report included possession of drug paraphernalia, additional driving offenses (most of which involved driving on a license suspended for his failure to take chemical tests), and, soon after his twenty-fifth birthday, taking a vehicle without the owner's consent.

On February 25, 2003, Judge Vaughn Walker of the United States District Court for the Northern District of California sentenced Gementera. The U.S. Sentencing Guidelines range was two to eight months incarceration; Judge Walker sentenced Gementera to the lower bound of the range, imposing two months incarceration and three years supervised release. He also imposed conditions of supervised release.

One such condition required Gementera to "perform 100 hours of community service," to consist of "standing in front of a postal facility in the city and county of San Francisco with a sandwich board which in large letters declares: 'I stole mail. This is my punishment.' " Gementera later filed a motion to correct the sentence by removing the sandwich board condition.

Judge Walker modified the sentence after inviting both parties to present "an alternative form or forms of public service that would better comport with the aims of the court." In lieu of the 100-hour signboard requirement, the district court imposed a four-part special condition in its stead. Three new terms, proposed jointly by counsel, mandated that the defendant observe postal patrons visiting the "lost or missing mail" window, write letters of apology to any identifiable victims of his crime, and deliver several lectures at a local school. It also included a scaled-down version of the signboard requirement:

> The defendant shall perform 1 day of 8 total hours of community service during which time he shall either (i) wear a two-sided sandwich board-style sign or (ii) carry a large two-sided sign stating, "I stole mail; this is my punishment," in front of a San Francisco postal facility identified by the probation officer. For the safety of defendant and general public, the postal facility designated shall be one that employs one or more security guards. Upon showing by defendant that this condition would likely impose upon defendant psychological harm or effect or

> result in unwarranted risk of harm to defendant, the public or postal employees, the probation officer may withdraw or modify this condition or apply to the court to withdraw or modify this condition. * * *

II

We first address Gementera's argument that the eight-hour sandwich board condition violates the Sentencing Reform Act.

The Sentencing Reform Act affords district courts broad discretion in fashioning appropriate conditions of supervised release, while mandating that such conditions serve legitimate objectives. * * * [A]ny condition must be "reasonably related" to "the nature and circumstances of the offense and the history and characteristics of the defendant." *See* 18 U.S.C. 3553(a)(1). Moreover, it must be both "reasonably related" to and "involve no greater deprivation of liberty than is reasonably necessary" to "afford adequate deterrence to criminal conduct," *see id.* at 3553(a)(2)(B), "protect the public from further crimes of the defendant," *see id.* at 3553(a)(2)(C), and "provide the defendant with needed educational or vocational training, medical care, or other correctional treatment in the most effective manner." *See id.* at 3553(a)(2)(D). Accordingly, the three legitimate statutory purposes of deterrence, protection of the public, and rehabilitation frame our analysis. *E.g., United States v. Rearden,* 349 F.3d 608, 618 (9th Cir. 2003).

Within these bounds, we have recognized the flexibility and considerable discretion the district courts exercise to impose conditions of supervised release, up to and including limits upon the exercise of fundamental rights. *See United States v. Bolinger,* 940 F.2d 478, 480 (9th Cir. 1991). This reflects, in part, their greater knowledge of and experience with the particular offenders before them. We have, for example, upheld conditions barring possession of sexually stimulating material, *United States v. Bee,* 162 F.3d 1232, 1234 (9th Cir. 1998), contact with minors, *id.,* association or membership in "motorcycle clubs," *Bolinger,* 940 F.2d at 480, and access to the internet, *Rearden,* 349 F.3d at 620.

Of course, the district court's discretion, while broad, is limited—most significantly here, by the statute's requirement that any condition reasonably relate to a legitimate statutory purpose. "This test is applied in a two-step process; first, this court must determine whether the sentencing judge imposed the conditions for permissible purposes, and then it must determine whether the conditions are reasonably related to the purposes." *United States v. Terrigno,* 838 F.2d 371, 374 (9th Cir. 1988). Gementera's appeal implicates both steps of the analysis.

A

Gementera first urges that the condition was imposed for an impermissible purpose of humiliation. He points to certain remarks of the district court at the first sentencing hearing:

> [H]e needs to understand the disapproval that society has for this kind of conduct, and that's the idea behind the humiliation. And it should be humiliation of having to stand and be labeled in front of people coming and going from a post office as somebody who has stolen the mail.

According to Gementera, these remarks, among others, indicate that the district court viewed humiliation as an end in itself and the condition's purpose.

Reading the record in context, however, we cannot but conclude that the district court's stated rationale aligned with permissible statutory objectives. At the second sentencing hearing, when the sentence was amended to what is now before us, the court explained: "[U]ltimately, the objective here is, one, to deter criminal conduct, and, number two, to rehabilitate the offender so that after he has paid his punishment, he does not reoffend, and a public expiation of having offended is, or at least it should be, rehabilitating in its effect." Although, in general, criminal punishment "is or at least should be humiliating," the court emphasized that "[h]umiliation is not the point." * * *

The court expressed particular concern that the defendant did not fully understand the gravity of his offense. Mail theft is an anonymous crime and, by "bring[ing] home to defendant that his conduct has palpable significance to real people within his community," the court aimed to break the defendant of the illusion that his theft was victimless or not serious. In short, it explained:

> While humiliation may well be—indeed likely will be—a feature of defendant's experience in standing before a post office with such a sign, the humiliation or shame he experiences should serve the salutary purpose of bringing defendant in close touch with the real significance of the crime he has acknowledged committing. Such an experience should have a specific rehabilitative effect on defendant that could not be accomplished by other means, certainly not by a more extended term of imprisonment.

Moreover, "[i]t will also have a deterrent effect on both this defendant and others who might not otherwise have been made aware of the real legal consequences of engaging in mail theft."

Read in its entirety, the record unambiguously establishes that the district court imposed the condition for the stated and legitimate statutory purpose of rehabilitation and, to a lesser extent, for general deterrence and for the protection of the public. We find no error in the condition's purpose.

B

Assuming the court articulated a legitimate purpose, Gementera asserts, under the second prong of our test, that humiliation or so-called "shaming" conditions are not "reasonably related" to rehabilitation. * * *

1

In evaluating probation and supervised release conditions, we have emphasized that the "reasonable relation" test is necessarily a "very flexible standard," and that such flexibility is necessary because of "our uncertainty about how rehabilitation is accomplished." [*United States v. Consuelo-Gonzalez,* 521 F.2d 259, 264 (9th Cir. 1975).] While our knowledge of rehabilitation is limited, we have nonetheless explicitly held that "a public apology may serve a rehabilitative purpose." *United States v. Clark,* 918 F.2d 843, 848 (9th Cir. 1990). Of course, for Gementera to prevail, introducing mere uncertainty about whether the condition aids rehabilitation does not suffice; rather, he must persuade us that the condition's supposed relationship to rehabilitation is unreasonable.

We considered a similar question in *Clark,* a case involving two police officers convicted of perjury in a civil rights lawsuit they brought against their department. In a deposition, the officers lied about a past episode in which they had falsely phoned in sick while actually en route to a vacation. As a probation condition, the court required them to publish a detailed apology in the local newspaper and in the police department newsletter. Though they challenged the condition based upon the First Amendment, we applied the same test applicable here, concluding that "[b]ecause the probation condition was reasonably related to the permissible end of rehabilitation, requiring it was not an abuse of discretion." *Id.* at 848.

Both *Clark* and *Gementera* involve defendants who seemingly failed to confront their wrongdoing, and the defendants in each case faced public expiation and apology. In *Clark,* the defendants had neither admitted guilt nor taken responsibility for their actions. Here, by contrast, the defendant pled guilty. His plea decision is unremarkable, though, given that he had been apprehended red-handed. Reflecting upon the defendant's criminal history, the court expressed concern that he did not fully understand the consequences of his continued criminality, and had not truly accepted responsibility. The court explained:

> [T]his is a young man who needs to be brought face-to-face with the consequences of his conduct. He's going down the wrong path in life. At age 24, committing this kind of an offense, he's already in a criminal history category 4, two-thirds of the way up the criminal history scale. He needs a wake-up call.

The court also determined that Gementera needed to be educated about the seriousness of mail crimes in particular, given that they might appear to be victimless:

> * * * He needs to be shown that stealing mail has victims; that there are people who depend upon the integrity and security of the mail in very important ways and that a crime of the kind

> that he committed abuses that trust which people place in the mail. He needs to see that there are people who count on the mails and integrity of the mails. How else can he be made to realize that than by coming face-to-face with people who use the postal service? That's the idea.

As with *Clark,* the district court concluded that public acknowledgment of one's offense—beyond the formal yet sterile plea in a cloistered courtroom—was necessary to his rehabilitation.

2 * * *

Gementera and amicus [Federal Public Defender for the Northern District of California] contend that shaming conditions cannot be rehabilitative because such conditions necessarily cause the offender to withdraw from society or otherwise inflict psychological damage, and they would erect a per se bar against such conditions. *See* Toni Massaro, *Shame, Culture, and American Criminal Law,* 89 MICH. L. REV. 1880, 1920–21 (1991) ("When it works, it redefines a person in a negative, often irreversible way" and the "psychological core" it affects cannot thereafter be rebuilt.). Though the district court had no scientific evidence before it, as Gementera complains, we do not insist upon such evidence in our deferential review. Moreover, the fact is that a vigorous, multifaceted, scholarly debate on shaming sanctions' efficacy, desirability, and underlying rationales continues within the academy. *See, e.g.,* Dan M. Kahan & Eric A. Posner, *Shaming White-Collar Criminals: A Proposal for Reform of the Federal Sentencing Guidelines,* 42 J. L. & ECON. 365, 371 (1999) (urging use of stigmatic punishments for white-collar criminals); Stephen P. Garvey, *Can Shaming Punishments Educate?,* 65 U. CHI. L. REV. 733, 738–39 (1998); Dan M. Kahan, *What Do Alternative Sanctions Mean?,* 63 U. CHI. L. REV. 591 (1996) (arguing that shaming sanctions reinforce public norms against criminality). By no means is this conversation one-sided.

Criminal offenses, and the penalties that accompany them, nearly always cause shame and embarrassment. Indeed, the mere fact of conviction, without which state-sponsored rehabilitation efforts do not commence, is stigmatic. The fact that a condition causes shame or embarrassment does not automatically render a condition objectionable; rather, such feelings generally signal the defendant's acknowledgment of his wrongdoing. * * * [T]he tendency to cause shame is insufficient to extinguish a condition's rehabilitative promise, at least insofar as required for our flexible reasonable relation test.

3

While the district court's sandwich board condition was somewhat crude, and by itself could entail risk of social withdrawal and stigmatization, it was coupled with more socially useful provisions, including lecturing at a high school and writing apologies, that might loosely be understood to promote the offender's social reintegration. *See*

Note, *Shame, Stigma, and Crime: Evaluating the Efficacy of Shaming Sanctions in Criminal Law,* 116 HARV. L. REV. 2186 (2003) (proposing how shaming sanctions may be structured to promote social reintegration most effectively); John Braithwaite, *Crime, Shame and Reintegration* 55 (1989) ("The crucial distinction is between shaming that is reintegrative and shaming that is disintegrative (stigmatization). Reintegrative shaming means that expressions of community disapproval, which may range from mild rebuke to degradation ceremonies, are followed by gestures of reacceptance into the community of law-abiding citizens."). We see this factor as highly significant. In short, here we consider not a stand-alone condition intended solely to humiliate, but rather a comprehensive set of provisions that expose the defendant to social disapprobation, but that also then provide an opportunity for Gementera to repair his relationship with society—first by seeking its forgiveness and then by making, as a member of the community, an independent contribution to the moral formation of its youth. These provisions, tailored to the specific needs of the offender, counsel in favor of concluding that the condition passes the threshold of being reasonably related to rehabilitation. * * *

5

Accordingly, we hold that the condition imposed upon Gementera reasonably related to the legitimate statutory objective of rehabilitation. In so holding, we are careful not to articulate a principle broader than that presented by the facts of this case. With care and specificity, the district court outlined a sensible logic underlying its conclusion that a set of conditions, including the signboard provision, but also including reintegrative provisions, would better promote this defendant's rehabilitation and amendment of life than would a lengthier term of incarceration. * * *

III

Gementera also urges that the sandwich board condition violates the Constitution. * * *

We turn then to the Eighth Amendment, which forbids the infliction of "cruel and unusual punishments." * * *

The Amendment's prohibition extends beyond those practices deemed barbarous in the 18th century, however. "[T]he words of the Amendment are not precise, and [ ] their scope is not static. The Amendment must draw its meaning from the evolving standards of decency that mark the progress of a maturing society." *Trop,* 356 U.S. at 100–01. * * *

The parties have offered no evidence whatsoever, aside from bare assertion, that shaming sanctions violate contemporary standards of decency. But the occasional imposition of such sanctions is hardly unusual, particularly in our state courts. *See, e.g.,* Stephen P. Garvey, *Can Shaming Punishments Educate?,* 65 U. CHI. L. REV. 733, 734 (1998) (describing proliferation of unorthodox and creative shaming punishments). Aside from a single case presenting concerns not at issue here,[17] we are aware of no case holding that contemporary shaming sanctions violate our Constitution's prohibition against cruel and unusual punishment.

We do, however, note that *Blanton v. N. Las Vegas,* 489 U.S. 538 (1989), is instructive, if only indirectly. In *Blanton,* the Court considered whether a Nevada DUI defendant was entitled to a jury trial pursuant to the Sixth Amendment. The inquiry into whether the offense constituted a petty crime not subject to the Sixth Amendment trial provision required the Court to evaluate the severity of the maximum authorized penalty. The statute provided a maximum sentence of six months or, alternatively, forty-eight hours of community service while dressed in distinctive garb identifying the defendant as a DUI offender, payment of a \$200–\$1000 fine, loss of driving license, and attendance at an alcohol abuse course. The Court wrote:

> We are also unpersuaded by the fact that, instead of a prison sentence, a DUI offender may be ordered to perform 48 hours of community service dressed in clothing identifying him as a DUI offender. Even assuming the outfit is the source of some embarrassment during the 48-hour period, such a penalty will be less embarrassing and less onerous than six months in jail.

Id. at 544. Just as the Court concluded that 48 hours of service dressed in distinctive DUI garb was less onerous than six months imprisonment, it would stretch reason to conclude that eight hours with a signboard, in lieu of incarceration, constitutes constitutionally cruel and unusual punishment. * * *

NOTES & QUESTIONS

1. **The Shaming Debate.** Shaming punishments were famously part of early American criminal justice—think scarlet letters and the pillory, which held defendants immobile and subject to ridicule in a public space.

---

[17] Gementera points to *Williams v. State,* 234 Ga.App. 37, 505 S.E.2d 816 (1998), in which a defendant convicted of soliciting sodomy was ordered to walk for ten days, between 7 p.m. and 11 p.m. each day, along that portion of the street where the solicitation occurred, holding a large sign stating, "BEWARE HIGH CRIME AREA." The police were to be notified in advance in order to monitor his performance and provide an appropriate level of safety. *Id.* at 817. While the court commended the trial judge for his "initiative" in developing a "new and creative form of sentencing which might very well have a positive effect on [the defendant] and be beneficial to the public," and explained that shaming punishments are not forbidden, it nonetheless found that the condition exposed the defendant to a constitutionally impermissible danger. *Id.* at 818.

* * * The condition in *Gementera* does not expose the defendant to any significant risk of danger. By contrast with *Williams,* the *Gementera* signboard is worn during eight hours of daylight during the business day, not at night; in front of a United States Post Office, not a "high crime" neighborhood where criminal solicitation occurs; and the sign's message does not provoke violence by threatening the criminal livelihood of those who illegally trade sex in a red light district, as the *Williams* sign might. Moreover, the district court in *Gementera* explicitly included a provision allowing for withdrawal of the condition upon a showing that the condition would impose a safety risk upon the defendant. Gementera made no such showing.

Such punishments fell into disuse in the nineteenth century. However, by the late twentieth century, shaming seemed to stage a comeback, fueled in part by popular appreciation for the "gotcha" value of subjecting criminal offenders to public ridicule. Examples include:

- A California defendant who was made to wear a t-shirt that read, "My record plus two-six packs equal four years," and on the back, "I am on felony probation for theft." *People v. Hackler,* 13 Cal. App. 4th 1049 (1993).
- An Illinois DWI defendant who was required to take out a newspaper ad with an apology and his mug shot. *People v. Johnson,* 528 N.E.2d 1360 (Ill. Ct. App. 1988).
- A New York DWI defendant who was made to affix a fluorescent sign to his license plate stating "CONVICTED DWI." *People v. Letterlough,* 655 N.E.2d 146 (N.Y. 1995).

Such requirements were frequently imposed as conditions of probation.

The reemergence of shaming provoked a lively academic debate, with some of the leading law review articles cited by the *Gementera* court.[13] Proponents of shaming advanced two major arguments. First, shaming was said to be a low-cost method of adding to the burdens of punishment, especially when compared to the expense of incarceration—in other words, deterrence on the cheap.[14] Indeed, because of the inherent tendency of shaming punishments to publicize themselves, such penalties might convey a deterrent message to a much wider audience than other punishments would. For instance, it is likely that many more people learned of Gementera's punishment by viewing him with his sandwich board than would have heard of the case if a more conventional sentence had been used. Second, because shaming enlists the public in condemnation of the offense, the punishment conveys the message that the offense was not merely a technical violation of the law, but also a violation of the community's sense of right and wrong. It was argued that the direct experience of condemnation by the community might promote an internalization of the moral norm that was violated—in other words, rehabilitation.

Opponents of shaming raised several practical and ethical objections. For instance, some shaming sanctions might endanger the defendant's safety by enabling and perhaps even implicitly encouraging public violence against the defendant. More important, though, has been the argument that shaming is not effective at reducing crime and may actually prove counterproductive. Shaming sanctions, it turns out, may provoke different psychological responses in the defendant than proponents assume. Psychological researchers distinguish between feelings of "guilt" and

---

[13] For a more elaborate recapitulation of the academic debate, see MICHAEL O'HEAR, PRISONS AND PUNISHMENT IN AMERICA: EXAMINING THE FACTS 62–64 (2018). For the recantation of a leading advocate of shaming, see Dan Kahan, *What's Really Wrong With Shaming Sanctions,* 84 TEX. L. REV. 2075 (2006).

[14] As noted in Chapter 1, the pertinent costs of incarceration might not be limited to the fiscal burdens imposed on taxpayers, but might also extend to third parties who are harmed by a defendant's removal from the community, e.g., minor children who depend on the defendant's caregiving or financial support.

"shame." June Price Tangney et al., *Relation of Shame and Guilt to Constructive Versus Disruptive Responses to Anger Across the Lifespan*, 70 J. PERSONALITY & SOC. PSYCHOL. 797 (1996). Feelings of guilt focus on a specific act, while shame is a negative feeling about one's whole self. Some individuals are more prone to guilt, and others to shame. A shaming punishment may produce varying degrees of guilt and shame in different defendants. Feelings of shame should be of concern, though, because they are associated with anger and hostility—responses that seem inconsistent with rehabilitation. Indeed, some research finds a connection between an individual's difficulty in managing feelings of shame and engaging in behaviors like bullying and repeat-offending. Nathan Harris, *Shame in Criminological Theory*, *in* ENCYCLOPEDIA OF CRIMINOLOGY AND CRIMINAL JUSTICE (Gerben Bruinsma & David Weisburd eds., 2013).

In light of the risk that sanctions might make some offenders *more* likely to reoffend, a leading proponent of shaming, John Braithwaite, has distinguished between "reintegrative" and "disintegrative" shaming. CRIME, SHAME AND REINTEGRATION 55 (1989). Disintegrative shaming stigmatizes and isolates the offender, diminishing the likelihood of reform and improvement. By contrast, "reintegrative shaming means that expressions of community disapproval, which may range from mild rebuke to degradation ceremonies, are followed by gestures of reacceptance into the community of law-abiding citizens." Reintegration, another commenter observes, "can be seen to have occurred when shaming is respectful, distinguishes between the person and their actions, [and] concludes with forgiveness or decertification of deviance." Harris, *supra*. Put differently, reintegrative shaming tries to elicit feelings of guilt, rather than feelings of shame. This may allow the defendant to take responsibility for his or her actions without developing deeply negative self-perceptions that might increase recidivism risk. Indeed, some research does support the prediction that reintegrative shaming may help to reduce recidivism rates. Alana Saulnier & Diane Sivasubramaniam, *Restorative Justice: Underlying Mechanisms and Future Directions*, 18 NEW CRIM. L. REV. 510, 520 (2015).

What aspects of Gementera's sentence led the Ninth Circuit to characterize it as reintegrative? What role did the characterization play in the court's decision to affirm the sentence? Are you convinced by the court's reasoning?

2. **Who Has What Burden?** Did the Ninth Circuit conclude that Gementera most likely would be rehabilitated by his sandwich board condition? What exactly is the legal test for appellate review of a release condition? Is this too deferential to sentencing judges who come up with their own non-standard conditions—and who may or may not have any understanding of the research literature on rehabilitation?

3. **Cruel and Unusual?** Like Gementera, defendants sometimes challenge idiosyncratic conditions as a violation of the Eighth Amendment. Why did Gementera lose on his constitutional claim? How did the Ninth Circuit distinguish the *Williams* case from Georgia (see footnote 17)? How was the Supreme Court's decision in *Blanton*, which was not an Eighth Amendment case, relevant to the Ninth Circuit's analysis?

A persistent challenge for defendants appealing their release conditions is the assumption that freedom in the community—no matter the strings attached—is almost inherently a less severe punishment than incarceration. If the defendant could have been locked up (or, in Gementera's case, locked up for longer), how can the defendant possibly complain about any of the conditions of his or her release?

Do you find this line of thinking persuasive?

4. **Cases Going the Other Way.** Conditions of release are occasionally rejected as not adequately justified. For instance, in each of the three cases cited in note 1 above (*Hackler*, *Johnson*, and *Letterlough*), the challenged condition was overturned on appeal.

Or, moving outside the shaming context, consider *United States v. Hamilton*, 986 F.3d 413 (4th Cir. 2021). After his conviction for possession of child pornography, the defendant was sentenced to prison and a lifetime term of supervised release, including the condition that he "must not work in any type of employment without the prior approval of the probation officer." The district judge apparently wished to give the PO an ability to block Hamilton from working in places where he would have access to children. On appeal, however, the Fourth Circuit found the condition overbroad and lacking a sufficient nexus to Hamilton's offense. "There must be some tailoring of the condition to the circumstances of the case," the court held. *Id.* at 420. The Fourth Circuit further objected to the condition's vesting of "completely unguided discretion" in the PO. "Unlike an employment condition that prohibits certain types of employment or jobs that involve interacting with certain groups of people, this condition provides Hamilton's probation officer with no bounds on how to exercise his discretion." *Id.* However, the court suggested that the condition might have been affirmed if it had contained a directive for the PO "to approve employment opportunities that pose minimal risk of problematic contact with children." *Id.* at 420–21. Additionally, the court did affirm two other conditions placed on Hamilton: (1) "You must not access the Internet except for reasons approved in advance by the probation officer," and (2) "You must not go to, or remain at, any place where you know children under the age of 18 are likely to be, including parks, schools, playgrounds, ball fields, childcare facilities, movies, and arcades."

Hamilton illustrates a trend toward more onerous special conditions of release for individuals convicted of sexual offenses, which are often, but not always, affirmed on appeal. *Hamilton* provides a helpful summary of the mixed case law on Internet bans, which have generated considerable litigation. *Id.* at 421–23. Is it truly possible in our contemporary society for a returning prisoner to achieve "reintegration" without being able to use the Internet? *Cf. Packingham v. North Carolina,* 137 S. Ct. 1730, 1737 (2017) (invalidating on First Amendment grounds state law making it a felony for convicted sex offender to access the Internet; "Even convicted criminals—and in some instances especially convicted criminals—might receive legitimate benefits from these means for access to the world of ideas, in particular if they seek to reform and to pursue lawful and rewarding lives.").

5. **Fundamental Rights.** As the *Gementera* court indicated, the deference shown to the sentencing judge's choice of conditions generally extends even to those conditions that restrict the exercise of fundamental rights, such as the right to associate with others and the right to possess First-Amendment-protected materials. A much-discussed example is *State v. Oakley*, 629 N.W.2d 200 (Wis. 2001). Oakley, a father of nine children, was convicted of intentionally failing to pay child support. As a condition of his probation, the sentencing judge ordered Oakley not to have any more children unless he could show that he was supporting his existing offspring and would also be able to support the new child.

On appeal, Oakley argued that the condition violated his fundamental right to procreate. The Wisconsin Supreme Court first rejected Oakley's argument that his no-procreation condition was subject to strict scrutiny. The court observed, "[G]iven that a convicted felon does not stand in the same position as someone who has not been convicted of a crime, we have previously stated that conditions of probation may impinge upon constitutional rights as long as they are not overly broad and are reasonably related to the person's rehabilitation." *Id.* at 210 (citation and internal quotation marks omitted). The court then held this test was satisfied by the no-procreation condition:

> [T]he condition is reasonably related to the goal of rehabilitation. A condition is reasonably related to the goal of rehabilitation if it assists the convicted individual in conforming his or her conduct to the law. Here, Oakley was convicted of intentionally refusing to support his children. The condition at bar will prevent him from adding victims if he continues to intentionally refuse to support his children. As the State argues, the condition essentially bans Oakley from violating the law again. Future violations of the law would be detrimental to Oakley's rehabilitation, which necessitates preventing him from continuing to disregard its dictates.

Id. at 213 (citations omitted). The court further observed that the sentencing judge had "preserved much of Oakley's liberty by imposing probation with conditions rather than the more punitive option of imprisonment." *Id.* at 212–13. Again, we see the suggestion that, where a constitutionally permissible sentence of incarceration was also on the table, the defendant can hardly complain that the more limited restrictions of probation are overbroad.

The Supreme Court has also indicated that Fourth Amendment protections may be limited by supervision conditions. *See, e.g., Samson v. California*, 547 U.S. 843 (2006) (upholding against Fourth Amendment challenge a California law requiring, as condition of parole, that parolee must "agree in writing to be subject to search or seizure by a parole officer or other peace officer at any time of the day or night, with or without a search warrant and with or without cause"). The Court has also held that that the Fourth Amendment exclusionary rule does not apply in revocation proceedings. *Pa. Bd. of Prob. & Parole v. Scott*, 524 U.S. 357 (1998). Thus, a person's supervision may be revoked on the basis of evidence that was obtained in violation of the person's Fourth Amendment rights.

PROBLEM 8-1: A SANDWICH BOARD FOR BANK ROBBERY?

Recall *United States v. Blake*, the bank robbery case discussed in Problem 1-1 in Chapter 1. The judge imposed a probationary sentence. Imagine that the judge included, as a condition, that Blake stand outside the bank she robbed for eight hours wearing a sandwich board that read, "I robbed this bank. This is my punishment." Assume that you are defense counsel. Based on *Gementara*, how might you argue on appeal that the condition should be overturned? How do you think the appellate court would respond to these arguments?

2. SUPERVISION

The PO plays a crucial role in determining the quality of the defendant's experience on supervision. Different POs have different styles, with some most heavily emphasizing the enforcement of conditions and others focused more on motivation and support—the classic dichotomy of cop versus social worker. Whatever their priorities, though, POs are apt to feel constrained by inadequate time and resources to do all that they would like to do with their charges. Additionally, POs operate within correctional bureaucracies, subject to the oversight of supervisors who have their own priorities and management styles, which may impose further constraints on what the field agents can accomplish.

Even acknowledging such limitations, it must be said that POs exercise a great deal of power over the lives of their supervisees. Agents give practical meaning to the sometimes vague conditions imposed by the judge or parole board, e.g., "remain on good behavior." They make decisions about how closely to monitor their supervisees, e.g., through unannounced home visits; whether to investigate possible violations; and the rigor with which conditions are enforced. *See* Fiona Doherty, *Obey All Laws and Be Good: Probation and the Meaning of Recidivism*, 104 GEO. L. J. 291, 347 (2016) (noting that "probation officers arguably inhabit the roles of victim, witness, investigator, prosecutor, and judge, all in the same case"); Cecelia Klingele, *Rethinking the Use of Community Supervision*, 103 J. CRIM. L. & CRIMINOLOGY 1015, 1035–40 (2013).

Many of the policy questions that we have invited you to consider regarding the judge's role at sentencing could also be raised with respect to the PO's role in supervision. What safeguards should be in place, if any, to ensure similar treatment for similar cases? How can the effects of implicit bias be minimized in discretionary decisionmaking? Where should the balance be struck between efficiency and due process? How much recidivism risk is tolerable? To what extent does a paternalistic desire to improve a defendant's life justify intrusions into what is normally considered the sphere of private choice? And, when it comes to reducing recidivism risk, what actually works?

The following excerpt summarizes some of the key research on the latter question.

Edward J. Latessa & Myrinda Schweitzer, Community Supervision and Violent Offenders: What the Research Tells Us and How to Improve Outcomes

103 MARQ. L. REV. 911 (2020)

[W]hat does the research tell us about traditional community supervision? Bonta and his colleagues provided some answers with preliminary results from a meta-analysis of the effects of community supervision on recidivism.[40] Examining fifteen studies, they found that decreases in recidivism were extremely small, and findings for violent offenders were even worse. They concluded that "[o]n the whole, community supervision does not appear to work very well." To further explore this issue, they examined traditional probation and parole officer interactions with offenders and concluded that there are several reasons community supervision is often not effective:

- They are too brief to have an impact.
- Conversations focus almost exclusively on monitoring compliance with conditions (and therefore emphasize external controls on behavior rather than developing an internal rationale for pro-social behavior).
- The relationship is often more confrontational and authoritarian in nature than helpful.
- What is targeted for change is not always based on assessment.
- The more areas discussed, the less effective the contact.

Figures 3(a) and 3(b) illustrate these points by showing the effects of time spent on compliance and criminogenic needs on recidivism. As seen in this figure, the more time spent on compliance the higher the failure rates. Conversely, as time spent discussing criminogenic needs increased, recidivism rates decreased. Recognizing the value in these results, scholars proposed that community supervision agencies adopt the Risk, Need, Responsivity Model, a model derived from the principles of effective intervention.

[40] *See generally* James Bonta, Tanya Rugge, Terri-Lynne Scott, Guy Bourgon & Annie K. Yessine, *Exploring the Black Box of Community Supervision*, 47 J. OFFENDER REHABILITATION 248 (2008).

Figure 3(A): Recidivism Rate and Time Spent on Compliance

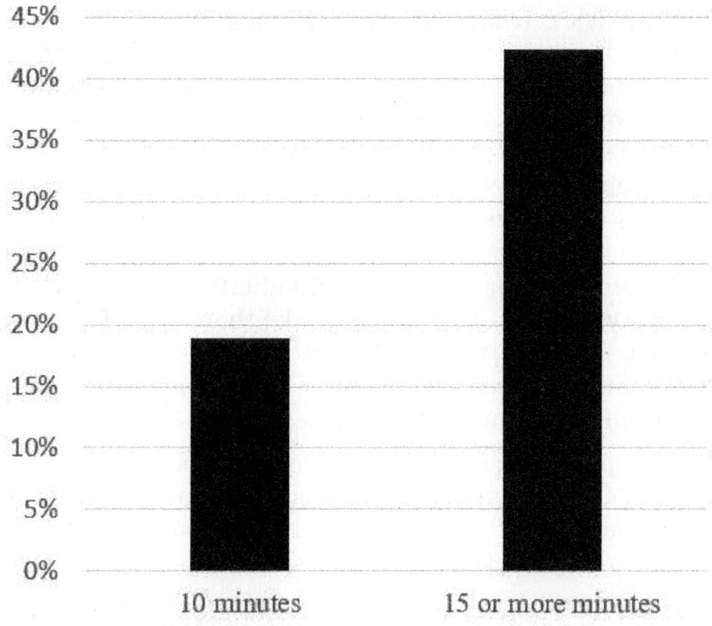

Figure 3(B): Recidivism Rate and Time Spent on Criminogenic Needs

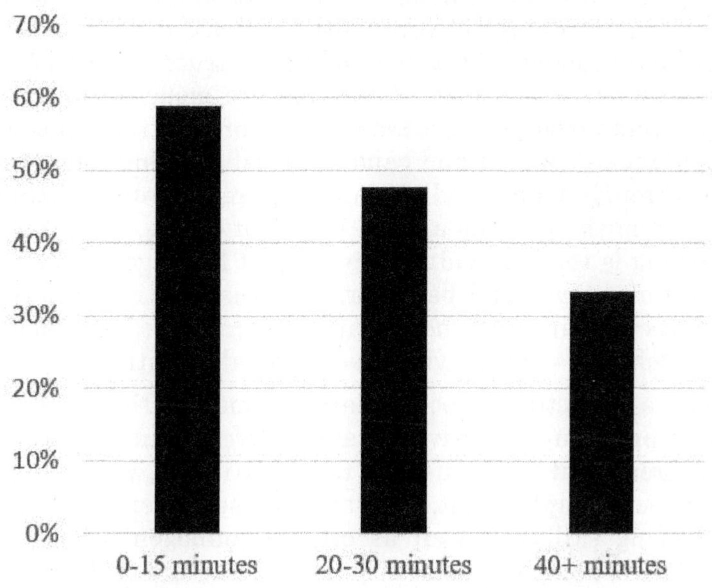

IV. THE RISK, NEED AND RESPONSIVITY MODEL

Nearly thirty years of research has indicated that the most effective programs are based on some principles of effective intervention, commonly referred to as the RNR model (Risk, Need and Responsivity). In this context, risk refers to the risk or probability of reoffending. The risk principle focuses on "who" should be the focus of intensive programming and services. The essence of the risk principle is that we should reserve our more intensive programs for higher risk offenders, and that intensive interventions can increase recidivism for lower risk individuals. There are several reasons why intensive programs can have a negative effect on low risk people. First, an exposure or contamination effect can occur when low risk offenders are mixed in with higher risk offenders. Second, placing low risk individuals in intensive programs takes them away from the things that make them low risk to begin with (e.g., their jobs, school, pro-social family members, and friends). Third, increased surveillance and supervision conditions can lead to more technical violations and subsequent revocations. * * *

The second principle, the need principle, helps us identify "what" to target for behavioral change—that is, dynamic risk factors (i.e. criminogenic needs) that are highly correlated with criminal conduct. The need principle states that programs should assess and target crime-producing needs, such as antisocial attitudes, anti-social peer associations, substance abuse, impulsivity, lack of problem-solving skills, and self-control, just to name a few. Thus, programs should ensure that most interventions are focused on these factors.

The third principle, responsivity, helps us determine "how" to deliver treatment by using behavioral interventions in a way that matches offenders' personalities, abilities, and motivation levels, while ensuring programs and services are delivered with fidelity. Examples of behavioral programs would include those that follow a structured social learning approach where new skills and behaviors are modeled, practiced, and consistently reinforced. Social learning is one of the strongest theories we have to explain how we act and behave. Social learning refers to several processes through which individuals acquire attitudes, behavior, or knowledge from the persons around them. Of course, the problem with social learning is that individuals do not just learn good behavior from others; they also learn bad behavior, which is why it is referred to as *structured* social learning, where staff are formally taught how to both model new behaviors and provide instrumental conditioning.

Within a structured social learning model, the most effective approach is providing cognitive behavioral treatment (CBT). Cognitive behavioral treatment can be used to target attitudes, values and beliefs, anti-social peers, employment, substance abuse, anger, impulsivity, and problem-solving skills, as well as other criminogenic needs. If done properly, CBT not only helps participants restructure their thinking, but it is also a vehicle for teaching new skills. The principles of CBT are that thinking affects behavior; anti-social, distorted, unproductive irrational thinking can lead to antisocial and unproductive behavior; thinking can be influenced; and we can change how we feel and behave by changing what we think. The advantages of using a CBT approach is that it can be done in any setting and in groups or one-on-one sessions; existing staff can be trained; it is relatively affordable to deliver; and there are a wide range of curricula available, including several that are free to use. There is also a great deal of research that demonstrates that cognitive behavioral programs can reduce recidivism. For example, according to the National Institute of Justice, "[c]ognitive behavioral therapy has been found to be effective with juvenile and adult offenders; substance abusing and violent offenders; and probationers, prisoners, and parolees. It is effective in various criminal justice settings, both in institutions and in the community, and addresses a host of problems associated with criminal behavior."[62] * * *

VI. PRACTICE RECOMMENDATIONS

As agencies adopt evidence-based decision-making, policies will begin to shape who is served and what needs are targeted, as well as what interventions are used to increase public safety and decrease recidivism. Here, the practical application of the RNR model takes priority. * * *

A. *Improve Assessment*

Community supervision agencies should assess offenders with a validated risk and need assessment tool. For individuals under supervision for a violent charge, this means officers should assess their risk for both violent and general recidivism. Once assessed, officers should use the results of the assessment to identify those higher risk offenders most appropriate for services and supervision and minimize services for those identified as low risk to reoffend.

B. *Improve Supervision Practices*

For those identified as appropriate for services and supervision, the results of the assessment tool(s) should also help determine what problem areas are targeted for change. In this way, for each offender on an officer's caseload, the officer should prioritize the criminogenic needs that the validated risk/needs assessment indicated are contributing to the likelihood that the offender will engage in future criminal behavior. * * *

Once the criminogenic needs are prioritized, officers should apply techniques that are known to impact behavior change and do so in a way that meets the individual characteristics of the offender. As noted above, cognitive-behavioral approaches grounded in social learning theory have been found to be the most effective with correctional populations. Therefore, officers should use CBT interventions during contact sessions

[62] [Patrick Clark, *Preventing Future Crime with Cognitive Behavioral Therapy*, NAT'L INST. JUST. J., Apr. 2010, at 22.]

to target criminogenic needs. Officers should also refer offenders to providers in the community that use CBT to focus on needs that cannot be fully met during contact sessions. Further, officers should attempt to address any barriers that may prevent the offender from complying with treatment or supervision. For example, an officer may work with an offender to increase motivation to change before referring the offender to a treatment program.

C. *Improve the Delivery of Services for Specific Groups*

Research suggests that even violent offenders benefit from cognitive-behavioral interventions. The same is true of sexual offenders. To successfully reduce the risk to reoffend for specific populations, interventions should target the thinking behind the behavior, provide practice opportunities for new thinking and new behaviors, and reinforce the use of newly developed attitudes, thoughts, and behaviors. * * *

D. *Monitor Internal and External Service Delivery*

Translating research into practice is an ongoing challenge for community supervision agencies and officers. While many agencies have been able to implement bits and pieces of the RNR model, few are able to consistently adhere to the principles. Therefore, it is important for agencies to monitor both the internal and external delivery of services. For example, agencies should measure incremental changes in offender behavior through drug tests, treatment attendance, adherence to court conditions, and reassessment of risk and need tool(s). Agencies should also measure staff performance through group and contact session observation, inter-rater reliability methods, file reviews, client satisfaction surveys, and other feedback mechanisms.

E. *Core Correctional Practices*

As community supervision agencies begin to translate the RNR model into practice, research suggests that training officers in core correctional practices can influence offender outcomes. Core Correctional Practices (CCP) are a combination of techniques that corrections professionals can use to more effectively interact with people and manage behavior. These practices include anti-criminal modeling, effective reinforcement and disapproval, use of authority, and quality interpersonal relationships. CCP skills to support individual change include cognitive restructuring, problem-solving techniques, and structured skill building. Prior research has shown these strategies support the implementation of correctional interventions and play a critical role in creating a learning environment for individual change. Moreover, these techniques are consistent with the principles of risk, need, and responsivity, and when implemented properly, equip professionals with tools to be effective agents of long-term behavior change. Figure 8 shows the results from a meta-analysis that examined the effects of using CCPs. As seen, trained officers were more effective in reducing recidivism than those that were not.[90]

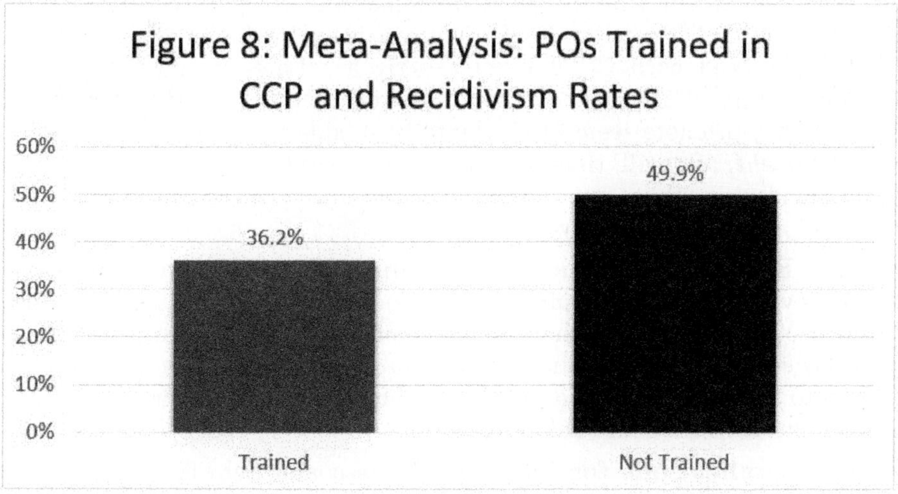

Incorporating CCP into supervision and treatment requires probation and parole officers to move from a control-oriented approach to one that is designed to facilitate behavioral change by *teaching* offenders' new ways to behave, rather than simply relying on external controls. Considering the above practice implications, scholars have recently challenged officers to consider themselves a coach, rather than a referee.[92] Lovins, Cullen, Latessa, and Jonson suggest that being a coach requires a different approach to community supervision where the officer aims to help the person under supervision not only adhere to the rules of supervision but also change their behavior to stay out of trouble. With this approach, officers are trained to help individuals under supervision develop new skills to anticipate and manage high risk situations successfully. This requires officers to develop and refine the skills described above. Lovins, Cullen, Latessa, and Jonson suggest that "[s]uch an identity is important because it organizes our action, motivates our choices, and provides meaning to our lives." We see this in the world of sports where the identity as a coach carries with it status, expertise, obligation, purpose, and accountability. Similarly, having officers build an identity as a coach has the potential to open new ways of envisioning their role and how they can be effective.

---

[90] [Nick Chadwick, Angela DeWolf & Ralph Serin, *Effectively Training Community Supervision Officers: A Meta-Analytic Review of the Impact on Offender Outcome*, 42 CRIM. JUST. & BEHAV. 977, 985–86 (2015).]

[92] *See* Brian K. Lovins, Francis T. Cullen, Edward F. Latessa, & Cheryl Lero Jonson, *Probation Officer as a Coach: Building a New Professional Identity*, FED. PROB., June 2018, at 13, 13.

NOTES & QUESTIONS

1. **RNR and CCP.** The recommendations of Latessa and Schweitzer are grounded in the concepts of Risk, Need, and Responsivity (RNR) and Core Correctional Practices (CCP). We considered RNR in Chapter 1, but what is involved with CCP? What exactly are Latessa and Schweitzer's recommendations, and how do they flow from RNR? Does the correctional mindset they promote seem fundamentally at odds with the principle that it is *punishment*, after all, that is being administered? For instance, did their recommendation that supervision agencies utilize "client satisfaction surveys" seem dissonant to you?

2. **Effectiveness and Intrusiveness.** Latessa and Schweitzer's article is very much in the spirit of the broader movement toward "evidence-based decisionmaking" in the criminal justice system. As we noted in the previous section, an increasing reliance on research and data may help the system to achieve lower recidivism rates, but potentially at the cost of much greater intrusiveness into defendants' lives.

3. **Implications for Lawyers.** Latessa and Schweitzer's article is addressed more to supervision agencies than to lawyers and judges, but do the research findings they discuss also have implications for legal practitioners? For instance, should prosecutors and defense lawyers try to familiarize themselves with the policies and practices of the community supervision agencies in the jurisdictions where they practice? Might this affect the positions they take and arguments they make with respect to the appropriateness of a supervision sentence, or the terms and conditions of supervision sentences?

4. **Treated Like "Children" . . . or "Animals"?** In 2016–2017, researchers at Robina Institute of Criminal Law and Criminal Justice at the University of Minnesota Law School conducted a series of focus groups with probationers and POs in six jurisdictions located in four different states. Michelle S. Phelps & Ebony L. Ruhland, *Governing Marginality: Coercion and Care in Probation*, ___ SOC. PROBLEMS ___ (2021). Their findings included the following:

> POs spoke at length about how much they "cared" about "clients," detailing how they provided social work services * * *. Yet this care was braided with the coercion of the criminal justice system—one of the ways officers "helped" was providing "accountability," using the threat of sanctions to force adults to become "responsible for their actions." * * * Other officers implicitly and explicitly referred to clients as their "children" * * * Other POs more explicitly pushed back against the rhetoric of probation as social work, adopting a law enforcement framework to argue that POs were poorly equipped, untrained, and not compensated to be social workers.
>
> Perhaps reflecting this variation in approaches, the focus groups with adults on probation demonstrated a huge degree of variation in evaluating supervisory relationships as care. * * *
>
> In the worst cases participants experienced treatment from POs as not just infantilizing, but dehumanizing. When one man

said, "They treat us like animals," there was vocal agreement in his focus group.

5. **Resource Constraints.** On average, states spend about twenty-three times more per prisoner than they do per probationer. Ronald Corbett, *The Burdens of Leniency: The Changing Face of Probation*, 99 MINN. L. REV. 1697 (2015). Miserly budgets may undermine the effectiveness of community supervision. For instance, while a caseload of thirty supervisees per PO has traditionally been regarded as ideal, actual caseloads of 100:1 are not uncommon, and caseloads of 200:1 or even 300:1 are not unheard of.[15] The MPC:S reporters observe, "Symptoms of shortfalls in funding include such practices as 'bunker' probation (where line probation officers seldom or never leave their offices) and 'kiosk' probation (where probationers can satisfy reporting requirements by interacting with an ATM-like machine)." *Id.*

A 2006 survey of state parole supervision agencies found that 14% of parolees were required to have a weekly face-to-face meeting with a PO and 54% only a monthly meeting. THOMAS P. BONCZAR, U.S. DEP'T OF JUSTICE, CHARACTERISTICS OF STATE PAROLE SUPERVISING AGENCIES, 2006, at 4 (2008). An additional 13% had no regular reporting requirement at all. Through some combination of necessity and design, it is apparent that many of the individuals who are formally on supervision are in practice left more-or-less to their own devices. Should this reality allay concerns regarding conditions that are vague or seem excessively intrusive?

A few states have experimented with incentive-based funding for supervision agencies, reportedly with some success. Incentive-based funding provides financial rewards to agencies that succeed in improving outcomes of interest, such as reduced revocations or recidivism. PEW CHARITABLE TRUSTS, POLICY REFORMS CAN STRENGTHEN COMMUNITY SUPERVISION 54–55 (2020).

3. VIOLATIONS & REVOCATION

a. POTENTIAL RESPONSES TO VIOLATIONS

Revocations of probation and parole have contributed significantly to mass incarceration in the United States. Revocations are thought to account for about half of jail admissions and one-third of prison admissions. Cecilia Klingele, *Rethinking Community Supervision*, 103 J. CRIM. L. & CRIMINOLOGY 1015, 1019 (2013). "These statistics suggest that rather than serving as an alternative, community supervision often is no more than a deferred sentence of incarceration." *Id.* Given the high social costs of revocations—to taxpayers, to defendants, and to their families—it would seem desirable for alternatives to revocation to be given careful consideration as a response to many or most violations of

[15] MPC:S § 6.03 rptrs. note b. Comprehensive national data on supervision practices are hard to come by. A 2006 national survey of parole-only supervision agencies found an average of forty-nine parolees per PO. THOMAS P. BONCZAR, U.S. DEP'T OF JUSTICE, CHARACTERISTICS OF STATE PAROLE SUPERVISING AGENCIES, 2006, at 3 (2008).

release conditions. Consider the federal framework for responding to violations.

18 U.S.C. § 3565. Revocation of probation

(a) Continuation or revocation.—If the defendant violates a condition of probation at any time prior to the expiration or termination of the term of probation, the court may, after a hearing pursuant to Rule 32.1 of the Federal Rules of Criminal Procedure, and after considering the factors set forth in section 3553(a) to the extent that they are applicable—

> **(1)** continue him on probation, with or without extending the term or modifying or enlarging the conditions; or
>
> **(2)** revoke the sentence of probation and resentence the defendant under subchapter A.

(b) Mandatory revocation for possession of controlled substance or firearm or refusal to comply with drug testing.—If the defendant—

> **(1)** possesses a controlled substance in violation of the condition set forth in section 3563(a)(3);
>
> **(2)** possesses a firearm, as such term is defined in section 921 of this title, in violation of Federal law, or otherwise violates a condition of probation prohibiting the defendant from possessing a firearm;
>
> **(3)** refuses to comply with drug testing, thereby violating the condition imposed by section 3563(a)(4); or
>
> **(4)** as a part of drug testing, tests positive for illegal controlled substances more than 3 times over the course of 1 year;

the court shall revoke the sentence of probation and resentence the defendant under subchapter A to a sentence that includes a term of imprisonment.

United States Sentencing Guidelines (2021)

§ 7B1.1. Classification of Violations (Policy Statement)

(a) There are three grades of probation and supervised release violations:

> (1) Grade A Violations—conduct constituting (A) a federal, state, or local offense punishable by a term of imprisonment exceeding one year that (i) is a crime of violence, (ii) is a controlled substance offense, or (iii) involves possession of a firearm or destructive device of a type described in 26 U.S.C. § 5845(a); or (B) any other federal, state, or local offense punishable by a term of imprisonment exceeding twenty years;

(2) Grade B Violations—conduct constituting any other federal, state, or local offense punishable by a term of imprisonment exceeding one year;

(3) Grade C Violations—conduct constituting (A) a federal, state, or local offense punishable by a term of imprisonment of one year or less; or (B) a violation of any other condition of supervision. * * *

§ 7B1.3. Revocation of Probation or Supervised Release (Policy Statement)

(a) (1) Upon a finding of a Grade A or B violation, the court shall revoke probation or supervised release.

(2) Upon a finding of a Grade C violation, the court may (A) revoke probation or supervised release; or (B) extend the term of probation or supervised release and/or modify the conditions of supervision.

NOTES & QUESTIONS

1. **Alternatives to Revocation.** Under 18 U.S.C. § 3565, the judge is not always required to respond to a probation violation by revoking probation. In many cases, the judge would be permitted instead to extend the term of probation, to add new conditions, or to do nothing at all. Given what you have already learned about probation conditions, you should appreciate that the judge's authority to add new conditions effectively gives the judge a vast range of non-revocation sanctions for violations. If the probationer leaves the jurisdiction without permission, for instance, the judge might order electronic monitoring (ankle bracelet) as a new condition. If the probationer violates a no-alcohol condition, the judge might order the probationer to avoid even entering any establishments that serve or sell alcohol. If the probationer missed a required *monthly* meeting with the PO, the probationer might be shifted to a *weekly* meeting requirement.

The general statutory rule of discretion is limited by the mandatory revocation provisions of 18 U.S.C. § 3565(b).[16] Do these seem sensible policy? Additionally, the sentencing guidelines indicate that probation should be revoked whenever the violation constitutes a new felony offense (i.e., punishable by a term of imprisonment exceeding one year). Note that a *conviction* is not required—the guidelines call for revocation when the *judge* finds a new felony using the same preponderance-of-the-evidence standard that is normally used for fact-finding in the guidelines system.

2. **Supervised Release.** The statutory framework for responding to supervised release violations is almost identical to that for responding to probation violations.[17] *See* 18 U.S.C. §§ 3583(e), (g). Indeed, as you may have

[16] Note that a bit of flexibility is established for failed drug tests under 18 U.S.C. § 3563(e), which directs the court to "consider whether the availability of appropriate substance abuse treatment programs, or an individual's current or past participation in such programs, warrants an exception in accordance with United States Sentencing Commission guidelines from the rule of section 3565(b), when considering any action against a defendant who fails a drug test."

[17] One notable difference concerns individuals who are required to register under the Sex Offender Registration and Notification Act (discussed in more detail in Chapter 11). These

noted in the excerpts above, the sentencing guidelines generally make no distinction between these two types of violations.

3. **Violations in the Federal System—by the Numbers.** Based on data from 2013–2017, about 17% of the individuals on federal supervision are found to be in violation of a release condition each year, with district-specific figures ranging from a low of 4.5% (Connecticut) to a high of 42.1% (Southern California). Black defendants accounted for 24% of the supervised population, but 34% of those found to be in violation of a release condition. A majority of violations (54.9%) were in the "Grade C" category, with only 13.6% in Grade A. In the overwhelming majority of cases (86.1%), the judge responded to the violation by imposing a term of imprisonment. U.S. SENT'G COMM'N, FEDERAL PROBATION AND SUPERVISED RELEASE VIOLATIONS (2020).

4. **PO Discretion.** Guidelines § 7B1.2 indicates that the PO "shall promptly report to the court any alleged Grade A or B violation," but authorizes the PO not to report a Grade C violation if "the officer determines: (1) that such violation is minor, and not part of a continuing pattern of violations; and (2) that non-reporting will not present an undue risk to an individual or the public or be inconsistent with any directive of the court relative to the reporting of violations."

5. **MPC:S.** The MPC:S does not provide for mandatory revocation in any circumstances, but, rather, specifies that the PO or judge should "impose the least severe consequence needed to address the violation and the risks posed by the offender in the community, in light of the purpose for which the condition was originally imposed." § 6.15(4). Which approach do you think represents better policy, federal or MPC:S?

6. **State Law—Probation.** In most states, any violation of a condition of probation may result in revocation, although a few states require additional findings beyond the fact of a violation alone, e.g., that the probationer presents a danger to public safety. However, states generally also provide for the possibility of lesser sanctions, with sanctioning discretion vested in the sentencing court and/or the supervising agency or officer. Most often, the ultimate sanction, revocation, is left for the court to impose, as in the MPC:S. Some states have developed guidelines to regulate sanctioning decisions. KELLY LYN MITCHELL ET AL., UNIV. OF MINN., PROFILES IN PROBATION REVOCATION: EXAMINING THE LEGAL FRAMEWORK IN 21 STATES (2014).

7. **State Law—Parole.** In most states that have retained discretionary parole release, it is the parole board, not the court, that determines whether parole should be revoked. Most commonly, parole can be revoked on the basis of any violation, although a few states require additional findings. Lesser sanctions are typically available at the decisionmaker's discretion. In most states, the revocation decisionmaker is now required to take into account actuarial risk-assessment scores and/or sanctioning guidelines. EBONY L. RUHLAND ET AL., UNIV. OF MINN., THE

---

individuals are subject to mandatory revocation of supervised release if they commit certain new felony offenses identified in 18 U.S.C. § 3583(k).

CONTINUING LEVERAGE OF RELEASING AUTHORITIES: FINDINGS FROM A NATIONAL SURVEY (2017).

8. **Reducing Revocations.** Several states have undertaken reforms in recent years that are intended to reduce revocation rates. The reforms respond to concerns about the fiscal burden of imprisoning large numbers of revoked individuals, as well as the possibility that unnecessary revocations may actually *increase* recidivism risk. In some states, legislatures have enacted new restrictions on revocations for so-called "technical" violations—that is, violations of release conditions that are not themselves criminal in nature. Thus, for instance, revocation might be precluded as a sanction for missing an appointment with a PO, at least if the behavior is not repeated. Additionally, some supervision agencies have adopted new guidelines that codify the principle of graduated sanctions, encouraging or requiring POs to try mild sanctions initially and then move to progressively more serious sanctions as violations continue. Klingele, *supra*, at 1048–51.

Note, however, that in many states, a short term of incarceration (up to ninety days in some places) may be used as an alternative sanction to full-blown revocation. Revocation-reducing reforms may not achieve all of their expected benefits if they lead to an increased use of non-revocation jailing as an alternative sanction, which may contribute to jail overcrowding and prove quite disruptive to defendants' efforts at reintegration. *See id.* at 1049.

9. **HOPE and Deterrence.** In 2004, Steven Alm, a trial judge in Honolulu, developed a new community supervision program called Hawaii Opportunity Probation with Enforcement, or "HOPE." Alm's goal was to reorganize probation around the principle of "swift, certain, fair" sanctions for violations, replacing an established system in which sanctions were infrequently imposed for a defendant's first several violations. By contrast, in HOPE, violations would be consistently met with arrest and short-term jailing—even for relatively minor violations like missing an appointment with a PO or failing a drug test. Steven Alm, *HOPE Probation and the New Drug Court: A Powerful Combination*, 99 MINN. L. REV. 1665 (2015). The results seemed quite encouraging, with a randomized controlled study finding lower rates of violations and arrests for new offenses among the HOPE group than those handled through conventional probation. Daniel Nagin, *Project HOPE: Does It Work?*, 15 CRIMINOLOGY & PUB. POL'Y 1005 (2016). National publicity followed, and dozens of jurisdictions then implemented their own HOPE experiments. However, results outside of Hawaii have not been as consistently positive. Pamela Lattimore et al., *Outcome Findings from the HOPE Demonstration Field Experiment: Is Swift, Certain, and Fair an Effective Supervision Strategy?*, 15 CRIMINOLOGY & PUB. POL'Y 1103 (2016).

The HOPE model seems to rest primarily on a deterrence theory. Cecelia Klingele, *What Are We Hoping For? Defining Purpose in Deterrence-Based Correctional Programs*, 99 MINN. L. REV. 1631 (2015). Do you see why HOPE might be expected to function better from a deterrence standpoint than conventional probation? On the other hand, can you imagine some of the reasons why HOPE might not ultimately succeed better than conventional probation in reducing recidivism rates?

Do you think jailing is necessary to deter future violations? Consistent with the HOPE model, a Wyoming supervision program requires a sanction for all violations but gives the PO discretion in choosing between jailing and community-based sanctions like community service or electronic monitoring. Eric J. Wodahl, John H. Boman IV & Brett E. Garland, *Responding to Probation and Parole Violations: Are Jail Sanctions More Effective Than Community-Based Graduated Sanctions?*, 43 J. CRIM. JUST. 242 (2015). Researchers sought to determine whether the use of jail as a sanction would produce better subsequent performance for the violating defendant than use of a community-based sanction. However, after controlling for various risk factors, the researchers found no significant differences in a defendant's likelihood of success based on the type of sanction experienced. Surprising outcome?

10. **Exiting Supervision—by the Numbers.** In 2019, nearly 1.8 million individuals exited probation in the United States. Putting aside about 400,000 whose status was unclear, more than 16% of the exits were to incarceration. By contrast, nearly 69% of the exiting probationers had satisfactorily completed probation. The same year, about 410,000 individuals exited parole. Putting aside 38,000 whose status was unclear, about 29% exited to incarceration, while about 63% completed parole satisfactorily. BARBARA OUDEKERK & DANIELLE KAEBLE, U.S. DEP'T OF JUSTICE, PROBATION AND PAROLE IN THE UNITED STATES, 2019, at 24, 31 (2021).

11. **Revocations for Technical Violations.** As noted above, recent efforts to reduce revocation rates have been motivated, in large part, by concerns over revocations for "technical" violations, that is, violations for behavior that is not criminal in itself, such as missing an appointment with a PO. However, it is difficult to know precisely how common such revocations are. One common benchmark is the number of returns to prison that are made with a new sentence. For instance, in 2019, about 28% of the probationers and parolees who were moved from supervision to incarceration were noted as having a new sentence. In other words, they were not simply being incarcerated on the basis of the original conviction and sentence. Does that mean that the remaining 72% of exits to incarceration were revocations for technical violations only? Not necessarily. In many cases, if a supervisee is being revoked because of the commission of a new crime, a prosecutor will decide that it is unnecessary to initiate a fresh prosecution for the new offense; the revocation provides sufficient punishment. This suggests that the true number of technical revocations may be far less than 72%. On the other hand, shouldn't there also be concerns about revocations that are based on low-level criminal conduct that does not normally result in incarceration, such as simple possession of illegal drugs for personal use?

b. CONSEQUENCES OF REVOCATION

Revocation normally implies incarceration, but for how long? Different jurisdictions have adopted quite different frameworks.

In the federal system, revocation of *probation* leads to a resentencing on the underlying offense, with the full range of original sentencing options back on the table. 18 U.S.C. § 3565. However, if *supervised release* is revoked, the resulting prison term is normally capped at one, two, three, or five years, depending on the seriousness of the underlying offense. 18 U.S.C. § 3583(e)(3). A new term of supervised release may also be imposed for when the defendant is released from the new term of imprisonment. *Id.* § 3583(h).

The U.S. Sentencing Commission has included within the federal sentencing guidelines directives as to the length of post-revocation terms of incarceration. The Commission has characterized its general approach this way:

> [A] violation resulting from a defendant's failure to follow the court-imposed conditions of probation or supervised release [should be considered] as a "breach of trust." While the nature of the conduct leading to the revocation [sh]ould be considered in measuring the extent of the breach of trust, imposition of an appropriate punishment for any new criminal conduct [sh]ould not be the primary goal of a revocation sentence. Instead, the sentence imposed upon revocation [sh]ould be intended to sanction the violator for failing to abide by the conditions of the court-ordered supervision, leaving the punishment for any new criminal conduct to the court responsible for imposing the sentence for that offense.

§ 7A3(a). Doesn't this approach lead to an inefficient need for a second criminal case that could, in effect, be folded into the sanctioning proceeding in the first case?

The Commission's general approach is reflected in §§ 7B1.3 and 7B1.4 of the guidelines. Section 7B1.4 contains a two-dimensional grid that is similar to the one used for calculating an original sentencing range. Using this grid, a presumptive incarceration range can be determined based on the grade of the violation (A, B, or C) and the defendant's criminal history category. In some circumstances, § 7B1.3 permits the sanctioning court to substitute community confinement or home detention for some or all of the recommended incarceration time.

Over the years 2013–2017, the average term of imprisonment was twenty-one months for a Grade A violation, twelve months for a Grade B, and eight months for a Grade C. U.S. SENT'G COMM'N, FEDERAL PROBATION AND SUPERVISED RELEASE VIOLATIONS 35 (2020). Nearly 60% of the revocation sentences were within the recommended guidelines range.

In many state systems, probation revocation sentences are handled quite differently than in the federal system. When initially imposing a probationary sentence, the judge is permitted or (in some states) required to impose and suspend an incarceration sentence. In some such states, when revocation occurs, the original suspended sentence is activated and must be served without modification. However, in other suspended-sentence states, the judge is permitted to impose either the suspended sentence or a lesser sentence. KELLY LYN MITCHELL ET AL., UNIV. OF MINN., PROFILES IN PROBATION REVOCATION: EXAMINING THE LEGAL FRAMEWORK IN 21 STATES (2014). From a policy standpoint, what do you think might said for and against the former approach—that is, requiring the original suspended incarceration term to be served without modification? If you were a revoked defendant, would you rather face a mandatory suspended sentence or (as in the federal system and some state systems) a fresh sentencing proceeding?

In states that retain discretionary parole release, the parole board (not the court) typically decides the term of reimprisonment in cases of revocation, although some states prescribe the term by law. In many states, the parole board has discretion to return a revoked parolee to parole with the same or modified conditions, to place the revoked parolee in a short-term confinement facility (jail), or to utilize intermediate sanctions like electronic monitoring. EBONY L. RUHLAND ET AL., UNIV. OF MINN., THE CONTINUING LEVERAGE OF RELEASING AUTHORITIES: FINDINGS FROM A NATIONAL SURVEY 43–44 (2017).

PROBLEM 8-2: RESPONDING TO PROBATION VIOLATIONS

A probation term of five years was imposed in *United States v. Blake* (Problem 1-1). The judge imposed all of the mandatory statutory conditions (see 18 U.S.C. § 3563(a), *supra*), plus a requirement that Blake "remain in therapy for the duration of her term unless directed otherwise by her probation officer."

Imagine a similar defendant who is given an identical sentence for a similar crime. After six months on probation, she is arrested for DUI, resulting in a misdemeanor conviction in state court. At the subsequent revocation hearing in federal court, she expresses remorse and states that was out celebrating a friend's birthday at a bar, had a few drinks, and then "stupidly" tried to drive home.

1. Does driving under the influence of alcohol constitute a violation of her probation?

2. Is the judge now required to revoke her probation? *See* 18 U.S.C. § 3565(b), *supra*.

3. What grade was the violation? *See* Guidelines § 7B1.1(a), *supra*.

4. Assuming that the defendant reported the DUI to her PO, was the PO then obligated to report the violation to the court? *See* Guidelines § 7B1.2.

5. How do you think the court should handle this violation?

6. Assume that the court responds to the DUI by imposing an alcohol condition under 18 U.S.C. § 3563(b)(7). Six months later, the defendant is convicted in state court of the misdemeanor offense of driving with a suspended license. At the revocation hearing, she explains that her license had been suspended as a result of her DUI and that she could not afford the reinstatement fee. She further states that she needed to drive to get to her

place of employment. How do you think the court should handle this latest violation?

7. Assume that the court responds by prohibiting the defendant from driving until her license is reinstated. Six months later, her therapist reports to the court that she has missed her last five weekly sessions. At the revocation hearing, she states, "I was no longer getting any benefit from these sessions, and it had gotten very hard to fit them in around my work schedule and childcare responsibilities, especially since I now need to use public transportation to get anywhere." How do you think the court should handle this violation?

8. If the defendant's probation were revoked, what is the maximum sentence that might be imposed? *See* 18 U.S.C. § 3565(a)(2), *supra*. If you think that revocation was appropriate for any of the three hypothetical violations, what term of incarceration do you think should have been imposed?

c. DUE PROCESS

Morrissey v. Brewer

408 U.S. 471 (1972)

■ BURGER, C.J.

We granted certiorari in this case to determine whether the Due Process Clause of the Fourteenth Amendment requires that a State afford an individual some opportunity to be heard prior to revoking his parole.

Petitioner Morrissey was convicted of false drawing or uttering of checks in 1967 pursuant to his guilty plea, and was sentenced to not more than seven years' confinement. He was paroled from the Iowa State Penitentiary in June 1968. Seven months later, at the direction of his parole officer, he was arrested in his home town as a parole violator and incarcerated in the county jail. One week later, after review of the parole officer's written report, the Iowa Board of Parole revoked Morrissey's parole, and he was returned to the penitentiary located about 100 miles from his home. Petitioner asserts he received no hearing prior to revocation of his parole.

The parole officer's report on which the Board of Parole acted shows that petitioner's parole was revoked on the basis of information that he had violated the conditions of parole by buying a car under an assumed name and operating it without permission, giving false statements to police concerning his address and insurance company after a minor accident, obtaining credit under an assumed name, and failing to report his place of residence to his parole officer. The report states that the officer interviewed Morrissey, and that he could not explain why he did not contact his parole officer despite his effort to excuse this on the ground that he had been sick. Further, the report asserts that Morrissey admitted buying the car and obtaining credit under an assumed name, and also admitted being involved in the accident. The parole officer recommended that his parole be revoked because of "his continual violating of his parole rules."

The situation as to petitioner Booher is much the same. Pursuant to his guilty plea, Booher was convicted of forgery in 1966 and sentenced to a maximum term of 10 years. He was paroled November 14, 1968. In August 1969, at his parole officer's direction, he was arrested in his home town for a violation of his parole and confined in the county jail several miles away. On September 13, 1969, on the basis of a written report by his parole officer, the Iowa Board of Parole revoked Booher's parole and Booher was recommitted to the state penitentiary, located about 250 miles from his home, to complete service of his sentence. Petitioner asserts he received no hearing prior to revocation of his parole.

The parole officer's report with respect to Booher recommended that his parole be revoked because he had violated the territorial restrictions of his parole without consent, had obtained a driver's license under an assumed name, operated a motor vehicle without permission, and had violated the employment condition of his parole by failing to keep himself in gainful employment. The report stated that the officer had interviewed Booher and that he had acknowledged to the parole officer that he had left the specified territorial limits and had operated the car and had obtained a license under an assumed name "knowing that it was wrong." The report further noted that Booher had stated that he had not found employment because he could not find work that would pay him what he wanted—he stated he would not work for $2.25 to $2.75 per hour—and that he had left the area to get work in another city. * * *

I

Before reaching the issue of whether due process applies to the parole system, it is important to recall the function of parole in the correctional process.

During the past 60 years, the practice of releasing prisoners on parole before the end of their sentences has become an integral part of the penological system. Rather than being an ad hoc exercise of clemency, parole is an established variation on imprisonment of convicted criminals. Its purpose is to help individuals reintegrate into society as constructive individuals as soon as they are able, without being confined for the full term of the sentence imposed. It also serves to alleviate the costs to society of keeping an individual in prison. The essence of parole is release from prison, before the completion of sentence, on the condition that the prisoner abide by certain rules during the balance of the sentence. * * *

The enforcement leverage that supports the parole conditions derives from the authority to return the parolee to prison to serve out the balance of his sentence if he fails to abide by the rules. * * *

Implicit in the system's concern with parole violations is the notion that the parolee is entitled to retain his liberty as long as he substantially abides by the conditions of his parole. The first step in a revocation decision thus involves a wholly retrospective factual question: whether the parolee has in fact acted in violation of one or more conditions of his parole. Only if it is determined that the parolee did violate the conditions does the second question arise: should the parolee be recommitted to prison or should other steps be taken to protect society and improve chances of rehabilitation? The first step is relatively simple; the second is more complex. The second question involves the application of expertise by the parole authority in making a prediction as to the ability of the individual to live in society without committing antisocial acts. This part of the decision, too, depends on facts, and therefore it is important for the board to know not only that some violation was committed but also to know accurately how many and how serious the violations were. Yet this second step, deciding what to do about the violation once it is identified, is not purely factual but also predictive and discretionary.

If a parolee is returned to prison, he usually receives no credit for the time "served" on parole. Thus, the returnee may face a potential of substantial imprisonment.

II

We begin with the proposition that the revocation of parole is not part of a criminal prosecution and thus the full panoply of rights due a defendant in such a proceeding does not apply to parole revocations. Parole arises after the end of the criminal prosecution, including imposition of sentence. Supervision is not directly by the court but by an administrative agency, which is sometimes an arm of the court and sometimes of the executive. Revocation deprives an individual, not of the absolute liberty to which every citizen is entitled, but only of the conditional liberty properly dependent on observance of special parole restrictions.

We turn, therefore, to the question whether the requirements of due process in general apply to parole revocations. As Mr. Justice Blackmun has written recently, "this Court now has rejected the concept that constitutional rights turn upon whether a governmental benefit is characterized as a 'right' or as a 'privilege.'" *Graham v. Richardson*, 403 U.S. 365, 374 (1971). Whether any procedural protections are due depends on the extent to which an individual will be "condemned to suffer grievous loss." *Joint Anti-Fascist Refugee Committee v. McGrath*, 341 U.S. 123, 168 (Frankfurter, J., concurring), *quoted in Goldberg v. Kelly*, 397 U.S. 254, 263 (1970). The question is not merely the "weight" of the individual's interest, but whether the nature of the interest is one within the contemplation of the "liberty or property" language of the Fourteenth Amendment. *Fuentes v. Shevin*, 407 U.S. 67 (1972). Once it is determined that due process applies, the question remains what process is due. It has been said so often by this Court and others as not to require citation of authority that due process is flexible and calls for such procedural protections as the particular situation demands. "(C)onsideration of what procedures due process may require under any given set of circumstances must begin with a determination of the precise nature of the government function involved as well as of the private interest that has been affected by governmental action." *Cafeteria & Restaurant Workers Union v. McElroy*, 367 U.S. 886, 895 (1961). * * *

We turn to an examination of the nature of the interest of the parolee in his continued liberty. The liberty of a parolee enables him to do a wide range of things open to persons who have never been convicted of any crime. The parolee has been released from prison based on an evaluation that he shows reasonable promise of being able to return to society and function as a responsible, self-reliant person. Subject to the conditions of his parole, he can be gainfully employed and is free to be with family and friends and to form the other enduring attachments of normal life. Though the State properly subjects him to many restrictions not applicable to other citizens, his condition is very different from that of confinement in a prison. He may have been on parole for a number of years and may be living a relatively normal life at the time he is faced with revocation. The parolee has relied on at least an implicit promise that parole will be revoked only if he fails to live up to the parole conditions. In many cases, the parolee faces lengthy incarceration if his parole is revoked.

We see, therefore, that the liberty of a parolee, although indeterminate, includes many of the core values of unqualified liberty and its termination inflicts a "grievous loss" on the parolee and often on others. It is hardly useful any longer to try to deal with this problem in terms of whether the parolee's liberty is a "right" or a "privilege." By whatever name, the liberty is valuable and must be seen as within the protection of the Fourteenth Amendment. Its termination calls for some orderly process, however informal.

Turning to the question what process is due, we find that the State's interests are several. The State has found the parolee guilty of a crime against the people. That finding justifies imposing extensive restrictions on the individual's liberty. Release of the parolee before the end of his prison sentence is made with the recognition that with many prisoners there is a risk that they will not be able to live in society without committing additional antisocial acts. Given the previous conviction and the proper imposition of conditions, the State has an overwhelming interest in being able to return the individual to imprisonment without the burden of a new adversary criminal trial if in fact he has failed to abide by the conditions of his parole.

Yet, the State has no interest in revoking parole without some informal procedural guarantees. Although the parolee is often formally described as being "in custody," the argument cannot even be made here that summary treatment is necessary as it may be with respect to controlling a large group of potentially disruptive prisoners in actual custody. Nor are we persuaded by the argument that revocation is so totally a discretionary matter that some form of hearing would be administratively intolerable. A simple factual hearing will not interfere with the exercise of discretion. Serious studies have suggested that fair treatment on parole revocation will not result in fewer grants of parole.

This discretionary aspect of the revocation decision need not be reached unless there is first an appropriate determination that the individual has in fact breached the conditions of parole. The parolee is not the only one who has a stake in his conditional liberty. Society has a stake in whatever may be the chance of restoring him to normal and useful life within the law. Society thus has an interest in not having parole revoked because of erroneous information or because of an erroneous evaluation of the need to revoke parole, given the breach of parole conditions. And society has a further interest in treating the parolee with basic fairness: fair treatment in parole revocations will enhance the chance of rehabilitation by avoiding reactions to arbitrariness.

Given these factors, most States have recognized that there is no interest on the part of the State in revoking parole without any procedural guarantees at all. What is needed is an informal hearing structured to assure that the finding of a parole violation will be based on verified facts and that the exercise of discretion will be informed by an accurate knowledge of the parolee's behavior.

III

We now turn to the nature of the process that is due, bearing in mind that the interest of both State and parolee will be furthered by an effective but informal hearing. In analyzing what is due, we see two important stages in the typical process of parole revocation.

(a) Arrest of Parolee and Preliminary Hearing. The first stage occurs when the parolee is arrested and detained, usually at the direction of his parole officer. The second occurs when parole is formally revoked. There is typically a substantial time lag between the arrest and the eventual determination by the parole board whether parole should be revoked. Additionally, it may be that the parolee is arrested at a place distant from the state institution, to which he may be returned before the final decision is made concerning revocation. Given these factors, due process would seem to require that some minimal inquiry be conducted at or reasonably near the place of the alleged parole violation or arrest and as promptly as convenient after arrest while information is fresh and sources are available. Such an inquiry should be seen as in the nature of a "preliminary hearing" to determine whether there is probable cause or reasonable ground to believe that the arrested parolee has committed acts that would constitute a violation of parole conditions.

In our view, due process requires that after the arrest, the determination that reasonable ground exists for revocation of parole should be made by someone not directly involved in the case. It would be unfair to assume that the supervising parole officer does not conduct an interview with the parolee to confront him with the reasons for revocation before he recommends an arrest. It would also be unfair to assume that the parole officer bears hostility against the parolee that destroys his neutrality; realistically the failure of the parolee is in a sense a failure for his supervising officer. However, we need make no assumptions one way or the other to conclude that there should be an uninvolved person to make this preliminary evaluation of the basis for believing the conditions of parole have been violated. The officer directly involved in making recommendations cannot always have complete objectivity in evaluating them. * * *

This independent officer need not be a judicial officer. The granting and revocation of parole are matters traditionally handled by administrative officers. In *Goldberg*, the Court pointedly did not require that the hearing on termination of [welfare] benefits be conducted by a judicial officer or even before the traditional "neutral and detached" officer; it required only that the hearing be conducted by some person other than one initially dealing with the case. * * *

With respect to the preliminary hearing before this officer, the parolee should be given notice that the hearing will take place and that its purpose is to determine whether there is probable cause to believe he has committed a parole violation. The notice should state what parole violations have been alleged. At the hearing the parolee may appear and speak in his own behalf; he may bring letters, documents, or individuals who can give relevant information to the hearing officer. On request of the parolee, [a] person who has given adverse information on which parole revocation is to be based is to be made available for questioning in his presence. However, if the hearing officer determines that an informant would be subjected to risk of harm if his identity were disclosed, he need not be subjected to confrontation and cross-examination.

The hearing officer shall have the duty of making a summary, or digest, of what occurs at the hearing in terms of the responses of the parolee and the substance of the documents or evidence given in support of parole revocation and of the parolee's position. Based on the information before him, the officer should determine whether there is probable cause to hold the parolee for the final decision of the parole board on revocation. Such a determination would be sufficient to warrant the parolee's continued detention and return to the state correctional institution pending the final decision. As in *Goldberg*, "the decision maker should state the reasons for his determination and indicate the evidence he relied on . . ." but it should be remembered that this is not a final determination calling for "formal findings of fact and conclusions of law." 397 U.S., at 271. No interest would be served by formalism in this process; informality will not lessen the utility of this inquiry in reducing the risk of error.

(b) The Revocation Hearing. There must also be an opportunity for a hearing, if it is desired by the parolee, prior to the final decision on revocation by the parole authority. This hearing must be the basis for more than determining probable cause; it must lead to a final evaluation of any contested relevant facts and consideration of whether the facts as determined warrant revocation. The parolee must have an opportunity to be heard and to show, if he can, that he did not violate the conditions, or, if he did, that circumstances in mitigation suggest that the violation does not warrant revocation. The revocation hearing must be tendered within a reasonable time after the parolee is taken into custody. A lapse of two months, as respondents suggest occurs in some cases, would not appear to be unreasonable.

We cannot write a code of procedure; that is the responsibility of each State. Most States have done so by legislation, others by judicial decision usually on due process grounds. Our task is limited to deciding the minimum requirements of due process. They include (a) written notice of the claimed violations of parole; (b) disclosure to the parolee of evidence against him; (c) opportunity to be heard in person and to present witnesses and documentary evidence; (d) the right to confront and cross-examine adverse witnesses (unless the hearing officer specifically finds good cause for not allowing confrontation); (e) a "neutral and detached" hearing body such as a traditional parole board, members of which need not be judicial officers or lawyers; and (f) a written statement by the factfinders as to the evidence relied on and reasons for revoking parole. We emphasize there is no thought to equate this second stage of parole revocation to a criminal prosecution in any sense. It is a narrow inquiry; the process should be flexible enough to consider evidence including letters, affidavits, and other material that would not be admissible in an adversary criminal trial.

We do not reach or decide the question whether the parolee is entitled to the assistance of retained counsel or to appointed counsel if he is indigent. * * *

In the peculiar posture of this case, given the absence of an adequate record, we conclude the ends of justice will be best served by remanding the case to the Court of Appeals for its return of the two consolidated cases to the District Court with directions to make findings on the procedures actually followed by the Parole Board in these two revocations.

NOTES & QUESTIONS

1. **"Some Orderly Process, However Informal."** In *Morrissey,* the Supreme Court held that the Due Process Clause requires "some orderly

process" in connection with parole revocation, but also made clear that this process may be far short of a full-blown criminal trial. What did the Court mean by asserting that "the interest of both State and parolee will be furthered by an effective but informal hearing?" What exactly did the Court indicate was constitutionally required for the revocation process? Would you have struck the balance any differently?

2. ***Gagnon v. Scarpelli*—Probation & Counsel.** The year after *Morrissey*, the Supreme Court extended *Morrissey*'s due process requirements from parole to probation in *Gagnon v. Scarpelli*, 411 U.S. 778, 782 (1973). *Gagnon* also took up the right-to-counsel question that *Morrissey* reserved. In the end, the Court adopted a case-by-case approach, rather than a categorical rule:

> [T]he effectiveness of the rights guaranteed by *Morrissey* may in some circumstances depend on the use of skills which the probationer or parolee is unlikely to possess. Despite the informal nature of the proceedings and the absence of technical rules of procedure or evidence, the unskilled or uneducated probationer or parolee may well have difficulty in presenting his version of a disputed set of facts where the presentation requires the examining or cross-examining of witnesses or the offering or dissecting of complex documentary evidence.
>
> By the same token, we think that the Court of Appeals erred in accepting respondent's contention that the State is under a constitutional duty to provide counsel for indigents in all probation or parole revocation cases. While such a rule has the appeal of simplicity, it would impose direct costs and serious collateral disadvantages without regard to the need or the likelihood in a particular case for a constructive contribution by counsel. In most cases, the probationer or parolee has been convicted of committing another crime or has admitted the charges against him. And while in some cases he may have a justifiable excuse for the violation or a convincing reason why revocation is not the appropriate disposition, mitigating evidence of this kind is often not susceptible of proof or is so simple as not to require either investigation or exposition by counsel.
>
> The introduction of counsel into a revocation proceeding will alter significantly the nature of the proceeding. If counsel is provided for the probationer or parolee, the State in turn will normally provide its own counsel; lawyers, by training and disposition, are advocates and bound by professional duty to present all available evidence and arguments in support of their clients' positions and to contest with vigor all adverse evidence and views. The role of the hearing body itself, aptly described in *Morrissey* as being "predictive and discretionary" as well as factfinding, may become more akin to that of a judge at a trial, and less attuned to the rehabilitative needs of the individual probationer or parolee. In the greater self-consciousness of its quasi-judicial role, the hearing body may be less tolerant of

> marginal deviant behavior and feel more pressure to reincarcerate than to continue nonpunitive rehabilitation. Certainly, the decisionmaking process will be prolonged, and the financial cost to the State—for appointed counsel, counsel for the State, a longer record, and the possibility of judicial review—will not be insubstantial.
>
> In some cases, these modifications in the nature of the revocation hearing must be endured and the costs borne because, as we have indicated above, the probationer's or parolee's version of a disputed issue can fairly be represented only by a trained advocate. But due process is not so rigid as to require that the significant interests in informality, flexibility, and economy must always be sacrificed. * * *
>
> We thus find no justification for a new inflexible constitutional rule with respect to the requirement of counsel. We think, rather, that the decision as to the need for counsel must be made on a case-by-case basis in the exercise of a sound discretion by the state authority charged with responsibility for administering the probation and parole system. Although the presence and participation of counsel will probably be both undesirable and constitutionally unnecessary in most revocation hearings, there will remain certain cases in which fundamental fairness—the touchstone of due process—will require that the State provide at its expense counsel for indigent probationers or parolees.

Id. at 786–90. Does the Court's approach here strike you as sound?

In a portion of *Gagnon* not reprinted above, the Court distinguished revocation proceedings from criminal trials—in which there is a categorical right to appointed counsel—based in part on the fact that the state is represented by a PO at the revocation hearing, not a prosecutor. *Id.* at 789. The Court characterized the PO's orientation as essentially rehabilitative and benign. "The parole agent," said the Court, "ordinarily defines his role as representing his client's best interests as long as these do not constitute a threat to public safety." *Id.* at 784 (quoting FRANK REMINGTON ET AL., CRIMINAL JUSTICE ADMINISTRATION, MATERIALS AND CASES 910–11 (1969)). However, since the time that *Gagnon* was decided, many commentators have observed a general shift in supervision philosophy in the United States from case-management and rehabilitation to surveillance and rules-enforcement. *See, e.g.*, Christine S. Scott-Hayward, *The Failure of Parole: Rethinking the Role of the State in Reentry*, 41 N.M. L. REV. 421, 438–39 (2011). Given this shift, should the Court reconsider its rejection of a categorical right to counsel?

3. ***Apprendi* and Revocation.** As discussed in Chapter 3, *Apprendi v. New Jersey* and its progeny generally give to defendants a right to a jury trial using the beyond-a-reasonable-doubt evidentiary standard as to those facts that increase either the maximum permissible or the minimum required sentence. In *United States v. Haymond*, 139 S. Ct. 2369 (2019), the

Supreme Court considered the application of the *Apprendi* doctrine to an unusually harsh, but narrowly targeted, federal revocation law.

Convicted by a jury of possessing child pornography, Haymond faced a potential prison sentence of zero to ten years. The judge imposed a sentence of about three years, which Haymond served, followed by a term of supervised release. While he was on release, a search of Haymond's phone and computers revealed the presence of additional child pornography, although there was some question as to whether he knowingly possessed these images. At a revocation hearing, a judge determined by a preponderance of the evidence that Haymond was guilty of knowing possession and revoked his release. Under the basic federal revocation statute, 18 U.S.C. § 3583(e)(3), Haymond faced a revocation sentencing range of zero to two years in prison. However, another statute, 18 U.S.C. § 3583(k), set a revocation sentencing range of five years to life for certain defendants who had been convicted of sexual offenses and were then found while on release to have committed one of a number of specified new offenses—including knowing possession of child pornography. Since his original offense was covered by § 3583(k), Haymond was thus subject to the enhanced five-to-life range based on the judge's fact-finding about the new offense at his revocation hearing.

On appeal, a fractured Supreme Court determined that Haymond's *Apprendi* rights had been violated. Writing for himself and three colleagues in a plurality opinion, Justice Gorsuch observed that the revocation judge's fact-finding had increased Haymond's minimum prison term from the original zero that had been authorized by the jury verdict to five years. Gorsuch saw no convincing way to distinguish this enhanced minimum from the enhanced minimum in *Alleyne v. United States* that the Court had previously found to trigger *Apprendi* rights.

Justice Alito authored a dissenting opinion that was also joined by three colleagues. Alito pointed out that *Morrissey* and *Gagnon* had rejected the suggestion that parole and probation revocation proceedings were part of the "criminal prosecution" to which the Sixth Amendment applied. *Id.* at 2394 (Alito, J., dissenting). Although neither precedent had dealt with supervised release, Alito could see no practical difference in the revocation of different forms of conditional liberty. In his view, any revocation deals with the *administration*, not the *imposition*, of a sentence. It is the imposition of the sentence that terminates the criminal prosecution and, hence, the defendant's rights under the *Apprendi* doctrine. Alito decried what he saw as the plurality's attempt to broaden the definition of "criminal prosecution" to include post-sentencing proceedings, which he argued would cause the "the whole concept of supervised release [to] come crashing down" because of the number of jury trials that would be necessitated. *Id.* at 2388.

Were Alito and the dissenters correct about the "revolutionary" implications of the plurality opinion? *See id.* at 2386. That may depend on whether there is a convincing way to distinguish § 3583(k) from § 3583(e)(3) for *Apprendi* purposes. The former is a narrowly targeted revocation statute that is infrequently applied; the latter is a general revocation statute that applies broadly—adding a jury-trial right to *its* use might plausibly have a large effect on federal supervised release practices. The plurality suggested a possible distinction between the two statutes insofar as the former includes a mandatory minimum prison term, while the latter does not. Indeed, the plurality took care to focus its analysis on the five-year minimum of § 3583(k) and not the life maximum. *See id.* at 2379 n.4 ("Because we hold that this mandatory minimum rendered Mr. Haymond's sentence unconstitutional in violation of *Alleyne*, we need not address the constitutionality of the statute's effect on his maximum sentence under *Apprendi*."). However, since *Alleyne*, the *Apprendi* doctrine has not generally distinguished between enhanced maximums and enhanced minimums. Thus, the logic of the plurality opinion might not be easily cabined to § 3583(k).

Alito and the dissenters described the effect of extending the plurality's reasoning to § 3583(e)(3) as follows:

> [A]doption of the rule toward which the plurality opinion seems to point would make a big difference in many cases. Under that rule, a term of supervised release could never be ordered for a defendant who is sentenced to the statutory maximum term of imprisonment, and only a short period of supervised release could be ordered for a defendant sentenced to a term of imprisonment that is close to the statutory maximum. Moreover, in many cases, a judge, before beginning a supervised-release revocation proceeding, would have to anticipate the period of additional confinement that the judge would find appropriate if a particular violation or set of violations was shown. For example, suppose that the statutory maximum term of certain confinement authorized by the offense of conviction is 10 years and that a prisoner is sentenced to and serves eight years. Suppose that the term of supervised release imposed at the time of sentencing is five years. Before starting a supervised-release revocation proceeding in this hypothetical case, the judge would have to decide whether to rule out the possibility of sending the defendant back to prison for more than two years. Unless the judge was willing to do this—without knowing all the facts—the judge would have to convene a jury.

Id. at 2390–91 (Alito, J., dissenting).

The plurality countered, "In most cases (including this one), combining a defendant's initial and post-revocation sentences issued under § 3583(e) will not yield a term of imprisonment that exceeds the statutory maximum term of imprisonment the jury has authorized for the original crime of conviction. That's because courts rarely sentence defendants to the statutory maxima, and revocation penalties under § 3583(e)(3) are only a small fraction of those available under § 3583(k)." *Id.* at 2384 (citation and internal quotation marks omitted) (citing data indicating that only about 1% of defendants receive the statutory maximum).

For the time being, whether the plurality's approach would prove "revolutionary" will likely remain an academic question. Justice Breyer, who supplied the crucial fifth vote in favor of Haymond, concurred in judgment only. "In light of the potentially destabilizing consequences," he stated, "I would not transplant the *Apprendi* line of cases to the supervised-release context." *Id.* at 2385 (Breyer, J., concurring in judgment). However, he saw three aspects of § 3583(k) that led him

> to think it is less like ordinary revocation and more like punishment for a new offense, to which the jury right would typically attach. *First,* § 3583(k) applies only when a defendant commits a discrete set of federal criminal offenses specified in the statute. *Second,* § 3583(k) takes away the judge's discretion to decide whether violation of a condition of supervised release should result in imprisonment and for how long. *Third,* § 3583(k) limits the judge's discretion in a particular manner: by imposing a mandatory minimum term of imprisonment of "not less than 5 years" upon a judge's finding that a defendant has "commit[ted] any" listed "criminal offense."

Id. at 2386. Breyer's opinion indicates that there is likely at least a five-Justice majority that would resist extending *Apprendi* rights to § 3583(e)(3) revocations.[18] However, Breyer's reasoning suggests some possibility that *Apprendi* rights may be triggered by other targeted revocation laws—federal or state—that mandate a minimum term of incarceration for the commission of given criminal acts by a person on supervision.

4. **Lesser Sanctions.** The Supreme Court has not addressed whether a defendant has constitutional due process rights in relation to sanctions short of revocation, such as an extension of the term of supervision or the addition of new conditions. A number of lower courts have held that no such rights exist, distinguishing *Morrissey* and *Gagnon* on the ground that the defendant's loss is qualitatively different and less severe than the loss of liberty that accompanies revocation. *See, e.g., State v. Smith,* 769 A.2d 698, 704 (Conn. 2001) (citing cases). *But see State v. Korzuch,* 920 P.2d 312 (Ariz. 1996) (holding constitutional due process rights apply to extension of probation term).

5. **Subconstitutional Due Process.** In the federal system, the revocation process is governed by Federal Rule of Criminal Procedure 32.1, which mostly tracks the constitutional requirements laid out by *Morrissey* and *Gagnon*. One notable difference, however, is that both stages of the revocation process (preliminary and final hearing) are conducted before a judicial officer. As a matter of constitutional law, *Morrissey* permits administrative officers to handle these proceedings, rather than judges. If you were a defendant facing revocation, do you think you would prefer a return to court, as in the federal system?

Within the framework of constitutional requirements, state processes vary in some important respects. Counsel, for instance, is provided in some states, but not in others. States also differ in their use of judicial versus nonjudicial decisionmakers, with variation even within some states between

---

[18] Since *Haymond,* several lower courts have treated Justice Breyer's opinion as controlling and rejected the argument that *Apprendi* rights are triggered when the sum of an original sentence and a revocation sentence exceed the statutory maximum for the underlying offense. *See, e.g., United States v. Henderson,* 998 F.3d 1071 (9th Cir. 2021).

probation and parole, and between preliminary and final hearing. Most states seem to conduct distinct preliminary and final hearings, but a few combine the hearings into a single proceeding. Additionally, states vary on such matters as the victim's right to participate in revocation hearings, the defendant's ability utilize an expert witness, attendance and participation by the defendant's family, and observation by the media. EBONY L. RUHLAND ET AL., UNIV. OF MINN., THE CONTINUING LEVERAGE OF RELEASING AUTHORITIES: FINDINGS FROM A NATIONAL SURVEY 39–41 (2017); KELLY LYN MITCHELL ET AL., UNIV. OF MINN., PROFILES IN PROBATION REVOCATION: EXAMINING THE LEGAL FRAMEWORK IN 21 STATES 7 (2014).

6. **Burden of Proof and Collateral Estoppel.** As illustrated in *Haymond, supra*, the burden of proof for revocation is typically preponderance of the evidence. Because of the lower burden of proof, most courts hold that the constitutional collateral estoppel doctrine does not preclude a defendant from being revoked on the basis of criminal conduct of which the defendant was acquitted. *See United States v. Frederickson*, 988 F.3d 76, 86 (1st Cir. 2021) ("[W]e conclude, as have several of our sister circuits, that the government's use of acquitted conduct to prove assault by a preponderance of the evidence at revocation does not violate principles of collateral estoppel." (citing cases)). *But see Commonwealth v. Brown*, 469 A.2d 1371, 1378 (Pa. 1983) (holding that revocation based on acquitted conduct would be "fundamentally unfair"). Moreover, because of the different nature of a revocation proceeding from a criminal trial, most courts have also declined to apply collateral estoppel going in the other direction, that is, from a decision not to revoke to a subsequent criminal case based on the same conduct that was alleged as a violation in the revocation proceeding. *See State v. Waters*, 560 S.W.3d 651 (Tex. Crim. App. 2018) (citing cases).

4. MODIFICATION OF TERMS AND CONDITIONS

If a defendant is doing *poorly* on community supervision, we have already noted that the term may be lengthened or new conditions added. How about if the defendant is doing *well*—can the term be reduced or conditions lifted in recognition of the defendant's success? Similarly, the defendant might like to modify conditions in order to accommodate new circumstances in his or her life. For instance, a defendant with a 9:00 p.m. curfew might like to have that restriction changed to take advantage of a new third-shift employment opportunity.

In general, to the extent that term length or conditions of release were matters of discretion at the start, they can be modified later to reflect changed circumstances. In the federal system, modification is expressly authorized by 18 U.S.C. §§ 3563(c) (probation) and 3583(e) (supervised release). Such provisions are also common features of state law.

Other than revocation, the biggest change to a term of community supervision might be early discharge. For instance, in the federal system, 18 U.S.C. § 3564(c) provides:

> The court, after considering the factors set forth in section 3553(a) to the extent that they are applicable, may, pursuant to the provisions of the Federal Rules of Criminal Procedure relating to the modification of probation, terminate a term of probation previously ordered and discharge the defendant at any time in the case of a misdemeanor or an infraction or at any time after the expiration of one year of probation in the case of a felony, if it is satisfied that such action is warranted by the conduct of the defendant and the interest of justice.

Section 3583(e)(1) provides similarly for early discharge from supervised release. However, only a small proportion of federal defendants are awarded an early discharge.[19]

At least 38 states also provide for early discharge from probation, parole, or both. PEW CHARITABLE TRUSTS, POLICY REFORMS CAN STRENGTHEN COMMUNITY SUPERVISION 30 (2020). However, this option is thought to be underutilized. As we noted earlier in this chapter, recidivism risk is at its highest in the first year or two of the supervision term. Even if it is assumed that supervision helpfully addresses recidivism risk at first, as time passes without serious incident, the costs of supervision—both to the supervision agency and to the supervised individual—are increasingly likely to outweigh any public safety benefits. Additionally, with more time on supervision, there is a greater likelihood of revocation for technical violations. Yet, the supervised individual is not normally actively represented by counsel during the term of supervision, especially if it proceeds smoothly. Without a lawyer's assistance, the individual may not be able to take advantage, or even be aware, of early discharge opportunities. As a practical matter, robust early discharge might require POs to proactively identify and support good candidates. However, overtaxed POs with large caseloads may not have the time or inclination for such initiatives.[20] One possible solution, which has been tried in a few states, is to establish presumptive discharge rules that would result in a supervised person's automatic discharge after a given period of time with no violations, unless there is an objection from a prosecutor or PO. *Id.*

More broadly, many states have been experimenting in recent years with programs that provide positive incentives for probationers and parolees to comply with their conditions of release and to engage with rehabilitative programming. Traditionally, community supervision has been all stick and no carrot. As an illustration of the "carrot" approach, at least nineteen states have now adopted "earned compliance" credits.

---

[19] In 2008, about 12% of supervised release cases were closed through early discharge. U.S. SENT'G COMM'N, FEDERAL OFFENDERS SENTENCED TO SUPERVISED RELEASE 62 (2010). On average, the defendants served more than 60% of their supervision terms before achieving discharge.

[20] The plausible early-discharge candidates would tend to be the easiest clients on a PO's docket. A PO might be reluctant to discharge an easy client, knowing that the opening on his or her docket would likely be taken by a more challenging client.

Id. at 26. These function analogously to "good time" credits for prisoners—shortening the term of supervision by a given amount as a reward for a given period of time violation-free. For instance, in a "30-for-30" structure, a defendant's supervision term would be automatically shortened by thirty days for each full calendar month that the defendant spends in the community without a violation. *Id.* at 27. Similarly, some states provide credit based on the completion of specified rehabilitative programs. In Texas, for instance, individuals on supervision can reduce their terms by thirty days if they complete a parenting, anger management, or life skills course. *Id.* It is hoped that such positive incentives will lead to more constructive use of the person's time on supervision.

C. INTERMEDIATE SANCTIONS

The term "intermediate sanctions" refers to sentencing options that are more restrictive or demanding than regular probation, but that do not involve 24-7 incarceration in a prison or similar facility. Familiar examples include:

- home detention,
- community service,
- electronic monitoring,
- boot camp, and
- halfway house.

An intermediate sanction may be formally recognized in the law as a sentencing option in its own right. More commonly, though, intermediate sanctions are utilized as a condition of community supervision. For instance, a defendant might have to complete 100 hours of community service or submit to electronic monitoring as a condition of probation. In addition to being incorporated into original sentences, intermediate sanctions are also used as responses to violations of probation and parole.

In the federal system, intermediate sanctions have been woven into the "zones" system of the guidelines grid. If you examine the sentencing table reprinted in Chapter 2, you will see that the cells are divided into four zones, lettered A–D. As one moves up in the zones from A to D, the offense severity and/or criminal history scores become more aggravated. As we noted earlier in this chapter, probation is freely available in Zone A. However, in Zone B, if probation or a term of incarceration below the guidelines range is imposed, the guidelines call for the use of intermediate sanctions. More specifically, the judge is expected to impose a term of intermittent confinement, community confinement (halfway house), or home detention, either as a condition of probation or as a component of supervised release after the defendant is released from incarceration. § 5C1.1(c). In Zone C, the guidelines indicate that a sentence of imprisonment should be imposed, but the term may be reduced to some extent if community confinement or home detention are made conditions of supervised release. § 5C1.1(d).

Proponents of intermediate sanctions have often described them as a "best of both worlds" sentencing option. In comparison with incarceration, intermediate sanctions tend to be less expensive to the state and less disruptive to the life of the defendant. In comparison with regular probation, intermediate sanctions may offer greater protection of public safety and more meaningful punishment for desert or deterrence purposes. In practice, however, intermediate sanctions have often fallen short of expectations.

We have already discussed some important intermediate sanctions: victim-offender mediation and conferencing based on restorative justice principles (Chapter 1) and problem-solving courts (Chapter 3). Shaming, discussed earlier in this chapter, might also be considered a type of intermediate sanction. In the remainder of this section, we consider a few additional intermediate sanctions in more detail.[21]

1. HOME DETENTION AND ELECTRONIC MONITORING

Home detention (a.k.a. home confinement or house arrest) requires the defendant to remain in his or her home for a period of time, often with limited privileges to leave for work, school, or other approved purposes. Home detention allows the defendant to fulfill his or her family responsibilities and maintain other positive activities and relationships in the community, while keeping the defendant out of social environments that would present dangerous temptations or expose the defendant to negative influences. By way of illustration, you may recall the *Bueno* case from Chapter 4, in which the defendant was sentenced to home detention in lieu of incarceration so that the defendant could care for his ailing spouse.

The restrictions of home detention are often enforced through electronic monitoring ("EM"). EM does not necessarily have to be coupled with home detention—for instance, it can also be used to enforce release conditions that prohibit individuals convicted of sex offenses from going near schools or playgrounds—but the two intermediate sanctions are often found together.[22]

---

[21] What should be included in the category of "intermediate sanctions" is not a matter of complete clarity or consensus. For instance, jail is sometimes characterized as an intermediate option because jail terms are normally much shorter than prison terms and usually keep the inmate much closer to home, sometimes with release options for work, education, treatment, or family needs. In this section, we do not attempt a comprehensive survey of all sentencing options that might plausibly fit under the "intermediate" heading but focus instead on a handful of options that are of practical importance in many jurisdictions and would be broadly recognized as intermediate.

[22] The use of EM with individuals convicted of sexual offenses is discussed further in Chapter 11.

The main EM technology for many years was the radio frequency system, in which the defendant wears a transmitter while a receiver is maintained in the home. If the defendant moves too far from the receiver, the connection with the transmitter is broken, and the supervising agency is automatically notified. Since 2000, the radio frequency technology has been eclipsed by GPS-based systems, which permit continuous tracking of the defendant's location. GPS monitoring is much more adaptable to enforcing restrictions on where an offender can go outside the home, which has contributed to a rapid increase in EM use. From 2005 to 2015, the number of individuals on EM increased from about 53,000 to more than 125,000. PEW CHARITABLE TRUSTS, USE OF ELECTRONIC OFFENDER-TRACKING DEVICES EXPANDS SHARPLY (2016). Meanwhile, the GPS portion of the EM market ballooned from less than 6% to more than 70%. *See also* Chaz Arnett, *Decarceration to E-Carceration*, 41 CARDOZO L. REV. 641 (2019).

EM is primarily based on a deterrence theory. If EM makes it more likely that undesired behavior will be detected, then it seems plausible that there will be less of that behavior. However, evaluations of the effectiveness of EM have been mixed. A 2005 meta-analysis found no convincing evidence that EM reduces crime. Marc Renzema & Evan Mayo-Wilson, *Can Electronic Monitoring Reduce Crime for Moderate to High-Risk Offenders?*, 1 J. EXPERIMENTAL CRIMINOLOGY 215 (2005). On the other hand, that study covered only the older radio frequency technology. A more recent study in Florida found a higher success rate with GPS than radio frequency devices, and determined that, overall, individuals who were on EM were 30% less likely to be revoked than similar individuals who were being supervised without EM. WILLIAM BALES ET AL., A QUANTITATIVE AND QUALITATIVE ASSESSMENT OF ELECTRONIC MONITORING (2010). For discussion of the Fourth Amendment implications of long-term electronic monitoring, see Kate Weisberg, *Sentenced to Surveillance: Fourth Amendment Limits on Electronic Monitoring*, 98 N.C. L. REV. 717 (2020).

2. DAY REPORTING CENTERS

Participants in a day reporting center ("DRC") spend the day in a correctional facility but return home in the evening. In effect, this is a sort of part-time incarceration. DRCs typically offer participants a range of rehabilitative programs and social services. A number of studies have attempted to evaluate the effectiveness of DRCs, but results have varied. *See* DOUGLAS J. BOYLE ET AL., OUTCOMES OF A RANDOMIZED TRIAL OF AN INTENSIVE COMMUNITY CORRECTIONS PROGRAM—DAY REPORTING CENTERS—FOR PAROLEES 10–12 (2011) (citing studies). At present, there is no consensus as to whether DRCs can reduce recidivism, save money for the criminal justice system, or achieve other desired outcomes.

3. BOOT CAMPS

Boot camps became a popular intermediate sanction in the 1990s, especially for younger defendants. The idea was to substitute a term of imprisonment with a shorter term in a specialized correctional facility that aimed to replicate aspects of the classic military boot camp experience, including military drill and ceremony, demanding physical exercise, and rigid enforcement of rules. Many defendants seem to come from family backgrounds lacking in discipline and structure. The boot camp aimed to fill that deficit.

Ninety-five correctional boot camps were established in the United States by 2000, holding nearly 13,000 inmates. SAMUEL WALKER, SENSE AND NONSENSE ABOUT CRIME, DRUGS, AND COMMUNITIES 267 (2011). However, for the most part, boot camps have not lived up to expectations. There is little evidence that efforts to instill military-style discipline and structure result in lower recidivism rates. Notably, the boot camps that have had some demonstrable success tend to be ones that emphasize treatment services and close post-release supervision, rather than the militaristic aspects of the experience. *Id.* at 268.

4. COMMUNITY SERVICE

A defendant who is sentenced to community service must spend a certain number of hours working at no pay for a public or charitable purpose. Examples include picking up trash in public spaces, working in a hospital emergency room, repairing roads or playgrounds, and speaking to school groups about the dangers of drugs. Because of the public nature of many community service experiences, they might be thought of, in part, as a species of shaming sanction. Even beyond that, the burdens of community service may have deterrent and retributive value. Additionally, it is sometimes suggested that community service may also advance rehabilitative ends insofar as it instills in defendants a better appreciation of the needs of others and of the satisfaction of contributing to the common good.

Community service has become a frequent add-on to probation sentences. In 2009, in large urban counties, nearly one-quarter of the defendants who were convicted of a felony and placed on probation were ordered to perform community service. BRIAN A. REAVES, U.S. DEPT. OF JUSTICE, FELONY DEFENDANTS IN LARGE URBAN COUNTIES, 2009—STATISTICAL TABLES 32 (2013). However, as with most other intermediate sanctions, evaluations of community service do not find consistent evidence of recidivism reduction. Hilde Wermink et al., *Comparing the Effects of Community Service and Short-Term Imprisonment on Recidivism: A Matched Samples Approach*, 6 J. EXPERIMENTAL CRIMINOLOGY 325 (2010).

5. INTENSIVE SUPERVISION

Edward J. Latessa & Myrinda Schweitzer, Community Supervision and Violent Offenders: What the Research Tells Us and How to Improve Outcomes

103 MARQ. L. REV. 911 (2020)

The most widely used alternative intermediate sanction involves some form of intensive supervision program (ISP). This sanction is sometimes combined with electronic monitoring (EM) or other interventions, and usually includes the requirement of more office and field contacts, frequent drug testing, and more stringent enforcement of conditions. In some instances, it can also include the requirement that the offender attend treatment programs.

There is a significant body of research on the effectiveness of intensive supervision that dates back to the early 1960s, when the first generation of ISPs were based on the assumption that reduced caseload would lead to more contacts and services, which in turn would result in lower recidivism rates. While contacts and services appeared to increase, reductions in recidivism did not. The second generation of ISPs started in the 1980s and were grounded in the belief that prison populations could be reduced by diverting higher risk offenders from prison to ISP. The assumption was that by providing close surveillance and control, ISP would deter offenders from future criminal behavior. This model of ISP was much less concerned with providing treatment and services and more focused on a control and surveillance-oriented approach. This form of ISP was consistent with the "get tough" approach of the 1980s and 90s, the failure of which is well documented. Finally, a third generation of ISPs was promoted by the American Probation and Parole Association, which called for a prototypical model that advocated a balanced approach to supervision, where increased supervision would be combined with more treatment and services. Although many agencies purport to support this model, there is some evidence that many still adhere to a deterrence-based approach. A summary of findings from this research has concluded:

- ISPs increase technical violations.
- ISPs have failed to reduce prison crowding.
- Most studies show no significant differences between recidivism rates for ISP and comparison groups.
- There appears to be a relationship between greater participation in treatment and lower recidivism rates.

Essentially, an ISP without treatment does not appear to work with most offenders * * *

NOTES & QUESTIONS

1. **Regular Versus Intensive Supervision.** There is no clear dividing line between what counts as "regular" and "intensive" supervision. A range of different supervision practices may be grouped under the "intensive" heading, although programs carrying this label tend to be marked by lower client-to-PO ratios and more frequent client-PO contacts (e.g., weekly instead of monthly). Intensive supervision programs (ISPs) are normally intended for higher-risk supervisees who might otherwise be incarcerated.

2. **Cost-Savings and Net-Widening.** Absent a robust treatment component, there is little evidence that an ISP—or, for that matter, just about any other type of intermediate sanction—will reliably reduce recidivism. Nonetheless, such programs might still be worth having if they save money. An ISP might save money if it successfully diverted a substantial number of defendants from prison, given that ISP placements are generally less expensive for the state than incarceration. In practice, however, ISPs—like intermediate sanction options more generally—have often drawn defendants who would have otherwise been given conventional probation, rather than the prison-bound population. For instance, a sentencing judge might be reluctant to "take a chance" keeping any high-risk defendant in the community, regardless of the supervision intensity, but might welcome the opportunity to channel low- and medium-risk defendants into a sentence that seems tougher (and/or offers more services) than conventional probation. This phenomenon of diverting lower-risk defendants into a sentence that was intended for higher-risk—sometimes called "net-widening"—tends to undermine cost-saving expectations. For one thing, the per-client costs of an ISP may be twice or more the per-client costs of conventional probation. For another, as Latessa and Schweitzer indicate, the closer supervision of an ISP often leads to more sanctioning of technical violations. Thus, the lower-risk defendants in an ISP may face an increased likelihood of revocation than they would in conventional probation—potentially leading to an overall *increase* in incarceration.

Can you think of any ways that net-widening might be minimized? In other words, what might be done to ensure that most ISP slots are occupied by defendants who would otherwise be prison-bound?

3. **HOPE.** The HOPE probation model, which was discussed earlier in this chapter, might be thought of as a species of ISP. Recall that HOPE emphasizes "swift, certain, fair" sanctions for all probation violations, in contrast with the traditional tendency to overlook or only minimally sanction a defendant's first few technical violations. Although seemingly quite successful when first implemented in Hawaii, the HOPE model has produced mixed results when imitated by other jurisdictions. Notably, while drug treatment was an important component of HOPE in its original form, subsequent versions have tended to emphasize its "zero-tolerance" philosophy over expanded treatment opportunities. Daniel Nagin, *Project HOPE: Does It Work?,* 15 CRIMINOLOGY & PUB. POL'Y 1005 (2016).

4. **Treatment Versus Containment/Surveillance.** Intermediate sanctions differ from one another in their relative emphasis on treatment versus surveillance. EM, for instance, is plainly all about surveillance, while DRCs tend to focus on programming and rehabilitation. As Latessa and Schweitzer indicate, some ISP proponents favor a balanced treatment-surveillance approach, but, in practice, many ISPs have prioritized surveillance.

The research tends to find better outcomes with intermediate sanctions that include treatment, in comparison with those that focus exclusively on surveillance and sanctioning. *See, e.g.*, Francis Cullen et al., *Nothing Works Revisited: Deconstructing Farabee's* Rethinking Rehabilitation, 4 VICTIMS & OFFENDERS 101 (2009); Doris L. MacKenzie & David P. Farrington, *Preventing Future Offending of Delinquents and Offenders: What Have We Learned From Experiments and Meta-Analyses?,* 13 J. EXPERIMENTAL CRIMINOLOGY 565 (2015). In light of the research, why do you suppose that there is not a robust treatment component in all ISPs, or a heavier reliance on DRCs and other intermediate sanctions that emphasize treatment?

5. **The Low-Risk Conundrum.** When considering the potential for wider use of treatment-oriented intermediate sanctions, it is important to bear in mind the "risk principle" from the RNR model, which indicates that rehabilitative programming for low-risk defendants is apt to prove ineffective or even counterproductive. Enhanced *surveillance* for low-risk defendants is also problematic insofar as it may lead to the discovery of more technical violations and needless revocations. The Hippocratic Oath for physicians famously includes the admonition, "First, do no harm." In the Hippocratic spirit, many low-risk defendants might be good candidates for the MPC:S's sentence of "unconditional discharge," or for passive or near-passive supervision mechanisms (e.g., "kiosk probation"). For some offenses, though, these options may seem unacceptable from the standpoint of desert or deterrence, no matter how low-risk the perpetrator. Might community service or home detention do the trick? Fines might be another appealing alternative when low-risk individuals commit crimes involving substantial culpability, but, as we will discuss in the next chapter, economic sanctions can present difficult administrative challenges in a system in which the great majority of defendants are poor.

6. **Who Pays?** The average per-defendant cost of ISPs and other intermediate sanctions tend to be much lower than the cost of incarceration. This creates the possibility of substantial long-run cost-savings for a jurisdiction that implements new intermediate options. However, the expectation of long-run fiscal benefits does not cover the start-up or initial operating costs of a new intermediate sanction program. Indeed, due to net-widening, the hoped-for cost-savings may never materialize.[23] Thus,

[23] Recapturing saved incarceration costs to pay for intermediate sanctions may also present a level-of-government problem. In state criminal justice systems, intermediate sanctions may be administered and paid for at either the state or local level. If an intermediate option is administered by a state agency, e.g., the state department of corrections, but mostly diverts defendants who were otherwise bound for jail, which is normally funded by local government, then the cost-savings will be enjoyed at the "wrong" level and will not readily flow to the agency that bears the costs of the intermediate option. A similar problem would be

jurisdictions often look to the defendant-participants themselves to defray the costs of EM, enhanced drug-testing, new treatment programs, and so forth. What is to be done, though, with the many defendants who are too poor to take on intermediate-sanction fees? Exclude them entirely from the costlier intermediate options? Excuse them from paying the fees—and, if so, by what formula, and to whom will their expenses be shifted? Or put them on extended payment plans—thus raising the need for protracted monitoring and enforcement, including the potential for revocation if payments are missed?

7. **How Far Should Surveillance-Based Sanctions Go?** Professors Mirko Bagaric, Dan Hunter, and Gabrielle Wolf have proposed what they call "technological incarceration," but what might just as easily be characterized as the ultimate ISP on steroids. *Technological Incarceration and the End of the Prison Crisis*, 108 J. CRIM L. & CRIMINOLOGY 73 (2018). Their proposal incorporates EM but adds a requirement that individuals "wear a series of remote sensors—including those for sound, video, and movement—that are connected to central computer systems that can detect unauthorized behavior." *Id.* at 78. The sensors would be similar to the body cams that are increasingly worn by police officers in the field. If the computer system, monitoring the individual's actions in real time, detected "unauthorized" behavior, it would be able to administer an immobilizing electroshock to the individual through Taser-like technology. Does this strike you as a promising new intermediate sanction?

8. **Let a Thousand Flowers Bloom?** Imagine two adjoining counties that have similar demographics, crime rates, and criminal justice budgetary resources. County A—let's call it Chocolate and Vanilla—puts its criminal justice money into a jail and a no-frills community-supervision agency. County B—let's call it 31 Flavors—has a jail and a community-supervision agency but has also invested in a plethora of intermediate sentencing options: multiple problem-solving courts (let's say, drug treatment, mental health, and veterans' courts); a day-reporting center; an ISP; and a restorative-justice center with a full-time coordinator. What might be said for and against each county's approach? If you were asked to predict which county's approach would prove more successful over the long run, what additional information would you like to have?

---

presented by the converse scenario—an intermediate option that is funded locally, but that mostly diverts from *prison*, which is funded by the state.

CHAPTER 9

ECONOMIC SANCTIONS

Economic sanctions include fines, restitution, forfeiture, and fees. Use of such sanctions has been on the rise, often as a supplement, rather than an alternative, to incarceration or probation. In many cases, multiple types of economic sanctions are layered on top of one another, e.g., fine *plus* restitution *plus* fees. Between 2001 and 2014, the total amount of outstanding criminal debt in the United States quintupled from about $20 billion to $100 billion. Claire Greenberg, Marc Meredith & Michael Morse, *The Growing and Broad Nature of Legal Financial Obligations: Evidence from Alabama Court Records*, 48 CONN. L. REV. 1079 (2016). The burden on poor defendants and their families has become a matter of growing concern. Indeed, some research indicates that "legal financial obligations" (another common term for economic sanctions) may sometimes become criminogenic.[1]

In this chapter, we will explore the different types of economic sanctions in more detail, consider general issues in their enforcement, and discuss constitutional limitations on their use. As you read this material, you might think about three important policy questions. First, in light of all of the contemporary concerns regarding mass incarceration and mass supervision, should there be greater use of economic sanctions as an *alternative*, as opposed to a *supplement*, to liberty-depriving punishments? Second, is it possible for a robust system of economic sanctions to be administered fairly and effectively when most criminal defendants have very limited assets (while a small minority have quite substantial resources)? Third, do some types of economic sanctions warp the priorities of law enforcement agencies, leading them to pursue revenue for their own benefit without regard to the harmful, and sometimes even criminogenic, effects on the lives of those who become the system's involuntary debtors? You may recall that we touched on the latter issue in the discussion of "collateral" purposes of punishment in Chapter 1.

[1] *See* Alexes Harris, Heather Evans & Katherine Beckett, *Drawing Blood from Stones: Legal Debt and Social Inequality in the Contemporary United States*, 115 AM. J. SOCIOLOGY 1753 (2010) (noting instances of defendants committing crimes to try to pay off economic sanctions); Alex Piquero & Wesley Jennings, *Research Note: Justice System-Imposed Financial Penalties Increase the Likelihood of Recidivism in a Sample of Juvenile Offenders*, 15 YOUTH VIOLENCE & JUSTICE 325 (2016) (finding association between imposition of economic sanctions on juveniles and increased recidivism).

A. TYPES

1. FINES

From the start of American history, small fines have been the sentence of choice for the very lowest level of criminal violations, such as public intoxication or routine traffic offenses. Larger fines are also generally authorized for more serious offenses, but controversy swirls around their use. Some contend that fines should be used more frequently as a more socially cost-effective and less intrusive alternative to incarceration or intermediate sanctions. Others, focusing on the harmful impact of fines on poor defendants and their families, argue that fines should not be used at all—or at least should be more carefully calibrated to the defendant's ability to pay than is currently the norm in American practice.

The statutes that define crimes often specify a maximum permissible—and sometimes a minimum required—fine for the commission of the crime, much as they establish a maximum and sometimes a minimum term of incarceration. *See, e.g.,* 21 U.S.C. § 841(b)(1)(A) (authorizing fine for individual defendant of up to $10,000,000 for certain serious drug trafficking offenses). If a statute authorizes a fine without specifying an amount, a generic fine statute may establish the permissible range. For instance, in the federal system, 18 U.S.C. § 3571(b) establishes a general maximum fine of $250,000 for felony offenses, unless a higher limit is set by the statute defining the offense. In any event, the sentencing judge will typically have discretion to select a fine amount from within an authorized range. Analytically, the judge's decisions about whether to impose a fine and, if so, the amount of the fine, may be analogized to the judge's decisions about whether to impose a term of incarceration and, if so, the length of the term. In principle, a fine seems most likely to advance desert or deterrence purposes of punishment. As with incarceration sentences, it may be appropriate for the judge to consider the potential for a fine to be criminogenic (e.g., if the fine impedes the defendant's ability to secure stable housing) or to harm innocent third parties (e.g., the defendant's children who depend on the defendant's financial support).

Consider how these factors are balanced in the federal fine guideline.

United States Sentencing Guidelines (2021)

§ 5E1.2. Fines for Individual Defendants

(a) The court shall impose a fine in all cases, except where the defendant establishes that he is unable to pay and is not likely to become able to pay any fine.

(b) The applicable fine guideline range is that specified in subsection (c) below. * * *

[*Fines table omitted. The recommended ranges are based exclusively on offense level. They vary from $200–$9,500 (offense level 3 and below) to $50,000–$500,000 (offense level 38 and above).*]

(d) In determining the amount of the fine, the court shall consider:

(1) the need for the combined sentence to reflect the seriousness of the offense (including the harm or loss to the victim and the gain to the defendant), to promote respect for the law, to provide just punishment and to afford adequate deterrence;

(2) any evidence presented as to the defendant's ability to pay the fine (including the ability to pay over a period of time) in light of his earning capacity and financial resources;

(3) the burden that the fine places on the defendant and his dependents relative to alternative punishments;

(4) any restitution or reparation that the defendant has made or is obligated to make;

(5) any collateral consequences of conviction, including civil obligations arising from the defendant's conduct;

(6) whether the defendant previously has been fined for a similar offense;

(7) the expected costs to the government of any term of probation, or term of imprisonment and term of supervised release imposed; and

(8) any other pertinent equitable considerations.

The amount of the fine should always be sufficient to ensure that the fine, taken together with other sanctions imposed, is punitive.

(e) If the defendant establishes that (1) he is not able and, even with the use of a reasonable installment schedule, is not likely to become able to pay all or part of the fine required by the preceding provisions, or (2) imposition of a fine would unduly burden the defendant's dependents, the court may impose a lesser fine or waive the fine. In these circumstances, the court shall consider alternative sanctions in lieu of all or a portion of the fine, and must still impose a total combined sanction that is punitive. Although any additional sanction not proscribed by the guidelines is permissible, community service is the generally preferable alternative in such instances.

NOTES & QUESTIONS

1. **"Shall Impose."** The basic federal fine statute indicates that the imposition of a fine is discretionary. *See* 18 U.S.C. § 3571(a) ("A defendant who has been found guilty of an offense *may* be sentenced to pay a fine." (emphasis added)). However, the guidelines specify that the judge "shall impose a fine in all cases," other than in cases of economic hardship. Under *Booker*, of course, federal judges have regained some of their discretion as to this and other guidelines mandates.

Despite the "shall impose" language, federal judges routinely waive fines. In FY2020, only 6.6% of sentenced federal defendants were ordered to pay a fine. U.S. SENT'G COMM'N, 2020 SOURCEBOOK OF FEDERAL SENTENCING STATISTICS tbl. 16. The average (mean) fine was $26,350. *Id.* tbl. 17.

2. **What About Criminal History?** As you know, the guidelines recommendations for incarceration are based on a combination of offense severity and criminal history (see the guidelines matrix reprinted in Chapter 2). By contrast, the fines table is based exclusively on offense severity. Why do you think that is?

3. **"Combined Sentence."** Section 5E1.2(d)(1) indicates that the fine amount should not be set independently from other aspects of the sentence; rather, the total burden of all parts of the sentence should be considered together to ensure that the combined sentence is sufficient, but not excessive, in light of the purposes of punishment. Does this imply that two defendants of equal culpability might appropriately receive different prison terms if one is able to pay a hefty fine and the other is not? Would such an outcome necessarily be objectionable?

4. **Gain-Stripping.** Under § 5E1.2(d)(1), one factor to consider in setting the fine is the amount of the defendant's gain from the offense. The application notes further indicate that an upward departure may be warranted where the top of the fine range does not equal at least twice the defendant's gain. Similarly, the fine statute expressly authorizes a fine of twice the defendant's gain, even where that amount is greater than the otherwise applicable maximum. 18 U.S.C. § 3571(d). Do you see how these provisions reflect deterrence theory? Why not simply mandate that the fine be made equivalent to the defendant's gain? What is the significance of the mandate that "the fine should always be sufficient to ensure that the fine, taken together with other sanctions imposed, is punitive?"

5. **Organizations.** Section 5E1.2 applies only to individual defendants. Since organizational defendants (e.g., a corporation that defrauded consumers) cannot be incarcerated, fines play an especially important role in their sentencing. Corporate sentencing is discussed in Chapter 10 below.

6. **Proving Hardship.** The guidelines place on the defendant the burden of proving an inability to pay or an undue burden on dependents. However, the application notes indicate that the "inability of a defendant to post bail bond (having otherwise been determined eligible for release) and the fact that a defendant is represented by (or was determined eligible for) assigned counsel are significant indicators of present inability to pay any fine. In conjunction with other factors, they may also indicate that the defendant is not likely to become able to pay any fine."

In assessing a defendant's ability to pay, federal judges benefit from the routine preparation of PSRs (presentence reports) in federal cases. As noted in Chapter 3, however, PSRs are much less frequently available in many state court systems, especially in lower-level cases. The absence of good information about defendant finances may discourage judges from using fines as an alternative to incarceration. *See* R. Barry Ruback & Mark H.

Bergstrom, *Economic Sanctions in Criminal Justice: Purposes, Effects, and Implications*, 33 CRIM. JUST. & BEHAVIOR 242, 263 (2006) ("Judges' single biggest complaint with regard to setting economic sanctions is that at sentencing, they lack complete information about offenders' economic circumstances, including employment income (net of taxes), other sources of income (e.g., welfare, unemployment), residence expenses, and number of dependents." (citing studies)).

If a federal defendant does establish hardship, § 5E1.2(e) indicates that the court should consider other sanctions that would substitute for the fine, with community service identified as "the generally preferable alternative." Might a blood donation be considered a form of community service that an indigent defendant can be ordered to undertake in lieu of a fine? In an episode that achieved some national notoriety, one Alabama judge threatened jail for defendants who were unable to pay their fines unless they made a blood donation. Campbell Robertson, *For Offenders Who Can't Pay, It's a Pint of Blood or Jail Time*, N.Y. TIMES, Oct. 19, 2015.

7. **Problem: *United States v. Smith.*** Taking into account the criteria in Guidelines § 5E1.2(d), *supra*, what fine, if any, do you think ought to be imposed in the hypothetical *Smith* case (PSR in Chapter 3)? You may assume that the recommended range under the Guidelines is $35,000–$350,000.

8. **Hardship in the MPC:S.** The MPC:S aims to protect defendants and their families from undue hardship caused by economic sanctions. The language is somewhat stronger than in the federal guidelines. The key provisions are contained in MPC:S § 6.04:

> (6) No economic sanction may be imposed unless the offender would retain sufficient means for reasonable living expenses and family obligations after compliance with the sanction.
>
> (7) If the court refrains from imposing an economic sanction because of the limitation in subsection (6), the court may not substitute incarceration for the unavailable economic sanction.

In explaining these limitations, the commentary states, "Much like bankruptcy law, a primary goal of the sentencing system should be to position ex-offenders so they may become productive and successful participants in the law abiding economy."

9. **Fine Maximums—State Law.** State laws are extraordinarily varied when it comes to the maximum size of fines that may be imposed, ranging from $5,000 in one state to $1 million in another. MPC:S § 6.04B cmmnt. b. The MPC:S favors relatively high maximums "to allow states room for the prosecution and punishment of major financial crimes." *Id.* The commentary observes, "In many such cases, the dollar amounts at stake are far greater than for average 'street' crime, and some offenders will have the means to pay large fine amounts . . . ."

As in federal law, many states also include as an alternative maximum an amount equal to two (or, in one state, three) times the defendant's gain from the offense or the victim's loss. MPC:S § 6.04B rptr. note b.

10. **Day Fines.** A handful of European nations utilize what is called the "day-fine" system. In such a system, the severity of the offense is assessed to determine an appropriate number of "day-fine units." The value of each unit is then established based on the defendant's wealth and income. Martin H. Pritikin, *Fine-Labor: The Symbiosis Between Monetary and Work Sanctions,* 81 U. COLO. L. REV. 343, 353 (2010). In this way, two defendants who committed similar crimes might receive fines of very different absolute value, but of comparable real economic "bite" in light of each defendant's personal economic circumstances. The system may help to protect poor defendants from excessive fines, but also operates to ensure large fines for wealthy defendants. In theory, similar results can be achieved in the United States through the exercise of judicial discretion on a case-by-case basis when fine ranges are large and adequate information about defendant finances is available, but the day-fine system is designed to provide greater consistency and coherence in the way that a defendant's economic circumstances are handled.

Some of the nations that implemented day fines in the mid- to late twentieth century came to rely far more on fines as a standard punishment, even in relatively serious cases, with a corresponding decrease in reliance on incarceration. *Id.* at 354. It is thought that day fines may have more credibility than traditional fines as an alternative sanction insofar as day fines are capable of avoiding two important problems: (1) unrealistically high fines for poor defendants, which are effectively uncollectable and hence seen as an empty gesture; and (2) excessively low fines for well-off defendants, which may fail to deter or deliver just deserts. Might importation of the day-fine system help to reduce mass incarceration in the U.S. by making economic sanctions a more attractive alternative to incarceration? Note that a few U.S. jurisdictions have experimented with day fines, but they have not caught on more broadly. What do you think the obstacles are?

The MPC:S endorses what it calls "means-based fines." These "are fines that are adjusted in amount in relation to the wealth and/or income of defendants, so that the punitive force of financial penalties will be comparable for offenders of varying economic means. One example . . . is the 'day fine,' which assigns fine amounts with reference to units of an offender's daily net income." § 6.04B(3).

11. **Perverse Incentives.** The fines collected by municipal (lower-level) criminal courts are often used to fund local government operations—including police and the courts themselves. Should we be concerned that such fiscal arrangements may create incentives for overly aggressive ticketing and fining? This was one of the chief criticisms leveled against the police and courts in Ferguson, Missouri, by the U.S. Department of Justice Civil Rights Division in its investigation of the causes of civil unrest in the city following the killing of Michael Brown. CIV. RIGHTS DIV., U.S. DEP'T OF JUSTICE, INVESTIGATION OF THE FERGUSON POLICE DEPARTMENT (2015). As one of us recently summarized the results of the investigation:

> Many residents saw Ferguson police as a "collection agency," felt regarded "less as constituents to be protected than as potential offenders and sources of revenue," and feared venturing outside for

> risk of being targeted and arrested due to a single missed payment. To generate revenue, police issued massive numbers of summons for alleged municipal code violations such as "Manner of Walking in the Roadway" and "Failure to Comply" with police, with revenue for the resulting LFOs allocated to local budgets (not the state, which would be required if parallel state provisions were utilized). The Department concluded that aggressive targeting of Ferguson's residents, who were predominantly poor and African-American, was not intended to provide better services or promote public safety but to secure more revenue, resulting in widespread distrust and dislike of police.

Wayne A. Logan, *What the Feds Can Do to Rein in Local Mercenary Justice*, 2018 U. ILL. L. REV. 1731, 1741 (citations omitted).

12. **An Expressiveness Deficit?** In trying to account for why fines are not used more frequently as an alternative to incarceration, Professor Dan Kahan has argued that fines are "insufficiently expressive of condemnation." *What Do Alternative Sanctions Mean?*, 63 U. CHI. L. REV. 591, 620 (1996). Kahan invokes the distinction made by Robert Cooter, a law and economics scholar, between a "sanction" ("a detriment imposed for doing what is *forbidden*") and a "price" (a detriment that must be borne "in order to do what is *permitted*"). *Id.* at 621 (quoting Robert Cooter, *Prices and Sanctions*, 84 COLUM. L. REV. 1523, 1524, 1525 (1984)). Prison, Kahan observes,

> is clearly a sanction; because liberty is so universally and intensely valued, taking it is our society's most potent symbol of moral condemnation. Fines condemn much more ambivalently. . . . [W]hen fines are used as a substitute for imprisonment the message is likely to be that the offenders' conduct is being priced rather than sanctioned.
>
> . . . Imprisonment, as a sanction, invariably condemns; fines, when viewed as prices, do not. Accordingly, when it lacks this signification, a fine, no matter how large, won't be viewed as an adequate substitute for an appropriate term of imprisonment.

Id. Does this line of thinking suggest that efforts to increase fine use relative to incarceration in the United States are doomed to failure?

13. **Fiscal Benefits?** From the standpoint of public policy, a commonly cited advantage of fines over incarceration is that fines generate revenue for the state, while incarceration is simply an expense. However, the fiscal advantage of fines may be largely offset by all of the effort that must go into collecting them. For instance, one study in Washington State found that, over a two-year time period, $21.6 million in fines and other legal financial obligations were collected, but at a direct cost of $16 million. Katherine Beckett & Alexes Harris, *On Cash and Conviction: Monetary Sanctions as Misguided Policy*, 10 CRIMINOLOGY & PUB. POL'Y 509, 527–28 (2011). For instance, one county alone had seven full-time employees working on collections. Moreover, the researchers pointed out, there were a variety of

additional indirect costs that could not be assessed, such as the cost of jailing individuals for nonpayment.

2. RESTITUTION

Restitution is compensation paid by the defendant to the victim. It is closely analogous to the damages a civil defendant might be required to pay to a plaintiff in a tort suit but enlists the aid of the state in obtaining and enforcing the judgment through standard criminal processes. Like fines, restitution may serve desert and deterrence purposes. However, much more clearly and directly than fines, restitution may also serve the purpose of victim restoration. Additionally, it is sometimes claimed that restitution serves rehabilitative purposes "because it forces the defendant to confront, in concrete terms, the harm his or her actions have caused. Such a penalty will affect the defendant differently from a traditional fine paid to the state as an abstract and impersonal entity, and often calculated without regard to the harm the defendant has caused." *Kelly v. Robinson*, 479 U.S. 36, 49 n.10 (1986).

As an aspect of criminal sentencing, restitution grew in importance as probation became a routine disposition in the late nineteenth and early twentieth centuries. Alan T. Harland, *Monetary Remedies for the Victims of Crime: Assessing the Role of the Criminal Courts*, 30 UCLA L. REV. 52 (1982). In setting conditions for release, many judges saw victim compensation as an appropriate requirement. In this way, restitution became established through the exercise of judicial sentencing discretion without explicit statutory authorization. In the latter half of the twentieth century, legislatures also began to provide for victim compensation, motivated in part by the rise of a politically powerful victims' rights movement. First came requirements that defendants contribute to state-administered victim compensation funds. However, these legislative schemes did not tie defendants' financial obligations to the harms suffered by their specific victims. Later came statutes that codified discretionary restitution or established mandatory restitution.

By the early 2000s, about one-third of American states, plus the federal government, had adopted mandatory restitution laws. AM. BAR ASS'N, RESTITUTION FOR CRIME VICTIMS: A NATIONAL STRATEGY (2004). Excerpts of the federal statute covering most violent and property offenses are reprinted below. Several additional federal statutes cover a variety of other offenses. There is also a more broadly encompassing *discretionary* restitution statute, 18 U.S.C. § 3663, that authorizes restitution for most victimizing offenses that are not covered by a mandatory restitution law.

Mandatory Victims Restitution Act of 1996 (as codified)

18 U.S.C. § 3663A. Mandatory restitution to victims of certain crimes

(a) (1) Notwithstanding any other provision of law, when sentencing a defendant convicted of an offense described in subsection (c), the court shall order, in addition to, or in the case of a misdemeanor, in addition to or in lieu of, any other penalty authorized by law, that the defendant make restitution to the victim of the offense or, if the victim is deceased, to the victim's estate.

(2) For the purposes of this section, the term "victim" means a person directly and proximately harmed as a result of the commission of an offense for which restitution may be ordered * * *.

(b) The order of restitution shall require that such defendant—

(1) in the case of an offense resulting in damage to or loss or destruction of property of a victim of the offense—

(A) return the property to the owner of the property or someone designated by the owner; or

(B) if return of the property under subparagraph (A) is impossible, impracticable, or inadequate, pay an amount equal to—

(i) the greater of—

(I) the value of the property on the date of the damage, loss, or destruction; or

(II) the value of the property on the date of sentencing, less

(ii) the value (as of the date the property is returned) of any part of the property that is returned;

(2) in the case of an offense resulting in bodily injury to a victim—

(A) pay an amount equal to the cost of necessary medical and related professional services and devices relating to physical, psychiatric, and psychological care, including nonmedical care and treatment rendered in accordance with a method of healing recognized by the law of the place of treatment;

(B) pay an amount equal to the cost of necessary physical and occupational therapy and rehabilitation; and

(C) reimburse the victim for income lost by such victim as a result of such offense;

(3) in the case of an offense resulting in bodily injury that results in the death of the victim, pay an amount equal to the cost of necessary funeral and related services; and

(4) in any case, reimburse the victim for lost income and necessary child care, transportation, and other expenses incurred during participation in the investigation or prosecution of the offense or attendance at proceedings related to the offense.

(c) (1) This section shall apply in all sentencing proceedings for convictions of, or plea agreements relating to charges for, any offense—

(A) that is—

(i) a crime of violence * * * ;

(ii) an offense against property under this title * * * and

(B) in which an identifiable victim or victims has suffered a physical injury or pecuniary loss.

(2) In the case of a plea agreement that does not result in a conviction for an offense described in paragraph (1), this section shall apply only if the plea specifically states that an offense listed under such paragraph gave rise to the plea agreement.

(3) This section shall not apply in the case of an offense described in paragraph (1)(A)(ii) * * * if the court finds, from facts on the record, that—

(A) the number of identifiable victims is so large as to make restitution impracticable; or

(B) determining complex issues of fact related to the cause or amount of the victim's losses would complicate or prolong the sentencing process to a degree that the need to provide restitution to any victim is outweighed by the burden on the sentencing process.

18 U.S.C. § 3664. Procedure for issuance and enforcement of order of restitution

(a) For orders of restitution under this title, the court shall order the probation officer to obtain and include in its presentence report, or in a separate report, as the court may direct, information sufficient for the court to exercise its discretion in fashioning a restitution order. * * *

(e) Any dispute as to the proper amount or type of restitution shall be resolved by the court by the preponderance of the evidence. The burden of demonstrating the amount of the loss sustained by a victim as a result of the offense shall be on the attorney for the Government. The burden of demonstrating the financial resources of the defendant and the financial needs of the defendant's dependents, shall be on the defendant. The burden of demonstrating such other matters as the court deems appropriate shall be upon the party designated by the court as justice requires.

(f)(1)(A) In each order of restitution, the court shall order restitution to each victim in the full amount of each victim's losses as determined by the court and without consideration of the economic circumstances of the defendant. * * *

(2) Upon determination of the amount of restitution owed to each victim, the court shall, pursuant to section 3572, specify in the restitution order the manner in which, and the schedule according to which, the restitution is to be paid, in consideration of—

(A) the financial resources and other assets of the defendant, including whether any of these assets are jointly controlled;

(B) projected earnings and other income of the defendant; and

(C) any financial obligations of the defendant; including obligations to dependents.

(3) (A) A restitution order may direct the defendant to make a single, lump-sum payment, partial payments at specified intervals, in-kind payments, or a combination of payments at specified intervals and in-kind payments.

(B) A restitution order may direct the defendant to make nominal periodic payments if the court finds from facts on the record that the economic circumstances of the defendant do not allow the payment of any amount of a restitution order, and do not allow for the payment of the full amount of a restitution order in the foreseeable future under any reasonable schedule of payments. * * *

(h) If the court finds that more than 1 defendant has contributed to the loss of a victim, the court may make each defendant liable for payment of the full amount of restitution or may apportion liability among the defendants to reflect the level of contribution to the victim's loss and economic circumstances of each defendant. * * *

(j) (1) If a victim has received compensation from insurance or any other source with respect to a loss, the court shall order that restitution be paid to the person who provided or is obligated to provide the compensation, but the restitution order shall provide that all restitution of victims required by the order be paid to the victims before any restitution is paid to such a provider of compensation.

(2) Any amount paid to a victim under an order of restitution shall be reduced by any amount later recovered as compensatory damages for the same loss by the victim in—

(A) any Federal civil proceeding; and

(B) any State civil proceeding, to the extent provided by the law of the State.

NOTES & QUESTIONS

1. **Ability to Pay.** The MVRA requires that the restitution order cover the full amount of victim losses, "without consideration of the economic

circumstances of the defendant." 18 U.S.C. § 3664(f)(1)(A). This marked a change in federal law, which had previously directed sentencing judges to consider the defendant's ability to pay. CATHARINE M. GOODWIN, JAY E. GRENIG & NATHAN A. FISHBACH, FEDERAL CRIMINAL RESTITUTION § 2:16 (2008). The MVRA may thus result in large restitution awards that a poor defendant is highly unlikely ever to be able to pay. Does that seem a sound policy choice? Note that the seeming rigidity of the law is softened to some extent by the sentencing judge's ability to consider economic circumstances in determining the payment schedule under § 3664(f)(2) or order nominal payments under § 3664(f)(3).

By contrast to the MVRA, and as noted in the earlier discussion of fines, MPC:S § 6.04(6) prohibits the imposition of any economic sanction, including restitution, that would deprive the defendant of "sufficient means for reasonable living expenses and family obligations." States are divided on whether restitution may be denied or limited on the basis of the defendant's inability to pay. MPC:S § 6.04A rptr. note h.

2. **Limited by Conviction Offense.** In *Hughey v. United States*, 495 U.S. 411 (1990), the Supreme Court considered whether a defendant might be required to pay restitution for harms caused by offenses of which the defendant was not formally convicted. Hughey was charged in a multicount indictment of stealing and unlawfully using several credit cards. Pursuant to a deal with the government, Hughey pled guilty to one count charging him with the unlawful use of one credit card; in return, the government dropped the remaining counts. However, at sentencing, the government sought, and won, restitution covering all of the losses resulting from Hughey's use of twenty-one different credit cards. This amounted to $90,431—in comparison with the $10,412 in losses from the one card that was the subject of the count to which Hughey pled guilty.

Interpreting the applicable pre-MVRA federal restitution statute, the Supreme Court overturned the restitution award. The Court held that the statute "authorize[d] an award of restitution only for the loss caused by the specific conduct that is the basis of the offense of conviction." *Id.* at 413. Through subsequent legislative changes to the restitution law, Congress has preserved the *Hughey* limitation. GOODWIN, GRENIG & FISHBACH, *supra*, § 5:8. Wouldn't it be fairer and more efficient, though, to allow all of a defendant's victims to recover through a single criminal proceeding, regardless of how the case was charged or pled out? Otherwise, the other victims are left only with civil litigation remedies. Civil litigation tends to drag out longer than criminal, and by the time the other victims obtain a civil judgment, the defendant's assets may already be gone—lost to legal fees, criminal restitution awards, fines, and other economic sanctions.

Consistent with *Hughey*, the MPC:S limits restitution to losses resulting from the offense of conviction, but states are divided on this question. MPC:S § 6.04A rptr. note d. If restitution is permitted for losses from other offenses, some commentators contend that any necessary fact-finding regarding the other offenses triggers the defendant's *Apprendi* rights, but such arguments have not found success in the lower courts. *Id.*

Note that § 3663(c)(2), *supra,* provides a way for the government, with the defendant's agreement, to circumvent the *Hughey* limitation. Do you think that prosecutors should normally insist on restitution for all victims as a plea-bargaining condition? You may recall from the discussion of the Crime Victims' Rights Act in Chapter 3 that federal prosecutors are statutorily obligated to "make their best efforts to see that crime victims are . . . accorded" their rights under the Act—one of which is the "right to full and timely restitution as provided in law." 18 U.S.C. § 3773(a)(6), (c)(1). Does this suggest that prosecutors ought to prioritize restitution for all victims in their charging and plea-bargaining decisions?

3. **Recoverable Losses: Physical Versus Psychological Injury.** Under § 3663A(b)(2), *supra,* a defendant who suffers "bodily injury" is entitled to restitution not only for the cost of treatment of the physical harm, but also of the psychological harm. In the absence of bodily injury, however, the MVRA makes no express provision for the costs of psychological care. Yet, doesn't it seem that some offenses may cause severe psychological trauma for victims even when there is no physical injury? Recall, for instance, *United States v. Blake,* the bank robbery case from Chapter 1. Only one bank employee was stabbed, but others may well have been terrified by the experience. Most courts indicate, though, that a need for psychological care, in and of itself, is not a basis for recovery under the MVRA. *See, e.g., United States v. King,* 414 F.3d 1329 (11th Cir. 2005) (reversing portion of restitution award in bank robbery case representing cost of providing grief counseling to bank employees). *But cf. United States v. Breshers,* 684 F.3d 699, 703 (7th Cir. 2012) ("[T]he MVRA's use of the undefined term 'bodily injury' is at best unclear on the question whether it includes mental injury."). Do you see any justification for limiting restitution in this way?

The MPC:S, like the law of many states, provides a more generous definition of recoverable losses, including compensation for mental-health care with or without physical injury. MPC:S § 6.04A rptr. note g. However, restitution is normally limited to the victim's liquidated, out-of-pocket economic losses, such as money spent on physical or psychological treatment, and excludes recovery for "pain and suffering"—even though such damages are commonly recoverable in civil tort litigation.

Why not make restitution replicate tort damages as closely as possible? Wouldn't it be more efficient to provide full recovery to the victim in a single proceeding, rather than placing on the victim the burden of pursuing additional damages through a separate civil case?

4. **Problem: *United States v. Blake.*** Review the facts in *Blake* (Problem 1-1). Which of the losses suffered by Sheron Nauzo, if any, would Blake be required to pay compensation for under the MVRA?

5. **Multiple Defendants.** Sometimes multiple individuals jointly cause a harm, as when a coordinated group commits a robbery or perpetrates an investment scam. Assuming all are later convicted, what does § 3664(h), *supra,* indicate about each defendant's restitution liability? When each defendant is made liable for the full amount, this is called "joint and several liability." In federal practice, joint and several liability is probably more

common than the alternative (apportionment). GOODWIN, GRENIG & FISHBACH, *supra*, § 13:14. Joint and several liability tends to lead to the wealthiest defendants bearing most or all of the restitution burden—even if there are poorer defendants who were equally or even more responsible for the victim's loss. Why do you suppose the law permits such unfairness as between the defendants?

Does joint and several liability under § 3664(h) permit victims the windfall of multiple recoveries for the same loss? Although the statute does not expressly address this question, courts have interpreted the MVRA such that multiple recoveries are precluded—once the full amount of restitution ordered by the court has been paid, the victim may recover no more. *See, e.g., United States v. Nucci*, 364 F.3d 419 (2d Cir. 2004). This approach may be consistent with the common law of torts, but does it best serve the purposes of *criminal* law? Recall, for instance, the view that restitution advances rehabilitation by "forc[ing] the defendant to confront, in concrete terms, the harm his or her actions have caused." *Kelly v. Robinson*, 479 U.S. 36, 49 n.10 (1986). On that view, shouldn't each defendant be required to pay compensation for the full amount of the harm, regardless of whether the victim thereby receives a windfall?

Like the MVRA, the MPC:S gives the trial judge discretion to choose between apportionment and joint and several liability. However, some states mandate that liability must be joint and several. MPC:S § 6.04A rptr. note j.

6. **Burden of Proof.** For purposes of determining the amount of losses and other restitution-specific fact-finding, 18 U.S.C. § 3664(e), *supra*, specifies that the civil preponderance-of-the-evidence standard should be used. This is consistent with the MPC:S and the law of most states. MPC:S § 6.04A rptr. note k.

7. **Double-Recovery in Civil and Criminal Proceedings.** The MVRA aims to prevent double-recovery for the same losses by offsetting civil recoveries against the defendant's restitution obligations. 18 U.S.C. § 3664(j)(2), *supra*. The MPC:S and most states take a similar position. MPC:S § 6.04A rptr. note *l*.

8. **Restitution Versus Fine.** If a defendant only has the capacity to pay restitution *or* a fine, but not both, which should take precedence? Federal statutes point to a higher priority for restitution. First, in cases covered by the MVRA, restitution is made mandatory, whereas the general fine statute, 18 U.S.C. § 3571(a), makes fines discretionary. Second, a separate statute, 18 U.S.C. § 3612(c), directs the Attorney General to apply payments from defendants first to satisfy restitution awards, and only after restitution is paid in full to cover fine obligations.

The MPC:S similarly prioritizes restitution over fines, which is consistent with the law in some, but not all, states. MPC:S § 6.04 rptr. note *l*.

9. **Victim's Litigation Strategy.** Imagine that you represent a person who has been victimized in a manner that would be covered by the MVRA if a federal criminal case were filed. You have already filed a civil tort suit against the victimizer. The local United States Attorney's Office is either

unaware of the matter or is ambivalent about filing criminal charges. Would you press federal prosecutors to take the case—which would likely result in a stay of the civil proceedings—or would you prefer to focus on moving ahead with the civil litigation? Such scenarios present complicated strategic questions. *See* GOODWIN, GRENIG & FISHBACH, *supra*, §§ 17:18–17:22. Due to the time constraints imposed by the Speedy Trial Act, a criminal case is apt to be completed more quickly than a civil case, which may mean a quicker payout to the victim. Additionally, the victim need not pay legal fees for the work performed on his or her behalf by a prosecutor, or by the PO in obtaining the defendant's financial information. Moreover, if facing the prospect of significant incarceration, a criminal defendant may not bother litigating restitution issues much—or might see cooperation on the restitution front as a helpful way to curry favor with the prosecutor or judge. On the other hand, as suggested above, restitution is in some important respects more limited than tort damages, which can include compensation for pain and suffering and punitive damages. Also, the victim will have less control over the conduct of the criminal litigation, including settlement strategy, than he or she would over the civil litigation. And, of course, the burden of proof is higher to establish criminal than civil liability. Are there any other strategic considerations that strike you as potentially important?

10. **Community Restitution.** Section 3663A, *supra*, covers cases in which an "identifiable victim or victims has suffered a physical injury or pecuniary loss." § 3663A(c)(1). Sometimes, however, crime causes more inchoate harms for a community as a whole. For instance, open-air drug trafficking on a particular city block may draw crime-prone substance abusers into the neighborhood, cause residents to become fearful about leaving their homes, and generally demoralize the community. Congress made restitution available, but not mandatory, in such situations through § 3663(c). Under the latter statute, a person who has been convicted of certain drug offenses may be required to pay an amount equal to the "public harm" caused by the offense. Money collected under § 3663(c) goes to the state victim assistance fund and substance abuse grants. However, the statute also specifies that fines and forfeitures take precedence over community restitution; only if the defendant has some additional ability to pay should community restitution be awarded. This may help to explain why community restitution is only infrequently ordered. GOODWIN, GRENIG & FISHBACH, *supra*, § 4:20.

11. **By the Numbers.** In FY2020, 10.9% of sentenced federal defendants were ordered to pay restitution. U.S. SENT'G COMM'N, 2020 SOURCEBOOK OF FEDERAL SENTENCING STATISTICS tbl. 16. The average (mean) restitution award was $995,382. *Id.* tbl. 17. Restitution awards are thus more common, and on average larger, than fines, which may, in part, reflect the lesser role of ability to pay as a factor in restitution determinations.

12. **Restitution and Structural Reform of the Criminal Justice System.** In Chapter 1, we noted the provocative argument by law professor Randy Barnett that restitution should become *the* standard form of punishment used by the criminal justice system, with other sanctions

relegated to a secondary role to enforce restitution awards. Even if you are not prepared to go that far, it may strike you that restitution is a more constructive and appropriate punishment for most crimes than incarceration and should be used with much greater frequency. Wider use of the "community restitution" concept might be part of such an agenda. However, in the current criminal justice context, the economic disadvantage of most defendants would make it difficult to expand the use of restitution in ways that would be practically meaningful. (As noted in the previous section, the same objection is made to expanding the use of fines.)

Can you think of any reforms to the system that might support broader use of restitution? Consider, for instance, the following:

- Greater use of intermediate sanctions (e.g., halfway house or home detention with work-release privileges) relative to full-blown incarceration, so that defendants would better be able to obtain or retain employment while serving their sentences.
- Increased availability of vocational training and institutional employment for incarcerated persons.
- Extension of minimum wage laws to incarcerated persons.
- Elimination of supervision conditions that interfere with employment, e.g., required in-person meetings with POs or drug tests during regular work hours.
- Elimination of other economic sanctions that take money that would otherwise be available for restitution.
- Elimination of the collateral consequences that restrict employment for many convicted persons (see Chapter 11 below).

13. **Who Is a "Victim"?** The MVRA defines a "victim" as "a person directly and proximately harmed as a result of the commission of an offense for which restitution may be ordered." 18 U.S.C. § 3663A(a)(2). Victimhood, for MVRA purposes, thus turns on the legal concept of proximate causation. As we saw in Chapter 3, the Crime Victims' Rights Act similarly makes use of proximate causation in its definition of victim. In most cases, the causation standard seems to present no particular difficulties, but in some cases it raises complex legal or factual problems. In the CVRA discussion in Chapter 3, for instance, we noted the *Hunter* case, involving an illegally sold firearm that was later used in a mass shooting. In that case, the district court determined that the parent of a child killed by the buyer was not a "victim" of the seller. The Supreme Court confronted a different causation problem in the case that follows.

Paroline v. United States

572 U.S. 434 (2014)

■ KENNEDY, J.

This case presents the question of how to determine the amount of restitution a possessor of child pornography must pay to the victim whose childhood abuse appears in the pornographic materials possessed. The relevant statutory provisions are set forth at 18 U.S.C. § 2259. Enacted as a component of the Violence Against Women Act of 1994, § 2259 requires district courts to award restitution for certain federal criminal offenses, including child-pornography possession.

Petitioner Doyle Randall Paroline pleaded guilty to such an offense. He admitted to possessing between 150 and 300 images of child pornography, which included two that depicted the sexual exploitation of a young girl, now a young woman, who goes by the pseudonym "Amy" for this litigation. The question is what causal relationship must be established between the defendant's conduct and a victim's losses for purposes of determining the right to, and the amount of, restitution under § 2259.

I

Three decades ago, this Court observed that "the exploitive use of children in the production of pornography has become a serious national problem." *New York v. Ferber,* 458 U.S. 747, 749 (1982). The demand for child pornography harms children in part because it drives production, which involves child abuse. The harms caused by child pornography, however, are still more extensive because child pornography is "a permanent record" of the depicted child's abuse, and "the harm to the child is exacerbated by [its] circulation." *Id.,* at 759. Because child pornography is now traded with ease on the Internet, "the number of still images and videos memorializing the sexual assault and other sexual exploitation of children, many very young in age, has grown exponentially." United States Sentencing Comm'n, P. Saris et al., Federal Child Pornography Offenses 3 (2012) (hereinafter Sentencing Comm'n Report).

One person whose story illustrates the devastating harm caused by child pornography is the respondent victim in this case. When she was eight and nine years old, she was sexually abused by her uncle in order to produce child pornography. Her uncle was prosecuted, required to pay about $6,000 in restitution, and sentenced to a lengthy prison term. The victim underwent an initial course of therapy beginning in 1998 and continuing into 1999. By the end of this period, her therapist's notes reported that she was " 'back to normal' "; her involvement in dance and other age-appropriate activities, and the support of her family, justified an optimistic assessment. Her functioning appeared to decline in her teenage years, however; and a major blow to her recovery came when, at the age of 17, she learned that images of her abuse were being trafficked on the Internet. The digital images were available nationwide and no doubt worldwide. Though the exact scale of the trade in her images is unknown, the possessors to date easily number in the thousands. The knowledge that her images were circulated far and wide renewed the victim's trauma and made it difficult for her to recover from her abuse.

As she explained in a victim impact statement submitted to the District Court in this case:

> Every day of my life I live in constant fear that someone will see my pictures and recognize me and that I will be humiliated all over again. It hurts me to know someone is looking at them—at me—when I was just a little girl being abused for the camera. I did not choose to be there, but now I am there forever in pictures that people are using to do sick things. I want it all erased. I want it all stopped. But I am powerless to stop it just like I was powerless to stop my uncle. . . . My life and my feelings are worse now because the crime has never really stopped and will never really stop. . . . It's like I am being abused over and over and over again.

The victim says in her statement that her fear and trauma make it difficult for her to trust others or to feel that she has control over what happens to her. * * *

Petitioner Paroline is one of the individuals who possessed this victim's images. In 2009, he pleaded guilty in federal court to one count of possession of material involving the sexual exploitation of children in violation of 18 U.S.C. § 2252. Paroline admitted to knowing possession of between 150 and 300 images of child pornography, two of which depicted the respondent victim. The victim sought restitution under § 2259, asking for close to $3.4 million, consisting of nearly $3 million in lost income and about $500,000 in future treatment and counseling costs. She also sought attorney's fees and costs. The parties submitted competing expert reports. They stipulated that the victim did not know who Paroline was and that none of her claimed losses flowed from any specific knowledge about him or his offense conduct.

After briefing and hearings, the District Court declined to award restitution. The District Court observed that "everyone involved with child pornography—from the abusers and producers to the end-users and possessors—contribute[s] to [the victim's] ongoing harm." But it concluded that the Government had the burden of proving the amount of the victim's losses "directly produced by Paroline that would not have occurred without his possession of her images." The District Court found that, under this standard, the Government had failed to meet its burden of proving what losses, if any, were proximately caused by Paroline's offense. It thus held that "an award of restitution is not appropriate in this case."

The victim sought a writ of mandamus, asking the United States Court of Appeals for the Fifth Circuit to direct the District Court to order Paroline to pay restitution in the amount requested. * * *

II

Title 18 U.S.C. § 2259(a) provides that a district court "shall order restitution for any offense" under Chapter 110 of Title 18, which covers a number of offenses involving the sexual exploitation of children and child pornography in particular. Paroline was convicted of knowingly possessing child pornography under § 2252, a Chapter 110 offense.

Section 2259 states a broad restitutionary purpose: It requires district courts to order defendants "to pay the victim . . . the full amount of the victim's losses as determined by the court," § 2259(b)(1), and expressly states that "[t]he issuance of a restitution order under this section is mandatory," § 2259(b)(4)(A). * * *

The threshold question the Court faces is whether § 2259 limits restitution to those losses proximately caused by the defendant's offense conduct. * * *

As a general matter, to say one event proximately caused another is a way of making two separate but related assertions. First, it means the former event caused the latter. This is known as actual cause or cause in fact. The concept of actual cause "is not a metaphysical one but an ordinary, matter-of-fact inquiry into the existence . . . of a causal relation as laypeople would view it." 4 F. Harper, F. James, & O. Gray, Torts § 20.2, p. 100 (3d ed. 2007).

Every event has many causes, however, and only some of them are proximate, as the law uses that term. So to say that one event was a proximate cause of another means that it was not just any cause, but one with a sufficient connection to the result. The idea of proximate cause, as distinct from actual cause or cause in fact, defies easy summary. It is "a flexible concept," *Bridge v. Phoenix Bond & Indemnity Co.,* 553 U.S. 639, 654 (2008), that generally "refers to the basic requirement that . . . there must be 'some direct relation between the injury asserted and the injurious conduct alleged,'" *CSX Transp., Inc. v. McBride,* 131 S. Ct. 2630, 2645 (2011) (ROBERTS, C.J., dissenting) (quoting *Holmes v. Securities Investor Protection Corporation,* 503 U.S. 258, 268 (1992)). The concept of proximate causation is applicable in both criminal and tort law, and the analysis is parallel in many instances. 1 W. LaFave, Substantive Criminal Law § 6.4(c), p. 471 (2d ed. 2003) (hereinafter LaFave). Proximate cause is often explicated in terms of foreseeability or the scope of the risk created by the predicate conduct. See, *e.g., ibid.*; 1 Restatement (Third) of Torts: Liability for Physical and Emotional Harm § 29, p. 493 (2005) (hereinafter Restatement). A requirement of proximate cause thus serves, *inter alia,* to preclude liability in situations where the causal link between conduct and result is so attenuated that the consequence is more aptly described as mere fortuity.

All parties agree § 2259 imposes some causation requirement. The statute defines a victim as "the individual harmed as a result of a commission of a crime under this chapter." § 2259(c). The words "as a result of" plainly suggest causation. And a straightforward reading of § 2259(c) indicates that the term "a crime" refers to the offense of conviction. Cf. *Hughey v. United States,* 495 U.S. 411, 416 (1990). So if the defendant's offense conduct did not cause harm to an individual, that individual is by definition not a "victim" entitled to restitution under § 2259.

As noted above, § 2259 requires a court to order restitution for "the full amount of the victim's losses," which the statute defines to include "any costs incurred by the victim" for six enumerated categories of expense, § 2259(b)(3). The reference to "costs incurred by the victim" is most naturally understood as costs stemming from the source that qualifies an individual as a "victim" in the first place—namely, ones arising "as a result of" the offense. Thus, as is typically the case with criminal restitution, § 2259 is intended to compensate victims for losses caused by the offense of conviction. This is an important point, for it means the central concern of the causal inquiry must be the conduct of the particular defendant from whom restitution is sought.

But there is a further question whether restitution under § 2259 is limited to losses proximately caused by the offense. As noted, a requirement of proximate cause is more restrictive than a requirement of factual cause alone. Even if § 2259 made no express reference to proximate causation, the Court might well hold that a showing of proximate cause was required. Proximate cause is a standard aspect of causation in criminal law and the law of torts. See 1 LaFave § 6.4(a), at 464–466; W. Keeton, D. Dobbs, R. Keeton, & D. Owen, Prosser and Keeton on Law of Torts § 41, p. 263 (5th ed. 1984) (hereinafter Prosser and Keeton). Given proximate cause's traditional role in causation analysis, this Court has more than once found a proximate-cause requirement built into a statute that did not expressly impose one.

Here, however, the interpretive task is easier, for the requirement of proximate cause is in the statute's text. The statute enumerates six categories of covered losses. § 2259(b)(3). These include certain medical services, § 2259(b)(3)(A); physical and occupational therapy, § 2259(b)(3)(B); transportation, temporary housing, and child care, § 2259(b)(3)(C); lost income, § 2259(b)(3)(D); attorney's fees and costs, § 2259(b)(3)(E); and a final catchall category for "any other losses suffered by the victim as a proximate result of the offense," § 2259(b)(3)(F). * * *

Reading the statute to impose a general proximate-cause limitation accords with common sense. As noted above, proximate cause forecloses liability in situations where the causal link between conduct and result is so attenuated that the so-called consequence is more akin to mere fortuity. For example, suppose the traumatized victim of a Chapter 110 offender needed therapy and had a car accident on the way to her therapist's office. The resulting medical costs, in a literal sense, would be a factual result of the offense. But it would be strange indeed to make a defendant pay restitution for these costs. * * *

III

There remains the difficult question of how to apply the statute's causation requirements in this case. The problem stems from the somewhat atypical causal process underlying the losses the victim claims here. It is perhaps simple enough for the victim to prove the aggregate losses, including the costs of psychiatric treatment and lost income, that stem from the ongoing traffic in her images as a whole. (Complications may arise in disaggregating losses sustained as a result of the initial physical abuse, but those questions may be set aside for present purposes.) These losses may be called, for convenience's sake, a victim's "general losses." The difficulty is in determining the "full amount" of those general losses, if any, that are the proximate result of the offense conduct of a particular defendant who is one of thousands who have possessed and will in the future possess the victim's images but who has no other connection to the victim.

In determining the amount of general losses a defendant must pay under § 2259 the ultimate question is how much of these losses were the "proximate result," § 2259(b)(3)(F), of that individual's offense. But the most difficult aspect of this inquiry concerns the threshold requirement of causation in fact. To be sure, the requirement of proximate causation, as distinct from mere causation in fact, would prevent holding any possessor liable for losses caused in only a remote sense. But the victim's costs of treatment and lost income resulting from the trauma of knowing that images of her abuse are being viewed over and over are direct and foreseeable results of child-pornography crimes, including possession, assuming the prerequisite of factual causation is satisfied. The primary problem, then, is the proper standard of causation in fact.

A

The traditional way to prove that one event was a factual cause of another is to show that the latter would not have occurred "but for" the former. This approach is a familiar part of our legal tradition, and no party disputes that a showing of but-for causation would satisfy § 2259's factual-causation requirement. Sometimes that showing could be made with little difficulty. For example, but-for causation could be shown with ease in many cases involving producers of child pornography; parents who permit their children to be used for child-pornography production; individuals who sell children for such purposes; or the initial distributor of the pornographic images of a child.

In this case, however, a showing of but-for causation cannot be made. The District Court found that the Government failed to prove specific losses caused by Paroline in a but-for sense and recognized that it would be "incredibly difficult" to do so in a case like this. That finding has a solid foundation in the record, and it is all but unchallenged in this Court. From the victim's perspective, Paroline was just one of thousands of anonymous possessors. To be sure, the victim's precise degree of trauma likely bears a relation to the total number of offenders; it would probably be less if only 10 rather than thousands had seen her images. But it is not possible to prove that her losses would be less (and by how much) but for one possessor's individual role in the large, loosely connected network through which her images circulate. Even without Paroline's offense, thousands would have viewed and would in the future view the victim's images, so it cannot be shown that her trauma and attendant losses would have been any different but for Paroline's offense. That is especially so given the parties' stipulation that the victim had no knowledge of Paroline.

Recognizing that losses cannot be substantiated under a but-for approach where the defendant is an anonymous possessor of images in wide circulation on the Internet, the victim and the Government urge the Court to read § 2259 to require a less restrictive causation standard, at least in this and similar child-pornography cases. They are correct to note that courts have departed from the but-for standard where circumstances warrant, especially where the combined conduct of multiple wrongdoers produces a bad outcome.

The victim and the Government look to the literature on criminal and tort law for alternatives to the but-for test. The Court has noted that the "most common" exception to the but-for causation requirement is applied where "multiple sufficient causes independently . . . produce a result," [*Burrage v. United States*, 571 U.S. 204, 214 (2014)]. This exception is an ill fit here, as all parties seem to recognize. Paroline's possession of two images of the victim was surely not sufficient to cause her entire losses from the ongoing trade in her images. Nor is there a practical way to isolate some subset of the victim's general losses that Paroline's conduct alone would have been sufficient to cause.

Understandably, the victim and the Government thus concentrate on a handful of less demanding causation tests endorsed by authorities on tort law. One prominent treatise suggests that "[w]hen the conduct of two or more actors is so related to an event that their combined conduct, viewed as a whole, is a but-for cause of the event, and application of the but-for rule to them individually would absolve all of them, the conduct of each is a cause in fact of the event." Prosser and Keeton § 41, at 268. The Restatement adopts a similar exception for "[m]ultiple sufficient causal sets." 1 Restatement § 27, Comment *f*, at 380–381. This is where a wrongdoer's conduct, though alone "insufficient . . . to cause the plaintiff's harm," is, "when combined with conduct by other persons," "more than sufficient to cause the harm." *Ibid*. The Restatement offers as an example a case in which three people independently but simultaneously lean on a car, creating enough combined force to roll it off a cliff. Even if each exerted too little force to move the car, and the force exerted by any two was sufficient to the move the car, each individual is a factual cause of the car's destruction. * * *

These alternative causal tests are a kind of legal fiction or construct. If the conduct of a wrongdoer is neither necessary nor sufficient to produce an outcome, that conduct cannot in a strict sense be said to have caused the outcome. Nonetheless, tort law teaches that alternative and less demanding causal standards are necessary in certain circumstances to vindicate the law's purposes. It would be anomalous to turn away a person harmed by the combined acts of many wrongdoers simply because none of those wrongdoers alone caused the harm. And it would be nonsensical to adopt a rule whereby individuals hurt by the combined wrongful acts of many (and thus in many instances hurt more badly than otherwise) would have no redress, whereas individuals hurt by the acts of one person alone would have a remedy. Those are the principles that underlie the various aggregate causation tests the victim and the Government cite, and they are sound principles.

These alternative causal standards, though salutary when applied in a judicious manner, also can be taken too far. That is illustrated by the victim's suggested approach to applying § 2259 in cases like this. The victim says that under the strict logic of these alternative causal tests, each possessor of her images is a part of a causal set sufficient to produce her ongoing trauma, so each possessor should be treated as a cause in fact of all the trauma and all the attendant losses incurred as a result of the entire ongoing traffic in her images. * * *

The striking outcome of this reasoning—that each possessor of the victim's images would bear the consequences of the acts of the many thousands who possessed those images—illustrates why the Court has been reluctant to adopt aggregate causation logic in an incautious manner, especially in interpreting criminal statutes where there is no language expressly suggesting Congress intended that approach. * * *

And there is special reason not to do so in the context of criminal restitution. Aside from the manifest procedural differences between criminal sentencing and civil tort lawsuits, restitution serves purposes that differ from (though they overlap with) the purposes of tort law. See, *e.g., Kelly v. Robinson,* 479 U.S. 36, 49, n. 10 (1986) (noting that restitution is, *inter alia,* "an effective rehabilitative penalty"). Legal fictions developed in the law of torts cannot be imported into criminal restitution and applied to their utmost limits without due consideration of these differences. * * *

It is unclear whether it could ever be sensible to embrace the fiction that this victim's entire losses were the "proximate result" of a single possessor's offense. Paroline's contribution to the causal process underlying the victim's losses was very minor, both compared to the combined acts of all other relevant offenders, and in comparison to the contributions of other individual offenders, particularly distributors (who may have caused hundreds or thousands of further viewings) and the initial producer of the child pornography. Congress gave no indication that it intended its statute to be applied in the expansive manner the victim suggests, a manner contrary to the bedrock principle that restitution should reflect the consequences of the defendant's own conduct, not the conduct of thousands of geographically and temporally distant offenders acting independently, and with whom the defendant had no contact.

The victim argues that holding each possessor liable for her entire losses would be fair and practical, in part because offenders may seek contribution from one another. If that were so, it might mitigate to some degree the concerns her approach presents. But there is scant authority for her contention that offenders convicted in different proceedings in different jurisdictions and ordered to pay restitution to the same victim may seek contribution from one another. There is no general federal right to contribution. Nor does the victim point to any clear statutory basis for a right to contribution in these circumstances. * * *

The reality is that the victim's suggested approach would amount to holding each possessor of her images liable for the conduct of thousands of other independently acting possessors and distributors, with no legal or practical avenue for seeking contribution. That approach is so severe it might raise questions under the Excessive Fines Clause of the Eighth Amendment. To be sure, this Court has said that "the Excessive Fines Clause was intended to limit only those fines directly imposed by, and payable to, the government." *Browning-Ferris Industries of Vt., Inc. v. Kelco Disposal, Inc.,* 492 U.S. 257, 268 (1989). But while restitution under § 2259 is paid to a victim, it is imposed by the Government "at the culmination of a criminal proceeding and requires conviction of an underlying" crime, *United States v. Bajakajian,* 524 U.S. 321, 328 (1998). Thus, despite the differences between restitution and a traditional fine, restitution still implicates "the prosecutorial powers of government," *Browning-Ferris, supra,* at 275. The primary goal of restitution is remedial or compensatory, but it also serves punitive purposes. That may be "sufficient to bring [it] within the purview of the Excessive Fines Clause," *Bajakajian, supra,* at 329, n. 4. And there is a real question whether holding a single possessor liable for millions of dollars in losses collectively caused by thousands of independent actors might be excessive and disproportionate in these circumstances. These concerns offer further reason not to interpret the statute the way the victim suggests.

B

The contention that the victim's entire losses from the ongoing trade in her images were "suffered . . . as a proximate result" of Paroline's offense for purposes of § 2259 must be rejected. But that does not mean the broader principles underlying the aggregate causation theories the Government and the victim cite are irrelevant to determining the proper outcome in cases like this. The cause of the victim's general losses is the trade in her images. And Paroline is a part of that cause, for he is one of those who viewed her images. While it is not possible to identify a discrete, readily definable incremental loss he caused, it is indisputable that he was a part of the overall phenomenon that caused her general losses. Just as it undermines the purposes of tort law to turn away plaintiffs harmed by several wrongdoers, it would undermine the remedial and penological purposes of § 2259 to turn away victims in cases like this.

With respect to the statute's remedial purpose, there can be no question that it would produce anomalous results to say that no restitution is appropriate in these circumstances. It is common ground that the victim suffers continuing and grievous harm as a result of her knowledge that a large, indeterminate number of individuals have viewed and will in the future view images of the sexual abuse she endured. Harms of this sort are a major reason why child pornography is outlawed. * * *

Denying restitution in cases like this would also be at odds with the penological purposes of § 2259's mandatory restitution scheme. In a sense, every viewing of child pornography is a repetition of the victim's abuse. One reason to make restitution mandatory for crimes like this is to impress upon offenders that their conduct produces concrete and devastating harms for real, identifiable victims. It would be inconsistent with this purpose to apply the statute in a way that leaves offenders with the mistaken impression that child-pornography possession (at least where the images are in wide circulation) is a victimless crime.

If the statute by its terms required a showing of strict but-for causation, these purposes would be beside the point. But the text of the statute is not so limited. Although Congress limited restitution to losses that are the "proximate result" of the defendant's offense, such unelaborated causal language by no means requires but-for causation by its terms. As the authorities the Government and the victim cite show, the availability of alternative causal standards where circumstances warrant is, no less than the but-for test itself as a default, part of the background legal tradition against which Congress has legislated. It would be unacceptable to adopt a causal standard so strict that it would undermine congressional intent where neither the plain text of the statute nor legal tradition demands such an approach.

In this special context, where it can be shown both that a defendant possessed a victim's images and that a victim has outstanding losses caused by the continuing traffic in those images but where it is impossible to trace a particular amount of those losses to the individual defendant by recourse to a more traditional causal inquiry, a court applying § 2259 should order restitution in an amount that comports with the defendant's relative role in the causal process that underlies the victim's general losses. The amount would not be severe in a case like this, given the nature of the causal connection between the conduct of a possessor like Paroline and the entirety of the victim's general losses from the trade in her images, which are the product of the acts of thousands of offenders. It would not, however, be a token or nominal amount. The required restitution would be a reasonable and circumscribed award imposed in recognition of the indisputable role of the offender in the causal process underlying the victim's losses and suited to the relative size of that causal role. * * *

There remains the question of how district courts should go about determining the proper amount of restitution. At a general level of abstraction, a court must assess as best it can from available evidence the significance of the individual defendant's conduct in light of the broader causal process that produced the victim's losses. This cannot be a precise mathematical inquiry and involves the use of discretion and sound judgment. But that is neither unusual nor novel, either in the wider context of criminal sentencing or in the more specific domain of restitution. It is well recognized that district courts by necessity "exercise . . . discretion in fashioning a restitution order." § 3664(a). Indeed, a district court is expressly authorized to conduct a similar inquiry where multiple defendants who have "contributed to the loss of a victim" appear before it. § 3664(h). In that case it may "apportion liability among the defendants to reflect the level of contribution to the victim's loss . . . of each defendant." Assessing an individual defendant's role in the causal process behind a child-pornography victim's losses does not involve a substantially different or greater exercise of discretion.

There are a variety of factors district courts might consider in determining a proper amount of restitution, and it is neither necessary nor appropriate to prescribe a precise algorithm for determining the proper restitution amount at this point in the law's development. Doing so would unduly constrain the decisionmakers closest to the facts of any given case. But district courts might, as a starting point, determine the amount of the victim's losses caused by the continuing traffic in the victim's images (excluding, of course, any remote losses like the hypothetical car accident described above), then set an award of restitution in consideration of factors that bear on the relative causal significance of the defendant's conduct in producing those losses. These could include the number of past criminal defendants found to have contributed to the victim's general losses; reasonable predictions of the number of future offenders likely to be caught and convicted for crimes contributing to the victim's general losses; any available and reasonably reliable estimate of the broader number of offenders involved (most of whom will, of course, never be caught or convicted); whether the defendant reproduced or distributed images of the victim; whether the defendant had any connection to the initial production of the images; how many images of the victim the defendant possessed; and other facts relevant to the defendant's relative causal role. * * *

The victim also argues that this approach would consign her to "piecemeal" restitution and leave her to face "decades of litigation that might never lead to full recovery," which "would convert Congress's promise to child pornography victims into an empty gesture." But Congress has not promised victims full and swift restitution at all costs.

To be sure, the statute states a strong restitutionary purpose; but that purpose cannot be twisted into a license to hold a defendant liable for an amount drastically out of proportion to his own individual causal relation to the victim's losses.

Furthermore, an approach of this sort better effects the need to impress upon defendants that their acts are not irrelevant or victimless. As the Government observes, it would undermine this important purpose of criminal restitution if the victim simply collected her full losses from a handful of wealthy possessors and left the remainder to pay nothing because she had already fully collected. Of course the victim should someday collect restitution for all her child-pornography losses, but it makes sense to spread payment among a larger number of offenders in amounts more closely in proportion to their respective causal roles and their own circumstances so that more are made aware, through the concrete mechanism of restitution, of the impact of child-pornography possession on victims. * * *

[The dissenting opinions of CHIEF JUSTICE ROBERTS and JUSTICE SOTOMAYOR are omitted.]

NOTES & QUESTIONS

1. **General and Specific Restitution Statutes.** Federal law, like the law in many states, includes both broadly applicable restitution statutes (the MVRA and its predecessor, the Victim and Witness Protection Act) and additional restitution statutes that are specific to certain types of offenses. *Paroline* dealt with a specific restitution statute that covers certain sexual and other offenses against children. The statute was enacted as part of the Violence Against Women Act of 1994 (VAWA).

The different federal restitution statutes differ in some respects, e.g., in the specific losses that are recoverable, but tend to employ many of the same procedures and legal standards. Note, for instance, that the key concept from the VAWA that the *Paroline* Court had to interpret, proximate causation, is also contained in the MVRA. Thus, the Court's analysis in *Paroline* may in some respects be more broadly applicable to federal restitution under the general statute, too.

2. **Victim Compensation When "But-For" Causation Cannot Be Proven.** *Paroline* presented, in the restitution context, a sort of causation problem that has bedeviled tort law for many years in cases dealing with exposure to toxic substances that might have come from any of a number of different sources. For instance, a person with asbestos-related lung disease might have been exposed to asbestos products manufactured by several different companies, making it impossible for the person to prove by a preponderance of the evidence that any given company caused his or her injury. Similarly, in *Paroline*, "Amy" could not prove that Paroline—who was only one of the thousands of individuals who viewed her images—had personally "caused" her to suffer any harm, at least not in the "but-for" sense of causation that has traditionally been used in both tort and criminal law.

But, as in the toxic tort context, strict application of traditional views of causation leads to an unsatisfactory conclusion: because no one defendant can be proven to have been the cause of the injury, *all* defendants escape financial liability—and an indisputably injured victim walks away with nothing.

In the torts context, some courts have developed workarounds to permit recovery by plaintiffs—what the *Paroline* Court called "alternative causal standards"—but these workarounds are not universally accepted even for torts, and the Court was evidently reluctant to extend these approaches to criminal restitution. Do you agree that the distinctive purposes of criminal punishment justify the Court's refusal to make Paroline liable for the full amount of Amy's losses?

The arguments in *Paroline* echo the policy debate over joint and several liability for codefendants. Jurisdictions that mandate joint and several liability effectively elevate the goal of efficient, complete compensation for victims over the competing objective of tying each defendant's financial liability to his or her relative culpability. If you favor joint and several liability, shouldn't you also support the alternative causal standard that was being proposed in *Paroline*?

3. **Excessive Fines Clause.** The *Paroline* Court suggested that the proposed causal standard might lead to such disproportionately large restitution judgments against some defendants that the Eighth Amendment's Excessive Fines Clause would be violated. We will consider the Clause in more depth later in this chapter.

4. **The Goldilocks Solution.** If the Court found it unacceptable to hold Paroline fully responsible for the millions of dollars that Amy sought in restitution, the Court also seemed to find it equally unacceptable that Amy should walk away emptyhanded. The Court settled on a middleground approach, in which the trial court "should order restitution in an amount that comports with the defendant's relative role in the causal process that underlies the victim's general losses." Does it seem to you there is any statutory basis for the Court's solution? (Chief Justice Roberts, writing in dissent, thought not.) Note that the Court carefully limited its holding to the "this special context, where it can be shown both that a defendant possessed a victim's images and that a victim has outstanding losses caused by the continuing traffic in those images but where it is impossible to trace a particular amount of those losses to the individual defendant by recourse to a more traditional causal inquiry."

5. **Enforcement by the Victim.** As you may recall from Chapter 3, the Crime Victims' Rights Act endows victims with some ability to enforce their rights—including the right to restitution—independently of the prosecutor. In *Paroline*, Amy took advantage of one of the CVRA's special enforcement provisions by seeking a writ of mandamus against the district court in the Fifth Circuit.

6. **Proximate and Actual Causation.** Suppose the uncle in *Paroline* took pornographic photographs of Amy for his exclusive personal use, storing the images on his laptop. Imagine, however, that his laptop was stolen, and

that it was the *thief* who disseminated Amy's images on the Internet. Based on the Court's discussion of causation in *Paroline*, should the uncle be liable for the full $3.4 million that Amy sought in restitution? What arguments do you see on both sides of the question?

3. FORFEITURE

Forfeiture orders transfer ownership to the government of specified items of property that were connected to the commission of an offense. Typically, the property is either the proceeds of the offense (e.g., money obtained through an illegal drug sale), or an instrumentality of the offense (e.g., a car or boat that was used to transport drugs). Depriving a person of the proceeds of an offense fits neatly into the deterrence paradigm—much of the incentive for committing certain kinds of offenses is taken away if the prospective offender knows that he or she is unlikely to retain any tangible benefit from the offense. For its part, instrumentality forfeiture may also serve an incapacitation-like purpose by taking from a defendant an item of property that might otherwise facilitate a repeat-offense. And, of course, taking any type of property from a defendant may also serve desert purposes.

As with other types of economic sanctions, however, concerns are raised that forfeitures may impede rehabilitation by creating or exacerbating difficult economic circumstances for the defendant. For instance, if a defendant is dependent on his or her car to be able to drive to work, and the car is forfeited because it was also used to transport drugs, the defendant might fall into unemployment, which tends to increase recidivism risk. Also, as with other economic sanctions, forfeitures may harm innocent third parties, especially family members of the defendant. Finally, like fines, but unlike restitution, forfeitures deliver an economic benefit to the government, which may warp law enforcement priorities.

Forfeitures may be accomplished through conventional criminal processes, in which case the forfeiture order would effectively be part of the sentence. Alternatively, forfeitures may be obtained through civil litigation, in which case there is no requirement of a criminal conviction of the property owner. Civil forfeiture has thus been controversial because the owner may be deprived of his or her property without the full panoply of due process protections that are normally afforded in a criminal case.

In this section, we first consider civil forfeiture and then take up its criminal counterpart.

a. CIVIL FORFEITURE

Civil forfeiture laws permit the government to seize and take ownership of property without the need to prove anyone's guilt beyond a reasonable doubt. Indeed, as a formal matter, it is the property itself that is named as the defendant in the civil forfeiture action—not the human being whose legal interest in the property the government is seeking to extinguish. This convention results in odd-looking case names, like *United States v. Mercedes-Benz 2000 Model S400* or *United States v. $23,000 in U.S. Currency*.

Thanks to a lower burden of proof and other relaxed procedural protections, civil forfeiture is far more common than criminal in federal practice. The principal civil forfeiture statutes cover drug, money-laundering, fraud, customs, and immigration offenses. Below, we excerpt the drug law, followed by another statute containing procedural requirements that apply to civil forfeitures more generally, and then an illustrative case.

21 U.S.C. § 881

(a) Subject property

The following shall be subject to forfeiture to the United States and no property right shall exist in them:

(1) All controlled substances which have been manufactured, distributed, dispensed, or acquired in violation of this subchapter.

(2) All raw materials, products, and equipment of any kind which are used, or intended for use, in manufacturing, compounding, processing, delivering, importing, or exporting any controlled substance or listed chemical in violation of this subchapter. * * *

(4) All conveyances, including aircraft, vehicles, or vessels, which are used, or are intended for use, to transport, or in any manner to facilitate the transportation, sale, receipt, possession, or concealment of property described in paragraph (1) [or (2)]. * * *

(6) All moneys, negotiable instruments, securities, or other things of value furnished or intended to be furnished by any person in exchange for a controlled substance or listed chemical in violation of this subchapter, all proceeds traceable to such an exchange, and all moneys, negotiable instruments, and securities used or intended to be used to facilitate any violation of this subchapter.

(7) All real property, including any right, title, and interest (including any leasehold interest) in the whole of any lot or tract of land and any appurtenances or improvements, which is used, or intended to be used, in any manner or part, to commit, or to facilitate the commission of, a violation of this subchapter punishable by more than one year's imprisonment. * * *

(e) Disposition of forfeited property

(1) Whenever property is civilly or criminally forfeited under this subchapter the Attorney General may—

(A) retain the property for official use or, in the manner provided with respect to transfers under section 1616a of Title

19, transfer the property to any Federal agency or to any State or local law enforcement agency which participated directly in the seizure or forfeiture of the property;

(B) * * * sell, by public sale or any other commercially feasible means, any forfeited property which is not required to be destroyed by law and which is not harmful to the public; * * *

(3) The Attorney General shall assure that any property transferred to a State or local law enforcement agency under paragraph (1)(A)—

(A) has a value that bears a reasonable relationship to the degree of direct participation of the State or local agency in the law enforcement effort resulting in the forfeiture, taking into account the total value of all property forfeited and the total law enforcement effort with respect to the violation of law on which the forfeiture is based; and

(B) will serve to encourage further cooperation between the recipient State or local agency and Federal law enforcement agencies. * * *

18 U.S.C. § 983

(c) Burden of proof.—In a suit or action brought under any civil forfeiture statute for the civil forfeiture of any property—

(1) the burden of proof is on the Government to establish, by a preponderance of the evidence, that the property is subject to forfeiture; * * *

(3) if the Government's theory of forfeiture is that the property was used to commit or facilitate the commission of a criminal offense, or was involved in the commission of a criminal offense, the Government shall establish that there was a substantial connection between the property and the offense.

(d) Innocent owner defense.—

(1) An innocent owner's interest in property shall not be forfeited under any civil forfeiture statute. The claimant shall have the burden of proving that the claimant is an innocent owner by a preponderance of the evidence.

(2)(A) With respect to a property interest in existence at the time the illegal conduct giving rise to forfeiture took place, the term "innocent owner" means an owner who—

(i) did not know of the conduct giving rise to forfeiture; or

(ii) upon learning of the conduct giving rise to the forfeiture, did all that reasonably could be expected under the circumstances to terminate such use of the property. * * *

(3)(A) With respect to a property interest acquired after the conduct giving rise to the forfeiture has taken place, the term "innocent owner" means a person who, at the time that person acquired the interest in the property—

(i) was a bona fide purchaser or seller for value (including a purchaser or seller of goods or services for value); and

(ii) did not know and was reasonably without cause to believe that the property was subject to forfeiture. * * *

(5) If the court determines, in accordance with this section, that an innocent owner has a partial interest in property otherwise subject to forfeiture, or a joint tenancy or tenancy by the entirety in such property, the court may enter an appropriate order—

(A) severing the property;

(B) transferring the property to the Government with a provision that the Government compensate the innocent owner to the extent of his or her ownership interest once a final order of forfeiture has been entered and the property has been reduced to liquid assets; or

(C) permitting the innocent owner to retain the property subject to a lien in favor of the Government to the extent of the forfeitable interest in the property. * * *

United States v. Funds in the Amount of One Hundred Thousand & One Hundred Twenty Dollars ($100,120.00)

901 F.3d 758 (7th Cir. 2018)

■ MANION, J.

In December 2002, law enforcement seized $100,120 in United States currency from a passenger on an Amtrak train. The federal government initiated a civil forfeiture proceeding against the currency. The passenger and the owner of the funds, neither of whom were ever charged with committing any crime related to the funds, joined the suit as claimants. After fourteen years and two appeals, the case went to a jury. The jury found the currency was substantially connected to a drug transaction and entered a verdict for the government. The claimants filed multiple post-trial motions, all of which the district court denied. The case now comes to us for the third time. We affirm.

I

A. Background * * *

On December 6, 2002, Officer Eric Romano of the Amtrak Police (a member of the Drug Enforcement Administration Chicago Transportation Interdiction Taskforce) arrived at work at Union Station in Chicago and pulled up the manifests for the long-distance trains leaving that day. One reservation that caught his eye was Vincent Fallon's. Fallon was traveling to Seattle, a city Officer Romano knew as a source for drugs. Also, Fallon had used cash to purchase a one-way ticket, with a private bedroom, only two days earlier. Because Fallon's conduct fit a drug-courier profile, Officer Romano decided to question him.

Officer Romano and Officer Sterling Terry of the Chicago Police Department approached Fallon in his bedroom on the train. Officer Romano noticed Fallon had two bags: a duffel bag and a briefcase. After introducing himself, Officer Romano asked Fallon why he was traveling to Seattle. Fallon said he was going to see "a lady friend." Officer Romano asked Fallon if he was carrying weapons, drugs, or large amounts of currency. Fallon responded he was not.

The conversation turned to Fallon's bags. Officer Romano asked Fallon what was inside the briefcase, which was locked. Fallon, who was sweating and trembling, said it contained personal items and that he had packed it, but he did not have a key. When pressed on its contents, Fallon said the briefcase contained $50,000. Officer Romano asked him again why he was going to Seattle, and this time Fallon said he was potentially going to put a down payment on a house.

Officer Romano decided he was going to take the briefcase for further investigation at the Amtrak Police office. A drug dog was summoned. Before it arrived, Officer Romano opened the briefcase and observed it contained United States currency. When the dog arrived, Officer Romano spoke with the dog's handler and hid the briefcase in the office's roll-call room. The handler gave the dog the instruction to "fetch dope," and the dog ultimately found and alerted on the briefcase. Officer Romano picked the bag up from the floor, and he and Officer Terry counted out nineteen bundles of cash. They placed the cash in an evidence bag and handed Fallon, who had accompanied them to the office, a receipt. Fallon was then free to go.

The money was taken to the DEA headquarters in Chicago and placed in an evidence vault. The seizure had taken place on a Friday, so on the following Monday Officers Romano and Terry took the currency to LaSalle National Bank to have it counted. The bank counted out $100,120 and issued a cashier's check to the government in that amount. The physical currency was not retained.

B. Procedural History

On May 28, 2003, the United States filed a civil complaint seeking forfeiture of the funds. Fallon and Nicholas Marrocco, the undisputed actual owner of the funds, joined the action as claimants. * * *

[The district court ruled against the government on a Fourth Amendment issue, but the Seventh Circuit reversed. The district court then granted summary judgment to the government, but the Seventh Circuit once against reversed.]

The trial began on January 25, 2016. In the government's case in chief, the jury heard testimony from Officer Romano about the events of December 6, 2002, which we recounted above. The jury also heard testimony on drug-dog training and testimony that the drug dog involved in this case had a perfect record in 116 searches, including a failure to alert to currency not tainted with drugs.

The government also called Marrocco to the stand. He testified the money was his—the result of saving cash he had earned working various jobs. But the government presented evidence suggesting that, based on his income as stated on tax documents and his expenses as stated in a discovery response, he could not have saved that much money. He claimed to have kept the money as cash because he did not have a bank account. He testified that credit-card issues from when he was in college (he was thirty-two years old at the time of the seizure) had prevented him from opening an account.

About why he put his purported savings in Fallon's hands to take to Seattle on a train, Marrocco said he wanted to invest in a restaurant or bar on the West Coast. He testified there were "specific places" he was looking at, but said nothing more definite than that. Marrocco testified he put $127,000 in the briefcase and gave it to Fallon the day before the seizure. The plan was for Fallon to take the money to Seattle and place it in a safety-deposit box. * * *

* * * The claimants then put on their case. The claimants presented testimony from Dr. Lawrence Myers, the founder and director of the Institute for Biological Detection Systems at Auburn University, and David Kroyer, a dog trainer from Texas. Both questioned the reliability of the drug dog's alert. * * *

Before closing arguments, the court instructed the jury. The instructions stated the government was required to prove by a preponderance of the evidence that the $100,120 was substantially connected to an unlawful drug transaction. The instructions also stated the government was not required to prove a connection to a specific drug transaction, only a connection to "some" transaction, and the government was not required to prove the claimants themselves were involved in any unlawful conduct. * * *

The jury returned a verdict for the government. * * *

II

A. New Trial

We address first the claimants' motion for a new trial. * * *

The claimants focus their attack [on the jury instructions] on the interplay between three instructions. The claimants do not contest the first instruction, the "elements instruction," which

> requir[ed] the jury to find both a substantial connection between the funds and an unlawful controlled substance ***and*** that the

> funds were (1) furnished or intended to be furnished in exchange for a controlled substance; (2) the proceeds from the sale of a controlled substance; or (3) monies used or intended to be used to facilitate a controlled substances transaction.

Instead, their dispute is with two instructions that followed the elements instruction: the "transaction" instruction and the "offense" instruction. The transaction instruction stated the "government did not need to link the funds to a specific controlled substance transaction at a given time and place, but only to some unidentified unlawful controlled substance transaction." The offense instruction told the jury "the government was not required to prove that the claimants committed a controlled substance offense and that the fact the claimants did not directly participate in illegal activity is not a defense to the forfeiture."

The claimants contend the transaction and offense instructions confused the jury, but we are not convinced. The transaction instruction accurately stated the law: the government was not required to prove the existence of a specific drug transaction. It is enough that the government showed a connection to *some* transaction—the details are not necessary.

Turning to the offense instruction, the claimants maintain it conflicts with the "innocent owner" defense to forfeiture. Put simply, if a claimant can show he is an "innocent owner (in other words, that he did not know about the illegal use of his property)," he can avoid the forfeiture. *United States v. $271,080*, 816 F.3d 903, 908 (7th Cir. 2016). The claimants argue the offense instruction negates that defense by stating the government need not prove the claimant was personally involved in any criminal activity, and so it confused the jury and there should be a new trial.

The claimants are wrong. First, the instruction is generally correct in that the government need not prove a claimant's culpability for unlawful conduct to obtain a forfeiture. Civil forfeiture is a proceeding *in rem*, wherein the "inanimate [property] is treated as being itself guilty of the wrongdoing, regardless of its owner's conduct." *United States v. One 1976 Mercedes Benz 280S*, 618 F.2d 453, 454 (7th Cir. 1980). And even where the innocent owner defense is raised, it is the *claimant's* burden to prove his innocence, not the government's to prove his guilt. *See* 18 U.S.C. § 983(d)(1). Second, the claimants were not prejudiced here because they never raised the innocent-owner defense at trial—their argument all along was that the funds were not related to an unlawful drug transaction, not that they were innocent owners of corrupted currency. Not having raised the defense, they cannot claim to be prejudiced by the instruction. * * *

B. Judgment as a Matter of Law

Federal Rule of Civil Procedure 50(a) allows a court to enter judgment against a party at the close of that party's case in chief in a jury trial if "the court finds that a reasonable jury would not have a legally sufficient evidentiary basis to find for the party." If, as happened here, the court denies that motion, "the movant may file a renewed motion for judgment as a matter of law," after trial. Fed. R. Civ. P. 50(b). * * *

The government based its case for forfeiture on 21 U.S.C. § 881(a)(6), which makes subject to forfeiture "[a]ll moneys . . . furnished or intended to be furnished by any person in exchange for a controlled substance or listed chemical in violation of this subchapter, all proceeds traceable to such an exchange, and all moneys . . . used or intended to be used to facilitate any violation of this subchapter." As discussed above, the instructions at trial required the government to prove "by a preponderance of the evidence" that the money fit into one of those categories and that "there was a substantial connection between the [money] and the offense."

Having reviewed the record, we conclude it was not irrational for the jury to find the $100,120 was subject to forfeiture. First, the evidence at trial showed Fallon had purchased a one-way ticket, with cash, just two days before his trip. He had reserved a private room. And he was traveling to a city known as a source for drugs. All of this conduct fit the contours of a drug-courier profile. Certainly, such profiles are subject to legitimate criticism. But the jury was entitled to credit it as some evidence that the currency was connected with drug trafficking.

There is also evidence of the drug dog's alert. The claimants sought to undermine the dog sniff on a number of grounds, including suggesting that all currency is tainted with trace amounts of illegal drugs. But the jury heard evidence that this dog had a perfect record: 116 out of 116, including not alerting to untainted currency. It was entirely rational for the jury to reject the claimants' suggestions and accept the dog sniff as evidence the currency had been in contact with drugs.

Finally, adding to the drug-courier profile and the drug dog's alert are the inconsistent and implausible explanations the claimants gave for why Fallon found himself on the train that December day. When he was first stopped on the train, Fallon said he was going to Seattle to visit "a lady friend" and he was not carrying large amounts of currency. As the encounter with law enforcement unfolded, he said he was carrying $50,000 to "maybe put a down payment on a house." The claimants point to no evidence Fallon ever told law enforcement about a safety-deposit box or investing in a restaurant on the West Coast.

Then, Marrocco testified the money actually represented his savings, though the government presented evidence suggesting Marrocco could not have legitimately saved that much money. Marrocco said he had entrusted the money to Fallon to take it to the West Coast to place it in a safety-deposit box so that it could be used to invest in an unidentified restaurant or bar. To top it all off, Marrocco claimed that he, a then thirty-two year old who was supposedly sophisticated enough to invest in a restaurant or bar approximately 2,000 miles away, was unable to open a bank account due to credit problems from his college days. The jury was certainly allowed to disbelieve that testimony and consider it evidence of the money's connection to something unlawful. Considering these implausible and conflicting explanations coupled with Fallon's suspicious conduct and the drug dog's alert, it was not irrational for the jury to find, by the low standard of a preponderance, that the currency was substantially connected with an unlawful drug transaction and fit within one of § 881(a)(6)'s categories.

III

Civil forfeiture is a much maligned practice, *see, e.g.*, *United States v. $506,231*, 125 F.3d 442, 454 (7th Cir. 1997) ("We are certainly not the first court to be 'enormously troubled by the government's increasing and virtually unchecked use of the civil forfeiture statutes and the disregard for . . . due process that is buried in those statutes.' " (quoting *United States v. All Assets of Statewide Auto Parts, Inc.*, 971 F.2d 896, 905 (2d Cir. 1992))), and this case certainly has characteristics suggesting why. The claimants, who lose $100,120, have not been charged with, let alone convicted of, any crime relating to that $100,120. The government, who gets to keep the $100,120 for itself, seized the drug-contaminated currency on a Friday and deposited it the following Monday without chemically testing, or even saving, a single bill. And both sides have now been engaged in a legal battle that has stretched over fifteen years.

But it is not our role to decide whether the government should be pursuing these kinds of cases. Our responsibility is solely to decide whether the law as it stands was followed. We conclude it was.

NOTES & QUESTIONS

1. **"A Much Maligned Practice."** In *$100,120*, the Seventh Circuit seemed rather critical of the government's use of civil forfeiture. Do you think that Marrocco and Fallon were treated unfairly? Do you think that that government could have gotten a criminal conviction against them based on the evidence presented at the forfeiture trial? Do you think that the government should have pursued criminal charges in this case?

Civil asset forfeiture has attracted considerable criticism in recent years, with critics sounding alarm over the lack of procedural protections (e.g., one need not even have been charged with, let alone convicted of, a crime before one's property is taken) and the incentivization of some law enforcement activities (e.g., drug enforcement) at the expense of other activities that are less "profitable" for police but perhaps more important from a public-safety standpoint (e.g., investigation of violent crimes). *See generally* Adam Crepelle, *Probable Cause to Plunder: Civil Asset Forfeiture and the Problems It Creates*, 7 WAKE FOREST J.L. & POL'Y 315, 315–16 (2017); Sarah Stillman, *Taken*, NEW YORKER, Aug. 5, 2013.

2. **Innocent Owners.** Review the innocent-owner defense in 18 U.S.C. § 983(d). This provision might come into play, for instance, if a rented home were used by the tenant for drug distribution; the landlord might invoke the defense to block forfeiture of the home. In *$100,120*, the claimants

argued that the "offense" instruction given to the jury in their trial was in conflict with the innocent-owner defense. There is at least some tension between the instruction and the defense, isn't there? Why did the claimants not win a new trial on this basis?

3. **Seizure.** In *$100,120*, the government did not wait to secure a forfeiture judgment before seizing the money. Such prejudgment seizures are commonplace. Do you see why the government might not want to wait for the conclusion of the litigation process?

Procedures for prejudgment seizure are set forth in 18 U.S.C. § 981(b) (not reprinted above). Seizures may be conducted pursuant to a judicial warrant, or, in some circumstances, without a warrant. In cases of demonstrated hardship, however, 18 U.S.C. § 983(f) provides for the release of seized property, as, for instance, when the seizure will cause a person to lose his or her job or become homeless.

Section 983(j) also provides for a variety of other mechanisms besides seizure to ensure that forfeitable property is not concealed, dissipated, or misused before judgment is entered: "the court may enter a restraining order or injunction, require the execution of satisfactory performance bonds, create receiverships, appoint conservators, custodians, appraisers, accountants, or trustees, or take any other action to seize, secure, maintain, or preserve the availability of property subject to civil forfeiture."

4. **Jury Trial.** Note that *$100,120* was tried to a jury. Civil forfeiture proceedings are not subject to the Sixth Amendment jury-trial right, but courts have generally held that the *Seventh* Amendment jury-trial right (or a state constitutional analog) covers these cases. *State v. Items of Real Prop. Owned &/or Possessed by Chilinski*, 383 P.3d 236, 243 (Mont. 2016); JIMMY GURULÉ, SANDRA GUERRA-THOMPSON & MICHAEL O'HEAR, THE LAW OF ASSET FORFEITURE § 3–1(k) (2d ed. 2004).

5. **A Weaker Case?** Despite the low burden of proof, the government does not always prevail in civil forfeiture actions. Consider, for instance, *United States v. $48,100.00 in U.S. Currency*, 756 F.3d 650 (8th Cir. 2014), which bore some factual similarities to *$100,120*. John Nelson, age 22, was stopped by a state trooper while driving his parents' RV from Colorado to his parents' home in Wisconsin. After Nelson admitted to the trooper that he was in possession of marijuana for personal use, the trooper searched the RV, finding a small quantity of the drug and $48,100 in cash. Nelson was not criminally charged, but the government sought civil forfeiture of the money. At the forfeiture trial, Nelson presented evidence that the money had come from lawful sources, which the government did not dispute. Rather, the government argued that Nelson had traveled from Wisconsin to Colorado with the intent of purchasing drugs in Denver, a distribution hub city, for resale in Wisconsin. The government contended that the deal had fallen apart for some unknown reason, leading Nelson to return to Wisconsin with the money unspent—but still subject to forfeiture. As in *$100,120*, the government relied on evidence that Nelson acted nervous during the traffic stop and initially lied about the purpose of his travel (snowboarding). For his part, Nelson stated that he had taken the RV and money to Denver with the

intent of relocating there but decided against it after learning that the city had an ordinance that would prevent him from keeping his pit bull. The government won in the district court, but the Eighth Circuit reversed, finding the evidence insufficient to prove that Nelson intended to use the money for a drug transaction. Does it seem to you that the government's case was any stronger in *$100,120*?

6. **"Follow the Money."** What will happen to the money in *$100,120* now that the government has obtained clear title to it? *See* 21 U.S.C. § 881(e), *supra*. Note that the investigation was conducted by an Amtrak police officer and another officer from the Chicago Police Department, apparently working under the auspices of a DEA taskforce. Such multi-agency efforts are common in the field of drug enforcement. When they result in a forfeiture under federal law, the proceeds are typically distributed among the participating agencies—a practice known as "equitable sharing." Seen in a positive light, equitable sharing encourages (and subsidizes) greater effort and collaboration by diverse agencies in furtherance of national drug-control policies. *See* 21 U.S.C. § 881(e)(3)(B), *supra*. Seen less positively, equitable sharing coopts state and local agencies, distorting their priorities and reducing their accountability to state and local legislatures.

Some state forfeiture laws mirror the federal law in permitting law-enforcement agencies to keep forfeiture proceeds; other states direct that some or all forfeiture proceeds must go to other specified purposes, such as education or drug treatment. GURULÉ, GUERRA-THOMPSON & O'HEAR, *supra*, § 13–1(c). *See also* Jefferson E. Holcomb, Tomislav V. Kovandzic & Marian R. Williams, *Civil Asset Forfeiture, Equitable Sharing, and Policing for Profit in the United States*, 39 J. CRIM. JUST. 273, 276 (2011) (finding that twenty-six states gave 100% of forfeiture proceeds to law enforcement; in remaining states, amount for law enforcement varied from 0% to 95%). In states that limit the direct benefit of forfeiture to law enforcement, agencies may be tempted to circumvent state law by taking seized assets to federal officials for forfeiture proceedings in federal court (a practice known as "federal adoption") and equitable sharing. *See id* at 282 (finding negative correlation between amount of equitable sharing in a state and proportion of forfeiture proceeds that go to law enforcement under state law). A few states have prohibited such federal-state collaborations—reforms that seem, not surprisingly, to result in sharp reductions in the number of forfeiture proceedings. GURULÉ, GUERRA-THOMPSON & O'HEAR, *supra*, § 13–1(c).

Whether good policy or not, federal forfeiture and equitable sharing have become important sources of law-enforcement funding. In FY2020, nearly $244 million in payments were distributed by the federal government to state and local agencies, while an additional $314 million went to foreign agencies through an analogous program that supports international cooperation in drug enforcement. Meanwhile, federal agencies placed more than $2 million in forfeited assets into federal law-enforcement service, including vehicles, firearms, and electronic equipment. An additional 58 vehicles were turned over to local police departments and sheriff's offices. U.S. Dep't of Justice, *FY2020 Asset Forfeiture Fund Reports to Congress*, https://www.justice.gov/afms/fy2020-asset-forfeiture-fund-reports-congress.

It is reported that some local agencies rely on forfeitures for up to one-third of their budgets. Holcomb, Kovandzic & Williams, *supra*, at 275.

State forfeiture laws can also be lucrative for law-enforcement agencies. One recent report found that Florida's agencies led the nation with $266 million in forfeitures in 2018, of which $246 million came through state forfeiture proceedings. Monivette Cordeiro, *Florida Police Lead Nation with $266M in Property Seizures*, ORLANDO SENTINEL, Dec. 18, 2020.

7. **Administrative Forfeiture.** Federal law provides for administrative forfeiture—that is, forfeiture without any judicial proceedings—for property valued at $500,000 or less, other than real property.[2] Administrative forfeiture is accomplished by seizure of the asset, publication of notice of intent to forfeit the property, and written notice to parties who appear to have an interest in the property. If no party files a claim to the property within certain time limits, the property may be declared forfeited by the seizing agency, which has the same legal effect as a judicial forfeiture order. However, if a timely claim is filed, then the seizing agency must refer the matter to the Department of Justice for the initiation of judicial forfeiture proceedings. Do you think it is fair to put the onus on a property owner to file a claim to the property in order to prevent administrative forfeiture?

8. **Constitutional Innocent Owner Defense.** Federal law currently provides for a statutory innocent owner defense in 18 U.S.C. § 983(d), *supra*, but forfeiture laws have not always done so. If property is taken from an innocent owner, and no statutory defense is available, does the owner have a constitutional claim? The Supreme Court considered this question in *Bennis v. Michigan*, 516 U.S. 442 (1996).

Tina and John Bennis were joint owners of an automobile. John was arrested after he was observed engaging in sexual activity in the car with a prostitute, and the car was declared forfeited under Michigan law. Tina had no prior knowledge of John's plan to use the family car for this purpose, but the state courts declined to provide any compensation to her for her interest in the car. On appeal to the U.S. Supreme Court, Tina argued that the uncompensated forfeiture violated the Due Process and Takings Clauses. However, in a 5–4 decision, the Court ruled against her. Although the Court had stated in an earlier case that "it would be difficult to reject the constitutional claim of . . . an owner who proved not only that he was uninvolved in and unaware of the wrongful activity, but also that he had done all that reasonably could be expected to prevent the proscribed use of his property," *Calero-Toledo v. Pearson Yacht Leasing Co.*, 416 U.S. 663, 689 (1974), the *Bennis* Court characterized the language as mere *dicta*. The Court also noted that Tina had not shown that she had undertaken any affirmative efforts to prevent the illegal use of her car—she was simply in the "unaware" category. *Bennis*, 516 U.S. at 450. The Court did not

[2] The rules for administrative forfeiture in the customs context are set forth at 19 U.S.C. §§ 1607–09. Under 21 U.S.C. § 881(d), these rules are also made applicable to drug forfeitures. Certain time limits and notice requirements are set forth at 18 U.S.C. § 983(a).

categorically foreclose the possibility of a constitutional innocent owner defense but made clear that such a defense would be quite narrow.

The *Bennis* decision provoked considerable public criticism, leading Michigan and other states that did not previously have an innocent owner statutory defense to adopt one. Holcomb, Kovandzic & Williams, *supra*, at 277.

9. **Double Jeopardy.** The Double Jeopardy Clause generally prohibits successive prosecutions for the "same offence." Does this preclude a criminal prosecution following a civil forfeiture action when both are based on the same illegal acts? For instance, following the conclusion of ***$100,120,*** *supra*, might Marrocco then be charged criminally with conspiracy to distribute drugs based on the same alleged plot to acquire drugs in Seattle? Alternatively, if Marrocco had been convicted criminally first, could the civil forfeiture action still proceed?

The Double Jeopardy analysis turns on whether the civil proceeding is actually punitive character. In *United States v. Ursery*, the Court applied a two-part test to determine whether forfeitures under 21 U.S.C. §§ 881(a)(6)–(7) are punitive, first examining congressional intent, and then considering "whether the proceedings are so punitive in fact as to persuade us that [they] may not legitimately be viewed as civil in nature, despite Congress' intent." 518 U.S. 267, 288 (1996) (internal quotation marks and citation omitted). The Court found a clear Congressional intent for § 881 proceedings to be civil, and no basis for overcoming that intent. While acknowledging some "punitive aspects" to § 881, the Court characterized as "remedial" the statute's aim to "encourage[ ] property owners to take care in managing their property and ensure[ ] that they will not permit that property to be used for illegal purposes." *Id.* at 290. The Court further concluded, "To the extent that § 881(a)(6) applies to 'proceeds' of illegal drug activity, it serves the additional nonpunitive goal of ensuring that persons do not profit from their illegal acts." *Id.* at 291. Because civil forfeitures under §§ 881(a)(6)–(7) are not considered punitive for double-jeopardy purposes, the government may pursue such forfeitures either before or after a criminal case based on the same underlying acts.

10. **Uniform Controlled Substances Act and State Law.** In 1970, the National Conference of Commissioners of Uniform State Laws promulgated the Uniform Controlled Substances Act, which included civil forfeiture provisions that closely tracked federal drug forfeiture law. GURULÉ, GUERRA-THOMPSON & O'HEAR, *supra*, § 13–2(a). Thereafter, forty states adopted drug forfeiture laws modeled on the Uniform Act. Some subsequent amendments to the federal statutes were also adopted by the Uniform Act and by state lawmakers. As a result, the drug forfeiture laws in many, but not all, states tend to mirror federal law in many, but not all, respects.

An important area of division in state law is the treatment of lower-level drug offenses, such as those involving only marijuana or only personal-use quantities of a drug. For instance, does a car become subject to forfeiture if the owner drove the car to purchase cocaine for the owner's personal use?

Different states would answer the question differently. *Id.* § 13–2(a)(3). Another important area of division concerns the forfeitability of real property. Most states follow federal law in permitting such forfeitures, but a significant minority do not, while still other states impose special restrictions, such as a heightened burden of proof on the government. *Id.* § 13–2(b)(1). Even if real property is generally forfeitable in a state, the state may have special protections in place for family homes. *Id.* § 13–4(b).

To the extent that a state's law is more restrictive than federal law, law-enforcement agencies in the state will have an incentive to take their forfeiture cases to the federal authorities for adoption and equitable sharing (see note 6 above). For instance, one study has found more equitable sharing in those states that are more favorable to defendants on burden of proof or the requirements of the innocent-owner defense. Holcomb, Kovandzic & Williams, *supra*, at 282.

The Uniform Act and the many state statutes on which it is modeled deal with drug forfeitures. Some states do not provide for forfeiture outside the drug context. Other states identify a variety of other specific offenses for which forfeiture is authorized. A handful provide broadly for forfeiture of proceeds and/or instrumentalities of *all* criminal offenses, or at least all felony offenses. *Id.* § 13–2(e). If civil forfeiture seems a good policy for combatting drug crime, why not extend it more broadly?

The MPC:S does not have a civil forfeiture provision and suggests that state legislatures consider eliminating civil forfeiture altogether, thus leaving forfeiture to the criminal process. § 6.04C. Does that strike you as a good idea?

b. CRIMINAL FORFEITURE

Criminal forfeiture, in contrast to civil forfeiture, requires a criminal conviction. The forfeiture order is then, in effect, an aspect of the sentence. In terms of the substance of what is forfeitable, the major federal criminal forfeiture statutes overlap to a considerable extent with the major civil forfeiture statutes. In particular, in the drug area, forfeitable property includes both the proceeds of any drug felony and any property that was used or intended to be used to facilitate a drug felony. 21 U.S.C. § 853(a)(1)–(2). The statute makes these forfeitures mandatory following conviction.

The criminal litigation context dictates some significant differences between the federal civil and criminal forfeiture processes, but they also share some broad similarities. For instance, in the criminal process, like the civil, the government may seize assets or obtain a protective order at the outset of the case to ensure that the assets will be available when judgment is entered.[3] 21 U.S.C. §§ 853(e)–(f). Similarly, most courts hold

[3] Criminal forfeiture law provides an additional mechanism by which the government may protect itself from a defendant's concealment or dissipation of forfeitable assets. The court must order forfeiture of a *substitute* asset of the defendant's if "as a result of any act or omission of the defendant," a forfeitable asset "(A) cannot be located upon the exercise of due diligence; (B) has been transferred or sold to, or deposited with, a third party; (C) has been placed beyond

that the burden of proof for forfeiture-specific facts is the civil preponderance standard.[4] Further, the Federal Rules of Criminal Procedure provide for a jury trial on forfeiture. FED. R. CRIM. P. 32.2(b)(5). Criminal forfeiture is also subject to much the same rules regarding the disposition of forfeited assets, including equitable sharing. 21 U.S.C. § 853(i)(4).

Although the innocent owner defense of 18 U.S.C. § 983(d), *supra*, only applies to civil forfeiture, criminal forfeiture laws have other mechanisms to protect the interests of innocent third parties. In particular, if forfeitable property has been transferred by the defendant, the transferee may be able to avoid forfeiture if he or she was "a bona fide purchaser for value of such property who at the time of purchase was reasonably without cause to believe that the property was subject to forfeiture." 21 U.S.C. § 853(c). A property owner may also be able to avoid forfeiture by showing that, at the time of the underlying criminal offense, he or she had a "right, title, or interest" in the property that was superior to the defendant's. 21 U.S.C. § 853(n)(6)(A).

In criminal cases, the Sixth Amendment right to counsel includes not only the right of indigent defendants to court-appointed counsel, but also the right of non-indigent defendants to retain a lawyer of their own choosing. However, the latter right may be undermined by forfeiture laws that deny the defendant access to funds needed to pay for a lawyer. The Supreme Court considered this tension in *Caplin & Drysdale, Chartered v. United States*, 491 U.S. 617 (1989). Christopher Reckmeyer was charged with drug trafficking in federal court, and the indictment sought forfeiture of specified assets—apparently, in fact, practically everything he had. The court entered a pretrial restraining order forbidding Reckmeyer from transferring any of these assets. Meanwhile, Reckmeyer had retained Caplin & Drysdale to provide his legal representation, and eventually entered into a plea agreement with the government. In conjunction with his sentencing, the district court granted the government's forfeiture requests, but allocated $170,000 of the assets to pay Caplin & Drysdale's legal fees. The government appealed, arguing that the district court had no discretion to reduce its forfeiture award in this way. For its part, Caplin & Drysdale contended that an exception for attorneys' fees was constitutionally required. The Supreme Court sided with the government. The Court reasoned,

> A defendant has no Sixth Amendment right to spend another person's money for services rendered by an attorney, even if those funds are the only way that that defendant will be able to

---

the jurisdiction of the court; (D) has been substantially diminished in value; or (E) has been commingled with other property which cannot be divided without difficulty." 21 U.S.C. § 853(p) (drug forfeiture law); 18 U.S.C. § 1963(m) (RICO); 18 U.S.C. § 982(b)(1)(A) (money-laundering).

[4] The principal federal criminal forfeiture statutes are not entirely clear about burden of proof. The lower courts have consistently, but not quite uniformly, adopted the preponderance standard over proof beyond a reasonable doubt. GURULÉ, GUERRA-THOMPSON & O'HEAR, *supra*, § 4–2(b). This approach follows the normal burden of proof for sentencing fact-finding.

> retain the attorney of his choice. A robbery suspect, for example, has no Sixth Amendment right to use funds he has stolen from a bank to retain an attorney to defend him if he is apprehended. The money, though in his possession, is not rightfully his; the Government does not violate the Sixth Amendment if it seizes the robbery proceeds and refuses to permit the defendant to use them to pay for his defense.

Id. at 626. The Court could see no valid distinction between the hypothetical robber's use of robbery proceeds to pay legal fees, and Reckmeyer's use of drug proceeds for the same purpose.

The MPC:S includes a general criminal forfeiture provision covering all felony offenses, in contrast to the specific federal laws for drugs, money-laundering, and so forth. § 6.04C. In the MPC:S, forfeiture is discretionary, not mandatory, and is subject (like all economic sanctions) to the requirement that defendants be left with sufficient means for "reasonable living expenses and family obligations." § 6.04(6). The MPC:S forbids law-enforcement agencies from retaining forfeited assets for their own use, including assets obtained through equitable sharing. § 6.04C(5). The MPC:S also includes broad protections for innocent partial or joint owners of instrumentality-type assets—think Tina Bennis and the family car. § 6.04C(4).

4. COSTS, FEES, ASSESSMENTS, SURCHARGES, AND THE LIKE

In addition to fines, restitution, and forfeitures, many jurisdictions have adopted a bewildering array of additional economic sanctions going by a variety of different names—costs, fees, assessments, and so forth. These sanctions are often loosely framed as ways of shifting the costs of administering one aspect or another of the criminal justice system from the public to the defendant, whose criminal actions caused the system to bear the costs in first place. In a sense, then, these sanctions may be conceptualized as a sort of restitution to the government and might arguably be justified on the same grounds as restitution is more generally. On the other hand, these sanctions raise concerns about the harsh (and potentially criminogenic) burdens they may place on poor defendants and their families, as well as the perverse incentives that are created when legal agencies derive financial benefits from their official actions. Moreover, the amount of these sanctions often seems arbitrary and disconnected from the actual costs generated by any given defendant.

Consider the following description of what have been called legal financial obligations, or "LFOs."

Wayne A. Logan & Ronald F. Wright, Mercenary Criminal Justice

2014 U. ILL. L. REV. 1175

Post-judgment LFOs go by many different names, many different actors assess and collect them, and they serve many different avowed purposes.

1. Investigation, Prosecution, and Court Costs

Criminal courts in all but a few states have the power to assess costs against convicted offenders, and the majority of states have legislation mandating assessments after conviction. A smaller number of states permit assessment of costs as a discretionary matter. Local governments in some states have the express authority to impose assessments on their own. The variety of costs and the amounts they entail have increased significantly over time, often serving as a major fiscal benefit for governments.

Consider first the LFOs that apply across the board to all offenders. In Florida, such assessments include a mandatory court cost ranging from $60 (traffic offenses) to $225 (felonies), and a mandatory minimum $50 assessment for the "cost of prosecution" payable to the "State Attorneys Revenue Trust Fund." This is in addition to a non-waivable $50 cost payable to the "Crimes Compensation Trust Fund," a $20 court cost for "crime stoppers" programs, and a $3 cost directed to the "Additional Court Cost Clearing Trust Fund" (required even when prosecution is withheld). Defendants might also be required to pay for investigative costs incurred by law enforcement agencies, including the salaries of permanent employees and prosecutors and $100 allocated to the "Operating Trust Fund of the Department of Law Enforcement" to help finance state crime laboratories. The state also allows counties with "teen courts" to require anyone convicted of any nontraffic offense to pay $3 to help fund the court.

Other states have similar laws. In Illinois, for instance, a $10 medical assessment is levied on persons convicted of crimes, regardless of whether the individual receives any medical treatment in the corrections system. The California legislature, to "maintain adequate funding for court facilities," assesses $30 for misdemeanor and felony convictions and $35 for each infraction, and extracts a $20 "court security fee" for every conviction. In Alabama, increased court fees allow the judiciary to hire additional courtroom personnel.

Second, consider the cost assessments that are tied to particular kinds of cases. Colorado, for instance, targets convicted sex offenders with "surcharges," ranging from $150 for a class three misdemeanor to $3000 for a class two felony. States also extract fees when they require convicted sex offenders to register. With drug cases, jurisdictions commonly seek payment for laboratory services. State pension funds for police officers and court clerks in Georgia receive state contributions based on the number of police officer traffic tickets that result in convictions.

If an offender is late in paying a LFO, a penalty can be imposed, based on a flat rate or a percentage of the amount owed. Late payment can also get private collection agencies involved, who themselves impose charges. Separate charges for extended payment plans can also ratchet up payments, with penalties again attaching to late payments.

2. "Pay-to-Stay": Detention LFOs

Assessments are also very commonly imposed upon offenders sentenced to prison or jail terms. Despite the typically limited financial means of inmates, state and local governments usually charge offenders for the costs of incarceration. Michigan, for instance, allows counties to recover up to $60 per day from inmates, and Arizona authorizes a $2 monthly electric utility fee. The total amounts collected can be substantial: New York State, for example, collected $22 million between 1995 and 2003.

Charges for telephone calls are also a significant moneymaker. The charges—paid by recipients of "collect" calls from inmates, based on rates far above the prevailing market—generate millions of dollars annually, with most of the money going to contractors.

3. Probation and Parole Fees

Jurisdictions also increasingly impose fees for community corrections services, with amounts tied to the duration of supervision. In Maryland, the parole supervision fee is $40 per month, which can amount to several hundred dollars during a parole term. In Pennsylvania, prisoners are ineligible for probation, parole, or accelerated disposition unless they pay a $60 fee, not subject to waiver for indigents. In many states supervision periods can be extended for failure or inability to pay.

It is also common for profit-oriented private firms to contract with the government to provide probation services. A court, for example, might place an offender on probation for public drunkenness and assess a fine of $270. The private probation company will then add a $15 enrollment fee and $39 per month for supervision and services. Use of Global Positioning System devices to track probationers, parolees, and others (typically convicted sex offenders "off-paper"), and operation of halfway houses are other ways for private contractors to get involved. When individuals are sentenced to community service, they can be required to buy an insurance policy from a private provider. Finally, as with costs, governments frequently outsource the collection of supervision-related fees and allow private firms to levy significant additional surcharges.

NOTES & QUESTIONS

1. **Pre-Judgment LFOs.** In addition to the post-judgment LFOs described above, the authors also note a number of common pre-judgment

LFOs, including booking fees, fees imposed by prosecutors in connection with pretrial diversions, and application fees for defense counsel.

2. **Judicial Regulation.** The Supreme Court has indicated, on constitutional due process grounds, that judicial officers may not be granted a direct, personal financial benefit for each conviction entered. *Tumey v. State of Ohio*, 273 U.S. 510 (1927). The Court has also rejected a system in which a village mayor, with executive responsibility for village finances, acts as a municipal judge—and in such capacity imposes fines that flow directly into village coffers. The Court stated, "[T]he test is whether the mayor's situation is one which would offer a possible temptation to the average man as a judge to forget the burden of proof required to convict the defendant, or which might lead him not to hold the balance nice, clear, and true between the state and the accused." *Ward v. Vill. of Monroeville, Ohio*, 409 U.S. 57, 60 (1972) (citation and internal quotation marks and alteration omitted). These cases thus suggest that LFOs may be unconstitutional if they create a sufficiently high risk to the neutrality of a judicial officer. The Court has further indicated that financial incentives for *prosecutors* may in some circumstances also violate the Due Process Clause, although the constitutional standards for prosecutorial neutrality are probably less demanding than for judicial neutrality. *Marshall v. Jerrico, Inc.*, 446 U.S. 238, 239 (1980).

A survey of the lower-court caselaw found inconsistent application of the Supreme Court's neutrality principle:

> At times, judges intervene to insist on impartiality, especially when the LFO enforcer is also the recipient of revenue. Yet . . . courts can often remain indifferent to indirect and systemic conflicts of interest. Placing weight on the designation of an enforcer as "judicial" or "non-judicial," however, may not reflect practical realities on the ground. In the local courthouse culture of "working groups," the full-time professionals are aware of what their co-workers need, even if they carry different titles and perform different phases of the work. Such an environment creates powerful reasons for one set of officials (say, judges) to make choices that protect the entire courthouse staff.

Logan & Wright, *supra*, at 1203.

Beyond the neutrality principle, the authors also found that lower courts sometimes overturn fees on constitutional or statutory grounds if the fees are not closely enough connected to the defendant's conduct. *Id.* at 1205. For instance, in *State v. Lanclos*, 980 So. 2d 643 (La. 2008), the Louisiana Supreme Court rejected a $5 fee imposed for all traffic violations that was used to supplement police budgets. The court held that "police salaries and uniform equipment and maintenance is too far attenuated from the 'administration of justice,' to be considered a legitimate court cost." *Id.* at 654. Still, such cases are unusual. Courts more typically defer to legislative judgments about the appropriateness of specific costs or fees. Logan & Wright, *supra*, at 1207. For an argument that defendants may have a constitutional jury-trial right with respect to the imposition of some fees, see

Laura I Appleman, *Nickel and Dimed into Incarceration: Cash-Register Justice in the Criminal System,* 57 B.C. L. REV. 1483 (2016).

3. **Lawyer and Judge Roles.** Lawyers and judges may be only dimly aware of the full range of costs and fees to which defendants are subject, especially the costs and fees that are assessed outside the regular sentencing process by correctional or other agencies. Yet, costs and fees may be an important part of the overall burden of a conviction on a defendant, particularly in lower-level cases in which lengthy incarceration is unlikely.[5] Ideally, defense lawyers should be familiar with costs and fees so that they can provide complete information to their clients about the consequences of a guilty plea. Prosecutors and judges should also have this information so that they can ensure that the total burdens of a conviction are not disproportionately severe or beyond the defendant's ability to pay. On the other hand, it may be quite difficult for judges and lawyers to obtain complete information about costs and fees, which can vary dramatically even from county to county within a single state. One study of Pennsylvania found 2,371 different county-level fees and costs assessed across sixty-seven counties. R. Barry Ruback & Valerie Clark, *Economic Sanctions in Pennsylvania: Complex and Inconsistent*, 49 DUQ. L. REV. 751, 767 (2011). These were in addition to state-mandated fees and costs.

In order to bring greater transparency to LFOs, Professors Logan and Wright recommend that a sentencing commission or other appropriate body in each state create and publish an inventory of each LFO in use in the state, whether on a local or state-wide basis. Logan & Wright, *supra*, at 1217. They argue that greater transparency about LFOs would not only support better public policymaking, but also help the lawyers and judges fill their plea-bargaining roles in a fairer, more effective manner. *Id.* at 1224–25.

4. **Abolition?** The MPC:S recommends the abolition of all "costs, fees, and assessments." § 6.04D. What arguments do you see for and against this position? The commentary states, "[P]ersons convicted of crimes should not be regarded as a special class of taxpayers called upon to make up for inadequate legislative appropriations for criminal justice agencies and programming."

As an alternative to full abolition, the MPC:S supports some significant limitations on the amount and use of costs, fees, and assessments:

- They may not "plac[e] a substantial burden on the defendant's ability to reintegrate into the law-abiding community."
- They may not "be imposed by any agency or entity in the absence of approval by the sentencing court."
- They may not "be imposed in excess of actual expenditures in the offender's case."

---

[5] In order to illustrate the magnitude of costs and fees, a report by New York University's Brennan Center for Justice reprinted a docket sheet from Pennsylvania listing twenty-six different fees imposed on a single defendant totaling $2,464, which was about three times the combined amount of fines and restitution in the case. ALICIA BANNON, MITALI NAGRECHA & REBEKAH DILLER, N.Y.U. SCHOOL OF LAW, CRIMINAL JUSTICE DEBT: A BARRIER TO REENTRY 9 (2010).

Alternative §§ 6.04D(2)–(4). Additionally, as with all economic sanctions in the MPC:S, costs, fees, and assessments are subject to further limitations, including the preservation of sufficient means for reasonable living expenses and family support, § 6.04(6) and (in order to mitigate conflicts of interest) a prohibition on retention of the collected funds by the collecting agency, § 6.04(8).

In recent years, a few local jurisdictions, including San Francisco City and County and Alameda County in California, have acted to sharply reduce the imposition of fines and fees that are not mandated by state law. PEW CHARITABLE TRUSTS, POLICY REFORMS CAN STRENGTHEN COMMUNITY SUPERVISION 39 (2020). A few states have also adopted new limitations on, or expanded opportunities for relief from, fees based on inability to pay. *Id.* at 40–41. And, in 2017, California repealed the authority of counties to assess fees in the *juvenile* system. Jeffrey Selbin, *Juvenile Fee Abolition in California: Early Lessons and Challenges for the Debt-Free Justice Movement*, 98 N.C. L. REV. 401, 410 (2020).

5. **LFOs for Sexual Offenses.** Individuals who have been convicted of sexual offenses may face especially onerous LFOs. These individuals are often subject to close monitoring regimens when on community supervision (e.g., electronic monitoring and regular polygraph testing), mandatory treatment, and registration requirements—all of which may trigger fees. For instance, in twenty-eight states, individuals on the sex offender registry are assessed costs for their initial registration and followup visits that can range from $5 to $250. Beth M. Huebner et al., *The Price of a Sex Offense Conviction: A Comparative Analysis of the Costs of Community Supervision*, 60 CRIMINOLOGY 159 (2022). One study of supervised individuals in Missouri found that those convicted of sexual offenses were obligated to pay an average of more than $2000 per year for supervision-related costs, while those convicted of other offenses faced an average of only $360 in annual costs. *Id.* at 170. The researchers also found that the particular stigma connected to sexual offenses made it harder for some individuals who were convicted of these offenses to obtain financial support from family members. *Id.* at 172. In Chapter 11, we consider in more detail the many collateral consequences that can follow from conviction of a sexual offense.

B. ENFORCEMENT OF ECONOMIC SANCTIONS

Although economic sanctions are often conceptualized as a form of punishment that is distinct from community supervision, the two types of sanctions are deeply intertwined in practice. This results from the fact that community supervision is routinely utilized to enforce fines, restitution, and other economic sanctions. Given the economic circumstances of most defendants, it cannot be assumed that they will simply write a check to cover their financial obligations immediately after sentencing and drop it off in the clerk's office on the way out of the courthouse. Recognizing that payments will frequently have to be made in bits and pieces over time—not uncommonly by a defendant who is unable or unwilling to stick to a regular payment schedule—the fulfillment of legal financial obligations is often made a condition of community supervision; the familiar tools used to enforce compliance with conditions, including revocation and incarceration, can then be deployed to ensure the satisfaction of the criminal legal debts.

Note that this practice gives a privileged status to criminal legal debts. If you fall behind on your car or credit-card payments, for instance, your creditor cannot normally hold a threat of incarceration over your head. Is this privileged status justifiable? Why not put legal financial obligations on the same footing as any other debt for enforcement purposes?

To be sure, revocation is not the only possible response to payment problems, and indeed, as we will see in the next section, its use with poor defendants who are unable to pay can raise constitutional problems. Thus, federal law suggests a number of alternatives to revocation:

> (1) Upon a finding that the defendant is in default on a payment of a fine or restitution, the court may, pursuant to section 3565, revoke probation or a term of supervised release, modify the terms or conditions of probation or a term of supervised release, resentence a defendant pursuant to section 3614, hold the defendant in contempt of court, enter a restraining order or injunction, order the sale of property of the defendant, accept a performance bond, enter or adjust a payment schedule, or take any other action necessary to obtain compliance with the order of a fine or restitution.
>
> (2) In determining what action to take, the court shall consider the defendant's employment status, earning ability, financial resources, the willfulness in failing to comply with the fine or restitution order, and any other circumstances that may have a bearing on the defendant's ability or failure to comply with the order of a fine or restitution.[6]

18 U.S.C. § 3613A(a).

Should defendants be revoked for failure to pay off criminal justice debt? On the one hand, a failure to use all available means to enforce ordered payments may undermine the credibility of the supervising agency or the court. On the other hand, in many cases the social costs of incarceration will be as great or greater than the money that is owed.[7]

---

[6] In cases in which lump-sum payment of a fine "would have an unduly severe impact" on the defendant or his or her dependents, the federal sentencing guidelines recommend that the court establish a payment schedule. § 5E1.2(f). However, this may be of limited benefit to financially stressed defendants because the guidelines also indicate that the "length of the installment schedule generally should not exceed twelve months," and that the "defendant should be required to pay a substantial installment at the time of sentencing." The guidelines also indicate that the "court may impose a condition prohibiting the defendant from incurring new credit charges or opening additional lines of credit unless he is in compliance with the payment schedule."

[7] One random-assignment study from New Jersey found that increased *threats* of incarceration, delivered in the form of a violation notice for missed payments, seemed to generate increased compliance. However, the researchers also noted an irony. In order for

Moreover, even if incarceration increases a defendant's *motivation* to pay, it may simultaneously decrease the defendant's *capacity* to pay, for instance, if the defendant loses his or her job as a result of being locked up. Consequently, judges are often quite reluctant to revoke. Indeed, a desire to avoid this dilemma in the first place may significantly discourage use of economic sanctions.

The federal statute, like the law in many states, authorizes an extension of the term of community supervision as an alternative sanction for nonpayment. If a defendant is otherwise performing satisfactorily on supervision, do you think it would be wise to the extend the person's supervision based solely on missed payments? If the term expires with criminal justice debt unpaid, that debt may remain enforceable on the same basis as ordinary civil debts.

As they are increasingly charged with the responsibility to enforce economic sanctions, probation and parole offices may become, in effect, little more than collection agencies. In some probation departments, officers are rated based on the amount of money they collect. Francis T. Cullen, Cheryl Lero Johnson & Daniel P. Mears, *Reinventing Community Corrections*, 46 CRIME & JUST. 27, 51 (2017). POs report frustration over the "conflict among their roles of counselor, monitor, and collection agent." R. Barry Ruback & Mark H. Bergstrom, *Economic Sanctions in Criminal Justice: Purposes, Effects, and Implications*, 33 CRIM. JUST. & BEHAVIOR 242, 266 (2006). In Chapter 8, we noted that large caseloads mean that many POs have very limited time during one-on-one meetings with clients. Each minute spent on collections takes a minute from other supervision or counseling topics that might conceivably be more productive from a risk-reduction standpoint. Moreover, the PO's efforts to pressure the client into making more or larger payments may undermine the client's trust in the PO.

Concerns about overburdening POs have led some jurisdictions to establish separate collection offices. However, some research suggests that POs are more successful than specialized offices in maximizing collections, perhaps because they are better able to understand and address underlying causes of nonpayment, e.g., childcare issues conflicting with employment. *Id.* at 266–67. As discussed in Chapter 8, POs vary in the extent to which they are willing and able to assume a social-worker (as opposed to a law-enforcer) role, but sometimes the

threats of incarceration to maintain their effectiveness, defendants who do not prove responsive to violation notices must actually be incarcerated. Yet, the average amount of additional money paid by defendants in the enhanced "threat" group was less than $100—a rather small amount relative to the costs of incarceration. Indeed, the researchers doubted whether the added money was even sufficient to offset the increased paperwork burdens on POs of handling all of the additional violations. David Weisburd, Tomer Einat & Matt Kowalski, *The Miracle of the Cells: An Experimental Study of Interventions to Increase Payment of Court-Ordered Financial Obligations*, 7 CRIMINOLOGY & PUB. POL'Y 9, 29–30 (2008).

social-work approach may be the most effective way to get a client on a regular payment schedule.[8]

As supervision offices determine how much priority should be placed on collections, there may be conflict-of-interest issues to the extent that clients' debt includes fees related to supervision. Indeed, some agencies are dependent on fees for as much as half of their budgets. Cullen, Johnson & Mears, *supra*, at 51. Agencies' budgetary self-interest may not only affect how collections are prioritized relative to other agency functions, but also the prioritization of some LFOs over others. Research suggests that POs tend to be more concerned with the collection of supervision fees (which go to their own agencies) than with fines (which typically go into the state's general revenue) or restitution (which goes to victims). Ruback & Bergstrom, *supra*, at 266.

Criminal justice debt can escalate if not promptly paid. One survey found that in thirteen of fifteen states studied, individuals could be charged interest or late fees if they fell behind in payments. ALICIA BANNON, MITALI NAGRECHA & REBEKAH DILLER, N.Y.U. SCHOOL OF LAW, CRIMINAL JUSTICE DEBT: A BARRIER TO REENTRY 17 (2010). Additionally, some states charged fees for individuals even to go on a payment plan, and some referred delinquent cases to private collection agencies that charged collection fees of 30–40% of the money owed. *Id.* at 17–18.

In several states, a person's driver's license may be suspended for missed payments on criminal justice debt. *Id.* at 24. Does this seem a sound policy? What should a person with a suspended license do if he or she must drive to work?

A person's wages may be garnished in order to enforce criminal justice debts. However, this may create a disincentive for work. Some defendants think it is just not "worth it" to seek employment since their income would be so diminished by garnishment. Katherine Beckett & Alexes Harris, *On Cash and Conviction: Monetary Sanctions as Misguided Policy*, 10 CRIMINOLOGY & PUB. POL'Y 509, 518 (2011). Additionally, employers may "dislike hiring those whose wages are garnished because of the cumbersome bureaucratic processes this entails." *Id.*

In some states, but not all, judges or supervision agencies have the ability to convert criminal justice debt into community service, although this appears infrequently done in practice. BANNON, NAGRECHA & DILLER, *supra*, at 15. Can you see any reasons why this might be so?

For enforcement purposes, the MPC:S recommends that carrots be used, not merely sticks:

[8] One study of restitution and procedural justice in Pennsylvania found a correlation between the amount of restitution paid by a defendant and the defendant's perception of fair treatment by probation staff. Andrew S. Gladfelter, Brendan Lantz & R. Barry Ruback, *Beyond Ability to Pay: Procedural Justice and Offender Compliance with Restitution Orders*, 62 INT'L J. OFFENDER THERAPY & COMP. CRIMINOLOGY 4314 (2018).

> The courts are encouraged to offer incentives to offenders who meet identified goals towards satisfaction of economic sanctions, such as payment of installments within a designated time period. Incentives contemplated by this subsection include shortening of probation or postrelease-supervision term, removal or lightening of sentence conditions, and full or partial forgiveness of economic sanctions [other than victim restitution].

§ 6.04(9).

Even outside the context of an incentive program, the MPC:S permits the court to modify or remove economic sanctions "at any time." § 6.04(10). In light of reintegration and rehabilitation concerns, it may be advisable to provide defendants with relief from criminal justice debts that are unlikely to be paid any time in the foreseeable future. Criminal justice debt may adversely affect a defendant's credit history, which may, in turn, make it harder for the defendant to obtain housing and employment. BANNON, NAGRECHA & DILLER, *supra*, at 27. Moreover, to the extent that unpaid debt is treated as a supervision violation, such violations can disqualify a person from a variety of welfare programs. *Id.* at 28. Additionally, in some states, unpaid criminal justice debt may affect a person's right to vote. *Id.* at 29.

C. CONSTITUTIONAL LIMITATIONS

Constitutional law imposes various limitations on the imposition and enforcement of economic sanctions. For instance, in the section on costs and fees above, we noted the due-process doctrine of *Tumey v. Ohio*, 273 U.S. 510 (1927), which limits the extent to which criminal justice actors may derive personal or institutional benefits from the economic sanctions they impose, especially if they are acting in a judicial role.

You may also recall from Chapter 3 that the *Apprendi* doctrine has been extended to fact-finding that increases the maximum possible fine in a case. *Southern Union v. United States*, 567 U.S. 343 (2012). The Supreme Court has not yet determined whether the doctrine applies to other economic sanctions, although Justices Gorsuch and Sotomayor recently indicated a desire for the Court to address the application of *Apprendi* to restitution. *Hester v. United States*, 139 S. Ct. 509 (2019) (Gorsuch, J., dissenting from denial of *certiorari*).

In the remainder of this section, we consider the impact of two additional constitutional constraints: safeguards for indigent defendants and the Excessive Fines Clause.

1. SAFEGUARDS FOR INDIGENT DEFENDANTS

Bearden v. Georgia

461 U.S. 660 (1983)

■ O'CONNOR, J.

The question in this case is whether the Fourteenth Amendment prohibits a State from revoking an indigent defendant's probation for failure to pay a fine and restitution. Its resolution involves a delicate balance between the acceptability, and indeed wisdom, of considering all relevant factors when determining an appropriate sentence for an individual and the impermissibility of imprisoning a defendant solely because of his lack of financial resources. We conclude that the trial court erred in automatically revoking probation because petitioner could not pay his fine, without determining that petitioner had not made sufficient bona fide efforts to pay or that adequate alternative forms of punishment did not exist. * * *

I

In September 1980, petitioner was indicted for the felonies of burglary and theft by receiving stolen property. He pleaded guilty, and was sentenced on October 8, 1980. Pursuant to the Georgia First Offender's Act, the trial court did not enter a judgment of guilt, but deferred further proceedings and sentenced petitioner to three years on probation for the burglary charge and a concurrent one year on probation for the theft charge. As a condition of probation, the trial court ordered petitioner to pay a $500 fine and $250 in restitution. Petitioner was to pay $100 that day, $100 the next day, and the $550 balance within four months.

Petitioner borrowed money from his parents and paid the first $200. About a month later, however, petitioner was laid off from his job. Petitioner, who has only a ninth grade education and cannot read, tried repeatedly to find other work but was unable to do so. The record indicates that petitioner had no income or assets during this period.

Shortly before the balance of the fine and restitution came due in February 1981, petitioner notified the probation office he was going to be late with his payment because he could not find a job. In May 1981, the State filed a petition in the trial court to revoke petitioner's probation because he had not paid the balance. After an evidentiary hearing, the trial court revoked probation for failure to pay the balance of the fine and restitution, entered a conviction and sentenced petitioner to serve the remaining portion of the probationary period in prison. * * *

II

This Court has long been sensitive to the treatment of indigents in our criminal justice system. Over a quarter-century ago, Justice Black declared that "there can be no equal justice where the kind of trial a man gets depends on the amount of money he has." *Griffin v. Illinois,* 351 U.S. 12, 19 (1956) (plurality opinion). *Griffin*'s principle of "equal justice," which the Court applied there to strike down a state practice of granting appellate review only to persons able to afford a trial transcript, has been applied in numerous other contexts. Most relevant to the issue here is the holding in *Williams v. Illinois,* 399 U.S. 235 (1970), that a State cannot subject a certain class of convicted defendants to a period of imprisonment beyond the statutory maximum solely because they are too poor to pay the fine. *Williams* was followed and extended in *Tate v. Short,* 401 U.S. 395 (1971), which held that a State cannot convert a fine imposed under a fine-only statute into a jail term solely because the defendant is indigent and cannot immediately pay the fine in full. But the Court has also recognized limits on the principle of protecting indigents in the criminal justice system. * * *

Due process and equal protection principles converge in the Court's analysis in these cases. Most decisions in this area have rested on an equal protection framework, although Justice Harlan in particular has insisted that a due process approach more accurately captures the competing concerns. * * *

The question presented here is whether a sentencing court can revoke a defendant's probation for failure to pay the imposed fine and restitution, absent evidence and findings that the defendant was somehow responsible for the failure or that alternative forms of punishment were inadequate. The parties, following the framework of *Williams* and *Tate,* have argued the question primarily in terms of equal protection, and debate vigorously whether strict scrutiny or rational basis is the appropriate standard of review. There is no doubt that the State has treated the petitioner differently from a person who did not fail to pay the imposed fine and therefore did not violate probation. To determine whether this differential treatment violates the Equal Protection Clause, one must determine whether, and under what circumstances, a defendant's indigent status may be considered in the decision whether to revoke probation. This is substantially similar to asking directly the due process question of whether and when it is fundamentally unfair or arbitrary for the State to revoke probation when an indigent is unable to pay the fine. Whether analyzed in terms of equal protection or due process,[8] the issue cannot be resolved by resort to easy slogans or pigeonhole analysis, but rather requires a careful inquiry into such factors as "the nature of the individual interest affected, the extent

---

[8] A due process approach has the advantage in this context of directly confronting the intertwined question of the role that a defendant's financial background can play in determining an appropriate sentence. When the court is initially considering what sentence to impose, a defendant's level of financial resources is a point on a spectrum rather than a classification. Since indigency in this context is a relative term rather than a classification, fitting "the problem of this case into an equal protection framework is a task too Procrustean to be rationally accomplished," *North Carolina v. Pearce,* 395 U.S. 711, 723 (1969). The more appropriate question is whether consideration of a defendant's financial background in setting or resetting a sentence is so arbitrary or unfair as to be a denial of due process.

to which it is affected, the rationality of the connection between legislative means and purpose, [and] the existence of alternative means for effectuating the purpose . . . ." *Williams v. Illinois, supra,* 399 U.S., at 260 (Harlan, J., concurring).

In analyzing this issue, of course, we do not write on a clean slate, for both *Williams* and *Tate* analyzed similar situations. The reach and limits of their holdings are vital to a proper resolution of the issue here. In *Williams,* a defendant was sentenced to the maximum prison term and fine authorized under the statute. Because of his indigency he could not pay the fine. Pursuant to another statute equating a $5 fine with a day in jail, the defendant was kept in jail for 101 days beyond the maximum prison sentence to "work out" the fine. The Court struck down the practice, holding that "[o]nce the State has defined the outer limits of incarceration necessary to satisfy its penological interests and policies, it may not then subject a certain class of convicted defendants to a period of imprisonment beyond the statutory maximum solely by reason of their indigency." 399 U.S., at 241–42. In *Tate v. Short,* 401 U.S. 395 (1971), we faced a similar situation, except that the statutory penalty there permitted only a fine. [W]e reasoned that "the same constitutional defect condemned in *Williams* also inheres in jailing an indigent for failing to make immediate payment of any fine, whether or not the fine is accompanied by a jail term and whether or not the jail term of the indigent extends beyond the maximum term that may be imposed on a person willing and able to pay a fine." 401 U.S., at 398.

The rule of *Williams* and *Tate,* then, is that the State cannot "impos[e] a fine as a sentence and then automatically conver[t] it into a jail term solely because the defendant is indigent and cannot forthwith pay the fine in full." *Tate, supra,* at 398. In other words, if the State determines a fine or restitution to be the appropriate and adequate penalty for the crime, it may not thereafter imprison a person solely because he lacked the resources to pay it. Both *Williams* and *Tate* carefully distinguished this substantive limitation on the imprisonment of indigents from the situation where a defendant was at fault in failing to pay the fine. * * *

This distinction, based on the reasons for non-payment, is of critical importance here. If the probationer has willfully refused to pay the fine or restitution when he has the means to pay, the State is perfectly justified in using imprisonment as a sanction to enforce collection. Similarly, a probationer's failure to make sufficient bona fide efforts to seek employment or borrow money in order to pay the fine or restitution may reflect an insufficient concern for paying the debt he owes to society for his crime. In such a situation, the State is likewise justified in revoking probation and using imprisonment as an appropriate penalty for the offense. But if the probationer has made all reasonable efforts to pay the fine or restitution, and yet cannot do so through no fault of his own, it is fundamentally unfair to revoke probation automatically without considering whether adequate alternative methods of punishing the defendant are available. * * *

The State, of course, has a fundamental interest in appropriately punishing persons—rich and poor—who violate its criminal laws. A defendant's poverty in no way immunizes him from punishment. Thus, when determining initially whether the State's penological interests require imposition of a term of imprisonment, the sentencing court can consider the entire background of the defendant, including his employment history and financial resources. * * *

The decision to place the defendant on probation, however, reflects a determination by the sentencing court that the State's penological interests do not require imprisonment. A probationer's failure to make reasonable efforts to repay his debt to society may indicate that this original determination needs reevaluation, and imprisonment may now be required to satisfy the State's interests. But a probationer who has made sufficient bona fide efforts to pay his fine and restitution, and who has complied with the other conditions of probation, has demonstrated a willingness to pay his debt to society and an ability to conform his conduct to social norms. * * *

[T]he State argues that its interests in punishing the lawbreaker and deterring others from criminal behavior require it to revoke probation for failure to pay a fine or restitution. The State clearly has an interest in punishment and deterrence, but this interest can often be served fully by alternative means. As we said in *Williams,* 399 U.S., at 244, and reiterated in *Tate,* "[t]he State is not powerless to enforce judgments against those financially unable to pay a fine." For example, the sentencing court could extend the time for making payments, or reduce the fine, or direct that the probationer perform some form of labor or public service in lieu of the fine. Justice Harlan appropriately observed in his concurring opinion in *Williams* that "the deterrent effect of a fine is apt to derive more from its pinch on the purse than the time of payment." *Ibid.,* 399 U.S., at 265. Indeed, given the general flexibility of tailoring fines to the resources of a defendant, or even permitting the defendant to do specified work to satisfy the fine, a sentencing court can often establish a reduced fine or alternate public service in lieu of a fine that adequately serves the State's goals of punishment and deterrence, given the defendant's diminished financial resources. Only if the sentencing court determines that alternatives to imprisonment are not adequate in a particular situation to meet the State's interest in punishment and deterrence may the State imprison a probationer who has made sufficient bona fide efforts to pay.

We hold, therefore, that in revocation proceedings for failure to pay a fine or restitution, a sentencing court must inquire into the reasons for the failure to pay. If the probationer willfully refused to pay or failed to make sufficient bona fide efforts legally to acquire the resources to pay, the court may revoke probation and sentence the defendant to imprisonment within the authorized range of its sentencing authority. If the probationer could not pay despite sufficient bona fide efforts to acquire the resources to do so, the court must consider alternate measures of punishment other than imprisonment. Only if alternate measures are not adequate to meet the State's interests in punishment and deterrence may the court imprison a probationer who has made sufficient bona fide efforts to pay. To do otherwise would deprive the probationer of his conditional freedom simply because, through no fault of his own, he cannot pay the fine. Such a deprivation would be contrary to the fundamental fairness required by the Fourteenth Amendment.

III

We return to the facts of this case. At the parole revocation hearing, the petitioner and his wife testified about their lack of income and assets and of his repeated efforts to obtain work. While the sentencing court commented on the availability of odd jobs such as lawn-mowing, it made no finding that the petitioner had not made sufficient bona fide efforts to find work, and the record as it presently stands would not justify such a finding. * * *

We do not suggest by our analysis of the present record that the State may not place the petitioner in prison. If, upon remand, the Georgia courts determine that petitioner did not make sufficient bona fide efforts to pay his fine, or determine that alternate punishment is not adequate to meet the State's interests in punishment and deterrence, imprisonment would be a permissible sentence. Unless such determinations are made, however, fundamental fairness requires that the petitioner remain on probation. * * *

[The opinion of JUSTICE WHITE, concurring in judgment, is omitted.]

NOTES & QUESTIONS

1. **From *Williams* and *Tate* to *Bearden*.** The two key precursors to *Bearden* were *Williams* and *Tate*. Based on the discussion in *Bearden*, what were the holdings of the two cases? How did *Bearden* extend or modify the *Williams/Tate* doctrine? How much protection, really, does *Bearden* provide to indigent defendants?

2. **Incarceration of Indigent Defendants for Nonpayment of Criminal Justice Debt.** Despite the protections adopted by *Bearden*, it is hardly uncommon for poor defendants to be incarcerated based, at least in part, on missed LFO payments. Professors Katherine Beckett and Alexes Harris observe,

> First, debtors might spend time in jail pending an "ability to pay" or violation hearing. In addition, debtors are frequently arrested and incarcerated not for nonpayment, but rather for (civil) contempt of court stemming from failure to comply with a court order to pay. . . . Similarly, failure to respond to a summons issued

in response to nonpayment is a violation of a court order (failure to appear) that might trigger incarceration.

Finally, in some cases, a correctional officer or judge does consider evidence regarding whether a debtors' nonpayment is "willful." Yet it seems that "willful" is a highly elastic concept, one that fails to create a meaningful barrier to the incarceration of indigent debtors. For example, one community corrections officer told us that in his view, "all nonpayment is willful" because felons "can always go out and get a day job." Judges sometimes accept this reasoning. . . .

In some jurisdictions, debtors are presented with the "option" of paying off their debt by going to jail. In Washington State, this is called the "pay or stay" option and is authorized by state statute.

On Cash and Conviction: Monetary Sanctions as Misguided Policy, 10 CRIMINOLOGY & PUB. POL'Y 509, 524–25 (2011). It has been suggested that such contemporary practices amount to a return of the "debtors' prison." Nino C. Monea, *A Constitutional History of Debtors' Prisons*, 14 DREXEL L. REV. ___ (2021). Imprisonment for debt had been a common practice in early American history but was banned in most state constitutions by the end of the nineteenth century. Of course, in its contemporary form, imprisonment for (legal) debt means that the debtor will likely have only very limited opportunities to earn money—a reality that seems at cross-purposes with the state's goal of obtaining payment of LFOs.

3. **The Flipside Scenario.** *Bearden* deals with the use of incarceration as a penalty for nonpayment. A Maryland case, *Reddick v. State*, 608 A.2d 1246 (Md. 1992), presents the reverse situation: a judge offered to *reduce* incarceration as an *incentive* for payment. After his conviction of second-degree murder, Reddick was sentenced to thirty years in prison. However, at sentencing, the judge offered to reduce Reddick's prison term by five years if he paid $6,000 in restitution to the victim's family. Since he was unable to pay this amount, Reddick appealed on equal protection grounds—a wealthier defendant in his situation, he argued, would have gotten a more lenient sentence. Maryland's high court agreed. Citing *Bearden*, the court held that "Reddick is entitled to the sentence that a defendant with the financial wherewithal to make the payment would have received under the same circumstances," i.e., twenty-five years. *Id.* at 1248.[9]

---

[9] *Reddick* may be contrasted with *Hutchison v. State*, 150 S.W.3d 292 (Mo. 2004). Hutchison, Lopez, and a third defendant were each charged with first-degree murder in connection with a double-killing. While the case was pending, Lopez's sister won a large cash prize in a lottery. With the aid of these funds, Lopez negotiated a civil settlement with the victims' family; in return for $230,000, the family agreed to recommend a ten-year sentence for Lopez in the criminal case. Payment to the family was made contingent on Lopez actually receiving a sentence of no more than ten years. Meanwhile, Hutchison went to trial. Lopez was the state's main witness against Hutchison, who was convicted and sentenced to death. Lopez himself negotiated a plea deal with the state and received the requested ten years. On appeal, Hutchison objected that Lopez effectively purchased a reduced sentence in violation of the state constitution, and that his own far more severe sentence violated the Equal Protection Clause insofar as it resulted from his inability to pay off the victims' family as Lopez had. However, the Missouri Supreme Court disagreed. The court did not see Lopez's sentence as one that was impermissibly purchased because the trial judge had discretion to reject both Lopez's plea deal

4. **Application to Prosecutors.** May a prosecutor condition dismissal of charges on payment of a monetary penalty? The Mississippi Supreme Court considered the question in *State v. Moody,* 716 So. 2d 562 (Miss. 1998). In bad check cases, the practice of a particular DA's office in Jones County was to obtain an indictment and then offer to drop the charges if the defendant paid a $500 fine and restitution. Presented with this choice, Moody was unable to take advantage of the offer because of her financial status. After her conviction, she appealed, challenging the DA's practice on equal protection grounds.

Citing *Bearden,* the Mississippi high court ruled in Moody's favor:

> [O]ne who is unable to pay will always be in a position of facing a felony conviction and jail time, while those with adequate resources will not. The automatic nature of the fine is what makes it discriminating to the poor, in that only the poor will face jail time. We hold that an indigent's equal protection rights are violated when all potential defendants are offered one way to avoid prosecution and that one way is to pay a fine, and there is no determination as to an individual's ability to pay such a fine. Subjecting one to a jail term merely because he cannot afford to pay a fine, due to no fault of his own, is unconstitutional.

Id. at 565.

2. EXCESSIVE FINES CLAUSE

United States v. Bajakajian

524 U.S. 321 (1998)

■ THOMAS, J.

Respondent Hosep Bajakajian attempted to leave the United States without reporting, as required by federal law, that he was transporting more than $10,000 in currency. Federal law also provides that a person convicted of willfully violating this reporting requirement shall forfeit to the Government "any property . . . involved in such offense." 18 U.S.C. § 982(a)(1). The question in this case is whether forfeiture of the entire $357,144 that respondent failed to declare would violate the Excessive Fines Clause of the Eighth Amendment. We hold that it would, because full forfeiture of respondent's currency would be grossly disproportional to the gravity of his offense.

I

On June 9, 1994, respondent, his wife, and his two daughters were waiting at Los Angeles International Airport to board a flight to Italy;

---

and the family's lenient sentence recommendation. Meanwhile, the Equal Protection claim was turned aside because Hutchison was not similarly situated to Lopez. Since Lopez cooperated with police and prosecutors, and since Hutchison had been the one who actually shot the victims (at least based on Lopez's self-serving testimony), there were nonfinancial grounds for treating the two defendants differently. Are you persuaded that this case really should have come out differently than *Reddick*?

their final destination was Cyprus. Using dogs trained to detect currency by its smell, customs inspectors discovered some $230,000 in cash in the Bajakajians' checked baggage. A customs inspector approached respondent and his wife and told them that they were required to report all money in excess of $10,000 in their possession or in their baggage. Respondent said that he had $8,000 and that his wife had another $7,000, but that the family had no additional currency to declare. A search of their carry-on bags, purse, and wallet revealed more cash; in all, customs inspectors found $357,144. The currency was seized and respondent was taken into custody.

A federal grand jury indicted respondent on three counts. Count One charged him with failing to report, as required by 31 U.S.C. § 5316(a)(1)(A), that he was transporting more than $10,000 outside the United States, and with doing so "willfully," in violation of § 5322(a). Count Two charged him with making a false material statement to the United States Customs Service, in violation of 18 U.S.C. § 1001. Count Three sought forfeiture of the $357,144 pursuant to 18 U.S.C. § 982(a)(1), which provides:

> "The court, in imposing sentence on a person convicted of an offense in violation of section . . . 5316, . . . shall order that the person forfeit to the United States any property, real or personal, involved in such offense, or any property traceable to such property." 18 U.S.C. § 982(a)(1).

Respondent pleaded guilty to the failure to report in Count One; the Government agreed to dismiss the false statement charge in Count Two; and respondent elected to have a bench trial on the forfeiture in Count Three. After the bench trial, the District Court found that the entire $357,144 was subject to forfeiture because it was "involved in" the offense. The court also found that the funds were not connected to any other crime and that respondent was transporting the money to repay a lawful debt. The District Court further found that respondent had failed to report that he was taking the currency out of the United States because of fear stemming from "cultural differences": Respondent, who had grown up as a member of the Armenian minority in Syria, had a "distrust for the Government."

Although § 982(a)(1) directs sentencing courts to impose full forfeiture, the District Court concluded that such forfeiture would be "extraordinarily harsh" and "grossly disproportionate to the offense in question," and that it would therefore violate the Excessive Fines Clause. The court instead ordered forfeiture of $15,000, in addition to a sentence of three years of probation and a fine of $5,000—the maximum fine under the Sentencing Guidelines—because the court believed that the maximum Guidelines fine was "too little" and that a $15,000 forfeiture would "make up for what I think a reasonable fine should be."

The United States appealed, seeking full forfeiture of respondent's currency as provided in § 982(a)(1). * * *

II

The Eighth Amendment provides: "Excessive bail shall not be required, nor excessive fines imposed, nor cruel and unusual punishments inflicted." This Court has had little occasion to interpret, and has never actually applied, the Excessive Fines Clause. We have, however, explained that at the time the Constitution was adopted, "the word 'fine' was understood to mean a payment to a sovereign as punishment for some offense." *Browning-Ferris Industries of Vt., Inc. v. Kelco Disposal, Inc.,* 492 U.S. 257, 265 (1989). The Excessive Fines Clause thus "limits the government's power to extract payments, whether in cash or in kind, 'as punishment for some offense.' " *Austin v. United States,* 509 U.S. 602, 609–10 (1993). Forfeitures—payments in kind—are thus "fines" if they constitute punishment for an offense.

We have little trouble concluding that the forfeiture of currency ordered by § 982(a)(1) constitutes punishment. The statute directs a court to order forfeiture as an additional sanction when "imposing sentence on a person convicted of" a willful violation of § 5316's reporting requirement. The forfeiture is thus imposed at the culmination of a criminal proceeding and requires conviction of an underlying felony, and it cannot be imposed upon an innocent owner of unreported currency, but only upon a person who has himself been convicted of a § 5316 reporting violation.

The United States argues, however, that the forfeiture of currency under § 982(a)(1) "also serves important remedial purposes." The Government asserts that it has "an overriding sovereign interest in controlling what property leaves and enters the country." It claims that full forfeiture of unreported currency supports that interest by serving to "dete[r] illicit movements of cash" and aiding in providing the Government with "valuable information to investigate and detect criminal activities associated with that cash." Deterrence, however, has traditionally been viewed as a goal of punishment, and forfeiture of the currency here does not serve the remedial purpose of compensating the Government for a loss. Although the Government has asserted a loss of information regarding the amount of currency leaving the country, that loss would not be remedied by the Government's confiscation of respondent's $357,144.[4]

The United States also argues that the forfeiture mandated by § 982(a)(1) is constitutional because it falls within a class of historic forfeitures of property tainted by crime. In so doing, the Government relies upon a series of cases involving traditional civil *in rem* forfeitures

[4] We do not suggest that merely because the forfeiture of respondent's currency in this case would not serve a remedial purpose, other forfeitures may be classified as nonpunitive (and thus not "fines") if they serve some remedial purpose as well as being punishment for an offense. Even if the Government were correct in claiming that the forfeiture of respondent's currency is remedial in some way, the forfeiture would still be punitive in part. (The Government concedes as much.) This is sufficient to bring the forfeiture within the purview of the Excessive Fines Clause.

that are inapposite because such forfeitures were historically considered nonpunitive.

The theory behind such forfeitures was the fiction that the action was directed against "guilty property," rather than against the offender himself. Historically, the conduct of the property owner was irrelevant; indeed, the owner of forfeited property could be entirely innocent of any crime. * * *

Traditional *in rem* forfeitures were thus not considered punishment against the individual for an offense. Because they were viewed as nonpunitive, such forfeitures traditionally were considered to occupy a place outside the domain of the Excessive Fines Clause. Recognizing the nonpunitive character of such proceedings, we have held that the Double Jeopardy Clause does not bar the institution of a civil, *in rem* forfeiture action after the criminal conviction of the defendant.[6]

The forfeiture in this case does not bear any of the hallmarks of traditional civil *in rem* forfeitures. The Government has not proceeded against the currency itself, but has instead sought and obtained a criminal conviction of respondent personally. The forfeiture serves no remedial purpose, is designed to punish the offender, and cannot be imposed upon innocent owners. * * *

The Government specifically contends that the forfeiture of respondent's currency is constitutional because it involves an "instrumentality" of respondent's crime.[8] According to the Government, the unreported cash is an instrumentality because it "does not merely facilitate a violation of law," but is "the very *sine qua non* of the crime." The Government reasons that "there would be no violation at all without the exportation (or attempted exportation) of the cash."

Acceptance of the Government's argument would require us to expand the traditional understanding of instrumentality forfeitures. This we decline to do. Instrumentalities historically have been treated as a form of "guilty property" that can be forfeited in civil *in rem* proceedings. In this case, however, the Government has sought to punish respondent by proceeding against him criminally, *in personam,* rather than proceeding *in rem* against the currency. It is therefore irrelevant

---

[6] It does not follow, of course, that all modern civil *in rem* forfeitures are nonpunitive and thus beyond the coverage of the Excessive Fines Clause. Because some recent federal forfeiture laws have blurred the traditional distinction between civil *in rem* and criminal *in personam* forfeiture, we have held that a modern statutory forfeiture is a "fine" for Eighth Amendment purposes if it constitutes punishment even in part, regardless of whether the proceeding is styled *in rem* or *in personam*. See *Austin v. United States, supra,* at 621–22 (although labeled *in rem,* civil forfeiture of real property used "to facilitate" the commission of drug crimes was punitive in part and thus subject to review under the Excessive Fines Clause).

[8] Although the term "instrumentality" is of recent vintage, it fairly characterizes property that historically was subject to forfeiture because it was the actual means by which an offense was committed. "Instrumentality" forfeitures have historically been limited to the property actually used to commit an offense and no more. A forfeiture that reaches beyond this strict historical limitation is *ipso facto* punitive and therefore subject to review under the Excessive Fines Clause.

whether respondent's currency is an instrumentality; the forfeiture is punitive, and the test for the excessiveness of a punitive forfeiture involves solely a proportionality determination.[9]

III

Because the forfeiture of respondent's currency constitutes punishment and is thus a "fine" within the meaning of the Excessive Fines Clause, we now turn to the question whether it is "excessive."

A

The touchstone of the constitutional inquiry under the Excessive Fines Clause is the principle of proportionality: The amount of the forfeiture must bear some relationship to the gravity of the offense that it is designed to punish. Until today, however, we have not articulated a standard for determining whether a punitive forfeiture is constitutionally excessive. We now hold that a punitive forfeiture violates the Excessive Fines Clause if it is grossly disproportional to the gravity of a defendant's offense.

The text and history of the Excessive Fines Clause demonstrate the centrality of proportionality to the excessiveness inquiry; nonetheless, they provide little guidance as to how disproportional a punitive forfeiture must be to the gravity of an offense in order to be "excessive." Excessive means surpassing the usual, the proper, or a normal measure of proportion. See 1 N. Webster, American Dictionary of the English Language (1828); S. Johnson, A Dictionary of the English Language 680 (4th ed. 1773). The constitutional question that we address, however, is just how proportional to a criminal offense a fine must be, and the text of the Excessive Fines Clause does not answer it.

Nor does its history. The Clause was little discussed in the First Congress and the debates over the ratification of the Bill of Rights. * * *

We must therefore rely on other considerations in deriving a constitutional excessiveness standard, and there are two that we find particularly relevant. The first, which we have emphasized in our cases interpreting the Cruel and Unusual Punishments Clause, is that judgments about the appropriate punishment for an offense belong in the first instance to the legislature. See, *e.g.*, *Solem v. Helm*, 463 U.S. 277, 290 (1983). The second is that any judicial determination regarding the gravity of a particular criminal offense will be inherently imprecise. Both of these principles counsel against requiring strict proportionality between the amount of a punitive forfeiture and the gravity of a criminal

---

[9] The currency in question is not an instrumentality in any event. The Court of Appeals reasoned that the existence of the currency as a "precondition" to the reporting requirement did not make it an "instrumentality" of the offense. We agree; the currency is merely the subject of the crime of failure to report. Cash in a suitcase does not facilitate the commission of that crime as, for example, an automobile facilitates the transportation of goods concealed to avoid taxes. In the latter instance, the property is the actual means by which the criminal act is committed.

offense, and we therefore adopt the standard of gross disproportionality articulated in our Cruel and Unusual Punishments Clause precedents.

In applying this standard, the district courts in the first instance, and the courts of appeals, reviewing the proportionality determination *de novo,* must compare the amount of the forfeiture to the gravity of the defendant's offense. If the amount of the forfeiture is grossly disproportional to the gravity of the defendant's offense, it is unconstitutional.

B

Under this standard, the forfeiture of respondent's entire $357,144 would violate the Excessive Fines Clause.[11] Respondent's crime was solely a reporting offense. It was permissible to transport the currency out of the country so long as he reported it. Section 982(a)(1) orders currency to be forfeited for a "willful" violation of the reporting requirement. Thus, the essence of respondent's crime is a willful failure to report the removal of currency from the United States. Furthermore, as the District Court found, respondent's violation was unrelated to any other illegal activities. The money was the proceeds of legal activity and was to be used to repay a lawful debt. Whatever his other vices, respondent does not fit into the class of persons for whom the statute was principally designed: He is not a money launderer, a drug trafficker, or a tax evader. And under the Sentencing Guidelines, the maximum sentence that could have been imposed on respondent was six months, while the maximum fine was $5,000. Such penalties confirm a minimal level of culpability.

The harm that respondent caused was also minimal. Failure to report his currency affected only one party, the Government, and in a relatively minor way. There was no fraud on the United States, and respondent caused no loss to the public fisc. Had his crime gone undetected, the Government would have been deprived only of the information that $357,144 had left the country. The Government and the dissent contend that there is a correlation between the amount forfeited and the harm that the Government would have suffered had the crime gone undetected. We disagree. There is no inherent proportionality in such a forfeiture. It is impossible to conclude, for example, that the harm respondent caused is anywhere near 30 times greater than that caused by a hypothetical drug dealer who willfully fails to report taking $12,000 out of the country in order to purchase drugs.

Comparing the gravity of respondent's crime with the $357,144 forfeiture the Government seeks, we conclude that such a forfeiture would be grossly disproportional to the gravity of his offense. It is larger

[11] The only question before this Court is whether the full forfeiture of respondent's $357,144 as directed by § 982(a)(1) is constitutional under the Excessive Fines Clause. We hold that it is not. The Government petitioned for certiorari seeking full forfeiture, and we reject that request. * * * Nor, indeed, do we address in *any* respect the validity of the forfeiture ordered by the District Court * * * .

than the $5,000 fine imposed by the District Court by many orders of magnitude, and it bears no articulable correlation to any injury suffered by the Government. * * *

[The dissenting opinion of JUSTICE KENNEDY is omitted.]

NOTES & QUESTIONS

1. **What Is a "Fine"?** The Excessive Fines Clause, by its terms, applies only to "fines." As *Bajakajian* makes clear, courts are not bound by legislative labels in determining what counts as a fine for constitutional purposes. Instead, the Court indicated that a "payment to a sovereign" would be treated as a fine if it had, at least in part, a punitive purpose—even if it also had, in part, a remedial purpose (see footnote 4). When it came to the forfeiture at issue in *Bajakajian,* the Court had "little trouble" finding a punitive purpose, emphasizing in particular that it was a *criminal* forfeiture—imposed through criminal processes and requiring a conviction.

What about *civil* forfeitures? In an earlier case, *Austin v. United States,* 509 U.S. 602 (1993), the Court held that a civil forfeiture might indeed have a sufficiently punitive purpose to count as a "fine," notwithstanding the use of civil litigation processes. In footnote 6, *Bajakajian* affirmed that *Austin* was still good law on this point.[10]

Thus, for both criminal and civil forfeitures, the key question for determining whether the Excessive Fines Clause applies is whether the forfeiture at issue is purely remedial or at least partly punitive.[11] In answering that question, the legislature's choice of civil versus criminal processes may play an important role but is not necessarily dispositive. Another important factor might be the existence of an "innocent owner" defense, which indicates that the legislature wished to tie forfeiture to culpability—a sign of a punitive purpose. *Austin*, 509 U.S. at 619.

Left uncertain by *Bajakajian* is whether there might be certain types of forfeitures categorically excluded from Excessive Fines Clause coverage because of their historical pedigree or otherwise. "Instrumentality" forfeitures are of particular interest in this regard. The government argued that Bajakajian's undeclared currency should be seen as an instrumentality of his offense. The Court acknowledged the long tradition of *civil* instrumentality forfeitures but held it to be inapplicable since the government in this case had used *criminal* forfeiture. The Court also seemed to adopt a narrow definition of "instrumentality" (footnote 9). *See United States v. Ferro*, 681 F.3d 1105, 1111–12, 1114 (9th Cir. 2012) (discussing uncertain status of civil instrumentality forfeitures after *Bajakajian*; holding that "all types of civil forfeitures—save perhaps forfeitures of contraband,

[10] There is thus an inconsistency in the analysis under the Excessive Fines and Double Jeopardy Clauses. As you may recall from the earlier discussion of civil forfeiture, the Supreme Court has indicated that proceeds and instrumentality forfeitures under 21 U.S.C. §§ 881(a)(6)–(7) are *not* punitive for double-jeopardy purposes. *United States v. Ursery*, 518 U.S. 267 (1996).

[11] The Court has equated punitive purposes with deterrence and retribution, which were contrasted with the remedial purposes of removing dangerous or illegal items from society or compensating the government for the costs of law enforcement activity. *Austin*, 509 U.S. at 621.

such as unregistered hand grenades or illegal drugs—are subject to review for excessiveness.").

Another notable forfeiture category not addressed at all by *Bajakajian* was offense proceeds, e.g., the money earned from an illegal sale of drugs. Most federal circuits have since decided that proceeds forfeitures are, by definition, not punitive and hence are beyond the reach of constitutional excessiveness review. *See, e.g., United States v. Betancourt,* 422 F.3d 240, 250 (5th Cir. 2005) (citing cases). For instance, it was for this reason that a constitutional excessiveness claim was rejected in the *$100,120* case excerpted earlier in this chapter. 901 F.3d at 772. However, not all circuits are in accord. *See United States v. Jalaram, Inc.,* 599 F.3d 347 (4th Cir. 2010).

Bajakajian and *Austin* considered the application of the Excessive Fines Clause to forfeiture. How about restitution? As a form of damages for the victim, restitution would seem to fall squarely on the remedial side of the remedial/punitive divide. However, as you may recall from *United States v. Paroline* (excerpted earlier in this chapter), the Court has suggested that a large restitution award that is disproportionate to the defendant's actual contribution to the victim's injury might run afoul of the Excessive Fines Clause. However, the Court has not expressly so decided and lower courts are divided on the question. Nathaniel Amann, Note, *Restitution and the Excessive Fines Clause*, 58 AM. CRIM. L. REV. 205 (2021). For an argument that restitution today is punitive, rather than compensatory, and thus requires additional constitutional protections, see Courtney Lollar, *What Is Criminal Restitution?*, 100 IOWA L. REV. 93 (2014).

How about fees and costs? Again, these economic sanctions are often framed as reimbursement for the costs incurred by criminal justice agencies and hence as remedial. But, as we have seen, the amount of fees imposed on individual defendants can seem quite arbitrary in some cases, which might perhaps give rise to a colorable Excessive Fines Clause claim. *See, e.g.,* Kristen M. Haight, Note, *Paying for the Privilege of Punishment: Reinterpreting Excessive Fines Clause Doctrine to Allow State Prisoners to Seek Relief from Pay-to-Stay Fees,* 62 WM. & MARY L. REV. 287 (2020) (arguing that room-and-board fees charged to inmates in some jurisdictions might qualify as "fines" for constitutional purposes).

2. **What Is "Excessive"?** Once it is determined that an economic sanction counts as a "fine," it is necessary to determine whether the fine is excessive. *Bajakajian* adopted a "gross disproportionality" test, as the Court also uses in assessing the constitutionality of prison sentences under the Cruel and Unusual Punishments Clause (see Chapter 6). The test embodies deference to legislative decisions on penal policy, although, as *Bajakajian* itself illustrates, the deference is not unlimited. What factors did the Court take into account in deciding that $357,144 was a grossly disproportionate forfeiture in relation to Bajakajian's offense?

Note that the defendant's ability to pay was *not* among the considerations discussed by the Court. But doesn't this seem an important factor in determining whether any economic sanction is excessive?

3. **Home Is Where the Hemp Is.** Although *Austin* and *Bajakajian* opened the door to constitutional review of forfeitures for disproportionality, lower courts have not often rejected forfeitures on this ground. Occasionally, though, claimants are successful. For instance, in *von Hofe v. United States*, 492 F.3d 175 (2d Cir. 2007), police executed a search warrant in the family home of Mr. and Mrs. von Hofe and discovered a marijuana growing operation involving sixty-five plants in the basement. In state court, Mr. von Hofe pled guilty to a trafficking offense and Mrs. von Hofe to simple possession. At the same time, the federal government sought civil forfeiture of the entire home as an instrumentality of a drug offense. Both spouses, who jointly owned the home, asserted a claim to the property in the civil proceeding, with Mrs. von Hofe advancing an innocent owner defense. The case went to trial, and the government won. The von Hofes appealed, arguing that loss of their entire home for a relatively small marijuana production operation would violate the Excessive Fines Clause.

The Second Circuit agreed—in part. Based on *Bajakajian* and circuit precedent, the court determined that the "excessiveness inquiry" required consideration of the following factors:

> (1) the harshness, or gross disproportionality, of the forfeiture in comparison to the gravity of the offense, giving due regard to (a) the offense committed and its relation to other criminal activity, (b) whether the claimant falls within the class of persons for whom the statute was designed, (c) the punishments available, and (d) the harm caused by the claimant's conduct; (2) the nexus between the property and the criminal offenses, including the deliberate nature of the use and the temporal and spatial extent of the use; and (3) the culpability of each claimant.

Id. at 186. In light of Mr. von Hofe's active involvement in production of the marijuana, the court found no excessiveness in the forfeiture of his one-half interest in the property. However, while Mrs. von Hofe's knowledge of the marijuana precluded her use of the innocent-owner defense, her merely passive acquiescence to her husband's activities did not justify the complete loss of her one-half interest. Like the Supreme Court in *Bajakajian*, the Second Circuit declined to state how much of a forfeiture would be constitutional, but simply ruled that the full amount sought by the government was too much.

4. **Statutory Codification.** In the wake of *Bajakajian*, Congress codified constitutional proportionality review for civil forfeitures in 18 U.S.C. § 983(g). The statute specifies that "the claimant shall have the burden of establishing that the forfeiture is grossly disproportional by a preponderance of the evidence at a hearing conducted by the court without a jury."

5. **Incorporation.** The Supreme Court has only relatively recently held that the Excessive Fines Clause is incorporated into the Fourteenth Amendment's Due Process Clause and is thereby binding on the states. *Timbs v. Indiana*, 139 S. Ct. 682, 691 (2019). The holding may open the door for new constitutional challenges to the vast array of fees, costs, and the like that are increasingly imposed in state courts across the country. For

discussion of *Timbs*, see Wayne A. Logan, Timbs v. Indiana: *Toward the Regulation of Mercenary Criminal Justice*, 32 FED. SENT'G RPTR. 2 (2019).

CHAPTER 10

SENTENCING OF CORPORATIONS

"Some will rob you with a six-gun/And some with a fountain pen."
Woody Guthrie, *The Ballad of Pretty Boy Floyd*[1]

In previous chapters, the focus was the sentencing of individuals. In this chapter, focus shifts to the sentencing of corporations.[2] Corporate criminal liability and sentencing are the subject of an expansive, intellectually rich literature. Among the most basic issues is this: how can a corporation, a legal fiction, be found criminally liable and punished, when it has "no soul to damn, no body to kick"?[3]

Due to this artificiality, the sentencing options available in the punishment of corporations are limited and often distinct. A corporation can be fined, as can a human actor; however, when a corporation is fined, it is shareholders, who may well be oblivious to the detected criminal activity, who feel the financial pain (despite perhaps benefitting from the criminality). At the same time, a fine might be thought appropriate when the corporation engages in financial crime, such as health care-related fraud or money laundering. But does a fine satisfy sentencing purposes and goals when corporate criminal activity results in the physical harm or death of individuals? Or when corporate activity despoils the environment? Ultimately, as well, is there a risk that a fine will be internalized by a corporation—regarded as simply "a cost of doing business" (i.e., a "price," not a "sanction")?

On the other side of the balance, unlike the application of substantive criminal law to human actors, corporations can be held vicariously liable for the acts (and omissions) of their employees acting within the scope of their employment and who were motivated, at least

[1] Woody Guthrie, *The Ballad of Pretty Boy Floyd*, Dust Bowl Records (1940).

[2] Although the term corporation is used, as a general matter the discussion here pertains to other business entities such as partnerships, sole proprietorships, and unincorporated associations, as well as governments.

[3] John C. Coffee, Jr., *"No Soul to Damn: No Body to Kick": An Unscandalized Inquiry into the Problem of Corporate Punishment*, 79 MICH. L. REV. 386 (1981). Often, individual corporate directors, officers, or employees are joined as co-defendants in prosecutions. The sentencing of these natural-person defendants poses interesting theoretical and practical challenges, which, while often distinct in some respects, share much with the challenges of sentencing individuals addressed in other chapters. The failure of prosecutors to criminally charge individuals holding high-level positions in corporate entities has been the subject of pointed criticism. *See, e.g.*, Jed S. Rakoff, *The Financial Crisis: Why Have No High-Level Executives Been Prosecuted?*, N.Y. REV. OF BOOKS, Jan. 9, 2014. In the fall of 2015, the U.S. Department of Justice adopted a new policy dedicated to focusing on the investigation and prosecution of individuals, known as the Yates Memo (named after then-Deputy Attorney General Sally Yates). To date, the policy appears to have had little impact. *See* Brandon L. Garrett, *Declining Corporate Prosecutions*, 57 AM. CRIM. L. REV. 109, 112, 131–35 (2020). For more on the Yates Memo, see Gideon Mark, *The Yates Memorandum*, 51 U.C. DAVIS L. REV. 1589 (2018).

in part, by an intent to benefit the corporation.[4] Liability can also attach when individual corporate actors, such as officers and directors, prioritize their self-interest over that of the corporation (what is known as the "agency" problem). In such instances, is it fair to punish the corporation and therefore shareholders[5] and employees (and perhaps the public, if the corporation passes along costs to consumers)?[6]

One example of this broader effect is found in the prosecution and eventual collapse of the energy, commodities, and services provider Enron Corporation in 2001, which resulted in the loss of 4500 jobs and over $1 billion in investments. Sebastian Bellum, Note, *A Dual System of Justice: Financial Institutions and White-Collar Criminal Enforcement*, 96 NOTRE DAME L. REV. 2007, 2013 (2021). The occurrence has given rise to the "Too-Big-to-Jail" problem—that "some corporations may be so valuable to the economy that prosecutors will not hold them accountable for crime." BRANDON L. GARRETT, TOO BIG TO JAIL: HOW PROSECUTORS COMPROMISE WITH CORPORATIONS 252 (2014). Prosecutors might also be reluctant to sanction harshly businesses in sectors of major national importance, such as defense and intelligence sector contractors, aerospace, and telecommunications. Moreover, corporate prosecutions are apt to be very resource-intensive, with expensive and expansive multi-prong investigations running for years, followed by complicated trials that can last weeks and even months.

In addition to these practical issues, sanctioning corporate misconduct raises a wealth of interesting and important theoretical issues. In terms of penal justification, for instance, how can retribution be served when liability is based on agency principles and punishment will impact innocents? Veronica Martinez, *The Government's Prioritization of Information Over Sanction: Implications for Compliance*, 83 LAW & CONTEMP. PROBS. 85, 90 (2020). At the same time, deterrence is more complicated with corporations. It can be the case that a corporate defendant, rather than experiencing a harm, actually secures reputational benefit from a prosecution. It can, for instance, publicly communicate that by complying with government sanctions it "is trying to change and correct misconduct from within by being transparent." W.

---

[4] *See* United States v. Agosto-Vega, 617 F.3d 541, 552–53 (1st Cir. 2010) (citations omitted) ("The test is whether the agent is performing acts of the kind which he is authorized to perform and those acts are motivated—at least in part—by an intent to benefit the corporation."); United States v. Singh, 518 F.3d 236, 249–50 (4th Cir. 2008) (citations omitted) ("a corporate accused is liable for the criminal acts of its 'employees and agents' acting 'within the scope of their employment' for the 'benefit [of] the corporation,' and such liability arises if the employee or agent has acted for his own benefit as well as that of his employer.").

[5] Although arguably problematic in principle, the actual amount of this pass-along cost to shareholders can be modest. For instance, Deutsche Bank, a global public corporation, was fined $150 million for its involvement in facilitating the criminal misconduct of client Jeffery Epstein, which had "the ultimate effect of fining each individual shareholder just over seven cents." Sebastian Bellum, Note, *A Dual System of Justice: Financial Institutions and White-Collar Criminal Enforcement*, 96 NOTRE DAME L. REV. 2007, 2010 (2021).

[6] For a retort to many of the standard objections to corporate criminal liability, see Sara Sun Beale, *A Response to the Critics of Corporate Criminal Liability*, 46 AM. CRIM. L. REV. 148 (2009).

Robert Thomas, *Corporate Criminal Law Is Too Broad—Worse, It's Too Narrow*, 53 ARIZ. ST. L.J. 99, 101 n.93 (2021). Also, corporate misconduct often implicates parallel criminal and civil prohibitions, such as those found in the Racketeering Influenced and Corrupt Organizations Act (RICO), and laws addressing securities, health care, and mail and wire fraud. The availability of a civil remedy can affect prosecutorial charging decisions, channeling cases away—at least to some extent—from the criminal justice system, which can obscure the criminal deterrence signal.

Today, corporate entities like Enron are synonymous with major financial wrongdoing causing billions of dollars in losses to economies and individuals. Staggering as the sums are, however, there is reason to believe that the true financial impact is actually understated—both because sophisticated technologies allow harms to go undetected and because organizations can be reluctant to acknowledge losses that attract regulators' attention and diminish market reputation. Meanwhile, corporate entities have facilitated worldwide criminal activities, including narcotics trafficking, by engaging in money-laundering, and bribed foreign officials in their business dealings.

The chapter begins with a brief overview of the history of corporate criminal liability and then discusses modern-era sentencing data, along with several important changes in prosecutorial practices that have shifted corporate cases away from the traditional criminal adjudicative process.[7] The chapter concludes with a discussion of the pertinent U.S. Sentencing Guideline provisions and the role of the federal judiciary in overseeing plea deals brokered by the government and corporations.

A. THEORETICAL BACKGROUND

At common law, a corporation was considered incapable of committing an indictable criminal offense. As Blackstone wrote, "a corporation cannot commit treason, or felony, or other crime in its corporate capacity: though its members may, in their distinct individual capacities." 1 WILLIAM BLACKSTONE, COMMENTARIES ON THE LAWS OF ENGLAND 464. This was because, as Chief Justice John Marshall put it, "[a] corporation is an artificial being, invisible, intangible, and existing only in contemplation of law." *Dartmouth College v. Woodward*, 17 U.S. (4 Wheat.) 518, 636 (1819). Although municipal corporations were at times found criminally liable for non-feasance of statutory duties, such as failure to maintain roads or bridges, corporations were generally deemed legally incapable of committing intentional criminal acts. *See generally* Kathleen F. Brickey, *Corporate Criminal Accountability: A Brief History and Observation*, 60 WASH. U. L.Q. 393, 401–05 (1982).

---

[7] Although states can and do criminally prosecute and sentence corporate entities, the focus here mainly will be on federal cases.

In the U.S., the liability landscape changed in the early twentieth century. In its landmark decision *N.Y. Cent. & Hudson River R.R. Co. v. United States*, 212 U.S. 481 (1909), the Supreme Court upheld the convictions of a railroad company and one of its employees for payment of rebates for shipments in violation of federal law. In finding liability, the Court reviewed the evolution of tort liability of corporations for the acts of employees within the scope of their employment (i.e., respondeat superior). The Court observed that:

> This is the rule when the act is done by the agent in the course of his employment, although done wantonly or recklessly or against the express orders of the principal. In such cases the liability is not imputed because the principal actually participates in the malice or fraud, but because the act is done for the benefit of the principal, while the agent is acting within the scope of his employment in the business of the principal.

Id. at 493. After finding that the fixing of rates was within the scope of authority of the defendant's employee, the Court elaborated on why criminal liability for the corporation itself was proper:

> We see no valid objection in law, and every reason in public policy, why the corporation, which profits by the transaction, and can only act through its agents and officers, shall be held punishable by fine because of the knowledge and intent of its agents to whom it has intrusted authority to act in the subject-matter . . . and whose knowledge and purposes may well be attributed to the corporation for which the agents act.

Id. at 495. Mindful of the increasingly central role played by corporations in American society, and the consequences of shielding corporations from criminal liability, the Court added that

> [The law] cannot shut its eyes to the fact that the great majority of business transactions in modern times are conducted through [corporations], and particularly that interstate commerce is almost entirely in their hands, and to give them immunity from all punishment because of the old and exploded doctrine that a corporation cannot commit a crime would virtually take away the only means of effectually controlling the subject-matter and correcting the abuses aimed at.

Id. at 495–96.[8]

Thirty years later, sociologist Edwin Sutherland popularized the term "white collar crime." In drawing the distinction, Sutherland highlighted the significant societal harms resulting from corporate criminal activity, and a new kind of criminal actor—one seeking financial and professional benefit within the corporate context. Today, the notion

[8] For full discussion of the intellectual history behind the evolution, see W. Robert Thomas, *How and Why Corporations Became (and Remain) Persons Under Criminal Law*, 45 FLA. ST. U. L. REV. 479 (2018).

that only "white collar" actors commit what is considered white collar crime is outmoded, much like the distinction drawn between crime "in the suites" and crime "in the streets." As Professor Samuel Buell has observed, today "[m]any white collar offenses, maybe even most of them, are committed by pedestrian hucksters." Samuel W. Buell, *Is the White Collar Offender Privileged?*, 63 DUKE L.J. 823, 830–31 (2014).

Although harms imposed by corporations are very often financial in nature, corporate action (and inaction) can result in the death of individuals, whether employees or members of the public. Historically, however, authorities trying to hold corporations liable for homicide have faced challenges. For instance, laws might refer to a "human being" or "person" fatally harming another, which resulted in homicide prosecutions mainly being brought against "small companies in which ownership and management were united in the same individuals, who were also charged individually." James W. Harlow, Note, *Corporate Criminal Liability for Homicide: A Statutory Framework*, 61 DUKE L.J. 123, 126 (2011).

Legal definitions have been amended over time to encompass corporate actors, increasing the wherewithal of prosecutors to bring homicide cases (typically involving involuntary manslaughter or criminally negligent or reckless homicide charges). In the early 1970s, for instance, the Ford Motor Company was successfully prosecuted for deaths relating to the operation of its Pinto automobile, based on a corporate cost-benefit decision to locate a fuel tank in a dangerous location (the rear-end).[9] More recent examples of homicide prosecutions are those of Massey Energy for the deaths of twenty-nine coal miners in one of its mines in 2010, and BP (formerly British Petroleum) for the deaths of eleven of its workers on one of its offshore oil rigs (the Deepwater Horizon) that exploded and caught fire, also in 2010.

B. MODERN TRENDS

As discussed in Chapters 2 and 3, federal sentencing law has undergone significant change in the last several decades. Prior to 1987, federal courts had significant discretion in all sentences they imposed, with little appellate oversight. In 1987, however, this changed with the introduction of the U.S. Sentencing Guidelines, which sought to reduce disparities in federal sentences among individuals. Four years later, in 1991, the Organizational Sentencing Guidelines came into effect, which like those concerning individuals, mandated more or less fixed sentences within specified ranges, based on base offense level, defendant culpability, and the appropriateness of any possible departures (increases or decreases). Of course, the landscape changed in 2005 when

[9] More recently, in 2017, General Motors admitted liability in a federal prosecution in a case involving a similar cost-benefit decision concerning a faulty ignition switch resulting in the deaths of 124 individuals. Veronica R. Martinez, *Complex Compliance Investigations*, 120 COLUM. L. REV. 249, 252–53 (2020).

the Supreme Court in *United States v. Booker*, 543 U.S. 220 (2005), held that the Guidelines were not mandatory, but rather advisory, and later issued a number of other decisions that restored considerable discretionary sentencing authority to judges.

More recently, the sentencing landscape shifted again, reflecting broader political currents and attendant shifts in the charging decisions of the U.S. Department of Justice and federal prosecutors. To a greater extent than ever before, corporate criminal misconduct is addressed by use of "deferred prosecution agreements" and "non-prosecution agreements," and sentencing discounts are provided for self-instituted corporate monitoring and compliance programs. Corporations, in short, often escape charges—and the public notoriety that they bring—by settling with government officials before or during investigations. *See generally* JOHN C. COFFEE, JR., CORPORATE CRIME AND PUNISHMENT: THE CRISIS OF UNDERENFORCEMENT (2020); BRANDON GARRETT, TOO BIG TO JAIL: HOW PROSECUTORS COMPROMISE WITH CORPORATIONS (2014).

Since 2000, the calamitous financial wrongdoing of corporate giants such as Enron, and the deaths and catastrophic environmental damage caused by BP Oil as a result of the massive Deepwater Horizon oil spill, have attracted major public attention.

The publicity generated, however, belies the fact that corporate criminal cases are in fact surprisingly rare. In fiscal year 2020, for instance, only 94 cases were reported to the U.S. Sentencing Commission (as opposed to 132 cases in 2016).[10] In 2020, the most common offenses were fraud (32%) and environmental crimes (28%). Here are some other facts of note:

- most organizations were closely-held or private corporations (64%) or limited liability companies (23%);
- 9% were publicly traded companies;
- 66% employed fewer than 50 workers (10% employed 1,000 employees or more);
- 12% of defendants had a history of misconduct, including previous criminal or civil adjudications or had pending charges; and
- 62% of the cases involved at least one related individual who was separately prosecuted in addition to the organization

    –of these individuals, 57% were not high level officials; 19% were managers/supervisors; 13% were owners; and 11% were board members in the organization.

[10] In his study of recent data, Professor Brandon Garrett noted a significant decline in federal corporate prosecutions from the Obama to Trump presidential administrations, both in number and the amount of fines imposed. Brandon L. Garrett, *Declining Corporate Prosecutions*, 57 AM. CRIM. L. REV. 109, 114–15 (2020).

In terms of the punishment imposed:

- 70% were sentenced to probation;
- 30% were ordered to develop a compliance and ethics program, usually as a condition of probation;
- 69% had a fine imposed. The median fine amount was $4,000,000 and average fine amount was $6.6 million;
- 29% were ordered to pay restitution. The median restitution ordered was $28,500 and the average restitution amount was $7.7 million; and
- 13% were ordered to forfeit money. The median forfeiture amount was $1.3 million and the average forfeiture amount was $6.7 million.

U.S. Sent'ng. Comm'n, *Quick Facts: Organizational Offenders, Fiscal Year 2020*, https://www.ussc.gov/sites/default/files/pdf/research-and-publications/quick-facts/Organizational-Offenders_FY20.pdf.

The foregoing data, while interesting, tell only part of the story. This is because the Commission only collects data on organizations that are convicted, most (94%) by a plea of guilty. The Commission data fail to reflect the predominant role now played by other dispositions, most notably "nonprosecution" and "deferred prosecution" agreements, the advent of which has been called "arguably the most profound development in corporate white collar practice" in recent memory. Peter Spivack & Sujit Raman, *Regulating the "New Regulators": Current Trends in Deferred Prosecution Agreements*, 45 AM. CRIM. L. REV. 159, 159 (2008).

1. NONPROSECUTION AGREEMENTS (NPAS)

NPAs are negotiated agreements between prosecutors and corporate entities that formalize a decision to withhold criminal charges in exchange for a financial penalty and other conditions. The agreement is not filed with a court, nor is it reviewed by a court. The appeal to a corporate defendant is obvious: it "can truthfully assert that it was never prosecuted for the misconduct." Peter J. Henning, *The Organizational Guidelines: R.I.P.?*, 116 YALE L.J. POCKET PART 312, 314 n.9 (2007). With an NPA, the entity is typically required to publicly acknowledge wrongdoing, comply with a sanction (e.g., pay a fine), agree to satisfy any other required conditions, and cooperate with the government's ongoing investigation. The agreement is memorialized without a formal guilty plea or conviction, and without judicial oversight, allowing the corporate defendant to accept public responsibility for its wrongdoing, without being subject to formal criminal charges. If the terms are not satisfied, the government reserves the right to void the agreement and file charges.

2. DEFERRED PROSECUTION AGREEMENTS (DPAS)

DPAs are also negotiated by the government and corporate entities, but, unlike NPAs, are used after charges have been filed. With DPAs, generally, the corporate entity must admit wrongdoing, cooperate with the government, comply with a sanction, and strengthen corporate compliance programs to avoid future misconduct. In exchange, the government agrees to withhold prosecution for a specified period (usually several years), providing the entity an opportunity to fulfill the terms of the agreement. If the provisions of the DPA are fulfilled, the government will discontinue the prosecution. If not, the government can pursue the previously filed charges. According to the U.S. Department of Justice, DPAs "occupy an important middle ground between declining prosecution and obtaining the conviction of a corporation." U.S. DEP'T OF JUSTICE, UNITED STATES ATTORNEYS' MANUAL § 9–28.200 (2015), https://www.justice.gov/usam/usam-9-28000-principles-federal-prosecution-business-organizations#9-28.200.

Proponents of DPAs point to a number of advantages. These advantages include:

- speedy and efficient dispute resolution;
- implementation of improved corporate compliance programs inside companies;
- imposition of monetary penalties for alleged corporate misconduct;
- fewer collateral consequences suffered by innocent third parties (including employees, customers, and shareholders); and
- increased cooperation by companies during government investigations.

Peter R. Reilly, *Sweetheart Deals, Deferred Prosecution, and Making a Mockery of the Criminal Justice System: U.S. Corporate DPAs Rejected on Many Fronts*, 50 ARIZ. ST. L.J. 1113, 1120 (2018) (citations omitted).

DPAs, however, have been the subject of frequent pointed critique. Their disadvantages include:

- a focus on addressing institutional instead of individual misconduct;
- excessive government bargaining power in the negotiation process;
- the appearance that alleged wrongdoers can "essentially buy their way out of a conviction";
- the creation of company-specific internal reform measures by government attorneys who sometimes lack training and expertise in corporate governance;

- a decrease in public access to information because DPAs resolve matters without public trials, published court decisions, or binding judicial precedent; and
- possible decreases in public involvement, transparency of the judicial process, and adherence to rule-of-law and separation-of-power principles.

Id. at 1121 (citations omitted).

The latter cluster of concerns in significant part stems from the fact that judges play little or no role in approving, rejecting, or modifying DPAs. In contrast to their role with guilty plea agreements, which entails review and approval of the terms of the agreement, judges play no oversight role.[11] With the current dominance of DPAs, Professor Jennifer Arlen has written, the justice system "has effectively granted authority to individual prosecutors' offices to use [DPAs] to create duties, interpret them, and enforce them, without either adequate constraint on their authority to create duties or effective oversight, internal or external." Jennifer Arlen, *Prosecuting Beyond the Rule of Law: Corporate Mandates Imposed Through Deferred Prosecution Agreements*, 8 J. LEG. ANALYSIS 191, 231 (2016).

* * *

Despite the criticisms of DPAs and NPAs,[12] they remain popular because of the negative collateral effects occurring when a corporate entity is forced to dissolve, such as experienced by the accounting firm Arthur Andersen LLP for its role in the Enron case. After its federal conviction for fraud in 2002, Andersen was prohibited from auditing public companies, a core part of its business, and the firm soon collapsed, resulting in the loss of thousands of jobs. Thereafter, the Department of Justice adopted a policy requiring consideration of the collateral effects of a conviction, in particular the negative impact on individuals dependent on the corporation who were uninvolved in its misconduct. GARRETT, TOO BIG TO FAIL, *supra*, at 6–7, 14–16. *See also* MARY K. RAMIREZ & STEVEN A. RAMIREZ, THE CASE FOR THE CORPORATE DEATH PENALTY: RESTORING LAW AND ORDER ON WALL STREET (2017). *Cf.* W. Robert Thomas, *Incapacitating Criminal Corporations*, 72 VAND. L. REV. 905 (2019).

Whether the internal self-regulation and monitoring required by NPAs and DPAs is effective in reducing corporate criminal behavior is open to question. *See, e.g.,* Veronica R. Martinez, *Complex Compliance Investigations*, 120 COLUM. L. REV. 249, 252–55 (2020) (noting several

[11] *See* United States v. HSBC Bank USA, 863 F.3d 125, 143 (2d Cir. 2017) (Poole, J., concurring) (noting that with DPAs "the prosecution exercises the core judicial functions of adjudicating guilt and imposing sentence with no meaningful oversight by the courts").

[12] In 2009, the federal Government Accountability Office criticized the Department of Justice for the lack of explicit criteria used in deciding whether a company should receive an NPA or DPA. As Professor Brandon Garrett has recently noted, however, "little has changed." *Declining Corporate Prosecutions*, 57 AM. CRIM. L. REV. 109, 143 (2020).

high-profile recent internal compliance failures by large companies). "[D]espite a great deal of time, effort, and money to enact structural reforms and improvements within organizations' compliance programs, every year brings a new, more stunning example of how organizations' attempts to rein in misconduct often fail to prevent even the most extensive compliance failures within industries and firms." *Id.* at 255. *See also* Brandon L. Garrett & Gregory Mitchell, *Testing Compliance*, 83 L. & CONTEMP. PROBS. 47, 50 (2020) ("[I]t is a pervasive problem that we lack metrics to evaluate whether compliance programs—the focus of so much litigation and regulation—actually reduce underlying violations."). Emblematic of the concern is the behavior of Deutsche Bank, "a symbol of corporate recidivism," which has paid more than $9 billion in fines since 2008, for crimes including manipulating interest rates, failing to prevent money laundering, evading sanctions on Iran and other nations, and fraud. James B. Stewart, *These Are the Deutsche Bank Executives Responsible for Serving Jeffrey Epstein*, N.Y. TIMES, July 13, 2020.

C. ORGANIZATIONAL SENTENCING GUIDELINES

In the federal system, organizations convicted of criminal misconduct, by plea or verdict, are punished on the basis of Chapter Eight of the U.S. Sentencing Guidelines, in particular a lengthy section entitled Sentencing of Organizations ("Organizational Guidelines"). Since *United States v. Booker*, 543 U.S. 220 (2005), the Guidelines are no longer mandatory, yet because courts must still consult the Guidelines they retain importance.

The Guidelines define an "organization" as "a person other than an individual." Thus, the Organizational Guidelines apply to "corporations, partnerships, associations, joint-stock companies, unions, trusts, pension funds, unincorporated organizations, governments and political subdivisions thereof, and nonprofit organizations." U.S. SENT'G COMM'N, GUIDELINES MANUAL § 8A1.1. The Guidelines apply to federal felonies and Class A misdemeanors committed by organizations and authorize three general types of sanctions.

Like DPAs and NPAs, the Guidelines reflect a "carrot" approach. As the Introductory Commentary of the Guidelines states:

> These guidelines offer incentives to organizations to reduce and ultimately eliminate criminal conduct by providing a structural foundation from which an organization may self-police its own conduct through an effective compliance and ethics program. The prevention and detection of criminal conduct, facilitated by an effective compliance and ethics program, will assist an organization in encouraging ethical conduct and in complying fully with all applicable laws.

Id. ch. 8, intro. comment.

The Guidelines allow for several sentencing outcomes.[13]

1. FINES

A fine can be imposed. GUIDELINES MANUAL ch. 8, pt. C. The calculation of a fine is the product of the seriousness of the offense and the culpability of the defendant. Offense seriousness is reflected in a "base fine," which mainly consists of the pecuniary gain to the organization from the misconduct and the pecuniary loss caused. Culpability is based on a "culpability score," which depends inter alia upon any history of similar misconduct or obstructed justice during the investigation. Points can be deducted for several reasons, including if the misconduct occurred despite the existence of a compliance and ethics program. After the culpability score is calculated, a chart in the Guidelines provides for an associated "multiplier" and a "maximum multiplier." The multipliers are then applied to the base fine amount, resulting in a fine range.

The Guidelines prescribe the factors a court should consider in determining the fine within the applicable guideline range. These include any nonpecuniary loss caused or threatened by the misconduct and any prior criminal record of high-ranking personnel in the organization. The court is not to consider as an offset any civil penalties or other adverse collateral monetary damages as a basis for reduction. Finally, the court can decide whether to depart upward or downward from the computed guideline range. When doing so, the court can consider mitigating facts, for instance any help provided to the government in investigating or prosecuting another organization, and aggravating facts, matters such as threats to a market flowing from the offense.[14]

Under the Guidelines, a firm can mitigate its sentence if it has an "effective compliance and ethics program," or if it demonstrates "self-reporting, cooperation, or acceptance of responsibility." GUIDELINES MANUAL ch. 8, intro. comment. To qualify, a compliance program must be "reasonably designed, implemented, and enforced so that [it] is generally effective in preventing and detecting criminal conduct," although a "failure to prevent or detect the instant offense does not necessarily mean that the program is not generally effective." *Id.* § 8B2.1.

---

[13] Much as with NPAs and DPAs, discussed above, the effectiveness of the organizational guidelines has been questioned. *See, e.g.*, Jennifer Arlen, *The Failure of the Organizational Sentencing Guidelines*, 66 U. MIAMI L. REV. 321 (2012) (concluding that the Guidelines provide insufficient mitigation to effectively incentivize entities to detect, self-report, and cooperate with investigations).

[14] In *Southern Union Co. v. United States*, 567 U.S. 343 (2012), the Supreme Court, relying on its prior decision in *Apprendi v. New Jersey* (2000), held that a jury may be required to determine the amount of a criminal fine. A key aspect of the fine amount in *Southern Union* turned on the duration of the violation, which the district court judge determined at sentencing. However, the Court held that the calculation must be done by a jury because the finding had the possible effect of increasing the fine (a punishment) beyond the statutory maximum made possible by the conviction alone.

Moreover, the Guidelines impose heightened penalties when a defendant tolerates, encourages, or condones misconduct. *Id.* §§ 8C2.5–8C2.7.

As a result of this approach, in recent years corporations have significantly ramped up their compliance and ethics programs:

> Firms annually spend tens of billions of dollars on compliance and ethics programs. Even if a firm does not imminently face an enforcement action, it has good reason to invest in an "effective" compliance program because doing so will earn it credit in the form of a lighter penalty, or even a declination, should a violation occur and be disclosed. In other words, contemporary enforcement policy offers firms a unilateral deal: if you implement a compliance program that will prevent violations or detect them if they do occur and report detected violations to the government, then you will receive credit.

Andrew K. Jennings, *Follow-up Enforcement*, 70 DUKE L.J. 1569, 1597–99 (2021) (citations omitted).

When an organization is found to have "operated primarily for a criminal purpose or primarily by criminal means," the Guidelines authorize what is known as the corporate "death penalty." Examples of such organizations

> include a front for a scheme that was designed to commit fraud or an organization established to participate in the illegal manufacture, importation, or distribution of a controlled substance. An example of an organization that operates primarily by criminal means would be a hazardous waste disposal business that had no legitimate means of disposing of hazardous waste.

U.S. SENT'G COMM'N, PRIMER: FINES FOR SENTENCING ORGANIZATIONS 5 (2021). The death penalty requires that the court impose a fine calculated "to divest [an] organization of all its net assets." GUIDELINES MANUAL § 8C1.1.

In less egregious cases, several rules apply. One is that if it appears that the corporation cannot pay restitution, no fine will be imposed because restitution has priority. Another is that a fine cannot exceed any statutory-based maximum that might apply. Also, the organizational guidelines mainly apply to offenses involving pecuniary loss that can be more readily quantified, such as fraud. They do not apply to other offenses, including bribery and misconduct relating to food, drugs, and agricultural and consumer products; fines for these kinds of misconduct are governed by other provisions in the U.S. Code.

2. RESTITUTION

Regardless of the culpability of the organization, the court must first order the organization to remedy any harm caused by its offense, either through restitution or by other means. GUIDELINES MANUAL ch. 8, pt. B. As the introductory notes to the Guidelines state, "[T]he resources expended to remedy the harm should not be viewed as punishment, but rather as a means of making victims whole for the harm caused." *Id.* ch. 8, intro. comment. Restitution is not required when the organization independently has compensated its victims, where compensation is impracticable given either the number of victims or the difficulty in identifying them, or where the complex fact-finding required would so delay the sentencing process that the burden imposed would outweigh the value of restitution. *Id.* § 8B1.1(b).

3. PROBATION

Probation, covered by Part D of Chapter 8, may be imposed to "ensure that another sanction will be fully implemented, or to ensure that steps will be taken within the organization to reduce the likelihood of future criminal conduct." *Id.* ch. 8, intro. comment. For instance, probation might be imposed to ensure that restitution, if not immediately required, is ultimately paid.

For a felony, probation must last at least one year, but not exceed five years, and must include a prohibition of any further offenses during the probation period. The court may also "order the organization, at its expense and in the format and media specified by the court, to publicize the nature of the offense committed, the fact of conviction, and the nature of the punishment imposed, and the steps that will be taken to prevent the occurrence of similar offenses." *Id.* § 8D1.4(a). The court can also order that the organization submit to regular or unannounced examinations of its records and questioning of individuals within it. *Id.* § 8D1.4(b)(5).

A court may order community service when such a remedy "is reasonably designed to repair the harm caused by the offense." *Id.* § 8B1.3. Community service may be an especially effective remedy when a "convicted organization possesses knowledge, facilities, or skills that uniquely qualify it to repair damage caused by the offense." *Id.* § 8B1.3, comment. background. Otherwise, court-ordered community service is a form of punishment that is considered a "less desirable" remedy than "a direct monetary sanction." *Id.*

4. FORFEITURE

The Guidelines also allow for the forfeiture of property, as provided by statute. *Id.* §§ 8E1.1, 5E1.4.

D. THE JUDICIAL ROLE

The following case is one of the comparatively rare instances where a federal court is asked to sign off on a plea negotiated by the government and a corporate defendant.

United States v. Aegerion Pharmaceuticals, Inc.

280 F. Supp. 3d 217 (D. Mass. 2017)

■ YOUNG, J.

Let's see if I've got this straight.

Aegerion Pharmaceuticals, Inc. ("Aegerion") developed an effective medicine, called Juxtapid, to treat high cholesterol in people with a rare genetic disease. The treatment did not come cheap. "At market launch in January 2013, Juxtapid cost roughly $295,000 per patient per year. The annual cost of Juxtapid later increased to over $330,000 per patient per year."

Thereafter Aegerion engaged in a series of unfair and deceptive acts, including outright fraud, which pervaded corporate management, all designed to increase the use of Juxtapid in circumstances where such treatment was not medically indicated. Aegerion wrongfully received a great deal of money from this corporate criminal conduct. Still more important, it appears that Aegerion knowingly induced the prescription of Juxtapid to many patients for which it would do no good, thus crowding out more promising therapies. Indeed, "[n]umerous HeFH, statin-intolerant, and diabetic patients, including elderly and pediatric patients suffered adverse events, including liver toxicity and gastrointestinal distress, and had to discontinue use of Juxtapid."

Facing two misdemeanor counts of introducing misbranded drugs into interstate commerce, Aegerion now seeks to plead guilty, pursuant to Fed. R. Crim. P. 11(c)(1)(C) (the " 'C' plea"). Under a "C" plea, the judge's choice at sentencing is limited to imposing the sentence agreed between the government and the offender or rejecting the plea altogether. The judge, of course, is forbidden from engaging in the plea bargaining itself. These two requirements conflict whenever a court is inclined to reject a "C" plea since an unexplained rejection smacks of personal fiat and any explanation sounds like court interference in the parties' good faith bargaining. There is no easy course. Seeking to avoid this difficulty, this Court in *United States v. Orthofix, Inc.*, 956 F. Supp. 2d 316 (D. Mass. 2013), thoroughly considered the issues and explained its conclusion that the "C" plea has no place, save in the rarest circumstances, in the context of corporate criminal pleas.

As this case illustrates, the issues presented by the "C" plea in the corporate context are more disquieting than I had originally thought.

To begin:

Here, there is much to commend the proffered plea; unfortunately much of it remains sealed so as not to compromise on-going criminal investigations. It suffices here to say that Aegerion's top management has undergone a near complete makeover and that its cooperation with the government's law enforcement efforts is truly extraordinary.

That said, in light of the larger issues discussed below, it is the duty of this Court candidly to explain the issues it has with this proffered "C" plea. This Court is not bargaining with the parties. None of these points—singly or together—is necessarily a deal breaker. Each one is a consideration—and perhaps I may well not yet have considered every relevant issue.

Oh, Aegerion amended "C" plea—

How do I dislike thee?

Let me count the ways:

- The government agrees that sentencing may take place immediately upon this Court's acceptance of the "C" plea even without the preparation of a Pre-Sentence Report. Why? One can readily understand why Aegerion wants its plea and sentence to be a one-day story, soon forgotten. Why does the government agree? Isn't it better to permit the Court to obtain a thorough Pre-Sentence Report from its own Probation Office the better to understand this complex case?
- Are the Sentencing Guidelines properly calculated? Why is there no enhancement for vulnerable victims? U.S.S.G. § 3A1.1(b)(1). One would think that the marketing of misbranded drugs to a patient population in need of appropriate treatment would meet the quintessential definition of vulnerable victims. Is there no enhancement for the use of sophisticated means to commit the crimes? After all, the scheme here involved falsely marketing Juxtapid for off-label uses to sophisticated physicians. One can readily infer that such false marketing was itself sophisticated.
- Assuming without concluding that the Sentencing Guidelines are properly calculated, the recommended fine range is not less than \$18,542,192 to \$30,903,653. Even so, the "C" plea calls for a fine of only \$6,200,000 paid in installments and forfeiture of \$1,000,000. The parties justify the downward variance by pointing to the extraordinary cooperation of Aegerion's new management and its present precarious financial condition.

What is left unexplained is why the government does not simply let Aegerion collapse in disgrace. Surely Aegerion is not too big to fail. After all, its stock apparently is now owned by Novelion, Inc., an innocent investor but one knowledgeable of Aegerion's criminal conduct at the time of its investment. Couldn't an asset sale to Novelion fund the civil settlement, the fine, and the forfeiture? Couldn't Novelion pick up Aegerion's employees? After all, Juxtapid is an FDA approved medicine with an appropriate therapeutic value.

Perhaps these questions do not make economic, real world sense. The point is, I do not know and the proffered "C" plea does not begin to explain the financial picture in detail. Apparently the parties think their representations suffice. They do not. I have a job to do—an independent judicial responsibility I may not delegate to others.

- Most problematic, this "C" plea provides not one cent of restitution to the actual victims. This result is justified say the parties by the multi-million dollar proposed settlement between Aegerion and the third-party payors, federal and state, who were fleeced into paying for misbranded drugs. Thus, governmental actors (who inferentially provided most of the purloined funds) get partial repayment but the actual victims, many of whom suffered medical complications and physical and emotional harm, get nothing.

How can I possibly justify such a result? The parties aver "that the complication and prolongation of the sentencing process that would result from an attempt to fashion a proper restitution order under 18 U.S.C. § 3663 outweighs the need to provide restitution to any non-governmental victims in this case." Really?

Why? The parties are utterly silent on this point. Indeed, in light of this Court's management of the *In Re Relafen Antitrust Litigation*, 231 F.R.D. 52, 64 (D. Mass. 2005), it hardly seems an insurmountable burden to find out who got Juxtapid when such medication was not clinically indicated. After all, the parties agree Aegerion's gross gain is $15,451,827.

- This "C" plea obligates the government not to undertake any further prosecution of Aegerion. What is the government trading away here? Why? What other companies may be implicated? None of this information is provided. Are we not concerned we may be foisting misbranded drugs on innocent and unsuspecting victims in other nations without adequate notification to their regulatory authorities?
- This Court has already commended the new management of Aegerion for its truly remarkable cooperation. It appears to go far beyond the cooperation required in the plea agreement. Why, then, is the cooperation agreement portion of the proffered "C" plea so pallid? The language of the proffered "C" plea is hardly a template for other cases. It obligates the corporate defendant to do little more than could be required by a proper subpoena.
- The proffered "C" plea includes a comprehensive—and in this Court's mind adequate—internal compliance and review program to prevent any recurrence of this

wrongdoing. The problem is that the proposed program is entirely **internal**. There is no provision for the Court's personnel (or some independent employee) **independently** to examine compliance much like an on-site bank examiner. Even with strict compliance, independent evaluation provides valuable insight. * * *

- While the amended "C" plea now includes a period of probation, it still prohibits this Court from setting any special conditions beyond those set forth in the agreement.
- Perhaps Aegerion's plea is premature. Maybe the Court ought stay its hand until the other criminal investigations have run their course. In that way, the Court fairly could evaluate the actual value of Aegerion's cooperation. *Cf.* U.S.S.G. 5K1.1. * * *

The Larger Issue—A Two-Tier Criminal Justice System

District judges throughout the United States play two vital roles in our constitutional polity. They try cases and sentence offenders. These two functions lie at the very heart and core of the judicial function. Upon their proper and dispassionate discharge rests much of the moral authority of the third branch of our government. * * *

The "C" plea displaces the common law adversarial proceeding and thus directly affects the judicial role. * * *

Aware of the concern for promoting justice, Aegerion advances three reasons why this Court ought nevertheless here take a pass and accept this proffered "C" plea.

First, Aegerion argues that times have changed since Orthofix, Inc. Look, it says, today we have the "Yates Memo" within the Department of Justice "emphasizing the importance of prosecuting the individuals responsible for the underlying wrongdoing when combatting corporate crime." Such prosecutions depend on corporate cooperation, Aegerion claims, and therefore "C" pleas must be granted to garner such cooperation. These are questionable premises. There has been no uptick in the prosecution of criminal executives since the issuance of the "Yates Memo" in 2015. Moreover, no responsible analysis suggests that, given the government's extensive powers to secure cooperation, granting "C" pleas plays any role in aiding its law enforcement goals.

Second, Aegerion posits that "[e]ntering into a Rule 11(c)(1)(C) plea is often a corporation's only option to resolve criminal charges as the uncertainty in sentencing inherent in Rule 11(c)(1)(B) pleas causes too great a risk to innocent employees, shareholders, investors, and other interested parties." Say what? Why is a "C" plea often a corporation's **only** option to resolve criminal charges? Does Aegerion think district judges simply are not competent to sentence corporate criminals? Or is it that the interests of drug dealers' innocent wives, children, neighbors, and colleagues are somehow less important than those of a corporation's shareholders and investment bankers? A "C" plea is never a corporation's **only** option—it has the option of a fair and impartial trial before an American jury, the purest and most incorruptible justice humankind has ever conceived.

Finally, Aegerion argues forcefully that rejecting its "C" plea would result in impermissible disparity in our sentencing regime. It notes, with apparent accuracy, "[t]he vast majority of corporate criminal charges involve (C) pleas. Since Orthofix pled guilty in December 2012, at least 85 companies have had (C) pleas accepted by federal courts." Aegerion supports this general statement with a footnote carefully limited to detailing the practice concerning criminal pharmaceutical corporations in this district. * * *

Reduced to its essence, Aegerion's argument goes like this: Look at this roster of criminal pharmaceutical corporations sentenced in Massachusetts [roster of firms omitted]. * * *

Like these corporations, we [Aegerion] are a criminal pharmaceutical corporation. They **all** got "C" pleas. Therefore we should too—it's forbidden disparity if we don't.

This argument is silly—complete balderdash. The disparity addressed by the Sentencing Reform Act of 1984 and the jurisprudence that follows it deals with unwarranted disparity among sentences actually imposed, not the analyses the judges used to get there.

Aegerion has, however, proved a different type of unwarranted disparity—the shocking disparity between the treatment of corporations and individuals in our criminal justice system. I am ashamed I had not recognized this glaring inequity until this case. Passing without further comment the truly breathtaking extent of pharmaceutical corporate criminality revealed by the "roster" above, Aegerion proves beyond peradventure that a forbidden two-tier system pervades our courts. Corporations routinely get "C" pleas after closed door negotiations with the executive branch while individual offenders but rarely are afforded the advantages of a "C" plea. Instead, they plead guilty and face a truly independent judge. This is neither fair nor just; indeed, it mocks our protestations of "equal justice under law."

It's not hard to understand why corporations facing criminal charges seek "C" pleas. It gives them various advantages, including the most effective damage control.

Save when they are themselves on the attack, seeking to enforce their own property rights, corporations today seek to avoid the legal system altogether. * * * They have been enormously successful. The insurance industry found it could largely immunize itself from suit due to the Employee Retirement Income Security Act ("ERISA"). In light of Supreme Court jurisprudence, many corporations found that through mandatory anti-consumer arbitration they could largely lock the little guy out of the courthouse. Moreover, corporations frequently found they could make peace with many executive agencies without admitting liability (thus exposing them to related civil litigation) and, even more important, could compel the imprimatur of the courts thereon.

Small wonder, then, that corporations seek the same cozy model (and act as though it is their due) even when facing serious criminal charges. Consider the advantages to the corporation of the "C" plea: All negotiations are private. No charges are brought until the plea deal is finalized so the risk of investigative journalism is minimized. All aspects of the sanction are negotiated so there will be no surprises from the judiciary. As the record here makes clear, the likelihood of the judge turning down the "C" plea is virtually non-existent. In a best case scenario, the court will perform the plea colloquy with a lower level functionary and will immediately impose the agreed upon sanction. Case over—in the vernacular of the days of the print journalism, "a one day story, second section, below the fold."

What is far more difficult to fathom is why the government negotiates a "C" plea with a corporation. In my experience, individuals are afforded "C" pleas only when the government's case is weak and it is trying to lock in the plea or when it is trying to flip an implicated co-defendant and obtain evidence against others. Neither of these concerns apply in most corporate criminal prosecutions. A corporation has no Fifth Amendment privilege * * * and it cannot testify. In my experience, the government never even commences a criminal prosecution against a corporation unless it has a very strong case.

So why does the government uniformly buckle on this point? Knowledgeable commentators have levelled harsh criticisms against prosecutors for such risk aversion. * * * Lacking sufficient knowledge, this Court expresses no opinion.

I can, however, offer two observations prosecutors ought always keep in mind.

First, **trials matter**. "Every lawsuit—whether it is a dispute arising out of a contract, the purchase of a defective product, or the conduct of a government official—has the potential to change the rules that govern behavior going forward." Alexandra Lahav, In Praise of Litigation 6 (Oxford Univ. Press, 2017). The verdict of an American jury has a moral force incomparably greater than any plea. That's why corporations are so desperate to avoid them. Corporate pleas involve well-educated elites talking to other equally well-educated elites. Things are said, sanctions imposed, nothing really happens. Prices do not come down. Consumers gain no perceptible benefit. Corporations march on, apparently impervious to government regulation or the law itself.

Contrast an actual trial: every trial is a public morality play—perhaps a story of greed and avarice or amoral chicanery, all of it played out live upon actual understandable evidence before twelve public judges largely chosen at random. The result is the fairest, most incorruptible, democratic expression of justice humankind has ever known. "[L]itigation is a social good [which] enables people to promote the rule of law and affirms our citizen-centered political system." *Id.* at 1. * * * Prosecutors ought not lightly bargain away the compelling societal advantages of a trial simply to insure a determination of corporate guilt.

Second, every corporate "C" plea diminishes the legitimacy of our independent judiciary. Even when prosecutors agree to bargain for a plea, why make it a "C" plea? What does a "C" plea add to the public good where prosecutors have a sound case? Face it, if used in strong cases the "C" plea delegitimizes the central role of the trial judge.

Any injustice rankles Americans, systemic injustice rankles them profoundly. Those of us who occupy the constitutional offices of the United States—in whatever branch we serve—must humbly acknowledge that there exists in America today a deep and pervasive sense of injustice. * * *

CONCLUSION

Upon this record and against this background, accepting this "C" plea simply is not in the public interest. There are just too many unknowns here and the "C" plea process itself unduly hobbles this Court's sworn constitutional duty to "do equal right to the poor and to the rich." 28 U.S.C. § 453.

I end as I began. I am not bargaining with anyone. The problem is the "C" plea process itself. Indeed, as I have already said, there is much in the proffered plea agreement to commend. Moreover, there is here not a scintilla of evidence of collusion among the parties. This does not appear to be a sweetheart deal. Were this Court to have a free hand, I might well sentence Aegerion to virtually the same sentence as the parties here urge on the Court (that's what happened in Orthofix)—or I might not. I simply do not know because, as yet, the parties have deprived me of that responsibility, perpetuating an improper and unjust two-tier system that erodes public confidence in the sentence to be imposed in violation of 18 U.S.C. 3553(a) (if indeed it does not violate the Equal Protection clause of the 14th Amendment to the U.S. Constitution).

This case will stand for trial as previously ordered.

NOTES & QUESTIONS

1. **Too Much or the Right Degree of Oversight?** Clearly, Judge Young was not pleased with the proposed plea, expressing concern over matters including the lack of restitution, the presence of vulnerable victims, the relatively low fine proposed, and the foregoing of future criminal action against the defendant. To your mind, did Judge Young (who was appointed by President Reagan and has served on the bench since 1985) exercise too much or the right amount of judicial oversight? Why?

2. **Broader Repercussions?** If you agree with Judge Young's reasoning and his view of his institutional role, do potential concerns arise?

For instance, does the *Aegerion* opinion possibly encourage yet more DPAs and NPAs—because the government and defendants will be wary of subjecting their negotiated pleas, likely the result of considerable time and effort, to critical scrutiny in such a public forum? If so, will this not simply further empower prosecutors, leading to less public transparency and accountability, a main concern of Judge Young? Or, perhaps the decision will be a roadmap for prosecutors, shedding light on aspects of a negotiated plea that might be problematic for a judge?

3. **Why Be So Generous?** What might possibly explain why the government backed certain aspects of the plea, such as the lack of consideration for vulnerable victims?

4. **Carrots and Sticks.** Reflecting on the materials in this chapter, do you think the current approach to sanctioning organizations is appropriate? Or does it rely too much on "carrots" and not enough on "sticks"? Why is it that corporations can avail themselves of NPAs and DPAs, yet individual "street" criminal defendants cannot? What accounts for the differences?

5. **"Andersen Effect."** Should the "Andersen effect"—government concern over the negative collateral effects on innocents, such as corporate employees—remain a paramount factor in prosecutorial decisions, or should the criminal accountability chips fall where they may: without regard for harms experienced by third parties—as is typically the case with the sentencing of non-organizational defendants? For an argument that the sentencing of individuals should more closely resemble that of corporations, including with respect to concern over the adverse collateral effects suffered by third parties, see Rachel E. Barkow, *Using the Corporate Prosecution and Sentencing Model for Individuals: The Case for a Unified Approach*, 83 LAW & CONTEMP. PROBS. 159 (2020).

CHAPTER 11

COLLATERAL CONSEQUENCES OF CONVICTION

Of late, major public attention has focused on the nation's decades-long penchant for incarceration and its very serious adverse human and financial consequences. While the importance of the issue cannot—and should not—be downplayed or ignored, the focus on incarceration alone ignores another very significant adverse impact experienced by convicted individuals: the vast array of "collateral consequences" they experience because of their conviction.[1] Examples include loss of the right to vote, hold public office, serve on a jury, and own or possess a firearm, as well as disabilities such as ineligibility for occupational licensure and being subject to deportation.[2] The consequences, which result from felony and misdemeanor convictions alike, can be imposed automatically or result from the exercise of discretion.

Although the term "collateral" is used, the consequences—which can last a lifetime—often have a greater personal impact than a "direct" consequence of conviction, such as incarceration, and exacerbate the already difficult path toward successful reentry. A guilty plea, perhaps hastily entered into to get out of jail or secure what otherwise seems to be a good deal, can trigger significant life-impairing collateral consequences, constituting what has been called a form of "invisible punishment." Moreover, it is important to keep in mind that collateral consequences attach even when no sentence of incarceration is imposed, affecting many more thousands of individuals.[3] In short, as one commentator has noted, "[t]here is no such thing as a low-stakes misdemeanor" because today even low-level offenses can trigger burdensome collateral consequences. Jenny Roberts, *Informed Misdemeanor Sentencing*, 46 HOFSTRA L. REV. 171, 171 (2017).

In many respects, the effects of collateral consequences today resemble the "civil death" in England and colonial America whereby all political and property rights were permanently extinguished,[4] adding to

---

[1] Over time, other phrases have been employed, including "civil disabilities" and "indirect consequences," and more recently "enmeshed consequences."

[2] For a discussion of the full scope of collateral consequences, as well as their history and recent legal developments expanding opportunities for relief, see MARGARET COLGATE LOVE, JENNY ROBERTS & WAYNE A. LOGAN, COLLATERAL CONSEQUENCES OF CRIMINAL CONVICTION: LAW, POLICY AND PRACTICE (4th ed. 2021–2022).

[3] The category of collateral consequences also includes the wide range of informal consequences of convictions, such as housing and employment discrimination. *See* Wayne A Logan, *Informal Collateral Consequences*, 88 WASH. L. REV. 1103 (2013).

[4] Gabriel Chin, *The New Civil Death: Rethinking Punishment in the Era of Mass Conviction*, 160 U. PENN. L. REV. 1789 (2012). As Professor Chin notes, civil death was considered a transitional status in that execution usually occurred subsequent to a felony

the significant burdens already flowing from a criminal conviction.[5] And, like incarceration, concern exists about the racially disparate impact of collateral consequences on African-Americans.[6]

Although collateral consequences have been imposed since the nation's origin, the last several decades, in keeping with the advent of "tough-on-crime" policies more generally, witnessed a radical increase in their number and severity. In 2010, the Supreme Court shined a spotlight on collateral consequences with its decision in *Padilla v. Kentucky*, 559 U.S. 356 (2010), where the Court held that a noncitizen defendant had a Sixth Amendment right to be told by his lawyer about a likely collateral consequence of his guilty plea—deportation.

After *Padilla*, several national organizations dedicated resources and attention to various aspects of collateral consequences. In a crucial first step, the American Bar Association conducted a national census of collateral consequences contained in state and federal laws, resulting in the National Inventory of the Collateral Consequences of Conviction, which by 2020 contained over 46,000 entries. As the leading treatise on collateral consequences observes with respect to their expansive and variegated nature, nested in state, federal, and local codes:

> Unlike the penalties imposed by the court at sentencing that are generally set forth in orderly fashion in the criminal code, collateral penalties have been promulgated with little coordination in disparate sections of state and federal statutes, in municipal ordinances, and in agency regulations, making it difficult for anyone to identify all of the penalties and disabilities that apply to a particular offense. Few jurisdictions have made any effort to collect them or match them up with their triggering crimes. To the extent they are imposed outside of the sentencing process, collateral consequences take effect without judicial consideration of their appropriateness in the specific case.

LOVE, ROBERTS, & LOGAN, *supra*, at 5.

This chapter surveys the most significant of the myriad collateral consequences that are imposed on individuals today. Thereafter, discussion turns to important aspects of advocacy for prosecutors and defense counsel, as well as the institutional role of judges in the imposition of collaterals. The chapter closes with discussion of the

---

conviction, and was not intended to be, as it is today, "a condition applicable potentially for decades." *Id.* at 1792.

5 *See* Parker v. Ellis, 362 U.S. 574, 593–94 (1960) (Warren, C.J., dissenting) (noting that "[c]onviction of a felony imposes a status upon a person which . . . seriously affects his reputation and economic opportunities"). The impact of criminal records has been magnified over time as data have been digitized. On this development more generally, see JAMES B. JACOBS, THE ETERNAL CRIMINAL RECORD (2015); SARAH E. LAGESON, DIGITAL PUNISHMENT: PRIVACY, STIGMA, AND THE HARMS OF DATA-DRIVEN CRIMINAL JUSTICE (2020).

6 *See, e.g.*, Michael Pinard, *Collateral Consequences of Criminal Convictions: Confronting Issues of Race and Dignity*, 85 N.Y.U. L. REV. 457 (2010).

various means of mitigating or removing collateral consequences, which while increasingly available, very often remain inaccessible or ineffective.

A. THE BROADER LANDSCAPE

1. CIVIL AND POLITICAL RIGHTS

a. VOTING

One of the better known civil rights lost as the result of a conviction is the right to vote, a remnant of "civil death." Laws preventing political participation by convicted individuals have proven controversial in recent years, prompting their relaxation. Aside from what many regard as a principled objection to banning voting in a democracy, critics point to the disparate effect disenfranchisement has on African-Americans in particular, functioning as a core impact of the system famously referred to by Michelle Alexander as the "New Jim Crow."[7] Also, because of the sheer size of the population targeted, over five million in 2020, the laws can affect electoral outcomes, which itself generates public debate and controversy.

Over time, disenfranchisement has been justified on a variety of bases, including it being a rightful sanction for the violation of the social contract that a criminal conviction represents (defending the "purity of the voting box"), preventing "subversive" voting (reflecting a concern that individuals will vote as a bloc for policies that undermine crime control and the rule of law), and diminishing the likelihood of electoral fraud (even though the laws sweep far beyond that particular offense).

Richardson v. Ramirez

418 U.S. 24 (1974)

■ REHNQUIST, J.

The three individual respondents in this case were convicted of felonies and have completed the service of their respective sentences and paroles. They filed a petition for a writ of mandate in the Supreme Court of California to compel California county election officials to register them as voters. They claimed, on behalf of themselves and others similarly situated, that application to them of the provisions of the California Constitution and implementing statutes which disenfranchised persons convicted of an 'infamous crime' denied them the right to equal protection of the laws under the Federal Constitution. * * *

---

[7] *See* MICHELLE ALEXANDER, THE NEW JIM CROW: MASS INCARCERATION IN THE AGE OF COLORBLINDNESS (2010).

II

Unlike most claims under the Equal Protection Clause, for the decision of which we have only the language of the Clause itself as it is embodied in the Fourteenth Amendment, respondents' claim implicates not merely the language of the Equal Protection Clause of s 1 of the Fourteenth Amendment, but also the provisions of the less familiar s 2 of the Amendment:

> 'Representatives shall be apportioned among the several States according to their respective numbers, counting the whole number of persons in each State, excluding Indians not taxed. But when the right to vote at any election for the choice of electors for President and Vice President of the United States, Representatives in Congress, the Executive and Judicial officers of a State, or the members of the Legislature thereof, is denied to any of the male inhabitants of such State, being twenty-one years of age, and citizens of the United States, or in any way abridged, *except for participation in rebellion, or other crime*, the basis of representation therein shall be reduced in the proportion which the number of such male citizens shall bear to the whole number of male citizens twenty-one years of age in such State.' (Emphasis supplied.)

Petitioner contends that the italicized language of s 2 expressly exempts from the sanction of that section disenfranchisement grounded on prior conviction of a felony. She goes on to argue that those who framed and adopted the Fourteenth Amendment could not have intended to prohibit outright in s 1 of that Amendment that which was expressly exempted from the lesser sanction of reduced representation imposed by s 2 of the Amendment. This argument seems to us a persuasive one unless it can be shown that the language of s 2, 'except for participation in rebellion, or other crime,' was intended to have a different meaning than would appear from its face.

The problem of interpreting the 'intention' of a constitutional provision is, as countless cases of this Court recognize, a difficult one. * * * The legislative history bearing on the meaning of the relevant language of s 2 is scant indeed. * * * Nonetheless, what legislative history there is indicates that this language was intended by Congress to mean what it says.

* * *

[R]espondents argue that our recent decisions invalidating other state-imposed restrictions on the franchise as violative of the Equal Protection Clause require us to invalidate the disenfranchisement of felons as well. They rely on [case cites omitted] to support the conclusions of the Supreme Court of California that a State must show a 'compelling state interest' to justify exclusion of ex-felons from the franchise and that California has not done so here.

As we have seen, however, the exclusion of felons from the vote has an affirmative sanction in s 2 of the Fourteenth Amendment, a sanction which was not present in the case of the other restrictions on the franchise which were invalidated in the cases on which respondents rely.

* * *

We hold that the understanding of those who adopted the Fourteenth Amendment, as reflected in the express language of s 2 and in the historical and judicial interpretation of the Amendment's applicability to state laws disenfranchising felons, is of controlling significance in distinguishing such laws from those other state limitations on the franchise which have been held invalid under the Equal Protection Clause by this Court. * * * Nor can we accept respondents' argument that because s 2 was made part of the Amendment "largely through the accident of political exigency rather than through the relation which it bore to the other sections of the Amendment," we must not look to it for guidance in interpreting s 1. It is as much a part of the Amendment as any of the other sections, and how it became a part of the Amendment is less important than what it says and what it means.

Pressed upon us by the respondents, and by amici curia, are contentions that these notions are outmoded, and that the more modern view is that it is essential to the process of rehabilitating the exfelon that he be returned to his role in society as a fully participating citizen when he has completed the serving of his term. We would by no means discount these arguments if addressed to the legislative forum which may properly weigh and balance them against those advanced in support of California's present constitutional provisions. But it is not for us to choose one set of values over the other. If respondents are correct, and the view which they advocate is indeed the more enlightened and sensible one, presumably the people of the State of California will ultimately come around to that view. And if they do not do so, their failure is some evidence, at least, of the fact that there are two sides to the argument.

We therefore hold that the Supreme Court of California erred in concluding that California may no longer, consistent with the Equal Protection Clause of the Fourteenth Amendment, exclude from the franchise convicted felons who have completed their sentences and paroles. * * *

■ MARSHALL, J., dissenting, with whom JUSTICE BRENNAN joins.

* * *

The Court construes s 2 of the Fourteenth Amendment as an express authorization for the States to disenfranchise former felons. Section 2 does except disenfranchisement for 'participation in rebellion, or other crime' from the operation of its penalty provision. As the Court notes, however, there is little independent legislative history as to the crucial words 'or other crime'; the proposed s 2 went to a joint committee containing only the phrase 'participation in rebellion' and emerged with 'or other crime' inexplicably tacked on.

* * *

It is clear that s 2 was not intended and should not be construed to be a limitation on the other sections of the Fourteenth Amendment. Section 2 provides a special remedy—reduced representation—to cure a particular form of electoral abuse—the disenfranchisement of Negroes. There is no indication that the framers of the provisions intended that special penalty to be the exclusive remedy for all forms of electoral discrimination.

* * *

[D]isenfranchisement for participation in crime was not uncommon in the States at the time of the adoption of the Amendment. Hence, not surprisingly, that form of disenfranchisement was excepted from the application of the special penalty provision of s 2. But because Congress chose to exempt one form of electoral discrimination from the reduction-of-representation remedy provided by s 2 does not necessarily imply congressional approval of this disenfranchisement.[24]

* * *

In my view, the disenfranchisement of ex-felons must be measured against the requirements of the Equal Protection Clause of s 1 of the Fourteenth Amendment. That analysis properly begins with the observation that because the right to vote 'is of the essence of a democratic society, and any restrictions on that right strike at the heart of representative government,' voting is a 'fundamental' right.

* * *

The State has the heavy burden of showing, first, that the challenged disenfranchisement is necessary to a legitimate and substantial state interest; second, that the classification is drawn with precision—that it does not exclude too many people who should not and need not be excluded; and, third, that there are no other reasonable ways to achieve the State's goal with a lesser burden on the constitutionally protected interest.

I think it clear that the State has not met its burden of justifying the blanket disenfranchisement of former felons presented by this case. There is certainly no basis for asserting that ex-felons have any less interest in the democratic process than any other citizen. Like everyone

[24] To say that s 2 of the Fourteenth Amendment is a direct limitation on the protection afforded voting rights by s 1 leads to absurd results. If one accepts the premise that s 2 authorizes disenfranchisement for any crime, the challenged California provision could * * * require disenfranchisement for seduction under promise of marriage, or conspiracy to operate a motor vehicle without a muffler. Disenfranchisement extends to convictions for vagrancy in Alabama or breaking a water pipe in North Dakota, to note but two examples. Note, *Disenfranchisement of Ex-felons: A Reassessment*, 25 STAN. L. REV. 845, 846 (1973). Even a jaywalking or traffic conviction could conceivably lead to disenfranchisement, since s 2 does not differentiate between felonies and misdemeanors.

else, their daily lives are deeply affected and changed by the decisions of government. As the Secretary of State of California observed in his memorandum to the Court in support of respondents in this case:

> 'It is doubtful . . . whether the state can demonstrate either a compelling or rational policy interest in denying former felons the right to vote. The individuals involved in the present case are persons who have fully paid their debt to society. They are as much affected by the actions of government as any other citizens, and have as much of a right to participate in governmental decision-making. Furthermore, the denial of the right to vote to such persons is a hindrance to the efforts of society to rehabilitate former felons and convert them into law-abiding and productive citizens.

It is argued that disenfranchisement is necessary to prevent vote frauds. Although the State has a legitimate and, in fact, compelling interest in preventing election fraud, the challenged provision is not sustainable on that ground. First, the disenfranchisement provisions are patently both overinclusive and underinclusive. The provision is not limited to those who have demonstrated a marked propensity for abusing the ballot by violating election laws. Rather, it encompasses all former felons and there has been no showing that ex-felons generally are any more likely to abuse the ballot than the remainder of the population. In contrast, many of those convicted of violating election laws are treated as misdemeanants and are not barred from voting at all. It seems clear that the classification here is not tailored to achieve its articulated goal, since it crudely excludes large numbers of otherwise qualified voters.

Moreover, there are means available for the State to prevent voting fraud which are far less burdensome on the constitutionally protected right to vote. * * * [T]he State 'has at its disposal a variety of criminal laws that are more than adequate to detect and deter whatever fraud may be feared.'

* * *

Another asserted purpose is to keep former felons from voting because their likely voting pattern might be subversive of the interests of an orderly society.

* * *

Although, in the last century, this Court may have justified the exclusion of voters from the electoral process for fear that they would vote to change laws considered important by a temporal majority, I have little doubt that we would not countenance such a purpose today. The process of democracy is one of change. Our laws are not frozen into immutable form, they are constantly in the process of revision in response to the needs of a changing society. The public interest, as conceived by a majority of the voting public, is constantly undergoing reexamination. * * * Voters who opposed the repeal of prohibition could have disenfranchised those who advocated repeal 'to prevent persons from being enabled by their votes to defeat the criminal laws of the country.' Today, presumably those who support the legalization of marihuana could be barred from the ballot box for much the same reason. The ballot is the democratic system's coin of the realm. To condition its exercise on support of the established order is to debase that currency beyond recognition.

* * *

I think it clear that measured against the standards of this Court's modern equal protection jurisprudence, the blanket disenfranchisement of ex-felons cannot stand.

NOTES & QUESTIONS

1. **Extent of Prohibition.** Today, millions of Americans are disenfranchised as the result of a criminal conviction (usually but not always a felony). The voting prohibition manifests in a variety of ways in different jurisdictions. As of 2021:

- 21 bar voting during prison;
- 16 bar voting during prison, probation, and parole;
- 11 bar voting during, prison, probation, parole, and post sentence (for some offenders or all); and
- 4 (Maine, Vermont, D.C., and Puerto Rico) impose no prohibitions at all

Sentencing Project, *Voting Rights in an Era of Mass Incarceration: A Primer* tbl. 1, https://www.sentencingproject.org/wp-content/uploads/2015/08/Voting-Rights-in-the-Era-of-Mass-Incarceration-A-Primer.pdf (visited Feb. 4, 2022).

The effect on individuals can be significant. In her book the *New Jim Crow: Mass Incarceration in the Age of Colorblindness* (2010), Michelle Alexander relates the story of an individual who described his frustration over his lack of a vote:

> I have no right to vote on the school referendums . . . that will affect my children. I have no right to vote on how my taxes [sic] is going to be spent or used, which I have to pay whether I'm a felon or not, you know? So basically I've lost all voice or control over my government. . . . I get mad because I can't say anything because I don't have a voice.

Id. at 161. Another individual, with marijuana possession convictions from the early 1990s, learned that he could not vote until he paid a $900 debt to the court. This individual, a veteran, was unable to vote because of this outstanding debt, despite serving his sentence and completing parole. In his words,

> I'm not able to vote. They say I owe $900 in fines. To me, that's a poll tax. You've got to pay to vote. It's "restitution," they say. I came off parole on October 13, 1999, but I'm still not allowed to vote. . . .

> I know a lot of friends got the same cases I got, not able to vote. A lot of guys doing the same things like I was doing. Just marijuana. They treat marijuana in Alabama like you committed treason or something. I was on the 1965 voting rights march from Selma. I was fifteen years old. At eighteen, I was in Vietnam fighting for my country. And now? Unemployed and they won't allow me to vote.

Id. at 159–60.

Do such personal testimonies affect your view of felon disenfranchisement laws?

2. **Supporting Rationales.** Simply because the Fourteenth Amendment allows for it, does not mean that a state must disenfranchise its citizens, and, as noted, jurisdictions have adopted a range of restraints (from none, in a few jurisdictions, to potentially life-long in others). From the time *Richardson* was decided, in 1974, to 2016, the number of disenfranchised individuals has risen from less than two million to more than six million. CHRISTOPHER UGGEN, RYAN LARSON & SARAH SHANNON, SENT'G PROJECT, 6 MILLION LOST VOTERS: STATE-LEVEL ESTIMATES OF FELONY DISENFRANCHISEMENT 9 fig.5 (2016).

As noted at the outset, and elaborated upon in Justice Marshall's dissent, disenfranchisement is justified by several rationales. Are some rationales more persuasive than others? If so, why? Professor Mary Sigler recently argued in support of disentrancement that it

> is best conceptualized not as a form of punishment but as a means of regulating electoral eligibility in a liberal-democratic polity. On this view, offenders who commit serious felonies are subject to regulatory disenfranchisement because they have violated the civic trust that makes liberal democracy possible.

Mary Sigler, *Defensible Disenfranchisement*, 99 IOWA L. REV. 1725, 1728 (2014). Other commentators posit that persons convicted are simply "less trustworthy and responsible than non-convicted citizens." Roger Clegg et al., *The Case Against Felon Voting*, 2 U. ST. THOMAS J.L. & PUB. POL'Y 1, 18 (2008). At the end of his dissent, Justice Marshall rejects the "voting bloc" rationale, drawing a perhaps prescient analogy between alcohol prohibition and marijuana legalization. Do you agree or disagree with his view?

3. **A Comparative Take.** Much like its status with incarceration, the U.S. is an international outlier with respect to disenfranchisement. The decision of the Supreme Court of Canada in *Sauve v. Canada*, 3 S.C.R. 519 (2002) highlights this distinctiveness. In *Sauve*, the Court invalidated a statute that denied the vote to individuals serving prison sentences of two years of longer while they were incarcerated. In doing so, the Court interpreted a provision of the Canadian Charter of Rights and Freedoms that accords the right to vote subject to "reasonable limits" that are "demonstrably justified in a free and democratic society." One of the proffered justifications was that disenfranchisement served an educational purpose, teaching inmates and the public at-large about the importance of being law-abiding. The Court reasoned that the policy had the opposite effect, "send[ing] the unacceptable message that democratic values are less

important than punitive measures ostensibly designed to promote order." *Id.* at 548. Another argument rejected was that disenfranchisement was a legitimate method of punishment. According to the Chief Justice, the author of the Court's onion:

> [t]he argument, stripped of its rhetoric, proposes that it is open to the Parliament to add a new tool to its arsenal of punitive implements—denial of constitutional rights. I find this notion problematic. . . . Could Parliament justifiably pass a law removing the right of all penitentiary prisoners to be protected from cruel and unusual punishment? I think not. What of freedom of expression or religion? Why, one asks, is the right to vote different?

Id. at 550, 552–53.

Note that the Court was deeming invalid the prohibition of voting *while incarcerated,* let alone after confinement. Do you agree?

4. **A Troubling History.** Despite the constitutional provenance of disenfranchisement, it has a troubling history. By 1869, 29 of the nation's 37 states had enacted such laws, with several Southern states tailoring their laws to bar African-American male voters by singling out as a basis for disqualification offenses thought most frequently committed by African-Americans (e.g., vagrancy). The president of the Alabama constitutional convention in 1901 stated at its opening "And what is it that we want to do? Why it is within the limits imposed by the Federal Constitution, to establish white supremacy in this State." The convention that year amended the Alabama Constitution to add "any . . . crime involving moral turpitude" to the list of enumerated crimes that resulted in disenfranchisement upon conviction. Neely Baugh-Dash, Note, *Criminal Disenfranchisement: Deconstructing Its Justifications and Crafting Its State-Centered Solutions,* 7 BELMONT L. REV. 123, 129–30 (2019).

In *Hunter v. Underwood*, 471 U.S. 222 (1985), a unanimous Supreme Court invalidated Alabama's felon disenfranchisement law on equal protection grounds, distinguishing it from the California prohibition upheld in *Richardson*. Although the Alabama provision was race-neutral on its face, trial testimony established that the Convention drafted its law with the intent to disenfranchise African-Americans, and the law continued to have disproportionate racial impact. To date, this is the only time the Supreme Court has declared a felon disenfranchisement law unconstitutional.

Should the absence of direct evidence of racial bias preclude a viable challenge? Should evidence of disparate racial impact suffice to validate a challenge?

5. **Possible Impact on Elections.** Efforts to re-enfranchise individuals have generated controversy. In Florida, for instance, in 2018 voters by a large margin backed a constitutional amendment that restored the voting rights of most people who had completed their "sentences" (individuals convicted of murder or sexual offenses were excepted). Thereafter, the state legislature made restoration conditional on an individual's payment of all "fines and fees associated with their sentence," meaning that only people who have paid all legal financial obligations were

eligible to vote. The Sentencing Project estimates that almost 900,000 people owe legal financial obligations and remain disenfranchised in the state. Sentencing Project, *Voting Rights in an Era of Mass Incarceration: A Primer* 2, https://www.sentencingproject.org/wp-content/uploads/2015/08/Voting-Rights-in-the-Era-of-Mass-Incarceration-A-Primer.pdf (visited Feb. 4, 2022).[8] Florida is not alone in its approach—three other states (Alabama, Arizona, and Tennessee) also condition eligibility on full payment of monies owed. *Id.*

As Chapter 9 discussed, "legal financial obligations" have proliferated in recent years, saddling many thousands of convicted individuals—who already face major financial challenges—with debt that they might not be able to pay. At times, it is very difficult if not possible to determine precisely how much money one owes. In Florida, for instance, there is no central database, interest and late fees dramatically accrue over time, and some convictions are so old that no records can be located. Jesse Wagman & Damon Winter, *When It Costs $53,000 to Vote*, N.Y. TIMES, Oct. 10, 2021. As a policy matter, should "paying" one's debt to society encompass only prison, jail, a fine, and satisfaction of any community supervision requirements? *See* Beth Colgan, *Wealth-Based Penal Disenfranchisement*, 72 VAND. L. REV. 55 (2019).

b. JURY SERVICE

There is no mistaking that juries (trial and grand jury) figure centrally in the nation's constitutional structure, appearing both in the Constitution (Article III, section 2) and the Bill of Rights (the Fifth and Sixth Amendments).[9] Like voting, jury service is regarded as an integral part of participatory democracy. However, as any student of history knows, for much of the nation's history the right (or, some might say, the obligation) to sit on a jury was not equally shared. Only white, male property owners were entrusted, excluding from eligibility, for instance, African-Americans and women.

Today, of course, such formal limits are no longer in place. Yet, much as with the electoral process, today it is very often the case that individuals convicted of crimes (including, at times, misdemeanors) are excluded from the jury system. Collectively, state laws ban twenty million people from jury service, with a disproportionate impact on

---

[8] According to Professors Jeff Manza and Christopher Uggen, disenfranchisement had an outcome-determinative impact in the 2000 election between Republican George W. Bush and Democrat Al Gore. Bush won Florida by 537 votes, a margin Manza and Uggen contend would have been significantly overtaken if the over 600,000 disenfranchised Floridians had been able to vote. JEFF MANZA & CHRISTOPHER UGGEN, LOCKED OUT: FELON DISENFRANCHISEMENT AND AMERICAN DEMOCRACY 192 (2006).

[9] *See also* Williams v. Florida, 399 U.S. 78, 100 (1970) ("[T]he essential feature of a jury obviously lies in the interposition between the accused and his accuser of the commonsense judgment of a group of laymen, and in the community participation and shared responsibility that results from that group's determination of guilt or innocence."); Baldwin v. New York, 399 U.S. 66, 72 (1970) ("[T]he primary purpose of the jury is to prevent the possibility of oppression by the Government; the jury interposes between the accused and his accuser the judgment of laymen who . . . are less likely to function or appear as but another arm of the Government that has proceeded against them.").

African-Americans. Ginger Jackson-Gleich, Prison Policy Initiative, *Rigging the Jury: How Each State Reduces Jury Diversity By Excluding People with Criminal Records*, Feb. 18, 2021, https://www.prisonpolicy.org/reports/juryexclusion.html. In urban areas especially, where African-Americans can comprise a major part of the population, the prohibition undercuts the expectation that a jury is to be composed of a "representative cross section" of the community, *Taylor v. Louisiana*, 419 U.S. 522 (1975), or more colloquially, of "one's peers."

Like disenfranchisement, the exclusion has several justifications. One is that persons with convictions are "bad" and/or that the stigma of their conviction will taint the integrity of the jury. Do you agree—does a conviction, for any and all felonies and some misdemeanors, reflect an intrinsic character flaw? Or, could it be that the under-inclusiveness cuts the other way: it undermines the demographic representativeness of juries and therefore undermines the integrity of the criminal justice process?

Another justification is that a convicted individual would be biased against the government and distort jury deliberations and verdicts. While such bias might be present in some cases, is total exclusion warranted? Does the opportunity for individual voir dire guard against its infiltration, based on successful peremptory challenges or strikes for cause? Ultimately, an individual might be predisposed to the government's case, wishing to please the prosecutor if the individual is on probation or parole, or might adopt a cynical view about protestations of innocence. Brian C. Kalt, *The Exclusion of Felons from Jury Service*, 53 AM. U. L. REV. 65, 107 (2003).

Lifting the prohibition, some argue, would have practical benefit. Again, much as with voting, allowing individuals with convictions to serve on juries might promote reintegration and provide an opportunity for civic participation, reducing the attractiveness of relapsing into anti-social behavior? In addition to promoting a sense of having a stake in lawful society, and reducing "otherness," jury participation might have educative benefit: it "teaches jurors about life and law, engages them in self-government, and forces them into a serious civic interchange with their fellows." *Id.* at 128.

Professor Anna Roberts asserts that excluding individuals with convictions can deprive the jury system of insights gained by "direct experience" with the criminal justice system:

> The judging of criminal cases may suffer from the absence of those with direct experience of the criminal justice system, since its workings are often not intuitive. . . . If a layperson tries to imagine him- or herself in a suspect's position, for example, it might defy common sense to imagine that a suspect would "confess" in the absence of guilt. Yet interrogation techniques are often designed to defy common sense, by making it appear as if giving a statement would be in the suspect's best

> interest. . . . Those who have been through the criminal justice system as defendants may be able to understand those pressures in a way inaccessible to others. In addition, the common sense of the uninitiated may suggest that those sworn to uphold the law—prosecutors and police—can be relied upon to act with integrity, and indeed laypersons generally place tremendous confidence in the integrity of prosecutors and police. Research into prosecutorial and police misconduct indicates that such confidence is often misplaced.

Anna Roberts, *Casual Ostracism: Jury Exclusion on the Basis of Criminal Convictions*, 98 MINN. L. REV. 592, 606–07 (2013) (footnotes omitted).

In order to regain the right to serve on a jury, individuals may be required to obtain a formal pardon from the governor or the governor's designee (in the case of state offenses), a pardon from the president (in the case of federal offenses), or a restoration of rights from the governor or state pardoning authority. *Id.* at 595–601.

2. EMPLOYMENT AND LICENSURE

Although it is accepted that having stable employment is a major predictor of successful reentry, having a criminal conviction can be a major obstacle to getting a job. It is for this reason that multiple employers, cities, counties, states, and the federal government have adopted "ban the box" laws. The "box" referred to is the part of a job application that asks whether the applicant has been convicted of a crime, allowing individuals with criminal records to display their qualifications before being asked about their criminal records (and therefore disqualified at the outset). *See generally* Dallan F. Flake, *Do Ban-the-Box Laws Work?*, 104 IOWA L. REV. 1079 (2019) (answering the article's query in the affirmative, countering criticisms that the laws merely postpone job refusals and might harm racial minorities by prompting employers to assume all minority applicants have a criminal record because of their higher arrest and conviction rates).

The ban the box movement, however, does nothing to limit the large number of provisions that can bar individuals with convictions from entire industries. For instance, one might be barred from working as a barber or beautician, electrician, nurse, plumber, street vendor, home health care worker, real estate appraiser, or teacher. It is estimated that, nationwide, there are many thousands of public and private sector provisions that preclude eligibility for occupational or professional licensure. Chidi Umez & Joshua Gaines, Council of State Governments, *After the Sentence, More Consequences: A National Report of Barriers to Work* 9 (2021), https://csgjusticecenter.org/publications/after-the-sentence-more-consequences/national-report/. As a result, it not unusual for an individual to be provided a skill in a penal institution for work, such as being a barber, yet not be able to practice the trade lawfully outside prison walls.

Although at times prohibitions might reflect a sensible connection, such as barring childcare work when a person has been convicted of child abuse, it is very often the case that no such connection is evident, for instance when a drug conviction bars a person from getting an electrician's license. Sometimes the prohibitions are mandatory and at other times discretionary, based on administrative decisions. Most often the limits are permanent or indefinite (83%), *id.* at 17, requiring an individual to secure a form of relief, which can be difficult to secure (discussed later in this chapter).

Military service might be precluded as an option (for juveniles and adults) because of a conviction. The armed forces are forbidden from allowing enlistment of individuals with a felony conviction, although an exception can be made in "meritorious cases." 10 U.S.C. § 504(a).

Can being rejected for a job be the basis for an employment discrimination claim? Title VII of the Civil Rights Act of 1964 prohibits employment discrimination based on race and the federal Equal Opportunity Employment Opportunity Commission has stated that denial of employment due to a criminal record can have a disparate impact on African-American and Latinx individuals. EEOC Enforcement Guidance No. 915.002, *Consideration of Arrest and Conviction Records in Employment Decisions Under Title VII of the Civil Rights Act of 1964* § V.A.2. 9 (2012). Disparate impact violates the Act unless an employer establishes that the exclusion from the particular position was "job related" and "consistent with business necessity." *Id.* § 2–000e–2(k)(1)(A). *Cf. Schware v. Bd. of Bar Examiners*, 353 U.S. 232, 239 (1957) (holding that due process requires a "rational connection" between the job applied for and the reason for the applicant's rejection).

3. GOVERNMENT BENEFITS

A conviction can also result in loss of government benefits. Among myriad examples is that contained in 21 U.S.C. § 862a(a), which prevents individuals convicted of a felony drug crime from receiving food stamps and Temporary Assistance for Needy Families benefits. Other examples include ineligibility for student financial assistance, subsidized public housing, social security benefits, and business loans. Unlike the loss of other, more individualized benefits, housing bans can, and often do, result in homelessness for entire households. *See generally* McKayla Stokes, Comment, *Families Belong Together: The Path to Family Sanctity in Public Housing*, 15 NW. J. L. & SOC. POL'Y 224 (2020).

What do you see as the arguments for and against the bans? Are some more sensible and justified than others?

4. DRIVERS' LICENSES

It stands to reason that a conviction for drunk or reckless driving, and for deaths or injuries related to driving more generally, might lead to driver's license suspension or revocation. However, it is very common for states to take such action as the result of nonpayment of fines and costs for less serious driving convictions (and non-appearance) and other non-traffic related misconduct. Congress has fueled the proliferation of state bans by tying receipt of federal highway funds to a state's willingness to suspend the licenses of individuals convicted of drug offenses.[10] William E. Crozier & Brandon L. Garrett, *Driven to Failure: An Empirical Analysis of Driver's License Suspension in North Carolina*, 69 DUKE L.J. 1585, 1592–93 (2020). The impact of suspensions is very substantial:

> Those with suspended licenses face a variety of impediments, such as limited employment prospects—both because they cannot transport themselves to work and because many employers in industries such as truck driving and food service require a driver's license—as well as difficulty obtaining medical care and reduced ability to participate meaningfully in society, particularly in places in which public transport is limited. One study found that 42 percent of respondents to a survey lost employment following a driver's license suspension. Since driving is such an important means of transportation, there is evidence that most who have suspended licenses continue to drive. . . . Those drivers are then more likely to be convicted of driving on a suspended or revoked license, which can lead to still more serious fines and criminal charges, including felony charges in some states. In three years in Texas, there were four hundred thousand prosecutions for driving with a suspended license.

Id. at 1600 (citations omitted). Laws requiring payment of debt are not designed to promote public safety, "but rather to use suspension to induce payment and compliance. In that context, driver's license suspension is a state-employed debt-collection tool. Existing data suggest that at least eleven million Americans, and perhaps far more, have suspended licenses." *Id.* at 1588.[11]

Of late, several jurisdictions, facing legal challenges and critiques that license suspension is counterproductive and disparately affects poor and minority communities, have eased or rescinded policies, particularly regarding failure to pay debt for offenses unrelated to dangerous driving. However, forty-four U.S. states still require suspension of driver's

---

[10] The law, however, allows states to opt out of the automatic suspension requirement. 23 U.S.C. § 159(a)(3)(B).

[11] Individuals convicted of a variety of crimes can also lose commercial drivers' licenses. *See, e.g.*, 49 U.S.C. § 31310(d) (allowing lifetime disqualification for using a commercial vehicle to transport drugs with intent to manufacture or distribute).

licenses for non-driving-related reasons—indefinitely in thirty-nine states. *Id.*

5. FIREARMS

In recent years, the Supreme Court has held that the Second Amendment ensures the right of individuals to possess firearms. *See McDonald v. City of Chicago*, 561 U.S. 742 (2010); *District of Columbia v. Heller*, 554 U.S. 570 (2008). In these decisions the Court acknowledged, however, that laws preventing the right to own or possess a firearm because of a felony conviction were "longstanding" and "presumptively lawful." *Heller*, 554 U.S. at 626 & 627 n.26.

Today, the federal government and every state other than Vermont limit the right to possess at least some types of firearms (e.g., handguns) after conviction of at least some felonies (and in some instances violent misdemeanors), for at least some period of time, and impose criminal penalties for violation of the restriction.[12] Federal law also makes gun possession illegal for any person convicted of a state, federal, or tribal misdemeanor crime of domestic violence. 18 U.S.C. § 922(d)(9). Of the laws more generally, it is recognized that

> state laws restricting firearm possession tend to be more narrowly tailored than the analogous federal provisions, distinguishing between categories of convicted persons, specifying the types of firearms that are prohibited and for how long, and sometimes even grading the periods of prohibition based on the seriousness of the disqualifying offense.

LOVE, ROBERTS, & LOGAN, *supra*, at 120. More specifically, with respect to state laws:

> in 28 states a person convicted of any felony loses the right to possess any firearm. A few of these 28 states extend dispossession to violent misdemeanors or domestic violence convictions. In 12 other states and the District of Columbia, only people convicted of specific crimes (usually violent, drug or sex crimes) lose any firearms rights. In 6 states (Alabama, Alaska, Connecticut, Indiana, Oklahoma, and South Carolina) only handgun rights are ever lost. In 3 states (Louisiana, New Jersey, and Tennessee) there are different rules for dispossession of long guns and handguns.

Id. at 120–21. In most states, the prohibition is indefinite, and individuals must petition a court for discretionary relief or secure a pardon. *Id.* at 121.

---

[12] For a survey of current state and federal laws, see Collateral Consequences Resource Center, *50-State Comparison: Loss & Restoration of Civil/Firearms Rights*, https://ccresourcecenter.org/state-restoration-profiles/chart-1-loss-and-restoration-of-civil-rights-and-firearms-privileges/.

In the wake of *Heller* and *McDonald,* Second Amendment challenges have been mounted against conviction-based firearm bans,[13] with some courts entertaining "as applied" challenges to categorical bans, for instance, regarding convictions for misdemeanor domestic violence. *See, e.g., Harley v. Wilkinson,* 988 F.3d 766 (4th Cir. 2021) (denying claim).[14] Federal courts, to date, have held that the federal ban does not violate the Second Amendment on its face. *See, e.g., United States v. Bogle,* 717 F.3d 281, 292 (7th Cir. 2013). At least one state court, however, has relied on its state constitution analog to the Second Amendment in refusing to apply a newly categorical ban to an individual whose conviction was decades old, when his firearm rights had been restored under an earlier law, and he had long since demonstrated rehabilitation. *Britt v. State,* 681 S.E.2d 320 (N.C. 2009).

An abiding question in these cases concerns the rationales of the prohibition. The prohibition is intended to "keep guns out of the hands of presumptively risky people," *United States v. Yancey,* 621 F.3d 681, 683–84 (7th Cir. 2010), and a felony conviction supports this presumption, *Kanter v. Barr,* 919 F.3d 437, 448 (7th Cir. 2019). In response to this rationale one commentator reasons that

> as a predictor of an individual's violent tendencies or his risk to the public, the felon label is patently overinclusive. Indeed, the term "felony" is regularly applied to a wide array of nonviolent conduct. This includes, for example, mail fraud or marijuana possession, offenses that seemingly have little bearing on one's ability to be a responsible gun owner. And as the list of felonies in state and federal criminal codes continues to grow, the range of nonviolent conduct that can potentially disqualify the average citizen from ever possessing a firearm under [the federal felon-in-possession prohibition] has expanded in equal measure.

Sherwood, *supra,* at 1451–52.

Provisions for regaining lost firearms rights vary widely, ranging from automatic restoration upon completion of sentence to the requirement of a full pardon. In a minority of states, dispossession is

---

[13] Some scholars have questioned the historical accuracy of the Court's statement that firearm prohibitions are "longstanding." *See, e.g.* Alexander C. Barrett, *Taking Aim at Felony Possession,* 93 B.U. L. REV. 163 (2013). Also, the felon carve-out for firearms, in *Heller,* is regarded as dictum by some judges. *See, e.g.,* United States v. McCane, 573 F.3d 1037, 1049 (10th Cir. 2009) (Tymkovich, J., concurring).

[14] According to one author:

> Five [federal] circuits have foreclosed such challenges entirely, meaning that the felon-in-possession ban is constitutional as applied to violent and nonviolent ex-felons alike, "regardless of their individual circumstances or the nature of their offenses." Six other circuits have left open the possibility of as-applied challenges, with a challenger's success depending largely on whether he has committed an offense "serious" enough to render him an "unvirtuous citizen" who is beyond the Second Amendment's scope. Yet in these six circuits, only once has a court of appeals held the federal felon-in-possession ban unconstitutional as applied to a particular defendant.

Zach Sherwood, Note, *Time to Reload: The Harms of the Federal Felon-in-Possession Ban in a Post-*Heller *World,* 70 DUKE L.J. 1429, 1441–42 (2021) (citations omitted).

time-limited and restoration is automatic for at least some types of convictions. In Montana, the only people not allowed to have firearms when they complete their sentences are those who used a dangerous weapon in their crime. In North Dakota, even people whose offense involved "violence or intimidation" automatically regain their firearms rights ten years after completion of sentence. But in most states, firearms dispossession is indefinite, and all who lost rights must petition a court for discretionary relief or ask for a pardon. The only relief from the federal firearms bar is a presidential pardon. LOVE, ROBERTS, & LOGAN, *supra*, at 121.

QUESTION

1. **Breadth of Prohibition.** Do you believe that a categorical ban tied to all felony convictions is too broad? *Heller* recognized the right to possess a firearm for self-defense in one's home; why should a person with a felony conviction (or qualifying misdemeanor, for that matter) be denied the right? Or are you persuaded that the right should only be enjoyed by "law-abiding, responsible citizens"?

6. IMMIGRATION

For non-citizens, surely one of the most significant consequences of conviction is deportation (or "removal") from the U.S. to the individual's country of origin. Most felony and many misdemeanor convictions can trigger deportation, a decision later made by an immigration judge or agency rather than a criminal court.[15] As the Supreme Court stated in its landmark decision *Padilla v. Kentucky*, 559 U.S. 356, 360 (2010), "While once there was only a narrow class of deportable offenses and judges wielded broad discretionary authority to prevent deportation, immigration reforms over time have expanded the class of deportable offenses and limited the authority of judges to alleviate the harsh consequences of deportation."

According to the Department of Homeland Security, in fiscal year 2019 more than 40% of total removals from the United States were based on a prior criminal conviction.[16] The important connection between convictions and adverse immigration consequences (deportation, inadmission, or bars to naturalization, which often depend on an individual's formal immigration status) is such that it has given rise to a specialized field: "crimmigration."

---

[15] In immigration proceedings, unlike criminal court, no Sixth Amendment right to court-appointed counsel exists. *See* Daniel Kanstroom, *The Right to Deportation Counsel in* Padilla v. Kentucky*: The Challenging Construction of the Fifth-and-a-Half Amendment*, 58 UCLA L. REV. 1461, 1494–1500, 1504–1513 (2011) (describing history of Sixth Amendment right to counsel as applied to immigration proceedings and proposing an "Amendment V 1/2" right to immigration counsel).

[16] U.S. Dept. of Homeland Security, *2019 Yearbook of Immigration Statistics* tbl. 41, https://www.dhs.gov/immigration-statistics/yearbook/2019/table4.

Immigration consequences are a matter of federal law, mainly the Immigration and Nationality Act (INA). In *Padilla*, the Supreme Court acknowledged that "[i]mmigration law can be complex, and it is a legal specialty of its own." *Padilla*, 559 U.S. at 369. For one of the several lengthy treatises on the subject, see MARY E. KRAMER, IMMIGRATION CONSEQUENCES OF CRIMINAL ACTIVITY (9th ed. 2021).

A broad range of convictions can trigger deportation, including those involving "moral turpitude." 8 U.S.C. § 1227(a)(2)(A)(i). Another major category encompasses what is regarded as an "aggravated felony," with the law often adopting a broad understanding of the phrase. *See, e.g.*, 8 U.S.C. § 1101(a)(43)(G) (including in definition of "aggravated felony" any "theft offense . . . for which the term of imprisonment [sic] at least one year"). A third category is a "controlled substance" offense, a category that can overlap with the aggravated felony category. For discussion of the often intricate analysis involved in deciding whether an offense fits within one or more of the categories, see Alina Das, *The Immigration Penalties of Criminal Convictions: Resurrecting Categorical Analysis in Immigration Law*, 86 N.Y.U. L. REV. 1669 (2011).

To determine whether a conviction for a particular offense is eligible, the "categorical approach" is usually used, a methodology that compares the elements of an individual's state crime of conviction to the elements of the federal crime specified in the INA. Rather than addressing the specific facts of a conviction, the categorical approach focuses on the statute and the acts it encompasses. The approach seeks to ensure that immigration consequences result from convictions, rather than an individual's acts in a particular case, in theory thereby providing a more consistent and equitable administration of immigration law. Much of the approach is incorporated into immigration law from the criminal context, where courts have analyzed the underlying conviction to determine whether sentencing enhancements under the Armed Career Criminal Act apply (see Chapter 4).

Deportation can be avoided by the granting of a "full and unconditional pardon by the President of the United States or by the Governor of any of the several States." *See* 8 U.S.C. § 1227(a)(2)(A)(vi).

B. SEX OFFENDER SPECIFIC COLLATERAL CONSEQUENCES

The next sections focus in particular on collateral consequences targeting individuals convicted of sex offenses. Starting in the early 1990s, state, local, and federal governments enacted a number of unique and often quite onerous laws targeting convicted sex offenders, often in the wake of widely publicized victimizations, especially those involving children. Very often, the laws were quickly enacted by overwhelming legislative majorities, and today affect the lives of hundreds of thousands of individuals.

1. INVOLUNTARY COMMITMENT

In the 1930s, amid what has since been termed a "sex crime panic," many states enacted laws allowing for the involuntary, indefinite civil commitment of "sexual psychopaths." The laws, which cast a wide net of inclusion, including males engaged in consensual homosexual relations, subjected individuals to commitment in lieu of prison, ostensibly for treatment. The laws fell into disuse and were abandoned by the mid 1980s, but later served as a template for a new wave of laws, first enacted in 1990 (in Washington State). New-generation laws, known as "sexually violent predator" (SVP) laws, differed from their predecessors in two chief respects. First, they targeted individuals with a history of criminal sexual behavior, along with a "mental abnormality" or other condition. Second, they allowed for indefinite commitment in addition to, not in lieu of, a term of imprisonment. The following decision addressed the constitutionality of a new-generation SVP law enacted by Kansas.

Kansas v. Hendricks

521 U.S. 346 (1997)

■ THOMAS, J.

In 1994, Kansas enacted the Sexually Violent Predator Act, which establishes procedures for the civil commitment of persons who, due to a "mental abnormality" or a "personality disorder," are likely to engage in "predatory acts of sexual violence." The State invoked the Act for the first time to commit Leroy Hendricks, an inmate who had a long history of sexually molesting children, and who was scheduled for release from prison shortly after the Act became law. Hendricks challenged his commitment on, inter alia, "substantive" due process, double jeopardy, and ex post facto grounds. The Kansas Supreme Court invalidated the Act, holding that its precommitment condition of a "mental abnormality" did not satisfy what the court perceived to be the "substantive" due process requirement that involuntary civil commitment must be predicated on a finding of "mental illness." The State of Kansas petitioned for certiorari. Hendricks subsequently filed a cross-petition in which he reasserted his federal double jeopardy and ex post facto claims. We granted certiorari on both the petition and the cross-petition, and now reverse the judgment below.

I

A

The Kansas Legislature enacted the Sexually Violent Predator Act (Act) in 1994 to grapple with the problem of managing repeat sexual offenders. Although Kansas already had a statute addressing the involuntary commitment of those defined as "mentally ill," the legislature determined that existing civil commitment procedures were inadequate to confront the risks presented by "sexually violent predators." * * * As a result, the legislature found it necessary to establish "a civil commitment procedure for the long-term care and treatment of the sexually violent predator." *Ibid.* The Act defined a "sexually violent predator" as:

> any person who has been convicted of or charged with a sexually violent offense and who suffers from a mental abnormality or personality disorder which makes the person likely to engage in the predatory acts of sexual violence.

A "mental abnormality" was defined, in turn, as a "congenital or acquired condition affecting the emotional or volitional capacity which predisposes the person to commit sexually violent offenses in a degree constituting such person a menace to the health and safety of others."

As originally structured, the Act's civil commitment procedures pertained to: (1) a presently confined person who, like Hendricks, "has been convicted of a sexually violent offense" and is scheduled for release; (2) a person who has been "charged with a sexually violent offense" but has been found incompetent to stand trial; (3) a person who has been found "not guilty by reason of insanity of a sexually violent offense"; and (4) a person found "not guilty" of a sexually violent offense because of a mental disease or defect.

The initial version of the Act, as applied to a currently confined person such as Hendricks, was designed to initiate a specific series of procedures. The custodial agency was required to notify the local prosecutor 60 days before the anticipated release of a person who might have met the Act's criteria. The prosecutor was then obligated, within 45 days, to decide whether to file a petition in state court seeking the person's involuntary commitment. If such a petition were filed, the court was to determine whether "probable cause" existed to support a finding that the person was a "sexually violent predator" and thus eligible for civil commitment. Upon such a determination, transfer of the individual to a secure facility for professional evaluation would occur. After that evaluation, a trial would be held to determine beyond a reasonable doubt whether the individual was a sexually violent predator. If that determination were made, the person would then be transferred to the custody of the Secretary of Social and Rehabilitation Services (Secretary) for "control, care and treatment until such time as the person's mental abnormality or personality disorder has so changed that the person is safe to be at large."

In addition to placing the burden of proof upon the State, the Act afforded the individual a number of other procedural safeguards. In the case of an indigent person, the State was required to provide, at public expense, the assistance of counsel and an examination by mental health care professionals. The individual also received the right to present and cross-examine witnesses, and the opportunity to review documentary evidence presented by the State.

Once an individual was confined, the Act required that "[t]he involuntary detention or commitment . . . shall conform to constitutional requirements for care and treatment." Confined persons were afforded three different avenues of review: First, the committing court was obligated to conduct an annual review to determine whether continued detention was warranted. Second, the Secretary was permitted, at any time, to decide that the confined individual's condition had so changed that release was appropriate, and could then authorize the person to petition for release. Finally, even without the Secretary's permission, the confined person could at any time file a release petition. If the court found that the State could no longer satisfy its burden under the initial commitment standard, the individual would be freed from confinement.

B

In 1984, Hendricks was convicted of taking "indecent liberties" with two 13-year-old boys. After serving nearly 10 years of his sentence, he was slated for release to a halfway house. Shortly before his scheduled release, however, the State filed a petition in state court seeking Hendricks' civil confinement as a sexually violent predator. On August 19, 1994, Hendricks appeared before the court with counsel and moved to dismiss the petition on the grounds that the Act violated various federal constitutional provisions. Although the court reserved ruling on the Act's constitutionality, it concluded that there was probable cause to support a finding that Hendricks was a sexually violent predator, and therefore ordered that he be evaluated at the Larned State Security Hospital.

Hendricks subsequently requested a jury trial to determine whether he qualified as a sexually violent predator. * * *

Hendricks admitted that he had repeatedly abused children whenever he was not confined. He explained that when he "get[s] stressed out," he "can't control the urge" to molest children. Although Hendricks recognized that his behavior harms children, and he hoped he would not sexually molest children again, he stated that the only sure way he could keep from sexually abusing children in the future was "to die." Hendricks readily agreed with the state physician's diagnosis that he suffers from pedophilia and that he is not cured of the condition; indeed, he told the physician that "treatment is bull____."

The jury unanimously found beyond a reasonable doubt that Hendricks was a sexually violent predator. The trial court subsequently determined, as a matter of state law, that pedophilia qualifies as a "mental abnormality" as defined by the Act, and thus ordered Hendricks committed to the Secretary's custody.

Hendricks appealed, claiming, among other things, that application of the Act to him violated the Federal Constitution's Due Process, Double Jeopardy, and Ex Post Facto Clauses. * * *

II

A

Kansas argues that the Act's definition of "mental abnormality" satisfies "substantive" due process requirements. We agree. Although freedom from physical restraint "has always been at the core of the liberty protected by the Due Process Clause from arbitrary governmental action," *Foucha v. Louisiana*, 504 U.S. 71, 80 (1992), that liberty interest is not absolute. The Court has recognized that an individual's constitutionally protected interest in avoiding physical restraint may be overridden even in the civil context:

> [T]he liberty secured by the Constitution of the United States to every person within its jurisdiction does not import an absolute right in each person to be, at all times and in all circumstances, wholly free from restraint. There are manifold restraints to which every person is necessarily subject for the common good. On any other basis organized society could not exist with safety to its members.

Jacobson v. Massachusetts, 197 U.S. 11, 26 (1905). Accordingly, States have in certain narrow circumstances provided for the forcible civil detainment of people who are unable to control their behavior and who thereby pose a danger to the public health and safety. We have consistently upheld such involuntary commitment statutes provided the confinement takes place pursuant to proper procedures and evidentiary standards. It thus cannot be said that the involuntary civil confinement of a limited subclass of dangerous persons is contrary to our understanding of ordered liberty.

The challenged Act unambiguously requires a finding of dangerousness either to one's self or to others as a prerequisite to involuntary confinement. Commitment proceedings can be initiated only when a person "has been convicted of or charged with a sexually violent offense," and "suffers from a mental abnormality or personality disorder which makes the person likely to engage in the predatory acts of sexual violence." The statute thus requires proof of more than a mere predisposition to violence; rather, it requires evidence of past sexually violent behavior and a present mental condition that creates a likelihood of such conduct in the future if the person is not incapacitated. As we have recognized, "[p]revious instances of violent behavior are an important indicator of future violent tendencies."

A finding of dangerousness, standing alone, is ordinarily not a sufficient ground upon which to justify indefinite involuntary commitment. We have sustained civil commitment statutes when they have coupled proof of dangerousness with the proof of some additional factor, such as a "mental illness" or "mental abnormality." These added statutory requirements serve to limit involuntary civil confinement to those who suffer from a volitional impairment rendering them dangerous beyond their control. The Kansas Act is plainly of a kind with these other civil commitment statutes: It requires a finding of future dangerousness, and then links that finding to the existence of a "mental abnormality" or "personality disorder" that makes it difficult, if not impossible, for the person to control his dangerous behavior. The precommitment requirement of a "mental abnormality" or "personality disorder" is consistent with the requirements of these other statutes that we have upheld in that it narrows the class of persons eligible for confinement to those who are unable to control their dangerousness.

Hendricks nonetheless argues that our earlier cases dictate a finding of "mental illness" as a prerequisite for civil commitment. * * * He then asserts that a "mental abnormality" is not equivalent to a "mental illness" because it is a term coined by the Kansas Legislature, rather than by the psychiatric community. Contrary to Hendricks' assertion, the term "mental illness" is devoid of any talismanic significance. Not only do "psychiatrists disagree widely and frequently on what constitutes mental illness," but the Court itself has used a variety of expressions to describe the mental condition of those properly subject to civil confinement.

Indeed, we have never required state legislatures to adopt any particular nomenclature in drafting civil commitment statutes. Rather, we have traditionally left to legislators the task of defining terms of a medical nature that have legal significance. As a consequence, the States have, over the years, developed numerous specialized terms to define mental health concepts. Often, those definitions do not fit precisely with the definitions employed by the medical community. The legal definitions of "insanity" and "competency," for example, vary substantially from their psychiatric counterparts. Legal definitions, however, which must "take into account such issues as individual responsibility . . . and competency," need not mirror those advanced by the medical profession. American Psychiatric Association, Diagnostic and Statistical Manual of Mental Disorders xxiii, xxvii (4th ed. 1994).

To the extent that the civil commitment statutes we have considered set forth criteria relating to an individual's inability to control his dangerousness, the Kansas Act sets forth comparable criteria and Hendricks' condition doubtless satisfies those criteria. The mental health professionals who evaluated Hendricks diagnosed him as suffering from pedophilia, a condition the psychiatric profession itself classifies as a serious mental disorder. Hendricks even conceded that, when he becomes "stressed out," he cannot "control the urge" to molest children. This admitted lack of volitional control, coupled with a prediction of future dangerousness, adequately distinguishes Hendricks from other dangerous persons who are perhaps more properly dealt with exclusively through criminal proceedings. Hendricks' diagnosis as a pedophile, which qualifies as a "mental abnormality" under the Act, thus plainly suffices for due process purposes.

B

We granted Hendricks' cross-petition to determine whether the Act violates the Constitution's double jeopardy prohibition or its ban on ex post facto lawmaking. The thrust of Hendricks' argument is that the Act establishes criminal proceedings; hence confinement under it necessarily constitutes punishment. He contends that where, as here, newly enacted "punishment" is predicated upon past conduct for which he has already been convicted and forced to serve a prison sentence, the Constitution's Double Jeopardy and Ex Post Facto Clauses are violated. We are unpersuaded by Hendricks' argument that Kansas has established criminal proceedings.

The categorization of a particular proceeding as civil or criminal "is first of all a question of statutory construction." We must initially ascertain whether the legislature meant the statute to establish "civil" proceedings. If so, we ordinarily defer to the legislature's stated intent. Here, Kansas' objective to create a civil proceeding is evidenced by its placement of the Act within the Kansas probate code, instead of the criminal code, as well as its description of the Act as creating a "civil commitment procedure." Nothing on the face of the statute suggests that the legislature sought to create anything other than a civil commitment scheme designed to protect the public from harm.

Although we recognize that a "civil label is not always dispositive," we will reject the legislature's manifest intent only where a party challenging the statute provides "the clearest proof" that "the statutory scheme [is] so punitive either in purpose or effect as to negate [the State's] intention" to deem it "civil." In those limited circumstances, we will consider the statute to have established criminal proceedings for constitutional purposes. Hendricks, however, has failed to satisfy this heavy burden.

As a threshold matter, commitment under the Act does not implicate either of the two primary objectives of criminal punishment: retribution or deterrence. The Act's purpose is not retributive because it does not affix culpability for prior criminal conduct. Instead, such conduct is used solely for evidentiary purposes, either to demonstrate that a "mental abnormality" exists or to support a finding of future dangerousness. We have previously concluded that an Illinois statute was nonpunitive even though it was triggered by the commission of a sexual assault, explaining that evidence of the prior criminal conduct was "received not to punish past misdeeds, but primarily to show the accused's mental condition and to predict future behavior." In addition, the Kansas Act does not make a criminal conviction a prerequisite for commitment—persons absolved of criminal responsibility may nonetheless be subject to confinement under the Act. An absence of the necessary criminal responsibility suggests that the State is not seeking retribution for a past misdeed. Thus, the fact that the Act may be "tied to criminal activity" is "insufficient to render the statut[e] punitive."

Moreover, unlike a criminal statute, no finding of scienter is required to commit an individual who is found to be a sexually violent predator; instead, the commitment determination is made based on a "mental abnormality" or "personality disorder" rather than on one's criminal intent. The existence of a scienter requirement is customarily an important element in distinguishing criminal from civil statutes. *See Kennedy v. Mendoza-Martinez*, 372 U.S. 144, 168 (1963). The absence of such a requirement here is evidence that confinement under the statute is not intended to be retributive.

Nor can it be said that the legislature intended the Act to function as a deterrent. Those persons committed under the Act are, by definition, suffering from a "mental abnormality" or a "personality disorder" that prevents them from exercising adequate control over their behavior. Such persons are therefore unlikely to be deterred by the threat of confinement. And the conditions surrounding that confinement do not suggest a punitive purpose on the State's part. The State has represented that an individual confined under the Act is not subject to the more restrictive conditions placed on state prisoners, but instead experiences essentially the same conditions as any involuntarily committed patient in the state mental institution. Because none of the parties argues that people institutionalized under the Kansas general civil commitment statute are subject to punitive conditions, even though they may be involuntarily confined, it is difficult to conclude that persons confined under this Act are being "punished."

Although the civil commitment scheme at issue here does involve an affirmative restraint, "the mere fact that a person is detained does not inexorably lead to the conclusion that the government has imposed punishment." *United States v. Salerno*, 481 U.S. 739, 746 (1987). The State may take measures to restrict the freedom of the dangerously mentally ill. This is a legitimate nonpunitive governmental objective and has been historically so regarded. The Court has, in fact, cited the confinement of "mentally unstable individuals who present a danger to the public" as one classic example of nonpunitive detention. If detention for the purpose of protecting the community from harm necessarily constituted punishment, then all involuntary civil commitments would have to be considered punishment. But we have never so held.

Hendricks focuses on his confinement's potentially indefinite duration as evidence of the State's punitive intent. That focus, however, is misplaced. Far from any punitive objective, the confinement's duration is instead linked to the stated purposes of the commitment, namely, to hold the person until his mental abnormality no longer causes him to be a threat to others. If, at any time, the confined person is adjudged "safe to be at large," he is statutorily entitled to immediate release.

Furthermore, commitment under the Act is only potentially indefinite. The maximum amount of time an individual can be incapacitated pursuant to a single judicial proceeding is one year. If

Kansas seeks to continue the detention beyond that year, a court must once again determine beyond a reasonable doubt that the detainee satisfies the same standards as required for the initial confinement. *Ibid.* This requirement again demonstrates that Kansas does not intend an individual committed pursuant to the Act to remain confined any longer than he suffers from a mental abnormality rendering him unable to control his dangerousness.

Hendricks next contends that the State's use of procedural safeguards traditionally found in criminal trials makes the proceedings here criminal rather than civil. In *Allen,* we confronted a similar argument. There, the petitioner "place[d] great reliance on the fact that proceedings under the Act are accompanied by procedural safeguards usually found in criminal trials" to argue that the proceedings were civil in name only. We rejected that argument, however, explaining that the State's decision "to provide some of the safeguards applicable in criminal trials cannot itself turn these proceedings into criminal prosecutions." The numerous procedural and evidentiary protections afforded here demonstrate that the Kansas Legislature has taken great care to confine only a narrow class of particularly dangerous individuals, and then only after meeting the strictest procedural standards. That Kansas chose to afford such procedural protections does not transform a civil commitment proceeding into a criminal prosecution.

Finally, Hendricks argues that the Act is necessarily punitive because it fails to offer any legitimate "treatment." Without such treatment, Hendricks asserts, confinement under the Act amounts to little more than disguised punishment. Hendricks' argument assumes that treatment for his condition is available, but that the State has failed (or refused) to provide it. The Kansas Supreme Court, however, apparently rejected this assumption, explaining:

> It is clear that the overriding concern of the legislature is to continue the segregation of sexually violent offenders from the public. Treatment with the goal of reintegrating them into society is incidental, at best. The record reflects that treatment for sexually violent predators is all but nonexistent. The legislature concedes that sexually violent predators are not amenable to treatment under [the existing Kansas involuntary commitment statute]. If there is nothing to treat under [that statute], then there is no mental illness. In that light, the provisions of the Act for treatment appear somewhat disingenuous.

It is possible to read this passage as a determination that Hendricks' condition was untreatable under the existing Kansas civil commitment statute, and thus the Act's sole purpose was incapacitation. Absent a treatable mental illness, the Kansas court concluded, Hendricks could not be detained against his will.

Accepting the Kansas court's apparent determination that treatment is not possible for this category of individuals does not obligate us to adopt its legal conclusions. We have already observed that, under the appropriate circumstances and when accompanied by proper procedures, incapacitation may be a legitimate end of the civil law. Accordingly, the Kansas court's determination that the Act's "overriding concern" was the continued "segregation of sexually violent offenders" is consistent with our conclusion that the Act establishes civil proceedings, especially when that concern is coupled with the State's ancillary goal of providing treatment to those offenders, if such is possible. While we have upheld state civil commitment statutes that aim both to incapacitate and to treat, we have never held that the Constitution prevents a State from civilly detaining those for whom no treatment is available, but who nevertheless pose a danger to others. A State could hardly be seen as furthering a "punitive" purpose by involuntarily confining persons afflicted with an untreatable, highly contagious disease. Similarly, it would be of little value to require treatment as a precondition for civil confinement of the dangerously insane when no acceptable treatment existed. To conclude otherwise would obligate a State to release certain confined individuals who were both mentally ill and dangerous simply because they could not be successfully treated for their afflictions.

Alternatively, the Kansas Supreme Court's opinion can be read to conclude that Hendricks' condition is treatable, but that treatment was not the State's "overriding concern," and that no treatment was being provided (at least at the time Hendricks was committed). Even if we accept this determination that the provision of treatment was not the Kansas Legislature's "overriding" or "primary" purpose in passing the Act, this does not rule out the possibility that an ancillary purpose of the Act was to provide treatment, and it does not require us to conclude that the Act is punitive. Indeed, critical language in the Act itself demonstrates that the Secretary, under whose custody sexually violent predators are committed, has an obligation to provide treatment to individuals like Hendricks. Other of the Act's sections echo this obligation to provide treatment for committed persons. Thus, * * * "the State has a statutory obligation to provide 'care and treatment for [persons adjudged sexually dangerous] designed to effect recovery,' " and we may therefore conclude that "the State has ... provided for the treatment of those it commits."

Although the treatment program initially offered Hendricks may have seemed somewhat meager, it must be remembered that he was the first person committed under the Act. That the State did not have all of its treatment procedures in place is thus not surprising. What is significant, however, is that Hendricks was placed under the supervision of the Kansas Department of Health and Social and Rehabilitative Services, housed in a unit segregated from the general prison population and operated not by employees of the Department of Corrections, but by other trained individuals. And, before this Court, Kansas declared "[a]bsolutely" that persons committed under the Act are now receiving in the neighborhood of "31-½ hours of treatment per week."

Where the State has "disavowed any punitive intent"; limited confinement to a small segment of particularly dangerous individuals; provided strict procedural safeguards; directed that confined persons be segregated from the general prison population and afforded the same status as others who have been civilly committed; recommended treatment if such is possible; and permitted immediate release upon a showing that the individual is no longer dangerous or mentally impaired, we cannot say that it acted with punitive intent. We therefore hold that the Act does not establish criminal proceedings and that involuntary confinement pursuant to the Act is not punitive. Our conclusion that the Act is nonpunitive thus removes an essential prerequisite for both Hendricks' double jeopardy and ex post facto claims.

1

The Double Jeopardy Clause provides: "[N]or shall any person be subject for the same offence to be twice put in jeopardy of life or limb." Although generally understood to preclude a second prosecution for the same offense, the Court has also interpreted this prohibition to prevent the State from "punishing twice, or attempting a second time to punish criminally, for the same offense." Hendricks argues that, as applied to him, the Act violates double jeopardy principles because his confinement under the Act, imposed after a conviction and a term of incarceration, amounted to both a second prosecution and a second punishment for the same offense. We disagree.

Because we have determined that the Kansas Act is civil in nature, initiation of its commitment proceedings does not constitute a second prosecution. Moreover, as commitment under the Act is not tantamount to "punishment," Hendricks' involuntary detention does not violate the Double Jeopardy Clause, even though that confinement may follow a prison term. . .If an individual otherwise meets the requirements for involuntary civil commitment, the State is under no obligation to release that individual simply because the detention would follow a period of incarceration. * * *

2

Hendricks' ex post facto claim is similarly flawed. The Ex Post Facto Clause, which " 'forbids the application of any new punitive measure to a crime already consummated,' " has been interpreted to pertain exclusively to penal statutes. As we have previously determined, the Act does not impose punishment; thus, its application does not raise ex post facto concerns. Moreover, the Act clearly does not have retroactive effect. Rather, the Act permits involuntary confinement based upon a determination that the person currently both suffers from a "mental abnormality" or "personality disorder" and is likely to pose a future danger to the public. To the extent that past behavior is taken into account, it is used, as noted above, solely for evidentiary purposes. Because the Act does not criminalize conduct legal before its enactment, nor deprive Hendricks of any defense that was available to him at the time of his crimes, the Act does not violate the Ex Post Facto Clause.

III

We hold that the Kansas Sexually Violent Predator Act comports with due process requirements and neither runs afoul of double jeopardy principles nor constitutes an exercise in impermissible ex post facto lawmaking. Accordingly, the judgment of the Kansas Supreme Court is reversed.

[Concurring opinion of JUSTICE KENNEDY omitted, as is the dissenting opinion of JUSTICE BREYER, which was joined by JUSTICES STEVENS and SOUTER and in part by JUSTICE GINSBURG.]

NOTES & QUESTIONS

1. **Punitive Sanction in Disguise?** Today, twenty states, the District of Columbia, and the federal government have SVP commitment laws. Although they can vary in their particulars, all require that individuals reside in secure facilities for an indefinite period time, pending an affirmative determination that they pose sufficiently low public-safety risk to warrant release. As of 2016, there were 5,355 SVP committees across the country, with an additional 1,001 detained pending involuntary commitment. Tamara Lave & Franklin Zimring, *Assessing the Real Risk of Sexually Violent Predators: Doctor Padilla's Dangerousness Data*, 55 AM. CRIM. L. REV. 705, 706 (2018).

SVP laws have been the subject of considerable critical scrutiny. Concerns include: (i) the difficulty of conducting reliable risk assessments of individuals, and identifying those thought sufficiently "likely" to reoffend; (ii) vague criteria used in making such determinations; (iii) inadequate procedural protections available in proceedings; and (iv) the breadth of potential legal bases for commitment, which can include nonviolent offenses.

Another concern is what might be seen as the built-in bias of SVP system decision makers. With respect to the front-end commitment stage, one study of two hundred mock jurors found that almost 75% voted to civilly commit before any evidence was presented. Nicholas Scurich & Daniel Kruss, *The Presumption of Dangerousness in Sexually Violent Predator Commitment Proceedings*, 13 LAW, PROB. & RISK 91 (2014). With respect to the back-end, it stands to reason that those in charge of deciding whether to release a "committee" will be risk-averse: they do not want to be proved wrong when a released individual commits another sexual offense in the community. The intuition is supported by the data: relatively few individuals are released. The results would appear to heighten the concern expressed by Justice Kennedy in his *Hendricks* concurrence that "[i]f the civil system is used simply to impose punishment after the State makes an improvident plea bargain on the criminal side, then it is not performing its proper function." *Hendricks*, 521 U.S. at 373 (Kennedy, J., concurring).

In *Hendricks*, the state's SVP law did not provide Hendricks with any treatment until after his release date from prison and only inadequate treatment thereafter. *Hendricks*, 521 U.S. at 384 (Breyer, J., dissenting). Also, Hendricks presumably could have been imprisoned for a very long time, based on his criminal history, but was not, and the Kansas SVP law was enacted on the eve of his departure from prison. Do these additional facts lend support to Justice Kennedy's concern, militating in favor of deeming the Kansas law punitive for ex post facto and double jeopardy purposes? Do you find the following concluding statement of Justice Breyer, in his dissent (joined by Justices Stevens, Souter, and Ginsburg), persuasive?

> The statutory provisions before us do amount to punishment primarily because, as I have said, the legislature did not tailor the statute to fit the nonpunitive civil aim of treatment, which it concedes exists in Hendricks' case. The Clause in these circumstances does not stand as an obstacle to achieving important protections for the public's safety; rather it provides an assurance that, where so significant a restriction of an individual's basic freedoms is at issue, a State cannot cut corners. Rather, the legislature must hew to the Constitution's liberty-protecting line. *See* The Federalist No. 78, p. 466 (C. Rossiter ed. 1961) (A. Hamilton).

Id. at 396 (Breyer, J., dissenting).

2. **"As Applied" Challenge.** Four years after *Hendricks*, the Court decided *Seling v. Young*, 531 U.S. 250 (2001), which involved a challenge to a Washington State SVP commitment law. The Court rejected Seling's argument that the law was being implemented in a punitive manner in violation of ex post facto and double jeopardy principles. The Court, after assuming that the Washington law was civil in its intent, rejected the "as applied" challenge, concluding that as applied challenges would be unworkable because conditions of confinement change: "The civil nature of a confinement scheme cannot be altered based merely on vagaries in the implementation of the authorizing statute." *Id.* at 263. In its next term, the Court decided *Kansas v. Crane*, 534 U.S. 407 (2002), which held that to justify involuntary commitment the government need only show that the individual in question has a "mental abnormality" or "personality disorder" that causes him "serious difficulty in controlling [his] behavior." *Id.* at 413. Taken together, the decisions impose major limits on the wherewithal of committees to secure release.

3. **Societal Self-Defense.** In *Hendricks*, the state conceded that Hendricks's condition was treatable. *See Hendricks*, 521 U.S. at 378 (Breyer, J., dissenting). What if by all accounts an individual is not amenable to treatment? Is a SVP law defensible as a matter of societal self-defense? In support of governmental authority in this regard, the *Hendricks* majority quoted from *Jacobson v. Massachusetts*, 197 U.S. 11 (1905), which upheld compulsory smallpox vaccination laws (backed by criminal sanction), stating

that "the liberty secured by the Constitution . . . to every person within its jurisdiction does not import an absolute right in each person to be, at all times and in all circumstances, wholly free from restraint." *Id.* at 356–57 (citation omitted). Are SVP laws an example of the "manifold restraints to which every person is necessarily subject for the common good?" *Id.*

4. **Preventive Detention?** SVP laws are by definition forward-looking: unlike criminal sentences, which punish what a person *has* done, SVP laws deprive individuals of liberty for what they *might* do. Does this trouble you in principle? Is there justified worry that the preventive regime—what has been termed a regime designed to "fill the gap between traditional criminal and civil confinement"[17]—will be extended to other sub-populations such as violent offenders and burglars? In a provocative article, Professor Paul Robinson argued that the system should separate punishment from prevention by using short prison sentences to punish and more extensive use of civil confinement for prevention. In support, he reasons:

> Life terms without the possibility of parole may be common and acceptable in a criminal justice system, in which horrible crimes deserve severe punishment. But life commitment with no further dangerousness review for a property offense [e.g., the 25 years to life sentence in *Ewing v. California*] would be preposterous on its face in a civil preventive system.

Paul H. Robinson, *Punishing Dangerousness: Cloaking Preventive Detention as Criminal Justice*, 114 HARV. L. REV. 1429, 1456 (2001). Do you agree?

5. **Program Outcomes.** From a purely practical perspective, it is hard to say with certainty whether SVP laws represent sound public policy. This is so for several reasons. First, assessing recidivism among committees is challenging because they are usually held for long periods of time and only a relative handful have been released. One study of 31 Florida SVP committees released into the community, for instance, found that just 3% committed a new sexual offense within 2.54 years of release, a recidivism rate considerably below that predicted by an actuarial risk instrument. Whether the program "worked" in reducing recidivist propensity, or the risk assessment conducted at the time of commitment exaggerated the subjects' actual risk, was unclear. Robin J. Wilson et al., *Comparing Sexual Offenders at the Regional Treatment Centre (Ontario) and the Florida Civil Commitment Center*, 57 INTL. J. OFFENDER THER. & COMP. CRIMINOLOGY 377 (2013). *See also, e.g.*, Jason Ryberg, *Civil Commitment and Risk Assessment in Perspective*, 16 CRIMINOLOGY & PUB. POL'Y 937 (2017). Another factor hindering definitive conclusions about the benefit of SVP laws derives from methodological challenges researchers face, such as controlling for variations in SVP programs and state sex offender policies more generally.

Finally, even if SVP laws are effective to some degree in reducing sexual offending, their implementation is very costly. For example, in New York State the cost to house an inmate in prison in 2017 was estimated at $190

[17] Stephen J. Morse, *Fear of Danger, Flight from Culpability*, 4 PSYCH. PUB. POL'Y & L. 250, 256 (1998).

per day, compared to $894 per day to civilly commit such an individual. As a consequence, the average annual cost of civil commitment in New York ($326,445) is almost five times higher than the cost of prison ($69,000). In Kansas, civil commitment is more than three times the cost of prison ($100,000 per year vs. $30,000 per year, respectively), and in Virginia, it is more than four times the cost ($125,000 vs. $30,000). Barbara Koppel, *Sex Crimes and Criminal Justice: Formerly Incarcerated Sex Offenders Say Civil Commitment Programs Deny Proper Rehabilitation*, WASH. SPECTATOR, May 4, 2018. Given the finite nature of government resources, to critics such costs typically come at the expense of other, perhaps more broadly efficacious, community-based strategies targeting sexual reoffending.

2. REGISTRATION AND COMMUNITY NOTIFICATION

In the early 1930s, localities in the Los Angeles area adopted laws requiring that individuals convicted of crimes register with law enforcement. Spurred in significant part by concern that "gangsters" from the Midwest were anonymously infiltrating their communities, as the result of increasing access to transportation and urbanization, the laws targeted a broad range of serious and non-serious criminal activity.[18]

In time, the strategy spread to multiple localities nationwide, until the Supreme Court in *Lambert v. California*, 355 U.S. 225 (1957), found constitutional fault with the laws. In *Lambert*, the petitioner had previously been convicted of forgery, a felony, but was unaware that a Los Angeles city ordinance required that felons register if they remained in the city for more than five days. Under the law, violators were to be fined $500 and sentenced to up to six months in jail for every day they remained unregistered in the city after the five-day limit. Lambert was convicted and appealed, arguing that the law violated due process because she lacked notice of the registration requirement.

The Supreme Court agreed, holding that knowledge or probability of knowledge of a statute is required to convict an individual. Writing for the five-member majority, Justice William O. Douglas reasoned that "[w]here a person did not know of the duty to register and where there was no proof of the probability of such knowledge, he may not be convicted consistently with due process." *Id.* at 229–30. While a win for the defense, *Lambert* did not invalidate registration laws in principle. Elsewhere in his opinion Justice Douglas stated:

> Registration laws are common, and their range is wide. Many such laws are akin to licensing statutes in that they pertain to the regulation of business activities. But the present ordinance is entirely different. Violation of its provisions is unaccompanied by any activity whatever, mere presence in the city being the

[18] For more on the early history of registration laws, see WAYNE A. LOGAN, KNOWLEDGE AS POWER: CRIMINAL REGISTRATION AND COMMUNITY NOTIFICATION LAWS IN AMERICA 20–48 (2009).

> test. Moreover, circumstances which might move one to inquire as to the necessity of registration are completely lacking. At most, the ordinance is but a law enforcement technique designed for the convenience of law enforcement agencies through which a list of the names and addresses of felons then residing in a given community is compiled. The disclosure is merely a compilation of former convictions already publicly recorded in the jurisdiction where obtained.
>
> Nevertheless, this appellant, on first becoming aware of her duty to register, was given no opportunity to comply with the law and avoid its penalty, even though her default was entirely innocent. She could but suffer the consequences of the ordinance, namely, conviction with the imposition of heavy criminal penalties thereunder. We believe that actual knowledge of the duty to register or proof of the probability of such knowledge and subsequent failure to comply are necessary before a conviction under the ordinance can stand.

Id. at 229.

Lambert, while notable because it essentially held that ignorance of the law is an excuse, had no effect on state (as opposed to local) registration laws, which by the early 1950s had taken root. California adopted the nation's first statewide registration law, in 1947, targeting convicted sex offenders exclusively, and other states thereafter followed suit. Illinois and New Jersey, for instance, required individuals convicted of drug offenses to register.

In subsequent years, the laws fell into disuse and remained so until the early 1990s when registration experienced a dramatic surge in reinterest. A critically important catalyst came in May 1989 in Tacoma, Washington, when a seven-year-old boy was kidnapped, sexually mutilated, and left to die in the woods. The boy, who survived, identified his assailant as Earl Shriner. Shriner, who had been released from prison five months before and had a long record of sexually abusing children, was well known to authorities. Indeed, state prison officials had been aware of the risk Shriner posed and unsuccessfully tried to have him involuntarily committed.

Upon learning of Shriner's alleged involvement, and that authorities allowed his release into the community when aware of the risk he posed, an outraged group of citizens demanded change. The Legislature responded: in addition to enacting the first modern-era SVP commitment law, lawmakers in 1990 instituted the state's first registration law, which had a new feature. In contrast to earlier registration laws, which expressly prohibited public disclosure of registrants' identifying information, the new law expressly permitted law enforcement to provide such information to the community in the name of allowing them to help monitor registrants and engage in self-protection.

After 1990, multiple states adopted sex offender registration and community notification laws, in significant part as the result of federal threats to withhold criminal justice funding if they did not. State and lower federal courts were thereafter inundated with challenges. The following decision, addressing an ex post facto challenge, paved the way for the continued use of registration and community laws, which over time have grown significantly in their coverage, requirements, and impact on those targeted.

Smith v. Doe

538 U.S. 84 (2003)

■ KENNEDY, J.

The Alaska Sex Offender Registration Act requires convicted sex offenders to register with law enforcement authorities, and much of the information is made public. We must decide whether the registration requirement is a retroactive punishment prohibited by the Ex Post Facto Clause.

I

A

The State of Alaska enacted the Alaska Sex Offender Registration Act (Act) on May 12, 1994. Like its counterparts in other States, the Act is termed a "Megan's Law." Megan Kanka was a 7-year-old New Jersey girl who was sexually assaulted and murdered in 1994 by a neighbor who, unknown to the victim's family, had prior convictions for sex offenses against children. The crime gave impetus to laws for mandatory registration of sex offenders and corresponding community notification. In 1994, Congress passed the Jacob Wetterling Crimes Against Children and Sexually Violent Offender Registration Act, which conditions certain federal law enforcement funding on the States' adoption of sex offender registration laws and sets minimum standards for state programs. By 1996, every State, the District of Columbia, and the Federal Government had enacted some variation of Megan's Law.

The Alaska law, which is our concern in this case, contains two components: a registration requirement and a notification system. Both are retroactive. The Act requires any "sex offender or child kidnapper who is physically present in the state" to register, either with the Department of Corrections (if the individual is incarcerated) or with the local law enforcement authorities (if the individual is at liberty). Prompt registration is mandated. If still in prison, a covered sex offender must register within 30 days before release; otherwise he must do so within a working day of his conviction or of entering the State. The sex offender must provide his name, aliases, identifying features, address, place of employment, date of birth, conviction information, driver's license number, information about vehicles to which he has access, and postconviction treatment history. He must permit the authorities to photograph and fingerprint him.

If the offender was convicted of a single, nonaggravated sex crime, he must provide annual verification of the submitted information for 15 years. If he was convicted of an aggravated sex offense or of two or more sex offenses, he must register for life and verify the information quarterly. The offender must notify his local police department if he moves. A sex offender who knowingly fails to comply with the Act is subject to criminal prosecution.

The information is forwarded to the Alaska Department of Public Safety, which maintains a central registry of sex offenders. Some of the data, such as fingerprints, driver's license number, anticipated change of address, and whether the offender has had medical treatment afterwards, are kept confidential. The following information is made available to the public: "the sex offender's or child kidnapper's name, aliases, address, photograph, physical description, description[,] license [and] identification numbers of motor vehicles, place of employment, date of birth, crime for which convicted, date of conviction, place and court of conviction, length and conditions of sentence, and a statement as to whether the offender or kidnapper is in compliance with [the update] requirements . . . or cannot be located." The Act does not specify the means by which the registry information must be made public. Alaska has chosen to make most of the nonconfidential information available on the Internet.

B

Respondents John Doe I and John Doe II were convicted of sexual abuse of a minor, an aggravated sex offense. . .Both were released from prison in 1990 and completed rehabilitative programs for sex offenders. Although convicted before the passage of the Act, respondents are covered by it. After the initial registration, they are required to submit quarterly verifications and notify the authorities of any changes. Both respondents, along with respondent Jane Doe, wife of John Doe I, brought an action under 42 U.S.C. § 1983, seeking to declare the Act void as to them under the Ex Post Facto Clause of Article I, § 10, cl. 1, of the Constitution and the Due Process Clause of § 1 of the Fourteenth Amendment. * * *

II

This is the first time we have considered a claim that a sex offender registration and notification law constitutes retroactive punishment forbidden by the Ex Post Facto Clause. The framework for our inquiry, however, is well established. We must "ascertain whether the legislature meant the statute to establish 'civil' proceedings." If the intention of the legislature was to impose punishment, that ends the inquiry. If, however, the intention was to enact a regulatory scheme that is civil and nonpunitive, we must further examine whether the statutory scheme is

" 'so punitive either in purpose or effect as to negate [the State's] intention' to deem it 'civil.' " Because we "ordinarily defer to the legislature's stated intent," " 'only the clearest proof' will suffice to override legislative intent and transform what has been denominated a civil remedy into a criminal penalty."

A

Whether a statutory scheme is civil or criminal "is first of all a question of statutory construction." We consider the statute's text and its structure to determine the legislative objective. A conclusion that the legislature intended to punish would satisfy an ex post facto challenge without further inquiry into its effects, so considerable deference must be accorded to the intent as the legislature has stated it.

The courts "must first ask whether the legislature, in establishing the penalizing mechanism, indicated either expressly or impliedly a preference for one label or the other." Here, the Alaska Legislature expressed the objective of the law in the statutory text itself. The legislature found that "sex offenders pose a high risk of reoffending," and identified "protecting the public from sex offenders" as the "primary governmental interest" of the law. The legislature further determined that "release of certain information about sex offenders to public agencies and the general public will assist in protecting the public safety." * * * "[A]n imposition of restrictive measures on sex offenders adjudged to be dangerous is "a legitimate nonpunitive governmental objective and has been historically so regarded." In this case, * * * "[n]othing on the face of the statute suggests that the legislature sought to create anything other than a civil . . . scheme designed to protect the public from harm."

Respondents seek to cast doubt upon the nonpunitive nature of the law's declared objective by pointing out that the Alaska Constitution lists the need for protecting the public as one of the purposes of criminal administration. As the Court stated in *Flemming v. Nestor*, rejecting an ex post facto challenge to a law terminating benefits to deported aliens, where a legislative restriction "is an incident of the State's power to protect the health and safety of its citizens," it will be considered "as evidencing an intent to exercise that regulatory power, and not a purpose to add to the punishment." * * * These precedents instruct us that even if the objective of the Act is consistent with the purposes of the Alaska criminal justice system, the State's pursuit of it in a regulatory scheme does not make the objective punitive.

Other formal attributes of a legislative enactment, such as the manner of its codification or the enforcement procedures it establishes, are probative of the legislature's intent. In this case these factors are open to debate. The notification provisions of the Act are codified in the State's "Health, Safety, and Housing Code," confirming our conclusion that the statute was intended as a nonpunitive regulatory measure. The Act's registration provisions, however, are codified in the State's criminal procedure code, and so might seem to point in the opposite direction.

These factors, though, are not dispositive. The location and labels of a statutory provision do not by themselves transform a civil remedy into a criminal one. * * *

The same rationale applies here. Title 12 of Alaska's Code of Criminal Procedure (where the Act's registration provisions are located) contains many provisions that do not involve criminal punishment, such as civil procedures for disposing of recovered and seized property. * * * Although some of these provisions relate to criminal administration, they are not in themselves punitive. The partial codification of the Act in the State's criminal procedure code is not sufficient to support a conclusion that the legislative intent was punitive. * * *

We conclude, as did the District Court and the [Ninth Circuit] Court of Appeals, that the intent of the Alaska Legislature was to create a civil, nonpunitive regime.

B

In analyzing the effects of the Act we refer to the seven factors noted in *Kennedy v. Mendoza-Martinez*, 372 U.S. 144, 168–169 (1963), as a useful framework. These factors, which migrated into our ex post facto case law from double jeopardy jurisprudence, have their earlier origins in cases under the Sixth and Eighth Amendments, as well as the Bill of Attainder and the Ex Post Facto Clauses. Because the *Mendoza-Martinez* factors are designed to apply in various constitutional contexts, we have said they are "neither exhaustive nor dispositive," but are "useful guideposts." The factors most relevant to our analysis are whether, in its necessary operation, the regulatory scheme: has been regarded in our history and traditions as a punishment; imposes an affirmative disability or restraint; promotes the traditional aims of punishment; has a rational connection to a nonpunitive purpose; or is excessive with respect to this purpose.

A historical survey can be useful because a State that decides to punish an individual is likely to select a means deemed punitive in our tradition, so that the public will recognize it as such. The Court of Appeals observed that the sex offender registration and notification statutes "are of fairly recent origin," which suggests that the statute was not meant as a punitive measure, or, at least, that it did not involve a traditional means of punishing. Respondents argue, however, that the Act—and, in particular, its notification provisions—resemble shaming punishments of the colonial period.

Some colonial punishments indeed were meant to inflict public disgrace. Humiliated offenders were required "to stand in public with signs cataloguing their offenses." At times the labeling would be permanent: A murderer might be branded with an "M," and a thief with a "T." The aim was to make these offenders suffer "permanent stigmas, which in effect cast the person out of the community." The most serious offenders were banished, after which they could neither return to their original community nor, reputation tarnished, be admitted easily into a new one. Respondents contend that Alaska's compulsory registration and notification resemble these historical punishments, for they publicize the crime, associate it with his name, and, with the most serious offenders, do so for life.

Any initial resemblance to early punishments is, however, misleading. Punishments such as whipping, pillory, and branding inflicted physical pain and staged a direct confrontation between the offender and the public. Even punishments that lacked the corporal component, such as public shaming, humiliation, and banishment, involved more than the dissemination of information. They either held the person up before his fellow citizens for face-to-face shaming or expelled him from the community. By contrast, the stigma of Alaska's Megan's Law results not from public display for ridicule and shaming but from the dissemination of accurate information about a criminal record, most of which is already public. Our system does not treat dissemination of truthful information in furtherance of a legitimate governmental objective as punishment. On the contrary, our criminal law tradition insists on public indictment, public trial, and public imposition of sentence. Transparency is essential to maintaining public respect for the criminal justice system, ensuring its integrity, and protecting the rights of the accused. The publicity may cause adverse consequences for the convicted defendant, running from mild personal embarrassment to social ostracism. In contrast to the colonial shaming punishments, however, the State does not make the publicity and the resulting stigma an integral part of the objective of the regulatory scheme.

The fact that Alaska posts the information on the Internet does not alter our conclusion. It must be acknowledged that notice of a criminal conviction subjects the offender to public shame, the humiliation increasing in proportion to the extent of the publicity. And the geographic reach of the Internet is greater than anything which could have been designed in colonial times. These facts do not render Internet notification punitive. The purpose and the principal effect of notification are to inform the public for its own safety, not to humiliate the offender. Widespread public access is necessary for the efficacy of the scheme, and the attendant humiliation is but a collateral consequence of a valid regulation.

The State's Web site does not provide the public with means to shame the offender by, say, posting comments underneath his record. An individual seeking the information must take the initial step of going to the Department of Public Safety's Web site, proceed to the sex offender registry, and then look up the desired information. The process is more analogous to a visit to an official archive of criminal records than it is to a scheme forcing an offender to appear in public with some visible badge of past criminality. The Internet makes the document search more efficient, cost effective, and convenient for Alaska's citizenry.

We next consider whether the Act subjects respondents to an "affirmative disability or restraint." Here, we inquire how the effects of the Act are felt by those subject to it. If the disability or restraint is minor and indirect, its effects are unlikely to be punitive. The Act imposes no physical restraint, and so does not resemble the punishment of imprisonment, which is the paradigmatic affirmative disability or restraint. The Act's obligations are less harsh than the sanctions of occupational debarment, which we have held to be nonpunitive. The Act does not restrain activities sex offenders may pursue but leaves them free to change jobs or residences.

The Court of Appeals * * * [reasoned that] "the procedures employed under the Alaska statute are likely to make [respondents] completely unemployable" because "employers will not want to risk loss of business when the public learns that they have hired sex offenders." This is conjecture. Landlords and employers could conduct background checks on the criminal records of prospective employees or tenants even with the Act not in force. The record in this case contains no evidence that the Act has led to substantial occupational or housing disadvantages for former sex offenders that would not have otherwise occurred through the use of routine background checks by employers and landlords. The Court of Appeals identified only one incident from the 7-year history of Alaska's law where a sex offender suffered community hostility and damage to his business after the information he submitted to the registry became public. *Id.*, at 987–988. This could have occurred in any event, because the information about the individual's conviction was already in the public domain.

Although the public availability of the information may have a lasting and painful impact on the convicted sex offender, these consequences flow not from the Act's registration and dissemination provisions, but from the fact of conviction, already a matter of public record. The State makes the facts underlying the offenses and the resulting convictions accessible so members of the public can take the precautions they deem necessary before dealing with the registrant.

The Court of Appeals reasoned that the requirement of periodic updates imposed an affirmative disability. In reaching this conclusion, the Court of Appeals was under a misapprehension, albeit one created by the State itself during the argument below, that the offender had to update the registry in person. The State's representation was erroneous. The Alaska statute, on its face, does not require these updates to be made in person. And, as respondents conceded at the oral argument before us, the record contains no indication that an in-person appearance requirement has been imposed on any sex offender subject to the Act.

The Court of Appeals held that the registration system is parallel to probation or supervised release in terms of the restraint imposed. This argument has some force, but, after due consideration, we reject it. Probation and supervised release entail a series of mandatory conditions and allow the supervising officer to seek the revocation of probation or release in case of infraction. By contrast, offenders subject to the Alaska statute are free to move where they wish and to live and work as other citizens, with no supervision. Although registrants must inform the authorities after they change their facial features (such as growing a beard), borrow a car, or seek psychiatric treatment, they are not required to seek permission to do so. A sex offender who fails to comply with the reporting requirement may be subjected to a criminal prosecution for that failure, but any prosecution is a proceeding separate from the individual's original offense. Whether other constitutional objections can be raised to a mandatory reporting requirement, and how those questions might be resolved, are concerns beyond the scope of this opinion. It suffices to say the registration requirements make a valid regulatory program effective and do not impose punitive restraints in violation of the Ex Post Facto Clause.

The State concedes that the statute might deter future crimes. Respondents seize on this proposition to argue that the law is punitive, because deterrence is one purpose of punishment. This proves too much. Any number of governmental programs might deter crime without imposing punishment. "To hold that the mere presence of a deterrent purpose renders such sanctions 'criminal' . . . would severely undermine the Government's ability to engage in effective regulation."

The Court of Appeals was incorrect to conclude that the Act's registration obligations were retributive because "the length of the reporting requirement appears to be measured by the extent of the wrongdoing, not by the extent of the risk posed." The Act, it is true, differentiates between individuals convicted of aggravated or multiple offenses and those convicted of a single nonaggravated offense. The broad categories, however, and the corresponding length of the reporting requirement, are reasonably related to the danger of recidivism, and this is consistent with the regulatory objective.

The Act's rational connection to a nonpunitive purpose is a "[m]ost significant" factor in our determination that the statute's effects are not punitive. As the Court of Appeals acknowledged, the Act has a legitimate nonpunitive purpose of "public safety, which is advanced by alerting the public to the risk of sex offenders in their communit[y]." Respondents concede, in turn, that "this alternative purpose is valid, and rational." They contend, however, that the Act lacks the necessary regulatory connection because it is not "narrowly drawn to accomplish the stated purpose." A statute is not deemed punitive simply because it lacks a close or perfect fit with the nonpunitive aims it seeks to advance. The imprecision respondents rely upon does not suggest that the Act's nonpunitive purpose is a "sham or mere pretext."

In concluding the Act was excessive in relation to its regulatory purpose, the Court of Appeals relied in large part on two propositions: first, that the statute applies to all convicted sex offenders without regard to their future dangerousness; and, second, that it places no limits on the number of persons who have access to the information. Neither argument is persuasive.

Alaska could conclude that a conviction for a sex offense provides evidence of substantial risk of recidivism. The legislature's findings are consistent with grave concerns over the high rate of recidivism among convicted sex offenders and their dangerousness as a class. The risk of recidivism posed by sex offenders is "frightening and high."

The Ex Post Facto Clause does not preclude a State from making reasonable categorical judgments that conviction of specified crimes should entail particular regulatory consequences. We have upheld against ex post facto challenges laws imposing regulatory burdens on individuals convicted of crimes without any corresponding risk assessment. * * * The State's determination to legislate with respect to convicted sex offenders as a class, rather than require individual determination of their dangerousness, does not make the statute a punishment under the Ex Post Facto Clause. * * *

The duration of the reporting requirements is not excessive. Empirical research on child molesters, for instance, has shown that, "[c]ontrary to conventional wisdom, most reoffenses do not occur within the first several years after release," but may occur "as late as 20 years following release."

The Court of Appeals' reliance on the wide dissemination of the information is also unavailing. The Ninth Circuit highlighted that the information was available "world-wide" and "[b]roadcas[t]" in an indiscriminate manner. As we have explained, however, the notification system is a passive one: An individual must seek access to the information. The Web site warns that the use of displayed information "to commit a criminal act against another person is subject to criminal prosecution." Given the general mobility of our population, for Alaska to make its registry system available and easily accessible throughout the State was not so excessive a regulatory requirement as to become a punishment.

The excessiveness inquiry of our ex post facto jurisprudence is not an exercise in determining whether the legislature has made the best choice possible to address the problem it seeks to remedy. The question is whether the regulatory means chosen are reasonable in light of the nonpunitive objective. The Act meets this standard.

The two remaining *Mendoza-Martinez* factors—whether the regulation comes into play only on a finding of scienter and whether the behavior to which it applies is already a crime—are of little weight in this case. The regulatory scheme applies only to past conduct, which was, and is, a crime. This is a necessary beginning point, for recidivism is the statutory concern. The obligations the statute imposes are the responsibility of registration, a duty not predicated upon some present or repeated violation.

Our examination of the Act's effects leads to the determination that respondents cannot show, much less by the clearest proof, that the effects of the law negate Alaska's intention to establish a civil regulatory scheme. The Act is nonpunitive, and its retroactive application does not violate the Ex Post Facto Clause. The judgment of the Court of Appeals for the Ninth Circuit is reversed, and the case is remanded for further proceedings consistent with this opinion.

[Concurring opinions of JUSTICES THOMAS and SOUTER omitted.]

■ STEVENS, J., dissenting.

* * *

The statutes impose significant affirmative obligations and a severe stigma on every person to whom they apply. In Alaska, an offender who has served his sentence for a single, nonaggravated crime must provide local law enforcement authorities with extensive personal information—including his address, his place of employment, the address of his employer, the license plate number and make and model of any car to which he has access, a current photo, identifying features, and medical treatment—at least once a year for 15 years. If one has been convicted of an aggravated offense or more than one offense, he must report this same information at least quarterly for life. Moreover, if he moves, he has one working day to provide updated information. Registrants may not shave their beards, color their hair, change their employer, or borrow a car without reporting those events to the authorities. Much of this registration information is placed on the Internet. In Alaska, the registrant's face appears on a webpage under the label "Registered Sex Offender." His physical description, street address, employer address, and conviction information are also displayed on this page.

The registration and reporting duties imposed on convicted sex offenders are comparable to the duties imposed on other convicted criminals during periods of supervised release or parole. And there can be no doubt that the "[w]idespread public access," to this personal and constantly updated information has a severe stigmatizing effect. In my judgment, these statutes unquestionably affect a constitutionally protected interest in liberty.

It is also clear beyond peradventure that these unique consequences of conviction of a sex offense are punitive. They share three characteristics, which in the aggregate are not present in any civil sanction. The sanctions (1) constitute a severe deprivation of the offender's liberty, (2) are imposed on everyone who is convicted of a relevant criminal offense, and (3) are imposed only on those criminals. Unlike any of the cases that the Court has cited, a criminal conviction under these statutes provides both a sufficient and a necessary condition for the sanction. * * *

No matter how often the Court may repeat and manipulate multifactor tests that have been applied in wholly dissimilar cases involving only one or two of these three aspects of these statutory sanctions, it will never persuade me that the registration and reporting obligations that are imposed on convicted sex offenders and on no one else as a result of their convictions are not part of their punishment. In my opinion, a sanction that (1) is imposed on everyone who commits a criminal offense, (2) is not imposed on anyone else, and (3) severely impairs a person's liberty is punishment.

It is therefore clear to me that the Constitution prohibits the addition of these sanctions to the punishment of persons who were tried and convicted before the legislation was enacted. As the Court recognizes, "recidivism is the statutory concern" that provides the supposed justification for the imposition of such retroactive punishment. That is the principal rationale that underlies the "three strikes" statute that the Court has upheld in *Ewing v. California*, 538 U.S. 11 (2003). Reliance on that rationale here highlights the conclusion that the retroactive application of these statutes constitutes a flagrant violation of the protections afforded by the Double Jeopardy and Ex Post Facto Clauses of the Constitution.

I think it equally clear, however, that the State may impose registration duties and may publish registration information as a part of its punishment of this category of defendants. Looking to the future, these aspects of their punishment are adequately justified by two of the traditional aims of punishment—retribution and deterrence. Moreover, as a matter of procedural fairness, Alaska requires its judges to include notice of the registration requirements in judgments imposing sentences on convicted sex offenders and in the colloquy preceding the acceptance of a plea of guilty to such an offense. Thus, I agree with the Court that these statutes are constitutional as applied to postenactment offenses.

Accordingly, I would hold that the Alaska statute violates the constitutional prohibition on ex post facto laws. * * *

■ GINSBURG, J., dissenting, joined by JUSTICE BREYER.

* * *

Measured by the *Mendoza-Martinez* factors, I would hold Alaska's Act punitive in effect. Beyond doubt, the Act involves an "affirmative disability or restraint." * * * Alaska's Act imposes onerous and intrusive obligations on convicted sex offenders; and it exposes registrants, through aggressive public notification of their crimes, to profound humiliation and community-wide ostracism.

Furthermore, the Act's requirements resemble historically common forms of punishment. Its registration and reporting provisions are comparable to conditions of supervised release or parole; its public notification regimen, which permits placement of the registrant's face on a webpage under the label "Registered Sex Offender," calls to mind shaming punishments once used to mark an offender as someone to be shunned.

Telling too, * * * past crime alone, not current dangerousness, is the "touchstone" triggering the Act's obligations. This touchstone adds to the impression that the Act retributively targets past guilt. * * *

Tending the other way, I acknowledge, the Court has ranked some laws civil and nonpunitive although they impose significant disabilities or restraints. The Court has also deemed some laws nonpunitive despite "punitive aspects."

What ultimately tips the balance for me is the Act's excessiveness in relation to its nonpunitive purpose. As respondents concede, the Act has a legitimate civil purpose: to promote public safety by alerting the public to potentially recidivist sex offenders in the community. But its scope notably exceeds this purpose. The Act applies to all convicted sex offenders, without regard to their future dangerousness. And the duration of the reporting requirement is keyed not to any determination of a particular offender's risk of reoffending, but to whether the offense of conviction qualified as aggravated. The reporting requirements themselves are exorbitant: The Act requires aggravated offenders to engage in perpetual quarterly reporting, even if their personal information has not changed. And meriting heaviest weight in my judgment, the Act makes no provision whatever for the possibility of rehabilitation: Offenders cannot shorten their registration or notification period, even on the clearest demonstration of rehabilitation or conclusive proof of physical incapacitation. However plain it may be that a former sex offender currently poses no threat of recidivism, he will remain subject to long-term monitoring and inescapable humiliation. * * *

Satisfied that the Act is ambiguous in intent and punitive in effect, I would hold its retroactive application incompatible with the Ex Post Facto Clause, and would therefore affirm the judgment of the Court of Appeals.

NOTES & QUESTIONS

1. **Mapping Registrants.** Today, sex offender registration and community notification (SORN) laws are in effect nationwide, sweeping up hundreds of thousands of individuals, very often for their lifetimes. They require that individuals register with authorities, update their registry information whenever it changes (e.g., growth of a beard or driving another car), and verify its continued accuracy as often as every three months (usually in person). Before proceeding, take a few moments to visit the registry concerning your jurisdiction. Here is a website operated by the U.S. Department of Justice that allows for access to registries: https://www.nsopw.gov/en/Registry/AllRegistries. Were you surprised to learn that a registrant lives nearby?

2. **Approaches.** SORN laws fall into two general categories, which determine the duration of registration and aspects of its onerousness (e.g.,

being subject to community notification and how often information must be verified): those based on the offense of conviction (e.g., Florida and South Carolina) and those based on an individualized risk evaluation (e.g., Minnesota and New York). The conviction-based approach is by far the most popular.

In a decision handed down the same term as *Smith v. Doe*, the Court upheld against a procedural due process challenge Connecticut's SORN law, which was triggered solely on the basis of a conviction for a legislatively specified offense. *See Conn. Dep't of Pub. Safety v. Doe*, 538 U.S. 1 (2003). Writing for the Court, Chief Justice Rehnquist reasoned that even assuming that the registrant had a protectable "liberty interest" (e.g., in informational privacy), and "could prove that he is not likely to be currently dangerous, Connecticut has decided that the registry information on all sex offenders—currently dangerous or not—must be publicly disclosed. . . . [A]ny hearing on current dangerousness [would be] a bootless exercise." *Id.* at 7–8.

Registrants, in short, receive all the procedural due process they are due when they were lawfully convicted of a registerable offense. Connecticut's website expressly stated that authorities had not determined if any registrant was currently dangerous. Should this disclaimer matter? Florida's conviction-based registry, for instance, provides no disclaimer.

3. **Privacy and Other Questions.** Are you convinced by the *Smith* majority's view that registries simply display "public" information—such as the home and work addresses of registrants, their photos, their vehicles, any identifying marks or scars, and offense history? Courts have regularly rejected privacy-based claims on this basis. Is it relevant, as a practical matter, that it would be very difficult, if not impossible, to actually gather from multiple sources the registry information posted on one's own? Are you persuaded by the dissent's view that SORN is the modern-era equivalent of colonial era public shaming?

4. **Research Regarding SORN.** SORN laws have grown exponentially over time, only very rarely being ratcheted back (usually for specific offenses, such as "Romeo and Juliet" sexual relationships). They have grown despite the lack of empirical evidence supporting their effectiveness in reducing sexual offending, and the possibility that they might actually foster recidivism because of the hardships they impose on registrants (e.g., finding a place to live). For a comprehensive review of the social science research on SORN, see SEX OFFENDER REGISTRATION AND COMMUNITY NOTIFICATION LAWS: AN EMPIRICAL EVALUATION (Wayne A. Logan & J.J. Prescott eds., 2021).

SORN laws themselves, moreover, are based on several questionable premises. First is that most sexual offending, including that involving child victims, is committed by strangers, which supports the rationale of community notification; in fact, however, most victims know their assailants, for one reason or another (e.g., a soccer coach). Second is that individuals required to register should be the focus of particular vigilance and concern, when in reality research shows that first-time offenders account for the majority of sexual offending. (The two aforementioned data points underlie the criticism that SORN laws create a false sense of security regarding non-registrants.) Third, the Court's repeated reference to sex offender recidivism as being "frightening and high" has been disputed. Although some offense subgroups do recidivate at higher rates, in general sex offenders have lower recidivism rates than other offender populations. Furthermore, the phrase was based on a non-refereed article in *Popular Psychology*, the quality and reliability of which has since been debunked. *See* Ira Ellman & Tara Ellman, *"Frightening and High": The Supreme Court's Crucial Error About Sex Crime Statistics*, 30 CONST. COMMENT. 495 (2015).

Finally, the conviction-based approach to SORN (versus assessing individual risk), followed in most states (and urged by the federal government in the Adam Walsh Act, 2006), is of questionable merit. The temporal scope of coverage can date back many years, as the result of retroactive application of SORN provisions, and states often afford very little opportunity for individuals to exit registries before their (possibly lifelong) registration period ends. *See* Wayne A. Logan, *Database Infamia: Exit from the Sex Offender Registries*, 2015 WIS. L. REV. 219. Lifetime and decades-long registration, however, has been challenged by recent research. Summarizing work done to date on offending histories, several leading researchers concluded that:

> After 10 to 15 years, most individuals will have desisted from sex offending, and virtually all will have desisted by 20 years. For example, even very high risk offenders [ ] can be expected to have less than a 2% risk for sexual recidivism after 18 years if they are able to remain in the community without reoffending. This rate is comparable to the rate of spontaneous out-of-the-blue sexual offenses by individuals with a criminal conviction but no prior history of sexual offending. Maintaining individuals on a registry who no longer present a risk for sexual offending wastes resources, risks harming the individuals on the registry (and their family and friends), and provides no public protection benefits.

David Thornton et al., *Estimating Lifetime and Residual Risk for Individuals Who Remain Sexual Offense Free in the Community: Practical Applications*, 33 SEXUAL ABUSE 3, 4 (2021) (citation omitted).

An important study of the conviction-based classification policy highlights its questionable accuracy as a recidivism risk-predictor. The study compared registrants in New York, which classifies registrants in terms of individual risk, who were instead hypothetically classified under the Adam Walsh Act's conviction-based approach. Researchers discovered that registrants statutorily classified as low risk under the Adam Walsh Act were rearrested for both sexual and nonsexual offenses more than registrants classified under the Adam Walsh Act as medium-and high risk. Summarizing their results, the authors stated that a conviction-based approach:

> may give community members a false sense of security. That is, community members may believe they are safe if no Tier 3 offenders (the highest risk) are residing in their neighborhood

> when, in fact, Tier 3 offenders are not at increased risk to reoffend. As such, [the Adam Walsh Act] appears unable to accurately identify high-risk offenders and, therefore, increase public safety.

Naomi J. Freeman & Jeffrey C. Sandler, *The Adam Walsh Act: A False Sense of Security or an Effective Policy Initiative?*, 21 CRIM. JUST. POL'Y REV. 31, 43 (2010).

Despite the foregoing, SORN laws remain very popular with the public, as well as legislators. Why do you think that they have persisted, indeed expanded over time? Could one reason be that they are often named after particular victims, such as "Megan's Law"? For more on this issue see Wayne A. Logan, Symposium, *Megan's Laws: A Case Study in Political Stasis*, 61 SYRACUSE L. REV. 371 (2011).

5. **Expanding the Scope.** Increasingly, jurisdictions have gravitated toward utilizing registration and community notification with individuals convicted of non-sexual offenses, including arson, murder, animal abuse, child abuse, elder abuse, and methamphetamine-related offenses. Elizabeth R. Platt, *Gangsters to Greyhounds: The Past, Present, and Future of Offender Registration*, 37 N.Y.U. REV. L. & SOC. CHANGE 727, 738–39 (2013). Kansas, for instance, has its Offender Registration Act, which encompasses individuals convicted of sex, drug, and violent offenses (including involuntary manslaughter). Yet even sex offender-oriented registration regimes can use non-sexual qualifying offenses—for instance, kidnapping and false imprisonment of a minor (with no sexual contact). *See, e.g.*, Rainer v. State, 690 S.E.2d 827 (Ga. 2010) (deeming valid a registration requirement for an 18 year-old who pled guilty to robbery and false imprisonment of a 17-year-old).

6. **State Court Decisions.** After *Smith v. Doe*, several state courts (including Alaska's), applying the U.S. Constitution and/or analogous provisions in their state constitutions, have invalidated SORN laws, reasoning that the laws are punitive and their retroactive application violates ex post facto principles. Often, but not always, the laws include new features making them more onerous, or require the registration of adjudicated juveniles (not only juveniles convicted in adult court). *See* Wayne A. Logan, *Challenging the Punitiveness of "New Generation" SORN Laws*, 21 NEW CRIM. L. REV. 426 (2018). One court, the Colorado Supreme Court, recently held that requiring lifetime registration of juveniles with several juvenile adjudications constituted cruel and unusual punishment under the Eighth Amendment. *See In the Interest of T.B.*, 489 P.3d 752 (Colo. 2021).

7. **Double Collaterals.** A notable aspect of SORN is that it can generate other consequences: in effect, collateral consequences of a collateral consequence. For instance, International Megan's Law requires that the passports of registrants be stamped with "[t]he bearer was convicted of a sex offense against a minor," and that registrants report their intent to travel internationally twenty-one days before departure. U.S. Dep't of State, *Passports and Megan's Law*, https://travel.state.gov/content/travel/en/passports/legal-matters/passports-and-international-megans-law.html. Violation results in a fine, up to ten years in prison, or both. 18 U.S.C. § 2250(b)(3).

In the domestic context, several states require that registrants obtain a state identification card or driver's license, which is stamped with various signifiers indicating registrant status. The identification which must be carried at all times, with violations typically resulting in a felony, is shown to others on a far more regular basis (e.g., when renting a car or cashing a check). *See, e.g.*, Okla. Stat. tit. 47 § 6–111 (requiring that card bear the words "Sex Offender"). Challenges to the branding requirement have achieved some success. *See, e.g.*, *State v. Hill*, ___ So. 3d ___, 2020 WL 6145294 (La. 2020), *cert. denied*, 141 S. Ct. 311 (2021) (invalidating on First Amendment compelled speech grounds requirement that card be stamped "SEX OFFENDER" in orange lettering, reasoning that a less intrusive signifier could be used).

Another strategy adopted by jurisdictions involves the placement of warning signs on the front lawns of registrants' homes during Halloween. In one recent case, local law enforcement posted a sign stating "STOP WARNING STOP NO TRICK-OR-TREAT AT THIS ADDRESS!! A COMMUNITY SAFETY MESSAGE FROM BUTTS COUNTY SHERIFF GARY LONG." The Eleventh Circuit deemed the signs a form of invalid government-compelled speech in violation of the First Amendment. *McClendon v. Long*, 22 F.4th 1330 (11th Cir. 2022).

Next, we examine yet another outgrowth of SORN (also a "double collateral"): laws prohibiting registrants from living in certain areas.

3. RESIDENCE EXCLUSION ZONES

During the past twenty years multiple localities and a majority of states have enacted laws prohibiting registrants, especially those with child victims, from living within a specified distance of locations where children might congregate, such as schools, playgrounds, and recreation centers. Violation of the prohibition typically results in a felony conviction.[19]

Residence exclusion laws have been challenged in the courts on a variety of constitutional bases, including vagueness (regarding, for instance, how to measure distances), freedom of association (especially regarding family), equal protection of the law, retroactive punishment, and takings of property by the government. Although the U.S. Supreme Court has yet to address their constitutionality, the laws typically withstand challenges in state and federal courts. What follows is one such example.

---

[19] Laws also often prohibit registrants from visiting certain locations, such as public libraries. *See, e.g.*, Doe v. City of Albuquerque, 667 F.3d 1111, 1122 (10th Cir. 2012) (granting relief to petitioner, stating that "the City's public libraries constitute designated public fora . . . the ban can survive constitutional scrutiny only if the City . . . ma[d]e a showing that the ban [wa]s narrowly tailored to serve a significant governmental interest and le[ft] open ample alternative channels of communication"). *See also generally* Jennifer Ekblaw, Comment, *Not in My Library: An Examination of State and Local Bans on Sex Offenders from Public Libraries*, 44 IND. L. REV. 919 (2011).

Doe v. Miller

405 F.3d 700 (8th Cir. 2005)

■ COLLOTON, J.

In 2002, in an effort to protect children in Iowa from the risk that convicted sex offenders may reoffend in locations close to their residences, the Iowa General Assembly passed, and the Governor of Iowa signed, a bill that prohibits a person convicted of certain sex offenses involving minors from residing within 2000 feet of a school or a registered child care facility. The district court declared the statute unconstitutional on several grounds. * * *

Because we conclude that the Constitution of the United States does not prevent the State of Iowa from regulating the residency of sex offenders in this manner in order to protect the health and safety of the citizens of Iowa, we reverse the judgment of the district court. We hold unanimously that the residency restriction is not unconstitutional on its face. A majority of the panel further concludes that the statute does not amount to unconstitutional ex post facto punishment of persons who committed offenses prior to July 1, 2002, because the appellees have not established by the "clearest proof," as required by Supreme Court precedent, that the punitive effect of the statute overrides the General Assembly's legitimate intent to enact a nonpunitive, civil regulatory measure that protects health and safety.

I.

Iowa Senate File 2197, now codified at Iowa Code § 692A.2A, took effect on July 1, 2002. It provides that persons who have been convicted of certain criminal offenses against a minor, including numerous sexual offenses involving a minor, shall not reside within 2000 feet of a school or registered child care facility. The law does not apply to persons who established a residence prior to July 1, 2002, or to schools or child care facilities that are newly located after July 1, 2002. * * * Violations of the statute are punishable as aggravated misdemeanors.

Almost immediately after the law took effect, three named plaintiffs—sex offenders with convictions that predate the law's effective date—filed suit asserting that the statute is unconstitutional on its face. * * * The named plaintiffs, identified as various "John Does," had committed a range of sexual crimes, including indecent exposure, "indecent liberties with a child," sexual exploitation of a minor, assault with intent to commit sexual abuse, lascivious acts with a child, and second and third degree sexual abuse, all of which brought them within the provisions of the residency restriction. * * *

During a two-day bench trial, plaintiffs presented evidence concerning the enforcement of § 692A.2A, including maps that had been produced by several cities and counties identifying schools and child care facilities and their corresponding restricted areas. After viewing these maps and hearing testimony from a county attorney, the district court found that the restricted areas in many cities encompass the majority of the available housing in the city, thus leaving only limited areas within city limits available for sex offenders to establish a residence. In smaller towns, a single school or child care facility can cause all of the incorporated areas of the town to be off limits to sex offenders. The court found that unincorporated areas, small towns with no school or child care facility, and rural areas remained unrestricted, but that available housing in these areas is "not necessarily readily available."

Plaintiffs also presented evidence of their individual experiences in seeking to obtain housing that complies with the 2000-foot restriction. Several of the plaintiffs * * * have friends or relatives with whom they would like to live, but whose homes are within 2000 feet of a school or child care facility. Many * * * live in homes that are currently compliant, either because they were established prior to July 1, 2002, or because the homes are outside the 2000-foot restricted areas. These plaintiffs, however, testified that they would like to be able to move into a restricted area. Still others are living in non-compliant residences that they wish to maintain.

Plaintiffs testified that in many cases they had a difficult time obtaining housing that was not within 2000 feet of a school or child care center. John Doe VII testified that he investigated 40 residences, but was unable to find any housing that would not place him in violation of § 692A.2A. * * *

In addition to evidence regarding the burden that § 692A.2A places on sex offenders, both plaintiffs and defendants presented expert testimony about the potential effectiveness of a residency restriction in preventing offenses against minors. The State presented the testimony of Mr. Allison, a parole and probation officer who specialized in sex offender supervision. * * * According to Allison, restrictions on the proximity of sex offenders to schools or other facilities that might create temptation to reoffend are one way to minimize the risk of recidivism. In the parole and probation context, Allison also has authority to limit offenders' activities in more specific ways, and he testified that he attempts to remove temptation by preventing offenders from working in jobs where they would have contact with potential victims or from living near parks or other areas where children might spend time unsupervised. In addition to the limits that he imposes on offenders under his supervision, Allison also testified that there is "a legitimate public safety concern" in where unsupervised sex offenders reside. In Allison's view, reoffense is "a potential danger forever." * * *

The State also introduced the transcript of hearing testimony by Dr. William McEchron, a psychologist with a general practice that includes sex offender patients. * * * Dr. McEchron testified that there is no cure for sex offenders and that "there are never any guarantees that they might not reoffend." In his view, the "biggest risk is what's going on inside the individual," but reducing the opportunity and the temptation to reoffend is extremely important to treatment. He explained that because there are "very high rates of re-offense for sex offenders who had offended against children," he believed it would be appropriate to restrict places where sex offenders might come into contact with children. He thought the appropriateness of such a restriction was "common sense," although he said there were insufficient data to know "where to draw the marks." Dr. McEchron also testified, however, that in his view, life-long restrictions like § 692A.2A do not aid in the treatment process, and could even foster negative attitudes toward authority and depression in offenders who view the law as unfair.

The plaintiffs offered the testimony of Dr. Luis Rosell, a psychologist with experience in sex offender treatment. * * * Dr. Rosell testified that reducing a specific sex offender's access to children was a good idea, and that "if you remove the opportunity, then the likelihood of reoffense is decreased." He did not believe, however, that "residential proximity makes that big of a difference." Moreover, Dr. Rosell thought that a 2000-foot limit was "extreme." Like Dr. McEchron, he worried that the law might be counterproductive to the offender's treatment goals by causing depression and potentially removing the offender from his "support system."

After hearing the testimony of all three experts and of the individual plaintiffs, the district court declared that § 692A.2A was unconstitutional. * * * Having found the statute unconstitutional, the district court issued a permanent injunction against enforcement.

II.

We first address the contention that § 692A.2A violates the rights of the covered sex offenders to due process of law under the Fourteenth Amendment. The appellees (to whom we will refer as "the Does") argue that the statute is unconstitutional because it fails to provide adequate notice of what conduct is prohibited, and because it does not require an individualized determination whether each person covered by the statute is dangerous. This claim relies on what is known as "procedural due process." * * *

[T]he Does contend that they are deprived of notice required by the Constitution because some cities in Iowa are unable to provide sex offenders with information about the location of all schools and registered child care facilities, and because it is difficult to measure the restricted areas, which are measured "as the crow flies" from a school or child care facility. We disagree that these potential problems render the statute unconstitutional on its face. A criminal statute is not vague on its face unless it is "impermissibly vague in all of its applications," and the possibility that an individual might be prosecuted in a particular case in a particular community despite his best efforts to comply with the restriction is not a sufficient reason to invalidate the entire statute. * * * Due process does not require that independently elected county attorneys enforce each criminal statute with equal vigor, and the existence of different priorities or prosecution decisions among jurisdictions does not violate the Constitution.

The Does also argue that § 692A.2A unconstitutionally forecloses an "opportunity to be heard" because the statute provides no process for individual determinations of dangerousness. * * *

We * * * conclude that the Iowa residency restriction does not contravene principles of procedural due process under the Constitution. The restriction applies to all offenders who have been convicted of certain crimes against minors, regardless of what estimates of future dangerousness might be proved in individualized hearings. Once such a legislative classification has been drawn, additional procedures are unnecessary, because the statute does not provide a potential exemption for individuals who seek to prove that they are not individually dangerous or likely to offend against neighboring schoolchildren. * * * Thus, the absence of an individualized hearing in connection with a statute that offers no exemptions does not offend principles of procedural due process.

III.

The Does also assert that the residency restriction is unconstitutional under the doctrine of substantive due process. * * * The Does argue that several "fundamental rights". * * * The Does first invoke "the right to personal choice regarding the family." * * *

We do not believe that the residency restriction of § 692A.2A implicates any fundamental right of the Does that would trigger strict scrutiny of the statute. * * * Unlike the precedents cited by the Does, the Iowa statute does not operate directly on the family relationship. Although the law restricts where a residence may be located, nothing in the statute limits who may live with the Does in their residences. * * *

While there was evidence that one adult sex offender in Iowa would not reside with his parents as a result of the residency restriction, that another sex offender and his wife moved 45 miles away from their preferred location due to the statute, and that a third sex offender could not reside with his adult child in a restricted zone, the statute does not directly regulate the family relationship or prevent any family member from residing with a sex offender in a residence that is consistent with the statute. We therefore hold that § 692A.2A does not infringe upon a constitutional liberty interest relating to matters of marriage and family in a fashion that requires heightened scrutiny.

The Does also assert that the residency restrictions interfere with their constitutional right to travel. The modern Supreme Court has recognized a right to interstate travel in several decisions [and has] * * * explained that the federal guarantee of interstate travel "protects interstate travelers against two sets of burdens: 'the erection of actual barriers to interstate movement' and 'being treated differently' from intrastate travelers." * * *

The Does argue that § 692A.2A violates this right to interstate travel by substantially limiting the ability of sex offenders to establish residences in any town or urban area in Iowa. They contend that the constitutional right to travel is implicated because the Iowa law deters previously convicted sex offenders from migrating from other States to Iowa. The district court agreed, reasoning that the statute "effectively bans sex offenders from residing in large sections of Iowa's towns and cities."

We respectfully disagree with this analysis. The Iowa statute imposes no obstacle to a sex offender's entry into Iowa, and it does not erect an "actual barrier to interstate movement." There is "free ingress and regress to and from" Iowa for sex offenders, and the statute thus does not "directly impair the exercise of the right to free interstate movement." Nor does the Iowa statute violate principles of equality by treating nonresidents who visit Iowa any differently than current residents, or by discriminating against citizens of other States who wish to establish residence in Iowa. We think that to recognize a fundamental right to interstate travel in a situation that does not involve any of these circumstances would extend the doctrine beyond the Supreme Court's pronouncements in this area. That the statute may deter some out-of-state residents from traveling to Iowa because the prospects for a convenient and affordable residence are less promising than elsewhere does not implicate a fundamental right recognized by the Court's right to travel jurisprudence.

The Does also assert that § 692A.2A infringes upon a fundamental constitutional right to intra state travel. The Supreme Court has not decided whether there is a fundamental right to intrastate travel. * * * Some of our sister circuits have recognized a fundamental right to intrastate travel. * * *

We find it unnecessary in this case to decide whether there is a fundamental right to intrastate travel under the Constitution, because assuming such a right is recognized, it would not require strict scrutiny of § 692A.2A. * * * [W]e believe that any fundamental right to intrastate travel would likely be "correlative" to the right to interstate travel discussed in *Saenz*, or would consist of a "right to travel locally through public spaces and roadways." Therefore, the Iowa statute would not implicate a right to intrastate travel for the same reasons that it does not implicate the right to interstate travel. The Iowa residency restriction does not prevent a sex offender from entering or leaving any part of the State, including areas within 2000 feet of a school or child care facility, and it does not erect any actual barrier to intrastate movement. * * *

The Does also urge that we recognize a fundamental right "to live where you want." This ambitious articulation of a proposed unenumerated right calls to mind the Supreme Court's caution that we should proceed with restraint in the area of substantive due process, because "[b]y extending constitutional protection to an asserted right or liberty interest, we, to a great extent, place the matter outside the arena of public debate and legislative action." Some thirty years ago, our court said "we cannot agree that the right to choose one's place of residence is necessarily a fundamental right," and we see no basis to conclude that the contention has gained strength in the intervening years. * * * [And] the Does have not developed any argument that the right to "live where you want" is "deeply rooted in this Nation's history and tradition," or "implicit in the concept of ordered liberty," such that "neither liberty nor justice would exist if [it] were sacrificed." We are thus not persuaded that the Constitution establishes a right to "live where you want" that requires strict scrutiny of a State's residency restrictions.

Because § 692A.2A does not implicate a constitutional liberty interest that has been elevated to the status of "fundamental right," we review the statute to determine whether it meets the standard of "rationally advancing some legitimate governmental purpose." The Does acknowledge that the statute was designed to promote the safety of children, and they concede that this is a legitimate state interest. They also allow that perhaps "certain identifiable sex offenders should not live right across the street from a school or perhaps anywhere else where there are children." The Does contend, however, that the statute is irrational because there is no scientific study that supports the legislature's conclusion that excluding sex offenders from residing within 2000 feet of a school or child care facility is likely to enhance the safety of children.

We reject this contention because we think it understates the authority of a state legislature to make judgments about the best means to protect the health and welfare of its citizens in an area where precise statistical data is unavailable and human behavior is necessarily unpredictable. * * * There can be no doubt of a legislature's rationality in believing that "[s]ex offenders are a serious threat in this Nation," and that "[w]hen convicted sex offenders reenter society, they are much more likely than any other type of offender to be re-arrested for a new rape or sexual assault." The only question remaining is whether, in view of a rationally perceived risk, the chosen residency restriction rationally advances the State's interest in protecting children.

We think the decision whether to set a limit on proximity of "across the street" (as appellees suggest), or 500 feet or 3000 feet (as the Iowa Senate considered and rejected, see S. Journal 79, 2d Sess., at 521 (Iowa 2002)), or 2000 feet (as the Iowa General Assembly and the Governor eventually adopted) is the sort of task for which the elected policymaking officials of a State, and not the federal courts, are properly suited. * * *

The record does not support a conclusion that the Iowa General Assembly and the Governor acted based merely on negative attitudes toward, fear of, or a bare desire to harm a politically unpopular group

[and] * * * we are not persuaded that the means selected to pursue the State's legitimate interest are without rational basis. * * *

V.

A final, and narrower, challenge advanced by the Does is that § 692A.2A is an unconstitutional ex post facto law because it imposes retroactive punishment on those who committed a sex offense prior to July 1, 2002. * * * In determining whether a state statute violates the Ex Post Facto Clause by imposing such punishment, we apply the framework outlined in *Smith v. Doe*, 538 U.S. 84, 92 (2003). * * *

The district court found that in passing the residency restriction of § 692A.2A, the Iowa General Assembly intended to create "a civil, non-punitive statutory scheme to protect the public." The Does do not dispute this conclusion on appeal, and we agree that the legislature's intent was not punitive. * * *

We must next consider whether the Does have established that the law was nonetheless so punitive in effect as to negate the legislature's intent to create a civil, non-punitive regulatory scheme. * * *

Turning first to any historical tradition regarding residency restrictions, the Does argue that § 692A.2A is the effective equivalent of banishment, which has been regarded historically as a punishment. * * *

While banishment of course involves an extreme form of residency restriction, we ultimately do not accept the analogy between the traditional means of punishment and the Iowa statute. Unlike banishment, § 692A.2A restricts only where offenders may reside. It does not "expel" the offenders from their communities or prohibit them from accessing areas near schools or child care facilities for employment, to conduct commercial transactions, or for any purpose other than establishing a residence. * * * We thus conclude that this law is unlike banishment in important respects, and we do not believe it is of a type that is traditionally punitive.

The second factor that we consider is whether the law promotes the traditional aims of punishment—deterrence and retribution. * * * We agree with the district court that the law could have a deterrent effect, but we do not agree that the deterrent effect provides a strong inference that the restriction is punishment. The primary purpose of the law is not to alter the offender's incentive structure by demonstrating the negative consequences that will flow from committing a sex offense. The Iowa statute is designed to reduce the likelihood of reoffense by limiting the offender's temptation and reducing the opportunity to commit a new crime. * * *

The statute's "retributive" effect is similarly difficult to evaluate. * * * While any restraint or requirement imposed on those who commit crimes is at least potentially retributive in effect, we believe that § 692A.2A, like the registration requirement in *Smith v. Doe*, is consistent with the legislature's regulatory objective of protecting the health and safety of children.

The next factor we consider is whether the law "imposes an affirmative disability or restraint." * * *

Iowa Code § 692A.2A is more disabling than the sex offender registration law at issue in *Smith v. Doe*. * * * The residency restriction is certainly less disabling, however, than the civil commitment scheme at issue in Hendricks, which permitted complete confinement of affected persons. * * *

This final factor—whether the regulatory scheme has a "rational connection to a nonpunitive purpose"—is the "most significant factor" in the ex post facto analysis. The requirement of a "rational connection" is not demanding. * * * In light of the high risk of recidivism posed by sex offenders, the legislature reasonably could conclude that § 692A.2A would protect society by minimizing the risk of repeated sex offenses against minors. * * *

The Does also urge that the law is excessive in relation to its regulatory purpose because there is no scientific evidence that a 2000-foot residency restriction is effective at preventing sex offender recidivism. * * * In this case, there was expert testimony that reducing the frequency of contact between sex offenders and children is likely to reduce temptation and opportunity, which in turn is important to reducing the risk of reoffense. None of the witnesses was able to articulate a precise distance that optimally balanced the benefit of reducing risk to children with the burden of the residency restrictions on sex offenders, and the Does' expert acknowledged that "[t]here is nothing in the literature that has addressed proximity." * * *

We believe the legislature's decision to select a 2000-foot restriction, as opposed to the other distances that were considered and rejected, is reasonably related to its regulatory purpose. * * *

The judgment of the district court is reversed, and the case is remanded with directions to enter judgment in favor of the defendants.

■ MELLOY, J., concurring and dissenting.

I join in the majority's opinion, sections I through IV. However, I dissent as to section V because I believe section 692A.2A is an unconstitutional ex post facto law. * * *

I agree with the majority that the purpose of section 692A.2A is to protect the public. This purpose is nonpunitive, so we must determine if the statute "is so punitive either in purpose or effect as to negate the State's intention to deem it civil." * * *

Though I believe a rational connection exists between the residency restriction and a nonpunitive purpose, I would find that the restriction is excessive in relation to that purpose. The statute limits the housing choices of all offenders identically, regardless of their type of crime, type of victim, or risk of re-offending. The effect of the requirement is quite dramatic: many offenders cannot live with their families and/or cannot live in their home communities because the whole community is a restricted area. This leaves offenders to live in the country or in small, prescribed areas of towns and cities that might offer no appropriate, available housing. In addition, there is no time limit to the restrictions. * * *

[T]he severity of residency restriction, the fact that it is applied to all offenders identically, and the fact that it will be enforced for the rest of the offenders' lives, makes the residency restriction excessive. * * * Because the imposition of the residency requirement " 'changes the punishment, and inflicts a greater punishment, than the law annexed to the crime, when committed,' " I would find Section 692A.2A is an unconstitutional ex post facto law that cannot be applied to persons who committed their offenses before the law was enacted.

NOTES & QUESTIONS

1. **NIMBY?** Residence exclusion laws are on the books in a majority of states and multiple localities (sometimes in conjunction with state laws, adding to their restrictions, for instance, by lengthening distances). The laws vary in their particulars, with the distance prohibitions ranging from 500 to 3000 feet. Some laws bar registrants from living near places "intended" for minors, while others impose the broader "congregate" standard.[20]

Perhaps predictably, the laws are very popular with the public. It is not unusual to see laws enacted in domino-like fashion, based on a NIMBY ("not in my backyard") mentality as one jurisdiction, fearful of an influx of registrants, adopts a law in reaction to that adopted in an adjacent jurisdiction. Amy P. Meek, *Street Vendors, Taxicabs, and Exclusion Zones: The Impact of Collateral Consequences of Criminal Convictions at the Local Level*, 75 OHIO ST. L.J. 1, 24 & 26 (2014). *See also* Debra Hunter & Paul Sharman, *Sexual Offenses: Change Provisions Relating to Sexual Offenders*, 23 GA. ST. U. L. REV. 11, 19 (2006) (quoting "candid[ ]"comment during state legislative hearing that restrictions in proposed Georgia law would force registrants "in many cases [to] have to move to another state, and that's the greatest protection I think any of us can offer our kids"). There have also been reported incidents of neighborhoods purposefully seeking to facilitate exclusion by creating a "pocket park" or other exclusion anchor point. Ian Lovett, *Neighborhoods Seek to Banish Sex Offenders by Building Parks*, N.Y. TIMES, Mar. 13, 2013.

The Eighth Circuit in *Doe v. Miller* rejected an array of constitutional challenges: substantive due process (vagueness); procedural due process; substantive due process (abridgement of a fundamental right); and ex post facto. Are any of the claims more persuasive than others? For instance, do you agree that the law challenged did not limit the fundamental right

[20] The laws impose limits distinct from other laws prohibiting registrants from entering, loitering, or working within particular distances from specified sites, and the more traditional spatial limits imposed on probationers and parolees (i.e., individuals "on paper").

concerning one's family? While the court noted that several Does were prohibited from living with family, within zones, the court held that "the statute does not directly regulate the family relationship or prevent any family member from residing with a sex offender that is consistent with the statute." *Doe*, 405 F.3d at 711. "Although the law restricts where a residence may be located, nothing in the statute limits who may live with the Does in their residences." *Id.* at 710. Do you agree?

2. **Majority or Dissent?** After finding no fundamental right jeopardized, the *Miller* majority had no difficulty finding that the law satisfied rational basis scrutiny, dismissing the Does' contention that the statute was irrational because no social scientific data supported that the prohibition enhanced the safety of children. To the court, the Does' position "understate[ed] the authority of a state legislature to make judgments about the best means to protect the health and welfare of its citizens in an area where precise statistical data [are] unavailable and human behavior is necessarily unpredictable." *Id.* at 714.

Similarly, in rejecting the ex post facto claim, the majority held that the Iowa law had a " 'rational connection to a nonpunitive purpose' " and was not excessive. This was so even though "none of the state's witnesses "was able to articulate a precise distance that optimally balanced the benefit of reducing risk to children with the burden of the residency restrictions." *Id.* at 722. In short, "the legislature's decision to select a 2000-foot restriction as opposed to the other distances that were considered and rejected, is reasonably related to its regulatory purposes . . . ." *Id.* at 723. Judge Melloy, in a partial dissent, however, concluded that the law, while having a rational connection with a nonpunitive purpose, was "excessive in relation to that purpose. . . . [T]he severity of the residency restriction, the fact that it is applied to offenders identically, and the fact that it will be enforced for the rest of offenders' lives, makes the residency restriction excessive." *Id.* at 726 (Melloy, J., dissenting in part).

Who has the better of the argument—the majority or Judge Melloy? Also, with respect to the ex post facto claim, the majority rejected the "analogy" to banishment, because the Iowa law "restrict[ed] only where offenders may reside. . . . It did not 'expel' the offenders from their communities . . . ." *Id.* at 719. Do you agree?

3. **Social Science Findings.** Residence exclusion laws are motivated by the intuition that preventing registrants from living near playgrounds, schools, and the like will reduce child sexual victimization because registrants will have no opportunity to be in the presence of minors. Considerable evidence, however, casts doubt on the accuracy of this intuition. Research shows by far the greatest percentage of sex crimes against children are committed by familiars, such as athletic coaches and family members, not opportunistic strangers. Moreover, studies have failed to find any nexus between residence location and child sexual victimization. *See generally* Joanne Savage & Casey Windsor, *Sex Offender Residence Restrictions and Sex Crimes Against Children: A Comprehensive Review*, 43 AGGRESSION & VIOL. BEHAV. 13 (2018). Reflecting the aforementioned research, one study funded by the U.S. Department of Justice advised

against adoption of the laws. Christopher Lobanov-Rostovsky, *Research in Brief, Adult Sex Offender Management* 4 (2015), https://smart.ojp.gov/sites/g/files/xyckuh231/files/media/document/adultsexoffendermanagement.pdf. Would the foregoing likely change the *Miller* majority's deferential view of legislative decision making?

4. **Homelessness.** Another concern with residence exclusion laws is that they can be at cross-purposes with broader governmental public safety aims. For instance, having stable housing is an acknowledged contributor to successful re-entry, yet residence laws make finding lawful housing—already a challenge for individuals with a conviction (let alone for a sexual offense)—very difficult or impossible. *See* Deanna Cann & Deanna Isom Scott, *Sex Offender Residence Restrictions and Homelessness: A Critical Look at South Carolina*, 31 CRIM. JUST. POL'Y REV. 1119 (2020). Homelessness is a major problem for anyone, but homeless registrants face distinct difficulties. For instance, they might be required to report to a government office in person with greater frequency to verify their sleeping location (e.g., "Behind the gas station at 125 Lincoln Ave."). Failure to comply often results in felony prosecution. Elizabeth Esser-Stuart, Note, *"The Irons Are Always in the Background": The Unconstitutionality of Sex Offender Post-Release Laws as Applied to the Homeless*, 96 TEX. L. REV. 811, 812 (2018).

And when housing is available for registrants, it is very often located on the outskirts of town or in rural areas, where public transportation is lacking. This worsens already scarce employment options and limits access to reentry services such as therapy and counseling, as well as social and family support systems, raising concern that the laws promote recidivism within a subpopulation already facing major reentry hurdles.

5. **First Amendment Concern?** A consequence that might not come to immediate mind is that residence exclusion laws can prevent registrants from attending church, a place where minors are present or congregate. In rejecting a First Amendment free exercise claim, the New Hampshire Supreme Court reasoned:

> Here, the defendant's freedom of belief has not been restricted. He may still practice his religion in ways that do not violate the condition of his sentences, including the use of books and video and audio recordings. He may also arrange bible study with elders from his congregation and attend meetings at a congregation where minors are not present.

State v. Perfetto, 7 A.3d 1179, 1183 (N.H. 2010). In response to the foregoing, Professor Christopher Lund recently wrote,

> The court emphasizes that, despite these restrictions, sex offenders can still believe what they want. But freedom of religion is not mere freedom of belief. The court says that sex offenders can still read books and watch videos by themselves. But doing those things alone in one's house is a transparently pathetic substitute for religious study, worship, and fellowship with other human beings.

Christopher C. Lund, *Sex Offenders and the Free Exercise of Religion*, 96 NOTRE DAME L. REV. 1025, 1042–43 (2021). Of the laws more generally, Professor Lund maintains that they create "a bitter irony":

> For while they are still inside prison, sex offenders can go to church freely with others. But once outside prison's walls, everything changes, and sex offenders find themselves locked out of religious life. When it comes to their religious options, as strange as it sounds, sex offenders are better off in prison. . . . [T]his seriously undermines the attempt to reintegrate sex offenders back into society. Churches can be, and often are, valuable sites of rehabilitation and redemption for people earnestly trying to get their lives back on track. It is bad enough that the law contributes so little to the rehabilitative project. The least the law could do, one would think, is get out of the way.

Id. at 1028.

Given the hardships imposed by the laws, can you see why a registrant might be disinclined to provide accurate residence information, which is at odds with the basic knowledge-based premise of SORN—that law enforcement and the public know where a registrant lives?

6. **Constitutional Challenges.** As mentioned at the outset, the laws usually withstand constitutional attack. Like the Eighth Circuit, most all courts deem the laws non-punitive, allowing them to be imposed retroactively, consistent with ex post facto principles. *See, e.g., Shaw v. Patton*, 823 F.3d 556 (10th Cir. 2016). Other constitutional claims have similarly met with defeat. *See, e.g., Vasquez v. Foxx*, 895 F.3d 515 (7th Cir. 2018) (substantive and procedural due process); *Duarte v. City of Lewisville*, 858 F.3d 348, 352–56 (5th Cir. 2017) (procedural due process and equal protection); *Weems v. Little Rock Police Dep't.*, 453 F.3d 1010, 1015–17 (8th Cir. 2006) (substantive due process, equal protection, constitutional right to travel).

A few challenges, however, have had some success.[21] In *In re Taylor*, 343 P.3d 867 (Cal. 2015), for instance, the California Supreme Court unanimously invalidated blanket application of the state's law preventing petitioners, registered sex offenders on parole, from living within 2,000 feet of a school or park where children regularly gather. The Court held that eligible individuals could be subject to the law on a case-by-case basis, but that blanket application was problematic because it

> severely restricted [petitioners'] ability to find housing in compliance with the statute, greatly increased the incidence of homelessness among them, and hindered their access to medical

[21] *See, e.g.,* Doe v. Miami-Dade County, Florida, 846 F.3d 1180 (11th Cir. 2017) (reversing dismissal of claims based on state and federal ex post facto provisions); Evenstad v. City of West St. Paul, 306 F. Supp. 3d 1086 (D. Minn. 2018) (granting preliminary injunction against local law); Hoffman v. Village of Pleasant Prairie, 249 F. Supp. 3d 951 (E.D. Wis. 2017) (holding that local ordinance violated federal Ex Post Facto Clause); State v. Pollard, 908 N.E.2d 1145 (Ind. 2009) (deeming restriction punitive based on Indiana ex post facto provision); Commonwealth v. Baker, 295 S.W.3d 437 (Ky. 2009) (deeming restriction punitive under both state and federal ex post facto provisions).

> treatment, drug and alcohol dependency services, psychological counseling and other rehabilitative social services available to all parolees, while further hampering the efforts of parole authorities and law enforcement officials to monitor, supervise, and rehabilitate them in the interests of public safety.

Id. at 869. Even under deferential rational basis review the law was unconstitutional because it imposed harsh and severe restrictions and disabilities on the petitioners'

> liberty and privacy rights, however limited, while producing conditions that hamper, rather than foster, efforts to monitor, supervise, and rehabilitate these persons. Accordingly, it bears no rational relationship to advancing the state's legitimate goal of protecting children from sexual predators, and has infringed the affected parolees' basic constitutional right to be free of official action that is unreasonable, arbitrary, and oppressive.

Id. at 879.

7. **Vagueness.** Vagueness challenges also often face defeat in the courts. For instance, a registrant might challenge the statutory language barring residence near where minors "congregate" or "frequent." Aligning itself with other courts rejecting such claims, the Vermont Supreme Court held that "the phrase 'where children congregate' is descriptive enough to put a defendant on notice that it includes all places where children are likely to be found in large numbers." *State v. Gauthier*, 145 A.3d 840 (Vt. 2016). What qualifies as "in large numbers" went unelaborated. Another possible uncertainty centers on the important question of how the specified distance is to be measured. Most commonly, as in *Miller*, an "as the crow flies" measurement is used, but not specified in the statute. This is so even though it results in disqualifying numerous residences that, as a practical matter, would be well over the prescribed distance because a freeway or other large obstruction stands between the two locations.

8. **Takings Claim.** Typically, as with the Iowa provision, the laws contain a grandfather clause, allowing registrants to remain in a residence purchased before enactment of the prohibition. An exception involved Georgia's law, which had no such clause, resulting in the state demanding that a registrant move after a childcare center located near his home. The Georgia Supreme Court held that the law qualified as an unconstitutional regulatory taking under the Georgia and U.S. Constitutions. *Mann v. Dep't of Corrections*, 653 S.E.2d 740 (Ga. 2007).

9. **A Successful Challenge.** It is important to note that exclusion laws can figure in challenges asserting that SORN, in tandem with residence exclusion, imposes distinct burdens. In *Does #1–5 v. Snyder*, 834 F.3d 696 (6th Cir. 2016), *cert. denied*, 138 S. Ct. 55 (2017), the Sixth Circuit Court of Appeals invalidated on federal ex post facto grounds Michigan's registry regime, which included a provision prohibiting registrants from living, working, or loitering within 1000 feet of a school. The court stated that the law's effects "resemble[ ], in some respects at least, the ancient punishment of banishment," with "very burdensome [effects], especially in densely

populated areas," likening the restrictions to acknowledged punitive sanctions of probation and parole. *Id.* at 703. On the issue of whether the law imposed an "affirmative disability or restraint," the court reasoned that "surely something is not 'minor and indirect' just because no one is actually being lugged off in cold irons bound. Indeed, those irons are always in the background since failure to comply with these restrictions carries with it the threat of serious punishment, including imprisonment." *Id.*

After stating that the Supreme Court's decision in *Smith v. Doe* should not "be understood as writing a blank check to states to do whatever they please in this arena," the court found that

> [a] regulatory regime that severely restricts where people can live, work, and "loiter," that categorizes them into tiers ostensibly corresponding to present dangerousness without any individualized assessment thereof, and that requires time-consuming and cumbersome in-person reporting, all supported by—at best—scant evidence that such restrictions serve the professed purpose of keeping Michigan communities safe, is something altogether different from and more troubling than Alaska's first-generation registry law. SORA brands registrants as moral lepers solely on the basis of a prior conviction. It consigns them to years, if not a lifetime, of existence on the margins, not only of society, but often, as the record in this case makes painfully evident, from their own families, with whom, due to school zone restrictions, they may not even live. It directly regulates where registrants may go in their daily lives and compels them to interrupt those lives with great frequency in order to appear in person before law enforcement to report even minor changes to their information.

Id. at 705.

4. OTHER SANCTIONS

a. ELECTRONIC MONITORING

Amid ongoing concerns over the massive expense of traditional brick-and-mortar confinement, combined with anxiety over and disdain for those convicted of sex offenses, jurisdictions have gravitated toward lifetime community supervision over such individuals.[22] Following Florida's lead in 2005, several dozen states have started using global positioning satellite (GPS) or other tracking technology to monitor people convicted of sex offenses after their release from confinement. While most laws are limited in their application to probation and parole periods, several subject individuals to lifetime electronic monitoring and require reimbursement of monitoring costs.

[22] For more on this shift, see generally Chaz Arnett, *From Decarceration to E-Carceration*, 41 CARDOZO L. REV. 641 (2019); Michelle Alexander, *The Newest Jim Crow*, N.Y. TIMES, Nov. 18, 2018.

In *Grady v. North Carolina,* 575 U.S. 306 (2015), the Supreme Court held that monitoring by means of the required wearing of an ankle bracelet constitutes a search under the Fourth Amendment but remanded for determination of whether the search itself was reasonable. According to the *Grady* Court, whether use of a tracking device is reasonable in a given case "depends on the totality of the circumstances, including the nature and purpose of the search and the extent to which the search intrudes upon personal privacy." *Id.* at 310. In the wake of *Grady*, courts have disagreed on the Fourth Amendment reasonableness question in particular instances.[23]

To date, courts have differed on the viability of ex post facto claims,[24] yet at least one court granted relief on due process grounds.[25] With respect to ex post facto, the Seventh Circuit has held that monitoring is non-punitive, reasoning that "[h]aving to wear the monitor is a bother, an inconvenience, an annoyance, but no more is punishment than being stopped by a police officer on the highway and asked to show your driver's license is punishment." *Belleau v. Wall*, 811 F.3d 929, 944 (7th Cir. 2016). The court further reasoned that "if civil commitment is not punishment, as the Supreme Court has ruled [in *Kansas v. Hendricks*], then a fortiori neither is having to wear an ankle monitor." *Id.*[26]

Monitoring is typically either "active" or "passive." With the former, authorities receive real-time information regarding location. With passive monitoring, locational information is collected and then transmitted at particular times (e.g., once per day). Of late, as well, microchip implant technology, which involves outpatient surgical implantation of a rice grain-sized "chip," usually between the thumb and forefinger, is being employed to locate (but not yet track) subject individuals, ensuring, for instance, that they are at home. Because the strategy enables authorities to monitor location, it can operate in tandem with exclusion zones, which prohibit registrants from living in or visiting designated areas (e.g., a school or swimming pool). The technology also can determine whether an individual is where they should be at an appointed time, such as at work or a treatment session.

---

[23] *See, e.g.,* Park v. State, 825 S.E.2d 147 (Ga. 2019) (deeming unreasonable law subjecting sexually violent predators to lifetime GPS monitoring and requiring them to pay for it); H.R. v. N.J. State Parole Bd., 231 A.3d 617 (N.J. 2020) (deeming valid monitoring of designated high risk individual); State v. Ross, 815 S.E.2d 754 (S.C. 2018) (deeming unreasonable automatic imposition of lifetime monitoring based on conviction for a failure to maintain registry information). *See also generally* Kate Weisburd, *Sentenced to Surveillance: Fourth Amendment Limits on Electronic Monitoring*, 98 N.C. L. REV. 717 (2020).

[24] *Compare, e.g.,* Belleau v. Wall, 811 F.3d 929 (7th Cir. 2016) (rejecting ex post facto claim), *and* State v. Bowditch, 700 S.E.2d 1 (N.C. 2010), *with* Riley v. N.J. State Parole Bd., 98 A.3d 544 (N.J. 2014) (granting relief on ex post facto grounds).

[25] State v. Dykes, 744 S.E.2d 505 (S.C. 2013).

[26] For an overview of the significant personal impact on individuals required to wear monitors, suggesting that the Seventh Circuit in *Belleau* gave the impact short shrift, see State v. Grady, 831 S.E.2d 542, 536–38 (N.C. 2019) (noting inter alia that the petitioner must wear a "half-pound ankle monitor at all times and respond to any of its repeating voice messages," and remain "tethered to a wall for what amounts to one month out of every year").

Monitoring technology can have drawbacks, however. At times, the signal can be blocked in certain areas such as in metal enclosures like trains. The tracking devices can also fail, for instance, because of battery failure, and be thwarted by various methods (e.g., covering them in tinfoil). More fundamentally, knowing where an individual is located does not reveal what they are doing. This recognition becomes particularly significant in light of the empirical reality that most sexual offending is committed by individuals who are known to their victims, prompting concern that monitoring promotes a false sense of security. Also, operational costs, paid for or defrayed by the individuals monitored, can be substantial, adding to the criminal justice debt discussed in Chapter 9.

b. INTERNET AND SOCIAL MEDIA LIMITS

Acting on the presumption that persons convicted of sex offenses will, upon release into the community, utilize the internet and social media sites to again engage in criminal sexual activity, governments have enacted laws limiting or banning their use. To date, courts often have been receptive to First Amendment constitutional challenges to the laws. This includes the U.S. Supreme Court, which in *Packingham v. North Carolina*, 137 S. Ct. 1730 (2017), unanimously held that a state law making it a felony for a registrant to utilize social media websites violated the First Amendment right to free speech. After noting that the ban prohibited access to a broad range of websites, the Court stated:

> By prohibiting sex offenders from using those websites, North Carolina with one broad stroke bars access to what for many are the principal sources for knowing current events, checking ads for employment, speaking and listening in the modern public square, and otherwise exploring the vast realms of human thought and knowledge. These websites can provide perhaps the most powerful mechanisms available to a private citizen to make his or her voice heard. They allow a person with an Internet connection to "become a town crier with a voice that resonates farther than it could from any soapbox."
>
> In sum, to foreclose access to social media altogether is to prevent the user from engaging in the legitimate exercise of First Amendment rights. It is unsettling to suggest that only a limited set of websites can be used even by persons who have completed their sentences. Even convicted criminals—and in some instances especially convicted criminals—might receive legitimate benefits from these means for access to the world of ideas, in particular if they seek to reform and to pursue lawful and rewarding lives.

Id. at 1737 (citation omitted). In so holding, however, the Court emphasized that it would not necessarily invalidate more circumscribed prohibitions:

> Though the issue is not before the Court, it can be assumed that the First Amendment permits a State to enact specific, narrowly tailored laws that prohibit a sex offender from engaging in conduct that often presages a sexual crime, like contacting a minor or using a website to gather information about a minor.

Id.[27]

Courts have been less receptive to challenges against laws requiring that registrants disclose their internet personal identifiers. *See, e.g.*, *State v. Aschbrenner*, 926 N.W.2d 240 (Iowa 2019) (rejecting First Amendment challenge to law requiring disclosure of internet identifiers, such as names used on social media, and citing other similarly decided cases).

C. ADVOCACY

Given the very significant, potentially life-long adverse impact of collateral consequences, it behooves defense counsel to be mindful of whether they will be imposed as the result of a conviction. In *Padilla v. Kentucky*, 559 U.S. 356 (2010), noted earlier, the Supreme Court constitutionalized this expectation, holding that the Sixth Amendment right to effective assistance of counsel requires that defense counsel inform a client that a guilty plea would render him subject to deportation. Padilla, born in Honduras and a lawful permanent resident, pled guilty to transporting a large amount of marijuana in his tractor-trailer after his lawyer failed to advise him that the plea might result in deportation and related that he " 'did not have to worry about immigration status since he had been in the country so long.' " As it turned out, deportation under federal law was "virtually mandatory." The *Padilla* Court held that defense counsel has an obligation not only to refrain from providing affirmative misadvice, such as in Padilla's case,[28] but also to inform a client when a plea "carries a risk of deportation." *Id.* at 369, 374.

In *Padilla*, the Court was aware of the complexity of immigration law and that defense counsel, public or private, might not be well versed in it, and that the counseling duty might therefore vary:

> There will, therefore, undoubtedly be numerous situations in which the deportation consequences of a particular plea are unclear or uncertain. The duty of the private practitioner in such cases is more limited. When the law is not succinct and straightforward . . . , a criminal defense attorney need do no

---

[27] *Cf.* United States v. Holena, 906 F.3d 288 (3d Cir. 2018) (vacating sentence that banned a defendant from possessing or using a computer or other electronic communication device and prohibited him from using the internet without his probation officer's approval).

[28] *See Padilla*, 559 U.S. at 368–69 ("In the instant case, the terms of the relevant immigration statute are succinct, clear, and explicit in defining the removal consequence for Padilla's conviction. . . . Padilla's counsel could have easily determined that his plea would make him eligible for deportation simply from reading the text of the statute. . . . Instead, Padilla's counsel provided him false assurance that his conviction would not result in his removal from this country. This is not a hard case in which to find deficiency.").

> more than advise a noncitizen client that pending criminal charges may carry a risk of adverse immigration consequences. But when the deportation consequence is truly clear, as it was in this case, the duty to give correct advice is equally clear.

Id. at 369.

The Court closed by recognizing what it saw as the broader institutional benefits of disclosure in the all-important plea-bargaining process:

> [I]nformed consideration of possible deportation can only benefit both the State and noncitizen defendants during the plea-bargaining process. By bringing deportation consequences into this process, the defense and prosecution may well be able to reach agreements that better satisfy the interests of both parties. As in this case, a criminal episode may provide the basis for multiple charges, of which only a subset mandate deportation following conviction. Counsel who possess the most rudimentary understanding of the deportation consequences of a particular criminal offense may be able to plea bargain creatively with the prosecutor in order to craft a conviction and sentence that reduce the likelihood of deportation, as by avoiding a conviction for an offense that automatically triggers the removal consequence. At the same time, the threat of deportation may provide the defendant with a powerful incentive to plead guilty to an offense that does not mandate that penalty in exchange for a dismissal of a charge that does.

Id. at 373.

Although courts have long drawn a distinction between direct and collateral consequences, requiring that counsel advise a client only of the former, the Court passed up the opportunity to delineate the categories, stating that it "need not consider [the question] in this case because of the unique nature of deportation," which it described as a "particularly severe 'penalty,' " albeit not a criminal one. *Id.* at 365. "Although removal proceedings are civil in nature, "deportation is nevertheless intimately related to the criminal process. Our law has enmeshed criminal convictions and the penalty of deportation for nearly a century." *Id.* at 365–66 (citations omitted).[29]

Padilla, not surprisingly, has required courts to address arguments that other collateral consequences are similarly "enmeshed" and therefore subject to Sixth Amendment requirements. For instance, some

[29] *See also Padilla*, 559 U.S. at 366 ("Deportation as a consequence of a criminal conviction is, because of its close connection to the criminal process, uniquely difficult to classify as either a direct or a collateral consequence. The collateral versus direct distinction is thus ill suited to evaluating a [Sixth Amendment] claim concerning the specific risk of deportation. We conclude that advice regarding deportation is not categorically removed from the ambit of the Sixth Amendment right to counsel.").

courts find that SORN requires counsel advisement yet others do not[30]; likewise with involuntary commitment as a "sexually violent predator."[31] The uncertainty has prompted Professor Jenny Roberts to advocate for a defense counsel duty to inform "whenever a reasonable person in the defendant's situation would deem knowledge of the consequences, penal or otherwise, to be a significant factor in deciding whether to plead guilty." Jenny Roberts, *The Mythical Divide Between Collateral and Direct Consequences of a Criminal Conviction: Involuntary Commitment of "Sexually Violent Predators,"* 93 MINN. L. REV. 670, 674 (2008). Do you agree? Does it matter whether defense counsel, typically saddled with an enormous caseload and little time, will actually be able to properly advise a client when faced with the thousands of collateral consequences, contained in far-flung parts of state, federal, and local codes?

Courts, when taking a guilty plea, are not required to advise a defendant of collateral consequences flowing from the conviction. *See, e.g., State v. Fisher*, 877 N.W.2d 676, 682 (Iowa 2016). In Florida, however, a court must advise a defendant of potential deportation, involuntary commitment as a "sexually violent predator," and suspension or revocation of a driver's license. Fla. R. Crim. P. Rule 3.172(c)(8)(9)(10).

Arguably, the Sixth Amendment right to effective assistance of counsel is not the only constitutional right implicated by the onerous effects of collateral consequences. What of the Sixth Amendment right to counsel? The Supreme Court has held that the right attaches only when "actual imprisonment" is imposed. *Argersinger v. Hamlin*, 407 U.S. 25, 37 (1972). As a result, one day in jail will trigger the right, allowing indigents to have publicly appointed counsel to contest a conviction, yet a non-carceral sentence, with likely more damaging life-long collateral consequences (e.g., deportation, lost access to public housing) does not? And what of the Sixth Amendment right to a jury? The Supreme Court has held that an offense that threatens more than six months of imprisonment triggers the right. *Baldwin v. New York*, 399 U.S. 66, 68 (1970). Yet, again, the personal impact of collateral consequences imposed as the result of a conviction can far exceed that of a six-month period of incarceration.[32] And, does the Supreme Court's decision in

---

[30] *Compare* Commw. v. Thompson, 548 S.W.3d 892 (Ky. 2018) (yes), *with* State v. Trotter, 330 P.3d 1267 (Utah 2014) (no).

[31] *Compare* People v. Hughes, 983 N.E.2d 439 (Ill. 2012) (yes), *with* State v. LeMere, 879 N.W.2d 580 (Wis. 2016) (no).

[32] *But see* Bado v. United States, 186 A.3d 1243 (D.C. 2018) (holding that a defendant facing deportation has a right to a jury trial); People v. Suazo, 118 N.E.3d 168 (N.Y. 2018) (same).

The Court held in a case after *Baldwin* that an authorized sentence of six months or less can trigger a jury right (more specifically, rebut the presumption that no right extends because an offense is "petty"), if a defendant "can demonstrate that any additional statutory penalties, viewed in conjunction with the maximum authorized period of incarceration, are so severe that they clearly reflect a legislative determination that the offense in question is a 'serious' one." Blanton v. City of North Las Vegas, 489 U.S. 538, 543 (1989). In practice, however, courts routinely refuse to take collateral consequences into account. Paul T. Crane, *Incorporating Collateral Consequences into Criminal Procedure*, 54 WAKE FOREST L. REV. 1, 27 (2019). *But see* Fushek v. State, 183 P.3d 536, 543 (Ariz. 2008) (allowing jury right and noting that "the

Apprendi v. New Jersey require jury findings on whether SORN should be imposed on a particular defendant (e.g., determining if the offense in question was "sexually motivated" and therefore subject to SORN)? Most courts conclude in the negative, reasoning that SORN is non-punitive. *See, e.g., State v. Trujillo*, 462 P.3d 550 (Ariz. 2020).

Should collateral consequences figure in Eighth Amendment proportionality analysis, or should a court at least consider their impact when determining a proper sentence? The American Bar Association has urged that the latter occur. *See* AM. BAR ASS'N., CRIMINAL JUSTICE STANDARDS, COLLATERAL SANCTIONS AND DISCRETIONARY DISQUALIFICATION OF CONVICTED PERSONS, Stnd. 19–2.4 (3d ed. 2004). The ABA Commentary elaborates that "the sentencing court should ensure that the totality of the penalty is not unduly severe and that it does not give rise to undue disparity." *Id.* comt. at 29.[33]

In recent years, "holistic lawyering" has been advanced as an approach to advocacy that does not regard "success" only as securing a "good deal," resulting in no prison time, but as one having an awareness of the broader formal and informal (such as social stigma) collateral consequences of conviction, which might be avoided or mitigated. *See generally* McGregor Smyth, *Holistic Is Not a Bad Word: A Criminal Defense Attorney's Guide to Using Invisible Punishments as an Advocacy Strategy*, 36 U. TOL. L. REV. 479 (2005).

In one of the *Padilla* passages quoted above, the Court recognized the importance of transparency of collateral consequences vis-à-vis the plea-bargaining process. Prosecutors in particular have largely unlimited charging authority and can therefore determine whether and what collateral consequences might result for a particular defendant. Of this power Professor Eisha Jain has written that

> prosecutors have powerful incentives to "prosecute" collateral consequences. . . . In some cases, this dynamic may be justified, such as where the collateral consequence is closely related to the underlying criminal conduct and it has a demonstrable and proportionate deterrent effect. But this dynamic also necessarily allows prosecutors to influence collateral consequences in more far-reaching circumstances.

Eisha Jain, *Prosecuting Collateral Consequences*, 104 GEO. L.J. 1197, 1200 (2016). In some instances, Jain suggests, a prosecutor might seek a "harsher criminal penalty in exchange for avoiding a collateral outcome.

---

potential of sex offender registration reflects a legislative determination that [the defendant] has been charged with serious crimes" and lending weight to the obligations and restraints associated with registration).

[33] For an example of a judge putting this view into effect, see United States v. Nesbeth, 188 F. Supp. 3d 179, 194–95 (E.D.N.Y. 2016) ("I have imposed a one-year term of probation. In fixing this term, I have also considered the collateral consequences Ms. Nesbeth would have faced with a longer term of probation, such as the curtailment of her right to vote and the inability to visit her father and grandmother in Jamaica because of the loss of her passport during her probationary term.").

Thus a defendant who seeks an immigration-safe plea might be required to 'plead' up to a more severe crime or serve a longer prison sentence." *Id.* at 1201.

D. BASES FOR RELIEF FROM COLLATERAL CONSEQUENCES

Mindful of the serious impediments collateral consequences impose, recent years have witnessed a proliferation of mechanisms for relief, allowing individuals to regain some or all of their rights lost as the result of a conviction, and to remove disabilities.

As briefly mentioned earlier, one area of significant reform concerns occupational prohibitions and limits on licensure. Testament to the known positive impact employment has on successful reentry (thereby increasing the number of law-abiding, tax-paying citizens), employment-focused efforts enjoy support across the political spectrum. California's "certificate of rehabilitation," for instance, limits consideration of felony convictions by licensing boards and serves as the first step in the executive pardon process. *See* Gabriel J. Chin & Eliza Hirsch, *Building a Functional Framework of Rights*, 30 FED. SENT'G REP. 282 (2018). In Ohio, a "certificate of qualification for employment" creates a rebuttable presumption that the person's criminal convictions are insufficient evidence that the person is unfit for the license, employment opportunity, or certification in question. Ohio Rev. Code Ann. §§ 2953.25, 2961.21–.24.

Certificates, which are used in roughly a dozen jurisdictions, can also mitigate or head-off other collateral consequences. In New York, for example, courts are authorized to grant "certificates of relief from disabilities" and "certificates of good conduct," allowing a broad range of relief. *See* Joy Radice, *Administering Justice: Removing Statutory Barriers to Reentry*, 83 U. COLO. L. REV. 715 (2012) (providing history of the certificates). Certificates have been backed by the American Law Institute in its Model Penal Code: Sentencing, the Uniform Law Commission, and the American Bar Association.

Research on certificates shows positive results in removing employment and housing disabilities. *See* Cara Suvall, *Certifying Second Chances*, 42 CARDOZO L. REV. 1175, 1191–96 (2021). Some research, however, suggests that the certificates have less positive impact, at least on removing employment barriers. *Id.* For this reason, some advocates for reform favor expungement and sealing, which do not rely "on the good will of employers, licensing boards, and landlords to give them effect." LOVE, ROBERTS, & LOGAN, *supra*, at 598.

Jurisdictions have also adopted laws and regulations more generally affecting employment and licensure. Many jurisdictions, for instance, have required government agencies to limit disqualifications to convictions "directly related" to particular occupations; rescinded vague "good moral character" criteria; and required justification of employment denials with written reasons that can be contested on appeal. *Id.* at 555–56.

Pardons can also play an important role in securing relief from collateral consequences, although they have been granted with decreasing frequency in recent years (see Chapter 12). Pardons can vary in their form and effect. An unconditional pardon will relieve all or most all collateral consequences. In Connecticut, a "provisional pardon" may "be limited to one or more enumerated barriers or forfeitures or may relieve the eligible offender of all barriers and forfeitures." Conn. Gen. Stat. § 54–130e(b). North Carolina has three types of pardon: pardon of forgiveness (useful in seeking employment); pardon of innocence; and unconditional pardon ("granted primarily to restore an individual's right to own or possess a firearm"). In many jurisdictions, pardons will relieve some collateral consequences but not others (e.g., the right to possess a firearm might need to be specifically restored). It can be the case, moreover, that pardons do not automatically expunge a record of criminal conviction, allowing it to be later considered, for instance, by a court.

In many jurisdictions pardons are the only way to remove a disability—for instance, with respect to the right to serve on a jury. And in jurisdictions without an opportunity for expungement, or where its availability is limited, pardon can be the only option. LOVE, ROBERTS, & LOGAN, *supra*, at 555.[34]

Recent years have also witnessed a surge of interest in mitigating the harmful effects of a criminal record more generally—"record relief," not only with respect to convictions. In addition to "ban the box" efforts, discussed earlier, jurisdictions are expanding opportunities for the expungement and sealing of criminal records. Although jurisdictions vary on the practical meaning of expungement and sealing, expungement often means that criminal records (including in electronic form) are destroyed, whereas sealing allows limited access but the records are preserved and can be used for some purposes (e.g., by law enforcement and courts). Jurisdictions can vary regarding who is eligible for expungement or sealing; for instance, only individuals convicted of non-violent crimes might be eligible, and those with more than one felony conviction might be barred.[35]

Of late, in the wake of marijuana legalization and decriminalization in multiple jurisdictions, there has been a flurry of activity directed at liberating the many thousands of individuals with marijuana conviction records. A few mechanisms expunge automatically and many others do

---

[34] In some states, governors lack the pardon authority for local offenses, and the collateral consequences they can trigger, prompting one commentator to advocate more robust local pardoning authority. *See* Hayato Watanabe, Note, *The Municipal Pardon Power*, 118 MICH. L. REV. 687, 700–05 (2020).

[35] For an up-to-date overview of current state and federal practices, see Collateral Consequences Resource Center, Restoration of Rights Project, *50-State Comparison: Expungement, Sealing & Other Record Relief*, https://ccresourcecenter.org/state-restoration-profiles/50-state-comparisonjudicial-expungement-sealing-and-set-aside/.

so by means of a general or specific petition. Stephanie Zimmermann, *Expungement Haze*, 106 A.B.A. J. 16 (April/May 2020).

Although expungement and sealing efforts are viewed by many as a positive development, some controversy exists. One concern is that although it might be charitable to "forgive" a criminal conviction, society need and should not "forget." Expungement and sealing, under this view, are inapt because they allow for concealment of criminal responsibility. Should it matter that the behavior underlying the conviction is no longer criminalized in a jurisdiction, such as with marijuana or consensual homosexual sodomy? Or should it only matter that the behavior was criminalized when the behavior was prosecuted?

Another concern is that, as a practical matter, securing record relief can pose major challenges for individuals. Petition procedures can be complicated and take considerable time and resources. As a result, according to one study of Michigan expungement, only 6.5% of individuals eligible for expungement successfully completed the state's application process within five years of eligibility (either because they did not apply or were not approved). *See* J.J. Prescott & Sonja B. Starr, *Expungement of Criminal Convictions: An Empirical Study*, 133 HARV. L. REV. 2460 (2020).[36] However, the study also found that expungement recipients had extremely low recidivism rates, compared to the general population, and major increases in wage and employment. *Id.* As a result, some jurisdictions have moved away from petition-based laws and adopted a "clean slate" strategy allowing for automatic sealing of many misdemeanors. These changes notwithstanding, concern exists that even the most ambitious efforts are no match for the far-flung and often indelible records reposed in digital databases. *See* Alessandro Corda & Sarah E. Lageson, *Disordered Punishment: Workaround Technologies of Criminal Records Disclosure and the Rise of a New Penal Entrepreneurialism*, 60 BRIT. J. CRIMINOLOGY 245 (2020).

The federal system has no established relief mechanism other than presidential pardons, which as noted have been granted at dramatically lower rates in recent years. The absence has prompted criticism from federal judges. *See, e.g., Doe v. United States*, 168 F. Supp. 3d 427, 446 (E.D.N.Y. 2016) (expressing frustration and issuing a "federal certificate of rehabilitation," hoping that it will prove "useful to present to landlords, benefits providers, and any others to whom her conviction is significant. If her attorney decides to make an application for a pardon from the President, I believe the certificate will help her make a strong case.").

---

[36] Research shows a similar disconnect between eligibility and relief with non-conviction records (e.g., regarding arrests). Multiple millions of individuals have records that are clearable under existing law but have not been cleared. *See* Colleen V. Chien, *America's Paper Prisons: The Second Chance Gap*, 119 MICH. L. REV. 519 (2020).

PROBLEM 11-1: INTER-JURISDICTIONAL CONSIDERATIONS

Larry Lanier was convicted of a sexual offense in the State of Justicia and was therefore subject to the registration and communication (SORN) laws of Justicia. After satisfying the 25-year requirement of registration and committing no other crimes (sexual or otherwise), Lanier decided to move to the State of Wonder. Out of an abundance of caution, on the very day that he arrived in Wonder, Lanier checked with law enforcement authorities to confirm that he would not be subject to the SORN laws of Wonder, which require lifetime registration of individuals with a conviction for the same offense as that committed by Lanier. Does Wonder have to "honor" the fact that Lanier was freed of SORN in Justicia? Would it matter if Lanier was instead unconditionally pardoned by the Governor of Justicia and therefore no longer subject to SORN in Justicia? What about other collateral consequences, such the right to vote or possess a firearm? For discussion of the issue, see Wayne A. Logan, *"When Mercy Seasons Justice": Interstate Recognition of Ex-Offender Rights*, 49 U.C. DAVIS L. REV. 1 (2016).

CHAPTER 12

SENTENCE REVIEW & MODIFICATION

Once a sentence is imposed in a case, there may still be many important decisions to make in the administration of that sentence, e.g., decisions by corrections officials about where precisely a prison term will be served or by the parole board as to when the defendant will be released. Such decisions, however, do not formally alter the judge's sentencing order, which continues to establish key parameters regarding the nature and duration of the defendant's punishment. Are there any ways, you might wonder, that the sentence itself might be changed? Broadly speaking, there are three pathways for sentence modification: judicial correction of a sentence that was erroneously imposed; judicial modification of a sentence based on new circumstances that were not present at the time of the original sentencing; or executive modification through clemency or otherwise. In this chapter, we consider each pathway in turn.

In general, the legal system has given great weight to the value of finality in criminal cases—once judgment is entered in the trial court, various doctrines and practices make it difficult to alter that outcome. There are, of course, certain efficiency advantages to this approach. It is also asserted that finality benefits victims and may even speed along the defendant's rehabilitation by minimizing the distraction and uncertainty created by ongoing legal proceedings. On the other hand, no sentencing judge can claim infallibility. Sentencing decisions may, for instance, be based on incomplete information, or reached through a rushed process, or excessively influenced by emotional testimony. In such cases, taking a second look at a later time may produce outcomes that better serve the recognized purposes of punishment. Moreover, even if a sentencing decision was thoughtful and well-informed at the time it was made, the defendant's circumstances may change in important and unforeseen ways before the sentence term is complete; revisiting the sentence in such cases may also better serve the purposes of punishment. There might also be an intervening change in some relevant body of law, such as with the recent legalization of marijuana in several states. Additionally, careful review of sentences by a centralized authority, such as an appellate court, may help to smooth out some of the unwarranted disparities that can result from the idiosyncrasies of individual judges.

In short, there seems a need to balance the virtues of finality against those of review and adjustment. As you read the material in this chapter, consider whether you think American law gets the balance right.

A. CORRECTION OF ERRONEOUSLY IMPOSED SENTENCES

Putting to one side states with presumptive guidelines systems, the choice of a sentence within a statutory range is generally treated as a decision that is committed to the discretion of the sentencing judge. As such, the sentencing decision is reviewed with a high degree of deference on appeal. Michael O'Hear, *Appellate Review of Sentences: Reconsidering Deference*, 51 WM. & MARY L. REV. 2123 (2010). Appellate courts typically employ some variation of the abuse-of-discretion standard of review, which has led to a steady stream of summary affirmances. The following decision is unusual for its self-conscious effort to clarify and strengthen abuse-of-discretion review, although the ultimate outcome may strike you as still quite reflective of the deference that normally prevails in this area of appellate practice.

State v. Gallion

678 N.W.2d 197 (Wis. 2004)

■ BRADLEY, J.

> In all Anglo-American jurisprudence a principal obligation of the judge is to explain the reasons for his actions. His decisions will not be understood by the people and cannot be reviewed by the appellate courts unless the reasons for decisions can be examined. It is thus apparent that requisite to a prima facie valid sentence is a statement by the trial judge detailing his reasons for selecting the particular sentence imposed.

McCleary v. State, 49 Wis. 2d 263, 280–81, 182 N.W.2d 512 (1971).

Those words are as true today as they were when they first appeared in *McCleary*. Yet, sentencing courts have strayed from the directive. Instead, for some, merely uttering the facts, invoking sentencing factors, and pronouncing a sentence is deemed sufficient. Such an approach confuses the exercise of discretion with decision-making.

As the *McCleary* court instructed, evidence of the exercise of discretion must be set forth on the record: "there must be evidence that discretion was in fact exercised. Discretion is not synonymous with decision-making. Rather, the term contemplates a process of reasoning."

Now, in the wake of truth-in-sentencing legislation, we reinvigorate the *McCleary* directive that the exercise of sentencing discretion must be set forth on the record. Although we do not change the appellate standard of review, appellate courts are required to more closely scrutinize the record to ensure that "discretion was in fact exercised and the basis of that exercise of discretion [is] set forth." * * *

Curtis Gallion seeks review of a published court of appeals decision that affirmed a judgment convicting him of homicide by intoxicated use of a motor vehicle. He asserts that the circuit court [i.e., the trial court] erroneously exercised its discretion in failing to provide an adequate explanation for the sentence given, citing *McCleary*. * * *

On March 3, 2000, at about 1:30 a.m., Gallion was drunk and driving his car at a high rate of speed in Milwaukee. He ran a red light and collided with another vehicle, crashing into its side. Vanessa Brown, a passenger in the other car, was killed by the collision. * * *

I

Two months later, Gallion entered a plea of guilty to homicide by intoxicated use of a motor vehicle. * * *

At sentencing, the circuit court heard testimony from Brown's mother, father, teacher, and employer. The court also received several letters from her relatives and associates. Both the witnesses and writers addressed Brown's admirable qualities along with the impact her death had on their lives.

[The court] sentenced Gallion to 21 years of confinement followed by 9 years of extended supervision. The maximum penalty for the offense was 40 years of confinement, followed by 20 years of extended supervision. * * *

II

It is a well-settled principle of law that a circuit court exercises discretion at sentencing. On appeal, review is limited to determining if discretion was erroneously exercised. When discretion is exercised on the basis of clearly irrelevant or improper factors, there is an erroneous exercise of discretion.

On review, "in any instance where the exercise of discretion has been demonstrated, [the appellate court] follows a consistent and strong policy against interference with the discretion of the trial court in passing sentence." *McCleary*, 49 Wis. 2d at 281. "Sentencing decisions of the circuit court are generally afforded a strong presumption of reasonability because the circuit court is best suited to consider the relevant factors and demeanor of the convicted defendant." *State v. Borrell*, 167 Wis. 2d 749, 781 (1992). "Appellate judges should not substitute their preference for a sentence merely because, had they been in the trial judge's position, they would have meted out a different sentence." *McCleary*, 49 Wis. 2d at 281.

The *McCleary* court summarized the reasoning process necessary to facilitate appellate review:

> The term [discretion] contemplates a process of reasoning. This process must depend on facts that are of record or that are reasonably derived by inference from the record and a conclusion based on a logical rationale founded upon proper legal standards.

Id. at 277.

III * * *

We believe that *McCleary* was and still is one of the best statements addressing how a circuit court should exercise its discretion. As we noted, there has been a regrettable disconnect, however, between its principles as-stated and its principles as-applied. This disconnect has resulted in a more mechanical form of sentencing: as long as the sentencing transcript reflects that the circuit court enunciates the primary sentencing factors and discusses the facts, followed by the imposition of an ultimate sentence, it has properly exercised its discretion.

Apparently concerned with this approach, the court of appeals recently asked this court to "clarify the showing necessary to overcome the presumption that a trial court has properly exercised its sentencing discretion." Certification by Court of Appeals of Wisconsin, *State v. Crouthers,* 2000 WI 121, p. 1. The court explained:

> The collective memory of the panel members assigned to this appeal could not produce any ready examples of cases since [*McCleary*] in which an appellate court overturned a sentence determination, absent the use of an improper factor or other illegality. . . .
>
> There appears to be some truth to the appellant's contention that a trial court that articulates the magic words "seriousness of the offense," "character of the offender" and "need to protect the public" will avoid any meaningful review of the sentence it imposes.

Id. at 2. * * *

With the advent of truth-in-sentencing [i.e., the abolition of discretionary parole release in 1998], we recognize a greater need to articulate on the record the reasons for the particular sentence imposed. Under the old, indeterminate system, sentencing discretion was shared among all three branches of government. The legislature set the maximum penalty and the manner of its enforcement; the courts imposed an indeterminate term; and the executive branch, through the parole board, determined how much of that term was going to be served. Under truth-in-sentencing legislation, the executive role has been diminished with the elimination of parole. The legislative role is limited to setting the parameters of the penalty. As a result, the judiciary's responsibility for ensuring a fair and just sentence has significantly increased. * * *

Previously the sentencing court had only modest control over the length of time actually spent in prison. Judges were thought to possess inadequate information to address the future progress of the inmate. Instead, only prison officials with sustained contacts with the inmate were thought to be in a position to determine if the rehabilitative efforts had been successful. Likewise, if the inmate was determined to be incorrigible over the years, it was thought that the on-the-scene prison officials advising the parole board were better positioned to assess the inmate's dangerousness and commensurate need for additional prison time.

Parole boards, in essence, served as a check on sentencing courts' exercise of discretion. Under truth-in-sentencing legislation, parole is abolished and that check is removed. * * *

In light of the increased responsibility placed upon the sentencing court, we reaffirm *McCleary*'s sentencing standards and reexamine the manner in which they are to be applied. What has previously been satisfied with implied rationale must now be set forth on the record. * * *

A basic framework for this process of reasoning that demonstrates the exercise of sentencing discretion has previously been set forth for sentencing courts. Circuit courts are required to specify the objectives of the sentence on the record. These objectives include, but are not limited to, the protection of the community, punishment of the defendant, rehabilitation of the defendant, and deterrence to others.

Courts are to identify the general objectives of greatest importance. These may vary from case to case. In some cases, punishment and protection of the community may be the dominant objectives. In others, rehabilitation of the defendant and victim restitution may be of greater import. Still others may have deterrence or a restorative justice approach as a primary objective.

Courts are to describe the facts relevant to these objectives. Courts must explain, in light of the facts of the case, why the particular component parts of the sentence imposed advance the specified objectives.

Courts must also identify the factors that were considered in arriving at the sentence and indicate how those factors fit the objectives and influence the decision. * * *

In each case, the sentence imposed shall "call for the minimum amount of custody or confinement which is consistent with the protection of the public, the gravity of the offense and the rehabilitative needs of the defendant." *McCleary,* 49 Wis. 2d at 276. Accordingly, the circuit courts should consider probation as the first alternative. Probation should be the disposition unless: confinement is necessary to protect the public, the offender needs correctional treatment available only in confinement, or it would unduly depreciate the seriousness of the offense.

If a circuit court imposes probation, it shall explain why the conditions of probation should be expected to advance the objectives it has specified. Likewise, if a circuit court imposes jail or prison, it shall explain why the duration of incarceration should be expected to advance the objectives it has specified. * * *

Because we recognize the difficulty in providing a reasoned explanation in isolation, we encourage circuit courts to refer to information provided by others. Courts may use counsels' recommendations for the nature and duration of the sentence and the recommendations of the presentence report as touchstones in their reasoning. Courts may also consider information about the distribution of sentences in cases similar to the case before it. * * *

We are mindful that the exercise of discretion does not lend itself to mathematical precision. The exercise of discretion, by its very nature, is not amenable to such a task. As a result, we do not expect circuit courts to explain, for instance, the difference between sentences of 15 and 17 years. We do expect, however, an explanation for the general range of the sentence imposed. This explanation is not intended to be a semantic trap for circuit courts. It is also not intended to be a call for more "magic words." Rather, the requirement of an on-the-record explanation will serve to fulfill the *McCleary* mandate that discretion of a sentencing judge be exercised on a "rational and explainable basis." This will assist appellate courts in determining whether the circuit court properly exercised its discretion. * * *

The rule of law suffers when the sentencing judge's discretion is unguided and unchecked. The rationale for sentencing decisions must be made knowable and subject to review. * * *

IV

* * * Gallion's first claim is that the circuit court committed error in not providing an adequate explanation for the sentence imposed. Specifically, he contends that re-sentencing is required in light of the circuit court's failure to describe the comparative weight given to the factors it identified, or to explain why the sentence constitutes the minimum amount of necessary confinement. Gallion complains, "almost any number of years in prison could be plugged in [the sentence imposed]." He further asserts that, "the court never stated how much incarceration was needed to accomplish rehabilitation/protection, or how, or why, 21 years of incarceration was needed . . . ." * * *

Accordingly, we examine the circuit court's actions under the law as it has been understood since *McCleary*. That law emphasized the delineation of the primary sentencing factors to the particular facts of the case. Here, the circuit court's explanation, which spans 20 pages of transcript, provides ample evidence of that.

With respect to the gravity of the offense, the circuit court focused on the recklessness of Gallion's behavior and the consequences of his actions. It stated:

> What brings you here today is a vehicular homicide. You drank and drank and drank to excess. You were almost two and a half times the legal limit. You got behind the wheel of a car. You drove it recklessly, irresponsibly, excessively, like your drinking. You went through the intersection of 35th and Locust, struck the car that Vanessa Brown was riding in and extinguished her life.

The court further impressed upon Gallion that his crime would forever affect the victim's friends, co-workers, and family, especially her three-year-old son.

In considering Gallion's character, the circuit court again discussed particularized facts. It stated that Gallion was a young man with limited education and employment history. Additionally, it recognized that he suffered from a severe drug and alcohol dependency. After examining his prior criminal record, however, the court concluded that Gallion did not have a good track record in trying to turn around his life. It seemed especially concerned with the fact that he had not taken advantage of the treatment options offered to him in the past.

Finally, the circuit court took into account the need to protect the public from Gallion and others like him. It determined that the defendant could best accomplish his rehabilitation in an institutional setting. The court also observed that society has an interest in punishing Gallion so that his sentence might serve as a general deterrence against drunk driving.

After considering these factors, the circuit court identified the recommendations of the defense counsel and presentence report writer. It further recognized that it was imposing a truth-in-sentencing disposition. The court then arrived at a sentence it believed was fair and just "given the nature of this specific crime, given who [Gallion is], and the interest of the community as a whole." Upon examining the circuit court's actions under the law as it has been understood since *McCleary*, we are satisfied that the circuit court properly exercised its discretion. * * *

NOTES & QUESTIONS

1. **Process and Substance.** As *Gallion* illustrates, in practice, abuse-of-discretion review tends to collapse into an assessment of the sentencing judge's reasoning *process*, as set forth on the record. At one level, by criticizing the practice of affirming sentences whenever the trial judge mumbles "magic words" like "seriousness of the offense" or "character of the offender," the court seemed to be straining against purely procedural understandings of abuse-of-discretion review. Yet, when articulating what sentencing judges *should* be doing—and, by extension, what appellate courts should be looking for when reviewing their handiwork—the *Gallion* court seemed to fall back on a set of procedural requirements. Based on *Gallion*, appellate courts might reasonably envision their role in terms of a checklist:

- Did the sentencing judge state a permissible purpose for the sentence?
- Did the sentencing judge explicitly identify any case-specific factors relevant to that purpose?
- Did the sentencing judge state a reason for the general severity of the sentence?

- Did the sentencing judge avoid mentioning any impermissible purposes or factors?

The court's application of its general principles seems to underscore their essentially procedural character. Does it seem to you that the court offered a meaningful response to Gallion's charge that "almost any number of years in prison could [have been] plugged" into the judge's pronouncement of the sentence? Couldn't the trial judge's reasoning as easily support a prison term half as long or twice as long as Gallion actually got? As long as some reasoning is stated on the record, *Gallion* suggests, appellate courts need not worry much about how persuasively the reasoning justifies the specific sentence imposed.

Absent from *Gallion* is any indication that appellate courts should review the proportionality of sentences, which would be a form of substantive evaluation. As we saw in Chapter 6, the Supreme Court has developed a test of sorts for constitutional proportionality review—although it is so deferential as to have little practical importance outside the context of capital or, to a much lesser extent, life-without-parole sentences. In principle, more rigorous forms of proportionality review *might* be woven into the abuse-of-discretion analysis, but courts have shied away from doing so. Why do you suppose that is? Similarly, from a utilitarian standpoint, appellate courts *might* assess whether sentences are substantively cost-benefit-justified but have generally refrained from doing so.

2. **Demeanor.** As appellate courts commonly do, the *Gallion* court justified deference to the sentencing judge based, in part, on the judge's access to demeanor evidence. Why do you think demeanor might matter in the selection of a sentence?

Demeanor evidence is sometimes said to help the sentencing judge determine whether the defendant is genuinely remorseful or not. Michael O'Hear, *Appellate Review of Sentences: Reconsidering Deference*, 51 WM. & MARY L. REV. 2123, 2125 (2010). The relevance of demeanor might thus depend on the relevance of remorse, which is a contested matter, as you may recall from the discussion of post-offense conduct in Chapter 4. Even assuming remorse is relevant, how helpful is demeanor to assessing remorse, as opposed, for instance, to concrete actions like making voluntary restitution? *See id.* at 2142–47 (discussing psychological evidence suggesting that judges may not be able to evaluate demeanor evidence reliably). *See also* M. Eve Hanan, *Remorse Bias*, 83 MO. L. REV. 301, 306 (2018) ("Because the decision whether to believe a defendant's expression of remorse is profoundly subjective, it is a fertile area in which implicit bias can flourish and lead to sentencing disparity.").

If demeanor evidence has little value to the sentencing decision, are there any other persuasive justifications for appellate deference?

3. **Parole and Appellate Review.** Traditions of appellate deference became entrenched during the time when discretionary parole was a ubiquitous feature of the American correctional system. As *Gallion* points out, the parole board could function, very loosely, as a sort of appellate tribunal. In making release decisions, the board could reevaluate the same

factors considered by the sentencing judge, as well as take into account new information regarding the prisoner's rehabilitative progress (or backsliding). Moreover, as a centralized body, the board might smooth out judge-to-judge sentencing disparities by ensuring some consistency in the time-to-release of similarly situated defendants.

The subsequent abolition of discretionary parole (in some states) and restrictions on board discretion (in others) have limited the ability of many parole boards to serve as a check on the sentencing judge. Do these developments call for more rigorous review of sentences by appellate courts?

4. **Benchmarks.** Substantive review of a sentence is difficult without benchmarks for comparison. *Gallion* suggested a few possible benchmarks for use by trial judges: "Courts may use counsels' recommendations for the nature and duration of the sentence and the recommendations of the presentence report as touchstones in their reasoning. Courts may also consider information about the distribution of sentences in cases similar to the case before it." Do these strike you as appropriate benchmarks? Why do you suppose the *Gallion* court did not make use of any of these benchmarks in its own review of Gallion's sentence?

Another benchmark of sorts is suggested by the court's indication that probation should always be considered as the first alternative. This principle might usefully anchor the analysis in many cases at both the trial- and appellate-court levels. It seems less helpful, however, in cases like *Gallion* itself, where the severity of the crime makes probation an unlikely disposition and requires the choice of a prison term from within a very wide range (anything up to forty years).

5. **Common Law.** *Gallion* (faintly) echoes the call of many commentators for a more robust "common law of sentencing." *See, e.g.*, Douglas A. Berman, *A Common Law for This Age of Federal Sentencing: The Opportunity and Need for Judicial Lawmaking*, 11 STAN. L. & POL'Y REV. 93 (1999). Much as appellate courts have historically developed, elaborated, clarified, and modified key principles of tort and contract law through the time-honored process of case-by-case adjudication, they might do the same for sentencing law. Consider, for instance, the many, varied statements about defendant personal characteristics (age, family responsibilities, military service, etc.) that are included in the federal sentencing guidelines (see Chapter 4). In a state without sentencing guidelines, it is possible to imagine the appellate courts making a similar set of pronouncements through case decisions over time, categorizing various sentencing factors as prohibited, generally permissible, or discouraged and limited to unusual circumstances. Doing so might help to bring greater consistency and coherence to sentencing practice in the state. However, outside a few guidelines jurisdictions, the common law of sentencing tends to be anemic at best.

Should legislatures encourage the development of a common law in this area? One possibility might be to adopt a provision of the MPC:S that expressly authorizes appellate courts to review sentences for proportionality. This subconstitutional proportionality review is intended to be more rigorous than the deferential proportionality review under the Eighth Amendment. MPC:S § 7.09 cmmnt. f(2). Appellate courts engaged in this substantive analysis might over time develop a body of case law that has legal force and that provides more meaningful sentencing guidance for lower courts.

6. **Appellate Review in Presumptive Guidelines States.** Appellate review can take on a quite different character in jurisdictions that have presumptive sentencing guidelines. The guidelines become the crucial benchmark against which sentences are assessed. Appellate courts may play an active role in policing compliance with the guidelines by ensuring that "departures" are adequately justified. Indeed, when a sentencing judge offers a ground for departure that is not enumerated in the relevant statutes or guidelines, appellate courts generally treat the propriety of that ground as a question of law that is reviewed de novo (i.e., with no deference). MPC:S § 7.09 rptrs. note (f)(1). The appellate courts in different states have varied in their receptivity to new departure grounds, with the Washington Supreme Court reputed to be the most restrictive. *Id.* However, if a permissible ground for departure is identified, sentencing decisions are normally reviewed deferentially, as are decisions *not* to depart. The standards of review in these cases are often framed as abuse of discretion or something similar. *See id.* note (f)(4) (citing examples).

7. **Appellate Review in the Post-*Booker* Federal System.** In Chapter 3, we considered the impact of the Supreme Court's decision in *United States v. Booker*, 543 U.S. 220 (2005), on appellate review in the federal system. Key features of the post-*Booker* system include:

- Sentences are reviewed for "reasonableness," which the Supreme Court has associated with the abuse-of-discretion standard.
- The appellate court must first ensure that the district court committed no significant procedural error, e.g., miscalculating the advisory guidelines range, treating the guidelines as mandatory, or failing to explain the chosen sentence.
- The appellate court must then review the substantive reasonableness of the sentence. In so doing, the appellate court may—but is not required to—accord a presumption of reasonableness to a sentence within a properly calculated guidelines range. However, a sentence outside the range may not be treated as presumptively unreasonable.
- For a sentence outside the range, the appellate court may take into account the extent of the deviation from the range in assessing the sentence's reasonableness.

See Rita v. United States, 552 U.S. 85 (2007); *Gall v. United States*, 552 U.S. 38 (2007).

These principles apply specifically to the federal system but may also have some relevance to state systems insofar as they have been developed under the shadow of the *Apprendi* doctrine. If a state appellate court engages in more rigorous appellate review than the Supreme Court has approved for the federal system—and particularly if the state court establishes more definite limits on the severity of sentences that can be imposed in the absence of specific aggravating factors—then the state court risks triggering the right of defendants to jury fact-finding beyond a reasonable doubt as to those factors.

8. **Government Appeals.** The Double Jeopardy Clause prohibits the government from appealing an acquittal. However, the Clause generally permits the government to appeal what it perceives to be unduly lenient sentences. *United States v. DiFrancesco*, 449 U.S. 117 (1980). As the Supreme Court has observed, "The imposition of a particular sentence usually is not regarded as an 'acquittal' of any more severe sentence that could have been imposed." *Bullington v. Missouri*, 451 U.S. 430, 438 (1981). Although government sentence appeals are restricted in a few states, they are permitted in the great majority of U.S. jurisdictions, including the federal system. MPC:S § 7.09 cmmnt. c.

9. **Sentence Appeal Waivers.** Other than the difficulties of reconciling appellate review with the *Apprendi* doctrine, the most controversial issue relating to sentence appeals in recent years has likely been the defendant's waiver of appellate rights through plea bargaining. In some jurisdictions, prosecutors routinely insist that defendants waive their right to appeal the sentence as a condition of entering into a plea agreement. Such waivers are usually defended on efficiency grounds. However, the criticisms have been many:

> Waivers are unconstitutional, opponents first argued, because there could be no knowing waiver of potential future errors that might occur at a proceeding that had yet to take place. Because sentencing had yet to take place, defendants could not possibly know and the judge at the plea proceeding could not describe what claims defendants were waiving. Opponents also protested that waiver is not a condition over which criminal defendants can bargain. They argued that to promote appeal waivers was to promote contracts of adhesion. Third, critics pointed out that trial judges and attorneys should not be encouraged to insulate from review their own past and future misconduct through waiver of direct and collateral review. Finally, waivers were assailed as bad policy because they undercut the function of appellate courts in regulating the sentencing process.

Nancy J. King & Michael E. O'Neill, *Appeal Waivers and the Future of Sentencing Policy*, 55 DUKE L.J. 209, 222–23 (2005) (citations and internal quotation marks omitted).

Despite these criticisms, appellate courts (self-servingly?) have generally upheld the validity of sentence appeal waivers—albeit sometimes with exceptions for certain types of claims, such as ineffective assistance of sentencing counsel. MPC:S § 7.09 cmmnt. e. The MPC:S includes a categorical ban on sentence appeal waivers. § 7.09(4).

10. **Forfeiture and Harmless Error.** Various general doctrines governing appellate practice may limit a party's ability to obtain relief for errors made by a sentencing judge. Two doctrines of particular importance

are the forfeiture and harmless error rules. First, if a party fails to make a timely objection to an error in the trial court, the issue is deemed forfeited; correction on appeal is only permitted if the error rises to the level of "plain error." The concept of "plain error" suffers from chronic ambiguity but is often understood to include both egregiousness (i.e., the error was beyond any reasonable debate) and adverse impact (i.e., the error led to an unfair outcome for the complaining party). *See* Brandon L. Garrett, *Accuracy in Sentencing*, 87 S. CAL. L. REV. 499, 520–21 (2014).

Second, even if a timely objection was raised regarding the sentencing judge's error, the error will not lead to a resentencing if the appellate court deems it "harmless." This is the jurisprudential equivalent of the old "no harm, no foul" rule of the playground. For instance, in the federal system, if a district judge miscalculates a defendant's sentencing guidelines range, the sentence will not be reversed on appeal if the district judge made sufficiently clear that the sentence would have been imposed regardless of the guidelines calculation. *See, e.g., United States v. Alvarez-Carvajal*, 2 F.4th 688 (7th Cir. 2021).

For a difficult case implicating both doctrines, consider the facts of *State v. Coffee*, 937 N.W.2d 579 (Wis. 2020). Coffee pled guilty to a set of charges arising from a pair of attempted armed robberies. At his sentencing, in arguing for a "substantial" prison term, the prosecutor reviewed Coffee's list of prior convictions and police contacts. In so doing, the prosecutor erroneously reported that Coffee had a prior arrest for *armed* robbery, when the arrest had actually been for unarmed robbery. However, Coffee's lawyer did not object or attempt to correct the error. Later in the hearing, the sentencing judge himself repeated the mistaken assertion about the prior armed robbery. On appeal, Coffee argued that he had been improperly sentenced on the basis of inaccurate information. The state countered that Coffee had forfeited the issue by failing to raise it at sentencing.

A fractured Wisconsin Supreme Court rejected the forfeiture argument. A majority of the justices agreed that "the forfeiture rule does not apply to previously unknown, inaccurate information first raised by the State at sentencing." *Id.* at 582 (plurality); *Id.* at 596 (Bradley, J., dissenting). The justices reasoned, "[I]f the forfeiture rule does not apply to challenges to this type of spontaneously raised information, then defense counsel has time to evaluate the information, discuss it with the defendant, determine if it is indeed inaccurate, and ascertain whether it was actually relied on at sentencing." *Id.* at 588 (plurality).

However, a different grouping of justices ruled, by a narrow 4–3 margin, that the sentencing judge's reliance on inaccurate information had been harmless. The majority observed that the sentencing judge had only referred twice to the inaccurate information and only in a preliminary phase of the proceeding. When actually imposing sentence, the judge emphasized several other considerations as justification for Coffee's thirteen-year prison term. The majority concluded "beyond a reasonable doubt that the State has met its burden to demonstrate that the circuit court's remarks and conclusions at Coffee's sentencing would have been the same absent the inaccurate information." *Id.* at 591.

Review question: If the inaccurate-information issue had been deemed forfeited, would Coffee have had a viable Sixth Amendment claim of ineffective assistance of counsel? See Chapter 3 for the two-part ineffectiveness test.

11. **Resentencing and Vindictiveness.** If a defendant prevails in a sentencing appeal, the result will typically be a return to the trial court for resentencing. Depending on the original sentence and the grounds for reversal, it might be possible for the defendant to receive an even longer sentence the second time around. For instance, if Gallion's sentence had been overturned for inadequate explanation, or Coffee's because it was based on inaccurate information, it is conceivable that either might have ended up with a longer prison term after remand. However, when a sentence is lengthened following a successful appeal, there may be concerns that the sentencing judge acted vindictively toward the defendant for the defendant's temerity in challenging the first judgment.

The Supreme Court has indicated that such vindictiveness at sentencing would violate constitutional due process requirements. The Court has not categorically prohibited a harsher outcome at resentencing, but has required an appropriate, non-vindictive explanation. More specifically, in *North Carolina v. Pearce*, 395 U.S. 711 (1969), the Court held:

> Due process of law, then, requires that vindictiveness against a defendant for having successfully attacked his first conviction must play no part in the sentence he receives after a new trial. And since the fear of such vindictiveness may unconstitutionally deter a defendant's exercise of the right to appeal or collaterally attack his first conviction, due process also requires that a defendant be freed of apprehension of such a retaliatory motivation on the part of the sentencing judge.
>
> In order to assure the absence of such a motivation, we have concluded that whenever a judge imposes a more severe sentence upon a defendant after a new trial, the reasons for his doing so must affirmatively appear. Those reasons must be based upon objective information concerning identifiable conduct on the part of the defendant occurring after the time of the original sentencing proceeding. And the factual data upon which the increased sentence is based must be made part of the record, so that the constitutional legitimacy of the increased sentence may be fully reviewed on appeal.

Id. at 725–26.

In order to avoid concerns about even an appearance of vindictiveness, appellate courts occasionally remand with instructions that a new judge should handle the resentencing. Sometimes, the concern may even be with perceived bias against the *prosecution*. For instance, in *United States v. Khan*, 997 F.3d 242 (5th Cir. 2021), the defendant was initially given a sentence below the guidelines range, and the government appealed. The Fifth Circuit reversed on procedural grounds, but on remand the district judge reimposed the same sentence. Again, the government appealed, and the Fifth Circuit reversed on grounds of substantive unreasonableness. The Fifth Circuit then remanded with instructions for reassignment "because of the judge's fixed and inflexible view of the case—and his statements evincing bias against the government as a party." *Id.* at 250.

12. **"May I Have a Refund?"** Shannon Nelson was convicted of various child-abuse offenses in Colorado state court. She was sentenced to prison and ordered to pay more than $8,000 in restitution, costs, and fees. Nelson began serving her prison term while her appeal was pending. The Colorado Department of Corrections withheld $702.10 from her inmate account as partial payment for her economic sanctions. Eventually, Nelson won her appeal. A new trial was ordered, and she was acquitted. She sought repayment of the $702.10 that had been taken from her account but was rebuffed. A state statute required her to file a civil claim for her refund and prove her innocence by clear and convincing evidence. Does that seem fair to you?

The U.S. Supreme Court thought not. The Court held that "[t]o comport with due process, a State may not impose anything more than minimal procedures on the refund of exactions dependent upon a conviction subsequently invalidated." *Nelson v. Colorado*, 137 S. Ct. 1249, 1258 (2017). Requiring the defendant to prove her innocence went beyond the "minimal procedures" that the state was permitted to impose.

13. **Mootness.** As illustrated by *Nelson*, defendants commonly begin to serve their sentences immediately after they are imposed, even if an appeal is anticipated. The law provides for the possibility of release pending appeal, but the standards are often much higher than they are for pretrial release. *See, e.g.*, 18 U.S.C. § 3143(b). As a result, if the sentence is unusually short or the appellate process unusually protracted, the defendant's sentence could be completed before there is a final decision in the case. In such circumstances, the appeal of the defendant's sentence *might* be dismissed as moot. However, because some collateral consequences and recidivism enhancements are tied to sentence length, the defendant might still be able to show that his or her sentence appeal presents a live issue despite completion of the sentence. *See United States v. Prophet*, 989 F.3d 231 (3d Cir. 2021).

14. **Collateral Attack.** What if a defendant appeals his or her *conviction*, but neglects to raise what might have been a meritorious sentencing issue? Or perhaps fails to file a timely direct appeal at all? If the sentencing judge committed an error, the defendant is usually best served by raising the issue as part of the direct appeal of the trial court's judgment. However, if the sentencing issue is not raised in a direct appeal, it may still be possible to do so through a "collateral" attack on the judgment. A collateral challenge normally begins in the same trial court that entered the judgment. Depending on the jurisdiction and the nature of the issues raised, the collateral challenge may take the form of a petition for a writ of habeas corpus or error coram nobis, or a motion under a modern statute that supersedes the common-law writs. For instance, a defendant who has been sentenced in federal court would normally make a motion under 28 U.S.C. § 2255 for collateral relief.

If a *state*-court sentencing judge has committed an error of constitutional dimensions, the defendant may undertake a collateral attack in federal court under 28 U.S.C. § 2254. However, the defendant is normally required to exhaust his or her state remedies first.

The procedural law governing collateral challenges is enormously complicated, and a detailed exploration lies well beyond the scope of this book. For present purposes, there are simply two points we would emphasize. First, the standards for obtaining relief through a collateral attack tend to be even higher than they are for winning a direct appeal. For instance, defendants are often required to show good cause for their failure to raise an issue on direct appeal or in an earlier collateral proceeding. *See, e.g.*, *Wainwright v. Sykes*, 433 U.S. 72 (1977).

Second, there is no federal constitutional right to counsel for collateral challenges. *Pennsylvania v. Finley*, 481 U.S. 551 (1987). As a result, habeas corpus petitions and the like are frequently filed by prisoners acting *pro se*. If a petition seems to have some possible merit, judges often have the power to appoint a lawyer to move the case forward. *See, e.g.*, 28 U.S.C. § 2255(g). But if a prisoner is unable on his or her own to indicate the legal and factual bases of a colorable claim in the initial petition—whether due to cognitive impairments, low educational attainment, poor access to law library resources, or otherwise—then the petition may be dismissed without the judge ever being aware of its potential merit. For this reason, a few states have chosen as a matter of state law to recognize a right to counsel at least for a person's first collateral challenge. *See, e.g.*, Pa. R. Crim. P. 904 ("[W]hen an unrepresented defendant satisfies the judge that the defendant is unable to afford or otherwise procure counsel, the judge shall appoint counsel to represent the defendant on the defendant's first petition for post-conviction collateral relief.").

B. JUDICIAL MODIFICATION BASED ON NEW CIRCUMSTANCES

In Chapter 8, we considered the normally quite broad discretion of sentencing judges to modify the terms and conditions of community supervision based on new circumstances. For instance, if a defendant who is on probation begins to miss required meetings with his or her PO, the judge might impose a new community service condition as a sanction. Or, if the difficulties stem from new demands on the defendant's schedule from, say, employment or childcare obligations, the judge might change the meeting condition so as to better accommodate those changed circumstances.

By contrast, judges have traditionally had much less discretion to modify terms of *incarceration* once they are imposed. These limitations may have seemed sensible enough when discretionary parole release was available in all states. After all, it was the parole board's job to evaluate new circumstances and decide whether release of the defendant was appropriate. A mechanism for judicial modification of the sentence might have seemed redundant and perhaps even a violation of the principle of separation of powers. Today, however, with discretionary parole abolished in many U.S. jurisdictions and sharply curtailed in many others, calls have arisen for strengthening the mechanisms of judicial sentence modification. As detailed in the following article, a small number of jurisdictions already have robust mechanisms in their laws, although these mechanisms are not necessarily utilized much in practice.

Cecelia Klingele, Changing the Sentence Without Hiding the Truth: Judicial Sentence Modification as a Promising Method of Early Release

52 WM. & MARY L. REV. 465 (2010)

* * *

In order to obtain more immediate cost savings and relief from overcrowding, many states have begun to question the necessity of long, predictable prison sentences. Through new legislation, many states have begun to ameliorate the effects of harsh prison sentences by reintroducing old forms of early release and developing new methods as well. The most common early release mechanisms in use today fall into three general categories: increased parole eligibility, reinstatement or expansion of sentence credit, and creation of infirmity-based release for geriatric and seriously ill prisoners. * * *

With rare exception, the early release mechanisms share a common feature: they are controlled by departments of corrections or parole boards. Allowing executive officials to administer early release provides several obvious benefits. Prison officials are uniquely aware of institutional capacity constraints and are therefore well positioned to award sentence credit or grant early release in ways that are targeted to the needs of the institution. Consequently, insofar as new laws are designed to provide relief to prisons in the form of cost savings and extra bed space, allowing executive agencies to control release decisions makes sense.

History demonstrates, however, that executive release decisions are subject to numerous criticisms. Their sensitivity to institutional concerns often comes at the expense of community worries about public safety and the legitimacy of sentencing decisions. Exacerbating lack of public trust is the absence of transparency in parole board and prison administrative decisions. * * *

III. An Alternative Mechanism: Judicial Sentence Modification * * *

A. Historical Roots

In its earliest form, sentence modification can be traced back to English common law. In the days when trial courts did not hold session year-round but instead divided their work into terms, as many courts of last resort do to this day, the rule was simple: when a court imposed sentence, or entered any other judicial order, for that matter, it retained unlimited power to change the disposition throughout the term in which the order was entered. So long as the term remained in session, the defendant's sentence could be altered. Once the term expired, however, the court lost jurisdiction over the sentence and could no longer modify any of its lawfully imposed provisions for any reason.

Over time, some jurisdictions abandoned the practice of holding terms at the trial court level. In jurisdictions where the practice of holding terms persisted, many courts began to modify the strict time limits traditionally associated with the common law rule, allowing trial courts to rule on timely filed motions for sentence modification even after the term had come to an end. In some cases, courts held these timely filed motions indefinitely, delaying modification until years after a defendant had begun serving his sentence. This practice, which was known colloquially as "bench parole," was criticized by prison officials and others who believed it constituted a judicial interference with the release power of executively controlled parole boards.

In 1946, the federal government enacted the first version of Federal Rule of Criminal Procedure 35(b), a rule that would later become the model for many state sentence modification provisions. In its original form, the rule provided that a court could reduce a sentence for any reason within sixty days of its imposition, either on motion by the defense or sua sponte. After sixty days, the court lost jurisdiction over the sentence entirely and could no longer change its length or conditions, regardless of whether the court's term had ended. At the time the law was enacted, legislators and prison officials alike expressed support for the provision, contending that it would "limit the time within which a court could exercise control over its judgments, reduce the potential for court infringement on Parole Commission authority over release determinations, and eliminate the overloading of court dockets with superfluous Rule 35(b) motions." Later, the statute was revised to expand the time for filing motions for sentence reduction from 60 to 120 days and to clarify that courts were required to rule on motions "within a reasonable time" after their filing.

Beginning shortly after Rule 35(b)'s original enactment, state courts around the country started to adopt versions of Rule 35. Like the original federal rule, these state analog statutes provided short time limits within which sentences could be reduced. Even after the federal system abandoned the original Rule 35(b) as part of its move to determinate sentencing in the 1980s, most states retained their analog statutes. As a result, most state courts are authorized to exercise jurisdiction to modify lawfully imposed sentences for a brief period ranging from thirty days to one year after a sentence is lawfully imposed.

B. Modern Use

Within the states that utilize Rule 35(b) analog statutes, data on the number of motions filed and granted is extremely difficult to obtain. There is no evidence that such motions are granted with any regularity, and it is easy to hypothesize why motions filed under Rule 35 analogs would rarely be successful. Given the brief amount of time between the original sentencing and the expiration of the trial court's jurisdiction to modify under these statutes, it is difficult to imagine circumstances in which relevant facts or circumstances would change in a way that would justify a principled alteration in the original sentence. * * *

Although it is true that early versions of Federal Rule of Criminal Procedure 35(b) and its later state analogs represent the most traditional form of judicial sentence modification, they are not the only form of the mechanism. While judicial sentence modification remains a fairly unusual phenomenon, courts and legislatures across the country have found ways to permit courts to retain jurisdiction over their sentences beyond the strict time limits provided by traditional Rule 35(b) statutes. * * *

1. The Rule 35 Motion Extended: Modification in Maryland

The State of Maryland is in many ways traditional, conferring jurisdiction on trial courts to modify sentences through its own Rule 35(b) analog, Maryland Rule of Court 4–345. As amended in 2005, the rule provides that

> [u]pon a motion filed within 90 days after imposition of a sentence . . . the court has revisory power over the sentence except that it may not revise the sentence after the expiration of five years from the date the sentence originally was imposed on the defendant and it may not increase the sentence.

The rule further specifies that a court may modify a sentence "only on the record in open court, after hearing from the defendant, the State, and from each victim or victim's representative who requests an opportunity to be heard." The rule leaves the grounds for modification wholly to the trial court's discretion.

Like most Rule 35 analog statutes, the Maryland rule limits the power of the court to modify an imposed sentence unless the defendant files a motion within a limited time period—in this case, ninety days. However, as the rule itself suggests, Maryland explicitly condones the practice of "bench parole" by permitting judges to hold timely filed motions in abeyance for up to five years. Commentators have observed that Maryland's willingness to allow judges to act on sentence modification motions "years after [they are] filed based on facts that were not in existence—or perhaps even contemplated—at the time of the motion, makes the Maryland procedure unique" in the modern era. Equally unique is the broad discretionary authority enjoyed by Maryland judges who can, and often do, modify sentences for a wide range of reasons. * * *

2. Inherent Jurisdiction: The Wisconsin Approach

In sharp contrast to Maryland and other states that premise ongoing trial court jurisdiction on state statutory authority, Wisconsin is one of the very few states that recognizes sentencing courts' inherent power to change and modify their own legally imposed sentences, even after those sentences have commenced. Although Wisconsin statutes provide that defendants must move for sentence modification within ninety days of sentencing when contending that their sentences are "unduly harsh," Wisconsin courts have held that their statutory time limits govern only the defendant's right to be heard by the court—not the court's discretionary power to hear the defendant's claims and to modify the sentence. In Wisconsin, therefore, a defendant may move for sentence modification at any time following the commencement of his sentence. When the defendant's motion is filed within the ninety-day time limit prescribed by statute, the court is obliged to entertain the motion. After those ninety days have passed, it is within the trial court's discretion to deny or hear the motion for modification.

In Wisconsin, motions for sentence modification can be made on two grounds: (1) that the sentence is unduly harsh, or (2) that the emergence of a "new factor" justifies modification of the original sentence. Modifications based on an alleged "new factor" must conform to strict common law rules governing what may and may not, as a matter of law, be considered a new factor. If a new factor can be shown to exist, it then falls within the discretion of the trial court to grant or deny modification of the sentence. Often the dispositive question is based on whether the new factor "frustrates the purpose of the original sentence." The trial court's decision to modify is subject to review for abuse only.

Over time, Wisconsin courts have identified specific categories of fact that may or may not constitute new factors. Facts that do not qualify include institutional compliance, the completion of rehabilitative programming, sentencing disparities between codefendants, and changes in maximum criminal penalties and classification of crime severity. As a result of these restrictions, the court's ability to modify a sentence is more restricted in Wisconsin than Maryland, even though the court's jurisdictional authority is inherent and continuing. Facts that have justified sentence modification include the correction of "inaccurate or incomplete information" relevant to the sentence imposed, judicial misunderstanding of relevant law or the collateral consequences of an imposed sentence, and a defendant's postconviction cooperation with law enforcement. * * *

3. Shared Decision Making: The Federal Model

Within the federal code, several statutes authorize judges to modify lawfully imposed sentences under certain conditions. One of these, 18

U.S.C. § 3582(c)(1)(A), is an obscure provision that permits judicial modification of federal sentences for "extraordinary and compelling reasons." Although the law places release decisions in the hands of sentencing courts, it puts a powerful constraint on the court's ability to exercise its discretion. Before a court may reduce a sentence under § 3582(c)(1)(A), the Bureau of Prisons must file a motion requesting sentence reduction and attesting to the extraordinary and compelling circumstances that justify the change in sentence. A defendant may not initiate the motion himself, nor can a court reduce a sentence sua sponte. Under this model, judicial sentence modification is the final step in a multibranch decision-making process that begins in the prison and ends in the courtroom.

Traditionally, the Bureau of Prisons has exercised its authority to file motions under § 3582(c)(1)(A) only in rare instances involving inmates with less than one year to live. Prompted in large part by pressure from advocacy groups that asserted the Bureau was abusing its discretion by interpreting the statute too narrowly, in 2007 the United States Sentencing Commission amended its guideline on the use of § 3582(c)(1)(A). The amendment clarified the Sentencing Commission's understanding that "extraordinary and compelling reasons exist" not only in cases involving terminally ill patients, but also when a defendant "suffer[s] from a permanent physical or medical condition, or is experiencing deteriorating physical or mental health because of the aging process, that substantially diminishes [his] ability . . . to provide self-care within the environment of a correctional facility and for which conventional treatment promises no substantial improvement." The Commission also explained that extraordinary and compelling reasons exist when "the defendant's only family member capable of caring for the defendant's minor child or minor children" dies or becomes incapacitated. The Commission made clear that these examples were not exhaustive, and that extraordinary and compelling reasons other than those delineated might warrant the filing of a motion for sentence modification.

These recent developments suggest the possibility of an expanding role for judicial sentence modification in the federal system. Since the passage of the 2007 amendments, however, the Bureau appears to have steadfastly adhered to its prior use of the federal statute: it appears not to have sponsored any motions for sentence modification involving nonterminally ill inmates. * * *

C. Advantages of Judicial Sentence Modification * * *

The possible advantages of judicial sentence modification are many. First, unlike the application of sentence credit or the decision to parole, judicial sentence modification decisions are transparent, occurring in open court and accompanied by an on-the-record explanation. Moreover, because the mechanism invites the original sentencing court to consider whether an offender may be safely returned to the community at a time earlier than originally anticipated, judicial sentence modification has the potential to enhance both offender accountability (by requiring the offender to justify his early release to the court and community that sentenced him) and judicial accountability (by checking the judge's original assessment of the proper sentence against the reality of the post-sentencing experience). Transparency and accountability are characteristics that respond directly to the concerns that led to the abolition of parole and other forms of early release in the 1980s and 1990s; therefore, to the degree they can be fully realized through the mechanism of judicial sentence modification, these advantages suggest the mechanism is worthy of greater consideration. * * *

NOTES & QUESTIONS

1. **Loosening the Traditional Constraints.** As Professor Klingele observes, judicial sentence modification is subject in most states to strict timing limitations, which greatly diminish the mechanism's practical utility. Do you think other states should follow the lead of Maryland and Wisconsin in extending or eliminating the traditional constraints?

It may seem to you that the answer depends on whether the state in question has a robust system of discretionary parole or other executive-branch mechanisms that already permit inmates to be released on the basis of new circumstances. If executive alternatives exist, then there would seem less need of a judicial mechanism, and greater risk of interbranch conflict if one is created. On the other hand, given the political pressures that often push against inmate releases, as well as the inertial tendencies that seem common across government agencies, perhaps there is something to be said in favor of having as many early release mechanisms as possible.

Is it clear to you, though, that there should *ever* be opportunities for inmates to obtain early release on the basis of new circumstances? Why might a retributivist be uncomfortable with early release? Do you see that there might even be utilitarian objections?

Assuming that *some* early release mechanism is desired, but only one is politically feasible, do you think it would be better to place that mechanism in the hands of the executive or judicial branch?

2. **Substantial Assistance.** The current version of Federal Rule of Criminal Procedure 35(b) permits sentence modification only on the basis of a defendant's substantial assistance to the government in investigating or prosecuting another person. Modification requires a motion from the government, which normally must be made within one year of sentencing. Substantial-assistance benefits under Rule 35(b) raise a similar set of policy issues as substantial-assistance departures under § 5K1.1 of the federal sentencing guidelines (see Chapter 4).

3. **"Extraordinary and Compelling Reasons."** In addition to Rule 35(b), 18 U.S.C. § 3582(c)(1)(A) provides another mechanism for sentence modification in the federal system. As enacted in 1984, the provision required "extraordinary and compelling reasons" for a new sentence, *and* the filing of a motion by the Bureau of Prisons. The latter requirement meant,

as Professor Klingele notes, that this sentence-modification authority was effectively shared by the executive and judicial branches. Additionally, the statute also gave a role to another agency by mandating that sentence reductions be "consistent with applicable policy statements issued by the Sentencing Commission."

Often characterized as a "compassionate release" provision, § 3582(c)(1)(A) was until recently used almost exclusively in cases of terminal illness. William W. Berry III, *Extraordinary and Compelling: A Re-Examination of the Justifications for Compassionate Release*, 68 MD. L. REV. 850, 853 (2009). Efforts by the Sentencing Commission to encourage broader use of the provision through a policy statement proved ineffectual. Finally, Congress intervened when it adopted the First Step Act of 2018. Shon Hopwood, *Second Looks & Second Chances*, 41 CARDOZO L. REV. 83, 106–07 (2019). The Act was intended to reduce the size and expense of the federal prison population. Among many other changes to federal law, the Act amended § 3582(c)(1)(A) by eliminating the requirement of a motion from the Bureau of Prisons. Prisoners are still required to *request* a motion from the Bureau but can now file a motion on their own if the Bureau refuses to file one or fails to act on a request within thirty days of receipt.

Congress eased the *procedural* hurdles for compassionate relief but retained the vague "extraordinary and compelling reasons" standard. In its policy statement, the Commission has identified several circumstances that would satisfy the standard:

- Terminal illness;
- A physical or mental condition "that substantially diminishes the ability of the defendant to provide self-care within the environment of a correctional facility and from which he or she is not expected to recover";
- Age, if the "defendant (i) is at least 65 years old; (ii) is experiencing a serious deterioration in physical or mental health because of the aging process; and (iii) has served at least 10 years or 75 percent of his or her term of imprisonment, whichever is less";
- "Death or incapacitation of the caregiver of the defendant's minor child or minor children"; or
- "Incapacitation of the defendant's spouse or registered partner when the defendant would be the only available caregiver for the spouse or registered partner."

Guidelines § 1B1.13, app. note 1. The policy statement also requires in all cases that "the defendant is not a danger to the safety of any other person or to the community."

The policy statement further indicates that its list of "extraordinary and compelling reasons" is not meant to be exhaustive; judges and the Bureau of Prisons might find other circumstances also qualify. However, pursuant to a Congressional directive in the 1984 Sentencing Reform Act, the policy statement specifies that "rehabilitation of the defendant is not, by itself, an extraordinary and compelling reason." *See* 28 U.S.C. § 994(t). Why do you think Congress imposed this limitation? Do you think it should be lifted?

In the wake of the First Step Act, many prisoners have attempted to take advantage of the liberalized procedures for compassionate release. Their efforts have raised a number of legal and practical questions with which courts continue to grapple. One difficulty is that the Commission's policy statement on compassionate release has not yet been updated based on the First Step Act and thus continues to indicate that Bureau support of compassionate release is required. *See United States v. Elias,* 984 F.3d 516 (6th Cir. 2021) (holding that district court not bound by policy statement in deciding motion brought directly by defendant). Another important question is whether compassionate release may be based on a post-sentencing change in the law that would have resulted in a lower sentence if the defendant had been sentenced later. For instance, the First Step Act itself relaxed aspects of a draconian mandatory minimum law, 18 U.S.C. § 924(c), that applies to certain offenses committed with a firearm. Should a defendant who was sentenced under the old version of the law be permitted to obtain compassionate release on the ground that he or she would have received a shorter prison term if sentenced for the same offense today? *See* Hopwood, *supra*, at 109–10 (arguing in the affirmative); *but see United States v. Hunter*, 12 F.4th 555, 568 (6th Cir. 2021) ("[N]on-retroactive changes in the law cannot be relied upon as 'extraordinary and compelling' explanations for a sentence reduction, regardless of whether the legal changes are offered alone or combined with other personal factors."). Another notable question is whether district courts may and should appoint counsel at government expense for compassionate-release petitioners who cannot afford private counsel of their own. *See* Siobhan A. O'Carroll, Note, *"Extraordinary and Compelling" Circumstances: Revisiting the Role of Compassionate Release in the Federal Criminal Justice System in the Wake of the First Step Act*, 98 WASH. U.L. REV. 1543, 1555–60 (2021).

4. **Compassionate Release in the States.** Almost all states have compassionate release laws of their own. One recent survey found that only Iowa was lacking in this regard. MARY PRICE, FAMILIES AGAINST MANDATORY MINIMUMS, EVERYWHERE AND NOWHERE: COMPASSIONATE RELEASE IN THE STATES (2018). State programs go by a variety of names, including, among others, medical parole, medical furlough, and medically recommended intensive supervision. In many states, the release decision is made by the parole board or the department of corrections, rather than the sentencing court. Whoever the decisionmaker may be, state laws tend to be far more substantively restrictive than the open-ended federal "extraordinary and compelling reasons" statute. In many states, compassionate release is limited to situations of terminal illness or other extremely serious medical conditions.

In 2020 and 2021, the threat of COVID-19 to medically compromised inmates in overcrowded prisons created pressure for the liberalization of compassionate release. Nationally, prison populations dropped somewhat during the pandemic, but it is not yet clear how much of this drop resulted from compassionate release. Eda Katharine Tinto & Jenny Roberts,

Expanding Compassion Beyond the COVID-19 Pandemic, 18 OHIO ST. J. CRIM. L. 575 (2021).

5. **Guidelines Changes.** If the Sentencing Commission makes a guideline more lenient, the Commission may choose whether and under what circumstances to make the amendment retroactive to defendants who were sentenced under the old guideline. If an amendment is made retroactive, an affected defendant may move for a sentence reduction in the original sentencing court, subject to any conditions imposed by the Commission. 18 U.S.C. § 3582(c)(2). The Commission has listed the amendments that can be used as the basis for a sentence reduction in § 1B1.10(d) of the guidelines. The sentencing court may, but is not required, to reduce the sentence in cases covered by the section. In most cases, the sentence may be reduced to the bottom of the revised guidelines range. § 1B1.10(b)(2).

A particularly important application of this provision occurred in 2014, when the Commission adopted an across-the-board reduction in drug offense levels. This resulted in more than 30,000 sentence reductions, with an average size of about two years. KIM STEVEN HUNT, DAVID RUTTER & TODD KOSTYSHAK, U.S. SENT'G COMM'N, RETROACTIVITY & RECIDIVISM: THE DRUGS MINUS TWO AMENDMENT (2020). Although opponents of retroactivity had expressed concern about the public-safety consequences of putting thousands of defendants on a faster track toward release, researchers at the Commission later found no statistically significant difference in the recidivism rates of those who were released early and other, similarly situated defendants who were required to complete their full terms.

The 2014 drug amendment reflected a large body of research indicating that long prison sentences for drug offenses are costly and ineffective. Patti B. Sarris, *A Generational Shift for Federal Drug Sentences*, 52 AM. CRIM. L. REV. 1 (2015). Does new research on, say, the deterrence, incapacitation, or rehabilitation effects of imprisonment seem an appropriate basis for modifying existing sentences? How about changes in public beliefs or priorities? For instance, public opinion surveys point to a growing public acceptance of marijuana use. Andrew Daniller, *Two-Thirds of Americans Support Marijuana Legalization*, PEW RESEARCH CENTER, Nov. 14, 2019. Does this shift suggest that individuals who are currently serving long prison terms for marijuana offenses should be considered for sentence modification?

6. **"Second-Look" Sentencing in the MPC:S.** In addition to an exceptionally broad compassionate-release provision (§ 305.7) and authorization for modifying sentences based on substantial assistance or changes in the law (§ 7.08), the MPC:S also includes an innovative "second-look" section that calls for periodic reconsideration of very long prison terms. More specifically, § 305.6 contemplates that prisoners will be able to request sentence modification after serving fifteen years. "The inquiry shall be whether the [general purposes of sentencing] would better be served by a modified sentence than the prisoner's completion of the original sentence." If a first request for modification is denied, the prisoner would be permitted to reapply at least once every ten years.

Section 305.6 is unusual as a sentence-modification mechanism inasmuch as modification requires no new circumstances, such as ill health, substantial assistance to the authorities, or changes in the law. Do you think there would ever be a good justification for simply reweighing the same considerations that led to the original sentencing decision?

7. **Second Look in the District of Columbia.** In a nationally notable legal development in early 2021, the District of Columbia adopted the Second Look Amendment Act, D.C. Act 23–568. Previously, District law had permitted individuals who had served at least fifteen years in prison for crimes committed before the age of eighteen to petition for resentencing. This opportunity had been created, in part, as a response to the Supreme Court's decision in *Miller v. Alabama* (Chapter 6) and was similarly based on scientific evidence regarding brain development during adolescence. The 2021 amendment then extended the District's original "second-look" provision to crimes committed before the age of twenty-five, based in part on evidence that important aspects of brain development often continue into a person's early twenties. NAZGOL GHANDNOOSH, SENT'G PROJECT, A SECOND LOOK AT INJUSTICE 22 (2021). Do you see why such evidence might arguably justify reconsideration of long prison terms?

As expanded in 2021, the District's second-look law is now perhaps the nation's most generous. In recent years, a handful of other states have adopted second-look reforms that more narrowly provide relief to defendants who had been victims of domestic abuse or that require a prosecutor's motion. *Id.* at 18, 21. A few states that retain discretionary parole have also recently liberalized the rules for parole eligibility for individuals who committed crimes in their late teens or early twenties. *Id.* at 27.

8. **Racial Disparities as Basis for Resentencing.** Adopted in the wake of national protests after the killing of George Floyd by a Minneapolis police officer, California's Racial Justice Act of 2020 (AB 2542) attempts to reduce the impact on criminal legal processes of race, ethnicity, and national origin bias. Among the Act's more notable provisions, defendants may now seek a resentencing on the basis of racial or other disparities in the county in which the sentencing took place. The Act also attempts to address disparities based on the *victim*'s characteristics. More specifically, in order to obtain relief, a defendant must show by a preponderance of the evidence either:

> (A) A longer or more severe sentence was imposed on the defendant than was imposed on other similarly situated individuals convicted of the same offense, and longer or more severe sentences were more frequently imposed for that offense on people that share the defendant's race, ethnicity, or national origin than on defendants of other races, ethnicities, or national origins in the county where the sentence was imposed [or]
>
> (B) A longer or more severe sentence was imposed on the defendant than was imposed on other similarly situated individuals convicted of the same offense, and longer or more severe sentences were more frequently imposed for the same offense on

> defendants in cases with victims of one race, ethnicity, or national origin than in cases with victims of other races, ethnicities, or national origins, in the county where the sentence was imposed.

Cal. Penal Code § 745(a)(4). "More frequently imposed" is defined to mean "that statistical evidence or aggregate data demonstrate a significant difference in seeking or obtaining convictions or in imposing sentences comparing individuals who have committed similar offenses and are similarly situated, and the prosecution cannot establish race-neutral reasons for the disparity." § 745(h)(1). Defendants may obtain discovery in support of a claim under the Act upon a showing of "good cause." § 745(d).

9. **Can the Government Obtain a Sentence *Increase*?** Our consideration of judicial sentence-modification has proceeded under the assumption that it is the *defendant* who is seeking a revised sentence. If the *government* were to seek an *increased* sentence after the defendant has already begun to serve a prison term, there might be serious double-jeopardy difficulties, although the relevant case law is quite sparse. Kingele, *supra*, at 522–24. The United States Supreme Court has suggested that such a post-sentencing upward modification would violate the Double Jeopardy Clause, but, thus far, only in *dicta*. *See United States v. Benz*, 282 U.S. 304, 307 (1931).

Note that the Double Jeopardy Clause does *not* bar an increased sentence if a conviction or sentence is overturned on appeal *at the defendant's behest*, resulting in a resentencing in the trial court. *North Carolina v. Pearce*, 395 U.S. 711, 721 (1969). Such an increase may, however, violate the Due Process Clause to the extent that it is vindictive, as discussed earlier in this chapter. Recall, further, that the Double Jeopardy Clause does not preclude civil commitment for a dangerous prisoner at the conclusion of the prisoner's term, as discussed in Chapter 11.

10. **Separation of Powers.** Judicial sentence-modification is sometimes seen as a violation of separation of powers, on the theory that it functionally gives to the judge a clemency or parole power that should be held exclusively by the executive branch of government. The Supreme Court rejected such an argument regarding the old version of Rule 35(b) in *United States v. Benz*, 282 U.S. 304 (1931). State courts have mostly, but not quite invariably, rejected similar separation-of-powers objections to state sentence-modification laws. Klingele, *supra*, at 525. However, to the extent that states continue the recent trend of adopting new sentence-modification laws that go beyond the traditional confines of the Rule 35(b) analogs, they may face a revival of separation-of-powers objections.

Although the separation-of-powers arguments in this area have mostly focused on encroachments by the judicial branch on the executive, some new laws have raised the opposite concern—encroachments by the executive on the judicial. More specifically, as a political compromise, some sentence-modification laws give prosecutors a veto power over sentence reductions. In at least one state, however, such a provision has been rejected as an unconstitutional encroachment on the judge's sentencing authority. *State v. Stenklyft*, 697 N.W.2d 769 (Wis. 2005).

C. ROLE OF THE EXECUTIVE BRANCH

Executive officials have the power to make a variety of decisions that may functionally—even if not formally—alter a sentence. Such decisions may affect the character, intensity, or duration of the punishment in ways that may not have been anticipated by the sentencing judge and that may even directly contravene the judge's intentions. The executive power in this regard with the deepest historical pedigree is the clemency power, which long antedates the use of imprisonment as a standard form of punishment in England or America. Before discussing clemency, however, we will first briefly review several other executive powers of note that have developed in conjunction with the use of imprisonment and that are exercised by parole boards or departments of corrections.

1. POWERS OF THE PAROLE BOARD & DEPARTMENT OF CORRECTIONS

In Chapter 8, we considered the crucial role played by parole boards and corrections officials in administering community-supervision sentences—for instance, in setting conditions for release from prison or determining how closely a defendant will be monitored in the community. Similarly, in Chapter 5, we noted the role of corrections officials in administering sentences of incarceration—for instance, in assigning defendants to particular institutions, from minimum security to super-max, or in rendering disciplinary responses to rules violations. Here, we focus on the executive role in determining release dates from prison.

In most states, for much of the twentieth century, the most visible executive power over release was that exercised by the parole board. And, even today, despite the late-twentieth-century trend toward its abolition or restriction, discretionary parole remains an important part of the criminal justice landscape in more than half of the states. Kevin R. Reitz & Edward E. Rhine, *Parole Release and Supervision: Crucial Drivers of American Prison Policy*, 3 ANN. REV. CRIMINOLOGY 281, 285 (2020). In Chapter 8, we noted the vagueness of the statutory criteria that are typically established for parole boards to apply; the informal, often hurried processes that are employed; and the longstanding criticisms that parole boards may be excessively political and risk-averse. We also noted reform efforts that have affected parole practices in many states in recent years, including the adoption of release guidelines and the incorporation of actuarial risk-assessment instruments into decisionmaking processes.

Should discretionary parole release be regarded as a form of sentence modification? If parole operates in a reasonably consistent, transparent fashion in a jurisdiction, then the judges in that jurisdiction are apt to have a pretty good idea of when most defendants will be released and can take that into account in fashioning sentences. Parole may then function more commonly in fulfillment than in derogation of the sentencing judge's intentions. By contrast, if parole is more arbitrary or obscure, then judges may often have the sense that the parole board is undermining their decisions, either by releasing too early or too late. Parole release may then functionally (though not formally) take on the character of a sort of executive sentence modification.

Good time and earned time are additional mechanisms that are routinely used in many jurisdictions in order to set or modify release dates. Good-time credits are accrued by prisoners on the basis of time spent in the institution without serious disciplinary violations. For instance, in the federal system, an inmate is awarded 54 days of credit for each year of his or her prison term in which he or she "display[s] exemplary compliance with institutional disciplinary regulations." 18 U.S.C. § 3624(b). In effect, good time reduces federal prison sentences by about 15 percent, assuming the maximum credit is awarded. In some states, good time can reduce prison terms by one-third or more, although individuals convicted of violent or sexual offenses are often subject to stricter good-time limitations than other inmates. Michael O'Hear, *Solving the Good-Time Puzzle: Why Following the Rules Should Get You Out of Prison Early*, 2012 WIS. L. REV. 195. A few states maintain "bad-time" systems that delay release on the basis of prison misconduct, rather than accelerating release on the basis of good behavior.

Earned-time credits are awarded on the basis of participation in or completion of certain programs or activities, such as employment in the institution, vocational training, drug treatment, or other educational or rehabilitative programs. For instance, through the First Step Act of 2018, Congress established a new earned-time program for federal prisoners. Under the program, a person may earn ten days of credit for every thirty days of "successful participation in evidence-based recidivism reduction programming or productive activities." 18 U.S.C. § 3632(d)(4)(A)(i). Certain low-risk individuals may qualify for even more credits, although other individuals are entirely excluded from earned time based on their offense of conviction. 18 U.S.C. § 3632(d)(4)(A), (D). As with good time, state earned-time rules vary widely in the amount of credits that may be earned. Note, too, that while an earned-time law may appear generous on its face, its actual practical impact may not be great if the state has relatively few slots available in the programs that qualify for credit.

Most states now offer good time and/or earned time to inmates. Michael O'Hear, *Solving the Good-Time Puzzle: Why Following the Rules Should Get You Out of Prison Early*, 2012 WIS. L. REV. 195, 197. In many of these jurisdictions, discretionary parole is also available. In such jurisdictions, the relationship between credits and parole consideration may be structured in a number of different ways. In some states, credits reduce the minimum term that must be served before a prisoner becomes eligible for parole. In other states, credits reduce the maximum term that must be served before mandatory release. In still others, credits are applied to both minimum and maximum terms.

Good time and earned time are probably less likely than parole to result in release dates that deviate sharply from the judge's (or, if well-advised by counsel, the defendant's) expectations at the time of sentencing. Good-time and earned-time credits are awarded formulaically, normally based on criteria that are more objective and transparent than those that are traditionally applied in parole decisions. Moreover, good time and earned time tend to create somewhat less variability in release dates than parole. For instance, in the federal system, good time creates variability as to only the final 15 percent of the prison term, but the old federal parole system permitted release anywhere from the one-third to the two-thirds mark of the sentence—and thus created variability affecting about 33 percent of the term. Additionally, some states impose caps on the total amount of credit that an inmate can obtain through good time, earned time, or both programs combined.

Still, it would be a mistake to think that there is no discretion or opportunity for arbitrariness in the administration of good time or earned time. Prison officials, for instance, often possess a great deal of discretion in determining how to respond to alleged or apparent violations of prison rules. While an aggressive approach to enforcement in one case might lead to a write-up that costs the inmate good time, a more lenient approach in another similar case might result in either no formal discipline or a finding of a lower-level violation that does not affect good time. Similarly, decisions by prison officials may affect an inmate's access to programming, employment, or other opportunities to accrue earned time. For instance, an inmate who is placed for disciplinary or administrative reasons into segregation may be required to remain in his or her cell on a nearly full-time basis. Additionally, most states give prison officials wide discretion to strip already-accrued credits from inmates as a sanction for misconduct.

Although good-time programs are not constitutionally required, the Supreme Court has indicated that a state's creation of such a program may endow inmates with a protectible liberty interest in their good-time credits, such that there must be at least some minimal due process accorded before credits are denied or taken away as a disciplinary sanction. *Wolff v. McDonnell,* 418 U.S. 539 (1974). However, the Court has indicated that due process in this context need not be even as extensive as that required for probation and parole revocations under *Morrissey v. Brewer* and *Gagnon v. Scarpelli* (Chapter 8). In particular, the Court has held that the constitutional requirements include "advance written notice of the claimed violation and a written statement of the factfinders as to the evidence relied upon and the reasons for the disciplinary action taken." *Wolff,* 418 U.S. at 563. The Court was "also of the opinion that the inmate facing disciplinary proceedings should be allowed to call witnesses and present documentary evidence in his defense when permitting him to do so will not be unduly hazardous to institutional safety or correctional goals." *Id.* at 566.

Discretionary parole, good time, and earned time are the most practically important mechanisms by which parole and corrections officials exercise control over release dates, but they are not the only such mechanisms. In the previous section, we noted the existence of "compassionate release" programs that permit early release for inmates on the basis of age, terminal illness, disability, or other serious mental or physical health conditions. Depending on the jurisdiction, control over compassionate release may be placed in the hands of the parole board, prison officials, the judiciary, or some combination of these actors. (Recall, for instance, the shared corrections-judicial authority that existed in the federal system prior to the First Step Act.) Prison officials may also be endowed with discretion to order "special action" releases in order to relieve overcrowding, provide furloughs in order to accommodate family or other special needs of inmates, or move inmates out of prisons and into halfway houses or other community-based "intermediate" sanctions.

PROBLEM 12-1: ISSUE SPOTTER—WHAT'S THE REAL LENGTH OF A PRISON TERM?

Imagine that you are an experienced criminal defense lawyer who has recently relocated and been admitted to the bar in a new state. One of your first clients in the new state faces a felony charge of simple possession of child pornography. His maximum sentence is twenty years, with no mandatory minimum. In return for a guilty plea by your client, the prosecutor offers to recommend a prison term of six years. When you present this offer to your client, he asks, "But what does that really mean? If I got six years, when would I get out? Can you at least give me best-case and worst-case scenarios?" You already know that your new state has discretionary parole, good time, and earned time, but you are still a little fuzzy on some of the technical details. In order to answer your client's questions, what information should you try to obtain?

2. CLEMENCY

Clemency is a broad category encompassing several forms of executive branch discretionary relief, with the two chief forms being pardons and commutations of sentence.[1]

Historically, pardons were bestowed by the king, and in the U.S. by governors and the president. A pardon is an act of mercy; it is "the equivalent of forgiveness for a crime; it does not declare the pardoned

[1] The Supreme Court has interpreted the Pardon Clause to include five forms of clemency: "pardons, commutations of sentence, reprieves, remissions of fines and penalties, and amnesties." Brian M. Hoffstadt, *Normalizing the Federal Clemency Power*, 79 TEX. L. REV. 561, 570 (2001) (citations omitted). The president's authority to commute sentences is understood to be included as a lesser power subsumed within the pardon power. *See, e.g.,* Ill. Cent. R.R. v. Bosworth, 133 U.S. 92, 103 (1890).

individual innocent of the crime." *R.J.L. v. State*, 887 So. 1268, 1281 (Fla. 2004).[2] Traditionally, pardon has been regarded as the most expansive vehicle for post-sentence relief, restoring to the individual "all his rights, civil and political, including the capacity or qualification to hold public office, as fully in every respect as though he had never committed the offense." *Ex parte Garland*, 71 U.S. 333, 339 (1867).

Today, all U.S. jurisdictions allow pardons to some extent, although they vary in their institutional approaches and their effect. In some states, the governor makes the pardon decision, in others the decision is made by an executive board, and in others still a hybrid approach is used. In the federal system, the president alone possesses the pardon power. *See* U.S. Const. art. II, § 2. Jurisdictions can also vary in their eligibility requirements, with many but not all, for instance, requiring waiting periods of crime-free years, which can vary with respect to felonies and misdemeanors.[3]

Pardons have been granted with markedly less frequency in recent years. One explanation for the decrease is that eligible individuals lack the ability, time, and resources to navigate the sometimes byzantine pardon process. Another is that political leaders (governors and presidents) are wary of appearing "soft on crime." *See generally* Margaret C. Love, *The Twilight of the Pardon Power*, 100 J. CRIM. L. & CRIMINOLOGY 1169 (2010). According to Professor Rachel Barkow, pardon authorities could avoid the potential negative political ramifications of pardons by adopting a more "surgical" approach:

> Pardons issued after an offender has served a sentence in full and has lived in society for some number of years without reoffending are certainly less risky than commutations that set someone free before the end of a judicially imposed sentence. To take the sliding scale further, it is also less risky to grant a former felon only a modest form of relief by reinstating his or her right to vote but granting no other relief.

Rachel E. Barkow, *The Politics of Forgiveness: Reconceptualizing Clemency*, 22 FED. SENT'G RPTR. 153, 154 (2009).

The overall decrease in pardons, it should be noted, masks important variation: fifteen jurisdictions have granted few or no pardons in the past twenty years (e.g., Kansas, Massachusetts, Oregon) and seventeen have granted pardons frequently (e.g., Alabama, Delaware, Pennsylvania). *See* Collateral Consequences Resource Center, Restoration of Rights Project, *50-State Comparison: Pardon Policy & Practice*, https://ccresourcecenter.

---

[2] Among the more notable pardons issued over time are those of blues-folk singer and songwriter Huddie William Ledbetter ("Lead Belly"), who, while serving a sentence for murder, secured a pardon from the governor of Texas in 1925, purportedly for his songwriting and singing ability, and President Richard Nixon, who in 1974 was pardoned by President Gerald Ford for any crimes he might have committed as president.

[3] For an argument that the power should be extended to localities regarding local offenses, even though it usually is not, see Hayato Watanabe, Note, *The Municipal Pardon Power*, 118 MICH. L. REV. 687 (2020).

org/state-restoration-profiles/50-state-comparisoncharacteristics-of-pardon-authorities-2/. Also, it can be the case that some individual governors grant pardons at far greater rates than others. *See* Barkow, *supra,* at 153 (noting high number of clemencies granted by former governor Mike Huckabee (Arkansas) and Timothy Kaine (Virginia), inferring that their "approach to clemency seems to have been driven in part by their religious faith and moral convictions").[4] Yet, as Professor Barkow notes, there is always the risk, and reality, of "one bad apple"—a pardoned individual who commits a serious crime, which can chill the willingness of political actors to be generous in their granting of pardons.

Commutations generally take the form of a sentence reduction (allowing immediate release or a shortened term) or the replacement of a death sentence with life imprisonment (versus a reprieve, which delays an execution). As summarized by one commentator, commutations are bestowed for any of several reasons, for instance when

> an offender's punishment differed greatly from the sentences received by others for the same offense or was unduly severe; the offender was elderly or facing death; the offender had performed some "meritorious service," such as assisting the government investigate, apprehend, or prosecute others that had not already been considered in his favor. Other "equitable factors" might also justify a commutation.

Paul J. Larkin, Jr., *Guiding Presidential Decision Making*, 18 GEO. J. L. & PUB. POL'Y 451, 464 (2020) (footnotes omitted). Unlike pardons, commutations do not remove the legal disabilities attaching to convictions, such as restrictions on civil or political rights. Also, unlike pardons, potential recipients cannot refuse a commutation so long as the terms are more lenient than the sentence that was originally imposed. James Russell Sunshine, *President Obama's Misunderstood Clemency Initiative,* 25 BERKELEY J. CRIM. L. 1, 8 (2020).

A recent example of commutation, on a rather large scale, is the "Clemency Initiative" undertaken by the Obama Administration. The Administration identified six factors to determine eligibility and guide decisions. Specifically, the applicant was required to:

> 1. Be currently serving a federal sentence in prison and, by operation of law, be likely to have received a substantially lower sentence if convicted of the same offense(s) at the time of the application;
>
> 2. Be a non-violent, low-level offender without significant ties to large scale criminal organizations, gangs, or cartels;
>
> 3. Have served at least 10 years of their prison sentence;

---

[4] Pardons, and the benefits they provide for persons of convicted of crime, are discussed at further length in Chapter 11, in relation to their role in removing or mitigating the collateral consequences of a conviction.

4. Not have a significant criminal history;

5. Have demonstrated good conduct in prison; and

6. Have no history of violence prior to or during the current term of imprisonment.

Id. at 17 (citation omitted). Ultimately, as a result of the initiative, the sentences of just under 1,700 federal inmates were commuted. *Id.* at 33.

Clemency, in principle and practice, has generated controversy. With respect to principle, clemency can be thought violative of equal protection: some individuals benefit from mercy while other, perhaps equally worthy, individuals do not. It also can be seen as unfair to crime victims. With respect to practice, evidence exists of clemency being granted in ways that reflect racial bias, result from personal or political connections, and appear arbitrary or random. For a review of the debates see, Chad Flanders, *Pardons and the Theory of the "Second Best,"* 65 FLA. L. REV. 1559 (2013). With respect to the exercise of clemency in the death penalty context in particular, see Michael Heise, *The Death of Death Row Clemency and the Evolving Politics of Unequal Grace*, 66 ALA. L. REV. 949 (2015).

INDEX

References are to Pages